THE TRUMP IMPEACHMENT REPORT

The House Judiciary Committee Report on the Impeachment of Donald J. Trump

Presented by

Celebrating 25 Years of Excellence

*Charity*Channel®

SILVER™

The Trump Impeachment Report: The Full House Judiciary Report on the Impeachment of Donald J. Trump

Published by

For the GENIUS Press, an imprint of CharityChannel LLC

POBox 14

Pleasant View, TN 37146-0014

CharityChannel.com

ISBN: 978-1-941050-53-8

13 12 11 10 9 8 7 6 5 4 3 2

Printed in the United States of America and certain other countries

Introduction

Here is the full Trump impeachment report, formally known as the *Report of the Committee on the Judiciary - House of Representatives on the Impeachment of Donald J. Trump, President of the United States.*

We publish the report, released to the public in redacted form December 16, 2019, without adding extraneous commentary, explanations, spin, or documents that aren't formally part of the report. We leave it to you, the intelligent reader, to make up your own mind.

Why is CharityChannel, the twenty-five-year-old community of nonprofit-sector professionals, publishing the Impeachment Report? Two reasons. First, it is important to disseminate this report as widely as possible because democracy thrives in the light. We believe that this report casts light that an informed American electorate should consider when electing its leaders, particularly its president. Second, many will appreciate the availability of this report in a book format. We had the means to rapidly produce the report in an 8 1/2" x 11" book and believe doing so performs a valuable public service.

We have preserved the original report's pagination, which is specific to the various sections, but also added our own through-pagination on the upper corner of each page.

So, if you want just the report without anything added or subtracted, you've found it.

116th Congress
1st Session }   HOUSE OF REPRESENTATIVES

IMPEACHMENT OF DONALD J. TRUMP PRESIDENT OF THE UNITED STATES

REPORT

OF THE

COMMITTEE ON THE JUDICIARY HOUSE OF REPRESENTATIVES

Jerrold Nadler, *Chairman*

TO ACCOMPANY
H. RES. 755

COMMITTEE ON THE JUDICIARY

JERROLD NADLER, New York, *Chairman*

ZOE LOFGREN, California
SHEILA JACKSON LEE, Texas
STEVE COHEN, Tennessee
HENRY C. "HANK" JOHNSON, JR., Georgia
THEODORE E. DEUTCH, Florida
KAREN BASS, California
CEDRIC L. RICHMOND, Louisiana
HAKEEM S. JEFFRIES, New York
DAVID N. CICILLINE, Rhode Island
ERIC SWALWELL, California
TED LIEU, California
JAMIE RASKIN, Maryland
PRAMILA JAYAPAL, Washington
VAL BUTLER DEMINGS, Florida
J. LUIS CORREA, California
MARY GAY SCANLON, Pennsylvania, *Vice-Chair*
SYLVIA R. GARCIA, Texas
JOE NEGUSE, Colorado
LUCY MCBATH, Georgia
GREG STANTON, Arizona
MADELEINE DEAN, Pennsylvania
DEBBIE MUCARSEL-POWELL, Florida
VERONICA ESCOBAR, Texas

DOUG COLLINS, Georgia, *Ranking Member*
F. JAMES SENSENBRENNER, JR. Wisconsin
STEVE CHABOT, Ohio
LOUIE GOHMERT, Texas
JIM JORDAN, Ohio
KEN BUCK, Colorado
JOHN RATCLIFFE, Texas
MARTHA ROBY, Alabama
MATT GAETZ, Florida
MIKE JOHNSON, Louisiana
ANDY BIGGS, Arizona
TOM MCCLINTOCK, California
DEBBIE LESKO, Arizona
GUY RESCHENTHALER, Pennsylvania
BEN CLINE, Virginia
KELLY ARMSTRONG, North Dakota
W. GREGORY STEUBE, Florida

Majority Staff

Amy Rutkin, Chief of Staff
Perry Apelbaum, Staff Director and Chief Counsel
John Doty, Senior Advisor
Aaron Hiller, Deputy Chief Counsel and Chief Oversight Counsel
Shadawn Reddick-Smith, Communications Director
Daniel Schwarz, Director of Strategic Communications
Moh Sharma, Director of Member Services and Outreach and Policy Advisor
David Greengrass, Senior Counsel
John Williams, Parliamentarian and Senior Counsel
Arya Hariharan, Deputy Chief Oversight Counsel
Barry Berke, Special Counsel
Norman Eisen, Special Counsel
Ted Kalo, Special Counsel
James Park, Chief Counsel of Constitution Subcommittee

Sophia Brill, Counsel
Milagros Cisneros, Counsel
Charles Gayle, Counsel
Maggie Goodlander, Counsel
Benjamin Hernandez-Stern, Counsel
Sarah Istel, Counsel
Danielle Johnson, Counsel
Joshua Matz, Counsel
Matthew Morgan, Counsel
Matthew N. Robinson, Counsel
Kerry Tirrell, Counsel

Madeline Strasser, Chief Clerk
Rachel Calanni, Professional Staff
Jordan Dashow, Professional Staff
William S. Emmons, Professional Staff
Julian Gerson, Professional Staff
Priyanka Mara, Professional Staff

Jessica Presley, Director of Digital Strategy
Kayla Hamedi, Deputy Press Secretary

Minority Staff

Brendan Belair, Staff Director, Counsel
Bobby Parmiter, Deputy Staff Director, Chief Counsel
Ashley Callen, Chief Oversight Counsel
Danny Johnson, Oversight Counsel
Jake Greenberg, Oversight Counsel
Paul Taylor, Chief Counsel, Constitution Subcommittee
Daniel Flores, Counsel
Ryan Breitenbach, Counsel
Jon Ferro, Parliamentarian, Counsel

Erica Barker, Deputy Parliamentarian
Ella Yates, Member Services Director
Andrea Woodard, Professional Staff Member
Jess Andrews, Communications Director
Amy Hasenberg, Press Secretary
Annie Richardson, Digital Director

G:\OFFICE\RAMSEYER\R16\RPT\HR755_V2A_RPT.XML

116TH CONGRESS *1st Session*	HOUSE OF REPRESENTATIVES	REPORT 116–

IMPEACHMENT OF DONALD JOHN TRUMP, PRESIDENT OF THE UNITED STATES

DECEMBER --, 2019.—Referred to the House Calendar and ordered to be printed

Mr. NADLER, from the Committee on the Judiciary,
submitted the following

R E P O R T

together with

DISSENTING VIEWS

[To accompany H. Res. 755]

The Committee on the Judiciary, to whom was referred the resolution (H. Res. 755) impeaching Donald John Trump, President of the United States, for high crimes and misdemeanors, having considered the same, reports favorably thereon pursuant to H. Res. 660 with an amendment and recommends that the resolution as amended be agreed to.

The amendment is as follows:

Strike all that follows after the resolving clause and insert the following:

That Donald John Trump, President of the United States, is impeached for high crimes and misdemeanors and that the following articles of impeachment be exhibited to the United States Senate:

Articles of impeachment exhibited by the House of Representatives of the United States of America in the name of itself and of the people of the United States of America, against Donald John Trump, President of the United States of America, in maintenance and support of its impeachment against him for high crimes and misdemeanors.

ARTICLE I: ABUSE OF POWER

The Constitution provides that the House of Representatives "shall have the sole Power of Impeachment" and that the President "shall be removed from Office on Impeachment for, and Conviction of, Treason, Bribery, or other high Crimes and Misdemeanors". In his conduct of the office of President of the United States—and in violation of his constitutional oath faithfully to execute the office of President of the United States and, to the best of his ability, preserve, protect, and defend the Constitution of the United States, and in violation of his constitutional duty to take care

G:\OFFICE\RAMSEYER\R16\RPT\HR755_V2A_RPT.XML

2

that the laws be faithfully executed—Donald J. Trump has abused the powers of the Presidency, in that:

Using the powers of his high office, President Trump solicited the interference of a foreign government, Ukraine, in the 2020 United States Presidential election. He did so through a scheme or course of conduct that included soliciting the Government of Ukraine to publicly announce investigations that would benefit his reelection, harm the election prospects of a political opponent, and influence the 2020 United States Presidential election to his advantage. President Trump also sought to pressure the Government of Ukraine to take these steps by conditioning official United States Government acts of significant value to Ukraine on its public announcement of the investigations. President Trump engaged in this scheme or course of conduct for corrupt purposes in pursuit of personal political benefit. In so doing, President Trump used the powers of the Presidency in a manner that compromised the national security of the United States and undermined the integrity of the United States democratic process. He thus ignored and injured the interests of the Nation.

President Trump engaged in this scheme or course of conduct through the following means:

(1) President Trump—acting both directly and through his agents within and outside the United States Government—corruptly solicited the Government of Ukraine to publicly announce investigations into—

(A) a political opponent, former Vice President Joseph R. Biden, Jr.; and

(B) a discredited theory promoted by Russia alleging that Ukraine—rather than Russia—interfered in the 2016 United States Presidential election.

(2) With the same corrupt motives, President Trump—acting both directly and through his agents within and outside the United States Government—conditioned two official acts on the public announcements that he had requested—

(A) the release of $391 million of United States taxpayer funds that Congress had appropriated on a bipartisan basis for the purpose of providing vital military and security assistance to Ukraine to oppose Russian aggression and which President Trump had ordered suspended; and

(B) a head of state meeting at the White House, which the President of Ukraine sought to demonstrate continued United States support for the Government of Ukraine in the face of Russian aggression.

(3) Faced with the public revelation of his actions, President Trump ultimately released the military and security assistance to the Government of Ukraine, but has persisted in openly and corruptly urging and soliciting Ukraine to undertake investigations for his personal political benefit.

These actions were consistent with President Trump's previous invitations of foreign interference in United States elections.

In all of this, President Trump abused the powers of the Presidency by ignoring and injuring national security and other vital national interests to obtain an improper personal political benefit. He has also betrayed the Nation by abusing his high office to enlist a foreign power in corrupting democratic elections.

Wherefore President Trump, by such conduct, has demonstrated that he will remain a threat to national security and the Constitution if allowed to remain in office, and has acted in a manner grossly incompatible with self-governance and the rule of law. President Trump thus warrants impeachment and trial, removal from office, and disqualification to hold and enjoy any office of honor, trust, or profit under the United States.

ARTICLE II: OBSTRUCTION OF CONGRESS

The Constitution provides that the House of Representatives "shall have the sole Power of Impeachment" and that the President "shall be removed from Office on Impeachment for, and Conviction of, Treason, Bribery, or other high Crimes and Misdemeanors". In his conduct of the office of President of the United States—and in violation of his constitutional oath faithfully to execute the office of President of the United States and, to the best of his ability, preserve, protect, and defend the Constitution of the United States, and in violation of his constitutional duty to take care that the laws be faithfully executed—Donald J. Trump has directed the unprecedented, categorical, and indiscriminate defiance of subpoenas issued by the House of Representatives pursuant to its "sole Power of Impeachment". President Trump has abused the powers of the Presidency in a manner offensive to, and subversive of, the Constitution, in that:

The House of Representatives has engaged in an impeachment inquiry focused on President Trump's corrupt solicitation of the Government of Ukraine to interfere in

G:\OFFICE\RAMSEYER\R16\RPT\HR755_V2A_RPT.XML

3

the 2020 United States Presidential election. As part of this impeachment inquiry, the Committees undertaking the investigation served subpoenas seeking documents and testimony deemed vital to the inquiry from various Executive Branch agencies and offices, and current and former officials.

In response, without lawful cause or excuse, President Trump directed Executive Branch agencies, offices, and officials not to comply with those subpoenas. President Trump thus interposed the powers of the Presidency against the lawful subpoenas of the House of Representatives, and assumed to himself functions and judgments necessary to the exercise of the "sole Power of Impeachment" vested by the Constitution in the House of Representatives.

President Trump abused the powers of his high office through the following means:

(1) Directing the White House to defy a lawful subpoena by withholding the production of documents sought therein by the Committees.

(2) Directing other Executive Branch agencies and offices to defy lawful subpoenas and withhold the production of documents and records from the Committees—in response to which the Department of State, Office of Management and Budget, Department of Energy, and Department of Defense refused to produce a single document or record.

(3) Directing current and former Executive Branch officials not to cooperate with the Committees—in response to which nine Administration officials defied subpoenas for testimony, namely John Michael "Mick" Mulvaney, Robert B. Blair, John A. Eisenberg, Michael Ellis, Preston Wells Griffith, Russell T. Vought, Michael Duffey, Brian McCormack, and T. Ulrich Brechbuhl.

These actions were consistent with President Trump's previous efforts to undermine United States Government investigations into foreign interference in United States elections.

Through these actions, President Trump sought to arrogate to himself the right to determine the propriety, scope, and nature of an impeachment inquiry into his own conduct, as well as the unilateral prerogative to deny any and all information to the House of Representatives in the exercise of its "sole Power of Impeachment". In the history of the Republic, no President has ever ordered the complete defiance of an impeachment inquiry or sought to obstruct and impede so comprehensively the ability of the House of Representatives to investigate "high Crimes and Misdemeanors". This abuse of office served to cover up the President's own repeated misconduct and to seize and control the power of impeachment—and thus to nullify a vital constitutional safeguard vested solely in the House of Representatives.

In all of this, President Trump has acted in a manner contrary to his trust as President and subversive of constitutional government, to the great prejudice of the cause of law and justice, and to the manifest injury of the people of the United States.

Wherefore, President Trump, by such conduct, has demonstrated that he will remain a threat to the Constitution if allowed to remain in office, and has acted in a manner grossly incompatible with self-governance and the rule of law. President Trump thus warrants impeachment and trial, removal from office, and disqualification to hold and enjoy any office of honor, trust, or profit under the United States.

CONTENTS

Introduction

The House Committee on the Judiciary has completed the consideration of two articles of impeachment against President Donald J. Trump. The first article charges that the President used the powers of his office to solicit and pressure a foreign government, Ukraine, to investigate his domestic political rival and interfere in the upcoming United States Presidential elections. The second article charges that the President categorically obstructed the Congressional impeachment inquiry into his conduct. Taken together, the articles charge that President Trump has placed his personal, political interests above our national security, our free and fair elections, and our system of checks and balances. He has engaged in a pattern of misconduct that will continue if left unchecked. Accordingly, President Trump should be impeached and removed from office.

This report proceeds in four parts.

First, it describes the process by which the Committee came to recommend that the House impeach the President of the United States. From start to finish, the House conducted its inquiry with a commitment to transparency, efficiency, and fairness. The Minority was present and able to participate at every stage. From September to November of this year, the House Permanent Select Committee on Intelligence, in coordination with the Committee on Oversight and Reform and the Committee on Foreign Affairs, collected evidence related to the charges against President Trump. The House Permanent Select Committee on Intelligence held public hearings to develop the evidence and share it with the American people. The committees then transmitted their evidence to the Judiciary Committee, together with a nearly 300-page public report and 123 pages of Minority views.

Consistent with House precedent, after the evidence arrived at the Judiciary Committee, the Committee invited President Trump and his counsel to participate in the process. Notably, and unlike past Presidents, President Trump declined to attend any hearings, question any witnesses, or recommend that the Committee call additional witnesses in his defense.

Second, the report discusses the standard for impeachment under the Constitution. The Framers were careful students of history and knew that threats to democracy could take many forms. Therefore, they adopted a standard for impeachment that captured a range of misconduct: "Treason, Bribery, or other high Crimes and Misdemeanors." A clear theme unified these constitutional wrongs: officials who abused, abandoned, or sought personal benefit from their public trust—and who threatened the rule of law if left in power—faced impeachment and removal. The Framers principally intended "other high Crimes and Misdemeanors" to include three forms of Presidential wrongdoing: (1) abuse of power, (2) betrayal of the national interest through foreign entanglements, and (3) corruption of office and elections. Any one of these violations of the public trust justifies impeachment. When combined in a single course of conduct, as is the case here, they state a powerful case for impeachment and removal from office.

Third, the report examines the facts underlying the first charge against President Trump: abuse of power. On July 25, 2019, when he spoke by telephone to President Zelensky of Ukraine, President Trump had the upper hand. President Zelensky had been recently elected. Ukraine was locked in an existential battle with Russia, which had invaded and illegally occupied eastern Ukraine more than five years earlier. The conflict was continuing and Ukraine needed our help—both in the form of vital military aid, which had already been appropriated by Congress because of our security interests in the region, and also in the form of an Oval Office meeting, to show the world that the United States continues to stand with our ally in resisting the aggression of our adversary.

On that July 25 call, President Zelensky expressed gratitude for past American defense support and indicated that he was ready to buy more anti-tank weapons from the United States. In response, President Trump immediately asked President Zelensky to "do us a favor, though." He asked Ukraine to announce two bogus investigations: one into former Vice President Joseph R. Biden, Jr., then his leading opponent in the 2020 election, and another to advance a conspiracy theory that Ukraine, not Russia, attacked our elections in 2016. One investigation was designed to help him gain an advantage in the 2020 election. The other was intended to help President Trump conceal the truth about the 2016 election. Neither investigation was supported by the evidence or premised on any legitimate national security or foreign policy interest.

After the call with President Zelensky, President Trump ratcheted up the pressure. He continued to dangle the offer of the Oval Office meeting and to withhold the $391 million in military aid. The evidence shows that, on the same day that the call took place, Ukrainian officials became aware that funding had been withheld. The President also deployed his private attorney and other agents, some acting outside the official and regular channels of diplomacy, to make his desires known.

These facts establish impeachable abuse of power. To the founding generation, abuse of power was a specific, well-defined offense. It occurs when a President exercises the powers of his office to obtain an improper personal benefit while injuring and ignoring the national interest. The evidence shows that President Trump leveraged his office to solicit and pressure Ukraine for a personal favor.

This unquestionably constitutes an impeachable offense, but the first article of impeachment also identifies two aggravating factors. When President Trump asked President Zelensky for a favor, he did so at the expense of both our *national security* and the *integrity of our elections*. As to the first, America has a vital national security interest in countering Russian aggression, and our strategic partner Ukraine is quite literally at the front line of resisting that aggression. When the President weakens a partner who advances American security interests, the President weakens America. As to election integrity, American democracy above all rests upon elections that are free and fair. When the President demands that a foreign government announce investigations targeting his domestic political rival, he corrupts our elections. To the Founders, this kind of corruption was especially pernicious, and plainly merited impeachment. American elections should be for Americans only.

Fourth and finally, the report describes the second charge against President Trump: obstruction of Congress. President Trump did everything in his power to obstruct the House's impeachment inquiry. Following his direction not to cooperate with the inquiry, the White House and other agencies refused to produce a single document in response to Congressional subpoenas. President Trump also attempted to muzzle witnesses, threatening to damage their careers if they agreed to testify, and even attacked one witness during her live testimony before Congress. To their great credit, many witnesses from across government--including from the National Security Council, the Department of State, and the Department of Defense--ignored the President's unlawful orders and cooperated with the inquiry. In the end, however, nine senior officials followed President Trump's direction and continue to defy duly authorized Congressional subpoenas. Other Presidents have recognized their obligation to provide information to Congress under these circumstances. President Trump's stonewall, by contrast, was categorical, indiscriminate, and without precedent in American history.

The Constitution grants the "sole Power of Impeachment" to the House of Representatives. Within our system of checks and balances, the President may not decide what constitutes a valid impeachment inquiry. Nor may he ignore lawful subpoenas for evidence and testimony or direct others to do so. If a President had such authority, he could block Congress from learning facts bearing upon impeachment in the House or trial in the Senate and could thus control a power that exists to restrain his own abuses. The evidence shows clearly that President Trump has assumed this power for himself and, left unchecked, the President will continue to obstruct Congress through unlawful means.

Although the 2020 election is less than a year away, Congress cannot wait for the next election to address the President's misconduct. President Trump has fallen into a pattern of behavior: this is not the first time he has solicited foreign interference in an election, been exposed, and attempted to obstruct the resulting investigation. He will almost certainly continue on this course. Indeed, in the same week that the Committee considered these articles of impeachment, the President's private attorney was back in Ukraine to promote the same sham investigations into the President's political rivals and, upon returning to the United States, rapidly made his way to the White House. We cannot rely on the next election as a remedy for presidential misconduct when the President is seeking to threaten the very integrity of that election. We must act immediately.

The Committee now transmits these articles of impeachment to the full House. By his actions, President Trump betrayed his office. His high crimes and misdemeanors undermine the Constitution. His conduct continues to jeopardize our national security and the integrity of our elections, presenting great urgency for the House to act. His actions warrant his impeachment and trial, his removal from office, and his disqualification to hold and enjoy any office of honor, trust, or profit under the United States.

The Impeachment Inquiry

I.   Introduction

The House of Representatives conducted a fair, thorough, and transparent impeachment inquiry under extraordinary circumstances. For the first time in modern history, committees of the House acted as original factfinders in a Presidential impeachment. Unlike in the previous impeachment inquiries into Presidents Richard M. Nixon and William J. Clinton, the House did not significantly rely on evidence obtained from other investigative bodies. Rather, committees of the House gathered evidence themselves. They did so fairly and efficiently, despite President Trump's concerted efforts to obstruct their work.

From September through November of this year, the House Permanent Select Committee on Intelligence (HPSCI), together with the Committees on Oversight and Reform and Foreign Affairs (collectively, "the Investigating Committees"), collected evidence that President Trump abused his office in soliciting and inducing foreign interference in the 2020 United States Presidential election. Despite the President's efforts to obstruct the Congressional investigation that followed, the Investigating Committees questioned seventeen current and former Trump Administration officials. In addition, although Executive Branch agencies, offices, and officials continue to defy subpoenas for documents at President Trump's direction, the Investigating Committees obtained from certain witnesses hundreds of text messages in their personal possession that corroborated their testimony, as well as reproductions of contemporaneous emails exchanged as the President's offenses were unfolding. Minority Members and their counsel participated equally in witness questioning, and the Investigating Committees released public transcripts of every deposition and interview, as well as significant documentary evidence upon which they relied. HPSCI then transmitted that evidence to the Judiciary Committee, together with a nearly 300-page public report documenting the Investigating Committees' findings, and a 123-page report containing the Minority's views.

The Judiciary Committee, consistent with House precedent, afforded ample opportunities for President Trump and his attorneys to participate as it considered articles of impeachment. Those opportunities were offered not as a matter of right, but as privileges typically afforded to Presidents pursuant to House practice. Article I of the Constitution vests the House with full discretion to structure impeachment proceedings, assigning to it both the "sole Power of Impeachment" and the authority to "determine the Rules of its Proceedings."[1] The purpose of such proceedings is not to conduct a full trial of offenses; it is "to gather evidence to determine whether the president may have committed an impeachable offense" and whether he ought to stand trial for that offense in the Senate.[2] In accordance with that purpose and House practice, President Trump was offered procedural privileges that were

---

[1] U.S. CONST. art. I, § 2, cl. 5; § 5, cl. 2.

[2] *Directing Certain Committees to Continue Their Ongoing Investigations as Part of the Existing House of Representatives Inquiry Into Whether Sufficient Grounds Exist for the House of Representatives to Exercise its Constitutional Power to Impeach Donald John Trump, President of the United States of America, and for Other Purposes*, H. Rep. No. 116-266 at 4 (2019) (hereinafter "*Rules Committee Report*"); *see also Staff of H. Comm. on the Judiciary, 116th Cong., Constitutional Grounds for Presidential Impeachment* 39 (Comm. Print 2019) (hereinafter "*Constitutional Grounds for Impeachment* (2019)").

equivalent to or exceeded those afforded to Presidents Nixon and Clinton.

II.   Background: Conduct of the House's Inquiry and Privileges Afforded to President Trump

A.   Proceedings Leading to Adoption of House Resolution 660

In early 2019, the Judiciary Committee began investigating potential abuses of office by President Trump, including obstruction of law enforcement investigations relating to Russia's interference in the 2016 United States Presidential election.[3] That investigation, which came to include consideration of whether to recommend articles of impeachment, was conducted in full public view and through public hearings. To the extent the Committee reviewed or obtained materials that it did not make available to the public, it did so in order to accommodate specific requests by the Executive Branch. The Committee also obtained responses to written questions from one fact witness and made those responses available to the public;[4] and it conducted one closed-door transcribed interview of a fact witness during which White House attorneys were present, then released a transcript of the interview the following day.[5] During this period, HPSCI also continued to investigate foreign intelligence and counterintelligence risks arising from efforts by Russia and other foreign powers to influence the United States political process during and since the 2016 election.[6]

Beginning in the spring and summer of 2019, evidence came to light that President Trump and his associates might have been seeking the assistance of another foreign government, Ukraine, to influence the upcoming 2020 election.[7] On September 9, 2019, the Investigating Committees announced they were launching a joint investigation and requested documents and records from the White House and the Department of State. In parallel, evidence emerged that the President may have attempted to cover up his actions and prevent the transmission of information to which HPSCI was entitled by law.[8] Given the gravity of these allegations and the immediacy of the threat to the next

---

[3] *See, e.g.*, *Resolution Recommending that the House of Representatives Find William P. Barr, Attorney General, U.S. Department of Justice, in Contempt of Congress for Refusal to Comply with a Subpoena Duly Issued by the Committee on the Judiciary*, H. Rep. No. 116-105, at 13 (June 6, 2019).

[4] *See* Responses by Ann Donaldson to Questions from the Committee on the Judiciary of the U.S. House of Representatives (July 5, 2019).

[5] *See Interview of Hope Hicks Before the H. Comm. on the Judiciary*, 116th Cong. (June 19, 2019).

[6] *See* App. of the Comm. on the Judiciary at 14 n.8, *In re App. of the Comm. on the Judiciary, U.S. House of Reps., for an Order Authorizing the Release of Certain Grand Jury Materials*, -- F. Supp. 3d --, 2019 WL 5485221 (D.D.C. Oct. 25, 2019) (hereinafter "*In re Rule 6(e) Application*"), *appeal pending*, No. 19-5288 (D.C. Cir.). In addition, in August 2019, Chairman Nadler requested that the chairs of five other committees investigating potential misconduct by President Trump share any materials with the Judiciary Committee that would be relevant to its consideration of impeachment. Letter from Jerrold Nadler, Chairman, H. Comm. on the Judiciary, to Adam Schiff, Chairman, H. Perm. Select Comm. on Intelligence, Maxine Waters, Chairwoman, H. Comm. on Financial Services, Elijah E. Cummings, Chairman, H. Comm. on Oversight and Reform, and Eliot L. Engel, Chairman, H. Comm. on Foreign Affairs (Aug. 22, 2019).

[7] *See* Kenneth P. Vogel, *Rudy Giuliani Plans Ukraine Trip to Push for Inquiries That Could Help Trump*, N.Y. TIMES, May 9, 2019.

[8] *See, e.g.*, Letter from Adam B. Schiff, Chairman, H. Perm. Select Comm. on Intelligence, to Joseph Maguire, Acting Dir. of Nat'l Intelligence (Sept. 10, 2019).

Presidential election, Speaker Nancy P. Pelosi announced on September 24, 2019 that the House would proceed with "an official impeachment inquiry," under which the Investigating Committees, the Judiciary Committee, and the Committees on Financial Services and Ways and Means would continue their investigations of Presidential misconduct.[9]

Following that announcement, the Investigating Committees issued additional requests and subpoenas for witness interviews and depositions and for documents in the possession of the Executive Branch.[10] The three committees "made clear that this information would be 'collected as part of the House's impeachment inquiry and shared among the Committees, as well as with the Committee on the Judiciary as appropriate.'"[11] However, as detailed further in the portion of this Report discussing obstruction of Congress, White House Counsel Pat A. Cipollone sent a letter on October 8, 2019 to Speaker Pelosi and Chairmen Adam B. Schiff, Eliot L. Engel, and Elijah E. Cummings stating that "President Trump and his Administration cannot participate in your partisan and unconstitutional inquiry."[12] As a result, the Administration refused—and continues to refuse—to produce any documents subpoenaed by the Investigating Committees as part of the impeachment inquiry, and nine current or former Administration officials remain in defiance of subpoenas for their testimony.[13]

Nevertheless, many other current and former officials complied with their legal obligations to appear for testimony, and the Investigating Committees conducted depositions or transcribed interviews of seventeen witnesses.[14] These depositions and interviews were conducted consistent with the Rules of the House and with longstanding procedures governing investigations by HPSCI and the other committees.[15] Members of the Minority previously advocated expanding these authorities, explaining that "[t]he ability to interview witnesses in private allows committees to gather information confidentially and in more depth than is possible under the five-minute rule governing committee

---

[9] Press Release, *Pelosi Remarks Announcing Impeachment Inquiry* (Sept. 24, 2019).

[10] *See The Trump-Ukraine Impeachment Inquiry Report: Report for the H. Perm. Select Comm. on Intelligence Pursuant to H. Res. 660 in Consultation with the H. Comm. on Oversight and Reform and the H. Comm. on Foreign Affairs* at 208, 116th Cong. (2019) (hereinafter "*Ukraine Report*").

[11] *Id.* (quoting Letter from Chairman Elijah E. Cummings, Chairman, H. Comm. on Oversight and Reform, Adam B. Schiff, Chairman, H. Perm. Select Comm. on Intelligence, and Eliot L. Engel, H. Comm. on Foreign Affairs, to Mick Mulvaney, Acting Chief of Staff, The White House (Oct. 4, 2019)).

[12] Letter from Pat A. Cipollone, Counsel to the President, to Nancy Pelosi, Speaker of the House, Adam B. Schiff, Chairman, H. Perm. Select Comm. on Intelligence, Eliot L. Engel, Chairman, H. Comm. on Foreign Affairs, and Elijah E. Cummings, Chairman, H. Comm. on Oversight and Reform (Oct. 8, 2019) (hereinafter "Oct. 8 Cipollone Letter").

[13] *Ukraine Report* at 30-31. Ten witnesses defied subpoenas for testimony, but the Investigating Committees subsequently withdrew their subpoena to one of the officials. *Id.* at 236.

[14] Depositions of four of the witnesses postdated the House's approval of H. Res. 660 on October 31.

[15] Rules governing the use of deposition authorities were issued at the beginning of the current Congress, just as they have been during previous Congresses. *See* H. Res. 6 § 103(a), 116th Cong. (2019) (providing authority for chairs of standing committees and chair of HPSCI to order the taking of depositions); *Regulations for Use of Deposition Authority*, 165 Cong. Rec. H1216-17 (daily ed. Jan. 25, 2019) (setting forth regulations pursuant to this provision).

hearings. This ability is often critical to conducting an effective and thorough investigation."[16]

All Members of the Investigating Committees were permitted to attend these depositions and interviews, along with Majority and Minority staff. Members and counsel for both the Majority and Minority were permitted equal time for questioning witnesses. Transcripts of all depositions and interviews were publicly released and made available through HPSCI's website on a rolling basis, subject to minimal redactions to protect classified or sensitive information.

B.   House Resolution 660 and Subsequent Proceedings

On October 31, 2019, the House voted to approve H. Res. 660, which directed the Judiciary Committee as well as HPSCI and the Committees on Oversight and Reform, Foreign Affairs, Financial Services, and Ways and Means to "continue their ongoing investigations as part of the existing . . . inquiry into whether sufficient grounds exist for the House of Representatives to exercise its Constitutional power to impeach Donald John Trump."[17] As the accompanying report by the Committee on Rules explained, HPSCI, in coordination with the Committees on Oversight and Reform and Foreign Affairs, was conducting an investigation that focused on three interrelated questions:

> 1. Did the President request that a foreign leader and government initiate investigations to benefit the President's personal political interests in the United States, including an investigation related to the President's political rival and potential opponent in the 2020 U.S. presidential election?
>
> 2. Did the President—directly or through agents—seek to use the power of the Office of the President and other instruments of the federal government in other ways to apply pressure on the head of state and government of Ukraine to advance the President's personal political interests, including by leveraging an Oval Office meeting desired by the President of Ukraine or by withholding U.S. military assistance to Ukraine?
>
> 3. Did the President and his Administration seek to obstruct, suppress or cover up information to conceal from the Congress and the American people evidence about the President's actions and conduct?[18]

The report explained that although a full House vote was by no means legally necessary, H. Res. 660 "provides a further framework for the House's ongoing impeachment inquiry."[19] That framework would be "commensurate with the inquiry process followed in the cases of President Nixon and President Clinton"—during which the House undertook various investigatory steps before voting to

---

[16] *Final Report of the H. Select Comm. on the Events Surrounding the 2012 Terrorist Attack in Benghazi*, H. Rep. No. 114-848 at 404-05 (2016) (footnote omitted).

[17] H. Res. 660, 116th Cong. (2019).

[18] *Rules Committee Report* at 2.

[19] *Id.* at 7.

authorize and structure proceedings for an impeachment inquiry.[20]

One significant difference, however, was that in this instance the House was conducting and would continue to conduct its own factfinding and collection of evidence through its investigative committees. As HPSCI has explained, "[u]nlike in the cases of Presidents Nixon and Clinton, the House conducted a significant portion of the factual investigation itself because no independent prosecutor was appointed to investigate President Trump's conduct."[21] Nevertheless, H. Res. 660 set forth detailed procedures that resulted in maximal transparency during the ongoing factfinding stage of the investigation and provided numerous privileges for President Trump and his counsel. The procedures entailed two stages for the public-facing phase of the impeachment inquiry: the first before HPSCI and the second before the Judiciary Committee.

First, HPSCI was authorized to conduct open hearings during which the Chairman and Ranking Member had extended equal time to question witnesses or permit their counsels to do so.[22] The Ranking Member was also permitted to identify and request witnesses and to issue subpoenas for documents and witness testimony with the concurrence of the Chairman, with the option to refer subpoena requests for a vote before the full Committee if the Chairman declined to concur.[23] H. Res. 660 further directed HPSCI to issue a report describing its findings and to make that report available to the public, and to transmit that report along with any supplemental materials and Minority views to the Judiciary Committee.[24]

Pursuant to H. Res. 660, HPSCI held five days of public hearings during which twelve current or former Trump Administration officials testified. These witnesses spoke in extensive detail about President Trump's repeated and prolonged efforts to pressure Ukraine into announcing and conducting baseless investigations into the President's political rival and into a discredited conspiracy theory that Ukraine, not Russia, interfered in the 2016 election. They also testified regarding United States policy interests regarding Ukraine, the value and strategic importance of the military and security assistance and the diplomatic visit to the White House that the President withheld from Ukraine, and the actions taken by individuals on the President's behalf in aid of his misconduct. In addition, the Investigating Committees received from certain witnesses hundreds of text messages as well as contemporaneous emails corroborating their testimony. The majority of witnesses maintained, however, that because they were government employees their documents and communications remained the property of Executive Branch offices and agencies. These offices and agencies, based on the President's direction, instructed officials not to provide any materials pursuant to the Investigating Committees' subpoenas.

Three of the witnesses who testified during the public hearings—Ambassador Kurt D. Volker,

---

[20] *Id.*

[21] *Ukraine Report* at 212-13.

[22] H. Res. 660 § 2(2).

[23] *Id.* § 2(4). In addition, the House's standing rules entitle committees of the House to issue subpoenas and to delegate subpoena authority to Committee chairs. *See* House Rule XI.2(m).

[24] H. Res. 660 § 2(6).

Undersecretary of State David M. Hale, and former National Security Council official Timothy A. Morrison—did so at the request of the Minority. As Chairman Schiff explained, however, the impeachment inquiry would not be permitted to serve as a means for conducting "the same sham investigations . . . that President Trump pressed Ukraine to conduct for his personal political benefit."[25] Chairman Schiff likewise made clear that he would not "facilitate efforts by President Trump and his allies in Congress to threaten, intimidate, and retaliate against the whistleblower who courageously raised the initial alarm."[26]

HPSCI's public hearings concluded on November 21, 2019. On December 3, 2019, in consultation with the Committees on Oversight and Reform and Foreign Affairs, HPSCI released and voted to adopt a report of nearly 300 pages detailing its extensive findings about the President's abuse of his office and obstruction of Congress. Chairman Schiff noted that although the investigation would continue, "[t]he evidence of the President's misconduct is overwhelming," and the need to submit an impeachment referral was too urgent to delay.[27] On December 6, 2019, and pursuant to H. Res. 660, the Investigating Committees transmitted a final version of that report, together with a report documenting the Minority's views and evidence upon which the report relied, to the Judiciary Committee.[28] The Committees on the Budget and Foreign Affairs transmitted certain materials to the Judiciary Committee as well.[29] In addition, HPSCI subsequently made a classified supplemental submission provided by one of its witnesses available for Judiciary Committee Members to review in a secure facility.[30]

With respect to proceedings before the Judiciary Committee, pursuant to H. Res. 660, the Rules Committee established "Impeachment Inquiry Procedures in the Committee on the Judiciary" that provided a host of procedural privileges for President Trump.[31] Those procedures required that President Trump's counsel be furnished with copies of all materials transferred to the Judiciary Committee by HPSCI and the other committees investigating the President's misconduct.[32] They

---

[25] Letter from Adam B. Schiff, Chairman, H. Perm. Select Comm. on Intelligence, to Devin Nunes, Ranking Member, H. Perm. Select Comm. on Intelligence (Nov. 9, 2019).

[26] *Id.*

[27] *Ukraine Report* at 9 (preface from Chairman Schiff).

[28] Letter from Adam B. Schiff, Chairman, H. Perm. Select Comm. on Intelligence, Carolyn B. Maloney, Chairwoman, H. Comm. on Oversight and Reform, and Eliot L. Engel, Chairman, H. Comm. on Foreign Affairs, to Jerrold Nadler, Chairman, H. Comm. on the Judiciary (Dec. 6, 2019); *see* H. Res. 660 §§ 2(6), 3.

[29] Letter from John Yarmuth, Chairman, H. Comm. on the Budget, to Jerrold Nadler, Chairman, H. Comm. on the Judiciary (Dec. 6, 2019); Letter from Eliot L. Engel, Chairman, H. Comm. on Foreign Affairs, to Jerrold Nadler, Chairman, H. Comm. on the Judiciary (Dec. 6, 2019).

[30] *See* Letter from Adam B. Schiff, Chairman, H. Perm. Select Comm. on Intelligence, to Jerrold Nadler, Chairman, H. Comm. on the Judiciary (Dec. 11, 2019).

[31] *Impeachment Inquiry Procedures in the Committee on the Judiciary*, submitted for printing in the Congressional Record, 165 Cong. Rec. E1357 (daily ed. October 29, 2019) (hereinafter "*Impeachment Inquiry Procedures*").

[32] Accordingly, after receiving these materials from the Investigating Committees, the Judiciary Committee transmitted them to the President on December 8, 2019, with limited exceptions for materials containing sensitive information. The Committee has made the materials containing sensitive information available for the President's counsel's review in a

afforded President Trump numerous opportunities to participate in the Judiciary Committee's proceedings through counsel. Those opportunities included the ability to present evidence orally or in writing; to question committee counsels presenting evidence; to attend all hearings of the Judiciary Committee, including those held in executive session; to raise objections during examinations of witnesses; to cross-examine any witness called before the Committee; and to request that additional witnesses be called.[33] In addition, as was the case for HPSCI, H. Res. 660 permitted the Ranking Member of the Judiciary Committee to issue subpoenas for documents and witness testimony with the concurrence of the Chairman, or to refer any such decision for a vote by the full Committee.[34]

On November 26, 2019, Chairman Nadler wrote to President Trump informing him of these procedures and the Committee's intention to hold a hearing the following week, on December 4, regarding constitutional grounds for impeachment. Chairman Nadler explained the purpose of the hearing and requested that President Trump indicate whether he and his counsel wished to participate and question the witness panel.[35] On November 29, 2019, Chairman Nadler wrote to President Trump further requesting that his counsel indicate whether he planned to participate in any of the Committee's upcoming proceedings and, if so, which privileges his counsel would seek to exercise.[36] On December 1, 2019, Mr. Cipollone responded that counsel for the President would not participate in the December 4 hearing, characterizing that process as "an after-the-fact constitutional law seminar."[37] On December 6, 2019, Mr. Cipollone sent Chairman Nadler another letter indicating the President would not avail himself of any other opportunities to participate in the Committee's proceedings, urging the Committee to "end this inquiry now and not waste even more time with additional hearings."[38] Mr. Cipollone quoted President Trump's recent statement that "if you are going to impeach me, do it now, fast, so we can have a fair trial in the Senate."[39]

On December 4, 2019, the Judiciary Committee held its public hearing on *Constitutional Grounds for Presidential Impeachment* and heard testimony from four constitutional experts, including one called by the Minority.[40] Consistent with the Judiciary Committee's proceedings during the

---

secure facility. *See* Letter from Jerrold Nadler, Chairman, H. Comm. on the Judiciary, to Pat A. Cipollone, Counsel to the President (Dec. 8, 2019).

[33] *Impeachment Inquiry Procedures* at (A)(3), (B)(2)-(3), (C)(1)-(2), (4).

[34] H. Res. 660 § 4(c)(2).

[35] Letter from Jerrold Nadler, Chairman, H. Comm. on the Judiciary, to Donald J. Trump, President of the United States (Nov. 26, 2019).

[36] Letter from Jerrold Nadler, Chairman, H. Comm. on the Judiciary, to Donald J. Trump, President of the United States (Nov. 29, 2019).

[37] Letter from Pat A. Cipollone, Counsel to the President, to Jerrold Nadler, Chairman, H. Comm. on the Judiciary (Dec. 1, 2019).

[38] Letter from Pat A. Cipollone, Counsel to the President, to Jerrold Nadler, Chairman, H. Comm. on the Judiciary (Dec. 6, 2019).

[39] *Id.*

[40] *The Impeachment Inquiry Into President Donald J. Trump: Constitutional Grounds for Presidential Impeachment Before the H. Comm. on the Judiciary*, 116th Cong. (Dec. 4, 2019) (hereafter "*Constitutional Grounds Hearing* (2019)").

impeachment of President Clinton, these experts discussed the kinds of conduct that amounts to "high Crimes and Misdemeanors" under the Constitution and whether the President's conduct met that standard.[41] The Chairman and Ranking Member were allotted equal periods of extended time for questioning, along with Majority and Minority counsel. On December 7, 2019, the Committee Majority staff released its report on this topic, outlining the grounds for impeachment as contemplated by the Founders and addressing certain arguments raised by the President.[42] The Minority staff published its own views as well, including the written testimony of its witness during the December 4 hearing.[43]

On December 9, 2019, in accordance with the "Impeachment Inquiry Procedures" promulgated pursuant to H. Res. 660, the Judiciary Committee conducted another public hearing to evaluate the evidence gathered by HPSCI.[44] Majority and Minority counsel for the Judiciary Committee presented opening statements, followed by presentations of the evidence from Majority and Minority counsel for HPSCI. The Chairman and Ranking Member were again allotted equal periods of extended time for questioning, with the ability to yield time for questioning by Majority and Minority counsels. The Majority counsel for HPSCI presented HPSCI's findings in detail and was subject to extensive questioning throughout the hearing's nine-hour duration. Minority counsel for HPSCI presented the Minority's views and was subject to questioning as well.

On December 10, 2019, Chairman Nadler introduced a resolution containing two articles of impeachment against President Trump for abuse of office and obstruction of Congress.[45] The Committee began debate the following evening and resumed debate throughout the day of December 12. On December 13, 2019, the Committee voted to report both articles of impeachment favorably to the House.

III.   The House's Inquiry Was Fully Authorized by House Rules and Precedent

The House's conduct of its impeachment inquiry—through which Committees of the House began investigating facts prior to a formal vote by the House—was fully consistent with the Constitution, the Rules of the House, and House precedent. The House's autonomy to structure its own proceedings for an impeachment inquiry is rooted in two provisions of Article I of the Constitution. First, Article I vests the House with the "sole Power of Impeachment."[46] It contains no other requirements as to how the House must carry out that responsibility. Second, Article I further states

---

This ratio of one Minority witness for every three Majority witnesses is consistent with other hearings conducted in the Judiciary Committee and in other committees.

[41] Cf. *Background and History of Impeachment: Hearing Before the Subcomm. on the Constitution, H. Comm. on the Judiciary*, 105th Cong. (1998).

[42] See *Constitutional Grounds for Impeachment* (2019).

[43] See *id.* at 53 (Minority Views).

[44] *The Impeachment Inquiry Into President Donald J. Trump: Presentations from H. Perm. Select Comm. on Intelligence and H. Comm. on the Judiciary*, 116th Cong. (Dec. 9, 2019) (hereinafter "*Presentation of Evidence Hearing* (2019)").

[45] H. Res. 755, 116th Cong. (2019).

[46] U.S. CONST. art I, § 2, cl. 5.

that the House is empowered to "determine the Rules of its Proceedings."[47] Taken together, these provisions give the House sole discretion to determine the manner in which it will investigate, deliberate, and vote upon grounds for impeachment.

The Rules of the House do not prescribe any particular manner in which the House or any of its committees must conduct impeachment inquiries. Although the Judiciary Committee has traditionally been "responsible for considering and potentially recommending articles of impeachment to the full House,"[48] it is not the exclusive factfinding body through which all evidence bearing on impeachment must be collected. To the contrary, as discussed further below, in the last two modern Presidential impeachments the Judiciary Committee relied on evidence obtained through prosecutors, grand juries, and (in the case of President Nixon) a committee of the Senate. In addition, the House Rules provide HPSCI and the standing committees with robust investigative authorities, including the power to issue subpoenas and take depositions.[49] Each of the three committees indisputably has oversight jurisdiction to investigate these matters.[50]

Throughout 2019, HPSCI continued to investigate Russia's interference in the 2016 election as well as ongoing efforts by Russia and other adversaries to interfere in upcoming elections. As allegations emerged that President Trump and his personal attorney, Rudolph Giuliani, were acting to solicit and pressure Ukraine to launch politically motivated investigations, the Investigating Committees announced publicly on September 9, 2019, that they were conducting a joint investigation of the President's conduct toward Ukraine.[51]

The principal objection by the President has consisted of a claim that no committee of the House was permitted to investigate Presidential misconduct for *impeachment* purposes unless or until the House enacted a resolution fully "authorizing" the impeachment inquiry.[52] That claim has no basis in the Constitution, any statutes, the House Rules, or House precedent. As already noted, the Constitution says nothing whatsoever about any processes or prerequisites governing the House's exercise of its "sole Power of Impeachment." To the contrary, the Constitution's Impeachment and Rulemaking Clauses indicate that it is only for the House itself to structure its impeachment investigations and proceedings. Yet the House Rules do not preclude committees from inquiring into potential grounds for impeachment. As a federal district court recently confirmed, the notion that a full House vote is

---

[47] U.S. CONST. art. I, § 5, cl. 2.

[48] *Rules Committee Report* at 7.

[49] House Rule XI.2(m); H. Res. 6 § 102(a).

[50] *See* House Rule X.1(i)(1), (10) (Committee on Foreign Affairs has jurisdiction regarding "[r]elations of the United States with foreign nations generally" and "[d]iplomatic service"); House Rule X.3(i), X.4(c)(2) (Committee on Oversight and Reform "shall review and study on a continuing basis the operation of Government activities at all levels, including the Executive Office of the President," and "may at any time conduct investigations of any matter" before other committees of the House); House Rule X.11(b)(1)(B) (HPSCI has jurisdiction regarding "[i]ntelligence and intelligence-related activities" of all "departments and agencies of the government").

[51] Press Release, *Three House Committees Launch Wide-Ranging Investigations into Trump-Giuliani Ukraine Scheme* (Sept. 9, 2019).

[52] *See* Oct. 8 Cipollone Letter.

required to authorize an impeachment inquiry "has no textual support in the U.S. Constitution [or] the governing rules of the House."[53]

Furthermore, House precedent makes manifestly clear that the House need *not* adopt a resolution authorizing or structuring an impeachment inquiry before such an inquiry can proceed. As *Jefferson's Manual* notes, "[i]n the House various events have been credited with setting an impeachment in motion," including charges made on the floor, resolutions introduced by members, or "facts developed and reported by an investigating committee of the House."[54] As Chief Judge Howell explained, the House has "[i]ndisputably initiated impeachment inquiries of federal judges without a House resolution 'authorizing' the inquiry."[55] One such inquiry involved a lengthy investigation of a sitting Supreme Court Justice.[56] Indeed, several "federal judges have been *impeached* by the House without a House resolution 'authorizing' an inquiry."[57] For example, the Judiciary Committee investigated grounds for the impeachment of Judge Walter Nixon following a referral by the United States Judicial Conference and the introduction of a resolution for his impeachment.[58] The Committee—without any direct authorization or instruction from the full House—subsequently adopted articles of impeachment, which were approved by a vote of the full House. The Senate later voted to convict Judge Nixon and remove him from office.[59] Similar proceedings occurred in impeachments of two other judges.[60] Indeed, as recently as the 114th Congress, the Judiciary Committee considered impeachment of the Commissioner of the Internal Revenue Service following a referral from another committee and absent a full vote of the House for an impeachment inquiry.[61]

In addition, in many prior instances in which the full House adopted resolutions authorizing and directing the Judiciary Committee to undertake impeachment inquiries, the resolutions served in part to provide the Committee with authorities it did not already have. For example, the 1974 resolution authorizing and directing the impeachment inquiry into President Nixon served to clarify the scope of the Committee's subpoena authority and authorized the Committee and its counsel to take depositions.[62] Today, the House Rules for standing committees and for HPSCI already provide these

---

[53] *In re Rule 6(e) Application*, 2019 WL 5485221, at *26.

[54] *Constitution, Jefferson's Manual, Rules of the House of Representatives of the United States*, H. Doc. No. 115-177 § 603 (2019 ed.) (hereinafter "*Jefferson's Manual*").

[55] *In re Rule 6(e) Application*, 2019 WL 5485221 at *26 (providing four examples).

[56] *Id.* (citing 3 *Deschler's Precedents of the United States House of Representatives* ch. 14 § 5 (1994) (hereinafter "Deschler").

[57] *In re Rule 6(e) Application*, 2019 WL 5485221 at *26 (emphasis in original).

[58] *Report of the Committee on the Judiciary, Impeachment of Walter L. Nixon, Jr.*, H. Rep. No. 101-36, at 13-16 (1989).

[59] *See Nixon v. United States*, 506 U.S. 224, 227-28 (1993).

[60] *See In re Rule 6(e) Application*, 2019 WL 5485221 at *26.

[61] *See Examining the Allegations of Misconduct Against IRS Commissioner John Koskinen (Part I): Hearing Before the H. Comm. on the Judiciary*, 114th Cong. 3 (2016) (statement by Rep. Darrell Issa describing the hearing as "an inquiry into the recommendation of impeachment" made by another committee).

[62] H. Res. 803 § 2(a)(1); *see* 3 Deschler ch. 14 § 6.2.

authorities.[63] Thus, as a practical matter, a full vote of the House is no longer needed to provide investigating committees with the kinds of authorities needed to conduct their investigations. Here, of course, the House did ultimately adopt H. Res. 660, which explicitly directed HPSCI and the Committees on the Judiciary, Oversight and Reform, Foreign Affairs, Financial Services, and Ways and Means to "continue their ongoing investigations" as part of the House's "existing" impeachment inquiry. Although the House was not obligated to enact such a resolution, H. Res. 660 affirmed the authority of the House and these committees to continue their investigations and provided further structure to govern the inquiry moving forward.

This sequence of events in the House's impeachment inquiry into President Trump bears substantial resemblance to the development of the House's impeachment inquiry into President Nixon. The Judiciary Committee's consideration of impeachment resolutions against President Nixon began in October 1973, when various resolutions calling for President Nixon's impeachment were introduced in the House and referred to the Judiciary Committee.[64] Over the next several months, the Committee investigated the Watergate break-in and coverup (among other matters) using its existing investigatory authorities.[65] The Committee also hired a special counsel and other attorneys to assist in these efforts, and the House adopted a resolution in November 1973 to fund the Committee's investigations.[66] As the Committee explained in a February 1974 staff report, its work up through that time included forming multiple task forces within the staff to gather evidence organized around various subjects of interest.[67] All of this occurred before the House approved a resolution directing the Judiciary Committee to investigate whether sufficient grounds existed to impeach President Nixon.[68]

So too here, committees of the House began investigating allegations of misconduct by President Trump before the House voted to approve H. Res. 660. That course of events is consistent not only with the House's impeachment inquiry against President Nixon but with common sense. After all, before voting to conduct an impeachment inquiry, the House must have some means of ascertaining the nature and seriousness of the allegations and the scope of the inquiry that may follow. It defies logic to suggest that House committees have no authority to begin examining the President's potentially impeachable misconduct unless or until the *full* House votes to conduct an impeachment inquiry.

IV.   President Trump Received Ample Procedural Protections

---

[63] *See* H. Res 6, 116th Cong. § 103(a), (2019); *Jefferson's Manual* § 805 (describing gradual expansion of these authorities).

[64] 3 Deschler ch. 14 § 15.1.

[65] *See id.* ch. 14 § 15.2 (Parliamentarian's Note); *Report of the H. Comm. on the Judiciary, Impeachment of Richard M. Nixon, President of the United States*, H. Rep. No. 93-1305 at 6 (1974) (hereinafter "*Committee Report on Nixon Articles of Impeachment* (1974)").

[66] *Committee Report on Nixon Articles of Impeachment* (1974) at 6.

[67] *Work of the Impeachment Inquiry Staff As of February 5, 1974: Report by the Staff of the H. Comm. on the Judiciary* at 2-3, 93d Cong. (1974) (hereinafter "*February 5, 1974 Progress Report*").

[68] H. Res. 803 § 1, 93d Cong. (1974).

A.   General Principles

As Chairman Rodino observed during this Committee's impeachment proceedings against President Nixon, "it is not a right but a privilege or a courtesy" for the President to participate through counsel in House impeachment proceedings.[69] An impeachment inquiry is not a trial; rather, it entails a collection and evaluation of facts before a trial occurs in the Senate. In that respect, the House acts analogously to a grand jury or prosecutor, investigating and considering the evidence to determine whether charges are warranted. Federal grand juries and prosecutors, of course, conduct their investigations in secret and afford little or no procedural rights to targets of investigations.[70] This type of confidentiality is necessary to (among other things) ensure freedom in deliberations, "prevent subornation of perjury or tampering with the witnesses who may testify," and "encourage free and untrammeled disclosures by persons who have [relevant] information."[71]

Nonetheless, in light of the gravity of the decision to impeach the President and the ramifications that such a decision has for the Nation as a whole, the House has typically provided a level of transparency in impeachment inquiries and has afforded the President certain procedural privileges. Although President Trump has at times invoked the notion of "due process," "an impeachment inquiry is not a criminal trial and should not be confused with one."[72] Rather, the task of the House—as part of the responsible exercise of its "sole Power of Impeachment"—is to adopt procedures that balance the need to protect the integrity of its investigations, the public interest in a full and fair inquiry, and the President's interest in telling his side of the story.

As discussed below, in past impeachment inquiries this has typically meant that the principal evidence relied upon by the Judiciary Committee is disclosed to the President and to the public—though some evidence in past proceedings has remained confidential. The President has also typically been afforded an opportunity to participate in the proceedings at a stage when evidence has been fully gathered and is presented to the Judiciary Committee. In addition, the President has been entitled to present his own evidence and to request that witnesses be called. He has not, however, been entitled to have counsel present during all interviews of witnesses. The procedures employed by the House here were tailored to these considerations and provided ample protections for President Trump.

B.   Processes Used in Modern Presidential Impeachments

The processes used in the House's impeachment inquiries into Presidents Nixon and Clinton shared certain common features that informed the House's consideration of how to structure its proceedings with respect to President Trump. In both the Nixon and Clinton impeachments, the House relied substantially on factual evidence collected through prior investigations. These prior investigations did not afford the President any particular procedural rights, such as the opportunity to

---

[69] *Impeachment Inquiry: Hearings Before the H. Comm. on the Judiciary*, 93d Cong. 497 (1974) (hereinafter "*Nixon Impeachment Hearings*").

[70] *See* Fed. R. Crim. P. 6(e).

[71] *United States v. Procter & Gamble Co.*, 356 U.S. 677, 681 n.6 (1958).

[72] *Rules Committee Report* at 8.

cross-examine witnesses, and many portions were conducted outside public view. At a later stage, when evidence was formally presented to the Judiciary Committee, the President's counsel was permitted to attend, present evidence and call witnesses, and cross-examine witnesses before the Committee.

1.   President Nixon

Impeachment proceedings in the House against President Nixon were conducted almost entirely behind closed doors, with the President's counsel afforded certain procedural privileges in later stages of the inquiry. As noted above, the Judiciary Committee began considering impeachment resolutions against President Nixon in October 1973, including by examining evidence in the public domain obtained from other investigations.[73] On February 6, 1974, the House adopted H. Res. 803, which authorized and directed the Committee to investigate "whether sufficient grounds exist for the House of Representatives to exercise its constitutional power to impeach Richard M. Nixon."[74] H. Res. 803 gave the Committee authority to subpoena documents and witnesses, to take depositions, and to issue interrogatories. This authority could be exercised by the Chairman or the Ranking Member, with each having the right to refer disagreements to the full Committee.[75] The Committee subsequently adopted procedures imposing tight restrictions on access to materials gathered during the course of its investigation, restricting access to the Chairman, the Ranking Member, and authorized staff.[76] In February and March 1974, the Committee met three times in closed executive sessions—without President Nixon's counsel in attendance—to hear updates from Committee staff.[77] In addition to reviewing information produced in other investigations, Committee staff conducted private interviews of fact witnesses.[78]

Much of the evidence relied upon by the Committee and gathered by staff was obtained through other investigations, including the investigation by the Senate Select Committee on Presidential Campaign Activities. Indeed, the Senate Select Committee's televised hearings are what typically come to mind when one thinks of Congress's investigation of Watergate. The Senate, of course, does not conduct impeachment inquiries; its constitutional function is "to try all Impeachments" if an officer of the United States is impeached by the House.[79] The Senate Select Committee was instead established pursuant to the Senate's general oversight and legislative authorities.[80] In the spring of 1973—before those televised hearings occurred—Select Committee staff interviewed hundreds of witnesses in

---

[73] *February 5, 1974 Progress Report* at 2.

[74] H. Res. 803 § 1, 93d Cong. (1974).

[75] *Id.* § 2(b)(1).

[76] *Procedures for Handling Impeachment Inquiry Material: H. Comm. on the Judiciary*, 93d Cong. (Comm. Print 1974); *see Committee Report on Nixon Articles of Impeachment* (1974) at 8.

[77] *Nixon Impeachment Hearings* at 53-78 (Feb. 5, 1974 briefing by staff); *id.* at 79-100 (Feb. 14, 1974 briefing by staff); *id.* at 131-59 (Mar. 5, 1974 briefing by staff).

[78] *See id.* at 96, 105, 206.

[79] U.S. CONST. art. I, § 3, cl. 6.

[80] *See Final Report of the S. Select Comm. on Presidential Campaign Activities*, S. Rep. No. 93-981, xxiii-xxiv (1974) (hereinafter "*Senate Select Committee Report*").

informal private settings or closed-door executive sessions of the Committee.[81] The Select Committee also met in numerous executive sessions to receive progress updates from staff.[82] Only later, beginning in May 1973 and lasting through the summer, did the Select Committee call witnesses to testify in public hearings.[83] Those hearings were not impeachment proceedings, President Nixon was not afforded any procedural privileges, such as the right to have counsel present and to question witnesses.

On February 7, 1974—the day after the House adopted its resolution directing an impeachment inquiry—the Senate Select Committee voted to transmit all of its files, including voluminous non-public files, to the House Judiciary Committee.[84] The Judiciary Committee relied on those non-public materials as it gathered evidence. For example, a March 1, 1974 progress report by Judiciary Committee staff noted that its "basic sources" included "the closed files of the [Senate Select Committee], including executive session testimony."[85] In March 1974, the Judiciary Committee also famously received the Watergate grand jury's "roadmap" describing evidence of potential offenses committed by President Nixon.[86] That report—which was not disclosed to the public until nearly 45 years later—described and appended evidence gathered through months of secret grand jury proceedings, during which counsel for defendants were not permitted to appear or question witnesses.

In the course of the Judiciary Committee's investigation, Committee staff also conducted interviews of witnesses in private settings in which no counsel for President Nixon was present. During a closed-door briefing in February 1974, Special Counsel John A. Doar made clear to members that counsel for the Minority would not necessarily be present for all interviews either, depending upon the circumstances.[87] In an effort to develop appropriate procedures governing the inquiry, Committee staff reviewed in detail the proceedings used in prior impeachment inquiries dating back to the eighteenth century. In a memorandum describing their findings, Committee staff noted they had found "[n]o record . . . of any impeachment inquiry in which the official under investigation participated in the investigation stage preceding commencement of Committee hearings."[88] Nor had Committee staff found any instance in which "the official under investigation . . . was granted access to the Committee's evidence before it was offered at a hearing."[89]

Later in the spring and early summer of 1974, the Committee held a series of closed-door meetings for formal presentations of evidence by Committee counsel. As relevant here, the procedures

---

[81] *Id.* at xxx.

[82] *Id.* at xviii.

[83] *Id.* at xxix.

[84] *Nixon Impeachment Hearings* at 95; *see also Senate Select Committee Report* at xxx.

[85] *Work of the Impeachment Inquiry Staff as of March 1, 1974* at 4, 93d Cong. (Comm. Print 1974).

[86] *See Haldeman v. Sirica*, 501 F.2d 714 (D.C. Cir. 1974).

[87] *Nixon Impeachment Hearings* at 96.

[88] Impeachment Inquiry Staff, H. Comm. on the Judiciary, *Memorandum: Presentation Procedures for the Impeachment Inquiry* at 11, 93d Cong. (Apr. 3, 1974).

[89] *Id.* at 18.

it adopted for those presentations allowed the President's counsel to attend strictly as an observer, to be provided with evidence as it was presented, and to present evidence orally or in writing afterward.[90] It was only in the final stages of the Judiciary Committee's inquiry—in late June and July 1974—that President Nixon's counsel was permitted to present evidence and to call and question witnesses.[91] These proceedings also occurred in closed executive sessions of the Committee, as did the questioning of additional witnesses called by the Committee.[92] In total, the Committee heard testimony from nine witnesses in these closed-door hearings, with the transcripts made available to the public afterward.[93] The sole public portions of the Committee's proceedings in which it considered the evidence were several days of debate between members about whether to recommend articles of impeachment.[94] The Committee ultimately voted on July 27, July 29, and July 30, 1974 to adopt three articles of impeachment,[95] and President Nixon resigned from office shortly afterward.

2.   President Clinton

The Judiciary Committee's impeachment inquiry concerning President Clinton occurred over a relatively brief period in late 1998 and relied almost entirely upon evidence collected by Independent Counsel Kenneth W. Starr. On September 9, 1998, Independent Counsel Starr notified the Speaker and Minority Leader of the House that his office had transmitted an impeachment referral and 36 sealed boxes of evidence to the Sergeant-at-Arms.[96] Two days later, the House approved H. Res. 525, requiring the Committee to review these materials and determine whether to recommend that the House proceed with an impeachment inquiry.[97] H. Res. 525 further directed that Independent Counsel Starr's report be published as a House document and called for all supporting documents and evidence to be released in the coming weeks, unless determined otherwise by the Committee.[98] Many of those materials, including grand jury materials, were released publicly on September 18 and 28, 1998; some, however, were withheld from the public and the President.[99]

---

[90] *See Nixon Impeachment Hearings* App. VI, "Impeachment Inquiry Procedures"; *e.g., id.* at 1189 (Chairman prohibited President Nixon's counsel from introducing a response to Committee's presentations at this stage).

[91] *Committee Report on Nixon Articles of Impeachment* (1974) at 9.

[92] *See Nixon Impeachment Hearings* at 1719-1866 (presentations by President Nixon's counsel); *id.* at 1867-79 (voting to conduct witness testimony in executive session).

[93] *See generally Testimony of Witnesses: Hearings Before the H. Comm. on the Judiciary*, 93d Cong. (1974).

[94] *Committee Report on Nixon Articles of Impeachment* (1974) at 9-10.

[95] *Id.* at 10.

[96] *See Impeachment of William J. Clinton, President of the United States: Report of the H. Comm. on the Judiciary*, H. Rep. No. 105-830, at 123 (hereinafter "*Committee Report on Clinton Articles of Impeachment* (1998)"). Independent Counsel Starr submitted this referral pursuant to 28 U.S.C. § 595(c), a provision of the now-expired Independent Counsel Act that required independent counsels to "advise the House of Representatives of any substantial and credible information . . . that may constitute grounds for an impeachment." *See id.* at 123-24.

[97] *Committee Report on Clinton Articles of Impeachment* (1998) at 125; *see* H. Res. 525, 105th Cong. (1998).

[98] H. Res. 525 § 2, 105th Cong. (1998).

[99] *Committee Report on Clinton Articles of Impeachment* (1998) at 125-26.

On October 8, 1998, the House adopted H. Res. 581, which authorized and directed the Judiciary Committee to investigate "whether sufficient grounds exist for the House of Representatives to exercise its constitutional power to impeach William Jefferson Clinton."[100] H. Res. 581 contained express authorization for the Committee to subpoena documents and witnesses and to issue interrogatories. As with the resolution governing the Nixon impeachment inquiry, H. Res. 581 specified that this authority could be exercised by the Chairman or Ranking Member, with each having the right to refer disagreements to the full Committee.[101]

The Committee's proceedings unfolded rapidly afterward. As in the Nixon impeachment proceedings, the Committee relied substantially during its investigation of President Clinton on evidence gathered from a prior investigation—that conducted by Independent Counsel Starr. Committee staff also conducted a limited number of depositions during which counsel for President Clinton was not present; additionally, Committee Majority staff conducted interviews which neither Minority staff nor counsel for the President attended. On two occasions in October and November 1998, White House attorneys wrote to Chairman Hyde and Committee Majority counsel expressing concern about their lack of an opportunity to participate in these depositions and interviews.[102] Majority counsel for the Committee responded by pointing to the Nixon-era staff memorandum as proof that counsel for the President has no right to attend depositions or interviews of witnesses. The President's contrary view, Committee counsel stated, was "on the wrong side of history."[103]

On November 19, 1998, Independent Counsel Starr testified in a public hearing before the Committee. He was the sole witness who presented factual evidence before the Committee, and his testimony consisted primarily of descriptions of evidence his office had gathered in the course of its investigation.[104] That evidence included tens of thousands of pages of grand jury testimony,[105] which by definition was taken in secret and without the opportunity for adversarial questioning. In addition, in November and December 1998, the Subcommittee on the Constitution and the full Committee, respectively, held open hearings on the background and history of impeachment and on the offense of

---

[100] H. Res. 581, 105th Cong. (1974).

[101] *Id.* § 2(b).

[102] Letter from Charles F.C. Ruff, Counsel to the President, Gregory B. Craig, Special Counsel to the President, and David E. Kendall, Special Counsel to the President, to Henry Hyde, Chairman, H. Comm. on the Judiciary (Oct. 23, 1998); Letter from Charles F.C. Ruff, Counsel to the President, to Thomas E. Mooney, Chief of Staff – General Counsel, H. Comm. on the Judiciary, and David P. Schippers, Chief Investigative Counsel, H. Comm. on the Judiciary (Nov. 20, 1998).

[103] Letter from Thomas E. Mooney, Chief of Staff – General Counsel, H. Comm. on the Judiciary, and David P. Schippers, Chief Investigative Counsel, H. Comm. on the Judiciary, to Charles F.C. Ruff, Counsel to the President, Gregory B. Craig, Special Counsel to the President, and David E. Kendall, Special Counsel to the President, at 2-3 (Nov. 9, 1998) (hereinafter "Mooney Letter").

[104] *See generally Impeachment Inquiry: William Jefferson Clinton, President of the United States: Hearing Before the H. Comm. on the Judiciary*, 105th Cong. (Nov. 19, 1998) (hereinafter "*Starr Hearing*"). President Clinton's counsel was permitted to question Independent Counsel Starr following questioning by Committee counsel and Members. *Id.* at 170-89.

[105] *See Committee Report on Clinton Articles of Impeachment* (1998) at 200 (Minority Views); *see also Starr Hearing* at 170.

perjury.[106] Finally, on December 8 and 9, 1998, President Clinton's legal counsel called multiple panels of outside legal experts and elicited testimony primarily on whether the President's alleged conduct rose to the level of impeachable offenses.[107]

Between December 10 to 12, 1998, the Committee debated and voted to adopt four articles of impeachment.[108] The following week, the articles were debated on the floor of the House over the course of two days. On December 19, 1998, the House voted to approve two of the articles and voted against two others.[109] Shortly after that vote, Ranking Member Conyers wrote to Chairman Hyde expressing concerns that Majority staff had conducted witness interviews without informing the Minority and provided summaries of those interviews to certain members while withholding them from the Minority. Chairman Conyers also raised concerns that members of the Majority had encouraged Members whose votes were still undecided to review certain evidence that had been withheld from the President and the public in an effort to sway those Members' decision-making.[110]

C.   The Procedural Protections Afforded to President Trump Met or Exceeded Those Afforded in Past Presidential Impeachment Inquiries

The House's impeachment inquiry provided President Trump procedural protections that were consistent with or in some instances exceeded those afforded to Presidents Nixon and Clinton. The House's inquiry was conducted with maximal transparency: transcripts of all interviews and depositions were made public, and HPSCI and the Judiciary Committee held seven days of public hearings. All documentary evidence relied on in HPSCI's report has been made available to President Trump, and much of it has been made public. Furthermore, during proceedings before the Judiciary Committee, President Trump was offered numerous opportunities to have his counsel participate, including by cross-examining witnesses and presenting evidence. The President's decision to reject these opportunities to participate affirms that his principal objective was to obstruct the House's inquiry rather than assist in its full consideration of all relevant evidence.

1.   The House's Inquiry Was Conducted with Maximal Transparency

The House's impeachment inquiry against President Trump was unique in its lack of reliance on the work of another investigative body. Instead, the Investigating Committees performed their own extensive investigative work—and they did so with abundant transparency. Twelve key witnesses

---

[106] *See Background and History of Impeachment: Hearing Before the H. Comm. on the Judiciary, Subcomm. on the Constitution*, 105th Cong. (Nov. 9, 1998); *The Consequences of Perjury and Related Crimes: Hearing Before the H. Comm. on the Judiciary*, 105th Cong. (Dec. 1, 1998).

[107] *Impeachment Inquiry: William Jefferson Clinton, President of the United States: Presentation on Behalf of the President: Hearing Before the H. Comm. on the Judiciary*, 105th Cong. (1998). President Clinton's counsel also called White House Counsel Charles F.C. Ruff to testify. *Id.* at 405-58.

[108] *Committee Report on Clinton Articles of Impeachment* (1998) at 128.

[109] 144 Cong. Rec. 28, 110-12 (1998).

[110] Letter from John Conyers, Jr., Ranking Member, H. Comm. on the Judiciary, to Henry J. Hyde, Chairman, H. Comm. on the Judiciary (Dec. 22, 1998).

critical to the Committees' investigation testified in publicly televised hearings. All transcripts for each of the seventeen witnesses interviewed or deposed have been made public and posted on HPSCI's website, subject to minimal redactions to protect classified or sensitive information. All documentary evidence relied on in HPSCI's report has been made available to the President and to the Judiciary Committee, and significant portions have been released to the public as well.

Those facts alone render this inquiry more transparent than those against Presidents Nixon and Clinton. As noted previously, during the House's impeachment inquiry into President Nixon, not a single evidentiary hearing took place in public. And although transcripts of closed-door witness hearings were subsequently released, notes or transcripts from private witness interviews were not. In addition, the Judiciary Committee relied on voluminous evidence that was obtained through other investigations, including investigations by prosecutors, a grand jury, and the Senate Select Committee. The Judiciary Committee amassed a collection of files from those investigations and maintained them under strict confidentiality procedures. With respect to President Clinton, the Judiciary Committee's impeachment inquiry was based almost solely upon evidence transmitted by Independent Counsel Starr. That evidence was collected in secret grand jury proceedings or through other law enforcement mechanisms. Even after the evidence was transmitted to the Judiciary Committee, not all of it was disclosed publicly. Furthermore, Committee staff conducted non-public depositions and interviews.

As the Majority counsel for HPSCI explained in his presentation to the Judiciary Committee, conducting witness interviews in a manner that does not allow witnesses to "line up their stories" is a "[b]est investigative practice."[111] Closed-door depositions in the present inquiry were necessary during earlier stages of the investigation to prevent witnesses from reviewing one another's testimony and tailoring their statements accordingly.[112] Indeed, the Judiciary Committee is unaware of any factfinding process—whether in criminal investigations or administrative proceedings—in which all witnesses are interviewed in full view of each other and of the person under investigation. Nevertheless, HPSCI released transcripts of the depositions it conducted on a rolling basis within weeks of their occurrence. In addition, the Judiciary Committee's proceedings were conducted in full public view.

2.   The President Was Afforded Meaningful Opportunities to Participate

At the investigative stage before HPSCI and the Committees on Oversight and Reform and Foreign Affairs, President Trump made concerted efforts to ensure that his closest advisors would not be heard from, including by ordering an across-the-board blockade of the House's inquiry and by directing multiple White House and other Executive Branch officials not to appear. Nonetheless, President Trump was offered—but declined—numerous opportunities to participate in the House's proceedings when they reached the Judiciary Committee.

Pursuant to the "Impeachment Inquiry Procedures in the Committee on the Judiciary" described

---

[111] *The Impeachment Inquiry into President Donald J. Trump: Presentations from the House Permanent Select Committee on Intelligence and House Judiciary Committee: Hearing Before the H. Comm. on the Judiciary,* 116th Cong. (2019) (testimony by Daniel Goldman).

[112] *Id.*

above, the President was given the opportunity to: have counsel attend any presentations of evidence before the Committee; have counsel ask questions during those presentations; respond orally or in writing to any evidence presented; request that additional witnesses be called; have counsel attend all other hearings in which witnesses were called; have counsel raise objections during those hearings; have counsel question any such witnesses; and have counsel provide a concluding presentation. For example, President Trump's counsel could have questioned counsel for HPSCI during his detailed presentation of evidence at the Committee's December 9 hearing. The President's counsel could also have questioned any of the four legal scholars who appeared during the Committee's December 4 hearing. The President could have submitted a statement in writing explaining his account of events— or he could have had his counsel make a presentation of evidence or request that other witnesses be called. President Trump did none of those things.

These privileges were equivalent to or exceeded those afforded to Presidents Nixon and Clinton. As noted previously, the Judiciary Committee conducted numerous closed-door briefings and took substantial investigative steps before affording any opportunities for President Nixon's counsel to participate, including conducting private interviews of witnesses. In addition, when President Nixon's counsel was later granted permission to attend closed-door presentations of evidence by Committee counsel, he could do so only as a passive observer. President Trump, by contrast, could have had his attorney cross-examine HPSCI's counsel during his presentation of evidence. That opportunity was also equivalent to the opportunity afforded to President Clinton to have his counsel cross-examine Independent Counsel Starr—which he did, at length.[113]

Furthermore, although President Trump has complained that his counsel was not afforded the opportunity to participate during HPSCI's proceedings, the proceedings against Presidents Nixon and Clinton demonstrate that in neither case was the President permitted to have counsel participate in the initial fact-gathering stages of the impeachment inquiry. As Committee staff explained during the Nixon impeachment inquiry—and then reiterated during the Clinton impeachment inquiry—there were no records from *any* prior impeachment inquiry of an "official under investigation participat[ing] in the investigation stage preceding commencement of committee hearings" or being offered access to Committee evidence "before it was offered at a hearing."[114] That is doubly true for the investigative proceedings that took place *before* the House began its impeachment inquiries against Presidents Nixon and Clinton. President Nixon certainly had no attorney present when prosecutors and grand juries began collecting evidence about Watergate and related matters, nor did he have an attorney present when the Senate Select Committee began interviewing witnesses and holding public hearings. Nor did President Clinton have an attorney present when prosecutors from the Office of Independent Counsel Kenneth Starr deposed witnesses and elicited their testimony before a grand jury.

Indeed, the proceedings before the Investigating Committees can be most closely analogized to the Senate Select Committee proceedings during Watergate. In both instances, Congressional bodies other than the House Judiciary Committee engaged in fact-finding investigations of grave Presidential

---

[113] *Starr Hearing* at 170-89.

[114] Mooney Letter at 3 (quoting Memorandum from Impeachment Inquiry Staff at 11, H. Comm. on the Judiciary (Apr. 3, 1974)); Memorandum from Impeachment Inquiry Staff, H. Comm. on the Judiciary at 18 (Apr. 3, 1974).

misconduct. Those investigations included private interviews and depositions followed by public hearings—after which all investigative files were provided to the House Judiciary Committee. The only difference is that in this case, transcripts of all interviews and depositions have been made public; all documentary evidence relied on by HPSCI in its report has been made available to the President; and the President's counsel could have participated and raised questions during presentations of evidence but chose not to.

3.   The President Was Not Entitled to Additional Procedural Rights

White House Counsel Pat A. Cipollone suggested in his October 8 letter on behalf of President Trump that the President was entitled to a host of additional due process rights during the House's impeachment inquiry, including "the right to see all evidence, to present evidence, to call witnesses, to have counsel present at all hearings, to cross-examine all witnesses, to make objections . . . , and to respond to evidence and testimony."[115] He also indicated that the President was entitled to review all favorable evidence and all evidence bearing on the credibility of witnesses.[116]

These are the types of procedural protections, however, typically afforded in criminal trials— not during preliminary investigative stages.[117] As HPSCI explained in its report, "there is no requirement that the House provide these procedures during an impeachment inquiry."[118] Rather, as Chairman Rodino stated during the Nixon impeachment inquiry, the President's participation "is not a right but a privilege or a courtesy."[119]

In any event, the core privileges described in Mr. Cipollone's letter *were* in fact offered to President Trump as courtesies during the Judiciary Committee's proceedings. The President was able to review "all evidence" relied on by the Investigating Committees, including evidence that the Minority's public report identified as favorable to him. During the Judiciary Committee's proceedings, the President had opportunities to present evidence, call witnesses, have counsel present to raise objections and cross-examine witnesses, and respond to the evidence raised against him. As the Rules Committee report accompanying H. Res. 660 noted, these privileges are "commensurate with the inquiry process followed in the cases of President Nixon and President Clinton."[120] President Trump simply chose not to avail himself of the procedural opportunities afforded to him.

D.   The Minority Was Afforded Full and Adequate Procedural Rights

Members of the Minority have also contended that they were not afforded the full procedural

---

[115] Oct. 8 Cipollone Letter.

[116] *Id.*

[117] *Cf., e.g., United States v. Calandra*, 414 U.S. 338, 350 (1974) (rejecting procedural protections that would "saddle a grand jury with minitrials and . . . assuredly impede its investigation").

[118] *Ukraine Report* at 212.

[119] *Nixon Impeachment Hearings* at 497.

[120] *Rules Committee Report* at 7.

rights provided to the Minority in prior impeachment inquiries and have raised a host of related objections to the proceedings. These claims lack merit.

First, the Minority has contended that it was deprived of the ability to subpoena witnesses and documentary evidence. However, the rules governing both the Nixon and Clinton impeachment inquiries rendered the Minority's subpoena authority equally contingent on the Majority. Under H. Res. 803 (governing the Nixon proceedings) and H. Res. 581 (governing the Clinton proceedings), the Chairman could refer a subpoena request by the Ranking Member for a vote by the full Committee if the Chairman disagreed with such a request.[121] So too here, H. Res. 660 authorized the Ranking Member to issue subpoenas with the Chairman's concurrence, or to refer such requests for a vote by the full Committee if the Chairman declined to concur.[122]

Second, the Minority has contended that the Committee should have heard testimony from additional witnesses they requested, including the whistleblower, various individuals with whom the whistleblower spoke, and even Chairman Schiff.[123] As an initial matter, during HPSCI's proceedings, the Minority called three witnesses of its choosing—Ambassador Volker, Undersecretary Hale, and Mr. Morrison. Ambassador Volker and Mr. Morrison testified on their own panel at length; and their testimony only served to corroborate other witnesses' accounts of the President's misconduct.[124] As to proceedings before the Judiciary Committee, the Minority called a witness of its choosing to present views during the Committee's December 4 hearing on *Constitutional Grounds for Presidential Impeachment*. Furthermore, Minority counsel had equal time to present arguments and evidence during the Committee's December 9 hearing. However, as Chairman Schiff stated and as Chairman Nadler reiterated, Congress has an imperative interest in protecting whistleblowers. And in this particular instance, Congress has an especially critical need to prevent the House's impeachment inquiry from being used to "facilitate the President's effort to threaten, intimidate, and retaliate against the whistleblower," which placed his or her personal safety at grave risk.[125] Furthermore, the whistleblower's allegations were not relied upon by HPSCI or the Judiciary Committee in reaching their conclusions, making his or her testimony "redundant and unnecessary."[126] Rather, HPSCI adduced

---

[121] H. Res. 803 § 2(b), 93d Cong. (1974); H. Res. 581 § 2(b), 105th Cong. (1998).

[122] H. Res. 660 § 4(c). The only distinction is that H. Res. 660 did not reciprocally allow the Ranking Member to refer subpoena requests by the Chairman for a full Committee vote. But that is because contemporary House Rules already permit the Judiciary Committee and other committees to delegate their subpoena authority to their chairs. House Rule XI.2(m)(3)(A)(i). It makes little sense to suggest that the subpoena authority of the Chairman of the Judiciary Committee should be *reduced* during an impeachment inquiry.

[123] *See* Letter from Doug Collins, Ranking Member, H. Comm. on the Judiciary, to Jerrold Nadler, Chairman, H. Comm. on the Judiciary (Dec. 6, 2019).

[124] *Impeachment Inquiry: Ambassador Kurt Volker and Timothy Morrison: Hearing Before the H. Perm. Select Comm. on Intelligence*, 116th Cong. (2019); *see, e.g.*, *Ukraine Report* at 123 (Ambassador Volker testified that Department of Justice did not make an official request for Ukraine's assistance in law enforcement investigations).

[125] Letter from Jerrold Nadler, Chairman, H. Comm. on the Judiciary, to Doug Collins, Ranking Member, H. Comm. on the Judiciary (Dec. 9, 2019).

[126] Letter from Adam B. Schiff, Chairman, H. Perm. Select Comm. on Intelligence, to Devin Nunes, Ranking Member, H. Perm. Select Comm. on Intelligence (Nov. 9, 2019).

independent and more direct evidence.[127]

In addition, the Ranking Member and all other Committee Members had the full opportunity to question HPSCI's lead investigative counsel during the Committee's December 9 hearing. Presentation of evidence by Committee counsel is consistent with the procedures followed during the Nixon impeachment inquiry—and in no impeachment inquiry has the House relied upon evidentiary presentations from another Member. Finally, the Ranking Member's request to hear testimony from other witnesses such as Hunter Biden was well outside the scope of the impeachment inquiry and would have allowed the President and his allies in Congress to propagate exactly the same kinds of misinformation that President Trump corruptly pressured Ukraine to propagate for his own political benefit. Such witnesses were entirely irrelevant to the question of whether President Trump abused his power for his personal gain.

Third, the Minority requested that it be entitled to a day of hearings pursuant to House Rule XI.2(j)(1), which entitles the Minority, upon request, to call witnesses to testify regarding any "measure or matter" considered in a committee hearing "during at least one day of hearing thereon." The Minority requested a hearing day on the subject of constitutional grounds for impeachment, as discussed at the Committee's December 4 hearing. However, as Chairman Nadler explained in ruling against the Ranking Member's point of order, this Rule does not require the Chairman "to schedule a hearing on a particular day," nor is the Chairman required "to schedule the hearing as a condition precedent to taking any specific legislative action."[128] Indeed, a report accompanying this provision when it was first promulgated stated that its purpose was not "an authorization for delaying tactics."[129] Chairman Nadler further explained that the Minority had been afforded the opportunity to have its views represented through its witness during the December 4 hearing, who testified at length. Additionally, the Chairman said he was willing to work with the Minority to schedule a Minority day for a hearing at an appropriate time.[130]

Fourth, the Minority has contended that the proceedings before the Judiciary Committee were inadequate because the Committee did not hear from "fact witnesses." The evidence in the House's impeachment inquiry consists of more than one hundred hours of deposition or interview testimony by seventeen witnesses, followed by five days of live televised hearings with twelve fact witnesses.[131] At bottom, the Minority's objection instead amounts to a claim that fact hearings do not count unless they occur before this Committee. That notion is inconsistent with both the Nixon and Clinton impeachment inquiries, in which the Judiciary Committee relied on, *inter alia*, public and private testimony before the Senate Select Committee in the case of President Nixon, and transcripts of grand jury proceedings in the case of President Clinton. In this instance, HPSCI and the Committees on Oversight and Reform

---

[127] *Id.*

[128] *H. Res. 755, Articles of Impeachment Against President Donald J. Trump: Markup Before H. Comm. on the Judiciary*, 116th Cong. (Dec. 11, 2019) (ruling on point of order by Chairman Nadler) (hereinafter "*H. Res. 755 Markup*").

[129] *Legislative Reorganization Act of 1970*, H. Rep. No. 91-1215, at 6 (1970).

[130] *H. Res. 755 Markup* (ruling on point of order by Chairman Nadler).

[131] *Ukraine Report* at 7.

and Foreign Affairs conducted their witness examinations ably and transparently, working within their subject matter areas of expertise. Furthermore, to the extent Judiciary Committee members wished to probe the evidentiary record, they had opportunities to do so when HPSCI's Majority and Minority counsels presented evidence before the Committee.

Finally, the Minority has repeatedly suggested that the House's impeachment inquiry has been rushed. The House's investigation of the President's conduct regarding Ukraine began in early September and has proceeded for more than three months. In addition, that investigation followed extensive investigations into the President's having welcomed foreign assistance from Russia during the 2016 United States Presidential election and then obstructing the law enforcement investigation that ensued. President Trump's efforts to enlist the assistance of another foreign government for the 2020 United States Presidential election therefore raised immediate alarm and required prompt action. As HPSCI's report states, "[w]ith this backdrop, the solicitation of new foreign intervention was the act of a president unbound."[132]

The House's investigation of President Trump's misconduct—which occupied a time frame commensurate with that for the impeachment inquiry against President Clinton—was fair and thorough. The Investigating Committees assembled a comprehensive record that was more than sufficient to provide them with a thorough picture of the facts. To the extent gaps remained, they resulted from President Trump's obstruction of Congress. The urgency posed by the President's abuse of his office, his invitation of foreign interference in the 2020 United States Presidential election, and his disregard for any mechanisms of accountability required concerted action by the House, not further delay.

V.   Conclusion

The House conducted a thorough and fair inquiry regarding President Trump's misconduct, notwithstanding the unique and extraordinary challenges posed by the President's obstruction. The Investigating Committees amassed thorough and irrefutable evidence that the President abused his office by pressuring a foreign government to interfere in the next election. When committees of the House—rather than a grand jury, a Senate committee, or an Independent Counsel—must serve as primary investigators in an impeachment inquiry, they have an obligation to balance investigative needs and best practices for collecting evidence with the President's interest in telling his story and the public interest in transparency. But that does not entitle the President to inject himself at each and every stage of the proceedings, thus confounding the House's inquiry.

Here, consistent with historical practice, the House divided its impeachment inquiry into two phases, first collecting evidence and then bringing that evidence before the Judiciary Committee for its consideration of articles of impeachment. The Judiciary Committee then evaluated the evidence in a process that afforded President Trump the same or more privileges of his predecessors who have faced impeachment inquiries. The President's refusal to comply with or participate in these proceedings only confirmed his intent to obstruct Congress in the performance of its essential constitutional functions.

---

[132] *Id.* at 10.

Constitutional Grounds for Presidential Impeachment

I.   Introduction

Our President holds the ultimate public trust. He is vested with powers so great that they frightened the Framers of our Constitution; in exchange, he swears an oath to faithfully execute the laws that hold those powers in check. This oath is no formality. The Framers foresaw that a faithless President could destroy their experiment in democracy. As George Mason warned at the Constitutional Convention, held in Philadelphia in 1787, "if we do not provide against corruption, our government will soon be at an end."[133] Mason evoked a well-known historical truth: when corrupt motives take root, they drive an endless thirst for power and contempt for checks and balances. It is then only the smallest of steps toward acts of oppression and assaults on free and fair elections. A President faithful only to himself—who will sell out democracy and national security for his own personal advantage— is a danger to every American. Indeed, he threatens America itself.

Impeachment is the Constitution's final answer to a President who mistakes himself for a monarch. Aware that power corrupts, our Framers built other guardrails against that error. The Constitution thus separates governmental powers, imposes an oath of faithful execution, prohibits profiting from office, and guarantees accountability through regular elections. But the Framers were not naïve. They knew, and feared, that someday a corrupt executive might claim he could do anything he wanted as President. Determined to protect our democracy, the Framers built a safety valve into the Constitution: A President can be removed from office if the House of Representatives approves articles of impeachment charging him with "Treason, Bribery, or other high Crimes and Misdemeanors," and if two-thirds of the Senate votes to find the President guilty of such misconduct after a trial.[134]

As Justice Joseph Story recognized, "the power of impeachment is not one expected in any government to be in constant or frequent exercise."[135] When faced with credible evidence of extraordinary wrongdoing, however, it is incumbent on the House to investigate and determine whether impeachment is warranted. On October 31, 2019, the House approved H. Res. 660, which, among other things, confirmed the preexisting inquiry "into whether sufficient grounds exist for the House of Representatives to exercise its Constitutional power to impeach Donald John Trump, President of the United States of America."[136]

The Judiciary Committee now faces questions of extraordinary importance. In prior impeachment inquiries addressing allegations of Presidential misconduct, the staff of the Judiciary

---

[133] 1 Max Farrand, ed., *The Records of the Federal Convention of 1787,* 392 (1911) (hereinafter, "*Records of the Federal Convention*").

[134] U.S. CONST. art. II, § 4; *id.* art. I, § 5, cl. 5; *id.* art. I, § 3, cl. 6.

[135] 2 Joseph Story, *Commentaries on the Constitution of the United States,* 221 (1833).

[136] H.Res. 660, 116th Cong. (2019).

Committee has prepared reports addressing relevant principles of constitutional law.[137] Consistent with that practice, and to assist the Committee and the House in working toward a resolution of the questions before them, the majority staff prepared the following report to explore the meaning of the words in the Constitution's Impeachment Clause: "Treason, Bribery, or other high Crimes and Misdemeanors." The report also describes the impeachment process and addresses several mistaken claims about impeachment that have recently drawn public notice.

II.   Summary of Principal Conclusions

Our principal conclusions are as follows.

The purpose of impeachment. As the Framers deliberated in Philadelphia, Mason posed a profound question: "Shall any man be above justice?"[138] By authorizing Congress to remove Presidents for egregious misconduct, the Framers offered a resounding answer. As Mason elaborated, "some mode of displacing an unfit magistrate is rendered indispensable by the fallibility of those who choose, as well as by the corruptibility of the man chosen."[139] Unlike Britain's monarch, the President would answer personally—to Congress and thus to the Nation—if he engaged in serious wrongdoing. Alexander Hamilton explained that the President would have no more resemblance to the British king than to "the Grand Seignior, to the khan of Tartary, [or] to the Man of the Seven Mountains."[140] Whereas "the person of the king of Great Britain is sacred and inviolable," the President of the United States could be "impeached, tried, and upon conviction . . . removed from office."[141] Critically, though, impeachment goes no further. It results only in loss of political power. This speaks to the nature of impeachment: it exists not to inflict punishment for past wrongdoing, but rather to save the Nation from misconduct that endangers democracy and the rule of law. Thus, the ultimate question in an impeachment is whether leaving the President in our highest office imperils the Constitution.[142]

Impeachable offenses. The Framers were careful students of history and knew that threats to democracy can take many forms. They feared would-be monarchs, but also warned against fake populists, charismatic demagogues, and corrupt kleptocrats. The Framers thus intended impeachment to reach the full spectrum of Presidential misconduct that menaced the Constitution. Because they could not anticipate and prohibit every threat a President might someday pose, the Framers adopted a standard sufficiently general and flexible to meet unknown future circumstances: "Treason, Bribery, or other high Crimes and Misdemeanors." This standard was proposed by Mason and was meant, in his words,

---

[137] *Staff of H. Comm. on the Judiciary, Constitutional Grounds for Presidential Impeachment 93d Cong.,* 4 (Comm. Print 1974) (hereinafter "*Staff Report on Constitutional Grounds for Presidential Impeachment (1974)*"); *Staff of H. Comm. on the Judiciary, Constitutional Grounds for Presidential Impeachment: Modern Precedents, 105th Cong.* (Comm. Print 1998) (hereinafter "*Staff Report on Constitutional Grounds for Presidential Impeachment: Modern Precedents (1998)*").

[138] 2 Farrand, *Records of the Federal Convention* at 65.

[139] 1 Farrand, *Records of the Federal Convention* at 86.

[140] Alexander Hamilton, *Federalist No. 69*, 444 (Benjamin Fletcher Wright ed., 2004).

[141] *Id.*

[142] *See* Laurence H. Tribe, *American Constitutional Law* 155 (3d ed. 2000).

to capture all manner of "great and dangerous offenses" against the Constitution.[143]

Treason and bribery. Applying traditional tools of interpretation puts a sharper point on this definition of "high Crimes and Misdemeanors." For starters, it is useful to consider the two impeachable offenses that the Framers identified for us. "Treason" is an unforgiveable betrayal of the Nation and its security. A President who levies war against the government, or lends aid and comfort to our enemies, cannot persist in office; a President who betrays the Nation once will most certainly do so again. "Bribery," in turn, sounds in abuse of power. Impeachable bribery occurs when the President offers, solicits, or accepts something of personal value to influence his own official actions. By rendering such bribery impeachable, the Framers sought to ensure that the Nation could expel a leader who would sell out the interests of "We the People" for his own personal gain.

In identifying "other high Crimes and Misdemeanors," we are guided by the text and structure of the Constitution, the records of the Constitutional Convention and state ratifying debates, and the history of impeachment practice. These sources demonstrate that the Framers principally intended impeachment for three overlapping forms of Presidential wrongdoing: (1) abuse of power, (2) betrayal of the nation through foreign entanglements, and (3) corruption of office and elections. Any one of these violations of the public trust justifies impeachment; when combined in a single course of conduct, they state the strongest possible case for impeachment and removal from office.

Abuse of power. There are at least as many ways to abuse power as there are powers vested in the President. It would thus be an exercise in futility to attempt a list of every abuse of power constituting "high Crimes and Misdemeanors." That said, impeachable abuse of power can be roughly divided into two categories: engaging in official acts forbidden by law and engaging in official action with motives forbidden by law. As James Iredell explained, "the president would be liable to impeachments [if] he had … acted from some corrupt motive or other."[144] This warning echoed Edmund Randolph's teaching that impeachment must be allowed because "the Executive will have great opportunitys of abusing his power."[145] President Richard Nixon's conduct has come to exemplify impeachable abuse of power: he acted with corrupt motives in obstructing justice and using official power to target his political opponents, and his decision to unlawfully defy subpoenas issued by the House impeachment inquiry was unconstitutional on its face.

Betrayal involving foreign powers. As much as the Framers feared abuse, they feared betrayal still more. That anxiety is shot through their discussion of impeachment—and explains why "Treason" heads the Constitution's list of impeachable offenses. James Madison put it simply: the President "might betray his trust to foreign powers."[146] Although the Framers did not intend impeachment for good faith disagreements on matters of diplomacy, they were explicit that betrayal of the Nation through schemes with foreign powers justified that remedy. Indeed, foreign interference in the

---

[143] 2 Farrand, *Records of the Federal Convention* at 550.

[144] Quoted in *Background and History of Impeachment: Hearing before the Subcomm. On the Constitution of the H. Comm on the Judiciary*, 105th Cong. 49 (1999) (hereinafter "*1998 Background and History of Impeachment Hearing*").

[145] 2 Farrand, *Records of the Federal Convention* at 67.

[146] *Id.* at 65-66.

American political system was among the gravest dangers feared by the Founders of our Nation and the Framers of our Constitution. In his farewell address, George Washington thus warned Americans "to be constantly awake, since history and experience prove that foreign influence is one of the most baneful foes of republican government."[147] And in a letter to Thomas Jefferson, John Adams wrote: "You are apprehensive of foreign Interference, Intrigue, Influence. So am I.—But, as often as Elections happen, the danger of foreign Influence recurs."[148]

Corruption. Lurking beneath the Framers' discussion of impeachment was the most ancient and implacable foe of democracy: corruption. The Framers saw no shortage of threats to the Republic, and sought to guard against them, "but the big fear underlying all the small fears was whether they'd be able to control corruption."[149] As Madison put it, corruption "might be fatal to the Republic."[150] This was not just a matter of thwarting bribes; it was a far more expansive challenge. The Framers celebrated civic virtue and love of country; they wrote rules to ensure officials would not use public power for private gain.

Impeachment was seen as especially necessary for Presidential conduct corrupting our system of political self-government. That concern arose in multiple contexts as the Framers debated the Constitution. The most important was the risk that Presidents would place their personal interest in re-election above our bedrock national commitment to democracy. The Framers knew that corrupt leaders concentrate power by manipulating elections and undercutting adversaries. They despised King George III, who "resorted to influencing the electoral process and the representatives in Parliament in order to gain [his] treacherous ends."[151] That is why the Framers deemed electoral treachery a central ground for impeachment. The very premise of the Constitution is that the American people govern themselves, and choose their leaders, through free and fair elections. When the President concludes that elections might threaten his grasp on power and abuses his office to sabotage opponents or invite inference, he rejects democracy itself and must be removed.

Conclusions regarding the nature of impeachable offenses. In sum, history teaches that "high Crimes and Misdemeanors" referred mainly to acts committed by public officials, using their power or privileges, that inflicted grave harm on our political order. Such great and dangerous offenses included treason, bribery, serious abuse of power, betrayal of the national interest through foreign entanglements, and corruption of office and elections. They were unified by a clear theme: officials who abused, abandoned, or sought personal benefit from their public trust—and who threatened the rule of law if left in power—faced impeachment. Each of these acts, moreover, should be plainly wrong to reasonable officials and persons of honor. When a political official uses political power in ways that substantially harm our political system, Congress can strip them of that power.

---

[147] *George Washington Farewell Address (1796), George Washington Papers, Series 2, Letterbooks 1754-1799: Letterbook 24, April 3, 1793 - March 3, 1797,* LIBRARY OF CONGRESS.

[148] *To Thomas Jefferson from John Adams, 6 December 1787,* Founders Online, NATIONAL ARCHIVES.

[149] Zephyr Teachout, *Corruption in America: From Benjamin Franklin's Snuff Box to Citizens United* 57 (2014).

[150] 2 Farrand, *Records of the Federal Convention* at 66.

[151] Gordon S. Wood, *The Creation of the American Republic, 1776-1787* 33 (1998).

Within these parameters, and guided by fidelity to the Constitution, the House must judge whether the President's misconduct is grave enough to require impeachment. That step must never be taken lightly. It is a momentous act, justified only when the President's full course of conduct, assessed without favor or prejudice, is "seriously incompatible with either the constitutional form and principles of our government or the proper performance of constitutional duties of the presidential office."[152] But when that high standard is met, the Constitution calls the House to action—and the House, in turn, must rise to the occasion. In such cases, a decision *not* to impeach can harm democracy and set an ominous precedent.

The criminality issue. It is occasionally suggested that Presidents can be impeached only if they have committed crimes. That position was rejected in President Nixon's case, and then rejected again in President Clinton's, and should be rejected once more. Offenses against the Constitution are different than offenses against the criminal code. Some crimes, like jaywalking, are not impeachable. And some forms of misconduct may offend both the Constitution and the criminal law. Impeachment and criminality must therefore be assessed separately—even though the President's commission of indictable crimes may further support a case for impeachment and removal. Ultimately, the House must judge whether a President's conduct offends and endangers the Constitution itself.

Fallacies about impeachment. In the final section, we briefly address six falsehoods about impeachment that have recently drawn public notice.

First, contrary to mistaken claims otherwise, we demonstrate that the current impeachment inquiry has complied in every respect with the Constitution, the Rules of the House, and historic practice and precedent of the House.

Second, we address several evidentiary matters. The House impeachment inquiry has compiled substantial direct and circumstantial evidence bearing on the issues at hand. Nonetheless, President Trump has objected that some of the evidence gathered by the House comes from witnesses lacking first-hand knowledge of his conduct. But in the same breath, he has unlawfully ordered many witnesses with first-hand knowledge to defy House subpoenas. As we show, President Trump's assertions regarding the evidence before the House are misplaced as a matter of constitutional law and common sense.

Third, we consider President Trump's claim that his actions are protected because of his right under Article II of the Constitution "to do whatever I want as president."[153] This claim is wrong, and profoundly so, because our Constitution rejects pretensions to monarchy and binds Presidents with law. That is true even of powers vested exclusively in the chief executive. If those powers are invoked for corrupt reasons, or wielded in an abusive manner harming the constitutional system, the President is

---

[152] *Report of the Committee on the Judiciary, Impeachment of Richard M. Nixon, President of the United States,* H.. Rep. No. 93-1305 8 (1974) (hereinafter "*Committee Report on Nixon Articles of Impeachment* (1974)").

[153] *Remarks by President Trump at Turning Point USA's Teen Student Action Summit 2019*, July 23, 2019, THE WHITE HOUSE.

subject to impeachment for "high Crimes and Misdemeanors." This is a core premise of the impeachment power.

Fourth, we address whether the House must accept at face value President Trump's claim that his motives were not corrupt. In short, no. When the House probes a President's state of mind, its mandate is to find the facts. That means evaluating the President's account of his motives to see if it rings true. The question is not whether the President's conduct *could have* resulted from permissible motives. It is whether the President's *real reasons*, the ones in his mind at the time, were legitimate. Where the House discovers persuasive evidence of corrupt wrongdoing, it is entitled to rely upon that evidence to impeach.

Fifth, we explain that attempted Presidential wrongdoing is impeachable. Mason himself said so at the Constitutional Convention, where he described "*attempts* to subvert the Constitution" as a core example of "great and dangerous offenses."[154] Moreover, the Judiciary Committee reached the same conclusion in President Nixon's case. Historical precedent thus confirms that ineptitude and insubordination do not afford the President a defense to impeachment. A President cannot escape impeachment just because his scheme to abuse power, betray the nation, or corrupt elections was discovered and abandoned.

Finally, we consider whether impeachment "nullifies" the last election or denies voters their voice in the next one. The Framers themselves weighed this question. They considered relying solely on elections—rather than impeachment—to remove wayward Presidents. That position was firmly rejected. No President is entitled to persist in office after committing "high Crimes and Misdemeanors," and no one who voted for him in the last election is entitled to expect he will do so. Where the President's misconduct is aimed at corrupting elections, relying on elections to solve the problem is no safeguard at all.

III.   The Purpose of Impeachment

Freedom must not be taken for granted. It demands constant protection from leaders whose taste of power sparks a voracious need for more. Time and again, republics have fallen to officials who care little for the law and use the public trust for private gain.

The Framers of the Constitution knew this well. They saw corruption erode the British constitution from within. They heard kings boast of their own excellence while conspiring with foreign powers and consorting with shady figures. As talk of revolution spread, they objected as King George III used favors and party politics to control Parliament, aided by men who sold their souls and welcomed oppression.

The Framers risked their freedom, and their lives, to escape that monarchy. So did their families and many of their friends. Together, they resolved to build a nation committed to democracy and the rule of law—a beacon to the world in an age of aristocracy. In the United States of America, "We the

---

[154] Cass R. Sunstein, *Impeachment: A Citizen's Guide* 47 (2017).

People" would be sovereign. We would choose our own leaders and hold them accountable for how they exercised power.

As they designed our government at the Constitutional Convention, however, the Framers faced a dilemma. On the one hand, many of them embraced the need for a powerful chief executive. This had been cast into stark relief by the failure of the Nation's very first constitution, the Articles of Confederation, which put Congress in charge at the federal level. The ensuing discord led James Madison to warn, "it is not possible that a government can last long under these circumstances."[155] The Framers therefore created the Presidency. A single official could lead the Nation with integrity, energy, and dispatch—and would be held personally responsible for honoring that immense public trust.

Power, though, is a double-edged sword. "The power to do good meant also the power to do harm, the power to serve the republic also meant the power to demean and defile it."[156] The President would be vested with breathtaking authority. If corrupt motives took root in his mind, displacing civic virtue and love of country, he could sabotage the Constitution. That was clear to the Framers, who saw corruption as "the great force that had undermined republics throughout history."[157] Obsessed with the fall of Rome, they knew that corruption marked a leader's path to abuse and betrayal. Mason thus emphasized, "if we do not provide against corruption, our government will soon be at an end." This warning against corruption—echoed no fewer than 54 times by 15 delegates at the Convention— extended far beyond bribes and presents. To the Framers, corruption was fundamentally about the misuse of a position of public trust for any improper private benefit. It thus went to the heart of their conception of public service. As a leading historian recounts, "a corrupt political actor would either purposely ignore or forget the public good as he used the reins of power."[158] Because men and women are not angels, corruption could not be fully eradicated, even in virtuous officials, but "its power can be subdued with the right combination of culture and political rules."[159]

The Framers therefore erected safeguards against Presidential abuse. Most famously, they divided power among three branches of government that had the means and motive to balance each other. "Ambition," Madison reasoned, "must be made to counteract ambition."[160] In addition, the Framers subjected the President to election every four years and established the Electoral College (which, they hoped, would select virtuous, capable leaders and refuse to re-elect corrupt or unpopular ones). Finally, the Framers imposed on the President a duty to faithfully execute the laws—and required him to accept that duty in a solemn oath.[161] To the Framers, the concept of faithful execution was profoundly important. It prohibited the President from taking official acts in bad faith or with corrupt

---

[155] Quoted in *id.* at 27.

[156] Arthur M. Schlesinger, Jr., *The Imperial Presidency* 415 (1973).

[157] Elizabeth B. Wydra & Brianne J. Gorod, *The First Magistrate in Foreign Pay*, THE NEW REPUBLIC, Nov. 11, 2019.

[158] Teachout, *Corruption in America* at 48.

[159] *Id.* at 47.

[160] James Madison, *Federalist No. 51* at 356.

[161] U.S. CONST. art. II, § 1, cl. 8.

intent, as well as acts beyond what the law authorized.[162]

A few Framers would have stopped there. This minority feared vesting any branch of government with the power to end a Presidency; as they saw it, even extreme Presidential wrongdoing could be managed in the normal course (mainly by periodic elections).

That view was decisively rejected. As Professor Raoul Berger writes, "the Framers were steeped in English history; the shades of despotic kings and conniving ministers marched before them."[163] Haunted by those lessons, and convening in the shadow of revolution, the Framers would not deny the Nation an escape from Presidents who deemed themselves above the law. So they turned to a mighty constitutional power, one that offered a peaceful and politically accountable method for ending an oppressive Presidency.

This was impeachment, a legal relic from the British past that over the preceding century had found a new lease on life in the North American colonies. First deployed in 1376—and wielded in fits and starts over the following 400 years—impeachment allowed Parliament to charge royal ministers with abuse, remove them from office, and imprison them. Over time, impeachment helped Parliament shift power away from royal absolutism and encouraged more politically accountable administration. In 1679, it was thus proclaimed in the House of Commons that impeachment was "the chief institution for the preservation of government."[164] That sentiment was echoed in the New World. Even as Parliamentary impeachment fell into disuse by the early 1700s, colonists in Maryland, Pennsylvania, and Massachusetts laid claim to this prerogative as part of their English birthright. During the revolution, ten states ratified constitutions allowing the impeachment of executive officials—and put that power to use in cases of corruption and abuse of power.[165] Unlike in Britain, though, American impeachment did not result in fines or jailtime. It simply removed officials from political power when their conduct required it.

Familiar with the use of impeachment to address lawless officials, the Framers offered a clear answer to Mason's question at the Constitutional Convention, "Shall any man be above justice"?[166] As Mason himself explained, "some mode of displacing an unfit magistrate is rendered indispensable by the fallibility of those who choose, as well as by the corruptibility of the man chosen."[167] Future Vice President Elbridge Gerry agreed, adding that impeachment repudiates the fallacy that our "chief magistrate could do no wrong."[168] Benjamin Franklin, in turn, made the case that impeachment is "the best way" to assess claims of serious wrongdoing by a President; without it, those accusations would

---

[162] *See* Andrew Kent, Ethan J. Leib & Jed Handelsman Shugerman, *Faithful Execution and Article II*, 132 HARV. L. REV. 2111- 2121 (2019).

[163] Raoul Berger, *Impeachment: The Constitutional Problems* 4 (1974).

[164] *Id.* at 1 n.2.

[165] Frank O. Bowman, III, *High Crimes and Misdemeanors: A History of Impeachment for the Age of Trump* 72 (2019).

[166] 2 Farrand, *Records of the Federal Convention* at 65-67.

[167] 1 Farrand, *Records of the Federal Convention* at 66.

[168] 2 Farrand, *Records of the Federal Convention* at 66.

fester unresolved and invite enduring conflict over Presidential malfeasance.[169]

Unlike in Britain, the President would answer personally—to Congress and thus to the Nation—for any serious wrongdoing. For that reason, as Hamilton later explained, the President would have no more resemblance to the British king than to "the Grand Seignior, to the khan of Tartary, [or] to the Man of the Seven Mountains."[170] Whereas "the person of the king of Great Britain is sacred and inviolable," the President could be "impeached, tried, and upon conviction ... removed from office."[171]

Of course, the decision to subject the President to impeachment was not the end of the story. The Framers also had to specify how this would work in practice. After long and searching debate they made three crucial decisions, each of which sheds light on their understanding of impeachment's proper role in our constitutional system.

First, they limited the consequences of impeachment to "removal from Office" and "disqualification" from future officeholding.[172] To the extent the President's wrongful conduct also breaks the law, the Constitution expressly reserves criminal punishment for the ordinary processes of criminal law. In that respect, "the consequences of impeachment and conviction go just far enough, and no further than, to remove the threat posed to the Republic by an unfit official."[173] This speaks to the very nature of impeachment: it exists not to inflict personal punishment for past wrongdoing, but rather to protect against future Presidential misconduct that would endanger democracy and the rule of law.[174]

Second, the Framers vested the House with "the sole Power of Impeachment."[175] The House thus serves in a role analogous to a grand jury and prosecutor: it investigates the President's misconduct and decides whether to formally accuse him of impeachable acts. As James Iredell explained during debates over whether to ratify the Constitution, "this power is lodged in those who represent the great body of the people, because the occasion for its exercise will arise from acts of great injury to the community."[176] The Senate, in turn, holds "the sole Power to try all Impeachments."[177] When the Senate sits as a court of impeachment for the President, each Senator must swear a special oath, the Chief Justice of the United States presides, and conviction requires "the concurrence of two thirds of the Members present."[178] By designating Congress to accuse the President and conduct his trial, the

---

[169] James Madison, *Notes on Debates in the Federal Convention of 1787* 332 (1987).

[170] Alexander Hamilton, *Federalist No. 69* at 444.

[171] *Id.*

[172] U.S. CONST. art. I, § 43, cl. 7.

[173] John O. McGinnis, *Impeachment: The Structural Understanding*, 67 GEO. WASH. L. REV. 650, 650 (1999).

[174] *See* Tribe, *American Constitutional Law* at 155.

[175] U.S. CONST. tart. I, § 2, cl. 5.

[176] 4 Jonathan Elliot, ed., *The Debates in the Several State Conventions on the Adoption of the Federal Constitution* 113 (1861) (hereinafter "*Debates in the Several State Conventions*").

[177] U.S. CONST. art. I, § 3, cl. 6.

[178] *Id.*

Framers confirmed—in Hamilton's words—that impeachment concerns an "abuse or violation of some public trust" with "injuries done immediately to the society itself."[179] Impeachment is reserved for offenses against our political system. It is therefore prosecuted and judged by Congress, speaking for the Nation.

Last, but not least, the Framers imposed a rule of wrongdoing. The President cannot be removed based on poor management, general incompetence, or unpopular policies. Instead, the question in any impeachment inquiry is whether the President has engaged in misconduct justifying an early end to his term in office: "Treason, Bribery, or other high Crimes and Misdemeanors."[180] This phrase had a particular legal meaning to the Framers. It is to that understanding, and to its application in prior Presidential impeachments, that we now turn.

IV.   Impeachable Offenses

As careful students of history, the Framers knew that threats to democracy can take many forms. They feared would-be monarchs, but also warned against fake populists, charismatic demagogues, and corrupt kleptocrats. In describing the kind of leader who might menace the Nation, Hamilton offered an especially striking portrait:

> When a man unprincipled in private life[,] desperate in his fortune, bold in his temper . . . known to have scoffed in private at the principles of liberty — when such a man is seen to mount the hobby horse of popularity — to join in the cry of danger to liberty — to take every opportunity of embarrassing the General Government & bringing it under suspicion — to flatter and fall in with all the non sense [sic] of the zealots of the day — It may justly be suspected that his object is to throw things into confusion that he may ride the storm and direct the whirlwind.[181]

This prophesy echoed Hamilton's warning, in *Federalist No. 1*, that "of those men who have overturned the liberties of republics, the greatest number have begun their career by paying an obsequious court to the people; commencing demagogues, and ending tyrants."[182]

The Framers thus intended impeachment to reach the full spectrum of Presidential misconduct that threatened the Constitution. They also intended our Constitution to endure for the ages. Because they could not anticipate and specifically prohibit every threat a President might someday pose, the Framers adopted a standard sufficiently general and flexible to meet unknown future circumstances. This standard was meant—as Mason put it—to capture all manner of "great and dangerous offenses" incompatible with the Constitution. When the President uses the powers of his high office to benefit himself, while injuring or ignoring the American people he is oath-bound to serve, he has committed

---

[179] Alexander Hamilton, *Federalist No. 65* at 426.

[180] U.S. CONST. art. II, § 4.

[181] Alexander Hamilton, *"Objections and Answers respecting the Administration of the Government,"* Founders Online, NATIONAL ARCHIVES.

[182] Alexander Hamilton, *Federalist No. 1* at 91.

an impeachable offense.

Applying the tools of legal interpretation, as we do below, puts a sharper point on this definition of "high Crimes and Misdemeanors." It also confirms that the Framers principally aimed the impeachment power at a few core evils, each grounded in a unifying fear that a President might abandon his duty to faithfully execute the laws. Where the President engages in serious abuse of power, betrays the national interest through foreign entanglements, or corrupts his office or elections, he has undoubtedly committed "high Crimes and Misdemeanors" as understood by the Framers. Any one of these violations of the public trust is impeachable. When combined in a scheme to advance the President's personal interests while ignoring or injuring the Constitution, they state the strongest possible case for impeachment and removal from office.

A.   Lessons from British and Early American History

As Hamilton recounted, Britain afforded "[t]he model from which the idea of [impeachment] has been borrowed."[183] That was manifestly true of the phrase "high Crimes and Misdemeanors." The Framers could have authorized impeachment for "crimes" or "serious crimes." Or they could have followed the practice of many American state constitutions and permitted impeachment for "maladministration" or "malpractice."[184] But they instead selected a "unique phrase used for centuries in English parliamentary impeachments."[185] To understand their choice requires a quick tour through history.

That tour offers two lessons. The first is that the phrase "high Crimes and Misdemeanors" was used *only* for parliamentary impeachments; it was never used in the ordinary criminal law.[186] Moreover, in the 400-year history of British impeachments, the House of Commons impeached many officials on grounds that did not involve any discernibly criminal conduct. Indeed, the House of Commons did so yet again just as the Framers gathered in Philadelphia. That same month, Edmund Burke—the celebrated champion of American liberty—brought twenty-two articles of impeachment against Warren Hastings, the Governor General of India. Burke charged Hastings with offenses including abuse of power, corruption, disregarding treaty obligations, and misconduct of local wars. Historians have confirmed that "none of the charges could fairly be classed as criminal conduct in any technical sense."[187] Aware of that fact, Burke accused Hastings of "[c]rimes, not against forms, but against those eternal laws of justice, which are our rule and our birthright: his offenses are not in formal, technical language, but in reality, in substance and effect, High Crimes and High Misdemeanors."[188]

Burke's denunciation of Hastings points to the second lesson from British history: "high Crimes

---

[183] Alexander Hamilton, *Federalist No. 65* at 427.

[184] Bowman, *High Crimes and Misdemeanors* at 65-72.

[185] *Constitutional Grounds for Presidential Impeachment* (1974) at 4.

[186] *See id.*

[187] Bowman, *High Crimes and Misdemeanors* at 41.

[188] *Id.*

and Misdemeanors" were understood as offenses against the constitutional system itself. This is confirmed by use of the word "high," as well as Parliamentary practice. From 1376 to 1787, the House of Commons impeached officials on seven general grounds: (1) abuse of power; (2) betrayal of the nation's security and foreign policy; (3) corruption; (4) armed rebellion [a.k.a. treason]; (5) bribery; (6) neglect of duty; and (7) violating Parliament's constitutional prerogatives.[189] To the Framers and their contemporaries learned in the law, the phrase "high Crimes and Misdemeanors" would have called to mind these offenses against the body politic.

The same understanding prevailed on this side of the Atlantic. In the colonial period and under newly-ratified state constitutions, most impeachments targeted abuse of power, betrayal of the revolutionary cause, corruption, treason, and bribery.[190] Many Framers at the Constitutional Convention had participated in drafting their state constitutions, or in colonial and state removal proceedings, and were steeped in this outlook on impeachment. Further, the Framers knew well the Declaration of Independence, "whose bill of particulars against King George III modeled what [we would] now view as articles of impeachment."[191] That bill of particulars did not dwell on technicalities of criminal law, but rather charged the king with a "long train of abuses and usurpations," including misuse of power, efforts to obstruct and undermine elections, and violating individual rights.[192]

History thus teaches that "high Crimes and Misdemeanors" referred mainly to acts committed by public officials, using their power or privileges, that inflicted grave harm on society itself. Such great and dangerous offenses included treason, bribery, abuse of power, betrayal of the nation, and corruption of office. They were unified by a clear theme: officials who abused, abandoned, or sought personal benefit from their public trust—and who threatened the rule of law if left in power—faced impeachment and removal.

B.   Treason and Bribery

For the briefest of moments at the Constitutional Convention, it appeared as though Presidential impeachment might be restricted to "treason, or bribery."[193] But when this suggestion reached the floor, Mason revolted. With undisguised alarm, he warned that such limited grounds for impeachment would miss "attempts to subvert the Constitution," as well as "many great and dangerous offenses."[194] Here he invoked the charges pending in Parliament against Hastings as a case warranting impeachment for reasons other than treason. To "extend the power of impeachments," Mason initially suggested adding "or maladministration" after "treason, or bribery."[195] Madison, however, objected that "so vague a term

---

[189] *Id.* at 46; Berger, *Impeachment* at 70.

[190] *See* Peter Charles Hoffer & N. E. H. Hull, *Impeachment in America, 1635-1805* 1-106 (1984).

[191] Laurence H. Tribe & Joshua Matz, *To End a Presidency: The Power of Impeachment* 7 (2018).

[192] *The Declaration of Independence, Thomas Jefferson, et al, July 4, 1776, Copy of Declaration of Independence,* LIBRARY OF CONGRESS.

[193] 2 Farrand, *Records of the Federal Convention* at 550.

[194] Id.

[195] Id.

will be equivalent to a tenure during the pleasure of the Senate."[196] In response, Mason substituted "other high Crimes and Misdemeanors."[197] Apparently pleased with Mason's compromise, the Convention accepted his proposal and moved on.

This discussion confirms that Presidential impeachment is warranted for all manner of great and dangerous offenses that subvert the Constitution. It also sheds helpful light on the nature of impeachable offenses: in identifying "*other* high Crimes and Misdemeanors," we can start with two that the Framers identified for us, "Treason" and "Bribery."

1.   **Impeachable Treason**

Under Article III of the Constitution, "treason against the United States, shall consist only in levying War against them, or in adhering to their Enemies, giving them Aid and Comfort."[198] In other words, a person commits treason if he uses armed force in an attempt to overthrow the government, or if he knowingly gives aid and comfort to nations (or organizations) with which the United States is in a state of declared or open war. At the very heart of "Treason" is deliberate betrayal of the nation and its security. Such betrayal would not only be unforgivable, but would also confirm that the President remains a threat if allowed to remain in office. A President who has knowingly betrayed national security is a President who will do so again. He endangers our lives and those of our allies.

2.   **Impeachable Bribery**

The essence of impeachable bribery is a government official's exploitation of his or her public duties for personal gain. To the Framers, it was received wisdom that nothing can be "a greater Temptation to Officers [than] to abuse their Power by Bribery and Extortion."[199] To guard against that risk, the Framers authorized the impeachment of a President who offers, solicits, or accepts something of personal value to influence his own official actions. By rendering such "Bribery" impeachable, the Framers sought to ensure that the Nation could expel a leader who would sell out the interests of "We the People" to achieve his own personal gain.

Unlike "Treason," which is defined in Article III, "Bribery" is not given an express definition in the Constitution. But as Justice Joseph Story explained, a "proper exposition of the nature and limits of this offense" can be found in the Anglo-American common law tradition known well to our Framers.[200] That understanding, in turn, can be refined by reference to the Constitution's text and the records of the Constitutional Convention.[201]

---

[196] Id.

[197] Id.

[198] U.S. CONST. art. III, § 3, cl. 1.

[199] William Hawkins, *A Treatise of Pleas to the Crown,* ch. 67, § 3 (1716).

[200] 2 Story, *Commentaries* at 263; *see also* H. Rep. No. 946 at 19 (1912).

[201] For example, while the English common law tradition principally addressed itself to *judicial* bribery, the Framers repeatedly made clear at the Constitutional Convention that they intended to subject the President to impeachment for bribery. They confirmed this intention in the Impeachment Clause, which authorizes the impeachment of "[t]he President,

To start with common law: At the time of the Constitutional Convention, bribery was well understood in Anglo-American law to encompass *offering*, *soliciting*, or *accepting* bribes. In 1716, for example, William Hawkins defined bribery in an influential treatise as "the receiving or offering of any undue reward, by or to any person whatsoever … in order to incline him to do a thing against the known rules of honesty and integrity."[202] This description of the offense was echoed many times over the following decades. In a renowned bribery case involving the alleged solicitation of bribes, Lord Mansfield agreed that "[w]herever it is a crime to take, it is a crime to give: they are reciprocal."[203] Two years later, William Blackstone confirmed that "taking bribes is punished," just as bribery is punishable for "those who offer a bribe, though not taken."[204] Soliciting a bribe—even if it is not accepted—thus qualified as bribery at common law. Indeed, it was clear under the common law that "the *attempt* is a crime; it is complete on *his* side who *offers* it."[205]

The Framers adopted that principle into the Constitution. As Judge John Noonan explains, the drafting history of the Impeachment Clause demonstrates that "'Bribery' was read both actively and passively, including the chief magistrate bribing someone and being bribed."[206] Many scholars of Presidential impeachment have reached the same conclusion.[207] Impeachable "Bribery" thus covers—inter alia—the *offer*, *solicitation*, or *acceptance* of something of personal value by the President to influence his own official actions.

This conclusion draws still more support from a closely related part of the common law. In the late-17th century, "bribery" was a relatively new offense, and was understood as overlapping with the more ancient common law crime of "extortion."[208] "Extortion," in turn, was defined as the "abuse of

---

Vice President and all civil Officers of the United States" for "Treason, Bribery, or other high Crimes and Misdemeanors." U.S. CONST., art. 2, § 4. It is therefore proper to draw upon common law principles and to apply them to the office of the Presidency.

[202] Hawkins, *A Treatise of Pleas to the Crown*, ch. 67, § 2 (1716).

[203] *Rex v. Vaughan*, 98 Eng. Rep. 308, 311 (K.B. 1769).

[204] William Blackstone, *Commentaries on the Laws of England, Vol. 2, Book 4, Ch. 10, § 17* (1771).

[205] *Rex v. Vaughan*, 98 Eng. Rep. 308, 311 (K.B. 1769). American courts have subsequently repeated this precise formulation. *See, e.g.*, *State v. Ellis*, 33 N.J.L. 102, 104 (N.J. Sup. Ct. 1868) ("The offence is complete when an offer or reward is made to influence the vote or action of the official."); *see also* William O. Russell, *A Treatise on Crimes and Misdemeanors* 239-240 (1st American Ed) (1824) ("The law abhors the least tendency to corruption; and up on the principle which has been already mentioned, of an attempt to commit even a misdemeanor, being itself a misdemeanor, (f) attempts to bribe, though unsuccessful, have in several cases been held to be criminal.").

[206] John T. Noonan, Jr., *Bribes: The Intellectual History of a Moral Idea* 430 (1984).

[207] As Professor Bowman writes, bribery was "a common law crime that developed from a narrow beginning" to reach "giving, and offering to give, [any] improper rewards." Bowman, *High Crimes & Misdemeanors* at 243; *see also, e.g.*, Tribe & Matz, *To End A Presidency* at 33 ("The corrupt exercise of power in exchange for a personal benefit defines impeachable bribery. That's self-evidently true whenever the president receives bribes to act a certain way. But it's also true when the president offers bribes to other officials—for example, to a federal judge, a legislator, or a member of the Electoral College … In either case, the president is fully complicit in a grave degradation of power, and he can never again be trusted to act as a faithful public servant.").

[208] *See* James Lindgren, *The Elusive Distinction Between Bribery and Extortion: From the Common Law to the Hobbs Act*,

public justice, which consists in any officer's unlawfully taking, by colour of his office, from any man, any money or thing of value, that is not due to him, or more than is due, or before it is due."[209] Under this definition, both bribery *and* extortion occurred when an official used his public position to obtain private benefits to which he was not entitled. Conduct which qualified as bribery was therefore "routinely punished as common law extortion."[210] To the Framers, who would have seen bribery and extortion as virtually coextensive, when a President acted in his official capacity to offer, solicit, or accept an improper personal benefit, he committed "Bribery."[211]

Turning to the nature of the improper personal benefit: because officials can be corrupted in many ways, the benefit at issue in a bribe can be anything of subjective personal value to the President. This is not limited to money. Indeed, given their purposes, it would have made no sense for the Framers to confine "Bribery" to the offer, solicitation, or acceptance of money, and they expressed no desire to impose that restriction. To the contrary, in guarding against foreign efforts to subvert American officials, they confirmed their broad view of benefits that might cause corruption: a person who holds "any Office of Profit or Trust," such as the President, is forbidden from accepting "any present, Office or Tile, of any kind whatever, from … a foreign State."[212] An equally pragmatic (and capacious) view applies to the impeachable offense of "Bribery." This view is further anchored in the very same 17th and 18th century common law treatises that were well known to the Framers. Those authorities used broad language in defining what qualifies as a "thing of value" in the context of bribery: "any undue reward" or any "valuable consideration."[213]

To summarize, impeachable "Bribery" occurs when a President offers, solicits, or accepts something of personal value to influence his own official actions. Bribery is thus an especially egregious and specific example of a President abusing his power for private gain. As Blackstone explained, bribery is "the genius of despotic countries where the true principles of government are never understood"—and where "it is imagined that there is no obligation from the superior to the inferior, no relative duty owing from the governor to the governed."[214] In our democracy, the Framers understood that there is no place for Presidents who would abuse their power and betray the public trust through bribery.

Like "Treason," the offense of "Bribery" is thus aimed at a President who is a continuing threat

---

35 UCLA L. REV. 815, 839 (1988).

[209] Blackstone, *Commentaries*, Vol. 2, Book 4, Ch. 10, § 22 (1771) (citing 1 Hawk. P. C. 170); *accord* Giles Jacob, A New Law-Dictionary 102 (1782) (defining "Extortion" as "an unlawful taking by an officer, &c. by colour of his office, of any money, or valuable thing, from a person where none at all is due, or not so much is due, or before it is due").

[210] Lindgren, *The Elusive Distinction*, 35 UCLA L. REV. at 839.

[211] For all the reasons given below in our discussion of the criminality issue, impeachable "Bribery" does not refer to the meaning of bribery under modern federal criminal statutes. *See also* Bowman, *High Crimes & Misdemeanors* at 243-44; Tribe & Matz, *To End A Presidency* at 31-33.

[212] U.S. CONST. art. I, § 9, cl.8.

[213] Hawkins, *A Treatise of Pleas to the Crown*, ch. 67, § 2 (1716).

[214] Blackstone, *Commentaries on the Laws of England*, Book 4, ch. 10 "Of Offenses Against Public Justice" (1765-1770).

to the Constitution. Someone who would willingly assist our enemies, or trade public power for personal favors, is the kind of person likely to break the rules again if they remain in office. But there is more: both "Treason" and "Bribery" are serious offenses with the capacity to corrupt constitutional governance and harm the Nation itself; both involve wrongdoing that reveals the President as a continuing threat if left in power; and both offenses are "plainly wrong in themselves to a person of honor, or to a good citizen, regardless of words on the statute books."[215] Looking to the Constitution's text and history—including the British, colonial, and early American traditions discussed earlier—these characteristics also define "other high Crimes and Misdemeanors."

C.   Abuse, Betrayal & Corruption

With that understanding in place, the records of the Constitutional Convention offer even greater clarity. They demonstrate that the Framers principally intended impeachment for three forms of Presidential wrongdoing: serious abuse of power, betrayal of the national interest through foreign entanglements, and corruption of office and elections. When the President engages in such misconduct, and does so in ways that are recognizably wrong and injurious to our political system, impeachment is warranted. That is proven not only by debates surrounding adoption of the Constitution, but also by the historical practice of the House in exercising the impeachment power.

1.   Abuse of Power

As Justice Robert Jackson wisely observed, "the purpose of the Constitution was not only to grant power, but to keep it from getting out of hand."[216] Nowhere is that truer than in the Presidency. As the Framers created a formidable chief executive, they made clear that impeachment is justified for serious abuse of power. Edmund Randolph was explicit on this point. In explaining why the Constitution must authorize Presidential impeachment, he warned that "the Executive will have great opportunitys of abusing his power."[217] Madison, too, stated that impeachment is necessary because the President "might pervert his administration into a scheme of ... oppression."[218] This theme echoed through the state ratifying conventions. Advocating that New York ratify the Constitution, Hamilton set the standard for impeachment at an "abuse or violation of some public trust."[219] In South Carolina, Charles Pinckney agreed that Presidents must be removed who "behave amiss or betray their public trust."[220] In Massachusetts, Reverend Samuel Stillman asked, "With such a prospect [of impeachment], who will dare to abuse the powers vested in him by the people."[221] Time and again, Americans who wrote and ratified the Constitution confirmed that Presidents may be impeached for abusing the power entrusted to them.

---

[215] Charles L. Black Jr. & Philip Bobbitt, *Impeachment: A Handbook, New Edition* 34 (2018).

[216] *Youngstown Sheet & Tube Co. v. Sawyer*, 343 U.S. 579, 640 (Jackson, J., concurring).

[217] 2 Farrand, *Records of the Federal Convention* at 67.

[218] *Id.* at 65-66.

[219] Alexander Hamilton, *Federalist No. 65* at 426.

[220] Berger, *Impeachment* at 94.

[221] 2 Elliot, *Debates in the Several State Conventions* at 169.

There are at least as many ways to abuse power as there are powers vested in the President. It would thus be an exercise in futility to attempt a list of every conceivable abuse constituting "high Crimes and Misdemeanors." That said, abuse of power was no vague notion to the Framers and their contemporaries. It had a very particular meaning to them. Impeachable abuse of power can take two basic forms: (1) the exercise of official power in a way that, on its very face, grossly exceeds the President's constitutional authority or violates legal limits on that authority; and (2) the exercise of official power to obtain an improper personal benefit, while ignoring or injuring the national interest. In other words, the President may commit an impeachable abuse of power in two different ways: by engaging in forbidden acts, or by engaging in potentially permissible acts but for forbidden reasons (*e.g.*, with the corrupt motive of obtaining a personal political benefit).

The first category involves conduct that is inherently and sharply inconsistent with the law—and that amounts to claims of monarchical prerogative. The generation that rebelled against King George III knew what absolute power looked like. The Framers had other ideas when they organized our government, and so they placed the chief executive within the bounds of law. That means the President may exercise only the powers expressly or impliedly vested in him by the Constitution, and he must also respect legal limits on the exercise of those powers (including the rights of Americans citizens). A President who refuses to abide these restrictions, thereby causing injury to society itself and engaging in recognizably wrongful conduct, may be subjected to impeachment for abuse of power.

That principle also covers conduct grossly inconsistent with and subversive of the separation of powers. The Framers knew that "[t]he accumulation of all powers, legislative, executive, and judiciary, in the same hands, ... may justly be pronounced the very definition of tyranny."[222] To protect liberty, they wrote a Constitution that creates a system of checks and balances within the federal government. Some of those rules are expressly enumerated in our founding charter; others are implied from its structure or from the history of inter-branch relations.[223] When a President wields executive power in ways that usurp and destroy the prerogatives of Congress or the Judiciary, he exceeds the scope of his constitutional authority and violates limits on permissible conduct. Such abuses of power are therefore impeachable. That conclusion is further supported by the British origins of the phrase "high Crimes and Misdemeanors": Parliament repeatedly impeached ministers for "subvert[ing] its conception of proper constitutional order in favor of the 'arbitrary and tyrannical' government of ambitious monarchs and their grasping minions."[224]

The Supreme Court advanced similar logic in *Ex Parte Grossman*, which held the President can pardon officials who defy judicial orders and are held in criminal contempt of court.[225] This holding raised an obvious concern: what if the President used "successive pardons" to "deprive a court of power

---

[222] James Madison, *Federalist No. 47* at 336.

[223] *See generally National Labor Relations Board v. Noel Canning, et al.*, 573 U.S. 513 (2014).

[224] Bowman, *High Crimes and Misdemeanors* at 109.

[225] *Ex Parte Grossman*, 267 U.S. 87 (1925).

to enforce its orders"?[226] That could fatally weaken the Judiciary's role under Article III of the Constitution. On behalf of a unanimous Court, Chief Justice William Howard Taft—who had previously served as President—explained that "exceptional cases like this ... would suggest a resort to impeachment."[227]

Two impeachment inquiries have involved claims that a President grossly violated the Constitution's separation of powers. The first was in 1868, when the House impeached President Andrew Johnson, who had succeeded President Abraham Lincoln following his assassination at Ford's Theatre. There, the articles approved by the House charged President Johnson with conduct forbidden by law: in firing the Secretary of War, he had allegedly violated the Tenure of Office Act, which restricted the President's power to remove cabinet members during the term of the President who had appointed them.[228] President Johnson was thus accused of a facial abuse of power. In the Senate, though, he was acquitted by a single vote—largely because the Tenure of Office Act was viewed by many Senators as likely unconstitutional (a conclusion later adopted by the Supreme Court in an opinion by Chief Justice Taft, who described the Act as "invalid"[229]).

Just over 100 years later, this Committee accused a second chief executive of abusing his power. In a departure from prior Presidential practice—and in contravention of Article I of the Constitution—President Nixon had invoked specious claims of executive privilege to defy Congressional subpoenas served as part of an impeachment inquiry. His obstruction centered on tape recordings, papers, and memoranda relating to the Watergate break-in and its aftermath. As the House Judiciary Committee found, he had interposed "the powers of the presidency against the lawful subpoenas of the House of Representatives, thereby assuming to himself functions and judgments necessary to exercise the sole power of impeachment vested by the Constitution in the House of Representatives."[230] Put simply, President Nixon purported to control the exercise of powers that belonged solely to the House and not to him—including the power of inquiry that is vital to any Congressional judgments about impeachment. In so doing, President Nixon injured the constitutional plan: "Unless the defiance of the Committee's subpoenas under these circumstances is considered grounds for impeachment, it is difficult to conceive of any President acknowledging that he obligated to supply the relevant evidence necessary for Congress to exercise its constitutional responsibility in an impeachment proceeding."[231] The House Judiciary Committee therefore approved an article of impeachment against President Nixon for abuse of power in obstructing the House impeachment inquiry.

But that was only part of President Nixon's impeachable wrongdoing. The House Judiciary Committee also approved two additional articles of impeachment against him for abuse of power, one

---

[226] *Id.* at 121.

[227] *Id.*

[228] *Articles of Impeachment Exhibited By The House Of Representatives Against Andrew Johnson, President of the United States*, 40th Cong. (1868).

[229] *Myers v. United States*, 272 U.S. 52, 108 (1926).

[230] *Committee Report on Nixon Articles of Impeachment* (1974) at 188.

[231] *Id.* at 213.

for obstruction of justice and the other for using Presidential power to target, harass, and surveil his political opponents. These articles demonstrate the second way in which a President can abuse power: by acting with improper motives.

This understanding of impeachable abuse of power is rooted in the Constitution's text, which commands the President to "faithfully execute" the law. At minimum, that duty requires Presidents "to exercise their power only when it is motivated in the public interest rather than in their private self-interest."[232] A President can thus be removed for exercising power with a corrupt purpose, even if his action would otherwise be permissible. As Iredell explained at the North Carolina ratifying convention, "the president would be liable to impeachments [if] he had … acted from some corrupt motive or other," or if he was "willfully abusing his trust."[233] Madison made a similar point at Virginia's ratifying convention. There, he observed that the President could be impeached for abuse of the pardon power if there are "grounds to believe" he has used it to "shelter" persons with whom he is connected "in any suspicious manner."[234] Such a pardon would technically be within the President's authority under Article II of the Constitution, but it would rank as an impeachable abuse of power because it arose from the forbidden purpose of obstructing justice. To the Framers, it was dangerous for officials to exceed their constitutional power, or to transgress legal limits, but it was equally dangerous (perhaps more so) for officials to conceal corrupt or illegitimate objectives behind superficially valid acts.

Again, President Nixon's case is instructive. After individuals associated with his campaign committee committed crimes to promote his reelection, he used the full powers of his office as part of a scheme to obstruct justice. Among many other wrongful acts, President Nixon dangled pardons to influence key witnesses, told a senior aide to have the CIA stop an FBI investigation into Watergate, meddled with Justice Department immunity decisions, and conveyed secret law enforcement information to suspects. Even if some of this conduct was formally within the scope of President Nixon's authority as head of the Executive Branch, it was undertaken with illegitimate motives. The House Judiciary Committee therefore included it within an article of impeachment charging him with obstruction of justice. Indeed, following President Nixon's resignation and the discovery of additional evidence concerning obstruction, all eleven members of the Committee who had originally voted against that article joined a statement affirming that "we were prepared to vote for his impeachment on proposed Article I had he not resigned his office."[235] Of course, several decades later, obstruction of justice was also the basis for an article of impeachment against President Clinton, though his conduct did not involve official acts.[236]

---

[232] Kent et al., *Faithful Execution* at 2120, 2179.

[233] *1998 Background and History of Impeachment Hearing* at 49.

[234] 3 Elliott, *Debates in the Several State Conventions* at 497-98.

[235] *Committee Report on Nixon Articles of Impeachment* (1974) at 361.

[236] In President Clinton's case, the House approved the article of impeachment for obstruction of justice. There was virtually no disagreement in those proceedings over whether obstructing justice can be impeachable; scholars, lawyers, and legislators on all sides of the dispute recognized that it can be. *See* Daniel J. Hemel & Eric A. Posner, *Presidential Obstruction of Justice*, 106 CAL. L. REV 1277, 1305-1307 (2018). Publicly available evidence does not suggest that the Senate's acquittal of President Clinton was based on the view that obstruction of justice is not impeachable. Rather, Senators who voted for acquittal appear to have concluded that some of the factual charges were not supported and that, even if

Yet obstruction of justice did not exhaust President Nixon's corrupt abuse of power. He was also accused of manipulating federal agencies to injure his opponents, aid his friends, gain personal political benefits, and violate the constitutional rights of American citizens. For instance, President Nixon improperly attempted to cause income tax audits of his perceived political adversaries; directed the FBI and Secret Service to engage in targeted (and unlawful) surveillance; and formed a secret investigative unit within the White House—financed with campaign contributions—that utilized CIA resources in its illegal covert activities. In explaining this additional article of impeachment, the House Judiciary Committee stated that President Nixon's conduct was "undertaken for his personal political advantage and not in furtherance of any valid national policy objective."[237] His abuses of executive power were thus "seriously incompatible with our system of constitutional government" and warranted removal from office.[238]

With the benefit of hindsight, the House's decision to impeach President Johnson is best understood in a similar frame. Scholars now largely agree that President Johnson's impeachment was motivated not by violations of the Tenure of Office Act, but on his illegitimate use of power to undermine Reconstruction and subordinate African-Americans following the Civil War.[239] In that period, fundamental questions about the nature and future of the Union stood unanswered. Congress therefore passed a series of laws to "reconstruct the former Confederate states into political entities in which black Americans enjoyed constitutional protections."[240] This program, however, faced an unyielding enemy in President Johnson, who declared that "white men alone must manage the south."[241] Convinced that political control by African-Americans would cause a "relapse into barbarism," President Johnson vetoed civil rights laws; when Congress overrode him, he refused to enforce those laws.[242] The results were disastrous. As Annette Gordon-Reed writes, "it would be impossible to exaggerate how devastating it was to have a man who affirmatively hated black people in charge of the program that was designed to settle the terms of their existence in post-Civil War America."[243] Congress tried to compromise with the President, but to no avail. A majority of the House finally determined that President Johnson posed a clear and present danger to the Nation if allowed to remain in office.

Rather than directly target President Johnson's faithless execution of the laws, and his illegitimate motives in wielding power, the House resorted to charges based on the Tenure of Office

---

Presidential perjury and obstruction of justice might in some cases justify removal, the nature and circumstances of the conduct at issue (including its predominantly private character) rendered it insufficiently grave to warrant that remedy.

[237] *Committee Report on Nixon Articles of Impeachment* (1974) at 139.

[238] *Id.*

[239] *See generally* Michael Les Benedict, *The Impeachment and Trial of Andrew Johnson* (1999).

[240] Jeffrey A. Engel, Jon Meacham, Timothy Naftali, & Peter Baker, *Impeachment: An American History* 48 (2018).

[241] *Id.* at 49.

[242] *Id.*

[243] *See* Annette Gordon-Reed, *Andrew Johnson: The American Presidents Series: the 17th President, 1865-1869* 12 (2011).

Act. But in reality, "the shaky claims prosecuted by [the House] obscured a far more compelling basis for removal: that Johnson's virulent use of executive power to sabotage Reconstruction posed a mortal threat to the nation—and to civil and political rights—as reconstituted after the Civil War … [T]he country was in the throes of a second founding. Yet Johnson abused the powers of his office and violated the Constitution to preserve institutions and practices that had nearly killed the Union. He could not be allowed to salt the earth as the Republic made itself anew."[244] Viewed from that perspective, the case for impeaching President Johnson rested on his use of power with illegitimate motives.

Pulling this all together, the Framers repeatedly confirmed that Presidents can be impeached for grave abuse of power. Where the President engages in acts forbidden by law, or acts with an improper motive, he has committed an abuse of power under the Constitution. Where those abuses inflict substantial harm on our political system and are recognizably wrong, they warrant his impeachment and removal.[245]

2.   Betrayal of the National Interest Through Foreign Entanglements

It is not a coincidence that the Framers started with "Treason" in defining impeachable offenses. Betrayal was no abstraction to them. They had recently waged a war for independence in which some of their fellow citizens remained loyal to the enemy. The infamous traitor, Benedict Arnold, had defected to Britain less than a decade earlier. As they looked outward, the Framers saw kings scheming for power, promising fabulous wealth to spies and deserters. The United States could be enmeshed in such conspiracies: "Foreign powers," warned Elbridge Gerry, "will intermeddle in our affairs, and spare no expense to influence them."[246] The young Republic might not survive a President who schemed with other nations, entangling himself in secret deals that harmed our democracy.

That reality loomed over the impeachment debate in Philadelphia. Explaining why the Constitution required an impeachment option, Madison argued that a President "might betray his trust to foreign powers."[247] Gouverneur Morris, who had initially opposed allowing impeachment, was convinced: "no one would say that we ought to expose ourselves to the danger of seeing the first

---

[244] Tribe & Matz, *To End a Presidency* at 55.

[245] In President Clinton's case, it was debated whether Presidents can be impeached for acts that do not involve their official powers. *See Staff Report on Constitutional Grounds for Presidential Impeachment: Modern Precedents (1998)* at 6-7; *Minority Staff of H. Comm. on the Judiciary, 105ᵗʰ Cong., Constitutional Grounds for Presidential Impeachment: Modern Precedents Minority Views* 3-4, 8-9, 13-16 (Comm. Print 1998). Many scholars have taken the view that such private conduct may be impeachable in extraordinary circumstances, such as where it renders the President unviable as the leader of a democratic nation committed to the rule of law. *See, e.g.*, Tribe & Matz, *To End A Presidency* at 10, 51; Black & Bobbitt, *Impeachment* at 35. It also bears mention that some authority supports the view that Presidents might be subject to impeachment not for *abusing* their official powers, but by *failing* to use them and thus engaging in gross dereliction of official duty. *See, e.g.*, Tribe & Matz, *To End A Presidency* at 50; Akhil Reed Amar, *America's Constitution: A Biography* 200 (2006); Black & Bobbitt, *Impeachment* at 34.

[246] Wydra & Gorod, *The First Magistrate in Foreign Pay*.

[247] 2 Farrand, *Records of the Federal Convention* at 65.

Magistrate in foreign pay, without being able to guard against it by displacing him."[248] In the same vein, Franklin noted "the case of the Prince of Orange during the late war," in which a Dutch prince reneged on a military treaty with France.[249] Because there was no impeachment power or other method of inquiry, the prince's motives were secret and untested, drastically destabilizing Dutch politics and giving "birth to the most violent animosities and contentions."[250]

Impeachment for betrayal of the Nation's interest—and especially for betrayal of national security and foreign policy—was hardly exotic to the Framers. "The history of impeachment over the centuries shows an abiding awareness of how vulnerable the practice of foreign policy is to the misconduct of its makers."[251] Indeed, "impeachments on this ground were a constant of parliamentary practice," and "a string of British ministers and royal advisors were impeached for using their official powers contrary to the country's vital foreign interests."[252] Although the Framers did not intend impeachment for genuine, good faith disagreements between the President and Congress over matters of diplomacy, they were explicit that betrayal of the Nation through plots with foreign powers justified removal.

In particular, foreign interference in the American political system was among the gravest dangers feared by the Founders of our Nation and the Framers of our Constitution. For example, in a letter to Thomas Jefferson, John Adams wrote: "You are apprehensive of foreign Interference, Intrigue, Influence. So am I.—But, as often as Elections happen, the danger of foreign Influence recurs."[253] And in *Federalist No. 68*, Hamilton cautioned that the "most deadly adversaries of republican government" may come "chiefly from the desire in foreign powers to gain an improper ascendant in our councils.[254]

The President's important role in foreign affairs does not disable the House from evaluating whether he committed impeachable offenses in that field. This conclusion follows from the Impeachment Clause itself but is also supported by the Constitution's many grants of power to Congress addressing foreign affairs. Congress is empowered to "declare War," "regulate Commerce with foreign Nations," "establish an uniform Rule of Naturalization," "define and punish Piracies and Felonies committed on the high Seas, and Offences against the Law of Nations," "grant Letters of Marque and Reprisal," and "make Rules for the Government and Regulation of the land and naval Forces."[255] Congress also has the power to set policy, define law, undertake oversight and investigations, create

---

[248] *Id.* at 68.

[249] *Id.* at 67-68.

[250] *Id.*

[251] Frank O. Bowman, III, *Foreign Policy Has Always Been at the Heart of Impeachment*, FOREIGN AFFAIRS (Nov 2019).

[252] Bowman, *High Crimes & Misdemeanors* at 48, 106.

[253] *To Thomas Jefferson from John Adams, 6 December 1787*, Founders Online, NATIONAL ARCHIVES.

[254] Alexander Hamilton, *Federalist No. 68* at 441.

[255] U.S. CONST., art. I, § 8.

executive departments, and authorize government funding for a slew of national security matters.[256] In addition, the President cannot make a treaty or appoint an ambassador without the approval of the Senate.[257] In those respects and many others, constitutional authority over the "conduct of the foreign relations of our Government" is shared between "the Executive and Legislative [branches]."[258] Stated simply, "the Executive is not free from the ordinary controls and checks of Congress merely because foreign affairs are at issue."[259] In these realms, as in many others, the Constitution "enjoins upon its branches separateness but interdependence, autonomy but reciprocity."[260]

Accordingly, where the President uses his foreign affairs power in ways that betray the national interest for his own benefit, or harm national security for equally corrupt reasons, he is subject to impeachment by the House. Any claims to the contrary would horrify the Framers. A President who perverts his role as chief diplomat to serve private rather than public ends has unquestionably engaged in "high Crimes and Misdemeanors"—especially if he invited, rather than opposed, foreign interference in our politics.

3.   Corruption of Office or Elections

As should now be clear, the Framers feared corruption most of all, in its many and shifting manifestations. It was corruption that led to abuse of power and betrayal of the Nation. It was corruption that ruined empires, debased Britain, and menaced American freedom. The Framers saw no shortage of threats to the Republic, and fought valiantly to guard against them, "but the big fear underlying all the small fears was whether they'd be able to control corruption."[261] This was not just a matter of thwarting bribes and extortion; it was a far greater challenge. The Framers aimed to build a country in which officials would not use public power for personal benefits, disregarding the public good in pursuit of their own advancement. This virtuous principle applied with special force to the Presidency. As Madison emphasized, because the Presidency "was to be administered by a single man," his corruption "might be fatal to the Republic."[262]

The Framers therefore sought to ensure that "corruption was more effectually guarded against, in the manner this government was constituted, than in any other that had ever been formed."[263] Impeachment was central to that plan. At one point the Convention even provisionally adopted "treason, bribery, or corruption" as the standard for impeaching a President. And no fewer than four delegates—

---

[256] *See* Lawrence Friedman & Victor Hansen, *There Is No Constitutional Impediment to an Impeachment Inquiry that Concerns National Security*, JUST SECURITY, Oct. 1, 2019.

[257] U.S. CONST., art. II, §2, cl. 2.

[258] *Medellin v. Texas*, 552 U.S. 491, 511 (2008).

[259] *Zivotofsky v. Kerry*, 135 S. Ct. 2076 (2015).

[260] *Youngstown Sheet & Tube Co. v. Sawyer*, 343 U.S. 579, 635 (1952) (Jackson, J., concurring).

[261] Teachout, *Corruption in America* at 57.

[262] Jonathan Elliot ed., *Debates on the Adoption of the Federal Constitution in the Convention Held at Philadelphia, in 1787* 341 (1861) (hereinafter "*Debates on the Adoption of the Federal Constitution*").

[263] 4 Elliot, *Debates in the Several State Conventions* at 302.

Morris, Madison, Mason, and Randolph—listed corruption as a reason why Presidents must be subject to removal. That understanding followed from history: "One invariable theme in [centuries] of Anglo-American impeachment practice has been corruption."[264] Treason posed a threat of swift national extinction, but the steady rot of corruption could destroy us from within. Presidents who succumbed to that instinct, serving themselves at the Nation's expense, forfeited the public trust.

Impeachment was seen as especially necessary for Presidential conduct corrupting our system of political self-government. That concern arose in two contexts: the risk that Presidents would be swayed to prioritize foreign over domestic interests, and the risk that they would place their personal interest in re-election above our abiding commitment to democracy. The need for impeachment peaks where both threats converge at once.

First was the risk that foreign royals would use wealth, power, and titles to seduce American officials. This was not a hypothetical problem. Just a few years earlier, and consistent with European custom, King Louis XVI of France had bestowed on Benjamin Franklin (in his capacity as American emissary) a snuff box decorated with 408 diamonds "of a beautiful water."[265] Magnificent gifts like this one could unconsciously shape how American officials carried out their duties. To guard against that peril, the Framers adopted the Foreign Emoluments Clause, which prohibits Presidents—among other federal officials—from accepting "any present, Emolument, Office, or Title, of any kind whatever, from any King, Prince, or foreign State" unless Congress affirmatively consents.[266]

The theory of the Foreign Emoluments Clause, based in history and the Framers' lived experience, "is that a federal officeholder who receives something of value from a foreign power can be imperceptibly induced to compromise what the Constitution insists be his exclusive loyalty: the best interest of the United States of America."[267] Rather than scrutinize every exchange for potential bribery, the Framers simply banned officials from receiving anything of value from foreign powers. Although this rule sweeps broadly, the Framers deemed it central to American self-governance. Speaking in Philadelphia, Charles Pinckney "urged the necessity of preserving foreign ministers, and other officers of the United States, independent of external influence."[268] At Virginia's convention, Randolph elaborated that "[i]t was thought proper, in order to exclude corruption and foreign influence, to prohibit any one in office from receiving or holding any *emoluments* from foreign states."[269] Randolph added that if the President violated the Clause, "he may be impeached."[270]

The Framers also anticipated impeachment if a President placed his own interest in retaining

---

[264] Bowman, *High Crimes & Misdemeanors* at 277.

[265] Teachout, *Corruption in America* at 1.

[266] U.S. CONST., art. I, § 9, cl. 8.

[267] Norman L. Eisen, Richard Painter & Laurence H. Tribe, *The Emoluments Clause: Its Text, Meaning, And Application To Donald J. Trump*, BROOKINGS, Dec. 16, 2016.

[268] Elliot, *Debates on the Adoption of the Federal Constitution* at 467.

[269] 3 Elliot, *Debates in the Several State Conventions* at 465.

[270] *Id.* at 201.

power above the national interest in free and fair elections. Several delegates were explicit on this point when the topic arose at the Constitutional Convention. By then, the Framers had created the Electoral College. They were "satisfied with it as a tool for picking presidents but feared that individual electors might be intimidated or corrupted."[271] Impeachment was their answer. William Davie led off the discussion, warning that a President who abused his office might seek to escape accountability by interfering with elections, sparing "no efforts or means whatever to get himself re-elected."[272] Rendering the President "impeachable whilst in office" was thus "an essential security for the good behaviour of the Executive."[273] The Constitution thereby ensured that corrupt Presidents could not avoid justice by subverting elections and remaining in office.

George Mason built on Davie's position, directing attention to the Electoral College: "One objection agst. Electors was the danger of their being corrupted by the Candidates; & this furnished a peculiar reason in favor of impeachments whilst in office. Shall the man who has practised corruption & by that means procured his appointment in the first instance, be suffered to escape punishment, by repeating his guilt?"[274] Mason's concern was straightforward. He feared that Presidents would win election by improperly influencing members of the Electoral College (*e.g.*, by offering them bribes). If evidence of such wrongdoing came to light, it would be unthinkable to leave the President in office—especially given that he might seek to avoid punishment by corrupting the next election. In that circumstance, Mason concluded, the President should face impeachment and removal under the Constitution. Notably, Mason was not alone in this view. Speaking just a short while later, Gouverneur Morris emphatically agreed that "the Executive ought therefore to be impeachable for … Corrupting his electors."[275] Although not articulated expressly, it is reasonable to infer that the concerns raised by Davie, Mason, and Morris were especially salient because the Constitution—until ratification of the Twenty-Second Amendment in 1951—did not limit the number of terms a President could serve in office.[276] A President who twisted or sabotaged the electoral process could rule for life, much like a king.

This commitment to impeaching Presidents who corruptly interfered with elections was anchored in lessons from British rule. As historian Gordon Wood writes, "[t]hroughout the eighteenth century the Crown had slyly avoided the blunt and clumsy instrument of prerogative, and instead had resorted to influencing the electoral process and the representatives in Parliament in order to gain its treacherous ends."[277] In his influential *Second Treatise on Civil Government*, John Locke blasted such manipulation, warning that it serves to "cut up the government by the roots, and poison the very

---

[271] Tribe & Matz, *To End A Presidency* at 4.

[272] 2 Farrand, *Records of the Federal Convention* at 64.

[273] *Id.*

[274] *Id.* at 65.

[275] *Id.* at 69.

[276] U.S. Const. Amend. XXII.

[277] Wood, *The Creation of the American Republic* at 33.

fountain of public security."[278] Channeling Locke, American revolutionaries vehemently objected to King George III's electoral shenanigans; ultimately, they listed several election-related charges in the Declaration of Independence. Those who wrote our Constitution knew, and feared, that the chief executive could threaten their plan of government by corrupting elections.

The true nature of this threat is its rejection of government by "We the People," who would "ordain and establish" the Constitution.[279] The beating heart of the Framers' project was a commitment to popular sovereignty. At a time when "democratic self-government existed almost nowhere on earth,"[280] the Framers imagined a society "where the true principles of representation are understood and practised, and where all authority flows from, and returns at stated periods to, the people."[281] That would be possible only if "those entrusted with [power] should be kept in dependence on the people."[282] This is why the President, and Members of Congress, must stand before the public for re-election on fixed terms. It is through free and fair elections that the American people protect their right to self-government, a right unforgivably denied to many as the Constitution was ratified in 1788 but now extended to all American citizens over the age of 18. When the President concludes that elections threaten his continued grasp on power, and therefore seeks to corrupt or interfere with them, he denies the very premise of our constitutional system. The American people choose their leaders; a President who wields power to destroy opponents or manipulate elections is a President who rejects democracy itself.

In sum, the Framers discussed the risk that Presidents would improperly conspire with foreign nations; they also discussed the risk that Presidents would place their interest in retaining power above the integrity of our elections. Both offenses, in their view, called for impeachment. That is doubly true where a President conspires with a foreign power to manipulate elections to his benefit—conduct that betrays American self-governance and joins the Framers' worst nightmares into a single impeachable offense.[283]

D.   Conclusion

Writing in 1833, Justice Joseph Story remarked that impeachable offenses "are of so various

---

[278] John Locke, *Second Treatise of Government* 112 (C.B. Macpherson ed. 1980).

[279] U.S. CONST. Pmbl.

[280] Amar, *America's Constitution* at 8.

[281] 4 Elliot, *Debates in the Several State Conventions* at 331; *see also* James Madison, *Federalist No. 14.*

[282] James Madison, *Federalist No. 37* at 268.

[283] In fact, the Framers were so concerned about improper foreign influence in the Presidency that they restricted that position to natural born citizens. U.S. CONST. art. II, § 1. As one commentator observed, "Considering the greatness of the trust, and that this department is the ultimately efficient power in government, these restrictions will not appear altogether useless or unimportant. As the President is required to be a native citizen of the United States, ambitious foreigners cannot intrigue for the office, and the qualification of birth cuts off all those inducements from abroad to corruption, negotiation, and war, which have frequently and fatally harassed the elective monarchies of Germany and Poland, as well as the pontificate at Rome." 1 James Kent, *Commentaries on American Law* 255 (1826).

and complex a character" that it would be "almost absurd" to attempt a comprehensive list.[284] Consistent with Justice Story's wisdom, "the House has never, in any impeachment inquiry or proceeding, adopted either a comprehensive definition of 'high Crimes and Misdemeanors' or a catalog of offenses that are impeachable."[285] Rather than engage in abstract, advisory or hypothetical debates about the precise nature of conduct that calls for the exercise of its constitutional powers, the House has awaited a "full development of the facts."[286] Only then has it weighed articles of impeachment.

In making such judgments, however, each Member of the House has sworn an oath to follow the Constitution, which sets forth a legal standard governing when Presidential conduct warrants impeachment. That standard has three main parts.

First, as Mason explained just before proposing "high Crimes and Misdemeanors" as the basis for impeachment, the President's conduct must constitute a "great and dangerous offense" against the Nation. The Constitution itself offers us two examples: "Treason" and "Bribery." In identifying "other" offenses of the same kind, we are guided by Parliamentary and early American practice, records from the Constitutional Convention and state ratifying conventions, and insights from the Constitution's text and structure. These sources prove that "high Crimes and Misdemeanors" involve misconduct that subverts and injures constitutional governance. Core instances of such misconduct by the President are serious abuse of power, betrayal of the national interest through foreign entanglements, and corruption of office and elections. The Framers included an impeachment power in the Constitution specifically to protect the Nation against these forms of wrongdoing.

Past practice of the House further illuminates the idea of a "great and dangerous offense." President Nixon's case is most helpful. There, as explained above, the House Judiciary Committee approved articles of impeachment on three grounds: (1) obstruction of an ongoing law enforcement investigation into unlawful acts by his presidential re-election campaign; (2) abuse of power in targeting his perceived political opponents; and (3) improper obstruction of a Congressional impeachment inquiry into his obstruction of justice and abuse of power. These articles of impeachment, moreover, were not confined to discrete acts. Each of them accused President Nixon of undertaking a course of conduct or scheme, and each of them supported that accusation with a list of discrete acts alleged to comprise and demonstrate the overarching impeachable offense.[287] Thus, where a President engages in a course of conduct involving serious abuse of power, betrayal of the national interest through foreign entanglements, or corruption of office and elections, impeachment is justified.

---

[284] 2 Story, *Commentaries* at 264.

[285] *1998 Background and History of Impeachment Hearing* at 2.

[286] *Staff Report on Constitutional Grounds for Presidential Impeachment* (1974) at 2.

[287] Consistent with that understanding, one scholar remarks that it is the "repetition, pattern, [and] coherence" of official misconduct that "tend to establish the requisite degree of seriousness warranting the removal of a president from office." John Labovitz, *Presidential Impeachment* 129-130 (1978); *see also, e.g.*, McGinnis, *Impeachment* at 659 ("[I]t has been well understood that the official's course of conduct as a whole should be the subject of judgment."); *Debate On Articles Of Impeachment: Hearing before the H. Comm. On the Judiciary*, 93rd Cong. (1974) (hereinafter "*Debate on Nixon Articles of Impeachment* (1974)") (addressing the issue repeatedly from July 24, 1974 to July 30, 1974).

Second, impeachable offenses involve wrongdoing that reveal the President as a continuing threat to the constitutional system if he is allowed to remain in a position of political power. As Iredell remarked, impeachment does not exist for a "mistake."[288] That is why the Framers rejected "maladministration" as a basis for impeachment, and it is why "high Crimes and Misdemeanors" are not simply unwise, unpopular, or unconsidered acts. Like "Treason" and "Bribery," they reflect decisions by the President to embark on a course of conduct—or to act with motives—inconsistent with our plan of government. Where the President makes such a decision, Congress may remove him to protect the Constitution, especially if there is reason to think that he will commit additional offenses if left in office (*e.g.*, statements by the President that he did nothing wrong and would do it all again). This forward-looking perspective follows from the limited consequences of impeachment. The question is not whether to punish the President; that decision is left to the criminal justice system. Instead, the ultimate question is whether to bring an early end to his four-year electoral term. In his analysis of the Constitution, Alexis de Tocqueville thus saw impeachment as "a preventive measure" which exists "to deprive the ill-disposed citizen of an authority which he has used amiss, and to prevent him from ever acquiring it again."[289] That is particularly true when the President injures the Nation's interests as part of a scheme to obtain personal benefits; someone so corrupt will again act corruptly.

Finally, "high Crimes and Misdemeanors" involve conduct that is recognizably wrong to a reasonable person. This principle resolves a potential tension in the Constitution. On the one hand, the Framers adopted a standard for impeachment that could stand the test of time. On the other hand, the structure of the Constitution—including its prohibition on bills of attainder and the *Ex Post Facto* Clause—implies that impeachable offenses should not come as a surprise.[290] Impeachment is aimed at Presidents who believe they are above the law, and who believe their own interests transcend those of the country and Constitution. Of course, as President Nixon proved, Presidents who have committed impeachable offenses may seek to confuse the public through manufactured ambiguity and crafty pretexts. That does not shield their misconduct from impeachment. The principle of a plainly wrong act is not about academic technicalities; it simply focuses impeachment on conduct that any person of honor would recognize as wrong under the Constitution.

To summarize: Like "Treason" and "Bribery," and consistent with the offenses historically considered by Parliament to warrant impeachment, "high Crimes and Misdemeanors" are great and dangerous offenses that injure the constitutional system. Such offenses are defined mainly by abuse of power, betrayal of the national interest through foreign entanglements, and corruption of office and elections. In addition, impeachable offenses arise from wrongdoing that reveals the President as a continuing threat to the constitutional system if allowed to remain in a position of power. Finally, they involve conduct that reasonable officials would consider to be wrong in our democracy.

Within these parameters, and guided by fidelity to the Constitution, the House must judge whether the President's misconduct is grave enough to require impeachment. That step must never be taken lightly. It is a momentous act, justified only when the President's full course of conduct, assessed

---

[288] Sunstein, *Impeachment* at 59.

[289] Alexis de Tocqueville, *Democracy in America and Two Essays on America* 124-30 (2003).

[290] *See* Black & Bobbitt, *Impeachment* at 29-30.

without favor or prejudice, is "seriously incompatible with either the constitutional form and principles of our government or the proper performance of constitutional duties of the presidential office."[291] When that standard is met, however, the Constitution calls the House to action. In such cases, a decision *not* to impeach has grave consequences and sets an ominous precedent. As Representative William Cohen remarked in President Nixon's case, "It also has been said to me that even if Mr. Nixon did commit these offenses, every other President … has engaged in some of the same conduct, at least to some degree, but the answer I think is that democracy, that solid rock of our system, may be eroded away by degree and its survival will be determined by the degree to which we will tolerate those silent and subtle subversions that absorb it slowly into the rule of a few."[292]

V.   The Criminality Issue

It is occasionally suggested that Presidents can be impeached only if they have committed crimes. That position was rejected in President Nixon's case, and then rejected again in President Clinton's, and should be rejected once more.[293]

Offenses against the Constitution are different in kind than offenses against the criminal code. Some crimes, like jaywalking, are not impeachable. Some impeachable offenses, like abuse of power, are not crimes. Some misconduct may offend both the Constitution and the criminal law. Impeachment and criminality must therefore be assessed separately—even though the commission of crimes may strengthen a case for removal.

A "great preponderance of authority" confirms that impeachable offenses are "not confined to criminal conduct."[294] This authority includes nearly every legal scholar to have studied the issue, as well as multiple Supreme Court justices who addressed it in public remarks.[295] More important, the House itself has long treated "high Crimes and Misdemeanors" as distinct from crimes subject to indictment. That understanding follows from the Constitution's history, text, and structure, and reflects the absurdities and practical difficulties that would result were the impeachment power confined to

---

[291] *Staff Report on Constitutional Grounds for Presidential Impeachment* (1974) at 27.

[292] *Debate on Nixon Articles of Impeachment* (1974) at 79.

[293] *Impeachment of William J. Clinton, President of the United States: Report of the H. Comm. on the Judiciary*, H. Rep. No. 105-830 at 64 (1998) (hereinafter "*Committee Report on Clinton Articles of Impeachment* (1998)") *Committee Report on Clinton Articles of Impeachment* (1998) at 64 ("Although, the actions of President Clinton do not have to rise to the level of violating the federal statute regarding obstruction of justice in order to justify impeachment."); *Staff Report on Constitutional Grounds for Presidential Impeachment* (1974) at 22-26.

[294] Berger, *Impeachment* at 58.

[295] *See, e.g.*, Black & Bobbitt, *Impeachment* at 33-37, 559-565; Bowman, *High Crimes and Misdemeanors* at 244-252; Tribe & Matz, *To End A Presidency* at 43-53; Sunstein, *Impeachment* at 117-134; Amar, *America's Constitution* at 200-20; Charles J. Cooper, *A Perjurer in the White House?: The Constitutional Case for Perjury and Obstruction of Justice as High Crimes and Misdemeanors*, 22 HARV. J. L. & PUB. POL'Y 619, 620 (1998-1999); Michael J. Gerhardt, *The Federal Impeachment Process: A Constitutional and Historical Analysis* 105-113 (2019); Berger, *Impeachment* at 58 (collecting sources); Merrill Otis, *A Proposed Tribunal: Is It Constitutional?*, 7 KAN. CITY. L. REV. 3, 22 (1938) (quoting Chief Justice Taft); Charles E. Hughes, *The Supreme Court of the United States* 19 (1928); 2 Henry Adams, *History of the United States of America* 223 (1962).

indictable crimes.

A.   History

"If there is one point established by … Anglo-American impeachment practice, it is that the phrase 'high Crimes and Misdemeanors' is not limited to indictable crimes."[296] As recounted above, impeachment was conceived in Parliament as a method for controlling abusive royal ministers. Consistent with that purpose, it was not confined to accusations of criminal wrongdoing. Instead, it was applied to "many offenses, not easily definable by law," such as abuse of power, betrayal of national security, corruption, neglect of duty, and violating Parliament's constitutional prerogatives.[297] Many officials were impeached for non-criminal wrongs against the British system of government; notable examples include the Duke of Buckingham (1626), the Earl of Strafford (1640), the Lord Mayor of London (1642), the Earl of Orford and others (1701), and Governor General Warren Hastings (1787).[298] Across centuries of use, the phrase "high Crimes and Misdemeanors" thus assumed a "special historical meaning different from the ordinary meaning of the terms 'crimes' and 'misdemeanors.'"[299] It became a term of art confined to impeachments, without "relation to whether an indictment would lie in the particular circumstances."[300]

That understanding extended to North America. Here, the impeachment process was used to address diverse misconduct by public officials, ranging from abuse of power and corruption to bribery and betrayal of the revolutionary cause.[301] As one scholar reports, "American colonists before the Revolution, and American states after the Revolution but before 1787, all impeached officials for non-criminal conduct."[302]

At the Constitutional Convention itself, no delegate linked impeachment to the technicalities of criminal law. On the contrary, the Framers invoked an array of broad, adaptable terms as grounds for removal—and when the standard was temporarily narrowed to "treason, or bribery," Mason objected that it must reach "great and dangerous" offenses against the Constitution. Here he cited Burke's call to impeach Hastings, whose acts were not crimes, but instead violated "those eternal laws of justice, which are our rule and our birthright."[303] To the Framers, impeachment was about abuse of power, betrayal of nation, and corruption of office and elections. It was meant to guard against these threats in every manifestation—known and unknown—that might someday afflict the Republic.

---

[296] Bowman, *High Crimes and Misdemeanors* at 44.

[297] 2 Story, *Commentaries* at 268.

[298] *See* Bowman, *High Crimes and Misdemeanors* at 44-47.

[299] *Staff Report on Constitutional Grounds for Presidential Impeachment* (1974) at 22.

[300] Berger, *Impeachment* at 62.

[301] Hoffer & Hull, *Impeachment in America* at 1-95.

[302] Bowman, *High Crimes and Misdemeanors* at 244.

[303] Edmund Burke, *Reflections on the Revolution in France and Other Writings* 409 (2015).

That view appeared repeatedly in the state ratifying debates. Delegates opined that the President could be impeached if he "deviates from his duty" or "dare[s] to abuse the power vested in him by the people."[304] In North Carolina, Iredell noted that "the person convicted [in an impeachment proceeding] is further liable to a trial at common law, and may receive such common-law punishment ... *if it be punishable by that law*" (emphasis added).[305] Similarly, in Virginia, George Nicholas declared that the President "will be absolutely disqualified [by impeachment] to hold any place of profit, honor, or trust, and liable to further punishment *if he has committed such high crimes as are punishable at common law*" (emphasis added).[306] The premise underlying this statement—and Iredell's—is that some Presidential "high Crimes and Misdemeanors" were *not* punishable by common law.

Leading minds echoed that position through the Nation's early years. In *Federalist No. 65*, Hamilton argued that impeachable offenses are defined by "the abuse or violation of some public trust."[307] In that sense, he reasoned, "they are of a nature which may with peculiar propriety be denominated POLITICAL, as they relate chiefly to injuries done immediately to the society itself."[308] A few years later, Constitutional Convention delegate James Wilson reiterated Hamilton's point: "Impeachments, and offences and offenders impeachable, come not ... within the sphere of ordinary jurisprudence. They are founded on different principles, are governed by different maxims, and are directed to different objects."[309] Writing in 1829, William Rawle described impeachment as reserved for "men whose treachery to their country might be productive of the most serious disasters."[310] Four years later, Justice Story emphasized that impeachable offenses ordinarily "must be examined upon very broad and comprehensive principles of public policy and duty."[311]

The American experience with impeachment confirms that lesson. A strong majority of the impeachments voted by the House since 1789 have included "one or more allegations that did not charge a violation of criminal law."[312] Several officials, moreover, have subsequently been convicted on non-criminal articles of impeachment. For example, Judge Robert Archbald was removed in 1912 for non-criminal speculation in coal properties, and Judge Halsted Ritter was removed in 1936 for the non-criminal offense of bringing his court "into scandal and disrepute."[313] As House Judiciary Committee Chairman Hatton Sumners stated explicitly during Judge Ritter's case, "We do not assume the responsibility ... of proving that the respondent is guilty of a crime as that term is known to criminal

---

[304] Quoted in Michael J. Gerhardt, *Impeachment: What Everyone Needs to Know* 60 (2018).

[305] *Staff Report on Constitutional Grounds for Presidential Impeachment* (1974) at 23.

[306] *Id.*

[307] Alexander Hamilton, *Federalist No. 65* at 426.

[308] *Id.*

[309] James Wilson, *Collected Works of James Wilson* 736 (Kermit L. Hall and Mark David Hall ed. 2007).

[310] William Rawle, *A View of the Constitution of the United States of America* 218 (1829).

[311] 2 Story, *Commentaries* at 234.

[312] *Staff Report on Constitutional Grounds for Presidential Impeachment* (1974) at 24.

[313] REPORT OF THE COMMITTEE ON THE JUDICIARY, ROBERT W. ARCHBALD, JUDGE OF THE UNITED STATES COMMERCE COURT, H. REP. NO. 62-946 (1912); H. RES. 422, 74th Cong. (1936).

jurisprudence."[314] The House has also applied that principle in Presidential impeachments. Although President Nixon resigned before the House could consider the articles of impeachment against him, the Judiciary Committee's allegations encompassed many non-criminal acts.[315] And in President Clinton's case, the Judiciary Committee report accompanying articles of impeachment to the House floor stated that "the actions of President Clinton do not have to rise to the level of violating the federal statute regarding obstruction of justice in order to justify impeachment."[316]

History thus affords exceptionally clear and consistent evidence that impeachable "high Crimes and Misdemeanors" are not limited to violations of the criminal code.

B.   Constitutional Text and Structure

That historical conclusion is bolstered by the text and structure of the Constitution. Starting with the text, we must assign weight to use of the word "high." That is true not only because "high Crimes and Misdemeanors" was a term of art with its own history, but also because "high" connotes an offense against the State itself. Thus, "high" treason in Britain was an offense against the Crown, whereas "petit" treason was the betrayal of a superior by a subordinate. The Framers were aware of this when they incorporated "high" as a limitation on impeachable offenses, signifying only constitutional wrongs.

That choice is particularly noteworthy because the Framers elsewhere referred to "crimes," "offenses," and "punishment" without using this modifier—and so we know "the Framers knew how to denote ordinary crimes when they wanted to do so."[317] For example, the Fifth Amendment requires a grand jury indictment in cases of a "capital, or otherwise infamous crime."[318] The Currency Clause, in turn, empowers Congress to "provide for the Punishment of counterfeiting the Securities and current Coin of the United States."[319] The Law of Nations Clause authorizes Congress to "define and punish Piracies and Felonies committed on the high Seas, and Offenses against the Law of Nations."[320] And the Interstate Extradition Clause provides that "[a] Person charged in any State with Treason, Felony, or other Crime" who flees from one state to another shall be returned upon request.[321] Only in the Impeachment Clause did the Framers refer to "high" crimes. By adding "high" in this one provision, while excluding it everywhere else, the Framers plainly sought to capture a distinct category of offenses against the state.[322]

---

[314] Berger, *Impeachment* at 60.

[315] *See generally Committee Report on Nixon Articles of Impeachment* (1974).

[316] *Committee Report on Clinton Articles of Impeachment* (1998) at 66.

[317] Tribe & Matz, *To End a Presidency* at 40.

[318] U.S. CONST. amend. V, § 1.

[319] U.S. CONST. art. I, § 8, cl. 6.

[320] U.S. CONST. art. I, § 8, cl. 10.

[321] U.S. CONST. art. IV, § 2, cl. 2.

[322] One might object that since "Treason" and "Bribery" are indictable crimes, the same must be true of "other high Crimes and Misdemeanors." But this argument would fail. Although it is true that "other high Crimes and Misdemeanors" share

That interpretation is also most consistent with the structure of the Constitution. This is true in three respects.

First, as explained above, the Impeachment Clause restricts the consequences of impeachment to removal from office and disqualification from future federal officeholding. That speaks to the fundamental character of impeachment. In Justice Story's words, it is "a proceeding purely of a political nature. It is not so much designed to punish an offender, as to secure the state against gross official misdemeanors. It touches neither his person, nor his property; but simply divests him of his political capacity."[323] Given that impeachment exists to address threats to the political system, applies only to political officials, and responds only by stripping political power, it makes sense to infer that "high Crimes and Misdemeanors" are offenses against the political system rather than indictable crimes.

Second, if impeachment were restricted to crimes, impeachment proceedings would be restricted to deciding whether the President had committed a specific crime. Such a view would create tension between the Impeachment Clause and other provisions of the Constitution. For example, the Double Jeopardy Clause protects against being tried twice for the same crime. Yet the Impeachment Clause contemplates that an official, once removed, can still face "Indictment, Trial, Judgment and Punishment, according to Law." It would be strange if the Framers forbade double jeopardy, yet allowed the President to be tried in court for crimes after Congress convicted him in a proceeding that necessarily (and exclusively) decided whether he was guilty of those very same crimes.[324] That oddity is avoided only if impeachment proceedings are seen "in noncriminal terms," which occurs if impeachable offenses are understood as distinct from indictable crimes.[325]

Finally, the Constitution was originally understood as limiting Congress's power to create a federal law of crimes. It would therefore be strange if the Framers restricted impeachment to criminal offenses, while denying Congress the ability to criminalize many forms of Presidential wrongdoing that they repeatedly described as requiring impeachment.

To set this point in context, the Constitution expressly authorizes Congress to criminalize only a handful of wrongful acts: "counterfeiting, piracy, 'offenses against the law of nations,' and crimes that occur within the military."[326] Early Congresses did not tread far beyond that core category of crimes, and the Supreme Court took a narrow view of federal power to pass criminal statutes. It was

---

certain characteristics with "Treason" and "Bribery," the key question is *which* characteristics unify them. And for all the reasons given here, it is wrong to conclude that criminality is the unifying principle of impeachable offenses. Moreover, if the Framers' goal was to limit impeachment to violations of the criminal law, it is passing strange that the Impeachment Clause uses a term of art—"high Crimes and Misdemeanors"—that appears neither in the criminal law itself nor anywhere else in the Constitution (which *does* elsewhere refer both to "crimes" and "offenses"). It would have been easy to write a provision limiting the impeachment power to serious crimes, and yet the Framers pointedly did not do so.

[323] 2 Story, *Commentaries* at 272.

[324] *See* Berger, *Impeachment* at 80.

[325] *Id.*

[326] William J. Stuntz, *The Collapse of American Criminal Justice* 99 (2011).

not until much later—in the twentieth century—that the Supreme Court came to recognize that Congress could enact a broader criminal code. As a result, early federal criminal statutes "covered relatively few categories of offenses."[327] Many federal offenses were punishable only when committed "in special places, and within peculiar jurisdictions, as, for instance, on the high seas, or in forts, navy-yards, and arsenals ceded to the United States."[328]

The Framers were not fools. They authorized impeachment for a reason, and that reason would have been gutted if impeachment were limited to crimes. It is possible, of course, that the Framers thought the common law, rather than federal statutes, would define criminal offenses. That is undeniably true of "Bribery": the Framers saw this impeachable offense as defined by the common law of bribery as it was understood at the time. But it is hard to believe that the Framers saw common law as the sole measure of impeachment. For one thing, the common law did not address itself to many wrongs that could be committed uniquely by the President in our republican system. The common law would thus have been an extremely ineffective tool for achieving the Framers' stated purposes in authorizing impeachment. Moreover, the Supreme Court held in 1812 that there is no federal common law of crimes.[329] If the Framers thought only crimes could be impeachable offenses, and hoped common law would describe the relevant crimes, then they made a tragic mistake—and the Supreme Court's 1812 decision ruined their plans for the impeachment power.[330]

Rather than assume the Framers wrote a Constitution full of empty words and internal contradictions, it makes far more sense to agree with Hamilton that impeachment is not about crimes. The better view, which the House itself has long embraced, confirms that impeachment targets offenses against the Constitution that threaten democracy.[331]

C.   The Purpose of Impeachment

The distinction between impeachable offenses and crimes also follows from the fundamentally different purposes that impeachment and the criminal law serve. At bottom, the impeachment power is "the first step in a remedial process—removal from office and possible disqualification from holding future office."[332] It exists "primarily to maintain constitutional government" and is addressed

---

[327] Tribe & Matz, *To End a Presidency* at 48.

[328] 2 Story, *Commentaries* at 264.

[329] *United States v. Hudson and Goodwin*, 11 U.S. 32 (1812).

[330] In the alternative, one might say that "high Crimes and Misdemeanors" occur when the president violates *state* criminal law. But that turns federalism upside down: invoking state criminal codes to supply the content of the federal Impeachment Clause would grant states a bizarre and incongruous primacy in the constitutional system. Especially given that impeachment is crucial to checks and balances *within* the federal government, it would be nonsensical for states to effectively control when this power may be wielded by Congress.

[331] Article III of the Constitution provides that "the Trial of all Crimes, except in Cases of Impeachment, shall be by Jury." Article III, §2. This provision recognizes that impeachable conduct *may* entail criminal conduct—and clarifies that in such cases, the trial of an impeachment still occurs in the Senate, not by jury.

[332] *Staff Report on Constitutional Grounds for Presidential Impeachment* (1974) at 24.

exclusively to abuses perpetrated by federal officeholders.[333] It is through impeachment proceedings that "a President is called to account for abusing powers that only a President possesses."[334] The criminal law, in contrast, "sets a general standard of conduct that all must follow."[335] It applies to all persons within its compass and ordinarily defines acts forbidden to everyone; in our legal tradition, the criminal code "does not address itself [expressly] to the abuses of presidential power."[336]

Indeed, "the early Congresses—filled with Framers—didn't even *try* to create a body of criminal law addressing many of the specific abuses that motivated adoption of the Impeachment Clause in the first place."[337] This partly reflects "a tacit judgment that it [did] not deem such a code necessary."[338] But that is not the only explanation. The Constitution vests "the sole Power of Impeachment" in the House; it is therefore doubtful that a statute enacted by one Congress (and signed by the President) could bind the House at a later date.[339] Moreover, any such effort to define and criminalize all impeachable offenses would quickly run aground. As Justice Story cautioned, impeachable offenses "are of so various and complex a character, so utterly incapable of being defined, or classified, that the task of positive legislation would be impracticable, if it were not almost absurd to attempt it."[340]

There are also general characteristics of the criminal law that make criminality inappropriate as an essential element of impeachable conduct. For example, criminal law traditionally forbids acts, rather than failures to act, yet impeachable conduct "may include the serious failure to discharge the affirmative duties imposed on the President by the Constitution."[341] In addition, unlike a criminal case focused on very specific conduct and nothing else, a Congressional impeachment proceeding may properly consider a broader course of conduct or scheme that tends to subvert constitutional government.[342] Finally, the application of general criminal statutes to the President may raise constitutional issues that have no bearing on an impeachment proceeding, the whole point of which is to assess whether the President has abused power in ways requiring his removal from office.[343]

For all these reasons, "[a] requirement of criminality would be incompatible with the intent of the framers to provide a mechanism broad enough to maintain the integrity of constitutional

---

[333] *Id.*

[334] *Id.*

[335] *Id.*

[336] *Id.*

[337] Tribe & Matz, *To End a Presidency* at 48-49.

[338] Berger, *Impeachment* at 78.

[339] *Committee Report on Nixon Articles of Impeachment* (1974) at 25.

[340] 2 Story, *Commentaries* at 264.

[341] *Staff Report on Constitutional Grounds for Presidential Impeachment* (1974) at 24

[342] *Id.* at 24-25.

[343] Special Counsel Robert S. Mueller, III, *Report On The Investigation Into Russian Interference In The 2016 Presidential Election,* Vol. II at 170-181 (March 2019).

government. Impeachment is a constitutional safety valve; to fulfill this function, it must be flexible enough to cope with exigencies not now foreseeable."[344]

D.   The Limited Relevance of Criminality

As demonstrated, the President can commit "high Crimes and Misdemeanors" without violating federal criminal law. "To conclude otherwise would be to ignore the original meaning, purpose and history of the impeachment power; to subvert the constitutional design of a system of checks and balances; and to leave the nation unnecessarily vulnerable to abusive government officials."[345] Yet the criminal law is not irrelevant. "Our criminal codes identify many terrible acts that would surely warrant removal if committed by the chief executive."[346] Moreover, the President is sworn to uphold the law. If he violates it while grossly abusing power, betraying the national interest through foreign entanglements, or corrupting his office or elections, that weighs in favor of impeaching him.

VI.   Addressing Fallacies About Impeachment

Since the House began its impeachment inquiry, a number of inaccurate claims have circulated about how impeachment works under the Constitution. To assist the Committee in its deliberations, we address six issues of potential relevance: (1) the law that governs House procedures for impeachment; (2) the law that governs the evaluation of evidence, including where the President orders defiance of House subpoenas; (3) whether the President can be impeached for the abuse of his executive powers; (4) whether the President's claims regarding his motives must be accepted at face value; (5) whether the President is immune from impeachment if he attempts an impeachable offense but is caught before he completes it; and (6) whether it is preferable to await the next election when a President has sought to corrupt that very same election.

A.   The Impeachment Process

It has been argued that the House has not followed proper procedure in its ongoing impeachment inquiry. We have considered those arguments and find that they lack merit.

To start with first principles, the Constitution vests the House with the "sole Power of Impeachment."[347] It also vests the House with the sole power to "determine the Rules of its Proceedings."[348] These provisions authorize the House to investigate potential "high Crimes and Misdemeanors," to draft and debate articles of impeachment, and to establish whatever rules and procedures it deems proper for those proceedings.[349]

---

[344] *Staff Report on Constitutional Grounds for Presidential Impeachment* (1974), at 25.

[345] Keith E. Whittington, *Must Impeachable Offenses Be Violations of the Criminal Code?*, LAWFARE, Nov. 19, 2019.

[346] Tribe & Matz, *To End a Presidency* at 51.

[347] U.S. CONST. art. I, § 2, cl. 5.

[348] U.S. CONST. art. I, § 5, cl. 2.

[349] *See* David Pozen, *Risk-Risk Tradeoffs in Presidential Impeachment*, TAKE CARE, Jun. 6, 2018 ("Both chambers of

When the House wields its constitutional impeachment power, it functions like a grand jury or prosecutor: its job is to figure out what the President did and why he did it, and then to decide whether the President should be charged with impeachable offenses. If the House approves any articles of impeachment, the President is entitled to present a full defense at trial in the Senate. It is thus in the Senate, and *not* in the House, where the President might properly raise certain protections associated with trials.[350]

Starting in May 2019, the Judiciary Committee undertook an inquiry to determine whether to recommend articles of impeachment against President Trump. The Committee subsequently confirmed, many times, that it was engaged in an impeachment investigation. On June 11, 2019, the full House approved a resolution confirming that the Judiciary Committee possessed "any and all necessary authority under Article I of the Constitution" to continue its investigation; an accompanying Rules Committee Report emphasized that the "purposes" of the inquiry included "whether to approve 'articles of impeachment with respect to the President.'"[351] As the Judiciary Committee continued with its investigation, evidence came to light that President Trump may have grossly abused the power of his office in dealings with Ukraine. At that point, the House Permanent Select Committee on Intelligence, and the House Oversight and Foreign Affairs Committees, began investigating potential offenses relating to Ukraine. On September 24, 2019, House Speaker Nancy Pelosi directed these committees, as well as the House Judiciary, Financial Services and Ways and Means Committees, to "proceed with their investigations under that umbrella of [an] impeachment inquiry."[352] Finally, on October 31, 2019, the full House approved H. Res. 660, which directed the six committees "to continue their ongoing investigations as part of the existing House of Representatives inquiry into whether sufficient grounds exist for the House of Representatives to exercise its Constitutional power to impeach Donald John Trump, President of the United States of America."[353]

This approach to investigating potential impeachable offenses adheres to the Constitution, the Rules of the House, and historical practice.[354] House Committees have frequently initiated and made substantial progress in impeachment inquiries before the full House considered a resolution formalizing their efforts. That is what happened in the cases of Presidents Johnson and Nixon, as well as in many

---

Congress enjoy vast discretion in how they run impeachment proceedings.").

[350] *Contra* Letter from Pat A. Cipollone, Counsel to the President, to Nancy Pelosi, Speaker of the House, Adam B. Schiff, Chairman, H. Perm. Select Comm. on Intelligence, Eliot L. Engel, Chairman, H. Comm. on Foreign Affairs, and Elijah E. Cummings, Chairman, H. Comm. on Oversight and Reform (Oct. 8, 2019); *Leader McCarthy Speech Against the Sham Impeachment Vote*, Kevin McCarthy, Republican Leader, Oct. 31, 2019.

[351] H. Res. 430, 116th Cong. (2019); *Authorizing the Committee on the Judiciary to Initiate or Intervene in Judicial Proceedings to Enforce Certain Subpoenas and for Other Purposes To Accompany H. Res. 430, H.* Rep. 116-108 at 21 (2019).

[352] Nancy Pelosi, Speaker of the House, *Pelosi Remarks Announcing Impeachment Inquiry,* Sep. 24 2019,.

[353] H. Res. 660, 116th Cong. (2019).

[354] *See generally* H. Rep. No. 116-108.

judicial impeachments (which are subject to the same constitutional provisions).[355] Indeed, numerous judges have been impeached without any prior vote of the full House authorizing a formal inquiry.[356] It is both customary and sensible for committees—particularly the Judiciary Committee—to investigate evidence of serious wrongdoing before decisions are made by the full House.

In such investigations, the House's initial task is to gather evidence. As is true of virtually any competent investigation, whether governmental or private, the House has historically conducted substantial parts of the initial fact-finding process out of public view to ensure more accurate and complete testimony.[357] In President Nixon's case, for instance, only the Judiciary Committee Chairman, Ranking Member, and Committee staff had access to material gathered by the impeachment inquiry in its first several months.[358] There was no need for similar secrecy in President Clinton's case, but only because the House did not engage in a substantial investigation of its own; it largely adopted the facts set forth in a report by Independent Counsel Kenneth Starr, who had spent years investigating behind closed doors.[359]

When grand juries and prosecutors investigate wrongdoing by private citizens and public officials, the person under investigation has no right to participate in the examination of witnesses and evidence that precedes a decision on whether to file charges. That is black letter law under the Constitution, even in serious criminal cases that threaten loss of life or liberty. The same is true in impeachment proceedings, which threaten only loss of public office. Accordingly, even if the full panoply of rights held by criminal defendants hypothetically were to apply in the non-criminal setting of impeachment, the President has no "due process right" to interfere with, or inject himself into, the House's fact-finding efforts. If the House ultimately approves articles of impeachment, any rights that the President might hold are properly secured at trial in the Senate, where he may be afforded an opportunity to present an evidentiary defense and test the strength of the House's case.

Although under no constitutional or other legal obligation to do so, but consistent with historical practice, the full House approved a resolution—H. Res. 660—that ensures transparency, allows effective public hearings, and provides the President with opportunities to participate. The privileges afforded under H. Res. 660 are even greater than those provided to Presidents Nixon and Clinton. They allow the President or his counsel to participate in House Judiciary Committee proceedings by presenting their case, responding to evidence, submitting requests for additional evidence, attending hearings (including non-public hearings), objecting to testimony, and cross-examining witnesses. In

---

[355] *See* 3 Hinds Ch. 75 § 2400 (President Johnson); 3 Deschler Ch. 14, § 15 (President Nixon); H. Rep. No. 101-36, at 13–16 (1988) (Judge Walter Nixon); H. Res. 320, 100th Cong. (Judge Alcee Hastings); H. Rep. No. 99-688, at 3–7 (1986) (Judge Harry Claiborne); 3 Deschler Ch. 14 § 5 (Justice William O. Douglas).

[356] *See* H. Res. 87, 101st Cong. (1989) (impeaching Judge Nixon); H. Res. 499, 100th Cong. (1988) (impeaching Judge Hastings); H. Res. 461, 99th Cong. (1986) (impeaching Judge Claiborne).

[357] *See* Tribe & Matz, *To End A Presidency* at 92 ("Historically, the House and Senate have investigated through their committees ... Critically, although they may involve occasional public hearings, most investigatory activities must be kept secret until they have nearly reached an end.").

[358] *Debate on Nixon Articles of Impeachment* (1974) at 86.

[359] *Committee Report on Clinton Articles of Impeachment* (1998) at 300.

addition, H. Res. 660 gave the minority the same rights to question witnesses that the majority has, as has been true at every step of this impeachment proceeding.

The impeachment inquiry concerning President Trump has thus complied in every respect with the Constitution, the Rules of the House, and historic practice of the House.

B.   Evidentiary Considerations and Presidential Obstruction

The House impeachment inquiry has compiled substantial direct and circumstantial evidence bearing on the question whether President Trump may have committed impeachable offenses. President Trump has objected that some of this evidence comes from witnesses lacking first-hand knowledge of his conduct. In the same breath, though, he has ordered witnesses with first-hand knowledge to defy House subpoenas for testimony and documents—and has done so in a categorical, unqualified manner. President Trump's evidentiary challenges are misplaced as a matter of constitutional law and common sense.

The Constitution does not prescribe rules of evidence for impeachment proceedings in the House or Senate. Consistent with its sole powers to impeach and to determine the rules of its proceedings, the House is constitutionally authorized to consider any evidence that it believes may illuminate the issues before it. At this fact-finding stage, "no technical 'rules of evidence' apply," and "[e]vidence may come from investigations by committee staff, from grand jury matter made available to the committee, or from any other source."[360] The House may thus "subpoena documents, call witnesses, hold hearings, make legal determinations, and undertake any other activities necessary to fulfill [its] mandate."[361] When deciding whether to bring charges against the President, the House is not restricted by the Constitution in deciding which evidence to consider or how much weight to afford it.

Indeed, were rules of evidence to apply anywhere, it would be in the Senate, where impeachments are tried. Yet the Senate does not treat the law of evidence as controlling at such trials.[362] As one scholar explains, "rules of evidence were elaborated primarily to hold *juries* within narrow limits. They have no place in the impeachment process. Both the House and the Senate ought to hear and consider *all* evidence which seems relevant, without regard to technical rules. Senators are in any case continually exposed to 'hearsay' evidence; they cannot be sequestered and kept away from newspapers, like a jury."[363]

---

[360] Black & Bobbitt, *Impeachment* at 9.

[361] Tribe & Matz, *To End a Presidency* at 129.

[362] Gerhardt, *The Federal Impeachment Process* at 42 ("[E]ven if the Senate could agree on such rules for impeachment trials, they would not be enforceable against or binding on individual senators, each of whom traditionally has had the discretion in an impeachment trial to follow any evidentiary standards he or she sees fit.").

[363] Black & Bobbitt, *Impeachment* at 18. *see also* Gerhardt, *The Federal Impeachment Process* at 117 ("Both state and federal courts require special rules of evidence to make trials more efficient and fair or to keep certain evidence away from a jury, whose members might not understand or appreciate its reliability, credibility, or potentially prejudicial effect.").

Instead of adopting abstract or inflexible rules, the House and Senate have long relied on their common sense and good judgment to assess evidence in impeachments. When evidence is relevant but there is reason to question its reliability, those considerations affect how much weight the evidence is given, not whether it can be considered at all.

Here, the factual record is formidable and includes many forms of highly reliable evidence. It goes without saying, however, that the record might be more expansive if the House had full access to the documents and testimony it has lawfully subpoenaed from government officials. The reason the House lacks such access is an unprecedented decision by President Trump to order a total blockade of the House impeachment inquiry.

In contrast, the conduct of prior chief executives illustrates the lengths to which they complied with impeachment inquiries. As President James Polk conceded, the "power of the House" in cases of impeachment "would penetrate into the most secret recesses of the Executive Departments," and "could command the attendance of any and every agent of the Government, and compel them to produce all papers, public or private, official or unofficial, and to testify on oath to all facts within their knowledge."[364] Decades later, when the House conducted an impeachment inquiry into President Johnson, it interviewed cabinet officials and Presidential aides, obtained extensive records, and heard testimony about conversations with Presidential advisors.[365] Presidents Grover Cleveland, Ulysses S. Grant, and Theodore Roosevelt each confirmed that Congress could obtain otherwise-shielded executive branch documents in an impeachment inquiry.[366] And in President Nixon's case—where the President's refusal to turn over tapes led to an article of impeachment—the House Judiciary Committee still heard testimony from his chief of staff (H.R. Haldeman), special counsel (Charles Colson), personal attorney (Herbert Kalmbach), and deputy assistant (Alexander Butterfield). Indeed, with respect to the Senate Watergate investigation, President Nixon stated: "All members of the White House Staff will appear voluntarily when requested by the committee. They will testify under oath, and they will answer fully all proper questions."[367] President Trump's categorical blockade of the House impeachment inquiry has no analogue in the history of the Republic.[368]

As a matter of constitutional law, the House may properly conclude that a President's obstruction of Congress is relevant to assessing the evidentiary record in an impeachment inquiry. For centuries, courts have recognized that "when a party has relevant evidence within his control which he

---

[364] H.R. Jour., 29th Cong., 1st Sess. 693 (1846); 4 James D. Richardson ed., *Messages and Papers of Presidents* 434-35 (1896).

[365] *See generally* Reports of Committees, Impeachment Investigation, 40th Cong., 1st Sess. 183-578 (1867).

[366] *See* Jonathan David Shaub, *The Executive's Privilege: Rethinking the President's Power to Withhold Information*, LAWFARE (Oct. 31, 2019).

[367] The White House, *Remarks by President Nixon* (Apr. 17, 1973) President Nixon initially stated that members of his "personal staff" would "decline a request for a formal appearance before a committee of the Congress," but reversed course approximately one month later., The White House, *Statement by the President, Executive Privilege* (Mar. 12, 1973).

[368] *See* Tribe & Matz, *To End A Presidency* at 129 ("Congress's investigatory powers are at their zenith in the realm of impeachment. They should ordinarily overcome almost any claim of executive privilege asserted by the president.").

fails to produce, that failure gives rise to an inference that the evidence is unfavorable to him."[369] Moreover, it is routine for courts to draw adverse inferences where a party acts in bad faith to conceal or destroy evidence or preclude witnesses from testifying.[370] Although those judicial rules do not control here, they are instructive in confirming that parties who interfere with fact-finding processes can suffer an evidentiary sanction. Consistent with that commonsense principle, the House has informed the administration that defiance of subpoenas at the direction or behest of the President or the White House could justify an adverse inference against the President. In light of President Trump's unlawful and unqualified direction that governmental officials violate their legal responsibilities to Congress, as well as his pattern of witness intimidation, the House may reasonably infer that their testimony would be harmful to the President—or at least not exculpatory. If this evidence were helpful to the President, he would not break the law to keep it hidden, nor would he engage in public acts of harassment to scare other witnesses who might consider coming forward.[371]

One noteworthy result of President Trump's obstruction is that the House has been improperly denied testimony by certain government officials who could have offered first-hand accounts of relevant events. That does not leave the House at sea: there is still robust evidence, both documentary and testimonial, bearing directly on his conduct and motives. But especially given the President's obstruction of Congress, the House is free under the Constitution to consider reliable testimony from officials who overheard—or later learned about—statements by the President to witnesses whose testimony he has blocked.[372]

---

[369] *Int'l Union, United Auto., Aerospace & Agr. Implement Workers of Am. (UAW) v. N. L. R. B.*, 459 F.2d 1329, 1336 (D.C. Cir. 1972); *see also Interstate Circuit v. United States*, 306 U.S. 208, 225–26 (1939); *Rossi v. United States*, 289 U.S. 89, 91–92 (1933); *Mammoth Oil Co. v. United States*, 275 U.S. 13, 51–53 (1927); *Burdine v. Johnson*, 262 F.3d 336, 366 (5th Cir. 2001) (collecting cases); *United States v. Pitts*, 918 F.2d 197, 199 (D.C. Cir. 1990) (holding that, where a missing witness has "so much to offer that one would expect [him] to take the stand," and where "one of the parties had some special ability to produce him," the law allows an inference "that the missing witness would have given testimony damaging to that party").

[370] *See, e.g., Bracey v. Grondin*, 712 F.3d 1012, 1018 (7th Cir. 2013); *Residential Funding Corp. v. DeGeorge Fin. Corp.*, 306 F.3d 99, 107 (2d Cir. 2002); *Nation-Wide Check Corp. v. Forest Hills Distributors, Inc.*, 692 F.2d 214, 217 (1st Cir. 1982); *see also* 2 *Jones on Evidence* § 13:12 & § 13:15 (7th ed. 2019 update).

[371] If the President could order all Executive Branch agencies and officials to defy House impeachment inquiries, and if the House were unable to draw any inferences from that order with respect to the President's alleged misconduct, the impeachment power would be a nullity in many cases where it plainly should apply.

[372] Under the Federal Rules of Evidence—which, again, are not applicable in Congressional impeachment proceedings— judges sometimes limit witnesses from offering testimony about someone else's out-of-court statements. They do so for reasons respecting reliability and with an eye to the unique risks presented by unsophisticated juries that may not properly evaluate evidence. But because hearsay evidence can in fact be highly reliable, and because it is "often relevant," *Tome v. United States*, 513 U.S. 150, 163 (1995), there are many circumstances in which such testimony is admissible in federal judicial proceedings. Those circumstances include, but are by no means limited to, recorded recollections, records of regularly conducted activity, records of a public office, excited utterances, and statements against penal or other interest. Moreover, where hearsay evidence bears indicia of reliability, it is regularly used in many other profoundly important contexts, including federal sentencing and immigration proceedings. *See, e.g., Arrazabal v. Barr*, 929 F.3d 451, 462 (7th Cir. 2019); *United States v. Mitrovic*, 890 F.3d 1217, 1222 (11th Cir. 2018); *United States v. Woods*, 596 F.3d 445, 448 (8th Cir. 2010). Ironically, although some have complained that hearings related to the Ukraine affair initially occurred out of public sight, one reason for that measure was to ensure the integrity of witness testimony. Where multiple witnesses testified

To summarize: just like grand jurors and prosecutors, the House is not subject to rigid evidentiary rules in deciding whether to approve articles. Members of the House are trusted to fairly weigh evidence in an impeachment inquiry. Where the President illegally seeks to obstruct such an inquiry, the House is free to infer that evidence blocked from its view is harmful to the President's position. It is also free to rely on other relevant, reliable evidence that illuminates the ultimate factual issues. The President has no right to defy an impeachment inquiry and then demand that the House turn back because it lacks the very evidence he unlawfully concealed. If anything, such conduct confirms that the President sees himself as above the law and may therefore bear on the question of impeachment.[373]

C.   Abuse of Presidential Power is Impeachable

The powers of the President are immense, but they are not absolute. That principle applies to the current President just as it applied to his predecessors. President Nixon erred in asserting that "when the President does it, that means it is not illegal."[374] And President Trump was equally mistaken when he declared he had "the right to do whatever I want as president."[375] The Constitution always matches power with constraint. That is true even of powers vested exclusively in the chief executive. If those powers are invoked for corrupt reasons, or in an abusive manner that threatens harm to constitutional governance, the President is subject to impeachment for "high Crimes and Misdemeanors."

This conclusion follows from the Constitution's history and structure. As explained above, the Framers created a formidable Presidency, which they entrusted with "the executive Power" and a host of additional authorities. For example, the President alone can confer pardons, sign or veto legislation, recognize foreign nations, serve as Commander in Chief of the armed forces, and appoint or remove principal officers. The President also plays a significant (though not exclusive) role in conducting diplomacy, supervising law enforcement, and protecting national security. These are daunting powers for any one person to wield. If put to nefarious ends, they could wreak havoc on our democracy.

The Framers knew this. Fearful of tyranny in all its forms, they saw impeachment as a necessary guarantee that Presidents could be held accountable for how they exercised executive power. Many delegates at the Constitutional Convention and state ratifying conventions made this point, including Madison, Randolph, Pinckney, Stillman, and Iredell. Their view was widely shared. As James Wilson observed in Pennsylvania, "we have a responsibility in the person of our President"—who is "possessed

---

to the same point in separate, confidential hearings, that factual conclusion may be seen as corroborated and more highly reliable.

[373] The President has advanced numerous arguments to justify his across-the-board defiance of the House impeachment inquiry. These arguments lack merit. As this Committee recognized when it impeached President Nixon for obstruction of Congress, the impeachment power includes a corresponding power of inquiry that allows the House to investigate the Executive Branch and compel compliance with its subpoenas.

[374] *Document: Transcript of David Frost's Interview with Richard Nixon,* TEACHING AMERICAN HISTORY. (1977).

[375] Michael Brice-Saddler, *While Bemoaning Mueller Probe, Trump Falsely Says the Constitution Gives Him 'The Right To Do Whatever I Want",* THE WASHINGTON POST, July 23, 2019..

of power"—since "far from being above the laws," he is "amenable to them … by impeachment."[376] Hamilton struck the same note. In *Federalist No. 70,* he remarked that the Constitution affords Americans the "greatest securities they can have for the faithful exercise of any delegated power," including the power to discover "with facility and clearness" any misconduct requiring "removal from office."[377] Impeachment and executive power were thus closely intertwined in the Framers' constitutional plan: the President could be vested with awesome power, but only because he faced removal from office for grave abuses.

The architects of checks and balances meant no exceptions to this rule. There is no power in the Constitution that a President can exercise immune from legal consequence. The existence of any such unchecked and uncheckable authority in the federal government would offend the bedrock principle that nobody is above the law. It would also upend the reasons why our Framers wrote impeachment into the Constitution: the *exact* forms of Presidential wrongdoing that they discussed in Philadelphia could be committed through use of executive powers, and it is unthinkable that the Framers left the Nation defenseless in such cases. In fact, when questioned by Mason in Virginia, Madison expressly stated that the President could be impeached for abuse of his exclusive pardon power—a view that the Supreme Court later echoed in *Ex Parte Grossman.*[378] By the same token, a President could surely be impeached for treason if he fired the Attorney General to thwart the unmasking of an enemy spy in wartime; he could impeached for bribery if he offered to divulge state secrets to a foreign nation, conditioned on regulatory exemptions for his family business.[379] Simply put, "the fact that a power is exclusive to the executive—that is, the president alone may exercise it—does not mean the power cannot be exercised in clear bad faith, and that Congress cannot look into or act upon knowledge of that abuse."[380]

The rule that abuse of power can lead to removal encompasses all three branches. The Impeachment Clause applies to "The President, Vice President and all civil Officers of the United States," including Article III judges.[381] There is no exception to impeachment for misconduct by federal judges involving the exercise of their official powers. In fact, the opposite is true: "If in the exercise of the powers with which they are clothed as ministers of justice, [judges] act with partiality, or maliciously, or corruptly, or arbitrarily, or oppressively, they may be called to an account by

---

[376] 2 Elliot, *Debates in the Several State Conventions* at 480.

[377] Alexander Hamilton, *Federalist No. 70* at 456.

[378] 3 Elliot, *Debates in the Several State Conventions* at 497-98; *Ex Parte Grossman,* 267 U.S. at 121. Madison adhered to this understanding after the Constitution was ratified. In 1789, he explained to his colleagues in the House that the President would be subject to impeachment for abuse of the removal power—which is held by the President alone—"if he suffers [his appointees] to perpetrate with impunity High crimes or misdemeanors against the United States, or neglects to superintend their conduct, so as to check their excesses." 1 *Annals of Congress* 387 (1789).

[379] Scholars have offered many examples and hypotheticals that they see as illustrative of this point. *See* Bowman, *High Crimes and Misdemeanors* at 258; Black & Bobbitt, *Impeachment* at 115; Hemel & Posner, *Presidential Obstruction of Justice* at 1297; Tribe & Matz, *To End a Presidency* at 61.

[380] Jane Chong, *Impeachment-Proof? The President's Unconstitutional Abuse of His Constitutional Powers,* LAWFARE, Jan. 2, 2018.

[381] U.S. CONST. art. II, § 4.

impeachment."[382] Similarly, if Members of Congress exercise legislative power abusively or with corrupt purposes, they may be removed pursuant to the Expulsion Clause, which permits each house of Congress to expel a member "with the Concurrence of two thirds."[383] *Nobody* is entitled to wield power under the Constitution if they ignore or betray the Nation's interests to advance their own.

This is confirmed by past practice of the House. President Nixon's case directly illustrates the point. As head of the Executive Branch, he had the power to appoint and remove law enforcement officials, to issue pardons, and to oversee the White House, IRS, CIA, and FBI. But he did not have any warrant to exercise these Presidential powers abusively or corruptly. When he did so, the House Judiciary Committee properly approved multiple articles of impeachment against him. Several decades later, the House impeached President Clinton. There, the House witnessed substantial disagreement over whether the President could be impeached for obstruction of justice that did *not* involve using the powers of his office. But it was universally presumed—and never seriously questioned—that the President could be impeached for obstruction of justice that *did* involve abuse of those powers.[384] That view rested firmly on a correct understanding of the Constitution.

Our Constitution rejects pretensions to monarchy and binds Presidents with law. A President who sees no limit on his power manifestly threatens the Republic.

D. Presidential Pretexts Need Not Be Accepted at Face Value

Impeachable offenses are often defined by corrupt intent. To repeat Iredell, "the president would be liable to impeachments [if] he had … acted from some corrupt motive or other," or if he was "willfully abusing his trust."[385] Consistent with that teaching, both "Treason" and "Bribery" require proof that the President acted with an improper state of mind, as would many other offenses described as impeachable at the Constitutional Convention. Contrary to occasional suggestions that the House may not examine the President's intent, an impeachment inquiry may therefore require the House to determine *why* the President acted the way he did. Understanding the President's motives may clarify whether he used power in forbidden ways, whether he was faithless in executing the laws, and whether he poses a continuing danger to the Nation if allowed to remain in office.

When the House probes a President's state of mind, its mandate is to find the facts. There is no room for legal fictions or lawyerly tricks that distort a clear assessment of the President's thinking. That means evaluating the President's explanations to see if they ring true. The question is not whether the President's conduct *could have* resulted from innocent motives. It is whether the President's *real reasons*—the ones actually in his mind as he exercised power—were legitimate. The Framers designed impeachment to root out abuse and corruption, even when a President masks improper intent with cover stories.

---

[382] *Bradley v. Fisher* 80 U.S. 335, 350 (1871).

[383] U.S. CONST. art. I, § 5, cl. 2.

[384] *See generally 1998 Background and History of Impeachment Hearing.*

[385] *Id.* at 49.

Accordingly, where the President's explanation of his motives defies common sense, or is otherwise unbelievable, the House is free to reject the pretextual explanation and to conclude that the President's false account of his thinking is itself evidence that he acted with corrupt motives. The President's honesty in an impeachment inquiry, or his lack thereof, can thus shed light on the underlying issue.[386]

President Nixon's case highlights the point. In its discussion of an article of impeachment for abuse of power, the House Judiciary Committee concluded that he had "falsely used a national security pretext" to direct executive agencies to engage in unlawful electronic surveillance investigations, thus violating "the constitutional rights of citizens."[387] In its discussion of the same article, the Committee also found that President Nixon had interfered with the Justice Department by ordering it to cease investigating a crime "on the pretext that it involved national security."[388] President Nixon's repeated claim that he had acted to protect national security could not be squared with the facts, and so the Committee rejected it in approving articles of impeachment against him for targeting political opponents.

Testing whether someone has falsely characterized their motives requires careful attention to the facts. In rare cases, "some implausible, fantastic, and silly explanations could be found to be pretextual without any further evidence."[389] Sifting truth from fiction, though, usually demands a thorough review of the record—and a healthy dose of common sense. The question is whether "the evidence tells a story that does not match the explanation."[390]

Because courts assess motive all the time, they have identified warning signs that an explanation may be untrustworthy. Those red flags include the following:

First, *lack of fit between conduct and explanation.* This exists when someone claims they were trying to achieve a specific goal but then engaged in conduct poorly tailored to achieving it.[391] For instance, imagine the President claims that he wants to solve a particular problem—but then he ignores many clear examples of that problem, weakens rules meant to stop it from occurring, acts in ways unlikely to address it, and seeks to punish only two alleged violators (both of whom happen to be his competitors). The lack of fit between his punitive conduct and his explanation for it strongly suggests that the explanation is false, and that he invented it as a pretext for corruptly targeting his competitors.

---

[386] *See* Tribe & Matz, *To End A Presidency* at 92 ("Does the president admit error, apologize, and clean house? Does he prove his innocence, or at least his reasonable good faith? Or does he lie and obstruct until the bitter end? Maybe he fires investigators and stonewalls prosecutors? … These data points are invaluable when Congress asks whether leaving the president in office would pose a continuing threat to the nation.").

[387] *Committee Report on Nixon Articles of Impeachment* (1974) at 146.

[388] *Id.* at 179.

[389] *Purkett v. Elem*, 514 U.S. 765, 776–77 (1995) (Stevens, J., dissenting).

[390] *Dep't of Commerce v. N.Y.*, No. 18-966, at 27 (U.S. Jun. 27, 2019).

[391] *See Romer v. Evans*, 517 U.S. 620, 632 (1996); *Albemarle Paper Co. v. Moody,* 422 U.S. 405, 425 (1975); *Miller-El v. Dretke,* 545 U.S. 231, 260 (2005).

Second, *arbitrary discrimination*. When someone claims they were acting for a particular reason, look to see if they treated similarly-situated individuals the same.[392] For example, if a President says that people doing business abroad should not engage in specific practices, does he punish everyone who breaks that rule, or does he pick and choose? If he picks and chooses, is there a good reason why he targets some people and not others, or does he appear to be targeting people for reasons unrelated to his stated motive? Where similarly-situated people are treated differently, the President should be able to explain why; if no such explanation exists, it follows that hidden motives are in play.

Third, *shifting explanations*. When someone repeatedly changes their story, it makes sense to infer that they began with a lie and may still be lying.[393] That is true in daily life and it is true in impeachments. The House may therefore doubt the President's account of his motives when he first denies that something occurred; then admits that it occurred but denies key facts; then admits those facts and tries to explain them away; and then changes his explanation as more evidence comes to light. Simply stated, the House is "not required to exhibit a naiveté from which ordinary citizens are free."[394]

Fourth, *irregular decisionmaking*. When someone breaks from the normal method of making decisions, and instead acts covertly or strangely, there is cause for suspicion. As the Supreme Court has reasoned, "[t]he specific sequence of events leading up the challenged decision" may "shed some light on the decisionmaker's purposes"—and "[d]epartures from the normal procedural sequence" might "afford evidence that improper purposes are playing a role."[395] There are many personnel and procedures in place to ensure sound decisionmaking in the Executive Branch. When they are ignored, or replaced by secretive irregular channels, the House must closely scrutinize Presidential conduct.

Finally, *explanations based on falsehoods*. Where someone explains why they acted a certain way, but the explanation depends on demonstrably false facts, then their explanation is suspect.[396] For example, if a President publicly states that he withheld funds from a foreign nation due to its failure to meet certain conditions, but the federal agencies responsible for monitoring those conditions certify that they were satisfied, the House may conclude that the President's explanation is only a distraction from the truth.

---

[392] *Flowers v. Mississippi*, 139 S. Ct. 2228, 2249 (2019); *Miller-El v. Cockrell*, 537 U.S. 322, 345 (2003).

[393] *See Foster v. Chatman*, 136 S. Ct. 1737, 1754 (2016); *Evans v. Sebelius*, 716 F.3d 617, 620–21 (D.C. Cir. 2013); *Geleta v. Gray*, 645 F.3d 408, 413–14 (D.C. Cir. 2011); *EEOC v. Sears Roebuck & Co.*, 243 F.3d 846, 853 (4th Cir.2001); *Dominguez–Cruz v. Suttle Caribe, Inc.*, 202 F.3d 424, 432 (1st Cir. 2000); *Thurman v. Yellow Freight Sys., Inc.*, 90 F.3d 1160, 1167 (6th Cir. 1996).

[394] *United States v. Stanchich*, 550 F.2d 1294, 1300 (2nd Cir. 1977) (Friendly, J.) (making a similar point about federal judges).

[395] *See Vill. of Arlington Heights v. Metro. Hous. Dev. Corp.*, 429 U.S. 252, 267 (1977).

[396] *See, e.g.*, *Reeves v. Sanderson Plumbing Products*, 530 U.S. 133, 147 (2000); *Geleta v. Gray*, 645 F.3d 408, 414 (D.C. Cir. 2011); *Czekalski v. Peters*, 475 F.3d 360, 366 (D.C. Cir. 2007); *Murray v. Gilmore*, 406 F.3d 708, 716 (D.C. Cir. 2005); *Salazar v. Wash. Metro. Transit Auth.*, 401 F.3d 504, 511–12 (D.C. Cir. 2005); *Anderson v. Zubieta*, 180 F.3d 329, 348 (D.C. Cir. 1999).

When one or more of these red flags is present, there is reason to doubt that the President's account of his motives is accurate. When they are all present simultaneously, that conclusion is virtually unavoidable. Thus, in examining the President's motives as part of an impeachment inquiry, the House must test his story against the evidence to see if it holds water. If it does not, the House may find that he acted with corrupt motives—and that he has made false statements as part of an effort to stymie the impeachment inquiry.

E.   Attempted Presidential Misconduct Is Impeachable

As a matter of settled constitutional law, and contrary to recent suggestions otherwise, attempted Presidential wrongdoing can be impeachable. This is clear from the records of the Constitutional Convention. In the momentous exchange that led to adoption of the "high Crimes and Misdemeanors" standard, Mason championed impeaching Presidents for any "great and dangerous offenses." It was therefore necessary, he argued, to avoid a narrow standard that would prevent impeachment for "*attempts* to subvert the Constitution" (emphasis added). Then, only minutes later, it was Mason himself who suggested "high Crimes and Misdemeanors" as the test for Presidential impeachment. The very author of the relevant constitutional text thus made clear it must cover "attempts."

The House Judiciary Committee reached this conclusion in President Nixon's case. Its analysis is compelling and consistent with Mason's reasoning:

> In some of the instances in which Richard M. Nixon abused the powers of his office, his unlawful or improper objective was not achieved. But this does not make the abuse of power any less serious, nor diminish the applicability of the impeachment remedy. The principle was stated by Supreme Court Justice William Johnson in 1808: "If an officer attempt[s] an act inconsistent with the duties of his station, it is presumed that the failure of the attempt would not exempt him from liability to impeachment. Should a President head a conspiracy for the usurpation of absolute power, it is hoped that no one will contend that defeating his machinations would restore him to innocence." *Gilchrist v. Collector of Charleston, 10 F.* Cas. 355, 365 (No. 5, 420) (C.C.D.S.C. 1808).

Adhering to this legal analysis, the Committee approved articles of impeachment against President Nixon that encompassed acts of attempted wrongdoing that went nowhere or were thwarted. That includes President Nixon's attempt to block an investigation by the Patman Committee into the Watergate break-ins,[397] his attempt to block testimony by former aides,[398] his attempt to "narrow and divert" the Senate Select Committee's investigation,[399] and his attempt to have the IRS open tax audits of 575 members of George McGovern's staff and contributors to his campaign, at a time when McGovern was President Nixon's political opponent in the upcoming 1972 presidential election.[400]

---

[397] *Committee Report on Nixon Articles of Impeachment* (1974) at 64.

[398] *Id.* at 120.

[399] *Id.*

[400] *Id.* at 143.

Moreover, the article of impeachment against President Nixon for abuse of power charged that he "attempted to prejudice the constitutional right of an accused to a fair trial."[401]

History thus confirms that defiance by his own aides do not afford the President a defense to impeachment. The Nation is not required to cross its fingers and hope White House staff will persist in ignoring or sidelining a President who orders them to execute "high Crimes and Misdemeanors." Nor can a President escape impeachment just because his corrupt plan to abuse power or manipulate elections was discovered and abandoned. It is inconceivable that our Framers authorized the removal of Presidents who engage in treason or bribery, but disallowed the removal of Presidents who attempt such offenses and are caught before they succeed. Moreover, a President who takes concrete steps toward engaging in impeachable conduct is not entitled to any benefit of the doubt. As one scholar remarks in the context of attempts to manipulate elections, "when a substantial attempt is made by a candidate to procure the presidency by corrupt means, we may presume that he at least thought this would make a difference in the outcome, and thus we should resolve any doubts as to the effects of his efforts against him."[402]

Common sense confirms what the law provides: a President may be impeached where he attempts a grave abuse of power, is caught along the way, abandons his plan, and subsequently seeks to conceal his wrongdoing. A President who attempts impeachable offenses will surely attempt them again. The impeachment power exists so that the Nation can remove such Presidents from power before their attempts finally succeed.

F.   Impeachment is Part of Democratic Governance

As House Judiciary Committee Chairman Peter Rodino emphasized in 1974, "it is under our Constitution, the supreme law of our land, that we proceed through the sole power of impeachment."[403] Impeachment is part of democratic constitutional governance, not an exception to it. It results in the President's removal from office only when a majority of the House, and then a super-majority of the Senate, conclude that he has engaged in sufficiently grave misconduct that his term in office must be brought to an early end. This process does not "nullify" the last election. No President is entitled to persist in office after committing "high Crimes and Misdemeanors," and no voter is entitled to expect that their preferred candidate will do so. Under the Constitution, when a President engages in great and dangerous offenses against the Nation—thus betraying their Oath of Office—impeachment and removal by Congress may be necessary to protect our democracy.

The Framers considered relying solely on elections, rather than impeachment, to remove wayward Presidents. But they overwhelmingly rejected that position. As Madison warned, waiting so long "might be fatal to the Republic."[404] Particularly where the President's misconduct is aimed at

---

[401] *Id.* at 3.

[402] Black & Bobbitt, *Impeachment* at 93.

[403] *Debate on Nixon Articles of Impeachment* (1974) at 2.

[404] Elliot, *Debates on the Adoption of the Federal Constitution* at 341.

corrupting our democracy, relying on elections to solve the problem is insufficient: it makes no sense to wait for the ballot box when a President stands accused of interfering with elections and is poised to do so again. Numerous Framers spoke directly to this point at the Constitutional Convention. Impeachment is the remedy for a President who will do anything, legal or not, to remain in office. Allowing the President a free pass is thus the wrong move when he is caught trying to corrupt elections in the final year of his first four-year term—just as he prepares to face the voters.

Holding the President accountable for "high Crimes and Misdemeanors" not only upholds democracy, but also vindicates the separation of powers. Representative Robert Kastenmeier explained this well in 1974: "The power of impeachment is not intended to obstruct or weaken the office of the Presidency. It is intended as a final remedy against executive excess … [a]nd it is the obligation of the Congress to defend a democratic society against a Chief Executive who might be corrupt."[405] The impeachment power thus restores balance and order when Presidential misconduct threatens constitutional governance.

VII.   Conclusion

As Madison recognized, "In framing a government which is to be administered by men over men, the great difficulty lies in this: You must first enable the government to control the governed; and in the next place oblige it control itself."[406] Impeachment is the House's last and most extraordinary resort when faced with a President who threatens our constitutional system. It is a terrible power, but only "because it was forged to counter a terrible power: the despot who deems himself to be above the law."[407] The consideration of articles of impeachment is always a sad and solemn undertaking. In the end, it is the House—speaking for the Nation as a whole—that must decide whether the President's conduct rises to the level of "high Crimes and Misdemeanors" warranting impeachment.

---

[405] *Debate on Nixon Articles of Impeachment* (1974) at 16.

[406] James Madison, *Federalist No. 51* at 356.

[407] Jill Lepore, *The Invention - And Reinvention – Of Impeachment,* THE NEW YORKER Oct. 21, 2019.

Article I: Abuse of Power

I.   The First Article of Impeachment

The Constitution provides that the House of Representatives "shall have the sole Power of Impeachment" and that the President "shall be removed from Office on Impeachment for, and Conviction of, Treason, Bribery, or other high Crimes and Misdemeanors". In his conduct of the office of President of the United States—and in violation of his constitutional oath faithfully to execute the office of President of the United States and, to the best of his ability, preserve, protect, and defend the Constitution of the United States, and in violation of his constitutional duty to take care that the laws be faithfully executed—Donald J. Trump has abused the powers of the Presidency, in that:

Using the powers of his high office, President Trump solicited the interference of a foreign government, Ukraine, in the 2020 United States Presidential election. He did so through a scheme or course of conduct that included soliciting the Government of Ukraine to publicly announce investigations that would benefit his reelection, harm the election prospects of a political opponent, and influence the 2020 United States Presidential election to his advantage. President Trump also sought to pressure the Government of Ukraine to take these steps by conditioning official United States Government acts of significant value to Ukraine on its public announcement of the investigations. President Trump engaged in this scheme or course of conduct for corrupt purposes in pursuit of personal political benefit. In so doing, President Trump used the powers of the Presidency in a manner that compromised the national security of the United States and undermined the integrity of the United States democratic process. He thus ignored and injured the interests of the Nation.

President Trump engaged in this scheme or course of conduct through the following means:

(1) President Trump—acting both directly and through his agents within and outside the United States Government—corruptly solicited the Government of Ukraine to publicly announce investigations into—

(A) a political opponent, former Vice President Joseph R. Biden, Jr.; and

(B) a discredited theory promoted by Russia alleging that Ukraine—rather than Russia—interfered in the 2016 United States Presidential election.

(2) With the same corrupt motives, President Trump—acting both directly and through his agents within and outside the United States Government—conditioned two official acts on the public announcements that he had requested—

(A) the release of $391 million of United States taxpayer funds that Congress had appropriated on a bipartisan basis for the purpose of providing vital military and security assistance to Ukraine to oppose Russian aggression and which President Trump had ordered suspended; and

(B) a head of state meeting at the White House, which the President of Ukraine sought to demonstrate continued United States support for the Government of Ukraine in the face of Russian aggression.

(3) Faced with the public revelation of his actions, President Trump ultimately released the military and security assistance to the Government of Ukraine, but has persisted in openly and corruptly urging and soliciting Ukraine to undertake investigations for his personal political benefit.

These actions were consistent with President Trump's previous invitations of foreign interference in United States elections.

In all of this, President Trump abused the powers of the Presidency by ignoring and injuring national security and other vital national interests to obtain an improper personal political benefit. He has also betrayed the Nation by abusing his high office to enlist a foreign power in corrupting democratic elections.

Wherefore President Trump, by such conduct, has demonstrated that he will remain a threat to national security and the Constitution if allowed to remain in office, and has acted in a manner grossly incompatible with self-governance and the rule of law. President Trump thus warrants impeachment and trial, removal from office, and disqualification to hold and enjoy any office of honor, trust, or profit under the United States.

II.   Introduction

The President is entrusted with extraordinary power and commanded to "take Care that the Laws be faithfully executed." At minimum, that means the President must use his office to serve and protect the American people. It is thus a grave violation of the Constitution for a President to betray the public by exercising power for his own personal gain while injuring and ignoring vital national interests. As the Framers confirmed, such abuse of power warrants impeachment.

President Donald J. Trump used the power of his office to solicit and pressure a foreign nation to interfere in the 2020 United States Presidential election. He did so not for any legitimate United States policy objective, but to obtain a personal political advantage and to harm a political opponent. His scheme involved directly soliciting the announcement of investigations related to former Vice President Joseph Biden and the 2016 United States Presidential election. It also involved leveraging military and security assistance to a fragile foreign ally, as well as a valuable White House meeting, as part of a pressure campaign to induce that sought-after announcement.

These corrupt efforts by President Trump to manipulate the next election in his favor harmed the national security of the United States and imperiled the integrity of our democratic system. But when President Trump was caught, he did not apologize or cease his misconduct. He instead persisted in urging foreign nations to investigate an American citizen who dared to oppose him politically. If President Trump is allowed to remain in office, he will unquestionably continue to pursue personal political benefits at the direct expense of our security and self-governance.

This conduct, and the risk posed by President Trump's pattern of misconduct, is the very definition of an impeachable offense. It captures the Framers' worst fears about how Presidents might someday abuse the powers of their office. To protect democracy and safeguard national security, the Committee on the Judiciary has no choice but to recommend that President Trump be impeached.

III. President Trump Committed "High Crimes and Misdemeanors" by Abusing the Powers of his Office

A.   Abuse of Power is an Impeachable "High Crime and Misdemeanor"

"[A]buse of power was no vague notion to the Framers and their contemporaries. It had a very particular meaning to them."[408] This meaning encompassed the use of official powers in a way that "on its very face grossly exceeds the President's constitutional authority or violates legal limits on that authority."[409] As relevant here, it also included "the exercise of official power to obtain an improper personal benefit, while ignoring or injuring the national interest."[410] This understanding is rooted in the Constitution's Take Care Clause, which commands the President to "faithfully execute" the law.[411] That duty requires Presidents "to exercise their power only when it is motivated in the public interest rather than in their private self-interest."[412]

Numerous Framers confirmed that a President can be impeached for exercising power with a corrupt purpose. As James Iredell explained, "the president would be liable to impeachments [if] he had … acted from some corrupt motive or other," or if he was "willfully abusing his trust."[413] Alexander Hamilton deemed impeachment proper for "offenses which proceed from the misconduct of public men, or, in other words, from the abuse or violation of some public trust."[414] In a similar vein, James Madison reasoned that the President could be impeached if there were "grounds to believe" he used his pardon power for the corrupt purpose of obstructing justice by "shelter[ing]" persons with whom he is connected "in any suspicious manner."[415] As these and many other historical authorities show, "to the Framers, it was dangerous for officials to exceed their constitutional power, or to transgress legal limits, but it was equally dangerous (perhaps more so) for officials to conceal corrupt or illegitimate objectives

---

[408] *See* Staff of H. Comm. on the Judiciary, 116th Cong., *Constitutional Grounds for Presidential Impeachment* 18 (Comm. Print 2019) (hereinafter "*Constitutional Grounds for Impeachment* (2019)").

[409] *Id.*

[410] *Id.* at 8.

[411] U.S. Const., art. II, § 3, cl. 5.

[412] Andrew Kent et al., *Faithful Execution and Article II*, 132 Harv. L. Rev. 2111, 2120, 2179 (2019).

[413] *Background and History of Impeachment: Hearing Before the Subcomm. On the Constitution of the H. Comm. on the Judiciary*, 105th Cong. 49 (1999) (statement of Michael J. Gerhardt).

[414] *The Federalist No. 65*, at 426 (Alexander Hamilton) (Benjamin Fletcher Wright ed., 2004).

[415] 3 Jonathan Elliot, ed., *The Debates in the Several State Conventions on the Adoption of the Federal Constitution* 497-98 (1861) (hereinafter "*Debates in the Several State Conventions*").

behind superficially valid acts."[416]

The proceedings against President Nixon confirm and exemplify the point. Two of the three articles against him—Article I (obstruction of justice) and Article II (abuse of power)—accused President Nixon of using his executive power for corrupt ends.[417] The second article principally addressed President Nixon's use of power, including powers vested solely in the Presidency, to aid political allies, harm political opponents, and gain improper personal political advantages. In explaining this article of impeachment, the House Committee on the Judiciary (the "Committee") stated that President Nixon's conduct was "undertaken for his personal political advantage and not in furtherance of any valid national policy objective."[418] His abuses of Presidential power were therefore "seriously incompatible with our system of constitutional government" and warranted removal from office.[419]

It is occasionally suggested that a President cannot be impeached for the use (or abuse) of powers vested in him by the Constitution. As the Framers made clear, and as President Nixon's case proves, that interpretation is plainly incorrect and, moreover, would eviscerate our system of checks and balances. The fact that a President is vested with powers does not mean he can exercise them with impunity. Nor does it mean he is free to set his own personal gain as the *de facto* policy of the United States. To the contrary, when the President wields power entrusted to him by the people of this Nation, he must honor and serve that public trust. Where a President betrays that obligation by corrupting his office, he is subject to impeachment.

B. The Framers Feared Presidents Would Abuse Their Power to Betray National Interests Through Foreign Entanglements and to Corrupt Elections

In warning against abuse of power, the Framers repeatedly returned to two very specific risks: betrayal of the national interest and corruption of elections. Informed by history, the Framers perceived these abuses as existential threats to the Republic. The United States could not survive if Presidents used their high office to conspire with foreign nations in pursuit of personal gain. And democracy would be in grave danger if Presidents used their powers to subvert elections. As John Adams warned in a letter to Thomas Jefferson, these risks were unavoidable and might sometimes overlap: "You are apprehensive of foreign Interference, Intrigue, Influence. So am I. ... [A]s often as Elections happen,

---

[416] *Constitutional Grounds for Impeachment* (2019), at 20. Many other Framers agreed that abuse of power is an impeachable offense. In explaining why the Constitution must authorize Presidential impeachment, Edmund Randolph warned that "the Executive will have great opportunit[ies] of abusing his power." 2 Max Farrand, ed., *The Records of the Federal Convention of 1787*, 67 (1911). Charles Pinckney agreed that Presidents must be removed who "behave amiss or betray their public trust." 4 *Debates in the Several State Conventions*, at 281. Reverend Samuel Stillman asked, "With such a prospect [of impeachment], who will dare to abuse the powers vested in him by the people?" 2 *Debates in the Several State Conventions*, at 169.

[417] *Report of the Committee on the Judiciary, Impeachment of Richard M. Nixon, President of the United States*, H. Rep. No. 93-1305, at 1-4 (1974) (hereinafter "*Committee Report on Nixon Articles of Impeachment (1974)*"). Obstruction of justice was also the basis for an article of impeachment against President Clinton, though his conduct did not involve official acts. *See* H. Res. 611, 105th Cong. (1998).

[418] *Committee Report on Nixon Articles of Impeachment (1974)* at 139.

[419] *Id.*

the danger of foreign Influence recurs."[420] In *Federalist No. 68*, Hamilton cautioned that the "most deadly adversaries of republican government" may come "chiefly from the desire in foreign powers to gain an improper ascendant in our councils."[421] The Framers sought to guard against this threat in the Impeachment Clause. If a President succumbed to temptation, placing his own personal interests above our national security and commitment to domestic self-governance, he faced impeachment and removal from his position of power.

Betrayal of national security was not an abstraction to the Framers, who had just waged a war for independence and knew the peril of corrupt foreign entanglements. "Foreign powers," warned Elbridge Gerry, "will intermeddle in our affairs, and spare no expense to influence them."[422] In explaining why the Constitution required an impeachment option, Madison argued that a President "might betray his trust to foreign powers."[423] Benjamin Franklin, in turn, referenced the Prince of Orange, who had reneged on a military treaty with France under suspicious circumstances, inciting "the most violent animosities and contentions" in Dutch politics.[424] These and other Framers made clear that impeachment was a safeguard against Presidents who betrayed vital national interests through plots with foreign powers. The President's broad authority in conducting foreign affairs makes it more important, not less, that he display unswerving loyalty to the United States.[425] "Accordingly, where the President uses his foreign affairs power in ways that betray the national interest for his own benefit, or harm national security for equally corrupt reasons, he is subject to impeachment by the House … A President who perverts his role as chief diplomat to serve private rather than public ends has unquestionably engaged in 'high Crimes and Misdemeanors'—especially if he invited, rather than opposed, foreign interference in our politics."[426]

This last point speaks to a distinct but related fear: that Presidents would improperly use the vast power of their office to ensure their own re-election. William Davie saw impeachment as "an essential security for the good behaviour of the Executive," who might otherwise spare "no efforts or means whatever to get himself re-elected."[427] George Mason agreed that the threat of electoral treachery "furnished a peculiar reason in favor of impeachments whilst in office": "Shall the man who has practised corruption & by that means procured his appointment in the first instance, be suffered to escape punishment, by repeating his guilt?"[428] Gouverneur Morris later added that "the Executive ought

---

[420] Papers of Thomas Jefferson, *To Thomas Jefferson from John Adams, 6 December 1787*, National Archives, Founders Online.

[421] *The Federalist No. 68*, at 441 (Alexander Hamilton).

[422] Brianne Gorod & Elizabeth Wydra, *The First Magistrate in Foreign Pay*, THE NEW REPUBLIC, Nov. 11, 2019.

[423] 2 Farrand, *Records of the Federal Convention*, at 66.

[424] *Id.* at 68.

[425] *Constitutional Grounds for Impeachment* (2019), at 45.

[426] *Id.* at 24. Thus, "[a]lthough the Framers did not intend impeachment for genuine, good faith disagreements between the President and Congress over matters of diplomacy, they were explicit that betrayal of the Nation through plots with foreign powers justified removal." *Id.* at 23.

[427] 2 Farrand, *Records of the Federal Convention*, at 64.

[428] *Id.* at 65.

therefore to be impeachable for … Corrupting his electors."[429] Based in their own experience under King George III, as well as the writings of John Locke and other luminaries, "those who wrote our Constitution knew, and feared, that the chief executive could threaten their plan of government by corrupting elections."[430] They included impeachment in the Constitution largely to thwart such treachery. As explained above, "The true nature of this threat is its rejection of government by 'We the People,' who would 'ordain and establish' the Constitution … When the President concludes that elections threaten his continued grasp on power, and therefore seeks to corrupt or interfere with them, he denies the very premise of our constitutional system. The American people choose their leaders; a President who wields power to destroy opponents or manipulate elections is a President who rejects democracy itself."[431]

These authorities make clear that a President commits "high Crimes and Misdemeanors" where he exercises official power to obtain an improper personal benefit, while ignoring or injuring the national interest. Such an abuse is especially abhorrent where it involves a betrayal of the national interest through foreign entanglements or an effort to corrupt our democracy. "Any one of these violations of the public trust justifies impeachment; when combined in a single course of conduct, they state the strongest possible case for impeachment and removal from office."[432]

C.   Key Findings of Fact

The complete evidentiary record bearing on President Trump's abuse of power is set forth in the Trump-Ukraine Impeachment Inquiry Report, (the "*Ukraine Report*"), and we rely on that Report and its findings here. Because we do not restate all of the facts contained in that Report which support the Committee's conclusions, we fully incorporate the *Ukraine Report* by reference here.[433]. On the basis of that full record, it is indisputable that President Trump engaged in abuse of power. The essential facts bearing on that judgment include the following:[434]

- Donald J. Trump, the 45th President of the United States—acting personally and through his agents within and outside of the U.S. government—solicited the interference of a foreign government, Ukraine, in the 2020 U.S. presidential election. The President engaged in this course of conduct for the benefit of his reelection, to harm the election prospects of a political opponent, and to influence our nation's upcoming presidential election to his advantage. In so doing, the President placed his personal political interests above the national interests of the

---

[429] *Id.* at 69.

[430] *See Constitutional Grounds for Impeachment* (2019), at 27.

[431] *Id.*

[432] *Id.* at 11.

[433] *The Trump-Ukraine Impeachment Inquiry Report: Report for the H. Perm. Select Comm. on Intelligence Pursuant to H. Res. 660 in Consultation with the H. Comm. on Oversight and Reform and the H. Comm. on Foreign Affairs* at 208, 116th Cong. (2019) (hereinafter "*Ukraine Report*").

[434] The facts that follow constitute the "key findings of fact" set forth in the *Ukraine Report. Id.* at 34-36.

United States, sought to undermine the integrity of the U.S. presidential election process, and endangered U.S. national security.

- In furtherance of this scheme, President Trump—directly and acting through his agents within and outside the U.S. government—sought to pressure and induce Ukraine's newly-elected president, Volodymyr Zelensky, to publicly announce unfounded investigations that would benefit President Trump's personal political interests and reelection effort. To advance his personal political objectives, President Trump encouraged the President of Ukraine to work with his personal attorney, Rudolph Giuliani.

- As part of this scheme, President Trump, acting in his official capacity and using his position of public trust, personally and directly requested from the President of Ukraine that the government of Ukraine publicly announce investigations into (1) the President's political opponent, former Vice President Joseph R. Biden, Jr. and his son, Hunter Biden, and (2) a baseless theory promoted by Russia alleging that Ukraine—rather than Russia—interfered in the 2016 U.S. election. These investigations were intended to harm a potential political opponent of President Trump and benefit the President's domestic political standing.

- To create additional leverage against Ukraine and force them to open these investigations, President Trump ordered the suspension of $391 million in vital military assistance urgently needed by Ukraine, a strategic partner, to resist Russian aggression. Because the aid was appropriated by Congress, on a bipartisan basis, and signed into law by the President, its expenditure was required by law. Acting directly and through his subordinates within the U.S. government, the President withheld from Ukraine this military assistance without any legitimate foreign policy, national security, or anticorruption justification. The President did so despite the longstanding bipartisan support of Congress, uniform support across federal departments and agencies for the provision to Ukraine of the military assistance, and his obligations under the Impoundment Control Act.

- President Trump used the power of the Office of the President and exercised his authority over the Executive Branch, including his control of the instruments of the federal government, to apply increasing pressure on the President of Ukraine and the Ukrainian government to announce the politically-motivated investigations desired by President Trump. Specifically, to advance and promote his scheme, the President withheld official acts of value to Ukraine and conditioned their fulfillment on actions by Ukraine that would benefit his personal political interests:

  - President Trump—acting through agents within and outside the U.S. government—conditioned a head of state meeting at the White House, which the President of Ukraine desperately sought to demonstrate continued United States support for Ukraine in the face of Russian aggression, on Ukraine publicly announcing the investigations that President Trump believed would aid his reelection campaign.

- To increase leverage over the President of Ukraine, President Trump, acting through his agents and subordinates, conditioned release of the vital military assistance he had suspended to Ukraine on the President of Ukraine's public announcement of the investigations that President Trump sought.

- President Trump's closest subordinates and advisors within the Executive Branch, including Acting Chief of Staff Mick Mulvaney, Secretary of State Mike Pompeo, Secretary of Energy Rick Perry, and other senior White House and Executive Branch officials had knowledge of, in some cases facilitated and furthered the President's scheme, and withheld information about the scheme from the Congress and the American public.

- In directing and orchestrating this scheme to advance his personal political interests, President Trump did not implement, promote, or advance U.S. anti-corruption policies. In fact, the President sought to pressure and induce the government of Ukraine to announce politically-motivated investigations lacking legitimate predication that the U.S. government otherwise discourages and opposes as a matter of policy in that country and around the world. In so doing, the President undermined U.S. support of anticorruption reform and the rule of law in Ukraine, and undermined U.S. national security.

- By withholding vital military assistance and diplomatic support from a strategic foreign partner government engaged in an ongoing military conflict illegally instigated by Russia, President Trump compromised national security to advance his personal political interests.

- Faced with the revelation of his actions, President Trump publicly and repeatedly persisted in urging foreign governments, including Ukraine and China, to investigate his political opponent. This continued solicitation of foreign interference in a U.S. election, as well as President Trump's other actions, present a clear and present danger that the President will continue to use the power of his office for his personal political gain.

D.   President Trump's Conduct Meets Each Element of Abuse of Power

The conduct set forth in the First Article of Impeachment unquestionably constitutes an "abuse of power" as that term was understood by the Framers. Indeed, it is falls within the heartland of the concerns raised at the Constitutional Convention as necessitating Presidential impeachment. It is the judgment of the Committee that President Trump has therefore committed "high Crimes and Misdemeanors."

1.   President Trump Exercised Official Power in Soliciting and Pressuring the Government of Ukraine to Publicly Announce Two Investigations

As explained above, a President commits an impeachable abuse of power where he exercises official power to obtain an improper personal benefit, while ignoring or injuring the national interest. The first requirement is satisfied here: President Trump exercised official power, entrusted to him by the Constitution, in soliciting and pressuring the Government of Ukraine to announce investigations that would benefit his reelection, harm the election prospects of a political opponent, and influence the 2020 United States Presidential election to his advantage.

This conclusion is straightforward. On his July 25, 2019 call with President Zelensky, President Trump was acting as our Nation's head of state and chief diplomat.[435] The call was itself an official act rooted in President Trump's powers under Article II of the Constitution. So, too, were many of the President's other acts throughout this scheme. It was only by virtue of his supervisory powers over the Executive Branch, as well as his power to appoint and remove certain officials,[436] that President Trump could order the Office of Management and Budget to block or allow the release of Congressionally-appropriated military and security assistance to Ukraine. Similarly, it was only by virtue of his executive powers—including his authority to "receive Ambassadors and other public Ministers"[437]—that President Trump could offer and then withhold a White House meeting (as well as the many other official governmental acts involved in such a high-stakes diplomatic visit). And it was only by virtue of his executive authority that President Trump could fire U.S. Ambassador to Ukraine Marie Yovanovitch (whom he knew would have stood in the way of his corrupt scheme), direct other administration officials in the execution of his agenda relating to Ukraine, and instruct United States officials to cooperate with his private attorney, Rudy Giuliani. The scheme or course of conduct described in the first Article of Impeachment is shot through with official acts.[438]

The official acts comprising the First Article of Impeachment, moreover, had the natural and foreseeable effect of obtaining a personal political benefit for President Trump. On January 20, 2017, President Trump filed initial paperwork to launch his re-election campaign with the Federal Election Commission.[439] On April 25, 2019, former Vice President Biden publicly announced his campaign for the Democratic nomination for President of the United States and launched his effort to unseat President Trump in the 2020 election.[440] President Trump and former Vice President Biden were widely recognized as political opponents for the 2020 United States Presidential election. In using the powers of his office to solicit and pressure the Government of Ukraine to publicly announce an investigation related to former Vice President Biden and his son—and into a discredited theory that Ukraine, not Russia, interfered with the 2016 United States Presidential election—President Trump sought an

---

[435] *See, e.g., Zivotofsky ex rel. Zivotofsky v. Kerry*, 135 S. Ct. 2076, 2086 (2015); *see also id.* at 2099 (finding that the "[e]arly practice of the founding generation also supports th[e] understanding of the President's "role of chief diplomat").

[436] *See id.* art. II, § 2 ("The President shall . . . appoint Ambassadors, other public Ministers and Consuls, Judges of the supreme Court, and all other Officers of the United States, whose Appointments are not herein otherwise provided for, and which shall be established by Law.").

[437] U.S. CONST. art. II, § 3.

[438] Those official acts include the President's public statements openly and corruptly urging and soliciting Ukraine to undertake investigations for his personal political benefit (which were made in his capacity as President and expressly directed to a foreign nation), as well as conduct undertaken by Mr. Giuliani while acting as the President's agent and facilitated by the President's implied or express direction that United States officials facilitate Mr. Giuliani's efforts.

[439] Donald J. Trump, FEC Form 99 Miscellaneous Text, Image No. 201701209041436569, filed January 20, 2017.

[440] Alexander Burns & Jonathan Martin, *Joe Biden Announces 2020 Run for President, After Months of Hesitation*, N.Y. TIMES, Apr. 25, 2019.

announcement that would help him politically. By its very nature, and on its face, the President's conduct thus involved an exercise of power to obtain a personal political benefit.

Although there can be no doubt that the abuse of power set forth in Article I involved the exercise of official power, it is helpful to closely consider the scheme at issue, as well as two of the means by which President Trump pursued it: specifically, his *solicitation* and *pressuring* of the Government of Ukraine to announce investigations that would result in a personal political benefit.

a.   The Scheme

Beginning in the Spring of 2019, President Trump and his agents undertook a scheme to pressure the newly-elected President of Ukraine to announce politically-motivated investigations related to former Vice President Joe Biden and the 2016 United States Presidential election. That scheme included extensive efforts by the President's personal attorney Mr. Giuliani, who sought to tarnish former Vice President Biden and pressed Ukrainian officials to initiate the investigations. Mr. Giuliani publicly confirmed that the President was aware of his efforts, which were undertaken not as part of official U.S. foreign policy but to help the President personally.[441]

But the task of carrying out this scheme was not limited to the President's personal attorney. On May 23, 2019, following the inauguration of Ukrainian president Volodymyr Zelensky, the President met with United States officials, including Ambassador to the European Union Gordon Sondland, Special Representative for Ukraine Negotiations Ambassador Kurt Volker, and Secretary of Energy Rick Perry.[442] These three officials, who would later dub themselves the "Three Amigos," reported their favorable impressions of Ukraine's new president, who had been elected on an anti-corruption platform, and recommended that President Trump invite President Zelensky to the White House.[443] President Trump reacted negatively. He expressed the view that Ukraine "tried to take [him] down" in 2016, and told the Three Amigos to "Talk to Rudy"—not U.S. diplomats and experts—about Ukraine.[444] Ambassador Sondland testified that "he understood the President's instruction to be a directive to work with Mr. Giuliani if [the delegation] hoped to advance relations with Ukraine."[445] Following that May 23 meeting, Mr. Giuliani made clear to Ambassadors Sondland and Volker, "who were directly communicating with the Ukrainians, that a White House meeting would not occur until Ukraine announced its pursuit of the two political investigations."[446]

---

[441] Kenneth P. Vogel, *Rudy Giuliani Plans Ukraine Trip to Push for Inquiries That Could Help Trump*, N.Y. Times, May 9, 2019 (hereinafter "Vogel Giuliani") (reporting on interview with Giuliani) ("Somebody could say it's improper. And this isn't foreign policy — I'm asking them to do an investigation that they're doing already and that other people are telling them to stop. And I'm going to give them reasons why they shouldn't stop it because that information will be very, very helpful to my client, and may turn out to be helpful to my government.").

[442] *Ukraine Report* at 16-17.

[443] *Id.*

[444] *Id.*

[445] *Id.* at 17.

[446] *Id.* at 19.

With these directives in mind, Ambassadors Sondland and Volker "worked to obtain the necessary assurance from President Zelensky that he would personally commit to initiate the investigations in order to secure both" the White House call and meeting.[447] On July 10, for example, "Ambassador Bolton hosted a meeting in the White House with two senior Ukrainian officials, several American officials, including Ambassadors Sondland and Volker, Secretary Perry, Dr. Fiona Hill, Senior Director for Europe and Russia at the NSC, and Lt. Col. Vindman."[448] When, as had become customary, the Ukrainians asked about the "long-delayed White House meeting," Ambassador Sondland revealed "an arrangement with Acting Chief of Staff Mick Mulvaney to schedule the White House visit after Ukraine initiated the 'investigations.'"[449] Despite Ambassador Bolton ending that meeting, Ambassador Sondland "ushered many of the attendees to the Ward Room downstairs to continue their discussion" and, at that meeting, Ambassador Sondland explained again "that he had an agreement with Mr. Mulvaney that the White House visit would come only after Ukraine announced the Burisma/Biden and 2016 Ukraine election interference investigations."[450]

Over the next two weeks, "Ambassadors Sondland and Volker worked closely with Mr. Giuliani and senior Ukrainian and American officials to ensure that," on the telephone call between President Trump and President Zelensky, President Zelensky would promise to undertake the investigations that Mr. Giuliani had been pushing on the President's behalf.[451] As Ambassador Sondland testified, "Mr. Giuliani was expressing the desires of the President of the United States, and we knew these investigations were important to the President."[452] The Ukrainians were reluctant to get involved, noting that they did not want to be "an instrument in Washington domestic, reelection politics."[453] Mr. Giuliani and the American officials made clear, however, that there would be no White House meeting without the investigations.

b.   The Solicitation

President Trump's official act of soliciting the investigations is apparent on the face of the transcript of his July 25 call with President Zelensky.[454] On that call, he requested that President

---

[447] *Id.* at 19.

[448] *Id.*

[449] *Id.*

[450] *Id.* "Following these discussions, Dr. Hill reported back to Ambassador Bolton, who told her to 'go and tell [the NSC Legal Advisor] that I am not part of whatever drug deal Sondland and Mulvaney are cooking up on this.' Both Dr. Hill and Lt. Col. Vindman separately reported the incident to the NSC Legal Advisor." *Id.*

[451] *Id.* at 18-20.

[452] Sondland Hearing Tr. at 18.

[453] *Ukraine Report* at 94.

[454] The White House, *Memorandum of Telephone Conversation: Telephone Conversation with President Zelenskyy of Ukraine* 3 (July 25, 2019) (hereinafter "July 25 Call Record"). That said, President Trump's solicitation was not confined

Zelensky investigate the widely debunked conspiracy theory that the Ukrainian government—and not Russia—was behind the hack of Democratic National Committee (DNC) computer network in 2016. According to this conspiracy theory, the American cybersecurity firm CrowdStrike moved a DNC server to Ukraine to prevent United States law enforcement from examining them. Here is how President Trump presented his solicitation:

> I would like you to find out what happened with this whole situation with Ukraine, they say Crowdstrike... I guess you have one of your wealthy people... The server, they say Ukraine has it. There are a lot of things that went on, the whole situation. I think you're surrounding yourself with some of the same people. I would like to have the Attorney General call you or your people and I would like you to get to the bottom of it. As you saw yesterday, that whole nonsense ended with a very poor performance by a man named Robert Mueller, an incompetent performance, but they say a lot of it started with Ukraine. Whatever you can do, it's very important that you do it if that's possible.[455]

Shortly thereafter, on the same phone call, President Trump expressly solicited an investigation into former Vice President Biden and his son. In so doing, he referenced former Vice President's Biden involvement in the removal of a corrupt former Ukrainian prosecutor:

> The other thing, There's a lot of talk about Biden's son, that Biden stopped the prosecution and a lot of people want to find out about that so whatever you can do with the Attorney General would be great. Biden went around bragging that he stopped the prosecution so if you can look into it... It sounds horrible to me.[456]

c.   The Pressure Campaign

As set forth in the First Article of Impeachment, "President Trump—acting both directly and through his agents within and outside the United States Government—conditioned two official acts on the public announcements that he had requested."[457] These two official acts were: (1) the release of vital military and security assistance to Ukraine that President Trump had ordered suspended; and (2) a valuable, strategically important head of state meeting with President Trump at the White House.

There is overwhelming evidence that President Trump made these official acts conditional on his sought-after announcements in order to pressure Ukraine. It is also clear that Ukrainian officials came to understand that they were being pressured in this manner. That evidence is comprehensively explained in the *Ukraine Report*; we will briefly summarize it here.

---

to the July 25 call, but rather was reiterated and conveyed continuously by his agents within and outside the United States Government (including Mr. Giuliani). *See, e.g., Ukraine Report* at 34-35, 147-49.

[455] *July 25 Call Record* at 3.

[456] *Id.* at 4.

[457] H. Res. 755, 116th Cong. (2019).

i.   The Military and Security Assistance

On July 18, 2019, OMB notified the agencies that President Trump had directed a hold on military and security assistance funding for Ukraine. No explanation was provided for that hold.[458] This was exceedingly irregular, given that the assistance had bipartisan Congressional support, was supported by the President's national security agencies and advisors (including the State Department, Department of Defense, and National Security Council), and was widely perceived as crucial to both Ukrainian and American security. Moreover, there were substantial concerns about the legality of the hold under the Impoundment Control Act.[459] Adding to the irregularity, a career civil servant at OMB with decades of experience in this arena (Mark Sandy) was deprived of sign off authority, which was shifted to a political appointee of President Trump (Michael Duffey) who had virtually no relevant experience or expertise and no history or stated interest in managing such issues.[460]

As early as July 25—the day that President Trump spoke by phone to President Zelensky—Ukrainian officials recognized and grew nervous about the delay in receiving their military and security assistance. That same day, Ukrainian officials contacted their American counterparts in Washington, D.C. to express those concerns.[461] Specifically, the Department of Defense received two e-mails from the State Department revealing that the Ukrainian Embassy was "asking about the security assistance" and knew about the "[security assistance] situation to an extent."[462] Former Ukrainian Deputy Foreign Minister, Olena Zerkal, also reported that her office, and the Ukrainian Presidential Administration, received a diplomatic cable from Ukrainian officials in Washington the week of the July 25 call, stating that the Trump administration had frozen military aid for Ukraine; she elaborated: "We had this information. … It was definitely mentioned there were some issues."[463]

In the weeks that followed, President Trump's top officials came to understand and communicated to Ukrainian officials that release of the assistance was in fact conditioned on President Zelensky publicly announcing the two investigations that President Trump had requested on his July 25 call. For example, on August 22, Ambassador Sondland e-mailed Secretary Pompeo, copying the State Department's Executive Secretary, Lisa Kenna, that to break the "logjam" on the assistance, President Zelensky should "look [President Trump] in the eye" and tell him he would "move forward publicly and with confidence on those issues of importance to Potus and to the U.S."[464] Ambassador Sondland testified that the "issues of importance to Potus" were the two investigations.[465]

---

[458] *Ukraine Report* at 72.

[459] *Id.* at 67-70.

[460] *Id.* at 78-80.

[461] *Id.* at 22.

[462] *Id.* at 81, 173 n.451.

[463] Andrew E. Kramer, *Ukraine Knew of Aid Freeze in July, Says Ex-Top Official in Kyiv*, N.Y. TIMES, Dec. 3, 2019.

[464] *Ukraine Report* at 127, 190 n.843 (quoting from written statement of Ambassador Sondland in *Impeachment Inquiry: Gordon Sonland: Hearing Before the H. Perm. Select Comm. on Intelligence*, 116th Cong. (Nov. 20, 2019)).

[465] *Id.* at 127; *see also* Sondland Hearing Tr. at 104.

Around this time, according to his testimony, Lt. Col. Vindman "was getting questions from Ukrainians about the status of the hold on security assistance."[466] By August 28, after *Politico* "first reported that President Trump had implemented a hold on nearly $400 million of U.S. military assistance to Ukraine that had been appropriated by Congress,"[467] Ukrainian officials "expressed alarm to their American counterparts."[468] Ambassador Taylor states that the Ukrainians were "just desperate" to receive the assistance, and that "American officials could provide little reassurance."[469]

On September 1, Ambassador Sondland stated to President Zelensky's aide, Mr. Yermak, that "the resumption of U.S. aid would likely not occur until Ukraine took some kind of action on the public statement that we had been discussing for many weeks."[470] National Security Council senior director Timothy Morrison also testified that he recalled this interaction. According to Mr. Morrison, he saw Ambassador Sondland and Mr. Yermak have a private conversation and, immediately after their conversation ended, Ambassador Sondland walked over to Mr. Morrison and reported that he had communicated to Mr. Yermak that a statement about the investigations was needed "to obtain release of the aid."[471] That same day, Ambassador Taylor texted Ambassador Sondland: "Are we now saying that security assistance and WH meeting are conditioned on investigations?" Ambassador Sondland then confirmed to Ambassador Taylor over the phone that President Trump wanted President Zelensky "in a public box," making a "public statement" about the investigations that President Trump had requested on July 25. Ambassador Sondland agreed that the United States position was that if President Zelensky did not announce those investigations, Ukraine was not "going to get" the assistance.[472]

On September 5, the *Washington Post* published an editorial exposing President Trump's scheme, entitled "Trump Tries to Force Ukraine to Meddle in the 2020 Election."[473] Two days later, on September 7, Ambassador Sondland called Mr. Morrison to report on a call he had just concluded with President Trump. Ambassador Sondland told Mr. Morrison that "there was no quid pro quo, but President Zelensky must announce the opening of the investigations and he should want to do it."[474] The following day, on September 8, Ambassador Sondland conveyed via text message to Ambassadors Volker and Taylor, too, that he had spoken with President Trump: "Guys multiple convos with Ze, Potus. Lets talk."[475] On the phone with Ambassador Taylor, Ambassador Sondland then "confirmed

---

[466] *Ukraine Report* at 82.

[467] Caitlin Emma & Connor O'Brien, *Trump Holds Up Ukraine Military Aid Meant to Confront Russia*, POLITICO, Aug. 28, 2019.

[468] *Ukraine Report* at 129.

[469] *Id.*

[470] *Id.* at 132.

[471] *Id.* at 180-81.

[472] *Id.* at 133-34.

[473] Editorial, *Trump Tries to Force Ukraine to Meddle in the 2020 Election*, WASH. POST, Sept. 5, 2019.

[474] *Ukraine Report* at 134.

[475] *Id.* at 135.

that he had talked to President Trump" and that "President Trump was adamant that President Zelensky himself had to clear things up and do it in public. President Trump said it was not a quid pro quo."[476] Ambassador Sondland added that, following his call with President Trump, he had told President Zelensky and Mr. Yermak that, "although this was not a quid pro quo, if President Zelensky did not clear things up in public, we would be at a stalemate." In response, President Zelensky agreed to make a public statement announcing the investigations in an interview on CNN.[477] Both Ambassadors Taylor and Sondland confirmed that the term "stalemate" referred to the hold on the security assistance to Ukraine.[478] Early the next morning on September 9, Ambassador Taylor texted Ambassadors Sondland and Volker: "As I said on the phone, I think it's crazy to withhold security assistance for help with a political campaign."

Ultimately, the connection between the assistance and the announcements was apparent to the relevant parties—including United States officials working with Ukraine and senior Ukrainian officials. Ambassador Sondland and Mr. Holmes both testified that President Trump's use of military and security assistance to secure his sought-after announcements became as clear as "two plus two equals four."[479] Moreover, at a press conference on October 17, Acting White House Chief of Staff Mick Mulvaney confirmed this equation. According to Mr. Mulvaney, President Trump "[a]bsolutely" mentioned "corruption related to the DNC server" in connection with the security assistance. Mr. Mulvaney also stated that the server was part of "why we held up the money." After a reporter attempted to clarify this explicit acknowledgement of a quid pro quo, Mr. Mulvaney replied: "We do that all the time with foreign policy." He added, "I have news for everybody: get over it. There is going to be political influence in foreign policy."[480]

ii.   The White House Visit

Turning to the White House visit, documentary evidence and testimony from multiple witnesses confirms that this official act—like the release of assistance—was conditional on Ukraine announcing investigations into former Vice President Biden and interference in the 2016 election.

As discussed above, prior to the July 25 call, President Trump's personal attorney repeatedly urged Ukraine to pursue investigations into "two matters of intense interest" to his client, President

---

[476] *Id.* at 135. Ambassador Sondland's recitation of his call with President Trump is the only evidence that President Trump suggested this was "not a quid pro quo." Moreover, Ambassador Sondland testified that President Trump made that statement, unprompted, on September 7—only after the White House had learned of a whistleblower complaint regarding the July 25 call and President Trump's efforts to pressure Ukraine, *and* the *Washington Post* had reported about the President's pressure campaign on Ukraine. In addition, President Trump immediately followed his stated denial of a quid pro quo by demanding that President Zelensky still make a public announcement, while the military assistance remained on an unexplained hold. For these reasons, and those detailed in the *Ukraine Report*, President Trump's self-serving denial of conditionality after he had been caught is not credible.

[477] *Id.* at 135.

[478] *Id.*

[479] *Ukraine Report* at 23; Sondland Hearing Tr. at 58.

[480] *Ukraine Report* at 139; The White House, *Press Briefing by Acting Chief of Staff Mick Mulvaney* (Oct. 17, 2019).

Trump: the "involvement of the former Vice President Joseph R. Biden Jr.'s son" on the board of a Ukrainian gas company and 2016 election interference.[481] In those statements, Mr. Giuliani clarified that "my only client is the President of the United States," and that this wasn't "foreign policy," but rather "information that will be very, very helpful" to President Trump.[482] Ambassadors Sondland and Volker were also enlisted by President Trump to work with Mr. Giuliani and "obtain the necessary assurance from President Zelensky that he would personally commit to initiate the investigations,"[483] and each had delivered their messages to the Ukrainians prior to the call. On July 2 in Toronto, Ambassador Volker "conveyed the message directly to President Zelensky, specifically referencing the 'Giuliani factor.'"[484] On July 19, Ambassador Sondland emailed several top Administration officials, confirming that Ambassador Sondland had "talked to Zelensky just now," and that President Zelensky was "prepared to receive Potus' call" and "assure [President Trump] that he intends to run a fully transparent investigation and will 'turn over every stone.'"[485] On the morning of the July 25 call, Ambassador Volker texted President Zelensky's aide: "Heard from White House—assuming President Z convinces trump he will investigate / 'get to the bottom of what happened' in 2016, we will nail down date for visit to Washington. Good luck!"[486]

On the July 25 call itself, when President Zelensky thanked President Trump for "great support in the area of defense" and raised the matter of purchasing anti-tank missiles from the United States, President Trump responded, "I would like you to do us a favor though." That "favor," President Trump then made clear, was for Ukraine to investigate the 2016 United States Presidential election, as well as former Vice President Biden and his son. These were the same two investigations that Mr. Giuliani had repeatedly, publicly stated in the preceding months were of "intense interest" to President Trump. President Zelensky understood what President Trump meant about the connection between a meeting and these investigations: "I also wanted to thank you for your invitation to visit the United States, specifically Washington D.C. *On the other hand*, I also want to ensure [sic] you that we will be very serious about the case and will work on the investigation."[487] President Zelensky also confirmed that his staff assistant had spoken to Mr. Giuliani, and President Trump reaffirmed that Mr. Giuliani "very much knows what's going on."

The pressure for the investigations continued after the call, as well. Several weeks later, on August 9, when discussing possible dates for a White House visit, Ambassador Sondland wrote to Ambassador Volker: "I think potus really wants the deliverable." The next day, President Zelensky's aide texted Ambassador Volker about setting a date for the meeting before making a statement

---

[481] *Vogel Giuliani*

[482] *Id.*

[483] *Id.* at 18.

[484] *Id.* at 19.

[485] Sondland Opening Statement at 21, Ex. 4.

[486] *Ukraine Report* at 20.

[487] *July 25 Call Record* at 5.

announcing the investigations, stating: "I think it's possible to make this declaration and mention all these things. Which we discussed yesterday. But it will be logic [sic] to do after we receive a confirmation of date. We inform about date of visit and about our expectations and our guarantees for future visit." Ambassador Volker replied: "Let's iron out statement and use that to get date and then PreZ [Zelensky] can go forward with it?" President Zelensky's aide responded, "[o]nce we have a date, will call for a press briefing, announcing upcoming visit and outlining vision for the reboot of US-UKRAINE relationship, including among other things Burisma and election meddling in investigations."[488] The day after that, Ambassador Sondland emailed Secretary of State Pompeo: "Kurt & I negotiated a statement from Ze [Zelensky] to be delivered for our review in a day or two. The contents will hopefully make the boss [i.e., President Trump] happy enough to authorize an invitation."[489]

Based on this and other evidence, it is clear that Ambassador Sondland spoke truthfully when he stated: "Was there a quid pro quo? As I testified previously with regard to the requested White House call and the White House meeting, the answer is yes."[490]

By making military and security assistance and a White House meeting conditional on announcing investigations that would benefit him politically, President Trump used official power to pressure Ukraine to make those announcements. Ukraine is at war with Russia and more than 13,000 Ukrainians have died in that conflict.[491] Ukraine relies heavily on the United States for military and security assistance and support on the global stage.[492] But as Ambassador Taylor described in his deposition, Ukraine is also "a young nation struggling to break free of its past, hopeful their new government will finally usher in a new Ukraine, proud of independence from Russia eager to join Western institutions and enjoy a more secure and prosperous life."[493] That is why, for weeks, Ukrainian officials expressed concern about President Trump's demands, advising United States officials that they did not want to be an "instrument in Washington domestic, reelection politics."[494] As Ukrainian Prosecutor General Ruslan Ryaboshapka stated, in an apparent reference to President Trump's demand for Ukrainian interference in United States elections, "[i]t's critically important for the west not to pull us into some conflicts between their ruling elites, but to continue to support so that we can cross the

---

[488] Text Message from Yermak to Ambassador Volker (Aug. 10, 2019, 5:42 PM).

[489] E-mail from Ambassador Sondland to Thomas Brechbuhl and Lisa Kenna (Aug. 11, 2019, 10:31 AM) (forwarded to Secretary of State Pompeo).

[490] Sondland Hearing Tr. at 26. While President Trump and President Zelensky met at the U.N. General Assembly on September 25, no White House visit date has been set. The fact of the White House visit, as confirmed in the *Ukraine Report*, is "critical" to President Zelensky, to show "U.S. support at the highest levels." *Ukraine Report* at 84 & n.456 (quoting Holmes Dep. Tr. at 18).

[491] John M. Donnelly, *Ukrainian Lives Hung in Balance as Trump Held Up Aid*, ROLL CALL, Oct. 24, 2019.

[492] *See id.*

[493] Taylor Dep. Tr. at 42-43.

[494] *See* Text Message from Ambassador William Taylor to Ambassador Sondland (July 20, 2019, 1:45 AM).

point of no return."[495] Nonetheless, as President Trump's pressure campaign continued, and as Ukraine contemplated the loss of military and security assistance necessary to defend itself in active hostilities with Russia, the Ukrainians became desperate.[496] So desperate, in fact, that, as Ambassador Sondland told the President, President Zelensky was willing to do *anything* that President Trump asked of him.[497] And, as set forth above, President Zelensky capitulated, and ultimately agreed to publicly announce the investigations in an interview on CNN.[498] President Zelensky canceled that interview only after President Trump's scheme was exposed and the assistance was released.[499]

To be sure, President Zelensky has subsequently denied that President Trump pressured him.[500] But although President Zelensky did not publicly announce the investigations, the power disparity between the United States and Ukraine remains unchanged, and President Zelensky thus remains under pressure from President Trump to this day. As Mr. Holmes testified, there are still things the Ukrainians want and need from President Trump, including a meeting with the President in the Oval Office; for these reasons, Mr. Holmes explained,

> I think [the Ukrainians are] being very careful. They still need us now going forward. In fact, right now, President Zelensky is trying to arrange a summit meeting with President Putin in the coming weeks, his first face to face meeting with him to try to advance the peace process. He needs our support. He needs President Putin to understand that America supports Zelensky at the highest levels. So this doesn't end with the lifting of the security assistance hold. Ukraine still needs us, and as I said, still fighting this war this very day.[501]

Ambassador Taylor likewise confirmed that, as President Zelensky is currently engaging in negotiations with President Putin concerning the war on their border, Russia is "watching closely to gauge the level of American support" for Ukraine.[502] The United States' public and unwavering support is therefore critical to Ukraine in approaching those negotiations from a position of strength. Indeed,

---

[495] Roman Olearchyk, *Cleaning Up Ukraine in the Shadow of Trump*, FIN. TIMES, Nov. 27, 2019 (interview with Ruslan Ryaboshapka) (hereinafter "Olearchyk").

[496] *See* Taylor Dep. Tr. at 137-38 ("Mr. Yermak and others were trying to figure out why this was . . . . They thought that there must be some rational reason for this being held up, and they just didn't—and maybe Washington they didn't understand how important this assistance was to their fight and to their armed forces. And so maybe they could figure–so they were just desperate.").

[497] Hill-Holmes Hearing Tr. 24, 54.

[498] Impeachment Inquiry: Ambassador William Taylor and Mr. George Kent: Hearing Before the H. Perm. Select Comm. on Intelligence, 116th Cong. 41 (Nov. 13, 2019).

[499] Andrew E. Kramer, *Ukraine's Zelensky Bowed to Trump's Demands, Until Luck Spared Him*, N.Y. TIMES, Nov. 7, 2019.

[500] Tara Law, *"Nobody Pushed Me." Ukrainian President Denies Trump Pressured Him to Investigate Biden's Son*, TIME, Sept. 25, 2019.

[501] *Ukraine Report* at 146-47.

[502] *Id.* at 129.

just last week on December 9, President Zelensky met with President Putin to discuss and negotiate an end to the war. President Zelensky's team was "discouraged by the absence of expected support" from President Trump in advance of that meeting, "as well as the lack of follow-through from the White House on a promised Oval Office meeting.[503] Moreover, the next day, on December 10, President Trump hosted the Russian foreign minister in the Oval Office.[504]

In addition, although the majority of the military and security assistance was ultimately released, certain of the funds to Ukraine remain unobligated,[505] and, moreover, in order to ensure that Ukraine "did not permanently lose $35 million of the critical military assistance frozen by the White House," Congress had to pass a provision to ensure that the military assistance could be spent.[506] "As of November 2019, Pentagon officials confirmed that the $35 million in security assistance originally held by the President and extended by Congress had still yet to be disbursed," and would not provide an explanation for the delay.[507]

The evidence thus demonstrates that President Trump used the powers of his office to make Ukraine an offer it had no real choice but to accept: Help me get re-elected or you will not get the military and security assistance and diplomatic support you desperately need from the United States of America. In other words, under these circumstances, it is understandable that President Zelensky has sought to serve his national interest by avoiding any statement or confession that might offend President Trump and also demonstrate his own weakness in dealings with the United States and on the world stage. But the record supports only one conclusion. President Trump took advantage of Ukraine's vulnerability and used his high office to solicit and pressure Ukraine to announce criminal investigations into a United States citizen. These investigations would clearly help President Trump's re-election campaign and harm a political opponent.

2. President Trump Exercised the Powers of his Office with the Corrupt Motive of Obtaining a Personal Political Benefit

In exercising official power to obtain a personal benefit, the President acted with motives forbidden by the Constitution. The first article of impeachment thus states: "President Trump engaged

[503] Kenneth P. Vogel & Andrew E. Kramer, *Ukraine's Leader, Wiser to Washington, Seeks New Outreach to Trump*, N.Y. TIMES (Dec. 13, 2019).

[504] *Id.*

[505] Molly O'Toole & Sarah D. Wire, *$35 Million in Pentagon Aid hasn't Reached Ukraine, Despite White House Assurances*, LOS ANGELES TIMES, Nov. 11, 2019.

[506] *Ukraine Report* at 145. Notably, "Ms. Cooper testified that such an act of Congress was unusual—indeed, she had never heard of funding being extended in this manner." *Id.*

[507] *Id.*

102   **Report of the Committee on the Judiciary - House of Representatives** ••••••••••••••••••••••••

in this scheme or course of conduct for corrupt purposes in pursuit of personal political benefit."[508]

To evaluate whether President Trump acted in pursuit of personal political advantage, the Committee has carefully considered the full evidentiary record, as well as arguments put forth by the Minority in its "Report of Evidence in the Democrats' Impeachment Inquiry in the House of Representatives" (the "Minority" or the "Minority Report") seeking to demonstrate that the President acted in pursuit of legitimate policy goals.[509] Consistent with past practice and constitutional requirements, the Committee has focused not on reasons that *could* have motivated the President's conduct, but rather on what the record shows about his *actual* motives. After all, "[t]he Framers designed impeachment to root out abuse and corruption, even when a President masks improper intent with cover stories."[510] The question is therefore whether "the evidence tells a story that does not match the [asserted] explanation."[511]

a.   The July 25 Call and its Background

On President Trump's July 25 phone call with President Zelensky, President Trump referenced two very specific investigations.[512] Then, in describing who he wanted Ukraine to investigate, President Trump mentioned only two people by name: former Vice President Biden and his son.[513] He also referred more generally to investigating the 2016 United States Presidential election, but reserved specificity for the Bidens.[514] He used their name three times on the call.

Any presumptions of good faith that the President might normally enjoy must be suspended when he calls a foreign leader and asks that leader to investigate a United States citizen who is also an announced candidate in the primaries for the next Presidential election. To be sure, the call summary "contains no reference to 2020 or President Trump's reelection bid."[515] But for good reason, multiple officials on the call immediately understood that President Trump was soliciting President Zelensky to announce an investigation into his political opponent. As Lieutenant Colonel Alexander Vindman testified, "I thought it was wrong. I thought it was wrong for the President of the United States to call for an investigation of -- call a foreign power to investigate a U.S. citizen."[516] Jennifer Williams, an

---

[508] H. Res. 755, 116th Cong. art. I (2019).

[509] *See Ukraine Report* at 47-49.

[510] *Id.* at 47.

[511] *Dep't of Com. v. New York*, 139 S. Ct. 2551, 2575 (2019).

[512] *July 25 Call Record* at 3.

[513] *Id.* at 3-4.

[514] *Id.*

[515] Republican Staff of the H. Perm. Select Comm. on Intelligence, 116th Cong., *Rep. on Evidence in the Democrats' Impeachment Inquiry in the House of Representatives* 12 (Comm. Print 2019) (hereinafter "Minority Report").

[516] Vindman Dep. Tr. at 152; *see also Impeachment Inquiry: Jennifer Williams and Alexander Vindman: Hearing Before the H. Perm. Select Comm. on Intelligence*, 116th Cong. 19 (Nov. 19, 2019) ("On July 25th, 2019, the call occurred. I listened in on the call in the Situation Room with White House colleagues. I was concerned by the call. What I heard was inappropriate, and I reported my concerns to Mr. Eisenberg. It is improper for the President of the United States to demand

96

advisor to Vice President Michael Pence, similarly testified that "it struck me as unusual and inappropriate."[517] She later added, "the references to specific individuals and investigations, such as former Vice President Biden and his son, struck me as political in nature."[518]

Events leading up to the July 25 call strongly support Ms. Williams's concern that President Trump's request was "political in nature." On May 2, 2019, President Trump retweeted a *New York Times* article entitled *Biden Faces Conflict of Interest Questions That Are Being Promoted by Trump and Allies*.[519] That article concluded that Mr. Giuliani's efforts underscored "the Trump campaign's concern about the electoral threat from the former vice president's presidential campaign" and noted that "Mr. Giuliani's involvement raises questions about whether Mr. Trump is endorsing an effort to push a foreign government to proceed with a case that could hurt a political opponent at home."[520] On May 9, 2019, it was reported that President Trump's private lawyer, Mr. Giuliani, planned to meet with President Zelensky "to urge him to pursue inquiries that allies of the White House contend could yield new information about two matters of intense interest to Mr. Trump."[521] Those matters were the same two investigations that President Trump raised on his July 25 call.[522] And as Mr. Giuliani stated in early May, "this isn't foreign policy."[523] Instead, Mr. Giuliani was seeking information that "will be very, very helpful to my client," namely "the President of the United States."[524] Again on May 9, Mr. Giuliani stated on *Fox News*, "I guarantee you, Joe Biden will not get to election day without this being investigated."[525] The next day, in an interview, upon learning that Mr. Giuliani was traveling to Ukraine to pursue investigations, President Trump responded, "I will speak to him about it before he leaves."[526]

a foreign government investigate a U.S. citizen and a political opponent. I was also clear that if Ukraine pursued an investigation -- it was also clear that if Ukraine pursued an investigation into the 2016 elections, the Bidens and Burisma, it would be interpreted as a partisan play.").

[517] Williams Dep. Tr. at 149.

[518] Vindman-Williams Hearing Tr. at 34.

[519] Donald J. Trump (@realDonaldTrump), Twitter (May 2, 2019, 6:21 AM) (retweeting Kenneth P. Vogel & Iuliia Mendel, *Biden Faces Conflict of Interest Questions That Are Being Promoted by Trump and Allies*, N.Y. TIMES, May 1, 2019) (online and searchable at http://www.trumptwitterarchive.com/archive).

[520] Vogel & Mendel, *Biden Faces Conflict of Interest Questions*.

[521] *See* Kenneth P. Vogel, *Rudy Giuliani Plans Ukraine Trip to Push for Inquiries That Could Help Trump*, N.Y. TIMES, May 9, 2019.

[522] *See id.*

[523] *Id.*

[524] In this interview, Mr. Giuliani stated: "My only client is the president of the United States . . . He's the only one I have an obligation to report to." *Id.* He also stated that the information he sought to gather "may turn out to be helpful to my government"—confirming that advancing his client's interests was all that mattered, and any incidental relation to United States public policy was secondary and incidental. *See id.*

[525] Ian Schwartz, *Giuliani: "Massive Collusion" Between DNC, Obama Admin, Clinton People & Ukraine to Create False Info About Trump*, REAL CLEAR POLITICS, May 10, 2019.

[526] Andrew Restuccia et al., *Transcript: POLITICO Interviews President Donald Trump on Joe Biden, Impeachment, Bill Barr, North Korea*, POLITICO, May 10, 2019.

Over the months that followed, Mr. Giuliani aggressively pursued his efforts to get Ukraine to investigate Mr. Biden. During these efforts—and subsequently—he claimed to act on behalf of his client, President Trump. On October 30, 2019, he tweeted, "All of the information I obtained came from interviews conducted as ... private defense counsel to POTUS, to defend him against false allegations."[527] On November 6, 2019, he tweeted, "The investigation I conducted concerning 2016 Ukrainian collusion and corruption, was done solely as a defense attorney to defend my client against false charges ..."[528] The *Ukraine Report* observes, "Numerous U.S. officials, including Ambassadors Sondland, Volker, and Bolton, as well as Lt. Col. Vindman and others, were well aware of Mr. Giuliani's efforts to push Ukraine to pursue these political investigations."[529]

As Mr. Giuliani worked hard to advance his client's personal and political interests—and *not* "foreign policy"—President Trump also required United States officials responsible for Ukraine to "talk with Rudy."[530] For example, Ambassador Sondland recalled that during a meeting in the Oval Office on May 23 with the U.S. officials who had attended the Ukrainian inauguration, President Trump "just kept saying: Talk to Rudy, talk to Rudy."[531] Ambassador Sondland explained that they "understood that talk with Rudy meant talk with Mr. Rudy Giuliani, the president's personal lawyer," and "if we did not talk to Rudy, nothing would move forward on Ukraine."[532] President Trump thus directed key U.S. officials to coordinate with and carry out the requests of his private lawyer, who was acting "solely" as President Trump's "defense attorney," regarding Ukraine.[533]

Mr. Giuliani's importance was not lost on the Ukrainians. By July 10, 2019, President Zelensky's top aide came to appreciate "that the key for many things is Rudi [sic] and I ready to talk with him at any time,"[534] and, as set forth above, key U.S. officials worked with Mr. Giuliani to convey messages to the Ukrainians and prepare President Zelensky for his July 25 call. Thus, on the July 25 call, President Zelensky preemptively mentioned that "we are hoping very much that Mr. Giuliani will be able to travel to Ukraine and we will meet once he comes to Ukraine."[535] President Trump replied, "I would like him to call you. I will ask him to call you along with the Attorney General. Rudy very much knows what's happening and he is a very capable guy. If you could speak to him that would be

---

[527] Rudolph Giuliani (@RudyGiuliani), Twitter (Oct. 30, 2019, 3:15 PM), https://twitter.com/RudyGiuliani/status/1189667099871981573; Rudolph Giuliani (@RudyGiuliani), Twitter (Oct. 30, 2019, 3:15 PM), https://twitter.com/RudyGiuliani/status/1189667101079932928.

[528] Rudolph Giuliani (@RudyGiuliani), Twitter (Nov. 6, 2019, 12:43 PM), https://twitter.com/RudyGiuliani/status/1192180680391843841.

[529] *Ukraine Report* at 90.

[530] *See* Sondland Hearing Tr. at 4.

[531] Sondland Dep. Tr. at 61-62.

[532] Sondland Hearing Tr. at 21, 71.

[533] Jordan Fabian, *Giuliani Says Ukraine Efforts 'Solely' for Trump's Legal Defense*, BLOOMBERG, Nov. 6, 2019.

[534] Text Message from Yermak to Ambassador Volker (July 10, 2019, 4:06 PM).

[535] *July 25 Call Record* at 3.

great."[536] Two sentences later, President Trump turned directly to his request that President Zelensky announce an investigation into the Bidens—and then, later in their discussion, confirmed that "I will have Mr. Giuliani give you a call and I am also going to have Attorney General Barr call …"[537] The call transcript thus confirms that President Trump saw Mr. Giuliani as his point person for organizing an investigation into the Bidens and the 2016 election, and that President Zelensky knew of Mr. Giuliani's role. Once again, it is therefore noteworthy that Mr. Giuliani has stated emphatically that he acted "solely" to advance his client's own interests—and that he was not engaged in "foreign policy."[538]

b.   Additional Evidence of Corrupt Intent

Many other considerations support the conclusion that President Trump's concerns had nothing to do with the legitimate foreign policy interests of the United States and everything to do with the President's personal political interests. *First*, after the removal of Ambasador Yovanovitch, President Trump's primary focus relating to Ukraine throughout this period was the announcement of two investigations that would benefit him politically. The day after the July 25 call, President Trump called Ambassador Sondland to ask whether President Zelensky "was going to do the investigation."[539] Ambassador Sondland stated that President Zelensky was "going to do it" and would do "anything you ask him to."[540] According to David Holmes, who overheard the conversation, Ambassador Sondland and President Trump spoke only about the investigation in their discussion about Ukraine.[541] The President made no mention of other major issues of importance in Ukraine, including President Zelensky's aggressive anti-corruption reforms and the ongoing war it was fighting against Russian-led forces in eastern Ukraine.[542] After Ambassador Sondland hung up the phone, he told Mr. Holmes that President Trump "did not give a shit about Ukraine."[543] Rather, he explained, the President cared only about "big stuff" that benefitted him personally, like "the Biden investigation that Mr. Giuliani was pitching."[544]

Second, in pursuit of these investigations, President Trump made it clear to Ambassador Sondland—who conveyed this message to Ambassador Taylor—that "everything was dependent on such an announcement, including security assistance."[545] Ambassador Sondland's admission confirms

---

[536] *Id.* at 3-4.

[537] *Id.* at 4.

[538] *See Vogel Giuliani.* In the months following the July 25 call, as President Trump through his agents continued to apply pressure on Ukraine to announce the investigations, call records confirm that Mr. Giuliani was in regular communication with the White House, Ambassadors Volker and Sondland, and members of President Zelensky's administration. *Ukraine Report* at 114-21 & nn.719-804.

[539] *See* Hill-Holmes Hearing Tr. at 29.

[540] *Id.*

[541] *See id.* at 29-30, 52.

[542] *See generally July 25 Call Record.*

[543] Holmes Dep. Tr. at 25; *see also* Hill-Holmes Hearing Tr. at 29.

[544] Holmes Dep. Tr. at 25; *see also* Hill-Holmes Hearing Tr. at 29-30.

[545] Taylor-Kent Hearing Tr. at 42.

that President Trump's actions were motivated only by the announcement of investigations. Ukraine is a key strategic partner of the United States. It had just elected a promising new leader who ran on an anti-corruption platform and was making strong progress in his reform agenda. But it had been invaded by Russia and depended heavily on United States support and assistance. The United States had provided such assistance on a bipartisan basis, with an overwhelming consensus in Congress and the national security community that this was vital to our own national interests.[546] To be sure, the President has broad latitude for certain policy judgments in foreign affairs in order to advance the national security interests of the country as a whole, but no witness interpreted the President's request for these investigations to be a change in policy, nor did his cabinet or Vice President.[547] This further supports the alternative and only plausible explanation that the President pressed for the public announcement of those investigations because they were of great personal political value to him.[548]

Third, the President's request for these investigations departed from established channels for making such a request. On the July 25 call, President Trump told President Zelensky that he should speak to Mr. Giuliani and Attorney General Barr.[549] But after the July 25 transcript was released, the Department of Justice publicly stated as follows:

> The President has not spoken with the Attorney General about having Ukraine investigate anything relating to former Vice President Biden or his son. The President has not asked the Attorney General to contact Ukraine—on this or any other matter. The Attorney General has not communicated with Ukraine—on this or any other subject. Nor has the Attorney General discussed this matter, or anything relating to Ukraine, with Rudy Giuliani.[550]

Ukraine's current Prosecutor General Ruslan Ryaboshapka, who assumed his new position in late August 2019, has since confirmed the Justice Department's account. He told *The Financial Times* in

---

[546] *Ukraine Report* at 68-70.

[547] *Id.* at 132 (describing Ms. Williams' testimony that during the September 1 meeting, the Vice President "assured President Zelensky that there was no change in U.S. policy in turns of our … full-throated support for Ukraine and its sovereignty and territorial integrity."); Williams Dep. Tr. at 83.

[548] That point is especially noteworthy given testimony indicating that President Trump did not actually care if the investigations occurred, but just wanted them to be announced. When asked by Chairman Schiff if President Zelensky "had to get those two investigations if [the White House meeting] was going to take place," Ambassador Sondland responded: "[President Zelensky] had to announce the investigations. He didn't actually have to do them, as I understood it." Sondland Hearing Tr. at 43.

The Minority Report claims that there is no evidence of corrupt intent because the U.S. "government did not convey the pause to the Ukrainians." *Minority Report* at ii. But, as explained above, this argument rests on a faulty premise. Ukraine did learn that the assistance had been withheld. And Ukrainian officials came to understand through their communications with United States officials that both the meeting and the military assistance depended on bowing to President Trump's demand for investigations.

[549] *July 25 Call Record* at 3-5.

[550] Statement of Kerri Kupec, Dep't of Just. (Sept. 25, 2019).

late November 2019 that Attorney General Barr had made no formal request regarding a potential investigation into allegations of wrongdoing by former Vice President Biden.[551]

Many Administration officials have also confirmed that there was no formal investigation into these matters within the Department of Justice or formal request to Ukraine for information in connection to the investigations and, moreover, that without going through the official process, the investigations were not proper. As Ambassador Volker testified, "[Mr. Yermak] said, and I think quite appropriately, that if they [Ukraine] are responding to an official request, that's one thing. If there's no official request, that's different. And I agree with that."[552] When Ambassador Volker discovered that no official request for investigations had been conveyed by the Department of Justice, he recalls thinking, "let's just not go there."[553]

In his testimony, Ambassador Taylor corroborated this account. He told the Committees that, on August 16, in a text message exchange with Ambassador Volker, he "learned that Mr. Yermak had asked that the United States submit an official request for an investigation into Burisma's alleged violations of Ukrainian law, if that is what the United States desired."[554] Ambassador Taylor noted that "a formal U.S. request to the Ukrainians to conduct an investigation based on violations of their own law" was "improper" and advised Ambassador Volker to "stay clear."[555] Mr. Kent similarly testified that on August 15, Ambassador Volker's special assistant asked him whether there was any precedent for the United States asking Ukraine to conduct investigations on its behalf. Mr. Kent replied: "[I]f you're asking me have we ever gone to the Ukrainians and asked them to investigate or prosecute individuals for political reasons, the answer is, I hope we haven't, and we shouldn't because that goes against everything that we are trying to promote in post-Soviet states for the last 28 years, which is the promotion of the rule of law."[556]

Fourth, the President's decision disregarded United States foreign policy towards Ukraine and did so abruptly and without explanation. To make a demand that benefits him personally, while endangering the rights of a United States citizen and political opponent is a bright red flag that supports only one conclusion—that the President was putting his own personal and political interests over the Nation's foreign policy interests. There is no dispute that President Trump's requested investigations were not part of any U.S. policy objectives relating to Ukraine, including its anti-corruption policies. Mr. Morrison, Lt. Col. Vindman, Mr. Kent, and Ambassador Taylor all confirmed that an investigation into the Bidens, or the 2016 election, was not a stated or recognized United States foreign policy

[551] *See Olearchyk*; *see also Ukraine Report* at 123. Moreover, with respect to election interference, the President's entire intelligence community had already concluded that Russia was responsible for interfering in the 2016 election and, as President Trump's former Homeland Security Advisor Tom Bossert made clear, the idea of Ukraine hacking the DNC server was "not only a conspiracy theory, it is completely debunked." *Id.* at 42.

[552] Volker Dep. Tr. at 198.

[553] *Id.* at 197.

[554] Taylor-Kent Hearing Tr. at 39.

[555] *Id.*

[556] Kent Dep. Tr. at 26.

objective.[557] Notably, President Trump was briefed on official policy prior to both calls that he had with President Zelensky—on April 21 and July 25.[558] Yet he chose not to follow talking points about corruption reform,[559] and instead decided on the July 25 call to go off-book and seek the criminal investigation of his political opponent.

Finally, President Trump's request was almost universally viewed by key United States and Ukrainian officials as improper, unusual, problematic, and, most importantly, purely political:

- Mr. Holmes: "I was shocked the requirement was so specific and concrete. While we had advised our Ukrainian counterparts to voice a commitment to following the rule of law and generally investigating credible corruption allegations, this was a demand that President Zelensky personally commit on a cable news channel to a specific investigation of President Trump's political rival."[560]

- Dr. Hill: "[Ambassador Sondland] was being involved in a domestic political errand, and we were being involved in national security foreign policy, and those two things had just diverged."[561]

- Lt. Col. Vindman: "What I was trying to do . . . was express my concerns about something that I viewed to be problematic."[562]

- Ambassador Taylor: "The Ukrainians did not owe President Trump anything. And holding up security assistance for domestic political gain was crazy."[563]

Other officials also voiced alarm. For example, Dr. Hill testified that Ambassador Bolton told her to "go and tell the [NSC Legal Advisor] that I am not part of whatever drug deal Sondland and Mulvaney

[557] *Impeachment Inquiry: Kurt Volker and Tim Morrison: Hearing Before the H. Perm. Select Comm. on Intelligence*, 116th Cong. 147 (Nov. 19, 2019) (confirming that he did not follow-up on the President's request to "investigate the Bidens" because he did "not understand it as a policy objective"); Vindman Hearing Tr. at 119 (confirming that he prepared the talking points for the call, that those talking points did not "contain any discussion of investigations into the 2016 election, the Bidens, or Burisma," and that he was not "aware of any written product from the National Security Council" suggesting those investigations were part of "the official policy of the United States"); Taylor-Kent Hearing Tr. at 179 ("Mrs. Demings[:] Was Mr. Giuliani promoting U.S. national interests or policy in Ukraine . . .? Ambassador Taylor[:] I don't think so, ma'am. . . . Mr. Kent[:] No, he was not. . . . Mrs. Demings[:] . . . What interest do you believe he was promoting. . . ? Mr. Kent[:] "I believe he was looking to dig up political dirt against a potential rival in the next election cycle. . . . Ambassador Taylor[:] I agree with Mr. Kent.").

[558] Vindman-Williams Hearing Tr. at 119.

[559] *Ukraine Report* at 52 (citing Deb Riechmann et al., *Conflicting White House Accounts of 1st Trump-Zelenskiy Call*, ASSOCIATED PRESS, Nov. 15, 2019).

[560] Hill-Holmes Hearing Tr. at 32.

[561] *Id.* at. 92.

[562] Vindman Dep. Tr. at 98.

[563] Taylor-Kent Hearing Tr. at 45 (statement of Ambassador Taylor).

are cooking up on this"; Dr. Hill explained that "drug deal" referred to Ambassador Sondland stating in a July 10 meeting, which included Ukrainian officials, that he had an agreement with Mr. Mulvaney for a White House meeting "if [Ukraine would] go forward with investigations."[564] On July 11, Dr. Hill "enlisted another NSC official who was present at the July 10 meeting" to attend a longer discussion with the NSC Legal Advisor about her concerns.[565] Similarly, although the Minority holds up his reaction as proof that nothing improper happened, Mr. Morrison immediately reported the July 25 call to the NSC legal advisor "to make sure that the package was reviewed by the appropriate senior level attention."[566] Further, Mr. Morrison tried to stay away from President Trump's requests because these investigations were not related to "the proper policy process that I was involved in on Ukraine," and "had nothing to do with the issues that the interagency was working on."[567]

Ukrainian officials, too, expressed similar reservations. On July 20, Ambassador Taylor spoke with Oleksandr Danyliuk, the Ukrainian national security advisor, who conveyed that President Zelensky "did not want to be used as a pawn in a U.S. reelection campaign."[568] As Ambassador Taylor testified, the "whole thrust" of the activities undertaken by Mr. Giuliani and Ambassador Sondland "was to get these investigations, which Danyliuk and presumably Zelensky were resisting because they didn't want to be seen to be interfering but also to be a pawn."[569] Further, as noted above, Ukrainian Prosecutor General Ruslan Ryaboshapka later stated—in apparent reference to President Trump's demands—that "it's critically important for the west not to pull us into some conflicts between their ruling elites, but to continue to support so that we can cross the point of no return."[570] In short, experienced officials on both sides of President Trump's scheme saw it for what it was: an effort to solicit Ukraine to assist his reelection campaign.

c. Alternative Explanations for President Trump's Course of Conduct Are Implausible and Inconsistent with the Evidence

Although the President has declined to participate in these proceedings, the Minority Report offers three alternative justifications for President Trump's conduct. The implausibility of these justifications, which are inconsistent with the evidence, only further proves that President Trump's motives were constitutionally improper.

i. Anti-Corruption

The Minority's principal contention is that President Trump denied a White House visit,

[564] *Ukraine Report* at 89.

[565] *Id.* at 90.

[566] Morrison Dep. Tr. at 61; *see* Volker-Morrison Hearing Tr. at 38.

[567] *Ukraine Report* at 106.

[568] *Id.* at 20.

[569] Taylor Dep. Tr. at 177.

[570] *Ukraine Report* at 55.

withheld military and security assistance, and demanded these two investigations due to his "deep-seated, genuine, and reasonable skepticism of Ukraine" for "pervasive corruption."[571] This after-the-fact contention is not credible.

To start, it is inconsistent with President Trump's own prior conduct respecting Ukraine. Under the previous Ukrainian administration of President Petro Poroshenko, which suffered from serious concerns about corruption issues, President Trump approved $510 million in aid in 2017 and $359 million in 2018; he also approved the sale of Javelin missiles to Ukraine in December 2017.[572] It was not until 2019, after Ukraine elected President Zelensky, who ran on a strong anti-corruption platform, that President Trump suddenly punished Ukraine by refusing a White House meeting and military and security assistance. If his goal were to fight corruption, President Trump would have withheld assistance from a corrupt leader and provided it to a reformer. Instead, he did the opposite, just a few months after former Vice President Biden announced his candidacy.

Nor did President Trump take any other steps one would expect to see if his concern were corruption. He was given extensive talking points about corruption for his April 21 and July 25 calls, yet ignored them both times and did not mention corruption on either call.[573] President Trump's staff uniformly agreed that President Zelensky was a credible anti-corruption reformer, yet President Trump suspended a White House meeting that his entire policy team agreed would lend support and cache to President Zelensky's anti-corruption agenda in Ukraine.[574] He withheld military and security assistance without any stated explanation, yet his own Department of Defense, in coordination with the Secretary of State, had certified in May that Ukraine satisfied all anti-corruption benchmarks necessary for that assistance to be released.[575] He continued to withhold the assistance, yet the White House never

---

[571] *Minority Report* at ii.

[572] USAID, *U.S. Foreign Aid by Country* (last updated Sept. 23, 2019); *Ukraine Report* at 100.

[573] *Ukraine Report* at 42 ("[C]ontrary to a public readout of the call originally issued by the White House, President Trump did not mention corruption in Ukraine, despite the NSC staff preparing talking points on that topic. Indeed, 'corruption' was not mentioned once during the April 21 conversation, according to the official call record."); Vindman-Williams Hearing Tr. at 24-25; *see July 25 Call Record*.

[574] *Ukraine Report* at 38 ("A new president [of Ukraine] had just been elected on an anti-corruption platform."); *id.* at 52 ("Mr. Zelensky's victory in April 2019 reaffirmed the Ukrainian people's strong desire to overcome an entrenched system of corruption and pursue closer partnership with the West."); *id.* at 63 ("Ambassador Sondland, Ambassador Volker, Secretary Perry, and Senator Johnson 'took turns' making their case 'that this is a new crowd, it's a new President' in Ukraine who was 'committed to doing the right things,' including fighting corruption. . . . They recommended that President Trump once again call President Zelensky and follow through on his April 21 invitation for President Zelensky to meet with him in the Oval Office."); *id.* at 65 ("On June 18, Ambassador Volker, Acting Assistant Secretary of State Ambassador Philip T. Reeker, Secretary Perry, Ambassador Sondland, and State Department Counselor T. Ulrich Brechbuhl participated in a meeting at the Department of Energy to follow up to the May 23 Oval Office meeting. Ambassador William Taylor . . . . participated by phone from Kyiv. The group agreed that a meeting between President Trump and President Zelensky would be valuable."); Hill-Holmes Hearing Tr. at 23 ("We at the Embassy also believed that a meeting was critical to the success of President Zelensky's administration and its reform agenda, and we worked hard to get it arranged.").

[575] Kent Dep. Tr. at 304-05 ("There was great confusion among the rest of us because we didn't understand why that had happened. . . . Since there was unanimity that this [aid] was in our national interest, it just surprised all of us."); Croft Dep. Tr. at 15 ("The only reason given was that the order came at the direction of the President."); Letter from John C. Rood, Under Sec'y of Defense for Policy, Dep't of Defense, to Eliot L. Engel, Chairman, House Comm. on Foreign Affairs (May 23, 2019) ("Ukraine has taken substantial actions to make defense institutional reforms for the purposes of decreasing

requested or independently conducted *any* subsequent review of Ukraine's anti-corruption policies—and the Defense Department adhered to its view that all anti-corruption benchmarks had already been satisfied.[576] He persisted in denying the public and his own staff any explanation, even though Congress and every agency other than OMB (headed by the President's Acting Chief of Staff) supported the provision of military and security assistance to Ukraine and strongly objected to President Trump's hold.[577] Tellingly, the President's purported concerns about corruption in Ukraine as a reason for placing the hold on security assistance were not conveyed at the time of the hold or any time prior to lifting the hold.

Moreover, as numerous United States officials observed, it would be squarely inconsistent with advancing an anti-corruption agenda for an American President to avoid official channels and demand that a foreign leader embroil themselves in our politics by investigating a candidate for President.[578] Yet President Trump made that very same demand. He also fired, without any explanation, an ambassador widely recognized as a champion in fighting corruption,[579] praised a corrupt prosecutor general in Ukraine,[580] and oversaw efforts to "cut foreign programs tasked with combating corruption

---

corruption. . . . [N]ow that this defense institution reform has occurred, we will use the authority provided...to support programs in Ukraine further."); *Ukraine Report* at 67.

[576] Cooper Dep. Tr. at. 92-93 ("Q: But DOD did not conduct any sort of review following this statement about whether Ukraine was making any sort of progress with regard to its anticorruption efforts in July or August or beginning of September. Is that right? A: That is correct. Q: Okay. And that's because, as a matter of process and law, all of those events took place precertification, pre-May? A: That is correct. And in the interagency discussions, DOD participants affirmed that we believed sufficient progress has been made. Q: Okay. And it wasn't just DOD participants who believed that these funds should flow to Ukraine during these interagency meetings, correct? A: That's correct. It was unanimous with the exception of the statements by OMB representatives, and those statements were relaying higher level guidance.").

[577] *Ukraine Report* at 67 ("In a series of interagency meetings, every represented agency other than OMB (which is headed by Mick Mulvaney, who is also the President's Acting Chief of Staff) supported the provision of assistance to Ukraine and objected to President Trump's hold. Ukraine experts at DOD, the State Department, and the National Security Council (NSC) argued that it was in the national security interest of the United States to continue to support Ukraine."); -Vindman-Williams Hearing Tr. at 125 ("Q. And from what you witnessed, did anybody in the National Security community support withholding the assistance? A. No."); Taylor-Kent Hearing Tr. at 35 ("I and others sat in astonishment. The Ukrainians were fighting Russians and counted on not only the training and weapons but also the assurance of U.S. support.").

[578] *Ukraine Report* at 149 ("When it became clear that President Trump was pressuring Ukraine to investigate his political rival, career public servants charged with implementing U.S. foreign policy in a non-partisan manner, such as Lt. Col. Vindman and Ambassador Taylor, communicated to President Zelensky and his advisors that Ukraine should avoid getting embroiled in U.S. domestic politics."); Hill-Holmes Hearing Tr. at 46 ("[O]ur longstanding policy is to encourage them [Ukraine] to establish and build rule of law institutions that are capable and that are independent and that can actually pursue credible allegations. That's our policy. We've been doing that for quite some time with some success. So focusing on particular[] cases, including [] cases where there is an interest of the President, it's just not part of what we've done. It's hard to explain why we would do that."); Taylor-Kent Hearing Tr. at 164 (concluding that President Trump's request "went against U.S. policy" and "would've undermined the rule of law and our longstanding policy goals in Ukraine, as in other countries, in the post-Soviet space").

[579] *Ukraine Report* at 38-50; *see also id.* at 49 ("There was a broad consensus that Ambassador Yovanovitch was successful in helping Ukraine combat pervasive and endemic corruption."); Holmes Dep. Tr. at 142; Hill-Holmes Hearing Tr. at 18-19.

[580] *July 25 Call Record* at 3.

in Ukraine and elsewhere overseas."[581]

Nothing about President Trump's conduct in the relevant period supports the theory that he was motivated by a "deep-seated, genuine, and reasonable skepticism of Ukraine" for "pervasive corruption." He gave Ukraine hundreds of millions of dollars under a regime that ultimately lost power because of mounting concerns about corruption and then punitively withheld funds when a reformer came to power. He launched a general attack on anti-corruption programs while growing closer with Vladimir Putin and other corrupt despots. His Administration *cut* anti-corruption programs in Ukraine during the relevant period.[582] And he ignored, defied, and confounded every office and agency within the Executive Branch seeking to promote anti-corruption programs, while demanding that Ukraine investigate his own domestic political rival. Even in the May 23 White House meeting with other U.S. officials, President Trump equated corruption in Ukraine with the false allegations that Ukraine tried to "take [him] down" in 2016, and directed his three senior U.S. government officials to assist "Mr. Giuliani's efforts, which, it would soon become clear, were exclusively for the benefit of the President's reelection campaign."[583]

In short, there is overpowering evidence that President Trump acted with corrupt intent. The after-the-fact claim that he asked for foreign investigations of his political rivals and withheld military aid because of a generalized concern about corruption defies all the evidence before us and common sense. The President's actions were unexplained and inexplicable, contradicted legal and factual findings reached by credible experts, and are indefensible given they involved soliciting a foreign power to open an investigation into an American citizen and rival political candidate.

ii.   Burden Sharing

We next consider the second justification proposed in the Minority Report: that President Trump has "been vocal about his skepticism of U.S. foreign aid and the need for European allies to shoulder more of the financial burden for regional defense."[584] This explanation is based largely on the fact that President Trump told President Zelensky on the July 25 call that European countries should be doing more to help Ukraine. But there is no evidence that this concern was the actual reason why he withheld a White House meeting, blocked the release of Congressionally approved military and security assistance, and requested the announcement of two investigations; in fact, the evidence available is inconsistent with that offered explanation.

To this day, President Trump has not explained why he withheld the valuable White House meeting. And until the whistleblower complaint was filed, there was no explanation for why President

---

[581] Erica Werner, *Trump Administration Sought Billions of Dollars in Cuts to Programs Aimed at Fighting Corruption in Ukraine and Elsewhere*, WASH. POST, Oct. 23, 2019 (hereinafter "Werner").

[582] *See Werner*.

[583] *Ukraine Report* at 17.

[584] *Minority Report* at ii.

Trump had blocked release of the military and security assistance.[585] This was extremely unusual. OMB Deputy Associate Director Mark Sandy, the senior budget official responsible for the Department of Defense portion of the aid to Ukraine, testified that he could not recall another instance in which a significant amount of assistance was held with no rationale provided.[586] Deputy Assistant George Kent testified that, upon learning of the hold on July 18, there was "great confusion" among representatives from the Department of Defense, State Department, and National Security Council because they "didn't understand why" the aid had been frozen.[587]

If the President's reason for ordering a hold was concern about Europe's contributions, he had no reason to keep that fact a secret from his own administration. Moreover, if that was his concern, the normal response would be to undertake a review process at the time of the hold. Yet, while Deputy Assistant Secretary of Defense Laura Cooper and other witnesses testified that they received some inquiries in late June about Ukraine security assistance, Ms. Cooper testified that there was no policy or interagency review process that she "participated in or knew of" in August 2019.[588] Ms. Cooper further testified that she had "no recollection of the issue of allied burden sharing coming up" in the three meetings she attended about the freeze on security assistance, or hearing about a lack of funding from Ukraine's allies as a reason for the freeze.[589] Under Secretary of State David Hale also testified that he did not hear about the lack of funding from Ukraine's allies as a reason for the security assistance hold.[590] And Ambassador Sondland, the ambassador to the European Union, testified that he was never asked to reach out to European countries to get them to contribute more.[591] Finally, President Trump ultimately released the military and security assistance without any further contributions from Europe. According to Lt. Col. Vindman, none of the "facts on the ground" had changed when this occurred.[592]

If the President's concern were genuinely about burden-sharing, it is implausible that he kept his own administration in the dark about that issue, never made any public statements about it, never ordered a review process focused on the question of burden sharing, never ordered his officials to push Europe to increase their contribution, and then released the aid without any change in Europe's

---

[585] *See, e.g., Ukraine Report* at 71-74; Vindman Dep. Tr. at 304-06; Hale Dep. Tr. at 105; Croft Dep. Tr. at 15; Holmes Dep. Tr. at 21; Kent Dep. Tr. at 304, 310; Sondland Hearing Tr. at 56, 80; Cooper Dep. Tr. at 44-45; Sandy Dep. Tr. at 91, 97; Morrison Dep. Tr. at 162-63. Mr. Morrison testified that, during a deputies' meeting on July 26, OMB stated that the "President was concerned about corruption in Ukraine, and he wanted to make sure that Ukraine was doing enough to manage that corruption." Morrison Dep. Tr. at 165. Mr. Morrison did not testify that concerns about Europe's contributions were raised during this meeting. In addition, Mr. Sandy testified that, as of July 26, despite its own statement, OMB did not actually have an understanding of the reason for the hold. *See* Sandy Dep. Tr. at 55-56.

[586] Sandy Dep. Tr. at 49.

[587] Kent Dep. Tr. at 304.

[588] Cooper Dep. Tr. at 91.

[589] *Impeachment Inquiry: Laura Cooper and David Hale: Hearing Before the H. Perm. Select Comm. on Intelligence*, 116th Cong. 75-76 (Nov. 20, 20190.

[590] *Id.* at 76.

[591] Sondland Dep. Tr. at 338.

[592] Vindman Dep. Tr. at 306.

contributions.

To be sure, after the whistleblower complaint was filed and the President became aware he had been caught, Mr. Sandy began receiving questions in September about burden sharing.[593] But that sequence only underscores the fact that this explanation was an after-the-fact justification to cover his tracks, as the hold had been in place for nearly two months without burden-sharing provided as a reason. Moreover, after Congress began investigating President Trump's conduct, the White House Counsel's Office reportedly conducted an internal review of "hundreds of documents," which "reveal[ed] extensive efforts to generate an after-the-fact justification" for the hold on assistance for Ukraine ordered by President Trump.[594] These documents reportedly included "early August email exchanges between acting chief of staff Mick Mulvaney and White House budget officials seeking to provide an explanation for withholding the funds after the president had already ordered a hold in mid-July on the nearly $400 million in security assistance."[595] Given the substantial evidence of irregular conduct at OMB—including, according to Mr. Sandy, the resignation of two OMB officials partly based on their objection to OMB's handling and rationale for the hold on assistance to Ukraine[596]—this effort to manufacture a pretext cannot reasonably be credited.

It also bears mention that European countries do, in fact, contribute substantial assistance to Ukraine. Since 2014, the European Union and European financial institutions have provided more than $16 billion in grants and loans to Ukraine, making the EU the largest donor to Ukraine.[597] This far exceeds the approximately $1.95 billion in assistance that the United States has provided during the same period, according to USAID.[598] Although the United States is the largest donor of military assistance to Ukraine, European countries also provide military aid to Ukraine through a NATO assistance package. For example, the United Kingdom has sent more than 1,300 soldiers to Ukraine since 2015 and has trained approximately 10,000 Ukrainian troops.[599]

iii.   Legitimate Investigations

The third and final justification that the Minority Report offers to explain President Trump's conduct is that he had a legitimate basis to request investigations into his political rival and the 2016

---

[593] Sandy Dep. Tr. at 44-45.

[594] Josh Dawsey et al., *White House Review Turns Up Emails Showing Extensive Effort to Justify Trump's Decision to Block Ukraine Military Aid*, WASH. POST, Nov. 24, 2019.

[595] *Id.* Because the White House has withheld these documents from Congress, the Committee is unable to verify the accuracy of the press reporting.

[596] Sandy Dep. Tr. at 149-56.

[597] European Union, *EU-Ukraine Relations – Fact Sheet* (Sept. 30, 2019).

[598] USAID, *U.S. Foreign Aid by Country* (last updated Sept. 23, 2019). According to Mr. Holmes, the United States has provided military and security assistance of about $3 billion since 2014. Hill-Holmes Hearing Tr. at 97.

[599] Ctr. for Strategic & Int'l Studies, *Not Contributing Enough? A Summary of European Military and Development Assistance to Ukraine Since 2014* (Sept. 26, 2019).

United States Presidential election.[600] Like the others conjectured by the Minority, this explanation is contradicted by the facts, the President's own statements, and common sense.

First, this theory presumes that the President was motivated by an overriding concern about events that occurred in 2015 and 2016—and that were widely reported at the time. Yet it was not until 2019 that the President requested these investigations and placed a hold on assistance to Ukraine. In other words, President Trump requested the investigations only after Vice President Biden had entered the 2020 presidential race and began beating him in the polls—thus giving him a personal and political motive to harm Vice President Biden publicly—and only after Special Counsel Robert Mueller's investigation affirmed the Intelligence Community Assessment's finding that Russia interfered in our election, and that it did so in a "sweeping and systematic" fashion in order to benefit President Trump.[601] The timing of President Trump's solicitation and pressure campaign, so shortly after Vice President Biden announced his candidacy and the Special Counsel Mueller's report was released, is powerful proof of the President's true motives for seeking the investigations.

Second, as explained above, had President Trump genuinely believed there was a legitimate basis to request Ukraine's assistance in law enforcement investigations, there are specific formal processes that he should have followed. Specifically, he could have instructed DOJ to make an official request for assistance through a Mutual Legal Assistance Treaty (MLAT).[602] But even though the United States and Ukraine have entered into an MLAT, multiple witnesses and DOJ itself have confirmed that there was never an official United States investigation into the Bidens' conduct in Ukraine, nor was there an official request to Ukraine for an investigation into its alleged interference in the 2016 United States Presidential election.[603] The President's failure to follow legitimate procedures is further proof that he was acting improperly.[604]

Third, the role of Mr. Giuliani also belies the suggestion that this was about legitimate United States investigations. Mr. Giuliani is not a representative of the United States government and had no formal role in facilitating Ukraine's involvement in United States criminal investigations. His

---

[600] *Minority Report* at 78-85.

[601] *See* Robert S. Mueller, III, *Report on the Investigation into Russian Interference in the 2016 Presidential Election*, Vol. I, 1 (March 2019) (hereinafter, "Mueller Report"); *see also Washington Post-ABC News poll, June 28-July 1, 2019*, WASH. POST, July 11, 2019 (poll showing Biden at 55, Trump at 41).

[602] *See* U.S. Dep't of Just., *Criminal Resource Manual* §§ 266-277 (describing the formal process for seeking international assistance in criminal investigations); *see also* Kent Dep. Tr. at 110-11, 158, 261; Yovanovitch Dep. Tr. at 192, 212; Holmes Dep. Tr. at 201-02; Taylor Dep. Tr. at 136.

[603] Kent Dep. Tr. at 111; Yovanovitch Dep. Tr. at 192; *see also* Matt Zapotosky et al., *Trump Wanted Barr to Hold News Conference Saying the President Broke No Laws in Call with Ukrainian Leader*, WASH. POST, Nov. 6, 2019.

[604] Although the President's supporters have noted that some Ukrainian officials made critical statements about President Trump during his campaign, as witnesses testified, witnesses explained that mere public comments are dramatically different than an orchestrated attempt to interfere in the level of election interference by the Ukrainian government. Moreover, those statements—which the Minority asserts became public in 2016 and early 2017—were not publicly raised by President Trump prior to 2019 nor during his call with President Zelensky, nor is there any evidence that President Trump was concerned about them. Rather, and quite irresponsibly, they have been raised by the President's political supporters in what appears to be an after-the-fact effort to manufacture a pretextual justification for the President's course of conduct.

involvement, as well as the lack of formal, official involvement by DOJ, provide ever more evidence that President Trump's actions were unrelated to legitimate United States criminal investigations, but rather about Giuliani's effort to "meddle in investigations" on behalf of his client, President Trump, as Giuliani told the New York Times in May.

Indeed, the record makes clear that President Trump was not seeking Ukrainian assistance in *United States* criminal investigations; rather, he wanted Ukraine to announce its own investigations of Vice President Biden and the 2016 United States Presidential election. This is clear from DOJ's non-involvement, as well as the President's public comments that Ukraine should "start a major investigation into the Bidens."[605] Multiple witnesses testified that it is extremely inappropriate and irregular for the United States to ask Ukraine to investigate a United States citizen—particularly when that citizen is a former Vice President and current political candidate.[606] For example, Lieutenant Colonel Vindman testified that he reported President Trump's July 25 call to legal counsel because he "did not think it was proper to demand that a foreign government investigate a U.S. citizen."[607] Ambassador Taylor echoed this concern, stating that "[a] formal U.S. request to the Ukrainians to conduct an investigation based on violations of their own law struck me as improper, and I recommended to Ambassador Volker that we stay clear."[608] Ambassador Volker, too, testified that "[t]o investigate the Vice President of the United States or someone who is a U.S. official. I don't think we should be asking foreign governments to do that. I would also say that's true of a political rival."[609] The President's improper request that Ukraine announce investigations varied from standard rules and norms; further demonstrating that it marked a dangerous abuse of power by the President.

Finally, both theories asserted by President Trump have been proven false. None of the 17 witnesses who appeared as part of this inquiry testified that they were aware of any factual basis to support the allegation that Ukraine interfered in the 2016 election; rather, multiple witnesses confirmed that these were false, debunked conspiracy theories.[610] As Dr. Fiona Hill testified, "[t]his is a fictional narrative that is being perpetrated and propagated by the Russian security services themselves."[611] Further, on December 9, 2019, FBI Director Christopher Wray stated, "We have no information that

---

[605] The White House, *Remarks by President Trump Before Marine One Departure*, Oct. 3, 2019.

[606] *See, e.g.*, Taylor-Kent Hearing Tr. at 159 ("it is not role of politicians to be involved in directing the judicial systems of … other countries"); Taylor Dep. Tr. at 32 ("A formal U.S. request to the Ukrainians to conduct an investigation based on violations of their own law struck me as improper, and I recommended to Ambassador Volker that we stay clear."); Volker-Morrison Hearing Tr. at 156 ("I don't believe it is appropriate for the President to [ask a foreign government to investigate a U.S. citizen]. If we have law enforcement concerns with a U.S. citizen generally, there are appropriate channels for that.").

[607] Vindman Dep. Tr. at 18.

[608] Taylor Dep. at 32.

[609] Volker Hearing Tr. at 103.

[610] Hill Dep. Tr. at 173, 175; Kent Dep. Tr. at 198; Vindman Dep. Tr. at 330-31; Hale Dep. Tr. at 121; Holmes Dep. Tr. at 128.

[611] Hill-Holmes Hearing Tr. at 40.

indicates that Ukraine interfered with the 2016 presidential election."[612] The Republican-led Senate Select Committee on Intelligence concluded the same.[613] It is therefore entirely not credible to suggest that the President's actions were based on a sincere belief that Ukraine interfered in the 2016 United States election or that the so-called "Crowdstrike theory" had any validity.[614]

Similarly, there is no legitimate basis for President Trump to claim former Vice President Biden behaved improperly in calling for the removal of Ukrainian prosecutor general Viktor Shokin. When he called for Mr. Shokin's removal, then-Vice President Biden acted in accordance with and in furtherance of an official United States policy and the broad consensus of various European countries and the International Monetary Fund.[615] Indeed, in late 2015, the International Monetary Fund threatened Ukraine that it would not receive $40 billion in international assistance unless Mr. Shokin was removed.[616] Vice President Biden was subsequently enlisted by the State Department to call for Mr. Shokin's removal—and in late 2015 and early 2016, he announced that the United States would withhold $1 billion in loan guarantees unless Mr. Shokin was dismissed.[617] Ultimately, in March 2016, Ukraine's parliament voted to dismiss Mr. Shokin.[618] Moreover, multiple witnesses confirmed that the removal of Mr. Shokin would have *increased* the likelihood that Burisma would be investigated for corruption, not the opposite, given that Mr. Shokin was widely considered to be both ineffective and

---

[612] Luke Barr & Alexander Mallin, *FBI Director Pushes Back on Debunked Conspiracy Theory About 2016 Election Interference*, ABC NEWS, Dec. 9, 2019.

[613] Natasha Bertrand, *Senate Panel Look into Ukraine Interference Comes Up Short*, POLITICO, Dec. 2, 2019.

[614] In fact, what President Trump raised on his call was a false conspiracy theory that Russia did not hack the Democratic National Committee ("DNC") servers in 2016 and that there is a DNC server hidden in Ukraine. As President Trump's own former Homeland Security Advisor Tom Bossert confirmed and previously advised President Trump, this theory has "no validity" and is "completely debunked." *See* Sheryl Gay Stolberg et al., *Trump Was Repeatedly Warned That Ukraine Conspiracy Theory Was 'Completely Debunked'*, N.Y. TIMES, Sept. 29, 2019. The theory appears to stem in part from an inaccurate suggestion by the President that Crowdstrike, an American cybersecurity firm retained by the DNC in 2016 to investigate the origins of Russia's hack on DNC servers, is owned by a Ukrainian. It is not. The intelligence communities have unanimously concluded that Russia interfered in the 2016 election, and the President has been repeatedly advised that the Crowdstrike theory is illegitimate. Dr. Hill testified that Mr. Bossert and National Security Advisor H.R. McMaster "spent a lot of time" in 2017 "trying to refute" the Crowdstrike theory and advised the President that the theory of Ukrainian interference was false. Hill Dep. Tr. at 234

[615] Multiple witnesses thus testified that Mr. Shokin was corrupt and failing to fulfill his duties as Prosecutor General. Mr. Kent, an expert on Ukraine and anti-corruption matters, described "a broad-based consensus" among the United States, European allies, and international financial institutions that Mr. Shokin was "a typical Ukraine prosecutor who lived a lifestyle far in excess of his government salary, who never prosecuted anybody known for having committed a crime" and who "covered up crimes that were known to have been committed." Kent Dep. Tr. at 45. In addition, Ukraine's former prosecutor general Yuriy Lutsenko who had perpetuated this allegation of wrongdoing by the Bidens has since recanted and stated that there is no evidence of wrongdoing by Vice President Biden or his son. *See Ukraine Report* at 42.

[616] Courtney Subramanian, *Explainer: Biden, Allies Pushed Out Ukrainian Prosecutor Because He Didn't Pursue Corruption Cases*, USA TODAY, Oct. 3, 2019; Neil Buckley, Roman Olearchyk, & Shawn Donnan, *IMF Warning Sparks Ukraine Pledge on Corruption and Reform*, FIN. TIMES, Feb. 10, 2016.

[617] Taylor-Kent Hearing Tr. at 93; Matt Viser & Paul Sonne, *Inside Joe Biden's Brawling Efforts to Reform Ukraine — Which Won Him Successes and Enemies*, WASH. POST, Oct. 19, 2019.

[618] Andrew E, Kramer, *Ukraine Ousts Viktor Shokin, Top Prosecutor, and Political Stability Hangs in the Balance*, N.Y. TIMES, Mar. 29, 2016.

corrupt.[619] Any suggestion that former Vice President Biden called for Mr. Shokin's removal in order to stop an investigation of Burisma, the company whose board Hunter Biden sat on, is inconsistent with these facts.[620]

iv.   Conclusion

The Committee does not lightly conclude that President Trump acted with corrupt motives. But the facts, including the uncontradicted and corroborated testimony and documents, as well as common sense once again, all support that inescapable conclusion. President Trump exercised his official powers to solicit and pressure Ukraine to launch investigations into former Vice President Biden and the 2016 election. He did so not for any legitimate reason, but to obtain an improper personal political benefit by aiding his reelection, harming the election prospects of a political opponent, and influencing the 2020 United States Presidential election to his advantage. In so doing, President Trump violated his Oath of Office and abused his public trust. The Framers could not have been clearer that Presidents who wield power for their own personal advantage are subject to impeachment, particularly when their private gain comes at the expense of the national interest.

3.   President Trump Ignored and Injured Vital National Interests

President Trump's abuse of power harmed the United States. It undermined our national security and weakened our democracy. There is no indication that the President attended to these concerns in pursuing his own political errand—and there is every indication that he purposely ignored them. This is exactly what the Framers feared, and it is why they authorized Presidential impeachment.

a.   National Security

While carrying out his corrupt scheme in Ukraine, President Trump ignored and injured the national security of the United States. He did so by threatening our safety and security, weakening democracy at home and abroad, undermining our efforts to promote the rule of law on a global stage, and tarnishing our reputation with allies. This is not a matter of policy disagreement. It is an objective assessment of the consequences of President Trump's conduct—an assessment that the House is entitled and required to make in these circumstances.

First, when he withheld military and security assistance from Ukraine (and did so for his own personal political benefit), President Trump threatened the safety and security of the United States.

---

[619] *Ukraine Report* at 42.

[620] Because Mr. Shokin failed to prosecute corruption in Ukraine, his removal made it *more*—not less—likely that Ukrainian authorities might investigate any allegations of wrongdoing at Burisma. In addition, Ukraine's former Prosecutor General Yuri Lutsenko who had perpetuated this allegation of wrongdoing by the Bidens has since recanted and stated that there is no evidence of wrongdoing by Vice President Biden or his son. *See* Tracy Wilkinson & Sergei L. Loiko, *Former Ukraine Prosecutor Says He Saw No Evidence of Wrongdoing by Biden*, L.A. TIMES, Sept. 29, 2019. For these reasons, the allegations that Vice President Biden inappropriately pressured Ukraine to remove Mr. Shokin in order to protect his son are baseless.

Ukraine is a "strategic partner of the United States."[621] By contrast, United States "national security policy" correctly identifies Russia as an adversary.[622] As multiple witnesses affirmed, the United States therefore has an interest in supporting Ukraine, to ensure it remains an independent and democratic country that can deter Russian influence, expansion, and military aggression. For example, Ambassador Yovanovitch explained in her testimony that "[s]upporting Ukraine is the right thing to do. It's also the smart thing to do. If Russia prevails and Ukraine falls to Russia dominion, we can expect to see other attempts by Russia to expand its territory and influence."[623] Mr. Morrison elaborated: "Russia is a failing power, but it is still a dangerous one. The United States aids Ukraine and her people so that they can fight Russia over there, and we don't have to fight Russia here."[624]

The military and security assistance that the United States has approved with bipartisan support to Ukraine since 2014 is critical to preventing Russia's expansion and aggression. Ukraine is on the front line of conflict with Russia; its forces defend themselves against Russian aggression every day, in an ongoing war.[625] When the United States provides assistance that allows Ukraine to equip itself with "radar and weapons and sniper rifles, that saves lives. It makes the Ukrainians more effective. It might even shorten the war. That's what our hope is, to show that the Ukrainians can defend themselves and the Russians, in the end, will say 'Okay, we're going to stop.'"[626] In addition, as Ambassador Taylor explained, the delay occurred "at a time when hostilities were still active in the east and when Russia was watching closely to gauge the level of American support for the Ukrainian Government."[627]

Above and beyond the security assistance itself, public support from the United States demonstrates to Russia that "we are Ukraine's reliable strategic partner."[628] In withholding not only assistance, but also a White House meeting, the President denied Ukraine a show of strength that could deter further Russian aggression and help Ukraine negotiate an end to its five-year war with Russia (a war that has already killed over 13,000 Ukrainians).[629] Indeed, the very fact of delayed assistance quite certainly emboldened our enemies and weakened our partner. President Trump's conduct continues to

---

[621] Taylor-Kent Hearing Tr. at 28.

[622] *Id.* at 53; *see also Worldwide Threat Assessment of the U.S. Intelligence Community Before S. Select Comm. on Intelligence*, 116th Cong. (Jan. 29, 2019) (testimony by Director Daniel R. Coats, Office of the Director of National Intelligence) ("We assess that Russia poses a cyber espionage, influence, and attack threat to the United States and our allies.").

[623] *Impeachment Inquiry: Marie Yovanovitch: Hearing Before the H. Perm. Select Comm. on Intelligence*, 116th Cong. 18 (Nov. 15, 2019). Mr. Holmes elaborated on the importance of Ukraine to our policy goals: "It's been said that without Ukraine, Russia is just a country, but with it, it's an empire." Hill-Holmes Hearing Tr. at 162.

[624] *Ukraine Report* at 69; Morrison-Volker Hearing Tr. at 11.

[625] *See, e.g., Ukraine Report* at 67-69; Kent. Dep. Tr. at 202, 338-339.

[626] *Ukraine Report* at 68; Taylor Dep. Tr. at 153.

[627] *Ukraine Report* at 129; Taylor-Kent Hearing Tr. at 40.

[628] *See Ukraine Report* at 83. Mr. Kent also testified to this point, explaining that a White House meeting was "also important for U.S. national security because it would have served to bolster Ukraine's negotiating position in peace talks with Russia. It also would have supported Ukraine as a bulwark against further Russian advances in Europe." *Id.* at 83-84.

[629] *Ukraine Report* at 68, 83-84.

exacerbate these dynamics; for example, the day after Presidents Zelensky and Putin met to negotiate an end to the war in their border region, on December 10, President Trump met with Russia's top envoy in the Oval Office, but has yet to schedule a White House meeting with President Zelensky.[630]

Second, our national security goals in support of Ukraine are part of a "broader strategic approach to Europe," whereby we seek to facilitate negotiation of conflicts in Europe, maintain peace and order in that region, and prevent further Russian aggression not just in Ukraine but in Europe and elsewhere.[631] Ambassador Taylor explained the importance of Ukraine to these policy goals in his testimony:

> Russians are violating all of the rules, treaties, understandings that they committed to that actually kept peace in Europe for nearly 70 years. Until they invaded Ukraine in 2014, they had abided by sovereignty of nations, of inviolability of borders. That rule of law, that order that kept the peace in Europe and allowed for prosperity as well as peace in Europe was violated by the Russians. And if we don't push back on that, on those violations, then that will continue. … [This] affects the kind of world that we want to see abroad. So that affects our national interests very directly. Ukraine is on the front line of that conflict.[632]

Third, President Trump's actions diminished President Zelensky's ability to advance his anti-corruption reforms in Ukraine—and, in turn, to help the United States promote our ideals abroad.

President Zelensky, who ran on a strong anti-corruption platform, was elected by a large majority of Ukrainians; subsequent to that election, Ukrainians voted to replace 80% of their Parliament to endorse a "platform consistent with our democratic values, our reform priorities, and our strategic interests."[633] Mr. Kent thus emphasized that President Zelensky's anti-corruption efforts could ensure that "the Ukrainian Government has the ability to go after corruption and effectively investigate, prosecute, and judge alleged criminal activities using appropriate institutional mechanisms, that is, to create and follow the rule of law."[634] Of course, it is always in our national security interest to help advance such democratic and anti-corruption platforms. At a time of shifting alliances, "Ukrainians and freedom loving people everywhere are watching the example we set here of democracy and rule of law."[635] "If Ukraine is able to enforce that anti-corruption agenda, it can serve as an example to other

---

[630] John Hudson & Anne Gearan, *Trump Meets Russia's Top Diplomat Amid Scrap Over Election Interference*, WASH. POST, Dec. 10, 2019.

[631] Taylor-Kent Hearing Tr. at 169-70.

[632] Taylor-Kent Hearing Tr. at 52-53.

[633] Hill-Holmes Hearing Tr. at 35.

[634] *Ukraine Report* at 149; Taylor-Kent Hearing Tr. at 24.

[635] Hill-Holmes Hearing Tr. at 36.

post-Soviet countries and beyond, from Moscow to Hong Kong."[636] "A secure, democratic, and free Ukraine [thus] serves not just the Ukrainian people, but the American people as well. That's why it was our policy and continues to be our policy to help the Ukrainians achieve their objectives. They match our objectives."[637]

As Mr. Holmes testified, a White House visit and U.S. support was "critical" to President Zelensky implementing his platform.[638] President Zelensky was a new leader, "looking to establish his bona fides as a regional and maybe even a world leader." In that context, a meeting with the United States—the most "powerful country in the world and Ukraine's most significant benefactor"—would have gone a long way in ensuring that President Zelensky had the credibility to implement his reforms.[639] Yet, to this day and as a result of President Trump's desire to obtain a personal political advantage in the upcoming election, no such meeting has occurred. This surely has not gone unnoticed by Ukraine, our democratic allies, or countries struggling to enforce similar democratic ideals. Indeed, Zelensky administration officials already are reportedly "now reconsidering their strategy on communication with and about the Trump administration."[640]

Fourth, President Trump's brazen use of official acts to pressure Ukraine to announce a politically motivated investigation undermined our credibility in promoting democratic values and the rule of law in Ukraine and elsewhere. As Ambassador Taylor underscored, "[o]ur credibility is based on a respect for the United States," and "if we damage that respect, then it hurts our credibility and makes it more difficult for us to do our jobs."[641] Mr. Kent, too, agreed that the President's request for investigations "went against U.S. policy" and "would've undermined the rule of law and our longstanding policy goals in Ukraine, as in other countries, in the post-Soviet space."[642]

Ukrainian officials' reaction to American requests following President Trump's demand illuminates this concern. When Ambassador Volker advised Mr. Yermak about "potential problems" with investigations that the Zelensky administration was contemplating into former Ukrainian President Petro Poroshenko, Mr. Yermak retorted, "what, you mean like asking us to investigate Clinton and Biden?"[643] Ambassador Volker did not respond.[644]

---

[636] *Id.* at 35.

[637] Yovanovitch Hearing Tr. at 17.

[638] Hill-Holmes Hearing Tr. at 23.

[639] *Id.* at 38-39.

[640] Betsy Swan, *Ukrainians: Trump Just Sent Us 'a Terrible Signal'*, DAILY BEAST, Dec. 11, 2019; *see also* Michael Birnbaum, *Ukraine Desperately Wants the U.S. on its Side. They Just Don't Know who has Trump's Ear Anymore*, WASH. POST, Nov. 22, 2019 (quoting a Zelensky ally who noted that the U.S. delay in military aid is "making us rethink how U.S. policy is operating").

[641] *Ukraine Report* at 150; Taylor-Kent Hearing Tr. at 165.

[642] *Ukraine Report* at 150; Taylor-Kent Hearing Tr. at 164.

[643] *Ukraine Report* at 150; Volker-Morrison Hearing Tr. at 139.

[644] *Id.*, at 139. President Trump's removal of Ambassador Yovanovitch following a discredited smear campaign on her character, and subsequent comments attacking her and telling a foreign leader that she would "go through some things,"

Finally, President Trump's conduct threatened to harm America's alliances more broadly. "The U.S. is the most powerful country in the history of the world in large part because of our values, and our values have made possible the network of alliances and partnerships that buttresses our own strength."[645] Yet President Trump's scheme—using Ukraine's desperation for military assistance and support to pressure our ally to announce an investigation into his political rival—shook Ukraine's "faith in us."[646] Even worse, it sent a message to our allies that the United States may withhold critical military and security assistance for our President's personal political benefit; if such conduct is allowed to stand, our allies will "constantly question the extent to which they can count on us."[647]

President Trump ignored and injured our national security when he corruptly abused the powers of his office for personal political gain. As Ambassador Yovanovitch summarized in her testimony, President Trump's "conduct undermines the U.S., exposes our friends, and widens the playing field for autocrats like President Putin. Our leadership depends on the power of our example and the consistency of our purpose. Both have now been opened to question."[648]

b. Free and Fair Elections

As explained at the outset, the Framers of our Constitution were particularly fearful that a President might someday abuse the powers of his office to undermine free and fair elections. The heart of the Framers' project was a commitment to popular sovereignty. In an age when "democratic self-government existed almost nowhere on earth,"[649] the Framers imagined a society "where the true principles of representation are understood and practi[c]ed, and where all authority flows from, and returns at stated periods to, the people."[650] But that would be possible only if "those entrusted with [power] should be kept in dependence on the people."[651] This is why the President, and Members of Congress, must stand before the public for re-election on fixed terms. Through free and fair democratic elections the American people protect their system of political self-government.

President Trump's conduct ignored and injured the Nation's fundamental interest in self-governance and free and fair elections. As Professor Pamela S. Karlan of Stanford Law School explained in her testimony before this Committee, "[t]he very idea that a President might seek the aid

---

contributed to this harm, as well. As she explained, "[i]f our chief representative is kneecapped it limits our effectiveness to safeguard the vital national security interests of the United States." *Ukraine Report* at 49; Yovanovitch Hearing Tr. at 22.

[645] Yovanovitch Hearing Tr. at 17.

[646] *Ukraine Report* at 136; Text Message from Ambassador Taylor to Ambassador Sondland (Sept. 9, 2019, 12:31 AM).

[647] Hill-Holmes Hearing Tr. at 175.

[648] Yovanovitch Hearing Tr. at 19.

[649] Akhil Reed Amar, *America's Constitution: A Biography* 8 (2006).

[650] 4 *Debates in the Several State Conventions*, at 331; *see also* James Madison, *Federalist No. 14*.

[651] James Madison, *Federalist No. 37*, at 268.

of a foreign government in his reelection campaign would have horrified [the Framers]."[652] Professor Karlan added:

> [O]ur elections become less free when they are distorted by foreign interference. What happened in 2016 was bad enough: there is widespread agreement that Russian operatives intervened to manipulate our political process. But that distortion is magnified if a sitting President abuses the powers of his office actually to invite foreign intervention … That is not politics as usual—at least not in the United States or any other mature democracy. It is, instead, a cardinal reason why the Constitution contains an impeachment power. Put simply, a candidate for president should resist foreign interference in our elections, not demand it.[653]

When asked to elaborate on her view that President Trump's conduct endangered the right to vote, which ranks among our most precious rights, Professor Karlan observed: "The way that it does it is exactly what President Washington warned about, by inviting a foreign government to influence our elections. It takes the right away from the American people and it turns that into a right that foreign governments decide to interfere for their own benefit. Foreign governments don't interfere in our elections to benefit us; they intervene to benefit themselves."[654]

Ultimately, the Constitution does not care whether President Trump, former Vice President Biden, or any other candidate wins the 2020 United States Presidential election. It is indifferent to political parties and individual candidates.[655] But it does care that we have free and fair elections. That is why foreigners can be excluded from activities of democratic self-government, including voting and contributing to political candidates.[656] And it is why a President who uses the powers of his office to invite foreign government interference in an election, all for his own personal political gain, is a President who has abandoned our constitutional commitment to democracy.[657]

4.   President Trump's Abuse of Power Encompassed Impeachable "Bribery" and Violations of Federal Criminal Law

The first Article of Impeachment charged President Trump with an abuse of power as that constitutional offense has long been understood. While there is no need for a crime to be proven in order for impeachment to be warranted, here, President Trump's scheme or course of conduct also

---

[652] *The Impeachment Inquiry into President Donald J. Trump: Constitutional Grounds for Presidential Impeachment Before the H. Comm. on the Judiciary*, 116th Cong. (Dec. 4, 2019) (written testimony of Professor Pamela S. Karlan).

[653] *Id.*

[654] *Id.* (testimony by Professor Pamela S. Karlan in response to question by Chairman Jerrold Nadler).

[655] The sole exception is a provision that restricts the Presidency to natural born citizens. U.S. CONST. art. II, § 1. As relevant here, this provision is intended to guard against improper foreign influence in American politics. *See* 1 James Kent, *Commentaries on American Law* 255 (1826).

[656] *See Bluman v. Fed. Election Comm'n*, 800 F. Supp. 2d 281 (D.D.C. 2011), *aff'd*, 565 U.S. 1104 (2012).

[657] *See Constitutional Grounds for Impeachment* (2019) at 24-28.

encompassed other offenses, both constitutional *and* criminal in character, and it is appropriate for the Committee to recognize such offenses in assessing the question of impeachment.

a.   Constitutional Bribery

"Bribery" under the Impeachment Clause occurs where a President corruptly offers, solicits, or accepts something of personal value to influence his own official actions.[658] In that respect, "Bribery is . . . an especially egregious and specific example of a President abusing his power for private gain."[659] Based on their lived experience, the Framers had good cause to view such conduct as grounds for impeachment. Bribery was considered "so heinous an Offence, that it was sometimes punished as High Treason."[660] And it was received wisdom in the late-17th century that nothing can be "a greater Temptation to Officers [than] to abuse their Power by Bribery and Extortion."[661]

Since the Founding, "[a] number of impeachments in the United States have charged individuals with misconduct that was viewed as bribery."[662] However, "the practice of impeachment in the United States has tended to envelop charges of bribery within the broader standard of 'other high Crimes and Misdemeanors'"[663] and, for the most part, "the specific articles of impeachment were framed as 'high crimes and misdemeanors' or an 'impeachable offense'" without ever "explicitly referenc[ing] bribery."[664] Here, the First Article of Impeachment alleges what is, among other things, a bribery scheme, whereby President Trump corruptly solicited things of value from a foreign power, Ukraine, to influence his own official actions—namely, the release of $391 million in Congressionally-authorized assistance and a head of state meeting at the White House.

The elements of impeachable bribery under the Constitution are not expressly set forth in our founding document. As Justice Joseph Story and other authorities have made clear, however, the Anglo-American common law tradition supplies a complete and "proper exposition of the nature and limits of the offense."[665] This Committee has reaffirmed for more than a century that "[t]he offense of bribery had a fixed status in the parliamentary law as well as the criminal law of England when our Constitution was adopted, and there is little difficulty in determining its nature and extent in the application of the law of impeachments in this country."[666] Indeed, the four legal experts who testified before this

---

[658] *Id.* at 3.

[659] *Id.* at 16.

[660] Giles Jacob, *A New Law-Dictionary* 95 (1729) (hereinafter "*A New Law-Dictionary*"); *see also* 1 W. Hawkins, *A Treatise of Pleas of the Crown*, ch. 67, § 6 (1716) (hereinafter "*Pleas of the Crown*") (noting that bribery "was sometimes viewed as High Treason").

[661] *Pleas of the Crown*, ch. 67, § 3.

[662] Cong. Research Serv., *Impeachment and the Constitution* 45 & n. 475 (Nov. 20, 2019).

[663] *Id.* at 46.

[664] *Id.* at 36 (describing impeachment proceedings against Judge G. Thomas Porteous Jr. and Judge Alcee L Hastings).

[665] 2 Joseph Story, *Commentaries on the Constitution* § 794 (1833).

[666] *Proceedings of the United States Senate and the House of Representatives in the Trial of Impeachment of Robert W. Archbald*, S. Doc. No. 1140, 62nd Cong., at 1695 (1913).

Committee agreed on the basic definition of common law bribery: it occurs where a President (1) offers, solicits, or accepts (2) something of personal value (3) to influence the official duties he is entrusted with exercising by the American people; (4) corruptly.[667] The experts also agreed that an impeachable offense need not be a crime.[668]

Two aspects of this definition merit special note. First, at the time of the Constitutional Convention, bribery was well understood in Anglo-American law to encompass *soliciting* bribes. As Judge John T. Noonan, Jr. explains, the drafting history of the Impeachment Clause demonstrates that "'Bribery' was read both actively and passively, including the chief magistrate bribing someone and being bribed."[669] In a renowned bribery case involving the alleged solicitation of bribes, Lord Mansfield explained that "[w]herever it is a crime to take, it is a crime to give: they are reciprocal."[670] William Blackstone likewise confirmed that "taking bribes is punished," just as bribery is punishable for "those who offer a bribe, though not taken."[671] In addition, at common law, soliciting a bribe—even if it is not accepted—completes the offense of bribery.[672] "[T]he *attempt* is a crime; it is complete on his side who offers it."[673]

Second, under common law, bribery occurred when the thing offered or solicited was of *personal* value to the recipient. Common law treatises explained that a bribe broadly encompassed "any

---

I. [667] *See The Impeachment Inquiry into President Donald J. Trump: Constitutional Grounds for Presidential Impeachment Before H. Comm. on the Judiciary*, 116th Cong. (2019) (hereinafter "Constitutional Grounds Hearing (2019)") (written testimony of Professor Jonathan Turley) ("Under the common law definition, bribery remains relatively narrow and consistently defined among the states. 'The core concept of a bribe is an inducement improperly influencing the performance of a public function meant to be gratuitously exercised.'") (quoting John T. Noonan, Jr., *Bribes: The Intellectual History of a Moral Idea* xi (1984)); *id.* (testimony by Professor Noah R. Feldman in response to question by Representative Jerrold L. Nadler) ("Bribery had a clear meaning to the Framers, it was -- when the President, using the power of his office, solicits or receives something of personal value from someone affected by his official powers."); *see also id.* (written testimony of Professor Pamela S. Karlan); *id.* (written testimony of Professor Michael J. Gerhardt) (similar).

[668] *See Constitutional Grounds Hearing (2019)* (written testimony of Professor Jonathan Turley); *id.* (written testimony of Professor Noah R. Feldman); *id.* (testimony by Professor Michael J. Gerhardt in response to question by Special Counsel Norman L. Eisen); *id.* (testimony by Professor Pamela S. Karlan in response to question by Special Counsel Norman L. Eisen); *see also Constitutional Grounds for Impeachment* (2019), at 31-38.

[669] Noonan, *Bribes*, at 430; *Pleas of the Crown*, ch. 67, § 2.

[670] *Rex v. Vaughan*, 98 Eng. Rep. 308, 311 (K.B. 1769).

[671] William Blackstone, *Commentaries on the Laws of England*, vol. 2, Book 4, ch. 10, § 17 (1771); *A New Law-Dictionary*, at 95 (defining "Bribery" as "the Receiving, or Offering, any undue Reward . . . to act contrary to his Duty.").

[672] *See* 4 William Blackstone, *Commentaries* *139; *Rex v. Plympton*, 2 Ld. Raym. 1377, 1379 (1724); *Rex v. Higgins*, 102 Eng. Rep. 269, 276 (1801) ("A solicitation or inciting of another, by whatever means it is attempted, is an act done"); *see also* John Marshall Gest, *The Writings of Sir Edward Coke*, 18 YALE L.J. 504, 522 (1909) ("Of bribery: 'They that buy will sell.'") (quoting Coke, C.J.) (citing 3 Inst. 148); Francis B. Sayre, *Criminal Attempts*, 41 HARV. L. REV. 821 (1928) (citing additional cases).

[673] *Vaughan*, 98 Eng. Rep. at 311. American courts subsequently repeated this principle; *see, e.g., State v. Ellis*, 33 N.J.L. 102, 103-04 (N.J. Sup. Ct. 1868) (importing the common law definition of bribery to include attempts); *see also* William O. Russell, *A Treatise on Crimes and Misdemeanors* 239-40 (1st U.S. ed. 1824).

undue Reward," "valuable thing," or valuable consideration, even where "the things were small."[674] The *value* of the thing was measured by its *value* to the public official who was offering, soliciting or receiving it.[675] Accordingly, as Professor Turley recognized in his testimony, the common law encompassed non-pecuniary things of value—even including, in the case of King Charles II (as would have been well known to the Framers), "a young French mistress."[676] Consistent with this broad understanding, in guarding against foreign efforts to corrupt American officials, the Constitution forbids any "Person holding *any* Office of Profit or Trust," from accepting "*any* present, Office or Title, of *any* kind whatever, from . . . a foreign State," unless Congress consents.[677] An equally capacious view applies to the impeachable offense of "Bribery."

Applying the constitutional definition of "Bribery" here, there can be little doubt that it is satisfied. President Trump solicited President Zelensky for a "favor" of great personal value to him[678]; he did so corruptly[679]; and he did so in a scheme to influence his own official actions respecting the release of military and security assistance and the offer of a White House meeting.[680]

b.   Criminal Bribery, 18 U.S.C. § 201

Although President Trump's actions need not rise to the level of a criminal violation to justify impeachment, his conduct here was criminal. In this section we address the federal statute banning bribery; in the next section we address the wire fraud statute. Both of these laws underscore the extent to which Congress and the American people have broadly condemned the use of a public position of trust for personal gain. As this Committee observed decades ago, "[n]othing is more corrosive to the fabric of good government than bribery."[681] The federal anti-bribery statute imposes up to fifteen years'

---

[674] *Pleas of the Crown*, ch. 67, § 2; Edward Coke, *The Third Part of the Institutes of the Laws of England: Concerning High Treason, and Other Pleas of the Crown, and Criminal Causes* 147 (1644).

[675] *A New Law-Dictionary*, at 734 (defining the "Value" of a thing to turn on "the *valuation* of the owner on it."); *see also Com. v. Callaghan*, 2 Va. Cas. 460 (1825) (holding that the "corrupt agreement" between two Justices of the Peace to trade votes qualified as a misdemeanor at Common Law).

[676] *Constitutional Grounds for Impeachment* (2019) (written testimony of Professor Jonathan Turley). This case was discussed on multiple occasions at the Constitutional Convention. *See, e.g., id.* ("Louis XIV bribed Charles II to sign the secret Treaty of Dover of 1670 with the payment of a massive pension and other benefits . . . . In return, Charles II not only agreed to convert to Catholicism, but to join France in a wartime alliance against the Dutch.") (citing George Clark, *The Later Stuarts (1660-1714)* 86-87, 130 (2d ed. 1956)); 5 *Debates in the Several State Conventions*, at 343 (recounting Morris's argument that the President should be removable through the impeachment process, noting concern that the President might "be bribed by a greater interest to betray his trust," and pointed to the example of Charles II receiving a bribe from Louis XIV).

[677] U.S. CONST., art. I, § 9, cl. 8 (emphasis added).

[678] *July 25 Call Record* at 3.

[679] *Ukraine Report* at 140 (referring to President Trump's "scheme" to condition release of military aid and White House meeting on favors to benefit his reelection campaign); *see supra* at Section III.D.2.

[680] *Id.; see supra* at Section III.D.1.c.

[681] *Bribery, Graft, and Conflicts of Interest*, H. Rep. No. 87-748, at 6 (1961).

imprisonment for public officials who solicit or obtain bribes.[682] The wire fraud statute, in turn, imposes up to twenty years imprisonment for public officials who breach the public trust by depriving them of their honest services.[683] President Trump's violation of both statutes is further evidence of the egregious nature of his abuse of power.

Starting with the federal anti-bribery statute, criminal bribery occurs when a public official (1) "demands [or] seeks" (2) "anything of value personally," (3) "in return for being influenced in the performance of any official act."[684] Additionally, the public official must carry out these actions (4) "corruptly."[685] We address the four statutory elements in turn.

i. "Demands" or "Seeks"

The evidence before the Committee makes clear that the President solicited from the President of Ukraine a public announcement that he would undertake two politically motivated investigations. That conduct satisfies the *actus reus* element of bribery under the federal criminal code.[686] Section 201 prohibits a wide variety of solicitations, including solicitations that are "indirect[]."[687] Courts have concluded that a bribe was solicited, for example, where a public official with authority to award construction contracts requested that a contractor "take a look at the roof" of the official's home.[688] Notably, where the other elements are met, the statutory offense of bribery is complete upon the demand—even if the thing of value is not provided.[689] That is because "the purpose of the statute is to discourage one from seeking an advantage by attempting to influence a public official to depart from conduct deemed essential to the public interest."[690]

President Trump solicited from President Zelensky a public announcement that he would conduct two politically motivated investigations into President Trump's political rival and into discredited claims about election interference in 2016. These demands easily constitute solicitation under federal law. To begin with, the President's improper solicitation is apparent in the record of his July 25 phone call with President Zelensky. As the record makes clear, after President Zelensky raised the issue of United States military assistance to Ukraine, President Trump immediately responded: "I

---

[682] 18 U.S.C. § 201(b)(2).

[683] 18 U.S.C §§ 1343, 1346.

[684] 18 U.S.C. § 201(b)(2).

[685] 18 U.S.C. § 201(b)(2)(A).

[686] As a threshold matter, the President is plainly a "public official" within the meaning of the criminal anti-bribery statute. *See* 18 U.S.C. § 201(a)(1) ("public official" includes "an officer . . . acting for or on behalf of the United States").

[687] 18 U.S.C. § 201(b)(2).

[688] *United States v. Repak*, 852 F.3d 230, 238 (3d Cir. 2017); *see also id.* at 251-52, 254.

[689] *United States v. Jacobs*, 431 F.2d 754, 759-60 (2d Cir. 1970) (reaffirming that statute "is violated even though the official offered a bribe is not corrupted, or the object of the bribe could not be attained, or it could make no difference if after the act were done it turned out that there had been actually no occasion to seek to influence any official conduct").

[690] *Id.* at 759.

would like you to do us a favor though[.]"[691] President Trump then explained the "favor," which involved the two demands for baseless investigations. In addition, the July 25 call "was neither the start nor the end" of these demands.[692] In the weeks leading up to it, for example, Ambassadors Volker and Sondland had both personally informed President Zelensky and his staff of the President's demands and advised the Ukrainian leader to agree to them.[693] These and other related actions by the President's subordinates were taken in coordination with Rudolph Giuliani, who was understood to be "expressing the desires of the President of the United States."[694] There can thus be no doubt that President Trump's conduct constituted a solicitation.

ii.   "Anything of Value Personally"

The next question is whether any of the "things" that President Trump solicited from President Zelensky count as a "things of value." Section 201 makes clear that bribery occurs when the thing offered or solicited is "anything of value *personally*" to the recipient[695]—and in this instance, President Trump placed significant personal value on the "favor[s]" demanded.

"The phrase 'anything of value' has been interpreted broadly to carry out the congressional purpose of punishing *the abuse of public office*."[696] It "is defined broadly to include 'the value which the defendant subjectively attaches to the items received.'"[697] For example, it has been held to include shares of stock that had "no commercial value" where the official receiving the bribe expected otherwise.[698] As the court in that case explained, "[c]orruption of office occurs when the officeholder agrees to misuse his office in the expectation of gain, whether or not he has correctly assessed the worth of the bribe."[699] The term "thing of value" encompasses intangible things of value as well. As used throughout the criminal code, it has been held to include (among other things): research work

---

[691] *July 25 Call Record* at 3.

[692] *Ukraine Report* at 9.

[693] *Id.* at 85-86.

[694] *Id.* at 19 (quoting Ambassador Sondland).

[695] 18 U.S.C. § 201(b)(2) (emphasis added).

[696] *United States v. Renzi*, 769 F.3d 731, 744 (9th Cir. 2014) (emphasis added) (quoting *United States v. Williams*, 705 F.2d 603, 623 (2d Cir. 1983)).

[697] *Id.* (quoting *United States v. Gorman*, 807 F.2d 1299, 1305 (6th Cir. 1986)).

[698] *Williams*, 705 F.2d at 622-23.

[699] *Id.* at 623.

product,[700] conjugal visits for a prison inmate,[701] confidential government files about informants,[702] information about the location of a witness,[703] a promise of future employment,[704] a promise to contact a public official,[705] "the amount of a confidential, competitive bid" for a government contract,[706] copies of grand jury transcripts provided to the target of an investigation,[707] and the testimony of a witness at a criminal trial.[708]

In this case, President Trump indisputably placed a subjective personal value on the announcement of investigations that he solicited from President Zelensky. The announcement of an investigation into President Trump's political rival would redound to President Trump's personal benefit; and the announcement of an investigation into purported Ukrainian interference in the 2016 election would vindicate the President's frequent denials that he benefitted from Russia's assistance. Mr. Giuliani recognized as much many times as he pursued his client's own interests in Ukraine.[709] Furthermore, Ambassador Sondland and others testified that President Trump's true priority was the public *announcement* of these investigations more than the investigations themselves.[710] This fact makes clear that "the goal was not the investigations, but the political benefit [President] Trump would derive from their announcement and the cloud they might put over a political opponent."[711] The

---

[700] *United States v. Croft*, 750 F.2d 1354, 1361-62 (7th Cir. 1984) (holding labor of government employee, whose research work product was appropriated by defendant for private gain, was "thing of value" under theft statute, 18 U.S.C. § 641). Courts have also explained that "'Congress's frequent use of the term 'thing of value' in various criminal statutes has evolved the phrase into a term of art'" and have therefore applied it broadly and consistently across various federal statutes. *United States v. Petrovic*, 701 F.3d 849, 858 (8th Cir. 2012) (quoting *United States v. Nilsen*, 967 F.2d 539, 542 (11th Cir. 1992) (per curiam)).

[701] *United States v. Marmolejo*, 89 F.3d 1185, 1191-93 (5th Cir. 1996).

[702] *United States v. Girard*, 601 F.2d 69, 71 (2d Cir. 1979) (holding that information was "thing of value" under federal theft statute, and listing cases in which the term was held to encompass "amusement," "the testimony of a witness," "the promise of sexual intercourse," "an agreement not to run in a primary election," and "a promise to reinstate an employee").

[703] *United States v. Sheker*, 618 F.2d 607, 608-09 (9th Cir. 1980) (per curiam).

[704] *Gorman*, 807 F.2d at 1305.

[705] *United States v. Scruggs*, 916 F. Supp. 2d 670 (N.D. Miss. 2012) (holding promise to contact public official constituted "anything of value" under bribery theory of honest services fraud, 18 U.S.C. §§ 1341, 1343, 1346).

[706] *United States v. Matzkin*, 14 F.3d 1014, 1020 (4th Cir. 1994).

[707] *United States v. Jeter*, 775 F.2d 670, 680 (6th Cir. 1985).

[708] *Nilsen*, 967 F.2d at 543; *see also* Off. of the Chair of the Fed. Election Comm'n, *The Law of a 'Thing of Value: Summary of the Sorts of Tangible and Intangible Goods and Services that Have Been Found to Have 'Value' by the Commission and Other U.S. Government Entities* 1 (2019) ("Federal courts have consistently applied an expansive reading to the term 'thing of value' in a variety of statutory contexts to include goods and services that have tangible, intangible, or even *merely perceived* benefits, for example: promises, information, testimony, conjugal visits, and commercially worthless stock.").

[709] *See Vogel Giuliani* (Giuliani acknowledging that investigations would produce "information [that] will be very, very helpful to my client").

[710] *See Ukraine Report* at 21.

[711] *Id.*; *see also id.* at 134 (Ambassador Taylor testified that according to information he had received, President Trump "insist[ed] that President Zelensky go to a microphone and say he is opening investigations of Biden and 2016 election interference").

promotion of these investigations and the political narratives behind them thus "served the [President's] personal political interests . . . because they would help him in his campaign for reelection in 2020."[712]

iii.   "In Return for Being Influenced in the Performance of any Official Act"

In Return for Being Influenced: This element of the criminal anti-bribery statute requires showing "a specific intent to give or receive something of value *in exchange* for an official act."—i.e., a *quid pro quo*.[713] As detailed above, the evidence satisfies this standard. President Trump sought an announcement of these investigations in return for performing two official acts. *First*, the President "conditioned release of [] vital military assistance . . . on [President Zelensky's] public announcement of the investigations."[714] *Second*, he "conditioned a head of state meeting at the White House . . . on Ukraine publicly announcing the investigations."[715]

Official Act: Federal anti-bribery law defines an "official act" as "any decision or action on any question, matter, cause, suit, proceeding or controversy" that may be pending or brought before a public official in that person's official capacity.[716] Both of the acts in question—releasing $391 million in approved military and security assistance, and hosting an official head-of-state diplomatic visit at the White House—plainly qualify as "official act[s]" within the meaning of the statute.

First, the release of much-needed assistance to Ukraine was unquestionably an official act. Release of these funds, totaling $391 million, involved a formal certification process by the Department of Defense regarding certain preconditions and an official notification to Congress, among other things.[717] In addition, President Trump's placement of a hold on the funds precipitated "a series of policy meetings involving increasingly senior officials" across numerous federal agencies.[718] These processes unmistakably involved "formal exercise[s] of government power" as defined by the Supreme Court in *McDonnell v. United States*.[719] Indeed, *McDonnell* confirmed that a decision to allocate funds obviously qualifies as an "official act."[720]

Second, when the President hosts a foreign head of state for an official diplomatic visit, he performs an official act specifically assigned to him by Article II of the Constitution. The President's

---

[712] *Id.* at 42.

[713] *United States v. Sun-Diamond Growers of Cal.*, 526 U.S. 398, 404-05 (1999) (emphasis in original).

[714] *Ukraine Report* at 35.

[715] *Id.*

[716] 18 U.S.C. § 201(a)(3).

[717] *Ukraine Report* at 17-18.

[718] *Id.* at 18.

[719] 136 S. Ct. 2355, 2368-70, 2372 (2016).

[720] *Id.* at 2370.

official functions include the duty to "receive Ambassadors and other public Ministers."[721] By receiving ambassadors and foreign heads of state under that authority, the President recognizes the legitimacy of their governments.[722] Furthermore, an official diplomatic visit by a head of state is an extensive governmental undertaking. During the type of visit sought here (an official "working" visit[723]), the visiting official is typically hosted at Blair House for several days, during which time the official meets with the President and attends a working luncheon at the White House, along with the Secretary of State.[724] Such engagements usually involve weeks of preparation and agenda-setting, at the end of which significant new policy initiatives may be announced.

For these reasons, it is beyond question that official White House visits constitute a "formal exercise of governmental power" within the meaning of *McDonnell*. In that case, the Supreme Court held that the former governor of Virginia did not perform "official acts" when he arranged meetings and hosted events for a benefactor. There, however, the actions in question were frequent and informal in nature. Official diplomatic visits to the White House, by contrast, are conducted pursuant to the President's express Article II authority, involve significant use of government resources, and entail extensive preparation. Indeed, the visiting official must even obtain a special kind of visa—a process that itself involves the performance of an official act.[725]

The context addressed by the Supreme Court in *McDonnell* also bears emphasis. The governor in that case "referred thousands of constituents to meetings with members of his staff and other government officials" and routinely hosted events for state businesses.[726] His arrangement of meetings was commonplace and casual, and the Court expressed deep concern about "chill[ing] federal officials' interactions with the people they serve" by bringing those interactions within the scope of anti-bribery laws.[727] The context here could not be more different, and there is no risk that applying anti-bribery laws to this context would chill diplomatic relations. Foreign nationals are already prohibited from donating to United States political campaigns[728]—or, for that matter, from giving any sorts of "presents" or "emoluments" to the President or other officials without Congress's express consent.[729] Application of anti-bribery laws in this context—*i.e.*, making it unlawful for the President to exchange official diplomatic visits for personal benefits—is therefore consistent with and compelled by the plain text of federal law.

---

[721] U.S. CONST., art. II, § 3.

[722] *See Zivotofsky*, 135 S. Ct. at 2086.

[723] *See* Sondland Deposition Tr. at 25; Sondland Hearing Tr. at 42.

[724] Julie Moffett, *World: How the U.S. Ranks the Visits of Foreign Heads of State*, RADIO FREE EUROPE, Aug. 6, 1997.

[725] *United States v. Jefferson*, 289 F. Supp. 3d 717, 738 (E.D. Va. 2017); *see* 9 Foreign Affairs Manual § 402.3-5 (2019) (explaining that diplomats and other foreign government officials traveling to the United States to engage solely in official duties or activities on behalf of their national government must obtain A-1 or A-2 visas prior to entering the United States).

[726] *McDonnell*, 136 S. Ct. at 2361-62.

[727] *Id.* at 2372 (internal quotation marks omitted).

[728] *See* 52 U.S.C. § 30121.

[729] U.S. CONST., art. I, § 9, cl. 8.

iv.   "Corruptly"

President Trump behaved corruptly throughout this course of conduct because he offered to perform official acts "in exchange for a *private* benefit," rather than for any public policy purpose.[730] Policymakers may of course trade support or assistance, and that type of "logrolling" does not constitute an exchange of bribes.[731] But that is entirely different from the President seeking an announcement of investigations to serve his personal and political interests, as he did here.[732] Indeed, and as detailed above, the record is clear that President Trump acted with corrupt motives, including that:

- President Trump's request for investigations on the July 25 call was not part of any official briefing materials or talking points he received in preparation for the call; nor were the investigations part of any U.S. official policy objective.

- President Trump's primary focus relating to Ukraine during the relevant period was the announcement of these two investigations that were not part of official U.S. policy objectives.

- There is no evidence that the President's request for the investigations was part of a change in official U.S. policy; that fact further supports the alternative and only plausible explanation that President Trump pressed the public announcements because there were of great *personal*, *political* value to him.

- President Trump's requests departed from established channels, including because he used his personal attorney, Mr. Giuliani, to press the investigations and never contacted the Department of Justice or made a formal request.

- President Trump's request was viewed by key United States and Ukrainian officials as improper, unusual, problematic, and, most importantly, purely political.

For all these reasons, President Trump's conduct satisfies the fourth and final element of the federal anti-bribery statute.

c.   Honest Services Fraud, 18 U.S.C § 1346

In addition to committing the crime of bribery, President Trump knowingly and willfully orchestrated a scheme to defraud the American people of his honest services as President of the United States. In doing so, he betrayed his position of trust and the duty he owed the citizenry to be an honest fiduciary of their trust. That offense is codified in the federal criminal code, which imposes up to twenty years' imprisonment for public officials who (by mail or wire fraud) breach the public trust by

---

[730] *United States v. Blagojevich*, 794 F.3d 729, 735 (7th Cir. 2015) (emphasis added).

[731] *Id.*

participating in a bribery scheme.[733] In *Skilling v. United States*, the Supreme Court confirmed that the statute governing "honest services fraud" applies to "bribes and kickbacks," and noted that this concept "draws content from" the federal anti-bribery statute.[734] As such, public officials who engage in bribery may also be charged with honest services fraud.[735]

Fundamentally, the President has deprived the American people of the honorable stewardship that the Nation expects and demands of its chief executive. Since *Skilling*, federal courts have looked to federal bribery statutes, paying particular attention to Section 201, to assess what constitutes willful participation in a scheme to defraud in the provision of "honest services."[736] As described above, President Trump engaged in conduct that constitutes a violation of Section 201. President Trump conditioned specific "official acts"—the provision of military and security assistance and a White House meeting—on President Zelensky announcing investigations that benefitted him personally, while harming national interests. In doing so, President Trump willfully set out to defraud the American people, through bribery, of his "honest services."

The underlying wire fraud statute, upon which the "honest services" crime is based, requires a transmission by "wire, radio, or television communication in interstate or foreign commerce any writings . . . for the purpose of executing [a] . . . scheme or artifice."[737] President Trump's July 25 call to President Zelensky, as well as his July 26 call to Ambassador Gordon Sondland both were foreign wire communications made in furtherance of an ongoing bribery scheme. Thus, the President's telephone calls on July 25th and July 26th lay bare the final element to find him criminally liable for his failure to provide "honest services" to the American people.

d. Conclusion

For the reasons given above, President Trump's abuse of power encompassed both the constitutional offense of "Bribery" and multiple federal crimes. He has betrayed the national interest, the people of this Nation, and should not be permitted to be above the law. It is therefore all the more vital that he be removed from office.

5. President Trump Poses a Continuing Threat if Left in Office

Impeachment exists "not to inflict personal punishment for past wrongdoing, but rather to protect against future Presidential misconduct that would endanger democracy and the rule of law."[738]

---

[733] *See* 18 U.S.C. §§ 1341, 1343, 1346.

[734] 561 U.S. 358, 412 (2010); *see also id.* at 404.

[735] Governor McDonnell, for example, was also charged for honest services fraud. *See McDonnell*, 136 S. Ct. at 2365. *See also, e.g., United States v. Nagin*, 810 F.3d 348, 351 (5th Cir. 2016).

[736] *See, e.g., United States v. Suhl*, 885 F.3d 1106, 1111 (8th Cir. 2018), *cert. denied*, 139 S. Ct. 172 (2018); *Woodward v. United States*, 905 F.3d 40, 44 (1st Cir. 2018).

[737] 18 U.S.C. § 1343.

[738] *Constitutional Grounds for Impeachment* (2019) at 10.

By virtue of the conduct encompassed by the First Article of Impeachment, President Trump "has demonstrated that he will remain a threat to national security and the Constitution if allowed to remain in office, and has acted in a manner grossly incompatible with self-governance and the rule of law." That is true in at least two respects: first, he has shown no remorse or regret, but rather insists that his conduct was "perfect" and continues to engage in misconduct; and second, the egregiousness and complexity of his scheme confirm his willingness to abuse the powers of his office for private gain.

a.   Lack of Remorse and Continued Misconduct

"It is true that the President has expressed regret for his personal misconduct. But he has never— he has never—accepted responsibility for breaking the law. He has never taken that essential step … He has stubbornly resisted any effort to be held accountable for his violations of the law, for his violations of his constitutional oath, and his violation of his duty as President. To this day, he remains adamantly unrepentant."[739]

Representative Charles Canady, serving as a House Manager, spoke those words while urging the Senate to uphold articles of impeachment against President Clinton. They apply here with full force and only one modification: it is *not* true "that the President has expressed regret for his personal misconduct." When President Trump, for his own personal political gain, asked for a favor from President Zelensky, he did exactly what our Framers feared most. He invited the influence of a foreign power into our elections—and used the powers of his office to secure that advantage at the direct expense of our national security. Yet President Trump has admitted to no wrongdoing. He maintains that he was always in the right and that his July 25 call with President Zelensky was "perfect."[740] President Trump has made it clear that he believes he is free to use his Presidential powers the same way, to the same ends, whenever and wherever he pleases.

Any doubt on that score is resolved by his conduct since the scheme came to light. He has made repeated false statements. He has stonewalled Congressional investigators and ordered others to do the same. He has argued that it is illegitimate for the House to investigate him. He has stayed in contact with Mr. Giuliani, his private lawyer, who remains hard at work advancing his client's personal interests in Ukraine. He has attacked Members of the House, as well as witnesses in House proceedings, who questioned his conduct. He has asserted and exercised the prerogative to urge foreign nations to investigate citizens who dare to challenge him politically.[741]

Indeed, even after the Speaker announced the impeachment inquiry, President Trump stated on October 2, "And just so you know, we've been investigating, on a personal basis—through Rudy and others, lawyers—corruption in the 2016 election."[742] The next day, President Trump went further: he

---

[739] *Proceedings of the U.S. Senate in the Impeachment Trial of President William Jefferson Clinton Vol. II: Floor Trial Proceedings*, 106th Cong. 1471 (1999) (statement of Rep. Charles Canady).

[740] *Ukraine Report* at 10.

[741] *See Ukraine Report* at 140-50; 207-60.

[742] The White House, *Remarks by President Trump and President Niinistö of the Republic of Finland in Joint Press Conference* (Oct. 2, 2019).

not only acknowledged that he wanted Ukraine to investigate former Vice President Biden, but also publicly suggested that China should do the same. When asked what he hoped President Zelensky would do about the Bidens, he stated as follows:

> Well, I would think that, if they were honest about it, they'd start a major investigation into the Bidens. It's a very simple answer. They should investigate the Bidens, because how does a company that's newly formed — and all these companies, if you look at — And, by the way, likewise, China should start an investigation into the Bidens, because what happened in China is just about as bad as what happened with — with Ukraine. So, I would say that President Zelensky — if it were me, I would recommend that they start an investigation into the Bidens. Because nobody has any doubt that they weren't crooked. That was a crooked deal — 100 percent. He had no knowledge of energy; didn't know the first thing about it. All of a sudden, he is getting $50,000 a month, plus a lot of other things. Nobody has any doubt. And they got rid of a prosecutor who was a very tough prosecutor. They got rid of him. Now they're trying to make it the opposite way. But they got rid — So, if I were the President, I would certainly recommend that of Ukraine.[743]

President Trump added that asking President Xi of China to investigate the Bidens "is certainly something we can start thinking about."[744] And the day after that, on October 4, in remarks before he departed on Marine One, the President stated:

> When you look at what Biden and his son did, and when you look at other people—what they've done. And I believe there was tremendous corruption with Biden, but I think there was beyond—I mean, beyond corruption—having to do with the 2016 campaign, and what these lowlifes did to so many people, to hurt so many people in the Trump campaign—which was successful, despite all of the fighting us. I mean, despite all of the unfairness.[745]

President Trump then once again reiterated his willingness to solicit foreign assistance related to his personal interests: "Here's what's okay: If we feel there's corruption, like I feel there was in the 2016 campaign—there was tremendous corruption against me—if we feel there's corruption, we have a right to go to a foreign country."

b.   The Egregiousness of the President's Conduct Confirms His Willingness to Abuse His Power for Personal Political Gain

The first Article of Impeachment does not seek President Trump's removal for an isolated error of judgment on the July 25 phone call, or for a mere series of related misjudgments in his public

---

[743] The White House, *Remarks by President Trump Before Marine One Departure* (Oct. 3, 2019).

[744] *Id.*

[745] The White House, *Remarks by President Trump Before Marine One Departure* (Oct. 4, 2019).

statements since then. The President's abuse of power involved a course of conduct in which he willfully chose, time and again, to place his own personal political gain above our national security and commitment to free and fair elections. He did so in ways large and small, using many Executive Branch agencies, offices, and officers to advance his corrupt agenda throughout 2019. Some may have joined knowingly; others, including several witnesses who testified before the Investigating Committees, only recognized the impropriety of the activity once the White House released the record of the President's July 25 call with President Zelensky or were dragooned against their will and resisted within the bounds of professional propriety. In the end, President Trump relied on a network of agents within and beyond the United States government to bend our Ukraine policy to use the powers of the presidency to harm a prominent political opponent, all at the expense of our security and democracy.

No private citizen could do this. Ordinary citizens cannot deny White House meetings, block Congressionally-appropriated military and security assistance, or condition such official acts on an agreement to sabotage their political opponents. These powers reside in the Office of the President. It was thus solely by virtue of powers entrusted to his office that President Trump could distort our foreign policy, and weaken our national security, to his own personal political gain. His conduct is thus an "abuse or violation of … public trust" and evokes the Framers' fear that "the Executive will have great opportunitys [sic] of abusing his power."[746] It also demonstrates that he will continue to engage in such abuses unless he is removed from office.

The Minority has objected that there is no such risk because the assistance to Ukraine was eventually released. But that is irrelevant. The fact that the President's scheme was discovered and disrupted does not cure his abuse of power or suggest that he will honor his Oath of Office in the future. That is true as a matter of law and as a matter of fact.

Starting with the law, as this Committee made clear in President Nixon's case, a President who tries and fails to abuse power remains subject to removal for his underlying wrong.[747] George Mason confirmed this principle at the Constitutional Convention, where he declared that "*attempts* to subvert the Constitution" rank as "great and dangerous offenses."[748] That is because attempts can still reveal the President as a threat to our society. Impeachment exists to save the Nation from such threats; we need not wait for harm to befall, or for the President to try again, before deeming his conduct impeachable.[749] This principle applies with added force where the President has insisted that he did nothing wrong and has unrepentantly continued his pattern of misconduct.

Turning to the facts, the military and security assistance was released to Ukraine only after President Trump got caught. On August 12, 2019, a whistleblower filed a complaint concerning the

---

[746] 2 Farrand, *Records of the Federal Convention,* at 67 (statement of Edmund Randolph).

[747] *See Nixon Impeachment Report* at 82-136.

[748] Cass R. Sunstein, *Impeachment: A Citizen's Guide* 47 (2017).

[749] As Professor Feldman testified, "If the President of the United States attempts to abuse his office, that is a complete impeachable offense. The possibility that the President might get caught in the process of attempting to abuse his office and then not be able to pull it off does not undercut in any way the impeachability of the act . . . . The attempt itself is the impeachable act." *Constitutional Grounds Hearing (2019).*

President's July 25 call and his actions towards Ukraine.[750] In late August, the President's counsel reportedly briefed President Trump about the complaint.[751] On September 5, *The Washington Post* published an editorial alleging that President Trump had withheld aid to Ukraine in an attempt "to force Mr. Zelensky to intervene in the 2020 U.S. presidential election by launching an investigation of the leading Democratic candidate, Joe Biden."[752] On September 9, several House Committees launched an investigation into "reported efforts by President Trump, the President's personal lawyer Rudy Giuliani, and possibly others to pressure the government of Ukraine to assist the President's reelection campaign."[753] On September 10, Intelligence Committee Chairman Adam Schiff requested that the complaint be provided to the Committee, as required by law.[754] Finally, on September 11, without any public explanation, President Trump abruptly ordered that the assistance be released to Ukraine; remarkably, he still has not held a White House meeting with President Zelensky.

This delay in releasing the assistance had significant real-world consequences. By the time the President ordered the release of security assistance to Ukraine, the Department of Defense was unable to spend approximately 14 percent of the funds appropriated by Congress for Fiscal Year 2019; as a result, Congress had to pass a new law to extend the funding in order to ensure the full amount could be used by Ukraine to defend itself.[755] Moreover, by delaying the assistance for purposes understood by United States and Ukrainian officials as corrupt, President Trump harmed our relationship with Ukraine, signaled vulnerability to Russia, and more broadly injured American credibility and national security. As Ambassador Taylor testified, President Vladimir Putin of Russia would "love to see the humiliation of President Zelensky at the hands of the Americans,"[756] which "would give the Russians a freer hand."[757] Ambassador Taylor further emphasized that the Ukrainians "counted on . . . the assurance of U.S. support" and so the hold on assistance had "shaken their faith in us."[758] President Zelensky echoed a similar sentiment in a recent interview with *Time*: "I don't want us to look like beggars. But you have to understand, we're at war. If you're our strategic partner, then you can't go

---

[750] Letter from Michael K. Atkinson, Inspector General of the Intelligence Community, to Adam Schiff, Chairman, H. Permanent Select Comm. on Intelligence, and Devin Nunes, Ranking Member, H. Permanent Select Comm. on Intelligence (Sept. 9, 2019).

[751] Michael S. Schmidt et al., *Trump Knew of Whistleblower Complaint When He Released Aid to Ukraine*, N.Y. TIMES, Nov. 26, 2019.

[752] Editorial, *Trump Tries to Force Ukraine to Meddle in the 2020 Election*, WASH. POST, Sept. 5, 2019.

[753] H. Perm. Select Comm. on Intelligence, *Three House Committees Launch Wide-Ranging Investigation into Trump-Giuliani Ukraine Scheme* (Sept. 9, 2019).

[754] Letter from Adam B. Schiff, Chairman, H. Perm. Select Comm. on Intelligence, to Joseph Maguire, Acting Director of Nat'l Intelligence (Sept. 10, 2019).

[755] Cooper-Hale Hearing Tr. at 13, 69; *see also* Continuing Appropriations Act, 2020, and Health Extenders Act of 2019, H.R. 4378, 116th Cong (2019).

[756] Taylor-Kent Hearing Tr. at 40.

[757] Taylor Dep. Tr. at 210.

[758] *Id.* at 28, 39.

blocking anything for us."[759]

The bottom line is that President Trump used for personal political gain the powers entrusted to his office. He did so knowingly, deliberately, and repeatedly. He involved parts of the Executive Branch in his scheme. He undermined American security and democracy to help ensure his re-election—and did not care. And after he was caught, President Trump not only insisted his conduct was acceptable and did everything in his power to obstruct Congress's investigation into his misconduct, he also sought to normalize and justify his behavior by publicly soliciting foreign powers to investigate a citizen who is challenging him in next year's election.

A President who acts this way believes he stands above the law. That belief is itself a guarantee that allowing him to remain in our highest office, vested with our mightiest political powers, poses a continuing threat to the Constitution. Unless he is stopped, President Trump will continue to erode our democracy and the fundamental values on which the Nation was founded.

6.   Consistency with Previous Conduct

The First Article of Impeachment impeaches President Trump for abuse of power relating to Ukraine. Yet, as noted in that Article, President Trump's conduct is "consistent with President Trump's previous invitations of foreign interference in United States elections." An understanding of those previous efforts, and the pattern of misconduct they represent, sheds light on the particular conduct set forth in that Article as sufficient grounds for the impeachment of President Trump.

These previous efforts include inviting and welcoming Russian interference in the 2016 United States Presidential election. On July 27, 2016, then-candidate Trump declared at a public rally: "Russia, if you're listening, I hope you're able to find the 30,000 emails that are missing. I think you will probably be rewarded mightily by our press."[760] The referenced emails were stored on a personal server used by then-candidate Trump's political opponent, Hillary Clinton. And Russia was listening. Within approximately five hours of Trump's statement, Russian hackers targeted Clinton's personal office and the referenced emails for the very first time.[761]

In the fall of 2016, as Election Day approached, WikiLeaks began publishing stolen emails that were damaging to the Clinton Campaign. WikiLeaks received these e-mails from the GRU, a Russian military group. Rather than condemn this interference in our elections, then-candidate Trump repeatedly praised and encouraged Wikileaks. For instance, he said on October 10, 2016: "This just came out. WikiLeaks! I love WikiLeaks!"[762] Two days later, he said: "This WikiLeaks stuff is

---

[759] Simon Shuster, *'I Don't Trust Anyone at All.' Ukrainian President Volodymyr Zelensky Speaks Out on Trump, Putin and a Divided Europe*, TIME, Dec. 2, 2019.

[760] *Mueller Report*, Vol. I at 49.

[761] *Id.*

[762] *Former Special Counsel Robert S. Mueller, III on the Investigation into Russian Interference in the 2016 Presidential Election: Hearing Before the H. Perm. Select Comm. on Intelligence*, 116th Cong. 49 (July 24, 2019) (hereinafter "HPSCI Mueller Hearing").

unbelievable. It tells you the inner heart, you gotta read it."[763] Similar statements from then-Candidate Trump continued over the following weeks. As the Special Counsel testified before House Committees, to call these statements "problematic" would be an "understatement" because they gave "hope or some boost to what is and should be illegal activity."[764]

During this period, senior members of the Trump Campaign were maintaining significant contacts with Russian nationals and seeking damaging information on candidate Hillary Clinton.[765] Among other evidence of such contacts, the Special Counsel's Report notes that President Trump somehow knew in advance about upcoming releases of stolen emails;[766] that the Trump Campaign's foreign policy adviser met repeatedly with Russian officials who claimed to have "dirt" on Clinton "in the form of thousands of emails";[767] and that Trump Campaign Chairman Paul Manafort caused internal campaign polling data to be shared with a Russian national.[768] There is no indication that anyone from the Trump Campaign, including the candidate, reported any of these contacts or offers of foreign assistance to U.S. law enforcement.[769]

A redacted version of the Special Counsel's Report was released to the public on April 18, 2019. The evidence obtained by the Special Counsel relating to this conduct, including Russia's attack on our elections, resulted in the criminal indictment of more than a dozen defendants.[770] It also indicated that the President had sought to thwart rather than advance the Special Counsel's investigation into Russian interference. When this Committee conducted its own investigation, President Trump similarly sought to thwart rather than advance those fact-finding efforts.

Since the release of the Special Counsel's report, President Trump has confirmed his willingness to welcome and invite foreign interference in our elections. For example, two months after the report was released and while President Trump was under congressional investigation, he admitted on live television that he would *still* welcome foreign interference. In an interview with George Stephanopoulos, President Trump disputed the idea that if a foreign government provided information on a political opponent—as Russia had done in 2016—it would be considered interference in our elections: "[I]t's not an interference, they have information—I think I'd take it if I thought there was something wrong, I'd go maybe to the FBI—if I thought there was something wrong. But when somebody comes up with oppo research, right, they come up with oppo research, 'oh let's call the FBI.'

---

[763] *Id.* at 48-49.

[764] *Id.*

[765] *Mueller Report*, Vol. I at 5-7, 66-144.

[766] *Id.* at 54.

[767] *Id.* at 5-6. This individual—George Papadopoulos has since been sentenced to 14 days in prison for lying to the F.B.I. about his contacts with Russian intermediaries during the 2016 presidential race. *See* Mark Mazzetti & Sharon LaFraniere, *George Papadopoulos, Ex-Trump Adviser, Is Sentenced to 14 Days in Jail*, N.Y. TIMES, Sept. 7, 2018.

[768] *Mueller Report*, Vol. I at 129. Mr. Manafort has since been sentenced to over 7 years in prison for various federal crimes, including conspiracy against the United States and obstruction of justice. *See id.*, Vol I at 129 n.838.

[769] *See HPSCI Mueller Hearing* Tr. at 29.

[770] *Mueller Report*, Vol. I at 14 n.4; *see also id.*, Vol. I at 174-75.

The FBI doesn't have enough agents to take care of it."[771]

On July 24, 2019, the Special Counsel testified before HPSCI and this Committee.[772] He affirmed his Report's evidence, which showed that—despite over 100 contacts between individuals associated with the Trump Campaign and Russian nationals or their agents while Russia was attacking our elections—no one from the Trump Campaign reported those contacts to law enforcement.[773] The Special Counsel emphasized to the Committees that reporting such information is something that Presidential campaigns "would and should do," not least because "knowingly accepting foreign assistance during a Presidential campaign" is a crime.[774]

The next day, however, President Trump did the opposite: he did not just accept and fail to report foreign interference in our elections, he *demanded* it on his July 25 call with President Zelensky. Moreover, this time he leveraged the powers of his presidential office, including military and security assistance and a White House visit, against a vulnerable foreign ally.

The Constitution creates a democracy that derives its power from the American people. Elections are crucial to that system of self-government. But the Framers knew that elections alone could "not guarantee that the United States would remain a republic" if "unscrupulous officials" rigged the process. President Trump has done just that. He has done it before, he has done it here, and he has made clear he will do it again. As Professor Karlan observes, what happened in "2016 was bad enough: there is a widespread agreement that Russian operatives intervened to manipulate our political process."[775] But "that distortion is magnified" when the President uses his official powers to procure and induce foreign intervention, all as part of a scheme to ensure his own re-election.[776]

Although the First Article of Impeachment addresses President Trump's solicitation and pressuring of Ukraine to announce two investigations for his own personal political benefit, as well as his persistence in such conduct since the scheme came to light, the consistency of this scheme with his broader pattern of welcoming and inviting foreign interference into our elections is relevant and striking.

E.   It is Necessary to Approve Articles of Impeachment Without Delay

There is an instinct in any investigation to seek more evidence, interview more witnesses, and

---

[771] Interview by George Stephanopoulos of President Donald Trump, ABC NEWS, Jun. 13, 2019.

[772] *Oversight of the Report on the Investigation into Russian Interference in the 2016 Presidential Election: Former Special Counsel Robert S. Mueller, III: Before the H. Comm. On the Judiciary*, 116th Cong. (July 24, 2019); *see also HPSCI Mueller Hearing.*

[773] *See* Karen Yourish & Larry Buchanan, *Mueller Report Shows Depth of Connections Between Trump Campaign and Russians*, N.Y. TIMES, Apr. 19, 2019.

[774] *HPSCI Mueller Hearing* Tr. at 30.

[775] *Constitutional Grounds Hearing (2019)* (written testimony of Professor Pamela S. Karlan).

[776] *Id.*

turn over every remaining stone. But there also comes a point when the evidence is powerful enough, and the danger of delay is great enough, that inaction is irresponsible. We have reached that point here. For all the reasons given above, President Trump will continue to threaten the Nation's security, democracy, and constitutional system if he is allowed to remain in office. That threat is not hypothetical. As noted above, President Trump has persisted *during this impeachment inquiry* in soliciting foreign powers to investigate his political opponent. The President steadfastly insists that he did nothing wrong and is free to do it all again. Every day that this Committee fails to act is thus another day that the President might use the powers of his office to rig the election while ignoring or injuring vital national interests. In Chairman Schiff's words: "The argument 'Why don't you just wait?' amounts to this: 'Why don't you just let him cheat in one more election? Why not let him cheat just one more time? Why not let him have foreign help just one more time?'"[777]

Members of the Minority have objected that the evidence is too thin; that it rests entirely on hearsay, speculation, and presumptions. That accusation is false. The evidentiary record developed by the Investigating Committees is extensive. The Committees heard more than 100 hours of deposition testimony from 17 witnesses with personal knowledge of key events. HPSCI heard an additional 30 hours of public testimony from 12 of those witnesses.[778] In addition, the Committees considered the records of President Trump's phone calls with President Zelensky. They obtained hundreds of text messages, which navigate the months-long efforts by Mr. Giuliani and United States officials to push Ukraine to make a public statement announcing the politically-motivated investigations sought by President Trump. They relied on hundreds of public statements, interviews, and tweets by the President and Mr. Giuliani, his personal attorney, unabashedly describing efforts to pursue investigations into former Vice President Biden prior to the 2020 election. And they relied on the press briefing by Mr. Mulvaney, who confirmed why the military and security assistance was withheld and then told Americans to "get over" it.[779]

The record contains extensive direct evidence—powerfully corroborated by circumstantial evidence—rendering the key facts indisputable. Most critically, the record includes the President's own words on the July 25 call, which by itself reveals his corrupt scheme. It includes testimony and contemporaneous text messages from Ambassadors Volker and Sondland, who were directed by the President to "Talk to Rudy,"[780] and who pushed Ukrainian officials to publicly announce the two investigations to "break the logjam" on assistance and a White House visit.[781] It includes the testimony of three first-hand witnesses to the July 25 phone call. It includes the testimony of Mr. Holmes, who overheard President Trump ask Ambassador Sondland whether President Zelensky was "going to do the investigation,"[782] and who was then told by Ambassador Sondland that President Trump cared only

[777] Allan Smith & Rebecca Shabad, *House Leaders Unveil Two Articles of Impeachment, Accusing Trump of 'High Crimes and Misdemeanors,'* NBC NEWS, Dec. 10, 2019 (quoting Chairman Schiff).

[778] *Ukraine Report* at 7.

[779] *Id.* at 12; The White House, *Press Briefing by Acting Chief of Staff Mick Mulvaney* (Oct. 17, 2019).

[780] Sondland Dep. Tr. at 62; Volker Dep. Tr. 305; Morrison-Volker Hearing Tr. at 39.

[781] Sondland Hearing Tr. at 29.

[782] Hill-Holmes Hearing Tr. at 29.

about the "big stuff" (namely, the investigations and nothing else relating to Ukraine).[783] It includes the testimony of Ambassador Sondland, a political appointee of the President who had multiple discussions with him—and who confirmed that there was a "quid pro quo" relating to the potential White House visit for President Zelensky, and that, in light of President Trump's statements and conduct, it became clear that assistance was also conditioned on an announcement of the investigations.[784]

Collectively, the evidence gathered by the Investigating Committees is consistent, reliable, well-corroborated, and derived from diverse sources. It paints a detailed picture of President Trump's scheme. To the extent that the Committees did not obtain additional documents—or additional testimony from witnesses with personal knowledge of the relevant events—that is a direct consequence of the President's unprecedented, categorical, and indiscriminate order that the entire Executive Branch unlawfully defy duly authorized Congressional subpoenas. As explained in the discussion of the Second Article of Impeachment, the President's obstruction of Congress is not cured by the possibility of judicial review, which, among other difficulties, would undoubtedly last well beyond the very election that President Trump seeks to corrupt. Given the President's unlawful cover up, and given the powerful evidence of a looming Presidential threat to the next election, this Committee cannot stand silent. Nor can it agree that the record is insufficient just because it could be broader. The record stands firmly on its own two feet. Indeed, President Trump has not stonewalled the entire impeachment inquiry so that he can protect a hidden trove of exculpatory evidence.

Put simply, President Trump's own words reveal that he solicited a foreign government to investigate his political rival. The President did so for his own political gain, rather than for foreign policy reasons. The testimony of experienced, expert officials in his own administration—including several of his own appointees—reveal that the President used his official powers as leverage to pressure a vulnerable strategic partner to do his bidding. And every indication, every piece of evidence, supports that the President will abuse his power again. Under these circumstances, Congress is duty-bound to invoke its "sole Power of Impeachment."

IV.   Conclusion

To the Framers of our Constitution, tyranny was no abstraction. They had suffered under King George III. They had studied republics that faltered when public virtue fell to private vice. They knew that freedom demands constant protection from leaders whose taste of power sparks a voracious need for more. So even as they created a powerful Presidency, they authorized Congress to impeach and remove Presidents whose persistence in office threatened the Constitution. As they designed this impeachment power, they turned repeatedly to three risks: corrupt abuse of power; betrayal of the nation through foreign entanglements; and corruption of free and fair elections.

President Trump has realized the Framers' worst nightmare. He has abused his power in soliciting and pressuring a vulnerable foreign nation to corrupt the next United States Presidential

---

[783] *Id.*

[784] Sondland Hearing Tr. at 26.

election by sabotaging a political opponent and endorsing a debunked conspiracy theory promoted by our adversary, Russia. President Trump has done all this for his own personal gain, rather than for any legitimate reason, and has compromised our national security and democratic system in the process. After he was caught, President Trump defiantly insisted his conduct was "perfect."

Democracy is fragile. Men and women have fought and died to protect ours—and for the right to participate in it. The President of the United States is a steward of that system, in which "We the People" are sovereign. His duty is to uphold the Constitution and protect our lives and liberty. But President Trump has betrayed that trust. He has placed his own interest in retaining power above our national security and commitment to self-governance. He has done so before, he has done so here, and he will undoubtedly do so again. To protect the Nation, and preserve our freedom, President Trump must be impeached by the House of Representatives for abuse of power.

Article II: Obstruction of Congress

I.   The Second Article of Impeachment

The Constitution provides that the House of Representatives "shall have the sole Power of Impeachment" and that the President "shall be removed from Office on Impeachment for, and Conviction of, Treason, Bribery, or other high Crimes and Misdemeanors." In his conduct of the office of President of the United States—and in violation of his constitutional oath faithfully to execute the office of President of the United States and, to the best of his ability, preserve, protect, and defend the Constitution of the United States, and in violation of his constitutional duty to take care that the laws be faithfully executed—Donald J. Trump has directed the unprecedented, categorical, and indiscriminate defiance of subpoenas issued by the House of Representatives pursuant to its "sole Power of Impeachment". President Trump has abused the powers of the Presidency in a manner offensive to, and subversive of, the Constitution, in that:

The House of Representatives has engaged in an impeachment inquiry focused on President Trump's corrupt solicitation of the Government of Ukraine to interfere in the 2020 United States Presidential election. As part of this impeachment inquiry, the Committees undertaking the investigation served subpoenas seeking documents and testimony deemed vital to the inquiry from various Executive Branch agencies and offices, and current and former officials.

In response, without lawful cause or excuse, President Trump directed Executive Branch agencies, offices, and officials not to comply with those subpoenas. President Trump thus interposed the powers of the Presidency against the lawful subpoenas of the House of Representatives, and assumed to himself functions and judgments necessary to the exercise of the "sole Power of Impeachment" vested by the Constitution in the House of Representatives.

President Trump abused the powers of his high office through the following means:

(1) Directing the White House to defy a lawful subpoena by withholding the production of documents sought therein by the Committees.

(2) Directing other Executive Branch agencies and offices to defy lawful subpoenas and withhold the production of documents and records from the Committees—in response to which the Department of State, Office of Management and Budget, Department of Energy, and Department of Defense refused to produce a single document or record.

(3) Directing current and former Executive Branch officials not to cooperate with the Committees—in response to which nine Administration officials defied subpoenas for testimony, namely John Michael "Mick" Mulvaney, Robert B. Blair, John A. Eisenberg, Michael Ellis, Preston Wells Griffith, Russell T. Vought, Michael Duffey, Brian McCormack, and T. Ulrich Brechbuhl.

These actions were consistent with President Trump's previous efforts to undermine United

States Government investigations into foreign interference in United States elections.

Through these actions, President Trump sought to arrogate to himself the right to determine the propriety, scope, and nature of an impeachment inquiry into his own conduct, as well as the unilateral prerogative to deny any and all information to the House of Representatives in the exercise of its "sole Power of Impeachment". In the history of the Republic, no President has ever ordered the complete defiance of an impeachment inquiry or sought to obstruct and impede so comprehensively the ability of the House of Representatives to investigate "high Crimes and Misdemeanors". This abuse of office served to cover up the President's own repeated misconduct and to seize and control the power of impeachment—and thus to nullify a vital constitutional safeguard vested solely in the House of Representatives.

In all of this, President Trump has acted in a manner contrary to his trust as President and subversive of constitutional government, to the great prejudice of the cause of law and justice, and to the manifest injury of the people of the United States.

Wherefore, President Trump, by such conduct, has demonstrated that he will remain a threat to the Constitution if allowed to remain in office, and has acted in a manner grossly incompatible with self-governance and the rule of law. President Trump thus warrants impeachment and trial, removal from office, and disqualification to hold and enjoy any office of honor, trust, or profit under the United States.

II. Introduction

This Nation has no kings. Unlike a monarch, whose every word is law, the President of the United States answers to the Constitution and the American people. He ordinarily does so through elections, legislative oversight, judicial review, and public scrutiny. In truly extraordinary cases, however, the Constitution empowers the House of Representatives to hold the President accountable through its "sole Power of Impeachment."[785] This power is not to be exercised lightly. It is one of the greatest powers in the Constitution. But when the House, in its own independent judgment, has cause to suspect the President of committing "high Crimes and Misdemeanors," it has the constitutional right and duty to investigate his conduct.[786] As Presidents, legislators, and judges have long recognized, that authority inheres in the "sole Power of Impeachment," which would be undermined if the House lacked a thorough power of inquiry.

In the history of the Republic, no President has ever claimed the unilateral prerogative to categorically and indiscriminately defy a House impeachment inquiry. Nor has any President ever directed his administration to do so. On the contrary, every President to address the issue has acknowledged that Congress possesses a broad and penetrating power of inquiry when investigating grounds for impeachment. Even President Richard M. Nixon, who resisted full personal compliance

---

[785] U.S. CONST., art. I, § 2, cl. 5.

[786] U.S. CONST., art. II, § 4.

139

with House subpoenas, instructed his staff to testify voluntarily in the Senate Watergate inquiry: "All members of the White House Staff will appear voluntarily when requested by the committee. They will testify under oath, and they will answer fully all proper questions."[787]

Presidents wield extraordinary power, but they do so under law. That law provides the House with sole authority to impeach Presidents. It does not allow Presidents to dictate the terms on which they will be impeached or investigated for impeachable offenses, to order subordinates to break the law by ignoring subpoenas, or to use executive power to orchestrate a cover up. The Constitution confirms that the House alone, and not the President, determines what documents and testimony are relevant to its exercise of the impeachment power.

If allowed to stand, President Trump's actions will undermine the Constitution's defenses against a tyrannical President. Over the past months, the House has engaged in an impeachment inquiry focused on President Trump's corrupt solicitation and inducement of Ukrainian interference in the 2020 United States Presidential Election. As part of this inquiry, the Investigating Committees served subpoenas on various Executive Branch agencies and offices, as well as current and former officials, seeking documents and testimony relevant to the investigation. President Trump responded by directing all Executive Branch agencies, offices, and officials not to cooperate with the impeachment inquiry. In so doing, he arrogated to himself the power to determine when and how an impeachment inquiry should be carried out. President Trump's direction has no precedent in American history. His order to the Executive Branch was categorical and indiscriminate. It did not allow for any case-by-case weighing of privacy or national security interests, nor did it permit any efforts at accommodation or compromise. Through his order, the President slammed the door shut.

Following President Trump's direction, and at his behest, the White House, the Department of State under Secretary Michael R. Pompeo, the Office of Management and Budget under Acting Director Russell T. Vought, the Department of Energy under Secretary James Richard "Rick" Perry, and the Department of Defense under Secretary Mark T. Esper refused to produce a single document or record in response to Congressional subpoenas. Moreover, adhering to President Trump's direction, nine Administration officials defied subpoenas for testimony, namely John Michael "Mick" Mulvaney, Robert B. Blair, John A. Eisenberg, Michael Ellis, Preston Wells Griffith, Russell T. Vought, Michael Duffey, Brian McCormack, and T. Ulrich Brechbuhl. In directing these agencies, offices, and officials to disobey subpoenas, President Trump prevented Congress from obtaining additional evidence highly pertinent to the House's impeachment inquiry. He did so, moreover, through an official direction lacking any valid cause or excuse—and that strikingly reflected his previous pattern of obstructing United States government investigations into foreign interference in our elections. By engaging in this conduct, President Trump grossly abused his power and sought to arrogate to himself the right to determine the propriety, scope, and nature of an impeachment inquiry into his own wrongdoing.

Despite President Trump's obstruction, the Investigating Committees gathered overwhelming evidence of his misconduct from courageous public servants who were willing to follow the law, comply with subpoenas, and tell the truth. On the basis of that formidable body of evidence, the House

---

[787] The White House, *Remarks by President Nixon* (Apr. 17, 1973).

Committee on the Judiciary recommends the adoption of the First Article of Impeachment.

Yet there can be no doubt that President Trump's blanket defiance of Congressional subpoenas, and his direction that many others defy such subpoenas, substantially interfered with the House's efforts to fulfill its constitutional responsibilities. "If left unanswered, President Trump's ongoing effort to thwart Congress' impeachment power risks doing grave harm to the institution of Congress, the balance of power between our branches of government, and the Constitutional order that the President and every Member of Congress have sworn to protect and defend."[788]

President Trump's obstruction of Congress does not befit the leader of a democratic society. It calls to mind the very claims of royal privilege against which our Founders rebelled. Nor is President Trump's obstruction mitigated by a veneer of legal arguments. Some conclusions are so obviously wrong that their premises cannot be taken seriously; that is true of President Trump's theory that he sets the terms of his own impeachment. Through this conduct, President Trump has shown his rejection of checks and balances. A President who will not abide legal restraint or supervision is a President who poses an ongoing threat to our liberty and security.

The Second Article of Impeachment reflects the judgment of the Committee that President Trump committed "high Crimes and Misdemeanors" in directing the unprecedented, categorical, and indiscriminate defiance of subpoenas issued by the House pursuant to its "sole Power of Impeachment." As the Article explains: "This abuse of office amounts to an effort by the President to seize and control the power of impeachment—and thus to nullify a vital constitutional safeguard vested solely in the House of Representatives."[789]

III.   President Trump Committed "High Crimes and Misdemeanors" in Directing Categorical and Indiscriminate Defiance of the House Impeachment Inquiry

Under our Constitution, the House is empowered to investigate grounds for impeachment and the President is required to cooperate with such investigations. Given the impeachment power's central role in protecting the Nation from Presidential wrongdoing—and as confirmed by historical practice and precedent—Congressional investigative authority is at its constitutional zenith during an impeachment inquiry. When the House takes up its "sole Power of Impeachment," the overwhelming presumption is that its subpoenas must be and will be obeyed, including by the President and all other recipients in the Executive Branch. In such cases, the House acts not only pursuant to its ordinary

---

[788]*The Trump-Ukraine Impeachment Inquiry Report: Report for the H. Perm. Select Comm. on Intelligence Pursuant to H. Res. 660 in Consultation with the H. Comm. on Oversight and Reform and the H. Comm. on Foreign Affairs* at 28, 116th Cong. (2019) (hereinafter "Ukraine Report").

[789]H. Res. *755, Articles of Impeachment Against President Donald J. Trump*, 116th Cong. (Dec. 11, 2019).

legislative powers, but also serves as a "grand inquest of the nation.'"[790] It is therefore presumed that "all the archives and papers of the Executive Departments, public or private, would be subject to . . . inspection" and "every facility in the power of the Executive [would] be afforded to enable [the House] to prosecute the investigation."[791]

In contravention of those settled principles, and in violation of the assignment of powers under the Constitution, President Trump has defied a subpoena served on the White House. He has also directed other agencies, offices, and officials across the Executive Branch to violate their own obligations under the law. His direction has been complete and wholly unqualified in nature. Rather than undertake a process of dialogue and accommodation, the President has stonewalled all investigative prerogatives and interests held by the House in an impeachment inquiry. Although the Justice Department and individual Executive Branch officials have additionally raised specific objections to certain subpoenas—none of which have merit—President Trump's general direction that the Executive Branch obstruct Congress has rendered those objections practically irrelevant. President Trump's unprecedented conduct thus raises a single question: Is it an impeachable offense under the Constitution for the President to direct the categorical and indiscriminate defiance of subpoenas issued pursuant to a House impeachment inquiry?

The Committee has undertaken a thorough survey of relevant authorities and concludes that the answer is plainly "yes." This is not a close case. President Trump has asserted and exercised the unilateral prerogative to direct complete defiance of every single impeachment-related subpoena served on the Executive Branch. He has purported to justify this obstruction by attacking the motives, procedures, and legitimacy of the House impeachment inquiry—in overt violation of our Constitution, which vests the House (and not the President) with the "sole Power of Impeachment."

Simply stated, these are not judgments for the President to make. His position would place Presidents in control of a power meant to restrain their own abuses. That is not what the Constitution provides. As Judiciary Committee Chairman Peter W. Rodino correctly explained to President Nixon in May 1974, "[u]nder the Constitution it is not within the power of the President to conduct an inquiry into his own impeachment, to determine which evidence, and what version or portion of that evidence, is relevant and necessary to such an inquiry. These are matters which, under the Constitution, the House has the sole power to determine."[792]

President Trump's direction to obstruct the House impeachment inquiry is thus grossly incompatible with, and subversive of, the Constitution. It marks a dangerous step toward debilitating the Impeachment Clause and unraveling the Framers' plan. This claim of Presidential power is also recognizably wrong—as every President in American history, except President Trump, has in fact recognized. Through his conduct, President Trump's has revealed himself as a continuing threat to

---

[790] Report of the Committee on the Judiciary, Impeachment of Richard M. Nixon, President of the United States, H. Rep. No. 93-1305 at 207 (1974) (quoting President Polk) (citations omitted) (hereinafter "*Committee Report on Nixon Articles of Impeachment (1974)*").

[791] *Id.*

[792] *Committee Report on Nixon Articles of Impeachment (1974)*, at 194.

constitutional governance if he remains in office. It is one thing for a President to use harsh rhetoric in criticizing an impeachment inquiry. It is something else entirely for that President to declare such an inquiry "illegitimate" and use his official powers to stonewall the House.[793] A President who declares himself above impeachment is a President who sees himself as above the law. That President is a monarch in all but name and imperils our democracy.[794]

To explain our judgment that President Trump's conduct constitutes "high Crimes and Misdemeanors," we first describe the House's power of inquiry, as well as its power to investigate grounds for impeachment. We next confirm the Committee's assessment from President Nixon's case that obstruction of a House impeachment inquiry is an impeachable offense. Finally, we apply the law to President Trump's conduct, consider his various excuses, and assess whether he remains a continuing threat to constitutional governance and democracy if allowed to remain in office.

A.   The House's Power of Inquiry

"[L]egislative subpoenas are older than our country itself."[795] They originated in the English Parliament, "when that body, as part of its campaign to 'challenge the absolute power of the monarch,' asserted 'plenary authority' to hold offending parties in contempt."[796] By the late 17th century, "[t]he privileges and powers of the [House of] Commons"—which include the linked powers of contempt and inquiry—"were naturally assumed to be an incident of the representative assemblies of the Thirteen Colonies."[797] In part for that reason, "[a]fter the Revolutionary War and the Constitutional Convention, the U.S. Congress wasted little time in asserting its power to use compulsory process to investigate matters of national—and potentially legislative—importance."[798] Such Congressional oversight activity was grounded in Article I of the Constitution, which grants Congress "[a]ll legislative Powers,"[799] and authorizes "[e]ach House [to] determine the Rules of its Proceedings."[800] Through these provisions, the Constitution vests the House with a "power of inquiry," including "process to

---

[793] Letter from Pat A. Cipollone, Counsel to the President, The White House, to Hon. Nancy Pelosi, Speaker of the House, Hon. Adam B. Schiff, Chairman, H. Perm. Select Comm. on Intelligence, Hon. Eliot L. Engel, Chairman, H. Foreign Affairs Comm., and Hon. Elijah E. Cummings, Chairman, H. Comm. on Oversight and Reform, at 8 (Oct. 8, 2019) (hereinafter, "*Oct. 8 Cipollone Letter*").

[794] *See* THE FEDERALIST NO. 69, at 444-45 (Alexander Hamilton) (Benjamin Fletcher Wright ed. 1961) ("The President of the United States would be liable to be impeached, tried, and, upon conviction of treason, bribery, or other high crimes or misdemeanors, removed from office; and would afterwards be liable to prosecution and punishment in the ordinary course of law. The person of the king of Great Britain is sacred and inviolable; there is no constitutional tribunal to which he is amenable; no punishment to which he can be subjected without involving the crisis of a national revolution.").

[795] *Trump v. Mazars USA, LLP*, 940 F.3d 710, 718 (D.C. Cir. 2019), *cert. granted*, No. 19-715, 2019 WL 6797734 (U.S. Dec. 13, 2019) ("*Mazars*").

[796] *Id.* (quoting *Watkins v. United States*, 354 U.S. 178, 188 (1957)).

[797] *Id.* (citations omitted).

[798] *Id.*; *see also M'Culloch v. State*, 17 U.S. 316, 401 (1819) ("[A] doubtful question . . . if not put at rest by the practice of the government, ought to receive a considerable impression from that practice.").

[799] U.S. CONST., art. I, § 1.

[800] *Id.* at § 5.

enforce it," as an "essential and appropriate auxiliary to the legislative function."[801]

"So long as the [House] is investigating a matter on which Congress can ultimately propose and enact legislation, the [House] may issue subpoenas in furtherance of its power of inquiry."[802] And the House's constitutional authority "to conduct investigations" is "broad."[803] "It encompasses inquiries concerning the administration of existing laws as well as proposed or possibly needed statutes," "[i]t includes surveys of defects in our social, economic or political system for the purpose of enabling the Congress to remedy them," and "[i]t comprehends probes into departments of the Federal Government to expose corruption, inefficiency or waste."[804] Congress may not usurp the constitutional functions of other branches of government, violate individual rights, engage in law enforcement, or investigate topics over which it cannot legislate.[805] But apart from these narrow limitations, "[a] legislative inquiry may be as broad, as searching, and as exhaustive as is necessary to make effective the constitutional powers of Congress."[806] Moreover, the ultimate outcome of oversight need not be apparent from the outset for it to be proper: "The very nature of the investigative function—like any research—is that it takes the searchers up some 'blind alleys' and into nonproductive enterprises. To be a valid legislative inquiry there need be no predictable end result."[807]

Consistent with Congress's role in checking the Executive Branch, "Presidents, too, have often been the subjects of Congress's legislative investigations."[808] "Historical examples stretch far back in time and broadly across subject matters," ranging from investigations of contract fraud under President Andrew Jackson, to allegations that President Abraham Lincoln was mishandling military strategy during the Civil War, to charges that President Franklin D. Roosevelt had incited the Japanese into bombing Pearl Harbor, to President Nixon and the Watergate scandal, to President Ronald W. Reagan's involvement in the Iran-Contra Affair, to President William J. Clinton and Whitewater, to the Benghazi investigation under President Barack H. Obama.[809]

As the Supreme Court has observed, "[w]ithout the power to investigate—including of course the authority to compel testimony, either through its own processes or through judicial trial—Congress could be seriously handicapped in its efforts to exercise its constitutional function wisely and

---

[801] *McGrain v. Daugherty*, 273 U.S. 135, 174 (1927).

[802] *Comm. on Judiciary, U.S. House of Representatives v. Miers*, 558 F. Supp. 2d 53, 77 (D.D.C. 2008).

[803] *Watkins*, 354 U.S. at 187; *accord Eastland v. U.S. Servicemen's Fund*, 421 U.S. 491, 504 n.15 (1975) ("[T]he power to investigate is necessarily broad."); *Barenblatt v. United States*, 360 U.S. 109, 111 (1959) (describing Congress's investigative power as "broad"); *Quinn v. United States*, 349 U.S. 155, 161 (1955) (same); *McGrain*, 273 U.S., at 173-74 (same).

[804] *Watkins*, 354 U.S. at 187.

[805] *See Mazars*, 940 F.3d at 723.

[806] *Townsend v. United States*, 95 F.2d 352, 361 (D.C. Cir. 1938); *accord Mazars*, 940 F.3d at 723.

[807] *Eastland*, 421 U.S. at 509.

[808] *Mazars*, 940 F.3d at 721.

[809] *See id.* at 721-22; *see also Ukraine Report*, at 205-206.

effectively."[810] Presidential obstruction of legislative subpoenas thus undermines Congress's constitutional function, offends the separation of powers, and effectively places the President above the law.

B.   The House's Power to Investigate Grounds for Impeachment

In light of the impeachment power's central role in our system of checks and balances, the House's investigative authority is at its peak during an impeachment inquiry. All three branches of the federal government have repeatedly confirmed this point.

When the Framers authorized the House to impeach Presidents, they necessarily empowered it to obtain and examine evidence deemed necessary to the exercise of that constitutional responsibility. This understanding follows directly from the Constitutional Convention. There, several delegates opposed including an impeachment power in the Constitution. They warned that it would be "destructive of [the executive's] independence."[811] The majority of delegates agreed that allowing impeachment would affect the separation of powers—but welcomed that result. As George Mason declared, "[n]o point is of more importance than that the right of impeachment should be continued."[812] Alexander Hamilton, in turn, later observed that "the powers relating to impeachments" are "an essential check in the hands of [Congress] upon the encroachments of the executive."[813] Many Americans in this period agreed that impeachment played an important role; it would keep Presidents in line and protect the Nation from abuse, betrayal, or corruption. Thus, even as the Constitution created a powerful presidency, it included a safety valve for emergencies.

Yet the impeachment power could not serve that role if the House were unable to investigate the facts necessary to make an informed impeachment determination, or if the President could liberally obstruct such efforts. This was recognized early on. In 1796, the House requested that President George Washington provide it with sensitive diplomatic materials relating to the Jay Treaty. President Washington famously declined this request on the ground that it exceeded the House's role and intruded upon his executive functions. But in that same letter, President Washington agreed that impeachment would change his calculus: "It does not occur that the inspection of the papers asked for can be relative to any purpose under the cognizance of the House of Representatives, *except that of an impeachment*, which the resolution has not expressed."[814] In the ensuing House debates, one Member noted that President Washington had "admitted, by implication, that where the House expresses an intention to impeach, the right to demand from the Executive all papers and information in his possession belongs

---

[810] *Quinn*, 349 U.S. at 160-61 (citations omitted).

[811] 2 Farrand, *Records of the Federal Convention*, at 67.

[812] 2 Farrand, *Records of the Federal* Convention, at 65.

[813] THE FEDERALIST NO. 66, at 431 (Alexander Hamilton) (Benjamin Fletcher Wright ed., 1961).

[814] George Washington, *Message to the House Regarding Documents Relative to the Jay Treaty* (Mar. 30, 1796) (emphasis added), (hereinafter "*Message on Jay Treaty*"); *see also* Laurence H. Tribe & Joshua Matz, *To End A Presidency: The Power of Impeachment* 153-155 (2018) (hereinafter "*To End A Presidency*") (discussing scattered calls in local newspapers for the impeachment of President Washington over his handling of the Jay Treaty).

to it."[815] And President Washington was right, because "the sole Power" of impeachment includes "a right to inspect every paper and transaction in any department, otherwise the power of impeachment could never be exercised with any effect."[816]

In 1833, Supreme Court Justice Joseph Story emphasized the House's broad investigatory power in impeachments—and the importance of not permitting the President to obstruct such inquiries. In his influential *Commentaries on the Constitution of the United States*, Justice Story addressed the interaction between impeachment and Presidential pardons. While doing so, he pointedly observed that "[t]he power of impeachment will generally be applied to persons holding high offices under the government; and *it is of great consequence that the President should not have the power of preventing a thorough investigation of their conduct*, or of securing them against the disgrace of a public conviction by impeachment."[817]

In 1842, amid ongoing strife between the House and President John Tyler, the House took substantial steps toward an impeachment inquiry.[818] During a dispute with President Tyler over the production of documents—which he ultimately provided—a Committee of the House confirmed its robust understanding of the power to investigate impeachable offenses:

> The House of Representatives has the sole power of impeachment. The President himself in the discharge of his most independent functions, is subject to the exercise of this power which implied the right of inquiry on the part of the House to the fullest and most unlimited extent. ... If the House possess the power to impeach, it must likewise possess all the incidents of that power—the power to compel the attendance of all witnesses and the production of all such papers as may be considered necessary to prove the charges on which impeachment is founded. If it did not, the power of impeachment conferred upon it by the Constitution would be nugatory. It could not exercise it with effect.[819]

Consistent with this precedent, President James K. Polk "cheerfully admitted" in 1846 the right of the House to investigate the conduct of all government officers with a view to exercising its impeachment power.[820] "In such a case," he wrote:

> [T]he safety of the Republic would be the supreme law, and the power of the

---

[815] *Frauds Upon Indians – Right of the President to Withhold Papers*, H.R. Rep. No. 27-271, at 12 (1843); *see also Message on Jay Treaty* ("It does not occur that the inspection of the papers asked for can be relative to any purpose under the cognizance of the House of Representatives, except that of an impeachment, which the resolution has not expressed.").

[816] *Committee Report on Nixon Articles of Impeachment* (1974) at 206 (citing 5 *Annals of Congress* 601 (1796)).

[817] 3 Joseph Story, *Commentaries on the Constitution of the United States* § 1495 at 352 (1833) (emphasis added).

[818] Tribe and Matz, To End A Presidency at 19-20.

[819] *Committee Report on Nixon Articles of Impeachment* (1974) at 206 (internal citations omitted).

[820] *Committee Report on Nixon Articles of Impeachment* (1974) at 207.

House in the pursuit of this object would penetrate into the most secret recesses of the Executive Departments. It could command the attendance of any and every agent of the Government, and compel them to produce all papers, public or private, official or unofficial, and to testify on oath to all facts within their knowledge.[821]

President Andrew Johnson conducted himself in accordance with this understanding when the Judiciary Committee undertook an initial inquiry into grounds for impeachment. During that investigation, which occurred in 1867, the Committee obtained executive and Presidential records; interviewed cabinet officers and Presidential aides about cabinet meetings and conversations with the President; and examined a number of Presidential decisions, including Presidential pardons, the issuance of executive orders, the implementation of Congressional Reconstruction, and the vetoing of legislation.[822] Multiple witnesses, moreover, answered questions about the opinions of the President, statements made by the President, and advice given to the President.[823] Significantly, as this Committee has previously summarized, "[t]here is no evidence that [President] Johnson ever asserted any privilege to prevent disclosure of presidential conversations to the Committee, or failed to comply with any of the Committee's requests."[824]

With only a few exceptions, invocations of the impeachment power largely subsided from 1868 to 1972.[825] Yet even in that period, while objecting to acts of ordinary legislative oversight, Presidents Ulysses S. Grant, S. Grover Cleveland, and Theodore Roosevelt each noted that Congress could obtain a broader set of Executive Branch documents in an impeachment inquiry.[826]

In 1973 and 1974, this Committee investigated whether President Nixon had committed "high Crimes and Misdemeanors." During that period, the Senate also investigated events relating to the Watergate break-in and its aftermath. Faced with these inquiries, President Nixon allowed senior administration officials to testify voluntarily in the Senate. As a result, many senior White House officials testified, including White House Counsel John W. Dean III, White House Chief of Staff H.R. "Bob" Haldeman, Deputy Assistant to the President Alexander P. Butterfield, and Chief Advisor to the

---

[821] *Committee Report on Nixon Articles of Impeachment* (1974) at 207 (internal citations omitted).

[822] *Committee Report on Nixon Articles of Impeachment* (1974) at 206 (internal citations omitted).

[823] When asked to disclose a conversation between himself and President Johnson regarding the preparation of a veto message, an advisor named Jeremiah Black thus agreed he was "bound in conscience to answer a question which that tribunal declares he ought to answer; that he is himself not the judge of what he ought to answer and what he ought not." *Committee Report on Nixon Articles of Impeachment* (1974) at 207.

[824] *Id.*

[825] Tribe and Matz, To End A Presidency at 156-169.

[826] *See* Staff of H. Comm. on the Judiciary, 116th Cong., Constitutional Grounds for Presidential Impeachment 42 (Comm. Print 2019) (citing Jonathan David Shaub, *The Executive's Privilege: Rethinking the President's Power to Withhold Information*, LAWFARE (Oct. 31, 2019)) (hereinafter "*Constitutional Grounds for Impeachment* (2019)").

President for Domestic Affairs John D. Ehrlichman.[827] President Nixon also produced numerous documents and records in response to Congressional subpoenas, including more than 30 transcripts of White House recordings and notes from meetings with the President.[828] This was consistent with prior practice. As the Judiciary Committee explained at the time: "Before the current inquiry, sixty-nine Federal officials had been the subject of impeachment investigations. With the possible exception of one minor official who invoked the privilege against self-incrimination, not one of them challenged the power of the committee conducting the investigation to compel the production of evidence it deemed necessary."[829]

However, President Nixon's production of records was incomplete in a very important respect: he did not produce key tape recordings of Oval Office conversations, and some of the transcripts of such recordings that he produced were heavily edited or inaccurate.[830] President Nixon claimed that his noncompliance with House subpoenas was necessary to protect the confidentiality of Presidential conversations. But as we explain further in the next section, this Committee rejected his arguments and approved an article of impeachment against President Nixon for obstruction of the House's impeachment inquiry.[831]

Twenty-four years later, the House undertook impeachment proceedings against President Clinton. Consistent with precedent, he "pledged to cooperate fully with the [impeachment] investigation."[832] And although the House engaged in very little independent fact-finding, President Clinton substantially cooperated, providing written responses to 81 interrogatories from the Judiciary Committee during the impeachment inquiry—as well as his own DNA.[833]

Thus, Presidents have long recognized that the House enjoys a nearly plenary power of inquiry while investigating grounds for impeachment. This conclusion is further supported by an additional

---

[827] *See, e.g.*, Senate Select Committee on Presidential Campaign Activities, Testimony of John Dean, Watergate and Related Activities, Phase I: Watergate Investigation, 93d Cong. (June 25, 1973); *Senate Select Committee on Presidential Campaign Activities, Testimony of H.R. Haldeman, Watergate and Related Activities, Phase I: Watergate Investigation*, 93d Cong. (July 30, 1973); *Senate Select Committee on Presidential Campaign Activities, Testimony of Alexander Butterfield, Watergate and Related Activities, Phase I: Watergate Investigation*, 93d Cong. (July 16, 1973); *Senate Select Committee on Presidential Campaign Activities, Testimony of John Ehrlichman, Watergate and Related Activities, Phase I: Watergate Investigation*, 93d Cong. (July 24, 1973); *see also Ukraine Report* at 206.

[828] *Committee Report on Nixon Articles of Impeachment* (1974) at 196.

[829] *Id.* at 206 (footnote omitted).

[830] *Id.* at 203.

[831] *Id.* at 382-83.

[832] Andrew Miga, *White House in Crisis*, Boston Herald, Oct. 9, 1998.

[833] *Impeachment of William Jefferson Clinton, President of the United States: Report of the Committee on the Judiciary*, H. Rep. No. 105-830 at 77 (1998) ("On November 5, 1998, the Committee presented President Clinton with 81 requests for admission.") (hereinafter "*Committee Report on Clinton Articles of Impeachment* (1998)"). The Judiciary Committee nevertheless concluded that President Clinton's failure to respond to certain written requests for admission, and his alleged perjurious, false, and misleading sworn statements in response to other requests, warranted impeachment. *Id.* at 76 (Article IV). This proposed article of impeachment, however, was voted down on the House floor. 144 Cong. Rec. H11975, 12042 (1998).

Executive Branch policy. In the current view of the Department of Justice (DOJ)—the accuracy of which we do not here opine upon—the President cannot be indicted or face criminal prosecution while in office.[834] As support for that view, DOJ has reasoned that a President "who engages in criminal behavior falling into the category of 'high Crimes and Misdemeanors'" is "always subject to removal from office upon impeachment by the House and conviction by the Senate."[835] DOJ adds that "the constitutionally specified impeachment process ensures that the immunity [of a sitting President from prosecution] would not place the President 'above the law.'"[836] Given DOJ's refusal to indict or prosecute a sitting President, impeachment and removal may be one of the few available mechanisms to hold a President immediately accountable for criminal conduct also constituting "high Crimes and Misdemeanors." On that view, the House must have broad access to evidence supporting or refuting allegations of impeachable misconduct, since an unduly narrow view of the House's authority would place the President beyond all legal constraint.

The Judiciary has similarly concluded that the House enjoys broad investigative power in an impeachment setting. In *Kilbourn v. Thompson*, for example, the Supreme Court invalidated a contempt order by the House, but emphasized that "the whole aspect of the case would have changed" were it an impeachment proceeding, since "[w]here the question of such impeachment is before either [House of Congress] acting in its appropriate sphere on that subject, we see no reason to doubt the right to compel the attendance of witnesses, and their answer to proper questions, in the same manner and by the use of the same means that courts of justice can in like cases."[837]

More recently, Judge John J. Sirica's influential opinion on the Watergate "road map" likewise emphasized the special and substantial weight assigned to legislative interests in an impeachment context: "[I]t should not be forgotten that we deal in a matter of the most critical moment to the Nation, an impeachment investigation involving the President of the United States. It would be difficult to conceive of a more compelling need than that of this country for an unswervingly fair inquiry based on all the pertinent information."[838] Sitting *en banc*, the United States Court of Appeals for the District of Columbia Circuit further recognized that the House has enhanced legal powers to obtain material from the President in an impeachment inquiry because "[t]he investigative authority of the Judiciary Committee with respect to presidential conduct has an express constitutional source."[839]

A spate of decisions from the 1980s further support the House's robust investigative powers during impeachment. In *Nixon v. Fitzgerald*, the Supreme Court announced a rule of absolute

---

[834] *See A Sitting President's Amenability to Indictment and Criminal Prosecution*, 24 Op. O.L.C. 222, 260 (2000).

[835] *Id.* at 257.

[836] *Id.*

[837] *Kilbourn v. Thompson*, 103 U.S. 168, 190, 194 (1880); *see also Barry v. U.S. ex rel. Cunningham*, 279 U.S. 597, 616 (1929) (recognizing that the Senate would have added power to compel witness testimony in an impeachment trial).

[838] *In re Report & Recommendation of June 5, 1972 Grand Jury Concerning Transmission of Evidence to House of Representatives*, 370 F. Supp. 1219, 1230 (D.D.C. 1974).

[839] *Senate Select Comm. on Presidential Campaign Activities v. Nixon*, 498 F.2d 725, 732 (D.C. Cir. 1974).

Presidential immunity from civil damages.[840] In so doing, it emphasized that this rule "will not leave the Nation without sufficient protection against misconduct on the part of the Chief Executive," since "there remains the constitutional remedy of impeachment."[841] The Court pointedly added that "[v]igilant oversight by Congress also may serve to deter Presidential abuses of office, as well as to make credible the threat of impeachment."[842] This statement constituted a recognition by the Court that the House cannot effectively exercise its impeachment power without the ability to undertake "vigilant oversight."[843]

Over the following years, several federal courts agreed. In 1984, the United States Court of Appeals for the Eleventh Circuit emphasized that impeachment inquiries require courts to place a heavy thumb on the scale in favor of turning over materials to Congressional investigators.[844] Three years later, a district judge elaborated that courts have limited power to constrain legislative investigations in an impeachment setting: "Ancillary to the sole power of impeachment vested in the House by the Constitution is the power to disclose the evidence that it receives as it sees fit. Again, recognition of the doctrine of separation of powers precludes the judiciary from imposing restrictions on the exercise of the impeachment power."[845] In affirming this decision, the Eleventh Circuit noted that "[p]ublic confidence in a procedure as political and public as impeachment is an important consideration justifying disclosure" of grand jury materials to Congress.[846]

More recent opinions have echoed these points. As one judge observed, when "subpoenas [are] issued in connection with an impeachment proceeding . . . . Congress's investigatory powers are at their peak."[847] Other judges have more broadly emphasized the public interest in obtaining Executive Branch

---

[840] *Nixon v. Fitzgerald*, 457 U.S. 731, 749 (1982) ("[W]e hold that petitioner, as a former President of the United States, is entitled to absolute immunity from damages liability predicated on his official acts.").

[841] *Id.* at 757.

[842] *Id.*

[843] *Id.*

[844] *See In re Petition to Inspect & Copy Grand Jury Materials*, 735 F.2d 1261, 1269–71 (11th Cir. 1984) ("Moreover, the question under investigation—whether an Article III judge should be recommended for impeachment by the Congress, otherwise disciplined, or granted a clean bill of health—is a matter of great societal importance. Given the character of an investigating committee and what is at stake—the public confidence in the judiciary, the independence and reputation of the accused judge—paragraph (c)(5) must in our view be read, with very few strings, as conferring authority to look into whatever is material to a determination of the truth or falsity of the charges.").

[845] *In re Grand Jury Proceedings of Grand Jury No. 81-1*, 669 F. Supp. 1072, 1078 (S.D. Fla. 1987).

[846] *In re Request for Access to Grand Jury Materials Grand Jury No. 81-1, Miami*, 833 F.2d 1438, 1445 (11th Cir. 1987).

[847] *Trump v. Deutsche Bank AG*, No. 19-1540, 2019 WL 6482561 at *38 n.1 (2d Cir. Dec. 3, 2019) (Livingston, J., concurring part and dissenting in part); *see also Comm. on the Judiciary, U.S. House of Representatives v. Donald F. McGahn II*, No. 19 Civ. 2379, 2019 WL 6463406 at *6 (D.D.C. Dec. 2, 2019) (emphasizing "the public's interest in thorough and well-informed impeachment proceedings."); *In re Application of Comm. on Judiciary, U.S. House of Representatives, for an Order Authorizing Release of Certain Grand Jury Materials*, No. 19-48, 2019 WL 5608827 at *3 (D.D.C. Oct. 29, 2019) ("'[A]n impeachment investigation involving the President of the United States is a matter of the most critical moment to the Nation' . . . Both HJC itself and the public, therefore, have an interest in HJC gaining immediate access to this grand jury material.") (citations and quotation marks omitted)).

records that may be relevant to an ongoing impeachment inquiry.[848]

"Long settled and established practice is a consideration of great weight in a proper interpretation of constitutional provisions regulating the relationship between Congress and the President."[849] Viewed together, the practices and express statements set forth above confirm that the House enjoys an exceedingly expansive power of inquiry when investigating grounds for impeachment. Because the House's interests in any such inquiry evoke the interests underlying the impeachment power itself, subpoenas issued by a House impeachment inquiry should overcome nearly any countervailing interest or privilege. Finally, by virtue of the plain language of Article I of the Constitution, which vests the House with the "sole Power of Impeachment" as a check against the Presidency, it is for the House—and not the President—to determine what documents and testimony are needed for its exercise of the impeachment power.

C.   Obstruction of Congress Is an Impeachable Offense

Impeachment is a cornerstone of the Constitution. When the House wields the impeachment power, it serves as a grand inquest of the Nation on behalf of the American people, charged with protecting our democracy. Because the premise of the Impeachment Clause is that the House must be able to act when the President has abused his power, betrayed the national interest, or corrupted elections, a President who obstructs House investigators has attacked the Constitution itself. Even when the President strenuously disagrees with the impeachment inquiry—and even when he doubts its motives—he must obey the law and allow others to meet their legal obligations. The absurdity of allowing Presidents to dictate the terms of impeachment inquiries is obvious. The danger of allowing Presidents to do so is manifest. For that reason, Presidential obstruction of an impeachment inquiry is itself an impeachable abuse of power under the Constitution.[850]

To be sure, Presidents may still raise privacy, national security, and other concerns in the course

---

[848] *See, e.g., Ctr. for Pub. Integrity v. U.S. Dep't of Def.*, No. 19 Civ. 3265, 2019 WL 6270921 at *3 (D.D.C. Nov. 25, 2019) ("Currently, the [House] is in the process of conducting impeachment proceedings concerning the same subject matter as the documents requested by Plaintiff. As such, the requested documents are sought in order to inform the public on a matter of extreme national concern. Only an informed electorate can develop its opinions and persuasively petition its elected officials to act in ways which further the aims of those opinions."); *Am. Oversight v. U.S. Dep't of State*, No. 19 Civ. 2934, 2019 WL 5665930 at *4 (D.D.C. Oct. 25, 2019) ("This is the extraordinary case where the public interest favors placing American Oversight's requests ahead of other requests in the State Department's FOIA queue. Presidential impeachment investigations are solemn affairs, which Congress thankfully has seen fit to undertake only a few times in the Nation's history. The records American Oversight seeks, if they exist, could directly inform the present investigation and the surrounding public debate. The public's interest in disclosure of responsive, non-exempt records is therefore high and outweighs any harm to other FOIA requesters that might result from a temporary diversion of the State Department's FOIA resources to accelerate processing of this request.").

[849] *N.L.R.B. v. Noel Canning*, 573 U.S. 513, 524 (2014) (quotation marks and citation omitted).

[850] *See, e.g.*, Frank O. Bowman III, *High Crimes & Misdemeanors: A History of Impeachment for the Age of Trump* 199 (2019) ("The subpoena power in impeachment cases arises directly from an explicit constitutional directive that the House conduct an adjudicative proceeding akin to a grand jury, the success of which is necessarily dependent on the availability of relevant evidence. Without the power to compel compliance with subpoenas and the concomitant right to impeach a president for refusal to comply, the impeachment power would be nullified.").

of an impeachment inquiry, to the extent they apply. There is room for inter-branch negotiation and accommodation—though there is an overwhelming presumption in favor of full disclosure and compliance with House subpoenas. But when a President abuses his office to defy House investigators on matters that they deem pertinent to their inquiry, and does so without lawful cause or excuse, his conduct may constitute an unconstitutional effort to seize and break the impeachment power vested solely in the House. In that respect, obstruction of Congress involves "the exercise of official power in a way that, on its very face, grossly exceeds the President's constitutional authority or violates legal limits on that authority."[851]

This is illustrated by President's Nixon case. As explained above, President Nixon allowed senior administration officials to testify and produced many documents. He did not direct anything approximating a categorical and indiscriminate blockade of the House's impeachment inquiry. But in response to the Judiciary Committee's eight subpoenas for recordings and materials related to 147 conversations, he produced only limited documents and edited transcripts of roughly 30 conversations; many of those transcripts were inaccurate or incomplete.[852] President Nixon claimed that his non-compliance was legally defensible, invoking the doctrine of executive privilege.[853]

The Judiciary Committee rejected these arguments and deemed President Nixon's conduct to be impeachable. It observed that his "statements that the institution of the Presidency is threatened when he is required to comply with a subpoena in an impeachment inquiry exaggerate both the likelihood of such an inquiry and the threat to confidentiality from it."[854] The Committee also emphasized that "the doctrine of separation of powers cannot justify the withholding of information from an impeachment inquiry."[855] After all, "[t]he very purpose of such an inquiry is to permit the House, acting on behalf of the people, to curb the excesses of another branch, in this instance the Executive."[856] Therefore, "[w]hatever the limits of legislative power in other contexts—and whatever need may otherwise exist for preserving the confidentiality of Presidential conversations—in the context of an impeachment proceeding the balance was struck in favor of the power of inquiry when the impeachment provision was written into the Constitution."[857]

Because "the refusal of [President Nixon] to comply with the subpoenas was an interference by him with the efforts of the Committee and the House of Representatives to fulfill their constitutional responsibilities," the Judiciary Committee deemed it impeachable.[858] The Committee reached that

---

[851] *Constitutional Grounds for Impeachment* (2019) at 18; *see also id.* (explaining that impeachable abuse of power was understood by the Framers as encompassing, *inter alia*, "conduct that is inherently and sharply inconsistent with the law—and that amounts to claims of monarchical prerogative").

[852] *Committee Report on Nixon Articles of Impeachment* (1974), at 203.

[853] *Id.* at 207-208.

[854] *Id.* at 210.

[855] *Id.* at 208.

[856] *Id.*

[857] *Id.* at 209.

[858] *Id.* at 188.

determination even though it had "been able to conduct an investigation and determine that grounds for impeachment exist," despite "the President's refusal to comply."[859] On that point, the Committee observed that President Nixon's obstruction "was not without practical import," since "[h]ad it received the evidence sought by the subpoenas, the Committee might have recommended articles structured differently or possible ones covering other matters."[860]

President Nixon's obstruction of the House impeachment inquiry featured in two of the three articles approved by the Judiciary Committee. Article II charged President Nixon with abuse of power, including "failing to act when he knew or had reason to know that his close subordinates endeavored to impede and frustrate lawful inquiries by duly constituted executive, judicial and *legislative* entities concerning the unlawful entry into the headquarters of the Democratic National Committee, and the cover-up thereof, and concerning other unlawful activities . . . ."[861]

More directly, Article III charged President Nixon with abusing his power by interfering with the discharge of the Judiciary Committee's responsibility to investigate fully and completely whether sufficient grounds existed to impeach him:

> In refusing to produce these papers and things, Richard M. Nixon, substituting his judgment as to what materials were necessary for the inquiry, interposed the powers of the Presidency against the lawful subpoenas of the House of Representatives, thereby assuming to himself functions and judgments necessary to the exercise of the sole power of impeachment vested by the Constitution in the House of Representatives.

> In all of this, Richard M. Nixon has acted in a manner contrary to his trust as President and subversive of constitutional government, to the great prejudice of the cause of law and justice, and to the manifest injury of the people of the United States . . . .[862]

President Nixon's case is thus persuasive authority that Presidential defiance of a House impeachment inquiry may constitute "high Crimes and Misdemeanors."

This Committee took the same view in President Clinton's case. The fourth article of impeachment against President Clinton charged that he had "impaired the due and proper administration of justice and the conduct of lawful inquiries, and contravened the authority of the legislative branch and the truth seeking purpose of a coordinate investigative proceeding."[863] Specifically, it accused him of failing to respond to certain written requests and making false and

---

[859] *Id*. at 189.

[860] *Id.*

[861] *Id*. at 3-4 (emphasis added).

[862] *Id.* at 4.

[863] *Committee Report on Clinton Articles of Impeachment* (1998) at 4.

misleading statements to Congress. To justify impeaching President Clinton on that basis, the Committee reasoned as follows:

> In responding in such a manner, the President exhibited contempt for the constitutional prerogative of Congress to conduct an impeachment inquiry. The impeachment duty is a solemn one vested exclusively in the House of Representatives as a check and balance on the President and the Judiciary. The Committee reached the unfortunate conclusion that the President, by giving perjurious, false, and misleading answers under oath to the Committee's requests for admission, chose to take steps to thwart this serious constitutional process.[864]

Ultimately, the House declined to approve this article. That decision, however, did not constitute a determination that obstruction of a House impeachment inquiry cannot be impeachable. Instead, it appears to reflect a judgment by the full House that President Clinton's conduct was not substantial, malicious, or obstructive enough to warrant an article of impeachment.

Applying these principles, a President commits "high Crimes and Misdemeanors" when he abuses his office to substantially obstruct House impeachment investigators on matters that it deems pertinent to its inquiry, and does so without lawful cause or excuse.

D.   President Trump Has Committed "[H]igh Crimes and Misdemeanors"

1.   President Trump Substantially Obstructed the Impeachment Inquiry

The evidentiary record bearing on President Trump's obstruction of the House impeachment inquiry is set forth in the *Ukraine Report* and incorporated by reference here.[865] On the basis of that record, it is indisputable that President Trump substantially obstructed the House impeachment inquiry. The essential facts bearing on that judgment include the following:

- From September through November 2019, the Investigating Committees served subpoenas on numerous Executive Branch agencies, offices, and officials. These subpoenas sought evidence and testimony regarding President Trump's efforts to solicit and pressure the Government of Ukraine to announce investigations into former Vice President Joseph R. Biden and a discredited conspiracy theory alleging Ukrainian interference in the 2016 United States Presidential election.[866]

---

[864] *Id.* at 77.

[865] *Ukraine Report* at 201-260 & nn.1-441.

[866] *Id.* at 216-42.

- At the time the Investigating Committees served these subpoenas, and continually since then, they were acting pursuant to a House impeachment inquiry under Article I of the Constitution.[867]

- Even before the House launched its Ukraine inquiry, President Trump rejected the authority of Congress to investigate his actions, stating, "We're fighting all the subpoenas,"[868] and "I have an Article [II], where I have the right to do whatever I want as President."[869]

- Writing "on behalf of President Donald J. Trump," White House Counsel Pat A. Cipollone sent a letter to senior House officials on October 8, 2019, confirming that President Trump had directed his entire Administration to defy the impeachment inquiry. Mr. Cipollone wrote: "President Trump cannot permit his Administration to participate in this partisan inquiry under these circumstances."[870]

- Two days later, President Trump agreed that Mr. Cipollone was conveying the President's direction in the October 8 letter. President Trump stated: "As our brilliant White House Counsel wrote to the Democrats yesterday, he said their highly partisan and unconstitutional effort threatens grave and lasting damage to our democratic institutions, to our system of free elections, and to the American people. That's what it is. To the American people. It's so terrible. Democrats are on a crusade to destroy our democracy. That's what's happening. We will never let it happen. We will defeat them."[871]

- President Trump's direction was *categorical* and *indiscriminate*: he directed all agencies, offices, and officials not to cooperate with the impeachment inquiry. In other words, President Trump directed officials throughout the Executive Branch to violate their own independent legal obligations.

---

[867] *See supra* The Impeachment Inquiry.

[868] Jeremy Diamond & Allie Malloy, *Trump at war with Democrats: 'We're fighting all the subpoenas'*, CNN, Apr. 24, 2019.

[869] *Remarks by President Trump at Turning Point USA's Teen Student Action Summit 2019*, THE WHITE HOUSE, July 23, 2019.

[870] *Oct. 8 Cipollone Letter* at 1, 4.

[871] *Speech: Donald Trump Holds a Political Rally in Minneapolis, Minnesota*, FACTBASE VIDEOS, Oct. 10, 2019.

Consistent with these statements, President Trump never negotiated in good faith with the Investigating Committees. He simply made one demand after another—each of them unjustified as a matter of law—and asserted that he would completely blockade the Investigating Committees if they did not concede. By no definition of the term is that a good faith negotiation. As Chief Judge Beryl Howell has observed in a related context, "The reality is that DOJ and the White House have been openly stonewalling the House's efforts to get information by subpoena and by agreement, and the White House has flatly stated that the Administration will not cooperate with congressional requests for information." *In re Application of Comm. on Judiciary, U.S. House of Representatives, for an Order Authorizing Release of Certain Grand Jury Materials*, 2019 WL 5485221, at *36 (citing the *Oct. 8 Cipollone Letter*).

- President Trump's direction was *unprecedented*: no President has ever issued such direction—or anything even approximating it—in response to an impeachment inquiry.

- President Trump's direction had the natural and foreseeable consequence of obstructing—and did, in fact, obstruct—the House impeachment inquiry:

    o Defying a subpoena, the White House refused to produce any information or records to the Investigating Committees as part of this inquiry.[872]

    o Defying subpoenas, the Department of State, the Office of Management and Budget, the Department of Energy, and the Department of Defense refused to produce a single record to the Investigating Committees as part of this inquiry.[873]

    o Defying subpoenas, nine Administration officials refused to testify before the Investigating Committees, namely Mick Mulvaney (Acting White House Chief of Staff), Robert B. Blair (Assistant to the President and Senior Advisor to the Chief of Staff), John A. Eisenberg (Deputy Counsel to the President for National Security Affairs and Legal Advisor, National Security Council), Michael Ellis (Senior Associate Counsel to the President and Deputy Legal Advisor, National Security Council), Preston Wells Griffith (Senior Director for International Energy and Environment, National Security Council), Russell T. Vought (Acting Director, Office of Management and Budget), Michael Duffey (Associate Director for National Security Programs, Office of Management and Budget), Brian McCormack (Associate Director for Natural Resources, Energy, and Science, Office of Management and Budget, and former Chief of Staff to Secretary of Energy Rick Perry), and T. Ulrich Brechbuhl (Counselor, Department of State).[874]

- The Investigating Committees concluded—with ample reason—that this defiance of their subpoenas resulted in the denial of evidence relevant to the inquiry. Numerous witnesses identified specific relevant documents that have been withheld, and there is substantial evidence that officials who followed President Trump's direction not to appear could have offered testimony bearing on President Trump's course of conduct regarding Ukraine.[875]

---

[872] *See Ukraine Report* at 217. The White House has not produced a single document in response to the subpoena. Instead, it has released to the public only two documents: call records from the President's phone calls with President Zelensky on April 21 and July 25, 2019. The public release of a mere two documents comes nowhere close to satisfying President Trump's obligations, or to mitigating the sheer scope and scale of his Administration-wide obstruction of Congress.

[873] *See Ukraine Report* at 219-227.

[874] *See Ukraine Report* at 231-244. "In addition to the President's broad orders seeking to prohibit all Executive Branch employees from testifying, many of these witnesses were personally directed by senior political appointees not to cooperate with the House's impeachment inquiry. These directives frequently cited or enclosed copies of Mr. Cipollone's October 8 letter conveying the President's order not to comply." *Id.* at 31, 243.

[875] *See Ukraine Report* at 216-227, 229.

- President Trump lacked lawful cause or excuse for issuing his direction that all Executive Branch officials defy their legal obligations in response to Congressional subpoenas.[876]

Despite President Trump's direction that the Executive Branch blockade the impeachment inquiry, the Investigating Committees found clear and overwhelming evidence of his misconduct. This includes powerful direct evidence, strengthened and supported by compelling circumstantial evidence, of President Trump's course of conduct and corrupt motivations in soliciting and pressuring the Government of Ukraine to interfere in the 2020 Presidential election. Some of the evidence before the Committee consists of testimony from officials who properly complied with their Congressional subpoenas, notwithstanding the President's contrary direction.[877] In response to such testimony, President Trump used the world's most powerful bully pulpit to attack, threaten, and intimidate numerous witnesses and potential witnesses.[878]

Ultimately, as in President Nixon's case, House Committees have "been able to conduct an investigation and determine that grounds for impeachment exist—even in the face of the President's refusal to comply."[879] But here, as there, the President's obstruction of the House impeachment inquiry was not "without practical import."[880] It may have prevented the House from learning the full extent of the President's misdeeds.

The President thus inflicted concrete harm on the House, which is duty-bound to inquire when it has cause to believe the President may have committed "high Crimes and Misdemeanors." The House made that judgment here when evidence emerged that President Trump had solicited and pressured a foreign power to interfere in our elections for his own personal political benefit. To discharge its constitutional obligations, the House—acting through its Committees—pursued an impeachment inquiry and subpoenaed relevant Executive Branch agencies, offices, and officials. In seeking to thwart the House in the faithful performance of that constitutional function, President Trump committed a

---

[876] *See Ukraine Report* at 211-215.

[877] *See Watkins*, 354 U.S. at 187-88 ("It is unquestionably the duty of all citizens to cooperate with the Congress in its efforts to obtain the facts needed for intelligent legislative action. It is their unremitting obligation to respond to subpoenas, to respect the dignity of the Congress and its committees and to testify fully with respect to matters within the province of proper investigation.").

[878] *See Ukraine Report* at 255-60. The Minority's dissenting views on the nature of impeachable offenses consist almost exclusively of testimony by Professor Turley, who contends that the President did not obstruct the inquiry because "many officials opted to testify, despite the orders from the President that they should decline." Minority Views, *Constitutional Grounds for Impeachment* (2019), attaching Written Statement of Jonathan Turley, Dec. 4, 2019, at 42. This is a curious argument. When the House issues subpoenas in an impeachment inquiry and the President orders total defiance, it is hardly a point in the President's favor that a handful of his subordinates disobey that unlawful order (even as most officials comply, and even as all agencies and offices comply). Professor Turley further notes that the officials who violated President Trump's directive "remain in federal service in good standing." *Id.* But the fact that President Trump has not (yet) fired or disciplined the witnesses who came forward in no respect ameliorates his unlawful order. His attempts at thwarting their testimony is itself grounds for impeachment—and, significantly, he *succeeded* in substantially obstructing the House impeachment inquiry as to the strong majority of documents and testimony sought.

[879] *Committee Report on Nixon Articles of Impeachment* (1974 at 189.

[880] *Id.*

gross abuse of power. Most immediately, this abuse involved ordering the defiance of Congressional subpoenas. That stands as "an affront to the mechanism for curbing abuses of power that the Framers carefully crafted for our protection."[881]

More fundamentally, President Trump's direction to defy House subpoenas constituted an assault on the Impeachment Clause itself—and thus on our Constitution's final answer to corrupt Presidents. As explained above, the "sole Power of Impeachment" authorizes the House to review information that resides within the very branch of government it is empowered to scrutinize. By engaging in substantial obstruction of a House impeachment inquiry, the President could effectively seek to control a check on his own abuses. That is exactly what happened here.

In President Nixon's case, this Committee concluded that "[u]nless the defiance of the [House] subpoenas … is considered grounds for impeachment, it is difficult to conceive of any President acknowledging that he is obligated to supply the relevant evidence necessary for Congress to exercise its constitutional responsibility in an impeachment proceeding."[882] The same lesson applies now, but with exponentially greater force. President Nixon authorized other officials and agencies to honor their legal obligations.[883] He also turned over many of his own documents, failing only to respond fully to eight subpoenas.[884] President Trump, in contrast, directed his entire Administration—every agency, office, and official in the Executive Branch—not to cooperate with the impeachment inquiry, including by disobeying duly authorized subpoenas. If this does not qualify as impeachable obstruction of Congress, then nothing does, and the House will have sent a dangerous invitation to future Presidents to defy impeachment inquiries.

2. President Trump's Obstruction of Congress Lacked Lawful Cause or Excuse and Involved Recognizably Wrongful Conduct

President Trump and his lawyers have offered various arguments to justify the President's complete defiance of the House impeachment inquiry. Those arguments are indefensible as a matter of law and come nowhere close to excusing the President's unprecedented obstruction of Congress. They amount to a claim that the President has the power to dictate the terms on which he is investigated for "high Crimes and Misdemeanors"—a claim that is fundamentally at odds with the Constitution.

The President's excuses consist mainly of complaints about the procedures adopted by the House and its Committees. For example, the President asserts that the full House needed to vote to authorize the impeachment inquiry at an earlier date; that the Investigating Committees were required to afford him a broad array of rights to intervene and participate in their proceedings as they engaged in fact finding; that the Investigating Committees were forbidden to conduct portions of their fact-

[881] *McGahn*, 2019 WL 6312011, at *28 (D.D.C. Nov. 25, 2019), *appeal docketed*, No. 19-5331 (D.C. Cir. Nov. 26, 2019).

[882] *Nixon Impeachment Report* (1974), at 213.

[883] *The President's Remarks Announcing Developments and Procedures to be Followed in Connection with the Investigation*, THE WHITE HOUSE, Apr. 17, 1973 ("All members of the White House Staff will appear voluntarily when requested by the committee. They will testify under oath, and they will answer fully all proper questions.").

[884] *Committee Report on Nixon Articles of Impeachment (1974)* at 478-82.

finding investigations behind closed doors; that the Investigating Committees were required to allow agency attorneys to attend depositions; that the Minority was entitled to certain subpoena powers; and that the House engaged in "threats and intimidation" by informing Executive Branch subpoena recipients of the legal consequences of their failure to comply with duly authorized Congressional subpoenas.[885]

The President has asserted many procedural arguments, but they all fail for similar reasons. *First*, the House—not the President—has the "sole Power of Impeachment"[886] and the sole power "to determine the Rules of its Proceedings."[887] President Trump's process complaints thus concern matters entrusted to the *exclusive* discretion of the House. His disagreement with how the House has organized its hearings and carried out its investigations offers no excuse for breaking the law and directing others to do so. *Second*, as already described, impeachment proceedings are not criminal in character and involve only the charging-style decision on whether to accuse the President of "high Crimes and Misdemeanors."[888] Thus, although President Trump has described his demands as seeking "due process," none of these procedures are "due" to him under the Constitution here. *Third*, President Trump's demands have no basis in history or prior practice, which cut against him.[889] *Finally*, in passing H. Res. 660, the House implemented procedural protections for the President that exceed (or are consistent with) those afforded to Presidents Nixon and Clinton.[890] The fact that President Trump declined to take advantage of these protections does not excuse his across-the-board stonewalling of

---

[885] *See Oct. 8 Cipollone Letter*. President Trump also raised arguments relating to "confidentiality interests" and the so-called doctrine of "absolute immunity." *Id.*; *see also, e.g., McGahn*, 2019 WL 6312011, at *34-45. As to the first argument, "[t]here is no basis in the law of executive privilege for declaring a categorical refusal to respond to any House subpoena. In an impeachment inquiry the House's need for information and its Constitutional authority are at their greatest, and the Executive's interest in confidentiality must yield." *Ukraine Report*, at 214. Moreover, although executive privilege could not excuse or justify the President's categorical and indiscriminate defiance, it bears notice that the President has not actually asserted executive privilege in the House's impeachment inquiry. Turning to the second argument, the House has never recognized the fictional theory of "absolute immunity" as a valid ground for defying an impeachment inquiry, and every federal court to consider the doctrine of "absolute immunity" has rejected it. *See McGahn*, 2019 WL 6312011, at *45; *Comm. on Judiciary, U.S. House of Representatives v. Miers*, 558 F. Supp. 2d 135-36 (D.D.C. 2008). It is inconceivable that this doctrine has lurked, in hiding, for centuries as a hidden excuse for Presidents to block untold numbers of current and former Executive Branch officials from giving any testimony whatsoever to the House. In any event, President Trump's direction that the Executive Branch undertake a total blockade of the House impeachment inquiry extends well beyond even the most extreme view of "absolute immunity," and so this doctrine neither excuses nor explains the President's position as articulated in Mr. Cipollone's letter.

[886] U.S. CONST. art. I, § 2.

[887] *Id.* at § 5.

[888] *See supra* The Impeachment Inquiry.

[889] *See supra* The Impeachment Inquiry.

[890] *See supra* The Impeachment Inquiry.

the House.[891]

President Trump's remaining arguments fare no better. Through Mr. Cipollone's letter, he asserts the prerogative to defy all House subpoenas because he has unilaterally decided that he did not do anything wrong.[892] He adds that the House must be acting with "partisan" and "illegitimate" motives.[893] Notably, the President did not simply make these points at a press conference or on Twitter. He had the White House Counsel include them in a letter to the House as part of his formal legal basis for directing obstruction of the House impeachment inquiry.[894]

To state the obvious, a President cannot obstruct a House impeachment inquiry because he believes his conduct was proper and sees no need for his acts to be investigated. Nor can he do so by impugning the House's motives or attacking its legitimacy. Once again, the Constitution vests the House with the "sole Power of Impeachment." These are judgments for the House alone to make, guided always by the Constitution. Otherwise, in contravention of the entire Anglo-American legal tradition, Presidents would truly be the judge of their own case.[895] That is why the Framers gave the impeachment power to Congress, not the President, and it is why the House and Senate, respectively, have "sole Power" to impeach and to adjudicate articles of impeachment.[896]

On this score, the Supreme Court's decision in *Walter Nixon v. United States* is instructive: "Judicial involvement in impeachment proceedings, even if only for purposes of judicial review, is counterintuitive because it would eviscerate the important constitutional check placed on the Judiciary by the Framers. [Judge] Nixon's argument would place final reviewing authority with respect to impeachments in the hands of the same body that the impeachment process is meant to regulate."[897] In

---

[891] President Trump's process objections are addressed individually, and at much greater length, in the *Ukraine Report*. We incorporate its reasoning and conclusions by reference. The October 8 letter from Mr. Cipollone raises two additional arguments, both of which fail for the reasons set forth above. First, the President cannot defy an impeachment inquiry just because he concludes that the minority has not been afforded sufficient subpoena rights in House committees; the House has both the "sole Power of Impeachment" and the sole power to "determine the Rules of its Proceedings." Nor can the President ignore Congressional subpoenas, or direct others to do so, by complaining that the House has informed subpoena recipients that it will treat non-compliance as evidence of obstruction. The House does not somehow forfeit its "sole Power of Impeachment" by pointing out that unlawful defiance of its duly-authorized Congressional subpoenas may have legal consequences or bear on the impeachment inquiry.

[892] *See Oct. 8 Cipollone Letter* at 6 ("It is transparent that you have resorted to such unprecedented and unconstitutional procedures because you know that a fair process would expose the lack of any basis for your inquiry. Your current effort is founded on a completely appropriate call on July 25, 2019, between President Trump and President Zelenskyy of Ukraine [. . .] That record clearly established that the call was completely appropriate, that the President did nothing wrong, and that there is no basis for an impeachment inquiry.").

[893] *Oct. 8 Cipollone Letter* at 7, 8.

[894] *See id.* at 5 ("In fact, your transparent rush to judgment, lack of democratically accountable authorization, and violation of basic rights in the current proceedings make clear the illegitimate, partisan purpose of this purported 'impeachment inquiry.'"); *see also* To End A Presidency at 64-66.

[895] *See Dr. Bonham's Case*, 8 Co. Rep. 114a, 118b, 77 Eng. Rep. 638, 654 (1610) (Coke, C.J.).

[896] U.S. CONST. art. I, §§ 2, 3.

[897] *Nixon v. United States*, 506 U.S. 224, 235 (1993) (quotation marks and citation omitted).

practice, President Trump would do what the Supreme Court has clearly warned against: place vital constitutional judgments about exercises of the impeachment power "in the hands of the same [President] that the impeachment process is meant to regulate."[898] Thus, while President Trump merely erred in asserting that the impeachment inquiry was unfounded, partisan, and "illegitimate," he moved from error to "high Crimes and Misdemeanors" in declaring that his self-determined innocence somehow justifies his scorched-earth obstruction campaign.

Throughout our history, impeachments—particularly of Presidents—have been rare. Moreover, in Judge Walter Nixon's case, the Supreme Court made clear its extreme wariness of intruding on powers of impeachment entrusted solely to Congress. As a result, impeachment proceedings against a President will inevitably raise questions of constitutional law that have not been definitively, specifically resolved by judicial precedent or past practice of the House. This leaves room for inter-branch negotiation. But it does not allow the President to seize on specious arguments, cobble them together, and use them in an effort to justify the unjustifiable: a Presidential direction that all House subpoenas be entirely defied under all circumstances. Such unyielding Presidential obstruction of an impeachment inquiry is plainly wrong. When the House investigates impeachable offenses, the President cannot cover up his misconduct by holding hostage all evidence contained within the Executive Branch. The Judiciary Committee made this clear in President Nixon's case and reaffirms that principle today.

Simply put, there are lines that a President cannot cross in an impeachment inquiry. Those lines exist to ensure that the Impeachment Clause can serve its fundamental purpose as a safeguard for the people of the United States. In comprehensively obstructing this House impeachment inquiry, President Trump crossed every one of these lines. He did so without any valid cause or excuse. He must therefore be impeached, lest future Presidents follow his example and persist in corruption, oppression, and abuse of power with little risk of discovery or accountability.

3.   Judicial Review is Unnecessary and Impractical Here

It has been suggested that the House cannot impeach President Trump for obstruction of Congress without seeking judicial enforcement of the subpoenas that he has ordered be defied. This claim is mistaken as a matter of constitutional law, precedent, and common sense.

As already explained, the Constitution vests the House—rather than the President or Judiciary—with "the sole Power of Impeachment." That "sole Power" includes the investigatory powers that the House has invoked in serving subpoenas as part of the current impeachment inquiry. This Committee therefore concluded in President Nixon's case that it would frustrate the constitutional plan for the House to depend entirely on the Judiciary to enforce subpoenas in impeachment proceedings.[899]   That would risk making the House subservient to courts in matters where the

---

[898] *Cf. id.*

[899] *Committee Report on Nixon Articles of Impeachment* (1974) at 210-212.

Constitution gives the House the final word.[900] It would also raise complexities in the case of a President who directed Executive Branch officials to defy House subpoenas—and then used his pardon power to immunize them from contempt orders if instructed by the Judiciary to honor those subpoenas.[901]

To be sure, judicial review may at first blush seem desirable because "it would be an independent determination by an entity with no interest in the proceedings."[902] But as this Committee has noted: "[T]he impeachment process itself provides an opportunity for such a determination— initially by the House in deciding whether to prosecute the Article of Impeachment, and, ultimately, by the Senate, the tribunal for an impeachment trial. Neither the Committee nor the House would be the final judge of the validity of the Committee's subpoenas. Whether noncompliance with the subpoenas is a ground for impeachment would ultimately be adjudicated in the Senate."[903]

Consistent with this understanding of the constitutional plan, the House has *never* before relied on litigation to compel witness testimony or the production of documents in a Presidential impeachment proceeding.[904] Some members of the Minority have suggested otherwise, but there is no law or practice to support such a theory.[905] As explained above, the history of House impeachment inquiries teaches a single lesson: compliance with subpoenas is the rule, defiance the exceedingly rare (and impeachable) exception. No President has ever issued a blanket ban on compliance with House subpoenas and challenged the House to find a way around his unlawful order. Under these strange and unprecedented circumstances, it is appropriate for the House to reach its own independent judgment that the President is obstructing the exercise of its constitutional impeachment power, rather than seeking judicial review.

Indeed, whereas the Minority suggests that recourse to litigation is *required*, President Trump has repeatedly argued that the House is *forbidden* to seek judicial enforcement of its subpoenas. In pending lawsuits filed by the House or its Committees, the Justice Department has raised jurisdictional arguments on behalf of President Trump that, if accepted, would hamper or negate the House's ability to enforce subpoenas in court.[906] Those arguments are mistaken and have already been rejected several

---

[900] *Id.* at 210 ("The Committee concluded that it would be inappropriate to seek the aid of the courts to enforce its subpoenas against the President. This conclusion is based on the constitutional provision vesting the power of impeachment solely in the House of Representatives and the express denial by the Framers of the Constitution of any role for the courts in the impeachment process.").

[901] *See id.* at 212.

[902] *Id.* at 212.

[903] *Id.*

[904] In President Nixon's case, the Special Prosecutor subpoenaed certain Oval Office tape recordings and then litigated the President's failure to comply with the subpoena. *See United States v. Nixon*, 418 U.S. 683, 686 (1974). The Judiciary Committee did not file suit when the President failed to comply fully with its own subpoenas.

[905] *H. Res. 755, Articles of Impeachment Against President Donald J. Trump: Markup Before the H. Comm. on the Judiciary*, 116th Cong. (2019) (Statement of Rep. James Sensenbrenner).

[906] Brief for Defendant-Appellant at 14-47, *Comm. on the Judiciary, U.S. House of Representatives v. Donald F. McGahn II*, No. 19-5331 (D.C. Cir. filed Dec. 9, 2019) (arguing courts lack jurisdiction to adjudicate subpoena enforcement suits by the House and that the House is not even injured for purposes of Article III standing when Executive Branch officials defy subpoenas); Memorandum of Points and Authorities in Support of Defendants' and Defendants-Intervenors' Motion

times,[907] but reflect the President's sustained and unwavering view that it is legally impermissible for the House to obtain judicial relief. Where the President orders total defiance of House subpoenas and vigorously argues that the courthouse door is locked, it is clear that he seeks to obstruct the House in the exercise of its impeachment power.

This conclusion comports with common sense. The President is under investigation for soliciting and pressuring a foreign power to interfere in an election that is less than a year away. The House has already received compelling evidence of his misconduct. Waiting any longer would thus be an abdication of duty—particularly given the extreme implausibility that litigation would soon bring new evidence to light. Consider three lawsuits filed by House Committees over the past two decades seeking to enforce subpoenas against senior Executive Branch officials:

- In *Committee on the Judiciary v. Miers*, this Committee sought to enforce a subpoena requiring former White House Counsel Harriet Miers to give testimony about the contentious firing of nine United States Attorneys. The Committee served that subpoena in June 2007, filed suit in March 2008, and won a favorable district court order in July 2008, but did not receive testimony from Miers until June 2009 due to the entry of a stay by the Court of Appeals and further negotiations between the parties.[908]
- In *Committee on Oversight and Reform v. Holder*, the Committee on Oversight and Reform (COR) sought to compel Attorney General Eric Holder to produce documents relating to Operation Fast and Furious. The committee served that subpoena in October 2011 and filed suit in August 2012. It then won a series of orders requiring the production of documents, but the first such order did not issue until August 2014.[909]
- In *Committee on the Judiciary v. McGahn*, this Committee seeks to enforce a subpoena requiring White House Counsel Donald F. McGahn II to give testimony regarding matters relating to the Special Counsel's investigation. The Committee served that subpoena in April 2019, filed suit in August 2019, and won a favorable district court order in November 2019, but the Court of Appeals has stayed that ruling and will not hear oral argument until January 2020.[910]

---

to Dismiss, *Comm. on Ways and Means, U.S. House of Representatives v. Dep't of Treasury*, No. 19 Civ. 1974 (D.D.C. filed Sept. 6, 2019).

[907] *See, e.g., United States v. Am. Tel. & Tel. Co.*, 551 F.2d 384, 391 (D.C. Cir. 1976) ("the House as a whole has standing to assert its investigatory power"); *McGahn*, 2019 WL 6312011 at *16-34 (D.D.C. Nov. 25, 2019) (rejecting DOJ's jurisdictional arguments); *Comm. on Oversight & Gov't Reform v. Holder*, 979 F. Supp. 2d 1 (D.D.C. 2013) (same); *Miers*, 558 F. Supp. 2d at 65-99 (same).

[908] *See Miers*, 558 F. Supp. 2d 53 (D.D.C. July 31, 2008) (holding Miers was required to testify); 542 F.3d 909 (D.C. Cir. Oct. 6, 2008) (staying decision pending appeal); Unopposed Motion for Voluntary Dismissal by Plaintiff at 3, *Miers* (D.D.C. filed Oct. 22, 2009) (Miers testified in a transcribed interview in June 2009).

[909] The district court rejected DOJ's motion to dismiss in September 2013, *see Holder*, 979 F. Supp. 2d 1; ordered production only of documents for which DOJ did not assert any privileges in August 2014, *see* 2014 WL 12662665 (D.D.C. Aug. 20, 2014); and did not order production of additional documents until January 2016, *see* 156 F. Supp. 3d 101 (D.D.C. Jan. 19, 2016).

[910] *McGahn*, 2019 WL 6312011; *see id.* at *4-6 (describing case history); *see* Order, No. 19-5331 (D.C. Cir. Nov. 27, 2019) (entering "administrative stay" and scheduling argument in January).

Even when the House urges expedition, it usually takes years—not months—to obtain documents or testimony through judicial subpoena enforcement proceedings. It would be unwise, indeed dangerous, to allow Presidents to defy all subpoenas in an impeachment inquiry and then assert that the House cannot impeach without exhausting judicial remedies. Particularly in a case like this one, where the President's misconduct is a constitutional crime in progress, waiting for the courts is the practical equivalent of inaction. This Committee will not stand idly by while the President abuses power by asking and pressuring foreign powers to corrupt the upcoming election.

4.   President Trump Poses a Continuing Threat if Left in Office

Impeachment exists "not to inflict personal punishment for past wrongdoing, but rather to protect against future Presidential misconduct that would endanger democracy and the rule of law."[911] By virtue of the conduct encompassed by Article II, President Trump "has demonstrated that he will remain a threat to the Constitution if allowed to remain in office, and has acted in a manner grossly incompatible with self-governance and the rule of law."[912] That is true in at least three respects: *first*, he has debased the impeachment remedy; *second*, he has broadly argued that no government entity in the United States has the legal power to investigate his official misconduct except on terms of his choosing; and *third*, his obstruction reflects a pattern of misconduct.

a.   Debasement of the Impeachment Remedy

The impeachment power exists for a reason. It is the Framers' final and most definitive answer to a fundamental question: "Shall any man be above Justice?"[913] Urging the necessity of allowing impeachments, Elbridge T. Gerry thus emphasized: "A good magistrate will not fear them. A bad one ought to be kept in fear of them."[914] In *Federalist Papers No. 69*, Alexander Hamilton affirmed that the Impeachment Clause separates Presidents from kings and khans.[915] Where a President abuses his power, betrays the public through foreign entanglements, or corrupts his office or elections, impeachment is our Nation's last line of defense against conduct "fatal to the Republic."[916] It was partly by virtue of this limit on malfeasance that the Framers entrusted Presidents with sweeping executive authority. A President who seeks to sabotage the impeachment power thus disorders our system of checks and balances, tilting it toward executive tyranny.

That is what President Trump did here. The point bears repetition: his conduct is unlike anything this Nation has ever seen. Other Presidents have disapproved of impeachments. Other Presidents have criticized the House and doubted its motives. Other Presidents have insisted they did nothing wrong.

---

[911] *Constitutional Grounds for Impeachment* (2019) at 10.

[912] H. Res. 755, 116th Cong. Art. II. (2019).

[913] 2 Farrand, *Records of the Federal Convention* at 65 (George Mason).

[914] *Id.* at 66 (Elbridge Gerry).

[915] THE FEDERALIST NO. 69 at 444-45 (Alexander Hamilton) (Benjamin Fletcher Wright ed. 1961).

[916] 2 Farrand, *Records of the Federal Convention* at 66 (James Madison).

But no President before this one has declared himself and his entire branch of government exempt from subpoenas issued by the House under its "sole Power of Impeachment." No President has made compliance with his every demand a condition of even considering whether to honor subpoenas. No President has directed his senior officials to violate their own legal obligations because an impeachment was "illegitimate." Indeed, every President in our Nation's history but one has done the opposite—and that President, Richard M. Nixon, faced an article of impeachment in this Committee for withholding key evidence from the House.

b.   Denial of Any Mechanism of Legal Oversight or Accountability

Approval of the Second Article of Impeachment is further supported by President Trump's apparent view that nobody in the United States government has the lawful authority to investigate any misconduct in which he engages. This view is evident in the legal positions he has taken while in office. To start, President Trump maintains that he is completely immune from criminal indictment and prosecution while serving as President.[917] He also claims that he cannot be investigated—under any circumstance—by state or federal law enforcement while in office.[918] He asserts the authority to terminate and control federal law enforcement investigations for any reason (or none at all), including when he is the subject of an investigation.[919] He insists that unfounded doctrines, such as absolute immunity, preclude testimony by many current and former officials who might shed light on any Presidential abuses.[920] He defies binding Congressional subpoenas on topics of national importance based on his own determination that they lack a legitimate purpose,[921] and then he sues to block third

---

[917] Memorandum of Law in Support of Plaintiff's Emergency Motion For a Temporary Restraining Order and a Preliminary Injunction, *Trump v. Vance, Jr.* No. 19 Civ. 08694, 2019 WL 5557333 (S.D.N.Y Sept. 20, 2019) ("Under Article II, the Supremacy Clause, and the structure of our Constitution, the President of the United States cannot be 'subject to the criminal process' while he is in office."); Ann E. Marimow & Jonathan O'Connell, *In Court Hearing, Trump Lawyer Argues a Sitting President Would be Immune from Prosecution Even If He Were to Shoot Someone*, WASH. POST, Oct. 23, 2019.

[918] *Trump v. Vance*, 941 F.3d 631, 640 (2d Cir. 2019) ("The President relies on what he described at oral argument as 'temporary absolute presidential immunity' – he argues that he is absolutely immune from all stages of state criminal process while in office, including pre-indictment investigation . . . .").

[919] Letter from John M. Dowd & Jay A. Sekulow to Robert S. Mueller, III (Jan. 29, 2018) ("It remains our position that the President's actions here, by virtue of his position as the chief law enforcement officer, could neither constitutionally nor legally constitute obstruction because that would amount to him obstructing himself, and that he could, if he wished, terminate the inquiry, or even exercise his power to pardon if he so desired.").

[920] *McGahn*, 2019 WL 6312011 at *34 ("DOJ asserts that current and former senior-level presidential aides have 'absolute testimonial immunity' from compelled congressional process, as a matter of law; therefore, if the President invokes 'executive privilege' over a current or former aides' testimony—as he has done with respect to McGahn—that aide need not accede to the lawful demands of Congress."). *See also, e.g., Ukraine Report* at 230 (President Trump ordered Acting Chief of Staff Mick Mulvaney to defy a subpoena for his testimony on grounds of "absolute immunity"); *id.* at 231 (same, with respect to White House advisor Robert Blair); *id.* at 232 (same, with respect to Deputy Counsel to the President for National Security Affairs John Eisenberg).

[921] *See Oct. 8 Cipollone Letter* at 2. *See also, e.g., Congressional Committee's Request for the President's Tax Returns*, 43 Op. O.L.C. __, 2019 WL 2563046 (supporting Department of the Treasury's decision to override plain statutory text requiring disclosure of the President's tax returns based on purported absence of a "legitimate legislative purpose").

parties from complying with such subpoenas.[922] Even as he pursues his own interests in court, his administration simultaneously argues that Congress is barred from obtaining judicial enforcement when Executive Branch officials disregard its subpoenas.[923]

Perhaps most remarkably, President Trump claims that the House cannot investigate his misconduct outside of an impeachment inquiry[924]—but also claims that it cannot investigate his misconduct as part of an impeachment inquiry if he deems it "illegitimate."[925] And an inquiry ranks as "illegitimate," in President Trump's view, if he thinks he did nothing wrong, doubts the motives of the House, or prefers a different set of Committee procedures. It is not hyperbole to describe this reasoning as better suited to George Orwell or Franz Kafka than the Office of the President.

Viewed in their totality, President Trump's positions amount to an insistence that he is above the law; that there is no governmental entity in the United States outside his direct control that can investigate him for official misconduct and hold him accountable for any wrongdoing. Even the House, wielding one of the mightiest powers in the Constitution—a power that exists *specifically* to address a rogue President—has no authority at all to investigate his official acts if he decides otherwise.

That is not our law. It never has been. The President is a constitutional officer. Unlike a despot, he answers to a higher legal authority. It is disconcerting enough that the President has attacked and resisted the House's explicit oversight authority in unprecedented ways. But it is worse, much worse, that he now claims the further prerogative to ignore a House impeachment inquiry.[926] The continuing threat posed by President Trump's conduct, as set forth in the Second Article of Impeachment, is thus exacerbated by his public and legal assertions that it is illegitimate and unlawful for anyone to

---

[922] *See, e.g., Mazars*, 940 F.3d at 717; *Trump v. Deutsche Bank AG*, -- F.3d --, 2019 WL 6482561 at *2 (2d Cir. Dec. 3, 2019).

[923] *McGahn*, 2019 WL 6312011, at *26 ("Here, as in *Miers*, DOJ attempts to shoehorn its emasculating effort to keep House committees from turning to the courts as a means of vindicating their constitutional interests into various categories of established legal arguments, some of which overlap substantially with jurisdictional contentions that the Court has already considered and rejected."). *Compare* Memorandum of Points and Authorities in Support of Defendants' and Defendant-Intervenors' Motion to Dismiss at 13, *Comm. on Ways and Means, U.S. House of Representatives v. Dep't of Treasury*, No. 19 Civ. 01974 (D.D.C. filed Sept. 6, 2019) (warning against "[t]he exertion of Federal judicial power to declare victors in inter-branch disputes of this nature"), *with* Brief for the United States as Amicus Curiae at 2, *Trump v. Deutsche Bank*, No. 19-1540 (2d Cir. filed Aug. 19, 2019) (encouraging the court to "engage in a searching evaluation of subpoenas directed at the President").

[924] *Mazars*, 940 F.3d at 750 (quoting DOJ's brief, "The House's impeachment power is an express authority whose exercise does not require a connection to valid legislation. But the Committee has asserted neither jurisdiction over, nor an objective of pursuing impeachment.").

[925] *Oct. 8 Cipollone Letter* at 8 ("For the foregoing reasons, the President cannot allow your constitutionally illegitimate proceedings to distract him and those in the Executive Branch from their work on behalf of the American people.").

[926] The President has accompanied this conduct with a series of public statements advocating the view that it is illegitimate for the House to investigate him. *See Ukraine Report* at 28-29 ("He has publicly and repeatedly rejected the authority of Congress to conduct oversight of his actions and has directly challenged the authority of the House to conduct an impeachment inquiry into his actions regarding Ukraine . . . . [President Trump's] rhetorical attacks appeared intended not just to dispute public reports of his misconduct, but to persuade the American public that the House lacks authority to investigate the President.").

investigate him for abuse of office except on his own terms.

c.   Consistency with Previous Conduct

The Second Article of Impeachment impeaches President Trump for obstructing Congress with respect to the House impeachment inquiry relating to Ukraine. Yet, as noted in that Article, President Trump's obstruction of that investigation is "consistent with [his] previous efforts to undermine United States Government investigations into foreign interference in United States elections."[927] An understanding of those previous efforts, and the pattern of misconduct they represent, sheds light on the particular conduct set forth in that Article as sufficient grounds for the impeachment of President Trump.[928]

These previous efforts include, but are not limited to, President Trump's endeavor to impede the Special Counsel's investigation into Russian interference with the 2016 United States Presidential election, as well as President Trump's sustained efforts to obstruct the Special Counsel after learning that he was under investigation for obstruction of justice.[929] There can be no serious doubt that the Special Counsel's investigation addressed an issue of extraordinary importance to our national security and democracy. As the Special Counsel concluded, "[t]he Russian government interfered in the 2016 presidential election in sweeping and systematic fashion."[930] This assessment accords with the consensus view of the United States intelligence community.[931]

Ultimately, although the Special Counsel "did not establish that members of the Trump Campaign conspired or coordinated with the Russian government in its election interference activities," he did conclude that "the Russian government perceived it would benefit from a Trump presidency and worked to secure that outcome, and that the Campaign expected it would benefit electorally from information stolen and released through Russian efforts."[932] Yet there is no indication in the Special Counsel's report that anyone from the Trump Campaign, including President Trump, reported to law enforcement any contacts or offers of foreign assistance. Instead, President Trump openly welcomed

---

[927] H. Res. 755, 116th Cong. Art. II (2019).

[928] This Committee has undertaken an investigation relating to the Special Counsel's report. That includes inquiring into President Trump's obstruction of the Special Counsel, as well as a review of other aspects of the Special Counsel's underlying work that the President obstructed. As part of this investigation, the Committee has sought to compel testimony by former White House Counsel Donald F. McGahn II, and to review certain grand jury materials relating to the Special Counsel's report. Should the Committee obtain the information, it would be utilized, among other purposes, in a Senate trial on these articles of impeachment, if any. The Committee, moreover, has continued and will continue those investigations consistent with its own prior statements respecting their importance and purposes.

[929] *See generally* Special Counsel Robert S. Mueller, III, *Report On The Investigation Into Russian Interference In The 2016 Presidential Election*, Vols. I and II (March 2019) (hereinafter, "*Mueller Report*").

[930] *Mueller Report* Vol. I at 1.

[931] *Ukraine Report* at 13 ("[T]he U.S. Intelligence Community had unanimously determined that Russia, not Ukraine, interfered in the 2016 election to help the candidacy of Donald Trump.").

[932] *Mueller Report* Vol. I at 5.

and invited Russian interference in the election.[933]

Rather than aid the Special Counsel's investigation into Russian interference, President Trump sought to thwart it—and used the powers of his office as part of that scheme.[934] Most notably, after learning that he was himself under investigation, President Trump among other things ordered the firing of the Special Counsel,[935] sought to curtail the Special Counsel's investigation in a manner exempting his own prior conduct,[936] instructed the White House Counsel to create a false record and make false public statements,[937] and tampered with at least two key witnesses in the Special Counsel's investigation.[938] Based on the Special Counsel's report, these acts were obstructive in nature, and there is evidence strongly supporting that President Trump acted with the improper (and criminal) purpose of avoiding potential liability and concealing information that he viewed as personally and politically damaging.[939]

The pattern is as unmistakable as it is unnerving. There, President Trump welcomed and invited a foreign nation to interfere in a United States Presidential election to his advantage; here, President Trump solicited and pressured a foreign nation to do so. There, Executive Branch law enforcement investigated; here, the House impeachment inquiry investigated. There, President Trump used the powers of his office to obstruct and seek to fire the Special Counsel; here, President Trump used the powers of his office to obstruct and embargo the House impeachment inquiry. There, while obstructing investigators, the President stated that he remained free to invite foreign interference in our elections; here, while obstructing investigators, President Trump in fact invited additional foreign interference. Indeed, President Trump placed his fateful July 25 call to President Zelensky just one day after the Special Counsel testified in Congress about his findings.

Viewed in this frame, it is apparent that President Trump sees no barrier to inviting (or inducing) foreign interference in our elections, using the powers of his office to obstruct anyone who dares to investigate such misconduct, and engaging in the same conduct with impunity all over again. Although the Second Article of Impeachment focuses on President Trump's categorical and indiscriminate obstruction of the House impeachment inquiry, the consistency of this obstruction with his broader pattern of misconduct is relevant and striking.[940]

---

[933] *See generally Mueller Report* Vol. II.

[934] *See id.*

[935] *See id.* at 77-90.

[936] *See id.* at 90-98.

[937] *See id.* at 113-20.

[938] *See id.* at 120-56.

[939] *See id.* at 87-90, 97-98, 118-20, 131-33, 153-56.

[940] The same point applies to President Trump's unjustified and improper obstruction of this Committee's efforts to investigate the evidence bearing on the question of whether President Trump committed obstruction of justice in his efforts to undermine the Special Counsel's investigation. *See, e.g., Nadler Statement on White House Obstruction of Dearborn, Porter & Lewandowski Testimony*, HOUSE COMMITTEE ON THE JUDICIARY, Sept. 16, 2019 (addressing White House obstruction of witness testimony on grounds of "absolute immunity"). Of course, several matters relating to that issue are

IV. Conclusion

As the Investigating Committees concluded, "it would be hard to imagine a stronger or more complete case of obstruction than that demonstrated by the President since the [impeachment] inquiry began."[941] In the history of our Republic, no President has obstructed Congress like President Trump. If President Nixon's obstruction of Congress raised a slippery slope concern, we now find ourselves at the bottom of the slope, surveying the damage to our Constitution.

That damage is extraordinary. As explained above, and as set forth in Article II, President Trump has "sought to arrogate to himself the right to determine the propriety, scope, and nature of an impeachment inquiry into his own conduct, as well as the unilateral prerogative to deny any and all information to the House of Representatives in the exercise of its 'sole Power of Impeachment.'"[942] This abuse of the Presidential office, moreover, "served to cover up the President's own repeated misconduct and to seize and control the power of impeachment—and thus to nullify a vital constitutional safeguard vested solely in the House of Representatives."[943] If President Trump is left unchecked, we will send an alarming message to future Presidents.

In word and deed, President Trump has sought to write the Impeachment Clause out of the Constitution. If his excuses for that conduct are accepted, then every future President can choose to ignore House subpoenas, and a bulwark against tyranny will be undone. This time, courageous and patriotic public servants defied the President's direction and offered testimony about his corrupt solicitation and inducement of foreign interference in our elections. Next time, we may not be so fortunate, and a President may perpetrate abuses that remain unknown or unprovable. That is exactly what the Framers feared most as they designed the Office of the President. It is what they warned against in their deliberations, and what they sought to prevent by authorizing impeachments. We are the inheritors of that legacy—of a Republic, if we can keep it.

---

currently pending before the courts. *See, e.g., McGahn*, 2019 WL 6312011, at *28 (D.D.C. Nov. 25, 2019), *appeal docketed*, No. 19-5331 (D.C. Cir. Nov. 26, 2019).

[941] *Ukraine Report* at 9.

[942] H. Res. 755, 116th Cong. Art. II (2019).

[943] *Id.*

HEARINGS

For the purposes of section 103(i) of H. Res. 6 of the 116th Congress and pursuant to H. Res. 660, the following hearings were used to develop H. Res. 755:

1. "The Impeachment Inquiry into President Donald J. Trump: Constitutional Grounds for Presidential Impeachment," held before the Judiciary Committee on December 4, 2019. During this hearing, the Committee heard testimony from: Noah Feldman, Felix Frankfurter Professor of Law and Director, Julis-Rabinowitz Program on Jewish and Israeli Law at Harvard Law School; Pamela S. Karlan, Kenneth and Harle Montgomery Professor of Public Interest Law and Co-Director, Supreme Court Litigation Clinic at Stanford Law School; Michael Gerhardt, Burton Craige Distinguished Professor of Jurisprudence at the University of North Carolina School of Law; and Jonathan Turley, J.B. and Maurice C. Shapiro Professor of Public Interest Law at the George Washington University Law School. In this hearing, the witnesses testified on the permissible grounds for presidential impeachment.

2. "The Impeachment Inquiry into President Donald J. Trump: Presentations from the House Permanent Select Committee on Intelligence and House Judiciary Committee," held before the Judiciary Committee on December 9, 2019. During this hearing, the Committee heard presentations from: Barry Berke, Majority Counsel for the House Committee on the Judiciary; Daniel Goldman, Majority Counsel for the House Permanent Select Committee on Intelligence; and Stephen Castor Minority Counsel for the House Committee on the Judiciary and the House Permanent Select Committee on Intelligence. Pursuant to H. Res. 660, in this hearing, Majority and Minority Counsels for the House Committee on the Judiciary presented

opening statements, followed by presentations of evidence from Majority and Minority

Counsels for the House Permanent Select Committee on Intelligence.

COMMITTEE CONSIDERATION

On December 11, 12, and 13, 2019, the Committee met in open session to consider H. Res.

755. On December 13, the Committee ordered the resolution favorably reported to the House with

an amendment. Pursuant to clause 5 of Rule XVI, the vote on reporting the resolution was divided

into separate votes on the articles. The Committee approved Article I (abuse of power) by a rollcall

vote of 23 to 17 and it approved Article II (obstruction of Congress) by a rollcall vote of 23 to 17, in

each case a quorum being present.

COMMITTEE VOTES

In compliance with clause 3(b) of rule XIII of the Rules of the House of Representatives, the

Committee advises that the following rollcall votes occurred during the Committee's consideration H.

Res. 755:

1.   A motion by Ms. Lofgren to lay on the table Mr. Collins' appeal of the ruling of the

chair that the Committee was not required to hold a minority hearing day before considering

articles of impeachment, was agreed to by a vote of 23 to 17.

Roll Call No. 1

Date: 12/12/19

COMMITTEE ON THE JUDICIARY
House of Representatives
116th Congress

Subject: Motion to table

	AYES	NOS	PRES.	
Jerrold Nadler (NY-10)	✓			
Zoe Lofgren (CA-19)	✓			
Sheila Jackson Lee (TX-18)	✓			
Steve Cohen (TN-09)	✓			
Hank Johnson (GA-04)	✓			
Ted Deutch (FL-22)	✓			
Karen Bass (CA-37)	✓			
Cedric Richmond (LA-02)	✓			
Hakeem Jeffries (NY-08)	✓			
David Cicilline (RI-01)	✓			
Eric Swalwell (CA-15)	✓			
Ted Lieu (CA-33)				
Jamie Raskin (MD-08)	✓			
Pramila Jayapal (WA-07)	✓			
Val Demings (FL-10)	✓			
Lou Correa (CA-46)	✓			
Mary Gay Scanlon (PA-05)	✓			
Sylvia Garcia (TX-29)	✓			
Joseph Neguse (CO-02)	✓			
Lucy McBath (GA-06)	✓			
Greg Stanton (AZ-09)	✓			
Madeleine Dean (PA-04)	✓			
Debbie Mucarsel-Powell (FL-26)	✓			
Veronica Escobar (TX-16)	✓			
	AYES	NOS	PRES	
Doug Collins (GA-27)		✓		
James F. Sensenbrenner (WI-05)		✓		
Steve Chabot (OH-01)		✓		
Louie Gohmert (TX-01)		✓		
Jim Jordan (OH-04)		✓		
Ken Buck (CO-04)		✓		
John Ratcliffe (TX-04)		✓		
Martha Roby (AL-02)		✓		
Matt Gaetz (FL-01)		✓		
Mike Johnson (LA-04)		✓		
Andy Biggs (AZ-05)		✓		
Tom McClintock (CA-04)		✓		
Debbie Lesko (AZ-08)		✓		
Guy Reschenthaler (PA-14)		✓		
Ben Cline (VA-06)		✓		
Kelly Armstrong (ND-AL)		✓		
Greg Steube (FL-17)		✓		
	AYES	NOS	PRES.	
TOTAL	23	17		

☑ PASSED

☐ FAILED

2. An amendment by Mr. Jordan to strike article I from the resolution, was defeated by a rollcall vote of 17 to 23.

Roll Call No. 2

Date: 12/12/19

COMMITTEE ON THE JUDICIARY
House of Representatives
116th Congress

Amendment # 1 ( ) to ANS H RES 755 offered by Rep. Jordan

	AYES	NOS	PRES.
Jerrold Nadler (NY-10)		✓	
Zoe Lofgren (CA-19)		✓	
Sheila Jackson Lee (TX-18)		✓	
Steve Cohen (TN-09)		✓	
Hank Johnson (GA-04)		✓	
Ted Deutch (FL-22)		✓	
Karen Bass (CA-37)		✓	
Cedric Richmond (LA-02)		✓	
Hakeem Jeffries (NY-08)		✓	
David Cicilline (RI-01)		✓	
Eric Swalwell (CA-15)		✓	
Ted Lieu (CA-33)			
Jamie Raskin (MD-08)		✓	
Pramila Jayapal (WA-07)		✓	
Val Demings (FL-10)		✓	
Lou Correa (CA-46)		✓	
Mary Gay Scanlon (PA-05)		✓	
Sylvia Garcia (TX-29)		✓	
Joseph Neguse (CO-02)		✓	
Lucy McBath (GA-06)		✓	
Greg Stanton (AZ-09)		✓	
Madeleine Dean (PA-04)		✓	
Debbie Mucarsel-Powell (FL-26)		✓	
Veronica Escobar (TX-16)		✓	
	AYES	NOS	PRES
Doug Collins (GA-27)	✓		
James F. Sensenbrenner (WI-05)	✓		
Steve Chabot (OH-01)	✓		
Louie Gohmert (TX-01)	✓		
Jim Jordan (OH-04)	✓		
Ken Buck (CO-04)	✓		
John Ratcliffe (TX-04)	✓		
Martha Roby (AL-02)	✓		
Matt Gaetz (FL-01)	✓		
Mike Johnson (LA-04)	✓		·
Andy Biggs (AZ-05)	✓		
Tom McClintock (CA-04)	✓		
Debbie Lesko (AZ-08)	✓		
Guy Reschenthaler (PA-14)	✓		
Ben Cline (VA-06)	✓		
Kelly Armstrong (ND-AL)	✓		
Greg Steube (FL-17)	✓		
	AYES	NOS	PRES.
TOTAL	17	23	

☐ PASSED

☑ FAILED

3. An amendment by Mr. Gaetz to replace a reference to the investigation into Joseph R.

Biden with Burisma and Hunter Biden, was defeated by a rollcall vote of 17 to 23.

Roll Call No. 3   Date: 12/12/19

COMMITTEE ON THE JUDICIARY
House of Representatives
116th Congress

Amendment # 2 ( ) to ANS HRes 755 offered by Rep. Gaetz

	AYES	NOS	PRES.
Jerrold Nadler (NY-10)		✓	
Zoe Lofgren (CA-19)		✓	
Sheila Jackson Lee (TX-18)		✓	
Steve Cohen (TN-09)		✓	
Hank Johnson (GA-04)		✓	
Ted Deutch (FL-22)		✓	
Karen Bass (CA-37)		✓	
Cedric Richmond (LA-02)		✓	
Hakeem Jeffries (NY-08)		✓	
David Cicilline (RI-01)		✓	
Eric Swalwell (CA-15)		✓	
Ted Lieu (CA-33)			
Jamie Raskin (MD-08)		✓	
Pramila Jayapal (WA-07)		✓	
Val Demings (FL-10)		✓	
Lou Correa (CA-46)		✓	
Mary Gay Scanlon (PA-05)		✓	
Sylvia Garcia (TX-29)		✓	
Joseph Neguse (CO-02)		✓	
Lucy McBath (GA-06)		✓	
Greg Stanton (AZ-09)		✓	
Madeleine Dean (PA-04)		✓	
Debbie Mucarsel-Powell (FL-26)		✓	
Veronica Escobar (TX-16)		✓	
	AYES	**NOS**	**PRES**
Doug Collins (GA-27)	✓		
James F. Sensenbrenner (WI-05)	✓		
Steve Chabot (OH-01)	✓		
Louie Gohmert (TX-01)	✓		
Jim Jordan (OH-04)	✓		
Ken Buck (CO-04)	✓		
John Ratcliffe (TX-04)	✓		
Martha Roby (AL-02)	✓		
Matt Gaetz (FL-01)	✓		
Mike Johnson (LA-04)	✓		
Andy Biggs (AZ-05)	✓		
Tom McClintock (CA-04)	✓		
Debbie Lesko (AZ-08)	✓		
Guy Reschenthaler (PA-14)	✓		
Ben Cline (VA-06)	✓		
Kelly Armstrong (ND-AL)	✓		
Greg Steube (FL-17)	✓		
	AYES	**NOS**	**PRES.**
TOTAL	17	23	

☐ PASSED

☑ FAILED

4. An amendment by Mr. Biggs to insert a section asserting foreign aid was released after President Zelensky signed anti-corruption measures into law, was defeated by a rollcall vote of 17 to 23.

Roll Call No. 4   Date: 12/12/19

COMMITTEE ON THE JUDICIARY
House of Representatives
116th Congress

Amendment # 3 ( ) to ANS HRes 755 offered by Rep. Biggs

	AYES	NOS	PRES.
Jerrold Nadler (NY-10)		✓	
Zoe Lofgren (CA-19)		✓	
Sheila Jackson Lee (TX-18)		✓	
Steve Cohen (TN-09)		✓	
Hank Johnson (GA-04)		✓	
Ted Deutch (FL-22)		✓	
Karen Bass (CA-37)		✓	
Cedric Richmond (LA-02)		✓	
Hakeem Jeffries (NY-08)		✓	
David Cicilline (RI-01)		✓	
Eric Swalwell (CA-15)		✓	
Ted Lieu (CA-33)			
Jamie Raskin (MD-08)		✓	
Pramila Jayapal (WA-07)		✓	
Val Demings (FL-10)		✓	
Lou Correa (CA-46)		✓	
Mary Gay Scanlon (PA-05)		✓	
Sylvia Garcia (TX-29)		✓	
Joseph Neguse (CO-02)		✓	
Lucy McBath (GA-06)		✓	
Greg Stanton (AZ-09)		✓	
Madeleine Dean (PA-04)		✓	
Debbie Mucarsel-Powell (FL-26)		✓	
Veronica Escobar (TX-16)		✓	
	AYES	NOS	PRES
Doug Collins (GA-27)	✓		
James F. Sensenbrenner (WI-05)	✓		
Steve Chabot (OH-01)	✓		
Louie Gohmert (TX-01)	✓		
Jim Jordan (OH-04)	✓		
Ken Buck (CO-04)	✓		
John Ratcliffe (TX-04)	✓		
Martha Roby (AL-02)	✓		
Matt Gaetz (FL-01)	✓		
Mike Johnson (LA-04)	✓		
Andy Biggs (AZ-05)	✓		
Tom McClintock (CA-04)	✓		
Debbie Lesko (AZ-08)	✓		
Guy Reschenthaler (PA-14)	✓		
Ben Cline (VA-06)	✓		
Kelly Armstrong (ND-AL)	✓		
Greg Steube (FL-17)	✓		
	AYES	NOS	PRES.
TOTAL	17	23	

☐ PASSED

☑ FAILED

5. An amendment by Mr. Reschenthaler to strike article II from the resolution, was defeated by a rollcall vote of 17 to 23.

Roll Call No. 5   Date: 12/12/19

COMMITTEE ON THE JUDICIARY
House of Representatives
116th Congress

Amendment # 4 ( ) to ANS H Res 755 offered by Rep. Reschenthaler

	AYES	NOS	PRES.
Jerrold Nadler (NY-10)		✓	
Zoe Lofgren (CA-19)		✓	
Sheila Jackson Lee (TX-18)		✓	
Steve Cohen (TN-09)		✓	
Hank Johnson (GA-04)		✓	
Ted Deutch (FL-22)		✓	
Karen Bass (CA-37)		✓	
Cedric Richmond (LA-02)		✓	
Hakeem Jeffries (NY-08)		✓	
David Cicilline (RI-01)		✓	
Eric Swalwell (CA-15)		✓	
Ted Lieu (CA-33)			
Jamie Raskin (MD-08)		✓	
Pramila Jayapal (WA-07)		✓	
Val Demings (FL-10)		✓	
Lou Correa (CA-46)		✓	
Mary Gay Scanlon (PA-05)		✓	
Sylvia Garcia (TX-29)		✓	
Joseph Neguse (CO-02)		✓	
Lucy McBath (GA-06)		✓	
Greg Stanton (AZ-09)		✓	
Madeleine Dean (PA-04)		✓	
Debbie Mucarsel-Powell (FL-26)		✓	
Veronica Escobar (TX-16)		✓	
	AYES	NOS	PRES
Doug Collins (GA-27)	✓		
James F. Sensenbrenner (WI-05)	✓		
Steve Chabot (OH-01)	✓		
Louie Gohmert (TX-01)	✓		
Jim Jordan (OH-04)	✓		
Ken Buck (CO-04)	✓		
John Ratcliffe (TX-04)	✓		
Martha Roby (AL-02)	✓		
Matt Gaetz (FL-01)	✓		
Mike Johnson (LA-04)	✓		
Andy Biggs (AZ-05)	✓		
Tom McClintock (CA-04)	✓		
Debbie Lesko (AZ-08)	✓		
Guy Reschenthaler (PA-14)	✓		
Ben Cline (VA-06)	✓		
Kelly Armstrong (ND-AL)	✓		
Greg Steube (FL-17)	✓		
	AYES	NOS	PRES.
TOTAL	17	23	

☐ PASSED

☑ FAILED

6. An amendment by Mr. Jordan to strike language asserting President Trump's conduct has demonstrated that he warrants "impeachment and trial, removal from office, and disqualification to hold and enjoy any office of honor, trust, or profit under the United States," was defeated by a rollcall vote of 17 to 23.

Roll Call No. **6**   Date: **12/12/19**

COMMITTEE ON THE JUDICIARY
House of Representatives
116th Congress

Amendment # **5** ( ) to ANS HRes 755 offered by Rep. **Jordan**

	AYES	NOS	PRES.
Jerrold Nadler (NY-10)		✓	
Zoe Lofgren (CA-19)		✓	
Sheila Jackson Lee (TX-18)		✓	
Steve Cohen (TN-09)		✓	
Hank Johnson (GA-04)		✓	
Ted Deutch (FL-22)		✓	
Karen Bass (CA-37)		✓	
Cedric Richmond (LA-02)		✓	
Hakeem Jeffries (NY-08)		✓	
David Cicilline (RI-01)		✓	
Eric Swalwell (CA-15)		✓	
Ted Lieu (CA-33)			
Jamie Raskin (MD-08)		✓	
Pramila Jayapal (WA-07)		✓	
Val Demings (FL-10)		✓	
Lou Correa (CA-46)		✓	
Mary Gay Scanlon (PA-05)		✓	
Sylvia Garcia (TX-29)		✓	
Joseph Neguse (CO-02)		✓	
Lucy McBath (GA-06)		✓	
Greg Stanton (AZ-09)		✓	
Madeleine Dean (PA-04)		✓	
Debbie Mucarsel-Powell (FL-26)		✓	
Veronica Escobar (TX-16)		✓	
	AYES	**NOS**	**PRES**
Doug Collins (GA-27)	✓		
James F. Sensenbrenner (WI-05)	✓		
Steve Chabot (OH-01)	✓		
Louie Gohmert (TX-01)	✓		
Jim Jordan (OH-04)	✓		
Ken Buck (CO-04)	✓		
John Ratcliffe (TX-04)	✓		
Martha Roby (AL-02)	✓		
Matt Gaetz (FL-01)	✓		
Mike Johnson (LA-04)	✓		
Andy Biggs (AZ-05)	✓		
Tom McClintock (CA-04)	✓		
Debbie Lesko (AZ-08)	✓		
Guy Reschenthaler (PA-14)	✓		
Ben Cline (VA-06)	✓		
Kelly Armstrong (ND-AL)	✓		
Greg Steube (FL-17)	✓		
	AYES	**NOS**	**PRES.**
TOTAL	**17**	**23**	

☐ PASSED

☑ FAILED

7. Upon demand that the vote to report the resolution, as amended, favorably to the House be divided into two propositions pursuant clause 5 of Rule XVI, Article I of the resolution (abuse of power) was agreed to by a rollcall vote of 23 to 17.

Roll Call No. 7

Date: 12/13/9

COMMITTEE ON THE JUDICIARY

House of Representatives
116th Congress

Final Passage on H. Res. 755 Article 1

☑ PASSED

☐ FAILED

	AYES	NOS	PRES.	
Jerrold Nadler (NY-10)	✓			
Zoe Lofgren (CA-19)	✓			
Sheila Jackson Lee (TX-18)	✓			
Steve Cohen (TN-09)	✓			
Hank Johnson (GA-04)	✓			
Ted Deutch (FL-22)	✓			
Karen Bass (CA-37)	✓			
Cedric Richmond (LA-02)	✓			
Hakeem Jeffries (NY-08)	✓			
David Cicilline (RI-01)	✓			
Eric Swalwell (CA-15)	✓			
Ted Lieu (CA-33)				
Jamie Raskin (MD-08)	✓			
Pramila Jayapal (WA-07)	✓			
Val Demings (FL-10)	✓			
Lou Correa (CA-46)	✓			
Mary Gay Scanlon (PA-05)	✓			
Sylvia Garcia (TX-29)	✓			
Joseph Neguse (CO-02)	✓			
Lucy McBath (GA-06)	✓			
Greg Stanton (AZ-09)	✓			
Madeleine Dean (PA-04)	✓			
Debbie Mucarsel-Powell (FL-26)	✓			
Veronica Escobar (TX-16)	✓			
	AYES	NOS	PRES	
Doug Collins (GA-27)		✓		
James F. Sensenbrenner (WI-05)		✓		
Steve Chabot (OH-01)		✓		
Louie Gohmert (TX-01)		✓		
Jim Jordan (OH-04)		✓		
Ken Buck (CO-04)		✓		
John Ratcliffe (TX-04)		✓		
Martha Roby (AL-02)		✓		
Matt Gaetz (FL-01)		✓		
Mike Johnson (LA-04)		✓		
Andy Biggs (AZ-05)		✓		
Tom McClintock (CA-04)		✓		
Debbie Lesko (AZ-08)		✓		
Guy Reschenthaler (PA-14)		✓		
Ben Cline (VA-06)		✓		
Kelly Armstrong (ND-AL)		✓		
Greg Steube (FL-17)		✓		
	AYES	NOS	PRES.	
TOTAL	23	17		

8. Upon demand that the vote to report the resolution, as amended, favorably to the House be divided into two propositions pursuant clause 5 of Rule XVI, Article II of the resolution (obstruction of Congress) was agreed to by a rollcall vote of 23 to 17.

Roll Call No. 8

Date: 12/13/19

COMMITTEE ON THE JUDICIARY
House of Representatives
116th Congress

Final Passage on H. Res. 755 Article II

☑ PASSED

☐ FAILED

	AYES	NOS	PRES.	
Jerrold Nadler (NY-10)	✓			
Zoe Lofgren (CA-19)	✓			
Sheila Jackson Lee (TX-18)	✓			
Steve Cohen (TN-09)	✓			
Hank Johnson (GA-04)	✓			
Ted Deutch (FL-22)	✓			
Karen Bass (CA-37)	✓			
Cedric Richmond (LA-02)	✓			
Hakeem Jeffries (NY-08)	✓			
David Cicilline (RI-01)	✓			
Eric Swalwell (CA-15)	✓			
Ted Lieu (CA-33)				
Jamie Raskin (MD-08)	✓			
Pramila Jayapal (WA-07)	✓			
Val Demings (FL-10)	✓			
Lou Correa (CA-46)	✓			
Mary Gay Scanlon (PA-05)	✓			
Sylvia Garcia (TX-29)	✓			
Joseph Neguse (CO-02)	✓			
Lucy McBath (GA-06)	✓			
Greg Stanton (AZ-09)	✓			
Madeleine Dean (PA-04)	✓			
Debbie Mucarsel-Powell (FL-26)	✓			
Veronica Escobar (TX-16)	✓			
	AYES	NOS	PRES	
Doug Collins (GA-27)		✓		
James F. Sensenbrenner (WI-05)		✓		
Steve Chabot (OH-01)		✓		
Louie Gohmert (TX-01)		✓		
Jim Jordan (OH-04)		✓		
Ken Buck (CO-04)		✓		
John Ratcliffe (TX-04)		✓		
Martha Roby (AL-02)		✓		
Matt Gaetz (FL-01)		✓		
Mike Johnson (LA-04)		✓		
Andy Biggs (AZ-05)		✓		
Tom McClintock (CA-04)		✓		
Debbie Lesko (AZ-08)		✓		
Guy Reschenthaler (PA-14)		✓		
Ben Cline (VA-06)		✓		
Kelly Armstrong (ND-AL)		✓		
Greg Steube (FL-17)		✓		
	AYES	NOS	PRES.	
TOTAL	23	17		

COMMITTEE OVERSIGHT FINDINGS

In compliance with clause 3(c)(1) of rule XIII of the Rules of the House of Representatives, the Committee advises that the findings and recommendations of the Committee, based on oversight activities under clause 2(b)(1) of rule X of the Rules of the House of Representatives, are incorporated in the descriptive portions of this report.

NEW BUDGET AUTHORITY AND TAX EXPENDITURES AND CONGRESSIONAL BUDGET OFFICE COST ESTIMATE

Clause 3(c)(2) of rule XIII of the Rules of the House of Representatives and section 308(a) of the Congressional Budget Act of 1974 and with respect to requirements of clause (3)(c)(3) of rule XIII of the Rules of the House of Representatives and section 402 of the Congressional Budget Act of 1974, are inapplicable because this resolution does not provide new budgetary authority or increased tax expenditures. Additionally, the Committee believes that the resolution will have no budget effect.

DUPLICATION OF FEDERAL PROGRAMS

No provision of H. Res. 755 establishes or reauthorizes a program of the federal government known to be duplicative of another federal program, a program that was included in any report from the Government Accountability Office to Congress pursuant to section 21 of Public Law 111-139, or a program related to a program identified in the most recent Catalog of Federal Domestic Assistance.

PERFORMANCE GOALS AND OBJECTIVES

The Committee states that pursuant to clause 3(c)(4) of rule XIII of the Rules of the House of Representatives, H. Res. 755 recommends articles of impeachment for President Donald J. Trump.

ADVISORY ON EARMARKS

In accordance with clause 9 of rule XXI of the Rules of the House of Representatives, H. Res. 755 does not contain any congressional earmarks, limited tax benefits, or limited tariff benefits as defined in clause 9(d), 9(e), or 9(f) of Rule XXI.

DISSENTING VIEWS

DISSENTING VIEWS

TABLE OF CONTENTS

I.   Introduction[1]

Impeachment of an American president demands the accuser prioritize legitimacy and thoroughness over expediency. In the impeachment inquiries for Presidents Johnson, Nixon, and Clinton, the facts had been established and agreed upon by the time Articles of Impeachment were considered. Due to years-long investigations into the allegations against Nixon and Clinton, the only question to answer was what Congress would do to confront the findings.

The evidence uncovered in this impeachment, by contrast, shows the case is not only weak but dangerously lowers the bar for future impeachments. The record put forth by the Majority is based on inferences built upon presumptions and hearsay. In short, the Majority has failed to make a credible, factually-based allegation against this president that merits impeachment.[2]

By deciding to pursue impeachment first and build a case second, the Majority has created a challenge for itself. In the face of new information that exculpates or exonerates the President, the Majority must choose: either accept that the impeachment inquiry's findings do not merit impeachment and face the political consequences or, alternatively, ignore those facts. Regrettably, the Majority has chosen the latter.

As detailed in Section III below, since the delivery of the Intelligence Committee's Reports (both Majority and Minority), new developments have emerged that further undermine the case for impeachment. The Majority's response to new exculpatory facts, as it has been since the day the President was elected, is to ignore them and press on.

The Majority has not only ignored exculpatory evidence but proclaims the facts are "uncontested." The facts are contested, and, in many areas, the Majority's claims are directly contradicted by the evidence. That assertion is further contradicted by the Articles of Impeachment themselves. Not one of the criminal accusations leveled at the President over the past year—including bribery, extortion, collusion/conspiracy with foreign enemies, or obstruction of justice—has found a place in the Articles. Some of these accusations are, in fact, holdovers from an earlier disingenuous attempt by the Majority to weaponize the Russia collusion investigations for political gain. The Majority has not made the case for impeachment in part due to its decision to impeach being rooted less in a concern for the nation than the debasement of the President.

History will record the impeachment of President Donald J. Trump as a signal that even the gravest constitutional remedy is not beyond political exploitation. The Articles of Impeachment alone, drafted by the Majority in haste to meet a self-imposed December deadline,

---

[1] As an initial matter, the Minority wishes to note for the record its unwavering commitment to security for the people and the nation of Ukraine. Throughout this process, the Minority has been cast variously as against foreign aid, pro-Russia, or unsympathetic to the plight of Ukrainians, who face unimaginable hardship in the face of Russian aggression. To the Ukrainian people, we say we categorically reject these characterizations and apologize that the Ukrainian democracy has been thrust into the spotlight besmirching both of our leaders. We congratulate you on your election of President Zelensky, whose commitment to fighting corruption and the Russian threat are values all decent Americans share with you.

[2] *See* Jonathan Turley, "The Impeachment Inquiry Into President Donald J. Trump: The Constitutional Basis For Presidential Impeachment," House Committee on the Judiciary, Written Statement, Dec. 4, 2019, at 4. ("I am concerned about lowering impeachment standards to fit a paucity of evidence and an abundance of anger. I believe this impeachment not only fails the standard of past impeachments but would create a dangerous precedent for future impeachments.").

underscore the Majority's anemic impeachment case. The Majority's actions are unprecedented, unjustifiable, and will only dilute the significance of the dire recourse that is impeachment. The ramifications for future presidents are not difficult to surmise. If partisan passions are not restrained, the House of Representatives will be thrown into an endless cycle of impeachment, foregoing its duty to legislate and usurping the place of the American people in electing their president.

II.   Procedural Background

Apart from those factual and evidentiary shortcomings referenced above, the Majority's dedication to impeaching the President at any cost was well-reflected by their willful disregard of House Rules and congressional precedent. Throughout the first session of the 116th Congress, Chairman Jerrold Nadler repeatedly violated any Rules that inconvenienced the Committee's ardent attempts to impeach the President. The Committee's impeachment-related activities during the first session of the 116th Congress should be viewed as a cautionary tale.

In 1974, Chairman Peter Rodino approached the question of presidential impeachment solemnly and with an eye towards fairness and thoroughness. He worked diligently to ensure that such a country-altering process was conducted with not only bipartisan support, but with the support of the American people. What has occurred in the halls of Congress over the final months of 2019 has been a sharp and unfortunate departure from Chairman Rodino's legacy. The institutional damage done to the House of Representatives by the Majority throughout this impeachment "process" can never be repeated.

A. Impeachment Proceedings Without Authorization

For most of 2019, the House Committee on the Judiciary (the "Committee" or the "Judiciary Committee") conducted various "impeachment" hearings outside the scope of its authority under Rule X of the Rules of the House. The Chairman's refusal to seek authorization by a vote of the full House of Representatives—as was done in 1974 and 1998—denied every Member of the House of Representatives the opportunity to determine whether such proceedings should commence.

Not only did the Majority fail to seek authorization from the House of Representatives, they insisted they did not need it. On multiple occasions, Speaker of the House Nancy Pelosi and the Chairman denied that a vote of the full House of Representatives was necessary prior to conducting an impeachment inquiry, arguing that House committees could conduct oversight pursuant to Rule X of the Rules of the House.[3] This is a manipulative reading of the Rules. Rule X prescribes – in list format – the specific topics over which each House committee may exercise jurisdiction. Impeachment is not listed in Rule X.[4] To add—even temporarily—to a committee's jurisdiction, the full House of Representatives must agree.[5]

B. The Bifurcation of Impeachment Inquiry Proceedings Under H. Res. 660

The adoption of H. Res. 660 diverged substantially, and without justification, from prior

---

[3] *Nadler: These are 'formal impeachment proceedings'*, CNN (Aug. 8, 2019); Susan Cornwall, *U.S. House Will Hold Off on Vote to Authorize Impeachment Probe: Pelosi*, REUTERS, (Oct. 15, 2019).;Lindsey McPherson, *McCarthy Asks Pelosi to Suspend Impeachment Inquiry Until She Defines Procedures*, ROLLCALL, (Oct. 3, 2019).
[4] Rules of the House of Representative, Rule X.
[5] Deschler-Brown's Precedents, Volume 3, Chapter 10. 94th Cong. 2042 (1994).

authorizations agreed to by the House of Representatives in 1974 and 1998. Most notably, it bifurcated impeachment proceedings, allowing the House Permanent Select Committee on Intelligence (the "Intelligence Committee") to usurp what has traditionally been the Committee's investigative role in presidential impeachment. To be clear, Members of the House of Representatives will soon have to vote on Articles of Impeachment reported by a Judiciary Committee that has barely reviewed the alleged evidence. After the Intelligence Committee "investigation," the Judiciary Committee held only one hearing and one presentation from staff on the impeachment inquiry. Not only was the Judiciary Committee almost completely shut out from the impeachment inquiry, it turned down the opportunity to examine all of the evidence collected by the Intelligence Committee or to hear testimony from even one fact witness.

The Majority allowed the entire investigative portion to take place in a committee that denied Minority-requested witnesses, would not allow the participation of the President's counsel to question fact witnesses, and censored Minority questions.[6] After the Intelligence Committee's one-sided investigation, the Judiciary Committee was unable to conduct a full review, leaving the American people in the dark.

C. Committee Proceedings Under H. Res. 660

1. Failure to Schedule a Minority Hearing Day

The Minority has a right to a minority day of hearings under clause 2(j)(1) of Rule XI of the Rules of the House.[7] The Rules set forth that a minority day of hearings must occur on the "measure or matter" under consideration at the time of the demand. On December 4, 2019, the Committee held a hearing titled "The Impeachment Inquiry into President Donald J. Trump: Constitutional Grounds for Presidential Impeachment."[8] It was during that hearing that a demand for a minority day of hearings was made. In fact, a demand for a minority day of hearings was made less than two minutes after the start of the hearing, which was the *first* Committee hearing designated pursuant to H. Res. 660.[9] Given the issue under consideration at the December 4 hearing, the Rules would require that the Chairman schedule a minority day of hearings on the impeachment inquiry into President Donald J. Trump, the matter under consideration at the time of the demand. Once the articles of impeachment were considered and adopted, the impeachment inquiry ended, and the necessity of the minority hearing day dissipated.

After the Chairman failed to acknowledge his obligation to schedule such a hearing during the December 4 hearing, Ranking Member Doug Collins sent a letter the following day reminding the Chairman that the requested minority hearing day must be scheduled before Committee consideration of any articles of impeachment.

The issue was again raised at the staff presentation hearing on December 9, 2019.[10] Each time the issue was raised directly to the Chairman, he said that he was still considering the

---

[6] Valerie Richardson, *Adam Schiff Rejects Hunter Biden, 'Whistleblower' as Impeachment Witnesses*, WASHINGTON TIMES (Nov. 10, 2019); Bob Fredericks & Aaron Feis, *Adam Schiff Blocks Republicans' Attempts to Question Impeachment Witnesses*, NEW YORK POST (Nov. 19, 2019).

[7] Rules of the House of Representative, Clause (2)(j)(1), Rule XI.

[8] The Impeachment Inquiry into President Donald J. Trump: Constitutional Grounds for Presidential Impeachment, Hearing Before the H. Comm. On the Judiciary, 116th Cong. (2019).

[9] *Id.* at 4.

[10] The Impeachment Inquiry into President Donald J. Trump: Presentations from the House Permanent Select Committee on Intelligence and House Judiciary Committee, Hearing Before the H. Comm. on the Judiciary, 116th Cong. 12 (2019).

request.[11] At the markup of articles of impeachment, a point of order was made against consideration of the articles for the Chairman's failure to schedule a minority hearing day. Instead of acknowledging his violation of the Rules, the Chairman ruled against the point of order, depriving Minority Members of their right to a minority day of hearings.

Such a blatant, intentional, and impactful violation of the Rules during consideration of a matter as course-altering as articles of impeachment has never occurred in the history of the House of Representatives.

2.   Staff Presentation

The staff "presentation" hearing held on Monday, December 9, 2019, could only be described as a bizarre, made-for-TV divergence from the precedent set during the impeachments of Presidents Nixon and Clinton. Staff presentations in 1974 and 1998 occurred as a means to assist Members of the Committee in sorting through dense volumes of evidence. The December 9 hearing was set up by the Majority as a means to functionally replace the participation of Members of Congress with paid, outside consultants, not to advise them.

To begin, an outside consultant to the Majority, Barry Berke, was permitted to make a presentation to the Committee without being sworn in or questioned by Members of the Committee.[12] He was later permitted forty-five minutes to cross-examine the Minority staff member (after said staffer had been sworn in) that had earlier presented the counter argument to his "presentation," which was in fact just thirty minutes of opinion.

This aspect of the hearing comported with the procedures of H. Res. 660, but we question any application of the Rules that would permit a private consultant to use Committee proceedings to cross examine a career staff member for forty-five minutes but only allow the majority of Members on the Committee five minutes to ask questions.

Future staff presentations of evidence during impeachment inquiries should be just that – presentations of evidence compiled and reviewed by the Committee. Instead, this Majority chose to prioritize TV ratings over meaningful Member participation and a greater understanding of the facts.

3.   Rejection of All Republican Witness Requests

H. Res. 660 provided that the Ranking Member could request that the Chairman subpoena witnesses. While H. Res. 660 provides no time constraints on such a request, the Chairman sent a letter requiring that the Ranking Member submit any such requests by December 6, 2019.[13] Despite the unjustifiably short time constraint, the Ranking Member sent a list of witnesses to the Chairman by the deadline. On Monday December 9, the Chairman rejected all of the Ranking Member's requests without justification beyond the Chairman's

[11] The Impeachment Inquiry into President Donald J. Trump: Presentations from the House Permanent Select Committee on Intelligence and House Judiciary Committee, Hearing Before the H. Comm. on the Judiciary, 116th Cong. 13 (2019).
[12] *Id.* at 74-5.
[13] Letter from the Honorable Jerrold Nadler, Chairman, H. Comm. on the Judiciary, to the Honorable Doug Collins, Ranking Member, H. Comm. on the Judiciary (Nov. 29, 2019).

unilateral determination that the witnesses were not relevant.[14] Considering that Articles of Impeachment were announced the very next morning, it is clear that the Chairman had no intention to provide the Minority Members with an opportunity to examine additional evidence or call additional witnesses.

III. Factual Background

From a substantive perspective, despite the Minority's efforts,[15] this Committee invited no fact witnesses to testify during this impeachment inquiry. Instead, it held one hearing with a panel of four academics, and one presentation with a panel of Congressional staffers.

Rather than conduct its own investigation, this Committee relied on the investigation conducted by the Intelligence Committee. The Intelligence Committee Majority produced a report. However, the Intelligence Committee's Minority Staff Report is the more complete document, describing in significant detail the evidentiary record.[16] The Intelligence Committee Minority Staff Report is incorporated into these Minority Views and attached as Appendix A. As that Minority Report shows, the Majority does not have evidence to support the allegations in the Articles of Impeachment.[17]

Since the conclusion of the Intelligence Committee's investigation and the provision of its reports, significant new facts have come to light that further contradict the Majority's primary allegation that the President conditioned U.S. security assistance on the initiation of Ukrainian investigations into a political rival. The Majority has ignored those facts. First, on December 2, President Zelensky repeated his earlier statements[18] that he was not pressured by President Trump. In fact, he said he was not aware of a *quid pro quo* involving U.S. security assistance.[19] Second, on December 10, a close aide to President Zelensky, Andriy Yermak, denied discussing a *quid pro quo* with Gordon Sondland, which, as discussed below, is the linchpin of the Majority's factual case.[20] It is difficult to conceive that a months-long pressure campaign existed when the alleged victims are not aware of it and deny being pressured. These exculpatory facts not only undercut the Majority's primary factual claims, they emphasize the problems with the rushed nature of the process.

IV. Article I Fails to Establish an Impeachable Offense

Impeachment is only warranted for conduct that constitutes "Treason, Bribery, or other high Crimes and Misdemeanors."[21] For months, the Majority claimed the President was guilty of

---

[14] Letter from the Honorable Jerrold Nadler, Chairman, H. Comm. on the Judiciary, to the Honorable Doug Collins, Ranking Member, H. Comm. on the Judiciary (Dec. 9, 2019).

[15] *See, e.g.*, Letter from the Honorable Doug Collins, Ranking Member, H. Comm. on the Judiciary, to the Honorable Jerrold Nadler, Chairman, H. Comm. on the Judiciary (December 6, 2019).

[16] *See* Appendix A, Report of Evidence in the Democrats' Impeachment Inquiry in the House of Representatives ("Intel. Comm. Minority Report") (Dec. 2, 2019).

[17] *Id.*

[18] Tara Law, *'Nobody Pushed Me.' Ukrainian President Denies Trump Pressured Him to Investigate Biden's Son*, TIME (Sep. 25, 2019).

[19] Simon Shuster, *'I Don't Trust Anyone at All,' Ukrainian President Volodymyr Zelensky Speaks Out on Trump, Putin and a Divided Europe*, TIME (Dec. 2, 2019).

[20] Simon Shuster, *Top Ukraine Official Andriy Yermak Casts Doubt on Key Impeachment Testimony*, TIME (Dec. 10, 2019).

[21] U.S. CONST. Art. II, § 4.

bribery, extortion, and a host of other common law and penal code crimes,[22] but the Articles of Impeachment do not include any of those specific offenses. In fact, the first Article in the resolution sponsored by Chairman Nadler alleges an amorphous charge of "abuse of power."[23]

Simply put, the Majority has included the vague "abuse of power" charge because they lack the evidence to prove bribery, extortion, or any other crimes. For example, during the Committee's markup of the articles of impeachment, Members from the Minority explained in detail why the Majority's claims that the President was guilty of bribery were erroneous.[24]

It is not the Minority's contention that an abuse of power can never form the basis for an impeachment. But an accusation of abuse of power must be based on a higher and more concrete standard than conduct that "ignored and injured the interests of the Nation."[25] The people, through elections, decide what constitutes the "interests of the nation." For an abuse of power charge, although "criminality is not required...clarity is necessary."[26]

Unfortunately, such clarity is utterly lacking in the Majority's articles. This is the first presidential impeachment in American history without the allegation of a crime, let alone a high crime or high misdemeanor. The absence of even an allegation of criminality, after months of claiming multiple crimes had been committed, reveals the Majority's inability to substantiate their claims.[27] The abuse of power charge in the first Article is vague, unprovable, and confined only by the impulses of the majority party in the House of Representatives. The Majority has failed to distinguish its definition of "abuse of power" from simple dislike or disagreement with the President's actions because this impeachment is inextricably tied to the Majority's dislike and disagreement with the President. That is not what the Founders intended.

The crux of the factual allegations in the first Article is that the President directed a months-long pressure campaign to force President Zelensky to announce particular investigations in exchange for U.S. security assistance or a White House meeting, in an effort to influence the 2020 election. The Intelligence Committee Minority Report demonstrates that these claims were not only unproven but, in fact, are undermined or contradicted by the primary actors in the alleged scheme.[28] Significantly, the alleged victims of the supposed pressure campaign were not even aware of any so-called pressure campaign.[29] Indeed, if the Majority had proof of bribery, they would have said so in the Articles.

---

[22] *See e.g.*, Mike DeBonis & Toluse Olorunnipa, *Democrats sharpen impeachment case, decrying 'bribery' as another potential witness emerges linking Trump to Ukraine scandal*, WASHINGTON POST (Nov. 14, 2019).
[23] H. Res. 775, 116th Cong. (2019).
[24] *See* Markup of H. Res 755, Articles of Impeachment Against President Donald J. Trump, Before the H. Comm. on the Judiciary, 116th Cong. 77-78, 167-68 (statements of Reps. Buck and Reschenthaler; specifically, that Democrats lacked the evidence to prove at least three elements of the crime of bribery).
[25] *Id.* at 110 (Article I, charging that the President abused his power because he "ignored and injured the interests of the nation.").
[26] Turley, *supra* note 2, at 11.
[27] *See* Appendix A (Intel. Comm. Minority Report), outlining the evidentiary deficiencies in the Majority's case.
[28] *Id.* at 32-64.
[29] Georgi Kantchev, *Ukrainian President Denies Trump Pressured Him During July Call*, WALL STREET JOURNAL (Oct. 10, 2019) (President Zelensky said, "There was no blackmail."); Matthias Williams, *U.S. envoy Sondland did not link Biden probe to aid: Ukraine minister*, REUTERS (Nov. 14, 2019) (Ukraine's Foreign Minister Vadym Prystaiko said Ambassador Sondland "did not tell us . . . about a connection between the assistance and the investigations."); Mark Moore, *Ukraine's Zelensky again denies quid pro quo during Trump phone call*, NY POST (Dec. 2, 2019) (President Zelensky again denies there was a *quid pro quo*); Simon Shuster, *Top Ukraine Official Andriy Yermak Casts Doubt on Key Impeachment Testimony*, TIME (Dec. 10, 2019) (Andriy Yermak denies discussing military assistance with Ambassador Sondland).

Because they do not have direct evidence of a pressure campaign against the Ukrainians, the Majority's allegations are based on presumptions, assumptions, hearsay, and inferences.[30] And its most critical assumptions and inferences have been contradicted by direct evidence from the primary actors in the alleged scheme.[31] It is no surprise the allegations shifted from *quid pro quo*, bribery, and extortion to settle on an undefined "abuse of power." The facts uncovered by the Intelligence Committee fail to approach the constitutional and historical standard for impeaching a president.[32] As Professor Jonathan Turley testified before this Committee, this is the "thinnest evidentiary record" in the history of presidential impeachments.[33] The reason the Majority has failed to seek information to substantiate that record, as Professor Turley and the Minority agree, is "an arbitrary deadline at the end of December."[34]

A. Impeachment in the House of Representatives Requires Clear and Convincing Evidence of Specific Impeachable Conduct. The Majority Has Not Met Its Burden.

Some in the Majority have argued that the House of Representatives is like a grand jury that should vote to impeach based on probable cause. This framing contradicts historical precedent. In the Clinton Impeachment Minority Views, House Democrats stated that the burden of proof, just as it was in the Nixon inquiry, should be "clear and convincing evidence."[35] Chairman Nadler elaborated on that standard when he said:

> At a bare minimum, [] the president's accusers must go beyond hearsay and innuendo and beyond demands that the president prove his innocence of vague and changing charges. They must provide clear and convincing evidence of specific impeachable conduct.[36]

The Majority should reflect upon Chairman Nadler's words.

The staff report on Constitutional Grounds for Impeachment filed during the Nixon impeachment further explains the high bar required for impeachment:

> Because impeachment of a President is a grave step for the nation, it is to be predicated only upon conduct seriously incompatible with either the constitutional form and principles of our government or the proper performance of constitutional duties of the presidential office.[37]

---

[30] *See* The Impeachment Inquiry into President Donald J. Trump: Testimony of Ambassador Gordon Sondland, Hearing Before the H. Perm. Sel. Comm. on Intelligence, 116th Cong. 148-51 (2019) (Ambassador Sondland testifying that his testimony about military was a "presumption" and that nobody told him the aid was linked to investigations); *see also* Appendix A (Intel. Comm. Minority Views) at 32-64.

[31] *See supra* note 29; Intel. Comm. Minority Views, at 43-44 (testimony of Ambassador Kurt Volker, the Special Envoy to Ukraine); Letter from Sen. Ron Johnson to the Honorable Jim Jordan, Ranking Member, H. Comm. on Oversight & Reform, and the Honorable Devin Nunes, Ranking Member, H. Perm. Sel. Comm. on Intelligence (Nov. 18, 2019).

[32] *See supra* note 10 (Opening Statement of Stephen R. Castor).

[33] Turley, *supra* note 2, at 4.

[34] *Id.* at 48.

[35] *See id.* at 211.

[36] Impeachment Inquiry: William Jefferson Clinton, President of the United States, 105th Cong., Consideration of Articles of Impeachment 78 (Comm. Print 1998) (statement of Rep. Jerrold Nadler).

[37] Staff of H. Comm. on the Judiciary, 93d Cong., Constitutional Grounds for Presidential Impeachment 4, at 27 (Comm. Print 1974) ("Nixon Constitutional Grounds for Presidential Impeachment").

As described below, the Majority's case fails to meet the burden of proof required.[38]

B. Abuse of Power Allegations Are Overbroad and Fail to Allege Specific Impeachable Conduct

Instead of alleging specific impeachable conduct, such as bribery or other high crimes, the Majority has alleged the vague and malleable charge of "abuse of power." While a consensus of scholars agree it is possible to impeach a president for non-criminal acts, the House of Representatives has never done so based "solely or even largely on the basis of a non-criminal abuse of power allegation."[39] That is because "[c]riminal allegations not only represent the most serious forms of conduct under our laws, but they also offer an objective source for measuring and proving such conduct."[40] No such objective measure has been articulated by the Majority.

The Majority claims its abuse of power standard is satisfied when a president injures "the interests of the nation" for a personal political benefit.[41] What constitutes an injury to the national interest has been left undefined. It can mean anything a majority in Congress wants it to mean. The opposition party almost unfailingly disagrees with a president on many issues and can always argue his or her actions injure the national interest. Here, for example, Majority Members have already begun to argue the abuse of power allegations in the first Article encompass conduct totally unrelated to the Ukraine allegations.[42] Moreover, nearly any action taken by a politician can result in a personal political benefit. When a certain standard can always be met by virtually all presidents, depending on partisan viewpoints, that standard has no limiting neutral principle and must be rejected. Simply stated, the Majority is advancing an impeachment based on policy differences with the President—a dangerous and slippery slope that our Founders cautioned against during discussions crafting the impeachment clause.

The Founders warned against such a vague and open-ended charge because it can be applied in a partisan fashion by a majority of the House of Representatives against an opposition president. Alexander Hamilton called partisan impeachment "regulated more by the comparative strength of parties, than by the real demonstrations of innocence or guilt" the "greatest danger."[43] Additionally, the Founders explicitly excluded the term "maladministration" from the impeachment clause because they did not want to subject presidents to the whims of Congress.[44] James Madison said, "So vague a term will be equivalent to a tenure during pleasure of the Senate."[45] As applied here, the Majority's abuse of power standard does precisely what the Founders rejected.

Thus, when the House of Representatives impeaches a president for non-criminal abuses of power, it must state with clarity how the harm to "national interests" is so egregious that it

---

[38] *See also* Appendix A (Intel Comm. Minority Report).

[39] Turley, *supra* note 2, at 47.

[40] *Id.* at 23.

[41] *See* H. Res. 755, 116th Cong. (2019) (Article I).

[42] *See, e.g.*, Rep. Rashida Tlaib, TWITTER, Dec. 10, 2019, 11:14am (stating that "abuse of power" standard includes the allegation that the "President targeted people solely based on their ethic [sic] background, their faith, disability, sexual orientation and even source of income.").

[43] THE FEDERALIST NO. 65 (Alexander Hamilton).

[44] 2 The Records of the Federal Convention of 1787, 550 (Max Farrand ed., 1937).

[45] *Id.*

merits usurping the will of the electorate.[46] The Majority has attempted to do that by equating a telephone conversation with election tampering. That argument is resoundingly unconvincing.

To prove an abuse of power, the accusation and the evidence against a president must "be sufficiently clear to assure the public that an impeachment is not simply an exercise of partisan creativity in rationalizing a removal of a president."[47] Here, specific impeachable conduct was not clearly identified because the Majority failed to prove its initial allegations of a *quid pro quo*, bribery, extortion, and other statutory crimes.

1.   Claims About the 2020 Election are Hyperbolic and Misleading

The injury to the national interest alleged against the President is harm to the integrity of the 2020 election. The Majority claims the President has engaged in a pattern of inviting foreign governments to intervene in American elections, and removal is the only option to preserve American democracy. Chairman Adam Schiff said not impeaching is equivalent to saying, "Why not let him cheat in one more election?"[48] That claim is hyperbolic and untrue.

First, the basis for the Majority's claimed pattern of conduct is a statement made in 2016 by then-candidate Trump during a public press conference, when he jokingly and mockingly asked Russia to find former Secretary of State Hillary Clinton's infamous 30,000 missing emails.[49] That statement has now been used as a basis to impeach the President because, the Majority argues, he invited a foreign power to intervene in the 2016 election and will do it again. This claim is specious for at least three reasons. First, the President was speaking publicly to fellow Americans. The remark was not, for example, caught on a hot microphone during a private conversation with the Russian president.[50] Second, the remark was made in jest in response to a question at a public press conference, following the news that 30,000 of Clinton's emails—potentially incriminating evidence—had mysteriously disappeared. Millions of Americans, including then-candidate Trump, were wondering what had happened. Finally, there is no evidence that the President actively sought to conspire with Russia to interfere in the election. The Majority simply does not like the comment.

The last point is particularly relevant. The Majority actively ignores the fact that the FBI and a special counsel spent nearly three years investigating the allegation that the President or his campaign colluded or conspired with the Russian government. Both concluded that the Trump-Russia collusion narrative was baseless.[51] The special counsel found no conspiracy and no collusion.[52] Indeed, on December 9, 2019—the same day the Committee received testimony from Chairman Schiff's staff, rather than Schiff himself—the Inspector General released a report outlining a myriad of egregious errors committed by the FBI during its Russia collusion

---

[46] Turley, *supra* note 2, at 11.

[47] *Id.* at 25.

[48] Allan Smith & Rebecca Shabad, *House leaders unveil two articles of impeachment, accusing Trump of 'high crimes and misdemeanors'*, NBC NEWS (Dec. 10, 2019) ("Remarks by Chairman Adam Schiff").

[49] *See* Ian Schwartz, Trump to Russia: I Hope You're Able to Find Clinton's 30,000 Missing Email, REAL CLEAR POLITICS (July 27, 2016).

[50] J. David Goodman, *Microphone Catches a Candid Obama*, NY TIMES (March 26, 2012).

[51] *See* Robert S. Mueller III, Report On The Investigation Into Russian Interference In The 2016 Presidential Election (March 2019) ("Mueller Report"); Michael Horowitz, A Review of Various Actions by the Federal Bureau of Investigation and Department of Justice in Advance of the 2016 Election (June 2018) ("Horowitz Report").

[52] *See* Mueller Report at 1.

investigation.[53] That the Majority included references to the Russia collusion narrative in these Articles of Impeachment illuminates the Majority's disregard for history, trivializes impeachment, and demonstrates an inability by the Majority to accept the inconvenient conclusions of those investigations—which, of course, the Majority previously lauded. It should be noted that the misconduct uncovered by the Department of Justice Inspector General largely occurred during President Obama's administration. As such, there is no basis to suspect President Trump's administration would allow the same election year abuses seen in 2016— which included the wiretapping of then-candidate Trump's campaign worker.[54]

Second, there was no invitation by President Trump for Ukraine to "intervene" in the 2020 election. By the Majority's standard, any action taken by any president that may affect an election is itself "intervention" in that election. Assuredly, every elected official eligible for reelection gives thought to how their actions will improve or harm their future campaign. Asking the president of Ukraine to "look into" potential corruption involving Hunter Biden's employment at a notoriously corrupt company in Ukraine is not "corrupting democratic elections."[55] Any request, however remote, that might benefit a politician politically is not an invitation to corrupt an election. To portray the President's request as corrupting the 2020 election is disingenuous, at best. As explained further below, the President did not ask for false information, and the fact that a key player in a corrupt Ukrainian company is the son of a politician does not transform a legitimate question into election interference.

Finally, the Majority argues that it must act now to prevent an ongoing "crime spree".[56] This is a spurious charge since the Articles of Impeachment do not allege *any* crimes, past or present. The Majority's argument that it must impeach the President to prevent future crimes, on the basis of past crimes not alleged in the Articles, is difficult to comprehend. Though impeachment is conceived of as prophylactic, the Majority would wield it on prognostication alone. The Majority must point to a high crime or other impeachable offense before claiming it is acting to protect future generations. It has completely failed to do so, instead relying on politically-motivated innuendo.

2.   Prior Presidential Impeachments Were All Based on Criminality

The Majority's Articles of Impeachment are unprecedented in American history because they are not based on criminality, as were all prior presidential impeachments. President Johnson was impeached by the House of Representatives in 1868 for violating the Tenure of Office Act.[57] The House Judiciary Committee approved Articles of Impeachment against President Nixon based on extensive and proven criminal conduct. As Professor Turley explained:

The allegations began with a felony crime of burglary and swept to encompass an array of other crimes involving political slush funds, payments of hush money, maintenance of an enemies list, directing tax audits of critics, witness intimidation, multiple instances of perjury, and even an alleged kidnapping. Ultimately, there were nearly 70 officials charged and four dozen of them found guilty. Nixon was also named as an unindicted

---

[53] *See* Horowitz Report at *i*.
[54] *Id.*
[55] H. Res. 755, 116th Cong. (2019) (Article I).
[56] *See supra* note 24, at 62.
[57] Turley, *supra* note 2, at 14-17.

conspirator by a grand jury. . . . The claim that the Ukrainian controversy eclipses Watergate is unhinged from history.[58]

The House of Representatives impeached President Clinton for the federal crime of lying under oath to deny justice to a fellow American.[59] While individual Articles of Impeachment have been passed against prior presidents that do not allege criminality, no president has been impeached solely on non-criminal accusations. This impeachment not only fails to satisfy the standard of past impeachments but would create a dangerous precedent because the alleged conduct is unproven.

3. This is the First Presidential Impeachment Where the Primary Allegations Have Not Been Proven.

The Majority has said repeatedly that the facts in this impeachment inquiry are not in dispute. That is false. Not only are the facts in dispute, the Majority's primary allegations are based on presumptions that are contradicted by direct evidence. Indeed, this is the first presidential impeachment where the primary allegations have not been proven.[60] In the Nixon impeachment, the Judiciary Committee had tapes and a host of proven crimes.[61] In the Clinton impeachment, there was physical evidence and a well-founded perjury claim that even President Clinton's supporters acknowledged was a felony, leaving them to argue that some felonies are not impeachable.[62] Here, all the Majority has presented connecting the hold on foreign security assistance to a request for investigations is a presumption by Ambassador Gordon Sondland.[63] But that presumption is contradicted by more credible direct evidence. Specifically, Ambassador Kurt Volker testified that there was no "linkage" between a White House meeting and Ukrainian actions to investigate President Trump's political rival.[64] During his public testimony, in an exchange with Rep. Mike Turner, Ambassador Volker reiterated that there was no linkage between foreign security assistance and investigations.[65]

There are four facts that will never change, making it impossible for the Majority to make any convincing case for the impeachment of the President on these facts. First, the President has publicly released the transcript of the July 25 call, which shows no conditionality for any official act.[66] Second, President Zelensky and his advisors did not know the aid was on hold until it was reported publicly at the end of August.[67] Third, both President Trump and President Zelensky have said repeatedly there was no pressure, no *quid pro quo*, and no linkage between the aid and investigations.[68] Fourth, the foreign security assistance funds were released without Ukraine

---

[58] *Id.* at 17-20.
[59] *See* H. Rept. 105-830, 105th Cong. (1998).
[60] Turley, *supra* note 2, at 22.
[61] *Id.*
[62] *See* Staff of H. Comm. on the Judiciary, 105th Cong., Constitutional Grounds for Presidential Impeachment: Modern Precedents, Minority Views, at 15 (1998) ("Clinton Impeachment Report").
[63] *See supra* note 30, at 148-151 (Testimony of Gordon Sondland stating that his testimony about security assistance was a "presumption" and that nobody told him the aid was linked to investigations).
[64] Transcribed Interview of Ambassador Kurt Volker (Oct. 3, 2019) at 35-36; 40.
[65] The Impeachment Inquiry into President Donald J. Trump: Testimony of Ambassador Kurt Volker and Mr. Timothy Morrison, Hearing Before the H. Perm. Sel. Comm. on Intelligence, 116th Cong. 106-108; 166 (2019).
[66] The White House, Memorandum of Telephone Conversation 1 (July 25, 2019).
[67] *See* Appendix A (Intel Comm. Minority Report), at 50 (citing testimony of Ambassadors Volker and Taylor).
[68] *See, e.g.,* Georgi Kantchev, *Ukrainian President Denies Trump Pressured Him During July Call*, WALL STREET JOURNAL (Oct. 10, 2019) (President Zelensky said "There was no blackmail."); Matthias Williams, *U.S. envoy Sondland did not link Biden probe to aid: Ukraine minister*, REUTERS (Nov. 14, 2019) (Ukraine's Foreign Minister Vadym Prystaiko said Ambassador Sondland "did not tell us . . . about a connection between the assistance and the

announcing or undertaking any investigations.

Additionally, Andriy Yermak, the only Ukrainian who allegedly was told about Ambassador Sondland's presumption, described in great detail his brief encounter with Ambassador Sondland that occurred when they were walking towards an escalator and said Ambassador Sondland never told him that U.S. security assistance was tied to investigations.[69] It defies logic to believe the President carefully orchestrated a months-long pressure campaign involving security assistance when the alleged victims of the supposed pressure campaign did not even know about it or about conditionality on any official act. Equally unconvincing is the assertion that everyone who disagrees with Ambassador Sondland's presumption is just lying.

Finally, the President was asked about Ambassador Sondland's presumption on two separate occasions, and both times President Trump said Sondland was wrong. After Ambassador Sondland told Senator Ron Johnson on August 30 about his presumption that U.S. security assistance was linked to investigations, Senator Johnson called the President on August 31 and asked if Ambassador Sondland's presumption was accurate.[70] The President said, "No way. I would never do that."[71] Senator Johnson and Senator Murphy subsequently met with President Zelensky. They discussed Ukraine's recent anti-corruption efforts and U.S. security assistance, but, not surprisingly, the question of investigations was not raised.[72] Likewise, when Ambassador Sondland asked President Trump what he wants from Ukraine, the President said, "I want nothing."[73] In fact, the President said he wanted President Zelensky to do what he ran on: root out corruption in Ukraine.[74]

Ultimately, Ukraine received the U.S. security assistance and a meeting with the President without announcing any investigations. There is no evidence that the President engaged in a pressure campaign or other scheme to condition security assistance on investigations. The Majority's case is built on a presumption that is contradicted by the evidence. The Intelligence Committee Minority Report provides further details about the flaws in the Majority's factual case. If the Majority proceeds with impeachment, it will be based on one presumption from one witness who amended his story multiple times.

C. The Majority Fails to Explain Why Asking About Hunter Biden's Role on Burisma Board of Directors is a High Crime or Misdemeanor

After failing to substantiate the allegations related to the U.S. security assistance, the Majority's remaining allegation is that the President committed the "high crime" of asking President Zelensky to look into potential corruption involving Hunter Biden's role on Burisma's board of directors.[75] This allegation is not a high crime or misdemeanor.

---

investigations."); Simon Shuster, *'I Don't Trust Anyone at All,' Ukrainian President Volodymyr Zelensky Speaks Out on Trump, Putin and a Divided Europe,"* TIME (Dec. 2, 2019) (President Zelensky again denies there was a *quid pro quo*).

[69] Simon Shuster, *Top Ukraine Official Andriy Yermak Casts Doubt on Key Impeachment Testimony,* TIME (Dec. 10, 2019).

[70] Letter from Sen. Ron Johnson to the Honorable Jim Jordan, Ranking Member, H. Comm. on Oversight & Reform, and the Honorable Devin Nunes, Ranking Member, H. Perm. Sel. Comm. on Intelligence, at 5 (Nov. 18, 2019).

[71] *Id.* at 6.

[72] *Id.* at 6-7.

[73] *See supra* note 30, at 148-151 (Testimony of Ambassador Gordon Sondland stating the President said "I want nothing.").

[74] *Id.*

[75] *See supra* note 69.

That question was the same question the American media had been asking for years. For example, on June 20, 2019, *ABC News* scrutinized Hunter Biden's involvement on the Burisma board of directors on a nationally televised news report.[76] The reporter asked whether "Hunter Biden profit[ed] off his Dad's work as vice-president, and did Joe Biden allow it?"[77] Numerous other publications have asked the same questions, including the Wall Street Journal as far back as 2015.[78] Former Vice President Biden himself, in a widely circulated video, explained his role in leveraging foreign aid to get a Ukrainian prosecutor who had investigated Burisma fired during a speech at the Council on Foreign Relations.[79] As the New York Times reported earlier this year, "Among those who had a stake in the outcome was Hunter Biden, Mr. Biden's younger son, who at the time was on the board of an energy company owned by a Ukrainian oligarch who had been in the sights of the fired prosecutor general."[80] Certainly, the questions surrounding the Bidens' role in Ukraine have been topics of interest for the media for a long time.

There is nothing untoward about a president asking a foreign government to investigate the same questions about potential corruption the American media was asking publicly. In fact, the United States has been party to a Mutual Legal Assistance Treaty (MLAT) with Ukraine since 2001.[81] The purpose of that MLAT includes "mutual assistance…in connection with the investigation, prosecution, and prevention of offenses, and in proceedings related to criminal matters."[82]

Furthermore, being a political campaign participant does not immunize anyone from scrutiny. The President did not ask for the creation of any false information. When Lt. Col. Vindman was asked "Would it ever be U.S. policy, in your experience, to ask a foreign leader to open a political investigation?" he replied, "…Certainly the President is well within his right to do that."[83]

V. Article II Fails to Establish an Impeachable Offense

The second Article of Impeachment, "Obstruction of Congress," appears to be a simple invective by the Majority against the constitutional reality of separation of powers.[84] The

---

[76] *Biden sidesteps questions about son's foreign work*, ABC NEWS (June 20, 2019).
[77] *Id.*
[78] Paul Sonne & Laura Mills, *Ukrainians See Conflict in Biden's Anticorruption Message*, WALL STREET JOURNAL (Dec. 7, 2015) (Quoting Ukrainian corruption expert stating: "If an investigator sees the son of the vice president of the United States is part of the management of a company … that investigator will be uncomfortable pushing the case forward."); *see also* James Risen, *Joe Biden, His Son and the Case Against a Ukrainian Oligarch*, NY TIMES (Dec. 8, 2015); Kenneth Vogel & Iuliia Mendel, *Biden Faces Conflict of Interest Questions that are being Promoted by Trump and Allies*, NY TIMES (May 1, 2019).
[79] Council on Foreign Relations, *Foreign Affairs Issue Launch with Former Vice President Joe Biden* (Jan. 23, 2018).
[80] Kenneth Vogel & Iuliia Mendel, *Biden Faces Conflict of Interest Questions that are being promoted by Trump and Allies*, NY TIMES (May 1, 2019).
[81] See Department of State, "Ukraine (12978) – Treaty on Mutual Legal Assistance in Criminal Matters".
[82] *Id.* at art. I cl. 1.
[83] The Impeachment Inquiry into President Donald J. Trump: Testimony of Ms. Jennifer Williams & Lt. Col. Alexander Vindman, Hearing Before the H. Perm. Sel. Comm. on Intelligence, 116th Cong. 120 (2019).
[84] *See* Montesquieu, Charles de Secondat, baron de, 1689-1755. *The Spirit of the Laws*. The Colonial Press, 1899 (New York). ("But should the legislative power usurp a share of the executive, the latter would be equally undone…Here, then, is the fundamental constitution of the government we are treating of. The legislative body being composed of two parts, they check one another by the mutual privilege of rejecting. They are both restrained by the executive power, as the executive is by the legislative.").

Majority's refusal to engage the Executive Branch in the traditional accommodations process,[85] or seek redress from the Judicial Branch, has rendered this Article as baseless as the first. The system of checks and balances is neither theoretical nor dispassionate; the Founders fully intended to put the three branches in conflict, and expected they would argue self-interestedly for their respective powers.[86] The inclusion of the second Article may be due to the Majority's reticence to propose only a single unsupported Article.

No president has been impeached for obstruction of Congress. The Majority seeks to impeach the President *not* for violating the Constitution but, instead, for asserting privileges that are part of its very structure. Though Legislative frustration with Executive resistance has previously inspired calls for impeachment and even the drafting of Articles of Impeachment, in this instance, the Majority is rushing to impeachment without attempting to engage available alternative avenues to obtain information. They have failed to do so because the Majority has set an arbitrary, politically-motivated deadline, by which it believes it must finish impeachment. Quite simply, further negotiations or the courts would take too long for the Majority's liking. This situation is truly unprecedented.

A. Obstruction of Congress Does Not Constitute a High Crime or High Misdemeanor While Further Recourse is Available

The obstruction of Congress allegations in this second Article do not meet the impeachable standard demanded by the Constitution. The Founders intended to create interbranch conflict. The fact that conflict exists here does not mean the President has committed either a high crime or a high misdemeanor. Most significantly, Congress has not pursued any of its many remedies to resolve interbranch disputes.

Congress has legislated remedies for itself to enforce its investigation requests, but it has not pursued those remedies.[87] Congress may also turn to the Judicial Branch to resolve interbranch disputes over subpoenas, as it has done many times in the past.[88] The Majority has neglected to do so. The Majority's claim that the current administration's "total" declination to participate in the effort to unseat him—either by the President himself or other Executive Branch officers—is somehow unprecedented is, simply, incorrect.[89] The Majority has engaged in a

---

[85] *Cf. U.S. v. Nixon*, 418 U.S. 683, 703 (1974) ("In the performance of assigned constitutional duties, each branch of the Government must initially interpret the Constitution, and the interpretation of its power by any branch is due great respect from the others.").

[86] THE FEDERALIST NO. 51 (James Madison) ("This policy of supplying, by opposite and rival interests, the defect of better motives, might be traced through the whole system of human affairs, private as well as public. We see it particularly displayed in all the subordinate distributions of power, where the constant aim is to divide and arrange the several offices in such a manner as that each may be a check on the other that the private interest of every individual may be a sentinel over the public rights…As the weight of the legislative authority requires that it should be thus divided, the weakness of the executive may require, on the other hand, that it should be fortified.").

[87] *See, e.g.,* 2 U.S.C. § 192.

[88] *See, e.g., H. Comm. on the Judiciary v. Miers*, 558 F. Supp. 2d (D.D.C. 2008).

[89] Many presidents have instructed Executive Branch officials not to comply with congressional demands. *See* Theodore Olson, History of Refusals By Executive Branch Officials to Provide Information Demanded by Congress, Part I, December 14, 1982, 6 Op. Off. Legal Counsel 751. The Olson OLC Opinion describes, for example, President Jackson stating, "It is now, however, my solemn conviction that I ought no longer, from any motive nor in any degree, to yield to these unconstitutional demands. Their continued repetition imposes on me, as the representative and trustee of the American people, the painful but imperious duty of resisting to the utmost any further encroachment on the rights of the Executive." President Theodore Roosevelt stated, "[I have] instructed the Attorney General not to respond to that portion of the resolution which calls for a statement of his reasons for nonaction." And President Eisenhower, in a May 17, 1954, letter to the Secretary of Defense said: "[Y]ou will

fundamentally unfair process and created a scenario in which the President's assertion of valid constitutional privileges is being used as a weapon against him.

The Intelligence Committee Majority served numerous subpoenas for documents and testimony. However, in at least one case, when the witness sought judicial review of the subpoena, the Majority withdrew it. Former Deputy National Security Advisor and Assistant to the President Charles Kupperman was one of the few people to listen in on the call between President Trump and President Zelensky on July 25 and received a subpoena to testify. When the White House instructed him to not testify, he asked the court to resolve "irreconcilable commands" from the Legislative and Executive Branches.[90] Inexplicably, the Majority promptly withdrew the subpoena and moved to dismiss the lawsuit.

Additionally, at least three subpoenas authorized and signed by Intelligence Committee Chairman Schiff were served prior to the passage of House Resolution 660 ("H. Res. 660").[91] Since H. Res. 660 gave Chairman Schiff jurisdiction to pursue this impeachment inquiry, an authorization he did not previously wield, it is likely these subpoenas would be defective and unenforceable since they were issued prior to its passage. Notably, the House of Representatives has chosen not to ask the federal judiciary to opine on such questions, instead rushing straight to impeachment without engaging the courts to resolve this interbranch dispute.

The federal judiciary's recent ruling that White House Counsel Don McGahn must appear before the Judiciary Committee demonstrates that assertions of privileges by the White House do not foreclose the House of Representatives' ability to hear testimony from relevant witnesses.[92] For the price of legitimacy, the Majority is only required to pay a small amount of patience and deference to the courts.

The Majority's claim that the courts are too slow or deliberative only demonstrates the Majority's pessimism about the merits of this case.[93] The Majority's actions show the American people disdain for working within the constitutional framework. Any case filed pursuant to an impeachment inquiry can be expedited in the courts. In the Nixon litigation, courts moved relevant cases quickly to and through the Supreme Court.[94] The decision to adopt an abbreviated schedule for the investigation and not to seek to compel testimony is a strategic choice by the Majority. It is not an appropriate justification for impeachment.

The feebleness of the Obstruction of Congress charge is rooted not only in the Majority's refusal to petition a court for enforcement of its subpoenas, but also the Majority's disregard for the typical process of accommodation that necessarily requires more time than the Majority has allowed. The "gold standard" of impeachment inquiries was with President Nixon.[95] But in that case the "Obstruction of Congress" Article of Impeachment authorized by the Judiciary

---

instruct employees of your Department that in all of their appearances before the Subcommittee of the Senate Committee on Government Operations regarding the inquiry now before it they are not to testify to any such conversations or communications, or to produce any such documents or reproductions."

[90] Brief of Plaintiff, Charles M. Kupperman, *Kupperman v. House of Representatives*, Case No: 1:19-cv-03224 at 2 (D.D.C. Oct. 25, 2019).

[91] Subpoena of Secretary of State Mike Pompeo (Sept. 27), Subpoena of Vice President Mike Pence (Oct. 4), and Subpoena of Acting White House Chief of Staff Mick Mulvaney (Oct. 4).

[92] *H. Comm. on the Judiciary v. McGahn*, Opinion of the Court, Case No: 1:19-cv-02379 (D.D.C. Nov. 25, 2019).

[93] *See supra* note 49.

[94] Two months elapsed between the ruling of Judge Sirica of the U.S. District Court for the District of Columbia and the Supreme Court's final decision.

[95] Turley, *supra* note 2, at 17.

Committee (but not voted on by the full House) was built upon a months-long negotiation with the White House, preceded by a years-long investigation by both houses of Congress.[96]

B. An Impeachment Inquiry Does Not Elevate the House of Representatives Above Fundamental Privileges

The Majority cites the "sole Power of Impeachment" five times in the two Articles of Impeachment. The recitation of Article I, Section 2, Clause 5 of the Constitution is correct, but it is utterly circular to assert the President deserves to be impeached because he defended himself from impeachment. The Constitution's grant of the impeachment power to the House of Representatives does not temporarily suspend the rights and powers of the other branches established by the Constitution. The initiation of impeachment proceedings does not entitle the House of Representatives automatic license to intrude into all corners of the federal government. For additional information regarding the unfair—and in fact, antagonistic—posture the Majority took during its investigation, refer to Section III of the Minority Views of the Intelligence Committee, attached as Appendix A.

The Majority's Articles also illustrate the risk of appropriating language from previous Articles of Impeachment never brought to a vote before the House of Representatives. Specifically, the Majority appears to have lifted from the Articles of Impeachment of President Nixon the language accusing the President of asserting privileges "without lawful cause or excuse."[97] But that is, of course, the heart of the argument in opposition to this Article. It is not for the Legislative Branch to determine unilaterally what is a "lawful cause or excuse." In fact, "[i]t is emphatically the duty of the Judicial Department to say what the law is."[98] The initiation of an impeachment inquiry does not change this calculus. The advantage an impeachment inquiry bestows to fact gatherers is the greater legitimacy of the Legislative Branch over the Executive Branch *before a Judicial Branch judge or magistrate*, which the Majority avoided altogether. The House of Representatives has no power to make laws by itself, and it has no mandate to determine to what privileges the Executive Branch is entitled. Though it may draft and pass Articles of Impeachment cloaking itself in the parlance of the judiciary, the House of Representatives is no substitute for the Judicial Branch. The adoption of such terminology further undermines the seriousness of this Article. In fact, it suggests the Majority is either unaware of the Nixon precedent, or seeks to deceive the American public about it.

---

[96] After requests were made to the White House on February 25, 1974, discussions were entered into to attempt to elicit further cooperation with the White House. Only after these negotiations failed was the first subpoena issued on April 11, 1974, authorized on a bipartisan basis by a vote of 33 to 3. President Nixon proceeded to release to the Committee and the public edited transcripts of 31 of the 42 subpoenaed recorded conversations. Finding the production insufficient and incompliant with the subpoena, the Committee authorized two additional subpoenas on May 15: the first, approved 37 to 1, demanded production of additional recorded telephone conversations which included President Nixon; the second, approved by separate but overwhelmingly bipartisan vote, demanded the "daily diaries" of President Nixon's calls for four specified periods. In a letter to Chairman Rodino on May 22, the President declined to produce the subject material of the May 15 subpoenas. On May 30, the Committee authorized a fourth subpoena, by a vote of 37 to 1, which demanded additional tape recordings and all papers relating to Watergate. By a vote of 28 to 10, the Committee also responded to President Nixon's failure to produce subpoenaed material, which was in turn was replied to by President Nixon on June 9. On June 24, the Committee authorized additional subpoenas into the ITT antitrust litigation and Kleindienst confirmation, domestic surveillance, governmental decisions affecting the dairy industry and campaign contributions, and alleged misuse of the IRS.
[97] *Cf.* Third Article Impeaching Richard M. Nixon, President of the United States. Approved by H. Comm. on the Judiciary (July 30, 1974).
[98] *Marbury v. Madison*, 5 U.S. 137 (1803).

C. The Majority's Failure to Conduct an Impeachment Inquiry in Accordance with Precedent has Led to Ex Post Facto Characterizations of that Inquiry

As detailed in Section II above, many of the Majority's obstruction allegations are due to the Majority's failure to conduct its inquiry in accordance with precedent. Fundamentally, the Majority has offered conflicting accounts of when the inquiry even began.

On September 24, Speaker of the House Nancy Pelosi announced the House of Representatives was "moving forward with an official impeachment inquiry."[99] The media generally reported that this was the commencement of impeachment proceedings, and the Majority purported to act pursuant to the Speaker's pronouncement.[100]

Nonetheless, over a month later, on October 31, the House of Representatives voted to authorize the impeachment inquiry that preceded these Articles, with the passage of H. Res. 660. This resolution directed the Committees on Financial Services, Foreign Affairs, the Judiciary, Oversight and Reform, and Ways and Means "to continue their ongoing investigations as part of the existing House of Representatives inquiry into whether sufficient grounds exist for the House of Representatives to exercise its Constitutional power to impeach Donald John Trump, President of the United States."[101]

Prior to the formal vote on October 31, serious and legitimate questions were raised as to whether the Executive Branch was being asked to comply with an impeachment inquiry, standard legislative oversight, or a novel hybrid of the two. The White House raised those concerns with the Majority on October 8, but no steps were taken to accommodate reasonable concerns about due process and fundamental fairness.[102]

The unnecessary confusion caused by the Majority about the status of its investigation calls into question the legitimacy of any subpoena issued prior to October 31 claiming to be part of an impeachment inquiry, because subpoenas issued before that date were not issued pursuant to a formal impeachment inquiry, congressional oversight, or any cognizable legislative purpose. A case addressing the validity of actions taken pursuant to Speaker Pelosi's edict is pending before the D.C. Circuit court.[103]

D. Assertions of Privilege by Previous Administrations Never Merited Impeachment

The Executive Branch has resisted congressional requests since the administration of President George Washington.[104] Resisting and asserting privileges in response to congressional demands has never formed the basis of impeachment.

For example, President Obama cited executive privilege and barred essential testimony

---

[99] *See supra* note 49 (Remarks by Speaker of the House Nancy Pelosi).

[100] *See, e.g.,* Nicholas Fandos, *Nancy Pelosi Announces Formal Impeachment Inquiry of Trump,* NY TIMES (Sep. 24, 2019).

[101] H. Res. 660, 116th Cong. (2019).

[102] Letter from Pat Cipollone, White House Counsel, to the Honorable Nancy Pelosi, Speaker of the House, et al. (Oct. 8, 2019).

[103] *See In re: Application of the H. Comm. on the Judiciary,* Department of Justice's Notice of Appeal, Case No: 1:19-gj-00048 BAH (D.C.C. Oct. 28, 2019).

[104] Washington famously declined to deliver to the House of Representatives documents recording the negotiations with Great Britain in what would be memorialized in the Jay Treaty of 1795.

and documents during the investigation of "Fast and Furious," a gunwalking operation in which the government arranged for the illegal sale of weapons to drug cartels in order to track their movement. The Obama administration argued that the courts had no authority over its denial of such witnesses and evidence to Congress. In *Committee on Oversight & Government Reform v. Holder*, Judge Amy Berman Jackson, ruled that "endorsing the proposition that the executive may assert an unreviewable right to withhold materials from the legislature would offend the Constitution more than undertaking to resolve the specific dispute that has been presented here. After all, the Constitution contemplates not only a separation, but a balance, of powers."[105] The position of the Obama Administration was extreme. It was also widely viewed as an effort to run the clock out on the investigation. Nevertheless, President Obama had every right to seek judicial review in the matter.

The subpoena campaign against the Trump Executive Branch began in earnest in September of this year, over a month before the impeachment inquiry had been authorized by the House of Representatives. In a letter to Secretary of State Michael Pompeo, the Committee on Foreign Affairs compelled the production of certain documents from the Department of State.[106] The subpoena issued by the Committee on Oversight and Reform to the White House on October 4, 2019, "compel[led] [the White House] to produce documents set forth in the accompanying schedule by October 18, 2019."[107] Any response less than immediate and total acquiescence, the letter stated, "shall constitute evidence of obstruction of the House's impeachment inquiry and may be used as an adverse inference against you and the President."[108] This refrain—a threat by any definition—has accompanied every subpoena issued to the Executive Branch and has needlessly created further tension between the Executive and Legislative Branches. From the commencement of this inquiry—whenever that may be definitively ascertained—the Majority has not been reluctant to voice its goal of impeaching the President.

VI.   Conclusion

Before the House of Representatives are two Articles of Impeachment against the President of the United States, Donald John Trump. To these Articles, the Minority dissents. The President has neither abused the power granted to him by the American people nor obstructed Congress. The Majority has failed to prove a case for impeachment. In fact, the paltry record on which the Majority relies is an affront to the constitutional process of impeachment and will have grave consequences for future presidents. The Majority's tactics and behavior—procedurally and substantively—emulate the charade impeachment of President Andrew Johnson, a president impeached because the House of Representatives did not agree with his policies.[109]

If President Nixon's impeachment proceedings are the "gold standard" for presidential impeachment inquiries, these proceedings, in stark contrast, will go down in history as the quintessential example of how such proceedings should *not* be conducted. The Majority Report and attendant documents will be viewed only as maps to the lowest depths of partisanship that no future Congress should follow. The quicker the Majority Report and the Majority's actions are

---

[105] *H. Comm. on Oversight & Gov't Reform v. Holder*, 979 F. Supp. 2d 1, 3 (D.D.C. 2013).

[106] This subpoena followed requests for documents from the Department of State made on September 9 and September 23 (prior to any vote authorizing an impeachment inquiry).

[107] Letter from the Honorable Elijah Cummings, Chairman, H. Comm. on Oversight & Reform, et al. to Pat Cipollone, White House Counsel (Oct. 4, 2019).

[108] *Id.*

[109] *See generally* Association of the Bar of New York, the Committee on Federal Legislation, *The Law of Presidential Impeachment* (1974).

forgotten, the better. As House Judiciary Republicans have repeatedly stated,[110] this institution should move on to working for the American people and forego this exercise of overturning 63 million of the votes cast on November 8, 2016.

---

[110] *See, e.g.*, Letter from H. Comm. on the Judiciary Republican Members to the Honorable Jerrold Nadler, Chairman, H. Comm. on the Judiciary (December 3, 2019).

forgotten, the better. As House Judiciary Republicans have repeatedly stated,[110] this institution should move on to working for the American people and forego this exercise of overturning 63 million of the votes cast on November 8, 2016.

Doug Collins
Ranking Member
House Committee on the Judiciary

---

[110] *See, e.g.,* Letter from H. Comm. on the Judiciary Republican Members to the Honorable Jerrold Nadler, Chairman, H. Comm. on the Judiciary (December 3, 2019).

REPORT OF EVIDENCE IN THE DEMOCRATS' IMPEACHMENT INQUIRY IN THE HOUSE OF REPRESENTATIVES

Republican Staff Report Prepared For

Devin Nunes
Ranking Member
Permanent Select Committee on Intelligence

Jim Jordan
Ranking Member
Committee on Oversight and Reform

Michael T. McCaul
Ranking Member
Committee on Foreign Affairs

December 2, 2019

EXECUTIVE SUMMARY

On November 8, 2016, nearly 63 million Americans from around the country chose Donald J. Trump to be the 45th President of the United States. Now, less than a year before the next presidential election, 231 House Democrats in Washington, D.C., are trying to undo the will of the American people.[*] As one Democrat admitted, the pursuit of this extreme course of action is because they want to stop President Trump's re-election.[†]

Democrats in the House of Representatives have been working to impeach President Trump since his election. Democrats introduced four separate resolutions in 2017 and 2018 seeking to impeach President Trump.[‡] In January 2019, on their first day in power, House Democrats again introduced articles of impeachment.[§] That same day, a newly elected Congresswoman promised to an audience of her supporters, "we're going to go in there and we're going to impeach the [expletive deleted]."[**] Her comments are not isolated. Speaker Nancy Pelosi called President Trump "an impostor" and said it is "dangerous" to allow American voters to evaluate his performance in 2020.[††]

The Democrats' impeachment inquiry is not the organic outgrowth of serious misconduct; it is an orchestrated campaign to upend our political system. The Democrats are trying to impeach a duly elected President based on the accusations and assumptions of unelected bureaucrats who disagreed with President Trump's policy initiatives and processes. They are trying to impeach President Trump because some unelected bureaucrats were discomforted by an elected President's telephone call with Ukrainian President Volodymyr Zelensky. They are trying to impeach President Trump because some unelected bureaucrats chafed at an elected President's "outside the beltway" approach to diplomacy.

The sum and substance of the Democrats' case for impeachment is that President Trump abused his authority to pressure Ukraine to investigate former Vice President Joe Biden, President Trump's potential political rival, for President Trump's benefit in the 2020 election. Democrats say this pressure campaign encompassed leveraging a White House meeting and the release of U.S. security assistance to force the Ukrainian President to succumb to President Trump's political wishes. Democrats say that Mayor Rudy Giuliani, the President's personal attorney, and a "shadow" group of U.S. officials conspired to benefit the President politically.

The evidence presented does not prove any of these Democrat allegations, and none of the Democrats' witnesses testified to having evidence of bribery, extortion, or any high crime or misdemeanor.

---

[*] H. Res. 660, 116th Cong. (2019) (Roll call vote 604).
[†] *Weekends with Alex Witt* (MSNBC television broadcast May 5 2019) (interview with Rep. Al Green).
[‡] H., Res. 705, 115th Cong. (2018); H. Res. 646, 115th Cong. (2017); H. Res. 621, 115th Cong. (2017); H. Res. 438, 115th Cong. (2017).
[§] H. Res. 13, 116th Cong. (2019).
[**] Amy B. Wong, *Rep. Rashida Tlaib profanely promised to impeach Trump. She's not sorry.*, Wash. Post, Jan. 4, 2019.
[††] Emily Tillett, *Nancy Pelosi says Trump's attacks on witnesses "very significant" to impeachment probe*, CBS News, Nov. 15, 2019; Dear Colleague Letter from Speaker Nancy Pelosi (Nov. 18, 2019).

i

The evidence does not support the accusation that President Trump pressured President Zelensky to initiate investigations for the purpose of benefiting the President in the 2020 election. The evidence does not support the accusation that President Trump covered up the summary of his phone conversation with President Zelensky. The evidence does not support the accusation that President Trump obstructed the Democrats' impeachment inquiry.

At the heart of the matter, the impeachment inquiry involves the actions of only two people: President Trump and President Zelensky. The summary of their July 25, 2019, telephone conversation shows no *quid pro quo* or indication of conditionality, threats, or pressure—much less evidence of bribery or extortion. The summary reflects laughter, pleasantries, and cordiality. President Zelensky has said publicly and repeatedly that he felt no pressure. President Trump has said publicly and repeatedly that he exerted no pressure.

Even examining evidence beyond the presidential phone call shows no *quid pro quo*, bribery, extortion, or abuse of power. The evidence shows that President Trump holds a deep-seated, genuine, and reasonable skepticism of Ukraine due to its history of pervasive corruption. The President has also been vocal about his skepticism of U.S. foreign aid and the need for European allies to shoulder more of the financial burden for regional defense. Senior Ukrainian officials under former President Petro Poroshenko publicly attacked then-candidate Trump during the 2016 campaign—including some senior Ukrainian officials who remained in their positions after President Zelensky's term began. All of these factors bear on the President's state of mind and help to explain the President's actions toward Ukraine and President Zelensky.

Understood in this proper context, the President's initial hesitation to meet with President Zelensky or to provide U.S. taxpayer-funded security assistance to Ukraine without thoughtful review is entirely prudent. Ultimately, President Zelensky took decisive action demonstrating his commitment to promoting reform, combatting corruption, and replacing Poroshenko-era holdovers with new leadership in his Administration. President Trump then released security assistance to Ukraine and met with President Zelensky in September 2019—all without Ukraine taking any action to investigate President Trump's political rival.

House Democrats allege that Ukraine felt pressure to bend to the President's political will, but the evidence shows a different reality. Ukraine felt good about its relationship with the United States in the early months of the Zelensky Administration, having had several high-level meetings with senior U.S. officials between July and September. Although U.S. security assistance was temporarily paused, the U.S. government did not convey the pause to the Ukrainians because U.S. officials believed the pause would get worked out and, if publicized, may be mischaracterized as a shift in U.S. policy towards Ukraine. U.S. officials said that the Ukrainian government in Kyiv never knew the aid was delayed until reading about it in the U.S. media. Ambassador Kurt Volker, the key American interlocutor trusted by the Ukrainian government, said the Ukrainians never raised concerns to him until after the pause became public in late August.

The Democrats' impeachment narrative ignores Ukraine's dramatic transformation in its fight against endemic corruption. President Trump was skeptical of Ukrainian corruption and his Administration sought proof that newly-elected President Zelensky was a true reformer. And after winning a parliamentary majority, the new Zelensky administration took rapid strides to crack down on corruption. Several high-level U.S. officials observed firsthand these anti-corruption achievements in Kyiv, and the security assistance was released soon afterward.

The Democrats' impeachment narrative also ignores President Trump's steadfast support for Ukraine in its war against Russian occupation. Several of the Democrats' witnesses described how President Trump's policies toward Ukraine to combat Russian aggression have been substantially stronger than those of President Obama—then under the stewardship of Vice President Biden. Where President Obama and Vice President Biden gave the Ukrainians night-vision goggles and blankets, the Trump Administration provided the Ukrainians with lethal defensive assistance, including Javelin anti-tank missiles.

The Democrats nonetheless tell a story of an illicit pressure campaign run by President Trump through his personal attorney, Mayor Giuliani, to coerce Ukraine to investigate the President's political rival by withholding a meeting and security assistance. There is, however, no direct, firsthand evidence of any such scheme. The Democrats are alleging guilt on the basis of hearsay, presumptions, and speculation—all of which are reflected in the anonymous whistleblower complaint that sparked this inquiry. The Democrats' narrative is so dependent on speculation that one Democrat publicly justified hearsay as "better" than direct evidence.[‡‡] Where there are ambiguous facts, the Democrats interpret them in a light most unfavorable to the President. In the absence of real evidence, the Democrats appeal to emotion—evaluating how unelected bureaucrats *felt* about the events in question.

The fundamental disagreement apparent in the Democrats' impeachment inquiry is a difference of world views and a discomfort with President Trump's policy decisions. To the extent that some unelected bureaucrats believed President Trump had established an "irregular" foreign policy apparatus, it was because they were not a part of that apparatus. There is nothing illicit about three senior U.S. officials—each with official interests relating to Ukraine—shepherding the U.S.-Ukraine relationship and reporting their actions to State Department and NSC leadership. There is nothing inherently improper with Mayor Giuliani's involvement as well because the Ukrainians knew that he was a conduit to convince President Trump that President Zelensky was serious about reform.

There is also nothing wrong with asking serious questions about the presence of Vice President Biden's son, Hunter Biden, on the board of directors of Burisma, a corrupt Ukrainian company, or about Ukraine's attempts to influence the 2016 presidential election. Biden's Burisma has an international reputation as a corrupt company. As far back as 2015, the Obama State Department had concerns about Hunter Biden's role on Burisma's board. Ukrainian anti-corruption activists noted concerns as well. Publicly available—and irrefutable—evidence shows how senior Ukrainian government officials sought to influence the 2016 U.S. presidential election in opposition to President Trump's candidacy, and that some in the Ukrainian embassy in Washington worked with a Democrat operative to achieve that goal. While Democrats reflexively dismiss these truths as conspiracy theories, the facts are indisputable and bear heavily on the Democrats' impeachment inquiry.

[‡‡] *"Impeachment Inquiry: Ambassador William B. Taylor and Mr. George Kent": Hearing before the H. Perm. Sel. Comm. on Intelligence*, 116th Cong. (2019) (statement of Rep. Mike Quigley).

* * *

In our system of government, power resides with the American people, who delegate executive power to the President through an election once every four years. Unelected officials and career bureaucrats assist in the execution of the laws. The unelected bureaucracy exists to serve the elected representatives of the American people. The Democrats' impeachment narrative flips our system on its head in service of their political ambitions.

The Democrats' impeachment inquiry, led by House Intelligence Committee Chairman Adam Schiff, is merely the outgrowth of their obsession with re-litigating the results of the 2016 presidential election. Despite their best efforts, the evidence gathered during the Democrats' partisan and one-sided impeachment inquiry does not support that President Trump pressured Ukraine to investigate his political rival to benefit the President in the 2020 presidential election. The evidence does not establish any impeachable offense.

But that is not for Democrats' want of trying.

For the first phase of the Democrats' impeachment inquiry, Chairman Schiff led the inquiry from his Capitol basement bunker, preventing transparency on the process and accountability for his actions. Because the fact-finding was unclassified, the closed-door process was purely for information control. This arrangement allowed Chairman Schiff—who had already publicly fabricated evidence and misled Americans about his interaction with the anonymous whistleblower—to selectively leak information to paint misleading public narratives, while simultaneously imposing a gag rule on Republican members. From his basement bunker, Chairman Schiff provided no due process protections for the President and he directed witnesses called by the Democrats not to answer Republican questions. Chairman Schiff also ignored Republican requests to secure the testimony of the anonymous whistleblower, despite promising earlier that the whistleblower would provide "unfiltered testimony."

When the Democrats emerged from the bunker for the public phase of their impeachment inquiry, Chairman Schiff continued to deny fundamental fairness and minority rights. Chairman Schiff interrupted Republican Members and directed witnesses not to answer Republican questions. Chairman Schiff refused to allow Republicans to exercise the limited procedural rights afforded to them. Chairman Schiff rejected witnesses identified by Republicans who would inject some semblance of fairness and objectivity. Chairman Schiff denied Republican subpoenas for testimony and documents, violating the Democrats' own rules to vote down these subpoenas with no notice to Republicans.

Speaker Pelosi, Chairman Schiff, and House Democrats seek to impeach President Trump—not because they have proof of a high crime or misdemeanor, but because they disagreed with the President's actions and his policies. But in our system of government, the President is accountable to the American people. The accountability to the American people comes at the ballot box, not in House Democrats' star chamber.

FINDINGS

Democrats allege that President Trump pressured Ukraine to initiate investigations into his political rival, former Vice President Biden, for the purpose of benefiting the President in the 2020 U.S. presidential election. The evidence does not support the Democrats' allegations. Instead, the findings outlined below are based on the evidence presented and information available in the public realm.

- President Trump has a deep-seated, genuine, and reasonable skepticism of Ukraine due to its history of pervasive corruption.

- President Trump has a long-held skepticism of U.S. foreign assistance and believes that Europe should pay its fair share for mutual defense.

- President Trump's concerns about Hunter Biden's role on Burisma's board are valid. The Obama State Department noted concerns about Hunter Biden's relationship with Burisma in 2015 and 2016.

- There is indisputable evidence that senior Ukrainian government officials opposed President Trump's candidacy in the 2016 election and did so publicly. It has been publicly reported that a Democratic National Committee operative worked with Ukrainian officials, including the Ukrainian Embassy, to dig up dirt on then-candidate Trump.

- The evidence does not establish that President Trump pressured Ukraine to investigate Burisma Holdings, Vice President Joe Biden, Hunter Biden, or Ukrainian influence in the 2016 election for the purpose of benefiting him in the 2020 election.

- The evidence does not establish that President Trump withheld a meeting with President Zelensky for the purpose of pressuring Ukraine to investigate Burisma Holdings, Vice President Joe Biden, Hunter Biden, or Ukrainian influence in the 2016 election.

- The evidence does not support that President Trump withheld U.S. security assistance to Ukraine for the purpose of pressuring Ukraine to investigate Burisma Holdings, Vice President Joe Biden, Hunter Biden, or Ukrainian influence in the 2016 election.

- The evidence does not support that President Trump orchestrated a shadow foreign policy apparatus for the purpose of pressuring Ukraine to investigate Burisma Holdings, Vice President Joe Biden, Hunter Biden, or Ukrainian influence in the 2016 election.

- The evidence does not support that President Trump covered up the substance of his telephone conversation with President Zelensky by restricting access to the call summary.

- President Trump's assertion of longstanding claims of executive privilege is a legitimate response to an unfair, abusive, and partisan process, and does not constitute obstruction of a legitimate impeachment inquiry.

TABLE OF CONTENTS

TABLE OF NAMES

Christopher Anderson	Foreign Service Officer, U.S. Department of State
Michael Atkinson	Inspector General of the Intelligence Community (May 2018–present)
Arsen Avakov	Ukrainian Minister of Internal Affairs (February 2014–present)
Hunter Biden	Board Member, Burisma Holdings (April 2014–October 2019)
Joseph R. Biden	Vice President of the United States (January 2009–January 2017)
Robert Blair	Senior Advisor to the White House Chief of Staff (January 2019–present)
Andriy Bohdan	Head of Ukrainian Office of Presidential Administration (May 2019–present)
John Bolton	U.S. National Security Advisor (April 2018–September 2019)
T. Ulrich Brechbuhl	Counselor to the U.S. Secretary of State, U.S. Department of State (May 2018–present)
Alexandra Chalupa	Former contractor, Democratic National Committee
Valeriy Chaly	Ukrainian Ambassador to the United States (July 2015–July 2019)
Laura Cooper	Deputy Assistant Secretary of Defense for Russia, Ukraine, and Eurasia, U.S. Department of Defense
Catherine Croft	Foreign Service Officer, U.S. Department of State Director for European Affairs, National Security Council (July 2017–July 2018)
Oleksandr Danylyuk	Secretary of the Ukrainian National Security and Defense Council (May 2019–September 2019)
Michael Duffey	Associate Director for National Security Programs, U.S. Office of Management and Budget (May 2019–present)
John Eisenberg	Legal Advisor, National Security Council (2017–present)
Michael Ellis	Deputy Legal Advisor, National Security Council (March 2017–present)
Rudy Giuliani	Mayor of New York City (1994–2001) Personal Attorney to President Trump (April 2018–present)
Preston Wells Griffith	Associate Director for Natural Resources, Energy & Science, U.S. Office of Management and Budget (April 2018–present)
David Hale	Under Secretary of State for Political Affairs, U.S. Department of State (August 2018–present)
Fiona Hill	Senior Director for European and Russian Affairs, National Security Council (April 2017–July 2019)
David Holmes	Political Counselor, U.S. Embassy Kyiv[§§] (August 2017–present)

[§§] Consistent with the U.S. Board on Geographic Names, this report spells the Ukrainian capital as "Kyiv" throughout.

Keith Kellogg	National Security Advisor to the Vice President (April 2018–present)
George Kent	Deputy Assistant Secretary of State, Bureau of European and Eurasian Affairs, U.S. Department of State (September 2018–present)
Igor Kolomoisky	Co-owner, PrivatBank Co-owner, 1+1 Media Group
Charles Kupperman	U.S. Deputy National Security Advisor (January 2019–September 2019)
Serhiy Leshchenko	Ukrainian Member of Parliament (November 2014–July 2019)
Yuriy Lutsenko	Prosecutor General of Ukraine (May 2016–August 2019)
Joseph Maguire	Acting U.S. Director of National Intelligence (August 2019–present)
Brian McCormack	Associate Director for Natural Resources, Energy & Science, U.S. Office of Management and Budget (September 2018–present)
Michael McKinley	Senior Advisor to the U.S. Secretary of State, U.S. Department of State (November 2018–October 2019)
Tim Morrison	Senior Director for European and Russian Affairs, National Security Council (July 2019–November 2019)
Mick Mulvaney	Director of the U.S. Office of Management and Budget (February 2017–present) Acting Chief of Staff to the President (January 2019–present)
Nellie Ohr	Contractor, Fusion GPS
Mike Pence	Vice President of the United States (January 2017–present)
Rick Perry	U.S. Secretary of Energy (March 2017–present)
Mike Pompeo	U.S. Secretary of State (April 2018–present)
Petro Poroshenko	President of Ukraine (June 2014–May 2019)
Vadym Prystaiko	Minister of Foreign Affairs of Ukraine (August 2019–present)
Philip Reeker	Acting Assistant Secretary of State, Bureau of European and Eurasian Affairs, U.S. Department of State (March 2019–present)
Mark Sandy	Deputy Associate Director for National Security, U.S. Office of Management and Budget (December 2013–present)
Viktor Shokin	Prosecutor General of Ukraine (February 2015–March 2016)
Oksana Shulyar	Deputy Chief of Mission, Embassy of Ukraine to the U.S.
Gordon Sondland	U.S. Ambassador to the European Union (July 2018–present)
William Taylor	U.S. Ambassador to Ukraine (June 2006–May 2009) U.S. Chargé d'Affaires, *a.i.*, U.S. Embassy Kyiv (June 2019–present)
Andrii Telizhenko	Political officer, Embassy of Ukraine to the U.S.
Donald J. Trump	President of the United States (January 2017–present)

Alexander Vindman   Director for European Affairs, National Security Council (July 2018–present)

Kurt Volker   U.S. Special Representative for Ukraine Negotiations, U.S. Department of State (July 2017–September 2019)

Russell Vought   Acting Director, U.S. Office of Management and Budget

Kathryn Wheelbarger   Acting Assistant Secretary of Defense for International Affairs, U.S. Department of Defense (November 2018–present)

Jennifer Williams   Special Adviser for Europe and Russia, Office of the Vice President

Viktor Yanukovych   President of Ukraine (February 2010–February 2014)

Arseniy Yatsenyuk   Prime Minister of Ukraine (February 2014–April 2016)

Andrey Yermak   Adviser to President of Ukraine Volodymyr Zelensky

Marie Yovanovitch   U.S. Ambassador to Ukraine (August 2016–May 2019)

Volodymyr Zelensky[***] President of Ukraine (May 2019–present)

Mykola Zlochevsky   Co-founder, Burisma Holdings (2002–present)
                        Ukrainian Minister of Ecology and Natural Resources (July 2010–April 2012)

[***] Although some sources use alternate spellings of the Ukrainian President's surname, this report uses the spelling "Zelensky" for consistency throughout.

I.   **The evidence does not establish that President Trump pressured the Ukrainian government to investigate his political rival for the purpose of benefiting him in the 2020 U.S. presidential election.**

Democrats have alleged that President Trump exerted pressure on Ukrainian President Zelensky to force the Ukrainian government to manufacture "dirt" or otherwise investigate a potential Democrat candidate in the 2020 U.S. presidential election for President Trump's political benefit.[1] Democrats allege that President Trump sought to use the possibility of a White House meeting with President Zelensky and release of U.S. security assistance to Ukraine as leverage to force Ukraine to help the President politically. Democrats allege that President Trump orchestrated a "shadow" foreign policy apparatus that worked to accomplish the President's political goals.

The evidence obtained in the Democrats' impeachment inquiry, however, does not support these Democrat allegations. In fact, witnesses called by the Democrats denied having any awareness of criminal activity or an impeachable offense. Rep. John Ratcliffe asked Ambassador Bill Taylor and Deputy Assistant Secretary George Kent whether they were "assert[ing] there was an impeachable offense in [the July 25] call."[2] Neither said there was.[3] Rep. Chris Stewart asked Ambassador Marie Yovanovitch if she had any information about President Trump's involvement in criminal activity.[4] Ambassador Yovanovitch said no.[5] Rep. Ratcliffe asked National Security Council (NSC) staff member LTC Alexander Vindman and Office of the Vice President special adviser Jennifer Williams if they have labeled the President's conduct as "bribery."[6] Both said no.[7] Rep. Elise Stefanik asked Ambassador Kurt Volker, the U.S. special envoy for Ukraine negotiations, and Tim Morrison, the NSC senior director for Europe, whether they saw any bribery, extortion, or *quid pro quo*.[8] Both said no.[9]

Contrary to Democrat assertions, the evidence does not show that President Trump pressured President Zelensky to investigate his political rival during the July 25 phone call. The best evidence of the conversation—the call summary—shows no evidence of conditionality, threats, or pressure. President Zelensky and President Trump have both said there was no

---

[1] *"Whistleblower Disclosure": Hearing of the H. Perm. Sel. Comm. on Intelligence*, 116th Cong. (2019) (statement of Rep. Adam Schiff, Chairman); Rep. Adam Schiff (@RepAdamSchiff), Twitter (Oct. 12, 2019, 2:53 p.m.), https://twitter.com/repadamschiff/status/1183138629130035200; *Lieu accuses Trump of asking Ukraine to "manufacture dirt" on Biden*, The Hill, Sept. 25, 2019.

[2] *"Impeachment Inquiry: Ambassador William B. Taylor and Mr. George Kent": Hearing before the H. Perm. Sel. Comm. on Intelligence*, 116th Cong. (2019).

[3] *Id.*

[4] *"Impeachment Inquiry: Ambassador Marie Yovanovitch": Hearing before the H. Perm. Sel. Comm. on Intelligence*, 116th Cong. (2019).

[5] *Id.*

[6] *"Impeachment Inquiry: LTC Alexander Vindman and Ms. Jennifer Williams": Hearing before the H. Perm. Sel. Comm. on Intelligence*, 116th Cong. (2019). This report abbreviates military titles consistent with the U.S. Government Printing Office style manual. *See* U.S. Gov't Printing Off., Style Manual 227 (2016).

[7] *Id.*

[8] *"Impeachment Inquiry: Ambassador Kurt Volker and Mr. Timothy Morrison": Hearing before the H. Perm. Sel. Comm. on Intelligence*, 116th Cong. (2019).

[9] *Id.*

pressure, the initial read-out from the State Department and the Ukrainian government reflected no concerns, and the NSC leadership saw no illegality or impropriety with the call.

The evidence does not show that President Trump withheld a meeting with President Zelensky to pressure Ukraine to investigate his political rival. The evidence shows that President Trump has a long-standing, deep-seated skepticism of Ukraine due to its history of pervasive corruption. President Zelensky was a political newcomer with untested views on anti-corruption and a close association with a Ukrainian oligarch. Even so, President Trump agreed to invite President Zelensky to the White House, and in the interim, Ukrainian officials had several high-level meetings with U.S. officials. President Trump and President Zelensky met in September 2019 without Ukraine ever taking any action on investigating President Trump's political rival.

In addition, the evidence does not show that President Trump withheld U.S. security assistance to Ukraine to pressure Ukraine to investigate his political rival. The evidence shows that President Trump has a skepticism of U.S. taxpayer-funded foreign aid and believes Europe should carry more financial burden for its regional defense. Although U.S. security assistance was paused temporarily, Democrats' witnesses denied there being any direct link to investigations of the President's political rival. Both the Ukrainian government and President Trump separately denied any linkage. U.S. officials did not tell the Ukrainian officials about the delay because they thought it would get worked out. Ambassador Volker, a senior U.S. diplomat and primary interlocutor with senior Ukrainian government officials, testified that the Ukrainians did not raise concerns to him about a delay in aid until after the pause was made public in late August 2019. The U.S. security assistance to Ukraine was ultimately disbursed without Ukraine taking any action to investigate President Trump's political rival.

The evidence does not show that President Trump established a "shadow" foreign policy apparatus to pressure Ukraine to investigate his political rival. The President has broad Constitutional authority over U.S. foreign policy, and President Trump is likely suspicious of the national security apparatus due to continual leaks of sensitive information and the resistance within the federal bureaucracy. The three U.S. officials who Democrats accuse of conducting an "irregular" foreign policy channel had legitimate responsibilities for Ukraine policy. They kept the State Department and NSC aware of their actions. To the extent Mayor Giuliani was involved, he was in communication with these officials and the Ukrainians did not see him as speaking on behalf of the President.

Although Democrats reflexively criticize President Trump for promoting "conspiracy theories" about Hunter Biden's role on Burisma's board or Ukrainian attempts to influence the 2016 election, evidence suggests there are legitimate questions about both issues. The Democrats' witnesses testified that it would be appropriate for Ukraine to investigate allegations of corruption in Ukraine.

Finally, there are fundamental flaws with the anonymous whistleblower complaint that initiated the Democrats' impeachment inquiry. The complaint contained inaccurate and misleading information that prejudiced the public understanding of President Trump's conversation with President Zelensky. The whistleblower had no firsthand knowledge of the events in question and a bias against President Trump. The whistleblower communicated with

Chairman Schiff or his staff prior to submitting the whistleblower complaint to the Inspector General of the Intelligence Community. Several witnesses contradicted assertions made by the anonymous whistleblower. The whistleblower's complaint did not accurately reflect the tone and substance of the phone call, which is unsurprising given the whistleblower's reliance on secondhand information that had likely already been colored by biases of the original sources.

A. The evidence does not establish that President Trump pressured President Zelensky during the July 25 phone call to investigate the President's political rival for the purpose of benefiting him in the 2020 election.

On July 25, 2019, President Trump and President Zelensky spoke by telephone.[10] This conversation would later serve as the basis for the anonymous whistleblower complaint and the spark for the Democrats' impeachment inquiry. Contrary to allegations that President Trump pressured Ukraine to investigate a domestic political rival during this call,[11] the evidence shows that President Trump did not pressure President Zelensky to investigate his political rival.

The call summary and initial read-outs of the conversation reflect no indication of conditionality, coercion, or intimidation—elements that would have been present if President Trump had used his authority to pressure President Zelensky to investigate his political rival. Importantly, both President Zelensky and President Trump have said publicly there was no pressure or anything inappropriate about their conversation. The anonymous whistleblower complaint—which sparked the impeachment inquiry—contains sensational rhetoric about the July 25 phone conservation that has prejudged subsequent views of the call.

1. The call summary does not reflect any improper pressure or conditionality to pressure Ukraine to investigate President Trump's political rival.

The best evidence of the telephone conversation between President Trump and President Zelensky is the contemporaneous summary prepared by the White House Situation Room. The Democrats' witnesses described how National Security Council (NSC) policy staffers and White House Situation Room duty officers typically listen in on presidential conversations with foreign leaders to transcribe the contents of the conversation.[12] This process occurred for President Trump's July 25 phone call with President Zelensky.

---

[10] President Trump had spoken with then-President-elect Zelensky on April 21, 2019, to congratulate him on his election. *See* The White House, *Memorandum of Telephone Conversation* (Apr. 21, 2019). This conversation too contained no indication of pressure, intimidation or threats. *See id.*

[11] *See, e.g.*, Josh Dawsey et al., *How Trump and Giuliani pressured Ukraine to investigate the President's rivals*, Wash. Post, (Sept. 20, 2019).

[12] *See, e.g.*, Deposition of Dr. Fiona Hill, in Wash., D.C., at 297-300 (Oct. 14, 2019) [hereinafter "Hill deposition"]. Although some have alleged that the presence of ellipses in the call summary connotes missing text, witnesses testified that call summaries often use ellipses to denote unfinished thoughts and not to "read too much" into the use of ellipses. *See, e.g., id.* at 307. LTC Vindman testified in his closed-door deposition that any editing decisions or missing words were not done maliciously. *See* Deposition of LTC Alexander Vindman, in Wash., D.C., at 253 (Oct. 29, 2019) [hereinafter "Vindman deposition"]. In his public testimony, LTC Vindman explained that although the summary did not mention the word "Burisma," it was "not a significant omission." *Impeachment Inquiry: LTC Alexander Vindman and Ms. Jennifer Williams, supra* note 6. Morrison testified in his deposition that he believed

As transcribed, the call summary denotes laughter, pleasantries, and compliments exchanged between President Trump and President Zelensky. The summary does not evince any threats, coercion, intimidation, or indication of conditionality. Democrats even acknowledged that the call summary reflected no *quid pro quo*.[13] The summary bears absolutely no resemblance to House Intelligence Committee Chairman Adam Schiff's self-described "parody" interpretation of the call, which the Chairman performed at a public hearing on September 26.[14]

The summary of the July 25 phone call begins by President Trump congratulating President Zelensky on a "great victory," a "terrific job," and a "fantastic achievement."[15] President Zelensky reciprocated by complimenting President Trump, saying:

> Well, yes, to tell you the truth, we are trying to work hard because we wanted to drain the swamp here in our country. We brought in many, many new people. Not the old politicians, not the typical politicians, because we want to have a new format and a new type of government. You are a great teacher for us and in that.[16]

President Trump expressed his concern that European countries were not providing their fair share in terms of assistance to Ukraine[17]—a topic about which President Trump has been vocal.[18] President Zelensky responded that President Trump was "absolutely right" and that he had expressed concerns to German Chancellor Angela Merkel and French President Emmanuel Macron.[19] President Zelensky thanked President Trump for U.S. military support and said Ukraine was "almost ready to buy more Javelins from the United States for defense purposes."[20]

President Trump then transitioned to discuss the allegation that some Ukrainian officials sought to influence the 2016 U.S. presidential election. Although Democrats have seized on the President's phrasing—"I would like you to do us a favor though"[21]—to accuse the President of pressuring President Zelensky to target his 2020 political rival for his political benefit,[22] they omit the remainder of his sentence. The full sentence shows that President Trump was not asking President Zelensky to investigate his political rival, but rather asking him to assist in "get[ting] to

---

the call memorandum was an "accurate and complete" reflection of the substance of the call. Deposition of Timothy Morrison, in Wash., D.C., at 60 (Oct. 31, 2019) [hereinafter "Morrison deposition"].

[13] *See, e.g., MSNBC Live with Craig Melvin* (MSNBC television broadcast Sept. 25, 2019) (interview with Rep. Ro Khanna) (saying evidence of a *quid pro quo* on the call summary is "irrelevant").

[14] *Whistleblower Disclosure, supra* note 1.

[15] The White House, *Memorandum of Telephone Conversation* 1 (July 25, 2019).

[16] *Id.* at 2.

[17] *Id.*

[18] *See infra* section I.C.2.

[19] *Memorandum of Telephone Conversation, supra* note 15, at 2.

[20] *Id.*

[21] *Id.* at 3.

[22] *See, e.g., Whistleblower Disclosure, supra* note 1 (statement of Rep. Adam Schiff, Chairman).

the bottom" of potential Ukrainian involvement in the 2016 election.[23] This reading is supported by President Trump's subsequent reference to Special Counsel Robert Mueller, who had testified the day before about his findings,[24] and to Attorney General William Barr, who had initiated an official inquiry into the origins of the U.S. government's 2016 Russia investigation.[25]

President Zelensky did not express any concern that President Trump had raised the allegations about Ukrainian influence in the 2016 election. In fact, President Zelensky responded by reiterating his commitment to cooperation between Ukraine and the United States and mentioning that he had recalled the Ukrainian Ambassador to the United States, Valeriy Chaly.[26] Ambassador Chaly had authored an op-ed in *The Hill* during the height of the presidential campaign in 2016 criticizing a statement that President Trump had made by Crimea.[27] President Zelensky said he planned to surround himself with "the best and most experienced people" and pledged that "as the President of Ukraine that all the investigations will be done openly and candidly."[28] President Zelensky also raised former New York Mayor Rudy Giuliani, saying "we are hoping very much that Mr. Giuliani will be able to travel to Ukraine and we will meet once he comes to Ukraine."[29]

The call summary shows that the discussion then intertwined several different topics. In response to President Zelensky's statement about new personnel, President Trump and President Zelensky discussed the position of prosecutor general.[30] President Zelensky did not express any discomfort discussing the prosecutor general position. He said the new prosecutor general would be "100% my person, my candidate" and said the prosecutor would look into the matters raised by President Trump to "mak[e] sure to restore the honesty" of the investigation.[31] President Zelensky later said "we will be very serious about the case and will work on the investigation."[32]

In response to President Zelensky's reference to Mayor Giuliani, President Trump said Mayor Giuliani is "a highly respected man" who "very much knows what's happening and he is a very capable guy."[33] President Trump said that he would ask Mayor Giuliani to call President Zelensky, along with Attorney General Barr, to "get to the bottom of it."[34] President Zelensky did not express any concern about Mayor Giuliani's engagement—in fact, President Zelensky, not President Trump, first referenced Mayor Giuliani in the conversation.

---

[23] *Memorandum of Telephone Conversation, supra* note 15, at 3. The President's reference to "Crowdstrike" during the conversation refers to a cybersecurity firm that examined the Democratic National Committee server following intrusion by the Russian government in 2016.
[24] *"Oversight of the Report on the Investigation into Russian Interference in the 2016 Presidential Election: Former Special Counsel Robert S. Mueller, III": Hearing before the H. Comm. on the Judiciary*, 116th Cong. (2019).
[25] *See, e.g.*, Adam Goldman et al., *Barr assigns U.S. Attorney in Connecticut to review origins of Russia inquiry*, N.Y. Times, May 13, 2019.
[26] *Memorandum of Telephone Conversation, supra* note 15, at 3.
[27] Valeriy Chaly, *Ukraine's ambassador: Trump's comments send wrong message to world*, The Hill, Aug. 4, 2016.
[28] *Memorandum of Telephone Conversation, supra* note 15, at 3.
[29] *Id.*
[30] *Id.* at 3-4.
[31] *Id.* at 4.
[32] *Id.* at 5.
[33] *Id.* at 3-4.
[34] *Id.* at 4.

President Trump then raised former U.S. Ambassador to Ukraine, Marie Yovanovitch, saying that she was "bad news" and "the people she was dealing with in the Ukraine were bad news."[35] President Zelensky did not express any hesitancy in discussing the ambassador. Contrary to Democrats' assertion that he felt obligated to agree with President Trump's assessment, President Zelensky stated his independent negative assessment of Ambassador Yovanovitch:

> Her attitude toward me was far from the best as she admired the previous President and she was on his side. She would not accept me as a new President well enough.[36]

President Trump also raised in passing—using the transition phrase "the other thing"—the topic of Vice President Joe Biden's son, Hunter Biden, referring to his position on the board of a Ukrainian energy company, Burisma, known for its corruption.[37] President Trump said "a lot of people want to find out about that so whatever you can do with the Attorney General would be great."[38] President Zelensky did not reply to President Trump's reference to the Bidens, and the two did not discuss the topic substantively.

The call concluded with President Zelensky raising energy cooperation between Ukraine and the United States and with President Trump reiterating his invitation for President Zelensky to visit the White House.[39]

Although some later expressed concern about the call, the call summary—the best evidence of the conversation—shows no indication of conflict, intimidation, or pressure. President Trump never conditioned a White House meeting on any action by President Zelensky. President Trump never mentioned U.S. security assistance to Ukraine. President Zelensky never verbalized any disagreement, hostility, or concern about any facet of the U.S.-Ukrainian relationship.

2. President Zelensky has publicly and repeatedly said he felt no pressure to investigate President Trump's political rival.

Since President Trump declassified and publicly released the content of his July 25 phone conversation with President Zelensky, President Zelensky and other senior Ukrainian officials have publicly and repeatedly asserted that President Zelensky felt no pressure to investigate President Trump's political rival. President Zelensky has variously asserted, "nobody pushed . . . me," "I was never pressured," and there was no "blackmail."

---

[35] *Id.*
[36] *Id.*
[37] *Id.*
[38] *Id.*
[39] *Id.* at 5.

On September 25, President Zelensky and President Trump met face-to-face for a bilateral meeting on the margins of the 74th United Nations (U.N.) General Assembly in New York. The presidents jointly participated in a media availability, during which President Zelensky asserted that he felt no pressure.[40] President Zelensky said then:

> Q. President Zelensky, have you felt any pressure from President Trump to investigate Joe Biden and Hunter Biden?
>
> A. I think you read everything. So I think you read text. I'm sorry, but I don't want to be involved to democratic, open elections — elections of USA. *No, you heard that we had, I think, good phone call. It was normal. We spoke about many things. And I — so I think, and you read it, that nobody pushed — pushed me.*[41]

President Zelensky again reiterated that he was not pressured to investigate President Trump's political rival during an interview with a Kyodo News, a Japanese media outlet, published on October 6. Kyodo News quoted President Zelensky as saying, "I was never pressured and there were no conditions being imposed" on a White House meeting or U.S. security assistance to Ukraine.[42] President Zelensky denied "reports by U.S. media that [President] Trump's requests were conditions" for a White House meeting or U.S. security assistance.[43]

On October 10, during an all-day media availability in Kyiv, President Zelensky again emphasized that he felt no pressure to investigate President Trump's political rival. President Zelensky said there was "no blackmail" during the conversation, explaining: "This is not corruption. It was just a call."[44]

In addition, on September 21—before President Trump had even declassified and released the call summary—Ukrainian Foreign Minister Vadym Prystaiko denied that President Trump had pressured President Zelensky to investigate President Trump's political rival.[45] Foreign Minister Prystaiko said:

> *I know what the conversation was about and I think there was no pressure.* There was talk, conversations are different, leaders have the right to discuss any problems that exist. This conversation was

[40] Press Release, The White House, Remarks by President Trump and President Zelensky of Ukraine Before Bilateral Meeting (Sept. 25, 2019), *available at* https://www.whitehouse.gov/briefings-statements/remarks-president-trump-president-zelensky-ukraine-bilateral-meeting-new-york-ny/.
[41] *Id.* (emphasis added).
[42] *Ukraine president denies being pushed by Trump to investigate Biden*, Kyodo News, Oct. 6, 2019.
[43] *Id.*
[44] *Ukraine's president says 'no blackmail' in Trump call*, BBC, Oct. 10, 2019.
[45] *"Trump did not pressure Zelenskyy, Ukraine is independent state" – Foreign Minister Prystaiko*, Hromadske, Sept. 21, 2019.

long, friendly, and it touched on a lot of questions, including those requiring serious answers.[46]

Similarly, Ambassador Bill Taylor explained that he had dinner with Oleksandr Danylyuk, then-Secretary of the National Security and Defense Council, the night of the phone conversation between President Trump and President Zelensky.[47] He explained that Danylyuk said that the Ukrainian government "seemed to think that the call went fine, the call went well. He wasn't disturbed by anything. He wasn't disturbed that he told us about the phone call."[48]

President Zelensky's repeated denials that President Trump pressured him to investigate domestic political rival—corroborated by Foreign Minister Prystaiko's similar denial—carry significant weight.

3. President Trump has publicly and repeatedly said he did not pressure President Zelensky to investigate his political rival.

Like President Zelensky, President Trump has repeatedly and publicly stated that he did not pressure President Zelensky to investigate his political rival. During the September 25 bilateral meeting with President Zelensky, President Trump said to the assembled members of the media: "There was no pressure. And you know there was—and, by the way, you know there was no pressure. All you have to do it see it, what went on the call."[49] When asked whether he wanted President Zelensky to "do more" to investigate Vice President Biden, President Trump responded: "No. I want him to do whatever he can. This was not his fault; he wasn't there. He's just been here recently. But whatever he can do in terms of corruption, because the corruption is massive."[50]

Despite the President's statements, some allege that an overheard conversation the day after President Trump's conversation with President Zelensky shows that the President sought to pressure President Zelensky. On July 26, following a meeting with President Zelensky, Ambassador Gordon Sondland, the U.S. Ambassador to the European Union, telephoned President Trump from Kyiv.[51] According to a subsequent account of David Holmes, a Political Counselor at U.S. Embassy Kyiv, Ambassador Sondland told the President that he was in Ukraine and stated President Zelensky "loves your ass."[52] Holmes recounted that President Trump asked Ambassador Sondland, "So he's going to do the investigation?"[53] Ambassador Sondland allegedly replied, "He's going to do it."[54]

---

[46] *Id.* (emphasis added).
[47] Deposition of Ambassador William B. Taylor, in Wash., D.C., at 80 (Oct. 22, 2019).
[48] *Id.*
[49] Remarks by President Trump and President Zelensky of Ukraine Before Bilateral Meeting, *supra* note 40.
[50] *Id.*
[51] Deposition of David Holmes, in Wash., D.C., at 23-25 (Nov. 15, 2019) [hereinafter "Holmes deposition"]. Ambassador Sondland did not mention this phone call in his deposition. *See generally* Deposition of Ambassador Gordon D. Sondland, in Wash., D.C. (Oct. 17, 2019) [hereinafter "Sondland deposition"].
[52] Holmes deposition, *supra* note 51, at 24
[53] *Id.*
[54] *Id.*

This conversation is not definitive evidence that President Trump pressured President Zelensky to investigate his political rival. First, according to Ambassador Sondland, it was not clear that President Trump meant an investigation into the Bidens. In his closed-door deposition, Ambassador Sondland testified that he only had "five or six" conversations with the President and did not mention this particular conversation.[55] In his public testimony, however, Ambassador Sondland suddenly recalled the conversation, saying that it "did not strike me as significant at the time" and that the primary purpose of the call was to discuss rapper A$AP Rocky, who was imprisoned in Sweden.[56] Ambassador Sondland testified that he has no recollection of discussing Vice President Biden or his son, Hunter Biden, with President Trump.[57]

Second, Holmes testified that although he disclosed Ambassador Sondland's conversation with the President to multiple friends on multiple occasions, he did not feel compelled to disclose it to the State Department or Congress until weeks into the impeachment inquiry.[58] Although Holmes testified that he told his boss, Ambassador Taylor, about the call on August 6 and received a "knowing" response, and that he referred to the call often in staff meetings, Ambassador Taylor testified publicly that he was "not aware of this information" at the time of his October 22 deposition, and that he only became aware of the Holmes account on November 8, 2019, two days after his hearing was publicly announced, at which point he referred it (for the first time) to the Legal Adviser for the Department of State.[59]

4. **Read-outs of the phone call from both the State Department and the Ukrainian government did not reflect that President Trump pressured President Zelensky to investigate his political rival.**

Immediately following the telephone conversation between President Trump and President Zelensky, senior U.S. and Ukrainian government officials provided read-outs of the conversation. According to witness testimony, none of these read-outs indicated that the conversation between the presidents was substantively concerning.

Ambassador Volker testified that he received informal read-outs of the call from both his State Department assistant and his high-level Ukrainian contacts.[60] These read-outs did not indicate any concern with the phone call. Ambassador Volker explained:

---

[55] Sondland deposition, *supra* note 51, at 56.

[56] *"Impeachment Inquiry: Ambassador Gordon Sondland": Hearing before the H. Perm. Sel. Comm. on Intelligence*, 116th Cong. (2019).

[57] *Id.*

[58] Holmes deposition, *supra* note 51, at 31, 158-62.

[59] *Id.* at 81-82, 121-22, 167; *see generally* Taylor deposition, *supra* note 47; *Impeachment Inquiry: Ambassador William B. Taylor and Mr. George Kent*, *supra* note 2.

[60] Transcribed interview of Ambassador Kurt Volker, in Wash., D.C., at 102-03 (Oct. 3, 2019) [hereinafter "Volker transcribed interview"]. Ambassador Volker's assistant at the time, Catherine Croft, testified that she only received a read-out of the phone call was based on what President Zelensky told Ambassador Volker, Ambassador Taylor, and Ambassador Sondland on July 26. Deposition of Catherine Croft, in Wash., D.C., at 16 (Oct. 30, 2019) [hereinafter "Croft deposition"].

A. I got an oral readout from the staffer who works for me in the State Department and our chargé, as well as from Andrey Yermak, who had been on the call in Ukraine himself.

Q. So you got two readouts?

A. Yeah.

Q. One from each side?

A. Correct.

Q. What was the top line message you got from the State Department?

A. Well, they were the same, actually, which is interesting. But the message was congratulations from the President to President Zelensky; President Zelensky reiterating that he is committed to fighting corruption and reform in the Ukraine; and President Trump reiterating an invitation for President Zelensky to visit him at the White House. That was it.[61]

In fact, in his public testimony, Ambassador Volker testified that President Zelensky was "very upbeat about the fact of the call."[62]

Ambassador Sondland received a summary of the phone call from his staff.[63] Ambassador Sondland testified that he was pleased to learn that it was a "good call."[64] George Kent, the Deputy Assistant Secretary of State covering Ukraine, testified that he received a readout of the call from NSC staffer LTC Alexander Vindman.[65] According to Kent, although LTC Vindman said the "atmospherics" of the conversation was cooler and reserved, LTC Vindman did not mention Vice President Biden's name or anything relating to 2016.[66]

In addition, the Office of the President of Ukraine issued an official statement following the phone call.[67] The official statement also signaled no concern about the call or any indication of coercion, intimidation, or pressure from President Trump. The statement read in full:

> President of Ukraine Volodymyr Zelensky had a phone conversation
> with President of the United States Donald Trump. President of the
> United States congratulated Ukraine on successful holding free and

---

[61] Volker transcribed interview, *supra* note 60, at 102-03.
[62] *Impeachment Inquiry: Ambassador Kurt Volker and Timothy Morrison, supra* note 8.
[63] Sondland deposition, *supra* note 51, at 116.
[64] *Id.*
[65] Deposition of George Kent, in Wash., D.C., at 163 (Oct. 15, 2019) [hereinafter "Kent deposition"].
[66] *Id.* at 163-65
[67] Press Release, Office of the President of Ukraine, Volodymyr Zelenskyy had a phone conversation with President of the United States (July 25, 2019), *available at* https://www.president.gov.ua/en/news/volodimir-zelenskij-proviv-telefonnu-rozmovu-z-prezidentom-s-56617.

democratic parliamentary elections as well as Volodymyr Zelensky with victory the Servant of the People Party.

Donald Trump is convinced that the new Ukrainian government will be able to quickly improve image of Ukraine, complete investigation of corruption cases, which inhibited the interaction between Ukraine and the USA.

He also confirmed continued support of the sovereignty and territorial integrity of Ukraine by the United States and the readiness of the American side to fully contribute to the implementation of a Large-Scale Reform Program in our country.

Volodymyr Zelensky thanked Donald Trump for US leadership in preserving and strengthening the sanctions pressure on Russia.

The Presidents agreed to discuss practical issues of Ukrainian-American cooperation during the visit of Volodymyr Zelensky to the United States.[68]

The initial read-outs of the July 25 telephone conversation between President Trump and President Zelensky provide compelling evidence that the key message conveyed during the conversation was about fighting corruption in Ukraine—and not about digging up dirt on President Trump's political rival for the President's political benefit.

5. The National Security Council leadership did not see the call as illegal or improper.

The evidence shows that the NSC leadership did not see the telephone conversation between President Trump and President Zelensky as improper. Timothy Morrison, who served as the Deputy Assistant to the President for National Security, listened in on the conversation.[69] He testified that he was concerned information from the call could leak, but he was not concerned that anything discussed on the call was illegal or improper.[70]

LTG Keith Kellogg, Vice President Pence's National Security Advisor, also listened in on the July 25 telephone conversation.[71] LTG Kellogg stated that like Morrison: "I heard nothing wrong or improper on the call. I had and have no concerns."[72] LTG Kellogg's subordinate, Jennifer Williams, testified that although she found the call to be "unusual," she did not raise

---

[68] *Id.*
[69] Morrison deposition, *supra* note 12, at 15.
[70] *Id.* at 16, 60-61.
[71] The White House, Statement from Lieutenant General Keith Kellogg, National Security Advisor to Vice President Mike Pence (Nov. 19, 2019) [hereinafter "Statement from Lieutenant General Kellogg"].
[72] *Id.*

concerns to LTG Kellogg.[73] LTG Kellogg similarly noted that Williams never raised concerns to him.[74]

Morrison's subordinate, LTC Vindman, listened in on the conversation.[75] At the time of the call, LTC Vindman handled Ukraine policy for the NSC.[76] He testified that he was concerned by the conversation and raised his concerns to the NSC's Legal Advisor, John Eisenberg.[77] Eisenberg, according to LTC Vindman, did not share the concern.[78] LTC Vindman did not raise any concerns to Morrison, his immediate supervisor.[79] In his public testimony, Morrison explained that he had concerns with LTC Vindman's judgment and deviation from the chain of command.[80]

The evidence suggests that any wider concerns about the July 25 phone call originated from LTC Vindman. Williams testified that she discussed the call with no one outside the NSC.[81] LTC Vindman, on the other hand, testified that he discussed the phone call with two people outside of the NSC, Deputy Assistant Secretary Kent and an unidentified intelligence community employee.[82] Deputy Assistant Secretary Kent explained that LTC Vindman felt "uncomfortable" and would not share the majority of the substance of the conversation.[83] According to Kent's recollection, LTC Vindman did not mention that the conversation included any reference to Vice President Biden.[84]

6. The anonymous, secondhand whistleblower complaint misstated details about the July 25 call, which has falsely colored the call's public characterization.

The anonymous whistleblower did not listen in on the July 25 call between President Trump and President Zelensky. The whistleblower's subsequent complaint about the conversation, compiled with secondhand information, misstated key details about the conversation.

The whistleblower sensationally alleged that President Trump "sought to pressure the Ukrainian leader to take actions to help the President's 2020 reelection bid."[85] The call summary, however, contains no reference to 2020 or President Trump's reelection bid.[86]

---

[73] Deposition of Jennifer Williams, in Wash., D.C., at 129 (Nov. 7, 2019) [hereinafter "Williams deposition"]; *Impeachment Inquiry: LTC Alexander Vindman and Ms. Jennifer Williams*, *supra* note 6.
[74] Statement from Lieutenant General Kellogg, *supra* note 71.
[75] Vindman deposition, *supra* note 12, at 18.
[76] *Id.* at 16.
[77] *Id.* at 96.
[78] *Id.* at 97, 258.
[79] Morrison deposition, *supra* note 12, at 59.
[80] *Impeachment Inquiry: Ambassador Kurt Volker and Mr. Timothy Morrison*, *supra* note 8.
[81] *Impeachment Inquiry: LTC Alexander Vindman and Ms. Jennifer Williams*, *supra* note 6.
[82] *Id.*
[83] Kent deposition, *supra* note 65, at 163-64.
[84] *Id.* at 165-66.
[85] Letter to Richard Burr, Chairman, S. Sel. Comm. on Intelligence, & Adam Schiff, Chairman, H. Perm. Sel. Comm. on Intelligence 2 (Aug. 12, 2019) [hereinafter "Whistleblower letter"].
[86] *Memorandum of Telephone Conversation*, *supra* note 15.

The whistleblower alleged that President Trump "pressured" President Zelensky to "initiate or continue an investigation into the activities of former Vice President Joseph Biden and his son, Hunter Biden."[87] The call summary, however, shows that President Trump referenced the Bidens only in passing and that the presidents did not discuss the topic substantively.[88]

The whistleblower alleged that President Trump "pressured" President Zelensky to "locate and turn over servers used by the Democratic National Committee (DNC) and examined by the U.S. cyber security firm Crowdstrike."[89] The call summary, however, demonstrates that while President Trump mentioned Crowdstrike and "the server," President Trump never made any request that President Zelensky locate or turn over any material.[90]

The whistleblower alleged that President Trump "praised Ukraine's Prosecutor General, Mr. Yuriy Lutsenko, and suggested that Mr. Zelensky might want to keep him in his position."[91] The call summary is not clear about which prosecutor general President Trump is referring to— Ambassador Volker testified he believed President Trump was referring to Lutsenko's predecessor, Viktor Shokin[92]—and President Trump never specifically referenced Lutsenko.[93] President Trump also never suggested or intimated that President Zelensky should "keep [Lutsenko] in his position."[94]

The whistleblower also alleged that T. Ulrich Brechbuhl, Counselor to Secretary of State Mike Pompeo, listened in on the July 25 phone call.[95] Subsequent reporting, confirmed by a letter sent by Brechbuhl's attorney, indicated that Brechbuhl was not on the call.[96]

* * *

Setting aside the whistleblower's mischaracterization of President Trump's phone call with President Zelensky, the best available evidence shows no coercion, threats, or pressure for Ukraine to investigate the President's political rival for the President's political benefit. The call summary shows no *quid pro quo*, the initial read-outs relayed no substantive concerns, and both President Zelensky and President Trump have repeatedly said publicly there was no pressure. These facts refute the Democrats' allegations.

---

[87] Whistleblower letter, *supra* note 85, at 2.
[88] *Memorandum of Telephone Conversation, supra* note 15.
[89] Whistleblower letter, *supra* note 85, at 2.
[90] *Memorandum of Telephone Conversation, supra* note 15, at 3.
[91] Whistleblower letter, *supra* note 85, at 3.
[92] Volker transcribed interview, *supra* note 60, at 355.
[93] *Memorandum of Telephone Conversation, supra* note 15.
[94] *Id.*
[95] Whistleblower letter, *supra* note 85, at 3.
[96] Christina Ruffini (@EenaRuffini), Twitter (Sept. 26, 2019, 12:41 p.m.), https://twitter.com/EenaRuffini/status/1177307225024544768; Letter from Ronald Tenpas to Adam Schiff, Chairman, H. Perm. Sel. Comm. on Intelligence (Nov. 5, 2019).

13

B. The evidence does not establish that President Trump withheld a meeting with President Zelensky to pressure Ukraine to investigate the President's political rival for the purpose of benefiting him in the 2020 election.

Democrats allege that President Trump withheld a meeting with President Zelensky as a way of pressuring Ukraine to investigate President Trump's political rival.[97] Here, too, the evidence obtained during the impeachment inquiry does not support this allegation. President Trump and President Zelensky met *without* Ukraine ever investigating Vice Present Biden or his son, Hunter Biden.

The evidence strongly suggests, instead, that President Trump was reluctant to meet with President Zelensky for a different reason—Ukraine's long history of pervasive corruption and uncertainty about whether President Zelensky would break from this history and live up to his anti-corruption campaign platform. The Democrats' witnesses described how President Trump has a deep-seated and genuine skepticism of Ukraine due to its corruption and that the President's view was reasonable. Because of President Trump's skepticism and because President Zelensky was a first-time candidate with relatively untested views, Ukraine and U.S. officials sought to convince President Trump that President Zelensky was the "real deal" on reform. President Trump ultimately signed a letter to President Zelensky on May 29 inviting him to the White House.

Although there were several months between President Trump's invitation on May 29 and the bilateral meeting on September 25, the evidence does not show the delay was intentional or aimed at pressuring President Zelensky. The Democrats' witnesses described the difficulty in scheduling high-level meetings and how an anticipated presidential meeting in Poland in early September was cancelled due to Hurricane Dorian. Nonetheless, U.S. foreign policy officials believed that the Ukrainian government felt good about its relationship with the Trump Administration because of several high-level bilateral meetings held between May and September 2019, including President Zelensky's meeting with Vice President Pence on September 1. Ultimately, of course, President Trump and President Zelensky met during the U.N. General Assembly in New York on September 25, without Ukraine taking steps to investigate President Trump's political rival.

1. Ukraine has a long history of pervasive corruption.

Since it became an independent nation following the collapse of the Soviet Union, Ukraine has been plagued by systemic corruption. *The Guardian* has called Ukraine "the most corrupt nation in Europe"[98] and Ernst & Young cites Ukraine among the three most-corrupt nations of the world.[99]

---

[97] *See, e.g.*, Karoun Demirjian et al., *Officials' texts reveals belief that Trump wanted probes as condition of Ukraine meeting*, Wash. Post, Oct. 4, 2019.

[98] Oliver Bullough, *Welcome to Ukraine, the Most Corrupt Nation in Europe*, Guardian, (Feb. 6, 2015).

[99] *See, e.g.*, *14th Global Fraud Survey*, Ernst & Young, (2016), https://www.ey.com/Publication/vwLUAssets/EY-corporate-misconduct-individual-consequences/$FILE/EY-corporate-misconduct-individual-consequences.pdf (noting that 88% of Ukrainian's agree that "bribery/corrupt practices happen widely in business in [Ukraine]"). *See also* Viktor Tkachuk, *People First: The Latest in the Watch on Ukrainian Democracy*, Kyiv Post, (Sept. 11, 2012),

The United States Agency for International Development (USAID) explained Ukraine's history of corruption in a 2006 report:

> From the early 1990s, powerful officials in [the Ukrainian] government and politics acquired and privatized key economic resources of the state. As well, shadowy businesses, allegedly close to organized crime, became powerful economic forces in several regions of the country. Over the course of the past decade, these business groupings—or clans—as they became called, grew into major financial-industrial structures that used their very close links with and influence over government, political parties, the mass media and the state bureaucracy to enlarge and fortify their control over the economy and sources of wealth. They used ownership ties, special privileges, relations with government and direct influence over the courts and law enforcement and regulatory organizations to circumvent weaknesses in governmental institutions.[100]

Corruption is so pervasive in Ukraine that in 2011, 68.8% of Ukrainian citizens reported that they had bribed a public official within the preceding twelve months.[101] Bribery and facilitation payments[102] are common schemes by which Ukrainian officials demand payment in exchange for ensuring public services are delivered either on time or at all.[103] Corruption also presents an obstacle to private and public business in Ukraine.[104] In 2011, then-President Petro Poroshenko estimated that 15%, or $7.4 billion, of the state budget "ends up in the pockets of officials" through corrupt public procurement practices.[105]

Pervasive corruption in Ukraine has been one of the primary impediments to Ukraine joining the European Union.[106] Corruption-related concerns also figure prominently in the E.U.-Ukrainian Association Agreement, the document establishing a political and economic

---

https://www.kyivpost.com/article/opinion/op-ed/people-first-the-latest-in-the-watch-on-ukrainian-democracy-5-312797.html.

[100] U.S. Agency for International Development, Final Report, Corruption Assessment: Ukraine (2006), https://pdf.usaid.gov/pdf_docs/PNADK247.pdf.

[101] *Fighting Corruption in Ukraine: Ukrainian Style*, Gorshenin Inst., (Mar. 7, 2011), http://gpf-europe.com/upload/iblock/333/round_table_eng.pdf.

[102] *See* Facilitation Payments, *Corruption Dictionary*, Ganintegrity.com, (last visited Oct. 23, 2019), https://www.ganintegrity.com/portal/corruption-dictionary/. Facilitation payments, also known as "grease payments," are a form of bribery made with the purpose of expediting or securing the performance of a routine action to which the payer is legally entitled. *Id.*

[103] *People & Corruption: Citizens' Voices from Around the World*, Transparency Int'l, (2017), https://www.transparency.org/whatwedo/publication/people_and_corruption_citizens_voices_from_around_the_world.

[104] *Id.*

[105] Mark Rachkevych, *Under Yanukovych, Ukraine Slides Deeper in Ranks of Corrupt Nations*, Kyiv Post, (Dec. 1, 2011).

[106] *See, e.g.*, Vladimir Isachenkov, *Ukraine's integration into West dashed by war and corruption*, Assoc. Press, Mar. 26, 2019.

association between the E.U. and Ukraine.[107] The Agreement was entered into with the intent of Ukraine committing to gradually conform to E.U. technical and consumer standards.

State Department witnesses called by the Democrats during the impeachment inquiry confirmed Ukraine's reputation for corruption. Deputy Assistant Secretary of State George Kent described Ukraine's corruption problem as "serious" and said corruption has long been "part of the high-level dialogue" between the United States and Ukraine.[108] Ambassador Bill Taylor said corruption in Ukraine is a "big issue."[109] Ambassador Kurt Volker testified that "Ukraine has a long history of pervasive corruption throughout the economy[,] throughout the country, and it has been incredibly difficult for Ukraine as a country to deal with this, to investigate it, to prosecute it."[110] He later elaborated:

> Ukraine had for decades a reputation of being just a corrupt place. There are a handful of people who own a disproportionate amount of the economy. Oligarchs, they use corruption as kind of the coin of the realm to get what they want, including influencing the Parliament, the judiciary, the government, state-owned industries. And so businessmen generally don't want to invest in Ukraine, even to this day, because they just fear that it's a horrible environment to be working in, and they don't want to put – expose themselves to that risk. I would have to believe that President Trump would be aware of that general climate.[111]

2. President Trump has a deep-seated, genuine, and reasonable skepticism of Ukraine due to its history of pervasive corruption.

Multiple Democrat witnesses offered firsthand testimony of President Trump's skeptical view of Ukraine, as far back as September 2017. Ambassador Volker explained: "President Trump demonstrated that he had a very deeply rooted negative view of Ukraine based on past corruption. And that's a reasonable position. Most people who would know anything about Ukraine would think that."[112] He elaborated that the President's concern about Ukraine was genuine,[113] and that this concern contributed to a delay in the meeting with President Zelensky. He explained:

---

[107] E.U.-Ukraine Ass'n Agreement, art. 14, Mar. 21, 2014, 57 Off. J. of the E.U. L161/3 ("In their cooperation on justice, freedom and security, the Parties shall attach particular importance to the consolidation of the rule of law and the reinforcement of institutions at all levels in the areas of administration in general and law enforcement and the administration of justice in particular. Cooperation will, in particular, aim at strengthening the judiciary, improving its efficiency, safeguarding its independence and impartiality, and combating corruption. Respect for human rights and fundamental freedoms will guide all cooperation on justice, freedom and security.").

[108] Kent deposition, *supra* note 65 at 105, 151.

[109] Taylor deposition, *supra* note 47, at 86.

[110] Volker transcribed interview, *supra* note 60, at 76.

[111] *Id.* at 148-49.

[112] *Id.* at 30.

[113] *Id.* at 295.

So the issue as I understood it was this deep-rooted, skeptical view of Ukraine, a negative view of Ukraine, preexisting 2019, you know, going back. When I started this, I had one other meeting with President Trump and [then-Ukrainian] President Poroshenko. It was in September of 2017. And at that time he had a very skeptical view of Ukraine. So I know he had a very deep-rooted skeptical view. And my understanding at the time was that even though he agreed in the [May23] meeting that we had with him, say, okay, I'll invite him, he didn't really want to do it. And that's why the meeting kept being delayed and delayed. [114]

Other testimony confirms Ambassador Volker's statements. Former U.S. Ambassador to Ukraine Marie Yovanovitch confirmed the President's skepticism, saying that she observed it during President Trump's meeting with President Poroshenko in September 2017.[115] She testified:

Q. Were you aware of the President's deep-rooted skepticism about Ukraine's business environment?

A. Yes.

Q. And what did you know about that?

A. That he—I mean, he shared that concern directly with President Poroshenko in their first meeting in the Oval Office.[116]

Dr. Fiona Hill, NSC Senior Director for Europe, also testified that President Trump was "quite publicly" skeptical of Ukraine and that "everyone has expressed great concerns about corruption in Ukraine."[117] Catherine Croft, a former NSC director, similarly attested to President's Trump skepticism when she staffed President Trump for two Ukraine matters in 2017, explaining: "Throughout both, I heard, directly and indirectly, President Trump described Ukraine as a corrupt country."[118]

3. Senior Ukrainian government officials publicly attacked President Trump during the 2016 campaign.

President Trump's skepticism about Ukraine was compounded by statements made by senior Ukrainian government officials in 2016 that were critical of then-candidate Trump and supportive of his opponent, former Secretary of State Hillary Clinton. Although Democrats have attempted to discredit these assertions as "debunked," the statements by Ukrainian leaders speak

---

[114] *Id.* at 41.
[115] Deposition of Ambassador Marie Yovanovitch, in Wash., D.C., at 142 (Oct. 11, 2019).
[116] *Id.*
[117] Hill deposition, *supra* note 12, at 118.
[118] Croft deposition, *supra* note 60, at 14.

for themselves and shed light on President Trump's mindset when interacting with President Zelensky in 2019.

In August 2016, less than three months before the election, Valeriy Chaly, then-Ukrainian Ambassador to the United States, authored an op-ed in the Washington-based publication *The Hill* criticizing candidate Trump for comments he made about Russia's occupation of Crimea.[119] Ambassador Chaly wrote that candidate Trump's comments "have raised serious concerns in [Kyiv] and beyond Ukraine."[120] Although President Zelensky dismissed Ambassador Chaly on July 19, 2019,[121] the ambassador's op-ed remains on the website of the Ukrainian Embassy in the U.S. as of the date of this report.[122]

Later that month, the *Financial Times* published an article asserting that Trump's candidacy led "Kyiv's wider political leadership to do something they would never have attempted before: intervene, however indirectly, in a US election."[123] The article quoted Serhiy Leshchenko, a Ukrainian Member of Parliament, to detail how the Ukrainian government was supporting Secretary Clinton's candidacy.[124] The article explained:

> Though most Ukrainians are disillusioned with the country's current leadership for stalled reforms and lackluster anti-corruption efforts, Mr. Leshchenko said events of the past two years had locked Ukraine on to a pro-western course. ***The majority of Ukraine's politicians, he added, are "on Hillary Clinton's side."***[125]

The *Financial Times* reported that during the U.S. presidential campaign, former Ukrainian Prime Minister Arseniy Yatsenyuk had warned on Facebook that candidate Trump "challenged the very values of the free world."[126] On Twitter, Ukrainian Internal Affairs Minister Arsen Avakov called Trump a "clown" who is "an even bigger danger to the US than terrorism."[127] In a Facebook post, Avakov called Trump "dangerous for Ukraine and the US" and said that Trump's Crimea comments were the "diagnosis of a dangerous misfit."[128] Avakov continues to serve in President Zelensky's government.

Multiple Democrat witnesses testified that these Ukrainian actions during the 2016 election campaign likely also colored President Trump's views of President Zelensky. Ambassador Volker said:

---

[119] *See* Chaly, *supra* note 27.
[120] *Id.*
[121] *Zelensky dismisses Valeriy Chaly from post of Ukraine's envoy to US*, Kyiv Post (July 19, 2019).
[122] Embassy of Ukraine in the United States of America, *Op-ed by Ambassador of Ukraine to the USA Valeriy Chaly for the Hill: "Trump's comments send wrong message to world,"* https://usa.mfa.gov.ua/en/press-center/publications/4744-posol-ukrajini-vislovlyuvannya-trampa-nadsilajuty-nevirnij-signal-svitu.
[123] Roman Olearchyk, *Ukraine's leaders campaign against 'pro-Putin' Trump*, Financial Times, Aug. 28, 2016.
[124] *Id.*
[125] *Id.* (emphasis added).
[126] *Id.*
[127] Kenneth P. Vogel & David Stern, *Ukrainian efforts to sabotage Trump backfire*, Politico, Jan. 11, 2017.
[128] *Id.*

Q. And you mentioned that the President was skeptical, had a deep-rooted view of the Ukraine. Is that correct?

A. That is correct.

Q. And that, whether fair or unfair, he believed there were officials in Ukraine that were out to get him in the run-up to his election?

A. That is correct.

Q. So, to the extent there are allegations lodged, credible or uncredible, if the president was made aware of those allegations, whether it was via The Hill or, you know, via Mr. Giuliani or via cable news, if the President was made aware of these allegations, isn't it fair to say that he may, in fact, have believed they were credible?

A. Yes, I believe so.[129]

Ambassador Sondland similarly testified:

Q. Did [President Trump] mention anything about Ukraine's involvement in the 2016 election?

A. I think he said: They tried to take me down. He kept saying that over and over.

Q. In connection with the 2016 election?

A. Probably, yeah.

Q. That was what your understanding was?

A. That was my understanding, yeah.[130]

4. U.S. foreign policy officials were split on President Zelensky, a political novice with untested views on anti-corruption and a close relationship with a controversial oligarch.

Evidence obtained during the Democrats' impeachment inquiry shows that the U.S. foreign policy apparatus was divided on the question of whether President Trump should meet with President Zelensky. President Zelensky was a first-time candidate and a newcomer to the Ukrainian political scene. Although President Zelensky ran on an anti-corruption and reform platform, the Democrats' witnesses explained that the State Department was unsure how he

---

[129] Volker transcribed interview, *supra* note 60, at 70-71.
[130] Sondland deposition, *supra* note 51, at 75.

would govern as president. In addition, others in the U.S. government worried about President Zelensky's association with Ukrainian oligarch Igor Kolomoisky.

President Zelensky won a landslide victory on April 21, 2019, defeating incumbent President Petro Poroshenko by a 73-24 percent margin.[131] The win came as a surprise to many.[132] At the time of his election, Mr. Zelensky was a comedic television personality. Ambassador Volker testified that "Zelensky kind of came up out of nowhere. . . . When he arose kind of meteorically, as an outside figure and a popular candidate, I think it did take everybody by surprise."[133]

Ambassador Yovanovitch also testified that Zelensky's election came as a surprise. She explained:

> And I think that there was, you know, as is true, I think, probably in any country during Presidential elections, a lot of – a lot of concerns among people. This was I think a big surprise for the political elite of Ukraine, which is relatively small. And so, I don't think they saw it coming really until the very end. And, so, there was surprise and, you know, all the stages of grief, anger, disbelief, how is this happening?[134]

Ambassador Yovanovitch agreed that President Zelensky was an "untried" politician:

> Q. And how did you feel about [Zelensky winning the election]? What were your views of Zelensky? Did you think he was going to be a good advocate for the anticorruption initiatives, as he was campaigning on?
>
> A. We didn't know. I mean, he was an untried politician. Obviously, he has a background as a comedian, as an actor, as a businessperson, but we didn't know what he would be like as a President.[135]

Ambassador Sondland testified that there was a difference in opinion regarding whether to schedule a call between Presidents Trump and Zelensky. Ambassador Sondland recalled that he, Ambassador Volker, and Secretary Perry advocated for a call between the presidents, while NSC officials disagreed.[136]

Evidence suggests that U.S. officials had concerns about some people surrounding President Zelensky. Ambassador Volker testified that President Zelensky's chief of presidential administration, Andriy Bohdan, had earlier been an attorney for "a very famous oligarch in

---

[131] *Ukraine election: Comedian Zelensky wins presidency by landside*, BBC News (Apr. 22, 2019*)*.

[132] *Id.*

[133] Volker transcribed interview, *supra* note 60 at 152-53.

[134] Yovanovitch deposition, *supra* note 115, at 73-74.

[135] *Id.* at 74.

[136] Sondland note 51, at 27-28.

Ukraine."[137] Senator Ron Johnson, who attended President Zelensky's inauguration in May 2019, recalled "concern over rumors that [President] Zelensky was going to appoint Andriy Bohdan, the lawyer for oligarch Igor Kolomoisky, as his chief of staff. The delegation [to the inauguration] viewed Bohdan's rumored appointment to be contrary to the goal of fighting corruption and maintaining U.S. support."[138] President Zelensky appointed Bohdan to be head of presidential administration in May 2019.[139]

In addition, Dr. Hill explained that the NSC had a concern about President Zelensky's relationship with Kolomoisky, an oligarch who had owned the television station on which Zelensky's comedy show aired.[140] Under the Poroshenko regime, the Ukrainian government had accused Kolomoisky of embezzling from PrivatBank, which he co-owned, causing Kolomoisky to flee Ukraine.[141] According to Ambassador Volker, "the Ukrainian taxpayer officially is bailing out the bank for the money that Kolomoisky stole. Because the IMF provides budgetary support to Ukraine, we [the U.S. taxpayers] actually ended up bailing out this bank."[142]

Ambassador Taylor testified that he discussed these concerns about Kolomoisky directly with President Zelensky:

> [T]he influence of one particular oligarch over Mr. Zelensky is of particular concern, and that's this fellow Kolomoisky, so – and Kolomoisky has growing influence. And this is one of the concerns that I have expressed to President Zelensky and his team on several occasions very explicitly, saying that, you know, Mr. President, Kolomoisky was not elected. You were elected and he, Mr. Kolomoisky, is increasing his influence in your government, which could cause you to fail. So I've had that conversation with him a couple of times.[143]

Kolomoisky returned to Ukraine following President Zelensky's victory.[144]

5. President Trump extended an invitation to the White House to President Zelensky on three occasions without conditions.

The evidence demonstrates that President Trump had a deep skepticism of Ukraine based on its history of pervasive corruption. This inherent skepticism, coupled with certain Ukrainian government officials' criticism of candidate Trump during the 2016 campaign and President Zelensky's untested views, contributed to President Trump's reticence to meet with President

---

[137] Volker transcribed interview, *supra* note 60, at 137.

[138] Letter from Sen. Ron Johnson to Jim Jordan, Ranking Member, H. Comm. on Oversight & Reform, & Devin Nunes, Ranking Member, H. Perm. Sel. Comm. on Intelligence 3 (Nov. 18, 2019).

[139] Roman Olearchyk, *Volodymyr Zelensky hires oligarch's lawyer as chief of staff*, Financial Times, May 22, 2019.

[140] Hill deposition, *supra* note 12, at 76-77.

[141] Andrew E. Kramer, *Oligarch's return raises alarm in Ukraine*, N.Y. Times, May 16, 2019.

[142] Volker transcribed interview, *supra* note 60, at 246.

[143] Taylor deposition, *supra* note 47, at 86.

[144] Kramer, *supra* note 141.

Zelensky. In spring and summer 2019, however, the President extended an invitation to the White House to President Zelensky on three occasions—without any conditions.

On April 21, 2019, President Trump placed a brief congratulatory call to President-elect Zelensky.[145] President Trump said: "When you're settled in and ready, I'd like to invite you to the White House."[146] The presidents did not discuss any investigations, and President Trump placed no conditions on his invitation.

On May 23, President Trump met with Ambassador Volker, Ambassador Sondland, Secretary Perry, and Senator Johnson—the senior U.S. officials who had comprised the official U.S. delegation to President Zelensky's inauguration days before. The delegation sought to convey to President Trump a positive impression of President Zelensky.[147] According to Ambassador Volker:

> President Trump demonstrated that he had a very deeply rooted negative view of Ukraine based on past corruption. And that's a reasonable position. Most people who would know anything about Ukraine would think that. That's why it was important that we wanted to brief him, because we were saying, it's different, this guy is different. But the President had a very deeply rooted negative view. We urged that he invite President Zelensky to meet with him at the White House. He was skeptical of that. We persisted. And he finally agreed, okay, I'll do it.[148]

Later in his transcribed interview, Ambassador Volker provided more context for the May 23 discussion:

> What I heard from President Trump in the meeting in the oval office was blanket, like, "this—these are terrible people, this is a corrupt country," you know, "I don't believe it." I made the argument that President Zelensky is the real deal, he is going to try to fix things, and, you know, he just did not believe it. He waved it off. So there's a general issue there.
>
> He did not mention investigations to me in that meeting, or call for investigations. I was not aware that he did so in the July 25th call later. His attitude towards Ukraine was just general and negative.[149]

Ambassador Sondland similarly testified that President Trump expressed negative views about Ukraine in this meeting and mentioned how "they tried to take me down" in 2016.[150]

---

[145] *Memorandum of Telephone Conversation, supra* note 10.
[146] *Id.*
[147] Hill deposition, *supra* note 12, at 320.
[148] Volker transcribed interview, *supra* note 60, at 30-31.
[149] *Id.* at 280.
[150] Sondland deposition, *supra* note 51, at 74-75.

Although Ambassador Sondland said he was discouraged by the President's viewpoint, he was pleased and surprised that the President later agreed to invite President Zelensky to the White House.[151]

Senator Johnson recalled that in this meeting, President Trump "expressed strong reservations about support for Ukraine. He made it crystal clear that he viewed Ukraine as a thoroughly corrupt country both generally and, specifically, regarding rumored meddling in the 2016 election."[152] Senator Johnson further explained:

> It was obvious that [the President's] viewpoint and reservations were strongly held, and that we would have a significant sales job ahead of us in getting him to change his mind. I specifically asked him to keep his viewpoint and reservations private and not to express them publicly until he had a chance to meet [President] Zelensky. He agreed to do so, but he added that he wanted [President] Zelensky to know exactly how he felt about the corruption in Ukraine prior to any future meeting.[153]

Senator Johnson recounted that he did not recall President Trump mentioning Burisma or the Bidens, but it was "obvious" that President Trump was aware of "rumors that corrupt actors in Ukraine might have played a part in helping create the false Russia collusion narrative."[154]

On May 29, President Trump wrote to President Zelensky to invite him to Washington, D.C. "as soon as we can find a mutually convenient time."[155] President Trump's letter did not mention any investigations and placed no conditions on President Zelensky's invitation to the White House. On July 25, during their phone conversation, President Trump reiterated his invitation to President Zelensky, again without conditions.[156]

6. Despite difficulty scheduling a face-to-face presidential meeting, senior Ukrainian officials interacted often with senior American officials between May and September 2019.

By late May 2019, President Trump had formally extended an invitation for President Zelensky to visit the White House. Although the two presidents did not meet face-to-face until September 25, the Democrats' witnesses testified that presidential meetings can often take time to schedule and that senior Ukrainian officials met frequently with American counterparts in the

---

[151] *Id.* at 74, 81, 85-87.
[152] Letter from Sen. Ron Johnson, *supra* note 138, at 4.
[153] *Id.*
[154] *Id.*
[155] Letter from President Donald J. Trump to His Excellency Volodymyr Zelenskyy, President of Ukraine (May 29, 2019). Dr. Hill testified that Ambassador Sondland claimed he had dictated the paragraph inviting President Zelensky to the White House, *see* Hill deposition, *supra* note 12, at 74; however, Ambassador Sondland testified that he had no role in drafting the letter. Sondland deposition, *supra* note 51, at 81.
[156] *Memorandum of Telephone Conversation*, *supra* note 15.

interim.[157] Ambassador Volker explained that the new Zelensky regime was "actually feeling pretty good by then" about its relationship with the Trump Administration.[158]

On June 4, President Zelensky attended an Independence Day dinner at the U.S. mission to the E.U. hosted by Ambassador Sondland and also attended by White House Senior Advisor Jared Kushner.[159]

On July 3, while in Toronto, Canada, for the Ukraine Reform Conference, President Zelensky met with Ambassador Volker and Deputy Assistant Secretary of State George Kent.[160]

On July 9, Oleksandr Danylyuk, then-Secretary of the National Security and Defense Council of Ukraine, and Andrey Yermak, a senior adviser to President Zelensky, met with LTG Keith Kellogg, Vice President Pence's National Security Advisor; Jennifer Williams, a special advisor covering European issues for Vice President Pence; and NSC staff member LTC Alexander Vindman.[161]

On July 10, Danylyuk and Yermak met at the White House with National Security Advisor John Bolton, Secretary Perry, Ambassador Volker, Ambassador Sondland, Dr. Hill, and LTC Vindman.[162]

On July 25, President Trump and President Zelensky spoke by telephone.[163]

On July 26, President Zelensky met with Ambassador Volker, Ambassador Sondland, and Ambassador Taylor in Kyiv.[164] Ambassador Volker testified that the meeting was scheduled before the presidents' phone call.[165] He said President Zelensky was "pleased that the call had taken place . . . . They thought it went well. And they were encouraged again because the President had asked them to pick dates for coming to the White House."[166]

On August 27, President Zelensky met with National Security Advisor Bolton in Kyiv.[167]

On September 1, President Zelensky met with Vice President Pence in Warsaw, Poland, after an event commemorating the 80th anniversary of the beginning of World War II.[168] President Trump had been scheduled to attend but was forced to cancel due to Hurricane

---

[157] Kent deposition, *supra* note 65, at 231; Volker transcribed interview, *supra* note 60, at 127.
[158] Volker transcribed interview, *supra* note 60, at 127.
[159] Sondland deposition, *supra* note 51, at 26-27, 148-49.
[160] Kent deposition, *supra* note 65, at 241; Volker transcribed interview, *supra* note 60, at 137.
[161] Williams deposition, *supra* note 73, at 51-53.
[162] Volker transcribed interview, *supra* note 60, at 66-67; Hill deposition, *supra* note 12, at 62-63.
[163] *Memorandum of Telephone Conversation, supra* note 15.
[164] Volker transcribed interview, *supra* note 60, at 312-33; Sondland deposition, *supra* note 51, at 29.
[165] Volker transcribed interview, *supra* note 60, at 102.
[166] *Id.* at 313.
[167] Taylor deposition, *supra* note 47, at 229-30.
[168] The White House, Readout of Vice President Mike Pence's Meeting with Ukrainian President Volodymyr Zelenskyy (Sept. 1, 2019); Taylor deposition, *supra* note 47, at 34-35.

Dorian.[169] According to Ambassador Taylor's testimony, Vice President Pence reiterated President Trump's views for "Europeans to do more to support Ukraine and that he wanted the Ukrainians to do more to fight corruption."[170]

On September 17, Secretary of State Pompeo had a telephone conversation with Ukrainian Foreign Minister Vadym Prystaiko.[171] According to a readout from the U.S. Embassy in Kyiv, Secretary Pompeo "affirmed U.S. support for Ukraine as it advances critical reforms to tackle corruption, strengthen the rule of law, and foster an economic environment that promotes competition and investment. The Secretary expressed unwavering U.S. support for Ukraine's sovereignty and territorial integrity."[172]

On September 18, President Zelensky and Vice President Pence spoke by telephone.[173] The two discussed President Zelensky's upcoming meeting with President Trump on the margins of the U.N. General Assembly and Ukraine's effort to address its corruption challenges.[174]

7. The evidence does not establish a linkage between a White House meeting and Ukrainian investigations into President Trump's political rival.

The evidence in the Democrats' impeachment inquiry does not show that a White House meeting was conditioned on Ukraine's willingness to investigate President Trump's political rival. Although the anonymous whistleblower, citing "multiple" secondhand sources, alleged that President Trump sought to withhold a meeting to pressure President Zelensky to "play ball,"[175] publicly available information contradicts the whistleblower's claim. For example, Andrey Yermak, a senior adviser to President Zelensky, admitted in an August 2019 *New York Times* article that he discussed with Mayor Giuliani both meeting between President Trump and President Zelensky and investigations.[176] The *Times* reported, however, that Yermak and Mayor Giuliani "did not discuss a link between the two."[177]

Other firsthand testimony obtained during the impeachment inquiry supports this finding. For example, Ambassador Volker, the key interlocutor with the Ukrainian government, clearly testified that there was no "linkage" between a White House meeting and Ukrainian actions to investigate President Trump's political rival. He explained:

> Q. Did the President ever withhold a meeting with President Zelensky
> until the Ukrainians committed to investigating those allegations?

---

[169] Volker transcribed interview, *supra* note 60, at 130; Taylor deposition, *supra* note 47, at 35.

[170] Taylor deposition, *supra* note 47, at 35.

[171] U.S. Embassy in Ukraine, Secretary Michael R. Pompeo's Call with Ukrainian Foreign Minister Vadym Prystayko (Sept. 17, 2019), https://ua.usembassy.gov/secretary-michael-r-pompeos-call-with-ukrainian-foreign-minister-vadym-prystayko/.

[172] *Id.*

[173] The White House, Readout of Vice President Mike Pence's Phone Call with President of Ukraine (Sept. 18, 2019).

[174] *Id.*; *see also* Volker transcribed interview, *supra* note 60, at 317-18.

[175] Whistleblower letter, *supra* note 85, at 7.

[176] Kenneth P. Vogel & Andrew E. Kramer, *Giuliani renews push for Ukraine to investigate Trump's political opponents*, N.Y. Times, Aug. 21, 2019.

[177] *Id.*

A. We had a difficult time scheduling a bilateral meeting between President Zelensky and President Trump.

Q. Ambassador Volker, that was a yes-or-no question.

A. Well, if I – can you repeat the question then?

Q. Sure. Did President Trump ever withhold a meeting with President Zelensky or delay a meeting with President Zelensky until the Ukrainians committed to investigate the allegations that you just described concerning the 2016 Presidential election?

A. The answer to the question is no, if you want a yes-or-no answer. But the reason the answer is no is we did have difficulty scheduling a meeting, but there was no linkage like that.[178]

***

Q. So before we move to the text messages, I want to ask you a clarifying question. You said that you were not aware of any linkage between the delay in the Oval Office meeting between President Trump and President Zelensky and the Ukrainian commitment to investigate the two allegations as you described them, correct?

A. Correct.[179]

Ambassador Sondland was the only witness to allege a *quid pro quo* with respect to a White House meeting. However, to the extent that Ambassador Sondland testified that he believed a White House meeting was conditioned on Ukrainian actions, his belief was that a meeting was conditioned on a public statement about anti-corruption—not on investigations into President Trump's political rival.[180] Ambassador Sondland testified in his closed-door deposition that "nothing about the request raised any red flags for me, Ambassador Volker, or Ambassador Taylor."[181] In his public testimony, Ambassador Sondland clarified that he *believed* there was linkage, but that President Trump had never discussed with him any preconditions for a White House visit by President Zelensky.[182]

In addition, there is conflicting testimony about what occurred during a July 10 meeting between two senior Ukrainian officials and senior U.S. officials in National Security Advisor John Bolton's office. Ambassador Volker, Ambassador Sondland, Secretary Perry joined

---

[178] Volker transcribed interview, *supra* note 60, at 35-36.
[179] *Id.* at 40.
[180] Sondland deposition, *supra* note 51, at 30, 331.
[181] *Id.* at 30.
[182] *Impeachment Inquiry: Ambassador Gordon Sondland, supra* note 56.

Ambassador Bolton to meet with Oleksandr Danylyuk, then-Secretary of Ukraine's National Security and Defense Council, and Andrey Yermak, an adviser to President Zelensky.[183] Dr. Hill and LTC Vindman from the NSC staff attended as well.[184]

Dr. Hill and LTC Vindman alleged that during the meeting, Ambassador Sondland raised potential Ukrainian actions on investigations, leading Ambassador Bolton to abruptly end the meeting.[185] Dr. Hill recounted that Ambassador Bolton told her to brief the NSC Legal Advisor, John Eisenberg, and said he would not be a part of what he termed a "drug deal."[186]

Although Dr. Hill testified that she confronted Ambassador Sondland over his discussion of investigations,[187] Ambassador Sondland testified in his closed-door deposition that "neither Ambassador Bolton, Dr. Hill, or anyone else on the NSC staff ever expressed any concerns to me about our efforts . . . or, most importantly, any concerns that we were acting improperly."[188] Ambassador Sondland testified in his deposition that he recalled no "unpleasant conversation" with Dr. Hill.[189] Likewise, although Ambassador Volker assessed that the meeting was "not good," he said it was because Danylyuk poorly conveyed the appropriate top-level message to Ambassador Bolton during the meeting.[190]

In his public testimony, Ambassador Volker acknowledged that Ambassador Sondland made a "general comment about investigations," but he disputed that the July 10 meeting ended abruptly.[191] He also testified that preconditions were not discussed during the meeting.[192] Although Ambassador Sondland denied in his closed-door depositions that he raised investigations during July 10 meeting,[193] he acknowledged that he did in his public testimony.[194] Even still, Ambassador Sondland denied that the July 10 meeting ended abruptly: "I don't recall any abrupt ending of the meeting or people storming out or anything like that. That would have been very memorable if someone had stormed out of a meeting, based on something I said."[195] He explained that Dr. Hill never raised concerns to him, and that any discussion of investigations did not mention specific investigations.[196] He testified:

> Q. And, in fact, after the meeting, you went out and you took a picture, right?

---

[183] Sondland deposition, *supra* note 51, at 27; Volker transcribed interview, *supra* note 60, at 50-51.

[184] Hill deposition, *supra* note 12, at 63; Vindman deposition, *supra* note 12, at 17-18.

[185] Hill deposition, *supra* note 12, at 67; Vindman deposition, *supra* note 12, at 17.

[186] Hill deposition, *supra* note 12, at 70-71.

[187] *Id.* at 68-71. Dr. Hill testified that she also had a "blow up" with Ambassador Sondland in June about Ukraine, saying that Ambassador Sondland got "testy." *Id.* at 113.

[188] Sondland deposition, *supra* note 51, at 28.

[189] *Id.* at 114.

[190] Volker transcribed interview, *supra* note 60, at 66.

[191] *Impeachment Inquiry: Ambassador Kurt Volker and Mr. Timothy Morrison, supra* note 8.

[192] *Id.*

[193] *Id.* at 109-10.

[194] *Impeachment Inquiry: Ambassador Gordon Sondland, supra* note 56.

[195] *Id.*

[196] *Id.*

A. Yeah. We – Ambassador Bolton – or his assistant indicated that he was out of time, that he needed – he had another meeting to attend. And we all walked out of the White House. Everyone was smiling, everyone was happy, and we took a picture on the lawn on a nice sunny day.

Q. Okay. Then did you retire to the Ward Room?

A. I think Secretary Perry asked to use the Ward Room to continue the conversation. And the real subject that was under debate – and it wasn't an angry debate, it was a debate – should the call from President Trump to President Zelensky be made prior to the parliamentary elections in Ukraine or after the parliamentary elections? And there was good reason for both. We felt – Ambassador Perry, Ambassador Volker, and I thought it would help President Zelensky to have President Trump speak to him prior to the parliamentary elections, because it would give President Zelensky more credibility, and ultimately he would do better with his people in the parliamentary elections. Others, I believe, pushed back and said, no, it's not appropriate to do it before. It should be done after. And ultimately, it was done after.

Q. Okay. There was no mention of Vice President Biden in the Ward Room?

A. Not that I remember, no.

Q. Or any specific investigation?

A. Just the generic investigations.[197]

Contemporaneous evidence contradicts the idea that there was serious discord during the meeting. Following the meeting, Ambassador Bolton retweeted a statement from Secretary Perry about the July 10 meeting, writing it was a "great discussion . . . on U.S. support for Ukrainian reforms and the peaceful restoration of Ukrainian territory."[198] The picture in the tweet of the U.S. and Ukrainian officials—taken immediately after the meeting in Ambassador Bolton's office[199]—shows smiling faces and no indication of hostility or discord between Ambassador Bolton and Ambassador Sondland.

---

[197] *Id.*
[198] John Bolton (@AmbJohnBolton), Twitter (July 10, 2019, 4:39 p.m.), https://twitter.com/AmbJohnBolton/status/1149100798632026112.
[199] Sondland deposition, *supra* note 51, at 110.

Figure 1: Ambassador Bolton tweet following July 10 meeting

Figure 2: Picture of smiling U.S. and Ukrainian officials following July 10 meeting

8. **The evidence does not establish that President Trump directed Vice President Pence not to attend President Zelensky's inauguration to pressure Ukraine to investigate the President's political rival.**

The evidence also does not establish that President Trump directed Vice President Pence not to attend President Zelensky's inauguration as a means of pressuring Ukraine to investigate the President's political rival. During their initial April 21 phone call, President Trump told President Zelensky that a "great" representative of the U.S. would attend the Zelensky inauguration.[200] The anonymous whistleblower alleged that President Trump later "instructed Vice President Pence to cancel his planned travel to Ukraine to attend President Zelensky's

---

[200] Memorandum of Telephone Conversation, *supra* note 10.

inauguration . . . . [I]t was also 'made clear' to them that the President did not want to meet with Mr. Zelensky until he saw how Zelensky 'chose to act' in office."[201] The evidence in the Democrats' impeachment inquiry does not support this assertion.

Although Jennifer Williams, a special adviser in the Office of the Vice President, testified in her closed-door deposition that a colleague told her that President Trump directed Vice President Pence not to attend the inauguration,[202] she had no firsthand knowledge of any such direction or the reasons given for any such direction.[203] Williams explained that the Office of the Vice President provided three dates—May 30, May 31 and June 1—during which Vice President Pence would be available to attend the inauguration.[204] Williams explained that "if it wasn't one of those dates it would be very difficult or impossible" for Vice President Pence to attend.[205] Neither the Secret Service nor advance teams deployed to Ukraine to prepare for Vice President Pence's travel.[206]

During this same period, Vice Present Pence was planning travel to Ottawa, Canada, on May 30 to promote the U.S.-Mexico-Canada Agreement (USMCA).[207] Williams acknowledged in her public testimony that the Office of the Vice President had "competing trips . . . for the same window."[208] Williams elaborated that due to international travel by President Trump and Vice President Pence, there was a "narrow window" within which Vice President Pence was able to attend President Zelensky's inauguration.[209] Dr. Hill explained that the President and Vice President cannot travel internationally at the same time, testifying that Vice President Pence's attendance at President Zelensky's inauguration was just dependent on scheduling and she had no knowledge that the Vice President was directed not to attend the inauguration.[210]

Ultimately, on May 16, the Ukrainian Parliament scheduled President Zelensky's inauguration for only four days later, May 20, which was a date not offered by the Vice President's Office.[211] Williams testified that this scheduling posed a problem: "To be honest, we hadn't looked that closely at the Vice President's schedule before the President's trip [to Japan]

---

[201] Whistleblower letter, *supra* note 85, at app. 1-2.

[202] Williams deposition, *supra* note 73, at 37.

[203] *Impeachment Inquiry: LTC Alexander Vindman and Ms. Jennifer Williams*, *supra* note 6.

[204] Williams deposition, *supra* note 73, at 58; *Impeachment Inquiry: LTC Alexander Vindman and Ms. Jennifer Williams*, *supra* note 6.

[205] Williams deposition, *supra* note 73, at 58.

[206] *Id.* at 59.

[207] *See* The White House, Joint Statement by Vice President Mike Pence and Canadian Prime Minister Justin Trudeau (May 30, 2019).

[208] *Impeachment Inquiry: LTC Alexander Vindman and Ms. Jennifer Williams*, *supra* note 6.

[209] *Id.*

[210] *"Impeachment Inquiry: Dr. Fiona Hill and Mr. David Holmes": Hearing before the H. Perm. Sel. Comm. on Intelligence*, 116th Cong. (2019); Hill deposition, *supra* note 12, at 185 ("It depended on the date. I mean, we were hoping, you know, if others couldn't attend that [Vice President Pence] could. I mean, I myself couldn't attend because of the date, that the way that it – again, there were several different dates, and then the date that was announced in May was very quickly announced."); *id.* at 316 ("And it was going to be very tight for the Vice President to make it for the inauguration. So I, you know, have no knowledge that he was actually ordered not to go, but it was going to be very difficult for him to go.").

[211] Kent deposition, *supra* note 65, at 189.

at the end of May just because we weren't expecting the Ukrainians to look at that timeframe."[212] Kent explained that this short notice sent the State Department "scrambl[ing]" to find a U.S. official to lead the delegation.[213] Secretary Pompeo was traveling, so the decision was made to ask Secretary Perry to lead the delegation.[214] On May 20, the day of President Zelensky's inauguration, Vice President Pence attended an event in Jacksonville, Florida, to promote the USMCA.[215]

9. President Trump and President Zelensky met during the United Nations General Assembly in September 2019 without any Ukrainian action to investigate President Trump's political rival.

On September 25, President Trump and President Zelensky met during the U.N. General Assembly in New York.[216] Ambassador Volker said that President Trump and President Zelensky had a "positive" meeting. He testified:

> Q. Turning back to President Trump's skepticism of Ukraine and the corruption there, do you think you made any inroads in convincing him that Zelensky was a good partner?
>
> A. I do. I do. I attended the President's meeting with President Zelensky in New York on, I guess it was the 25th of September. And I could see the body language and the chemistry between them was positive, and I felt that this is what we needed all along.[217]

Ambassador Taylor testified that the meeting was "good" and President Trump "left pleased that they had finally met face to face."[218] Ambassador Taylor said there was no discussion about investigations during the September 25 meeting.[219]

Notably, President Trump and President Zelensky met in New York without Ukraine ever investigating President Trump's political rival.

* * *

The evidence presented in the impeachment inquiry does not support the Democrats' assertion that President Trump sought to withhold a White House meeting to pressure the Ukrainian government to investigate the President's political rival. President Trump and President Zelensky met in September 2019 *without* Ukraine ever investigating Vice President Biden or Hunter Biden.

---

[212] Williams deposition, *supra* note 73, at 60.
[213] Kent deposition, *supra* note 65, at 190.
[214] *Id.* at 190-91.
[215] The White House, Remarks by Vice President Pence at America First Policies Event USMCA: A Better Deal for American Worker (May 20, 2019).
[216] Remarks by President Trump and President Zelensky of Ukraine Before Bilateral Meeting, *supra* note 40.
[217] Volker transcribed interview, *supra* note 60, at 87-88.
[218] Taylor deposition, *supra* note 47, at 288.
[219] *Id.*

Contrary to the assertions in the anonymous whistleblower complaint, the evidence shows that President Trump has a genuine, deep-seated, and reasonable skepticism of Ukraine given its history of pervasive corruption. In addition, U.S. foreign policy officials were divided on whether President Trump should meet with President Zelensky, in part due to President Zelensky's close association with an oligarch accused of embezzlement. In May 2019, President Trump formally invited President Zelensky to the White House. For several months, there were attempts to arrange a meeting between President Trump and President Zelensky. Although President Trump indicated during their July 25 call that they may meet in Warsaw in September, Hurricane Dorian forced President Trump to cancel. Vice President Pence met with President Zelensky instead. President Trump and President Zelensky ultimately met without Ukraine ever investigating any of President Trump's political rival.

C. The evidence does not establish that President Trump withheld U.S. security assistance to Ukraine to pressure Ukraine to investigate the President's political rival for the purpose of benefiting him in the 2020 election.

Democrats allege that President Trump conspired to withhold U.S. security assistance to Ukraine as a way of pressuring Ukraine to investigate President Trump's political rival.[220] Here, too, the evidence obtained during the impeachment inquiry does not support this allegation.

The evidence suggests a far less nefarious reality. Just as President Trump holds a deep-seated skepticism about Ukraine, the President is highly skeptical of foreign assistance. Any examination of the President's actions must consider this factor. President Trump has been vocal about his view that U.S. allies in Europe should contribute a fair share for regional security. As Ukrainian government officials worked with U.S. officials to convince President Trump that President Zelensky was serious about reform and worthy of U.S. assistance, they discussed a public statement conveying that commitment. Although the security assistance was paused in July, it is not unusual for U.S. foreign assistance to become delayed. Assistance to Ukraine has been delayed before. Most telling, the Trump Administration has been stronger than the Obama Administration in providing Ukraine with lethal defensive arms to deter Russian aggression.

The Democrats' witnesses testified that U.S. security assistance to Ukraine was not conditioned on Ukrainian action on investigations. U.S. officials did not raise the issue of the delay in security assistance with Ukrainian officials because they viewed it as a bureaucratic issue that would be resolved. The Ukrainian government in Kyiv was not even aware that the aid was paused until it was reported publicly, only two weeks before the aid was released, as senior U.S. officials confidently predicted it would be. Ultimately, the U.S. disbursed security assistance to Ukraine *without* Ukraine ever investigating Vice Present Biden or his son, Hunter Biden.

---

[220] *See, e.g.*, Rishika Dugyala, *Democratic Senator: 'No doubt' Ukraine 'felt pressure'*, Politico (Oct. 27, 2019).

1. President Trump has been skeptical about U.S. taxpayer-funded foreign assistance.

Evidence suggests that President Trump is generally skeptical of U.S. taxpayer-funded foreign assistance. President Trump's skepticism of U.S. taxpayer-funded foreign assistance is long-standing. On June 16, 2015, when President Trump announced his candidacy for president, he said:

> It is time to stop sending jobs overseas through bad foreign trade deals. We will renegotiate our trade deals with the toughest negotiators our country has… the ones who have actually read "The Art of the Deal" and know how to make great deals for our country.
>
> It is time to close loopholes for Wall Street and create far more opportunities for small businesses.
>
> It is necessary that we invest in our infrastructure, *stop sending foreign aid to countries that hate us and use that money to rebuild our tunnels, roads, bridges and schools—and nobody can do that better than me*.[221]

During the 2016 presidential campaign, then-candidate Trump continued to express his skepticism of U.S. taxpayer-funded foreign aid. In March 2016, he told the *Washington Post*, "I do think it's a different world today and I don't think we should be nation building anymore. I think it's proven not to work. And we have a different country than we did then. You know we have 19 trillion dollars in debt. . . . And I just think we have to rebuild our country."[222] That same month, then-candidate Trump told the *New York Times*, "We're going to be friendly with everybody, but we're not going to be taken advantage of by anybody. . . . I think we'll be very worldview [*sic*], but we're not going to be ripped off anymore by all of these countries."[223]

As president, President Trump has sought to reduce U.S. taxpayer-funded foreign assistance. In his fiscal year 2018 budget proposal, the President proposed "to reduce or end direct funding for international programs and organizations whose missions do not substantially advance U.S. foreign policy interests. The Budget also renews attention on the appropriate U.S. share of international spending . . . for many other global issues where the United States currently pays more than its fair share."[224] The President's 2020 budget proposal—submitted in March 2019—likewise "supports America's reliable allies, but reflects a new approach toward countries that have taken unfair advantage of the United States' generosity."[225] The President's

[221] Donald Trump, Announcement of Candidacy for President of the United States, in New York, N.Y. (June 16, 2015) (emphasis added).
[222] *A transcript of Donald Trump's meeting with the Washington Post editorial board*, Wash. Post, Mar. 21, 2016.
[223] Maggie Haberman & David Sanger, *Transcript: Donald Trump Expounds on His Foreign Policy Views*, N.Y. Times, Mar. 26, 2016.
[224] Budget of the U.S. Government Fiscal Year 2018 at 13 (May 23, 2017).
[225] Budget of the U.S. Government Fiscal Year 2020 at 71 (Mar. 11, 2019).

Budget specifically sought "greater accountability by international partners along with donor burden sharing that is more balanced."[226]

Testimony from the Democrats' witnesses reinforces the President's skepticism of foreign assistance. Ambassador Taylor, U.S. chargé *a.i.* in Kyiv, testified that on August 22, 2019, he had a phone conversation with NSC Senior Director for Europe Tim Morrison in which Morrison said that the "President doesn't want to provide any assistance at all."[227] Morrison testified that President Trump generally does not like giving foreign aid to other countries and believes U.S. "ought not" to be the only country providing security assistance.[228] LTC Vindman, the NSC director handling Ukraine policy, similarly testified that President Trump is skeptical of foreign aid.[229]

In fact, evidence suggests that President Trump sought to review U.S. taxpayer-funded foreign assistance across the board. Ambassador David Hale, the Under Secretary of State for Political Affairs, testified that the Trump Administration was undertaking a "review" of foreign assistance globally.[230] He testified:

> Q. You mentioned that there was a foreign assistance review undergoing –
>
> A. Yes.
>
> Q. – at that time. What can you tell us about that?
>
> A. Well, it had been going on for quite a while, and the concept, you know, the administration did not want to take a, sort of, business-as-usual approach to foreign assistance, a feeling that once a country has received a certain assistance package, it's a – it's something that continues forever. It's very difficult to end those programs and to make sure that we have a very rigorous measure of why we are providing the assistance.
>
> We didn't go to zero base, but almost a zero-based concept that each assistance program and each country that receives the program had to be evaluated that they were actually worthy beneficiaries of our assistance; that the program made sense; that we have embarked on, you know, calling everything that we do around the world countering violent extremism, but, rather, that's actually focused on tangible and proven means to deal with extremist problems; that we avoid nation-building strategies; and that we not provide assistance to countries that are lost to us in terms of policy, to our adversaries.

---

[226] *Id.* at 73.
[227] Taylor deposition, *supra* note 47, at 33.
[228] Morrison deposition, *supra* note 12, at 78-79, 132.
[229] *Impeachment Inquiry: LTC Alexander Vindman and Ms. Jennifer Williams*, *supra* note 6.
[230] Deposition of Ambassador David Hale, in Wash., D.C., at 80 (Nov. 6, 2019) [hereinafter "Hale deposition"].

Q. And do you know if the President also had concerns about whether the allies of Ukraine, in this example, were contributing their fair share?

A. That's another factor in the foreign affairs review is appropriate burden sharing. But it was not, in the deputies committee meeting, OMB [the U.S. Office of Management and Budget] did not really explain why they were taking the position other than they had been directed to do so.

Q. Okay. You are aware of the President's skeptical views on foreign assistance? Right?

A. Absolutely.

Q. And that's a genuinely held belief, correct?

A. It is what guided the foreign affairs review.

Q. Okay. It's not just related to Ukraine?

A. Absolutely not. It's global in nature.[231]

2. President Trump has been clear and consistent in his view that Europe should pay its fair share for regional defense.

Since his 2016 presidential campaign, President Trump has emphasized his view that U.S. foreign assistance should be spent wisely and cautiously. As President, he has continued to be critical of sending U.S. taxpayer dollars to foreign countries and asked our allies to share the financial burden for international stewardship.

In a March 2016 interview with the *New York Times*, then-candidate Trump said: "Now, I'm a person that—you notice I talk about economics quite a bit [in foreign policy] because it is about economics, because we don't have money anymore because we've been taking care of so many people in so many different forms that we don't have money."[232] Then-candidate Trump elaborated about the North Atlantic Treaty Organization (NATO), a collective defense alliance between the U.S., Canada, and European countries:

> I mean, we defend everybody. (Laughs.) We defend everybody. No matter who it is, we defend everybody. We're defending the world. But we owe, soon, it's soon to be $21 trillion. You know, it's 19 now but it's soon to be $21 trillion. But we defend everybody. When in doubt, come to the United States. We'll defend you. In some cases

---

[231] *Id.* at 81-83.
[232] Haberman & Sanger, *supra* note 223.

free of charge. And in all cases for a substantially, you know, greater amount. We spend a substantially greater amount than what the people are paying.[233]

That same month, candidate Trump spoke to CBS News about U.S. spending to NATO. He said then:

> NATO was set up when we were a richer country. We're not a rich country anymore. We're borrowing, we're borrowing all of this money . . . NATO is costing us a fortune and yes, we're protecting Europe with NATO but we're spending a lot of money. Number one, I think the distribution of costs has to be changed.[234]

As president, President Trump has continued to press European allies to contribute more NATO defense. For example, in a tweet on July 9, 2018, President Trump wrote:

> The United States is spending far more on NATO than any other Country. This is not fair, nor is it acceptable. While these countries have been increasing their contributions since I took office, they must do much more. Germany is at 1%, the U.S. is at 4%, and NATO benefits.......[235]

Jens Stoltenberg, the NATO Secretary-General, acknowledged in an interview that President Trump's message has "helped" NATO member countries to increase defense spending, commending the President on "his strong message on burden sharing."[236]

NSC Senior Director Tim Morrison explained the President's specific views about burden sharing regarding Ukraine during his public testimony. He testified:

> Q. And the President was also interested, was he not, in better understanding opportunities for increased burden sharing among the Europeans?
>
> A. Yes.
>
> Q. And what can you tell us about that?
>
> A. The President was concerned that the United States seemed to – to bear the exclusive brunt of security assistance to Ukraine. He wanted to see the Europeans step up and contribute more security assistance.

---

[233] *Id.*

[234] Shayna Freisleben, *A Guide to Trump's Past Comments about NATO*, CBS News, (Apr. 12, 2017).

[235] Donald J. Trump (@realDonaldTrump), Twitter (Jul. 9, 2018, 7:55 a m.), https://twitter.com/realDonaldTrump/status/1016289620596789248.

[236] David Greene, *After Trump's NATO Criticism, Countries Spend More on Defense*, NPR.org, (May 18, 2018).

Q. And was there any interagency activity, whether it be with the State Department for or the Defense Department, in coordination by the National Security Council, to look into that a little bit for the President?

A. We were surveying the data to understand who was contributing what and sort of in what categories.

Q. And so the President's evinced concerns, the interagency tried to address them?

A. Yes.[237]

In his public testimony, LTC Vindman confirmed the President's concerns about U.S. allies sharing the burden for mutual defense.[238]

3. U.S. foreign aid is often conditioned or paused, and U.S. security assistance to Ukraine has been paused before.

U.S. taxpayer-funded assistance to foreign governments is not an entitlement. The United States often conditions foreign aid on actions by recipient nations. In addition, foreign aid can, and often does, get delayed for various reasons. The pause of U.S. security assistance to Ukraine in this case is therefore not presumptive evidence of misconduct.

The United States conditions foreign assistance to a number of nations as a result of concerns about corruption, human rights abuses, or other issues. On October 31, 2019, the Trump Administration announced that it would withhold $105 million in security assistance for Lebanon shortly after the resignation of Lebanese Prime Minister Saad al-Hariri.[239] In September 2019, the State Department announced that it was withholding $160 million in aid from Afghanistan, citing corruption.[240] In June 2019, the Administration told Congress that it would reallocate $370 million in aid to Central American nations and suspend an additional $180 million in an effort to incentivize those countries to reduce the number of migrants reaching the U.S. border.[241] In 2017, President Trump froze $195 million in security assistance to Egypt—one of the largest recipients of U.S. aid—due to frustration with the country's poor track record on human rights and a recently enacted law regarding nongovernmental organizations.[242]

---

[237] *Impeachment Inquiry: Ambassador Kurt Volker and Mr. Timothy Morrison, supra* note 8.

[238] *Impeachment Inquiry: LTC Alexander Vindman and Ms. Jennifer Williams, supra* note 6.

[239] Patricia Zengerle & Mike Stone, *Exclusive: U.S. withholding $105 million in security aid for Lebanon- sources,* Reuters, Oct. 31, 2019.

[240] Tal Axelrod, *US withholds $160M in Afghan aid citing corruption,* The Hill, Sept. 9, 2019.

[241] Lesley Wroughton & Patricia Zengerle, *As promised, Trump slashes aid to Central America over migrants,* Reuters, Jun. 17, 2019.

[242] Gardiner Harris & Declan Walsh, *U.S. Slaps Egypt on Human Rights Record and Ties to North Korea,* N.Y. Times, Aug. 22, 2017.

The Democrats' witnesses explained that it is not unusual for foreign aid to be paused or even withheld. Ambassador Taylor testified that U.S. aid to foreign countries can be paused in various instances, such as a Congressional hold.[243] Ambassador Volker testified that foreign assistance can be delayed for a multitude of reasons and that "this hold on security assistance [to Ukraine] was not significant."[244] Ambassador Volker elaborated during his public testimony:

> Q. Ambassador Volker, you testified during your deposition that aid, in fact, does get held up from time-to-time for a whole assortment of reasons. Is that your understanding?
>
> A. That is true.
>
> Q. And sometimes the holdups are rooted in something at OMB, sometimes it's at the Defense Department, sometimes it's at the State Department, sometimes it's on the Hill. Is that correct?
>
> A. That is correct.
>
> Q. And so, when the aid was held up for 55 days for Ukraine, that didn't in and of itself strike you as uncommon?
>
> A. No. It's something that had happened in my career in the past. I had seen holdups of assistance. I just assumed it was part of the decision-making process. Somebody had an objection, and we had to overcome it.[245]

Ambassador David Hale, the Under Secretary of State for Political Affairs, agreed that U.S. taxpayer-funded aid has been paused from several countries around the world for various reasons and, in some cases, for unknown reasons.[246] Ambassador Hale elaborated:

> We've often heard at the State Department that the President of the United States wants to make sure that foreign assistance is reviewed scrupulously to make sure that it's truly in U.S. national interests, and that we evaluate it continuously, so that it meets certain criteria that the President has established.[247]

Ambassador Hale explained that the NSC launched a review of U.S. foreign assistance to ensure U.S. taxpayer money was spent efficiently and to advance "[t]he principle of burden sharing by allies and other like-minded states."[248] Dr. Hill, the NSC's Senior Director for Europe, testified that as she was leaving NSC in July 2019, "there had been more scrutiny" to assistance:

[243] Taylor deposition, *supra* note 47, at 170-71.
[244] Volker transcribed interview, *supra* note 60, at 78-80.
[245] *Impeachment Inquiry: Ambassador Kurt Volker and Mr. Timothy Morrison*, *supra* note 8.
[246] *"Impeachment Inquiry: Ms. Laura Cooper and Mr. David Hale": Hearing before the H. Perm. Sel. Comm. on Intelligence*, 116th Cong. (2019).
[247] *Id.*
[248] *Id.*

> As I understood them, there had been a directive for whole-scale review of our foreign policy, foreign policy assistance, and the ties between our foreign policy objectives and the assistance. This had been going on actually for many months. And in the period when I was wrapping up my time there, there had been more scrutiny than specific assistance to specific sets of countries as a result of that overall view – review.[249]

The Democrats' witnesses also described how U.S. foreign assistance to Ukraine has been delayed in the past. Dr. Hill testified that security assistance to Ukraine has been paused before "at multiple junctures" during her time at NSC, even with bipartisan support for the assistance.[250] Dr. Hill testified:

> Q. On the issue of the security assistance freeze, had assistance for Ukraine ever been held up before during your time at NSC?
>
> A. Yes.
>
> Q. For what – and when was that?
>
> A. At multiple junctures. You know, it gets back to the question that [Republican staff] asked before. There's often a question raised about assistance, you know, a range of assistance –
>
> Q. But for Ukraine specifically?
>
> A. Yeah, that's correct.
>
> Q. Okay. Even though there's been bipartisan support for the assistance?
>
> A. Correct.[251]

Catherine Croft, a former NSC director, offered an example in her deposition, explaining that OMB paused the sale of Javelin missiles to Ukraine in November or December 2017.[252] This pause, too, was eventually lifted and Ukraine received the missiles.[253]

---

[249] *Impeachment Inquiry: Dr. Fiona Hill and Mr. David Holmes, supra* note 210.
[250] Hill deposition, *supra* note 12, at 304.
[251] *Id.* at 303-04.
[252] Croft deposition, *supra* note 60, at 67.
[253] *Id.* at 68.

4. Despite President Trump's skepticism, the Trump Administration's policies have shown greater commitment and support to Ukraine than those of the Obama Administration.

Several of the Democrats' witnesses testified that President Trump has taken a stronger stance in supporting Ukraine. Dr. Hill testified that President Trump's decision to support Ukraine with lethal defensive weapons was a more robust policy than under the Obama Administration.[254] Ambassador Taylor characterized President Trump's policy as a "substantial improvement."[255] Ambassador Yovanovitch agreed, testifying:

> And I actually felt that in the 3 years that I was there, partly because of my efforts, but also the interagency team, and President Trump's decision to provide lethal weapons to Ukraine, that our policy actually got stronger over the three last 3 years [*sic*].[256]

She added:

> Q. Can you testify to the difference [to] the changes in aid to Ukraine with the new administration starting in 2017? The different initiatives, you know, as far as providing lethal weapons and –
>
> A. Yeah. Well, I think that most of the assistance programs that we had, you know, continued, and due to the generosity of the Congress actually were increased. And so that was a really positive thing, I think, for Ukraine and for us. In terms of lethal assistance, we all felt *it was very significant that this administration made the decision to provide lethal weapons to Ukraine*.[257]

Ambassador Volker also explained how President Trump's policies of providing lethal defensive assistance to Ukraine have been "extremely helpful" in deterring Russian aggression in Ukraine.[258] He explained:

> So there has been U.S. assistance provided to Ukraine for some time, under the Bush administration, Obama administration, and now under the Trump administration. I was particularly interested in the security assistance and lethal defensive weapons. The reason for this is this was something that the Obama administration did not approve. They did not want to send lethal defensive arms to Ukraine.
>
> I fundamentally disagreed with that decision. It is not my – you know, I was just a private citizen, but that's my opinion. I thought

---

[254] Hill deposition, *supra* note 12, at 196.

[255] Taylor deposition, *supra* note 47, at 155.

[256] Yovanovitch deposition, *supra* note 115, at 140-41 (emphasis added).

[257] *Id.* at 144.

[258] Volker transcribed interview, *supra* note 60, at 87.

that this is a country that is defending itself against Russian aggression. They had their military largely destroyed by Russia in 2014 and '15 and needed the help. And humanitarian assistance is great, and nonlethal assistance, you know, MREs and blankets and all, that's fine, but if you're being attacked with mortars and artilleries and tanks, you need to be able to fight back.

The argument against this assistance being provided, the lethal defensive assistance, was that it would be provocative and could escalate the fighting with Russia. I had a fundamentally different view that if we did not provide it, it's an inducement to Russia to keep up the aggression, and there's no deterrence of Russia from trying to go further into Ukraine. So I believed it was important to help them rebuild their defensive capabilities and to deter Russia. It's also a symbol of U.S. support.

So I argued very strongly from the time I was appointed by Secretary Tillerson that the rationale for why we were not providing lethal defensive assistance to me doesn't hold water and that is a much stronger rationale that we should be doing it.

That eventually became administration policy. It took a while, but Secretary Tillerson, you know, he wanted to think it through, see how that would play out. How would the allies react to this? How would Russia react to this? How would the Ukrainians handle it? And we managed those issues. Secretary Mattis was very much in favor. And they met. I did not meet with the President about this, but they met with the President and the President approved it.[259]

5. Although security assistance to Ukraine was paused in July 2019, several witnesses testified that U.S. security assistance was not linked to any Ukrainian action on investigations.

Several witnesses testified that U.S. security assistance was not linked to or conditioned on any Ukrainian action to investigate President Trump's political rival. Even after U.S. officials learned in early- to mid-July that the security assistance had been paused for unknown reasons, evidence suggests that there was not a link between U.S. security assistance and Ukrainian action to investigate President Trump's political rival.

LTC Vindman testified that he learned about a pause on security assistance on July 3.[260] Morrison said he learned of the pause around July 15.[261] According to Ambassador Taylor, he learned via conference call on July 18 that OMB had paused the security assistance to

---

[259] *Id.* at 84-86.
[260] Vindman deposition, *supra* note 12, at 178.
[261] Morrison deposition, *supra* note 12, at 16.

Ukraine.[262] Ambassador Taylor relayed that according to the OMB representative on the call, the pause was done at the direction of the President and the chief of staff.[263] Although a reason was not provided for the pause at the time, OMB official Mark Sandy testified that he learned in early September 2019 that the pause was related "to the President's concern about other countries contributing more to Ukraine."[264]

Despite the pause, testimony from the Democrats' witnesses suggests the assistance was not linked to Ukraine investigating President Trump's political rival. Ambassador Volker, the key intermediary between the Ukrainian government and U.S. officials, testified that he was aware of no *quid pro quo* and that the Ukrainian government never raised concerns to him about a *quid pro quo*.[265] He said that when Ambassador Taylor raised questions about the appearance of a *quid pro quo*, "I discussed with him that there is no linkage here. I view this as an internal thing, and we are going to get it fixed."[266] Ambassador Volker further explained that even if Ukrainians perceived the aid was linked to investigations, they "never raised" that possibility with him.[267] Ambassador Volker believed that given the trust he had developed with the Ukrainian government, the Ukrainians would have come to him with concerns about the security assistance.[268]

House Intelligence Committee Chairman Adam Schiff attempted to get Ambassador Volker to testify in his closed-door deposition that the Ukrainian government would have felt pressure to investigate President Trump's political rival once they learned that the security assistance was delayed.[269] Ambassador Volker refused to accept Chairman Schiff's conclusion. He testified:

> Q. The request is made. And even though the suspension may have occurred earlier, the request is made to investigate the Bidens, and then Ukraine learns, for mysterious reasons, hundreds of millions in military support is being withheld. Do I have the chronology correct?
>
> A. Yes.
>
> Q. At the point they learned that, wouldn't that give them added urgency to meet the President's request on the Bidens?
>
> A. I don't know the answer to that. The –

---

[262] Taylor deposition, *supra* note 47, at 27.

[263] *Id.* at 28.

[264] Deposition of Mark Sandy, in Wash., D.C., at 42 (Nov. 16, 2019). Sandy testified that in early September, OMB received "requests for information on what additional countries were contributing to Ukraine." *Id.* at 44. OMB provided that information sometime in the first week of September. *Id.* at 82.

[265] Volker transcribed interview, *supra* note 60, at 170, 300-01.

[266] *Id.* at 130.

[267] *Id.* at 284.

[268] *Id.* at 300-01.

[269] *Id.* at 124-28.

Q. Ambassador –

A. When that – no –

Q. – as a career diplomat, you can't venture –

A. But, Congressman, this is why I'm trying to the say the context is different, because at the time they learned that, if we assume it's August 29th, they had just had a visit from the National Security Advisor, John Bolton. That's a high level meeting already. He was recommending and working on scheduling the visit of President Zelensky to Washington. We were also working on a bilateral meeting to take place in Warsaw on the margins of a commemoration on the beginning of World War II. And in that context, I think the Ukrainians felt like things are going the right direction, and they had not done anything on – they had not done anything on an investigation, they had not done anything on a statement, and things were ramping up in terms of their engagement with the administration. So I think they were actually feeling pretty good by then.

Q. Ambassador, I find it remarkable as a career diplomat that you have difficulty acknowledging that when Ukraine learned that their aid had been suspended for unknown reasons, that this wouldn't add additional urgency to a request by the President of the United States. I find that remarkable.[270]

During his public testimony, in an exchange with Rep. Mike Turner, Ambassador Volker reiterated that there was no linkage between U.S. security assistance and investigations. He testified:

Q. Did the President of the United States ever say to you that he was not going to allow aid from the United States to go to the Ukraine unless there were investigations into Burisma, the Bidens, or the 2016 elections?

A. No, he did not.

Q. Did the Ukrainians ever tell you that they understood that they would not get a meeting with the President of the United States, a phone call with the President of the United States, military aid or foreign aid from the United States unless they undertook investigations of Burisma, the Bidens, or the 2016 elections?

A. No, they did not.

---

[270] *Id.* at 126-28 (question and answer with Chairman Adam Schiff).

Q. So I would assume, then, that the Ukrainians never told you that [Mayor] Giuliani had told them that, in order to get a meeting with the President, a phone call with the President, military aid or foreign aid from the United States, that they would have to do these investigations.

A. No.[271]

Similarly, Deputy Assistant Secretary Kent testified in his closed-door deposition that he also did not "associate" the security assistance to investigations."[272] Kent relayed how Ambassador Taylor had told him that Ambassador Sondland was "pushing" President Zelensky to give an interview during the Yalta European Strategy (YES) conference in Kyiv in mid-September.[273] Ambassador Taylor told Kent that the "hope" was if President Zelensky gave a public signal on investigations, the security assistance pause would lift; however, Ambassador Taylor asserted that "both Tim Morrison and Gordon Sondland said that they did not believe the two issues were linked."[274]

During his sworn deposition, Ambassador Sondland testified that he could not recall "any discussions with the White House about withholding U.S. security assistance from Ukraine in exchange for assistance with President Trump's 2020 election campaign."[275] Ambassador Sondland testified that he was "never" aware of any preconditions on the delay of security assistance to Ukraine, or that the aid was tied to Ukraine undertaking any investigations.[276]

Although media reports allege that Ambassador Sondland later recanted this testimony to "confirm" a *quid pro quo*,[277] those reports exaggerate the supplemental information that Ambassador Sondland later provided. In a written supplement to his deposition testimony, Ambassador Sondland asserted that by the beginning of September 2019, "in the absence of any credible explanation for the suspension of aid, [he] ***presumed*** that the aid suspension had become linked to the proposed anti-corruption statement."[278] Ambassador Sondland asserted that he spoke to Yermak in Warsaw on September 1 and conveyed that U.S. aid would not "likely" flow until Ukraine provided an anti-corruption statement.[279] Yermak, however, in an interview with *Bloomberg*, disputed Ambassador Sondland's account, saying that he "bumped into" Ambassador Sondland and "doesn't remember any reference to military aid."[280]

---

[271] *Impeachment Inquiry: Ambassador Kurt Volker and Mr. Timothy Morrison*, *supra* note 8.

[272] Kent deposition, *supra* note 65, at 323.

[273] *Id.* at 269.

[274] *Id.*; *see also id.* at 323.

[275] Sondland deposition, *supra* note 51, at 35.

[276] *Id.* at 197.

[277] *See, e.g.*, Andrew Desiderio & Kyle Cheney, *Sondland reverses himself on Ukraine, confirming quid pro quo*, Politico, Nov. 5, 2019.

[278] Declaration of Ambassador Gordon D. Sondland at ¶ 4 (Nov. 4, 2019) (emphasis added) [hereinafter "Sondland declaration"].

[279] *Id.* at ¶ 5.

[280] Stephanie Baker & Daryna Krasnolutska, *Ukraine's fraught summer included a rogue embassy in Washington*, Bloomberg, Nov. 22, 2019.

Ambassador Sondland's addendum does not prove a nefarious *quid pro quo*. At most, and even discounting Yermak's subsequent denial, the addendum shows that as of September 1, Ambassador Sondland assumed there was a connection and relayed this assumption to Yermak—an assumption that the President would later tell Ambassador Sondland was inaccurate.[281]

During his deposition, Ambassador Taylor testified that he spoke by phone with Ambassador Sondland on September 8.[282] Ambassador Taylor recounted how Ambassador Sondland told him that President Trump wanted President Zelensky to "clear things up and do it in public" but there was no "*quid pro quo*."[283]

On September 9, Ambassador Sondland texted Ambassador Volker and Ambassador Taylor: "The President has been crystal clear: no *quid pro quo*'s [*sic*] of any kind. The President is trying to evaluate whether Ukraine is truly going to adopt the transparency and reforms that President Zelensky promised during his campaign."[284] When asked about this text message during his transcribed interview, Ambassador Volker testified that "Gordon was repeating here what we all understood."[285]

In his public testimony, Ambassador Taylor clarified his statement from his closed-door deposition that he had "clear understanding" that Ukraine would not receive security assistance until President Zelensky committed to investigations.[286] He explained his "clear understanding" came from Ambassador Sondland, who acknowledged that he had *presumed* there to be a linkage. In an exchange with Rep. Jim Jordan, Ambassador Taylor testified:

> Q. So what I'm wondering is, where did you get this clear understanding?
>
> A. As I testified, Mr. Jordan, this came from Ambassador Sondland.
>
> ***
>
> Q. You said you got this from Ambassador Sondland.
>
> A. That is correct. Ambassador Sondland also said he had talked to President Zelensky and Mr. Yermak and had told them that, although this was not a *quid pro quo*, if President Zelensky did not clear things up in public, we would be at a stalemate. That was the – that was one point.
>
> ***

---

[281] *See infra* note 297 and accompanying text.
[282] Taylor deposition, *supra* note 47, at 39.
[283] *Id.*
[284] Text message from Gordon Sondland to William Taylor and Kurt Volker (Sept. 9, 2019, 5:19 a.m.) [KV00000053].
[285] Volker transcribed interview, *supra* note 60, at 170.
[286] *Impeachment Inquiry: Ambassador William B. Taylor and Mr. George Kent, supra* note 2.

Q. All right. So, again, just to recap, you had three meetings with President Zelensky; no linkage in those three meetings came up. Ambassador Zelensky didn't announce that he was going [to] do any investigation of the Bidens or Burisma before the aid was released. He didn't –

A. That was President –

Q. – do a tweet, didn't do anything on CNN, didn't do any of that. President Zelensky. Excuse me.

A. Yeah. Right.

Q. And then what you have in front of you is an addendum that Mr. Sondland made to his testimony that we got a couple weeks ago. It says, "Declaration of Ambassador Gordon Sondland. I, Gordon Sondland, do hereby swear and affirm as follows." I want to you look at point number two, bullet point number two, second sentence. "Ambassador Taylor recalls that Mr. Morrison told Ambassador Taylor that I told Mr. Morrison that I conveyed this message to Mr. Yermak on September 1st, 2019, in connection with Vice President Pence's visit to Warsaw and a meeting with President Zelensky." Now, this is his clarification. Let me read it one more time. "Ambassador Taylor recalls that Mr. Morrison told Ambassador Taylor that I told Mr. Morrison that I had conveyed this message to Mr. Yermak on September 1st, 2019, in connection with Vice President Pence's visit to Warsaw and a meeting with President Zelensky." We've got six people having four conversations in one sentence, and you just told me this is where you got your clear understanding, which – I mean, even though you had three opportunities with President Zelensky for him to tell you, "You know what? We're going to do these investigations to get the aid," he didn't tell you, three different times. Never makes an announcement, never tweets about it, never does the CNN interview. Ambassador, you weren't on the call, were you? The President – you didn't listen in on President Trump's call and President Zelensky's call?

A. I did not.

Q. You never talked with Chief of Staff Mulvaney.

A. I never did.

Q. You never met the President.

A. That's correct.

Q. You had three meetings again with Zelensky and it didn't come up.

A. And two of those, they had never heard about it, as far as I know, so there was no reason for it to come up.

Q. And President Zelensky never made an announcement. This is what I can't believe. And you're their star witness. You're their first witness.

A. Mr. Jordan –

Q. You're the guy. You're the guy based on this, based on – I mean, I've seen church prayer chains that are easier to understand than this.[287]

During his public testimony, Ambassador Sondland made clear that no one had ever told him that the security assistance was tied to Ukraine investigating the President's political rival. In particular, Ambassador Sondland explained that "President Trump never told me directly that the aid was conditioned on the meetings."[288] In an exchange with Rep. Turner, Ambassador Sondland elaborated:

Q. What about the aid? [Ambassador Volker] says that they weren't tied, that the aid was not tied—

A. And I didn't say they were conclusively tied either. I said I was presuming it.

Q. Okay. And so the President never told you they were tied.

A. That is correct.

Q. So your testimony and [Ambassador Volker's] testimony is consistent, and the President did not tie aid to investigations.

A. That is correct.

***

Q. So no one told you, not just the President. [Mayor] Giuliani didn't tell you. [Acting Chief of Staff] Mulvaney didn't tell you. Nobody— [Secretary] Pompeo didn't tell you. Nobody else on this planet told

---

[287] *Impeachment Inquiry: Ambassador William B. Taylor and Mr. George Kent, supra* note 2.
[288] *Impeachment inquiry: Ambassador Gordon Sondland, supra* note 56.

you that Donald Trump was tying aid to these investigations. Is that correct?

A. I think I already testified to that.

Q. No. Answer the question. Is it correct? No one on this planet told you that Donald Trump was tying aid to the investigations? Because if your answer is yes, then the chairman is wrong and the headline on CNN is wrong. No one on this planet told you that President Trump was tying aid to investigations, yes or no?

A. Yes.[289]

6. President Trump rejected any linkage between U.S. security assistance and Ukrainian action on investigations.

The evidence also shows that when President Trump was asked about a potential linkage between U.S. security assistance and Ukrainian investigations into the President's political rival, the President vehemently denied any connection. This evidence is persuasive because the President made the same denial twice to two separate senior U.S. officials in private, where there is no reason for the President to be anything less than completely candid.

In an interview with the *Wall Street Journal* and a detailed written submission to the impeachment inquiry, Senator Ron Johnson, the Chairman of the Senate Foreign Relations Subcommittee on Europe, disclosed that he spoke to President Trump on August 31, after learning from Ambassador Sondland that U.S. security assistance may be linked to Ukraine's willingness to demonstrate its commitment to fight corruption.[290] Senator Johnson explained that his purpose for calling President Trump was "to inform President Trump of my upcoming trip to Ukraine and to try to persuade him to authorize me to tell [President] Zelensky that the hold would be lifted on military aid."[291]

Senator Johnson recounted that President Trump was "not prepared" to lift the pause on security assistance to Ukraine, citing Ukrainian corruption and frustration that Europe did not share more of the burden.[292] Echoing his continual statements about U.S. allies sharing the financial burden for mutual defense, President Trump told Senator Johnson: "Ron, I talk to Angela [Merkel, German chancellor] and ask her, 'why don't you fund these things,' and she tells me, 'because we know you will.' We're schmucks, Ron. We're schmucks."[293]

When Senator Johnson raised the potential of a linkage between U.S. security assistance and investigations, President Trump vehemently denied it.[294] According to Senator Johnson,

---

[289] *Id.*

[290] Letter from Sen. Johnson, *supra* note 138, at 5; Siobhan Hughes & Rebecca Ballhaus, *Trump, in August call with GOP Senator, denied official's claim on Ukraine aid*, Wall St. J., Oct. 4, 2019.

[291] Letter from Sen. Johnson, *supra* note 138, at 5.

[292] *Id.*

[293] *Id.*

[294] *Id.*

Without hesitation, President Trump immediately denied such an arrangement existed. As reported in the *Wall Street Journal*, I quoted the President as saying, "[Expletive deleted]—No way. I would never do that. Who told you that?" *I have accurately characterized his reaction as adamant, vehement and angry* – there was more than one expletive that I have deleted.[295]

At the end of the phone call, President Trump circled back to Senator Johnson's request to release the pause on security assistance. President Trump said: "Ron, I understand your position. We're reviewing it now, and you'll probably like my final decision."[296] This conversation occurred on August 31, well before the Democrats initiated their impeachment inquiry, and undermines the assertion that the President fabricated legitimate reasons for the pause in security assistance in response to the Democrats' impeachment inquiry.

During his deposition, Ambassador Sondland testified that he called President Trump on September 9 and asked him "What do you want from Ukraine?" The President's response was "Nothing. There is no *quid pro quo*."[297] During his deposition, Ambassador Sondland testified:

> Q. So when you telephoned the President, tell us what happened.
>
> A. Well, from the time that the aid was help up until I telephoned the President there were a lot of rumors swirling around as to why the aid had been help up, including they wanted a review, they wanted Europe to do more. There were all kinds of rumors. And I know in my few previous conversations with the President he's not big on small talk to I would have one shot to ask him. And rather than asking him, "Are you doing X because of X or because of Y or because of Z?" *I asked him one open-ended question: What do you want from Ukraine? And as I recall, he was in a very bad mood. It was a very quick conversation. He said: I wanted nothing. I want no quid pro quo. I want Zelensky to do the right thing. And I said: What does that mean? And he said: I want him to do what he ran on.*[298]

When asked about his conversation with Senator Johnson—which prompted Senator Johnson to call President Trump—Ambassador Sondland testified that he was "speculating" about the linkage between security assistance and investigations.[299] He explained:

> I noticed in the media [Senator Johnson] had come out and said that he and I had a conversation on the phone about it. And he had said

[295] *Id.* (emphasis added).
[296] *Id.*
[297] Sondland deposition, *supra* note 51, at 106.
[298] *Id.* at 105-06 (emphasis added).
[299] *Id.* at 196.

that I told him – this is in the media report, and I haven't discussed this with him since that media report – that I had said there was a *quid pro quo*. And I don't remember telling him that because I'm not sure I knew that at that point. I think what I might have done is I might have been speculating – I hope there's no, I hope this isn't being held up for nefarious reasons.[300]

Although Democrats and some in the media believe that Acting Chief of Staff Mick Mulvaney confirmed the existence of a *quid pro quo* during an October 2019 press briefing,[301] a careful reading of his statements shows otherwise. Chief of Staff Mulvaney cited President Trump's concerns about Ukrainian corruption and foreign aid in general as the "driving factors" in the temporary pause on security assistance.[302] He explained that Ukraine's actions in the 2016 election "was part of the thing that [the President] was worried about in corruption with that nation."[303] Chief of Staff Mulvaney specified, however, that "the money held up had absolutely nothing to do with [Vice President] Biden."[304]

7. Senior U.S. officials never substantively discussed the delay in security assistance with Ukrainian officials before the July 25 call.

Evidence also suggests that the senior levels of the Ukrainian government did not know that U.S. security assistance was delayed until some point after the July 25 phone call between President Trump and President Zelensky. Although the assistance was delayed at the time of the July 25 call, President Trump never raised the assistance with President Zelensky or implied that the aid was in danger. As Ambassador Volker testified, because Ukrainian officials were unaware of the pause on security assistance, "there was no leverage implied."[305] This evidence undercuts the allegation that the President withheld U.S. security assistance to pressure President Zelensky to investigate his political rival.

Most of the Democrats' witnesses, including Ambassador Taylor, traced their knowledge of the pause to a July 18 interagency conference call, during which OMB announced a pause on security assistance to Ukraine.[306] However, the two U.S. diplomats closest the Ukrainian government—Ambassador Volker and Ambassador Taylor—testified that Ukraine did not know about the delay "until the end of August," six weeks later, after it was reported publicly by *Politico* on August 28.[307]

---

[300] *Id.*
[301] *Impeachment Inquiry: Dr. Fiona Hill and Mr. David Holmes, supra* note 210 (statement of Rep. Adam Schiff, Chairman); Aaron Blake, *Trump's acting chief of staff admits it: There was a Ukraine quid pro quo*, Wash. Post, Oct. 17, 2019.
[302] The White House, Press Briefing by Acting Chief of Staff Mick Mulvaney (Oct. 17, 2019).
[303] *Id.*
[304] *Id.*
[305] Volker transcribed interview, *supra* note 60, at 124-25.
[306] *See, e.g.*, Taylor deposition, *supra* note 47, at 27.
[307] Volker transcribed interview, *supra* note 60, at 125, 266-67; Taylor deposition, *supra* note 47, at 119-20.

Ambassador Volker, the chief interlocutor with the Ukrainian government, testified that he never informed the Ukrainians about the delay.[308] The Ukrainian government only raised the issue with Ambassador Volker after reading about the delay in *Politico* in late August.[309] Explaining why the delay was not "significant, Ambassador Volker testified:

> Q. Looking back on it now, is [the delayed security assistance] something, in the grand scheme of things, that's very significant? I mean, is this worthy of investigating, or is this just another chapter in the rough and tumble world of diplomacy and foreign assistance?
>
> A. In my view, this hold on security assistance was not significant. I don't believe – in fact, I am quite sure that at least I, Secretary Pompeo, the official representatives of the U.S., never communicated to Ukrainians that it is being held for a reason. We never had a reason. And I tried to avoid talking to Ukrainians about it for as long as I could until it came out in *Politico* a month later because I was confident we were going to get it fixed internally.[310]

During his public testimony, Ambassador Volker confirmed that he did not have any communication with the Ukrainian government about the pause on U.S. security assistance until they raised the topic with him.[311] Morrison likewise testified that he avoided discussing the pause on security assistance with the Ukrainian government.[312]

Ambassador Taylor similarly testified that the Ukrainian government was not aware of the pause on U.S. security assistance until late August 2019. In an exchange with Rep. Ratcliffe, he explained:

> Q. So, based on your knowledge, nobody in the Ukrainian government became aware of a hold on military aid until 2 days later, on August 29th.
>
> A. That's my understanding.
>
> Q. That's your understanding. And that would have been well over a month after the July 25th call between President Trump and President Zelensky.
>
> A. Correct.
>
> Q. So you're not a lawyer, are you, Ambassador Taylor?

---

[308] Volker transcribed interview, *supra* note 60, at 80.

[309] *Id*. at 80-81; Text message from Andrey Yermak to Kurt Volker, (Aug. 29, 2019, 03:06:14 AM), [KV00000020]; *see* Caitlin Emma & Connor O'Brien, *Trump holds up Ukraine military aid meant to confront Russia*, Politico, Aug. 28, 2019.

[310] Volker transcribed interview, *supra* note 60, at 80.

[311] *Impeachment Inquiry: Ambassador Kurt Volker and Mr. Timothy Morrison*, *supra* note 8.

[312] *Id.*

A. I am not.

Q. Okay. So the idea of a *quid pro quo* is it's a concept where there is a demand for an action or an attempt to influence action in exchange for something else. And in this case, when people are talking about a *quid pro quo*, that something else is military aid. So, if nobody in the Ukrainian government is aware of a military hold at the time of the Trump-Zelensky call, then, as a matter of law and as a matter of fact, there can be no *quid pro quo* based on military aid. I just want to be real clear that, again, as of July 25th, you have no knowledge of a *quid pro quo* involving military aid.

A. July 25th is a week after the hold was put on the security assistance. And July 25th, they had a conversation between the two presidents where it was not discussed.

Q. And to your knowledge, nobody in the Ukrainian government was aware of the hold?

A. That is correct.[313]

Likewise, Philip Reeker, the Acting Assistant Secretary of State for Europeans Affairs, testified that he was unaware of any U.S. official conveying to a Ukrainian official that President Trump sought political investigations.[314] Acting Assistant Secretary Reeker testified that he was not aware of whether Ambassador Volker or Ambassador Sondland had such conversations with the Ukrainians.[315]

Some witnesses testified that the Ukrainian embassy made informal inquiries about the status of the security assistance. LTC Vindman recalled receiving "light queries" from his Ukrainian embassy counterparts about the aid in either early- or mid-August, but he was unable to pinpoint specific dates, or even the week, that he had such conversations.[316] LTC Vindman testified that Ukrainian questions about the delay were not "substantive" or "definitive" until around the time of the Warsaw summit, on September 1.[317] State Department official Catherine Croft testified that two individuals from the Ukrainian embassy approached her about a pause on security assistance at some point before August 28, but Croft told them she "was confident that any issues in process would get resolved."[318] Deputy Assistant Secretary of Defense Laura Cooper testified publicly that her staff received inquiries from the Ukrainian embassy in July that "there was some kind of issue" with the security assistance; however, she did not know what the Ukrainian government knew at the time.[319]

[313] Taylor deposition, *supra* note 47, at 119-20.
[314] Deposition of Philip Reeker in Wash., D.C., at 149 (Oct. 26, 2019).
[315] *Id.* at 150.
[316] Vindman deposition, *supra* note 12, at 135-37, 189-90.
[317] *Id.* at 189-90.
[318] Croft deposition, *supra* note 60, at 86-87.
[319] *Impeachment Inquiry: Ms. Laura Cooper and Mr. David Hale, supra* note 246.

Although this evidence suggests that Ukrainian officials in Washington were vaguely aware of an issue with the security assistance before August 28, the evidence does not show that the senior leadership of Ukrainian government in Kyiv was aware of the pause until late August. A *New York Times* story claimed that unidentified Ukrainian officials were aware of a delay in "early August" 2019 but said there was no stated link between that delay and any investigative demands.[320] However, a subsequent *Bloomberg* story reported that President Zelensky "and his key advisers learned of [the pause on U.S. security assistance] only in a *Politico* report in late August."[321]

The *Bloomberg* story detailed how Ukraine's embassy in Washington—led by then-Ambassador Chaly, who had been appointed by President Zelensky's predecessor—went "rogue" in the early months of the Zelensky administration.[322] According to Andrey Yermak, a close adviser to President Zelensky, the Ukrainian embassy officials, who were loyal to former President Poroshenko, did not inform President Zelensky that there was any issue with the U.S. security assistance.[323] This information explains the conflicting testimony between witnesses like LTC Vindman and Deputy Assistant Secretary Cooper, who testified that the Ukrainian embassy raised questions about the security assistance, and Ambassador Volker and Ambassador Taylor, who testified that the Zelensky government did not know about any pause in security assistance.

According to the Ukrainian government, President Zelensky and his senior advisers only learned of the pause on security assistance from *Politico*—severely undercutting the idea that President Trump was seeking to pressure Ukraine to investigate his political rival.

8. The Ukrainian government denied any awareness of a linkage between U.S. security assistance and investigations.

Publicly available information also shows clearly that the Ukrainian government leadership denied any awareness of a linkage between U.S. security assistance and investigations into the President's political rival. The Ukrainian government leaders made this assertion following public reports that Ambassador Sondland had raised the potential connection in early September. This understanding is supported by information provided by Senator Johnson.

In Ambassador Sondland's addendum to his closed-door testimony, dated November 5, 2019, he wrote how he came to perceive a connection between security assistance and the investigations. He wrote:

> [B]y the beginning of September 2019, and in the absence of any credible explanation for the suspension of aid, I presumed that the aid suspension had become linked to the proposed anti-corruption

---

[320] Andrew E. Kramer & Kenneth P. Vogel, *Ukraine knew of aid freeze by early August, undermining Trump defense*, N.Y. Times, Oct. 23, 2019.
[321] Baker & Krasnolutska, *supra* note 280.
[322] *Id.*
[323] *Id.*

statement. . . . And it would have been natural for me to have voiced what I had presumed to Ambassador Taylor, Senator Johnson, the Ukrainians, and Mr. Morrison.[324]

Following media reports of Ambassador Sondland's addendum, Ukrainian Foreign Minister Prystaiko told the media that Ambassador Sondland had not linked the security assistance to Ukrainian action on investigations.[325] He said: "Ambassador Sondland did not tell us, and certainly did not tell me, about a connection between the assistance and the investigations."[326] Minister Prystaiko went further to say that he was never aware of any connection between security assistance and investigations: "***I have never seen a direct relationship between investigations and security assistance***. Yes, the investigations were mentioned, you know, in the conversation of the presidents. But there was no clear connection between these events."[327]

Senator Johnson explained that he had three meetings with senior Ukrainian government officials in June and July 2019.[328] Two of meetings were with Oleksandr Danylyuk, then-secretary of Ukraine's National Security and Defense Council, and Valeriy Chaly, then-Ukrainian Ambassador to the U.S.[329] Senator Johnson said that none of the these Ukrainian officials raised any concerns with him about security assistance or investigations: "At no time during those meetings did anyone from Ukraine raise the issue of the withholding of military aid or express concerns regarding pressure being applied by the president or his administration."[330]

9. **The Ukrainian government considered issuing a public anti-corruption statement to convey that President Zelensky was "serious and different" from previous Ukrainian regimes.**

Evidence shows that in light of President Trump's deep-rooted skepticism about Ukraine, and working in tandem with senior U.S. officials, the Ukrainian government sought to convince President Trump that the new regime took corruption seriously. This commitment took two potential forms: a public statement that Ukraine would investigate corruption or a media interview about investigations. Although the parties later discussed the inclusion of specific investigations proposed by Mayor Giuliani, U.S. officials explained that the intent of the statement was to convey a public commitment to anti-corruption reform and that they did not associate the statement with an investigation of the President's political rival.

Ambassador Volker explained the goal of having Ukraine convey President Zelensky's commitment to reform and fighting corruption in a public message. He testified:

    A. So the issue as I understood it was this deep-rooted, skeptical view of Ukraine, a negative view of Ukraine, preexisting 2019, you know,

---

[324] Sondland declaration, *supra* note 278, at ¶4.
[325] *U.S. envoy Sondland did not link Biden probe to aid: Ukraine minister*, Reuters, Nov. 14, 2019.
[326] *Id.*
[327] *Id.* (emphasis added).
[328] Letter from Sen. Ron Johnson, *supra* note 138, at 4.
[329] *Id.*
[330] *Id.* at 4-5.

going back. When I started this I had one other meeting with President Trump and President Poroshenko. It was in September of 2017. And at that time he had a very skeptical view of Ukraine. So I know he had a very deep-rooted skeptical view. And my understanding at the time was that even though he agreed in the [May 23] meeting that we had with him, say, okay, I'll invite him, he didn't really want to do it. And that's why the meeting kept being delayed and delayed. And we ended up at a point in talking with the Ukrainians – who we'll come to this, but, you know, who had asked to communicate with Giuliani – that they wanted to convey that they really are different. And we ended up talking about, well, then, make a statement about investigating corruption and your commitment to reform and so forth.

Q. Is that the statement that you discussed in your text messages –

A. Yes.

Q.   – around August of 2019?

A. Yes.

Q. Okay.

A. Yeah. To say make a statement along those lines. And *the thought behind that was just trying to be convincing that they are serious and different from the Ukraine of the past.*[331]

Ambassador Volker elaborated during his public testimony that a public statement is not unusual. He explained:

> I didn't find it that unusual. I think when you're dealing with a situation where I believe the President was highly skeptical about President Zelensky being committed to really changing Ukraine after his entirely negative view of the country, that he would want to hear something more from President Zelensky to be convinced that, "Okay, I'll give this guy a chance."[332]

The Democrats' witnesses explained how the idea of a public statement arose. Ambassador Volker testified that Andrey Yermak, a senior adviser to President Zelensky, sent him a draft statement following Yermak's meeting with Mayor Giuliani on August 2.[333] Ambassador Volker said that he believed the statement was "valuable for getting the Ukrainian

---

[331] Volker transcribed interview, *supra* note 60, at 41-42 (emphasis added).
[332] *Impeachment Inquiry: Ambassador Kurt Volker and Mr. Timothy Morrison*, *supra* note 8.
[333] Volker transcribed interview, *supra* note 60, at 71.

Government on the record about their commitment to reform and change and fighting corruption because I believed that would be helpful in overcoming this deep skepticism that the President had about Ukraine."[334] Ambassador Volker, however, did not see the statement as a "necessary condition" for President Zelensky securing a White House meeting.[335]

Ambassador Volker explained that although the statement evolved to include specific references to "Burisma" and "2016," the goal was still to show that President Zelensky was "different." He testified:

> Q. And the draft statement went through some iterations. Is that correct?
>
> A Yeah. It was pretty quick, though. I don't know the timeline exactly. We have it. But, basically, Andrey [Yermak] sends me a text. I share it with Gordon Sondland. We have a conversation with Rudy to say: The Ukrainians are looking at this text. Rudy says: Well, if it doesn't say Burisma and if it doesn't say 2016, what does it mean? You know, it's not credible. You know, they're hiding something. And so we talked and I said: So what you're saying is just at the end of the – same statement, just insert Burisma and 2016, you think that would be more credible? And he said: Yes. So I sent that back to Andrey, conveyed the conversation with him – because he had spoken with Rudy prior to that, not me – conveyed the conversation, and Andrey said that he was not – he did not think this was a good idea, and I shared his view.
>
> Q. You had testified from the beginning you didn't think it was a good idea to mention Burisma or 2016.
>
> A. Correct.
>
> Q. But then, as I understand it, you came to believe that if we're going to do the statement, maybe it's necessary to have that reference in there, correct?
>
> A. I'd say I was in the middle. I wouldn't say I thought it was necessary to have it in there because I thought the target here is not the specific investigations. The target is getting Ukraine to be seen as credible in changing the country, fighting corruption, introducing reform, that Zelensky is the real deal. You may remember that there was a statement that Rudy Giuliani made when he canceled his visit to Ukraine in May of 2019 that President Zelensky is surrounded by enemies of the United States. And I just knew that to be

---

[334] *Id.*

[335] *Impeachment Inquiry: Ambassador Kurt Volker and Mr. Timothy Morrison*, *supra* note 8

fundamentally not true. And so I think, when you talk about overcoming skepticism, that's kind of what I'm talking about, getting these guys out there publicly saying: We are different.[336]

Although subsequent reporting has connoted a connection between "Burisma" and the Bidens,[337] the Democrats' witnesses testified that they did not have that understanding while working with the Ukrainian government about a potential statement. Ambassador Volker explained that "there is an important distinction about Burisma" and that Vice President Biden or Hunter Biden were "never part of the conversation" with the Ukrainians.[338] He also testified that the Ukrainians did not link Burisma to the Bidens: "They never mentioned Biden to me."[339] Ambassador Volker also made clear that following his initial conversation with Mayor Giuliani in May 2019, Mayor Giuliani "never brought up Biden or Bidens with me again. And so when we talked or heard Burisma, I literally meant Burisma and that, not the conflation of that with the Bidens."[340]

Ambassador Sondland testified that he was unaware that "Burisma" may have meant "Biden" until the White House released the July 25th call transcript on September 25.[341] In fact, Ambassador Sondland testified that he recalled no discussions with any State Department or White House official about former Vice President Joe Biden or Hunter Biden.[342] Ambassador Sondland testified that he did not recall Mayor Giuliani ever discussing the Bidens with him.[343]

Testimony and text messages reflect that Ambassador Volker, Ambassador Sondland, and Ambassador Taylor communicated about Ukraine's commitment to fight corruption throughout the summer. Ambassador Taylor testified that in a phone conversation on June 27, Ambassador Sondland told him that President Zelensky "needed to make clear to President Trump that he, President Zelensky, was not standing in the way of 'investigations.'"[344] Ambassador Taylor said he did not know to what "investigations" Ambassador Sondland was referring, but that Ambassador Volker "intended to pass that message [to President Zelensky] in Toronto several days later."[345]

In early July, Ambassador Volker explained the dynamic directly to President Zelensky in Toronto, emphasizing the need to demonstrate a commitment to reform. Ambassador Volker testified:

---

[336] Volker transcribed interview, *supra* note 60, at 71-73.

[337] *See, e.g.*, Paul Sonne, Michael Kranish, & Matt Viser, *The gas tycoon and the vice president's son: The story of Hunter Biden's foray into Ukraine,* Wash. Post, Sept. 28, 2019.

[338] Volker transcribed interview, *supra* note 60, at 73.

[339] *Id.* at 193.

[340] *Id.* at 213.

[341] Sondland deposition, *supra* note 51, at 70.

[342] *Id.* at 33. Ambassador Sondland testified that Burisma was "one of many examples" of Ukrainian corruption. *Id.* Ambassador Sondland mentioned Naftogaz as another example of Ukrainian corruption and lack of transparency that "[came] up at every conversation." *Id.* at 71, 99.

[343] *Id.* at 33.

[344] Taylor deposition, *supra* note 47, at 25.

[345] *Id.* at 62-65.

I believe [Mayor Giuliani] was getting bad information, and I believe that his negative messaging about Ukraine would be reinforcing the President's already negative position about Ukraine. So I discussed this with President Zelensky when I saw him in Toronto on July 3rd, and I said I think this is a problem that we have Mayor Giuliani – so I didn't discuss his meeting with Lutsenko then. That came later. I only learned about that later. But I discussed even on July 3rd with President Zelensky that you have a problem with your message of being, you know, clean, reform, that we need to support you, is not getting – or is getting countermanded or contradicted by a negative narrative about Ukraine, that it is still corrupt, there's still terrible people around you. At this time, there was concern about his chief of presidential administration, Andriy Bohdan, who had been a lawyer for a very famous oligarch in Ukraine. And so I discussed this negative narrative about Ukraine that Mr. Giuliani seemed to be furthering with the President.[346]

On July 21, Ambassador Sondland sent a text message to Ambassador Taylor that read: "[W]e need to get the conversation started and the relationship built, irrespective of the pretext. I am worried about the alternative."[347] Ambassador Sondland testified that the word "pretext" concerned agreement on an interview or press statement and that the "alternative" was no engagement at all between President Trump and President Zelensky.[348] Ambassador Sondland testified that he viewed giving a press interview or making a press statement as different from pressuring Ukraine to investigate political rival.[349]

On August 9, Ambassador Sondland sent a text message to Ambassador Volker, writing in part: "I think potus [*sic*] really wants the deliverable."[350] Ambassador Sondland testified that "deliverable" referred to the Ukrainian press statement.[351] Ambassador Volker testified that President Trump wanted a public commitment to reform as a "deliverable":

Q. And what – yeah, what did you understand what the President wanted by deliverable?

A. That statement that had been under conversation.

Q. That was the deliverable from Zelensky that the President wanted before he would commit to –

---

[346] Volker transcribed interview, *supra* note 60, at 137.

[347] Text message from Gordon Sondland to Kurt Volker & William Taylor (July 21, 2019, 4:45 a m.) [KV00000037].

[348] Sondland deposition, *supra* note 51, at 183-84.

[349] *Id.* at 170-71.

[350] Text message from Gordon Sondland to Kurt Volker (Aug. 9, 2019, 5:47 p m.) [KV00000042].

[351] Sondland deposition, *supra* note 51, at 290.

A. *He wanted to see that they're going to come out publicly and commit to reform, investigate the past*, et cetera.[352]

According to Ambassador Taylor, on September 8, Ambassador Sondland relayed to Ambassador Taylor that he had told President Zelensky and Yermak that if President Zelensky "did not clear things up in public, we would be at a stalemate."[353] Ambassador Taylor interpreted Ambassador Sondland's use of "stalemate" to mean that there would be no security assistance to Ukraine.[354] Ambassador Taylor recounted that Ambassador Sondland said that President Trump is a businessman and businessmen ask for something before "signing a check."[355] Ambassador Taylor testified that he understood that "signing a check" related to security assistance.[356] Ambassador Sondland did not recall the conversation with Ambassador Taylor and denied making a statement about President Trump seeking something for signing a check to Ukraine.[357] He testified:

> Q. So you hadn't – did you ever, in the course of this, ever make a statement to the effect of, you know, we're cutting a big check to the Ukraine, you know, what should we get for his?
>
> A. That's not something I would have said. I don't remember that at all.
>
> Q. Okay. So you've never made a statement relating the aid to conditions that the Ukrainians ought to comply with?
>
> A. I don't remember that, no.
>
> Q. But if someone suggested that you made that statement, that would be out of your own character, you're saying?
>
> A. Yes.[358]

Although Ambassador Sondland's statements imply that the President personally sought a conditionality on the security assistance, other witnesses testified that Ambassador Sondland had a habit of exaggerating his interactions with President Trump.[359] Ambassador Sondland himself acknowledged that he only spoke with the President five or six times, one of which was a Christmas greeting.[360] It is not readily apparent that Ambassador Sondland was speaking on behalf of President Trump in this context.

---

[352] Volker transcribed interview, *supra* note 60, at 184 (emphasis added).
[353] Taylor deposition, *supra* note 47, at 39.
[354] *Id.*
[355] *Id.* at 40
[356] *Id.*
[357] Sondland deposition, *supra* note 51, at 198-99, 351.
[358] *Id.* at 198-99.
[359] Hill deposition, *supra* note 12, at 240-41; Kent deposition, *supra* note 65, at 257.
[360] Sondland deposition, *supra* note 51, at 56.

10. President Zelensky never raised a linkage between security assistance and investigations in his meetings with senior U.S. government officials.

Between July 18—the date on which OMB announced the pause on security assistance to Ukraine during an interagency conference call—and September 11—when the pause was lifted—President Zelensky had five separate meetings with high-ranking U.S. government officials. The evidence shows that President Zelensky never raised any concerns in those meeting that he felt pressure to investigate President Trump's political rival or that U.S. security assistance to Ukraine was conditioned on any such investigations.

On July 25, President Zelensky spoke by telephone with President Trump. Although President Zelensky noted a desire to purchase additional Javelin missiles from the United States—an expenditure separate from security assistance—the call summary otherwise does not show that the President discussed a pause on U.S. security assistance to Ukraine.[361]

On July 26, President Zelensky met in Kyiv with Ambassador Volker, Ambassador Taylor, and Ambassador Sondland.[362] According to Ambassador Sondland's closed-door deposition, President Zelensky did not raise any concern about a pause on security assistance or a linkage between the aid and investigations into President Trump's political rival.[363]

On August 27, President Zelensky met in Kyiv with President Trump's then-National Security Advisor John Bolton.[364] According to Ambassador Taylor, President Zelensky and Ambassador Bolton did not discuss U.S. security assistance.[365]

On September 1, President Zelensky met in Warsaw with Vice President Pence, after the existence of the security assistance pause became public. Tim Morrison, Senior Director at the NSC, testified that President Zelensky raised the security assistance directly with Vice President Pence during their meeting.[366] According to Morrison, Vice President Pence relayed President Trump's concern about corruption, the need for reform in Ukraine, and his desire for other countries to contribute more to Ukrainian defense.[367] As Jennifer Williams, senior adviser for Europe in the Office of the Vice President, testified:

> Once the cameras left the room, the very first question that President Zelensky had was about the status of security assistance. And the VP responded by really expressing our ongoing support for Ukraine, but wanting to hear from President Zelensky, you know, what the status of his reform efforts were that he could then convey back to

---

[361] *Memorandum of Telephone Conversation, supra* note 15.
[362] Taylor deposition, *supra* note 47, at 31; Sondland deposition, *supra* note 51, at 29.
[363] Sondland deposition, *supra* note 51, at 252.
[364] Taylor deposition, *supra* note 47, at 33.
[365] *Id.*
[366] Morrison deposition, *supra* note 12, at 131-34.
[367] *Id.*

the President, and also wanting to hear if there was more that European countries could do to support Ukraine.[368]

Vice President Pence did not discuss any investigations with President Zelensky.[369] Morrison said that Vice President Pence spoke to President Trump that evening, who was "still skeptical" due to the fact that U.S. allies were not adequately contributing to Ukraine.[370] Although Ambassador Sondland claimed in his public hearing that he informed Vice President Pence of his assumption of a link between security assistance and investigations in advance of the Vice President's meeting with President Zelensky,[371] the Vice President's office said Ambassador Sondland never raised investigations or conditionality on the security assistance.[372]

On September 5, President Zelensky met in Kyiv with Senator Ron Johnson, Senator Chris Murphy, and Ambassador Taylor.[373] President Zelensky raised the issue of the security assistance, and Senator Johnson relayed to him what President Trump had told Senator Johnson during their August 31 conversation.[374] Senator Murphy then warned President Zelensky "not to respond to requests from American political actors or he would risk losing Ukraine's bipartisan support."[375] Senator Johnson recalled that he did not comment on Senator Murphy's statement but began discussing a potential presidential meeting.[376] To help President Zelensky understand President Trump's mindset, Senator Johnson "tried to portray [President Trump's] strongly held attitude and reiterated the reasons President Trump consistently gave [Senator Johnson] for his reservations regarding Ukraine: endemic corruption and inadequate European support."[377] Senator Johnson recounted how President Zelensky raised no concerns about pressure:

> This was a very open, frank, and supportive discussion. There was no reason for anyone on either side not to be completely honest or to withhold any concerns. ***At no time during this meeting—or any other meeting on this trip—was there any mention by [President] Zelensky or any Ukrainian that they were feeling pressure to do anything in return for military aid***, not even after [Senator] Murphy warned them about getting involved in the 2020 election—which would have been the perfect time to discuss any pressure.[378]

---

[368] Williams deposition, *supra* note 73, at 81.
[369] *Impeachment Inquiry: Ambassador Kurt Volker and Mr. Timothy Morrison, supra* note 8; *Impeachment Inquiry: LTC Alexander Vindman and Ms. Jennifer Williams, supra* note 6. In fact, Williams testified that Vice President Pence has "never brought up" these investigations. *Impeachment Inquiry: LTC Alexander Vindman and Ms. Jennifer Williams, supra* note 6.
[370] Morrison deposition, *supra* note 12, at 133-34.
[371] *Impeachment Inquiry: Ambassador Gordon Sondland, supra* note 56.
[372] Office of the Vice President, Statement from VP Chief of Staff Marc Short (Nov. 20, 2019). In addition, the summary of President Trump's July 25 call with President Zelensky was not included in Vice President Pence's briefing book for his meeting with President Zelensky. Williams deposition, *supra* note 73, at 108.
[373] Sen. Johnson letter, *supra* note 138, at 6.
[374] *Id.*
[375] *Id.* at 7.
[376] *Id.*
[377] *Id.*
[378] *Id.* at 8 (emphasis added).

After Senator Johnson offered his perspective, Senator Murphy similarly provided an account of the September 5 meeting.[379] Senator Murphy did not dispute the facts as recounted by Senator Johnson, including that President Zelensky raised no concerns about feeling pressure to investigate the President's political rival.[380] Senator Murphy, however, interpreted President Zelensky's silence to mean that he felt pressure.[381] This "interpretation"—based on what President Zelensky did not say—is unpersuasive in light of President Zelensky's repeated and consistent statements that he felt no pressure.[382]

11. In early September 2019, President Zelensky's government implemented several anti-corruption reform measures.

Publicly available information shows that following the seating of Ukraine's new parliament, the Verkhovna Rada (Rada), on August 29, 2019, the Zelensky government initiated aggressive anti-corruption reforms. Almost immediately, President Zelensky appointed a new prosecutor general and opened Ukraine's Supreme Anti-Corruption Court.[383] On September 3, the Rada passed a bill that removed parliamentary immunity.[384] President Zelensky signed the bill on September 11.[385] On September 18, the Rada approved a bill streamlining corruption prosecutions and allowing the Supreme Anti-Corruption Court to focus on high-level corruption cases.[386]

Witnesses described how these legislative initiatives instilled confidence that Ukraine was delivering on anti-corruption reform. NSC staffer LTC Vindman testified that the Rada's efforts were significant.[387] In his deposition, Ambassador Taylor lauded President Zelensky for this demonstrable commitment to reform. He testified:

> President Zelensky was taking over Ukraine in a hurry. He had appointed reformist ministers and supported long-stalled anticorruption legislation. He took quick executive action, including opening Ukraine's High Anti-Corruption Court, which was established under previous Presidential administration but was never allowed to operate. . . . With his new parliamentary majority, President Zelensky changed the Ukrainian constitution to remove absolute immunity from Rada deputies, which had been the source of raw corruption for decades.[388]

---

[379] Letter from Sen. Chris Murphy to Adam Schiff, Chairman, H. Perm. Sel. Comm. on Intelligence, & Carolyn Maloney, Acting Chairwoman, H. Comm. on Oversight & Reform (Nov. 19, 2019).

[380] *Id.* at 5.

[381] *Id.*

[382] *See supra* Section I.A.2.

[383] Stefan Wolff & Tatyana Malyarenko, *In Ukraine, Volodymyr Zelenskiy must tread carefully or may end up facing another Maidan uprising*, The Conversation, Nov. 11, 2019.

[384] *Bill on lifting parliamentary immunity submitted to Zelensky for signature*, Unian, Sept. 4, 2019.

[385] *Zelensky signs law on stripping parliamentary immunity*, Interfax-Ukraine, Sept. 11, 2019.

[386] *Anti-corruption Court to receive cases from NABU, SAPO*, 112 UA, Sept. 18, 2019.

[387] *Impeachment Inquiry: LTC Alexander Vindman and Ms. Jennifer Williams*, *supra* note 6.

[388] Taylor deposition, *supra* note 47, at 22-23.

Likewise, NSC Senior Director Tim Morrison recalled that President Zelensky's team had literally been working through the night on anti-corruption reforms. He testified:

Q: And after the Rada was seated, do you know if President Zelensky made an effort to implement those [anti-corruption] reforms?

A: I do.

Q: And what reforms generally can you speak to?

A: Well, he named a new prosecutor general. That was something that we were specifically interested in. He had his party introduce a spate of legislative reforms, one of which was particularly significant was stripping Rada members of their parliamentary immunity. That passed fairly quickly, as I recall. Those kinds of things.

Q: And within what time period were some of those initial reforms passed?

A: Very, very quickly.

Q: Okay. So in the month of August?

A: When we were – when Ambassador Bolton was in Ukraine and he met with President Zelensky, we observed that everybody on the Ukrainian side of the table was exhausted, because they had been up for days working on, you know, reform legislation, working on the new Cabinet, to get through as much as possible on the first day.

Q: Remind me again of Ambassador Bolton's visit. Was that August, at the end of August?

A: It was at the end of August. It was between the G7 and the Warsaw commemoration

Q: So by Labor Day, for example?

A: I seem to recall we were – we – we were there on the opening day of the Rada. President – President Zelensky met with Ambassador Bolton on the opening day of the Rada, and they were in an all-night session. Yeah. So, I mean, things were happening that day.[389]

These actions by the Ukrainian government in early September 2019 are significant in demonstrating President Zelensky's commitment to fighting corruption. Although the

---

[389] Morrison deposition, *supra* note 12, at 128-29.

Department of Defense had certified Ukraine met its anti-corruption benchmarks in Spring 2019, that certification occurred before President Zelensky's inauguration.[390] Deputy Assistant Secretary of Defense Laura Cooper testified during her public hearing that the anti-corruption review examined the efforts of the Poroshenko administration and that President Zelensky had appointed a new Minister of Defense.[391]

As President Trump told Ambassador Sondland on September 9, he sought "nothing" from the Ukrainian government; he only wanted President Zelensky to "do what he ran on."[392] President Zelensky had run on an anti-corruption platform, and these early aggressive actions provided confirmation that he was the "real deal," as U.S. officials advised President Trump.

12. The security assistance was ultimately disbursed to Ukraine in September 2019 without any Ukrainian action to investigate President Trump's political rival.

On September 11, President Trump met with Vice President Pence, Senator Rob Portman, and Acting Chief of Staff Mick Mulvaney to discuss U.S. security assistance to Ukraine.[393] As recounted by NSC Senior Director Tim Morrison, the group discussed whether President Zelensky's progress on anti-corruption reform—which Vice President Pence discussed during his bilateral meeting with President Zelensky on September 1—was significant enough to justify releasing the aid.[394] He testified:

> I believe Senator Portman was relating, and I believe the Vice President as well, related their view of the importance of the assistance. The Vice President was obviously armed with his conversation with President Zelensky, and they were – they convinced the President that the aid should be disbursed immediately.[395]

Following this meeting, the President decided to lift the pause on U.S. security assistance to Ukraine.[396] The release was conveyed to the interagency the following morning.[397] The U.S. disbursed this assistance without Ukraine ever acting to investigate President Trump's political rival.

Democrats cannot show conclusively that the Trump Administration lifted the pause on security assistance only as a result of their impeachment inquiry. In a private conversation with Senator Johnson on August 31, President Trump signaled that the aid would be released, saying then: "We're reviewing it now, and you'll probably like my final decision."[398] A number of other

---

[390] Deposition of Laura Cooper, in Wash., D.C., at 19, 99 (Oct. 23, 2019).
[391] *Impeachment Inquiry: Ms. Laura Cooper and Mr. David Hale, supra* note 246.
[392] Sondland deposition, *supra* note 51, at 106.
[393] Morrison deposition, *supra* note 12, at 242-43.
[394] *Id.* at 243.
[395] *Id.*.
[396] *Id.* at 211.
[397] *Id.*
[398] Letter from Sen. Johnson, *supra* note 138, at 5.

events occurred within the same period. President Zelensky implemented serious anti-corruption reforms in Ukraine and OMB conducted a review of foreign assistance globally and provided data on what other countries contribute to Ukraine. Bipartisan senators contacted the White House, telling the Administration that the Senate would act legislatively to undo the pause on security assistance.[399] In fact, Senator Dick Durbin credited the release of the security assistance to the Senate's potential action.[400] Senator Durbin said, "It's beyond a coincidence that they released it the night before our vote in the committee."[401]

* * *

The evidence does not support the Democrats' allegation that President Trump sought to withhold U.S. security assistance to Ukraine to pressure President Zelensky to investigate his political rival for the President's political benefit. The Democrats' witnesses denied the two were linked. The U.S. officials never informed the Ukrainian government that the security assistance was delayed, and senior Ukrainian officials did not raise concerns to U.S. officials until after the delay was publicly reported. President Trump never raised the security assistance during his phone call with President Zelensky. President Zelensky never voiced concerns about pressure or conditionality on security assistance in any meetings he had with senior U.S. government officials. U.S. security assistance ultimately flowed to Ukraine without the Ukrainian government taking any action to investigate President Trump's political rival.

D. The evidence does not establish that President Trump set up a shadow foreign policy apparatus to pressure Ukraine to investigate the President's political rival for the purpose of benefiting him in the 2020 election.

Democrats allege that President Trump established an unauthorized, so-called "shadow" foreign policy apparatus to pressure Ukraine to investigate his political rival to benefit the President in the 2020 election.[402] Democrats also alleged that President Trump's recall of Ambassador Yovanovitch was a "politically motivated" decision to appease "allies of President Trump."[403] Although the Constitution gives the President broad authority to conduct the foreign policy of the United States, the Democrats say that President Trump abused his power by disregarding the traditional State Department bureaucratic channels for his personal political benefit. These allegations fall flat.

It is impossible to fairly assess the facts without appreciating the circumstances in which they occurred. From the very first days of the Trump Administration—indeed even before it began—the unelected bureaucracy rejected President Trump and his policies. The self-proclaimed "resistance" organized protests and parody social media accounts, while high-level

---

[399] *See* Byron York, *Why did Trump release Ukraine aid? The answer is simple*, Wash. Exam., Nov. 24, 2019.

[400] Caitlin Emma et al., *Trump administration backs off hold on Ukraine military aid*, Politico, Sept. 12, 2019.

[401] *Id.*

[402] Press Release, H. Comm. On Foreign Affairs, Engel Floor Remarks on Resolution for Open Hearings on Trump's Abuse of Power (Oct. 31, 2019); Adam Schiff (@RepAdamSchiff) (Nov. 6, 2019, 10:58 AM), https://twitter.com/RepAdamSchiff/status/1192154367199260672.

[403] Press Release, H. Comm. on Foreign Affairs, Engel & Hoyer Statement on U.S. Ambassador to Ukraine Masha Yovanovitch (May 7, 2019).

bureaucrats received praise from colleagues for openly defying the Administration's policies. Leaks of secret information became almost daily occurrence, including details about the President's sensitive conversations with foreign leaders. Meanwhile, the Department of Justice and FBI spent 22 months thoroughly investigating false allegations that the Trump campaign had colluded with the Russian government in the 2016 election.

The evidence shows that following President Zelensky's inauguration, the three senior U.S. officials who attended his inauguration—Ambassador Kurt Volker, Ambassador Gordon Sondland, and Secretary Rick Perry—assumed responsibility for shepherding the U.S.-Ukrainian relationship. Contrary to assertions of an "irregular" foreign policy channel, all three men were senior U.S. leaders who had important official interests in Ukraine. The three men maintained regular communication with the NSC and the State Department about their work in Ukraine.

Following President Zelensky's inauguration, Ambassador Volker, Ambassador Sondland, and Secretary Perry sought to convince President Trump of Ukraine's commitment to reform. In that meeting, President Trump referenced Mayor Rudy Giuliani, who had experience in Ukraine. When President Zelensky's adviser Andrey Yermak asked Ambassador Volker to connect him with Mayor Giuliani, Ambassador Volker did so because he believed it would advance U.S.-Ukrainian interests. Mayor Giuliani informed Ambassador Volker about his communications with Yermak. Volker and Yermak both have said that Mayor Giuliani did not speak on behalf of the President in these discussions.

Some pockets of the State Department and NSC grumbled that Ambassador Volker, Ambassador Sondland, and Secretary Perry had become so active in U.S-Ukraine policy. Others criticized Ambassador Marie Yovanovitch's recall or fretted about Mayor Giuliani's involvement. Yet, despite these bureaucratic misgivings, there is no evidence that the involvement of Ambassador Volker, Ambassador Sondland, Secretary Perry, or Mayor Giuliani was illegal or hurt U.S. strategic interests. There is also no evidence that President Trump made this arrangement or recalled Ambassador Yovanovitch for the purpose of pressuring Ukraine to investigate the President's political rival for his benefit in the 2020 presidential election.

1. The President has broad Constitutional authority to conduct the foreign policy of the United States.

The Constitution vests the President of the United States with considerable authority over foreign policy.[404] The President is the Commander-in-Chief of U.S. Armed Forces. The President has the power to make treaties with foreign nations, and he appoints and receives "Ambassadors and other public ministers."[405] The Supreme Court has explained that the Constitution gives the President "plenary and exclusive authority" over the conduct of foreign affairs.[406] The President is the "sole organ of the federal government" with respect to foreign affairs.[407]

---

[404] U.S. Const. Art. II.

[405] *Id.*

[406] United States v. Curtiss-Wright Export Corp., 299 U.S. 304, 320 (1936).

[407] *Id.* Although the President makes treaties with the advice and consent of the Senate; the President alone negotiates. *Cf.* H. Jefferson Powell, *The President's Authority Over Foreign Affairs: An Executive Branch Perspective*, 67 Geo. Wash. L. Rev. 527, 546-47 (1999). Dealings with foreign nations require "caution and unity of design," which depend on the President's authority to speak with "one voice" on behalf of U.S. interests. *Id.* at 546.

2. President Trump was likely skeptical of the established national security apparatus as a result of continual leaks and resistance from the federal bureaucracy.

In the wake of President Trump's electoral victory in 2016, he faced almost immediate intransigence from unelected—and often anonymous—federal employees. Since then, the "Resistance" has protested President Trump and leaked sensitive national security information about the Trump Administration's policies and objectives. In this context, one can see how President Trump would be justifiably skeptical of the national security apparatus.

Since the beginning of the Trump Administration, leaks of sensitive national security information have occurred at unprecedented rate. As the *Washington Post* noted, "[e]very presidential administration leaks. So far, the Trump White House has gushed."[408] According to an analysis from the Senate Homeland Security and Governmental Affairs Committee in May 2017, the Trump Administration faced about one national security leak per day—flowing seven times faster in the Trump Administration than during the Obama or Bush Administrations.[409] Unelected bureaucrats leaked details about President Trump's private conversations with world leaders and the investigation into Russian interference in the 2016 election.[410]

In Kimberley Strassel's book *Resistance (At All Costs)*, she described the Resistance as "the legions of Americans who were resolutely opposed to the election of Trump, and who remain angrily determined to remove him from office."[411] This resistance included anonymous federal employees who criticized President Trump and his policies on parody U.S. government social media accounts.[412] This resistance included high-level bureaucrats—including then-Acting Attorney General Sally Yates—who openly defied implementing Administration policies.[413] The resistance included an anonymous employee who published an op-ed in the *New York Times* in September 2018 titled, "I Am Part of the Resistance Inside the Trump Administration," detailing how he or she and other unelected bureaucrats were actively working at odds with the President.[414] The op-ed earned the anonymous employee a book deal.[415]

The "Resistance" extended to the U.S. national security apparatus as well, including FBI agents investigating unproven allegations of collusion between the Trump campaign and the Russian government.[416] An FBI lawyer working the investigation, and later assigned to Special Counsel Robert Mueller's office, texted another FBI employee, "Vive le resistance," in the

---

[408] Paul Farhi, *The Trump administration has sprung a leak. Many of them, in fact*, Wash. Post, Feb. 5, 2017.
[409] Maj. Staff on S. Comm. on Homeland Sec. & Gov't Affairs, 115th Cong., State Secrets: How An Avalanche Of Media Leaks Is Harming National Security (2017) [hereinafter "HSGAC report"].
[410] *Id.*
[411] Kimberley Strassel, Resistance (At All Costs): How Trump Haters Are Breaking America (2019).
[412] Kimberley A. Strassel, *Whistleblowers and the Real Deep State*, Wall St. J., Oct. 11, 2019.
[413] *Id.*
[414] *I Am Part of the Resistance Inside the Trump Administration*, N.Y. Times, Sep. 5, 2018.
[415] Alexa Diaz, *Anonymous Trump official who wrote 'resistance' op-ed to publish tell-all book*, L.A. Times, Oct. 22, 2019.
[416] Special Counsel Robert S. Mueller, III, *Report On The Investigation Into Russian Interference In The 2016 Presidential Election*, 1-2. Vol. 1 (2019) [hereinafter "Mueller report"].

month that President Trump was elected.[417] In the week after election night, FBI Agent Peter Strzok and FBI lawyer Lisa Page—who were both involved in the Russia collusion investigation—wrote to each other: "OMG THIS IS F*CKING TERRIFYING" and "I bought all the president's men. Figure I needed to brush up on watergate [*sic*]."[418]

The FBI surveilled Trump campaign associates using evidence delivered by Christopher Steele—a confidential human source funded by then-candidate Trump's political opponents and who admitted he was "desperate" that Donald Trump lose the election.[419] During her deposition, Dr. Hill testified that Steele's reporting was likely a bogus Russia misinformation campaign against Steele.[420] Yet, the FBI accepted Steele's information and used it to obtain surveillance warrants on Trump campaign associate Carter Page.[421] Ultimately, Special Counsel Mueller's report concluded that the Trump campaign did not conspire or coordinate with Russian election interference actions.[422] In considering the President's mindset, this context cannot be ignored.

3. The President has the constitutional authority to remove Ambassador Yovanovitch.

U.S. ambassadors are the President's representatives abroad, serving at the pleasure of the President. Every ambassador interviewed during this impeachment inquiry recognized and appreciated this fact.[423] Even Ambassador Yovanovitch understood that the President could remove any ambassador at any time for any reason, although she unsurprisingly disagreed with the reason for her removal.[424] The removal of Ambassador Yovanovitch, therefore, is not *per se* evidence of wrongdoing for the President's political benefit.

Evidence suggests that President Trump likely had concerns about Ambassador Yovanovitch's ability to represent him in Ukraine,[425] and that then-Ukrainian President

---

[417] Inspector Gen., Dep't of Justice, *A Review of Various Actions by the Federal Bureau of Investigation and Department of Justice in Advance of the 2016 Election*, 396, 419 (2018).

[418] *Id.* at 397, 400.

[419] F.B.I., Dep't of Just., 302 Interview with Bruce Ohr on Dec. 19, 2016 at 3.

[420] *See* Hill deposition, *supra* note 12, at 177-180 ("I think it was a rabbit hole . . . . The way that the Russians operate is that they will use whatever conduit they can to put out information that is both real and credible but that also masks a great deal of disinformation . . . .").

[421] Transcribed Interview of Sally Moyer, in Wash., D.C., at 162 (Oct. 23, 2018).

[422] Mueller report, *supra* note 416.

[423] Sondland deposition, *supra* note 51, at 19; Volker transcribed interview, *supra* note 60, at 88-89; Transcribed interview of Ambassador Michael McKinley, in Wash., D.C., at 37 (Oct. 16, 2019) [hereinafter "McKinley transcribed interview"]; Yovanovitch deposition, *supra* note 115, at 23; Taylor deposition, *supra* note 47, at 297; Hale deposition, *supra* note 230, at 38.

[424] Yovanovitch deposition, *supra* note 115, at 23. Evidence suggests that Ambassador Yovanovitch took steps to gain the President's trust. Deputy Assistant Secretary of State George Kent testified that Ambassador Yovanovitch taped videos in which she proclaimed support for the Trump Administration's foreign policies. Kent deposition, *supra* note 65, at 118-19. Ambassador Yovanovitch testified that she sought Ambassador Sondland's guidance on how to address negative news reports critical of her work as Ambassador to Ukraine. She said that Ambassador Sondland told her to "go big or go home" in publicly supporting the President. Yovanovitch deposition, *supra* note 115, at 267-28, 306-07. Ambassador Sondland, however, testified that he did not recall advising Ambassador Yovanovitch to make a public statement. Sondland deposition, *supra* note 51, at 58-59.

[425] Memorandum of Telephone Conversation, *supra* note 15.

Poroshenko had authorized an effort to criticize Ambassador Yovanovitch.[426] Ambassador Volker testified that he had no firsthand knowledge of Ambassador Yovanovitch criticizing the President; however, he said that "President Trump would understandably be concerned if that was true because you want to have trust and confidence in your Ambassadors."[427]

Despite recognizing the President's prerogative to dismiss ambassadors, some in the U.S. foreign policy apparatus voiced concerns about Ambassador Yovanovitch's removal. Ambassador McKinley testified that he resigned from the State Department because he believed that it failed to protect its diplomats.[428] However, Ambassador McKinley did not resign when he first learned that Ambassador Yovanovitch had been called home, despite knowing that she had been recalled.[429] He only resigned months later, after the whistleblower's account and the President's comments to President Zelensky about Ambassador Yovanovitch during the July 25 call transcript became public.[430]

Ambassador Yovanovitch testified that her removal from Kyiv had little effect on her career with the State Department. Her post was scheduled to end only a matter of weeks after her recall.[431] Although she had considered extending her tour, a decision had not been officially made.[432] Ambassador Yovanovitch explained that she had been planning to retire following her tour in Ukraine and "[s]o I don't think from a State Department point of view [the recall] has had any effect."[433] The recall also did not affect her compensation.[434] Ambassador Yovanovitch explained that the State Department was helpful in securing her a position with Georgetown University.[435]

4. Ambassador Volker, Ambassador Sondland, and Secretary Perry were all senior U.S. government officers with official interests in Ukraine policy.

Contrary to allegations that President Trump orchestrated a "shadow" foreign policy channel to pressure Ukraine to investigate his political rival, evidence shows that the U.S. interactions with Ukraine were led by senior U.S. officials. These officials, Ambassador Volker, Ambassador Sondland, and Secretary Perry, had attended President Zelensky's inauguration in May 2019 and all had official interests in U.S. policy toward Ukraine.

Ambassador Volker explained that "we viewed ourselves as having been empowered as a Presidential delegation to go there, meet, make an assessment [of whether President Zelensky was a legitimate anti-corruption reformer], and report" to President Trump.[436] He said that they

---

[426] Kent deposition, *supra* note 65, at 232.

[427] Volker transcribed interview, *supra* note 60, at 90.

[428] McKinley transcribed interview, *supra* note 423, at 20, 24-25.

[429] *Id.* at 33-34.

[430] *Id.* at 35-36. *See also* Karen DeYoung, *Senior adviser to Pompeo resigns*, Wash. Post, Oct. 10, 2019.

[431] Yovanovitch deposition, *supra* note 115, at 114-16, 140.

[432] *Id.* at 22, 114-16, 122.

[433] *Id.* at 139-40.

[434] *Impeachment Inquiry: Ambassador Marie Yovanovitch*, *supra* note 4.

[435] Yovanovitch deposition, *supra* note 115, at 139.

[436] Volker transcribed interview, *supra* note 60, at 206.

assumed responsibility to "shepherd this [U.S.-Ukrainian] relationship together as best we could."[437] The delegation assumed this responsibility at a time when the U.S. government lacked an experienced chief of mission in Kyiv.

Importantly, cutting against the idea of a "shadow" channel, each of these three men had an official role with respect to U.S. policy toward Ukraine.[438] Ambassador Volker described his role as the Special Representative for Ukraine Negotiations as "supporting democracy and reform in Ukraine, helping Ukraine better defend itself and deter Russian aggression, and leading U.S. negotiating efforts to end the war and restore Ukraine's territorial integrity."[439] As Ambassador to the European Union, Ambassador Sondland said that Ukraine issues were "central" to his responsibilities.[440] In addition, the Department of Energy, led by Secretary Perry, has significant equities in energy policies in Ukraine.[441]

In the absence of a seasoned chief of mission in Kyiv—before Ambassador Taylor's arrival—these three individuals assumed responsibility following President Zelensky's inauguration for shepherding U.S. engagement with President Zelensky's government. That each individual had an official interest in U.S. policy toward Ukraine undercuts the notion that they engaged in "shadow" diplomacy for illegitimate purposes.

5. Referencing Ukrainian corruption, President Trump told Ambassador Volker, Ambassador Sondland, and Secretary Perry to talk to Mayor Giuliani.

Evidence suggests that Mayor Giuliani's negative assessment of President Zelensky may have reinforced President Trump's existing skepticism about Ukraine and its history of corruption. In May 2019, Mayor Giuliani said that President-elect Zelensky was "surrounded by enemies" of President Trump.[442] When the U.S. delegation to President Zelensky's inauguration later tried to assure President Trump that President Zelensky was different, the President referenced Mayor Giuliani as someone knowledgeable about Ukrainian corruption and told the men to talk to Mayor Giuliani.[443] Testimony differs, however, on whether the President's reference to Mayor Giuliani was a direction or an aside. Either way, because President Trump—constitutionally, the nation's "sole organ of foreign affairs"[444]—raised Mayor Giuliani as

---

[437] *Id.* at 67.

[438] *See Impeachment Inquiry: Dr. Fiona Hill and Mr. David Holmes, supra* note 210.

[439] Volker transcribed interview, *supra* note 60, at 13.

[440] Sondland deposition, *supra* note 51, at 20. During her deposition, Dr. Hill testified that Ambassador Sondland told her that President Trump had "given him broad authority on all things related to Europe, that he was the President's point man on Europe." Hill deposition, *supra* note 12, at 60. Dr. Hill later acknowledged it that Ambassador Sondland could have been exaggerating, explaining that she often saw Ambassador Sondland coming out of West Wing saying he was seeing the President but she learned later that he was really seeing other staff. *Id.* at 204.

[441] James Osborne, *What Rick Perry was doing in Ukraine*, Houston Chronicle, Oct. 16, 2019.

[442] *See* Charles Creitz, *Giuliani cancels Ukraine trip, says he'd be 'walking into a group of people that are enemies of the US,'* Fox News, May 11, 2019.

[443] Sondland deposition, *supra* note 51, at 25. According to public reports, Mayor Giuliani has over a decade of experience working in Ukraine. *See, e.g.*, Rosalind S. Helderman et al., *Impeachment Inquiry Puts New Focus on Giuliani's Work for Prominent Figures in Ukraine,* Wash. Post, Oct. 2, 2019.

[444] *Curtiss-Wright Export Corp.*, 299 U.S. at 320.

someone knowledgeable about Ukraine, this arrangement is not evidence of an unsanctioned and nefarious "shadow" foreign policy apparatus.

On May 23, the U.S. delegation to President Zelensky's inauguration briefed President Trump about their impressions of President Zelensky. Ambassador Sondland testified that the President relayed concerns about Ukrainian corruption, saying "Ukraine is a problem," "tried to take me down," and "talk to Rudy."[445] During his transcribed interview, Ambassador Volker elaborated:

> Q. And can you describe the discussion –
>
> A. Yes.
>
> Q. – that occurred?
>
> A Yes. The President started the meeting and started with kind of a negative assessment of the Ukraine. As I've said earlier –
>
> Q. Yep.
>
> A. – it's a terrible place, all corrupt, terrible people, just dumping on Ukraine.
>
> Q. And they were out to get me in 2016.
>
> A. And they were out to get – and they tried to take me down.
>
> Q. In 2016?
>
> A. Yes. And each of us took turns from this delegation giving our point of view, which was that this is a new crowd, it's a new President, he is committed to doing the right things. I believe I said, he agrees with you. That's why he got elected. It is a terrible place, and he campaigned on cleaning it up, and that's why the Ukrainian people supported him.
>
> So, you know, we strongly encouraged him to engage with this new President because he's committed to fighting all of those things that President Trump was complaining about.
>
> Q. And how did the President react?
>
> A. He just didn't believe it. He was skeptical. And he also said, that's not what I hear. I hear, you know, he's got some terrible people

---

[445] Sondland deposition, *supra* note 51, at 61-62, 75.

around him. And he referenced that he hears from Mr. Giuliani as part of that.

Q. Can you explain a little bit more about what the President said about Rudy Giuliani in that meeting?

A. He said that's not what I hear. I hear a whole bunch of other things. And I don't know how he phrased it with Rudy, but it was – I think he said, not as an instruction but just as a comment, talk to Rudy, you know. He knows all of these things, and they've got some bad people around him. And that was the nature of it. It was clear that he also had other sources. It wasn't only Rudy Giuliani. I don't know who those might be, but he – or at least he said, I hear from people.[446]

In his public testimony, Ambassador Volker reiterated that he did not understand the President's comment, "talk to Rudy," to be a direction.[447] He explained:

I didn't take it as an instruction. I want to be clear about that. He said: That's not what I hear. You know, when we were giving him our assessment about President Zelensky and where Ukraine is headed: That's not what I hear. I hear terrible things. He's got terrible people around him. Talk to Rudy. And I understood, in that context, him just saying that's where he hears it from. I didn't take it as an instruction."[448]

Ambassador Sondland, however, in both his closed-door deposition and his public testimony, characterized the President's comment as a "direction."[449] In an interview with the *Wall Street Journal*, Energy Secretary Rick Perry stated that he called Mayor Giuliani following the May 23 meeting, and that Mayor Giuliani told him "to be careful with regards" to President Zelensky.[450] Secretary Perry said "he never heard the president, any of his appointees, Mr. Giuliani, or the Ukrainian regime discuss the possibility of specifically investigating former Vice President Joe Biden, a Democratic presidential contender, and his son Hunter Biden."[451]

---

[446] Volker transcribed interview, *supra* note 60, at 304-05. Deputy Assistant Secretary Kent testified that Dr. Hill relayed to him that President Trump had conversations with Viktor Orban, the Prime Minister of Hungary, and Vladimir Putin, the President of Russia, which he said may have also colored President Trump's view of Ukraine. Kent deposition, *supra* note 65, at 253-54.
[447] *Impeachment Inquiry: Ambassador Kurt Volker and Mr. Timothy Morrison*, *supra* note 8.
[448] *Id.*
[449] *Impeachment Inquiry: Ambassador Gordon Sondland*, *supra* note 56; Sondland deposition, *supra* note 51, at 25-26.
[450] Timothy Puko & Rebecca Ballhaus, *Rick Perry called Rudy Giuliani at Trump's direction on Ukraine concerns*, Wall St. J., Oct. 16, 2019.
[451] *Id.*

6. At the Ukrainian government's request, Ambassador Volker connected them with Mayor Giuliani to change his impression about the Zelensky regime.

Evidence shows that the Ukrainian government, and specifically Zelensky adviser Andrey Yermak, initiated contact with Mayor Giuliani—and not the other way around—to attempt to refute Mayor Giuliani's views about President Zelensky. Yermak later told *Bloomberg* that he had informed both Republicans and Democrats in Congress in July 2019 that he planned to engage with Mayor Giuliani and heard no objections.[452]

According to Ambassador Volker, in May 2019, he "became concerned that a negative narrative about Ukraine fueled by assertions made by Ukraine's departing prosecutor general" was reaching President Trump via Mayor Giuliani.[453] In July, Ambassador Volker shared his concerns with Yermak, who asked Ambassador Volker to connect him with Mayor Giuliani directly.[454] Ambassador Volker explained:

> After sharing my concerns with the Ukrainian leadership, an adviser to President Zelensky asked me to connect him to the President's personal lawyer, Mayor Rudy Giuliani. I did so. I did so solely because I understood that the new Ukrainian leadership wanted to convince those, like Mayor Giuliani, who believed such a negative narrative about Ukraine, that times have changed and that, under President Zelensky, Ukraine is worthy of U.S. support. I also made clear to the Ukrainians on a number of occasions that Mayor Giuliani is a private citizen and the President's personal lawyer and that he does not represent the United States Government.[455]

Ambassador Volker was clear during his transcribed interview that his action connecting Yermak with Mayor Giuliani was in the best interests of the United States. He testified:

> Q. And so any of the facts here, you connecting Mr. Giuliani with Mr. Yermak and to the extent you were facilitating Mr. Giuliani's communication with anybody in the Ukraine, you were operating under the best interests of the United States?
>
> A. Absolutely.
>
> Q. And to the extent Mr. Giuliani is tight with the President, has a good relationship with him, has the ability to influence him, is it fair to say that, at times, it was in the U.S.'s interest to have Mr. Giuliani connecting with these Ukrainian officials?

---

[452] Baker & Krasnolutska, *supra* note 280.
[453] Volker transcribed interview, *supra* note 60, at 18.
[454] *Id.*; *see also id.* at 137-38.
[455] *Id.* at 18.

A. Yes. I would say it this way: It was I think in the U.S. interest for the information that was reaching the President to be accurate and fresh and coming from the right people. And if some of what Mr. Giuliani believed or heard from, for instance, the former [Ukrainian] Prosecutor General Lutsenko was self-serving, inaccurate, wrong, et cetera, I think correcting that perception that he has is important, because to the extent that the President does hear from him, as he would, you don't want this dissonant information reaching the President.[456]

In an interview with *Bloomberg*, Yermak explained that he sought to engage with Mayor Giuliani to "dispel the notion that the new Ukraine government was corrupt."[457] Yermak said the Zelensky regime was "surprised" that Mayor Giuliani believed them to be "enemies of the U.S." and they sought to ask Mayor Giuliani directly why he believed that.[458] Yermak recounted how, before his engaged with Mayor Giuliani, he sought bipartisan feedback from Congress about this approach.[459] He said that he spoke with "the top national security advisers to the minority and majority leaders in both the U.S. House and Senate" and told them that "he planned to talk to [Mayor] Giuliani to explain the nation's reform agenda and to urge him not to communicate with Ukraine through the media."[460] Yermak recalled, "Everyone said: 'good idea.'"[461]

7. The Ukrainian government understood that Mayor Giuliani was not speaking on behalf of President Trump.

Ambassador Volker was the chief interlocutor with the Ukrainian government. He described himself as someone who had the Ukrainian government's trust and who offered them counsel on how to address the negative narrative about Ukrainian corruption.[462] Ambassador Volker testified that the Ukrainian government did not view Mayor Giuliani as President Trump's "agent" on whose behalf he spoke.[463] Instead, the Ukrainians saw Mayor Giuliani as a one-way method for conveying information to President Trump about President Zelensky's commitment to reform.

Under examination by House Intelligence Committee Chairman Adam Schiff in his closed-door deposition, Ambassador Volker was resolute that the Ukrainian government saw Mayor Giuliani as someone who "had the President's ear," not someone who spoke for the President. He explained:

Q. You understood that the Ukrainians recognized that Rudy Giuliani represented the President, that he was an agent of the President, that

---

[456] *Id.* at 69-70.
[457] Baker & Krasnolutska, *supra* note 280.
[458] *Id.*
[459] *Id.*
[460] *Id.*
[461] *Id.*
[462] Volker transcribed interview, *supra* note 60, at 168-69.
[463] *Id.* at 116.

he was a direct channel to the President. Ukrainian officials you were dealing with would have understood that, would they not?

A. ***I would not say that they thought of him as an agent***, but that he was a way of communicating, that you could get something to Giuliani and he would be someone who would be talking to the President anyway, so it would flow information that way.

Q. So this was someone who had the President's ear?

A. Yes. That's fair.[464]

In his public testimony, Ambassador Volker reiterated that Mayor Giuliani was not speaking on the President's behalf. He explained:

> I made clear to the Ukrainians that Mayor Giuliani was a private citizen, the President's personal lawyer, and not representing the U.S. Government. Likewise, in my conversations with Mayor Giuliani, I never considered him to be speaking on the President's behalf, or giving instructions. Rather, the information flow was the other way, from Ukraine to Mayor Giuliani, in the hopes that this would clear up the information reaching President Trump.[465]

During her closed-door deposition, Dr. Hill confirmed this assessment, explaining that she could not say that Mayor Giuliani was acting on President Trump's behalf.[466]

Andrey Yermak, in an August 2019 *New York Times* article, said it was also not clear to him whether Mayor Giuliani was speaking on behalf of President Trump.[467] According to the *Times*, Mayor Giuliani "explicitly stated that he was not" speaking on behalf of the President.[468] President Trump confirmed this fact in a November 2019 interview, explaining that he did not direct Mayor Giuliani's Ukraine activities.[469]

8. Ambassador Volker, Ambassador Sondland, and Secretary Perry kept the National Security Council and the State Department informed about their actions.

As Ambassador Volker, Ambassador Sondland, and Secretary Perry engaged with Ukrainian government officials, they maintained communications with the State Department and NSC. This coordination undercuts any notion that President Trump orchestrated a "shadow" foreign policy apparatus to work outside of the State Department or NSC.

---

[464] *Id.* (emphasis added).
[465] *Impeachment Inquiry: Ambassador Kurt Volker and Mr. Timothy Morrison, supra* note 8.
[466] Hill deposition, *supra* note 12, at 424-25.
[467] Kramer & Vogel, *supra* note 176.
[468] *Id.*
[469] Daniel Chaitin, *'I didn't direct him': Trump denies sending Giuliani to Ukraine*, Wash. Exam., Nov. 26, 2019.

Ambassador Volker testified that "while executing my duties, I kept my colleagues at the State Department and National Security Council informed and also briefed Congress about my actions."[470] Ambassador Volker and Ambassador Sondland also communicated regularly with Ambassador Bill Taylor once he became the chargé d'affaires, *a.i.*, in Kyiv.[471] These briefings went as high as the Counselor to the Secretary of State, Ulrich Brechbuhl.[472]

In his public testimony, Ambassador Sondland explained that it was "no secret" what he, Ambassador Volker, and Secretary Perry were doing. As he stated, "[w]e kept the NSC apprised of our efforts, including specifically our efforts to secure a public statement from the Ukrainians that would satisfy President Trump's concerns."[473] Ambassador Sondland testified that "everyone was in the loop," although he conceded that he "presumed" a connection between investigations and security assistance without speaking to President Trump, Acting Chief of Staff Mulvaney, or Mayor Giuliani.[474]

9. **Although some in the U.S. foreign policy establishment bristled, the roles of Ambassador Volker, Ambassador Sondland, and Secretary Perry and their interactions with Mayor Giuliani did not violate the law or harm national security.**

Evidence suggests that some in the U.S. foreign policy establishment disliked the involvement of Ambassador Volker, Ambassador Sondland, and Secretary Perry in the U.S.-Ukrainian relationship. Some also expressed discomfort with Mayor Giuliani's interactions with Ukrainian officials. However, the use of private citizens, such as Mayor Giuliani, to assist effectuating U.S. foreign policy goals on specific issues is not *per se* inappropriate and the Democrats' witnesses testified that the use of private citizens can sometimes beneficial. There is no evidence that the arrangement here violated any laws or harmed national security.

Some of the Democrats' witnesses criticized the non-traditional diplomacy. Ambassador Taylor testified about his concern for what he characterized as "two channels" of U.S. policy-making in Ukraine: a regular, State Department channel and an "irregular, informal" channel featuring Ambassador Volker, Ambassador Sondland, Secretary Perry, and Mayor Giuliani.[475] Deputy Assistant Secretary Kent testified that he was concerned that discussions were occurring outside the "formal policy process."[476]

Dr. Hill, too, disapproved of a non-traditional channel of communication, testifying that she disagreed with Ambassador Volker's decision to engage with Mayor Giuliani.[477] Dr. Hill

---

[470] Volker transcribed interview, *supra* note 60, at 19.
[471] *See* generally text messages exchanged between Kurt Volker and Gordon Sondland [KV00000036-39].
[472] Volker transcribed interview, *supra* note 60, at 59.
[473] *Impeachment Inquiry: Ambassador Gordon Sondland*, *supra* note 56.
[474] *Id.*
[475] Taylor deposition, *supra* note 47, at 23-24.
[476] Kent deposition, *supra* note 65, at 266-67.
[477] Hill deposition, *supra* note 12, at 113-14. Ambassador Sondland recounted that when he met with Dr. Hill prior to her departure from the White House in mid-July, she was "pretty upset about her role" in the Administration and

characterized Ambassador Sondland's conduct as a "domestic political errand."[478] However, by the time that Dr. Hill left the NSC on July 19, Ambassador Volker had only met with Mayor Giuliani once and Ambassador Sondland had never communicated with him.[479] Mayor Giuliani did not meet with the Ukrainian government until early August.[480]

Despite this criticism, Ambassador Volker said that Ambassador Taylor never raised concerns to him about an "irregular" foreign policy channel.[481] The Democrats' witnesses also explained that unorthodox foreign policy channels are not unusual and can actually be helpful to advance U.S. interests. Ambassador Taylor testified that non-traditional channels of diplomacy "can be helpful."[482] Ambassador Volker testified that he always operated with the best interests of the U.S. in mind and to advance "U.S. foreign policy goals with respect to Ukraine."[483]

The impeachment inquiry has uncovered no clear evidence that President Trump directed Ambassador Volker, Ambassador Sondland, and Secretary Perry to work with Mayor Giuliani for the purpose of pressuring Ukraine to investigate his political rival. In fact, the evidence suggests that the White House actively worked to stop potential impropriety. When Mayor Giuliani attempted to obtain a visa for former Ukrainian Prosecutor General Viktor Shokin to travel to the U.S. in January 2019, the White House shut down the effort.[484] The State Department had denied Shokin's visa and Mayor Giuliani apparently appealed to the White House.[485] According to Deputy Assistant Secretary Kent, in settling the matter, White House senior advisor Rob Blair said: "I heard what I need to know to protect the interest of the President."[486] Shokin did not receive a visa.

* * *

The evidence does not support the Democrats' allegation that President Trump set up a shadow foreign policy apparatus to pressure Ukraine to investigate the President's political rival for his political benefit in the 2020 election. The Constitution vests the President with broad authority over U.S. foreign relations. The U.S. officials accused of conducting "shadow" foreign policy—Ambassador Volker, Ambassador Sondland, and Secretary Perry—were all senior leaders with official interests in Ukraine who informed the State Department and NSC of their actions. Mayor Giuliani, whom President Trump referenced in the May 23 meeting with these three U.S. officials, also had experience in Ukraine.

---

so mad that Ambassador Sondland said he had "never seen anyone so upset." Sondland deposition, *supra* note 51, at 266-67, 307. In her public testimony, Dr. Hill explained that she was angry with Ambassador Sondland for not coordinating with her sufficiently. *Impeachment Inquiry: Dr. Fiona Hill and Mr. David Holmes, supra* note 210.
[478] *Impeachment Inquiry: Dr. Fiona Hill and Mr. David Holmes, supra* note 210.
[479] *Impeachment Inquiry: Ambassador Kurt Volker and Mr. Timothy Morrison, supra* note 8; *Impeachment Inquiry: Ambassador Gordon Sondland, supra* note 56.
[480] *Impeachment Inquiry: Ambassador Kurt Volker and Mr. Timothy Morrison, supra* note 8.
[481] *Impeachment Inquiry: Ambassador Kurt Volker and Mr. Timothy Morrison, supra* note 8.
[482] Taylor deposition, *supra* note 47, at 177.
[483] Volker transcribed interview, *supra* note 60, at 15, 69.
[484] Kent deposition, *supra* note 65, at 48-49.
[485] *Id.* at 48-49.
[486] *Id.* at 143.

The Ukrainian government asked Ambassador Volker to connect them with Mayor Giuliani to help change Mayor Giuliani's skeptical view of President Zelensky and "clear up" information flowing to the President. The Ukrainian government saw Mayor Giuliani as someone who had the President's ear but they did not see him as speaking on behalf of the President. While some in the U.S. foreign policy establishment disagreed with these actions, there is no indication it harmed national security or violated any laws. Notably, Ambassador Volker said he operated at all times with the U.S. national interest in mind. Ultimately, Ukraine took no actions to investigate President Trump's political rival.

E. President Trump is not wrong to raise questions about Hunter Biden's role with Burisma or Ukrainian government officials' efforts to influence the 2016 campaign.

Democrats allege that President Trump and Mayor Giuliani are spreading "conspiracy theories" by raising questions about Hunter Biden's role on the board of Burisma and certain Ukrainian government officials' efforts to influence the 2016 election.[487] The evidence available, however, shows that there are legitimate, unanswered questions about both issues. As Ukraine implements anti-corruption reforms, it is appropriate for the country to examine these allegations.

The Democrats' witnesses described how Burisma has long been a subject of controversy in Ukraine. The company's founder, Mykola Zlochevsky, was Ukraine's Minister of Ecology and Natural Resources from 2010 to 2012. In that role, he allegedly granted Burisma licenses for certain mineral deposits. Hunter Biden and other well-connected Democrats joined Burisma's board at a time when the company faced criticism. Hunter Biden's role on Burisma was concerning enough to the Obama State Department that it raised the issue with Vice President Biden's office and even prepared Ambassador Yovanovitch for a potential question on the topic at her confirmation hearing in 2016.

The extent of Ukraine's involvement in the 2016 election draws a much more visceral denial from Democrats, despite harsh rhetoric from prominent Democrats condemning foreign interference in U.S. election. It is undisputed that the then-Ukraine Ambassador to the U.S. authored an op-ed criticizing candidate Trump in U.S. media at the height of the presidential campaign. It is undisputed that senior Ukrainian officials made negative and critical comments about candidate Trump. In addition, a well-researched January 2017 article in *Politico* chronicles attempts by some Ukrainian government officials to harm candidate Trump. The article quotes a former DNC contractor and Ukrainian embassy staffer to show how the Ukrainian embassy worked with Democrat operatives and the media to hurt President Trump's candidacy.

1. It is appropriate for Ukraine to investigate allegations of corruption in its country.

As Ukraine adopts anti-corruption reforms, the United States has encouraged the country's leaders to investigate and prosecute corruption. Deputy Assistant Secretary of State for

---

[487] *See, e.g., Impeachment Inquiry: Ambassador Gordon Sondland, supra* note 56; *Impeachment Inquiry: Ambassador William B. Taylor and Mr. George Kent, supra* note 2;

European and Eurasian Affairs George Kent described Ukraine's corruption problem as "serious" and said corruption has long been "part of the high-level dialogue" between the United States and Ukraine.[488] Ambassador Marie Yovanovitch, the former U.S. Ambassador to Ukraine, testified that in Ukraine "corruption is not just prevalent, but frankly is the system."[489] Although Ukraine has established various anti-corruption prosecutors, courts, and investigative agencies to address the pervasive problem, corruption remains a problem.[490]

The Democrats' witnesses testified that it is appropriate for Ukraine to investigate allegations of corruption, including allegations about Burisma and 2016 election influence. Dr. Fiona Hill, Senior Director for Europe at the NSC, explained that it is "not actually . . . completely ridiculous" for President Zelensky's administration to investigate allegations of corruption arising from prior Ukrainian administrations.[491] Ambassador Volker testified that he "always thought [it] was fine" for Ukraine to investigate allegations about 2016 election influence.[492] Ambassador Yovanovitch testified:

> Q. Ambassador Volker mentioned the fact that to the extent there are corrupt Ukrainians and the United States is advocating for the Ukraine to investigate themselves, that certainly would be an appropriate initiative for U.S. officials to advocate for. Is that right?
>
> A. If that's what took place.[493]

With President Trump's deep-seated and genuine concern about corruption in Ukraine, it is not unreasonable that he would raise two examples of concern in a conversation with President Zelensky. Democrats are fundamentally wrong to argue that President Trump urged President Zelensky to "manufacture" or "dig up" "dirt" by raising these issues. As Ambassador Volker testified:

> Q. Would you say that President Trump in the phone call – and you've read the transcript and you're familiar with all the parties – was asking President Zelensky to manufacture dirt on the Bidens?
>
> A. No. And I've seen that phrase thrown around a lot. And I think there's a difference between the manufacture or dig up dirt versus finding out did anything happen in the 2016 campaign or did anything happen with Burisma. I think – or even if he's asking them to investigate the Bidens, it is to find out what facts there may be rather than to manufacture something.

[488] Kent deposition, *supra* note 65, at 105, 151.
[489] Yovanovitch deposition, *supra* note 115, at 18.
[490] *Id.* at 79-80.
[491] Hill deposition, *supra* note 12, at 394.
[492] Volker transcribed interview, *supra* note 60, at 146.
[493] Yovanovitch deposition, *supra* note 115, at 294.

Q. It is not an accurate statement of what the President was asking
Ukraine to sum it up as saying that President Trump was asking
Ukraine to manufacture dirt?

A. Yeah, I agree with that.[494]

2. There are legitimate concerns surrounding Hunter Biden's position on the board of Ukrainian energy company Burisma during his father's term as Vice President of the United States.

Burisma Holdings had a reputation in Ukraine as a corrupt company.[495] The company was founded by Mykola Zlochevsky, who served as Ukraine's Minister of Ecology and Natural Resources from 2010 to 2012.[496] During Zlochevsky's tenure in the Ukrainian government, Burisma received oil exploration licenses without public auctions.[497]

According to the *New York Times*, Hunter Biden and two other well-connected Democrats—Christopher Heinz, then-Secretary of State John Kerry's stepson, and Devon Archer—"were part of a broad effort by Burisma to bring in well-connected Democrats during a period when the company was facing investigations backed not just by domestic Ukrainian forces but by officials in the Obama administration."[498] Hunter Biden joined Burisma's board when his father, Vice President Joe Biden, acted as the Obama Administration's point person on Ukraine.[499]

The appearance of a conflict of interest raised concerns during the Obama Administration. In May 2014, the *Washington Post* reported "[t]he appointment of the vice president's son to a Ukrainian oil board looks nepotistic at best, nefarious at worst. No matter how qualified Biden is, it ties into the idea that U.S. foreign policy is self-interested, and that's a narrative Vladimir Putin has pushed during Ukraine's crisis."[500] The *Post* likened Hunter Biden's position with Burisma to "children of Russian politicians" who take "executive positions in companies at the top of the Forbes 500 list, and China's 'princelings' [who] have a similar habit."[501]

Deputy Assistant Secretary of State George Kent testified that while he served as acting Deputy Chief of Mission in Kyiv in early 2015, he raised concerns directly to Vice President Biden's office about Hunter Biden's service on Burisma's board.[502] Kent said that the "message"

---

[494] Volker transcribed interview, *supra* note 60, at 212-213.
[495] Kent deposition, *supra* note 65, at 83.
[496] Paul Sonne & Laura Mills, *Ukrainians see conflict in Biden's anticorruption message*, Wall St. J., Dec. 7, 2015.
[497] *Id.*
[498] Kenneth P. Vogel & Iuliia Mendel, *Biden faces conflicts of interest questions that are being promoted by Trump and allies*, N.Y. Times, May 1, 2019.
[499] Adam Taylor, *Hunter Biden's new job at a Ukrainian gas company is a problem for U.S. soft power*, Wash. Post, May 14, 2014.
[500] *Id.*
[501] *Id.*
[502] Kent deposition, *supra* note 65, at 226-27.

he received back was that because Vice President Biden's elder son, Beau, was dying of brain cancer at the time, there was no "bandwidth" to deal with any other family issues.[503]

In December 2015, the *Wall Street Journal* reported that Ukrainian anti-corruption activists complained that Vice President Biden's anti-corruption message "is being undermined as his son receives money" from Zlochevsky.[504] According to the *Journal*, "some anticorruption campaigners here [in Kyiv] worry the link with Mr. Biden may protect Mr. Zlochevsky from being prosecuted in Ukraine."[505]

Ambassador Yovanovitch testified that the Obama State Department actually prepared her to address Hunter Biden's role on Burisma if she received a question about it during her Senate confirmation hearing to be ambassador to Ukraine in June 2016. She explained:

> Q. And you may have mentioned this when we were speaking before lunch, but when did the issues related to Burisma first get to your attention? Was that as soon as you arrived in country?
>
> A. Not really. I first became aware of it when I was being prepared for my Senate confirmation hearing. So I'm sure you're familiar with the concept of questions and answer and various other things. And so there was one there about Burisma, and so, you know, that's when I first heard that word.
>
> Q. Were there any other companies that were mentioned in connection with Burisma?
>
> A. I don't recall.
>
> Q. And was it in the general sense of corruption, there was a company bereft with corruption?
>
> A. The way the question was phrased in this model Q&A was, what can you tell us about Hunter Biden's, you know, being named to the board of Burisma?
>
> ***
>
> Q. Did anyone at the State Department – when you were coming on board as the new ambassador, did anyone at the State Department brief you about this tricky issue, that Hunter Biden was on the board of this company and the company suffered from allegations of corruption, and provide you guidance?

---

[503] *Id.*
[504] Sonne & Mills, *supra*, note 496.
[505] *Id.*

A. Well, there was that Q&A that I mentioned.[506]

According to testimony, the Obama State Department actually took steps to prevent the U.S. government from associating with Burisma. In his closed-door deposition, Deputy Assistant Secretary Kent recounted a story about how he stopped a taxpayer-funded partnership with Burisma in mid-2016.[507] He said he learned that Burisma sought to cosponsor a U.S. Agency for International Development (USAID) program to encourage Ukrainian school children to develop ideas for clean energy.[508] Kent said he advised USAID not to work with Burisma due to its reputation for corruption.[509]

U.S. law enforcement in the past has examined employment arrangements in which a company hires a seemingly unqualified individual to influence government action. In 2016, the Obama Justice Department fined a Hong Kong subsidiary of a multinational bank for a scheme similar to Burisma's use of Hunter Biden and other well-connected Democrats.[510] There, the company hired otherwise unqualified candidates to "influence" officials toward favorable business outcomes.[511] At the time, then-Assistant Attorney General Leslie Caldwell explained that "[a]warding prestigious employment opportunities to unqualified individuals in order to influence government officials is corruption, plain and simple."[512]

During their public testimony, Democrat witnesses testified that Hunter Biden's role on Burisma's board of directors created the potential for the appearance of a conflict of interest. LTC Vindman testified that Hunter Biden did not appear qualified to serve on Burisma's board.[513] Deputy Assistant Secretary Kent explained that the issues surrounding Burisma were worthy of investigation by Ukrainian authorities.[514] Kent testified:

> Q. But given Hunter Biden's role on Burisma's board of directors, at some point, you testified in your deposition that you expressed some concern to the Vice President's office. Is that correct?
>
> A. That is correct.
>
> Q. And what did they do about that concern that you expressed?
>
> A. I have no idea. I reported my concern to the Office of the Vice President.

---

[506] Yovanovitch deposition, *supra* note 115, at 150-53.
[507] Kent deposition, *supra* note 65, at 88, 102-03.
[508] *Id.* at 103
[509] *Id.* at 102.
[510] Press Release, U.S. Dep't of Justice, JPMorgan's Investment Bank in Hong Kong Agrees to Pay $72 Million Penalty for Corrupt Hiring Scheme in China (Nov. 17, 2016), https://www.justice.gov/opa/pr/jpmorgan-s-investment-bank-hong-kong-agrees-pay-72-million-penalty-corrupt-hiring-scheme.
[511] *Id.*
[512] *Id.*
[513] *Impeachment Inquiry: LTC Alexander Vindman and Ms. Jennifer Williams, supra* note 6.
[514] *Impeachment Inquiry: Ambassador William B. Taylor and Mr. George Kent, supra* note 2.

Q. Okay. That was the end of it? Nobody –

A. Sir, you would have to ask people who worked in the Office of the Vice President during 2015.

Q. But after you expressed a concern of a perceived conflict of interest, at the least, the Vice President's engagement in the Ukraine didn't decrease, did it?

A. Correct, because the Vice President was promoting U.S. policy objectives in Ukraine.

Q. And Hunter Biden's role on the board of Burisma didn't cease, did it?

A. To the best of my knowledge, it didn't. And my concern was that there was the possibility of a perception of a conflict of interest.[515]

Similarly, in her public testimony, Ambassador Yovanovitch agreed that concerns about Hunter Biden's presence on Burisma's board were legitimate. In an exchange with Rep. Ratcliffe, she testified:

Q. You understood from Deputy Assistant Secretary George Kent's testimony, as it's been related to you that he testified a few days ago, do you understand that that arrangement, Hunter Biden's role on the Burisma board, caused him enough concern that, as he testified in his statement, that "in February of 2015, I raised my concern that Hunter Biden's status as a board member could create the perception of a conflict of interest." Then he went on to talk about the Vice President's responsibilities over the Ukraine – or over Ukraine – Ukrainian policy as one of those factors. Do you recall that?

A. Yes.

Q. Did you ever – do you agree with that?

A. Yes.

Q. That it was a legitimate concern to raise?

A. I think that it could raise the appearance of a conflict of interest.

***

---

[515] *Id.*

Q. But the legitimate concern about Hunter Biden's role was legitimate, correct?

A. I think it creates a concern that there could be an appearance of conflict of interest.[516]

During her public testimony, Dr. Hill testified:

Q. Dr. Hill, you told us during your deposition that, indeed, that there are perceived conflict of interest troubles when the child of a government official is involved with something that government official has an official policy role in, correct?

A. I think any family member of any member of the U.S. Government, Congress or the Senate, is open to all kinds of questions about optics and of perhaps undue outside influence, if they take part in any kind of activity that could be misconstrued as being related to their parent or the family member's work. So as a matter of course, yes, I do think that's the case.[517]

Despite this evidence, House Intelligence Committee Chairman Adam Schiff has prevented Republican Members from fully assessing the role of Hunter Biden on Burisma's board of directors. Chairman Schiff refused to invite Hunter Biden and Devon Archer to testify during public hearings.[518] Chairman Schiff declined to concur with a Republican subpoena for Hunter Biden to testify in a closed-door deposition.[519] Chairman Schiff declined to concur with a Republican subpoena for documents relating to Hunter Biden's role on Burisma.[520]

In addition to Burisma, there are questions about why the Ukrainian government fired then-Prosecutor General Shokin—according to Vice President Biden, at his insistence[521]—when it did not fire his successor, Prosecutor General Yuriy Lutsenko. Although Shokin and Lutsenko were both seen by State Department officials as corrupt and ineffective prosecutors, there was no effort to remove Lutsenko to the same degree or in the same way as there was with Shokin.[522] Ambassador Yovanovitch testified:

Q. And was he, in your experience – because you're very knowledgeable about the region, so when I ask you in your opinion, you have a very informed opinion – was Lutsenko better or worse than Shokin?

---

[516] *Impeachment Inquiry: Ambassador Marie Yovanovitch, supra* note 4.

[517] *Impeachment Inquiry: Dr. Fiona Hill and Mr. David Holmes, supra* note 210.

[518] *See, e.g.,* Allan Smith, *Democrats push back on GOP effort to have whistleblower, Hunter Biden testify*, NBC News, Nov. 10, 2019.

[519] *Impeachment Inquiry: Ms. Laura Cooper and Mr. David Hale, supra* note 246.

[520] *Id.*

[521] Council on Foreign Relations, Foreign Affairs Issue Launch with Former Vice President Joe Biden (Jan. 23, 2018).

[522] Kent deposition, *supra* note 65, at 90-98, 144-49.

A. I mean, honestly, I don't know. I mean, I think they're cut from the same cloth.

***

Q. There was never as much of a clamor to remove Lutsenko as there was Shokin. Is that fair to say?

A. Yeah, I think that's fair.

Q. And what do you account for that?

A. I would say that there was, I think, still a hope that one could work with Mr. Lutsenko. There was also that prospect of Presidential elections coming up, and as seemed likely by, you know, December, January, February, whatever the time was, that there would be a change of government. And I think we certainly hoped that Mr. Lutsenko would be replaced in the natural order of things, which is, in fact, what happened. We also had more leverage before. I mean, this was not easy. President Poroshenko and Mr. Shokin go way back. In fact, I think that they are godfathers to each other's children. So this was, you know, this was a big deal. But we had assistance, as did the IMF, that we could condition.[523]

Evidence suggests that Lutsenko's misconduct was not trivial. Deputy Assistant Secretary Kent explained that the U.S. government became disillusioned with Lutsenko in 2017 when he exposed an undercover investigator working to catch Ukrainian government officials selling fraudulent biometric passports.[524] Kent said that Lutsenko's actions could have resulted in terrorists obtaining fraudulent biometric passports.[525] Whereas Shokin only served for little over a year, Lutsenko served for years until President Zelensky removed him.[526] Although both prosecutors were regarded as ineffective and corrupt, the U.S. government only took an official position with respect to Shokin's removal and never as to Lutsenko's.[527]

3. There are legitimate questions about the extent to which Ukrainian government officials worked to oppose President Trump's candidacy in the 2016 election.

Democrats reflexively oppose any discussion about whether senior Ukrainian government officials worked to oppose President Trump's candidacy and support former Secretary Clinton during the 2016 election. Calling these allegations "debunked" and "conspiracy theories," Democrats ignore irrefutable evidence that is inconvenient for their

---

[523] Yovanovitch deposition, *supra* note 115, at 102-03.
[524] Kent deposition, *supra* note 65, at 145-47.
[525] *Id.* at 147-48.
[526] *Id.* at 95-103.
[527] *Id.* at 95.

political narrative. The facts, however, show outstanding questions about Ukrainian influence in the 2016 presidential election—questions that the Democrats' witnesses said would be appropriate for Ukraine to examine.

Prominent Democrats expressed concern about foreign interference in U.S. elections when they believed that the Russian government colluded with the Trump campaign in 2016. For example, in a 2017 hearing about Russian election interference, then-Ranking Member Schiff said that the "stakes are nothing less than the future of liberal democracy."[528] But where evidence suggests that Ukraine also sought to influence the election to the benefit of the Clinton campaign, now-Chairman Schiff and fellow Democrats have held their outrage.

Democrats have posited a false choice: that influence in the 2016 election is binary—it could have been conducted by Russia or by Ukraine, but not both. This is nonsense. Under then-Chairman Devin Nunes, Republicans on the House Intelligence Committee issued a report in March 2018 detailing Russia's active measures campaign against the United States.[529] But Russian interference in U.S. elections does not preclude Ukrainian officials from also attempting to influence the election. As Ambassador Volker testified during his public hearing, it is possible for more than one country to influence U.S. elections.[530]

Indisputable evidence shows that senior Ukrainian government officials sought to influence the 2016 election in favor of Secretary Clinton and against then-candidate Trump. In August 2016, then-Ukrainian Ambassador to the United States, Valeriy Chaly, wrote an op-ed in *The Hill* criticizing Trump's policies toward Ukraine.[531] The same month, the *Financial Times* reported that Trump's candidacy led "Kyiv's wider political leadership to do something they would never have attempted before: intervene, however indirectly, in a US election."[532] Ukrainian parliamentarian Serhiy Leshchenko explained that Ukraine was "on Hillary Clinton's side.[533] Other senior Ukrainian officials called candidate Trump a "clown," a "dangerous misfit," and "dangerous," and alleged that candidate Trump "challenged the very values of the free world."[534]

Other publicly available information reinforces the conclusion that senior Ukrainian government officials worked in 2016 to support Secretary Clinton. A January 2017 *Politico* article by current-*New York Times* reporter Ken Vogel detailed the Ukrainian effort to "sabotage" the Trump campaign.[535] Although Democrats reflexively dismiss the information presented in this article, neither *Politico* nor Vogel have retracted the story.

---

[528] *Open hearing on Russian Active Measures Campaign: Hearing before the H. Perm. Sel. Comm. on Intelligence*, 115th Cong. (2017)

[529] H. Perm. Sel. Comm. on Intelligence, Report on Russian Active Measures (Mar. 2018).

[530] *Impeachment Inquiry: Ambassador Kurt Volker and Mr. Timothy Morrison, supra* note 8

[531] *See* Chaly, *supra* note 27.

[532] Olearchyk, *supra* note 123.

[533] *Id.*

[534] *Id.*; Vogel & Stern, *supra* note 127.

[535] Vogel & Stern, *supra* note 127.

According to Vogel's reporting, the Ukrainian government worked with a Democrat operative and the media in 2016 to boost Secretary Clinton's candidacy and hurt President Trump's. Vogel wrote:

> Ukrainian government officials tried to help Hillary Clinton and undermine Trump by publicly questioning his fitness for office. They also disseminated documents implicating a top Trump aide in corruption and suggested they were investigating the matter, only to back away after the election. And they helped Clinton's allies research damaging information on Trump and his advisers, a *Politico* investigation found.[536]

Vogel reported how Alexandra Chalupa, a Ukrainian-American contractor paid by the DNC and working with the DNC and the Clinton campaign, "traded information and leads" about Paul Manafort, Trump's campaign manager, with staff at the Ukrainian embassy.[537] Chalupa also told Vogel that the Ukrainian embassy "worked directly with reporters researching Trump, Manafort, and Russia to point them in the right directions."[538] With the DNC's encouragement, Chalupa asked Ukrainian embassy staff "to try to arrange an interview in which [Ukrainian President] Poroshenko might discuss Manafort's ties to [Russia-aligned former Ukrainian President Viktor] Yanukovych."[539]

Vogel also spoke on the record to Andrii Telizhenko, a political officer in the Ukrainian Embassy under Ambassador Chaly, who corroborated Chalupa's account.[540] Telizhenko said that he was instructed by Ambassador Chaly's top aide, Oksana Shulyar, to "help Chalupa research connections between Trump, Manafort, and Russia" with the goal of generating a hearing in Congress.[541] Telizhenko also told Vogel that he was instructed not to speak to the Trump campaign:

> We had an order not to talk to the Trump team, because he was critical of Ukraine and the government and his critical position on Crimea and the conflict. I was yelled at when I proposed to talk to Trump. The ambassador said not to get involved – Hillary is going to win.[542]

---

[536] *Id.*

[537] *Id.* In April 2019, then-Ambassador Chaly issued a statement to *The Hill* denying that the Ukrainian embassy sought to influence the election. *See Official April 25, 2019 statement of the Ukrainian embassy in Washington to The Hill concerning the activities of Democratic National Committee Alexandra Chalupa during the 2016 U.S. election*, https://www.scribd.com/document/432699412/Ukraine-Chaly-Statement-on-Chalupa-042519.

[538] Vogel & Stern, *supra* note 127.

[539] *Id.* Interestingly, in August 2019, when Chairman Schiff tweeted an allegation that U.S. security assistance to Ukraine was tied up with Ukrainian investigations, Alexandra Chalupa replied that she had "a lot of information on this topic." *See* Adam Schiff (@RepAdamSchiff), Twitter (Aug. 28, 2019, 5:17 p.m.), https://twitter.com/RepAdamSchiff/status/1166867471862829056. It is unknown whether Chalupa ever provided information to Chairman Schiff or his staff.

[540] Vogel & Stern, *supra* note 127.

[541] *Id.*

[542] *Id.*

Vogel also reported on the actions of Ukrainian parliamentarian Leshchenko, who spoke out against Manafort, in part, to show that candidate Trump was a "pro-Russia candidate."[543] A separate congressional investigation in 2018 learned that Leshchenko was a source for Fusion GPS, the opposition research firm hired by the DNC's law firm, Perkins Coie, to gather information about candidate Trump.[544] Fusion GPS received information about Manafort that may have originated from Leshchenko.[545]

The Democrats' witnesses in the impeachment inquiry testified that the allegations of Ukrainian influence in the 2016 election were appropriate to examine.[546] Asked about the *Politico* reporting, Ambassador Taylor said that, if true, it is "disappointing" that some Ukrainian officials worked against President Trump. He testified:

> Q. So isn't it possible that Trump administration officials might have a good-founded belief, whether true or untrue, that there were forces in the Ukraine that were operating against them?
>
> A. [B]ased on this [January 2017] *Politico* article, which, again, surprises me, disappoints me because I think it's a mistake for any diplomat or any government official in one country to interfere in the political life of another country. That's disappointing.[547]

Ambassador Taylor testified that he was "surprise[ed] [and] disappoint[ed]" that Avakov, an influential member of the Ukrainian government—who still serves in President Zelensky's government—had criticized President Trump during the 2016 campaign.[548] He testified:

> Q. What do you know about Avakov?
>
> A. So he is the Minister of Internal Affairs and was the Minister of Internal Affairs under President Poroshenko as one of only two carryovers from the Poroshenko Cabinet to the Zelensky Cabinet. He, as I think I mentioned earlier when we were talking about Lutsenko, the Minister of Interior, which Avakov is now, controls the police, which gives him significant influence in the government.
>
> Q. Avakov, he's a relatively influential Minister. Is that right?
>
> A. That is correct.

---

[543] *Id.*; Olearchyk, *supra* note 123.
[544] Transcribed Interview of Nellie Ohr, in Wash., D.C., at 113-15 (Oct. 19, 2018).
[545] *Id.*
[546] *See, e.g.*, Volker transcribed interview, *supra* note 60, at 146.
[547] Taylor deposition, *supra* note 47, at 101.
[548] *Id.* at 98-99.

Q. Does it concern you that at one time he was being highly critical of candidate Trump?

A. It does.

Q. And did you ever have any awareness of that before I called your attention to this?

A. I haven't. This is surprising. Disappointing, but—[549]

Despite this testimony, Chairman Schiff has prevented Republican Members from fully assessing the nature and extent of Ukraine's influence in the 2016 election. Chairman Schiff refused to invite Alexandra Chalupa or Fusion GPS contractor Nellie Ohr to testify during public hearings.[550] Chairman Schiff declined to concur with a Republican subpoena for documents relating to the DNC's communications with the Ukrainian government.[551] Chairman Schiff declined to concur with a Republican subpoena for documents relating to the DNC's work with Alexandra Chalupa.[552]

* * *

There are legitimate concerns about Burisma's corruption and Hunter Biden's role on the company's board, and Ukrainian government officials' actions to support Secretary Clinton over President Trump in the 2016 election. Democrats reflexively dismiss these concerns because acknowledging them would require an admission that past U.S. assistance to Ukraine may have been misspent. As Ambassador Yovanovitch testified:

> I think most Americans believe that there shouldn't be meddling in our elections. And if Ukraine is the one that had been meddling in our elections, I think the support that all of you [in Congress] have provided to Ukraine over the last almost 30 years, I don't know that – I think people would ask themselves questions about that.[553]

Similarly, other career foreign service employees spoke about their emotional investment in U.S. foreign assistance to Ukraine. Speaking about his reaction to the recent events in Ukraine, Ambassador Taylor testified that he feels a strong "emotional attachment, bond, connection to this country and these people."[554] Deputy Assistant Secretary Kent, according to current State Department employee and former NSC staffer Catherine Croft, likewise "has a lot of emotion tied into" U.S. policy toward Ukraine, saying he "feels very strongly in all aspects of our policy

---

[549] *Id.*

[550] *See, e.g.*, Riley Beggin, *House Democrats deny Republicans' request for whistleblower testimony.* Vox, Nov. 10, 2019.

[551] *Impeachment Inquiry: Ms. Laura Cooper and Mr. David Hale, supra* note 246.

[552] *Id.*

[553] Yovanovitch deposition, *supra* note 115, at 137.

[554] Taylor deposition, *supra* note 47, at 273.

with regard to Ukraine."[555] President Trump's world view threatens these personal, subjective interests, which may explain why some are so eager to discount these allegations.

F. The anonymous whistleblower who served as the basis for the impeachment inquiry has no firsthand knowledge of events and a bias against President Trump.

Democrats built their impeachment inquiry on the foundation of the anonymous whistleblower complaint submitted to the Inspector General of the Intelligence Community on August 12. This foundation is fundamentally flawed.

The anonymous whistleblower acknowledged having no firsthand knowledge about the events he or she described. As a result, his or her complaint mischaracterized important facts and portrayed events in an inaccurate light. The anonymous whistleblower reportedly had a professional relationship with Vice President Joe Biden, which, if true, biases the whistleblower's impressions of the events as they relate to Vice President Biden. The anonymous whistleblower also reportedly communicated initially with House Intelligence Committee Chairman Adam Schiff, who has been an ardent and outspoken critic of President Trump, or his staff. Chairman Schiff's early secret awareness of the issue tainted the objectivity of the Democrats' impeachment inquiry.

To this day, only one Member of Congress—Chairman Schiff—knows the identity of the individual whose words sparked the impeachment of the President. Chairman Schiff has prevented any objective assessment of the whistleblower's credibility or knowledge. Chairman Schiff declined to invite the whistleblower to testify as part of the Democrats' impeachment inquiry, but only after Chairman Schiff's or his staff's communications with the whistleblower came to light.[556] Chairman Schiff rejected a Republican subpoena for documents relating to the drafting of the whistleblower complaint and the whistleblower's personal memorandum written shortly after the July 25 telephone conversation.[557]

The public reporting about the existence of a whistleblower and his or her sensational allegations about President Trump generated tremendous public interest. But Americans cannot assess the credibility, motivations, or biases of the whistleblower. This analysis is necessary because the whistleblower's inaccurate assertions, coupled with Chairman Schiff's selective leaks of cherry-picked information, have prejudiced the public narrative surrounding President Trump's telephone call with President Zelensky.

1. The anonymous whistleblower acknowledged having no firsthand knowledge of the events in question.

The anonymous whistleblower has no direct, firsthand knowledge of the events described in his or her complaint. In the complaint, the whistleblower acknowledged, "I was not a direct

---

[555] Croft deposition, *supra* note 60, at 105-06.
[556] *See, e.g.,* Beggin, *supra* note 550.
[557] *Impeachment Inquiry: Ms. Laura Cooper and Mr. David Hale, supra* note 246.

witness to most of the events described," and admitted that he or she was not on the July 25 call between President Trump and President Zelensky.[558] Instead, the anonymous whistleblower relied upon indirect, secondhand information provided by others—individuals who are also still unidentified. The whistleblower's lack of firsthand knowledge undermines the credibility of his or her accusations.

Testimony provided by officials with firsthand knowledge of the events rebuts the whistleblower's allegations. Ambassador Sondland testified that some of the concerns in the August 12 whistleblower complaint may be inaccurate or hyperbole.[559] For example, both Ambassador Volker and Ambassador Sondland testified that the whistleblower incorrectly alleged "that State Department officials, including Ambassadors Volker and Sondland, had spoken with Mr. Giuliani to 'contain the damage' to U.S. national security."[560] The ambassadors also disagreed with the whistleblower's statement that they helped Ukrainian leadership "'navigate' the demands" from President Trump.[561]

In addition, Ambassador Sondland took issue with the whistleblower's characterization of efforts to arrange a meeting between President Trump and President Zelensky. The whistleblower complaint stated:

> During this same timeframe, multiple U.S. officials told me [the anonymous whistleblower] that the Ukrainian leadership was led to believe that a meeting or phone call between the President and President Zelensky would depend on whether Zelensky showed willingness to "play ball" on the issues that had been publicly aired by Mr. Lutsenko and Mr. Giuliani.[562]

Ambassador Sondland testified that he never heard U.S. officials use the expression "play ball" in this context.[563]

2. Press reports suggest that the anonymous whistleblower acknowledged having a professional relationship with former Vice President Biden.

The anonymous whistleblower reportedly acknowledged having a professional relationship with Vice President Biden. This admission is important because Vice President Biden was referenced in passing on the July 25 call and is a potential opponent of President Trump in the 2020 presidential election. It stands to reason that a mention of Vice President Biden—no matter how brief or innocuous—could stir the passion of someone who had a professional relationship with him.

---

[558] Whistleblower letter, *supra* note 85, at 1; *see also* Letter from Hon. Michael Atkinson, Inspector Gen. of the Intelligence Cmty., to Hon. Joseph Maguire, Acting Dir. Of Nat'l Intelligence (Aug. 26, 2019).
[559] Sondland deposition, *supra* note 51, at 259-64, 311-14.
[560] Volker transcribed interview, *supra* note 60, at 100-01; Sondland deposition, *supra* note 51, at 261-62, 313.
[561] Volker transcribed interview, *supra* note 60, at 101; Sondland deposition, *supra* note 51, at 259-61, 311-12.
[562] Whistleblower letter, *supra* note 85, at 7.
[563] Sondland deposition, *supra* note 51, at 264.

On August 26, 2019, Inspector General Atkinson wrote to Acting Director of National Intelligence (DNI) Joseph Maguire stating that he found "some indicia of an arguable political bias on the part of the [anonymous whistleblower] in favor of a rival political candidate . . . ."[564] News reports later reported that the "rival political candidate" referenced in Atkinson's letter was a 2020 Democrat presidential candidate with whom that the whistleblower acknowledged having a "professional relationship."[565]

Subsequent news reports explained that the whistleblower is a CIA analyst who had been detailed to the NSC and would have worked closely with Vice President Biden's office.[566] This relationship is significant because President Obama relied upon Vice President Biden to be the Obama Administration's point person for Ukrainian policy.[567] This relationship suggests that aside from any partisan bias in support of Vice President Biden's 2020 presidential campaign, the whistleblower may also have had a bias in favor of Vice President Biden's Ukrainian policies instead of those of President Trump.

3. The anonymous whistleblower secretly communicated with Chairman Schiff or his staff.

According to an admission from Chairman Schiff, the anonymous whistleblower communicated with Chairman Schiff's staff prior to submitting his or her complaint. This early, secret involvement of Chairman Schiff severely prejudices the objectivity of the whistleblower's allegations, given Chairman Schiff's obsession with attacking President Trump for partisan gain.

Since 2016, Chairman Schiff has been a chief ringleader in Congress for asserting that President Trump colluded with Russia, going so far as to allege that he had secret evidence of collusion.[568] Now Chairman Schiff is the investigator-in-chief of President Trump's July 25 phone call with Ukrainian President Zelensky. Chairman Schiff led the investigation's first phase from behind the closed doors of his Capitol basement bunker, even though the depositions were all unclassified. Chairman Schiff did so purely for information control—allowing him to leak selected pieces of information to paint a misleading public narrative.

Chairman Schiff has publicly fabricated evidence about President Trump's July 25 phone call and misled the American public about his awareness of the whistleblower allegations. On September 26, at a public hearing of the House Intelligence Committee, Chairman Schiff opened the proceedings by fabricating the contents of President Trump's call with President Zelensky to

---

[564] Letter from Hon. Michael Atkinson, Inspector General of the Intelligence Community, to Hon. Joseph Maguire, Dir. Of Nat'l Intelligence, Office of the Dir. of Nat'l Intelligence (Aug. 26, 2019).
[565] Byron York, *Whistleblower Had 'Professional' Tie to 2020 Democratic Candidate,* Wash. Exam., Oct. 8, 2019.
[566] *See generally* Rob Crilly, Steven Nelson, & David Drucker, *Joe Biden Worked with Whistleblower When he was Vice President, Officials Reveal,* Wash. Exam., Oct. 10, 2019; Ben Feuerherd, *Whistleblower May Have Worked with Joe Biden in White House: Report,* N.Y. Post, Oct. 10, 2019; Julian Barnes, Michael Schmidt, Adam Goldman, & Katie Benner, *White House Knew of Whistleblower's Allegations Soon After Trump's Call with Ukraine Leader,* N.Y. Times, Sept. 26, 2019.
[567] Greg Myre, *What Were the Bidens Doing in Ukraine? 5 Questions Answered,* Nat'l Pub. Radio, Sept. 24, 2019.
[568] *See, e.g.,* Kelsey Tamborrino, *Warner: 'Enormous amounts of evidence' of possible Russia collusion,* Politico, Mar. 3, 2019.

make the conversation seem sinister.[569] Pretending to be President Trump, Chairman Schiff said in part:

> I hear what you want. I have a favor I want from you though. And I'm going to say this only seven times so you better listen good. I want you to make up dirt on my political opponent, understand. Lots of it.[570]

These words were never uttered by President Trump. When Chairman Schiff rightly faced criticism for his actions, he blamed others for not understanding that he was joking.[571] Republicans sought to hold Chairman Schiff accountable for his fabrication of evidence; however, Democrats prevented the House from voting on a censure resolution.[572]

In October 2019, the *New York Times* reported that the whistleblower contacted a staff member on the House Intelligence Committee—chaired by Chairman Schiff—after asking a colleague to convey his or her concerns about the July 25 call to the CIA's top lawyer.[573] Chairman Schiff, however, had denied ever communicating directly with the whistleblower,[574] and the whistleblower failed to disclose that he or she had contacted Chairman Schiff's staff when asked by the Intelligence Community Inspector General.[575] Chairman Schiff acknowledged his early awareness of the whistleblower's allegations only after he was caught.[576] The *Washington Post* gave Chairman Schiff "Four Pinocchios"—its worst rating—for "clearly ma[king] a statement that was false."[577]

Chairman Schiff's early awareness of the whistleblower complaint explains why he publicly posited a connection between paused U.S. security assistance and Ukrainian investigations well before the whistleblower complaint became public. On August 28, 2019, before the public became aware of the whistleblower complaint or any allegations that U.S. security assistance to Ukraine was linked to Ukraine investigating President Trump's political rival, Chairman Schiff made such a connection in a tweet.[578] According to the *New York Times*, Chairman Schiff knew "the outlines" of the anonymous whistleblower complaint at the time that he issued this tweet.[579]

---

[569] *Whistleblower disclosure, supra* note 1.

[570] *Id.*

[571] *Id.*

[572] Katherine Tully-McManus, *Republican effort to censure Adam Schiff halted*, Roll Call, Oct. 21, 2019.

[573] Julian Barnes, Michael Schmidt, & Matthew Rosenberg, *Schiff Got Early Account of Accusations as Whistleblower's Concerns Grew*, N.Y. Times, Oct. 2, 2019.

[574] *See, e.g.*, Glenn Kessler, *Schiff's false claim his committee had not spoken to the whistleblower*, Wash. Post, Oct. 4, 2019.

[575] Andrew O'Reilly, *Schiff Admits He Should Have Been 'Much More Clear' About Contact with Whistleblower*, Fox News, Oct. 13, 2019.

[576] *Schiff Got Early Account of Accusations as Whistleblower's Concerns Grew, supra* note 573.

[577] *Schiff's false claim his committee had not spoken to the whistleblower, supra* note 574.

[578] Adam Schiff (@RepAdamSchiff), Twitter, (Aug. 28, 2019, 8:17 PM), https://twitter.com/RepAdamSchiff/status/1166867471862829056.

[579] Barnes, Schmidt, & Rosenberg, *supra* note 573.

Figure 3: Chairman Schiff's August 28 tweet linking aid to investigations

Chairman Schiff's early awareness also explains why he pressured Inspector General Atkinson to produce the whistleblower's complaint to Congress, despite Acting DNI Maguire's determination that transmittal was not required because the complaint did not meet the legal definition of "urgent concern."[580]

* * *

The allegations of the anonymous whistleblower—the foundation for the Democrats' impeachment inquiry—are fundamentally flawed. The whistleblower acknowledged having no direct, firsthand knowledge of the events he or she described. The whistleblower reportedly acknowledged a professional relationship with Vice President Joe Biden, which, if true, suggests a bias toward Vice President Biden and against President Trump. Finally, the whistleblower secretly communicated with staff of Chairman Schiff, who subsequently misled the public about this communication.

If Democrats are serious about impeaching the President—about undoing the will of the American people—they cannot limit the evidence and information available to the House of Representatives. The motivations, biases, and credibility of the anonymous whistleblower are necessary aspects of any serious examination of the facts in question.

---

[580] U.S. Dep't of Justice, Office of Legal Counsel, "Urgent Concern" Determination by the Inspector General of the Intelligence Community 2 (2019).

II.   The evidence does not establish that President Trump engaged in a cover-up of his interactions with Ukrainian President Zelensky.

Democrats also argue that President Trump is engaged in a cover-up of his July 25 telephone conversation by hiding evidence of his alleged wrongdoing.[581] There is no basis for this allegation. The President has been transparent about the issues surrounding the anonymous whistleblower complaint and the telephone call with President Zelensky.

On September 24, Speaker Pelosi launched the impeachment inquiry based solely on reports of the telephone call between President Trump and President Zelensky. She had not listened to the conversation; she had not read the call summary or the whistleblower complaint. The following day, to offer unprecedented transparency and prove there was no *quid pro quo*, President Trump declassified the July 25 call summary for the American people to read for themselves. President Trump also released a redacted version of the anonymous whistleblower complaint and he released the summary of his April 21 telephone conversation with President Zelensky. Even the Democrats' best evidence of a "cover-up"—the restricted access to the call summary—is unpersuasive. Evidence suggests that the call summary was restricted not for a malicious intention but as a result of the proliferation of leaks by unelected bureaucrats, including leaks of President Trump's conversations with foreign leaders.

A. President Trump declassified and released publicly the summary of his July 25 phone call with President Zelensky.

On July 25, President Trump and President Zelensky spoke by telephone.[582] Normally, presidential conversations with foreign leaders are presumptively classified because "[t]he unauthorized disclosure of foreign government information is presumed to cause damage to the national security."[583] In fact, the call summary of President Trump's call with President Zelensky was initially marked as classified.[584]

On September 25, after questions arose about the contents of the phone call, President Trump chose to declassify and release the transcript in the interest of full transparency. He wrote on Twitter: "I am currently at the United Nations representing our Country, but have authorized the release tomorrow of the complete, fully declassified and unredacted transcript of my phone conversation with President Zelensky of Ukraine."[585] The President stressed his goal that Americans could read for themselves the contents of the call: "You will see it was a very friendly and totally appropriate call. No pressure unlike Joe Biden and his son, NO quid pro quo! This is

---

[581] *See, e.g.*, Speaker Nancy Pelosi, Transcript of Pelosi Weekly Press Conference (Sept. 26, 2019) ("The [whistleblower] complaint reports 'repeated abuse of an electronics record system designed to store classified, sensitive national security information, which the White House used to hide information of a political nature.' This is a cover-up. This is a cover-up.").

[582] Memorandum of Telephone Conversation, *supra* note 15.

[583] Exec. Order 13,526 (2009).

[584] *See* Memorandum of Telephone Conversation, *supra* note 15.

[585] Donald J. Trump (@realDonaldTrump), Twitter (Sept. 24, 2019, 11:12 a.m.), https://twitter.com/realdonaldtrump/status/1176559966024556544.

nothing more than a continuation of the Greatest and most Destructive Witch Hunt of all time."[586]

B. President Trump released a redacted version of the classified anonymous whistleblower complaint.

Like the call summary, the anonymous whistleblower complaint was initially classified. The complaint was reportedly "hand delivered . . . to Capitol Hill" hours after President Trump released the call summary.[587] Although a limited number of Members of Congress—like Chairman Schiff—could access the classified complaint, the American public could not. The President released a redacted version of the anonymous whistleblower complaint so that every American could read it for themselves.[588]

C. President Trump released publicly the summary of his April 21 phone call with President Zelensky.

President Trump first spoke by telephone with President Zelensky on April 21, 2019, the date on which President Zelensky won the Ukrainian presidential election.[589] On November 15, the President publicly released the summary of this April conversation.[590] President Trump explained that he chose to release the summary of this call to "continue being the most transparent President in history."[591]

D. The Trump Administration has experienced a surge in sensitive leaks, including details of the President's communications with foreign leaders.

The Trump Administration has experienced an unprecedented number of potentially damaging leaks from the U.S. national security apparatus.[592] According to a report from the Senate Homeland Security and Governmental Affairs Committee in May 2017, these leaks have flowed seven times faster under President Trump than during former Presidents Obama and Bush's administrations—averaging almost one per day.[593] The report explained:

---

[586] Donald J. Trump (@realDonaldTrump), Twitter (Sept. 24, 2019, 11:12 a m.),
https://twitter.com/realdonaldtrump/status/1176559970390806530.

[587] Dana Bash, et al, *Whistleblower complaint about Trump declassified and may be released Thursday*, CNN, Sept. 26, 2019.

[588] *Whistleblower complaint says White House tried to "lock down" Ukraine call records*, CBS News, Sept. 26, 2019.

[589] *Memorandum of Telephone Conversation*, *supra* note 10.

[590] Mark Mazzetti & Eileen Sullivan, *Rough transcript of Trump's first phone call with Ukrainian leader released*, N.Y. Times, Nov. 15, 2019.

[591] Donald J. Trump (@realDonaldTrump), Twitter (Nov. 11, 2019, 3:35 p.m.),
https://twitter.com/realDonaldTrump/status/1194035922066714625.

[592] HSGAC report, *supra* note 409.

[593] *Id.*

From the morning of President Trump's inauguration, when major newspapers published information about highly sensitive intelligence intercepts, news organizations have reported on an avalanche of leaks from officials across the U.S. government. Many disclosures have concerned the investigations of alleged Russian interference in the 2016 election, with the world learning details of whose communications U.S. intelligence agencies are monitoring, what channels are being monitored, and the results of those intercepts. All such revelations are potential violations of federal law, punishable by jail time.

But the leak frenzy has gone far beyond the Kremlin and has extended to other sensitive information that could harm national security. President Trump's private conversations with other foreign leaders have shown up in the press, while secret operations targeting America's most deadly adversaries were exposed in detail.

As *The New York Times* wrote in a candid self-assessment: "Journalism in the Trump era has featured a staggering number of leaks from sources across the federal government." No less an authority than President Obama's CIA director called the deluge of state secrets "appalling." These leaks do not occur in a vacuum. They can, and do, have real world consequences for national security.[594]

As the *Washington Post* explained, "Every presidential administration leaks. So far, the Trump White House has gushed."[595] Sensitive national security information—for which public disclosure could harm U.S. interests—found its way into mainstream news outlets such as the *New York Times*, the *Washington Post*, NBC, and *Associated Press*.[596] This unfortunate reality helps to explain the circumstances by which the NSC handled the summary of President Trump's July 25 telephone conversation with President Zelensky.

E. The evidence does not establish that access to the July 25 call summary was restricted for inappropriate reasons.

The anonymous whistleblower complaint alleged that NSC staffers deliberately placed the call summary of the July 25 call on a highly secure server to hide its contents.[597] This allegation has not been proven. In fact, the Democrats' witnesses testified that it was mistakenly place on a highly classified server. Evidence suggests that call summaries of the President's conversations with other foreign leaders have been subject to restricted access due to a pattern of leaks.

---

[594] *Id.*
[595] Paul Farhi, *The Trump administration has sprung a leak. Many of them, in fact*, Wash. Post, Feb. 5, 2017.
[596] HSGAC report, *supra* note 409.
[597] Whistleblower letter, *supra* note 85.

As the Trump Administration dealt with an unprecedented number of national security leaks, it sought to take appropriate precautions. Public reporting indicates that the NSC began restricting access to summaries of the President's communications with foreign leaders following the leak of President Trump's conversation in May 2017 with senior Russian officials.[598] Dr. Fiona Hill, the former NSC Senior Director for Europe, testified that a summary of this meeting was not initially restricted and that details of the conversation "seemed to immediately end up in the press."[599] Following this leak, the White House began a practice of restricting access to summaries of calls and meetings with foreign leaders.[600] Current and former White House officials said that it made sense to restrict access to calls given the number of leaks.[601]

With respect to the summary of President Trump's conversation with President Zelensky on July 25, NSC Senior Director Tim Morrison testified in his closed-door deposition that although he "was not concerned that anything illegal was discussed," he was concerned about a leak of the summary of President Trump's call with President Zelensky.[602] He explained that he was "concerned about how the contents [of the call summary] would be used in Washington's political process."[603] In his public testimony, Morrison elaborated:

> Q. And you were concerned about it leaking because you were worried about how it would play out in Washington's polarized political environment, correct?
>
> A. Yes.
>
> Q. And you were also worried how that would lead to the bipartisan support here in Congress towards Ukraine, right?
>
> A. Yes.
>
> Q. And you were also concerned that it might affect the Ukrainians' perception negatively.
>
> A. Yes.
>
> Q. And, in fact, all three of those things have played out, haven't they?
>
> A. Yes.[604]

---

[598] *See, e.g.,* Julian E. Barnes et al., *White House Classified Computer System is Used to Hold Transcripts of Sensitive Calls*, N.Y. Times, Sept. 29, 2019.
[599] Hill deposition, *supra* note 12, at 294.
[600] Barnes, et al., *supra* note 598.
[601] *Id.*
[602] Morrison deposition, *supra* note 12, at 16.
[603] *Id.* at 44.
[604] *Impeachment Inquiry: Ambassador Kurt Volker and Timothy Morrison, supra* note 8.

LTC Vindman—the NSC staffer who raised concerns about the contents of call—testified there was no "malicious intent" in restricting access to the summary.[605] Morrison also testified that call summary was mistakenly placed on a secure server with restricted access.[606] He explained:

> Q. And were you ever provided with an explanation for why [the call summary] was placed in the highly classified system?
>
> A. Yes.
>
> Q. What was the explanation you were given?
>
> A. It was a mistake.
>
> Q. It was a mistake?
>
> A. Yes.[607]

In his public testimony, Morrison reiterated that the placement of the call summary on a secure server was an administrative error.[608] He explained that NSC Legal Advisor John Eisenberg sought to restrict access to the summary, but that his direction was mistakenly interpreted to mean placing the summary on a secure server.[609] He testified:

> I spoke with the NSC Executive Secretariat staff, asked them why [the summary had been removed from the normal server]. And they did their research, and they informed me it had been moved to the higher classification system at the direction of John Eisenberg, whom I then asked why. I mean, that's – if that was the judgment he made, that's not necessarily mine to question, but I didn't understand it. And he essentially told me, "I gave no such direction." He did his own inquiry, and he represented back to me that it was – his understanding was that it was a kind of administrative error, that when he also gave direction to restrict access, the Executive Secretariat staff understood that as an apprehension that there was something in the content of the [call summary] that could not exist on the lower classification system.[610]

Morrison also explained that there was no malicious intent in moving the transcript to the secure server.[611]

---

[605] Vindman deposition, *supra* note 12, at 124.
[606] Morrison deposition, *supra* note 12, at 54-57.
[607] *Id.* at 54.
[608] *Impeachment Inquiry: Ambassador Kurt Volker and Timothy Morrison*, *supra* note 8.
[609] *Id.*
[610] *Id.*
[611] *Id.*

To the extent Democrats allege that President Trump sought to cover up his July 25 telephone conversation with President Zelensky, the facts do not support such a charge. Indeed, President Trump has declassified and publicly released the July 25 call summary. He has also released a redacted version of the classified anonymous whistleblower complaint and released the call summary of his first phone call with President Zelensky, on April 21. Although the July 25 call summary was located on a secure White House server prior to its public release, testimony shows that its placement on the server was an "administrative error." In light of substantial leaks of sensitive national security information—including the President's conversations with foreign leaders—testimony shows that the NSC Legal Advisor sought to restrict access to the summary. In attempting to carry out this direction, the NSC executive secretariat staff incorrectly placed the summary on a secure server. Taken, together, these facts do not establish that President Trump sought to cover up his interactions with President Zelensky.

III.   The evidence does not establish that President Trump obstructed Congress in the Democrats' impeachment inquiry.

Democrats allege that President Trump has obstructed Congress by declining to participate in Speaker Pelosi's impeachment inquiry.[612] Under any fair assessment of the facts, however, President Trump has not obstructed Congress. In fact, the President personally urged at least one witness to cooperate with the Democrats' impeachment inquiry and to testify truthfully.[613] But Democrats cannot and should not impeach President Trump for declining to submit himself to an abusive and unfair process.

In the Democrats' impeachment inquiry, fairness is not an asset guaranteed or even recognized. Democrats have told witnesses in the inquiry that a failure to adhere strictly to their demands "shall constitute evidence of obstruction of the House's impeachment inquiry and may be used as an adverse inference against the President."[614] Democrats have threatened to withhold the salaries for agency employees as punishment for not meeting Democrat demands.[615] As Chairman Schiff explained the Democrat logic, any disagreement with Democrats amounts to obstruction: "The failure to produce this witness, the failure to produce these documents, we consider yet additionally strong evidence of obstruction of the constitutional functions of Congress, a coequal branch of government."[616]

The Democrats' actions are fundamentally abusive. In any just proceeding, the President ought to be afforded an opportunity to raise defenses without Democrats considering it to be *de facto* evidence of obstruction. In any just proceeding, investigators would not impute the conduct of a witness to the President or use a witness's refusal to cooperate with an unfair process as an "adverse inference" against the President.

The Democrats' obstruction arguments are also divorced from historical precedent for House impeachment proceedings and basic legal concepts of due process and the presumption of innocence. Past bipartisan precedent for presidential impeachment inquiries guaranteed fundamental fairness by authorizing bipartisan subpoena authority; providing the President unrestricted access to information presented; and allowing the President's counsel to identify relevant witnesses and evidence, cross examine witnesses, and respond to evidence collected. These guarantees of due process and fundamental fairness are not present in the Democrats' impeachment resolution against President Trump.

Congressional oversight of the Executive Branch is an important and serious undertaking designed to improve the efficiency and accountability of the federal government. The White House has said that it is willing to work with Democrats on legitimate congressional oversight

[612] *See, e.g.*, Amber Phillips, *How the House Could Impeach Trump for Obstructing its Probe*, Wash. Post, Oct. 8, 2019.
[613] Sondland deposition, *supra* note 51, at 38.
[614] *See, e.g.*, letter from Eliot L. Engel, Chairman, H. Comm. on Foreign Affairs, et al. to John Eisenberg, Nat'l Sec. Council (Oct. 30, 2019).
[615] *See* letter from Eliot L. Engel, Chairman, H. Comm. on Foreign Affairs, et al. to John J. Sullivan, Dep. Sec'y, Dep't of State (Oct. 1, 2019).
[616] Phillips, *supra* note 612.

requests.[617] However, public statements from prominent Democrats suggest they are pursuing impeachment purely for partisan reasons—that they seeking to prevent President Trump's reelection in 2020.[618] The Democrats' unfair and abusive impeachment process confirms that they are not interested in pursuing a full understanding of the facts.

Even despite the Democrats' partisan rhetoric and unfair process, President Trump has been transparent about his interactions with Ukrainian President Zelensky. President Trump has released to the public documents directly relevant the subject matter and he has spoken publicly about the issues. Democrats cannot justly condemn President Trump for declining to submit to their abusive and fundamentally unfair process.

A. Democrats have abandoned long-standing precedent by failing to guarantee due process and fundamental fairness in their impeachment inquiry.

The two recent impeachment investigations into presidents by the House of Representatives were largely identical to each other despite the passage of two decades. In 1974, the House authorized an impeachment inquiry into President Nixon by debating and passing House Resolution 803.[619] This resolution authorized the Committee on the Judiciary to issue subpoenas, including those offered by the minority; to sit and act without regard to whether the House stood in recess; and to expend funds in the pursuit of the investigation.[620] In 1998, the House passed House Resolution 581, a nearly identical resolution authorizing an impeachment inquiry into President Clinton.[621]

In 1974, the House undertook this action because "the rule of the House defining the jurisdiction of committees does not place jurisdiction over impeachment matters in the Judiciary Committee. In fact, it does not place such jurisdiction anywhere."[622] Passing a resolution authorizing the inquiry was "a necessary step if we are to meet our obligations [under the Constitution]."[623] By passing the resolution, the House sought to make "[t]he committee's investigative authority . . . fully coextensive with the power of the House in an impeachment investigation . . . ."[624]

Notably, in empowering the Judiciary Committee to conduct the Nixon impeachment inquiry, the House granted subpoena power to the minority, an action that was "against all precedents" at the time.[625] During debate, Members made it "crystal clear that the authority given to the minority [ranking] member and to the chairman, the right to exercise authority [to issue a

---

[617] *See* letter from Pat A. Cipollone, Counsel to the President to Speaker Nancy Pelosi et al. 8 (Oct. 8, 2019).
[618] *See, e.g., Weekends with Alex Witt* (MSNBC television broadcast May 5 2019) (interview with Rep. Al Green).
[619] H. Res. 803, 93rd Cong. (1974).
[620] *See Id.*
[621] H. Res. 581, 105th Cong. (1998).
[622] 130 Cong. Rec. 2351 (Feb. 6, 1974) (statement of Rep. Hutchinson).
[623] *Id.* at 2350 (statement of Rep. Rodino).
[624] H.R. Rep. No. 93-774, at 3 (1974).
[625] 130 Cong. Rec. at 2352 (statement of Rep. Brooks).

subpoena], is essentially the same. It is the same. Both are subject to a veto by a majority of the membership of that committee."[626]

In 1998, the House similarly passed a resolution authorizing an impeachment inquiry because the "[Judiciary] Committee decided that it must receive authorization from the full House before proceeding . . . ."[627] The Judiciary Committee reached this conclusion "[b]ecause impeachment is delegated solely to the House of Representatives by the Constitution, [and therefore] the full House of Representatives should be involved in critical decision making regarding various stages of impeachment."[628]

In putting forth this resolution for consideration by the House, the Judiciary Committee made several commitments with respect to ensuring "procedural fairness" of the impeachment inquiry. For instance, the Judiciary Committee voted to allow the President or his counsel to be present at all executive sessions and open hearings and to allow the President's counsel to cross examine witnesses, make objections regarding relevancy, suggest additional evidence or witnesses that the committee should receive, and to respond to the evidence collected.[629]

The fundamental fairness and due process protections guaranteed in the Nixon and Clinton impeachment proceedings are missing from Speaker Pelosi's impeachment inquiry. The Democrats' impeachment inquiry offers a veneer of legitimacy that hides a deeply partisan and one-sided process. The impeachment resolution passed by Democrats in the House—against bipartisan opposition—allows Democrats to maintain complete control of the proceedings.[630] The resolution denies Republicans co-equal subpoena authority and requires the Democrat chairmen to concur with Republican subpoenas—unlike Democrat subpoenas, which the chairmen may issue with no Republican input.[631] The Democrat impeachment resolution requires Republicans to specifically identify and explain the need for witnesses 72 hours before the first impeachment hearing—without a similar requirement for Democrats.[632] Most importantly, the Democrats' resolution excludes the President's counsel from House Intelligence Committee Chairman Adam Schiff's proceedings and provides House Judiciary Committee Chairman Jerry Nadler with discretion to do the same.[633] In short, these partisan procedures dramatically contradict the bipartisan Nixon and Clinton precedents.

B. Democrats have engaged in an abusive process toward a pre-determined outcome.

Since the beginning of the 116 Congress, Democrats have sought to impeach President Trump. Just hours after her swearing in, Rep. Rashida Tlaib told a crowd at a public event that

---

[626] *Id.*
[627] H.R. Rep. No. 105-795, at 24 (1998).
[628] *Id.*
[629] *Id.* at 25-26.
[630] H. Res. 660, 116th Cong. (2019).
[631] *Id.*
[632] *Id.*
[633] *Id.*

"[Democrats are] going to go in there, and we're going to impeach the [expletive deleted]."[634] Rep. Brad Sherman introduced articles of impeachment against President Trump on the very first day of the Democrat majority.[635] Rep. Al Green separately introduced articles of impeachment in July 2019, and even forced the House to consider the measure.[636] The House tabled Rep. Green's impeachment resolution by an overwhelming bipartisan majority—332 ayes to 95 nays.[637]

Such a fervor to impeach a political opponent for purely partisan reasons was what Alexander Hamilton warned of as the "greatest danger" in Federalist No. 65: that "the decision [to impeach] will be regulated more by the comparative strength of parties, than by the real demonstrations of innocence or guilt."[638] Indicative of this partisan fervor, Democrats have already forced the House to consider three resolutions of impeachment—offered by Democrats after no investigation, report, or process of any kind—since President Trump took office.[639]

During the consideration of articles of impeachment against President Clinton, Democrats argued that "[i]f we are to impeach the President, it should be at the end of a fair process. . . . [and not through decisions] made on a strictly partisan basis."[640] Rep. Zoe Lofgren, now a senior member of the Judiciary Committee, testified then before the Rules Committee on the resolution authorizing the Clinton impeachment inquiry. She said:

> Under our Constitution, the House of Representatives has the sole power of impeachment. This is perhaps our single most serious responsibility short of a declaration of war. Given the gravity and magnitude of this undertaking, only a fair and bipartisan approach to this question will ensure that truth is discovered, honest judgments rendered, and the constitutional requirement observed. Our best yardstick is our historical experience. We must compare the procedures used today with what Congress did a generation ago when a Republican President was investigated by a Democratic House.[641]

However, Speaker Pelosi's impeachment inquiry has been divorced from historical experience and has borne no markings of a fair process. During the first several weeks, the Speaker asserted that a vote authorizing the inquiry was unnecessary.[642] This process allowed Chairman Schiff to conduct his partisan inquiry behind closed doors with only a limited group of Members present. It also allowed Chairman Schiff to selectively leak cherry-picked information

---

[634] Nicholas Fandos, *Rashida Tlaib's Expletive-Laden Cry to Impeach Trump Upends Democrats' Talking Points*, N.Y. Times, Jan. 4, 2019.

[635] H. Res. 13, 116th Cong. (2019).

[636] H. Res. 498, 116th Cong. (2019).

[637] *Id.* (Roll call vote 483).

[638] Federalist No. 65 (Alexander Hamilton).

[639] *See* H. Res. 646, 115th Cong. (2018); H. Res. 705, 115th Cong. (2018); H. Res. 498, 116th Cong. (2019).

[640] Impeachment Inquiry: William Jefferson Clinton, President of the United States, 105th Cong., Consideration of Articles of Impeachment 82 (Comm. Print 1998) (statement of Rep. Bobby Scott).

[641] *Hearing before the Committee on Rules on H. Res. 525*, 105th Cong., 2d Sess. 108 (1998).

[642] *See, e.g.*, Haley Byrd, *Kevin McCarthy Calls on Nancy Pelosi to Suspend Impeachment Inquiry*, CNN, Oct. 3, 2019.

to paint a misleading public narrative. Chairman Schiff failed to respond to Republican requests for witnesses,[643] and directed witnesses not to answer questions from Republicans.[644] Chairman Schiff even declined to share closed-door deposition transcripts with Republican Members.[645]

During the public hearings, despite the modicum of minority rights outlined in the Democrats' impeachment resolution, Chairman Schiff has continued to trample long-held minority rights. Chairman Schiff interrupted Republican Members during questioning and directed witnesses not to answer Republican questions.[646] Chairman Schiff declined to invite all the witnesses identified by Republicans as relevant to the inquiry.[647] Chairman Schiff declined to honor Republican subpoenas for documents and witnesses, and then violated House rules and the Democrats' impeachment resolution to vote down the subpoenas without sufficient notice or even any debate.[648]

This is the very sort of process that Democrats had previously decried as "what happens when a legislative chamber is obsessively preoccupied with investigating the opposition rather than legislating for the people who elected them to office."[649] Rep. Jerrold Nadler, now chairman of the Judiciary Committee, once argued that:

> The effect of impeachment is to overturn the popular will of voters as expressed in a national election. . . . ***There must never be a narrowly voted impeachment or an impeachment substantially supported by one of our major political parties and largely opposed by the other***. Such an impeachment would lack legitimacy and produce the divisiveness and bitterness in our politics for years to come and will call into question the very legitimacy of our political institutions.[650]

During the impeachment proceedings for President Clinton, Democrats warned against "dump[ing] mountains of salacious, uncross-examined and otherwise untested materials onto the Internet, and then . . . sorting through boxes of documents to selectively find support for a foregone conclusion."[651] But now, in Speaker Pelosi's impeachment inquiry, as conducted by Chairman Schiff, the Democrats' old warnings have become the very process by which their current impeachment inquiry has proceeded.

---

[643] Letter from Jim Jordan, Ranking Member, H. Comm. on Oversight & Reform, et al., to Adam Schiff, Chairman, H. Perm. Sel. Comm. on Intelligence (Oct. 23, 2019).
[644] *See, e.g.*, Vindman deposition, *supra* note 12, at 78-80, 103-05.
[645] *See, e.g.*, Deirdre Shesgreen & Bart Jansen, *House Republicans complain about limited access to closed-door House impeachment investigation sessions*, USA Today, Oct. 16, 2019.
[646] *See, e.g., Impeachment Inquiry: Ambassador William B. Taylor and Mr. George Kent, supra* note 2; *Impeachment Inquiry: Ambassador Marie Yovanovitch, supra* note 4.
[647] *See, e.g.*, Beggin, *supra* note 550.
[648] *Impeachment Inquiry: Ms. Laura Cooper and Mr. David Hale, supra* note 246.
[649] Impeachment Inquiry: William Jefferson Clinton, President of the United States, *supra* note 640, at 94 (statement of Rep. Zoe Lofgren).
[650] *Id.* at 77 (statement of Rep. Jerrold Nadler) (emphasis added).
[651] *Id.* at 82 (statement of Rep. Bobby Scott).

C. President Trump may raise privileges and defenses in response to unfair, abusive proceedings.

Speaker Pelosi's impeachment inquiry, as conducted by Chairman Schiff, has abandoned due process and the presumption of innocence that lies at the heart of western legal systems.[652] Due to this abusive conduct and the Democrats' relentless attacks on the Trump Administration, President Trump may be rightly concerned about receiving fair treatment from House Democrats during this impeachment inquiry.

During the Clinton impeachment proceedings, Rep. Bobby Scott, now a senior member of the Democrat caucus, argued that the impeachment process should "determine[], with a presumption of innocence, whether those allegations [against President Clinton] were true by using cross-examination of witnesses and other traditionally reliable evidentiary procedures."[653] Similarly, Rep. Jerrold Nadler argued then that "[w]e have been entrusted with the grave and awesome duty by the American people, by the Constitution and by history. We must exercise that duty responsibly. At a bare minimum, that means *the President's accusers must go beyond hearsay and innuendo and beyond demands that the President prove his innocence of vague and changing charges*."[654]

Furthermore, Democrats had previously argued that the assertion of privileges by a president does not constitute an impeachable offense. During the Clinton impeachment proceedings, Rep. Scott stated:

> At the hearing when I posed the question of whether any of the witnesses on the hearing's second panel believed that the count involving invoking executive privilege should be considered an impeachable offense, the clear consensus on the panel was that the charge was not an impeachable offense. In fact, one Republican witness said, I do not think invoking executive privilege even if frivolously, and I believe it was frivolous in these circumstances, that that does not constitute an impeachable offense.[655]

Despite this prior commitment to due process and a presumption of innocence, the Democrats now favor a presumption of guilt. Chairman Schiff has said publicly that the Trump Administration and witnesses asserting their constitutional rights and seeking to test the soundness of subpoenas have formed "a very powerful case against the president for obstruction, an article of impeachment based on obstruction."[656] Similarly, Chairman Schiff has made clear

---

[652] *See, e.g., Id.* at 102 (statement of Rep. Maxine Waters) ("As Members of Congress have sworn to uphold the Constitution, we must always insist on equal and just treatment under the law. The presumption of innocence until proven guilty is central and basic to our system of justice.").

[653] *Id.* at 82 (statement of Rep. Bobby Scott).

[654] *Id.* at 78 (statement of Rep. Jerrold Nadler) (emphasis added).

[655] *Id.* at 83 (statement of Rep. Bobby Scott).

[656] Kyle Cheney, *Trump Makes 'Very Powerful Case' for Impeachment Based on Obstruction, Schiff Warns*, Politico, Oct. 28, 2019.

that he will simply assume that a witness's testimony is adverse to the President when that witness or the President asserts a right or privilege.[657] These are not the hallmarks of a fair and transparent process; these are the tell-tale signs of a star chamber.

D. Although declining to submit to the Democrats' abusive and unfair process, President Trump has released information to help the American public understand the issues.

Just twenty-seven minutes after President Trump's inauguration on January 20, 2017, the *Washington Post* reported that the "campaign to impeach President Trump has begun."[658] As the *Post* reported:

> The effort to impeach President Donald John Trump is already underway. At the moment the new commander in chief was sworn in, a campaign to build public support for his impeachment went live at ImpeachDonaldTrumpNow.org, spearheaded by two liberal advocacy groups aiming to lay the groundwork for his eventual ejection from the White House. . . . The impeachment drive comes as Democrats and liberal activists are mounting broad opposition to stymie Trump's agenda.[659]

In 2017 and 2018, Democrats introduced four separation resolution in the House with the goal of impeaching President Trump.[660] On January 3, 2019, on the Democrats' first day in power, Rep. Al Green again introduced articles of impeachment.[661] That same day, Rep. Rashida Tlaib promised, "we're going to go in there and we're going to impeach the [expletive deleted]."[662]

In this context, it is difficult to see the Democrats' impeachment inquiry as anything other than a partisan effort to undo the results of the 2016 election. Rep. Green said on MSNBC in May 2019, "If we don't impeach this President, he will get re-elected."[663] Even as Democrats have conducted their impeachment inquiry, Speaker Pelosi has called President Trump "an impostor" and said it is "dangerous" to allow American voters to evaluate his performance in

---

[657] *See Id.* ("Schiff also argued that the president is seeking to block Kupperman because he is concerned about a high-level source corroborating damning testimony that Trump pressured Ukraine to open investigations of his political rivals—and condition military aid and a White House visit on bending the European ally to his will.").
[658] Matea Gold, *The campaign to impeach President Trump has begun*, Wash. Post, Jan. 20, 2017.
[659] *Id.*
[660] H., Res. 705, 115th Cong. (2018); H. Res. 646, 115th Cong. (2017); H. Res. 621, 115th Cong. (2017); H. Res. 438, 115th Cong. (2017).
[661] H. Res. 13, 116th Cong. (2019).
[662] Amy B. Wong, *Rep. Rashida Tlaib profanely promised to impeach Trump. She's not sorry.*, Wash. Post, Jan. 4, 2019.
[663] *Weekends with Alex Witt*, *supra* note 618.

2020.[664] The Democrats' impeachment process has mirrored this rhetoric, stacking the deck against the President.[665]

Even so, the President is not entirely unwilling to cooperate with the Democrats' demands. In October 2019, Pat A. Cipollone, the Counsel to the President, wrote to Speaker Pelosi and the chairmen of the three "impeachment" committees:

> If the Committees wish to return to the regular order of oversight requests, we stand ready to engage in that process as we have in the past, in a manner consistent with well-established bipartisan constitutional protections and a respect for the separation of powers enshrined in our Constitution.[666]

Speaker Pelosi did not respond to Mr. Cipollone's letter. President Trump explained that he would "like people to testify" but he is resisting the Democrats' unfair and abusive process "for future Presidents and the Office of the President."[667]

Although the Democrats' abusive and unfair process has prevented his cooperation with the Democrats' impeachment inquiry, President Trump has nonetheless been transparent about his conduct. On September 25, President Trump declassified and released to the public the summary of his July 25 phone conversation with President Zelensky, stressing his goal that Americans could read for themselves the contents of the call: "You will see it was a very friendly and totally appropriate call."[668] On November 15, President Trump released to the public the summary of this April 21 phone conversation with President Zelensky in the interest of transparency.[669] In addition, President Trump has spoken publicly about his actions, as has Acting Chief of Staff Mick Mulvaney.[670]

Congress has a serious and important role to play in overseeing the Executive Branch. When the House of Representatives considers impeachment of a president, bipartisan precedent dictates fundamental fairness and due process. In pursuing impeachment of President Trump, however, Democrats have abandoned those principles, choosing instead to use impeachment as a tool to pursue their partisan objectives. While the President has declined to submit himself to the Democrats' unfair and abusive process, he has still made an effort to be transparent with the Americans to whom he is accountable. Under these abusive and unfair circumstances, the Democrats cannot establish a charge of obstruction.

---

[664] Emily Tillett, *Nancy Pelosi says Trump's attacks on witnesses "very significant" to impeachment probe*, CBS News, Nov. 15, 2019; Dear Colleague Letter from Speaker Nancy Pelosi (Nov. 18, 2019).
[665] *See* H. Res. 660, 116th Cong. (2019).
[666] Letter from Pat A. Cipollone, *supra* note 617.
[667] Donald J. Trump (@realDonaldTrump), Twitter (Nov. 26, 2019, 7:43 a m.), https://twitter.com/realDonaldTrump/status/1199352946187800578.
[668] Donald J. Trump (@realDonaldTrump), Twitter (Sept. 24, 2019, 11:12 a.m.), https://twitter.com/realdonaldtrump/status/1176559970390806530.
[669] Donald J. Trump (@realDonaldTrump), Twitter (Nov. 11, 2019, 3:35 p.m.), https://twitter.com/realDonaldTrump/status/1194035922066714625.
[670] *See, e.g.*, The White House, Remarks by President Trump before Marine One Departure (Nov. 20, 2019); Press Briefing by Acting Chief of Staff Mick Mulvaney, *supra* note 302.

IV.   Conclusion

The impeachment of a president is one of the gravest and most solemn duties of the House of Representatives. For Democrats, impeachment is a tool for settling political scores and re-litigating election results with which they disagreed. This impeachment inquiry and the manner in which the Democrats are pursuing it sets a dangerous precedent.

The Democrats have not established an impeachable offense. The evidence presented in this report does not support a finding that President Trump pressured President Zelensky to investigate his political rival for the President's benefit in the 2020 election. The evidence does not establish that President Trump withheld a White House meeting to pressure President Zelensky to investigate his political rival to benefit him in the 2020 election. The evidence does not support that President Trump withheld U.S. security assistance to pressure President Zelensky to investigate his political rival for the President's benefit in the 2020 election. The evidence does not establish that President Trump orchestrated a shadow foreign policy apparatus to pressure President Zelensky to investigate his political rival to benefit him in the 2020 election.

The best evidence of President Trump's interaction with President Zelensky is the "complete and accurate" call summary prepared by the White House Situation Room staff. The summary shows no indication of conditionality, pressure, or coercion. Both President Trump and President Zelensky have denied the existence of any pressure. President Zelensky and his senior advisers in Kyiv did not even know that U.S. security assistance to Ukraine was paused until it was publicly reported in U.S. media. Ultimately, Ukraine received the security assistance and President Zelensky met with President Trump, all without Ukraine ever investigating President Trump's political rival. These facts alone severely undercut the Democrat allegations.

The evidence in the Democrats' impeachment inquiry shows that President Trump is skeptical about U.S. taxpayer-funded foreign assistance and strongly believes that European allies should shoulder more of the financial burden for regional defense. The President also has deeply-rooted, reasonable, and genuine concerns about corruption in Ukraine, including the placement of Vice President Biden's son on the board of a Ukrainian energy company notorious for corruption at a time when Vice President Biden was the Obama Administration's point person for Ukraine policy. There is also compelling and indisputable evidence that Ukrainian government officials—some working with a Democrat operative—sought to influence the U.S. presidential election in 2016 in favor of Secretary Clinton and in opposition to President Trump.

The Democrats' impeachment narrative ignores the President's state of mind and it ignores the specific and concrete actions that the new Zelensky government took to address pervasive Ukrainian corruption. The Democrats' case rests almost entirely on hearsay, presumption, and emotion. Where there are ambiguous facts, the Democrats interpret them in a light most unfavorable to the President. The Democrats also flatly disregard any perception of potential wrongdoing with respect to Hunter Biden's presence on the board of Burisma Holdings or Ukrainian influence in the 2016 election.

The evidence presented also does not support allegations that President Trump covered-up his conversation with President Zelensky by restricting access to it. In light of leaks of other presidential conversations with world leaders, the White House took reasonably steps to restrict access to the July 25 call summary. The summary was mistakenly placed on a secure server; however, the Democrats' witnesses explained that there was no nefarious conduct or malicious intent associated with this action.

Likewise, the evidence presented does not support allegations that President Trump obstructed the Democrats' impeachment inquiry by raising concerns about an unfair and abusive process. The Democrats deviated from prior bipartisan precedent for presidential impeachment and denied Republican attempts to inject basic fairness and objectivity into their partisan and one-sided inquiry. The White House has signaled that it is willing to work with Democrats but President Trump cannot be faulted for declining to submit himself to the Democrats' star chamber. Even so, President Trump has been transparent with the American people about his actions, releasing documents and speaking publicly about the subject matter.

The Democrats' impeachment inquiry paints a picture of unelected bureaucrats within the foreign policy and national security apparatus who fundamentally disagreed with President Trump's style, world view, and decisions. Their disagreements with President Trump's policies and their discomfort with President Trump's actions set in motion the anonymous, secondhand whistleblower complaint. Democrats seized on the whistleblower complaint to fulfill their years-old obsession with removing President Trump from office.

The unfortunate collateral damage of the Democrats' impeachment inquiry is the harm done to bilateral U.S.-Ukraine relations, the fulfillment of Russian President Vladimir Putin's desire to sow discord within the United States, and the opportunity costs to the American people. In the time that Democrats spent investigating the President, Democrats could have passed legislation to implement the U.S.-Mexico-Canada Agreement, lower the costs of prescription drugs, or secure our southern border. Instead, the Democrats' obsession with impeaching President Trump has paralyzed their already-thin legislative agenda. Less than a year before the 2020 election and Democrats in the House still cannot move on from the results of the last election.

Congressman Mike Johnson (LA-04)
Dissenting Views to H. Res. 755
December 13, 2019
WHY THIS IMPEACHMENT IS A SHAM

The founders of this country warned against a single party impeachment because they feared it would bitterly, and perhaps irreparably, divide our nation. This risk was openly acknowledged in years past by the very Democrats who are leading the single party impeachment charade today. Our radical liberal colleagues have vowed to impeach President Donald J. Trump since the day of his election, they have desperately created a fraudulent, unprecedented process to pursue that goal, and now they are pulling the trigger on what was described by the Minority's expert witness in our House Judiciary Committee as *"the shortest proceeding, with the thinnest evidentiary record, and the narrowest grounds ever used to impeach a president."'* This impeachment is a sham, and here is why.

Although every previous U.S. President has made unpopular decisions and even, at times, infuriated his political opponents, impeachments are—for good reason and by specific design—*exceedingly rare*. In the 243-year history of our nation, only two previous presidents (Andrew Johnson in 1868 and Bill Clinton in 1998) have been impeached by the House. Richard Nixon resigned in 1974 to avoid it. In each of those three previous impeachments, evidence clearly established that specific criminal acts were committed. **That is NOT the case here.**

House Democrats began efforts to impeach President Trump immediately upon his election. They introduced four separate impeachment resolutions while they were in the minority in 2017 and 2018, and a new resolution in January 2019. In all, as many as 95 House Democrats—including 17 of 24 Democrats serving on the Judiciary Committee—had voted to proceed with impeachment well before the famous phone call between Presidents Trump and Zelensky ever took place on July 25, 2019.

C:\P16\AOT\ARTICLES_FINAL.XML

2

1 its impeachment against him for high crimes and mis-
2 demeanors.
3   ARTICLE I: ABUSE OF POWER
4   The Constitution provides that the House of Rep-
5 resentatives "shall have the sole Power of Impeachment"
6 and that the President "shall be removed from Office on
7 Impeachment for, and Conviction of, Treason, Bribery, or
8 other high Crimes and Misdemeanors". In his conduct of
9 the office of President of the United States—and in viola-
10 tion of his constitutional oath faithfully to execute the of-
11 fice of President of the United States and, to the best of
12 his ability, preserve, protect, and defend the Constitution
13 of the United States, and in violation of his constitutional
14 duty to take care that the laws be faithfully executed—
15 Donald J. Trump has abused the powers of the Presi-
16 dency, in that:
17   Using the powers of his high office, President Trump
18 solicited the interference of a foreign government,
19 Ukraine, in the 2020 United States Presidential election.
20 He did so through a scheme or course of conduct that
21 **included soliciting the Government of Ukraine to publicly**
22 **announce investigations that would benefit his reelection,**
23 **harm the election prospects of a political opponent, and**
24 influence the 2020 United States Presidential election to
25 his advantage. President Trump also sought to pressure
26 the Government of Ukraine to take these steps by condi-

g:\VHLC\121019\121019.007 and   (752941 8)
December 10, 2019 (7:16 a.m.)

This is indeed the relevant language of U.S. Const., Art. II, Sec. 4, and it shows the inherent weakness of the current case.

Because Democrats found no evidence of treason or bribery against President Trump, but had already promised his impeachment to their liberal base, they felt they had no choice but to default to two amorphous articles: "abuse of power" and "obstruction of Congress."

"Abuse of power" is a non-criminal act, and it is significant that Democrats made this their first article. As Prof. Turley testified to Judiciary: "[This country] has never impeached a president solely or even largely on the basis of a non-criminal abuse of power allegation. There is good reason for that unbroken record. Abuses of power tend to be even less defined and more debatable as a basis for impeachment than [specified] crimes. …In this case, there needs to be clear and unequivocal proof of a *quid pro quo*."
That does NOT exist here.

Democrats know there is **zero direct evidence** in the record of these proceedings to show that President Trump engaged in any "scheme" of any kind, or that he intended in his dealings with Ukraine to "influence the 2020 United States Presidential election to his advantage." No impeachment should ever proceed on the basis of mere hearsay, speculation and conjecture that would not even be admissible in a local traffic court.

3

1 tioning official United States Government acts of signifi-
2 cant value to Ukraine on its public announcement of the
3 investigations. President Trump engaged in this scheme
4 or course of conduct for corrupt purposes in pursuit of
5 personal political benefit. In so doing, President Trump
6 used the powers of the Presidency in a manner that com-
7 promised the national security of the United States and
8 undermined the integrity of the United States democratic
9 process. He thus ignored and injured the interests of the
10 Nation.
11   President Trump engaged in this scheme or course
12 of conduct through the following means:
13   (1) President Trump—acting both directly and
14   through his agents within and outside the United
15   States Government—corruptly solicited the Govern-
16   ment of Ukraine to publicly announce investigations
17   into—
18   (A) a political opponent, former Vice Presi-
19   dent Joseph R. Biden, Jr.; and
20   (B) a discredited theory promoted by Rus-
21   sia alleging that Ukraine—rather than Rus-
22   sia— interfered in the 2016 United States Pres-
23   idential election.
24   (2) With the same corrupt motives, President
25   Trump—acting both directly and through his agents

Once again, Democrats include bold allegations that are completely unsupported by the evidentiary record. For example, Article I alleges "corrupt purposes" or intent at least eight times, but presents **zero proof** for the claim. There is also zero proof that, for example, President Trump was pursuing "personal benefit" or "ignored and injured the interests of the Nation." To the contrary, the record is clear that he had exactly the opposite in mind.

As summarized in the Minority Staff Report of Dec. 2: "The evidence shows that President Trump holds a deep-seated, genuine, and reasonable skepticism of Ukraine due to its history of pervasive corruption. . . and his Administration sought proof that newly-elected President Zelensky was a true reformer." President Trump wanted to ensure that American taxpayer-funded security assistance would not be squandered by what is reported to be the third most corrupt nation in the world. A glaring example that still concerns the president, and millions of Americans, is what who meddled with our 2016 elections, and how. The Trump/Ukraine discussions were never about what will happen in 2020, but rather what already happened in 2016.

G:\PU\AC\ARTICLES_FINAL.XML

4

1   within and outside the United States Government—

2   conditioned two official acts on the public announce-

3   ments that he had requested—

4   (A) the release of $391 million of United

5   States taxpayer funds that Congress had appro-

6   priated on a bipartisan basis for the purpose of

7   providing vital military and security assistance

8   to Ukraine to oppose Russian aggression and

9   which President Trump had ordered suspended;

10   and

11   (B) a head of state meeting at the White

12   House, which the President of Ukraine sought

13   to demonstrate continued United States support

14   for the Government of Ukraine in the face of

15   Russian aggression.

16   (3) Faced with the public revelation of his ac-

17   tions, President Trump ultimately released the mili-

18   tary and security assistance to the Government of

19   Ukraine, but has persisted in openly and corruptly

20   urging and soliciting Ukraine to undertake investiga-

21   tions for his personal political benefit.

22   These actions were consistent with President

23   Trump's previous invitations of foreign interference in

24   United States elections.

g:\VH\LC\121219\121219.007.xml   (75804408)
December 10, 2019 (7:10 a.m.)

There is **zero** evidence for any "condition." To the contrary, **four indisputable facts** in the record clearly destroy the Democrats' case theory:

1) Both President Trump and President Zelensky say there was <u>no pressure</u> exerted.
2) The July 25 call transcript shows <u>no</u> conditionality between aid funding and an investigation.
3) Ukraine was <u>not aware</u> that aid was delayed when the presidents spoke.
4) Ukraine <u>never opened an</u> investigation, but still received aid and a meeting with President Trump.

G:\PJ16\AOR\ARTICLES_FINAL.XML

5

1   In all of this, President Trump abused the powers
2 of the Presidency by ignoring and injuring national secu-
3 rity and other vital national interests to obtain an im-
4 proper personal political benefit. He has also betrayed the
5 Nation by abusing his high office to enlist a foreign power
6 in corrupting democratic elections.
7   Wherefore President Trump, by such conduct, has
8 demonstrated that he will remain a threat to national se-
9 curity and the Constitution if allowed to remain in office,
10 and has acted in a manner grossly incompatible with self-
11 governance and the rule of law. President Trump thus
12 warrants impeachment and trial, removal from office, and
13 disqualification to hold and enjoy any office of honor,
14 trust, or profit under the United States.
15   ARTICLE II: OBSTRUCTION OF CONGRESS
16   The Constitution provides that the House of Rep-
17 resentatives "shall have the sole Power of Impeachment"
18 and that the President "shall be removed from Office on
19 Impeachment for, and Conviction of, Treason, Bribery, or
20 other high Crimes and Misdemeanors". In his conduct of
21 the office of President of the United States—and in viola-
22 tion of his constitutional oath faithfully to execute the of-
23 fice of President of the United States and, to the best of
24 his ability, preserve, protect, and defend the Constitution
25 of the United States, and in violation of his constitutional
26 duty to take care that the laws be faithfully executed—

Two bases are summarized for the claim that President Trump abused his powers:

1) He "ignored and injured" the interests of the country "to obtain an improper personal political benefit;" and
2) He "betrayed the nation" to "enlist" Ukraine "in corrupting democratic elections."

Neither of those allegations is true or supported by a scintilla of evidence in the record.

The Democrats' second claim is that President Trump "obstructed Congress" by simply doing what virtually every other President in the modern era has ALSO done—to assert a legitimate executive privilege and legal immunity to avoid subpoenas issued to various White House officials. THERE IS NO EVIDENCE OF ANY IMPEACHABLE OFFENSE HERE. On every previous occasion of this assertion in the past, that natural impasse between the executive and legislative branches in our constitutional system has been easily and calmly resolved by either a good faith negotiation—or a simple filing with the THIRD branch of our government—the judicial branch.

G:\P\16\IMPEACH\ARTICLES_FINAL.XML

6

1 Donald J. Trump has directed the unprecedented, categor-
2 ical, and indiscriminate defiance of subpoenas issued by
3 the House of Representatives pursuant to its "sole Power
4 of Impeachment". President Trump has abused the pow-
5 ers of the Presidency in a manner offensive to, and subver-
6 sive of, the Constitution, in that.
7 The House of Representatives has engaged in an im-
8 peachment inquiry focused on President Trump's corrupt
9 solicitation of the Government of Ukraine to interfere in
10 the 2020 United States Presidential election. As part of
11 this impeachment inquiry, the Committees undertaking
12 the investigation served subpoenas seeking documents and
13 testimony deemed vital to the inquiry from various Execu-
14 tive Branch agencies and offices, and current and former
15 officials.
16 In response, without lawful cause or excuse, Presi-
17 dent Trump directed Executive Branch agencies, offices,
18 and officials not to comply with those subpoenas. Presi-
19 dent Trump thus interposed the powers of the Presidency
20 against the lawful subpoenas of the House of Representa-
21 tives, and assumed to himself functions and judgments
22 necessary to the exercise of the "sole Power of Impeach-
23 ment" vested by the Constitution in the House of Rep-
24 resentatives.

g:\VHLC\121019\121019.007.xml   (753244|2)
December 10, 2019 (7:16 a.m.)

Again, the presidential assertion of executive privilege and legal immunity to Congressional subpoenas is quite common in the modern era, and not "unprecedented."

In spite of their allegation, Democrats know the President Trump has "lawful cause ' to challenge their subpoenas in this matter. In this case, House Democrats are trying to impeach President Trump instead of simply seeking judicial review over whether the direct communications between high-ranking advisors and a president under these circumstances are privileged or must be disclosed. That case wouldbe expedited in the courts, but Democrats said they "don't have time for that." Why? Because they promised their base they would deliver an impeachment by Christmas!

G:\PK\MAOR\ARTICLES_FINAL.XML

7

1   President Trump abused the powers of his high office

2 through the following means:

3   (1) Directing the White House to defy a lawful

4   subpoena by withholding the production of docu-

5   ments sought therein by the Committees.

6   (2) Directing other Executive Branch agencies

7   and offices to defy lawful subpoenas and withhold

8   the production of documents and records from the

9   Committees—in response to which the Department

10   of State, Office of Management and Budget, Depart-

11   ment of Energy, and Department of Defense refused

12   to produce a single document or record.

13   (3) Directing current and former Executive

14   Branch officials not to cooperate with the Commit-

15   tees—in response to which nine Administration offi-

16   cials defied subpoenas for testimony, namely John

17   Michael "Mick" Mulvaney, Robert B. Blair, John A.

18   Eisenberg, Michael Ellis, Preston Wells Griffith,

19   Russell T. Vought, Michael Duffey, Brian McCor-

20   mack, and T. Ulrich Brechbuhl.

21   These actions were consistent with President

22   Trump's previous efforts to undermine United States Gov-

23   ernment investigations into foreign interference in United

24   States elections.

g:\VHLC\121219\121219.097.xml   (759324|42)
December 12, 2019 (7:16 a.m.)

It should be noted that President Trump has consistently cooperated with Congress in fulfilling its oversight and investigation responsibilities.

For example, over 25 Administration officials have testified before the House Oversight Committee this year, and over 20 have testified before the House Judiciary Committee. At the start of the Democrat's impeachment inquiry, the White House also produced more than 100,000 pages of documents to the Oversight Committee.

In spite of their allegation, Democrats know the President Trump has "lawful cause" to challenge these subpoenas because they involve direct communications between high-ranking advisors and a president, and most of these individuals are not related to the Ukraine matter at hand. Any objective observer would regard this as a mere "fishing expedition" and harassment of the Administration by Democrat committee chairs with a political agenda. That agenda does not allow them to proceed to a court to get this simple disagreement appropriately resolved.

G:\P14\AGD\ARTICLES_FINAL.XML

H

1   Through these actions, President Trump sought to
2   arrogate to himself the right to determine the propriety,
3   scope, and nature of an impeachment inquiry into his own
4   conduct, as well as the unilateral prerogative to deny any
5   and all information to the House of Representatives in the
6   exercise of its "sole Power of Impeachment". In the his-
7   tory of the Republic, no President has ever ordered the
8   complete defiance of an impeachment inquiry or sought
9   to obstruct and impede so comprehensively the ability of
10   the House of Representatives to investigate "high Crimes
11   and Misdemeanors". This abuse of office served to cover
12   up the President's own repeated misconduct and to seize
13   and control the power of impeachment—and thus to nul-
14   lify a vital constitutional safeguard vested solely in the
15   House of Representatives.
16   In all of this, President Trump has acted in a manner
17   contrary to his trust as President and subversive of con-
18   stitutional government, to the great prejudice of the cause
19   of law and justice, and to the manifest injury of the people
20   of the United States.
21   Wherefore, President Trump, by such conduct, has
22   demonstrated that he will remain a threat to the Constitu-
23   tion if allowed to remain in office, and has acted in a man-
24   ner grossly incompatible with self-governance and the rule
25   of law. President Trump thus warrants impeachment and

g:\VHLC\121019\121019.087.xml   (750846|8)
December 10, 2019 (7:45 a.m.)

Democrats know this is an absurd charge. The *truth* is, in the history of the Republic, there has never been a <u>single party, fraudulent impeachment process</u> deployed against a president like the one being used against Donald Trump.

Democrats are the ones here seeking to nullify our vital constitutional safeguards with this sham. Their ultimate objective is to nullify the votes of the 63 million Americans who voted to elect Donald Trump the President.

The "manifest injury to the people" and "threat to the Constitution" is what is being perpetuated by the House Democrats engaged in this charade.

G:\P16\AOP\ARTICLES_FINAL.XML

9

1   trial, removal from office, and disqualification to hold and

2   enjoy any office of honor, trust, or profit under the United

3   States.

g:\VHLC\121018\121018.207.xml   (798044|6)
December 10, 2018 (7:18 a.m.)

The REAL abuse of power here is on the part of the House Democrats, as they have recklessly pursued this impeachment—*20 times faster* than the impeachment investigation of Bill Clinton—to reach their predetermined political outcome. Along the way, they have steamrolled over constitutionally- guaranteed due process, House Rules and the Federal Rules of Civil Procedure. They have: ignored or blocked exculpatory evidence; intimidated witnesses; restricted Republican lines of questioning; denied defense witnesses and involvement of the president's counsel; restricted Republican review of evidence; denied a Minority hearing; and violated proper Minority notice and fairness at all stages.

Ironically, during the Clinton impeachment, the Democrats published a report which read: "As Rep. Barbara Jordan (D-Tx.) observed during the Watergate inquiry, impeachment not only mandates due process, but 'due process *quadrupled.*'" The Democrats of this Congress have done exactly the opposite—and everyone in this country can see that clearly. This impeachment will fail, and the Democrats will justly pay a heavy political price for it. But the Pandora's Box they have opened today will do irreparable damage to our country in the years ahead. God help us.

Mike Johnson
Ranking Member
House Judiciary Subcommittee on the Constitution, Civil Rights and Civil Liberties

Andy Biggs AZ 05
Dec 15, 2019

DISSENTING VIEWS
Congressman Andy Biggs

I concur with Ranking Member Doug Collins' dissenting views and submit my additional statements for the record.

Democrats have sought to remove or delegitimize President Donald J. Trump since the day he won the 2016 presidential election. Representative Al Green (D-TX) expressed his desire to impeach the President while Barack Obama was still President. Media outlets and others stoked this fire and have kept it going for three years.

Their efforts have been uneven and unsuccessful. The most notorious attempt was the Russian "collusion" allegations that consumed more than $30 million and took the time of 19 FBI agents and operatives, hundreds of interviews, and hundreds of thousands of pages of documents. The conclusion was that the Trump campaign did not conspire, coordinate, cooperate, or collude with the Russians to interfere in the 2016 election.

Even now, however, Representatives who sit on the House Judiciary Committee and House Permanent Select Committee on Intelligence (HPSCI or Intel) insist that they have evidence of "collusion."

In August 2019, a leaker, who had been told about a telephone conversation between President Trump and Ukraine President Zelensky, contacted HPSCI staff. Even though HPSCI Chairman Schiff publicly denied this contact, media accounts exposed that there had indeed been contact, and insinuated that there might have been assistance in drafting the "whistleblower's" complaint, which has launched this latest attack on President Trump.

Speaker Pelosi announced the opening of an impeachment inquiry based on the complaint. During her announcement she made representations of the contents of the complaint, as had Chairman Schiff.

The complaint was proven to be substantively false and utterly without merit when President Trump released a transcript of the phone call.

The testimony presented to the Judiciary Committee came in two hearings. In one hearing three law professors who despise this President urged impeachment. A fourth law professor, who did not and does not support President Trump, stated that this impeachment is based on "wafer thin" evidence which does not support Democrat allegations, in a process that is the fastest in the nation's history.

The only other "evidentiary" hearing consisted of the bizarre scenario where a Democrat staffer, who had testified for thirty minutes, left his spot at the witness table to sit next to Judiciary Chairman Nadler on the dais, and cross examine a Republican staffer for thirty minutes. All this strangeness took place in a hearing where each side was supposed to present its report on the closed-door proceedings of HPSCI.

The only facts adduced from those who have direct knowledge of the matters considered in this impeachment are:

1) Ukraine received U.S. aid in conformity with the law;
2) The aid was received without any preconditions other than those required by law;
3) During the period the release of aid was legally paused, Ukraine was not aware of the pause;
4) President Trump had a justified interest in Ukrainian corruption and a well-expressed antipathy toward any foreign aid.

In attempting to make their case Democrats have chosen to draw every inference from the scanty evidence in the most negative light possible against the President. Their obvious animus toward him has prevented them from giving, even one time, a benign interpretation of the evidence. And certainly, they would never accept an interpretation that might inure to the President's benefit.

Having watched and participated in the proceedings, even though limited by Chairman Schiff and the acquiescence of Chairman Nadler in that limitation, I have concluded that the Democrats' would never give a neutral interpretation of the facts (which they believe include rumor, gossip, and innuendo) where President Trump is concerned.

They have no facts. The law is against them. They have rigged the process. Why should the American public give the Democrats the benefit of the doubt?

ARTICLE I – ABUSE OF POWER

During their impeachment inquiry against President Trump, Democrats have dishonestly alleged that President Trump abused the powers of his office by soliciting "interference of a foreign government, Ukraine, in the 2020 United States Presidential election." There is no basis for this outlandish claim. Democrats have twisted facts, taken statements out of context, and lied to the American people all in the name of fulfilling their 2016-stated desire of removing President Trump from office.

The shaky foundation of the Democrat case is the July 25, 2019, call between President Donald Trump and Ukrainian President Volodymyr Zelensky. On this call, Democrats allege that President Trump conditioned future support for Ukraine on their agreement to "publicly announce investigations into…former Vice President Joseph R. Biden." This is not true.

There is no mention of the aid appropriated by the United States for Ukraine on the call. Additionally, there is no discussion of any precondition to release aid. This is the first of many examples of the Democrats twisting the facts to create their own narrative.

Democrats called in several witnesses hoping to confirm their narrative, most for sessions of closed-door testimony, and some of whose transcripts still have not been released. Not one testified of a *quid pro quo*.

Gordon Sondland, U.S. Ambassador to the European Union is the Democrats' star witness. He is mentioned more than 600 times in a 262-page report authored by Chairman Schiff, which purports to be a summary of the HPSCI hearings.
Ambassador Sondland was not on the July 25 call. He repeatedly testified that the only direct statement from President Trump was that President Trump wanted nothing from Ukraine except for it to clean up its corruption.

Other statements of Sondland, that there was a *quid pro quo*, and everyone was "in the loop," were simply assumptions he made. In fact, he acknowledged that "no one on earth" told him that there were any preconditions on release of aid. His only direct knowledge was the President's explicit contradiction of the entirety of Sondland's presumptions.

Presumptions cannot be the basis for an impeachment. All the presumptions in the world do not overcome the direct evidence of the President's statement. In a conversation with Ambassador Sondland, President Trump said, "I want nothing [from Ukraine]. I want no *quid pro quo*. I want Zelensky to do the right thing. I want him to do what he ran on." In this case, President Trump is referring to President Zelensky's campaign to root out corruption within the Ukrainian government. The President's statement directly contradicts Ambassador Sondland's presumption.

The appropriated aid was released to the Ukraine without any investigation or announcement of an investigation by Ukraine. But the Democrats even put their own spin on the ultimate reasoning for release.

Democrats infer that President Trump released the aid because the delay on delivery was made public and Ukraine was made aware. Because they have no direct evidence to substantiate this assertion, they have attempted to rely on a timeline that says the whistleblower complaint became public before President Trump released the money to Ukraine. That temporal coincidence is a pin prick through which they attempt to drive a truck. But their inference is wrong.

That timeline is their only evidence. While that timeline of events is in fact true, that the whistleblower complaint was made public prior to the aid being released, there is a stronger rationale for the President's release of aid. In late August 2019, the Ukraine legislature was working on strong anticorruption legislation, which even Democrat witnesses said would be a significant curb on rampant Ukrainian corruption.

President Trump released the aid the very same day that President Zelensky signed into law two anti-corruption measures: one that ended immunity for Ukrainian legislators and the reinstatement of a vigorous anticorruption court.

The United States had provided aid to Ukraine in 2017 and 2018, but aid was only paused in 2019. The Democrats assert this is because President Trump wanted Ukraine to investigate a political rival. In fact, several Democrats asked what changed between 2017, 2018, and 2019.

What changed? A new president who had run on an anticorruption platform who had been employed by a Ukrainian oligarch before election. President Zelensky was also surrounded by several of the previous corrupt regime's officials. A brief pause, consistent with the law, to determine the credibility of the new president's commitment to ending corruption was justified.

To that end, during the pause there were multiple high-level meetings between U.S. leaders and President Zelensky where the need to take anticorruption measures was emphasized. The aid was released the day the two anticorruption laws were executed.

The Democrats' accusation that President Trump asked for an investigation into his political rival is based on a presumption that is inconsistent with the facts. On the July 25 phone call, President Trump mentioned a set of circumstances in which former Vice President Joseph Biden appeared to have stopped a prosecution that might have implicated Biden's son, Hunter. President Trump asked President Zelensky to "look into" those circumstances. President Trump did not ask President Zelensky to investigate Biden or to "dig up dirt" on Biden, as Schiff brazenly misrepresented to the American people.

Investigating events is not the same as investigating people. It is apparent that this distinction is lost on the Democrats. They have been investigating President Trump for three years and have investigated every nook and cranny of his life. They have investigated his family, his friends and associates, his supporters, his businesses. Democrats always project what they are doing on everyone else. They have been assailing President Trump at every turn. They have been investigating the person, not the events.

Not one witness testified that President Trump ever mentioned politics or the upcoming election. The evidence is that he was motivated by his understanding of widespread corruption in Ukraine and the corrupt circumstances of the Biden's involvement with Burisma, a Ukrainian energy company that was considered by many to be a corrupt actor. A person who is involved with entities committing corrupt acts may end up being investigated in conjunction with the corrupt acts of that entity. Immunity is not granted simply because that person's father is a powerful American political figure.

The telephone call between the two presidents was considered a good, fruitful conversation. The evidence in this case is clear: Ukraine received the aid within the lawful time provided for distribution, provided nothing in return for the aid, and Ukrainian President Zelensky stated publicly on multiple occasions that he never discussed any form of *quid pro quo* with President Trump and he felt no pressure from the United States.

The real abuse of power is on the part of House Democrats, led by Speaker Nancy Pelosi, House Intelligence Committee Chairman Adam Schiff, and House Judiciary Committee Chairman Jerry Nadler. For months, they have run a Stalin-like court and failed to provide the due process fundamental to our nation. They used their platform to lie to the American people and to subvert the political will of 63 million American voters. Their efforts – which were stated in 2016, long before the call between President Trump and President Zelensky – are the real abuse of power.

ARTICLE II – OBSTRUCTION OF CONGRESS

Democrats' second Article is the most dubious, the "Obstruction of Congress" allegation. Obstruction of Congress is weaker than the obstruction of justice story they bandied about for several years. It certainly is not a crime of moral turpitude, nor a "high crime or misdemeanor." It is almost an admission that Democrats are aware of the paucity of evidence to support their claims that they bring this Article forward.

Democrats argue that President Trump's unwillingness to support their impeachment is, somehow, obstruction of Congress. Is the President required to acquiesce to process that is patently harassing and of dubious motivation? The principles of separation of powers and checks and balances demand that a president be permitted to resist orders of the legislative branch that are overly broad, burdensome, harassing, or violative of his constitutional privileges.

Democrats claim that by asserting his constitutional privilege President Trump usurped the constitutional imperative that the House has the sole power of impeachment. They demand obeisance to their commands. It is an absurdity to claim that by granting Congress the sole power of impeachment the president is required to cooperate in any and all congressional requests, no matter their merit. Disputes between our branches are a feature, not a bug, of our system. The branches typically engage in a process of accommodation to reach an agreement. When disputes between the legislative and executive branches cannot be resolved, the two can appeal to the courts to rule. Anything less threatens the separation of powers that is the very foundation of our Constitution.

Democrats choose instead to ignore both the accommodation process and the judicial process to resolve this impasse. With a certain degree of shamelessness, they assert that President Trump defied subpoenas issued by the House. President Trump chose to assert his executive privilege, a valid constitutional option. Democrats did not try to reach any accommodation with President Trump and refused to attempt to enforce their subpoenas in court. The courts would have determined the validity of the subpoenas and of President Trump's privilege claim. But Chairman Schiff and Chairman Nadler publicly stated that turning to the courts would take too long. Democrats are letting themselves be held hostage by the clock and the calendar rather than attempting to follow the constitutional structure that the Founders intended.

Democrats have argued that President Trump undermined the integrity of the democratic process by his efforts to ensure the new Ukrainian President addressed corruption. But really, it's Democrats relentless attacks on President Trump and attempts to overturn the 2016 election that are undermining the integrity of the democratic process.

Democrats spent months of their first year back in the majority focused on impeachment. Rather than address the real issues facing our nation—border security, mounting national debt, and skyrocketing health care prices, to name a few—they've spent all their energy and efforts perpetrating a sham impeachment. We should consider who is more of an obstruction to Congress – President Trump or House Democrats. It's safe to say, it's House Democrats.

BROKEN PROCESS

The Democrats and their adherents in the Left-wing media have propounded a seemingly endless parade of reasons to impeach President Trump. In a "tweet" he used the term "fake news" and some saw that as grounds for impeachment. They asserted he should be impeached for the Muslim Ban (upheld by the Supreme Court), exercising his legitimate constitutional power to pardon (someone they didn't like), his tweet about FBI and U.S. intelligence surveillance of his presidential campaign (confirmed by the 2019 Inspector General report), tweeting about NFL players disrespecting the Flag and law enforcement officers, and just about everything else. One congressman suggested he should be impeached for slavery.

All of these were either policy disputes or personality conflicts. Some were outlandish and nonsensical. But the media and Democrats often repeated them.

Democrats helped perpetuate the Russian collusion hoax and even suggested an invocation of the 25th Amendment to remove the President.

Is it any wonder that this impeachment process has been greeted with such skepticism? And, once the Schiff show in the top-secret basement bunker started, without the presence of the traditional committee of jurisdiction, the Judiciary Committee, the Democrats demonstrated that Americans' mistrust was justified.

The entire process was based on a foundation of deception. Chairman Schiff opened the informal impeachment – the first time in history an impeachment inquiry has been opened without a full vote of the House – by deceiving the American people into thinking a whistleblower expressed concern over the July 25 call between President Trump and President Zelensky. But Democrats' own *New York Times* broke the news that the whistleblower had communicated with Chairman Schiff's staff before coming forward publicly. To this day, it is still unclear whether Chairman Schiff himself met with the whistleblower or how his staff conspired to help craft his statement because Chairman Schiff and his staff refuse to answer questions about their dealings.

Once the transcript of the July 25 call was released by the White House and Chairman Schiff found that it did not support, and in fact, conflicted with his narrative, he created his own. After all, he needed some claim such as conditionality that would allow him to propound his false narrative.

Because there was no evidence of a this-for-that in the transcript of the call, Schiff wrote his own dialogue. He made up a conversation and told this fabrication to the world. He made it sound like President Trump directly asked President Zelensky for an investigation of his political opponent. But it was false. A lie. He had to make it up because the evidence he hoped for wasn't there. The oddest part is that Democrats quoted liberally from his report in the impeachment markup and Democrats continue to perpetuate the myth.

Next up, Democrats started calling witnesses to testify, hoping one of them would give them some facts to support their narrative. In violation of House rules, they held these interviews and depositions in a top-secret room in the basement of the Capitol, denying access to most members of Congress (including the Judiciary Committee) and prohibiting attending members from discussing the substance. The secret room and gag rules allowed Democrats to get their story

6

straight before presenting their sham to the American people. Transcripts of the interviews trickled out over time, though not all of them have been released, even to this day. Once again, I call upon Chairman Schiff to release the transcript of the deposition of the Intelligence Community Inspector General.

When Pelosi finally allowed a vote on the rules, H.Res.660 gave President Trump and the minority less due process than President Clinton received from the Republicans during his impeachment. The President's counsel was prevented from examining any fact witnesses, Republicans were denied the right to call their own witnesses, and Republicans didn't have subpoena authority of their own. Worse still, Democrats inappropriately used their subpoenas to gather phone records from the President's attorney, from members of Congress, and members of the press, each of which were cherry picked and published. Despite multiple requests for documents throughout the process, Democrats stonewalled until releasing 8,000 pages of records less than 48 hours before the Judiciary Committee's hearing on the report published by the HPSCI. Never has a majority party abused its power in such a shocking and appalling way.

During one of only two impeachment hearings held by the House Judiciary Committee in this impeachment process—the committee that has historically been tasked with overseeing impeachment inquiries—neither of which were attended by any fact witnesses, House Republicans, in accordance with the House rules, requested the opportunity to hold a minority hearing. Republicans, after all, deserve the opportunity to call additional witnesses and to seek the truth. House rules require the Chairman to hold the hearing once it's requested, presumably in a timely way. Consistent with their track record of denying minority rights, Chairman Nadler refused to approve the hearing before the Judiciary Committee voted to approve the impeachment articles.

After the two hearings at which there were only presentations, the House Judiciary Committee met for more than 12 hours to debate and amend the articles of impeachment. Throughout the entire day, and as they did throughout the entire impeachment process, Chairman Nadler refused to follow committee rules on points of order, recognizing Members, or parliamentary inquiries. These rules are how committees maintain their decorum and protect the rights of the minority. The majority's disregard of the rules has set a terrible precedent and might lead to justification for future abuses. And, quite frankly, the disregard was completely unnecessary. Democrats have a substantial majority and will win the final vote. Disregarding the rules prevents members from representing the tens of millions of Americans who elected them, all the while knowing that the outcome of the final impeachment vote was a *fait accompli*.

The penultimate disrespect of the minority occurred late into the evening. After many hours of debate, Chairman Nadler postponed voting on the articles until the following morning and recessed the committee. This was done with no consultation of the Ranking Member, no prior notification to Members on the committee, and no reason given for why the vote could not be held that evening. But it was observed that most of the media had departed.

The following morning, after the media had returned, the anticlimactic vote occurred, lasting all of 10 minutes.

During the Judiciary Committee markup, a Democrat Congressman stated, "Freedom from oppression, freedom from tyranny, freedom from abuse of power, freedom is in our DNA." A wiser man, President Ronald Reagan, counterargued that "Freedom is never more than one generation away from extinction. We didn't pass it to our children in the bloodstream. It must be fought for, protected, and handed on for them to do the same, or one day we will spend our sunset years telling our children and our children's children what it was once like in the United States where men were free." Democrats have tried to wrap themselves in the flag and say they are standing for the Constitution. But they are simply ignoring the clearly established facts and circumventing the rules to their advantage.

The American people see this process for what it is – a sham. This President, and all Americans deserve elected officials who have respect for their political will, for the foundations of our constitutional republic, and for the great responsibility that has been set before them. Democrats have damaged our representative republic with this impeachment.

DISSENTING VIEWS

On the Resolution and Report Recommending to the U.S. House of Representatives the Impeachment of President Donald J. Trump

December 13, 2019

On December 13, 2019, the Judiciary Committee advanced H.Res. 755, Articles of Impeachment Against Donald J. Trump, out of the Committee for consideration by the House of Representatives. My position on the Articles of Impeachment contained in H.Res. 755 is in concurrence with Ranking Member Doug Collins.

Tom McClintock

GUY RESCHENTHALER
14TH DISTRICT, PENNSYLVANIA

JUDICIARY COMMITTEE

FOREIGN AFFAIRS COMMITTEE

DISTRICT OFFICES:

700 PELLIS ROAD
SUITE 1
GREENSBURG, PA 15601
(724) 219-4200

14 SOUTH MAIN STREET
WASHINGTON, PA 15301
(724) 206-4800

Congress of the United States
House of Representatives
531 Cannon House Office Building
Washington, DC 20515-3814
(202) 225-2065

DISSENTING VIEWS

H.Res. 755

I agree with the views expressed by Ranking Member Doug Collins.

Sincerely,

Guy Reschenthaler
Member of Congress

Appendix

THE TRUMP-UKRAINE
IMPEACHMENT INQUIRY REPORT

Report of the House Permanent Select Committee on Intelligence,
Pursuant to H. Res. 660 in Consultation with the
House Committee on Oversight and Reform and the
House Committee on Foreign Affairs

December 2019

House Permanent Select Committee on Intelligence

Rep. Adam B. Schiff (CA), Chairman

Rep. Jim Himes (CT)
Rep. Terri Sewell (AL)
Rep. André Carson (IN)
Rep. Jackie Speier (CA)
Rep. Mike Quigley (IL)
Rep. Eric Swalwell (CA)
Rep. Joaquin Castro (TX)
Rep. Denny Heck (WA)
Rep. Peter Welch (VT)
Rep. Sean Patrick Maloney (NY)
Rep. Val Demings (FL)
Rep. Raja Krishnamoorthi (IL)

Rep. Devin Nunes (CA), Ranking Member
Rep. Mike Conaway (TX)
Rep. Michael Turner (OH)
Rep. Brad Wenstrup (OH)
Rep. Chris Stewart (UT)
Rep. Elise Stefanik (NY)
Rep. Will Hurd (TX)
Rep. John Ratcliffe (TX)
Rep. Jim Jordan (OH)

Majority Staff
Timothy S. Bergreen, Staff Director
Daniel S. Goldman, Director of Investigations
Maher Bitar, General Counsel
Rheanne Wirkkala, Deputy Director of Investigations
Patrick M. Boland, Communications Director

Impeachment Inquiry Investigative Staff

William M. Evans
Patrick Fallon
Sean A. Misko
Nicolas A. Mitchell

Daniel S. Noble
Diana Y. Pilipenko
Ariana N. Rowberry

Carly A. Blake, Deputy Staff Director
William Wu, Budget and Policy Director
Wells C. Bennett, Deputy General Counsel

Oversight Staff

Linda D. Cohen
Thomas Eager
Abigail C. Grace
Kelsey M. Lax
Amanda A. Rogers Thorpe

Lucian D. Sikorskyj
Conrad Stosz
Kathy L. Suber
Aaron A. Thurman
Raffaela L. Wakeman

Non-Partisan Security and Information Technology Staff

Kristin Jepson   Kimberlee Kerr   Claudio Grajeda

Ho se Commi ee on Oversight and Reform

Rep. Carolyn B. Maloney (NY), Chairwoman
Rep. Elijah E. Cummings (MD), Chairman

Rep. Eleanor Holmes Norton (DC)
Rep. Wm. Lacy Clay (MO)
Rep. Stephen Lynch (MA)
Rep. Jim Cooper (TN)
Rep. Gerald E. Connolly (VA)
Rep. Raja Krishnamoorthi (IL)
Rep. Jamie Raskin (MD)
Rep. Harley Rouda (CA)
Rep. Debbie Wasserman Schultz (FL)
Rep. John Sarbanes (MD)
Rep. Peter Welch (VT)
Rep. Jackie Speier (CA)
Rep. Robin Kelly (IL)
Rep. Mark DeSaulnier (CA)
Rep. Brenda Lawrence (MI)
Rep. Stacey Plaskett (VI)
Rep. Ro Khanna (CA)
Rep. Jimmy Gomez (CA)
Rep. Alexandria Ocasio-Cortez (NY)
Rep. Ayanna Pressley (MA)
Rep. Rashida Tlaib (MI)

Rep. Jim Jordan (OH), Ranking Member
Rep. Paul Gosar (AZ)
Rep. Thomas Massie (KY)
Rep. Virginia Foxx (NC)
Rep. Mark Meadows (NC)
Rep. Jody Hice (GA)
Rep. Glenn Grothman (WI)
Rep. James Comer (KY)
Rep. Michael Cloud (TX)
Rep. Bob Gibbs (OH)
Rep. Clay Higgins (LA)
Rep. Ralph Norman (SC)
Rep. Chip Roy (TX)
Rep. Carol Miller (WV)
Rep. Mark Green (TN)
Rep. Kelly Armstrong (ND)
Rep. Greg Steube (FL)
Rep. Fred Keller (PA)

Majority Staff
Dave Rapallo, Staff Director
Susanne Sachsman Grooms, Deputy Staff Director & Chief Counsel
Peter Kenny, Chief Investigative Counsel
Krista A. Boyd, General Counsel
Janet H. Kim, Chief Counsel for Investigations
Russell Anello, Chief Oversight Counsel
Aryele Bradford, Communications Director

Investigative Staff

S. Tori Anderson
Aaron D. Blacksberg
Chioma Chukwu
Cassie Fields
Greta Gao
Michael Gordon
Jessica L. Heller

Gina Kim
Jason Powell
Dan Rebnord
Ricardo Brandon Rios
Erinn L. Sauer, Detailee
Amish A. Shah
Laura Waters

Operations and Press Team

Zachary Barger, Intern   Elisa LaNier
Jamitress Bowden   Kellie Larkin
Kristen Charley, Intern   Olivia Letts, Intern
Kenyatta Collins   Anna Rose Marx, Intern
James Darlson, Intern   Courtney Miller
Emma Dulaney   Noah Steimel, Intern
Evan Elizabeth Freeman, Intern Travis Stoller, Intern
Christopher Godshall, Intern   Amy Stratton
Trinity Goss   Laura Trevisani, Intern
Brandon Jacobs   Joshua Zucker

House Committee on Foreign Affairs

Rep. Eliot L. Engel (NY), Chairman

Rep. Brad Sherman (CA)
Rep. Gregory Meeks (NY)
Rep. Albio Sires (NJ)
Rep. Gerald E. Connolly (VA)
Rep. Theodore Deutch (FL)
Rep. Karen Bass (CA)
Rep. William Keating (MA)
Rep. David Cicilline (RI)
Rep. Ami Bera (CA)
Rep. Joaquin Castro (TX)
Rep. Dina Titus (NV)
Rep. Adriano Espaillat (NY)
Rep. Ted Lieu (CA)
Rep. Susan Wild (PA)
Rep. Dean Phillips (MN)
Rep. Ilhan Omar (MN)
Rep. Colin Allred (TX)
Rep. Andy Levin (MI)
Rep. Abigail Spanberger (VA)
Rep. Chrissy Houlahan (PA)
Rep. Tom Malinowski (NJ)
Rep. David Trone (MD)
Rep. Jim Costa (CA)
Rep. Juan Vargas (CA)
Rep. Vicente Gonzalez (CA)

Rep. Michael McCaul (TX) *Ranking Member*
Rep. Christopher Smith (NJ)
Rep. Steve Chabot (OH)
Rep. Joe Wilson (SC)
Rep. Scott Perry (PA)
Rep. Ted Yoho (FL)
Rep. Adam Kinzinger (IL)
Rep. Lee Zeldin (NY)
Rep. James Sensenbrenner (WI)
Rep. Ann Wagner (MO)
Rep. Brian Mast (FL)
Rep. Francis Rooney (FL)
Rep. Brian Fitzpatrick (PA)
Rep. John Curtis (UT)
Rep. Ken Buck (CO)
Rep. Ron Wright (TX)
Rep. Guy Reschenthaler (PA)
Rep. Tim Burchett (TN)
Rep. Greg Pence (IN)
Rep. Steve Watkins (KS)
Rep. Michael Guest (MS)

Majority Staff
Jason Steinbaum, Staff Director
Doug Campbell, Deputy Staff Director
Janice Kaguyutan, Chief Counsel
Laura Carey, Senior Professional Staff Member, State Department Oversight
Tim Mulvey, Communications Director
Jacqueline Ramos, Senior Professional Staff Member, Europe and Russia

Operations and Press Staff

Evan Bursey
Jacqueline Colvett

Rachel Levitan

TABLE OF CONTENTS

PREFACE

This report reflects the evidence gathered thus far by the House Permanent Select Committee on Intelligence, in coordination with the Committee on Oversight and Reform and the Committee on Foreign Affairs, as part of the House of Representatives' impeachment inquiry into Donald J. Trump, the 45th President of the United States.

The report is the culmination of an investigation that began in September 2019 and intensified over the past three months as new revelations and evidence of the President's misconduct towards Ukraine emerged. The Committees pursued the truth vigorously, but fairly, ensuring the full participation of both parties throughout the probe.

Sustained by the tireless work of more than three dozen dedicated staff across the three Committees, we issued dozens of subpoenas for documents and testimony and took more than 100 hours of deposition testimony from 17 witnesses. To provide the American people the opportunity to learn and evaluate the facts themselves, the Intelligence Committee held seven public hearings with 12 witnesses—including three requested by the Republican Minority—that totaled more than 30 hours.

At the outset, I want to recognize my late friend and colleague Elijah E. Cummings, whose grace and commitment to justice served as our North Star throughout this investigation. I would also like to thank my colleagues Eliot L. Engel and Carolyn B. Maloney, chairs respectively of the Foreign Affairs and Oversight and Reform Committees, as well as the Members of those Committees, many of whom provided invaluable contributions. Members of the Intelligence Committee, as well, worked selflessly and collaboratively throughout this investigation. Finally, I am grateful to Speaker Nancy Pelosi for the trust she placed in our Committees to conduct this work and for her wise counsel throughout.

I also want to thank the dedicated professional staff of the Intelligence Committee, who worked ceaselessly and with remarkable poise and ability. My deepest gratitude goes to Daniel Goldman, Rheanne Wirkkala, Maher Bitar, Timothy Bergreen, Patrick Boland, Daniel Noble, Nicolas Mitchell, Sean Misko, Patrick Fallon, Diana Pilipenko, William Evans, Ariana Rowberry, Wells Bennett, and William Wu. Additional Intelligence Committee staff members also assured that the important oversight work of the Committee continued, even as we were required to take on the additional responsibility of conducting a key part of the House impeachment inquiry. Finally, I would like to thank the devoted and outstanding staff of the Committee on Oversight and Reform, including but not limited to Dave Rapallo, Susanne Sachsman Grooms, Peter Kenny, Krista Boyd, and Janet Kim, as well as Laura Carey from the Committee on Foreign Affairs.

* * *

In his farewell address, President George Washington warned of a moment when "cunning, ambitious, and unprincipled men will be enabled to subvert the power of the people and to usurp for themselves the reins of government, destroying afterwards the very engines which have lifted them to unjust dominion."

The Framers of the Constitution well understood that an individual could one day occupy the Office of the President who would place his personal or political interests above those of the nation. Having just won hard-fought independence from a King with unbridled authority, they were attuned to the dangers of an executive who lacked fealty to the law and the Constitution.

In response, the Framers adopted a tool used by the British Parliament for several hundred years to constrain the Crown—the power of impeachment. Unlike in Britain, where impeachment was typically reserved for inferior officers but not the King himself, impeachment in our untested democracy was specifically intended to serve as the ultimate form of accountability for a duly-elected President. Rather than a mechanism to overturn an election, impeachment was explicitly contemplated as a remedy of last resort for a president who fails to faithfully execute his oath of office "to preserve, protect and defend the Constitution of the United States."

Accordingly, the Constitution confers the power to impeach the president on Congress, stating that the president shall be removed from office upon conviction for "Treason, Bribery, or other high Crimes and Misdemeanors." While the Constitutional standard for removal from office is justly a high one, it is nonetheless an essential check and balance on the authority of the occupant of the Office of the President, particularly when that occupant represents a continuing threat to our fundamental democratic norms, values, and laws.

Alexander Hamilton explained that impeachment was not designed to cover only criminal violations, but also crimes against the American people. "The subjects of its jurisdiction," Hamilton wrote, "are those offenses which proceed from the misconduct of public men, or, in other words, from the abuse or violation of some public trust. They are of a nature which may with peculiar propriety be denominated political, as they relate chiefly to injuries done immediately to the society itself."

Similarly, future Associate Justice of the United States Supreme Court James Wilson, a delegate from Pennsylvania at the Constitutional Convention, distinguished impeachable offenses from those that reside "within the sphere of ordinary jurisprudence." As he noted, "impeachments are confined to political characters, to political crimes and misdemeanors, and to political punishments."

* * *

As this report details, the impeachment inquiry has found that President Trump, personally and acting through agents within and outside of the U.S. government, solicited the interference of a foreign government, Ukraine, to benefit his reelection. In furtherance of this scheme, President Trump conditioned official acts on a public announcement by the new Ukrainian President, Volodymyr Zelensky, of politically-motivated investigations, including one into President Trump's domestic political opponent. In pressuring President Zelensky to carry out his demand, President Trump withheld a White House meeting desperately sought by the Ukrainian President and critical U.S. military assistance to fight Russian aggression in eastern Ukraine.

The President engaged in this course of conduct for the benefit of his own presidential reelection, to harm the election prospects of a political rival, and to influence our nation's upcoming presidential election to his advantage. In doing so, the President placed his own personal and political interests above the national interests of the United States, sought to undermine the integrity of the U.S. presidential election process, and endangered U.S. national security.

At the center of this investigation is the memorandum prepared following President Trump's July 25, 2019, phone call with Ukraine's President, which the White House declassified and released under significant public pressure. The call record alone is stark evidence of misconduct; a demonstration of the President's prioritization of his personal political benefit over the national interest. In response to President Zelensky's appreciation for vital U.S. military assistance, which President Trump froze without explanation, President Trump asked for "a favor though": two specific investigations designed to assist his reelection efforts.

Our investigation determined that this telephone call was neither the start nor the end of President Trump's efforts to bend U.S. foreign policy for his personal gain. Rather, it was a dramatic crescendo within a months-long campaign driven by President Trump in which senior U.S. officials, including the Vice President, the Secretary of State, the Acting Chief of Staff, the Secretary of Energy, and others were either knowledgeable of or active participants in an effort to extract from a foreign nation the personal political benefits sought by the President.

The investigation revealed the nature and extent of the President's misconduct, notwithstanding an unprecedented campaign of obstruction by the President and his Administration to prevent the Committees from obtaining documentary evidence and testimony. A dozen witnesses followed President Trump's orders, defying voluntary requests and lawful subpoenas, and refusing to testify. The White House, Department of State, Department of Defense, Office of Management and Budget, and Department of Energy refused to produce a single document in response to our subpoenas.

Ultimately, this sweeping effort to stonewall the House of Representatives' "sole Power of Impeachment" under the Constitution failed because witnesses courageously came forward and testified in response to lawful process. The report that follows was only possible because of their sense of duty and devotion to their country and its Constitution.

Nevertheless, there remain unanswered questions, and our investigation must continue, even as we transmit our report to the Judiciary Committee. Given the proximate threat of further presidential attempts to solicit foreign interference in our next election, we cannot wait to make a referral until our efforts to obtain additional testimony and documents wind their way through the courts. The evidence of the President's misconduct is overwhelming, and so too is the evidence of his obstruction of Congress. Indeed, it would be hard to imagine a stronger or more complete case of obstruction than that demonstrated by the President since the inquiry began.

The damage the President has done to our relationship with a key strategic partner will be remedied over time, and Ukraine continues to enjoy strong bipartisan support in Congress. But the damage to our system of checks and balances, and to the balance of power within our three branches of government, will be long-lasting and potentially irrevocable if the President's ability to stonewall Congress goes unchecked. Any future President will feel empowered to resist an investigation into their own wrongdoing, malfeasance, or corruption, and the result will be a nation at far greater risk of all three.

* * *

The decision to move forward with an impeachment inquiry is not one we took lightly. Under the best of circumstances, impeachment is a wrenching process for the nation. I resisted calls to undertake an impeachment investigation for many months on that basis, notwithstanding the existence of presidential misconduct that I believed to be deeply unethical and damaging to our democracy. The alarming events and actions detailed in this report, however, left us with no choice but to proceed.

In making the decision to move forward, we were struck by the fact that the President's misconduct was not an isolated occurrence, nor was it the product of a naïve president. Instead, the efforts to involve Ukraine in our 2020 presidential election were undertaken by a President who himself was elected in 2016 with the benefit of an unprecedented and sweeping campaign of election interference undertaken by Russia in his favor, which the President welcomed and utilized.

Having witnessed the degree to which interference by a foreign power in 2016 harmed our democracy, President Trump cannot credibly claim ignorance to its pernicious effects. Even more pointedly, the President's July call with Ukrainian President Zelensky, in which he solicited an investigation to damage his most feared 2020 opponent, came the day after Special Counsel Robert Mueller testified to Congress about Russia's efforts to damage his 2016 opponent and his urgent warning of the dangers of further foreign interference in the next election. With this backdrop, the solicitation of new foreign intervention was the act of a president unbound, not one chastened by experience. It was the act of a president who viewed himself as unaccountable and determined to use his vast official powers to secure his reelection.

This repeated and pervasive threat to our democratic electoral process added urgency to our work. On October 3, 2019, even as our Committee was engaged in this inquiry, President Trump publicly declared anew that other countries should open investigations into his chief political rival, saying, "China should start an investigation into the Bidens," and "President Zelensky, if it were me, I would recommend that they start an investigation into the Bidens." When a reporter asked the President what he hoped Ukraine's President would do following the July 25 call, President Trump, seeking to dispel any doubt as to his continuing intention, responded: "Well, I would think that, if they were honest about it, they'd start a major investigation into the Bidens. It's a very simple answer."

By doubling down on his misconduct and declaring that his July 25 call with President Zelensky was "perfect," President Trump has shown a continued willingness to use the power of his office to seek foreign intervention in our next election. His Acting Chief of Staff, Mick Mulvaney, in the course of admitting that the President had linked security assistance to Ukraine to the announcement of one of his desired investigations, told the American people to "get over

10

it." In these statements and actions, the President became the author of his own impeachment inquiry. The question presented by the set of facts enumerated in this report may be as simple as that posed by the President and his chief of staff's brazenness: is the remedy of impeachment warranted for a president who would use the power of his office to coerce foreign interference in a U.S. election, or is that now a mere perk of the office that Americans must simply "get over"?

* * *

Those watching the impeachment hearings might have been struck by how little discrepancy there was between the witnesses called by the Majority and Minority. Indeed, most of the facts presented in the pages that follow are uncontested. The broad outlines, as well as many of the details of the President's scheme, have been presented by the witnesses with remarkable consistency. There will always be some variation in the testimony of multiple people witnessing the same events, but few of the differences here go to the heart of the matter. And so, it may have been all the more surprising to the public to see very disparate reactions to the testimony by the Members of Congress from each party.

If there was one ill the Founders feared as much as that of an unfit president, it may have been that of excessive factionalism. Although the Framers viewed parties as necessary, they also endeavored to structure the new government in such a way as to minimize the "violence of faction." As George Washington warned in his farewell address, "the common and continual mischiefs of the spirit of party are sufficient to make it the interest and duty of a wise people to discourage and restrain it."

Today, we may be witnessing a collision between the power of a remedy meant to curb presidential misconduct and the power of faction determined to defend against the use of that remedy on a president of the same party. But perhaps even more corrosive to our democratic system of governance, the President and his allies are making a comprehensive attack on the very idea of fact and truth. How can a democracy survive without acceptance of a common set of experiences?

America remains the beacon of democracy and opportunity for freedom-loving people around the world. From their homes and their jail cells, from their public squares and their refugee camps, from their waking hours until their last breath, individuals fighting human rights abuses, journalists uncovering and exposing corruption, persecuted minorities struggling to survive and preserve their faith, and countless others around the globe just hoping for a better life look to America. What we do will determine what they see, and whether America remains a nation committed to the rule of law.

As Benjamin Franklin departed the Constitutional Convention, he was asked, "what have we got? A Republic or a Monarchy?" He responded simply: "A Republic, if you can keep it."

Adam B. Schiff
Chairman, House Permanent Select Committee on Intelligence

EXECUTIVE SUMMARY

The impeachment inquiry into Donald J. Trump, the 45th President of the United States, uncovered a months-long effort by President Trump to use the powers of his office to solicit foreign interference on his behalf in the 2020 election. As described in this executive summary and the report that follows, President Trump's scheme subverted U.S. foreign policy toward Ukraine and undermined our national security in favor of two politically motivated investigations that would help his presidential reelection campaign. The President demanded that the newly-elected Ukrainian president, Volodymyr Zelensky, publicly announce investigations into a political rival that he apparently feared the most, former Vice President Joe Biden, and into a discredited theory that it was Ukraine, not Russia, that interfered in the 2016 presidential election. To compel the Ukrainian President to do his political bidding, President Trump conditioned two official acts on the public announcement of the investigations: a coveted White House visit and critical U.S. military assistance Ukraine needed to fight its Russian adversary.

During a July 25, 2019, call between President Trump and President Zelensky, President Zelensky expressed gratitude for U.S. military assistance. President Trump immediately responded by asking President Zelensky to "do us a favor though" and openly pressed for Ukraine to investigate former Vice President Biden and the 2016 conspiracy theory. In turn, President Zelensky assured President Trump that he would pursue the investigation and reiterated his interest in the White House meeting. Although President Trump's scheme intentionally bypassed many career personnel, it was undertaken with the knowledge and approval of senior Administration officials, including the President's Acting Chief of Staff Mick Mulvaney, Secretary of State Mike Pompeo, and Secretary of Energy Rick Perry. In fact, at a press conference weeks after public revelations about the scheme, Mr. Mulvaney publicly acknowledged that the President directly tied the hold on military aid to his desire to get Ukraine to conduct a political investigation, telling Americans to "get over it."

President Trump and his senior officials may see nothing wrong with using the power of the Office of the President to pressure a foreign country to help the President's reelection campaign. Indeed, President Trump continues to encourage Ukraine and other foreign countries to engage in the same kind of election interference today. However, the Founding Fathers prescribed a remedy for a chief executive who places his personal interests above those of the country: impeachment. Accordingly, as part of the House of Representatives' impeachment inquiry, the Permanent Select Committee on Intelligence, in coordination with the Committees on Oversight and Reform and Foreign Affairs, was compelled to undertake a serious, sober, and expeditious investigation into whether the President's misconduct warrants that remedy.

In response, President Trump engaged in an unprecedented campaign of obstruction of this impeachment inquiry. Nevertheless, due in large measure to patriotic and courageous public servants who provided the Committees with direct evidence of the President's actions, the Committees uncovered significant misconduct on the part of the President of the United States. As required under House Resolution 660, the Intelligence Committee, in consultation with the Committees on Oversight and Reform and Foreign Affairs, has prepared this report to detail the evidence uncovered to date, which will now be transmitted to the Judiciary Committee for its consideration.

SECTION I—THE PRESIDENT'S MISCONDUCT

The President Conditioned a White House Meeting and Military Aid to Ukraine on a Public Announcement of Investigations Beneficial to his Reelection Campaign

The President's Request for a Political Favor

On the morning of July 25, 2019, President Donald Trump settled in to the White House Executive Residence to join a telephone call with President Volodymyr Zelensky of Ukraine. It had been more than three months since President Zelensky, a political neophyte, had been swept into office in a landslide victory on a platform of rooting out corruption and ending the war between his country and Russia. The day of his election, April 21, President Zelensky spoke briefly with President Trump, who had called to congratulate him and invite him to a visit at the White House. As of July 25, no White House meeting had materialized.

As is typical for telephone calls with other heads of state, staff members from the National Security Council (NSC) convened in the White House Situation Room to listen to the call and take notes, which would later be compiled into a memorandum that would constitute the U.S. government's official record of the call. NSC staff had prepared a standard package of talking points for the President based on official U.S. policy. The talking points included recommendations to encourage President Zelensky to continue to promote anti-corruption reforms in Ukraine, a pillar of American foreign policy in the country as far back as its independence in the 1990s when Ukraine first rid itself of Kremlin control.

This call would deviate significantly from that script. Shortly before he was patched through to President Zelensky, President Trump spoke with Gordon Sondland, who had donated $1 million to President Trump's 2016 presidential inauguration and whom the President had appointed as the United States Ambassador to the European Union. Ambassador Sondland had helped lay the groundwork for a very different kind of call between the two Presidents.

Ambassador Sondland had relayed a message to President Zelensky six days earlier that "assurances to run a fully transparent investigation" and "turn over every stone" were necessary in his call with President Trump. Ambassador Sondland understood these phrases to refer to two investigations politically beneficial to the President's reelection campaign: one into former Vice President Joe Biden and a Ukrainian gas company called Burisma, of which his son sat on the board, and the other into a discredited conspiracy theory alleging that Ukraine, not Russia, interfered in the 2016 U.S. election. The allegations about Vice President Biden were without evidence, and the U.S. Intelligence Community had unanimously determined that Russia, not Ukraine, interfered in the 2016 election to help the candidacy of Donald Trump. Despite the falsehoods, Ambassador Sondland would make it clear to Ukrainian officials that the public announcement of these investigations was a prerequisite for the coveted White House meeting with President Trump, an effort that would help the President's reelection campaign.

The White House meeting was not the only official act that President Trump conditioned on the announcement of these investigations. Several weeks before his phone call with President Zelensky, President Trump ordered a hold on nearly $400 million of congressionally-

13

appropriated security assistance to Ukraine that provided Kyiv essential support as it sought to repel Russian forces that were occupying Crimea and inflicting casualties in the eastern region of the country. The President's decision to freeze the aid, made without explanation, sent shock waves through the Department of Defense (DOD), the Department of State, and the NSC, which uniformly supported providing this assistance to our strategic partner. Although the suspension of aid had not been made public by the day of the call between the two Presidents, officials at the Ukrainian embassy in Washington had already asked American officials about the status of the vital military assistance.

At the outset of the conversation on July 25, President Zelensky thanked President Trump for the "great support in the area of defense" provided by the United States to date. He then indicated that Ukraine would soon be prepared to purchase additional Javelin anti-tank missiles from the United States as part of this defense cooperation. President Trump immediately responded with his own request: "I would like you to do us a favor though," which was "to find out what happened" with alleged Ukrainian interference in the 2016 election.

President Trump then asked President Zelensky "to look into" former Vice President Biden's role in encouraging Ukraine to remove a prosecutor widely viewed by the United States and numerous European partners to be corrupt. In so doing, President Trump gave currency to a baseless allegation that Vice President Biden wanted to remove the corrupt prosecutor because he was investigating Burisma, a company on whose board the Vice President's son sat at the time.

Over the course of the roughly thirty-minute call, President Trump repeated these false allegations and pressed the Ukrainian President to consult with his personal attorney, Rudy Giuliani, who had been publicly advocating for months for Ukraine to initiate these specific investigations. President Zelensky promised that he would "work on the investigation of the case." Later in the call, he thanked President Trump for his invitation to join him at the White House, following up immediately with a comment that, "[o]n the other hand," he would "ensure" that Ukraine pursued "the investigation" that President Trump had requested.

During the call, President Trump also disparaged Marie Yovanovitch, the former U.S. ambassador to Ukraine, who championed anti-corruption reforms in the country, and whom President Trump had unceremoniously removed months earlier following a smear campaign waged against her by Mr. Giuliani and others. President Trump claimed that she was "bad news" and was "going to go through some things." He praised the current prosecutor at the time, who was widely viewed as corrupt and who helped initiate the smear campaign against her, calling him "very good" and "very fair."

Hearing the call as it transpired, several White House staff members became alarmed. Far from giving the "full-throated endorsement of the Ukraine reform agenda" that had been hoped for, the President instead demanded a political investigation into an American—the presidential candidate he evidently feared most, Joe Biden.

Lieutenant Colonel Alexander Vindman, an NSC staff member responsible for Ukraine policy who listened to the call, immediately reported his concerns to NSC lawyers. His supervisor, NSC Senior Director for Europe and Russia Timothy Morrison, also reported the call to the lawyers, worrying that the call would be "damaging" if leaked publicly. In response, the lawyers placed the memorandum summarizing the call onto a highly classified server, significantly limiting access to the materials.

The call record would not remain hidden forever. On September 25, 2019, facing immense public pressure to reveal the contents of the call and following the announcement the previous day of a formal impeachment inquiry in the House of Representatives into President Trump's actions toward Ukraine, the White House publicly released the memorandum of the July 25 call.

The record of the call would help explain for those involved in Ukraine policy in the U.S. government, the Congress, and the public why President Trump, his personal attorney, Mr. Giuliani, his hand-picked appointees in charge of Ukraine issues, and various senior Administration officials would go to great lengths to withhold a coveted White House meeting and critical military aid from Ukraine at a time when it served as a bulwark against Russian aggression in Europe.

The answer was as simple as it was inimical to our national security and election integrity: the President was withholding officials acts while soliciting something of value to his reelection campaign—an investigation into his political rival.

The story of that scheme follows.

* * *

The President Removed Anti-Corruption Champion Ambassador Yovanovitch

On April 24, 2019, President Trump abruptly called back to Washington the United States Ambassador to Ukraine, Marie "Masha" Yovanovitch, after a ruthless smear campaign was waged against her. She was known throughout Ukraine and among her peers for aggressively advocating for anti-corruption reforms consistent with U.S. foreign policy and only recently had been asked to extend her stay in Ukraine. Her effectiveness in anti-corruption efforts earned her enemies in Kyiv and in Washington. As Deputy Assistant Secretary of State George Kent testified in praising Ambassador Yovanovitch: "You can't promote principled anticorruption action without pissing off corrupt people."

Beginning on March 20, *The Hill* newspaper published several op-eds attacking Ambassador Yovanovitch and former Vice President Joe Biden, relying on information from a Ukrainian prosecutor, Yuriy Lutsenko, who was widely viewed to be corrupt. Mr. Lutsenko had served as the chief prosecutor in Ukraine under the then-incumbent president who lost to Volodymyr Zelensky in April 2019. Although he would later recant many of his allegations, Mr. Lutsenko falsely accused Ambassador Yovanovitch of speaking negatively about President Trump and giving Mr. Lutsenko a "do-not-prosecute list."

The attacks against Ambassador Yovanovitch were amplified by prominent, close allies of President Trump, including Mr. Giuliani and his associates, Sean Hannity, and Donald Trump Jr. President Trump tweeted the smears himself just a month before he recalled the Ambassador from Ukraine. In the face of attacks driven by Mr. Lutsenko and the President's allies, Ambassador Yovanovitch and other senior State Department officials asked Secretary of State Mike Pompeo to issue a statement of support for her and for the U.S. Embassy in Ukraine. The Secretary declined, fearing that President Trump might publicly undermine those efforts, possibly through a tweet.

Following a ceremony in which she presented an award of courage to the family of a young female anti-corruption activist killed in Ukraine for her work, Ambassador Yovanovitch received an urgent call from the State Department regarding her "security," and imploring her to take the first plane back to Washington. When she arrived, she was informed that she had done nothing wrong, but that the President had lost confidence in her. She was told to leave her post as soon as possible.

In her place, the President would designate three new agents to spearhead Ukraine policy, political appointees far more willing to engage in an improper "domestic political errand" than an ambassador known for her efforts to fight corruption.

The President's Hand-Picked Agents Began the Scheme

Just three days before Ambassador Yovanovitch's abrupt recall to Washington, President Trump had his first telephone call with President-elect Zelensky. During that conversation, President Trump congratulated the Ukrainian leader on his victory, complimented him on his country's Miss Universe Pageant contestants, and invited him to visit the White House. A White House meeting would help demonstrate the United States' strong support for Ukraine as it fought a hot war with Russia and attempted to negotiate an end to the conflict with Russian President Vladimir Putin, as well as to bolster President-elect Zelensky's standing with his own people as he sought to deliver on his promised anti-corruption agenda. Although the White House's public summary of the call included some discussion of a commitment to "root out corruption," President Trump did not mention corruption at all.

Shortly after the conversation, President Trump asked Vice President Mike Pence to attend President Zelensky's inauguration. Vice President Pence confirmed directly to President Zelensky his intention to attend during a phone conversation on April 23, and Vice President Pence's staff and the U.S. Embassy in Kyiv began preparations for the trip.

At the same time, President Trump's personal attorney, Mr. Giuliani, intensified his campaign to pressure Ukraine's newly-elected President to initiate investigations into Joe Biden, who had officially entered the race for the Democratic nomination on April 25, and the baseless conspiracy theory about Ukrainian interference in the 2016 election. On May 9, the *New York Times* published an article in which Mr. Giuliani declared that he intended to travel to Ukraine on behalf of his client, President Trump, in order to meddle in an investigation. After public backlash, Mr. Giuliani canceled the trip, blaming "some bad people" around President Zelensky. Days later, President Trump rescinded the plans for Vice President Pence to attend President

Zelensky's inauguration, which had not yet been scheduled. The staff member planning the trip was not provided an explanation for the about-face, but staff in the U.S. Embassy in Kyiv were disappointed that President Zelensky would not receive a "high level" show of support from the United States.

In Vice President Pence's stead, Secretary of Energy Rick Perry led the American delegation to the Ukrainian President's inauguration. Ambassador Sondland, Special Representative for Ukraine Negotiations Ambassador Kurt Volker, and Lt. Col. Vindman also attended. In comments that would foreshadow troubling events to come, Lt. Col. Vindman warned President Zelensky to stay out of U.S. domestic politics to avoid jeopardizing the bipartisan support Ukraine enjoyed in Congress.

The delegation returned to the United States impressed with President Zelensky, especially his focus on anti-corruption reforms. Ambassador Sondland quickly organized a meeting with President Trump in the Oval Office on May 23, attended by most of the other members of the delegation. The three political appointees, who would describe themselves as the "Three Amigos," relayed their positive impression of President Zelensky to President Trump and encouraged him to schedule the Oval Office meeting he promised in his April 21 phone call with the new leader.

President Trump reacted poorly to the suggestion, claiming that Ukraine "tried to take me down" in 2016. In order to schedule a White House visit for President Zelensky, President Trump told the delegation that they would have to "talk to Rudy." Ambassador Sondland testified that he understood the President's instruction to be a directive to work with Mr. Giuliani if they hoped to advance relations with Ukraine. President Trump directed the three senior U.S. government officials to assist Mr. Giuliani's efforts, which, it would soon become clear, were exclusively for the benefit of the President's reelection campaign.

As the Three Amigos were given responsibility over the U.S. government's Ukraine portfolio, Bill Taylor, a former Ambassador to Ukraine, was considering whether to come out of retirement to accept a request to succeed Ambassador Yovanovitch in Kyiv. As of May 26, Ambassador Taylor was "still struggling with the decision," and, in particular, whether anyone can "hope to succeed with the Giuliani-Biden issue swirling." After receiving assurances from Secretary Pompeo that U.S. policy toward Ukraine would not change, Ambassador Taylor accepted the position and arrived in Kyiv on June 17. Ambassador Taylor would quickly come to observe an "irregular channel" led by Mr. Giuliani that, over time, began to undermine the official channel of diplomatic relations with Ukraine. Mr. Giuliani would prove to be, as the President's National Security Advisor Ambassador John Bolton would tell a colleague, a "hand grenade that was going to blow everyone up."

The President Froze Vital Military Assistance

For fiscal year 2019, Congress appropriated and authorized $391 million in security assistance to Ukraine: $250 million in funds administered by DOD and $141 million in funds administered by the State Department. On June 18, DOD issued a press release announcing its intention to provide $250 million in taxpayer-funded security assistance to Ukraine following the certification that all legitimate conditions on the aid, including anti-corruption reforms, had been met. Shortly after this announcement, however, both the Office of Management and Budget (OMB) and DOD received inquiries from the President related to the funds. At that time, and throughout the next few months, support for Ukraine security assistance was overwhelming and unanimous among all of the relevant agencies and within Congress.

By July 3, OMB blocked a Congressional notification which would have cleared the way for the release of $141 million in State Department security assistance funds. By July 12, President Trump had placed a hold on all military support funding for Ukraine. On July 18, OMB announced the hold to all of the relevant agencies and indicated that it was directed by the President. No other reason was provided.

During a series of policy meetings involving increasingly senior officials, the uniform and consistent position of all policymaking agencies supported the release of funding. Ukraine experts at DOD, the State Department, and the NSC argued that it was in the national security interest of the United States to continue to support Ukraine. As Mr. Morrison testified, "The United States aids Ukraine and her people so that they can fight Russia over there, and we don't have to fight Russia here."

Agency officials also expressed concerns about the legality of President Trump's direction to withhold assistance to Ukraine that Congress had already appropriated for this express purpose. Two OMB career officials, including one of its legal counsels, would resign, in part, over concerns regarding the hold.

By July 25, the date of President Trump's call with President Zelensky, DOD was also receiving inquiries from Ukrainian officials about the status of the security assistance. Nevertheless, President Trump continued to withhold the funding to Ukraine without explanation, against the interests of U.S. national security, and over the objections of these career experts.

The President Conditioned a White House Meeting on Investigations

By the time Ukrainian officials were first learning about an issue with the anticipated military assistance, the President's hand-picked representatives to Ukraine had already informed their Ukrainian counterparts that President Zelensky's coveted White House meeting would only happen after Ukraine committed to pursuing the two political investigations that President Trump and Mr. Giuliani demanded.

Ambassador Sondland was unequivocal in describing this conditionality, testifying, "I know that members of this committee frequently frame these complicated issues in the form of a simple question: Was there a quid pro quo? As I testified previously with regard to the requested White House call and the White House meeting, the answer is yes." Ambassadors Sondland and Volker worked to obtain the necessary assurance from President Zelensky that he would personally commit to initiate the investigations in order to secure both.

On July 2, in Toronto, Canada, Ambassador Volker conveyed the message directly to President Zelensky, specifically referencing the "Giuliani factor" in President Zelensky's engagement with the United States. For his part, Mr. Giuliani made clear to Ambassadors Sondland and Volker, who were directly communicating with the Ukrainians, that a White House meeting would not occur until Ukraine announced its pursuit of the two political investigations. After observing Mr. Giuliani's role in the ouster of a U.S. Ambassador and learning of his influence with the President, Ukrainian officials soon understood that "the key for many things is Rudi [sic]."

On July 10, Ambassador Bolton hosted a meeting in the White House with two senior Ukrainian officials, several American officials, including Ambassadors Sondland and Volker, Secretary Perry, Dr. Fiona Hill, Senior Director for Europe and Russia at the NSC, and Lt. Col. Vindman. As had become customary each time Ukrainian officials met with their American counterparts, the Ukrainians asked about the long-delayed White House meeting. Ambassador Bolton demurred, but Ambassador Sondland spoke up, revealing that he had worked out an arrangement with Acting Chief of Staff Mick Mulvaney to schedule the White House visit after Ukraine initiated the "investigations." Ambassador Bolton "stiffened" and quickly ended the meeting.

Undaunted, Ambassador Sondland ushered many of the attendees to the Ward Room downstairs to continue their discussion. In the second meeting, Ambassador Sondland explained that he had an agreement with Mr. Mulvaney that the White House visit would come only after Ukraine announced the Burisma/Biden and 2016 Ukraine election interference investigations. At this second meeting, both Lt. Col. Vindman and Dr. Hill objected to intertwining a "domestic political errand" with official foreign policy, and they indicated that a White House meeting would have to go through proper channels.

Following these discussions, Dr. Hill reported back to Ambassador Bolton, who told her to "go and tell [the NSC Legal Advisor] that I am not part of whatever drug deal Sondland and Mulvaney are cooking up on this." Both Dr. Hill and Lt. Col. Vindman separately reported the incident to the NSC Legal Advisor.

The President's Agents Pursued a "Drug Deal"

Over the next two weeks, Ambassadors Sondland and Volker worked closely with Mr. Giuliani and senior Ukrainian and American officials to arrange a telephone call between President Trump and President Zelensky and to ensure that the Ukrainian President explicitly promised to undertake the political investigations required by President Trump to schedule the White House meeting. As Ambassador Sondland would later testify: "Mr. Giuliani was expressing the desires of the President of the United States, and we knew these investigations were important to the President."

On July 19, Ambassador Volker had breakfast with Mr. Giuliani and his associate, Lev Parnas, at the Trump Hotel in Washington, D.C. Mr. Parnas would subsequently be indicted for campaign finance violations as part of an investigation that remains ongoing. During the conversation, Ambassador Volker stressed his belief that the attacks being leveled publicly against Vice President Biden related to Ukraine were false and that the former Vice President was "a person of integrity." He counseled Mr. Giuliani that the Ukrainian prosecutor pushing the false narrative, Mr. Lutsenko, was promoting "a self-serving narrative to preserve himself in power." Mr. Giuliani agreed, but his promotion of Mr. Lutsenko's false accusations for the benefit of President Trump did not cease. Ambassador Volker also offered to help arrange an in-person meeting between Mr. Giuliani and Andriy Yermak, one of President Zelensky's most trusted advisors, which would later take place in Madrid, Spain in early August.

After the breakfast meeting at the Trump Hotel, Ambassador Volker reported back to Ambassadors Sondland and Taylor about his conversation with Mr. Giuliani, writing in a text message that, "Most impt [sic] is for Zelensky to say that he will help investigation—and address any specific personnel issues—if there are any," likely referencing President Zelensky's decision to remove Mr. Lutsenko as prosecutor general, a decision with which Mr. Giuliani disagreed. The same day, Ambassador Sondland spoke with President Zelensky and recommended that the Ukrainian leader tell President Trump that he "will leave no stone unturned" regarding the political investigations during the upcoming presidential phone call.

Ambassador Sondland emailed several top Administration officials, including Secretary of State Pompeo, Acting Chief of Staff Mulvaney, and Secretary Perry, stating that President Zelensky confirmed that he would "assure" President Trump that "he intends to run a fully transparent investigation and will 'turn over every stone.'" According to Ambassador Sondland, he was referring in the email to the Burisma/Biden and 2016 election interference investigations. Secretary Perry and Mr. Mulvaney responded affirmatively that the call would soon take place, and Ambassador Sondland testified later that "everyone was in the loop" on plans to condition the White House meeting on the announcement of political investigations beneficial to President Trump. The arrangement troubled the Ukrainian President, who "did not want to be used as a pawn in a U.S. reelection campaign."

The President Pressed President Zelensky to Do a Political Favor

On the morning of July 25, Ambassador Volker sent a text message to President Zelensky's top aide, Mr. Yermak, less than 30 minutes before the presidential call. He stated: "Heard from White House—assuming President Z convinces trump he will investigate / 'get to the bottom of what happened' in 2016, we will nail down date for visit to Washington. Good luck!" Shortly before the call, Ambassador Sondland spoke directly with President Trump.

President Zelensky followed this advice during his conversation with President Trump. President Zelensky assured that he would pursue the investigations that President Trump had discussed—into the Bidens and 2016 election interference—and, in turn, pressed for the White House meeting that remained outstanding.

The following day, Ambassadors Volker, Sondland, and Taylor met with President Zelensky in Kyiv. The Ukrainian President told them that President Trump had mentioned "sensitive issues" three times during the previous day's phone call. Following the meeting with the Ukrainian leader, Ambassador Sondland had a private, one-on-one conversation with Mr. Yermak in which they discussed "the issue of investigations." He then retired to lunch at an outdoor restaurant terrace with State Department aides where he called President Trump directly from his cellphone. The White House confirmed that the conversation lasted five minutes.

At the outset of the call, President Trump asked Ambassador Sondland whether President Zelensky "was going to do the investigation" that President Trump had raised with President Zelensky the day before. Ambassador Sondland stated that President Zelensky was "going to do it" and "would do anything you ask him to." According to David Holmes, the State Department aide sitting closest to Ambassador Sondland and who overheard the President's voice on the phone, Ambassador Sondland and President Trump spoke only about the investigation in their discussion about Ukraine. The President made no mention of other major issues of importance in Ukraine, including President Zelensky's aggressive anti-corruption reforms and the ongoing war it was fighting against Russian-led forces in eastern Ukraine.

After hanging up the phone, Ambassador Sondland explained to Mr. Holmes that President Trump "did not give a shit about Ukraine." Rather, the President cared only about "big stuff" that benefited him personally, like "the Biden investigation that Mr. Giuliani was pitching," and that President Trump had pushed for in his July 25 call with the Ukrainian leader. Ambassador Sondland did not recall referencing Biden specifically, but he did not dispute Mr. Holmes' recollection of the call with the President or Ambassador Sondland's subsequent discussion with Mr. Holmes.

The President's Representatives Ratcheted up Pressure on the Ukrainian President

In the weeks following the July 25 call, the President's hand-picked representatives increased the President's pressure campaign on Ukrainian government officials—in person, over the phone, and by text message—to secure a public announcement of the investigations beneficial to President Trump's reelection campaign.

In discussions with Ukrainian officials, Ambassador Sondland understood that President Trump did not require that Ukraine *conduct* investigations as a prerequisite for the White House meeting so much as publicly *announce* the investigations—making clear that the goal was not the investigations, but the political benefit Trump would derive from their announcement and the cloud they might put over a political opponent.

On August 2, President Zelensky's advisor, Mr. Yermak, traveled to Madrid to meet Mr. Giuliani in person. There, they agreed that Ukraine would issue a public statement, and they discussed potential dates for a White House meeting. A few days later, Ambassador Volker told Mr. Giuliani that it "would be good" if Mr. Giuliani would report to "the boss," President Trump, about "the results" of his Madrid discussion so that President Trump would finally agree to a White House visit by President Zelensky.

On August 9, Ambassador Volker and Mr. Giuliani spoke twice by phone, and Ambassador Sondland spoke twice to the White House for a total of about 20 minutes. In a text message to Ambassador Volker later that day, Ambassador Sondland wrote, "I think potus [sic] really wants the deliverable," which Ambassador Sondland acknowledged was the public statement announcing the two political investigations sought by President Trump and Mr. Giuliani.

The following day, Ambassador Sondland briefed State Department Counselor Ulrich Brechbuhl, a top advisor to Secretary Pompeo, on these discussions about President Zelensky issuing a statement that would include an announcement of the two political investigations. Ambassador Sondland also emailed Secretary Pompeo directly, copying the State Department's executive secretary and Mr. Brechbuhl, to inform them about the agreement for President Zelensky to give the press conference. He expected to see a draft of the statement, which would be "delivered for our review in a day or two." Ambassador Sondland noted his hope that the draft statement would "make the boss happy enough to authorize an invitation."

On August 12, Mr. Yermak sent the proposed statement to Ambassador Volker, but it lacked specific references to the two investigations politically beneficial to President Trump's reelection campaign. The following morning, Ambassadors Sondland and Volker spoke with Mr. Giuliani, who made clear that if the statement "doesn't say Burisma and 2016, it's not credible." Ambassador Volker revised the statement following this direction to include those references and returned it to the Ukrainian President's aide.

Mr. Yermak balked at getting drawn into U.S. politics and asked Ambassador Volker whether the United States had inquired about investigations through any appropriate Department of Justice channels. The answer was no, and several witnesses testified that a request to a foreign country to investigate a U.S. citizen "for political reasons" goes "against everything" the United States sought to promote in eastern Europe, specifically the rule of law. Ambassador Volker eventually agreed with Mr. Yermak that the announcement of the Biden/Burisma and 2016 elections investigations would "look like it would play into our domestic politics," so the statement was temporarily "shelved."

Nevertheless, Ambassador Sondland, in accordance with President Trump's wishes, continued to pursue the statement into early September 2019.

Ukrainians Inquired about the President's Hold on Security Assistance

Once President Trump placed security assistance on hold in July, "it was inevitable that it was eventually going to come out." On July 25, DOD officials learned that diplomats at the Ukrainian Embassy in Washington had made multiple overtures to DOD and the State Department "asking about security assistance." Separately, two different contacts at the Ukrainian Embassy approached Ambassador Volker's special advisor, Catherine Croft, to ask her in confidence about the hold. Ms. Croft was surprised at the effectiveness of their "diplomatic tradecraft," noting that they "found out very early on" that the United States was withholding critical military aid to Ukraine. By mid-August, before the freeze on aid became public, Lt. Col. Vindman had also received inquiries from an official at the Ukrainian Embassy.

The hold remained in place throughout August against the unanimous judgment of American officials focused on Ukraine policy. Without an explanation for the hold, which ran contrary to the recommendation of all relevant agencies, and with President Trump already conditioning a White House visit on the announcement of the political investigations, it became increasingly apparent to multiple witnesses that the military aid was also being withheld in exchange for the announcement of them. As both Ambassador Sondland and Mr. Holmes would later testify, it became as clear as "two plus two equals four."

On August 22, Ambassador Sondland emailed Secretary Pompeo again, recommending a plan for a potential meeting between President Trump and President Zelensky in Warsaw, Poland on September 1. Ambassador Sondland noted that President Zelensky should "look him in the eye" and tell President Trump that once new prosecutorial officials were in place in Ukraine, "Zelensky should be able to move forward publicly and with confidence on those issues of importance to Potus and the U.S." Ambassador Sondland testified that this was a reference to the political investigations that President Trump discussed on the July 25 call, which Secretary Pompeo had listened to. Ambassador Sondland hoped this would "break the logjam"—the hold on critical security assistance to Ukraine. Secretary Pompeo replied three minutes later: "Yes."

The President's Security Assistance Hold Became Public

On August 28, *Politico* published a story revealing President Trump's weeks-long hold on U.S. military assistance to Ukraine. Senior Ukrainian officials expressed grave concern, deeply worried about the practical impact on their efforts to fight Russian aggression, but also about the public message it sent to the Russian government, which would almost certainly seek to exploit any real or perceived crack in U.S. resolve toward Ukraine.

On August 29, at the urging of National Security Advisor Bolton, Ambassador Taylor wrote a first-person cable to Secretary Pompeo. This was the only first-person cable the Ambassador had ever sent in his decades of government service. He explained the "folly" of withholding security assistance to Ukraine as it fought a hot war against Russia on its borders. He wrote that he "could not and would not defend such a policy." Ambassador Taylor stated that Secretary Pompeo may have carried the cable with him to a meeting at the White House.

The same day that Ambassador Taylor sent his cable, President Trump cancelled his planned trip to Warsaw for a World War II commemoration event, where he was scheduled to meet with President Zelensky. Vice President Pence traveled in his place. Ambassador Sondland also traveled to Warsaw and, at a pre-briefing discussion with the Vice President before he met President Zelensky, Ambassador Sondland raised the issue of the hold on security assistance. He told Vice President Pence that he was concerned that the security assistance "had become tied to the issue of investigations" and that "everything is being held up until these statements get made." Vice President Pence nodded in response, apparently expressing neither surprise nor dismay at the linkage between the two.

At the meeting, President Zelensky expressed concern that even an appearance of wavering support from the United States for Ukraine could embolden Russia. Vice President Pence reiterated U.S. support for Ukraine, but could not promise that the hold would be lifted. Vice President Pence said he would relay his support for lifting the hold to President Trump so a decision could be made on security assistance as soon as possible. Vice President Pence spoke with President Trump that evening, but the hold was not lifted.

Following this meeting, Ambassador Sondland pulled aside President Zelensky's advisor, Mr. Yermak, to explain that the hold on security assistance was conditioned on the public announcement of the Burisma/Biden and the 2016 election interference investigations. After learning of the conversation, Ambassador Taylor texted Ambassador Sondland: "Are we now saying that security assistance and WH meeting are conditioned on investigations?"

The two then spoke by phone. Ambassador Sondland explained that he had previously made a "mistake" in telling Ukrainian officials that only the White House meeting was conditioned on a public announcement of the political investigations beneficial to President Trump. He clarified that "everything"—the White House meeting and hundreds of millions of dollars of security assistance to Ukraine—was now conditioned on the announcement. President Trump wanted President Zelensky in a "public box," which Ambassador Taylor understood to mean that President Trump required that President Zelensky make a public announcement about the investigations and that a private commitment would not do.

On September 7, President Trump and Ambassador Sondland spoke. Ambassador Sondland stated to his colleagues that the President said, "there was no quid pro quo," but that President Zelensky would be required to announce the investigations in order for the hold on security assistance to be lifted, "and he should want to do it." Ambassador Sondland passed on a similar message directly to President Zelensky and Mr. Yermak that, "although this was not a quid pro quo, if President Zelensky did not clear things up in public, we would be at a stalemate," referring to the hold on security assistance. Arrangements were made for the Ukrainian President to make a public statement during an interview on CNN.

After speaking with Ambassador Sondland, Ambassador Taylor texted Ambassadors Sondland and Volker: "As I said on the phone, I think it's crazy to withhold security assistance for help with a political campaign." Notwithstanding his long-held understanding that the White House meeting was conditioned on the public announcement of two political investigations desired by President Trump—and not broader anti-corruption concerns—Ambassador Sondland responded hours later:

Bill, I believe you are incorrect about President Trump's intentions. The President has been crystal clear: no quid pro quo's of any kind. The President is trying to evaluate whether Ukraine is truly going to adopt the transparency and reforms that President Zelensky promised during his campaign. I suggest we stop the back and forth by text. If you still have concerns, I recommend you give Lisa Kenna or [Secretary Pompeo] a call to discuss with them directly. Thanks.

Ambassador Sondland's subsequent testimony revealed this text to be a false exculpatory—an untruthful statement that can later be used to conceal incriminating information. In his public testimony, Ambassador Sondland testified that the President's direction to withhold a presidential telephone call and a White House meeting for President Zelensky were both quid pro quos designed to pressure Ukraine to announce the investigations. He also testified that he developed a clear understanding that the military aid was also conditioned on the investigations, that it was as simple as 2+2=4. Sondland confirmed that his clear understanding was unchanged after speaking with President Trump, which he then communicated to the Ukrainians—President Zelensky had to publicly announce the two investigations if he wanted to get the meeting or the military aid.

In Ambassador Sondland's testimony, he was not clear on whether he had one conversation with the President in which the subject of a quid pro quo came up, or two, or on precisely which date the conversation took place during the period of September 6 through 9. In one version of the conversation, which Ambassador Sondland suggested may have taken place on September 9, he claimed that the President answered an open question about what he wanted from Ukraine with an immediate denial—"no quid pro quo." In another, he admitted that the President told him that President Zelensky should go to a microphone and announce the investigations, and that he should want to do so—effectively confirming a quid pro quo.

Both Ambassador Taylor and Mr. Morrison, relying on their contemporaneous notes, testified that the call between Ambassador Sondland and President Trump occurred on September 7, which is further confirmed by Ambassador Sondland's own text message on September 8, in which he wrote that he had "multiple convos" with President Zelensky and President Trump. A call on September 9, which would have occurred in the middle of the night, is at odds with the weight of the evidence and not backed up by any records the White House was willing to provide Ambassador Sondland. Regardless of the date, Ambassador Sondland did not contest telling both Mr. Morrison and Ambassador Taylor of a conversation he had with the President in which the President reaffirmed Ambassador Sondland's understanding of the quid pro quo for the military aid.

As Ambassador Sondland acknowledged bluntly in his conversation with Mr. Holmes, President Trump's sole interest with respect to Ukraine was the "big stuff" that benefited him personally, such as the investigations into former Vice President Biden, and not President Zelensky's promises of transparency and reform.

The President's Scheme Unraveled

By early September, President Zelensky was ready to make a public announcement of the two investigations to secure a White House meeting and the military assistance his country desperately needed. He proceeded to book an interview on CNN, during which he could make such an announcement, but other events soon intervened.

On September 9, the House Permanent Select Committee on Intelligence, the Committees on Oversight and Reform, and the Committee on Foreign Affairs announced an investigation into the scheme by President Trump and his personal attorney, Mr. Giuliani, "to improperly pressure the Ukrainian government to assist the President's bid for reelection." The Committees sent document production and preservation requests to the White House and the State Department related to the investigation. NSC staff members believed this investigation might have had "the effect of releasing the hold" on Ukraine military assistance because it would have been "potentially politically challenging" to "justify that hold."

Later that day, the Inspector General of the Intelligence Community (ICIG) sent a letter to Chairman Schiff and Ranking Member Nunes notifying the Committee that a whistleblower had filed a complaint on August 12 that the ICIG had determined to be both an "urgent concern" and "credible." Nevertheless, the Acting Director of National Intelligence (DNI) took the unprecedented step of withholding the complaint from the Congressional Intelligence Committees, in coordination with the White House and the Department of Justice.

The White House had been aware of the whistleblower complaint for several weeks, and press reports indicate that the President was briefed on it in late August. The ICIG's notification to Congress of the complaint's existence, and the announcement of a separate investigation into the same subject matter, telegraphed to the White House that attempts to condition the security assistance on the announcement of the political investigations beneficial to President Trump— and efforts to cover up that misconduct—would not last.

On September 11, in the face of growing public and Congressional scrutiny, President Trump lifted the hold on security assistance to Ukraine. As with the implementation of the hold, no clear reason was given. By the time the President ordered the release of security assistance to Ukraine, DOD was unable to spend approximately 14 percent of the funds appropriated by Congress for Fiscal Year 2019. Congress had to pass a new law to extend the funding in order to ensure the full amount could be used by Ukraine to defend itself.

Even after the hold was lifted, President Zelensky still intended to sit for an interview with CNN in order to announce the investigations—indeed, he still wanted the White House meeting. At the urging of Ambassador Taylor, President Zelensky cancelled the CNN interview on September 18 or 19. The White House meeting, however, still has not occurred.

The President's Chief of Staff Confirmed Aid was Conditioned on Investigations

The conditioning of military aid to Ukraine on the investigations sought by the President was as clear to Ambassador Sondland as "two plus two equals four." In fact, the President's own Acting Chief of Staff, someone who meets with him daily, admitted that he had discussed security assistance with the President and that his decision to withhold it was directly tied to his desire to get Ukraine to conduct a political investigation.

On October 17, at a press briefing in the White House, Acting Chief of Staff Mick Mulvaney confirmed that President Trump withheld the essential military aid for Ukraine as leverage to pressure Ukraine to investigate the conspiracy theory that Ukraine had interfered in the 2016 U.S. election. As Dr. Hill made clear in her testimony, this false narrative has been promoted by President Putin to deflect away from Russia's systemic interference in our election and to drive a wedge between the United States and a key partner.

According to Mr. Mulvaney, President Trump "[a]bsolutely" mentioned "corruption related to the DNC server" in connection with the security assistance during his July 25 call. Mr. Mulvaney also stated that the server was part of "why we held up the money." After a reporter attempted to clarify this explicit acknowledgement of a quid pro quo, Mr. Mulvaney replied:

"We do that all the time with foreign policy." He added, "I have news for everybody: get over it. There is going to be political influence in foreign policy."

Ambassador Taylor testified that in his decades of military and diplomatic service, he had never seen another example of foreign aid conditioned on the personal or political interests of the President. Rather, "we condition assistance on issues that will improve our foreign policy, serve our foreign policy, ensure that taxpayers' money is well-spent," not specific investigations designed to benefit the political interests of the President of the United States.

In contrast, President Trump does not appear to believe there is any such limitation on his power to use White House meetings, military aid or other official acts to procure foreign help in his reelection. When asked by a reporter on October 3 what he had hoped President Zelensky would do following their July 25 call, President Trump responded: "Well, I would think that, if they were honest about it, they'd start a major investigation into the Bidens. It's a very simple answer."

SECTION II—THE PRESIDENT'S OBSTRUCTION OF THE HOUSE OF REPRESENTATIVES' IMPEACHMENT INQUIRY

The President Obstructed the Impeachment Inquiry by Instructing Witnesses and Agencies to Ignore Subpoenas for Documents and Testimony

An Unprecedented Effort to Obstruct an Impeachment Inquiry

Donald Trump is the first President in the history of the United States to seek to completely obstruct an impeachment inquiry undertaken by the House of Representatives under Article I of the Constitution, which vests the House with the "sole Power of Impeachment." He has publicly and repeatedly rejected the authority of Congress to conduct oversight of his actions and has directly challenged the authority of the House to conduct an impeachment inquiry into his actions regarding Ukraine.

President Trump ordered federal agencies and officials to disregard all voluntary requests for documents and defy all duly authorized subpoenas for records. He also directed all federal officials in the Executive Branch not to testify—even when compelled.

No other President has flouted the Constitution and power of Congress to conduct oversight to this extent. No President has claimed for himself the right to deny the House's authority to conduct an impeachment proceeding, control the scope of a power exclusively vested in the House, and forbid any and all cooperation from the Executive Branch. Even President Richard Nixon—who obstructed Congress by refusing to turn over key evidence—accepted the authority of Congress to conduct an impeachment inquiry and permitted his aides and advisors to produce documents and testify to Congressional committees.

Despite President Trump's unprecedented and categorical commands, the House gathered overwhelming evidence of his misconduct from courageous individuals who were willing to follow the law, comply with duly authorized subpoenas, and tell the truth. In response, the President engaged in a brazen effort to publicly attack and intimidate these witnesses.

If left unanswered, President Trump's ongoing effort to thwart Congress' impeachment power risks doing grave harm to the institution of Congress, the balance of power between our branches of government, and the Constitutional order that the President and every Member of Congress have sworn to protect and defend.

Constitutional Authority for Congressional Oversight and Impeachment

The House's Constitutional and legal authority to conduct an impeachment inquiry is clear, as is the duty of the President to cooperate with the House's exercise of this authority.

Article I of the U.S. Constitution gives the House of Representatives the "sole Power of Impeachment." The Framers intended the impeachment power to be an essential check on a President who might engage in corruption or abuse of power. Congress is empowered to conduct oversight and investigations to carry out its authorities under Article I. Because the impeachment power is a core component of the nation's Constitutional system of checks and balances, Congress' investigative authority is at its zenith during an impeachment inquiry.

The Supreme Court has made clear that Congress' authority to investigate includes the authority to compel the production of information by issuing subpoenas, a power the House has delegated to its committees pursuant to its Constitutional authority to "determine the Rules of its Proceedings."

Congress has also enacted statutes to support its power to investigate and oversee the Executive Branch. These laws impose criminal and other penalties on those who fail to comply with inquiries from Congress or block others from doing so, and they reflect the broader Constitutional requirement to cooperate with Congressional investigations.

Unlike President Trump, past Presidents who were the subject of impeachment inquiries—including Presidents Andrew Johnson, Richard Nixon, and Bill Clinton—recognized and, to varying degrees, complied with information requests and subpoenas.

President Nixon, for example, agreed to let his staff testify voluntarily in the Senate Watergate investigation, stating: "All members of the White House Staff will appear voluntarily when requested by the committee. They will testify under oath, and they will answer fully all proper questions." President Nixon also produced documents in response to the House's subpoenas as part of its impeachment inquiry, including more than 30 transcripts of White House recordings and notes from meetings with the President. When President Nixon withheld tape recordings and produced heavily edited and inaccurate records, the House Judiciary Committee approved an article of impeachment for obstruction.

The President's Categorical Refusal to Comply

Even before the House of Representatives launched its investigation regarding Ukraine, President Trump rejected the authority of Congress to investigate his actions, proclaiming, "We're fighting all the subpoenas," and "I have an Article II, where I have the right to do whatever I want as president."

When the Intelligence, Oversight and Reform, and Foreign Affairs Committees began reviewing the President's actions as part of the House's impeachment inquiry, the President repeatedly challenged the legitimacy of the investigation in word and deed. His rhetorical attacks appeared intended not only to dispute reports of his misconduct, but to persuade the American people that the House lacks authority to investigate the President.

On September 26, President Trump argued that Congress should not be "allowed" to impeach him under the Constitution and that there "should be a way of stopping it—maybe legally, through the courts." A common theme of his defiance has been his claims that Congress is acting in an unprecedented way and using unprecedented rules. However, the House has been following the same investigative rules that Republicans championed when they were in control.

On October 8, White House Counsel Pat Cipollone sent a letter to House Speaker Nancy Pelosi and the Chairmen of the investigating Committees confirming that President Trump directed his entire Administration not to cooperate with the House's impeachment inquiry. Mr. Cipollone wrote: "President Trump cannot permit his Administration to participate in this partisan inquiry under these circumstances."

Mr. Cipollone's letter advanced remarkably politicized arguments and legal theories unsupported by the Constitution, judicial precedent, and more than 200 years of history. If allowed to stand, the President's defiance, as justified by Mr. Cipollone, would represent an existential threat to the nation's Constitutional system of checks and balances, separation of powers, and rule of law.

The President's Refusal to Produce Any and All Subpoenaed Documents

Following President Trump's categorical order, not a single document has been produced by the White House, the Office of the Vice President, the Office of Management and Budget, the Department of State, the Department of Defense, or the Department of Energy in response to 71 specific, individualized requests or demands for records in their possession, custody, or control. These subpoenas remain in full force and effect. These agencies and offices also blocked many current and former officials from producing records directly to the Committees.

Certain witnesses defied the President's sweeping, categorical, and baseless order and identified the substance of key documents. For example, Ambassador Gordon Sondland attached ten exhibits to his written hearing testimony reflecting reproductions of certain communications with high-level Administration officials, including Acting White House Chief of Staff Mick Mulvaney, former National Security Advisor John Bolton, Secretary of State Mike Pompeo, and Secretary of Energy Rick Perry. Other witnesses identified numerous additional documents that the President and various agencies are withholding that are directly relevant to the impeachment inquiry.

Like the White House, the Department of State refused to produce a single document in response to its subpoena, even though there is no legal basis for the Department's actions. In fact, on November 22, the Department was forced to produce 99 pages of emails, letters, notes, timelines, and news articles to a non-partisan, nonprofit ethics watchdog organization pursuant to a court order in a lawsuit filed under the Freedom of Information Act (FOIA). Although limited in scope, this production affirms that the Department is withholding responsive documents from Congress without any valid legal basis.

The President's Refusal to Allow Top Aides to Testify

No other President in history has issued an order categorically directing the entire Executive Branch not to testify before Congress, including in the context of an impeachment inquiry. President Trump issued just such an order.

As reflected in Mr. Cipollone's letter, President Trump directed government witnesses to violate their legal obligations and defy House subpoenas—regardless of their offices or positions. President Trump even extended his order to former officials no longer employed by the federal government. This Administration-wide effort to prevent all witnesses from providing testimony was coordinated and comprehensive.

At President Trump's direction, twelve current or former Administration officials refused to testify as part of the House's impeachment inquiry, ten of whom did so in defiance of duly authorized subpoenas:

- Mick Mulvaney, Acting White House Chief of Staff
- Robert B. Blair, Assistant to the President and Senior Advisor to the Chief of Staff
- Ambassador John Bolton, Former National Security Advisor
- John A. Eisenberg, Deputy Counsel to the President for National Security Affairs and Legal Advisor, National Security Council
- Michael Ellis, Senior Associate Counsel to the President and Deputy Legal Advisor, National Security Council
- Preston Wells Griffith, Senior Director for International Energy and Environment, National Security Council
- Dr. Charles M. Kupperman, Former Deputy Assistant to the President for National Security Affairs, National Security Council
- Russell T. Vought, Acting Director, Office of Management and Budget
- Michael Duffey, Associate Director for National Security Programs, Office of Management and Budget
- Brian McCormack, Associate Director for Natural Resources, Energy, and Science, Office of Management and Budget
- T. Ulrich Brechbuhl, Counselor, Department of State
- Secretary Rick Perry, Department of Energy

These witnesses were warned that their refusal to testify "shall constitute evidence that may be used against you in a contempt proceeding" and "may be used as an adverse inference against you and the President."

The President's Unsuccessful Attempts to Block Other Key Witnesses

Despite President Trump's orders that no Executive Branch employees should cooperate with the House's impeachment inquiry, multiple key officials complied with duly authorized subpoenas and provided critical testimony at depositions and public hearings. These officials not only served their nation honorably, but they fulfilled their oath to support and defend the Constitution of the United States.

In addition to the President's broad orders seeking to prohibit all Executive Branch employees from testifying, many of these witnesses were personally directed by senior political appointees not to cooperate with the House's impeachment inquiry. These directives frequently cited or enclosed copies of Mr. Cipollone's October 8 letter conveying the President's order not to comply.

For example, the State Department, relying on President Trump's order, attempted to block Ambassador Marie Yovanovitch from testifying, but she fulfilled her legal obligations by appearing at a deposition on October 11 and a hearing on November 15. More than a dozen current and former officials followed her courageous example by testifying at depositions and public hearings over the course of the last two months. The testimony from these witnesses produced overwhelming and clear evidence of President Trump's misconduct, which is described in detail in the first section of this report.

The President's Intimidation of Witnesses

President Trump publicly attacked and intimidated witnesses who came forward to comply with duly authorized subpoenas and testify about his misconduct, raising grave concerns about potential violations of criminal laws intended to protect witnesses appearing before Congressional proceedings. For example, the President attacked:

- Ambassador Marie Yovanovitch, who served the United States honorably for decades as a U.S. diplomat and anti-corruption advocate in posts around the world under six different Presidents;

- Ambassador Bill Taylor, who graduated at the top of his class at West Point, served as an infantry commander in Vietnam, and earned a Bronze Star and an Air Medal with a V device for valor;

- Lieutenant Colonel Alexander Vindman, an active-duty Army officer for more than 20 years who earned a Purple Heart for wounds he sustained in an improvised explosive device attack in Iraq, as well as the Combat Infantryman Badge; and

- Jennifer Williams, who is Vice President Mike Pence's top advisor on Europe and Russia and has a distinguished record of public service under the Bush, Obama, and Trump Administrations.

The President engaged in this effort to intimidate these public servants to prevent them from cooperating with Congress' impeachment inquiry. He issued threats, openly discussed possible retaliation, made insinuations about their character and patriotism, and subjected them to mockery and derision—when they deserved the opposite. The President's attacks were broadcast to millions of Americans—including witnesses' families, friends, and coworkers.

It is a federal crime to intimidate or seek to intimidate any witness appearing before Congress. This prohibition applies to anyone who knowingly "uses intimidation, threatens, or corruptly persuades" another person in order to "influence, delay, or prevent the testimony of any person in an official proceeding." Violations of this law can carry a criminal sentence of up to 20 years in prison.

In addition to his relentless attacks on witnesses who testified in connection with the House's impeachment inquiry, the President also repeatedly threatened and attacked a member of the Intelligence Community who filed an anonymous whistleblower complaint raising an "urgent concern" that "appeared credible" regarding the President's conduct. The whistleblower filed the complaint confidentially with the Inspector General of the Intelligence Community, as authorized by the relevant whistleblower law. Federal law prohibits the Inspector General from revealing the whistleblower's identity. Federal law also protects the whistleblower from retaliation.

In more than 100 public statements about the whistleblower over a period of just two months, the President publicly questioned the whistleblower's motives, disputed the accuracy of the whistleblower's account, and encouraged others to reveal the whistleblower's identity. Most chillingly, the President issued a threat against the whistleblower and those who provided information to the whistleblower regarding the President's misconduct, suggesting that they could face the death penalty for treason.

The President's campaign of intimidation risks discouraging witnesses from coming forward voluntarily, complying with mandatory subpoenas for documents and testimony, and disclosing potentially incriminating evidence in this inquiry and future Congressional investigations.

KEY FINDINGS OF FACT

Based on witness testimony and evidence collected during the impeachment inquiry, the Intelligence Committee has found that:

I.   Donald J. Trump, the 45th President of the United States—acting personally and through his agents within and outside of the U.S. government—solicited the interference of a foreign government, Ukraine, in the 2020 U.S. presidential election. The President engaged in this course of conduct for the benefit of his reelection, to harm the election prospects of a political opponent, and to influence our nation's upcoming presidential election to his advantage. In so doing, the President placed his personal political interests above the national interests of the United States, sought to undermine the integrity of the U.S. presidential election process, and endangered U.S. national security.

II.   In furtherance of this scheme, President Trump—directly and acting through his agents within and outside the U.S. government—sought to pressure and induce Ukraine's newly-elected president, Volodymyr Zelensky, to publicly announce unfounded investigations that would benefit President Trump's personal political interests and reelection effort. To advance his personal political objectives, President Trump encouraged the President of Ukraine to work with his personal attorney, Rudy Giuliani.

III.   As part of this scheme, President Trump, acting in his official capacity and using his position of public trust, personally and directly requested from the President of Ukraine that the government of Ukraine publicly announce investigations into (1) the President's political opponent, former Vice President Joseph R. Biden, Jr. and his son, Hunter Biden, and (2) a baseless theory promoted by Russia alleging that Ukraine—rather than Russia—interfered in the 2016 U.S. election. These investigations were intended to harm a potential political opponent of President Trump and benefit the President's domestic political standing.

IV.   President Trump ordered the suspension of $391 million in vital military assistance urgently needed by Ukraine, a strategic partner, to resist Russian aggression. Because the aid was appropriated by Congress, on a bipartisan basis, and signed into law by the President, its expenditure was required by law. Acting directly and through his subordinates within the U.S. government, the President withheld from Ukraine this military assistance without any legitimate foreign policy, national security, or anti-corruption justification. The President did so despite the longstanding bipartisan support of Congress, uniform support across federal departments and agencies for the provision to Ukraine of the military assistance, and his obligations under the Impoundment Control Act.

V.   President Trump used the power of the Office of the President and exercised his authority over the Executive Branch, including his control of the instruments of the federal government, to apply increasing pressure on the President of Ukraine and the Ukrainian government to announce the politically-motivated investigations desired by President Trump. Specifically, to advance and promote his scheme, the President withheld official acts of value to Ukraine and conditioned their fulfillment on actions by Ukraine that would benefit his personal political interests:

A.   President Trump—acting through agents within and outside the U.S. government—conditioned a head of state meeting at the White House, which the President of Ukraine desperately sought to demonstrate continued United States support for Ukraine in the face of Russian aggression, on Ukraine publicly announcing the investigations that President Trump believed would aid his reelection campaign.

B.   To increase leverage over the President of Ukraine, President Trump, acting through his agents and subordinates, conditioned release of the vital military assistance he had suspended to Ukraine on the President of Ukraine's public announcement of the investigations that President Trump sought.

C.   President Trump's closest subordinates and advisors within the Executive Branch, including Acting Chief of Staff Mick Mulvaney, Secretary of State Mike Pompeo, Secretary of Energy J. Richard Perry, and other senior White House and Executive Branch officials had knowledge of, in some cases facilitated and furthered the President's scheme, and withheld information about the scheme from the Congress and the American public.

VI.   In directing and orchestrating this scheme to advance his personal political interests, President Trump did not implement, promote, or advance U.S. anti-corruption policies. In fact, the President sought to pressure and induce the government of Ukraine to announce politically-motivated investigations lacking legitimate predication that the U.S. government otherwise discourages and opposes as a matter of policy in that country and around the world. In so doing, the President undermined U.S. policy supporting anti-corruption reform and the rule of law in Ukraine, and undermined U.S. national security.

VII.   By withholding vital military assistance and diplomatic support from a strategic foreign partner government engaged in an ongoing military conflict illegally instigated by Russia, President Trump compromised national security to advance his personal political interests.

VIII.   Faced with the revelation of his actions, President Trump publicly and repeatedly persisted in urging foreign governments, including Ukraine and China, to investigate his political opponent. This continued solicitation of foreign interference in a U.S. election presents a clear and present danger that the President will continue to use the power of his office for his personal political gain.

IX.   Using the power of the Office of the President, and exercising his authority over the Executive Branch, President Trump ordered and implemented a campaign to conceal his conduct from the public and frustrate and obstruct the House of Representatives' impeachment inquiry by:

A.   refusing to produce to the impeachment inquiry's investigating Committees information and records in the possession of the White House, in defiance of a lawful subpoena;

B.   directing Executive Branch agencies to defy lawful subpoenas and withhold the production of all documents and records from the investigating Committees;

C.   directing current and former Executive Branch officials not to cooperate with the Committees, including in defiance of lawful subpoenas for testimony; and

D.   intimidating, threatening, and tampering with prospective and actual witnesses in the impeachment inquiry in an effort to prevent, delay, or influence the testimony of those witnesses.

In so doing, and despite the fact that the Constitution vests in the House of Representatives the "sole Power of Impeachment," the President sought to arrogate to himself the right to determine the propriety, scope, and nature of an impeachment inquiry into his own misconduct, and the right to deny any and all information to the Congress in the conduct of its constitutional responsibilities.

SECTION I.

THE PRESIDENT'S MISCONDUCT

1.   The President Forced Out the U.S. Ambassador to Ukraine

> *The President forced out the United States Ambassador to Ukraine, Marie Yovanovitch, following a baseless smear campaign promoted by President Trump's personal attorney, Rudy Giuliani, and others. The campaign publicized conspiracy theories that benefited the President's personal political interests and undermined official U.S. policy, some of which the President raised during his July 25 call with the President of Ukraine.*

Overview

On April 24, 2019, President Donald J. Trump abruptly recalled the U.S. Ambassador to Ukraine, Marie Yovanovitch. Ambassador Yovanovitch, an award-winning 33-year veteran Foreign Service officer, aggressively advocated for anti-corruption reforms in Ukraine consistent with U.S. foreign policy. President Trump forced her out following a baseless smear campaign promoted by his personal attorney, Rudy Giuliani, associates of Mr. Giuliani, and corrupt Ukrainians.

Ambassador Yovanovitch was told by the State Department that President Trump had lost confidence in her, but she was never provided a substantive justification for her removal. Her ouster set the stage for other U.S. officials appointed by President Trump to work in cooperation with Mr. Giuliani to advance a scheme in support of the President's reelection.

Mr. Giuliani and his associates promoted false conspiracy theories about Ukraine colluding with Democrats to interfere in the 2016 U.S. election. This false claim was promoted by Russian President Vladimir Putin in February 2017—less than a month after the unanimous U.S. Intelligence Community assessment that Russia alone was responsible for a covert influence campaign aimed at helping President Trump during the 2016 election. Mr. Giuliani also made discredited public allegations about former Vice President Joe Biden and his son, Hunter, in an apparent effort to hurt President Trump's political rival in the 2020 presidential election. Mr. Giuliani's associates, with their own ties to President Trump, also worked to enter into arrangements with current and former corrupt Ukrainian officials to promote these false allegations—the same unfounded allegations President Trump requested that Ukraine investigate on his July 25 call with Ukrainian President Volodymyr Zelensky.

President Trump amplified these baseless allegations by tweeting them just a month before he recalled Ambassador Yovanovitch. Despite requests from Ambassador Yovanovitch and other senior State Department officials, Secretary of State Mike Pompeo refused to issue a statement of support for the Ambassador or the U.S. Embassy in Ukraine for fear of being undermined by a tweet by President Trump.

The removal of Ambassador Yovanovitch left a vacuum in the leadership of the U.S. Embassy in Ukraine at an important time. A new president had just been elected on an anti-corruption platform, and the country was in a period of transition as it continued to defend itself against Russia-led military aggression in the east.

Anti-Corruption Ceremony Interrupted to Recall Anti-Corruption Ambassador

Ambassador Yovanovitch represented the United States of America as the U.S. Ambassador to Ukraine from 2016 to 2019. She is a non-partisan career public servant, first selected for the American Foreign Service in 1986. President George W. Bush named her as an Ambassador twice, to the Kyrgyz Republic and Armenia, and President Barack Obama nominated her for the posting in Kyiv.[1]

On the evening of April 24, Ambassador Yovanovitch approached a podium in front of gold drapes at the U.S. Ambassador's residence in Ukraine's capital city. She was hosting an event to present an award of courage to the father of Kateryna Handziuk, who was brutally murdered by people who opposed her efforts to expose and root out public corruption in Ukraine. In 2018, attackers threw sulfuric acid at Ms. Handziuk, burning more than 30 percent of her body. After months of suffering and nearly a dozen surgeries, she died at the age of 33.[2] Her attackers have still not been held to account.[3]

Ambassador Yovanovitch began her speech by noting that Ms. Handziuk "was a woman of courage who committed herself to speaking out against wrongdoing." She lamented how Ms. Handziuk had "paid the ultimate price for her fearlessness in fighting against corruption and for her determined efforts to build a democratic Ukraine." She pledged that the United States would "continue to stand with those engaged in the fight for a democratic Ukraine free of corruption, where people are held accountable" and commended Ukrainians who "have demonstrated to the world that they are willing to fight for a better system."[4]

Ambassador Yovanovitch concluded her remarks by holding Ms. Handziuk's story up as an inspiration to the many Ukrainians striving to chart a new course for their country in the face of Russian interference and aggression:

> I think we can all see what a remarkable woman Kateryna Handziuk was, but she continues to inspire all of us to fight for justice. She was a courageous woman, who wanted to make Ukraine a better place. And she is continuing to do so. And I'll just leave you with one thought that was expressed in Washington at the ceremony—that courage is contagious. I think we saw that on the Maidan in 2014, we see that on the front lines every day in the Donbas, we see it in the work that Kateryna Handziuk did here in Ukraine. And we see it in the work of all of you—day in, day out—fighting for Ukraine and the future of Ukraine.[5]

Ambassador Yovanovitch's evening was interrupted around 10:00 p.m. by a telephone call from the State Department's headquarters in Washington, D.C.

Director General of the Foreign Service and Director of Human Resources Ambassador Carol Perez warned that the Department's leaders had "great concern" and "were worried" about her. Ambassador Yovanovitch testified that it is "hard to know how to react to something like that." Ambassador Perez said she did not know what the concerns were but pledged she would "try to find out more" and would try to call back "by midnight."[6]

Finally, at 1:00 a.m. in Kyiv, Ambassador Perez called again: The "concerns" were from "up the street" at the White House. Ambassador Perez said that Ambassador Yovanovitch needed to "come home immediately, get on the next plane to the U.S." She warned that there were concerns about Ambassador Yovanovitch's "security." When Ambassador Yovanovitch asked if Ambassador Perez was referring to her physical safety, Ambassador Perez relayed that she "hadn't gotten that impression that it was a physical security issue," but that Ambassador Yovanovitch "needed to come home right away."[7]

Ambassador Yovanovitch asked Ambassador Perez specifically whether this order had anything to do with President Trump's personal attorney, Rudy Giuliani, who had been making unfounded allegations against her in the media. Ambassador Perez said she "didn't know."[8] Ambassador Yovanovitch argued that this order to return to Washington, D.C. was "extremely irregular" and that no one had provided her a reason.[9] In the end, however, Ambassador Yovanovitch swiftly returned to Washington.[10]

Rudy Giuliani, on Behalf of President Trump, Led a Smear Campaign to Oust Ambassador Yovanovitch

Ambassador Yovanovitch's recall followed a concerted smear campaign by Mr. Giuliani and his associates, promoted by President Trump. The campaign was largely directed by Mr. Giuliani, President Trump's personal attorney since early 2018.[11] A cast of supporting characters, which included corrupt Ukrainian prosecutors, now-indicted middlemen, conservative media pundits, and attorneys close to President Trump, assisted Mr. Giuliani. Among those associates were two U.S. citizens, Lev Parnas and Igor Fruman. Mr. Parnas and Mr. Fruman were Florida-based businessmen who were represented by Mr. Giuliani "in connection with their personal and business affairs" and who also "assisted Mr. Giuliani in connection with his representation of President Trump."[12] Both Mr. Parnas and Mr. Fruman were criminally indicted in the Southern District of New York in October and face charges of conspiring to violate the federal ban on foreign donations and contributions in connection with federal and state elections.[13] Dr. Fiona Hill, former Deputy Assistant to the President and Senior Director for Europe and Russia, National Security Council (NSC), learned from her colleagues that "these guys were notorious in Florida and that they were bad news."[14]

The campaign was also propelled by individuals in Ukraine, including two prosecutors general. Yuriy Lutsenko served as the Prosecutor General of Ukraine under former Ukrainian President Petro Poroshenko—the incumbent who lost to President Zelensky in April 2019—and previously was the head of President Poroshenko's faction in the Ukrainian parliament.[15] Viktor Shokin was Mr. Lutsenko's predecessor and was removed from office in 2016.[16] Mr. Shokin has been described as "a typical Ukraine prosecutor who lived a lifestyle far in excess of his government salary, who never prosecuted anybody known for having committed a crime," and "covered up crimes that were known to have been committed."[17]

In late 2018, Ukrainian officials informed Ambassador Yovanovitch about Mr. Giuliani's and Mr. Lutsenko's plans to target her. They told her that Mr. Lutsenko "was in communication with Mayor Giuliani" and that "they were going to, you know, do things, including to me."[18]

Soon thereafter, Ambassador Yovanovitch learned that "there had been a number of meetings" between Mr. Giuliani and Mr. Lutsenko, who was looking to "hurt" her "in the U.S."[19]

The allegations against Ambassador Yovanovitch, which later surfaced publicly, concerned false claims that she had provided a "do-not-prosecute list" to Mr. Lutsenko and made disparaging comments about President Trump.[20]

Ambassador Yovanovitch inferred that Mr. Lutsenko was spreading "falsehoods" about her because she was "effective at helping Ukrainians who wanted reform, Ukrainians who wanted to fight against corruption, and … that was not in his interest."[21] Anti-corruption reform was not in Mr. Lutsenko's interest because he himself was known to be corrupt.[22] David Holmes, Counselor for Political Affairs at the U.S. Embassy in Kyiv, Ukraine, explained that:

> In mid-March 2019, an Embassy colleague learned from a Ukrainian contact that Mr. Lutsenko had complained that Ambassador Yovanovitch had, quote, unquote, destroyed him, with her refusal to support him until he followed through with his reform commitments and ceased using his position for personal gain.[23]

Deputy Assistant Secretary of State George Kent similarly summarized Mr. Lutsenko's smear campaign against Ambassador Yovanovitch, which was facilitated by Mr. Giuliani and his associates, as motivated by revenge:

> Over the course of 2018 and 2019, I became increasingly aware of an effort by Rudy Giuliani and others, including his associates Lev Parnas and Igor Fruman, to run a campaign to smear Ambassador Yovanovitch and other officials at the U.S. Embassy in Kyiv. The chief agitators on the Ukrainian side of this effort were some of those same corrupt former prosecutors I had encountered, particularly Yuriy Lutsenko and Viktor Shokin. They were now peddling false information in order to extract revenge against those who had exposed their misconduct, including U.S. diplomats, Ukrainian anticorruption officials, and reform-minded civil society groups in Ukraine.[24]

Mr. Kent succinctly summarized, "[y]ou can't promote principled anti-corruption efforts without pissing off corrupt people."[25] By doing her job, Ambassador Yovanovitch drew Mr. Lutsenko's ire.

In late 2018 and early 2019, Mr. Lutsenko also risked losing his job as Prosecutor General, and risked possible criminal investigation, if then-candidate Volodymyr Zelensky won the presidency. Special Representative for Ukraine Negotiations, Ambassador Kurt Volker, explained:

> As is often the case in Ukraine, a change in power would mean change in prosecutorial powers as well, and there have been efforts in the past at prosecuting the previous government. I think Mr. Lutsenko, in my estimation, and I said this to Mayor Giuliani when I met with him, was interested in preserving his own position. He wanted to avoid being fired by a new government in order to prevent prosecution of himself, possible prosecution of himself.[26]

Officials in Ukraine have also speculated that Mr. Lutsenko cultivated his relationship with Mr. Giuliani in an effort to hold on to his position.[27] Ambassador Yovanovitch described Mr. Lutsenko as an "opportunist" who "will ally himself, sometimes simultaneously ... with whatever political or economic forces he believes will suit his interests best at the time."[28]

Mr. Lutsenko promoted debunked conspiracy theories that had gained traction with President Trump and Mr. Giuliani. Those debunked conspiracy theories alleged that the Ukrainian government—not Russia—was behind the hack of the Democratic National Committee (DNC) server in 2016, and that former Vice President Biden had petitioned for the removal of Mr. Shokin to prevent an investigation into Burisma Holdings, a Ukrainian energy company for which Vice President Biden's son, Hunter, served as a board member.

Both conspiracy theories served the personal political interests of President Trump because they would help him in his campaign for reelection in 2020. The first would serve to undercut Special Counsel Robert Mueller's investigation, which was still underway when Mr. Giuliani began his activities in Ukraine and was denounced as a "witch hunt" by the President and his supporters.[29] The second would serve to damage Democratic presidential candidate Vice President Biden.

These conspiracies lacked any basis in fact. The Intelligence Community, the Senate Select Committee on Intelligence, both the Majority and Minority of the House Permanent Select Committee on Intelligence, and the investigation undertaken by Special Counsel Robert Mueller concluded that Russia was responsible for interfering in the 2016 election.[30] President Trump's former Homeland Security Advisor, Tom Bossert, said that the idea of Ukraine hacking the DNC server was "not only a conspiracy theory, it is completely debunked."[31]

Russia has pushed the false theory that Ukraine was involved in the 2016 election to distract from its own involvement.[32] Mr. Holmes testified that it was to President Putin's advantage to promote the theory of Ukrainian interference in the 2016 U.S. elections for several reasons:

> First of all, to deflect from the allegations of Russian interference. Second of all, to drive a wedge between the United States and Ukraine which Russia wants to essentially get back into its sphere of influence. Thirdly, to besmirch Ukraine and its political leadership, [and] to degrade and erode support for Ukraine from other key partners in Europe and elsewhere.[33]

The allegations that Vice President Biden inappropriately pressured the Ukrainians to remove Mr. Shokin also are without merit. Mr. Shokin was widely considered to be ineffective and corrupt.[34] When he urged the Ukrainian government to remove Mr. Shokin, Vice President Biden was advocating for anti-corruption reform and pursuing official U.S. policy.[35] Moreover, Mr. Shokin's removal was supported by other countries, the International Monetary Fund, and the World Bank, and was "widely understood internationally to be the right policy."[36] In May 2019, even Mr. Lutsenko himself admitted that there was no credible evidence of wrongdoing by Hunter Biden or Vice President Biden.[37]

Nevertheless, Mr. Giuliani engaged with both Mr. Lutsenko and Mr. Shokin regarding these baseless allegations. According to documents provided to the State Department Office of Inspector General, in January 23, 2019, Mr. Giuliani, Mr. Parnas, and Mr. Fruman participated in a conference call with Mr. Shokin. According to notes of the call, Mr. Shokin made allegations about Vice President Biden and Burisma. Mr. Shokin also claimed that Ambassador Yovanovitch had improperly denied him a U.S. visa and that she was close to Vice President Biden.[38]

Mr. Giuliani separately met with Mr. Lutsenko in New York.[39] Over the course of two days, on January 25 and 26, Mr. Giuliani, Mr. Lutsenko, Mr. Parnas, and Mr. Fruman, reportedly discussed whether Ambassador Yovanovitch was "loyal to President Trump," as well as investigations into Burisma and the Bidens.[40] For his part, Mr. Lutsenko later said he "understood very well" that Mr. Giuliani wanted Mr. Lutsenko to investigate former Vice President Biden and his son, Hunter. "I have 23 years in politics," Mr. Lutsenko said. "I knew. … I'm a political animal."[41]

Mr. Giuliani later publicly acknowledged that he was seeking information from Ukrainians on behalf of his client, President Trump. On October 23, Mr. Giuliani tweeted "everything I did was to discover evidence to defend my client against false charges."[42] Then, in a series of tweets on October 30, Mr. Giuliani stated:

> All of the information I obtained came from interviews conducted as … private defense counsel to POTUS, to defend him against false allegations. I began obtaining this information while Mueller was still investigating his witch hunt and a full 5 months before Biden even announced his run for Pres.[43]

President Trump and Mr. Giuliani's efforts to investigate alleged Ukrainian interference in the 2016 U.S. election and Vice President Biden negatively impacted the U.S. Embassy in Kyiv. Mr. Holmes testified:

> Beginning in March 2019, the situation at the Embassy and in Ukraine changed dramatically. Specifically, the three priorities of security, economy, and justice and our support for Ukrainian democratic resistance to Russian aggression became overshadowed by a political agenda promoted by former New York City Mayor Rudy Giuliani and a cadre of officials operating with a direct channel to the White House.[44]

U.S. national interests in Ukraine were undermined and subordinated to the personal, political interests of President Trump.

The Smear Campaign Accelerated in Late March 2019

The smear campaign entered a more public phase in the United States in late March 2019 with the publication of a series of opinion pieces in *The Hill*.

On March 20, 2019, John Solomon penned an opinion piece quoting a false claim by Mr. Lutsenko that Ambassador Yovanovitch had given him a do-not-prosecute list.[45] Mr. Lutsenko later retracted the claim.[46] Mr. Solomon's work also included false allegations that Ambassador Yovanovitch had "made disparaging statements about President Trump."[47] Ambassador Yovanovitch called this allegation "fictitious," and the State Department issued a statement describing the allegations as a "fabrication."[48]

The Committees uncovered evidence of close ties and frequent contacts between Mr. Solomon and Mr. Parnas, who was assisting Mr. Giuliani in connection with his representation of the President. Phone records show that in the 48 hours before publication of *The Hill* opinion piece, Mr. Parnas spoke with Mr. Solomon.[49] In addition, *The Hill* piece cited a letter dated May 9, 2018, from Representative Pete Sessions (R-Texas) to Secretary Pompeo, in which Rep. Sessions accused Ambassador Yovanovitch of speaking "privately and repeatedly about her disdain for the current administration."[50] A federal criminal indictment alleges that in or about May 2018, Mr. Parnas sought a congressman's assistance to remove Ambassador Yovanovitch, at the request of one or more Ukrainian government officials.[51]

On March 20, 2019, the day *The Hill* opinion piece was published, Mr. Parnas again spoke with Mr. Solomon for 11 minutes.[52] Shortly after that phone call, President Trump promoted Mr. Solomon's article in a tweet.[53]

Following President Trump's tweet, the public attacks against Ambassador Yovanovitch were further amplified on social media and were merged with the conspiracy theories regarding both Ukrainian interference in the 2016 U.S. election and the Bidens. On March 22, 2019, Mr. Giuliani tweeted: "Hillary, Kerry, and Biden people colluding with Ukrainian operatives to make money and affect 2016 election." He also gave an interview to *Fox News* in which he raised Hunter Biden and called for an investigation.[54] Then, on March 24, Donald Trump, Jr. called Ambassador Yovanovitch a "joker" on Twitter and called for her removal.[55]

This campaign reverberated in Ukraine. Mr. Kent testified that "starting in mid-March" Mr. Giuliani was "almost unmissable" during this "campaign of slander" against Ambassador Yovanovitch.[56] According to Mr. Kent, Mr. Lutsenko's press spokeswoman retweeted Donald Trump, Jr.'s tweet attacking the Ambassador.[57]

Concerns About President Trump Kept State Department from Issuing Statement of Support

At the end of March, as this smear campaign intensified, Ambassador Yovanovitch sent Under Secretary of State for Political Affairs David Hale an email identifying her concerns with the false allegations about her and asking for a strong statement of support from the State Department. She explained that, otherwise, "it makes it hard to be a credible ambassador in a country."[58] Ambassador Hale had been briefed on the smears in a series of emails from Mr. Kent.[59] Ambassador Hale agreed that the allegations were without merit.[60]

Ambassador Yovanovitch was told that State Department officials were concerned that if they issued a public statement supporting her, "it could be undermined" by "[t]he President."[61] Ambassador Hale explained that a statement of support "would only fuel further negative reaction" and that "it might even provoke a public reaction from the President himself about the

Ambassador."[62] In short, State Department officials were concerned "that the rug would be pulled out from underneath the State Department."[63]

Ambassador Yovanovitch turned to the U.S. Ambassador to the European Union, Gordon Sondland, for advice. According to Ambassador Yovanovitch, Ambassador Sondland suggested that, in response to the smear campaign, she make a public statement in support of President Trump. She said Ambassador Sondland told her, "you need to go big or go home" and "tweet out there that you support the President, and that all these are lies and everything else."[64] Ambassador Yovanovitch said she felt that this "was advice that I did not see how I could implement in my role as an Ambassador, and as a Foreign Service officer."[65]

Ultimately, Secretary Pompeo refused to issue a public statement of support for Ambassador Yovanovitch. At the same time Secretary Pompeo was refusing to issue a statement, he was communicating with one of the individuals involved in the smear campaign against her. Records and witness testimony indicate that Secretary Pompeo spoke to Mr. Giuliani on March 26, 28, and 29, not long after Mr. Solomon's first article in *The Hill*.[66]

The Smear Campaign was a Coordinated Effort by Mr. Giuliani, His Associates, and One or More Individuals at the White House

In April, Mr. Solomon continued to publish opinion pieces about Ambassador Yovanovitch and other conspiracy theories being pursued by Mr. Giuliani on behalf of President Trump. Mr. Solomon was not working alone. As further described below, there was a coordinated effort by associates of President Trump to push these false narratives publicly, as evidenced by public statements, phone records, and contractual agreements.

On April 1, Mr. Solomon published an opinion piece in *The Hill* alleging that Vice President Biden had inappropriately petitioned for the removal of Mr. Shokin to protect his son, Hunter.[67] The opinion piece was entitled, "Joe Biden's 2020 Ukrainian Nightmare: A Closed Probe is Revived." Many of the allegations in the piece were based on information provided by Mr. Lutsenko. The following day, Donald Trump, Jr. retweeted the article.[68]

Phone records obtained by the Committees show frequent communication between key players during this phase of the scheme. Between April 1 and April 7, Mr. Parnas exchanged approximately 16 calls with Mr. Giuliani (longest duration approximately seven minutes) and approximately 10 calls with Mr. Solomon (longest duration approximately nine minutes).[69]

On April 7, Mr. Solomon followed up with another opinion piece. The piece accused Ambassador Yovanovitch of preventing the issuance of U.S. visas for Ukrainian officials who wished to travel to the United States to provide purported evidence of wrongdoing by "American Democrats and their allies in Kiev."[70] One of those Ukrainian officials allegedly denied a visa was Kostiantyn Kulyk, a deputy to Mr. Lutesenko. Mr. Kulyk participated in a "wide-ranging interview" with Mr. Solomon and was extensively quoted.[71]

These Ukrainian officials claimed to have evidence of wrongdoing about Vice President Biden's efforts in 2015 to remove Mr. Shokin, Hunter Biden's role as a Burisma board member,

Ukrainian interference in the 2016 U.S. election in favor of Hillary Clinton, and the misappropriation and transfer of Ukrainian funds abroad.[72] The opinion piece also made clear that Mr. Giuliani was pursuing these very same theories on behalf of the President:

> More recently, President Trump's private attorney Rudy Giuliani—former mayor and former U.S. attorney in New York City—learned about some of the allegations while, on behalf of the Trump legal team, he looked into Ukrainian involvement in the 2016 election.

According to Mr. Solomon's piece, Mr. Lutsenko was reported to have sufficient evidence, "particularly involving Biden, his family and money spirited out of Ukraine—to warrant a meeting with U.S. Attorney General William Barr."[73]

On the same day that Mr. Solomon published these allegations, Mr. Giuliani appeared on *Fox News*. Mr. Giuliani discussed how he learned about alleged Ukrainian interference in the 2016 U.S. elections and the Bidens' purported misconduct in Ukraine:

> Let me tell you my interest in that. I got information about three or four months ago that a lot of the explanations for how this whole phony investigation started will be in the Ukraine, that there were a group of people in the Ukraine that were working to help Hillary Clinton and were colluding really—[LAUGHTER]—with the Clinton campaign. And it stems around the ambassador and the embassy, being used for political purposes. So I began getting some people that were coming forward and telling me about that. And then all of a sudden, they revealed the story about Burisma and Biden's son ... [Vice President Biden] bragged about pressuring Ukraine's president to firing [sic] a top prosecutor who was being criticized on a whole bunch of areas but was conducting investigation of this gas company which Hunter Biden served as a director.[74]

The next day, April 8, Mr. Giuliani tweeted about Mr. Solomon's opinion piece.[75]

Over the course of the four days following the April 7 article, phone records show contacts between Mr. Giuliani, Mr. Parnas, Ranking Member Nunes, and Mr. Solomon. Specifically, Mr. Giuliani and Mr. Parnas were in contact with one another, as well as with Mr. Solomon.[76] Phone records also show contacts on April 10 between Mr. Giuliani and Ranking Member Nunes, consisting of three short calls in rapid succession, followed by a nearly three-minute call.[77] Later that same day, Mr. Parnas and Mr. Solomon had a four minute, 39 second call.[78]

Victoria Toensing, a lawyer who, along with her partner Joseph diGenova, once briefly represented President Trump in connection with Special Counsel Robert Mueller's investigation,[79] also was in phone contact with Mr. Giuliani and Mr. Parnas at the beginning of April.[80]

Beginning in mid-April, Ms. Toensing signed retainer agreements between diGenova & Toensing LLP and Mr. Lutsenko, Mr. Kulyk, and Mr. Shokin—all of whom feature in Mr. Solomon's opinion pieces.[81] In these retainer agreements, the firm agreed to represent Mr.

Lutsenko and Mr. Kulyk in meetings with U.S. officials regarding alleged "evidence" of Ukrainian interference in the 2016 U.S. elections, and to represent Mr. Shokin "for the purpose of collecting evidence regarding his March 2016 firing as Prosecutor General of Ukraine and the role of Vice President Biden in such firing, and presenting such evidence to U.S. and foreign authorities."[82] On July 25, President Trump would personally press President Zelensky to investigate these very same matters.

On April 23, Mr. Parnas had a call with Mr. Solomon, and multiple phone contacts with Mr. Giuliani.[83] On that same day, Mr. Giuliani had a series of short phone calls (ranging from 11 to 18 seconds) with a phone number associated with the White House, followed shortly thereafter by an eight minute, 28-second call with an unidentified number that called him.[84] Approximately half an hour later, Mr. Giuliani had a 48-second call with a phone number associated with Ambassador John Bolton, National Security Advisor to the President.[85]

That same day, Mr. Giuliani tweeted:

Hillary is correct the report is the end of the beginning for the second time...NO COLLUSION. Now Ukraine is investigating Hillary campaign and DNC conspiracy with foreign operatives including Ukrainian and others to affect 2016 election. And there's no Comey to fix the result.[86]

The next day, on the morning of April 24, Mr. Giuliani appeared on *Fox and Friends*, lambasting the Mueller investigation. Mr. Giuliani also promoted the false conspiracy theories about Ukraine and Vice President Biden:

And I ask you to keep your eye on Ukraine, because in Ukraine, a lot of the dirty work was done in digging up the information. American officials were used, Ukrainian officials were used. That's like collusion with the Ukrainians. And, or actually in this case, conspiracy with the Ukrainians. I think you'd get some interesting information about Joe Biden from Ukraine. About his son, Hunter Biden. About a company he was on the board of for years, which may be one of the most crooked companies in Ukraine. … And Biden bragged about the fact that he got the prosecutor general fired. The prosecutor general was investigating his son and then the investigation went south.[87]

Later that day, Mr. Giuliani had three phone calls with a number associated with OMB, and eight calls with a White House phone number.[88] One of the calls with the White House was four minutes, 53 seconds, and another was three minutes, 15 seconds.

Later that evening, the State Department phoned Ambassador Yovanovitch and abruptly called her home because of "concerns" from "up the street" at the White House.[89]

Ambassador Yovanovitch Was Informed That the President "Lost Confidence" in Her

When Ambassador Yovanovitch returned to the United States at the end of April, Deputy Secretary of State John Sullivan informed her that she had "done nothing wrong," but "there had been a concerted campaign" against her and that President Trump had "lost confidence" in her leadership.[90] He also told her that "the President no longer wished me to serve as Ambassador to Ukraine, and that, in fact, the President had been pushing for my removal since the prior summer."[91] Ambassador Philip T. Reeker, Acting Assistant Secretary of State for the Bureau of European and Eurasian Affairs, offered a similar assessment. He explained to Ambassador Yovanovitch that Secretary Pompeo had tried to "protect" her, but "was no longer able to do that."[92]

Counselor of the Department of State T. Ulrich Brechbuhl, who had been handling Ambassador Yovanovitch's recall, refused to meet with her.[93]

Ambassador Yovanovitch's final day as U.S. Ambassador to Ukraine was May 20, 2019. This was the same day as President Zelensky's inauguration, which was attended by Secretary of Energy Rick Perry, Ambassador Sondland, and Ambassador Volker.[94] Rather than joining the official delegation at the inaugural festivities, she finished packing her personal belongings and boarded an airplane for her final flight home. Three days later, President Trump met in the Oval Office with his hand-picked delegation and gave them the "directive" to "talk with Rudy [Giuliani]" about Ukraine.[95]

The President Provided No Rationale for the Recall of Ambassador Yovanovitch

Ambassador Yovanovitch testified that she was never provided a justification for why President Trump recalled her.[96] Only two months earlier, in early March 2019, Ambassador Yovanovitch had been asked by Ambassador Hale to extend her assignment as Ambassador to Ukraine until 2020.[97]

Ambassador Hale testified that Ambassador Yovanovitch was "an exceptional officer doing exceptional work at a very critical embassy in Kyiv."[98] He added, "I believe that she should've been able to stay at post and continue to do the outstanding work that she was doing."[99]

During her more than three-decade career, Ambassador Yovanovitch received a number of awards, including: the Presidential Distinguished Service Award, the Secretary's Diplomacy in Human Rights Award, the Senior Foreign Service Performance Award six times, and the State Department's Superior Honor Award five times.[100]

Career foreign service officer Ambassador P. Michael McKinley, former Senior Advisor to Secretary Pompeo, testified that Ambassador Yovanovitch's reputation was "excellent, serious, committed."[101] Ambassador Reeker described her as an "[o]utstanding diplomat," "very precise, very—very professional," "an excellent mentor," and "a good leader."[102]

Ambassador Yovanovitch Strongly Advocated for the U.S. Policy to Combat Corruption

Throughout the course of her career, and while posted to Kyiv, Ambassador Yovanovitch was a champion of the United States' longstanding priority of combatting corruption.

Mr. Kent described U.S. foreign policy in Ukraine as encompassing the priorities of "promoting the rule of law, energy independence, defense sector reform, and the ability to stand up to Russia."[103] Ambassador Yovanovitch testified that it "was—and remains—a top U.S. priority to help Ukraine fight corruption" because corruption makes Ukraine more "vulnerable to Russia."[104] Additionally, she testified that an honest and accountable Ukrainian leadership makes a U.S.-Ukrainian partnership more reliable and more valuable to the United States.[105]

Mr. Holmes testified that Ambassador Yovanovitch was successful in implementing anti-corruption reforms in Ukraine by achieving, for example, "the hard-fought passage of a law establishing an independent court to try corruption cases."[106] Mr. Holmes said Ambassador Yovanovitch was "[a]s good as anyone known for" combatting corruption.[107] The reforms achieved by Ambassador Yovanovitch helped reduce the problem faced by many post-Soviet countries of selective corruption prosecutions to target political opponents.[108]

There was a broad consensus that Ambassador Yovanovitch was successful in helping Ukraine combat pervasive and endemic corruption.

The President's Authority Does Not Explain Removal of Ambassador Yovanovitch

While ambassadors serve at the pleasure of the president, the manner and circumstances of Ambassador Yovanovitch's removal were unusual and raise questions of motive.[109]

Ambassador Yovanovitch queried "why it was necessary to smear my reputation falsely."[110] She found it difficult to comprehend how individuals "who apparently felt stymied by our efforts to promote stated U.S. policy against corruption" were "able to successfully conduct a campaign of disinformation against a sitting ambassador using unofficial back channels."[111]

Dr. Hill similarly testified that while the President has the authority to remove an ambassador, she was concerned "about the circumstances in which [Ambassador Yovanovitch's] reputation had been maligned, repeatedly, on television and in all kinds of exchanges." Dr. Hill "felt that that was completely unnecessary."[112]

The Recall of Ambassador Yovanovitch Threatened U.S.-Ukraine Policy

The smear campaign questioning Ambassador Yovanovitch's loyalty undermined U.S. diplomatic efforts in Ukraine, a key U.S. partner and a bulwark against Russia's expansion into Europe. As Ambassador Yovanovitch explained:

> Ukrainians were wondering whether I was going to be leaving, whether we really represented the President, U.S. policy, et cetera. And so I think it was—you know, it really kind of cut the ground out from underneath us.[113]

Summarizing the cumulative impact of the attacks, she emphasized: "If our chief representative is kneecapped it limits our effectiveness to safeguard the vital national security interests of the United States."[114]

President Trump's recall of Ambassador Yovanovitch left the U.S. Embassy in Ukraine without an ambassador at a time of electoral change in Ukraine and when the Embassy was also without a deputy chief of mission. Mr. Kent explained:

> During the late spring and summer of 2019, I became alarmed as those efforts bore fruit. They led to the outer [ouster] of Ambassador Yovanovitch and hampered U.S. efforts to establish rapport with the new Zelensky administration in Ukraine.[115]
> …
> One of the unfortunate elements of the timing was that we were also undergoing a transition in my old job as deputy chief of mission. The person who replaced me had already been moved early to be our DCM and Charge in Sweden, and so we had a temporary acting deputy chief of mission. So that left the embassy not only without—the early withdrawal of Ambassador Yovanovitch left us not only without an Ambassador but without somebody who had been selected to be deputy chief of mission.[116]

It was not until late May that Secretary Pompeo asked Ambassador Bill Taylor, who had previously served as Ambassador to Ukraine, to return to Kyiv as Chargé d'Affaires to lead the embassy while it awaited a confirmed Ambassador. Ambassador Taylor did not arrive in Kyiv until June 17, more than a month after Ambassador Yovanovitch officially left Kyiv.[117] His mission to carry out U.S. objectives there would prove challenging in the face of ongoing efforts by Mr. Giuliani and others—at the direction of the President—to secure investigations demanded by the President to help his reelection.

2.   The President Put Giuliani and the Three Amigos in Charge of Ukraine Issues

After President Trump recalled Ambassador Yovanovitch, his personal agent, Rudy Giuliani, intensified the President's campaign to pressure Ukraine's newly-elected president to interfere in the 2020 U.S. election. President Trump directed his own political appointees to coordinate with Mr. Giuliani on Ukraine, while National Security Council officials expressed alarm over the efforts to pursue a "domestic political errand" for the political benefit of the President. Officials at the highest levels of the White House and Trump Administration were aware of the President's scheme.

Overview

On April 21, 2019, the day that Ukrainian President Volodymyr Zelensky was elected as president of Ukraine, President Trump called to congratulate him. After a positive call—in which Mr. Zelensky complimented President Trump and requested that President Trump attend his inauguration—President Trump instructed Vice President Mike Pence to lead the U.S. delegation to the inauguration. However, on May 13—before the inauguration date was even set—President Trump instructed Vice President Pence not to attend.

Rudy Giuliani also announced a plan to visit Ukraine in mid-May 2019—not on official U.S. government business, but instead to pursue on behalf of his client, President Trump, the debunked conspiracy theories about alleged Ukrainian interference in the 2016 election and discredited claims about the Bidens. After public scrutiny in response to his announced visit, Mr. Giuliani cancelled his trip and alleged that President-elect Zelensky was surrounded by "enemies of the President."

Secretary of Energy Rick Perry, Ambassador to the European Union Gordon Sondland, and Ambassador Kurt Volker, Special Representative for Ukraine Negotiations, ultimately led the U.S. delegation to President Zelensky's inauguration. Upon returning to Washington, D.C., the three U.S. officials—who dubbed themselves the "Three Amigos"—debriefed the President in the Oval Office and encouraged him to engage with President Zelensky. Instead of accepting their advice, President Trump complained that Ukraine is "a terrible place, all corrupt, terrible people," and asserted that Ukraine "tried to take me down in 2016." The President instructed the "Three Amigos" to "talk to Rudy" and coordinate with him on Ukraine matters. They followed the President's orders.

Dr. Fiona Hill, Deputy Assistant to the President and Senior Director for Europe and Russia at the National Security Council, would later observe that Ambassador Sondland "was being involved in a domestic political errand, and we [the NSC staff] were being involved in national security foreign policy, and those two things had just diverged."

A Political Newcomer Won Ukraine's Presidential Election on an Anti-Corruption Platform

On April 21, popular comedian and television actor, Volodymyr Zelensky, won a landslide victory in Ukraine's presidential election, earning the support of 73 percent of voters and unseating the incumbent Petro Poroshenko. Mr. Zelensky, who had no prior political experience, told voters a week before his victory: "I'm not a politician. I'm just a simple person who came to break the system."[118] Five years earlier, in late 2013, Ukrainians had gathered in Kyiv and rallied against the corrupt government of former President Viktor Yanukovych, eventually forcing him to flee to the safety of Vladimir Putin's Russia. Mr. Zelensky's victory in April 2019 reaffirmed the Ukrainian people's strong desire to overcome an entrenched system of corruption and pursue closer partnership with the West.[119]

Following the election results, at 4:29 p.m. Eastern Time, President Trump was connected by telephone to President-elect Zelensky and congratulated him "on a job well done … a fantastic election." He declared, "I have no doubt you will be a fantastic president."[120]

According to a call record released publicly by the White House, President Trump did not openly express doubts about the newly-elected leader.[121] And contrary to a public readout of the call originally issued by the White House, President Trump did not mention corruption in Ukraine, despite the NSC staff preparing talking points on that topic.[122] Indeed, "corruption" was not mentioned once during the April 21 conversation, according to the official call record.[123]

In the call, President-elect Zelensky lauded President Trump as "a great example" and invited him to visit Ukraine for his upcoming inauguration—a gesture that President Trump called "very nice."[124] President Trump told Mr. Zelensky:

I'll look into that, and well—give us the date and, at a very minimum, we'll have a great representative. Or more than one from the United States will be with you on that great day. So, we will have somebody, at a minimum, at a very, very high level, and they will be with you.[125]

Mr. Zelensky persisted. "Words cannot describe our country," he went on, "so it would be best for you to see it yourself. So, if you can come, that would be great. So again, I invite you to come."[126] President Trump responded, "Well, I agree with you about your country and I look forward to it."[127] In a nod to his past experience working with Ukraine as a businessman, President Trump added, "When I owned Miss Universe … Ukraine was always very well represented."[128]

President Trump then invited Mr. Zelensky to the White House to meet, saying: "When you're settled in and ready, I'd like to invite you to the White House. We'll have a lot of things to talk about, but we're with you all the way." Mr. Zelensky promptly accepted the President's invitation, adding that the "whole team and I are looking forward to that visit."[129]

Mr. Zelensky then reiterated his interest in President Trump attending his inauguration, saying, "it will be absolutely fantastic if you could come and be with us." President Trump promised to let the Ukrainian leader know "very soon" and added that he would see Mr. Zelensky "very soon, regardless."[130]

Shortly after the April 21 call, Jennifer Williams, Special Advisor to the Vice President for Europe and Russia, learned that President Trump asked Vice President Pence to attend Mr. Zelensky's inauguration.[131] Ms. Williams testified that in a separate phone call between Vice President Pence and President-elect Zelensky two days later, "the Vice President accepted that invitation from President Zelensky, and looked forward to being able to attend ... if the dates worked out."[132] Ms. Williams and her colleagues began planning for the Vice President's trip to Kyiv.[133]

Rudy Giuliani and his Associates Coordinated Efforts to Secure and Promote the Investigations with Ukrainian President Zelensky

As previously explained in Chapter 1, Mr. Giuliani, acting on behalf of President Trump, had for months engaged corrupt current and former Ukrainian officials, including Ukrainian Prosecutor General Yuriy Lutsenko. The April election of Mr. Zelensky, however, raised the possibility that Mr. Lutsenko might lose his job as Prosecutor General once Mr. Zelensky took power.

In the immediate aftermath of President-elect Zelensky's election, Mr. Giuliani continued publicly to project confidence that Ukraine would deliver on investigations related to the Bidens. On April 24—before Ambassador Yovanovitch received calls abruptly summoning her back to Washington—Mr. Giuliani stated in an interview on *Fox and Friends* that viewers should,

> [K]eep your eye on Ukraine... I think you'd get some interesting information about Joe Biden from Ukraine. About his son, Hunter Biden. About a company he was on the board of for years, which may be one of the most crooked companies in Ukraine.[134]

Behind the scenes, however, Mr. Giuliani was taking steps to engage the new Ukrainian leader and his aides.

The day before, on April 23, the same day that Vice President Pence confirmed his plans to attend President-elect Zelensky's inauguration, Mr. Giuliani dispatched his own delegation—consisting of Lev Parnas and Igor Fruman—to meet with Ihor Kolomoisky, a wealthy Ukrainian with ties to President-elect Zelensky. Instead of going to Kyiv, they booked tickets to Israel, where they met with Mr. Kolomoisky.[135] Mr. Kolomoisky owned Ukraine's largest bank until 2016, when Ukrainian authorities nationalized the failing financial institution. Although he denied allegations of committing any crimes, Mr. Kolomoisky subsequently left Ukraine for Israel, where he remained until President Zelensky assumed power.[136]

Mr. Kolomoisky confirmed to the *New York Times* that he met with Mr. Parnas and Mr. Fruman in late April 2019. He claimed they sought his assistance in facilitating a meeting between Mr. Giuliani and President-elect Zelensky, and he told them, "you've ended up in the wrong place," and declined to arrange the requested meeting.[137]

Mr. Giuliani was not deterred.

During the time surrounding Ambassador Yovanovitch's recall, Mr. Giuliani and Mr. Parnas connected over a flurry of calls around a planned trip to Ukraine by Mr. Giuliani, which he would eventually cancel after growing public scrutiny. As previously described in Chapter 1, call records obtained by the Committees show a series of contacts on April 23 and 24 between Mr. Giuliani, the White House, Mr. Parnas, and John Solomon, among others.[138]

On April 25, 2019, former Vice President Biden publicly announced his campaign for the Democratic nomination for President of the United States and launched his effort to unseat President Trump in the 2020 election.[139]

That evening, Mr. Solomon published a new opinion piece in *The Hill* entitled, "How the Obama White House Engaged Ukraine to Give Russia Collusion Narrative an Early Boost." Like Mr. Solomon's previous work, this April 25 piece repeated unsubstantiated conspiracy theories about alleged Ukrainian interference in the 2016 U.S. presidential election.[140]

Meanwhile, in Kyiv, David Holmes, Counselor for Political Affairs at the U.S. Embassy, learned on April 25 that Mr. Giuliani had reached out to Mr. Zelensky's campaign chair, Ivan Bakanov, seeking a channel to the newly-elected leader. Mr. Bakanov told Mr. Holmes "that he had been contacted by, quote, someone named Giuliani, who said he was an advisor to the Vice President, unquote."[141] Mr. Holmes clarified that Mr. Bakanov was "speaking in Russian" and that he did not "know what he [Bakanov] meant" by his reference to the Vice President, "but that's what he [Bakanov] said."[142] Regardless of Mr. Bakanov's apparent confusion as to who Mr. Giuliani represented, Mr. Holmes explained that by this point in time, Ukrainian officials seemed to think that Mr. Giuliani "was a significant person in terms of managing their relationship with the United States."[143]

At 7:14 p.m. Eastern Time on April 25, Mr. Giuliani once again received a call from an unknown "-1" number, which lasted four minutes and 40 seconds.[144] Minutes later, Mr. Giuliani held a brief 36 second call with Sean Hannity, a *Fox News* opinion host.[145]

On the night of April 25, President Trump called into Mr. Hannity's prime time *Fox News* show. In response to a question about Mr. Solomon's recent publication, President Trump said:

> It sounds like big stuff. It sounds very interesting with Ukraine. I just spoke to the new president a little while ago, two days ago, and congratulated him on an incredible race. Incredible run. A big surprise victory. That's 75 percent of the vote. But that sounds like big, big stuff. I'm not surprised.[146]

As Mr. Holmes later learned on July 26 from Ambassador Sondland, President Trump did not care about Ukraine, he cared about this "big stuff"—such as the investigation into Vice President Biden.[147]

In the same *Fox News* interview, Mr. Hannity asked President Trump whether America needed to see the purported evidence possessed by the unnamed Ukrainians noted in Mr. Solomon's piece. The President replied, invoking Attorney General William P. Barr:

> Well, I think we do. And, frankly, we have a great new attorney general who has done an unbelievable job in a very short period of time. And he is very smart and tough and I would certainly defer to him. I would imagine he would want to see this. People have been saying this whole—the concept of Ukraine, they have been talking about it actually for a long time. You know that, and I would certainly defer to the attorney general. And we'll see what he says about it. He calls them straight. That's one thing I can tell you.[148]

Ukraine's current Prosecutor General Ruslan Ryaboshapka, who assumed his new position in late August 2019, told the *Financial Times* in late November 2019 that Attorney General Barr had made no contact regarding a potential investigation into allegations of wrongdoing by former Vice President Biden.[149] In an apparent reference to President Trump's demand for Ukrainian interference in U.S. elections, Mr. Ryaboshapka stated: "It's critically important for the west not to pull us into some conflicts between their ruling elites, but to continue to support so that we can cross the point of no return."[150]

President Trump Promoted False Information About Former Vice President Joe Biden

In early May, Mr. Giuliani continued his outreach to President-elect Zelensky and promoted the need for Ukrainian investigations into former Vice President Biden that served President Trump's political needs.

On May 2, at 6:21 a.m. Eastern Time, President Trump retweeted a link to an article in the *New York Times,* which assessed that Mr. Giuliani's efforts underscored "the Trump campaign's concern about the electoral threat from the former vice president's presidential campaign" and noted that "Mr. Giuliani's involvement raises questions about whether Mr. Trump is endorsing an effort to push a foreign government to proceed with a case that could hurt a political opponent at home."[151]

Later that evening, in an interview with *Fox News* at the White House, President Trump referenced the false allegations about the firing of a corrupt former Ukrainian prosecutor, Viktor Shokin, that Mr. Giuliani had been promoting. He was asked, "Should the former vice president explain himself on his feeling in Ukraine and whether there was a conflict … with his son's business interests?"[152] President Trump replied:

> I'm hearing it's a major scandal, major problem. Very bad things happened, and we'll see what that is. They even have him on tape, talking about it. They have Joe Biden on tape talking about the prosecutor. And I've seen that tape. A lot of people are talking about that tape, but that's up to them. They have to solve that problem.[153]

"The tape" President Trump referenced in his interview was a publicly available video of former Vice President Biden speaking in January 2018 at an event hosted by the Council on Foreign Relations (CFR), a nonpartisan think-tank focused on foreign policy matters. During an interview with the CFR president, Vice President Biden detailed how the United States—consistent with the policy of its European allies and the International Monetary Fund (IMF)—withheld $1 billion in loan guarantees until the Ukrainian government acceded to uniform American and international demands to fire the corrupt prosecutor.[154]

By late 2015, Ukrainians were agitating for Mr. Shokin's removal, and in March 2016, Ukraine's parliament voted to dismiss the prosecutor general.[155] Multiple witnesses testified that Mr. Shokin's dismissal in 2016 made it *more*—not less—likely that Ukrainian authorities might investigate any allegations or wrongdoing at Burisma or other allegedly corrupt companies.[156] Nonetheless, President Trump and his supporters sought to perpetuate the false narrative that Mr. Shokin should not have been removed from office and that Vice President Biden had acted corruptly in carrying out U.S. policy.

Rudy Giuliani Was "Meddling in an Investigation" on Behalf of President Trump

On May 7, 2019, Christopher Wray, the Director of the Federal Bureau of Investigation, testified before the U.S. Senate Appropriations Subcommittee on Commerce, Justice, Science, and Related Agencies regarding foreign interference in U.S. elections:

> My view is that, if any public official or member of any campaign is contacted by any nation-state or anybody acting on behalf of a nation-state about influencing or interfering with our election, then that is something that the FBI would want to know about. [157]

Mr. Giuliani nonetheless pressed forward with his plan to personally convey to President-elect Zelensky, on behalf of his client President Trump, the importance of opening investigations that would assist President Trump's reelection campaign.

On the morning of May 8, Mr. Giuliani called the White House Switchboard and connected for six minutes and 26 seconds with someone at the White House.[158] That same day, Mr. Giuliani also connected with Mr. Solomon for almost six minutes and separately with Mr. Parnas. Mr. Parnas connected for one minute 13 seconds and with Derek Harvey, a member of Ranking Member Nunes' staff on the Intelligence Committee, on the same day.[159]

During a meeting that same day, Ukraine Minister of Interior Arsen Avakov disclosed to Deputy Assistant Secretary of State George Kent that Mr. Parnas and Mr. Fruman would soon visit Kyiv "and that they were coming with their associate, the Mayor Giuliani."[160] Minister Avakov confided to Mr. Kent that "Mayor Giuliani had reached out to him and invited him to come and meet the group of them in Florida" in February 2019.[161] Although he declined that offer, Minister Avakov indicated that he intended to accept their new invitation to meet in Kyiv.[162]

The next day, on May 9, the *New York Times* publicized Mr. Giuliani's plan to visit Ukraine.[163] Mr. Giuliani confirmed that he planned to meet with President Zelensky and press the Ukrainians to pursue investigations that President Trump promoted only days earlier on *Fox News*.[164] The *New York Times* described Mr. Giuliani's planned trip as:

[P]art of a monthslong effort by the former New York mayor and a small group of Trump allies working to build interest in the Ukrainian inquiries. Their motivation is to…undermine the case against Paul Manafort, Mr. Trump's imprisoned former campaign chairman; and potentially to damage Mr. Biden, the early front-runner for the 2020 Democratic presidential nomination.[165]

Mr. Giuliani claimed, "We're not meddling in an election, we're meddling in an investigation, which we have a right to do."[166]

Only a few days after Director Wray's public comments about foreign interference in U.S. elections, Mr. Giuliani acknowledged that "[s]omebody could say it's improper" to pressure Ukraine to open investigations that would benefit President Trump. But, Mr. Giuliani argued:

[T]his isn't foreign policy—I'm asking them to do an investigation that they're doing already, and that other people are telling them to stop. And I'm going to give them reasons why they shouldn't stop it because that information will be very, very helpful to my client, and may turn out to be helpful to my government.[167]

Mr. Giuliani's "client" was President Trump, as Mr. Giuliani repeatedly stated publicly. According to Mr. Giuliani, the President fully supported putting pressure on Ukraine to open investigations that would benefit his 2020 reelection campaign.[168] Mr. Giuliani emphasized that President Trump "basically knows what I'm doing, sure, as his lawyer."[169] Underscoring his commitment to pressuring Ukraine until it opened the investigations President Trump promoted on *Fox News*, Mr. Giuliani told the *Washington Post* that he would "make sure that nothing scuttles the investigation that I want."[170]

On May 9, following public revelation of his trip by the *New York Times*, Mr. Giuliani connected in quick succession with Mr. Solomon and then Mr. Parnas for several minutes at a time.[171] Mr. Giuliani then made brief connections with the White House Switchboard and Situation Room several times, before connecting at 1:43 p.m. Eastern Time with someone at the White House for over four minutes.[172] He connected, separately, thereafter with Mr. Parnas several times in the afternoon and into the evening.[173]

That evening, Mr. Giuliani tweeted:

If you doubt there is media bias and corruption then when Democrats conspiring with Ukrainian officials comes out remember much of the press, except for Fox, the Hill, and NYT, has suppressed it. If it involved @realDonaldTrump or his son it would have been front page news for weeks.[174]

Shortly thereafter, on the night of May 9, he made an appearance on *Fox News* and reiterated that his trip to Ukraine was intended to further the President's personal and political interests by pressuring the Ukrainian government to investigate the Bidens:

57

It's a big story. It's a dramatic story. And I guarantee you, Joe Biden will not get to election day without this being investigated, not because I want to see him investigated. This is collateral to what I was doing.[175]

The next morning, on May 10, amidst the press coverage of his trip, Mr. Giuliani tweeted:

Explain to me why Biden shouldn't be investigated if his son got millions from a Russian loving crooked Ukrainian oligarch while He was VP and point man for Ukraine. Ukrainians are investigating and your fellow Dems are interfering. Election is 17 months away. Let's answer it now[176]

He then had another flurry of calls with Mr. Parnas. Shortly after 2:00 p.m., Eastern Time, Mr. Giuliani also spoke with Ambassador Volker on the phone.[177] Ambassador Volker had learned that Mr. Giuliani intended to travel to Ukraine "to pursue these allegations that Lutsenko had made, and he was going to investigate these things"—specifically, the debunked story that Vice President Biden had improperly pressured Ukraine to fire a corrupt prosecutor general, as well as the Russian-backed conspiracy that the Ukrainians interfered in the 2016 U.S. election.[178] Ambassador Volker testified that he had a simple warning for Mr. Giuliani: Prosecutor General Lutsenko "is not credible. Don't listen to what he is saying."[179] Call records obtained by the Committees reveal that their call lasted more than 30 minutes.[180]

Call records also show that around midday on May 10, Mr. Giuliani began trading aborted calls with Kashyap "Kash" Patel, an official at the National Security Council who previously served on Ranking Member Nunes' staff on the Intelligence Committee. Mr. Patel successfully connected with Mr. Giuliani less than an hour after Mr. Giuliani's call with Ambassador Volker. Beginning at 3:23 p.m., Eastern Time, Mr. Patel and Mr. Giuliani spoke for over 25 minutes.[181] Five minutes after Mr. Patel and Mr. Giuliani disconnected, an unidentified "-1" number connected with Mr. Giuliani for over 17 minutes.[182] Shortly thereafter, Mr. Giuliani spoke with Mr. Parnas for approximately 12 minutes.[183]

That same afternoon, President Trump conducted a 15-minute long phone interview with *Politico*. In response to a question about Mr. Giuliani's upcoming visit to Kyiv, the President replied, "I have not spoken to him at any great length, but I will … I will speak to him about it before he leaves."[184]

Recently, when asked what Mr. Giuliani was doing in Ukraine on his behalf, the President responded: "Well, you have to ask that to Rudy, but Rudy, I don't, I don't even know. I know he was going to go to Ukraine, and I think he canceled a trip."[185] Prior to that, on October 2, the President publicly stated: "And just so you know, we've been investigating, on a personal basis—through Rudy and others, lawyers—corruption in the 2016 election."[186] On October 4, the President publicly stated: "If we feel there's corruption, like I feel there was in the 2016 campaign—there was tremendous corruption against me—if we feel there's corruption, we have a right to go to a foreign country."[187]

By the evening of May 10, Mr. Giuliani appeared to have concerns about the incoming Ukrainian President. He appeared on *Fox News* and announced, "I'm not going to go" to Ukraine "because I think I'm walking into a group of people that are enemies of the President."[188] In a text message to *Politico*, Mr. Giuliani alleged the original offer for a meeting with President-elect Zelensky was a "set up" orchestrated by "several vocal critics" of President Trump who were advising President-elect Zelensky.[189] Mr. Giuliani declared that President-elect Zelensky "is in [the] hands of avowed enemies of Pres[ident] Trump."[190]

Like Mr. Giuliani, President Trump would express hostility toward Ukraine in the days and weeks to come.

Russian President Putin and Hungarian Prime Minister Orban Counseled President Trump on Ukraine

In early May, Mr. Giuliani was not the only person who conveyed his skepticism of Ukraine to President Trump. The President reportedly discussed Ukraine with Russian President Vladimir Putin when they spoke by phone on May 3. President Trump posted on Twitter that he "[h]ad a long and very good conversation with President Putin of Russia" and discussed "even the 'Russian Hoax'"—an apparent reference to the unanimous finding by the U.S. Intelligence Community that Russia interfered in the 2016 election with the aim of assisting President Trump's candidacy.[191] Mr. Kent subsequently heard from Dr. Hill, the NSC's Senior Director for Europe and Russia, that President Putin also expressed negative views about Ukraine to President Trump. He testified that President Putin's motivation in undercutting President-elect Zelensky was "very clear":

> He denies the existence of Ukraine as a nation and a country, as he told President Bush in Bucharest in 2008. He invaded and occupied 7 percent of Ukraine's territory and he's led to the death of 13,000 Ukrainians on Ukrainian territory since 2014 as a result of aggression. So that's his agenda, the agenda of creating a greater Russia and ensuring that Ukraine does not survive independently.[192]

On May 13, President Trump met one-on-one for an hour with Hungarian Prime Minister Viktor Orban. President Trump offered the leader a warm reception in the Oval Office and claimed Prime Minister Orban had "done a tremendous job in so many different ways. Highly respected. Respected all over Europe."[193] The European Union and many European leaders, however, have widely condemned Prime Minister Orban for undermining Hungary's democratic institutions and promoting anti-Semitism and xenophobia.[194]

Mr. Kent explained to the Committees that Prime Minister Orban's "animus towards Ukraine is well-known, documented, and has lasted now two years." Due to a dispute over the rights of 130,000 ethnic Hungarians who live in Ukraine, Mr. Kent noted that Prime Minister Orban "blocked all meetings in NATO with Ukraine at the ministerial level or above," undercutting U.S. and European efforts to support Ukraine in its war against Russia.[195] Nonetheless, President Trump told reporters prior to his meeting with Prime Minister Orban to not "forget they're a member of NATO, and a very good member of NATO."[196]

Commenting on what Dr. Hill shared with him following the May 3 call and May 13 meeting, Mr. Kent said he understood President Trump's discussions about Ukraine with President Putin and Prime Minister Orban "as being similar in tone and approach." He explained that "both leaders" had "extensively talked Ukraine down, said it was corrupt, said Zelensky was in the thrall of oligarchs" the effect of which was "negatively shaping a picture of Ukraine, and even President Zelensky personally."[197] The veteran State Department diplomat concluded, "[T]hose two world leaders [Putin and Orban], along with former Mayor Giuliani, their communications with President Trump shaped the President's view of Ukraine and Zelensky, and would account for the change from a very positive first call on April 21 to his negative assessment of Ukraine."[198]

President Trump Instructs Vice President Pence Not to Attend President Zelensky's Inauguration

On Monday, May 13, at approximately 11:00 a.m. Eastern Time, Ms. Williams received a call from an assistant to the Vice President's Chief of Staff.[199] President Trump, the assistant relayed, had "decided that the Vice President would not attend the inauguration in Ukraine," despite the fact that Vice President Pence previously had accepted the invitation.[200] Ms. Williams was never given a reason for the change in President Trump's decision.[201]

Mr. Holmes later testified that:

[The U.S. Embassy in Kyiv had] gone back and forth with NSC staff about proposing a list of potential members of the delegation. It was initially quite a long list. We had asked who would be the senior [U.S.] member of that delegation. We were told that Vice President Pence was likely to be that senior member, it was not yet fully agreed to. And so we were anticipating that to be the case. And then the Giuliani event happened, and then we heard that he was not going to play that role.[202]

Asked to clarify what he meant by "the Giuliani event," Mr. Holmes replied, "the interview basically saying that he had planned to travel to Ukraine, but he canceled his trip because there were, quote, unquote, enemies of the U.S. President in Zelensky's orbit."[203]

One of the individuals around President-elect Zelensky whom Mr. Giuliani publicly criticized was the oligarch Mr. Kolomoisky, who had refused to set up a meeting between Mr. Giuliani and President Zelensky. On May 18, Mr. Giuliani complained on Twitter that the oligarch "returned from a long exile and immediately threatened and defamed two Americans, Lev Parnas and Igor Fruman. They are my clients and I have advised them to press charges."[204]

Mr. Kolomoisky responded to Mr. Giuliani in a televised interview and declared, "Look, there is Giuliani, and two clowns, Lev Parnas and Igor Fruman, who were engaging in nonsense. They are Giuliani's clients." He added: "They came here and told us that they would organize a meeting with Zelensky. They allegedly struck a deal with [Prosecutor-General Yuriy] Lutsenko about the fate of this criminal case—Burisma, [former Vice President] Biden, meddling in the U.S. election and so on."[205] He warned that a "big scandal may break out, and not only in

Ukraine, but in the United States. That is, it may turn out to be a clear conspiracy against Biden."[206]

Despite Ukraine's significance to U.S. national security as a bulwark against Russian aggression and the renewed opportunity that President Zelensky's administration offered for bringing Ukraine closer to the United States and Europe, President Trump did not ask Secretary of State Michael Pompeo, Acting Secretary of Defense Patrick Shanahan, or National Security Advisor John Bolton to lead the delegation to President Zelensky's inauguration. Instead, according to Mr. Holmes, the White House "ultimately whittled back an initial proposed list for the official delegation to the inauguration from over a dozen individuals to just five."[207]

Topping that list was Secretary Perry. Accompanying him were Ambassador Sondland, U.S. Special Representative for Ukraine Negotiations Ambassador Volker, and NSC Director for Ukraine Lt. Col. Alexander Vindman.[208] Acting Deputy Chief of Mission (Chargé d'Affaires) of U.S. Embassy Kyiv Joseph Pennington joined the delegation, in place of outgoing U.S. Ambassador to Ukraine Marie Yovanovitch. U.S. Senator Ron Johnson also attended the inauguration and joined several meetings with the presidential delegation. When asked if this delegation was "a good group," Mr. Holmes replied that it "was not as senior a delegation as we [the U.S. embassy] might have expected."[209]

Secretary Perry, Ambassador Volker, and Ambassador Sondland subsequently began to refer to themselves as the "Three Amigos." During the delegation's meeting with President Zelensky, Mr. Holmes recounted that "Secretary Perry passed President Zelensky a list of, quote, 'people he trusts' from whom Zelensky could seek advice on energy sector reform, which was the topic of subsequent meetings between Secretary Perry and key Ukrainian energy sector contacts, from which Embassy personnel were excluded by Secretary Perry's staff."[210]

Mr. Holmes assessed that the delegation's visit proceeded smoothly, although "at one point during a preliminary meeting of the inaugural delegation, someone in the group wondered aloud about why Mr. Giuliani was so active in the media with respect to Ukraine."[211] Ambassador Sondland responded: "Dammit, Rudy. Every time Rudy gets involved he goes and effs everything up."[212] Mr. Holmes added: "He used the 'F' word."[213]

By the time of the inauguration, Mr. Holmes assessed that President Zelensky and the Ukrainians were already starting to feel pressure to conduct political investigations related to former Vice President Biden.[214] Lt. Col. Vindman also was concerned about the potentially negative consequences of Mr. Giuliani's political efforts on behalf of President Trump—both for U.S. national security and also Ukraine's longstanding history of bipartisan support in the U.S. Congress.[215]

During the U.S. delegation's meeting with President Zelensky on the margins of the inauguration, Lt. Col. Vindman was the last person to speak.[216] He "offered two pieces of advice" to President Zelensky. First, he advised the new leader, "be particularly cautious with regards to Russia, and its desire to provoke Ukraine."[217] And second, Lt. Col. Vindman warned, "stay out of U.S. domestic … politics."[218] Referencing the activities of Mr. Giuliani, Lt. Col Vindman explained:

[I]n the March and April timeframe, it became clear that there were—there were actors in the U.S., public actors, nongovernmental actors that were promoting the idea of investigations and 2016 Ukrainian interference. And it was consistent with U.S. policy to advise any country, all the countries in my portfolio, any country in the world, to not participate in U.S. domestic politics. So I was passing the same advice consistent with U.S. policy.[219]

U.S. Officials Briefed President Trump About their Positive Impressions of Ukraine

Ambassadors Volker and Sondland left Kyiv with "a very favorable impression" of the new Ukrainian leader.[220] They believed it was important that President Trump "personally engage with the President of Ukraine in order to demonstrate full U.S. support for him," including by inviting him to Washington for a meeting in the Oval Office.[221] It was agreed that the delegation would request a meeting with President Trump and personally convey their advice. They were granted time with President Trump on May 23.

According to Mr. Kent, the delegation was able to secure the Oval Office meeting shortly after the return from Kyiv because of Ambassador Sondland's "connections" to Acting White House Chief of Staff Mick Mulvaney and President Trump.[222] Christopher Anderson, Special Advisor to Ambassador Kurt Volker, also attributed the delegation's ability to quickly confirm a meeting with President Trump to Ambassador Sondland's "connections to the White House."[223]

At the May 23 meeting, Ambassadors Sondland and Volker were joined by Secretary Perry, Senator Johnson, and Dr. Charles M. Kupperman, the Deputy National Security Advisor. Mr. Mulvaney may have also participated.[224]

Lt. Col. Vindman, who had represented the White House at President Zelensky's inauguration, did not participate in the meeting. Dr. Hill directed him not to join, because she had learned that "there was some confusion" from the President "over who the director for Ukraine is."[225] Specifically, Dr. Hill testified that around the time of the May 23 debriefing in the Oval Office, she "became aware by chance and accident" that President Trump had requested to speak with the NSC's Ukraine director about unspecified "materials."[226] A member of the NSC executive secretary's staff stated that in response to the President's request, "we might be reaching out to Kash."[227]

Dr. Hill testified that she understood the staff to be referring to Mr. Patel, who then served as a director in the NSC's directorate of International Organizations and Alliances, not the directorate of Europe and Russia.[228] She subsequently consulted with Dr. Kupperman and sought to clarify if Mr. Patel "had some special … Ambassador Sondland-like representational role on Ukraine" that she had not been informed about, but "couldn't elicit any information about that."[229] All Dr. Kupperman said was that he would look into the matter.[230] Dr. Hill also testified that she never saw or learned more about the Ukraine-related "materials" that the President believed he had received from Mr. Patel, who maintained a close relationship with Ranking Member Nunes after leaving his staff to join the NSC.[231]

President Trump Put the Three Amigos in Charge of the United States' Ukraine Relationship and Directed Them to "Talk to Rudy" About Ukraine

According to witness testimony, the May 23 debriefing with the President in the Oval Office proved consequential for two reasons. President Trump authorized Ambassador Sondland, Secretary Perry, and Ambassador Volker to lead engagement with President Zelensky's new administration in Ukraine. He instructed them, however, to talk to and coordinate with his personal attorney, Mr. Giuliani.

Ambassador Sondland, Ambassador Volker, Secretary Perry, and Senator Johnson "took turns" making their case "that this is a new crowd, it's a new President" in Ukraine who was "committed to doing the right things," including fighting corruption.[232] According to Ambassador Sondland, the group "emphasized the strategic importance of Ukraine" and the value to the United States of strengthening the relationship with President Zelensky.[233] They recommended that President Trump once again call President Zelensky and follow through on his April 21 invitation for President Zelensky to meet with him in the Oval Office.[234]

President Trump reacted negatively to the positive assessment of Ukraine. Ambassador Volker recalled that President Trump said Ukraine is "a terrible place, all corrupt, terrible people" and was "just dumping on Ukraine."[235] This echoed Mr. Giuliani's public statements about Ukraine during early May.

According to both Ambassadors Volker and Sondland, President Trump also alleged, without offering any evidence, that Ukraine "tried to take me down" in the 2016 election.[236] The President emphasized that he "didn't believe" the delegation's positive assessment of the new Ukrainian President, and added "that's not what I hear" from Mr. Giuliani.[237] President Trump said that Mr. Giuliani "knows all of these things" and knows that President Zelensky has "some bad people around him."[238] Rather than committing to an Oval Office meeting with the Ukrainian leader, President Trump directed the delegation to "[t]alk to Rudy, talk to Rudy."[239]

Ambassador Sondland testified that the "Three Amigos" saw the writing on the wall and concluded "that if we did not talk to Rudy, nothing would move forward on Ukraine."[240] He continued:

> [B]ased on the President's direction we were faced with a choice. We could abandon the goal of a White House meeting for President Zelensky, which we all believed was crucial to strengthening U.S.-Ukrainian ties … or we could do as President Trump directed and talk to Mr. Giuliani to address the President's concerns. We chose the latter path.[241]

Ambassador Volker reached a similar conclusion. He believed "that the messages being conveyed by Mr. Giuliani were a problem, because they were at variance with what our official message to the President was, and not conveying that positive assessment that we all had. And so, I thought it was important to try to step in and fix the problem."[242] Ultimately, however, the "problem" posed by the President's instruction to coordinate regarding Ukraine with his personal attorney persisted and would become more acute.

After the May 23 meeting, Ambassador Sondland stayed behind with President Trump and personally confirmed that the Three Amigos "would be working on the Ukraine file."[243]

Multiple witnesses testified about this shift in personnel in charge of the Ukraine relationship.[244] Mr. Kent recalled that, after the Oval Office meeting, Secretary Perry, Ambassador Sondland, and Ambassador Volker began "asserting that, going forward, they would be the drivers of the relationship with Ukraine."[245] Catherine Croft, Special Advisor to Ambassador Kurt Volker, recalled that "Sondland, Volker, and sort of Perry, as a troika, or as the Three Amigos, had been sort of tasked with Ukraine policy" by President Trump.[246] Under Secretary of State for Political Affairs David Hale testified about his understanding of the meeting, "[I]t was clear that the President, from the readout I had received, the President had tasked that group, members of that delegation to pursue these objectives: the meeting, and the policy goals that I outlined earlier. So I was, you know, knowing I was aware that Ambassador Volker and Ambassador Sondland would be doing that."[247]

On a June 10 conference call with the Three Amigos, "Secretary Perry laid out for Ambassador Bolton the notion that" they "would assist Ambassador Taylor on Ukraine and be there to support" him as the U.S.-Ukraine relationship "move[ed] forward."[248]

This *de facto* change in authority was never officially communicated to other officials, including Dr. Hill, who had responsibility for Ukraine at the National Security Council.[249]

U.S. Officials Collaborated with Rudy Giuliani to Advance the President's Political Agenda

Ambassador Sondland testified that in the weeks and months after the May 23 Oval Office meeting, "everyone was in the loop" regarding Mr. Giuliani's role in advancing the President's scheme regarding Ukraine.[250] The "Three Amigos" did as the President ordered and began communicating with Mr. Giuliani. E-mail messages described to the Committees by Ambassador Sondland showed that he informed Mr. Mulvaney, Ambassador Bolton, and Secretaries Pompeo and Perry, as well as their immediate staffs, of his Ukraine-related efforts on behalf of the President.[251]

According to Ambassador Sondland, Secretary Perry agreed to reach out to Mr. Giuliani first "given their prior relationship."[252] Secretary Perry discussed with Mr. Giuliani the political concerns that President Trump articulated in the May 23 meeting.[253]

Dr. Hill testified that Ambassador Volker, Ambassador Sondland, and Secretary Perry "gave us every impression that they were meeting with Rudy Giuliani at this point, and Rudy Giuliani was also saying on the television, and indeed has said subsequently, that he was closely coordinating with the State Department."[254] These meetings ran counter to Ambassador Bolton's repeated declarations that "nobody should be meeting with Giuliani"[255]

Like Dr. Hill, Ambassador Bolton also closely tracked Mr. Giuliani's activities on behalf of the President. According to Dr. Hill, Ambassador Bolton closely monitored Mr. Giuliani's public statements and repeatedly referred to Mr. Giuliani as a "hand grenade that was going to blow everyone up."[256] During a meeting on June 13, Ambassador Bolton made clear that he supported more engagement with Ukraine by senior White House officials but warned that "Mr. Giuliani was a key voice with the President on Ukraine."[257] According to Ambassador Bolton, Mr. Giuliani's influence "could be an obstacle to increased White House engagement."[258] Ambassador Bolton joked that "every time Ukraine is mentioned, Giuliani pops up."[259]

Ambassador Bolton also reportedly joined Dr. Hill in warning Ambassador Volker against contacting Mr. Giuliani.[260] Dr. Hill was particularly concerned about engagement with Mr. Giuliani because "the more you engage with someone who is spreading untruths, the more validity you give to those untruths."[261] She further testified that she also discussed Mr. Giuliani's activities with Dr. Kupperman, specifically her concern that "Ukraine was going to be played by Giuliani in some way as part of the campaign."[262]

On June 18, Ambassador Volker, Acting Assistant Secretary of State Ambassador Philip T. Reeker, Secretary Perry, Ambassador Sondland, and State Department Counselor T. Ulrich Brechbuhl participated in a meeting at the Department of Energy to follow up to the May 23 Oval Office meeting.[263] Ambassador William Taylor, Chargé d'Affaires for U.S. Embassy in Kyiv, who had arrived in Ukraine just the day before, participated by phone from Kyiv.[264] The group agreed that a meeting between President Trump and President Zelensky would be valuable.[265] However, Ambassadors Volker and Sondland subsequently relayed to Ambassador Taylor that President Trump "wanted to hear from Zelensky before scheduling the meeting in the Oval Office."[266] Ambassador Taylor testified that he did not understand, at that time, what the President wanted to hear from his Ukrainian counterpart.[267] However, Ambassador Volker's assistant, Mr. Anderson, recalled "vague discussions" about addressing "Mr. Giuliani's continued calls for a corruption investigation."[268]

The quid pro quo—conditioning the Oval Office meeting that President Trump first offered the Ukrainian leader during their April 21 call on the Ukrainians' pursuit of investigations that would benefit President Trump politically—was beginning to take shape. As Ambassador Sondland testified, the conditions put on the White House meeting and on Ukraine's continued engagement with the White House would get "more insidious" with the passage of time.[269]

President Trump Invited Foreign Interference in the 2020 Election

As U.S. officials debated how to meet the President's demands as articulated by Mr. Giuliani, President Trump publicly disclosed on June 12 in an Oval Office interview with *ABC News* anchor George Stephanopoulos that there was "nothing wrong with listening" to a foreign power who offered political dirt on an opponent. The President added, "I think I'd want to hear it."

Mr. Stephanopoulos then pressed the President directly, "You want that kind of interference in our elections?" to which President Trump replied, "It's not an interference, they have information. I think I'd take it."[270] President Trump also made clear that he did not think a foreign power offering damaging information on an opponent was necessarily wrong, and said only that he would "maybe" contact the FBI "*if* I thought there was something wrong."[271]

President Trump's willingness to accept foreign interference in a U.S. election during his interview with Mr. Stephanopoulos was consistent with tweets and interviews by Mr. Giuliani at this time. For example, on June 21, Mr. Giuliani tweeted:

> New Pres of Ukraine still silent on investigation of Ukrainian interference in 2016 election and alleged Biden bribery of Pres Poroshenko. Time for leadership and investigate both if you want to purge how Ukraine was abused by Hillary and Obama people.[272]

On June 18, Dr. Hill met with Ambassador Sondland at the White House. She "asked him quite bluntly" what his role was in Ukraine. Ambassador Sondland replied that "he was in charge of Ukraine."[273] Dr. Hill was taken aback and a bit irritated. She prodded Ambassador Sondland again and asked, "Who put you in charge of Ukraine?" Dr. Hill testified: "And, you know, I'll admit, I was a bit rude. And that's when he told me the President, which shut me up."[274]

Dr. Hill tried to impress upon Ambassador Sondland the "importance of coordinating" with other national security officials in the conduct of Ukraine policy, including the NSC staff and the State Department. Ambassador Sondland "retorted" that he was "coordinating with the President" and Mr. Mulvaney, "filling in" Ambassador Bolton, and talking to State Department Counselor T. Ulrich Brechbuhl. Ambassador Sondland asked: "Who else did he have to inform?"[275]

Dr. Hill stated that, in hindsight, with the benefit of the sworn testimony by others during the impeachment inquiry and seeing documents displayed by witnesses, she realized that she and Ambassador Sondland were working on two fundamentally different tasks. Dr. Hill testified:

> But it struck me when yesterday, when you put up on the screen Ambassador Sondland's emails and who was on these emails, and he said, These are the people who need to know, that he was absolutely right. Because he was being involved in a domestic political errand, and we were being involved in national security foreign policy, and those two things had just diverged. So he was correct. And I had not put my finger on that at the moment, but I was irritated with him and angry with him that he wasn't fully coordinating. And I did say to him, Ambassador Sondland, Gordon, I think this is all going to blow up. And here we are. [276]

Reflecting on her June 18 conversation with Ambassador Sondland, Dr. Hill concluded:

> Ambassador Sondland is not wrong that he had been given a different remit than we had been. And it was at that moment that I started to realize how those things had diverged. And I realized, in fact, that I wasn't really being fair to Ambassador Sondland, because he was carrying out what he thought he had been instructed to carry out, and we were doing something that we thought was just as—or perhaps even more important, but it wasn't in the same channel.[277]

3.   The President Froze Military Assistance to Ukraine

> *The President froze military assistance to Ukraine against U.S. national security interests and over the objections of career experts.*

Overview

Since 2014, the United States has maintained a bipartisan policy of delivering hundreds of millions of dollars in security assistance to Ukraine each year. These funds benefit the security of the United States and Europe by ensuring that Ukraine is equipped to defend itself against Russian aggression. In 2019, that bipartisan policy was undermined when President Trump ordered, without justification, a freeze on military assistance to Ukraine.

For fiscal year 2019, Congress authorized and appropriated $391 million in security assistance: $250 million through the Department of Defense's (DOD) Ukraine Security Assistance Initiative and $141 million through the State Department's Foreign Military Financing program. In July 2019, however, President Trump ordered the Office of Management and Budget (OMB) to put a hold on all $391 million in security assistance to Ukraine.

The hold surprised experts from DOD and the State Department. DOD had already announced its intent to deliver security assistance to Ukraine after certifying that the country had implemented sufficient anti-corruption reforms, and the State Department was in the process of notifying Congress of its intent to deliver foreign military financing to Ukraine. In a series of interagency meetings, every represented agency other than OMB (which is headed by Mick Mulvaney, who is also the President's Acting Chief of Staff) supported the provision of assistance to Ukraine and objected to President Trump's hold. Ukraine experts at DOD, the State Department, and the National Security Council (NSC) argued that it was in the national security interest of the United States to continue to support Ukraine. Agency experts also expressed concerns about the legality of President Trump withholding assistance to Ukraine that Congress had already appropriated for this express purpose.

Despite these concerns, OMB devised a plan to implement President Trump's hold on the assistance. On July 25, 2019, OMB began using a series of footnotes in funding documents to notify DOD that the assistance funds were temporarily on hold to allow for interagency review. Throughout August and September, OMB continued to use this method and rationale to maintain the hold, long after the final interagency meeting on Ukraine assistance occurred on July 31. The hold continued despite concerns from DOD that the hold would threaten its ability to fully spend the money before the end of the fiscal year, as legally required.

On July 25—the same day as President Trump's call with President Zelensky—officials at Ukraine's embassy emailed DOD to ask about the status of the hold. By mid-August, officials at DOD, the State Department, and the NSC received numerous questions from Ukrainian officials about the hold. President Trump's hold on the Ukraine assistance was publicly reported on August 28, 2019.

Security Assistance to Ukraine is Important to U.S. National Security Interests

The United States has an interest in providing security assistance to Ukraine to support the country in its longstanding battle against Russian aggression and to shore it up as an independent and democratic country that can deter Kremlin influence in both Ukraine and other European countries. In early 2014, in what became known as the Revolution of Dignity, Ukrainian citizens demanded democratic reforms and an end to corruption, thereby forcing the ouster of pro-Kremlin Viktor Yanukovych as Ukraine's President. Shortly thereafter, Russian military forces and their proxies began an incursion into Ukraine that led to Russia's illegal annexation of the Crimean Peninsula of Ukraine, as well as the ongoing, Russian-led armed conflict in the Donbass region of eastern Ukraine. Approximately 13,000 people have been killed as a result of the conflict and over 1.4 million people have been displaced.[278]

Former U.S. Ambassador to the United Nations, Nikki Haley, noted that "militants in eastern Ukraine report directly to the Russian military, which arms them, trains them, leads them, and fights alongside them."[279] Similarly, then-Secretary of Defense James Mattis, during a visit to Ukraine in 2017, chided Russia, stating that "despite Russia's denials, we know they are seeking to redraw international borders by force, undermining the sovereign and free nations of Europe."[280]

In response to Russia's aggression, the international community imposed financial and visa sanctions on Russian individuals and entities, and committed to providing billions of dollars in economic, humanitarian, and security assistance to Ukraine to continue to support its sovereignty and democratic development.

The European Union is the single largest contributor of total foreign assistance to Ukraine, having provided €15 billion in grants and loans since 2014.[281] In addition to economic and humanitarian assistance, the United States has contributed a substantial amount of security assistance, mostly lethal and non-lethal military equipment and training, to Ukraine. In fact, the United States is the largest contributor of security assistance to Ukraine. Since 2014, the United States has delivered approximately $1.5 billion in security assistance to Ukraine.[282]

Multiple witnesses—including Ambassador William Taylor, Deputy Assistant Secretary of State George Kent, Lt. Col. Alexander Vindman, and Deputy Assistant Secretary of Defense Laura Cooper—testified that this security assistance to Ukraine is vital to the national security of the United States and Europe.[283] As Ambassador Taylor noted:

> [R]adar and weapons and sniper rifles, communication, that saves lives. It makes the Ukrainians more effective. It might even shorten the war. That's what our hope is, to show that the Ukrainians can defend themselves and the Russians, in the end, will say "Okay, we're going to stop."[284]

State Department Special Advisor for Ukraine, Catherine Croft, further emphasized that Ukrainians currently "face casualties nearly every day in defense of their own territory against Russian aggression."[285] Ambassador Taylor testified that American aid is a concrete demonstration of the United States' "commitment to resist aggression and defend freedom."[286]

Witnesses also testified that it is in the interest of the United States for Russian aggression to be halted in Ukraine. In the 20th century, the United States fought two bloody wars to resist the aggression of a hostile power that tried to change the borders of Europe by force. As Ambassador Taylor put it, Russian aggression in Ukraine "dismissed all the principles that have kept the peace and contributed to prosperity in Europe since World War II."[287]

Timothy Morrison, former Senior Director for Europe and Russia at the NSC, put the importance of U.S. assistance in stark terms:

Russia is a failing power, but it is still a dangerous one. The United States aids Ukraine and her people so that they can fight Russia over there, and we don't have to fight Russia here.[288]

Bipartisan Support for Security Assistance to Ukraine

Congressional support for security assistance to Ukraine has been overwhelming and bipartisan. Congress provided $391 million in security assistance to Ukraine for fiscal year 2019: $250 million through the DOD-administered Ukraine Security Assistance Initiative (USAI) and $141 million through the State Department-administered Foreign Military Financing program.

On September 26, 2018, Congress appropriated $250 million for the Ukraine Security Assistance Initiative, which is funded through DOD. The funding law made clear that the funding was only "available until September 30, 2019." President Trump signed the bill into law on September 28, 2018.[289]

The Ukraine Security Assistance Initiative—a Congressionally-mandated program codifying portions of the European Reassurance Initiative, which was originally launched by the Obama Administration in 2015—authorizes DOD to provide "security assistance and intelligence support, including training, equipment, and logistics support, supplies and services, to military and other security forces of the Government of Ukraine."[290] Recognizing that strengthening Ukraine's institutions, in addition to its military, is vital to helping it break free of Russia's influence, Congress imposed conditions upon DOD before it could spend a portion of the security assistance funds. Half of the money was held in reserve until the Secretary of Defense, in coordination with the Secretary of State, certified to Congress that Ukraine had undertaken sufficient anti-corruption reforms, such as in civilian control of the military and increased transparency and accountability.[291]

On February 28, 2019, John C. Rood, Under Secretary of Defense for Policy, notified Congress that DOD intended to deliver the first half ($125 million) of assistance appropriated in September 2018 to Ukraine, including "more than $50 million of assistance to deliver counter-artillery radars and defensive lethal assistance."[292] Congress cleared the Congressional notification, which enabled DOD to begin obligating (spending) funds.[293]

For Ukraine to qualify to receive the remaining $125 million of assistance, Congress required that the Secretary of Defense, in coordination with the Secretary of State, certify that the

Government of Ukraine had taken substantial anticorruption reform actions.[294] Ms. Cooper and others at DOD conducted a review to evaluate whether Ukraine had met the required benchmarks.[295] Ms. Cooper explained that the review involved "pulling in all the views of the key experts on Ukraine defense, and coming up with a consensus view," which was then run "up the chain in the Defense Department, to ensure we have approval."[296]

On May 23, 2019, Under Secretary Rood certified to Congress that Ukraine had completed the requisite defense institutional reforms to qualify for the remaining $125 million in funds. He wrote:

> On behalf of the Secretary of Defense, and in coordination with the Secretary of State, I have certified that the Government of Ukraine has taken substantial actions to make defense institutional reforms for the purposes of decreasing corruption, increasing accountability, and sustaining improvements of combat capability enabled by U.S. assistance.[297]

Congress then cleared the related Congressional notification, which enabled DOD to begin obligating the remaining $125 million in funds.[298]

On June 18, 2019, DOD issued a press release announcing its intention to provide $250 million in security assistance funds to Ukraine "for additional training, equipment, and advisory efforts to build the capacity of Ukraine's armed forces." DOD announced that the security assistance would provide Ukraine with sniper rifles, rocket-propelled grenade launchers, and counter-artillery radars, command and control, electronic warfare detection and secure communications, military mobility, night vision, and military medical treatment.[299]

On February 15, 2019, Congress also appropriated $115 million for Ukraine through the State Department-administered Foreign Military Financing Program (FMF).[300] The Foreign Military Financing Program is administered by the State Department and provides grants or loans to foreign countries to help them purchase military services or equipment manufactured by U.S. companies in the United States. In addition to the $115 million appropriated for fiscal year 2019, approximately $26 million carried over from fiscal year 2018.[301] Thus, the total amount of foreign military financing available for Ukraine was approximately $141 million.

Before a country receives foreign military financing, the State Department must first seek Congressional approval through a notification to Congress.[302] The State Department never sent the required Congressional notification to Congress in the spring or summer of 2019. As described below, OMB blocked the notification.[303]

President Trump Had Questions About Ukraine Security Assistance

The day after DOD issued its June 18 press release announcing $250 million in security assistance funds for Ukraine, President Trump started asking OMB questions about the funding for Ukraine. On June 19, Mark Sandy, Deputy Associate Director for National Security Programs at OMB, was copied on an email from his boss, Michael Duffey, Associate Director for National Security Programs at OMB, to Elaine McCusker, Deputy Under Secretary of

Defense (Comptroller) that said that "the President had questions about the press report and that he was seeking additional information."[304] Notably, the same day, President Trump gave an interview on *Fox News* where he raised the so-called "Crowdstrike" conspiracy theory that Ukraine, rather than Russia, had interfered in the 2016 election, a line he would repeat during his July 25 call with the Ukrainian president.[305]

On June 20, in response to the President's inquiry, Ms. McCusker responded to President Trump's inquiry by providing Mr. Sandy information on the security assistance program.[306] Mr. Sandy shared the document with Mr. Duffey, who had follow-up questions about the "financial resources associated with the program, in particular," the "history of the appropriations, [and] any more details about the intent of the program."[307] Mr. Sandy said that his staff provided the relevant information to Mr. Duffey, but he did not know whether Mr. Duffey shared the information with the White House.[308]

Ms. Cooper also recalled receiving an email inquiring about DOD-administered Ukraine security assistance a "few days" after DOD's June 18, 2019, press release.[309] The email was from the Secretary of Defense's Chief of Staff, "asking for follow-up on a meeting with the President." The email contained three questions:

> And the one question was related to U.S. industry. Did U.S—is U.S. industry providing any of this equipment? The second question that I recall was related to international contributions. It asked, what are other countries doing, something to that effect. And then the third question, I don't recall—I mean, with any of these I don't recall the exact wording, but it was something to the effect of, you know, who gave this money, or who gave this funding?[310]

Like Mr. Sandy, Ms. Cooper believed that the President's inquiries were spurred by DOD's June 18 press release. She testified, "we did get that series of questions just within a few days after the press release and after that one article that had the headline."[311] Ms. Cooper noted that it was "relatively unusual" to receive questions from the President, and that she and her staff at the DOD responded "as quickly" as they could.[312] According to Ms. Cooper, DOD officials included in their answers that security assistance funding "has strong bipartisan support," but never received a response.[313]

President Trump Froze Military Assistance

Despite the fact that DOD experts demonstrated that the security assistance was crucial for both Ukraine and U.S. national security and had strong bipartisan support in Congress, President Trump ordered OMB to freeze the funds in July.

On July 3, the State Department notified DOD and NSC staff that OMB was blocking the State Department from transmitting a Congressional notification for the provision of State Department-administered security assistance to Ukraine (the $141 million in foreign military financing).[314] Because the State Department is legally required to transmit such a notification to Congress before spending funds, blocking the Congressional notification effectively barred the State Department from spending the funding.[315] Ms. Williams testified that she saw the news in a draft email that was being prepared as part of the nightly update for the National Security Advisor.[316] She agreed that the hold came "out of the blue" because it had not been discussed previously by OMB or the NSC.[317]

On or about July 12, 2019, President Trump directed that a hold be placed on security assistance funding for Ukraine. That day, Robert Blair, Assistant to the President and Senior Advisor to the Chief of Staff, sent an email to Mr. Duffey at OMB about Ukraine security assistance.[318] Mr. Sandy, who was on personal leave at the time but later received a copy of the email from Mr. Duffey, testified that in the July 12 email, Mr. Blair communicated "that the President is directing a hold on military support funding for Ukraine."[319] The email mentioned no concerns about any other country, security assistance package, or aid of any sort.[320]

On or about July 15, Mr. Morrison learned from Deputy National Security Advisor Charles Kupperman "that it was the President's direction to hold the assistance."[321] On or about July 17 or 18, 2019, Mr. Duffey and Mr. Blair again exchanged emails about Ukraine security assistance.[322] Mr. Sandy later received a copy of the emails, which showed that when Mr. Duffey asked Mr. Blair about the reason for the hold, Mr. Blair provided no explanation and instead said, "we need to let the hold take place" and then "revisit" the issue with the President.[323]

On July 18 or 19, when he returned from two weeks of personal leave, Mr. Sandy learned for the first time that the President had placed a hold on Ukraine security assistance from Mr. Duffey.[324] According to Mr. Sandy, Mr. Duffey was not aware of the reason but "there was certainly a desire to learn more about the rationale" for the hold.[325]

Agency Experts Repeatedly Objected to the Hold on Security Assistance

Between July 18 and July 31, 2019, the NSC staff convened a series of interagency meetings, at which the hold on security assistance was discussed in varying degrees of detail. Over the course of these meetings, it became evident that:

- the President directed the hold through OMB;

- no justification was provided for the hold;

- with the exception of OMB, all represented agencies supported Ukraine security assistance because it was in the national security interests of the United States; and

- there were concerns about the legality of the hold.

The first interagency meeting was held on July 18 at the Deputy Assistant Secretary level (i.e., a "sub-Policy Coordination Committee"). It was supposed to be a "routine Ukraine policy meeting."[326] Ambassador Taylor, Lt. Col. Vindman, Ms. Croft, and Mr. Kent were among the attendees. Witnesses testified that OMB announced at the meeting that President Trump had directed a hold on Ukraine security assistance. Mr. Kent testified that at the meeting, an OMB staff person announced that Acting White House Chief of Staff Mick Mulvaney "at the direction of the President had put a hold on all security assistance to the Ukraine."[327] Ambassador Taylor testified that the "directive had come from the President to the Chief of Staff to OMB" and that when he learned of the hold on military assistance, he "realized that one of the key pillars of our strong support for Ukraine was threatened."[328]

According to Ms. Croft, when Mr. Kent raised the issue of security assistance, it "blew up the meeting."[329] Ambassador Taylor testified that he and others on the call "sat in astonishment" when they learned about the hold.[330] David Holmes, Political Counselor at the U.S. Embassy in Kyiv, was also on the call. He testified he was "shocked" and thought the hold was "extremely significant."[331] He thought the hold undermined what he had understood to be longstanding U.S. policy in Ukraine.[332]

Ms. Croft testified that "the only reason given was that the order came at the direction of the President."[333] Ms. Cooper, who did not participate but received a readout of the meeting, testified that the fact that the hold was announced without explanation was "unusual."[334] Mr. Kent testified that "[t]here was great confusion among the rest of us because we didn't understand why that had happened."[335] He explained that "[s]ince there was unanimity that this [security assistance to Ukraine] was in our national interest, it just surprised all of us."[336]

With the exception of OMB, all agencies present at the July 18 meeting advocated for the lifting of the hold.[337]

There was also a lack of clarity as to whether the hold applied only to the State Department-administered Foreign Military Financing to Ukraine or whether it also applied to the DOD-administered Ukraine Security Assistance Initiative funding.[338] Ms. Cooper and her colleagues at the DOD were "concerned" about the hold.[339] After the meeting, DOD sought further clarification from the NSC and State Department about its impact on the DOD-administered funding.[340] However, there was no "specific guidance for DOD at the time."[341]

The second interagency meeting to discuss the hold on Ukraine security assistance was held at the Assistant Secretary level (i.e., a "Policy Coordination Committee") on July 23, 2019.[342] The meeting was chaired by Mr. Morrison.[343] Ms. Cooper, who participated via secure video teleconference, testified that "the White House chief of staff ha[d] conveyed that the President has concerns about Ukraine and Ukraine security assistance."[344] Jennifer Williams, Special Advisor to Vice President Pence for Europe and Eurasia, who also attended the meeting on behalf of the Vice President, testified that the "OMB representative conveyed that they had been directed by the Chief of Staff, the White House Chief of Staff, to continue holding it [the Ukraine security assistance] until further notice."[345] Similar to the July 18 meeting, the July 23 meeting did not provide clarity about whether the President's hold applied to the DOD-administered funding or only to the funds administered by the State Department.[346]

Again, no reason was provided for the hold.[347] Mr. Sandy did not attend the July 23 meeting as the representative for OMB, but he received a readout that other agencies expressed concerns about the hold. Specifically, the concerns related to the lack of rationale for the hold, the hold's implications on U.S. assistance and "overall policy toward Ukraine," and "similar legal questions."[348]

Mr. Morrison also testified that there was a discussion at the July 23 meeting about the legality of the hold, and specifically whether it is "actually legally permissible for the President to not allow for the disbursement of the funding."[349] Mr. Morrison recalled that DOD raised concerns about possible violations of the Impoundment Control Act.[350] The Impoundment Control Act gives the President the authority to delay spending, or not spend, funds *only* if Congress is notified of those intentions and approves the proposed action (see below for further discussion of the act).[351]

With the exception of OMB, all agencies present at the July 23rd meeting advocated for the lifting of the hold.[352] Ambassador Taylor explained that the State Department "made a strong statement about the importance of this assistance" and that Ms. Cooper, on behalf of DOD, "made a very strong case and continued to make a very strong case for the effectiveness" of the security assistance.[353] Lt. Col. Vindman, who also attended the meeting, testified that there was agreement that the issue should be elevated to the Agency deputies "as quickly as possible to recommend a release of security assistance."[354]

The third interagency meeting, a Deputies Small Group meeting at the Cabinet Deputies level, was held on July 26, 2019. Mr. Duffey was the OMB representative, and Mr. Sandy prepared Mr. Duffey for the meeting.[355] Mr. Sandy explained that he prepared Mr. Duffey to get policy guidance on six critical issues: (1) the reason for the hold; (2) the extent of the hold; (3) the duration of the hold; (4) the Congressional affairs approach; (5) the public affairs approach; and (6) and the diplomatic approach.[356] Mr. Sandy testified that on July 26, OMB still did not have an understanding of the reason for the hold.[357] According to Mr. Sandy, at that time, there was no discussion within OMB about the amount of money that was being contributed to Ukraine by other countries, or whether that topic was the reason for the President's hold.[358]

Mr. Morrison, Lt. Col. Vindman, Ms. Cooper, Under Secretary of State for Political Affairs David Hale, and Mr. Duffey attended the July 26 meeting. At the meeting, OMB stated that "they had guidance from the President and from Acting Chief of Staff Mulvaney to freeze the assistance."[359] It also was "stated very clearly" that the hold applied to both the State Department and Defense Department security assistance funds.[360] Ambassador Hale, as the representative for the Department of State, "advocated strongly for resuming the assistance," as did representatives from all agencies other than OMB.[361]

Mr. Morrison testified that, at the meeting, "OMB represented that—and the Chief of Staff's Office was present—that the President was concerned about corruption in Ukraine, and he wanted to make sure that Ukraine was doing enough to manage that corruption."[362] Ms. Cooper had a similar recollection but received no further understanding of what OMB meant by "corruption."[363] Ms. Cooper recalled that the deputies did not consider corruption to be a legitimate reason for the hold because they unanimously agreed that Ukraine was making sufficient progress on anti-corruption reforms, as had been certified by DOD on May 23.[364]

President Trump Continued the Hold Despite Agency Concerns About Legality

Prior to the passage of the Impoundment Control Act, presidents had frequently impounded—i.e., refused to spend—Congressionally-appropriated funds to enforce their policy priorities when they diverged from Congress'. However, most of these impoundments were small (i.e., no more than a few percent of the total program budget) or temporary (i.e., funds were released in time for them to be spent before the end of the fiscal year) and rooted in policy, rather than political interests of the President. It was not until President Richard Nixon that presidential impoundment of funds would prompt Congress to take action citing constitutional concerns.[365]

Unlike his predecessors, President Nixon undertook impoundments that were both substantial and, in some cases, permanent, which raised concerns for Congress over its Article I powers. In fact, between 1969 and 1972, PresidentNixon impounded between 15% and 20% of Congressionally-appropriated funds in various accounts.[366]

To reassert Congressional authority over the budget, in 1973, Congress established the Joint Study Committee on Budget Control, which held a series of hearings and produced more than 4,600 pages of testimony and reports. The Joint Study Committee's findings ultimately led to the overwhelmingly bipartisan passage—over President Nixon's veto—of the Impoundment Control Act of 1974, one of a series of reform bills designed to reign in presidential power. Looking back at that moment in history, Rep. Bill Archer (R-TX), a fiscal conservative who served 30 years in the House of Representatives, including as the Chairman of the Ways and Means Committee, remarked, "the culture then was that the president had too much power…the president is abusing his power."[367]

In addition to establishing the Congressional Budget Committees and the independent Congressional Budget Office, the Impoundment Control Act also limits the circumstances under which a president can *legally* impound Congressionally-appropriated funds. According to the Act, although the President may request authority from Congress to withhold or permanently cancel the availability of budget authority, such an action is not allowed without Congressional approval. Any amount of budget authority proposed to be deferred (i.e., temporarily withheld) or rescinded (i.e., permanently withheld) must be made available for obligation unless Congress, within 45 legislative days, completes action on a bill rescinding all or part of the amount proposed for rescission.[368] The Impoundment Control Act does not permit the withholding of funds through their date of expiration, which would be a de facto rescission without Congressional approval.[369]

At the July 26 interagency meeting, senior agency officials raised serious concerns about the legality of the hold under the Impoundment Control Act. Ms. Cooper testified:

> A: Well, I'm not an expert on the law, but in that meeting immediately deputies began to raise concerns about how this could be done in a legal fashion because there was broad understanding in the meeting that the funding—the State Department funding related to an earmark for Ukraine and that the DOD funding was specific to Ukraine security assistance. So the comments in the room at the deputies' level reflected a sense that there was not an understanding of how this could legally play out. And at that meeting the deputies agreed to look into the legalities and to look at what was possible.

Q: Okay. So is it fair to say the deputies thought the President was not authorized to place a hold on these funds?

A: They did not use that term, but the expression in the room that I recall was a sense that there was not an available mechanism to simply not spend money that has been in the case of USAI [DOD security assistance] already notified to Congress.[370]

Lt. Col. Vindman testified that the issue needed to be "elevated to a PC [Principals Committee] as quickly as possible to release the hold on security assistance" so that the funds could be obligated before the end of the fiscal year.[371]

A Principals Committee meeting was never convened.[372] According to Mr. Morrison, National Security Advisor John Bolton "believed that it was unnecessary, that he already had a reasonable idea of where the principals were, and he wanted to get directly to the President as early as possible in the most effective way."[373] Ambassador Bolton understood that the principals "were all supportive of the continued disbursement of the aid."[374] As had been clear since the very first interagency meeting on July 18, the lifting of the hold was "the unanimous position of the entire interagency."[375] At this point, it remained unclear to many officials why the President continued to hold the funds.

On July 31, 2019, a fourth and final interagency meeting was held at the Policy Coordination Committee level. Ms. Cooper attended the meeting on behalf of DOD. According to Ms. Cooper, the agenda "was largely focused on just routine Ukraine business, postelection follow up," and "security assistance was not actually an explicit agenda item."[376] Ms. Cooper nevertheless raised security assistance and expressed her understanding, after consulting with DOD counsel, that there were only two legally available options to implement the hold: a Presidential rescission notice to Congress (i.e., requesting that Congress "take back" funds it had already appropriated) or for the Defense Department to do a reprogramming action (i.e., use Congressionally-appropriated funds for a different purpose).[377] In either case, the law requires that the Executive Branch notify, and seek approval from, Congress before taking any action.[378]

At the July 31 meeting, Ms. Cooper emphasized to the participants that because "there are only two legally available options and we do not have direction to pursue either," DOD would have to start obligating the funds on or about August 6.[379] She explained at her deposition that DOD would have had to begin obligating the funds by that date or risk violation of the Impoundment Control Act.[380]

The Administration, however, never proposed a rescission or reprogramming of funds for Ukraine security assistance and never notified Congress of its intent to withhold funds.[381]

OMB Used Unusual Process to Implement President's Hold, Skirting Legal Concerns

OMB plays a critical role in the release of security assistance funding. The Antideficiency Act requires that, before any department or agency may spend Congressionally-appropriated funding, the Director of OMB or his delegates must "apportion" (i.e., make available to spend) the funds in writing.[382] Through this mechanism, OMB has the ability to directly impact security assistance funding or funding of any kind that is appropriated by Congress.

In parallel with the interagency meetings that occurred during the latter half of July 2019, OMB devised a way to implement the President's hold on security assistance to Ukraine, notwithstanding DOD's Congressional notifications of February 28 and May 23. Over the course of his twelve-year career at OMB, Mr. Sandy could not recall any other time when a hold had been placed on security assistance after a Congressional notification had been sent.[383]

When speaking with Mr. Duffey on or about July 18 or 19, Mr. Sandy immediately raised concerns about how to implement the hold without violating the Impoundment Control Act, which required that the funds be obligated (i.e., spent) before they expired at the end of the fiscal year, on September 30.[384] In light of that legal requirement, the hold would have to be temporary.[385] An additional hurdle was the fact that OMB had already authorized DOD to spend the security assistance funds DOD administered for fiscal year 2019.[386] Therefore, when President Trump directed the hold in July, OMB scrambled to reverse that prior authorization.

From July 19 through July 24, Mr. Sandy consulted with the OMB Office of General Counsel as well as Ms. McCusker at DOD on how to legally implement a hold on the funds.[387] Mr. Sandy's staff at OMB also conferred with OMB's Budget Review Division.[388] Based on these consultations, OMB decided to implement the hold through a series of nine funding documents, known legally as "apportionments."[389] Apportionments typically are used to convey authority to an agency to spend funds, not to withhold funds; thus, in order to bar DOD from spending money, these particular apportionments included footnotes that would impose the holds while using creative language to skirt legal concerns. Mr. Sandy testified that "the purpose of the footnote was to preclude obligation for a limited period of time but enable planning and casework to continue."[390] He also testified that this use of footnotes was unusual and that in his 12 years of OMB experience, he could "not recall another event like it."[391]

On July 25, OMB issued the first funding document implementing the hold. In this document, the relevant footnote notified DOD that the Ukraine Security Assistance Initiative funds "are not available for obligation until August 5, 2019, to allow for an interagency process to determine the best use of such funds." The footnote also stated that:

> Based on OMB's communication with DOD on July 25, 2019, OMB understands from the Department that this brief pause in obligations will not preclude DOD's timely execution of the final policy direction. DOD may continue its planning and casework for the Initiative during this period.[392]

Mr. Sandy explained that the "interagency process" referenced in the footnote referred to the NSC-led interagency meetings convened during the latter half of July, and that the August 5 date provided a "reasonable timeframe for an interagency process" to produce "clear guidance" on the hold.[393] The August 5 date was determined in consultation with Mr. Duffey at OMB and Ms. McCusker at DOD.[394]

Mr. Sandy further testified that the second sentence in the footnote—which states, in relevant part, that "OMB understands from the Department that this brief pause in obligations will not preclude DOD's timely execution of the final policy direction"—was critical to the implementation of the hold:

> Well, that gets to the heart of that issue about ensuring that we don't run afoul of the Impoundment Control Act, which means that you have to allow for the timely execution. And this reflects my conversation with—conversations plural with Elaine McCusker that they can confirm that, during this brief period, they would not foresee any problem fully executing the program by the end of the fiscal year.[395]

The sentence, in effect, affirmed that if the hold remained in place only until August 5, DOD would still have sufficient time to spend all security assistance funds by September 30, 2019. President Trump, however, would continue the hold long past August 5.

Trump Appointee Took Over Signing Authority from Career Budget Expert

Since becoming Deputy Associate Director for National Security in 2013, Mr. Sandy was responsible for approving release of the funding for programs within his portfolio, including the Ukraine Security Assistance Initiative.[396] Mr. Sandy approved and signed the July 25 funding document.[397] On July 29, however, Mr. Duffey—a political appointee of President Trump whose prior position had been as Executive Director of the Republican Party of Wisconsin—told Mr. Sandy—a career civil servant with decades of experience in this area—that he would no longer be responsible for approving the release of funding for Ukraine Security Assistance Initiative.[398] Mr. Duffey also revoked the authority for approving the release of funding for Foreign Military Financing from Mr. Sandy's colleague at OMB.[399] Instead, Mr. Duffey would himself assume authority for the $250 million in DOD-administered Ukraine security assistance and authority for approving the release of funding for the $141 million in State Department-administered Foreign Military Financing to Ukraine.[400]

Mr. Duffey did not tell Mr. Sandy whether he requested this change in authority but did say that "it was in essence a joint decision reflecting both guidance from the Acting Director and also his support."[401] Over the course of several days, Mr. Duffey explained to Mr. Sandy and others in the National Security Division that "there was interest among the leadership in tracking the uses of moneys [sic] closely."[402] Mr. Duffey expressed an "interest in being more involved in daily operations" and "regarded this responsibility as a way for him to learn more about specific accounts within his area."[403]

Mr. Sandy testified that prior to July 29, he had never heard Mr. Duffey state any interest in approving the release of funding.[404] Furthermore, when they learned that Mr. Duffey was taking on this new responsibility, Mr. Sandy and other staff relayed their concerns to Mr. Duffey that it was a substantial workload.[405] Mr. Sandy also testified that "people were curious what he thought he would learn from apportionments about the accounts as opposed to the other, you know, sources of information."[406] Mr. Sandy agreed that there are more efficient ways of learning about accounts and programs, and that "I can think of other ways—other materials that I personally would find more informative."[407]

Mr. Sandy was not aware of any prior instance when a political appointee assumed this kind of funding approval authority.[408]

After the July 31 interagency meeting at which Ms. Cooper announced that DOD would have to start obligating the funds on or about August 6, Mr. Duffey sought clarification.[409] Ms. Cooper explained to Mr. Duffey that at a certain point DOD would not have sufficient time to fully obligate the funds before they expired at the end of the fiscal year. In response, Mr. Duffey "wanted more information on the precise nature of how long does it take to obligate, and how many cases, and that sort of thing."[410] Ms. Cooper referred Mr. Duffey to the DOD comptroller and to the Defense Security Cooperation Agency.[411] During the month of August, Mr. Duffey and Ms. McCusker communicated about the implementation of the hold on the Ukraine Security Assistance Initiative funds.[412]

On August 6 and August 15, Mr. Duffey approved two more funding documents that contained footnotes with language nearly identical to the footnote in the July 25 funding document that initiated the hold; the only difference was that the date funds would become available for spending was changed from August 5 to August 12.[413]

The August 6 and 15 footnotes, and all subsequent footnotes through September 10, continued to state that the hold was in place "to allow for an interagency process to determine the best use of such funds," even though the final interagency meeting regarding Ukraine security assistance occurred on July 31.[414] Not only was there no active interagency process after July, but Ms. Cooper also was not aware of any review of the funding conducted by DOD in July, August, or September.[415] In fact, Ms. Cooper noted that months before, DOD had completed its review of whether Ukraine "had made sufficient progress in meeting defense reform and anticorruption goals consistent with the NDAA," and certified to Congress in May 2019 that Ukraine had met the requirements to receive funding.[416] Similarly, Mr. Kent testified that the State Department did not conduct, and was never asked to conduct, a review of the security assistance funding administered by the State Department.[417]

At the same time that OMB was implementing the President's hold through the funding footnotes, officials inside OMB were advocating for release of the funds. On August 7, the National Security Division, International Affairs Division, and Office of Legal Counsel of OMB drafted and transmitted a memo on Ukraine security assistance to OMB Acting Director Vought "in anticipation of a principals-level discussion to address the topic."[418] The National Security Division's portion of the memorandum recommended to remove the hold because (1) the assistance was consistent with the national security strategy in terms of supporting a stable, peaceful Europe; (2) the aid countered Russian aggression; and (3) there was bipartisan support for the program.[419] Mr. Duffey approved the memorandum and agreed with the policy recommendation.[420]

Sometime in mid-August, DOD raised concerns that it might not be able to fully obligate the Defense Department-administered funds before the end of the fiscal year.[421] Ms. Cooper testified that the Defense Security Cooperation Agency estimated that $100 million of aid might not be obligated in time and was at risk.[422]

Because of this, DOD concluded that it could no longer support OMB's claim in the footnote that "this brief pause in obligations will not preclude DOD's timely execution of the final policy direction."[423] As mentioned above, Mr. Sandy testified that this sentence was at "the heart of that issue about ensuring that we don't run afoul of the Impoundment Control Act."[424]

As a result of DOD's concerns, all of the subsequent footnotes issued by OMB during the pendency of the hold—approved by Mr. Duffey on August 20, 27, and 31, and September 5, 6, and 10—removed the sentence regarding DOD's ability to fully obligate by the end of the fiscal year.[425] Each footnote extended the hold for a period of two to six days.[426]

Mr. Sandy and his staff "continued to express concerns [to Mr. Duffey] about the potential implications vis-à-vis the Impoundment Control Act,"[427] and advised Mr. Duffey to consult with OMB's Office of General Counsel "on every single footnote."[428] Mr. Sandy was copied on emails with the Office of General Counsel on these topics.[429] Although Mr. Sandy understood that the Office of General Counsel supported the footnotes, he noted that there were dissenting opinions within the Office of General Counsel.[430] Concerns about whether the Administration was bending, if not breaking, the law by holding back this vital assistance contributed to at least two OMB officials resigning, including one attorney in the Office of General Counsel.[431] Mr. Sandy testified that the resignation was motivated in part by concerns about the way OMB was handling the hold on Ukraine security assistance.[432] According to Mr. Sandy, the colleague disagreed with the Office of General Counsel about the application of the Impoundment Control Act to the hold on Ukraine security assistance.[433]

Nevertheless, at the direction of the President, OMB continued to implement the hold through September 11.

Senior Officials Failed to Convince President Trump to Release the Aid in August

Sometime prior to August 16, Ambassador Bolton had a one-on-one meeting with President Trump about the aid.[434] According to Mr. Morrison, at that meeting the President "was not yet ready to approve the release of the assistance."[435] Following the meeting, Ambassador Bolton instructed Mr. Morrison to look for opportunities to get the principals together "to have the direct, in-person conversation with the President about this topic."[436]

On or about August 13 or 14, Lt. Col. Vindman was directed to draft a Presidential Decision Memorandum for Ambassador Bolton and the other principals to present to President Trump for a decision on Ukraine security assistance.[437] The memorandum, finalized on August 15, recommended that the hold should be lifted, explained why, and included the consensus views from the July 26 meeting that the funds should be released.[438] Lt. Col. Vindman received conflicting accounts about whether the memorandum was presented to the President.[439]

Mr. Morrison, who was Lt. Col. Vindman's supervisor at the NSC and agreed with the recommendation to lift the hold, testified that the memorandum was never provided to the President.[440] Mr. Morrison explained that Ambassador Bolton intended to present the memorandum to the President during an unrelated meeting in Bedminster, New Jersey, on August 15, but the "other subject matter of that meeting consumed all the time."[441] However, while at Bedminster, the principals "all represented to Ambassador Bolton that they were prepared to tell the President they endorsed the swift release and disbursement of the funding."[442]

Mr. Morrison testified that he attempted to gather the "the right group of principals" to meet with the President but was unable to do so because of scheduling issues.[443] According to Mr. Morrison, the next possible opportunity was during a trip to Warsaw, Poland at the beginning of September, but President Trump did not end up making that trip.[444]

Ms. Cooper recalled receiving an email at the end of August from Secretary of Defense Esper referencing a meeting or discussion with the President, and that there was "no decision on Ukraine."[445]

Ukrainian Officials Learned About the Hold in July 2019

Witnesses testified that officials in the Ukraine government knew of President Trump's hold on security assistance before it was publicly reported in the press on August 28, 2019. Ms. Croft testified that after July 18—when the hold was announced by OMB at the interagency meeting—it was "inevitable that it was eventually going to come out."[446]

Two individuals from the Ukrainian Embassy in Washington, D.C., approached Ms. Croft approximately a week apart "quietly and in confidence to ask me about an OMB hold on Ukraine security assistance."[447] Ms. Croft could not precisely recall the dates of these conversations, but testified that she was "very surprised at the effectiveness of my Ukrainian counterparts' diplomatic tradecraft, as in to say they found out very early on or much earlier than I expected them to."[448]

Ms. Croft explained that the Ukrainian officials came to her quietly because they would not want the hold to become public:

> I think that if this were public in Ukraine it would be seen as a reversal of our policy and would, just to say sort of candidly and colloquially, this would be a really big deal, it would be a really big deal in Ukraine, and an expression of declining U.S. support for Ukraine.[449]

DOD also received questions from the Ukraine Embassy about the status of the military assistance. Ms. Cooper testified that those occurred on July 25, 2019—the same day as President Trump's call with President Zelensky:

> On July 25th, a member of my staff got a question from a Ukraine Embassy contact asking what was going on with Ukraine security assistance, because at that time, we did not know what the guidance was on USAI [DOD-administered funds]. The OMB notice of apportionment arrived that day, but this staff member did not find out about it until later. I was informed that the staff member told the Ukrainian official that we were moving forward on USAI, but recommended that the Ukraine Embassy check in with State regarding the FMF [State Department-administered funds].[450]

On July 25, Ms. Cooper's staff received two emails from the State Department revealing that the Ukrainian Embassy was "asking about security assistance" and that "the Hill knows about the FMF situation to an extent, and so does the Ukrainian Embassy."[451]

One of Ms. Cooper's staff members reported that sometime during the week of August 6, a Ukrainian Embassy officer stated that "a Ukrainian official might raise concerns about security assistance in an upcoming meeting," but that the issue was "not, in fact, raised."[452] Ms. Cooper's staff further reported that Ukrainian officials were aware of the hold on security assistance in August.[453]

Lt. Col. Vindman testified that, by mid-August, he too was getting questions from Ukrainians about the status of the hold on security assistance:

> So to the best of my knowledge, the Ukrainians, first of all, are in general pretty sophisticated, they have their network of, you know, Ukrainian interest groups and so forth. They have bipartisan support in Congress. And certainly there are—it was no secret, at least within government and official channels, that security assistance was on hold. And to the best of my recollection, I believe there were some of these light inquires in the mid-August timeframe.[454]

While numerous individuals, including Ukrainians, were aware of the hold, it did not become publicly known until a *Politico* report on August 28, 2019.[455]

4.   **The President's Meeting with the Ukrainian President Was Conditioned on An Announcement of Investigations**

> *President Trump demanded the public announcement by President Zelensky of investigations into President Trump's political rival and alleged Ukrainian interference in the 2016 U.S. election in exchange for an Oval Office meeting. The President's representatives made that quid pro quo clear to Ukrainian officials.*

Overview

After ordering the hold on security assistance to Ukraine against the unanimous advice of the relevant U.S. government agencies, President Trump used his hand-picked representatives to demand that Ukrainian leaders publicly announce investigations into his political rival, former Vice President Joe Biden, and into the debunked conspiracy theory that Ukraine, not Russia, interfered in the 2016 U.S. election. President Trump, through his agents, made clear that his demand needed to be met before a coveted White House meeting with Ukrainian President Volodymyr Zelensky would be scheduled. A face-to-face meeting with President Trump in the Oval Office would have conferred on the new Ukrainian leader much-sought prestige and would have signaled to Russia that Ukraine could continue to count on the support of the President of the United States, which was particularly important as Russia continued to wage war in eastern Ukraine.

To date, the White House meeting for President Zelensky has not occurred. Following the May 23 meeting in the Oval Office, President Trump's hand-picked representatives—the so-called "Three Amigos"—worked with the President's personal attorney, Rudy Giuliani, to pressure Ukrainian leaders to announce publicly investigations that would benefit the President's reelection campaign. Testimony of multiple witnesses and contemporaneous text messages exchanged between and among President Trump's representatives confirm that the White House meeting—and later the release of security assistance for Ukraine—was conditioned on Ukraine acquiescing to the President's demands.

In the weeks leading up to the July 25 call between President Trump and President Zelensky, President Trump's representatives repeatedly relayed the message of conditionality to Ukrainian government officials—including to President Zelensky himself—in meetings in Kyiv, Toronto, and Washington, D.C. President Zelensky and his advisors struggled to navigate these demands, recognizing that President Trump's desire that Ukraine announce these political investigations threatened to render Ukraine a "pawn" in U.S. domestic reelection politics.

An Oval Office Meeting for President Zelensky Was Important to Ukraine and U.S. National Security

A face-to-face meeting with the President of the United States in the Oval Office was critical to President Zelensky as the newly-elected Ukrainian leader sought U.S. support for his ambitious anti-corruption agenda and to repel Russian aggression. A White House meeting was also important for U.S. national security because it would have served to bolster Ukraine's negotiating position in peace talks with Russia. It also would have supported Ukraine as a bulwark against further Russian advances in Europe.

Multiple witnesses unanimously attested to the importance of a White House meeting for Ukraine and the United States. For example, David Holmes, the Political Counselor at the U.S. Embassy in Kyiv, testified that a White House meeting was "critical" to President Zelensky's ability to "encourage Russian President Putin to take seriously President Zelensky's peace efforts."[456] Likewise, Deputy Assistant Secretary George Kent explained that a White House meeting was "very important" for Ukrainians to demonstrate the strength of their relationship with "Ukraine's strongest supporter." He also said that it "makes sense" for the United States to meet with the Ukrainians as they were on "the front lines of Russian malign influence and aggression."[457]

Dr. Fiona Hill, Deputy Assistant to the President and Senior Director of Europe and Russia at the NSC, explained that a White House meeting would supply the new Ukrainian Government with "the legitimacy that it needed, especially vis-à-vis the Russians,"—and that the Ukrainians viewed a White House meeting as "a recognition of their legitimacy as a sovereign state."[458] Lt. Col. Alexander Vindman, the NSC Director for Ukraine, testified that a White House meeting would provide a "show of support" from "the most powerful country in the world and Ukraine's most significant benefactor," which would help the Ukrainian President "establish his bona fides" and "implement his agenda."[459]

Ambassador Kurt Volker, Special Representative for Ukraine Negotiations, also recognized that it was "a tremendous symbol of support" to have President Zelensky visit the White House.[460] He explained that a meeting "enhances [President Zelensky's] stature, that he is accepted, that he is seen at the highest level. The imagery you get from being at the White House is the best in the world, in terms of how it enhances someone's image."[461]

President Trump "Wanted to Hear from Zelensky" Before Scheduling Oval Office Meeting

Ambassador William B. Taylor, Jr. arrived in Ukraine as the new Chargé d'Affaires at the U.S. Embassy in Kyiv on June 17, 2019. After arriving, Ambassador Taylor worked to secure an Oval Office meeting between President Trump and President Zelensky. This was "an agreed-upon goal" of policymakers in both Ukraine and the United States.[462]

Ambassador Taylor worked with Ambassador Volker and Ambassador to the European Union Gordon Sondland—two of the Three Amigos—to try to schedule this meeting. Just days after beginning his new position, Ambassador Taylor learned that President Trump "wanted to hear from Zelensky" before scheduling the Oval Office meeting, but Ambassador Taylor did not understand what that meant at the time.[463] On June 27, Ambassador Sondland informed Ambassador Taylor that President Zelensky needed to "make clear" to President Trump that he, President Zelensky, was not "standing in the way of 'investigations.'"[464] Ambassador Taylor relayed this conversation to Mr. Holmes, who testified that he understood "investigations" in that context to mean the "Burisma-Biden investigations that Mr. Giuliani and his associates had been speaking about" publicly.[465]

On June 28, Secretary of Energy Rick Perry—the third of the Three Amigos—and Ambassadors Sondland, Volker, and Taylor participated in a conference call to prepare for a discussion later that day with President Zelensky. During this preparatory call, Ambassador Volker explained that he planned to be "explicit" with President Zelensky in an upcoming one-on-one meeting in Toronto, Canada. Specifically, Ambassador Volker intended to inform President Zelensky that President Trump would require Ukraine to address "rule of law, transparency, but also, specifically, cooperation on investigations to get to the bottom of things" in order to "get the meeting in the White House."[466]

For the subsequent call with President Zelensky on June 28, Ambassador Sondland sought to limit the number of U.S. government personnel listening in. According to Ambassador Taylor, Ambassador Sondland stated that he did not want to include "most of the regular interagency participants" and that "he wanted to make sure no one was transcribing or monitoring" the call when President Zelensky was patched in. Ambassador Taylor testified that he considered Ambassador Sondland's requests to be "odd."[467] During that call, President Zelensky and the U.S. officials discussed energy policy and the conflict with Russia in eastern Ukraine. The Ukrainian president also noted that he looked forward to the White House visit that President Trump had offered in a letter dated May 29.[468]

The exclusion of State Department staff and notetakers from the June 28 call was an early indication to Ambassador Taylor that separate channels of diplomacy related to Ukraine policy—an official channel and an irregular channel—were "diverging." Ambassador Taylor testified:

> This suggested to me that there were the two channels. This suggested to me that the normal channel, where you would have staff on the phone call, was being cut out, and the other channel, of people who were working, again, toward a goal which I supported, which was having a meeting to further U.S.-Ukrainian relations, I supported, but that irregular channel didn't have a respect for or an interest in having the normal staff participate in this call with the head of state.[469]

Given Ambassador Sondland's efforts to exclude staff on the June 28 call with President Zelensky, Ambassador Taylor asked Ambassadors Sondland and Volker by text message how they planned to handle informing other U.S. officials about the contents of the call. Ambassador Volker responded: "I think we just keep it among ourselves to try to build working relationship and just get the d*** date for the meeting!"[470] Ambassador Sondland then texted: "Agree with KV. Very close hold."[471] Nevertheless, Ambassador Taylor informed Mr. Kent about the call and wrote a memo for the record dated June 30 that summarized the conversation with President Zelensky.[472]

Ambassador Volker Pressed "Investigations" with President Zelensky in Toronto

On July 2, Ambassador Volker met with President Zelensky and his chief of staff on the sidelines of the Ukraine Reform Conference in Toronto. As he later texted to Ambassador Taylor, Ambassador Volker "pulled the two of them aside at the end and explained the Giuliani factor."[473] Ambassador Volker clarified that by "the Giuliani factor," he meant "a negative narrative about Ukraine" that was "being amplified by Rudy Giuliani" and was unfavorably impacting "Ukraine's image in the United States and our ability to advance the bilateral relationship."[474] Ambassador Volker later informed Ukraine's incoming Minister of Foreign Affairs, Vadym Prystaiko, about his pull-aside with President Zelensky in Toronto via text message: "I talked to him privately about Giuliani and impact on president T[rump]."[475]

On July 3, the day after his pull-aside with President Zelensky in Toronto, Ambassador Volker sent a message to Ambassador Taylor emphasizing that "The key thing is to tee up a phone call w potus and then get visit nailed down."[476] Ambassador Volker told Ambassador Taylor that during the Toronto conference, he counseled the Ukrainian president about how he could "prepare for the phone call with President Trump." Specifically, Ambassador Volker told the Ukrainian leader that President Trump "would like to hear about the investigations."[477] In his public testimony, Ambassador Volker confirmed that he mentioned "investigations" to President Zelensky in Toronto, explaining that he was "thinking of Burisma and 2016" in raising the subject, and that his "assumption" was that Ukrainian officials also understood his reference to "investigations" to be "Burisma/2016."[478]

Ambassador Volker's efforts to prepare President Zelensky for his phone call with President Trump appear to have borne fruit. As discussed further in Chapter 5, during the July 25 call, President Zelensky expressed his openness to pursuing investigations into President Trump's political rival, former Vice President Biden, and the conspiracy theory that Ukraine, rather than Russia, interfered in the 2016 U.S. election. President Zelensky also specifically referenced "Burisma" during the call.

Ambassadors Volker and Sondland Worked to Get Mr. Giuliani What He Needed

According to Ambassador Sondland, President Zelensky's commitment to make a public announcement about investigations into Burisma and the 2016 election was a "prerequisite[]" for the White House meeting.[479] In fact, Ambassador Sondland testified that the *announcement* of the investigations—and not the investigations themselves—was the price President Trump sought in exchange for a White House meeting with Ukrainian President Zelensky:

> Q: But he had to get those two investigations if that official act was going to take place, correct?
>
> A: He had to announce the investigations. He didn't actually have to do them, as I understood it.
>
> Q: Okay. President Zelensky had to announce the two investigations the President wanted, make a public announcement, correct?
>
> A: Correct.[480]

Ambassadors Sondland and Volker understood that they needed to work with Mr. Giuliani, who was publicly pressing for the announcement of investigations that would benefit President Trump politically. As discussed in Chapter 2, Ambassador Sondland testified that the key to overcoming President Trump's skepticism about Ukraine was satisfying the President's personal attorney. Sondland said, "Nonetheless, based on the President's direction, we were faced with a choice: We could abandon the efforts to schedule the White House phone call and a

White House visit" or "do as President Trump had directed and 'talk with Rudy'" because "it was the only constructive path open to us."[481]

Ambassador Volker discussed his intention to contact Mr. Giuliani with Mr. Kent. Ambassador Volker explained that he intended to reach out to Mr. Giuliani because it was clear that the former mayor "had influence" with President Trump "in terms of the way the President thought of Ukraine."[482]   Ukrainian officials also understood the importance of working through Mr. Giuliani, something that was underscored by his successful effort to smear and remove Ambassador Marie Yovanovitch from Kyiv in late April.[483]

In response to Ambassador Volker's stated intention to reach out to Mr. Giuliani, Mr. Kent raised concerns about Mr. Giuliani's "track record," including "asking for a visa for a corrupt former prosecutor," attacking Ambassador Yovanovitch, and "tweeting that the new President needs to investigate Biden and the 2016 campaign." Mr. Kent also warned Ambassador Volker that "asking another country to investigate a prosecution for political reasons undermines our advocacy of the rule of law."[484]

On July 10, Ambassador Taylor met with Ukrainian officials in Kyiv, before their Ukrainian colleagues were scheduled to meet with National Security Advisor John Bolton at the White House later that day. At the meeting in Kyiv, the Ukrainian officials expressed that they were "very concerned" because they had heard from former Prosecutor General Yuriy Lutsenko, who had learned from Mr. Giuliani, that President Trump had decided not to meet with President Zelensky.[485]

Ambassador Taylor texted Ambassador Volker to explain the situation and advised that he had also informed T. Ulrich Brechbuhl, Counselor of the Department of State:

Volker:	Good grief. Please tell Vadym to let the official USG representatives speak for the U.S. lutsenko has his own self-Interest here…
Taylor:	Exactly what I told them.
Taylor:	And I said that RG is a private citizen.
Taylor:	I briefed Ulrich this afternoon on this.[486]

Despite his text message to Ambassador Taylor that official U.S. government representatives should be allowed to "speak for the U.S.," and notwithstanding Mr. Kent's warnings about engaging with Mr. Giuliani, Ambassador Volker almost immediately reached out to Mr. Giuliani. Four minutes after sending the text message above, Ambassador Volker texted Mr. Giuliani to request a meeting to "update you on my conversations about Ukraine." He told Mr. Giuliani that he believed he had "an opportunity to get you what you need."[487]

One hour later, around 9:00 a.m. Eastern Time, Ambassador Volker met Ukrainian presidential aide Andriy Yermak for coffee at the Trump Hotel before they traveled down Pennsylvania Avenue to their afternoon meetings at the White House.[488] Over coffee, Mr. Yermak asked Ambassador Volker to connect him to Mr. Giuliani, thus further demonstrating the Ukrainians' understanding that satisfying Mr. Giuliani's demands was a key to getting what they wanted from President Trump, namely the Oval Office meeting.[489]

July 10 White House Meetings: Ambassador Sondland
Explicitly Communicated the "Prerequisite of Investigations" to Ukrainians

On July 10, during two separate meetings at the White House, Ambassador Sondland informed senior Ukrainian officials that there was a "prerequisite of investigations" before an Oval Office meeting between President Trump and President Zelensky would be scheduled.[490]

The first meeting took place in Ambassador Bolton's office. NSC officials, including Ambassador Bolton's staff responsible for Ukraine—Dr. Hill and Lt. Col. Vindman—attended, as did the Three Amigos: Secretary Perry, Ambassador Sondland, and Ambassador Volker. The Ukrainian delegation included Mr. Yermak, a senior aide to President Zelensky, and Oleksandr "Sasha" Danyliuk, the incoming Ukrainian National Security Advisor.[491] The purpose of the meeting was twofold. The Ukrainians were seeking advice and assistance from Ambassador Bolton about how to "revamp" the Ukrainian National Security Council, and they were also "very anxious to set up a meeting, a first meeting between President Zelensky and our President."[492]

Near the end of the meeting, the Ukrainian officials raised the scheduling of the Oval Office meeting for President Zelensky. According to Dr. Hill, Ambassador Sondland, who is "a fairly big guy, kind of leaned over" and then "blurted out: Well, we have an agreement with the [White House] Chief of Staff for a meeting if these investigations in the energy sector start." Dr. Hill described that others in the room looked up from their notes, thinking the comment was "somewhat odd." Ambassador Bolton "immediately stiffened" and ended the meeting. Dr. Hill recounted that Ambassador Bolton was polite but was "very abrupt. I mean, he looked at the clock as if he had, you know, suddenly another meeting and his time was up, but it was obvious he ended the meeting," she added.[493]

Lt. Col. Vindman similarly testified that the meeting in Ambassador Bolton's office "proceeded well" until Ukrainian officials raised the meeting between President Trump and President Zelensky. The Ukrainians stated that they considered the Oval Office meeting to be "critically important in order to solidify the support for their most important international partner." When Ambassador Sondland mentioned Ukraine "delivering specific investigations in order to secure the meeting with the President," Ambassador Bolton cut the meeting short.[494]

Although Ambassador Volker did not recall any mention of "investigations" during the July 10 meeting at his deposition,[495] he later testified at his public hearing, "As I remember, the meeting [in Ambassador Bolton's office] was essentially over when Ambassador Sondland made a general comment about investigations. I think all of us thought it was inappropriate" and "not what we should be talking about."[496]

After Ambassador Bolton ended the meeting in his office, Ambassador Sondland "went out into the office in front of Ambassador Bolton" and made "unusual" arrangements for the Ukrainians, Ambassador Volker, Secretary Perry, and others to go to a second meeting in the Ward Room of the White House, located near the secure spaces of the White House Situation Room. As Dr. Hill described it, the purpose of the Ward Room meeting was "to talk to the

Ukrainians about next steps" regarding the Oval Office meeting for President Zelensky.[497] As Dr. Hill was leaving Ambassador Bolton's office, he pulled her aside and directed her to attend the Ward Room meeting to "find out what they're talking about and come back" and report to him. Dr. Hill followed his instruction.[498]

During the Ward Room meeting, which occurred after a brief photo opportunity outside the West Wing, Ambassador Sondland was more explicit in pressing the Ukrainians to undertake the investigations in order to secure an Oval Office meeting for President Zelensky. Lt. Col. Vindman testified that when the group entered the Ward Room, Ambassador Sondland began to "review what the deliverable would be in order to get the meeting," and that "to the best of my recollection, he did specifically say 'investigation of the Bidens.'" Lt. Col. Vindman said the request "was explicit. There was no ambiguity" and that Ambassador Sondland also mentioned "Burisma."[499]

Dr. Hill entered the Ward Room as the discussion was underway. She testified that "Ambassador Sondland, in front of the Ukrainians, as I came in, was talking about how he had an agreement with Chief of Staff Mulvaney for a meeting with the Ukrainians if they were going to go forward with investigations. And my director for Ukraine [Lt. Col. Vindman] was looking completely alarmed."[500] Dr. Hill recalled that Ambassador Sondland mentioned "Burisma" in the presence of the Ukrainians, in response to which Mr. Danyliuk also appeared "very alarmed" and as if he did not know what was happening.[501]

Dr. Hill confronted Ambassador Sondland, informing him that Ambassador Bolton had sent her there to ensure that the U.S. officials did not commit "at this particular juncture" to a meeting between President Trump and President Zelensky. Ambassador Sondland responded that he and the Ukrainians already had an agreement that the meeting would go forward.[502] At Dr. Hill's urging, however, Ambassador Sondland excused the Ukrainian officials, who moved into the corridor near the White House Situation Room.

Dr. Hill then told Ambassador Sondland: "Look, I don't know what's going on here, but Ambassador Bolton wants to make it very clear that we have to talk about, you know, how are we going to set up this meeting. It has to go through proper procedures." Lt. Col. Vindman relayed his own concerns to Ambassador Sondland in the Ward Room.[503] He explained that "the request to investigate the Bidens and his son had nothing to do with national security, and that such investigations were not something that the NSC was going to get involved in or push."[504]

Ambassador Sondland responded that he had had conversations with Mr. Mulvaney and he also mentioned Mr. Giuliani. Lt. Col. Vindman confirmed that Ambassador Sondland described an agreement he had with Mr. Mulvaney about the Oval Office meeting: "I heard him say that this had been coordinated with White House Chief of Staff Mr. Mick Mulvaney … He just said that he had had a conversation with Mr. Mulvaney, and this is what was required in order to get a meeting."[505] Dr. Hill then cut the conversation short because she "didn't want to get further into this discussion at all." She testified that Ambassador Sondland "was clearly annoyed with this, but then, you know, he moved off. He said he had other meetings."[506]

Later on July 10, when Ambassador Taylor asked Ambassador Volker how the meetings went with the Ukrainian officials and whether they had resulted in a decision on a presidential call, Ambassador Volker replied: "Not good—lets talk."[507]

Following the July 10 White House meetings, Mr. Yermak followed up with Ambassador Volker by text message: "Thank you for meeting and your clear and very logical position. Will be great meet with you before my departure and discuss. I feel that the key for many things is Rudi and I ready to talk with him at any time."[508]

Concerned Officials Reported Details of This "Drug Deal" to White House Lawyers

After the Ward Room meeting, Dr. Hill returned to Ambassador Bolton's office and relayed what she had just witnessed. Ambassador Bolton was "very angry" and instructed her to report the conversation to John Eisenberg, Deputy Counsel to the President for National Security Affairs and the Legal Advisor to the National Security Council:

> And he told me, and this is a direct quote from Ambassador Bolton: You go and tell Eisenberg that I am not part of whatever drug deal Sondland and Mulvaney are cooking up on this, and you go and tell him what you've heard and what I've said.[509]

Dr. Hill explained that "drug deal" referred to Ambassador Sondland's and Mr. Mulvaney's conditioning of a White House meeting on investigations.[510] By this point, Dr. Hill explained, it was clear that investigations were "code, at least, for Burisma. Because that had been mentioned, you know, in the course of Mr. Giuliani's appearances on television."[511] Numerous U.S. officials, including Ambassadors Sondland, Volker, and Bolton, as well as Lt. Col. Vindman and others, were well aware of Mr. Giuliani's efforts to push Ukraine to pursue these political investigations.

Following the meeting with Ambassador Bolton, Dr. Hill reported what had occurred to Mr. Eisenberg. She conveyed to Mr. Eisenberg the details of the two meetings, including Ambassador Sondland's agreement with Mr. Mulvaney to provide the White House meeting if Ukraine agreed to pursue the investigations.[512] The initial conversation between Dr. Hill and Mr. Eisenberg was brief, and they scheduled a longer discussion for the next day.[513]

On July 11, Dr. Hill enlisted another NSC official who attended the July 10 meetings, Senior Director for International Energy and Environment P. Wells Griffith, to attend the longer discussion with Mr. Eisenberg.[514] Dr. Hill and Mr. Griffith went over the events of July 10 and further explained that Ambassador Sondland said that he had been communicating with Mr. Giuliani. Mr. Eisenberg was "very concerned" and stated that he would follow up. Dr. Hill understood that Mr. Eisenberg later discussed the issue with his "reporting authority," specifically, White House Counsel Pat Cipollone.[515]

Lt. Col. Vindman separately reported his concerns about the July 10 meetings to Mr. Eisenberg. He told Mr. Eisenberg that Ambassador Sondland had asked for investigations into "Bidens and Burisma," which he thought was "inappropriate."[516] Lt. Col. Vindman also reported that the investigation "Mr. Giuliani was pushing was now being pulled into a, you know, national security dialogue."[517] Mr. Eisenberg said that he would look into it and invited Lt. Col. Vindman to return if any further concerns arose. No one from the of the White House Counsel's Office, however, followed up with Lt. Col. Vindman on this issue.[518]

Dr. Hill and Lt. Col. Vindman discussed their reactions and alarm about the July 10 discussions with each other. They both believed that Ambassador Sondland's statements were inappropriate and "had nothing to do with national security," and that they would not get involved with the scheme.[519] On July 19, they also shared their concerns about Ambassador Sondland's comments during the July 10 meetings with Ambassador Taylor.[520]

Ambassador Sondland Coached President Zelensky on Investigations and Kept Senior White House and State Department Officials "In the Loop"

In mid-July, Dr. Hill was preparing to depart the NSC and transitioning her role to Timothy Morrison, who had been serving in another role at the NSC.[521] On July 13, Ambassador Sondland emailed Mr. Morrison, explaining that the "[s]ole purpose" of a presidential call was for President Zelensky to assure President Trump that, "Corruption ending, unbundling moving forward and any hampered investigations will be allowed to move forward transparently." In exchange, Ambassador Sondland wrote, the "Goal is for Potus to invite him to Oval. Volker, Perry, Bolton and I strongly recommend."[522] Later that evening, Mr. Morrison responded, "Thank you. Tracking."[523]

On July 19, a little over a week after the July 10 meetings at the White House, Ambassador Sondland spoke directly to President Zelensky about the upcoming call between the two presidents: "It was a short call. I think I said: It looks like your call is finally on, and I think it's important that you, you know, give President Trump—he wanted this—some kind of a statement about corruption."[524]

Following his call with President Zelensky, Ambassador Sondland emailed several senior Trump Administration officials, including Mr. Mulvaney, Secretary of State Michael Pompeo, Secretary Perry, and their staffs. The subject line of the July 19 email read: "I Talked to Zelensky just now." Ambassador Sondland wrote:

> He is prepared to receive Potus' call. Will assure him that he intends to run a fully transparent investigation and will "turn over every stone". He would greatly appreciate a call prior to Sunday so that he can put out some media about a "friendly and productive call" (no details) prior to Ukraine election on Sunday.[525]

Secretary Perry responded that Mr. Mulvaney had confirmed a call would be set up "for tomorrow by NSC,"[526] and Mr. Mulvaney also responded to confirm that he had asked the NSC to set up the call between the presidents for the following day, July 20.[527]

Ambassador Sondland explained that this email chain showed that "[e]veryone was in the loop" regarding his discussions with Ukrainian officials about the need for the Ukrainian leader to confirm to President Trump that he would announce the investigations. As Ambassador Sondland further testified:

It was no secret. Everyone was informed via email on July 19th, days before the Presidential call. As I communicated to the team, I told President Zelensky in advance that assurances to run a fully transparent investigation and turn over every stone were necessary in his call with President Trump.[528]

Call records reviewed by the Committees show repeated contact between Ambassador Sondland and the White House around this time. For example, on July 19, at 10:43 a.m. Eastern Time, a number associated with the White House dialed Ambassador Sondland. Four minutes later, at 10:47 a.m., Ambassador Sondland called a White House phone number and connected for approximately seven minutes.[529]

Later in the afternoon of July 19, Ambassador Sondland texted Ambassadors Volker and Taylor: "Looks like Potus call tomorrow. I spike [sic] directly to Zelensky and gave him a full briefing. He's got it."[530] Ambassador Volker replied: "Good. Had breakfast with Rudy this morning—teeing up call w Yermak Monday. Must have helped. Most impt is for Zelensky to say that he will help investigation—and address any specific personnel issues—if there are any."[531]

Mr. Giuliani Met with State Department Officials and Ukrainian Government Officials

As Ambassador Volker informed Ambassador Sondland in the above text message, on July 19, Ambassador Volker met Mr. Giuliani and his now-indicted associate Lev Parnas for breakfast at the Trump Hotel in Washington, D.C.[532] Ambassador Volker also texted Mr. Yermak to inform him that he and Mr. Giuliani were meeting that day: "Having our long anticipated breakfast today—will let you know and try to connect you directly."[533]

During the breakfast, Mr. Giuliani and Ambassador Volker discussed the discredited allegations against former Vice President Biden relating to Ukraine. Ambassador Volker testified that he pushed back against the allegations during his breakfast with Mr. Giuliani:

One of the things that I said in that breakfast that I had with Mr. Giuliani, the only time Vice President Biden was ever discussed with me, and he was repeating—he wasn't making an accusation and he wasn't seeking an investigation—but he was repeating all of the things that were in the media that we talked about earlier about, you know, firing the prosecutor general and his son being on the company and all that.

And I said to Rudy in that breakfast the first time we sat down to talk that it is simply not credible to me that Joe Biden would be influenced in his duties as Vice President by money or things for his son or anything like that. I've known him a long time, he's a person of integrity, and that's not credible.[534]

Ambassador Volker further advised Mr. Giuliani during the breakfast that the then-Ukrainian Prosecutor General, Yuriy Lutsenko, was promoting a "self-serving narrative to preserve himself in power." Mr. Giuliani agreed with Ambassador Volker and stated that he had come to that conclusion as well.[535]

Following the breakfast, Ambassador Volker connected Mr. Giuliani with Mr. Yermak by text message:

> Volker: Mr Mayor—really enjoyed breakfast this morning. As discussed, connecting you here with Andrey Yermak, who is very close to President Zelensky. I suggest we schedule a call together on Monday—maybe 10am or 11am Washington time? Kurt
>
> Giuliani: Monday 10 to 11
>
> Yermak: Ok, thank you
>
> Volker: I will set up call—10 am—thanks - Kurt
>
> Yermak: 👍[536]

On the morning of July 22, Mr. Yermak texted Ambassador Volker about the upcoming call with Mr. Giuliani, writing that it was "very good" that their discussion would take place before the call between President Trump and President Zelensky.[537] Later that day, the three men spoke by phone. Ambassador Volker described the July 22 discussion as merely an "introductory phone call,"[538] although phone records indicate that the call lasted for approximately 38 minutes.[539]

Ambassador Volker testified that during the call, Mr. Giuliani and Mr. Yermak discussed plans for an in-person meeting in Madrid in early August.[540] Afterward, Ambassador Volker texted Mr. Yermak that he thought the call had been "very useful" and recommended that Mr. Yermak send Mr. Giuliani a text message to schedule a date for the Madrid meeting.[541] Mr. Yermak texted Mr. Giuliani later that day about a plan to "take this relationship to a new level" and to meet in person as soon as possible.[542]

Later on July 22, Ambassador Volker updated Ambassador Sondland on the "great call" he "[o]rchestrated" between Mr. Giuliani and Mr. Yermak, noting that "Rudy is now advocating for phone call," an apparent reference to the call between President Trump and President Zelensky that would occur on July 25. Ambassador Volker also recommended that Ambassador Sondland inform Mr. Mulvaney that "Rudy agrees," and that he planned to convey the same information to Ambassador Bolton. Ambassador Sondland replied that Mr. Morrison of the White House NSC was also in support of the call.[543] Ambassador Volker also told Ambassador Sondland that Mr. Giuliani and Mr. Yermak would meet in person in Madrid within a couple of weeks.[544]

President Zelensky Feared Becoming "A Pawn" in U.S. Reelection Campaign

Around this time, senior Ukrainian officials informed U.S. officials that the new Ukrainian president did not want Ukraine to become enmeshed in U.S. domestic reelection politics.

On July 20, Ambassador Taylor spoke with Mr. Danyliuk, the Ukrainian national security advisor, who conveyed that President Zelensky "did not want to be used as a pawn in a U.S. reelection campaign."[545] Ambassador Taylor discussed President Zelensky's concern with Ambassador Volker and, the next day, texted Ambassador Sondland:

Taylor: Gordon, one thing Kurt and I talked about yesterday was Sasha Danyliuk's point that President Zelenskyy is sensitive about Ukraine being taken seriously, not merely as an instrument in Washington domestic, reelection politics.

Sondland: Absolutely, but we need to get the conversation started and the relationship built, irrespective of the pretext. I am worried about the alternative.[546]

Ambassador Taylor explained that his reference to "Washington domestic reelection politics" was "a reference to the investigations that Mr. Giuliani wanted to pursue."[547] According to Ambassador Taylor, President Zelensky understood what President Trump and Mr. Giuliani meant by "investigations," and "he did not want to get involved." Specifically, the Ukrainians understood that the "investigations were pursuant to Mr. Giuliani's request to develop information, to find information about Burisma and the Bidens. This was very well known in public. Mr. Giuliani had made this point clear in several instances in the beginning—in the springtime."[548] Ambassador Taylor also testified that the "whole thrust" of the activities undertaken by Mr. Giuliani and Ambassador Sondland "was to get these investigations, which Danyliuk and presumably Zelensky were resisting because they didn't want to be seen to be interfering but also to be a pawn."[549]

Despite the Ukrainian resistance, Ambassador Sondland said he believed that the public announcement of investigations would "fix" an impasse between the Ukrainian government and President Trump. When asked what he meant by "irrespective of the pretext" in his July 21 text message to Ambassador Taylor, Ambassador Sondland explained, "Well, the pretext being the agreed-upon interview or the agreed-upon press statement. We just need to get by it so that the two can meet, because, again, it was back to once they meet, all of this will be fixed."[550]

Witnesses Confirmed the President Conditioned an Oval Office Meeting on Investigations

Multiple witnesses testified that the conditioning of an Oval Office meeting on President Zelensky's announcement of investigations to benefit the President's reelection campaign came from the very top: President Trump.

Ambassador Sondland testified that he, Secretary Perry, and Ambassador Volker worked with Mr. Giuliani "at the express direction of the President of the United States."[551] Ambassador Sondland stated that "Mr. Giuliani was expressing the desires of the President of the United States, and we knew these investigations were important to the President."[552] Ambassador Sondland explained that he "followed the directions of the President" and that "we followed the President's orders."[553]

Ambassador Sondland further testified that President Trump expressed—both directly and through Mr. Giuliani—that he wanted "a public statement from President Zelensky committing to the investigations of Burisma and the 2016 election" as "prerequisites for the White House call and the White House meeting."[554] Ambassador Sondland explained:

> I know that members of this committee frequently frame these complicated issues in the form of a simple question: Was there a quid pro quo? As I testified previously with regard to the requested White House call and the White House meeting, the answer is yes.[555]

Ambassador Sondland also testified that knowledge of this quid pro quo was widespread among the President's advisers: "Everyone was in the loop" about the President's expectation that President Zelensky had to announce these specific investigations to secure an Oval Office meeting. As an example, Ambassador Sondland cited an email—copying Senior Advisor to the White House Chief of Staff Robert Blair, State Department Executive Secretary Lisa Kenna, Chief of Staff to the Secretary of Energy Brian McCormack, Mr. Mulvaney, Secretary Perry, and Secretary Pompeo—where "[e]veryone was informed."[556]

Other U.S. government officials also understood this scheme as a quid pro quo. Ambassador Taylor testified that as early as mid-July, it was "becoming clear" to him that "the meeting President Zelensky wanted was conditioned on investigations of Burisma and alleged Ukrainian influence in the 2016 elections" and that "this condition was driven by the irregular policy channel I had come to understand was guided by Mr. Giuliani."[557] Mr. Holmes similarly understood that by July, "it was made clear that some action on a Burisma/Biden investigation was a precondition for an Oval Office visit."[558] Dr. Hill testified that this quid pro quo was readily apparent after reading the July 25 call summary, explaining that it revealed that the White House meeting was used as "some kind of asset" that was "dangled out to the Ukrainian Government" to secure a political benefit.[559]

Final Preparation for Trump-Zelensky Call: Ambassador Volker Counseled Ukrainians and Ambassador Sondland Prepped President Trump

Ambassador Taylor testified that the call between President Trump and President Zelensky that ultimately occurred on July 25 was not confirmed until the last minute: "We were trying to schedule it for about a week in advance, that whole week. As I say, back and forth, yes, no, this time, that time. … it may have been about the day before that it was actually locked down, so about the 24th."[560] According to Ambassador Taylor, at least one person had prescient concerns about the call before it occurred: "Ambassador Bolton was not interested in having—

did not want to have the call because he thought it was going to be a disaster. He thought that there could be some talk of investigations or worse on the call."[561]

Before the call took place on July 25, Ambassador Volker had lunch with Mr. Yermak in Kyiv. Ambassador Volker followed up with a text message to Mr. Yermak approximately 30 minutes before the call, noting that a White House visit was still on the table if, during the call, President Zelensky convinced President Trump that Ukraine would "investigate" and "get to the bottom of what happened" in 2016:

> Volker: Good lunch – thanks. Heard from White House—assuming President Z convinces trump he will investigate / "get to the bottom of what happened" in 2016, we will nail down date for visit to Washington. Good luck! See you tomorrow - kurt

Ambassador Volker later informed Ambassador Sondland that he had relayed this "message" to Mr. Yermak, which Ambassador Sondland had conveyed to Ambassador Volker earlier that day:

> Volker: Hi Gordon - got your message. Had a great lunch w Yermak and then passed your message to him. He will see you tomorrow. Think everything in place[562]

Ambassador Sondland testified that the "message" that Ambassador Volker conveyed to Mr. Yermak in advance of the July 25 call likely originated from an earlier conversation that Ambassador Sondland had with President Trump:

> Q: So is it fair to say that this message is what you received from President Trump on that phone call that morning?
> A: Again, if he testified to that, to refresh my own memory, then, yes, likely I would have received that from President Trump.
> Q: But the sequence certainly makes sense, right?
> A: Yeah, it does.
> Q: You talked to President Trump.
> A: Yeah.
> Q: You told Kurt Volker to call you. You left a message for Kurt Volker. Kurt Volker sent this text message to Andriy Yermak to prepare President Zelensky and then President Trump had a phone call where President Zelensky spoke very similar to what was in this text message, right?
> A: Right.
> Q: And you would agree that the message in this—that is expressed here is that President Zelensky needs to convince Trump that he will do the investigations in order to nail down the date for a visit to Washington, D.C. Is that correct?
> A: That's correct.[563]

Ambassador Sondland testified that he spoke with President Trump before the call with President Zelensky.[564] Mr. Morrison also confirmed that President Trump and Ambassador

Sondland spoke before President Trump's call with President Zelensky.[565] Mr. Morrison stated that Ambassador Sondland emailed him on the morning of the call and listed "three topics that he was working on, the first of which was 'I spoke to the President this morning to brief him on the call.'"[566] According to Mr. Morrison, Ambassador Sondland "believed" that he helped to facilitate the July 25 call between President Trump and President Zelensky.[567]

On July 26, the day after the call between President Trump and President Zelensky, Ambassador Volker acknowledged his role in prepping President Zelensky for the call with President Trump in a text to Mr. Giuliani: "Hi Mr Mayor – you may have heard—the President has [sic] a great phone call with the Ukrainian President yesterday. Exactly the right messages as we discussed."[568]

5.   The President Asked the Ukrainian President to Interfere in the 2020 U.S. Election by Investigating the Bidens and 2016 Election Interference

> *During a call on July 25, President Trump asked President Zelensky of Ukraine to "do us a favor though" and investigate his political opponent, former Vice President Joe Biden, and a debunked conspiracy theory that Ukraine interfered in the 2016 U.S. election. The next day, Ambassador Gordon Sondland informed President Trump that President Zelensky "was gonna do the investigation" and "anything" President Trump asked of him.*

Overview

During a telephone call on July 25, 2019, President Donald J. Trump asked Ukrainian President Volodymyr Zelensky to investigate his political rival, former Vice President Joseph Biden, and a debunked conspiracy theory that Ukraine interfered in the 2016 U.S. election. President Trump also discussed the removal of Ambassador Marie Yovanovitch, former U.S. Ambassador to Ukraine, said that she was "bad news," and warned that she would "go through some things." Two witnesses who listened to the call testified that they immediately reported the details of the call to senior White House lawyers.

When asked by a reporter on October 3, 2019, what he had hoped President Zelensky would do following the call, President Trump responded: "Well, I would think that, if they were honest about it, they'd start a major investigation into the Bidens. It's a very simple answer."

Witnesses unanimously testified that President Trump's claims about former Vice President Biden and alleged Ukrainian interference in the 2016 U.S. election have been discredited. The witnesses reaffirmed that in late 2015 and early 2016, when former Vice President Biden advocated for the removal of a corrupt Ukrainian prosecutor, he acted in accordance with a "broad-based consensus" and the official policy of the United States, the European Union, and major international financial institutions. Witnesses also unanimously testified that the removal of that prosecutor made it more likely that Ukraine would investigate corruption, not less likely.

Dr. Fiona Hill, former Deputy Assistant to the President and Senior Director for Europe and Russia at the National Security Council, testified that the conspiracy theories about Ukrainian interference in the 2016 U.S. election touted by President Trump are a "fictional narrative that is being perpetrated and propagated by the Russian security services." She noted that President Trump's former Homeland Security Advisor Tom Bossert and former National Security Advisor H.R. McMaster repeatedly advised the President that the so-called "CrowdStrike" conspiracy theory that President Trump raised in the July 25 call is completely "debunked," and that allegations Ukraine interfered in the 2016 U.S. election are false.

Nonetheless, on July 26, 2019, U.S. Ambassador to the European Union Gordon Sondland met with senior Ukrainian officials in Kyiv and then informed President Trump that President Zelensky "was gonna do the investigation" into former Vice President Biden and alleged Ukrainian interference in the 2016 U.S. election. Ambassador Sondland added that President Zelensky would "do anything" President Trump asked of him. After the call, Ambassador Sondland told David Holmes, Counselor for Political Affairs at the U.S. Embassy in Kyiv, that President Trump "did not give a shit about Ukraine" and that he only cared about the "big stuff" that benefited his personal interests, like the "Biden investigation."

President Trump's Call with President Zelensky on July 25, 2019

On July 25, 2019, President Zelensky finally had a long-awaited phone call with Ukraine's most important international partner: The President of the United States.

It had been over three months since the two leaders first spoke. Despite a warm but largely non-substantive call on April 21, President Trump had since declined President Zelensky's invitation to attend his inauguration and directed Vice President Mike Pence not to attend either.[569] Ukrainian efforts to set a date for a promised Oval Office meeting with President Trump were stalled. As Mr. Holmes explained, following the April 21 call:

> President Zelensky's team immediately began pressing to set a date for that visit. President Zelensky and senior members of his team made clear that they wanted President Zelensky's first overseas trip to be to Washington, to send a strong signal of American support, and requested a call with President Trump as soon as possible.[570]

Before scheduling the July 25 call or a White House visit, President Trump met on June 28 with Russian President Vladimir Putin—whose armed forces were engaged in a war of attrition against U.S.-backed Ukrainian forces—on the sidelines of the G20 summit in Osaka, Japan.[571] During their meeting, President Trump and President Putin shared a joke about Russia's meddling in the 2016 U.S. election.[572]

On July 25, President Trump joined the call with President Zelensky from the Executive Residence at the White House, away from a small group of senior national security aides who would normally join him in the Oval Office for a conversation with a foreign head of state. President Trump and President Zelensky began to speak at 9:03 a.m. Washington time—4:03 p.m. in Kyiv. According to Tim Morrison, the newly-installed Senior Director for Europe and Russia on the NSC, President Zelensky spoke in Ukrainian and occasionally in "chopped English."[573] Translators interpreted the call on both sides.[574] American aides listening to the call from the White House Situation Room hoped that what was said over the next 30 minutes would provide President Zelensky with the strong U.S. endorsement he needed in order to successfully negotiate an end to the five-year-old war with Russia that had killed over 13,000 Ukrainian soldiers and to advance President Zelensky's ambitious anti-corruption initiatives in Ukraine.[575]

The Trump Administration's subject-matter experts, NSC Director for Ukraine Lt. Col. Alexander Vindman and Mr. Morrison, were both on the call.[576] They had prepared talking points for President Trump and were taking detailed notes of what both leaders said, so that they could promptly implement any agreed-upon actions.[577] They were joined by Lt. Gen. Keith Kellogg, National Security Advisor to the Vice President, and Jennifer Williams, Special Advisor to the Vice President for Europe and Russia. Assistant to the President Robert Blair, a senior aide to Acting Chief of Staff Mick Mulvaney, was also present, along with an NSC press officer.[578] Secretary of State Mike Pompeo listened from a different location, as did Dr. Charles M. Kupperman, the Deputy National Security Advisor.[579]

Notably, Secretary Pompeo did not reveal that he listened to the July 25 call when asked directly about it on *This Week* on September 22.[580] Neither Secretary Pompeo nor the State Department corrected the record until September 30, when "a senior State Department official" disclosed the Secretary of State's participation in the July 25 call.[581]

The two presidents first exchanged pleasantries. President Trump congratulated the Ukrainian leader on his party's parliamentary victory. In a nod to their shared experience as political outsiders, President Zelensky called President Trump "a great teacher" who informed his own efforts to involve "many many new people" in Ukraine's politics and "drain the swamp here in our country."[582]

The discussion turned to U.S. support for Ukraine. President Trump contrasted U.S. assistance to that of America's closest European allies, stating: "We spend a lot of effort and a lot of time. Much more than the European countries are doing and they should be helping you more than they are." The call then took a more ominous turn. President Trump stated that with respect to U.S. support for Ukraine, "I wouldn't say that it's reciprocal necessarily because things are happening that are not good but the United States has been very very good to Ukraine."[583]

President Zelensky, whose government receives billions of dollars in financial support from the European Union and its member states, responded that European nations were "not working as much as they should work for Ukraine," including in the area of enforcing sanctions against Russia.[584] He noted that "the United States is a much bigger partner than the European Union" and stated that he was "very grateful" because "the United States is doing quite a lot for Ukraine."[585]

President Zelensky then raised the issue of U.S. military assistance for Ukraine with President Trump: "I also would like to thank you for your great support in the area of defense"—an area where U.S. support is vital.[586] President Zelensky continued: "We are ready to continue to cooperate for the next steps specifically we are almost ready to buy more Javelins from the United States for defense purposes."[587] The Javelin anti-tank missiles, first transferred to Ukraine by the United States in 2018, were widely viewed by U.S. officials as a deterrent against further Russian encroachment into Ukrainian territory.[588]

Immediately after the Ukrainian leader raised the issue of U.S. military assistance to Ukraine, President Trump replied: "I would like you to do us a favor though because our country has been through a lot and Ukraine knows a lot about it."[589]

Request to Investigate 2016 Election

President Trump then explained the "favor" he wanted President Zelensky to do. He first requested that Ukraine investigate a discredited conspiracy theory aimed at undercutting the U.S. Intelligence Community's unanimous conclusion that the Russian government interfered in the 2016 U.S. election.[590] Specifically, President Trump stated:

> I would like you to find out what happened with this whole situation with Ukraine, they say Crowdstrike... I guess you have one of your wealthy people... The server, they say Ukraine has it. There are a lot of things that went on, the whole situation. I think you're surrounding yourself with some of the same people. I would like to have the Attorney General call you or your people and I would like you to get to the bottom of it. As you saw yesterday, that whole nonsense ended with a very poor performance by a man named Robert Mueller, an incompetent performance, but they say a lot of it started with Ukraine. Whatever you can do, it's very important that you do it if that's possible.[591]

President Trump was referencing the widely debunked conspiracy theory that the Ukrainian government—and not Russia—was behind the hack of Democratic National Committee (DNC) servers in 2016, and that the American cybersecurity firm CrowdStrike moved the DNC's servers to Ukraine to prevent U.S. law enforcement from examining them. This theory is often referred to in shorthand as "CrowdStrike" and has been promoted by the Russian government.[592]

For example, during a press conference in February 2017, just weeks after the U.S. Intelligence Community unanimously assessed in a public report that Russia interfered in the 2016 U.S. election to benefit the candidacy of Donald J. Trump, President Putin falsely asserted that "the Ukrainian government adopted a unilateral position in favour of one candidate. More than that, certain oligarchs, certainly with the approval of the political leadership, funded this candidate, or female candidate, to be more precise."[593] President Trump's reference in his July 25 telephone call to "one of your wealthy people" tracked closely with President Putin's accusations that "certain oligarchs" in Ukraine meddled in the 2016 U.S. election to support Democratic candidate Hillary Clinton.

Dr. Hill, an expert on Russia and President Putin, testified that the claim that "Russia and its security services did not conduct a campaign against our country and that perhaps, somehow for some reason, Ukraine did" is "a fictional narrative that is being perpetrated and propagated by the Russian security services themselves." Dr. Hill reaffirmed that the U.S. Intelligence Community's January 2017 conclusion that Russia interfered in the 2016 U.S. election is "beyond dispute, even if some of the underlying details must remain classified."[594]

Tom Bossert, President Trump's former Homeland Security Advisor, stated publicly that the CrowdStrike theory is "not only a conspiracy theory, it is completely debunked."[595] Dr. Hill testified that White House officials—including Mr. Bossert and former National Security Advisor H.R. McMaster—"spent a lot of time" refuting the CrowdStrike conspiracy theory to President Trump. Dr. Hill explained that Mr. Bossert and others "who were working on cybersecurity laid out to the President the facts about the interference." She affirmed that

President Trump was advised that "the alternative theory that Ukraine had interfered in the election was false."[596]

President Zelensky did not directly address President Trump's reference to CrowdStrike during the July 25 call, but he tried to assure President Trump that "it is very important for me and everything that you just mentioned earlier."[597]   President Zelensky committed to proceed with an investigation, telling President Trump that he had "nobody but friends" in the new Ukrainian presidential administration, possibly attempting to rebut Rudy Giuliani's earlier claims that President Zelensky was surrounded by "enemies" of President Trump.   President Zelensky then specifically noted that one of his assistants "spoke with Mr. Giuliani just recently and we are hoping very much that Mr. Giuliani will be able to travel to Ukraine and we will meet once he comes to Ukraine."[598]

Significantly, President Zelensky referenced Mr. Giuliani even before President Trump had mentioned him, demonstrating the Ukrainian leader's understanding that Mr. Giuliani represented President Trump's interests in Ukraine. The Ukrainian leader then reassured President Trump, "I also plan to surround myself with great people and in addition to that investigation" into the CrowdStrike conspiracy theory. He said, "I guarantee as the President of Ukraine that all the investigations will be done openly and candidly. That I can assure you."[599] President Trump replied, "Rudy very much knows what's happening and he is a very capable guy. If you could speak to him that would be great."[600]

Request to Investigate Bidens

President Trump then returned to his requested "favor," asking President Zelensky about the "[t]he other thing": that Ukraine investigate President Trump's U.S. political rival, former Vice President Biden, for allegedly ending an investigation into the Ukrainian energy company Burisma Holdings. Vice President Biden's son, Hunter Biden, served as a member of Burisma's board of directors. President Trump told President Zelensky:

> The other thing, There's a lot of talk about Biden's son, that Biden stopped the prosecution and a lot of people want to find out about that so whatever you can do with the Attorney General would be great. Biden went around bragging that he stopped the prosecution so if you can look into it... It sounds horrible to me.[601]

President Trump later continued, "I will have Mr. Giuliani give you a call and I am also going to have Attorney General Barr call and we will get to the bottom of it. I'm sure you will figure it out."[602]

In public remarks on October 3, 2019, a reporter asked President Trump, "what exactly did you hope Zelensky would do about the Bidens after your phone call? Exactly." President Trump responded: "Well, I would think that, if they were honest about it, they'd start a major investigation into the Bidens. It's a very simple answer."[603]

When President Trump asserted to President Zelensky during the July 25 call that former Vice President "Biden went around bragging that he stopped the prosecution," President Trump was apparently referring to Vice President Biden's involvement in the removal of the corrupt former Ukrainian prosecutor general, Viktor Shokin.

Multiple witnesses—including Dr. Hill, former U.S. Ambassador to Ukraine Marie Yovanovitch, Mr. Holmes, and Deputy Assistant Secretary of State George Kent—testified that they were not aware of any credible evidence to support the claim that former Vice President Biden acted inappropriately when he advocated for the removal of Mr. Shokin.[604] To the contrary, those witnesses confirmed that it was the official policy of the United States, the European Union, and major international financial institutions, to demand Mr. Shokin's dismissal. As Mr. Kent testified, there was "a broad-based consensus" that Mr. Shokin was "a typical Ukraine prosecutor who lived a lifestyle far in excess of his government salary, who never prosecuted anybody known for having committed a crime" and who "covered up crimes that were known to have been committed."[605] Mr. Kent further explained:

> What former Vice President Biden requested of former President of Ukraine Poroshenko was the removal of a corrupt prosecutor general, Viktor Shokin, who had undermined a program of assistance that we had spent, again, U.S. taxpayer money to try to build an independent investigator unit to go after corrupt prosecutors.[606]

As Ambassador Yovanovitch testified, the removal of a corrupt Ukrainian prosecutor general, who was not prosecuting enough corruption, increased the chance that alleged corruption in companies in Ukraine could be investigated.[607]

Mr. Shokin was a known associate of Mr. Giuliani. As described in Chapter 1, Mr. Giuliani had been communicating with Mr. Shokin since at least 2018.[608] Mr. Giuliani also lobbied the White House on behalf of Mr. Shokin to intervene earlier in 2019 when the State Department rejected a visa application for Mr. Shokin to visit the United States based upon Mr. Shokin's notorious corrupt conduct.[609] Ambassador Kurt Volker, U.S. Special Representative for Ukraine Negotiations, testified that he explicitly warned Mr. Giuliani—to no avail—against pursuing "the conspiracy theory that Vice President Biden would have been influenced in his duties as Vice President by money paid to his son."[610] Ambassador Volker affirmed that former Vice President Biden is "an honorable man, and I hold him in the highest regard."[611]

Attacks Against Ambassador Yovanovitch

During the July 25 call, President Trump also attacked Ambassador Yovanovitch, whom he had ousted as the U.S. Ambassador to Ukraine three months earlier after a concerted smear campaign perpetuated by Mr. Giuliani. As described in Chapter 1, Mr. Giuliani viewed Ambassador Yovanovitch—a decorated diplomat who had championed Ukrainian anti-corruption officials and activists—as an impediment to his activities in Ukraine.[612] President Trump told President Zelensky: "The former ambassador from the United States, the woman, was bad news and the people she was dealing with in the Ukraine were bad news so I just want to let you know that." He later added: "Well, she's going to go through some things."[613]

Ambassador Yovanovitch described her visceral reaction when she first read the call record, after the White House released it publicly on September 25, 2019. She testified, "I was shocked. I mean, I was very surprised that President Trump would—first of all, that I would feature repeatedly in a Presidential phone call, but secondly, that the President would speak about me or any ambassador in that way to a foreign counterpart."[614] When asked whether she felt "threatened" by President Trump's statement that "she's going to go through some things," Ambassador Yovanovitch answered that she did.[615]

Praise of Corrupt Former Ukrainian Prosecutor

After disparaging Ambassador Yovanovitch, who had an extensive record of combatting corruption, President Trump praised an unnamed former Ukrainian prosecutor general—referring to Yuriy Lutsenko—who was widely considered to be corrupt and had promoted false allegations against Ambassador Yovanovitch.[616] President Trump told President Zelensky: "Good because I heard you had a prosecutor who was very good and he was shut down and that's really unfair. A lot of people are talking about that, the way they shut your very good prosecutor down and you had some very bad people involved."[617] He later added, "I heard the prosecutor was treated very badly and he was a very fair prosecutor so good luck with everything."[618]

At the time of the July 25 call, Mr. Lutsenko—who was collaborating with Mr. Giuliani to smear Ambassador Yovanovitch and the Bidens—was still the Ukrainian prosecutor general. Mr. Holmes testified that Mr. Lutsenko "was not a good partner. He had failed to deliver on the promised reforms that he had committed to when he took office, and he was using his office to insulate and protect political allies while presumably enriching himself."[619] By July 2019, Mr. Holmes assessed that Mr. Lutsenko was "trying to angle to keep his job" under the new Zelensky Administration and that part of his strategy was "appealing to Rudy Giuliani and Donald Trump by pushing out these false theories about the Bidens and the 2016 election."[620]

Multiple witnesses testified that another former Ukrainian prosecutor, Mr. Shokin, was also considered to be corrupt. For example, Mr. Kent testified during his deposition that Mr. Lutsenko and Mr. Shokin were "corrupt former prosecutors" who were "peddling false information in order to extract revenge against those who had exposed their misconduct, including U.S. diplomats, Ukrainian anticorruption officials, and reform-minded civil society groups in Ukraine."[621] Ambassador Volker testified at his public hearing that Mr. Lutsenko was "not credible, and was acting in a self-serving capacity."[622] Mr. Holmes further noted that Mr. Lutsenko "resisted fully empowering truly independent anticorruption institutions that would help ensure that no Ukrainians, however powerful, were above the law."[623]

After the call, the White House press office issued a short and incomplete summary of the call, omitting major elements of the conversation. The press statement read:

> Today, President Donald J. Trump spoke by telephone with President Volodymyr Zelenskyy of Ukraine to congratulate him on his recent election. President Trump and President Zelenskyy discussed ways to strengthen the relationship between the United States and Ukraine, including energy and economic cooperation. Both leaders also expressed that they look forward to the opportunity to meet.[624]

Concerns Raised by Lieutenant Colonel Alexander Vindman

Prior to President Trump's July 25 call with President Zelensky, Lt. Col. Vindman had prepared—with Mr. Morrison's review and approval—a call briefing package, including talking points for President Trump's use. This was consistent with the NSC's regular process of preparing for the President's phone calls with foreign leaders.[625] The NSC-drafted talking points did not include any reference to Biden, Burisma, CrowdStrike, or alleged Ukrainian interference in the 2016 U.S. election.[626]

Lt. Col. Vindman testified during his deposition that, prior to the July 25 call, he was aware of concerns from former National Security Advisor John Bolton and other U.S. officials that President Trump might raise these discredited issues with President Zelensky.[627] Indeed, Ambassador Bolton had resisted scheduling the call because he believed it might be a "disaster."[628]

As he sat in the White House Situation Room listening to the leaders, Lt. Col. Vindman quickly recognized that the President's conversation was diverging from the talking points he helped prepare based on the interagency policy process, and "straying" into an "unproductive narrative" promoted by Mr. Giuliani and other "external and nongovernmental influencers"[629]— topics that Lt. Col. Vindman dubbed "stray voltage."[630]

Lt. Col. Vindman knew immediately that he had a duty to report the contents of the call to the White House lawyers. He explained, "I had concerns, and it was my duty to report my concerns to the proper—proper people in the chain of command."[631] Lt. Col. Vindman testified that President Trump's request that a foreign leader dependent on the United States open an investigation into his U.S. political opponent constituted a "demand" that President Zelensky had to meet in order to secure a White House meeting:

> So, Congressman, the power disparity between the President of the United States and the President of Ukraine is vast, and, you know, in the President asking for something, it became—there was—in return for a White House meeting, because that's what this was about. This was about getting a White House meeting. It was a demand for him to fulfill his—fulfill this particular prerequisite in order to get the meeting.[632]

Lt. Col. Vindman further testified that President Trump's demand of the Ukrainian leader was "inappropriate" and "improper," and that it would undermine U.S. national security:

> Chairman, as I said in my statement, it was inappropriate. It was improper for the President to request—to demand an investigation into a political opponent, especially a foreign power where there's, at best, dubious belief that this would be a completely impartial investigation, and that this would have significant implications if it became public knowledge, and it would be perceived as a partisan play. It would undermine our Ukraine policy, and it would undermine our national security.[633]

Within an hour of the call ending, Lt. Col. Vindman reported his concerns to John A. Eisenberg, the Deputy Counsel to the President for National Security Affairs and the Legal

Advisor to the NSC , and Michael Ellis, a Senior Associate Counsel to the President and the Deputy Legal Advisor to the NSC.[634] Lt. Col. Vindman recounted the content of the call based on his handwritten notes and told the lawyers that he believed it was "wrong" for President Trump to ask President Zelensky to investigate Vice President Biden.[635]

Concerns Raised by Timothy Morrison

After 17 years as a Republican Congressional staffer and approximately a year serving elsewhere on the NSC staff, Mr. Morrison assumed his position as the NSC's Senior Director for Europe and Russia on July 15, 2019, only 10 days before President Trump's call with President Zelensky.[636]

Before he transitioned into his new role, Mr. Morrison met with his predecessor, Dr. Hill. She advised him to stay away from efforts orchestrated by Mr. Giuliani and Ambassador Sondland to pressure Ukraine into investigating a "bucket of issues" that included "Burisma the company," and "Hunter Biden on the board."[637] Dr. Hill also warned Mr. Morrison before the July 25 call about the President's interest in alleged Ukrainian interference in the 2016 U.S. election related to the DNC server.[638]

Mr. Morrison testified that he had no knowledge of any investigations at the time, but after performing a Google search of "what is Burisma?" and seeing the name Hunter Biden, Mr. Morrison decided to "stay away."[639] Even though he was new to the portfolio, Mr. Morrison promptly concluded that because "Burisma" involved Hunter Biden, and because former Vice President Biden was running for President, such investigations could be a "problematic" area.[640] Mr. Morrison further explained that he tried to stay away from requests related to Burisma and the 2016 U.S. election because these investigations were not related to "the proper policy process that I was involved in on Ukraine," and "had nothing to do with the issues that the interagency was working on."[641]

With that background in mind, Mr. Morrison admitted he was "concerned" when, while listening to the call on July 25, he heard President Trump raise "issues related to the [DNC] server." Ultimately, Mr. Morrison said, "the call was not the full-throated endorsement of the Ukraine reform agenda that I was hoping to hear."[642]

In "fairly short order," Mr. Morrison reported the contents of the call to Mr. Eisenberg and Mr. Ellis, the NSC lawyers. He asked them to review the call, which he feared would be "damaging" if leaked.[643] Mr. Morrison stated that at the time of the call, he "did not have a view" on whether the call was "appropriate and proper."[644] He also stated that he "was not concerned that anything illegal was discussed."[645] During his deposition, however, Mr. Morrison clarified, "I did not then and I do not now opine … as to the legality" of what happened on the call.[646]

In a second meeting with Mr. Eisenberg, Mr. Morrison requested that access to the electronic files of the call record be restricted. This was an unusual request. Mr. Morrison confirmed to the Committee that he had never before asked the NSC Legal Advisor to restrict access to a presidential call record.[647] It was also unusual because Mr. Morrison raised restricting access with Mr. Eisenberg despite the fact that Mr. Morrison himself had the authority, as an NSC senior director, to recommend restrictions on the relevant files to the NSC's Executive Secretariat.

Lt. Col. Vindman also discussed restricting access to the July 25 call summary with Mr. Eisenberg and Mr. Ellis. At some point after the call, Lt. Col. Vindman discussed with the NSC lawyers the "sensitivity" of the matters raised on the call and "the fact that … there are constant leaks."[648] Lt. Col. Vindman explained that "[f]rom a foreign policy professional perspective, all of these types of calls would inherently be sensitive."[649] But the July 25 call was particularly sensitive because it could "undermine our relationship with the Ukrainians" given that it "would implicate a partisan play."[650] The NSC lawyers, therefore, believed that it was "appropriate to restrict access for the purpose of the leaks" and "to preserv[e] the integrity" of the transcript.[651] Lt. Col. Vindman recalled that Mr. Ellis raised the idea of placing the call summary on the NSC's server for highly classified information and Mr. Eisenberg "gave the go-ahead."[652]

Some weeks after his discussions with the NSC attorneys, Mr. Morrison could not locate the call record. He contacted the staff of the NSC's Executive Secretariat in search of an explanation and was informed that "John Eisenberg had directed it to be moved to a different server" utilized by the NSC staff for highly classified information.[653] This transfer occurred despite Mr. Morrison's view that the call record did not meet the requirements to be placed on the highly classified system.[654]

Mr. Eisenberg later told Mr. Morrison that the call record had been placed on the highly classified system by "mistake."[655] Even after Mr. Eisenberg stated that the call record was moved to the highly classified system by "mistake," it nevertheless remained on that system until at least the third week of September 2019, shortly before its declassification and public release by the White House.[656]

Concerns Raised by Jennifer Williams

Vice President Pence's advisor, Ms. Williams, had listened to nearly a dozen phone calls between President Trump and other heads of state prior to July 25, 2019, as well as Vice President Pence's April 23 call with President Zelensky.[657] As she sat listening to President Trump's July 25 call, she was struck by his requests relating to Vice President Biden. She stated that she believed that President Trump's comments were "unusual and inappropriate."[658]

Ms. Williams testified that she thought that "references to specific individuals and investigations, such as former Vice President Biden and his son" were "political in nature, given that the former Vice President is a political opponent of the President."[659] The comments struck her as "more specific to the President in nature, to his personal political agenda," as opposed to "a broader foreign policy objective of the United States."[660] She added, "it was the first time I had heard internally the President reference particular investigations that previously I had only heard about through Mr. Giuliani's press interviews and press reporting."[661]

Significantly, Ms. Williams, who had learned about the hold on security assistance for Ukraine on July 3, also said that the Trump-Zelensky call "shed some light on possible other motivations behind a security assistance hold."[662]

"Burisma" Omitted from Call Record

Mr. Morrison, Lt. Col. Vindman, and Ms. Williams all agreed that the publicly released record of the call was substantially accurate, but Lt. Col. Vindman and Ms. Williams both testified that President Zelensky made an explicit reference to "Burisma" that was not included in the call record. Specifically, Lt. Col. Vindman testified that his notes indicated President Zelensky used the word "Burisma"—instead of generically referring to "the company"—when discussing President Trump's request to investigate the Bidens.[663] Ms. Williams' notes also reflected that President Zelensky had said "Burisma" later in the call when referring to a "case."[664]

Lt. Col. Vindman indicated that President Zelensky's mention of "Burisma" was notable because it suggested that the Ukrainian leader was "prepped for this call." He explained that "frankly, the President of Ukraine would not necessarily know anything about this company Burisma." Lt. Col. Vindman continued, "he would certainly understand some of this—some of these elements because the story had been developing for some time, but the fact that he mentioned specifically Burisma seemed to suggest to me that he was prepped for this call."[665]

The Substance of the Call Remained Tightly Controlled

Ms. Williams testified that staff in the Office of the Vice President placed the draft call record in the Vice President's nightly briefing book on July 25.[666]

Separately, and following established protocols for coordinating U.S. government activities toward Ukraine, Lt. Col. Vindman provided Mr. Kent at the State Department with a readout. Because Mr. Kent had worked on Ukraine policy for many years, Lt. Col. Vindman sought Mr. Kent's "expert view" on the investigations requested by the President. Mr. Kent informed him that "there was no substance" behind the CrowdStrike conspiracy theory and "took note of the fact that there was a call to investigate the Bidens."[667] Recalling this conversation, Mr. Kent testified that Lt. Col. Vindman said "he could not share the majority of what was discussed [on the July 25 call] because of the very sensitive nature of what was discussed," but that Lt. Col. Vindman noted that the call "went into the direction of some of the most extreme narratives that have been discussed publicly."[668]

Ambassador Sondland Followed Up on President Trump's Request for Investigations

Soon after arriving in Kyiv from Brussels on July 25, Ambassador Sondland asked the U.S. Embassy to arrange a meeting the next day with Ukrainian presidential aide Andriy Yermak.[669]

On the morning of July 26, Ambassadors Sondland, Volker and Taylor—accompanied by Mr. Holmes, who acted as their official notetaker—went to the Presidential Administration

Building in central Kyiv for meetings with Ukrainian officials.[670] Contrary to standard procedure, Mr. Holmes and Ambassador Taylor did not receive readouts of the July 25 call, so they were unaware of what President Trump and President Zelensky had discussed.[671] Ambassador Volker also did not receive an official readout of the July 25 call from the NSC staff. He testified that Andriy Yermak, a senior aide to President Zelensky, simply characterized it as a "good call" in which "President Zelensky did reiterate his commitment to reform and fighting corruption in Ukraine."[672]

The first meeting on July 26 was with Chief of Staff to President Zelensky Andriy Bohdan.[673] Regarding the July 25 call, Mr. Holmes recalled Mr. Bohdan sharing that "President Trump had expressed interest … in President Zelensky's personnel decisions related to the Prosecutor General's office [PGO]."[674] Mr. Holmes further testified that Mr. Bohdan then "started asking … about individuals I've since come to understand they were considering appointing to different roles in the PGO."[675] Mr. Holmes explained that he "didn't understand it," and that "[i]t wasn't until I read the July 25th phone call transcript that I realized that the President [Trump] had mentioned Mr. Lutsenko in the call."[676]

Subsequently, Ambassadors Sondland, Taylor, and Volker met with President Zelensky and other senior officials. Mr. Holmes once again took notes.[677] He testified "During the meeting, President Zelensky stated that, during the July 25th call, President Trump had, quote, 'three times raised some very sensitive issues' and that he would have to follow up—he, Zelensky—would have to follow up on those issues when he and President Trump met in person."[678] After he read the transcript of the July 25 call, Mr. Holmes determined that President Zelensky's mention of "sensitive issues" was a reference to President Trump's demands for a "Burisma Biden investigation."[679]

Catherine Croft, Special Advisor to Ambassador Kurt Volker, was also in Kyiv on July 26. Although she did not attend the meeting with President Zelensky, she received a readout from Ambassadors Volker and Taylor later that day, as they were traveling in an embassy vehicle. Ms. Croft testified that her handwritten notes from that readout indicate "the President [Trump] had raised investigations multiple times" in his July 25 call with President Zelensky.[680] Ambassadors Sondland and Taylor told the Committee that they did not recall President Zelensky's comments about investigations.[681] Ambassador Volker similarly did not recall that the issue of investigations was discussed, but testified that he did not dispute the validity of "notes taken contemporaneously at the meeting."[682]

Ambassador Sondland Met One-on-One with Ukrainian Presidential Aide

The meeting with President Zelensky ended around noon.[683] After the meeting, Ambassadors Taylor and Volker departed the Presidential Administration building for a visit to the front lines of the war with Russia in eastern Ukraine.[684] Ambassador Sondland separately headed for Mr. Yermak's office. Mr. Holmes testified that, at the last minute, he received instruction from his leadership at the U.S. Embassy to join Ambassador Sondland.[685] By that point, Mr. Holmes recalled, he "was a flight of stairs behind Ambassador Sondland as he headed to meet with Mr. Yermak."[686] Mr. Holmes continued, "When I reached Mr. Yermak's office, Ambassador Sondland had already gone in to the meeting."[687] Mr. Holmes then "explained to

Mr. Yermak's assistant that I was supposed to join the meeting as the Embassy's representative and strongly urged her to let me in, but she told me that Ambassador Sondland and Mr. Yermak had insisted that the meeting be one on one with no note taker."[688] Mr. Holmes "then waited in the anteroom until the meeting ended, along with a member of Ambassador Sondland's staff and a member of the U.S. Embassy Kyiv staff."[689]

Ambassador Sondland's meeting with Mr. Yermak lasted approximately 30 minutes.[690] When it ended, Ambassador Sondland did not provide Mr. Holmes an explanation of what they discussed.[691] Ambassador Sondland later testified that he did not "recall the specifics" of his conversation with Mr. Yermak, but he believed "the issue of investigations was probably a part of that agenda or meeting."[692]

Call Between President Trump and Ambassador Sondland on July 26, 2019

After a busy morning of meetings with Ukrainian officials on July 26, Ambassador Sondland indicated that he wanted to get lunch. Mr. Holmes interjected that he would "be happy to join" Ambassador Sondland and two other State Department colleagues accompanying him "if he wanted to brief me out on his meeting with Mr. Yermak or discuss other issues."[693] Ambassador Sondland accepted the offer. The diplomats proceeded "to a nearby restaurant and sat on an outdoor terrace."[694] Mr. Holmes "sat directly across from Ambassador Sondland," close enough that they could "share an appetizer."[695]

Mr. Holmes recounted that "at first, the lunch was largely social. Ambassador Sondland selected a bottle of wine that he shared among the four of us, and we discussed topics such as marketing strategies for his hotel business."[696] Later during the meal, Ambassador Sondland "said that he was going to call President Trump to give him an update."[697] Ambassador Sondland then placed a call on his unsecure mobile phone. Mr. Holmes was taken aback. He told the Committee, "it was, like, a really extraordinary thing, it doesn't happen very often"—a U.S. Ambassador picking up his mobile phone at an outdoor cafe and dialing the President of the United States.[698]

Mr. Holmes, who was sitting directly opposite from Ambassador Sondland, said he "heard him announce himself several times, along the lines of, 'Gordon Sondland, holding for the President.' It appeared that he was being transferred through several layers of switchboards and assistants, and I then noticed Ambassador Sondland's demeanor changed and understood that he had been connected to President Trump."[699]

Mr. Holmes stated he was able to hear the first part of Ambassador Sondland's conversation with President Trump because it was "quite loud" and "quite distinctive" when the President began speaking. When President Trump started speaking, Ambassador Sondland "sort of winced and held the phone away from his ear," and "did that for the first couple exchanges."[700]

Recounting the conversation that followed, Mr. Holmes testified:

I heard Ambassador Sondland greet the President and explain he was calling from Kyiv. I heard President Trump then clarify that Ambassador Sondland was in Ukraine. Ambassador Sondland replied, yes, he was in Ukraine, and went on to state that President Zelensky, quote, "loves your ass." I then heard President Trump ask, "So he's going to do the investigation?" Ambassador Sondland replied that he is going to do it, adding that President Zelensky will do "anything you ask him to do."[701]

President Trump has denied that he spoke to Ambassador Sondland on July 26 and told reporters, "I know nothing about that."[702] But in his public testimony before the Committee, Ambassador Sondland noted that White House call records made available to his legal counsel confirmed that the July 26 call in fact occurred.[703] Ambassador Sondland further explained that Mr. Holmes's testimony—specifically, a "reference to A$AP Rocky"—refreshed his recollection about the July 26 call, which Ambassador Sondland had not originally disclosed to the Committee.[704]

Although Ambassador Sondland did not believe he mentioned the Bidens by name, he testified that with regard to the substance of his July 26 conversation with President Trump: "I have no reason to doubt that this conversation included the subject of investigations."[705] He added that he had "no reason" to doubt Mr. Holmes' testimony about the contents of the call, and that he would "have been more surprised if President Trump had not mentioned investigations, particularly given what we were hearing from Mr. Giuliani about the President's concerns."[706] Asked about his statement to President Trump that President Zelensky "loves your ass," Ambassador Sondland replied: "That sounds like something I would say. That's how President Trump and I communicate, a lot of four-letter words, in this case three letter."[707]

After the call between Ambassador Sondland and President Trump ended, Ambassador Sondland remarked to Mr. Holmes that "the President was in a bad mood," as "was often the case early in the morning."[708] Mr. Holmes, who had learned about the freeze on U.S. security assistance days earlier, was attempting to clarify the President's thinking, and said he "took the opportunity to ask Ambassador Sondland for his candid impression of the President's views on Ukraine":

> In particular, I asked Ambassador Sondland if it was true that the President did not give a shit about Ukraine. Ambassador Sondland agreed that the President did not give a shit about Ukraine. I asked, why not, and Ambassador Sondland stated, the President only cares about, quote, unquote, "big stuff." I noted there was, quote, unquote, big stuff going on in Ukraine, like a war with Russia. And Ambassador Sondland replied that he meant, quote, unquote, "big stuff" that benefits the President, like the, quote, unquote, "Biden investigation" that Mr. Giuliani was pushing. The conversation then moved on to other topics.[709]

Ambassador Sondland did not dispute the substance of Mr. Holmes' recollection of this discussion. He stated, "I don't recall my exact words, but clearly the President, beginning on May 23, when we met with him in the Oval Office, was not a big fan" of Ukraine. Asked whether President Trump "was a big fan of the investigations," Ambassador Sondland replied: "Apparently so."[710] Asked to clarify if, during his July 26 conversation with Mr. Holmes, he recalled "at least referring to an investigation that Rudy Giuliani was pushing," Ambassador Sondland replied, "I would have, yes."[711]

Mr. Holmes Informed U.S. Embassy Leadership about President Trump's Call with Ambassador Sondland

After the lunch, Mr. Holmes dropped off Ambassador Sondland at his hotel, the Hyatt Regency Kyiv. Mr. Holmes then returned to the U.S. Embassy.[712] Ambassador Taylor, the acting Ambassador in Kyiv, was still visiting the front line. So when he arrived at the Embassy, Mr. Holmes briefed his immediate supervisor, Kristina Kvien, Deputy Chief of Mission at U.S. Embassy Kyiv, about the President's call with Ambassador Sondland and Ambassador Sondland's subsequent description of President Trump's priorities for Ukraine.[713]

After taking a long-planned vacation from July 27 to August 5, Mr. Holmes told Ambassador Taylor about his lunch with Ambassador Sondland on the first day he returned to work, August 6.[714] Mr. Holmes told the Committee that he did not brief the call in detail to Ambassador Taylor because "it was obvious what the President was pressing for":

> Of course that's what's going on. Of course the President is pressing for a Biden investigation before he'll do these things the Ukrainians want. There was nodding agreement. So did I go through every single word in the call? No, because everyone by that point agreed, it was obvious what the President was pressing for.[715]

In October 2019, following the public release of testimony by several witnesses pursuant to the Committee's impeachment inquiry, Mr. Holmes reminded Ambassador Taylor about Ambassador Sondland's July 26 conversation with President Trump. Ambassador Taylor was preparing to return to Washington and testify publicly before the Committee. Mr. Holmes had been following news coverage of the inquiry and realized he had unique, firsthand evidence that "potentially bore on the question of whether the President did, in fact, have knowledge" of efforts to press the Ukrainian President to publicly announce investigations:

> I came to realize that I had firsthand knowledge regarding certain events on July 26 that had not otherwise been reported and that those events potentially bore on the question of whether the President did, in fact, have knowledge that those senior officials were using the levers of diplomatic power to influence the new Ukrainian President to announce the opening of a criminal investigation against President Trump's political opponent. It is at that point that I made the observation to Ambassador Taylor that the incident I had witnessed on July 26th had acquired greater significance, which is what he reported in his testimony last week and is what led to the subpoena for me to appear here today.[716]

Mr. Holmes testified that the July 26 call became "sort of a touchstone piece of information" for diplomats at the U.S. Embassy in Kyiv who "were trying to understand why we weren't able to get the meeting" between President Trump and President Zelensky and "what was going on with the security hold."[717] He elaborated:

I would refer back to it repeatedly in our, you know, morning staff meetings. We'd talk about what we're trying to do. We're trying to achieve this, that. Maybe it will convince the President to have the meeting. And I would say, 'Well, as we know, he doesn't really care about Ukraine. He cares about some other things. And we're trying to keep Ukraine out of our politics and so, you know, that's what we're up against.' And I would refer— use that repeatedly as a refrain.[718]

6.   The President Wanted Ukraine to Announce the Investigations Publicly

> *In the weeks following the July 25 call, President Trump's hand-picked representatives carried out his wishes to condition a coveted White House meeting for the Ukrainian President on the public announcement of investigations beneficial to President Trump. Top U.S. officials, including the Secretary of State and Secretary of Energy, were "in the loop."*

Overview

In the weeks following the July 25 call, during which President Trump had pressed Ukrainian President Volodymyr Zelensky to "do us a favor though," the President's representatives worked to secure from the Ukrainian President a public announcement about the requested investigations as a condition for the White House meeting.

That meeting would have conferred vital support on a new president who relied on the United States to help defend his nation militarily, diplomatically, and politically against Russian aggression. U.S. Ambassador to the European Union Gordon Sondland provided testimony and quoted from documents demonstrating that he kept everyone "in the loop" about the plan, including the Secretaries of State and Energy.

Ambassadors Sondland and Volker worked closely with Mr. Giuliani, the President's personal lawyer, to help draft Ukraine's public statement. They sought to ensure that President Zelensky explicitly used the words "Burisma"—a reference to allegations about former Vice President Biden and his son—and "2016 elections."

Ukrainian officials were "very uncomfortable" with the provision of this statement, which they understood to be a requirement and a "deliverable" demanded by President Trump. The Ukrainian President was elected on a platform of rooting out public corruption, and so he resisted issuing the statement. Instead, President Zelensky's aides asked whether an official request for legal assistance with investigations had been made through appropriate channels at the U.S. Department of Justice. No such formal request was ever made. Consequently, Ukrainian officials made clear to Ambassador Volker that they did not support issuing a public statement because it could "play into" U.S. domestic politics. Nevertheless, U.S. efforts to secure a public statement continued.

Giuliani Met with Ukrainian Presidential Aide Andriy Yermak in Madrid and Discussed a White House Meeting

On July 26, the day after the call between President Trump and President Zelensky, Ambassador Volker wrote to Mr. Giuliani to confirm that he would soon be meeting with Andriy Yermak, a Ukrainian presidential aide, to "help" efforts.[719]

Ambassador Volker texted: "Please send dates when you will be in Madrid. I am seeing Yermak tomorrow morning. He will come to you in Madrid. Thanks for your help! Kurt."[720]

Mr. Giuliani replied that he would travel to Spain from August 1 to 5, and Ambassador Volker affirmed that he would tell the Ukrainian presidential aide to "visit with you there."[721] Ambassador Volker kept himself apprised of plans, texting Mr. Yermak on August 1 to ensure that everything was "on track" for the meeting in Spain's capital. He also asked whether Mr. Yermak planned to visit Washington.[722]

On August 2, Mr. Yermak and Mr. Giuliani met in Madrid.[723] Ambassador Volker received a meeting summary from Mr. Yermak the same day: "My meeting with Mr. Mayor was very good." Mr. Yermak added: "We asked for White House meeting during week start [sic] 16 Sept. Waiting for confirmation. Maybe you know the date?"[724]

The Madrid meeting set off a "series of discussions" among Mr. Giuliani, Ambassador Volker, and Ambassador Sondland about the need for President Zelensky to issue a public statement about the investigations into Burisma and the 2016 election conspiracy theory in order to secure a White House meeting with President Trump.[725] Ambassador Volker first spoke to Mr. Giuliani, who said that he thought Ukraine "should issue a statement."[726] Ambassador Volker then spoke to Mr. Yermak, who affirmed that the Ukrainian leader was "prepared to make a statement" that "would reference Burisma and 2016 in a wider context of bilateral relations and rooting out corruption anyway."[727]

Mr. Giuliani, acting as President Trump's personal attorney, exerted significant influence in the process. On August 4, Mr. Yermak inquired again about the presidential meeting. Ambassador Volker replied that he would speak with Mr. Giuliani later that day and would call the Ukrainian aide afterward.[728] Ambassador Volker texted the former mayor about the Madrid meeting and asked for a phone call. Mr. Giuliani replied: "It was excellent I can call a little later."[729]

Phone records obtained by the Committees show a 16 minute call on August 5 between Ambassador Volker and Mr. Giuliani.[730] Ambassador Volker texted Mr. Yermak: "Hi Andrey—had a good long talk w Rudy—call anytime—Kurt."[731] During the same period, Ambassador Volker informed Ambassador Sondland that "Giuliani was happy with that meeting," and "it looks like things are turning around."[732]

"Potus Really Wants the Deliverable" Before Scheduling a White House Visit for President Zelensky

Things had not turned around by August 7. Ambassador Volker texted Mr. Giuliani to recommend that he report to "the boss"—President Trump—about his meeting with Mr. Yermak in Madrid. He wrote:

> Hi Rudy—hope you made it back safely. Let's meet if you are coming to DC. And would be good if you could convey results of your meeting in Madrid to the boss so we can get a firm date for a visit.[733]

The Committees did not find evidence that Mr. Giuliani responded to Ambassador Volker's text message.

However, call records show that the next day, on August 8, Mr. Giuliani connected with the White House Situation Room switchboard in the early afternoon, Eastern Time, for 42 seconds, and then again for one minute, 25 seconds.[734]

The same day, Mr. Giuliani texted several times with a number associated with the White House. The Committees were unable to identify the official associated with the phone number. In the mid-afternoon, someone using a telephone number associated with the Office of Management and Budget (OMB) called Mr. Giuliani, and the call lasted for nearly 13 minutes. Mr. Giuliani called the OMB number and the White House Situation Room several more times that evening, but each time connected for only a few seconds or not at all.

Rudy Giuliani Call History, August 8

Date	Connect-ing Time (EDT)	Duration of Call	Caller	Recipient
08/08/19	12:44:56	0:42	Giuliani, Rudy	White House Switchboard (Situation Room)[735]
08/08/19	12:45:38	1:25	Giuliani, Rudy	White House Switchboard (Situation Room)[736]
08/08/19	13:02:37	TEXT	Giuliani, Rudy	White House Number[737]
08/08/19	13:02:37	TEXT	Giuliani, Rudy	White House Number[738]
08/08/19	13:02:57	TEXT	Giuliani, Rudy	White House Number[739]
08/08/19	14:14:53	TEXT	White House Number	Giuliani, Rudy[740]
08/08/19	14:15:17	TEXT	Giuliani, Rudy	White House Number[741]
08/08/19	14:21:13	TEXT	Giuliani, Rudy	White House Number[742]
08/08/19	15:13:05	12:56	OMB Number	Giuliani, Rudy[743]
08/08/19	15:56:44	0:00	Giuliani, Rudy	OMB-Associated Number[744]
08/08/19	15:56:51	0:00	Giuliani, Rudy	OMB-Associated Number[745]
08/08/19	15:57:05	0:00	Giuliani, Rudy	OMB-Associated Number[746]
08/08/19	15:57:21	0:22	Giuliani, Rudy	White House Switchboard (Situation Room)[747]
08/08/19	17:20:33	0:17	Giuliani, Rudy	White House Switchboard (Situation Room)[748]
08/08/19	19:14:48	0:00	Giuliani, Rudy	White House Switchboard (Situation Room)[749]

Approximately 30 minutes after his text to Mr. Giuliani on August 7, Ambassador Volker received a text message from Mr. Yermak: "Do you have some news about White House meeting date?"[750] Ambassador Volker responded that he had asked Mr. Giuliani to "weigh in," presumably with the President, "following your meeting," and that Ambassador Sondland would be speaking with President Trump on Friday, August 9. Ambassador Volker added: "We are pressing this."[751] The next day, on August 8, Mr. Yermak texted Ambassador Volker to report that he had "some news."[752] Ambassador Volker replied that he was available to speak at that time.[753]

Later on the evening of August 8, Eastern Time, Mr. Giuliani sent a text message to a phone number associated with the White House. Approximately one hour 15 minutes later, someone using an unidentified number ("-1") dialed Mr. Giuliani three times in rapid succession. Less than three minutes later, Mr. Giuliani dialed the White House switchboard for the White House Situation Room. When the call did not connect, Mr. Giuliani immediately dialed another general number for the White House switchboard and connected for 47 seconds. Approximately 16 minutes later, someone using the "-1" number called Mr. Giuliani and connected for just over four minutes.[754]

Rudy Giuliani Call History, August 8, cont.

Date	Connect-ing Time (EDT)	Duration of Call	Caller	Recipient
08/08/19	20:53:13	TEXT	Giuliani, Rudy	White House Number[755]
08/08/19	22:09:31	0:00	"-1"	Giuliani, Rudy[756]
08/08/19	22:09:32	0:05	"-1"	Giuliani, Rudy[757]
08/08/19	22:09:46	0:00	"-1"	Giuliani, Rudy (Cell 2)[758]
08/08/19	22:09:47	0:02	"-1"	Giuliani, Rudy (Cell 2)[759]
08/08/19	22:10:08	0:05	"-1"	Giuliani, Rudy[760]
08/08/19	22:11:52	0:00	Giuliani, Rudy	OMB-Associated Number[761]
08/08/19	22:12:16	0:00	Giuliani, Rudy	White House Switchboard (Situation Room)[762]
08/08/19	22:12:25	0:47	Giuliani, Rudy	White House Switchboard[763]
08/08/19	22:28:51	4:06	"-1"	Giuliani, Rudy[764]

Late the next morning Washington time, on August 9, Ambassador Volker texted Mr. Giuliani and Ambassador Sondland:

> Hi Mr. Mayor! Had a good chat with Yermak last night. He was pleased with your phone call. Mentioned Z [President Zelensky] making a statement. Can we all get on the phone to make sure I advise Z [President Zelensky] correctly as to what he should be saying? Want to make sure we get this done right. Thanks![765]

It is unclear which "phone call" Ambassador Volker was referencing.

Text messages and call records obtained by the Committees show that Ambassador Volker and Mr. Giuliani connected by phone twice around noon Eastern Time on August 9 for several minutes each.[766] Following the calls with Mr. Giuliani, Ambassador Volker created a three-way group chat using WhatsApp that included Ambassador Volker, Ambassador Sondland, and Mr. Yermak.[767]

At 2:24 p.m. Eastern Time on August 9, Ambassador Volker texted the group: "Hi Andrey—we have all consulted here, including with Rudy. Can you do a call later today or tomorrow your afternoon time?"[768] Ambassador Sondland texted that he had a call scheduled for 3 p.m. Eastern Time "for the three of us. [State Department] Ops will call."[769]

Call records obtained by the Committees show that on August 9, Ambassador Sondland twice called numbers associated with the White House, once in early afternoon for approximately 18 minutes, and once in late afternoon for two minutes, 25 seconds with a number associated with OMB.[770]

By early evening, minutes after his second call with the OMB-associated number, Ambassador Volker and Ambassador Sondland discussed a breakthrough they had reached in obtaining a date for a White House visit, noting that President Trump really wanted "the deliverable":

Sondland:	[Tim] Morrison ready to get dates as soon as Yermak confirms.
Volker:	Excellent!! How did you sway him? :)
Sondland:	Not sure i did. I think potus really wants the deliverable
Volker:	But does he know that?
Sondland:	Yep
Sondland:	Clearly lots of convos going on
Volker:	Ok—then that's good it's coming from two separate sources[771]

Ambassador Sondland told the Committees that the "deliverable" required by President Trump was a press statement from President Zelensky committing to "do the investigations" pushed by President Trump and Mr. Giuliani.[772]

To ensure progress, immediately after their text exchange, Ambassador Sondland recommended to Ambassador Volker that Mr. Yermak share a draft of the press statement to "avoid misunderstandings" and so they would know "exactly what they propose to cover." Ambassador Sondland explained: "Even though Ze [President Zelensky] does a live presser [press event] they can still summarize in a brief statement." Ambassador Volker agreed.[773]

As they were negotiating the language that would appear in a press statement, "there was talk about having a live interview or a live broadcast" during which President Zelensky would make the agreed-upon statement.[774] Ambassador Sondland suggested reviewing a written summary of the statement because he was "concerned" that President Zelensky would "say whatever he would say on live television and it still wouldn't be good enough for Rudy, slash, the President [Trump]."[775]

"Everyone Was in the Loop" About Plan for Ukrainians to Deliver a Public Statement about Investigations in Exchange for a White House Visit

As negotiations continued, on August 10, Mr. Yermak texted Ambassador Volker in an attempt to schedule a White House meeting *before* the Ukrainian president made a public statement in support of investigations into Burisma and the 2016 election. He wrote:

> I think it's possible to make this declaration and mention all these things. Which we discussed yesterday. But it will be logic [sic] to do after we receive a confirmation of date. We inform about date of visit about our expectations and our guarantees for future visit. Let [sic] discuss it[776]

Ambassador Volker responded that he agreed, but that first they would have to "iron out [a] statement and use that to get [a] date," after which point President Zelensky would go forward with making the statement.[777] They agreed to have a call the next day, and to include Ambassador Sondland. Mr. Yermak texted:

> Excellent. Once we have a date, will call for a press briefing, announcing upcoming visit and outlining vision for the reboot of the US-UKRAINE relationship, including, among other things, Burisma and election meddling in investigations.[778]

Ambassador Volker forwarded the message to Ambassador Sondland, and they agreed to speak with Mr. Yermak the next day.[779]

Ambassador Sondland testified that "everyone was in the loop" regarding this plan.[780] Also on August 10, Ambassador Sondland informed Ambassador Volker that he briefed T. Ulrich Brechbuhl, Counselor of the Department of State, noting: "I briefed Ulrich. All good."[781] Ambassador Sondland testified that he "may have walked [Mr. Brechbuhl] through where we were."[782] When asked if Mr. Brechbuhl briefed Secretary Pompeo, Ambassador Sondland noted that it was Mr. Brechbuhl's "habit" to "consult with Secretary Pompeo frequently."[783]

Secretary of Energy Rick Perry was also made aware of efforts to pressure Ukraine to issue a public statement about political investigations in exchange for a White House meeting. Ambassador Sondland testified:

Mr. Giuliani conveyed to Secretary Perry, Ambassador Volker, and others that President Trump wanted a public statement from President Zelensky committing to investigations of Burisma and the 2016 election. Mr. Giuliani expressed those requests directly to the Ukrainians. Mr. Giuliani also expressed those requests directly to us. We all understood that these prerequisites for the White House call and the White House meeting reflected President Trump's desires and requirements.[784]

On August 11, Ambassador Volker requested a phone call with Ambassador Sondland and Mr. Giuliani, noting that he had heard from Mr. Yermak that the Ukrainians were "writing the statement now and will send to us."[785] According to call records obtained by the Committees, Ambassador Volker and Mr. Giuliani connected for 34 seconds.[786]

The same day, Ambassador Sondland updated Mr. Brechbuhl and Lisa Kenna, Executive Secretary of the State Department, about efforts to secure a public statement and a "big presser" from President Zelensky, which he hoped might "make the boss happy enough to authorize an invitation." He addressed the email to Secretary Pompeo:

> Mike,
> Kurt [Volker] and I negotiated a statement from Zelensky to be delivered for our review in a day or two. The contents will hopefully make the boss happy enough to authorize an invitation. Zelensky plans to have a big presser on the openness subject (including specifics) next week.[787]

Ambassador Sondland made clear in his hearing testimony that by "specifics," he meant the "2016 and the Burisma" investigations; "the boss" referred to "President Trump;" and "the invitation" referred to "the White House meeting."[788] Ms. Kenna replied to Ambassador Sondland that she would "pass to S [Secretary Pompeo]. Thank you."[789] Ambassador Sondland cited the email as evidence that "everyone was in the loop" on plans to condition a White House meeting on a public statement about political investigations.[790]

President Trump's Agents Negotiated a Draft Statement about the Investigations

In the evening of the next day, August 12, Mr. Yermak texted Ambassador Volker an initial version of the draft statement, which read:

> Special attention should be paid to the problem of interference in the political processes of the United States, especially with the alleged involvement of some Ukrainian politicians. I want to declare that this is unacceptable. We intend to initiate and complete a transparent and unbiased investigation of all available facts and episodes, which in turn will prevent the recurrence of this problem in the future.[791]

The draft statement did not explicitly mention Burisma or 2016 election interference, as expected.

On August 13, around 10 a.m. Eastern Time, Ambassador Volker texted Mr. Giuliani: "Mr mayor—trying to set up call in 5 min via state Dept. If now is not convenient, is there a time later today?"[792] Phone records show that, shortly thereafter, someone using a State

Department number called Mr. Giuliani and connected for more than nine minutes.[793] Ambassador Volker told the Committees that, during the call, Mr. Giuliani stated: "If [the statement] doesn't say Burisma and 2016, it's not credible, because what are they hiding?"[794] Ambassador Volker asked whether inserting references to "Burisma and 2016" at the end of the statement would make it "more credible." Mr. Giuliani confirmed that it would.[795]

Two minutes after the call ended, Ambassador Volker sent a WhatsApp message to Ambassador Sondland and Mr. Yermak: "Hi Andrey—we spoke with Rudy. When is good to call you?"[796] Ambassador Sondland replied that it was, "Important. Do you have 5 mins."[797] They agreed to a call approximately 10 minutes later.[798] When Ambassador Sondland suggested having his "operator" in Brussels dial in the group, Ambassador Volker asked if they could "do this one on what's App?"[799] Text messages and calls in the WhatsApp cell phone application are encrypted from end-to-end, ensuring that WhatsApp employees and third parties cannot listen in or retrieve deleted communications.[800]

Shortly before the call, Ambassador Volker sent a revised draft of the proposed statement to Ambassador Sondland. It had been edited to include reference to Burisma and the 2016 elections:

> Special attention should be paid to the problem of interference in the political processes of the United States, especially with the alleged involvement of some Ukrainian politicians. I want to declare that this is unacceptable. We intend to initiate and complete a transparent and unbiased investigation of all available facts and episodes **including those involving Burisma and the 2016 US elections**, which in turn will prevent the recurrence of this problem in the future.[801]

Ambassador Sondland replied: "Perfect. Lets send to Andrey after our call."[802]

Following the call, Ambassador Volker texted Ambassador Sondland and Mr. Yermak: "Andrey—good talking—following is text with insert at the end for the 2 key items."[803] Ambassador Volker then sent to them the revised statement that included the explicit references to "Burisma and 2016 elections."[804]

Comparison of Draft Statements

Yermak Draft August 12	Giuliani-Volker-Sondland Draft August 13
Special attention should be paid to the problem of interference in the political processes of the United States, especially with the alleged involvement of some Ukrainian politicians. I want to declare that this is unacceptable. We intend to initiate and complete a transparent and unbiased investigation of all available facts and episodes, which in turn will prevent the recurrence of this problem in the future.	Special attention should be paid to the problem of interference in the political processes of the United States, especially with the alleged involvement of some Ukrainian politicians. I want to declare that this is unacceptable. We intend to initiate and complete a transparent and unbiased investigation of all available facts and episodes, **including those involving Burisma and the 2016 US elections**, which in turn will prevent the recurrence of this problem in the future.

A "Quid Pro Quo" from "the President of the United States"

Ambassador Volker testified that the language reflected what Mr. Giuliani deemed necessary for the statement to be "credible."[805] Ambassador Sondland noted the language was "proposed by Giuliani."[806] Ambassador Sondland explained that the language was a clear quid pro quo that expressed "the desire of the President of the United States":

> Mr. Giuliani's requests were a quid pro quo for arranging a White House visit for President Zelensky. Mr. Giuliani demanded that Ukraine make a public statement announcing investigations of the 2016 election/DNC server and Burisma. Mr. Giuliani was expressing the desires of the President of the United States, and we knew that these investigations were important to the President.[807]

Shortly after Ambassador Volker sent the revised statement to Mr. Yermak on August 13, Ambassador Sondland called Mr. Giuliani and connected for nearly four minutes.

Ukrainian Officials and Career State Department Became Increasingly Concerned

On August 13—while Ambassador Volker, Ambassador Sondland, and Mr. Yermak were negotiating the draft statement about investigations—Mr. Yermak asked Ambassador Volker "whether any request had ever been made by the U.S. to investigate election interference in 2016." He appeared interested in knowing whether the U.S. Department of Justice had made an official request to Ukraine's law enforcement agency for legal assistance in such a matter.[808] When Ambassador Volker sent Mr. Giuliani's approved draft statement to Mr. Yermak, he stated that he would "work on official request."[809]

Ambassador Volker testified: "When I say official request, I mean law enforcement channels, Department of Justice to law enforcement in Ukraine, please investigate was there any effort to interfere in the U.S. elections."[810] Ambassador Volker explained:

> He [Yermak] said, and I think quite appropriately, that if they [Ukraine] are responding to an official request, that's one thing. If there's no official request, that's different. And I agree with that.[811]

According to Ambassador Volker, he was merely trying to "find out" if there was ever an official request made by the Department of Justice: "As I found out the answer that we had not, I said, well, let's just not go there."[812]

On September 25, within hours of the White House's public release of the record of the July 25 call between President Trump and President Zelensky, a Justice Department spokesperson issued a statement, apparently confirming that no such formal request had been made:

> The President has not spoken with the Attorney General about having Ukraine investigate anything relating to former Vice President Biden or his son. The President has not asked the Attorney General to contact Ukraine—on this or any other matter. The Attorney General has not communicated with Ukraine—on this or any other subject.[813]

Ukraine's current Prosecutor General Ruslan Ryaboshapka, who assumed his new position in late August 2019, confirmed the Justice Department's account. He told the *Financial Times* in late November 2019 that Attorney General Barr had made no formal request regarding a potential investigation into allegations of wrongdoing by former Vice President Biden.[814] In an apparent reference to President Trump's demand that Ukraine interfere in U.S. elections, Mr. Ryaboshapka added: "It's critically important for the west not to pull us into some conflicts between their ruling elites, but to continue to support so that we can cross the point of no return."[815]

Neither Ambassador Taylor in Ukraine nor Deputy Assistant Secretary George Kent in Washington were aware of the efforts by Ambassadors Sondland and Volker, in coordination with Mr. Giuliani, to convince Ukrainian officials to issue a statement in real time. Ambassador Taylor told the Committees that, on August 16, in a text message exchange with Ambassador Volker, he "learned that Mr. Yermak had asked that the United States submit an official request for an investigation into Burisma's alleged violations of Ukrainian law, if that is what the United States desired."[816] Ambassador Taylor noted that "a formal U.S. request to the Ukrainians to conduct an investigation based on violations of their own law" was "improper" and advised Ambassador Volker to "stay clear."[817]

Nevertheless, Ambassador Volker requested Ambassador Taylor's help with the matter.[818] "To find out the legal aspects of the question," Ambassador Taylor gave Ambassador Volker the name of an official at the Department of Justice "whom I thought would be the proper point of contact for seeking a U.S. referral for a foreign investigation."[819]

On August 15, Ambassador Volker texted Ambassador Sondland that Mr. Yermak wanted to "know our status on asking them to investigate."[820] Two days later, Ambassador Volker wrote: "Bill [Taylor] had no info on requesting an investigation—calling a friend at DOJ." Ambassador Volker testified that he was not able to connect with his contact at the Department of Justice.[821]

Mr. Kent testified that on August 15, Catherine Croft, Ambassador Volker's special assistant, approached him to ask whether there was any precedent for the United States asking Ukraine to conduct investigations on its behalf. Mr. Kent advised Ms. Croft:

> [I]f you're asking me have we ever gone to the Ukrainians and asked them to investigate or prosecute individuals for political reasons, the answer is, I hope we haven't, and we shouldn't because that goes against everything that we are trying to promote in post-Soviet states for the last 28 years, which is the promotion of the rule of law.[822]

Mr. Kent testified that the day after his conversation with Ms. Croft, he spoke with Ambassador Taylor, who "amplified the same theme" and told Mr. Kent that "Yermak was very uncomfortable" with the idea of investigations and suggested that "it should be done officially and put in writing." As a result, it became clear to Mr. Kent in mid-August that Ukraine was being pressured to conduct politically-motivated investigations. Mr. Kent told Ambassador Taylor "that's wrong, and we shouldn't be doing that as a matter of U.S. policy."[823]

After speaking to Ms. Croft and Ambassador Taylor, Mr. Kent wrote a memo to file on August 16 documenting his "concerns that there was an effort to initiate politically motivated prosecutions that were injurious to the rule of law, both in Ukraine and U.S."[824] Mr. Kent testified:

> At the time, I had no knowledge of the specifics of the [July 25] call record, but based on Bill Taylor's account of the engagements with Andriy Yermak that were engagements of Yermak with Kurt Volker, at that point it was clear that the investigations that were being suggested were the ones that Rudy Giuliani had been tweeting about, meaning Biden, Burisma, and 2016.[825]

On August 17, Mr. Yermak reached out to both Ambassador Sondland and Ambassador Volker.[826] Ambassador Sondland texted Ambassador Volker that "Yermak just tapped on me about dates. Havent responded. Any updates?"[827] Ambassador Volker responded that "I've got nothing" and stated that he was contacting the Department of Justice to find out about requesting an investigation.[828]

Ambassador Sondland then asked: "Do we still want Ze [Zelensky] to give us an unequivocal draft with 2016 and Boresma [sic]?" Ambassador Volker replied: "That's the clear message so far ... ." Ambassador Sondland said that he would ask that Mr. Yermak "send us a clean draft," to which Ambassador Volker replied that he had spoken to Mr. Yermak and suggested that he and Ambassador Sondland speak the following day, August 18, to discuss "all the latest."[829]

Ambassador Volker claimed that he "stopped pursuing" the statement from the Ukrainians around this time because of concerns raised by Mr. Yermak that Yuriy Lutsenko was still the Prosecutor General. Mr. Lutsenko was likely to be replaced by President Zelensky, and because Mr. Lutsenko was alleging the same false claims that President Trump and Mr. Giuliani were demanding of President Zelensky, Ukrainian officials "did not want to mention Burisma or 2016."[830] Ambassador Volker testified that he "agreed" and advised Mr. Yermak that "making those specific refences was not a good idea" because making those statements might "look like it would play into our domestic politics."[831]

Mr. Yermak agreed and, according to Ambassador Volker, plans to put out a statement were "shelved."[832] Ambassador Volker reasoned that the plan for a public statement did not materialize partly because of "the sense that Rudy was not going to be convinced that it meant anything, and, therefore, convey a positive message to the President if it didn't say Burisma and 2016."[833] He added:

> I agreed with the Ukrainians they shouldn't do it, and in fact told them just drop it, wait till you have your own prosecutor general in place. Let's work on substantive issues like this, security assistance and all. Let's just do that. So we dropped it.[834]

Ambassador Volker testified that, "From that point on, I didn't have any further conversations about this statement."[835] Nevertheless, efforts to secure a presidential statement announcing the two investigations into the Bidens and the 2016 U.S. election interference continued well into September.

On August 19, Ambassador Sondland told Ambassador Volker that he "drove the 'larger issue' home" with Mr. Yermak: that this was bigger than just a White House meeting and was about "the relationship per se."[836] Ambassador Volker told the Committees that he understood this referred to "the level of trust that the President has with President Zelensky. He has this general negative assumption about everything Ukraine, and that's the larger issue."[837] That negative assumption would prove difficult to overcome as Ukrainian and U.S. officials sought to finally obtain a White House meeting and shake free from the White House hundreds of millions of dollars in Congressionally-approved security assistance for Ukraine.

7.   **The President's Conditioning of Military Assistance and a White House Meeting on Announcement of Investigations Raised Alarm**

Following the public disclosure in late August 2019 of a hold on U.S. security assistance to Ukraine, President Trump made clear that "everything"—an Oval Office meeting and the release of taxpayer-funded U.S. security assistance—was contingent on the Ukrainian president announcing investigations into former Vice President Joe Biden and a debunked conspiracy theory about Ukrainian interference in the 2016 U.S. election. President Trump wanted the Ukrainian leader "in a public box," even as Ambassador Bill Taylor warned that it was "crazy to withhold security assistance for help with a political campaign."

Overview

On August 28, 2019, *Politico* first reported that President Trump was withholding hundreds of millions of dollars of Congressionally-appropriated U.S. security assistance from Ukraine, a fact that had been previously suspected by Ukrainian officials in July. Public revelations about the freeze raised questions about the U.S. commitment to Ukraine and harming efforts to deter Russian influence and aggression in Europe.

Around this time, American officials made clear to Ukrainians that a public announcement about investigations into Ukrainian interference in the 2016 election and former Vice President Joe Biden was a pre-condition—not only to obtain a White House meeting for President Zelensky, but also to end the freeze on military and other security assistance for Ukraine.

In early September, Ambassador Gordon Sondland conveyed President Trump's demands to both U.S. and Ukrainian officials. On September 1, he informed a senior Ukrainian official that the military aid would be released if the "prosecutor general would to go the mike [sic]" and announce the investigations. Later, on September 7, President Trump informed Ambassador Sondland that he wanted President Zelensky—not the Prosecutor General—in a "public box" and demanded that the Ukrainian president personally announce the investigations to "clear things up." Only then would Ukraine end the "stalemate" with the White House related to security assistance. President Zelensky proceeded to schedule an interview on CNN in order to announce the investigations and satisfy President Trump.

The President's efforts to withhold vital military and security assistance in exchange for political investigations troubled U.S. officials. NSC Senior Director for Europe and Russia Timothy Morrison twice reported what he understood to be the President's requirement of a quid pro quo to National Security Advisor John Bolton, who advised him to "make sure the lawyers are tracking." Ambassador Bill Taylor expressed his concerns to Ambassador Sondland, stating plainly that it was "crazy to withhold security assistance for help with a political campaign."

Secretary Pompeo and Ambassador Sondland Worked to "Break the Logjam"

President Trump's hold on security assistance persisted throughout August, without explanation to U.S. officials and contrary to the consensus recommendation of the President's national security team. At the same time, President Trump refused to schedule a coveted White House visit for President Zelensky until he announced two investigations that could benefit President Trump's reelection prospects. The confluence of those two circumstances led some American officials, including Ambassador Sondland and David Holmes, Counselor for Political Affairs at the U.S. Embassy in Kyiv, to conclude that the military assistance was conditioned on Ukraine's public announcement of the investigations.[838]

On August 20, Ambassador Kurt Volker met with Deputy Assistant Secretary of Defense Laura Cooper. Ms. Cooper and Ambassador Volker agreed that if the hold on security assistance was not lifted, "it would be very damaging to the relationship" between the U.S. and Ukraine.[839] During this meeting, Ambassador Volker mentioned that he was talking to an advisor to President Zelensky about making a statement "that would somehow disavow any interference in U.S. elections and would commit to the prosecution of any individuals involved in election interference."[840] Ambassador Volker indicated that if his efforts to get a statement were successful, the hold on security assistance might be lifted.[841]

Although he did not mention that conversation during his deposition, Ambassador Volker had a similar recollection, during his public testimony, of the meeting with Ms. Cooper. Ambassador Volker recalled discussing with Ms. Cooper the draft statement that had been coordinated with Ukrainian presidential aide Andriy Yermak—which included reference to the two investigations that President Trump demanded in the July 25 call—and that such a statement "could be helpful in getting a reset of the thinking of the President, the negative view of Ukraine that he had" which might, in turn, "unblock[] whatever hold there was on security assistance."[842]

Around this time, Ambassador Sondland sought to "break the logjam" on the security assistance and the White House meeting by coordinating a meeting between the two Presidents through Secretary of State Mike Pompeo. On August 22, Ambassador Sondland emailed Secretary Pompeo, copying the State Department's Executive Secretary, Lisa Kenna:

> Should we block time in Warsaw for a short pull-aside for POTUS to meet Zelensky? I would ask Zelensky to look him in the eye and tell him that once Ukraine's new justice folks are in place (mid-Sept) Ze should be able to move forward publicly and with confidence on those issues of importance to Potus and to the US. Hopefully, that will break the logjam.[843]

Secretary Pompeo replied, "Yes."[844]

Ambassador Sondland testified that when he referenced "issues of importance to Potus," he meant the investigation into the false allegations about Ukrainian interference in the 2016 election and the investigation into the Bidens.[845] He told the Committee that his goal was to "do what was necessary to get the aid released, to break the logjam."[846] Ambassador Sondland believed that President Trump would not release the aid until Ukraine announced the two investigations the President wanted.[847]

Ambassador Sondland testified: "Secretary Pompeo essentially gave me the green light to brief President Zelensky about making those announcements."[848] He explained:

This was a proposed briefing that I was going to give President Zelensky, and I was going to call President Zelensky and ask him to say what is in this email. And I was asking essentially ... [Secretary] Pompeo's permission to do that, which he said yes.[849]

He then forwarded the email to Ms. Kenna, seeking confirmation of "10-15 min on the Warsaw sched[ule]" for the pull-aside meeting. The Ambassador stated that he was seeking confirmation in order to brief President Zelensky. Ms. Kenna replied, "I will try for sure."[850]

On August 24, Ukraine celebrated its Independence Day. According to Mr. Holmes, Ukrainian Independence Day presented "another good opportunity to show support for Ukraine."[851] However, nobody senior to Ambassador Volker attended the festivities, even though Secretary of Defense James Mattis attended in 2017 and Ambassador Bolton attended in 2018.[852]

Two days later, on August 26, Ambassador Bolton's office requested Mr. Giuliani's contact information from Ambassador Sondland. Ambassador Sondland sent Ambassador Bolton the information directly.[853] Ambassador Sondland testified that he had "no idea" why Ambassador Bolton requested the contact information.[854]

Ambassador Bolton Visited Kyiv

On August 27, Ambassador Bolton arrived in Kyiv for an official visit. Ambassador Bolton emphasized to Andriy Bohdan, President Zelensky's chief of staff, that an upcoming meeting between Presidents Trump and Zelensky, scheduled for September 1 in Warsaw, Poland, would be "crucial to cementing their relationship."[855] Mr. Holmes, who accompanied Ambassador Bolton in Kyiv, testified that he also heard "Ambassador Bolton express to Ambassador Taylor and Mr. Morrison his frustration about Mr. Giuliani's influence with the President, making clear there was nothing he could do about it."[856]

Prior to Ambassador Bolton's departure from Kyiv, Ambassador Taylor asked to meet with him privately. Ambassador Taylor expressed his "serious concern about the withholding of military assistance to Ukraine while the Ukrainians were defending their country from Russian aggression."[857] During the conversation, Ambassador Bolton "indicated that he was very sympathetic" to Ambassador's Taylor's concerns.[858] He advised that Ambassador Taylor "send a first-person cable to Secretary Pompeo directly relaying my concerns" about the withholding of military assistance.[859]

Mr. Holmes testified that Ambassador Bolton advised during his trip that "the hold on security assistance would not be lifted prior to the upcoming meeting between President Trump and President Zelensky in Warsaw, where it would hang on whether Zelensky was able to favorably impress President Trump."[860]

Ukrainian Concern Over Military Aid Intensified After First Public Report of Hold

On August 28, 2019, *Politico* first reported that President Trump had implemented a hold on nearly $400 million of U.S. military assistance to Ukraine that had been appropriated by Congress.

Almost immediately after the news became public, Ukrainian officials expressed alarm to their American counterparts. Mr. Yermak sent Ambassador Volker a link to the *Politico* story and then texted: "Need to talk with you."[861] Other Ukrainian officials also expressed concerns to Ambassador Volker that the Ukrainian government was being "singled out and penalized for some reason."[862]

On August 29, Mr. Yermak also contacted Ambassador Taylor to express that he was "very concerned" about the hold on military assistance.[863] Mr. Yermak and other Ukrainian officials told Ambassador Taylor that they were "just desperate" and would be willing to travel to Washington to raise with U.S. officials the importance of the assistance. Ambassador Taylor described confusion among Ukrainian officials over the hold on military aid:

> I mean, the obvious question was, "Why?" So Mr. Yermak and others were trying to figure out why this was … They thought that there must be some rational reason for this being held up, and they just didn't—and maybe in Washington they didn't understand how important this assistance was to their fight and to their armed forces. And so maybe they could figure—so they were just desperate.[864]

Without any official explanation for the hold, American officials could provide little reassurance to their Ukrainian counterparts. Ambassador Taylor continued, "And I couldn't tell them. I didn't know and I didn't tell them, because we hadn't—we hadn't—there'd been no guidance that I could give them."[865]

Ambassador Taylor's First-Person Cable Described the "Folly" in Withholding Military Aid

The same day that Ambassador Taylor heard from Mr. Yermak about his concerns about the hold on military aid, Ambassador Taylor transmitted his classified, first-person cable to Washington. It was the first and only time in Ambassador Taylor's career that he sent such a cable to the Secretary of State.[866] The cable described "the folly I saw in withholding military aid to Ukraine at a time when hostilities were still active in the east and when Russia was watching closely to gauge the level of American support for the Ukrainian Government."[867]

Ambassador Taylor worried about the public message that such a hold on vital military assistance would send in the midst of Ukraine's hot war with Russia: "The Russians, as I said at my deposition, would love to see the humiliation of President Zelensky at the hands of the Americans. I told the Secretary that I could not and would not defend such a policy."[868]

The cable also sought to explain clearly "the importance of Ukraine and the security assistance to U.S. national security," according to Mr. Holmes.[869] However, Mr. Holmes worried that the national security argument might not achieve its purpose given the reasons he suspected for the hold on military aid. His "clear impression" at the time was that "the security assistance hold was likely intended by the President either as an expression of dissatisfaction with the Ukrainians, who had not yet agreed to the Burisma/Biden investigation, or as an effort to increase the pressure on them to do so."[870] Mr. Holmes viewed this as "the only logical conclusion."[871] He had "no other explanation for why there was disinterest in this [White House] meeting that the President had already offered" and there was a "hold of the security assistance with no explanation whatsoever."[872]

Ambassador Taylor never received a response to his cable, but was told that Secretary Pompeo carried it with him to a White House meeting about security assistance to Ukraine.[873]

Ambassador Sondland Told Senator Johnson That Ukraine Aid Was Conditioned on Investigations

The next day, on August 30, Republican Senator Ron Johnson spoke with Ambassador Sondland to express his concern about President Trump's decision to withhold military assistance to Ukraine. According to Senator Johnson, Ambassador Sondland told him that if Ukraine would commit to "get to the bottom of what happened in 2016—if President Trump has that confidence, then he'll release the military spending."[874]

On August 31, Senator Johnson spoke by phone with President Trump regarding the decision to withhold aid to Ukraine.[875] President Trump denied the quid pro quo that Senator Johnson had learned of from Ambassador Sondland.[876] At the same time, however, President Trump refused to authorize Senator Johnson to tell Ukrainian officials that the aid would be forthcoming.[877]

The message that Ambassador Sondland communicated to Senator Johnson mirrored that used by President Trump during his July 25 call with President Zelensky, in which President Trump twice asked that the Ukrainian leader "get to the bottom of it," including in connection to an investigation into the debunked conspiracy theory that Ukraine interfered in the 2016 election to help Hillary Clinton.[878] To the contrary, the U.S. Intelligence Community unanimously assessed that Russia interfered in the 2016 election to help Donald Trump, as did Special Counsel Robert Mueller.[879]

In a November 18 letter to House Republicans, Senator Johnson confirmed the accuracy of the *Wall Street Journal*'s account of his August 30 call with Ambassador Sondland.[880]

Ambassador Sondland testified that he had "no reason to dispute" Senator Johnson's recollection of the August 30 call and testified that by late August 2019, he had concluded that "if Ukraine did something to demonstrate a serious intention to fight corruption, and specifically addressing Burisma and the 2016, then the hold on military aid would be lifted."[881]

Ambassador Sondland Raised the Link Between Investigations and Security Assistance to Vice President Pence Before Meeting with President Zelensky

On September 1, President Trump was scheduled to meet President Zelensky in Warsaw, Poland during an event commemorating World War II. Citing the approach of Hurricane Dorian towards American soil, the President canceled his trip just days beforehand. Vice President Mike Pence traveled to Warsaw instead.[882]

Jennifer Williams, Special Advisor to the Vice President for Europe and Russia, learned of the change in the President's travel plans on August 29 and "relied heavily on the NSC briefing papers" originally prepared for President Trump. Ms. Williams recalled that "prior to leaving, [National Security Advisor to the Vice President] General Kellogg had asked, at the request of the Vice President, for an update on the status of the security assistance that was at that time still on hold." Given the public reporting about the hold on August 29, White House officials expected that President Zelensky would seek further information on the status of the funds.[883]

The delegation arrived in Warsaw and gathered in a hotel room to brief the Vice President shortly before his engagement with President Zelensky. Ambassador Bolton, who had just arrived from Kyiv, led the Ukraine briefing. He updated Vice President Pence on President Zelensky's efforts to combat corruption and explained "what the security assistance was for." Advisors in the room "agreed on the need to get a final decision on that security assistance as soon as possible so that it could be implemented before the end of the fiscal year."[884]

Before the bilateral meeting between Vice President Pence and President Zelensky, Ambassador Sondland attended a "general briefing" for the Vice President.[885] Ambassador Sondland testified that he raised concerns that the delay in security assistance had "become tied to the issue of investigations."[886] The Vice President "nodded like, you know, he heard what I said."[887]

During Ambassador Sondland's public testimony, Vice President Pence's office issued a carefully worded statement claiming that the Vice President "never had a conversation with Gordon Sondland about investigating the Bidens, Burisma, or the conditional release of financial aid to Ukraine based upon potential investigations," and that "Ambassador Gordon Sondland was never alone with the Vice President on the September 1 trip to Poland."[888] Ambassador Sondland did not testify that he specifically mentioned the Bidens, Burisma, or the conditional release of financial aid to Ukraine during his discussion with Vice President Pence, nor did he testify that he was alone with the Vice President.

Before Vice President Pence's meeting with President Zelensky, Ukrainian National Security Advisor Oleksandr "Sasha" Danyliuk wrote Ambassador Taylor, incorrectly describing the failure to provide security assistance as a "gradually increasing problem."[889] In the hours before Vice President Pence's meeting with President Zelensky, Ambassador Taylor replied, clarifying that "the delay of U.S. security assistance was an all-or-nothing proposition, in the sense that if the White House did not lift the hold prior to the end of the fiscal year, September 30th, the funds would expire and Ukraine would receive nothing."[890] Ambassador Taylor wanted to make sure Mr. Danyliuk understood that if the assistance was not provided "by the end of the fiscal year, then it goes away."[891]

President Zelensky Immediately Asked Vice President Pence About Security Assistance

As expected, at the outset of the bilateral meeting, President Zelensky immediately asked Vice President Pence about the status of U.S. security assistance. It was "the very first question" that he raised.[892] President Zelensky emphasized the multifold importance of American assistance, stating that "the symbolic value of U.S. support in terms of security assistance ... was just as valuable to the Ukrainians as the actual dollars."[893] President Zelensky also expressed concern that "any hold or appearance of reconsideration of such assistance might embolden Russia to think that the United States was no longer committed to Ukraine."[894]

According to Ms. Williams, the Vice President "assured President Zelensky that there was no change in U.S. policy in terms of our ... full-throated support for Ukraine and its sovereignty and territorial integrity."[895] Vice President Pence also assured the Ukrainian delegation that he would convey to President Trump the details of President Zelensky's "good progress on reforms, so that hopefully we could get a decision on the security assistance as soon as possible."[896]

The reassurance proved to be ineffective. The *Washington Post* later reported that one of President Zelensky's aides told Vice President Pence: "You're the only country providing us military assistance. You're punishing us."[897]

Mr. Holmes testified that President Trump's decision to cancel his Warsaw trip effectively meant that "the hold [on security assistance] remained in place, with no clear means to get it lifted."[898]

Ambassador Sondland Informed President Zelensky's Advisor that Military Aid Was Contingent on Ukraine Publicly Announcing the Investigations

After the bilateral meeting between Vice President Pence and President Zelensky, Ambassador Sondland briefly spoke to President Zelensky's aide, Mr. Yermak. Ambassador Sondland conveyed his belief that "the resumption of U.S. aid would likely not occur until Ukraine took some kind of action on the public statement that we had been discussing for many weeks" regarding the investigations that President Trump discussed during the July 25 call.[899]

Immediately following the conversation, Ambassador Sondland told Mr. Morrison what had transpired during his aside with Mr. Yermak. Mr. Morrison recounted to the Committees that Ambassador Sondland told Mr. Yermak "what could help them move the aid was if the prosecutor general would go to the mike [sic] and announce that he was opening the Burisma investigation."[900]

Mr. Morrison Reported Ambassador Sondland's Proposal to Get Ukrainians "Pulled Into Our Politics" to White House Officials and Ambassador Taylor

Mr. Morrison felt uncomfortable with "any idea that President Zelensky should allow himself to be involved in our politics."[901] He promptly reported the conversation between Ambassador Sondland and Mr. Yermak to Ambassador Bolton. Mr. Morrison had concerns with "what Gordon was proposing about getting the Ukrainians pulled into our politics."[902] Ambassador Bolton told Mr. Morrison—consistent with his own "instinct"—to "make sure the lawyers are tracking."[903] Upon his return to Washington, Mr. Morrison reported his concerns to NSC lawyers John Eisenberg and Michael Ellis.[904]

Mr. Morrison testified that, in speaking to the NSC legal advisors, he wanted to ensure "that there was a record of what Ambassador Sondland was doing, to protect the President."[905] At this point, Mr. Morrison was not certain that the President had authorized Ambassador Sondland's activities, but Mr. Morrison agreed that if the President had been aware of Ambassador Sondland's activities, the effect could be to create a paper trail that incriminated President Trump.[906]

Mr. Morrison also reported the conversation to Ambassador Taylor "because I wanted him to be in a position to advise the Ukrainians not to do it."[907] Ambassador Taylor said that he was "alarmed" to hear about the remarks to Mr. Yermak.[908] He explained that "this was the first time that I had heard that the security assistance, not just the White House meeting, was conditioned on the investigations."[909] To Ambassador Taylor, "It's one thing to try to leverage a meeting in the White House. It's another thing, I thought, to leverage security assistance … to a country at war, dependent on both the security assistance and the demonstration of support."[910]

President Trump Wanted President Zelensky in a "Public Box," and Said "Everything" Depended on Announcing the Investigations

Upon hearing from Mr. Morrison about the conditionality of the military aid on Ukraine publicly announcing the two investigations, Ambassador Taylor sent a text message to Ambassador Sondland: "Are we now saying that security assistance and WH meeting are conditioned on investigations?" Ambassador Sondland responded, "Call me."[911]

Ambassador Sondland confirmed over the phone to Ambassador Taylor that "everything"—the Oval Office meeting and the security assistance—was dependent on the Ukrainian government publicly announcing the political investigations President Trump requested on July 25. Informed by a review of contemporaneous notes that he took during his phone call, Ambassador Taylor testified:

> During that phone call, Ambassador Sondland told me that President Trump had told him that he wants President Zelensky to state publicly that Ukraine will investigate Burisma and alleged Ukrainian interference in the 2016 election. Ambassador Sondland also told me that he now recognized that he had made a mistake by earlier telling Ukrainian officials that only a White House meeting with President Zelensky was dependent on a public announcement of the investigations. In fact, Ambassador Sondland said,

everything was dependent on such an announcement, including security assistance. He said that President Trump wanted President Zelensky in a public box, by making a public statement about ordering such investigations.[912]

By this point, Ambassador Taylor's "clear understanding" was that President Trump would withhold security assistance until President Zelensky "committed to pursue the investigation."[913] He agreed that the U.S. position was "if they don't do this," referring to the investigations, "they are not going to get that," referring to the security assistance.[914] Ambassador Taylor also concurred with the statement that "if they don't do this, they are not going to get that" was the literal definition of a quid pro quo.[915]

Ambassador Taylor testified that his contemporaneous notes of the phone call with Ambassador Sondland reflect that Ambassador Sondland used the phrase "public box" to describe President Trump's desire to ensure that the initiation of his desired investigations was announced publicly.[916] Ambassador Sondland, who did not take contemporaneous notes of any of his conversations, did not dispute that he used those words.[917] He also testified that, when he spoke to Mr. Yermak, he believed that it would be sufficient to satisfy the requirements of President Trump and Mr. Giuliani if the new Ukrainian prosecutor general issued a statement about investigations, but his understanding soon changed.[918]

President Trump Informed Ambassador Sondland that President Zelensky Personally "Must Announce the Opening of the Investigations"

On September 7, Ambassador Sondland called Mr. Morrison to report that he had just concluded a call with President Trump. Mr. Morrison testified that Ambassador Sondland told him "that there was no quid pro quo, but President Zelensky must announce the opening of the investigations and he should want to do it."[919] This led Mr. Morrison to believe that a public announcement of investigations by the Ukrainian president—and not the prosecutor general— was a prerequisite for the release of the security assistance.[920] He reported the conversation to Ambassador Bolton, who once again instructed him to "tell the lawyers," which Mr. Morrison did.[921]

Later on September 7, Mr. Morrison relayed the substance of Ambassador Sondland's conversation with President Trump to Ambassador Taylor. Ambassador Taylor explained:

I had a conversation with Mr. Morrison in which he described a phone conversation earlier that day between Ambassador Sondland and President Trump. Mr. Morrison said that he had a sinking feeling after learning about this conversation from Ambassador Sondland. According to Mr. Morrison, President Trump told Ambassador Sondland he was not asking for a quid pro quo, but President Trump did insist that President Zelensky go to a microphone and say he is opening investigations of Biden and 2016 election interference and that President Zelensky should want to do this himself. Mr. Morrison said that he told Ambassador Bolton and the NSC lawyers of this phone call between President Trump and Ambassador Sondland.[922]

The following day, on September 8, Ambassador Sondland texted Ambassadors Volker and Taylor: "Guys multiple convos with Ze, Potus. Lets talk." Ambassador Taylor responded one minute later, "Now is fine with me."[923] On the phone, Ambassador Sondland "confirmed that he had talked to President Trump" and that "President Trump was adamant that President Zelensky himself had to clear things up and do it in public. President Trump said it was not a quid pro quo."[924] Ambassador Sondland also shared that he told President Zelensky and Mr. Yermak that, "although this was not a quid pro quo, if President Zelensky did not clear things up in public, we would be at a stalemate."[925]

Ambassador Taylor testified that he understood "stalemate" to mean that "Ukraine would not receive the much-needed military assistance."[926] During his public testimony, Ambassador Sondland did not dispute Ambassador Taylor's recollection of events and agreed that the term "stalemate" referred to the hold on U.S. security assistance to Ukraine.[927]

Although Ambassador Sondland otherwise could not independently recall any details about his September 7 conversation with President Trump, he testified that he had no reason to dispute the testimony from Ambassador Taylor or Mr. Morrison—which was based on their contemporaneous notes—regarding this conversation.[928] Ambassador Sondland, however, did recall that President Zelensky agreed to make a public announcement about the investigations into Burisma and the Bidens and the 2016 election in an interview on CNN."[929]

According to Ambassador Taylor, Ambassador Sondland explained that President Trump was a "businessman," and that when "a businessman is about to sign a check to someone who owes him something, the businessman asks that person to pay up before signing the check."[930] Ambassador Taylor was concerned that President Trump believed Ukraine "owed him something" in exchange for the hundreds of millions of dollars in taxpayer-funded U.S. security assistance.[931] He argued to Ambassador Sondland that "the explanation made no sense. The Ukrainians did not owe President Trump anything. And holding up security assistance for domestic political gain was crazy."[932] Ambassador Sondland did not recall this exchange specifically, but did not dispute Ambassador Taylor's testimony.[933]

Ambassador Taylor Texted Ambassador Sondland that "It's Crazy to Withhold Security Assistance for Help with a Political Campaign"

Ambassador Taylor remained concerned by the President's directive that "everything" was conditioned on President Zelensky publicly announcing the investigations. He also worried that, even if the Ukrainian leader did as President Trump required, the President might continue to withhold the vital U.S. security assistance in any event. Ambassador Taylor texted his concerns to Ambassadors Volker and Sondland stating: "The nightmare is they give the interview and don't get the security assistance. The Russians love it. (And I quit.)"[934]

Ambassador Taylor testified:

"The nightmare" is the scenario where President Zelensky goes out in public, makes an announcement that he's going to investigate the Burisma and the ... interference in 2016 election, maybe among other things. He might put that in some series of investigations.

But ... the nightmare was he would mention those two, take all the heat from that, get himself in big trouble in this country and probably in his country as well, and the security assistance would not be released. That was the nightmare.[935]

Early in the morning in Europe on September 9, Ambassador Taylor reiterated his concerns about the President's "quid pro quo" in another series of text messages with Ambassadors Volker and Sondland:

Taylor:	The message to the Ukrainians (and Russians) we send with the decision on security assistance is key. With the hold, we have already shaken their faith in us. Thus my nightmare scenario.
Taylor:	Counting on you to be right about this interview, Gordon.
Sondland:	Bill, I never said I was "right". I said we are where we are and believe we have identified the best pathway forward. Lets hope it works.
Taylor:	As I said on the phone, I think it's crazy to withhold security assistance for help with a political campaign.[936]

By "help with a political campaign," Ambassador Taylor was referring to President Trump's 2020 reelection effort.[937] Ambassador Taylor testified: "The investigation of Burisma and the Bidens was clearly identified by Mr. Giuliani in public for months as a way to get information on the two Bidens."[938]

Ambassador Taylor framed the broader national security implications of President Trump's decision to withhold vital security assistance from Ukraine. He said:

[T]he United States was trying to support Ukraine as a frontline state against Russian attack. And, again, the whole notion of a rules-based order was being threatened by the Russians in Ukraine. So our security assistance was designed to support Ukraine. And it was not just the United States; it was all of our allies.[939]

Ambassador Taylor explained:

[S]ecurity assistance was so important for Ukraine as well as our own national interests, to withhold that assistance for no good reason other than help with a political campaign made no sense. It was counterproductive to all of what we had been trying to do. It was illogical. It could not be explained. It was crazy.[940]

Ambassador Sondland Repeated the President's Denial of a "Quid Pro Quo" to Ambassador Taylor, While He and President Trump Continued to Demand Public Investigations

In response to Ambassador Taylor's text message that it was "crazy to withhold security assistance for help with a political campaign," Ambassador Sondland denied that the President had demanded a "quid pro quo."

At approximately 5:17 a.m. Eastern Time, Ambassador Sondland responded to Ambassador Taylor:

> Bill, I believe you are incorrect about President Trump's intentions. The President has been crystal clear: no quid pro quo's of any kind. The President is trying to evaluate whether Ukraine is truly going to adopt the transparency and reforms that President Zelensky promised during his campaign. I suggest we stop the back and forth by text. If you still have concerns, I recommend you give Lisa Kenna or S [Secretary Pompeo] a call to discuss them directly. Thanks.[941]

Notably, Ambassador Sondland recalled that President Trump raised the possible existence of a quid pro quo entirely on his own, without any prompting. Ambassador Sondland asked President Trump what he affirmatively wanted from Ukraine, yet President Trump reportedly responded by asserting what was not the case:

> Q: Okay. During that telephone conversation with President Trump, you didn't ask the President directly if there was a quid pro quo, correct?
> A: No. As I testified, I asked the question open ended, what do you want from Ukraine?
> Q: President Trump was the first person to use the word "quid pro quo," correct?
> A: That is correct.[942]

In contrast, Ambassador Sondland testified unequivocally there was a quid pro quo in connection to a telephone call between President Trump and President Zelensky, as well as a White House meeting for President Zelensky.[943] He acknowledged that the reference to "transparency and reforms" in his text message to Ambassador Taylor "was my clumsy way of saying he wanted these announcement to be made."[944]

Ambassador Sondland also testified that President Trump immediately followed his stated denial of a quid pro quo by demanding that President Zelensky still make a public announcement, while the military assistance remained on an unexplained hold. Ambassador Sondland agreed that President Trump said that he wanted President Zelensky to "clear things up and do it in public," as Ambassador Taylor had testified.[945] Ambassador Sondland testified that nothing on his call with President Trump changed his understanding of a quid pro quo and, at least as of September 8, he was "absolutely convinced" the White House meeting and President Trump's release of the military assistance were conditioned on the public announcement of the investigations President Trump sought.[946]

After hearing from President Trump, Ambassador Sondland promptly told the Ukrainian leader and Mr. Yermak that "if President Zelensky did not clear things up in public, we would be at a stalemate."[947] President Zelensky responded to the demand relayed by Ambassador Sondland, by agreeing to make an announcement of investigations on CNN.[948]

Regardless of when the call between President Trump and Ambassador Sondland occurred, both that phone call and Ambassador's Sondland text message denying any quid pro quo occurred *after* the White House had been informed of the whistleblower complaint discussing the hold on security assistance. The White House first received notice of the whistleblower complaint alleging wrongdoing concerning the President's July 25 call with President Zelensky on August 26—over a week before the "no quid pro quo" denial.[949] In addition, Ambassador Sondland wrote his text message on September 9, the same day that the ICIG informed the Committee of the existence of a "credible" and "urgent" whistleblower complaint that was later revealed to be related to Ukraine.[950] The Administration received prior notice of the ICIG's intent to inform the Committee.[951]

Ambassador Sondland's Testimony is the Only Evidence the Committees Received Indicating That President Trump Denied Any "Quid Pro Quo" on the Phone on September 9

Ambassador Sondland testified in his deposition that he sent a text message to Ambassador Taylor after speaking directly with President Trump on September 9. However, testimony from other witnesses and documents available to the Committees do not confirm that Ambassador Sondland and President Trump spoke on that day.

Ambassador Sondland's own testimony indicated some ambiguity in his recollection of the timing of the call. At a public hearing on November 20, Ambassador Sondland testified that he "still cannot find a record of that call [on September 9] because the State Department and the White House cannot locate it."[952] While Ambassador Sondland testified that "I'm pretty sure I had the call on that day,"[953] he acknowledged that he might have misremembered the date of the September 9 call—"I may have even spoken to him on September 6th"—and that without his call records, he could not be certain about when he spoke to President Trump.[954]

After the deposition transcripts of Ambassador Taylor and Mr. Morrison were made public, including their detailed accounts of the September 7 conversation that Ambassador Sondland had with President Trump, Ambassador Sondland submitted a written addendum to his deposition based on his "refreshed" recollection.[955] In that addendum, Ambassador Sondland amended his testimony and stated, "I cannot specifically recall if I had one or two phone calls with President Trump in the September 6-9 time frame."[956]

Furthermore, the conversation recalled by Ambassador Sondland as having taken place on September 9 is consistent with a conversation that Ambassador Sondland relayed to Mr. Morrison and Ambassador Taylor during the previous two days. Both Mr. Morrison and Ambassador Taylor, after reviewing their contemporaneous written notes, provided detailed testimony about Ambassador Sondland's description of his call with President Trump. For example, Ambassador Sondland shared with Ambassador Taylor that even though President Trump asserted that "there is no quid pro quo," President Trump "did insist that President Zelensky go to a microphone and say he is opening investigations of Biden and 2016 election interference."[957] Mr. Morrison and Ambassador Taylor both testified that this conversation occurred on September 7.[958] Ambassador Sondland acknowledged that he had no basis to dispute the recollections of Mr. Morrison and Ambassador Taylor.[959] Ambassador Sondland, who testified that he does not take notes, stated: "If they have notes and they recall that, I don't have any reason to dispute it."[960]

Text messages produced to the Committees also indicate that Ambassador Sondland spoke to President Trump prior to September 8. On September 4, Ambassador Volker texted Mr. Yermak that Ambassador Sondland planned to speak to President Trump on September 6 or 7. Ambassador Volker wrote: "Hi Andrey. Reports are that pence liked meeting and will press trump on scheduling Ze visit. Gordon will follow up with pence and, if nothing moving, will have a chance to talk with President on Saturday [September 7]."[961] Ambassador Volker then corrected himself: "Sorry—on Friday [September 6]."[962]

On Sunday, September 8, at 11:20 a.m. Eastern Time, Ambassador Sondland texted Ambassadors Taylor and Volker: "Guys multiple convos with Ze, Potus. Lets talk."[963] Shortly after this text, Ambassador Taylor testified that he spoke to Ambassador Sondland, who recounted his conversation with President Trump on September 7, as well as a separate conversation that Ambassador Sondland had with President Zelensky.

The timing of the text messages also raises questions about Ambassador Sondland's recollection. If Ambassador Sondland spoke to President Trump after receiving Ambassador Taylor's text message on September 9, and before he responded, then the timing of the text messages would mean that President Trump took Ambassador Sondland's call in the middle of the night in Washington, D.C. Ambassador Taylor sent his message on September 9 at 12:47 a.m. Eastern Time, and Ambassador Sondland responded less than five hours later at 5:19 a.m. Eastern Time.[964]

In any event, President Trump's purported denial of the "quid pro quo" was also contradicted when Acting Chief of Staff Mick Mulvaney publicly admitted that security assistance was withheld in order to pressure Ukraine to conduct an investigation into the 2016 election.

On October 17, at a press briefing in the White House, Mr. Mulvaney confirmed that President Trump withheld the essential military aid for Ukraine as leverage to pressure Ukraine to investigate the conspiracy theory that Ukraine had interfered in the 2016 U.S. election, which was also promoted by Vladimir Putin.[965] Mr. Mulvaney confirmed that President Trump "absolutely" mentioned "corruption related to the DNC server. ... No question about that."[966] When the White House press corps attempted to clarify this acknowledgement of a quid pro quo related to security assistance, Mr. Mulvaney replied: "We do that all the time with foreign policy." He continued. "I have news for everybody: get over it."[967]

8.   The President's Scheme Was Exposed

> *President Trump lifted the hold on U.S. military assistance to Ukraine on September 11 after it became clear to the White House and President Trump that his scheme was exposed.*

Overview

As news of the President's hold on military assistance to Ukraine became public on August 28, Congress, the press, and the public increased their scrutiny of President Trump's actions regarding Ukraine, which risked exposing President Trump's scheme. By this date, the White House had learned that the Inspector General of the Intelligence Community (ICIG), Michael Atkinson, had determined that a whistleblower complaint related to the same Ukraine matters was "credible" and an "urgent concern," and, pursuant to the applicable statute, recommended to the Acting Director of National Intelligence (DNI), Joseph Maguire, that the complaint should be transmitted to Congress.

In early September, bipartisan Members of both houses of Congress—publicly, and privately—expressed concerns to the White House about the hold on military assistance. On September 9, after months of internal discussion due to growing concern about the activity of President Trump's personal attorney, Rudy Giuliani, regarding Ukraine, the Chairs of the Permanent Select Committee on Intelligence, the Committee on Foreign Affairs, and the Committee on Oversight and Reform announced a joint investigation into efforts by President Trump and Mr. Giuliani, "to improperly pressure the Ukrainian government to assist the President's bid for reelection," including by withholding Congressionally-appropriated military assistance.

Later that same day, the ICIG notified Chairman Schiff and Ranking Member Nunes that, despite uniform past practice and a statutory requirement that credible, "urgent concern" complaints be provided to the intelligence committees, the Acting DNI was nevertheless withholding the whistleblower complaint from Congress. The Acting DNI later testified that his office initially withheld the complaint on the advice of the White House, with guidance from the Department of Justice.

Two days later, on September 11, the President lifted the hold on the military assistance to Ukraine. Numerous witnesses testified that they were never aware of any official reason for why the hold was either implemented or lifted.

Notwithstanding this ongoing inquiry, President Trump has continued to urge Ukraine to investigate his political rival, former Vice President Biden. For example, when asked by a journalist on October 3 what he hoped Ukraine's President would do about the Bidens in response to the July 25 call, President Trump responded: "Well, I would think that, if they were honest about it, they'd start a major investigation into the Bidens. It's a very simple answer." President Trump reiterated his affinity for the former Prosecutor General of Ukraine, Yuriy Lutsenko, whom numerous witnesses described as inept and corrupt: "And they got rid of a prosecutor who was a very tough prosecutor. They got rid of him. Now they're trying to make it the opposite way."

Public Scrutiny of President Trump's Hold on Military Assistance for Ukraine

After news of the President's freeze on U.S. military assistance to Ukraine became public on August 28, both houses of Congress increased their ongoing scrutiny of President Trump's decision.[968] On September 3, a bipartisan group of Senators, including Senator Rob Portman and Senator Ron Johnson, sent a letter to Acting White House Chief of Staff Mick Mulvaney expressing "deep concerns" that the "Administration is considering not obligating the Ukraine Security Initiative funds for 2019."[969] The Senators' letter urged that the "vital" funds be obligated "immediately."[970] On September 5, the Chairman and Ranking Member of the House Foreign Affairs Committee sent a letter to Mr. Mulvaney and Acting Director of the OMB Russell Vought expressing "deep concern" about the continuing hold on security assistance funding for Ukraine.[971]

On September 5, the *Washington Post* editorial board reported concerns that President Trump was withholding military assistance for Ukraine and a White House meeting in order to force President Zelensky to announce investigations of Mr. Biden and purported Ukrainian interference in the 2016 U.S. election. The *Post* editorial board wrote:

> [W]e're reliably told that the president has a second and more venal agenda: He is attempting to force Mr. Zelensky to intervene in the 2020 U.S. presidential election by launching an investigation of the leading Democratic candidate, Joe Biden. Mr. Trump is not just soliciting Ukraine's help with his presidential campaign; he is using U.S. military aid the country desperately needs in an attempt to extort it.

It added:

> The White House claims Mr. Trump suspended Ukraine's military aid in order for it [sic] be reviewed. But, as CNN reported, the Pentagon has already completed the study and recommended that the hold be lifted. Yet Mr. Trump has not yet acted. If his recalcitrance has a rationale, other than seeking to compel a foreign government to aid his reelection, the president has yet to reveal it.[972]

On the same day that the *Washington Post* published its editorial, Senators Christopher Murphy and Ron Johnson visited Kyiv, and met with President Zelensky. They were accompanied by Ambassador Bill Taylor and Counselor for Political Affairs David Holmes of U.S. Embassy Kyiv. President Zelensky's "first question to the Senators was about the withheld security assistance."[973] Ambassador Taylor testified that both Senators "stressed that bipartisan support for Ukraine in Washington was Ukraine's most important strategic asset and that President Zelensky should not jeopardize that bipartisan support by getting drawn into U.S. domestic politics."[974]

As Senator Johnson and Senator Murphy later recounted, the Senators sought to reassure President Zelensky that there was bipartisan support in Congress for providing Ukraine with military assistance for Ukraine and that they would continue to urge President Trump to lift the hold—as Senator Johnson had already tried, unsuccessfully, before traveling to Ukraine.[975]

Three Committees Announced Joint Investigation of President's Scheme

On September 9, the Chairs of the House Intelligence Committee, the Committee on Foreign Affairs, and the Committee on Oversight and Reform publicly announced a joint investigation of the scheme by President Trump and Mr. Giuliani "to improperly pressure the Ukrainian government to assist the President's bid for reelection."[976] The Committees had been planning and coordinating this investigation since early summer, after growing public scrutiny of Mr. Giuliani's activities in Ukraine and questions about Ambassador Yovanovitch's abrupt removal following a public smear campaign targeting her.

In a letter sent to White House Counsel Pat Cipollone the same day, the three Chairs stated that President Trump and Mr. Giuliani "appear to have acted outside legitimate law enforcement and diplomatic channels to coerce the Ukrainian government into pursuing two politically-motivated investigations under the guise of anti-corruption activity"—investigations into purported Ukrainian interference in the 2016 election and Vice President Biden and his son.[977]

With respect to the hold on Ukraine military assistance, the Chairs observed that "[i]f the President is trying to pressure Ukraine into choosing between defending itself from Russian aggression without U.S. assistance or leveraging its judicial system to serve the ends of the Trump campaign, this would represent a staggering abuse of power, a boon to Moscow, and a betrayal of the public trust."[978] The Chairs requested that the White House preserve all relevant records and produce them by September 16, including the transcript of the July 25 call between President Trump and President Zelensky.[979]

On the same day, the Chairs of the three Committees sent a similar letter to Secretary of State Mike Pompeo seeking the preservation and production of all relevant records at the Department of State by September 16.[980] To date, and as explained more fully in Section II, Secretary Pompeo has not produced a single document sought by the Committees pursuant to a lawful subpoena.

NSC Senior Director for Russia and Europe Timothy Morrison recalled seeing a copy of the letter that was sent by the three Chairs to the White House.[981] He also recalled that the three Committees' Ukraine investigation was discussed at meeting of senior-level NSC staff soon after it was publicly announced.[982] The NSC's legislative affairs staff issued a notice of the investigation to NSC staff members, although it is unclear exactly when.[983] NSC Director for Ukraine Alexander Vindman recalled discussions among NSC staff members, including Mr. Morrison's deputy, John Erath, that the investigation "might have the effect of releasing the hold" on Ukraine military assistance because it would be "potentially politically challenging" for the Administration to "justify that hold" to the Congress.[984]

Inspector General Notified Intelligence Committee that the Administration Was Withholding Whistleblower Complaint

Later that same day, September 9, Inspector General Atkinson sent a letter to Chairman Schiff and Ranking Member Nunes notifying them that an Intelligence Community whistleblower had filed a complaint with the ICIG on August 12.[985] Pursuant to a statute governing whistleblower disclosures, the Inspector General—after a condensed, preliminary review—had determined that the complaint constituted an "urgent concern" and that its allegations appeared to be "credible."[986] The Inspector General's September 9 letter did not disclose the substance or topic of the whistleblower complaint.

Contrary to uniform past practice and the clear requirements of the whistleblower statute, Acting DNI Maguire withheld the whistleblower complaint based on advice from the White House.[987] Acting DNI Maguire also relied upon an unprecedented intervention by the Department of Justice into Intelligence Community whistleblower matters to overturn the ICIG's determination based on a preliminary investigation.[988]

The White House had been aware of the whistleblower complaint weeks prior to the ICIG's letter of September 9.[989] Acting DNI Maguire testified that, after receiving the whistleblower complaint from the Inspector General on August 26, his office contacted the White House Counsel's Office for guidance.[990]

Consistent with Acting DNI Maguire's testimony, the *New York Times* reported that in late August, Mr. Cipollone and National Security Council Legal Advisor John Eisenberg personally briefed President Trump about the complaint's existence—and explained to the President that they believed the complaint could be withheld on executive privilege grounds.[991] The report alleged that Mr. Cipollone and Mr. Eisenberg "told Mr. Trump they planned to ask the Justice Department's Office of Legal Counsel to determine whether they had to disclose the complaint to lawmakers."[992]

On September 10, Chairman Schiff wrote to Acting DNI Maguire to express his concern about the Acting DNI's "unprecedented departure from past practice" in withholding the whistleblower complaint from the Congressional intelligence committees notwithstanding his "express obligations under the law" and the Inspector General's determination.[993] Chairman Schiff observed that the "failure to transmit to the Committee an urgent and credible whistleblower complaint, as required by law, raises the prospect that an urgent matter of a serious nature is being purposefully concealed from the Committee."[994]

Also on September 10, Ambassador John Bolton resigned from his position as National Security Advisor. Ambassador Bolton's deputy, Dr. Charles Kupperman, became the Acting National Security Advisor. The Committee was unable to determine if Ambassador Bolton's departure related to the matters under investigation because neither he nor Dr. Kupperman agreed to appear for testimony as part of this inquiry.

On September 13, the Office of the Director of National Intelligence (ODNI) General Counsel informed the Committee that DOJ had overruled the ICIG's determination, and that the

ODNI could not transmit the complaint to the Committee at its discretion because it involved "potentially privileged communications by persons outside the Intelligence Community"— presumably presidential communications.[995] In response, Chairman Schiff issued a subpoena to the Acting DNI on September 13 and announced to the public that ODNI was withholding a "credible" whistleblower complaint of "urgent concern."[996] Following intense pressure from the public and Congress, on September 25, the White House released the complaint to the intelligence committees and the July 25 call record to the public.[997]

President Trump Lifted the Hold on Military Assistance for Ukraine

On September 11—two days after the three Committees launched their investigation into President Trump's scheme, and one day after Chairman Schiff requested that Acting DNI Maguire produce a copy of the whistleblower complaint—President Trump lifted the hold on military assistance for Ukraine.

On the evening of September 11, prior to lifting the hold, President Trump met with Vice President Mike Pence, Mr. Mulvaney, and Senator Portman to discuss the hold.[998] Around 8:00 p.m. on September 11, the Chief of Staff's office informed Dr. Kupperman that the hold had been lifted.[999]

Just like there was no official explanation for why the hold on Ukraine security assistance was implemented, numerous witnesses testified that they were not provided with a reason for why the hold was lifted on September 11.[1000] For example, Deputy Assistant Secretary of Defense Laura Cooper testified that President Trump's lifting of the hold "really came quite out of the blue… It was quite abrupt."[1001] Jennifer Williams, Special Advisor to the Vice President for Europe and Russia, testified that from the time when she first learned about the hold on July 3 until it was lifted on September 11, she never came to understand why President Trump ordered the hold.[1002]

OMB Deputy Associate Director of National Security Programs Mark Sandy, who was the senior career official overseeing the administration of some of the Ukraine military assistance, only learned of a possible rationale for the hold in early September—after the Acting DNI had informed the White House about the whistleblower complaint.[1003] Mr. Sandy testified that he could not recall another instance "where a significant amount of assistance was being held up" and he "didn't have a rationale for as long as I didn't have a rationale in this case."[1004] However, in "early September," approximately two months after President Trump had implemented the hold, and several weeks after the White House learned of the whistleblower complaint, Mr. Sandy received an email from OMB Associate Director of National Security Programs Michael Duffey. For the first time, it "attributed the hold to the President's concern about other countries not contributing more to Ukraine" and requested "information on what additional countries were contributing to Ukraine."[1005]

Mr. Sandy testified that he was not aware of any other countries committing to provide more financial assistance to Ukraine prior to the lifting of the hold on September 11.[1006] According to Lt. Col. Vindman, none of the "facts on the ground" changed before the President lifted the hold.[1007]

After the Hold was Lifted, Congress was Forced to Pass a Law to Ensure All of the Military Aid Could Be Distributed to Ukraine

The lengthy delay created by the hold on Ukraine military assistance prevented the Department of Defense from spending all of the Congressionally-appropriated funds by the end of the fiscal year, which meant that the funds would expire on September 30 because unused funds do not roll over to the next fiscal year.[1008] This confirmed the fears expressed by Ms. Cooper, Mr. Sandy, and others related to the illegal impoundment of Congressionally-mandated funding—concerns that were discussed in some depth within the relevant agencies in late July and throughout August.[1009]

Prior to the release of the funds, DOD's internal analysis raised concerns that up to $100 million of military assistance could go unspent as a result of the hold imposed by the President.[1010] Ultimately, approximately $35 million of Ukraine military assistance—14% of the total funds—remained unspent by the end of fiscal year 2019.[1011] Typically, DOD averages between 2 and 5 percent unspent funds for similar programs, substantially less than the 14 percent left unspent in this case.[1012]

In order to ensure that Ukraine did not permanently lose $35 million of the critical military assistance frozen by the White House,[1013] Congress passed a provision on September 27—three days before funds were set to expire—to ensure that the remaining $35 million in 2019 military assistance to Ukraine could be spent.[1014] Ms. Cooper testified that such an act of Congress was unusual—indeed, she had never heard of funding being extended in this manner.[1015]

As of November 2019, Pentagon officials confirmed that the $35 million in security assistance originally held by the President and extended by Congress had still yet to be disbursed. When asked for an explanation, the Pentagon only confirmed that the funds had not yet been spent but declined to say why.[1016]

Pressure to Announce Investigations Continued After the Hold was Lifted

Before President Trump lifted the hold on security assistance, Ukrainian officials had relented to the American pressure campaign to announce the investigations and had scheduled President Zelensky to appear on CNN.[1017] Even after President Trump lifted the hold on September 11, President Zelensky did not immediately cancel his planned CNN interview.[1018]

On September 12, Ambassador Taylor personally informed President Zelensky and the Ukrainian foreign minister that President Trump's hold on military assistance had been lifted.[1019] Ambassador Taylor remained concerned, however, that "there was some indication that there might still be a plan for the CNN interview in New York" during which President Zelensky would announce the investigations that President Trump wanted Ukraine to pursue.[1020] Ambassador Taylor testified that he "wanted to be sure that that didn't happen, so I addressed it with Zelensky's staff."[1021]

On September 13, a staff member at the U.S. Embassy in Kyiv texted Mr. Holmes to relay a message that "Sondland said the Zelensky interview is supposed to be today or Monday, and they plan to announce that a certain investigation that was 'on hold' will progress."[1022] The Embassy Kyiv staffer stated that he "did not know if this was decided or if Sondland was advocating for it. Apparently he's been discussing this with Yermak."[1023]

On September 13, during a meeting in President Zelensky's office, Ukrainian presidential aide Andriy Yermak "looked uncomfortable" when Ambassador Taylor sought to confirm that there were no plans for President Zelensky to announce the investigations during a CNN interview.[1024] Although President Zelensky's National Security Advisor Oleksandr Danyliuk indicated that there were no plans for President Zelensky to do the CNN interview, Ambassador Taylor was still concerned after he and Mr. Holmes saw Mr. Yermak following the meeting.[1025] According to Ambassador Taylor, Mr. Yermak's "body language was such that it looked to me like he was still thinking they were going to make that statement."[1026] Mr. Holmes also recalled that when he and Ambassador Taylor ran into Mr. Yermak following the meeting, Ambassador Taylor "stressed the importance of staying out of U.S. politics and said he hoped no interview was planned," but "Mr. Yermak shrugged in resignation and did not answer, as if to indicate he had no choice."[1027]

That same day, September 13, President Zelensky reportedly met with CNN's Fareed Zakaria, who was in Kyiv to moderate the Yalta European Strategy Conference.[1028] During the meeting with Mr. Zakaria, President Zelensky did not cancel his planned CNN interview.[1029]

Conflicting advice prompted the Ukrainian foreign minister to observe in a meeting with Ambassador Volker, Ambassador Taylor, and Deputy Assistant Secretary of State George Kent, "You guys are sending us different messages in different channels."[1030]

For example, at a September 14 meeting in Kyiv attended by Ambassador Volker, Mr. Yermak, and the Ukrainian foreign minister, Ambassador Volker stated that when the two Presidents finally meet, "it's important that President Zelensky give the messages that we discussed before," apparently referring to President Zelensky's "willingness to open investigations in the two areas of interest to the President and that had been pushed previously by Rudy Giuliani."[1031] Ambassador Taylor, however, replied: "Don't do that."[1032]

On September 18 or 19, President Zelensky cancelled his scheduled interview with CNN.[1033] Although President Zelensky did not publicly announce the investigations that President Trump wanted, he remains under pressure from President Trump, particularly because he requires diplomatic, financial, and military backing from the United States, the most powerful supporter of Ukraine. That pressure continues to this day. As Mr. Holmes testified:

> [A]lthough the hold on the security assistance may have been lifted, there were still things they wanted that [the Ukrainians] weren't getting, including a meeting with the President in the Oval Office. Whether the hold—the security assistance hold continued or not, Ukrainians understood that that's something the President wanted, and they still wanted important things from the President.

And I think that continues to this day. I think they're being very careful. They still need us now going forward. In fact, right now, President Zelensky is trying to arrange a summit meeting with President Putin in the coming weeks, his first face to face meeting with him to try to advance the peace process. He needs our support. He needs President Putin to understand that America supports Zelensky at the highest levels. So this doesn't end with the lifting of the security assistance hold. Ukraine still needs us, and as I said, still fighting this war this very day.[1034]

Vice President Pence Spoke to President Zelensky

On September 18, approximately one week before President Trump was scheduled to meet with President Zelensky at the United Nations General Assembly in New York, Vice President Pence spoke with President Zelensky by telephone.[1035] According to Ms. Williams, during the call, Vice President Pence "reiterat[ed] the release of the funds" and "ask[ed] a bit more about … how Zelensky's efforts were going."[1036]

On November 26, Ms. Williams submitted a classified addendum to her hearing testimony on November 19 related to this telephone call. According to Ms. Williams' counsel, the Office of the Vice President informed Ms. Williams' counsel that certain portions of the September 18 call, including the additional information in Ms. Williams' addendum, are classified. The Committee has requested that the Office of the Vice President conduct a declassification review so that the Committee may share this additional information regarding the substance of the September 18 call publicly. On October 9, Vice President Pence told reporters, "I'd have no objection" to the White House releasing the transcript of his calls with President Zelensky and said that "we're discussing that with White House counsel as we speak."[1037] In a November 7 interview with *Fox Business*, Vice President Pence reiterated, "I have no objection at all" to releasing records of his calls.[1038]

President Trump and Rudy Giuliani, Undeterred, Continued to Solicit Foreign Interference in Our Elections

On September 19, Rudy Giuliani was interviewed by Chris Cuomo on CNN. During the interview, Mr. Giuliani confirmed that he had urged Ukraine to investigate "the allegations that there was interference in the election of 2016, by the Ukrainians, for the benefit of Hillary Clinton[.]" When asked specifically if he had asked Ukraine to look into Vice President Biden, Mr. Giuliani replied immediately, "of course I did."

Seconds later, Mr. Giuliani attempted to clarify his admission, insisting that he had not asked Ukraine to investigate Vice President Biden but instead "to look into the allegations that related to my client [President Trump], which tangentially involved Joe Biden in a massive bribery scheme." Mr. Giuliani insisted that his conduct was appropriate, telling Mr. Cuomo later in the interview that "it is perfectly appropriate for a President to say to a leader of a foreign country, investigate this massive bribe … that was paid by a former Vice President."[1039]

President Trump also has continued to publicly urge President Zelensky to launch an investigation of Vice President Biden and alleged 2016 election interference by Ukraine. On September 23, in a public press availability, President Trump stated:

> I put no pressure on them whatsoever. I could have. I think it would probably, possibly, have been okay if I did. But I didn't. I didn't put any pressure on them whatsoever. You know why? Because they want to do the right thing.[1040]

On September 24, in public remarks upon arriving at the opening session of the U.N. General Assembly, President Trump stated: "What Joe Biden did for his son, that's something they should be looking at."[1041]

On September 25—in a joint public press availability with President Zelensky—President Trump stated that "I want him to do whatever he can" in reference to the investigation of the Biden family. He added, "Now, when Biden's son walks away with millions of dollars from Ukraine, and he knows nothing, and they're paying him millions of dollars, that's corruption." President Trump added, "He [President Zelensky] was elected—I think, number one—on the basis of stopping corruption, which unfortunately has plagued Ukraine. And if he could do that, he's doing, really, the whole world a big favor. I know—and I think he's going to be successful."[1042]

On September 30, during his remarks at the swearing-in ceremony of Labor Secretary Eugene Scalia, President Trump stated:

> Now, the new President of Ukraine ran on the basis of no corruption. That's how he got elected. And I believe that he really means it. But there was a lot of corruption having to do with the 2016 election against us. And we want to get to the bottom of it, and it's very important that we do.[1043]

On October 2, in a public press availability, President Trump discussed the July 25 call with President Zelensky and stated that "the conversation was perfect; it couldn't have been nicer." He added:

> The only thing that matters is the transcript of the actual conversation that I had with the President of Ukraine. It was perfect. We're looking at congratulations. We're looking at doing things together. And what are we looking at? We're looking at corruption. And, in, I believe, 1999, there was a corruption act or a corruption bill passed between both— and signed—between both countries, where I have a duty to report corruption. And let me tell you something: Biden's son is corrupt, and Biden is corrupt.[1044]

On October 3, in remarks before he departed on Marine One, President Trump expressed his "hope" that Ukraine would investigate Mr. Biden and his son. Specifically, President Trump stated that he had hoped—after his July 25 conversation—that Ukraine would "start a major investigation into the Bidens." The President also stated that "by the way, likewise, China should start an investigation into the Bidens, because what happened in China is just about as bad as what happened with—with Ukraine." He addressed the corrupt prosecutor general, Yuriy

Lutsenko, who had recently been removed by Parliament: "And they got rid of a prosecutor who was a very tough prosecutor. They got rid of him. Now they're trying to make it the opposite way.[1045]

The next day, on October 4, in remarks before he departed on Marine One, the President again said:

> When you look at what Biden and his son did, and when you look at other people — what they've done. And I believe there was tremendous corruption with Biden, but I think there was beyond—I mean, beyond corruption—having to do with the 2016 campaign, and what these lowlifes did to so many people, to hurt so many people in the Trump campaign—which was successful, despite all of the fighting us. I mean, despite all of the unfairness.[1046]

President Trump reiterated his willingness to solicit foreign assistance related to his personal interests: "Here's what's okay: If we feel there's corruption, like I feel there was in the 2016 campaign—there was tremendous corruption against me—if we feel there's corruption, we have a right to go to a foreign country."[1047] President Trump added that asking President Xi of China to investigate the Bidens "is certainly something we can start thinking about."[1048]

Consistent with the President's remarks after this inquiry began, Ambassador Volker understood that references to fighting "corruption" in Ukraine, when used by President Trump and Mr. Giuliani, in fact referred to the two investigations into "Burisma"—and former Vice President Biden—and the 2016 election interference that President Trump sought to benefit his reelection efforts.[1049]

The President's Scheme Undermined U.S. Anti-Corruption Efforts in Ukraine

Rather than combatting corruption in Ukraine, President Trump's ongoing efforts to urge Ukraine to pursue an investigation into former Vice President Biden undermine longstanding U.S. anti-corruption policy, which encourages countries to refrain from using the criminal justice system to investigate political opponents. When it became clear that President Trump was pressuring Ukraine to investigate his political rival, career public servants charged with implementing U.S. foreign policy in a non-partisan manner, such as Lt. Col. Vindman and Ambassador Taylor, communicated to President Zelensky and his advisors that Ukraine should avoid getting embroiled in U.S. domestic politics.[1050]

Mr. Kent, an anti-corruption and rule of law expert, explained that U.S. anti-corruption efforts prioritize "building institutional capacity so that the Ukrainian Government has the ability to go after corruption and effectively investigate, prosecute, and judge alleged criminal activities using appropriate institutional mechanisms, that is, to create and follow the rule of law.[1051]

Mr. Holmes concurred:

> [O]ur longstanding policy is to encourage them [Ukraine] to establish and build rule of law institutions, that are capable and that are independent and that can actually pursue

credible allegations. That's our policy. We've been doing that for quite some time with some success. So focusing on [particular] cases, including [] cases where there is an interest of the President, it's just not part of what we've done. It's hard to explain why we would do that.[1052]

Mr. Kent emphasized that when foreign government officials "hear diplomats on the ground saying one thing, and they hear other U.S. leaders saying something else," it raises concerns about the United States' credibility on anti-corruption efforts.[1053] Ambassador Taylor agreed, stating that "[o]ur credibility is based on a respect for the United States" and "if we damage that respect, then it hurts our credibility and makes it more difficult for us to do our jobs."[1054]

Mr. Kent, like many other witnesses, explained that urging Ukraine to engage in "selective politically associated investigations or prosecutions" undermined the rule of law more generally:

> As a general principle, I do not believe the United States should ask other countries to engage in selective politically associated investigations or prosecutions against opponents of those in power because such selective actions undermine the rule of law, regardless of the country.[1055]

Mr. Kent agreed that pressuring Ukraine to conduct political investigations is not a part of U.S. foreign policy to promote the rule of law in Ukraine and around the world.[1056] Mr. Kent concluded that the President's request for investigations "went against U.S. policy" and "would've undermined the rule of law and our longstanding policy goals in Ukraine, as in other countries, in the post-Soviet space."[1057]

These conflicting messages came to a head at a September 14 meeting between American and Ukrainian officials in Kyiv. During that meeting, Ambassador Volker advised Mr. Yermak about the "potential problems" with investigations that the Zelensky administration was contemplating into former Ukrainian President Petro Poroshenko.[1058] Mr. Yermak retorted, "what, you mean like asking us to investigate Clinton and Biden?"[1059] Ambassador Volker did not respond.[1060]

SECTION I ENDNOTES

[1] Yovanovitch Hearing Tr. at 16-17.

[2] *Kateryna Handziuk, Ukrainian Activist, Dies From Acid Attack*, New York Times (Nov. 5, 2018) (online at www.nytimes.com/2018/11/05/world/europe/kateryna-handziuk-dies-ukraine.html).

[3] Yovanovitch Hearing Tr. at 30-31.

[4] U.S. Embassy in Ukraine, Department of State, *Ambassador Yovanovitch's Remarks at a Women of Courage Reception in Honor of Kateryna Handziuk* (Apr. 24, 2019) (online at https://ua.usembassy.gov/ambassador-yovanovitchs-remarks-at-a-women-of-courage-reception-in-honor-of-kateryna-handziuk/).

[5] U.S. Embassy in Ukraine, Department of State, *Ambassador Yovanovitch's Remarks at a Women of Courage Reception in Honor of Kateryna Handziuk* (Apr. 24, 2019) (online at https://ua.usembassy.gov/ambassador-yovanovitchs-remarks-at-a-women-of-courage-reception-in-honor-of-kateryna-handziuk/).

[6] Yovanovitch Hearing Tr. at 31.

[7] *Id.* at 31-32.

[8] *Id.* at 32.

[9] *Id.* at 31.

[10] *Id.* at 31-32.

[11] *Giuliani to Join Trump's Legal Team*, New York Times (April 19, 2018) (online at www.nytimes.com/2018/04/19/us/politics/giuliani-trump.html).

[12] Letter from John M. Dowd, Counsel to Igor Fruman and Lev Parnas, to Committee Staff (Oct. 3, 2019).

[13] Department of Justice, *Lev Parnas and Igor Fruman Charged with Conspiring to Violate Straw and Foreign Donor Bans* (Oct. 10, 2019) (online at www.justice.gov/usao-sdny/pr/lev-parnas-and-igor-fruman-charged-conspiring-violate-straw-and-foreign-donor-bans).

[14] Hill Dep. Tr. at 59.

[15] Yovanovitch Dep. Tr. at 28-29.

[16] *Ukraine Ousts Victor Shokin, Top Prosecutor, and Political Stability Hangs in the Balance*, New York Times (Mar. 29, 2016) (online at www.nytimes.com/2016/03/30/world/europe/political-stability-in-the-balance-as-ukraine-ousts-top-prosecutor.html).

[17] Kent Dep. Tr. at 45.

[18] Yovanovitch Dep. Tr. at 27-28.

[19] *Id.* at 31-32.

[20] *Id.* at 21.

[21] *Id.* at 32-33, 38 ("I think that he felt that I and the embassy were effective at helping Ukrainians who wanted reform, Ukrainians who wanted to fight against corruption, and he did not – you know, that was not in his interest.").

[22] *Id.* at 30.

[23] Holmes Dep. Tr. at 14.

[24] Kent-Taylor Hearing Tr. at 25.

[25] *Id.* at 132.

[26] Morrison-Volker Hearing Tr. at 27.

[27] Nickolay Kapitonenko, an advisor to the Ukrainian Parliament's Foreign Policy Committee, described Giuliani as a "mythical link to the U.S." who is viewed as "an extension of Trump." *Giuliani Sits at the Center of the Ukraine Controversy*, Wall Street Journal (Sept. 26, 2019) (online at www.wsj.com/articles/giuliani-sits-at-the-center-of-the-ukraine-controversy-11569546774); David Sakvarelidze, a former Ukrainian deputy prosecutor general, stated, "Lutsenko was trying to save his political skin by pretending to be Trumpist at the end of his career." *Meet the Ukrainian Ex-Prosecutor Behind the Impeachment Furor*, New York Times (Oct. 5, 2019) (online at www.nytimes.com/2019/10/05/world/europe/ukraine-prosecutor-trump.html).

[28] Yovanovitch Dep. Tr. at 30.

[29] Donald J. Trump, Twitter (Jan. 17, 2019) (online at https://twitter.com/realdonaldtrump/status/1086096691613323265) ("Gregg Jarrett: 'Mueller's prosecutors knew the 'Dossier' was the product of bias and deception.' It was a Fake, just like so much news coverage in our Country. Nothing but a Witch Hunt, from beginning to end!").

[30] Office of the Director of National Intelligence, *Background to "Assessing Russian Activities and Intentions in Recent US Elections": The Analytic Process and Cyber Incident Attribution* (Jan. 6, 2017) (online at www.dni.gov/files/documents/ICA_2017_01.pdf); Senate Select Committee on Intelligence, *Russian Active Measures Campaigns and Interference in the 2016 U.S. Election* (May 8, 2018) (online at www.intelligence.senate.gov/publications/report-select-committee-intelligence-united-states-senate-russian-active-measures); House Permanent Select Committee on Intelligence, *Report on Russian Active Measures* (Mar. 22, 2018) (online at https://docs.house.gov/meetings/IG/IG00/20180322/108023/HRPT-115-1_1-p1-U3.pdf); House Permanent Select Committee on Intelligence, *Minority Views* (Mar. 26, 2018) (online at https://intelligence.house.gov/uploadedfiles/20180411_-_final_-_hpsci_minority_views_on_majority_report.pdf).

[31] *President Trump's Former National Security Advisor 'Deeply Disturbed' by Ukraine Scandal: 'Whole World Is Watching,'* ABC News (Sept. 29, 2019) (online at https://abcnews.go.com/Politics/president-trumps-national-security-advisor-deeply-disturbed-ukraine/story?id=65925477).

[32] *Charges of Ukrainian Meddling? A Russian Operation, U.S. Intelligence Says*, New York Times (Nov. 22, 2019) (online at www.nytimes.com/2019/11/22/us/politics/ukraine-russia-interference.html).

[33] Hill-Holmes Hearing Tr. at 56-57.

[34] Kent Dep. Tr. at 45.

[35] Volker Transcribed Interview Tr. at 330.

[36] *Id.* at 330; *Explainer: Biden, Allies, Pushed Out Ukrainian Prosecutor Because He Didn't Pursue Corruption Cases*, USA Today (Oct. 3, 2019) (online at www.usatoday.com/story/news/politics/2019/10/03/what-really-happened-when-biden-forced-out-ukraines-top-prosecutor/3785620002/).

[37] *See, e.g.*, *Ukraine Prosecutor Says No Evidence of Wrongdoing by Bidens*, Bloomberg (May 16, 2019) (online at www.bloomberg.com/news/articles/2019-05-16/ukraine-prosecutor-says-no-evidence-of-wrongdoing-by-bidens) ("Hunter Biden did not violate any Ukrainian laws -- at least as of now, we do not see any wrongdoing. A company can pay however much it wants to its board … Biden was definitely not involved … We do not have any grounds to think that there was any wrongdoing starting from 2014.").

[38] Notes of Call with Viktor Shokin (Jan. 23, 2019); *Ukraine Prosecutor Says No Evidence of Wrongdoing by Bidens*, Bloomberg (May 16, 2019) (online at www.bloomberg.com/news/articles/2019-05-16/ukraine-prosecutor-says-no-evidence-of-wrongdoing-by-bidens).

[39] *Giuliani Pursued Business in Ukraine While Pushing for Inquiries for Trump*, New York Times (Nov. 27, 2019) (online at www.nytimes.com/2019/11/27/nyregion/giuliani-ukraine-business-trump.html); *Ukraine Prosecutor Says No Evidence of Wrongdoing by Bidens*, Bloomberg (May 16, 2019) (online at www.bloomberg.com/news/articles/2019-05-16/ukraine-prosecutor-says-no-evidence-of-wrongdoing-by-bidens).

[40] Notes of Meeting with Yuriy Lutsenko (Jan. 25, 2019); *Ukraine Prosecutor Says No Evidence of Wrongdoing by Bidens*, Bloomberg (May 16, 2019) (online at www.bloomberg.com/news/articles/2019-05-16/ukraine-prosecutor-says-no-evidence-of-wrongdoing-by-bidens).

[41] *Giuliani Pursued Business in Ukraine While Pushing for Inquiries for Trump*, New York Times (Nov. 27, 2019) (online at www.nytimes.com/2019/11/27/nyregion/giuliani-ukraine-business-trump.html).

[42] Rudy Giuliani, Twitter (Oct. 23, 2019) (online at https://twitter.com/RudyGiuliani/status/1187168034835894272).

[43] Rudy Giuliani, Twitter (Oct. 30, 2019) (online at https://twitter.com/RudyGiuliani/status/1189667101079932928).

[44] Hill-Holmes Hearing Tr. at 19.

[45] *As Russia Collusion Fades, Ukrainian Plot to Help Clinton Emerges*, The Hill (Mar. 20, 2019) (online at https://thehill.com/opinion/campaign/435029-as-russia-collusion-fades-ukrainian-plot-to-help-clinton-emerges).

[46] *Ukraine Prosecutor General Lutsenko Admits U.S. Ambassador Didn't Give Him a Do Not Prosecute List*, The Ukrainian (Apr. 18, 2019) (online at www.unian.info/politics/10520715-ukraine-prosecutor-general-lutsenko-admits-u-s-ambassador-didn-t-give-him-a-do-not-prosecute-list.html).

[47] *As Russia Collusion Fades, Ukrainian Plot to Help Clinton Emerges*, The Hill (Mar. 20, 2019) (online at https://thehill.com/opinion/campaign/435029-as-russia-collusion-fades-ukrainian-plot-to-help-clinton-emerges).

[48] Yovanovitch Dep. Tr. at 21, 37.

[49] AT&T Document Production, Bates ATTHPSCI_20190930_00768- ATTHPSCI_20190930_00772, ATTHPSCI_20190930_00775. The Committee did not subpoena the call detail records of any member of Congress or staff, including Ranking Member Devin Nunes, nor of any journalist, including John Solomon. To the extent that congressional members or staff, or journalists, appear in the report, call records indicate that they were in contact with individuals of interest to the investigation. A subpoena served to the White House requesting certain call records was obstructed in full by President Trump. Nevertheless, the Committee's investigation into these and other call records remains ongoing.

[50] *As Russia Collusion Fades, Ukrainian Plot to Help Clinton Emerges*, The Hill (Mar. 20, 2019) (online at https://thehill.com/opinion/campaign/435029-as-russia-collusion-fades-ukrainian-plot-to-help-clinton-emerges).

[51] Department of Justice, *Lev Parnas and Igor Fruman Charged with Conspiring to Violate Straw and Foreign Donor Bans* (Oct. 10, 2019) (online at www.justice.gov/usao-sdny/pr/lev-parnas-and-igor-fruman-charged-conspiring-violate-straw-and-foreign-donor-bans) (alleging that in May and June 2018, Mr. Parnas sought the assistance of an unnamed congressman in causing the removal or recall of the then-U.S. ambassador to Ukraine).

[52] AT&T Document Production, Bates ATTHPSCI_20190930_00775.

[53] Donald J. Trump, Twitter (Mar. 20, 2019) (online at https://twitter.com/realdonaldtrump/status/1108559080204001280).

[54] Rudy Giuliani, Twitter (Mar. 22, 2019) (online at https://twitter.com/RudyGiuliani/status/1109117167176466432); *Giuliani Slams Mueller Leak*, Fox News (Apr. 7, 2019) (online at https://www.foxnews.com/transcript/giuliani-slams-mueller-leak).

[55] Donald Trump, Jr., Twitter (Mar. 24, 2019) (online at https://twitter.com/donaldjtrumpjr/status/1109850575926108161).

[56] Kent Dep. Tr. at 57-58.

[57] *Id*. at 178.

[58] Yovanovitch Dep. Tr. at 62.

[59] Hale Dep. Tr. at 37-38.

[60] *Id*. at 99-100.

[61] Yovanovitch Dep. Tr. at 63-64.

[62] Hale Dep. Tr. at 27.

[63] Yovanovitch Dep. Tr. at 124.

[64] *Id.* at 267-268.

[65] *Id.* at 268.

[66] Email from [Redacted] to S_All (Mar. 26, 2019) (online at www.americanoversight.org/wp-content/uploads/2019/11/AO_State_Ukraine_Docs_11-22.pdf); Email from Operations Center to [Redacted] (Mar. 29, 2019) (online at www.americanoversight.org/wp-content/uploads/2019/11/AO_State_Ukraine_Docs_11-22.pdf). (The same State Department records show that Secretary Pompeo was scheduled to have a secure call with Rep. Nunes on April 1, 2019.); Email from Operations Center to [Redacted] (Mar. 29, 2019) (online at www.americanoversight.org/wp-content/uploads/2019/11/AO_State_Ukraine_Docs_11-22.pdf); Email from [Redacted] to S_Scheduling (Mar. 28, 2019) (online at www.americanoversight.org/wp-content/uploads/2019/11/AO_State_Ukraine_Docs_11-22.pdf); Hale Dep. Tr. at 34 (stating that Secretary Pompeo spoke with Mr. Giuliani on March 28 and March 29); AT&T Document Production, Bates ATTHPSCI_20190930_02034- ATTHPSCI_20190930_02053, ATTHPSCI_20190930_03538-ATTHPSCI_20190930_03539.

[67] *Joe Biden's 2020 Ukrainian Nightmare: A Closed Probe is Revived*, The Hill (Apr. 1, 2019) (online at https://thehill.com/opinion/white-house/436816-joe-bidens-2020-ukrainian-nightmare-a-closed-probe-is-revived).

[68] Donald Trump, Jr., Twitter (Apr. 2, 2019) (online at https://twitter.com/donaldjtrumpjr/status/1113046659456528385).

[69] AT&T Document Production, Bates ATTHPSCI_20190930_00848-ATTHPSCI_20190930_00884. Mr. Parnas also had an aborted call that lasted 5 seconds on April 5, 2019 with an aide to Rep. Devin Nunes on the Intelligence Committee, Derek Harvey. *Id.* at Bates ATTHPSCI_20190930_00876. Call records obtained by the Committees show that Mr. Parnas and Mr. Harvey had connected previously, including a four minute 42 second call on January 31, 2019, a one minute 7 second call on February 4, and a one minute 37 second call on February 7, 2019. *Id.* at Bates ATTHPSCI_20190930_00617, ATTHPSCI_20190930_00630, ATTHPSCI_20190930_00641. As explained later in this Chapter, Rep. Nunes would connect separately by phone on April 10 and 11 with Mr. Giuliani, and on April 12 with Mr. Parnas. *Id.* at Bates ATTHPSCI_20190930_00913-ATTHPSCI_20190930_00914; ATTHPSCI_20190930-02125, ATTHPSCI_20190930-02129.

[70] *Ukrainian to US Prosecutors: Why Don't You Want Our Evidence on Democrats?*, The Hill (Apr. 7, 2019) (online at https://thehill.com/opinion/white-house/437719-ukrainian-to-us-prosecutors-why-dont-you-want-our-evidence-on-democrats).

[71] *Id.*

[72] *Id.*

[73] *Id.*

[74] *Giuliani Slams Mueller Leak*, Fox News (Apr. 7, 2019) (online at www.foxnews.com/transcript/giuliani-slams-mueller-leak).

[75] Rudy Giuliani, Twitter (Apr. 8, 2019) (online at https://twitter.com/RudyGiuliani/status/1115171828618731520).

[76] Specifically, between April 8 and April 11, phone records show the following phone contacts:

- at least six calls between Mr. Giuliani and Mr. Parnas (longest duration approximately five minutes), AT&T Document Production, Bates ATTHPSCI_20190930-02115-ATTHPSCI_20190930-02131.
- at least four calls between Mr. Giuliani and Mr. Solomon (all on April 8, longest duration approximately one minute, 30 seconds) AT&T Document Production, Bates ATTHPSCI_20190930-02114-ATTHPSCI_20190930-02115;
- at least nine calls between Mr. Parnas and Mr. Solomon (longest duration four minutes, 39 seconds) AT&T Document Production, Bates ATTHPSCI_20190930-00885-ATTHPSCI_20190930-00906; and
- at least three calls between Mr. Parnas and Ms. Toensing (longest duration approximately six minutes), AT&T Document Production, Bates ATTHPSCI_20190930-00885-ATTHPSCI_20190930-00905.

The Committee did not subpoena the call detail records of any member of Congress or staff, including Ranking Member Devin Nunes, nor of any journalist, including John Solomon. To the extent that congressional members or staff, or journalists, appear in the report, records indicate that they were in contact with individuals of interest to the investigation. A subpoena served to the White House requesting certain call records was obstructed in full by President Trump. Nevertheless, the Committee's investigation into these and other call records remains ongoing.

[77] *Id.* at Bates ATTHPSCI_20190930-02125, ATTHPSCI_20190930-03236.

Date	Connecting Time (ET)	Duration of Call	Caller	Recipient
04/10/19	12:00:36	0:35	Giuliani, Rudy	Nunes, Devin
04/10/19	12:10:35	0:00	Nunes, Devin	Giuliani, Rudy
04/10/19	12:10:37	0:31	Nunes, Devin	Giuliani, Rudy
04/10/19	12:11:10	SMS	UNKNOWN	Giuliani, Rudy
04/10/19	12:12:35	2:50	Giuliani, Rudy	Nunes, Devin
04/10/19	12:15:38	0:00	Giuliani, Rudy	Nunes, Devin

[78] *Id.* Bates ATTHPSCI_20190930-00902.

[79] Jay Sekulow, personal counsel to President Trump, stated that the President was disappointed that Mr. diGenova and Ms. Toensing had to withdraw due to a conflict of interest, but noted that "those conflicts do not prevent them from assisting the President in other legal matters. The President looks forward to working with them." *Trump's Legal Team Remains in Disarray as New Lawyer Will No Longer Represent Him in Russia Probe*, Washington Post (Mar. 25, 2018) (online at www.washingtonpost.com/politics/in-another-blow-to-trumps-efforts-to-combat-russia-probe-digenova-will-no-longer-join-legal-team/2018/03/25/8ac8c8d2-3038-11e8-94fa-32d48460b955_story.html).

[80] For example, between April 1 and April 7, Ms. Toensing exchanged at least five calls with Mr. Parnas and two calls with Mr. Giuliani. ATTHPSCI_20190930-02089-ATTHPSCI_20190930-02110; ATTHPSCI_20190930-00871-ATTHPSCI_20190930-00884. In addition, on April 10, Ms. Toensing and Mr. Giuliani spoke for approximately six minutes, 19 seconds. AT&T Document Production, Bates ATTHPSCI_20190930-02126. Mr. diGenova and Ms. Toensing were also very active on social media in promoting these conspiracy theories as well as the false accusations against Ambassador Yovanovitch. *See, e.g.,* Ryan Saavedra, Twitter (Mar. 23, 2019) (online at https://twitter.com/RealSaavedra/status/1109546629672009728); Victoria Toensing, Twitter (Mar. 21, 2019) (online at https://twitter.com/VicToensing/status/1108751525239762944); Victoria Toensing, Twitter (Mar. 24, 2019) (online at https://twitter.com/VicToensing/status/1109882728101625856).

[81] Retainer Letter, diGenova & Toensing, LLP, Yuriy Lutsenko, and Kostiantyn Kulyk (Apr. 12, 2019); Retainer Letter, diGenova & Toensing, LLP, Viktor Shokin (Apr. 15, 2019).

[82] On April 12, less than a week after the latest piece in *The Hill*, Ms. Toensing signed a retainer agreement between diGenova & Toensing, LLP, Mr. Lutsenko, and his former deputy Kostiantyn Kulyk, two of the primary sources for Mr. Solomon's articles. The Committees obtained a copy of this document which is not signed by the Ukrainians, but a spokesman for Ms. Toensing and Mr. diGenova confirmed that the firm represented Mr. Lutsenko. *See Giuliani Weighed Doing Business with Ukrainian Government*, Wall Street Journal (Nov. 27, 2019) (online at www.wsj.com/articles/giuliani-weighed-doing-business-with-ukrainian-government-11574890951).

The first paragraph of the retainer agreement sets forth the services to be provided by diGenova & Toensing, LLP to their Ukrainian clients:

> Yurii Lutsenko and Kostiantyn Kulyk ("Clients") hereby engage the firm of diGenova & Toensing, LLP ("Firm" or "Attorneys") to represent them in connection with recovery and return to the Ukraine government of funds illegally embezzeled from that country and providing assistance to meet and discuss with United States government officials the evidence of illegal conduct in Ukraine regarding the United States, for example, interference in the 2016 U.S. elections.

See Retainer Letter, diGenova & Toensing, LLP, Yuriy Lutsenko, and Kostiantyn Kulyk (Apr. 12, 2019).

The scope of representation—which includes representing Mr. Lutsenko and Mr. Kulyk in meetings with U.S. officials regarding Ukrainian interference in the 2016 U.S. elections—mirrors the allegations reported in *The Hill*, pursued by Mr. Giuliani on behalf of President Trump, and pushed by the President on his July 25 call with President Zelensky. According to the retainer agreement, Mr. Lutsenko was to pay diGenova & Toensing, LLP $25,000 per month, plus costs, for four months for this work. *See* Retainer Letter, diGenova & Toensing, LLP, Yuriy Lutsenko, and Kostiantyn Kulyk (Apr. 12, 2019).

On April 12, the same day Ms. Toensing signed the retainer agreement with Mr. Lutsenko, phone records show contacts between Ms. Toensing, Mr. Giuliani, and Mr. Parnas, as well as contacts between Mr. Parnas and Mr. Solomon, and Mr. Parnas and Rep. Nunes. In addition, among these calls are contacts between Mr. Giuliani and a phone number associated with the Office of Management and Budget (OMB), an unidentified number ("-1"), and a phone number associated with the White House:

Date	Connecting Time (ET)	Duration of Call	Caller	Recipient	Source
04/12/19	9:48:57	0:24	Toensing, Victoria	Parnas, Lev	AT&T Document Production, Bates ATTHPSCI_20190930-00908
04/12/19	10:40:19	3:25	Parnas, Lev	Toensing, Victoria	AT&T Document Production, Bates ATTHPSCI_20190930-00909
04/12/19	11:05:25	0:03	OMB-Associated Phone Number	Giuliani, Rudy	AT&T Document Production, Bates ATTHPSCI_20190930-02134
04/12/19	11:05:39	12:10	"-1"	Giuliani, Rudy	AT&T Document Production, Bates ATTHPSCI_20190930-02134
04/12/19	13:13:49	0:12	Giuliani, Rudy	White House Phone Number	AT&T Document Production, Bates ATTHPSCI_20190930-02135
04/12/19	13:18:46	0:07	Toensing, Victoria	Giuliani, Rudy	AT&T Document Production, Bates ATTHPSCI_20190930-02135
04/12/19	13:26:54	0:24	Giuliani Partners	Parnas, Lev	AT&T Document Production, Bates ATTHPSCI_20190930-00911

04/12/19	14:11:22	0:03	"-1"	Giuliani, Rudy	AT&T Document Production, Bates ATTHPSCI_20190930-02136
04/12/19	14:11:27	0:03	OMB-Associated Phone Number	Giuliani, Rudy	AT&T Document Production, Bates ATTHPSCI_20190930-02136
04/12/19	14:17:46	0:07	Toensing, Victoria	Parnas, Lev	AT&T Document Production, Bates ATTHPSCI_20190930-00912
04/12/19	15:09:22	0:02	Parnas, Lev	Giuliani, Rudy	AT&T Document Production, Bates ATTHPSCI_20190930-00912
04/12/19	15:09:32	0:01	Parnas, Lev	Giuliani, Rudy	AT&T Document Production, Bates ATTHPSCI_20190930-00912
04/12/19	15:16:09	1:38	Parnas, Lev	Solomon, John	AT&T Document Production, Bates ATTHPSCI_20190930-00912
04/12/19	15:48:09	0:03	OMB-Associated Phone Number	Giuliani, Rudy	AT&T Document Production, Bates ATTHPSCI_20190930-02137
04/12/19	16:10:49	0:00	Parnas, Lev	Giuliani, Rudy	AT&T Document Production, Bates ATTHPSCI_20190930-00913
04/12/19	16:10:51	0:02	Parnas, Lev	Giuliani, Rudy	AT&T Document Production, Bates ATTHPSCI_20190930-00913
4/12/19	16:12:53	1:00	Parnas, Lev	Nunes, Devin	AT&T Document Production, Bates ATTHPSCI_20190930-00913
04/12/19	16:54:11	0:00	Nunes, Devin	Parnas, Lev	AT&T Document Production, Bates ATTHPSCI_20190930-00913
04/12/19	16:54:13	0:02	Nunes, Devin	Parnas, Lev	AT&T Document Production, Bates ATTHPSCI_20190930-00913
04/12/19	17:07:20	1:27	Parnas, Lev	Giuliani, Rudy	AT&T Document Production, Bates ATTHPSCI_20190930-00913

04/12/19	17:17:36	7:52	Sekulow, Jay	Giuliani, Rudy	AT&T Document Production, Bates ATTHPSCI_20190930-03565
04/12/19	17:24:05	1:49	Parnas, Lev	Solomon, John	AT&T Document Production, Bates ATTHPSCI_20190930-00914
04/12/19	17:26:48	0:28	Parnas, Lev	Solomon, John	AT&T Document Production, Bates ATTHPSCI_20190930-00914
04/12/19	17:30:19	8:34	Parnas, Lev	Nunes, Devin	AT&T Document Production, Bates ATTHPSCI_20190930-00914
04/12/19	17:39:25	0:53	Parnas, Lev	Solomon, John	AT&T Document Production, Bates ATTHPSCI_20190930-00914
04/12/19	19:56:43	5:03	Giuliani, Rudy	White House Phone Number	AT&T Document Production, Bates ATTHPSCI_20190930-02139

As part of the investigation, the Committees uncovered contact between Mr. Giuliani and a landline number with a prefix associated with the Office of Management and Budget within the Executive Office of the President, according to public directories. This number appears to obscure the identity of outgoing calls, but does not itself accept incoming calls. The Committees continue to investigate the originator(s) of these calls, including to determine whether other offices or landlines within the White House may also show up with the same landline number when outgoing calls are made and to clarify who at the White House spoke to Mr. Giuliani at these key points in time under investigation. A subpoena served to the White House requesting certain call records was obstructed in full by President Trump. Nevertheless, the Committee's investigation into these and other call records remains ongoing.

Mr. Lutsenko and Mr. Kulyk were not the only Ukrainians who appear to have engaged with diGenova & Toensing, LLP. On April 15, Ms. Toensing signed another retainer agreement between diGenova & Toensing, LLP and former Prosecutor General Viktor Shokin. Again, the Committees' copy is not signed by Mr. Shokin. A spokesman for Ms. Toensing and Mr. diGenova acknowledged that the firm represented "Ukrainian whistleblowers," but claimed that the identities of those clients (other that Mr. Lutsenko) are protected by attorney-client privilege. *See Giuliani Weighed Doing Business with Ukrainian Government*, Wall Street Journal (Nov. 27, 2019) (online at www.wsj.com/articles/giuliani-weighed-doing-business-with-ukrainian-government-11574890951).

The first paragraph of the retainer agreement outlined the services to be rendered:

Viktor Shokin ("Client") hereby engaged the firm diGenova & Toensing, LLP ("Firm" or "Attorneys") to represent him for the purpose of collecting evidence regarding his March 2016 firing as Prosecutor General of Ukraine and the role of then-Vice President Joe Biden in such firing, and presenting such evidence to U.S. and foreign authorities.

See Retainer Letter, diGenova & Toensing, LLP, Viktor Shokin (Apr. 15, 2019).

The subject matter of the agreement—the activities of Vice President Biden—again echo Mr. Solomon's pieces in *The Hill*, conspiracy theories spread by Mr. Giuliani on behalf of President Trump, and the President's statements about Vice President Biden on his July 25 call with President Zelensky.

[83] AT&T Document Production, Bates ATTHPSCI_20190930-00947-ATTHPSCI_20190930-00950.

[84] *Id. at* Bates ATTHPSCI_20190930-02222-ATTHPSCI_20190930-02223.

Date	Connecting Time (ET)	Duration of Call	Caller	Recipient
04/23/19	14:00:56	1:50	Giuliani. Rudy	Parnas. Lev
04/23/19	14:15:18	0:18	Giuliani. Rudy	White House Phone Number
04/23/19	14:15:43	0:11	Giuliani. Rudy	White House Phone Number
04/23/19	15:20:17	0:11	Giuliani. Rudy	White House Phone Number
04/23/19	15:50:23	8:28	"-1"	Giuliani. Rudy

[85] AT&T Document Production, Bates ATTHPSCI_20190930-02224.

[86] Rudy Giuliani, Twitter (Apr. 23, 2019) (online at https://twitter.com/RudyGiuliani/status/1120798794692612097).

[87] *Giuliani Fires Back at Hillary Clinton's Remarks on Mueller Probe*, Fox News (Apr. 24, 2019) (online at www.youtube.com/watch?v=FDtg8z12Q7s&feature=youtu.be).

[88] AT&T Document Production. Bates ATTHPSCI_20190930-02229- ATTHPSCI_20190930-02237.

Date	Connecting Time (ET)	Duration of Call	Caller	Recipient
04/24/19	7:17:48	0:42	OMB-Associated Phone Number	Giuliani. Rudy
04/24/19	7:47:57	0:37	Giuliani. Rudy	White House Phone Number
04/24/19	7:48:39	0:21	Giuliani. Rudy	White House Phone Number
04/24/19	7:49:00	0:31	OMB-Associated Phone Number	Giuliani. Rudy
04/24/19	7:49:00	0:20	Giuliani. Rudy	White House Phone Number
04/24/19	7:49:35	4:53	Giuliani. Rudy	White House Phone Number
04/24/19	7:54:52	0:24	Giuliani. Rudy	White House Phone Number
04/24/19	13:03:50	13:44	OMB-Associated Phone Number	Giuliani. Rudy
04/24/19	16:42:52	8:00	Parnas. Lev	Giuliani. Rudy
04/24/19	18:38:57	0:44	Giuliani. Rudy	White House Phone Number
04/24/19	18:42:43	8:42	"-1"	Giuliani. Rudy

| 04/24/19 | 20:09:14 | 0:06 | Giuliani, Rudy | White House Phone Number |
| 04/24/19 | 20:12:08 | 3:15 | White House Phone Number | Giuliani, Rudy |

[89] Yovanovitch Hearing Tr. at 31-32.

[90] Yovanovitch Dep. Tr. at 22.

[91] Yovanovitch Hearing Tr. at 21-22.

[92] Yovanovitch Dep. Tr. at 129.

[93] *Id.* at 139.

[94] Yovanovitch Hearing Tr. at 28.

[95] Sondland Hearing Tr. at 21.

[96] Yovanovitch Hearing Tr. at 131-132.

[97] Hale Dep. Tr. at 16-17, 112-113; Yovanovitch Hearing Tr. at 21.

[98] Cooper-Hale Hearing Tr. at 63 ("I only met her when I took this job, but immediately I understood that we had an exceptional officer doing exceptional work at a very critical embassy in Kyiv. And during my visits to Kyiv, I was very impressed by what she was doing there, to the extent that I asked her if she'd be willing to stay, if that was a possibility, because we had a gap coming up.").

[99] *Id.* at 64.

[100] *Biography of Marie L. Yovanovitch*, Department of State (online at https://2009-2017.state.gov/r/pa/ei/biog/261588.htm).

[101] McKinley Transcribed Interview Tr. at 37.

[102] Reeker Dep. Tr. at 26.

[103] Kent Dep. Tr. at 188-189.

[104] Yovanovitch Hearing Tr. at 18-19.

[105] *Id.*

[106] Hill-Holmes Hearing Tr. at 18-19, 45-46.

[107] Holmes Dep. Tr. at 142.

[108] *What "Corruption" Means in the Impeachment Hearings*, New Yorker (Nov. 16, 2019) (online at www.newyorker.com/news/our-columnists/the-corruption-of-the-word-corruption-and-so-much-else-amid-the-impeachment-hearings).

[109] 22 U.S.C. § 3941.

[110] Yovanovitch Hearing Tr. at 110-111.

[111] Ambassador Yovanovitch said: "Although then and now I have always understood that I served at the pleasure of the President, I still find it difficult to comprehend that foreign and private interests were able to undermine U.S. interests in this way. Individuals who apparently felt stymied by our efforts to promote stated U.S. policy against corruption, that is, to do our mission, were able to successfully conduct a campaign of disinformation against a sitting ambassador using unofficial back channels. As various witnesses have recounted, they shared baseless allegations with the President and convinced him to remove his ambassador despite the fact that the State Department fully understood that the allegations were false and the sources highly suspect." Yovanovitch Hearing Tr. at 22.

[112] Hill-Holmes Hearing Tr. at 78-79.

[113] Yovanovitch Dep. Tr. at 313-314.

[114] Yovanovitch Hearing Tr. at 22.

[115] Kent-Taylor Hearing Tr. at 25.

[116] Kent. Dep. Tr. at 131-132.

[117] Kent-Taylor Hearing Tr. at 31-32.

[118] *Comedian Volodymyr Zelensky Unseats Incumbent in Ukraine's Presidential Election, Exit Polls Show*, Washington Post (Apr. 21, 2019) (online at www.washingtonpost.com/world/as-ukraine-votes-in-presidential-runoff-a-comedian-looks-to-unseat-the-incumbent/2019/04/21/b7d69a38-603f-11e9-bf24-db4b9fb62aa2_story.html).

[119] *Id.*

[120] The White House, *Memorandum of Telephone Conversation* (Apr. 21, 2019) (online at https://assets.documentcloud.org/documents/6550349/First-Trump-Ukraine-Call.pdf).

[121] *Id.*

[122] *Conflicting White House accounts of 1st Trump-Zelenskiy call*, Associated Press (Nov. 15, 2019) (online at https://apnews.com/2f3c9910e0a14ec08d6d76ed93148059).

[123] The White House, *Memorandum of Telephone Conversation* (Apr. 21, 2019) (online at https://assets.documentcloud.org/documents/6550349/First-Trump-Ukraine-Call.pdf).

[124] *Id.*

[125] *Id.*

[126] *Id.*

[127] *Id.*

[128] *Id.*

[129] *Id.*

[130] *Id.*

[131] Williams Dep. Tr. at 36.

[132] *Id.* at 37.

[133] *Id.* at 36.

[134] *Fox & Friends*, Fox News (Apr. 24, 2019) (online at www.youtube.com/watch?v=FDtg8z12Q7s#action=share).

[135] *Why Giuliani Singled Out 2 Ukrainian Oligarchs to Help Look for Dirt*, New York Times (Nov. 25, 2019) (online at www.nytimes.com/2019/11/25/us/giuliani-ukraine-oligarchs.html).

[136] *Ukraine's Unlikely President, Promising a New Style of Politics, Gets a Taste of Trump's Swamp*, New Yorker (Oct. 25, 2019) (online at www.newyorker.com/magazine/2019/11/04/how-trumps-emissaries-put-pressure-on-ukraines-new-president).

[137] *Why Giuliani Singled Out 2 Ukrainian Oligarchs to Help Look for Dirt*, New York Times (Nov. 25, 2019) (online at www.nytimes.com/2019/11/25/us/giuliani-ukraine-oligarchs.html).

[138] AT&T Document Production, Bates ATTHPSCI_20190930_00947; ATTHPSCI_20190930_00949; ATTHPSCI_20190930_02222; ATTHPSCI_20190930_02223.

[139] *Joe Biden Announces 2020 Run for President, After Months of Hesitation*, New York Times (Apr. 25, 2019) (online at www.nytimes.com/2019/04/25/us/politics/joe-biden-2020-announcement.html).

[140] *How the Obama White House Engaged Ukraine to Give Russia Collusion Narrative an Early Boost*, The Hill (Apr. 25, 2019) (online at https://thehill.com/opinion/white-house/440730-how-the-obama-white-house-engaged-ukraine-to-give-russia-collusion).

[141] Holmes Dep. Tr. at 17.

[142] *Id*. at 116.

[143] *Id*.

[144] AT&T Document Production, Bates ATTHPSCI_20190930_02245.

[145] *Id*.

[146] *Sean Hannity Interviews Trump on Biden, Russia Probe, FISA Abuse, Comey*, Fox News (Apr. 26, 2019) (online at www.realclearpolitics.com/video/2019/04/26/full_video_sean_hannity_interviews_trump_on_biden_russia_probe_fisa_abuse_comey html).

[147] Holmes Dep. Tr. at 55-56.

[148] *Sean Hannity Interviews Trump on Biden, Russia Probe, FISA Abuse, Comey*, Fox News (Apr. 26, 2019) (online at www.realclearpolitics.com/video/2019/04/26/full_video_sean_hannity_interviews_trump_on_biden_russia_probe_fisa_abuse_comey html). As discussed later in this report, on the morning of September 25, 2019, the Department of Justice would quickly issue a statement after President Trump released the record of his July 25 call with President Zelensky. The statement asserted that that Attorney General Barr had not engaged on Ukraine matters at the President's request:

> The President has not spoken with the Attorney General about having Ukraine investigate anything relating to former Vice President Biden or his son. The President has not asked the Attorney General to contact Ukraine—on this or any other matter. The Attorney General has not communicated with Ukraine—on this or any other subject.

[149] *Cleaning Up Ukraine in the Shadow of Trump*, Financial Times (Nov. 28, 2019) (online at www ft.com/content/eb8e4004-1059-11ea-a7e6-62bf4f9e548a).

[150] *Id*.

[151] *Biden Faces Conflict of Interest Questions That Are Being Promoted by Trump and Allies*, New York Times (May 1, 2019) (online at www.nytimes.com/2019/05/01/us/politics/biden-son-ukraine.html).

[152] *Transcript: Fox News Interview with President Trump*, Fox News (May 7, 2019) (online at www.foxnews.com/politics/transcript-fox-news-interview-with-president-trump).

[153] *Id*.

[154] *Foreign Affairs Issue Launch with Former Vice President Joe Biden*, Council on Foreign Relations (Jan. 23, 2018) (online at: www.cfr.org/event/foreign-affairs-issue-launch-former-vice-president-joe-biden).

[155] *Ukraine Ousts Viktor Shokin, Top Prosecutor, and Political Stability Hangs in the Balance*, New York Times (Mar. 29, 2016) (online at www.nytimes.com/2016/03/30/world/europe/political-stability-in-the-balance-as-ukraine-ousts-top-prosecutor.html).

[156] Yovanovitch Hearing Tr. at 50; Kent-Taylor Hearing Tr. at 115.

[157] *Trump Says He'd Consider Accepting Information from Foreign Governments on His Opponents*, Washington Post (June 12, 2019) (online at www.washingtonpost.com/politics/trump-says-hed-consider-accepting-dirt-from-foreign-governments-on-his-opponents/2019/06/12/b84ba860-8d5c-11e9-8f69-a2795fca3343_story.html).

[158] AT&T Document Production, Bates ATTHPSCI_20190930_02313.

[159] *Id*. at Bates ATTHPSCI_20190930_02314; ATTHPSCI_20190930_02316; ATTHPSCI_20190930_02318; ATTHPSCI_20190930_01000.

[160] Kent Dep. Tr. at 137.

[161] *Id.*

[162] *Id.*

[163] *Rudy Giuliani Plans Ukraine Trip to Push for Inquiries That Could Help Trump*, New York Times (May 9, 2019) (online at www.nytimes.com/2019/05/09/us/politics/giuliani-ukraine-trump.html).

[164] *Id.*

[165] *Id.*

[166] *Id.*

[167] *Id.*

[168] *Id.*

[169] *Id.*

[170] *Trump's Interest in Stirring Ukraine Investigations Sows Confusion in Kiev*, Washington Post (May 11, 2019) (online at www.washingtonpost.com/world/europe/trumps-interest-stirring-ukraine-investigations-sows-confusion-in-kiev/2019/05/11/cb94f7f4-73ea-11e9-9331-30bc5836f48e_story.html).

[171] AT&T Document Production, Bates ATTHPSCI_20190930_02321; ATTHPSCI_20190930_02322.

[172] AT&T Document Production, Bates ATTHPSCI_20190930_02320, 02321, 02322, 02323, 03612.

[173] AT&T Document Production, Bates ATTHPSCI_20190930_03614; ATTHPSCI_20190930_02326; ATTHPSCI_20190930_02327; ATTHPSCI_20190930_03614.

[174] Rudy Giuliani, Twitter (May 9, 2019) (online at https://twitter.com/RudyGiuliani/status/1126701386224156673).

[175] *Giuliani: "Massive Collusion" Between DNC, Obama Admin, Clinton People & Ukraine To Create False Info About Trump*, Real Clear Politics (May 10, 2019) (online at www.realclearpolitics.com/video/2019/05/10/giuliani_massive_collusion_between_dnc_obama_admin_clinton_people__ukraine_to_create_false_info_about_trump.html).

[176] Rudy Giuliani, Twitter (May 10, 2019) (online at https://twitter.com/rudygiuliani/status/1126858889209831424?lang=en).

[177] AT&T Document Production, Bates ATTHPSCI_20190930_02334.

[178] Volker Transcribed Interview Tr. at 227; *see also id.* at 32-33, 36 (describing the allegations).

[179] *Id.* at 227.

[180] AT&T Document Production, Bates ATTHPSCI_20190930_02334.

[181] AT&T Document Production, Bates ATTHPSCI_20190930_02335.

[182] *Id.*

[183] *Id.*

[184] *Trump: Discussing a Biden Probe with Barr Would Be 'Appropriate,'* Politico (May 10, 2019) (online at www.politico.com/story/2019/05/10/trump-biden-ukraine-barr-1317601).

[185] *Trump Denies Sending Rudy Giuliani to Ukraine to Push Biden, Election Probes*, CNBC (Nov. 27, 2019) (online at www.cnbc.com/2019/11/27/trump-denies-sending-rudy-giuliani-to-ukraine-to-push-biden-election-probes.html).

[186] *Remarks by President Trump and President Niinistö of the Republic of Finland in Joint Press Conference*, The White House (Oct. 2, 2019) (online at www.whitehouse.gov/briefings-statements/remarks-president-trump-president-niinisto-republic-finland-joint-press-conference/).

[187] *Remarks by President Trump before Marine One Departure*, The White House (Oct. 4, 2019) (online at www.whitehouse.gov/briefings-statements/remarks-president-trump-marine-one-departure-68/).

[188] *Giuliani: I Didn't Go to Ukraine to Start an Investigation, There Already Was One*, Fox News (May 11, 2019) (online at https://video.foxnews.com/v/6035385372001/#sp=show-clips).

[189] *Trump: Discussing a Biden Probe with Barr Would Be 'Appropriate'*, Politico (May 10, 2019) (online at www.politico.com/story/2019/05/10/trump-biden-ukraine-barr-1317601) (documenting Giuliani text message).

[190] *Id.*

[191] Donald J. Trump, Twitter (May 3, 2019) (online at https://twitter.com/realDonaldTrump/status/1124359594418032640)

[192] Kent Dep. Tr. at 338-339.

[193] *Remarks by President Trump and Prime Minister Orban of Hungary Before Bilateral Meeting*, The White House (May 13, 2019) (online at www.whitehouse.gov/briefings-statements/remarks-president-trump-prime-minister-orban-hungary-bilateral-meeting/).

[194] *In Hungary, a Freewheeling Trump Ambassador Undermines U.S. Diplomats*, New York Times (Oct. 22, 2019) (online at www.nytimes.com/2019/10/22/world/europe/david-cornstein-hungary-trump-orban.html); *Hungarian Prime Minister Earns Rare Rebuke from European Bloc that Has Long Backed Him*, Washington Post (Mar. 20, 2019) (online at www.washingtonpost.com/world/europe/hungarys-orban-earns-rare-rebuke-from-european-bloc-that-has-long-backed-him/2019/03/20/83be110a-4b17-11e9-8cfc-2c5d0999c21e_story.html).

[195] Kent Dep. Tr. at 339.

[196] *Remarks by President Trump and Prime Minister Orban of Hungary Before Bilateral Meeting*, The White House (May 13, 2019) (online at www.whitehouse.gov/briefings-statements/remarks-president-trump-prime-minister-orban-hungary-bilateral-meeting/).

[197] Kent Dep. Tr. at 253.

[198] *Id.* at 254.

[199] Williams Dep. Tr. at 37-38.

[200] Vindman-Williams Hearing Tr. at 14. Other witnesses testified that Vice President Pence may not have been able to attend on account of scheduling issues. *See* Hill Dep. Tr. at 316 ("there was a lot of scheduling issues" regarding the attempts to schedule the Vice President's participation in the delegation); Kent Dep. Tr. at 189-191 (Vice President Pence was not available); Volker Transcribed Interview Tr. at 288-290, 293 (Volker "wasn't surprised" Pence could not make it and assumed it was a matter of scheduling). However, Ms. Williams was the only staff member in the Office of the Vice President to testify before the Committees, and the only witness to testify to having heard an explanation from Vice President Pence's staff about why Vice President Pence did not attend the inauguration.

[201] Williams Dep. Tr. at 39.

[202] Holmes Dep. Tr. at 37.

[203] *Id.*

[204] Rudy Giuliani, Twitter (May 18, 2019) (online at https://twitter.com/RudyGiuliani/status/1129761193755910144)

[205] *Kolomoisky: We Called Varkuch and Asked: 'Do You Support Zelensky or No?'*, Pravda (May 27, 2019) (online at www.pravda.com.ua/rus/articles/2019/05/27/7216183/).

[206] *Id.*

[207] Holmes Dep. Tr. at 16.

[208] Volker Transcribed Interview Tr. at 288-290; Vindman Dep. Tr. at 125.

[209] Holmes Dep. Tr. at 101.

[210] *Id.* at 18.

[211] *Id.* 17-18.

[212] *Id.* at 18.

[213] *Id.*

[214] Hill-Holmes Hearing Tr. at 61.

[215] Vindman-Williams Hearing Tr. at 26.

[216] Hill-Holmes Hearing Tr. at 61.

[217] Vindman-Williams Hearing Tr. at 26.

[218] *Id.*

[219] *Id.*; David Holmes separately testified that Lt. Col. Vindman "made a general point about the importance of Ukraine to our national security, and he said it's very important that the Zelensky administration stay out of U.S. domestic politics." Hill-Holmes Hearing Tr. at 61.

[220] Volker Transcribed Interview Tr. at 30.

[221] *Id.* at 29-30.

[222] Kent Dep. Tr. at 193.

[223] Anderson Dep. Tr. at 15, 54. Ambassador Sondland testified that he did not specifically recall who arranged the May 23 meeting and conjectured that "either Rick Perry or I reached out to someone at the NSC saying: Doesn't the President want a briefing about the inauguration. And I think—I think it was Perry, if I recall correctly, that got it nailed down." Sondland Dep. Tr. at 87.

[224] Volker Transcribed Interview Tr. at 29, 303; Vindman Dep. Tr. at 168.

[225] Hill Dep. Tr. at 311.

[226] *Id.* at 308.

[227] *Id.*

[228] *Id.* at 309-310.

[229] *Id.*

[230] *Id.*

[231] *Nunes Ally Kash Patel Who Fought Russia Probe Gets Senior White House National Security Job*, The Daily Beast (July 31, 2019) (online at www.thedailybeast.com/kash-patel-devin-nunes-ally-who-fought-russia-probe-gets-senior-white-house-national-security-job).

[232] Volker Transcribed Interview Tr. at 304.

[233] Sondland Dep. Tr. at 25.

[234] *Id.*

[235] Volker Transcribed Interview Tr. at 304.

[236] Sondland Dep. Tr. at 337; Volker Transcribed Interview Tr. at 304; Hill Dep. Tr. at 320-321 (describing Volker's readout); Croft Dep. Tr. at 90 (describing Volker's readout); Anderson Dep. Tr. at 57 (describing Volker's readout).

[237] Volker Transcribed Interview Tr. at 305.

[238] *Id.*

[239] Sondland Dep. Tr. at 62; Volker Transcribed Interview Tr. 305; Morrison-Volker Hearing Tr. at 40.

[240] Sondland Hearing Tr. at 71.

[241] Sondland Dep. Tr. at 26. *See also id.* at 87-90.

[242] Morrison-Volker Hearing Tr. at 131.

[243] Sondland Hearing Tr. at 167.

[244] In addition to the testimony cited in this paragraph, *see also* Hill Dep. Tr. at 113; Hale Dep. Tr. at 90; Taylor Dep. Tr. at 58, 285; and Reeker Dep. Tr. at 148.

[245] Kent Dep. Tr. at 195.

[246] Croft Dep. Tr. at 91.

[247] Hale Dep. Tr. at 73.

[248] Sondland Dep. Tr. at 151-152.

[249] Hill Dep. Tr. at 59-60.

[250] Sondland Hearing Tr. at 24, 27, 123-124, 125-126.

[251] *Id.* at 27-30.

[252] *Id.* at 22.

[253] Sondland Dep. Tr. at 77-78.

[254] Hill-Holmes Hearing Tr. at 94.

[255] Hill Dep. Tr. at 127. According to call records obtained by the Committees, Mr. Giuliani connected with Ambassador Bolton's office three times for brief calls of under a minute between April 23 and May 10, 2019—a time period that corresponds with the recall of Ambassador Yovanovitch and the acceleration of Mr. Giuliani's efforts, on behalf of President Trump, to pressure Ukraine into opening investigations that would benefit his reelection campaign. AT&T Document Production, Bates ATTHPSCI_20190930_02224, 02322, 02330.

[256] Hill Dep. Tr. at 127.

[257] Anderson Dep. Tr. at 15.

[258] *Id.*

[259] *Id.* at 101.

[260] Hill Dep. Tr. at 127-128.

[261] *Id.* at 116-117.

[262] *Id.* at 130.

[263] Anderson Dep. Tr. at 16.

[264] *Id.*; Taylor Dep. Tr. at 24-25, 167.

[265] Taylor Dep. Tr. at 25.

[266] *Id.*

[267] *Id.*

[268] Anderson Dep. Tr. at 16-17.

[269] Sondland Dep. Tr. at 240.

[270] *ABC News' Oval Office Interview with President Trump*, ABC News (June 13, 2019) (online at https://abcnews.go.com/Politics/abc-news-oval-office-interview-president-donald-trump/story?id=63688943).

[271] *ABC News' Oval Office Interview with President Trump*, ABC News (June 13, 2019) (online at https://abcnews.go.com/Politics/abc-news-oval-office-interview-president-donald-trump/story?id=63688943) (emphasis added).

[272] Rudy Giuliani, Twitter (June 21, 2019) (online at https://twitter.com/RudyGiuliani/status/1142085975230898176)

[273] Hill-Holmes Hearing Tr. at 77.

[274] *Id.* at 91.

[275] Hill Dep. Tr. at 222-223.

[276] Hill-Holmes Hearing Tr. at 92.

[277] *Id.* at 93.

[278] Office of the United Nations High Commissioner for Human Rights, *Report on the Human Rights Situation in Ukraine: 16 November 2018 to 15 February 2019* (online at www.ohchr.org/Documents/Countries/UA/ReportUkraine16Nov2018-15Feb2019.pdf); Office of the United Nations High Commissioner for Human Rights, *Report on the Human Rights Situation in Ukraine: 16 August to 15 November 2017* (online at www.ohchr.org/Documents/Countries/UA/UAReport20th_EN.pdf); Office of the United Nations High Commissioner for Human Rights, *Conflict in Ukraine Enters its Fourth Year with No End in Sight* (June 13, 2017) (online at www.ohchr.org/EN/NewsEvents/Pages/DisplayNews.aspx?NewsID=21730&LangID=E). These figures do not include the 298 civilians of 13 different nationalities killed aboard Malaysia Airlines Flight 17, which a Dutch-led joint investigation found was shot down by a Russian missile system from a Russian military unit, a conclusion supported by U.S. intelligence. *See* Dutch Safety Board, *Report on the Crash of Malaysia Airlines Flight MH17* (Oct. 13, 2015) (online at www.onderzoeksraad.nl/en/page/3546/crash-mh17-17-july-2014); *U.S. Discloses Intelligence on Downing of Malaysian Jet*, Washington Post (July 22, 2014) (online at www.washingtonpost.com/world/national-security/us-discloses-intelligence-on-downing-of-malaysian-jet/2014/07/22/b178fe58-11e1-11e4-98ee-daea85133bc9_story.html).

[279] Ambassador Nikki Haley, United States Mission to the United Nations, *Remarks at a U.N. Security Council Briefing on Ukraine* (May 29, 2018) (online at https://usun.usmission.gov/remarks-at-a-un-security-council-briefing-on-ukraine-2/).

[280] Department of Defense, *Secretary of Defense James Mattis Remarks with President Petro Poroshenko* (Aug. 24, 2017) (online at www.defense.gov/Newsroom/Speeches/Speech/Article/1291430/secretary-of-defense-james-mattis-remarks-with-president-petro-poroshenko/).

[281] European Union External Action, *EU-Ukraine Relations Factsheet* (Sept. 30, 2019) (online at https://eeas.europa.eu/headquarters/headQuarters-homepage/4081/eu-ukraine-relations-factsheet_en); NATO, *Fact Sheet: NATO's Support to Ukraine* (Nov. 2018) (www.nato.int/nato_static_fl2014/assets/pdf/pdf_2018_11/20181106_1811-factsheet-nato-ukraine-support-eng.pdf).

[282] *DOD Announces $250M to Ukraine*, U.S. Department of Defense (June 18, 2019) (online at www.defense.gov/Newsroom/Releases/Release/Article/1879340/dod-announces-250m-to-ukraine/).

[283] Kent-Taylor Hearing Tr. at 21, 28-29, 50; Vindman Dep. Tr. at 40-41, 113; Cooper Dep. Tr. at 15-16.

[284] Taylor Dep. Tr. at 153.

[285] Croft Dep. Tr. at 16.

[286] Kent-Taylor Hearing Tr. at 30.

[287] Taylor Dep. Tr. at 20.

[288] Morrison-Volker Hearing Tr. at 11.

[289] Department of Defense and Labor, Health and Human Services, and Education Appropriations Act, 2019 and Continuing Appropriations Act, 2019, Pub. L. No. 115-245, § 9013 (2018).

[290] National Defense Authorization Act for Fiscal Year 2016, Pub. L. 114-92, § 1250 (2015), amended by the National Defense Act Authorization Act for Fiscal Year 2018, Pub. L. No. 115-91, § 1234 (2017), and most recently amended by the John S. McCain National Defense Authorization Act for Fiscal Year 2019, Pub. L. No. 115-232, § 1246 (2018).

[291] National Defense Authorization Act for Fiscal Year 2017, Pub. L. No. 114-328, § 1237 (2016); National Defense Authorization Act for Fiscal Year 2018, Pub. L. No. 115-91, § 1234 (2018); John S. McCain National Defense Authorization Act for Fiscal Year 2019, Pub. L. No. 115-232, § 1246 (2018).

[292] Letter from John C. Rood, Under Secretary of Defense for Policy, Department of Defense, to Chairman Eliot L. Engel, House Committee on Foreign Affairs (Feb. 28, 2019).

[293] Cooper Dep. Tr. at 27-28.

[294] National Defense Authorization Act for Fiscal Year 2016, Pub. L. No. 114-92, § 1250 (2015), as amended by the National Defense Act Authorization Act for Fiscal Year 2018, Pub. L. No. 115-91, § 1234 (2017), and most recently amended by the John S. McCain National Defense Authorization Act for Fiscal Year 2019, Pub. L. No. 115-232, § 1246 (2018).

[295] Cooper Dep. Tr. at 24.

[296] *Id.*

[297] Letter from John C. Rood, Under Secretary of Defense for Policy, Department of Defense, to Chairman Eliot L. Engel, House Committee on Foreign Affairs (May 23, 2019).

[298] Cooper Dep. Tr. at 31-32.

[299] *DOD Announces $250M to Ukraine*, Department of Defense (June 18, 2019) (online at www.defense.gov/Newsroom/Releases/Release/Article/1879340/dod-announces-250m-to-ukraine/).

[300] Consolidated Appropriations Act, 2019, Pub. L. No. 116-6, §7046(a)(2) (2019); Conference Report to Accompany Consolidated Appropriations Act, 2019, H.R. Rep. No. 116-9, p. 869 (2019).

[301] Consolidated Appropriations Act, 2018, Pub. L. No. 115-141, Title VIII (2017).

[302] Consolidated Appropriations Act, 2019, Pub. L. No. 116-6, §7015(c) (2019); Consolidated Appropriations Act, 2018, Pub. L. No. 115-141, § 7015(c) (2017).

[303] OMB Circular No. A-11, § 22.3 (2019) (requiring that the State Department receive clearance from OMB before notifying Congress).

[304] Sandy Dep. Tr. at 25; *DOD Announces $250M to Ukraine*, Department of Defense (June 18, 2019) (online at www.defense.gov/Newsroom/Releases/Release/Article/1879340/dod-announces-250m-to-ukraine/).

[305] *Sean Hannity Interviews Donald Trump via Telephone*, Fox News (June 19, 2019) (transcript at https://factba.se/transcript/donald-trump-interview-sean-hannity-fox-telephone-june-19-2019).

[306] Sandy Dep. Tr. at 26-27.

[307] *Id.* at 27-28.

[308] *Id.* at 29-30.

[309] Cooper Dep. Tr. at 33-34.

[310] *Id.* at 33.

[311] *Id.* at 34.

[312] *Id.* at 38.

[313] *Id.* at 37-38.

[314] Cooper-Hale Hearing Tr. at 14; Vindman Dep. Tr. at 178-179. *See also Stalled Ukraine Military Aid Concerned Members of Congress for Months,* CNN (Sept. 30, 2019) (online at www.cnn.com/2019/09/30/politics/ukraine-military-aid-congress/index.html) (suggesting that the State Department sought OMB's approval for $141 million in FMF funds on June 21, 2019).

[315] OMB Circular No. A-11, § 22.3 (2019) (requiring that the State Department receive clearance from OMB before notifying Congress).

[316] Williams Dep. Tr. at 54-55.

[317] *Id.* at 55.

[318] Blair previously served as Associate Director of National Security Programs at OMB (Blair was Duffey's predecessor), and left OMB for the White House Office of Chief of Staff with Mick Mulvaney. Sandy Dep. Tr. at 36-38.

[319] Sandy Dep. Tr. at 38-39.

[320] *Id*. at 39.

[321] Morrison Dep. Tr. at 161.

[322] Sandy Dep. Tr. at 141-142.

[323] *Id*. at 142.

[324] *Id*. at 31-32.

[325] *Id*. at 41-42.

[326] Cooper Dep. Tr. at 40; *see also* Croft Dep. Tr. at 83 ("very routine low-level business").

[327] Kent Dep. Tr. at 303-305.

[328] Taylor Dep. Tr. at 27-28.

[329] Croft Dep. Tr. at 83.

[330] Taylor Dep. Tr. at 27.

[331] Holmes Dep. Tr. at 154.

[332] *Id*.

[333] Croft Dep. Tr. at 15.

[334] Cooper Dep. Tr. at 45.

[335] Kent Dep. Tr. at 304.

[336] *Id*. at 305.

[337] Sandy Dep. Tr. at 99; Vindman Dep. Tr. at 182.

[338] Cooper Dep. Tr. at 40. Morrison, who did not attend the sub-PCC meeting but received a readout, testified that he thought OMB announced at the July 18th meeting that the hold "covered all dollars, DOD and Department of State, and it was—it was beyond funds not yet obligated to include funds that had, in fact, been obligated but not yet expended." Morrison Dep. Tr. at 161.

[339] Cooper Dep. Tr. at 40.

[340] *Id*. at 44-45.

[341] *Id*. at 40.

[342] Kent Dep. Tr. at 307-308.

[343] Morrison Dep. Tr. at 162.

[344] Cooper Dep. Tr. at 46.

[345] Williams Dep. Tr. at 91-92; *see also* Morrison Dep. Tr. at 162 (testifying that representatives from OMB stated that the hold "had been imposed by the chief of staff's office" and that the hold "was at the direction of the President").

[346] Cooper Dep. Tr. at 46.

[347] Morrison Dep. Tr. at 162-163; Kent Dep. Tr. at 310; Sandy Dep. Tr. at 91.

[348] Sandy Dep. Tr. at 91.

[349] Morrison Dep. Tr. at 163.

[350] *Id.*

[351] 2 U.S.C. § 601 *et seq.*

[352] Williams Dep. Tr. at 91-92; Vindman Dep. Tr. at 182; Morrison Dep. Tr. at 162; Sandy Dep. Tr. at 99.

[353] Taylor Dep. Tr. at 195.

[354] Vindman Dep. Tr. at 182.

[355] Sandy Dep. Tr. at 54.

[356] *Id.* at 54, 96-98.

[357] *Id.* at 97.

[358] *Id.* at 97.

[359] Hale Dep. Tr. at 81.

[360] Cooper Dep. Tr. at 47.

[361] Hale Dep. Tr. at 81; *see also* Vindman Dep. Tr. at 184 ("It was unanimous consensus on the approach that we had laid out in expanding engagement, the areas of cooperation that we wanted to focus on, and that this should be elevated to a PC as quickly as possible to release the hold on security assistance because we're talking about the end of July, and time these funds were set to expire September 30th, so there was some urgency to it."); Cooper Dep. Tr. at 49 ("Although each member went around to talk about how important it [security assistance] was and how they assessed the future in Ukraine based on the recent election results.").

[362] Morrison Dep. Tr. at 165.

[363] Cooper Dep. Tr. at 93.

[364] *Id.* at 49, 93.

[365] *Nixon's Presidency: Crisis for Congress*, New York Times (Mar. 5, 1973) (online at www.nytimes.com/1973/03/05/archives/nixons-presidency-crisis-for-congress-this-is-the-second-of-a html).

[366] Congressional Research Service, The Congressional Budget Act of 1974 (P.L. 93-344) Legislative History and Analysis (Feb. 26, 1975) (online at https://budgetcounsel files.wordpress.com/2018/05/added-crs-the-congressional-budget-act-of-1974-p-l-93-344-legislative-history-and-analysis-order-code-75-94-s-february-26-1975.pdf).

[367] Calvin Coolidge Presidential Foundation, *The History of the 1921 and 1974 Budget Acts* (Nov. 26, 2014); *So... this is Nixon's Fault?*, Politico (Oct. 21, 2015) (online at www.politico.com/agenda/story/2015/10/richard-nixon-congressional-budget-control-act-history-000282).

[368] 2 U.S.C. § 683.

[369] U.S. Government Accountability Office, *Impoundment Control Act—Withholding of Funds through Their Date of Expiration* (Dec. 10, 2018) (online at www.gao.gov/assets/700/695889.pdf).

[370] Cooper Dep. Tr. at 47-48. With regard to interagency discussions about the legality of the hold, Vindman testified "[s]o I'm not a legal expert, but there was a sufficient amount of—a significant amount of work done to determine whether it was legal for OMB to be able to place the hold. ... I think at the—so my recollection in the [July 18th] sub-PCC was that the matter was raised; at the [July 23rd] PCC, it was tasked for further development; and I think by the time it got to our [July 26th] DSG it was determined that, you know, there was a legal basis to hold." Vindman Dep. Tr. at 185.

[371] Vindman Dep. Tr. at 184.

[372] Morrison Dep. Tr. at 165.

[373] *Id.* at 264.

[374] *Id.*

[375] *Id.*

[376] Cooper Dep. Tr. at 51.

[377] *Id.*; *see also id.* at 113 (explaining that she relied on a conversation with DOD legal to form her understanding of the two proper legal mechanisms).

[378] 2 U.S.C. § 683.

[379] Cooper Dep. Tr. at 58-59.

[380] *Id.* at 114.

[381] *Id.* at 51, 57; Sandy Dep. Tr. at 147-148.

[382] 31 U.S.C. §§ 1511-1516.

[383] Sandy Dep. Tr. at 87, 163.

[384] *Id.* at 34-35.

[385] *Id.* at 51.

[386] *Id.* at 23.

[387] *Id.* at 33-35, 51-52.

[388] *Id.* at 86.

[389] *Id.* at 86-87.

[390] *Id.* at 86.

[391] *Id.* at 87-88.

[392] SF-132 Apportionment Schedule FY 2019, OMB Footnote A4 (July 25, 2019).

[393] Sandy Dep. Tr. at 94.

[394] *Id.*

[395] *Id.* at 94-95; SF-132 Apportionment Schedule FY 2019, OMB Footnote A4 (July 25, 2019).

[396] Sandy Dep. Tr. at 87.

[397] SF-132 Apportionment Schedule FY 2019, OMB Footnote A4 (July 25, 2019); Sandy Dep. Tr. at 92.

[398] Sandy Dep. Tr. at 101.

[399] *Id.* at 102.

[400] *Id.* at 96-97, 102.

[401] *Id.* at 101-102.

[402] *Id.* at 63.

[403] *Id.*

[404] *Id.* at 102.

[405] *Id.* at 64-65.

[406] *Id.* at 65.

[407] *Id.* at 108-109.

[408] *Id.* at 104, 119-120.

[409] Cooper Dep. Tr. at 58-59.

[410] *Id.*

[411] *Id.* at 59.

[412] Sandy Dep. Tr. at 74-75, 127-128.

[413] SF-132 Apportionment Schedule FY 2019, OMB Footnote A4 (August 6, 2019); SF-132 Apportionment Schedule FY 2019, OMB Footnote A4 (August 15, 2019). Because of a drafting error in which OMB forgot to extend the date, the footnotes technically did not restrict DOD from spending funds between August 12 and August 20 (the date of the subsequent funding document reinstating the hold). However, Sandy testified that the hold was still in place and that the direction from the President remained unchanged. Sandy Dep. Tr. at 124-126.

[414] SF-132 Apportionment Schedule FY 2019, OMB Footnote A4 (August 6, 2019); SF-132 Apportionment Schedule FY 2019, OMB Footnote A4 (August 15, 2019); SF-132 Apportionment Schedule FY 2019, OMB Footnote A4 (August 20, 2019); SF-132 Apportionment Schedule FY 2019, OMB Footnote A4 (August 27, 2019); SF-132 Apportionment Schedule FY 2019, OMB Footnote A4 (August 31, 2019); SF-132 Apportionment Schedule FY 2019, OMB Footnote A4 (Sept. 5, 2019); SF-13; SF-132 Apportionment Schedule FY 2019, OMB Footnote A4 (Sept. 6, 2019); Apportionment Schedule FY 2019, OMB Footnote A4 (Sept. 10, 2019).

[415] Cooper Dep. Tr. at 91-92.

[416] *Id.* at 92.

[417] Kent Dep. Tr. at 318-319.

[418] Sandy Dep. Tr. at 56-61.

[419] *Id.* at 59-60.

[420] *Id.* at 60-61.

[421] *Id.* at 75, 127-128; Cooper Dep. Tr. at 57-58; *see also id.* at 59 ("And along the way, [the] Defense Security Cooperation Agency was expressing doubt that they could do it.").

[422] Cooper Dep. Tr. at 80-81. Ultimately, as described below, DOD was able to obligate all but approximately $35 million in USAI funds by September 30th. Sandy Dep. Tr. at 146-147.

[423] Sandy Dep. Tr. at 127-128.

[424] *Id.* at 95.

[425] SF-132 Apportionment Schedule FY 2019 (August 20, 2019); SF-132 Apportionment Schedule FY 2019 (August 27, 2019); SF-132 Apportionment Schedule FY 2019 (August 31, 2019); SF-132 Apportionment Schedule FY 2019 (September 5, 2019); SF-132 Apportionment Schedule FY 2019 (September 6, 2019); SF-132 Apportionment Schedule FY 2019 (September 10, 2019).

[426] SF-132 Apportionment Schedule FY 2019 (August 20, 2019) (funds not available for obligation until August 26); SF-132 Apportionment Schedule FY 2019 (August 27, 2019) (funds not available for obligation until August 31); SF-132 Apportionment Schedule FY 2019 (August 31, 2019) (funds not available for obligation until September 5); SF-132 Apportionment Schedule FY 2019 (September 5, 2019) (funds not available for obligation until September 7); SF-132 Apportionment Schedule FY 2019 (September 6, 2019) (funds not available for obligation until September 11); SF-132 Apportionment Schedule FY 2019 (September 10, 2019) (funds not available for obligation until September 12).

[427] Sandy Dep. Tr. at 131.

[428] *Id.* at 136-137.

[429] *Id.* at 136.

[430] *Id.* at 135-137, 150-155.

[431] *Id.* at 149-152.

[432] *Id.* at 152.

[433] *Id.* at 150-156.

[434] Morrison Dep. Tr. at 266-267.

[435] *Id.* at 268.

[436] *Id.* at 267.

[437] Vindman Dep. Tr. at 186.

[438] *Id.*

[439] *Id.* at 187-188.

[440] Morrison Dep. Tr. at 167-168.

[441] *Id.* at 170-171.

[442] *Id.* at 265-266.

[443] *Id.* at 172, 266.

[444] *Id.* at 266.

[445] Cooper Dep. Tr. at 68.

[446] Croft Dep. Tr. at 86.

[447] *Id.* at 86-87.

[448] *Id.* at 86-87, 101.

[449] *Id.* at 97-98.

[450] Cooper-Hale Hearing Tr. at 14.

[451] *Id.* at 13-14.

[452] *Id.* at 14.

[453] *Id.* at 15.

[454] Vindman Dep. Tr. at 221-222.

[455] *Trump Holds Up Ukraine Military Aid Meant to Confront Russia*, Politico (Aug. 28, 2019) (online at www.politico.com/story/2019/08/28/trump-ukraine-military-aid-russia-1689531).

[456] Holmes Dep. Tr. at 18 ("It is important to understand that a White House visit was critical to President Zelensky. He needed to demonstrate U.S. support at the highest levels, both to advance his ambitious anti-corruption agenda at home and to encourage Russian President Putin to take seriously President Zelensky's peace efforts.").

[457] Kent Dep. Tr. at 202 ("The President of the United States is a longtime acknowledged leader of the free world, and the U.S. is Ukraine's strongest supporter. And so in the Ukraine context, it's very important to show that they can establish a strong relationship with the leader of the United States. That's the Ukrainian argument and desire to have a meeting. The foreign policy argument is it's a very important country in the front lines of Russian malign influence and aggression. And the U.S. spends a considerable amount of our resources supporting Ukraine and therefore it makes sense.").

[458] Hill Dep. Tr. at 158 ("He was just generally concerned about actually not having a meeting because he felt that this would deprive Ukraine, the new Ukrainian Government of the legitimacy that it needed, especially vis-a-vis the Russians. So this gets to, you know, the heart of our national security dilemma. You know, the Ukrainians at this point, you know, are looking at a White House meeting or looking at a meeting with the President of the United States as a recognition of their legitimacy as a sovereign state.").

[459] Vindman Hearing Tr. at 38-39 ("The show of support for President Zelensky, still a brand-new President, frankly, a new politician on the Ukrainian political scene, looking to establish his bona fides as a regional and maybe even a world leader, would want to have a meeting with the United States, the most powerful country in the world and Ukraine's most significant benefactor, in order to be able to implement his agenda.").

[460] Volker Transcribed Interview Tr. at 59.

[461] *Id.* at 328.

[462] Taylor Dep. Opening Statement at 5 ("In late June, one of the goals of both channels was to facilitate a visit by President Zelensky to the White House for a meeting with President Trump, which President Trump had promised in his congratulatory letter of May 29. The Ukrainians were clearly eager for the meeting to happen. During a conference call with Ambassador Volker, Acting Assistant Secretary of State for European and Eurasian Affairs Phil Reeker, Secretary Perry, Ambassador Sondland, and Counsel of the U.S. Department of State Ulrich Brechbuhl on June 18, it was clear that a meeting between the two presidents was an agreed-upon goal.").

[463] *Id.* at 25 ("[D]uring my subsequent communications with Ambassadors Volker and Sondland, they relayed to me that the President 'wanted to hear from Zelensky' before scheduling the meeting in the Oval Office. It was not clear to me what this meant.").

[464] *Id.*

[465] Holmes Dep. Tr. at 20.

[466] Taylor Dep. Tr. at 25-26.

[467] *Id.* at 25. *See also id.* at 128.

Q: But Ambassador Sondland made it clear not only that he didn't wish to include most of the regular interagency participants but also that no one was transcribing or monitoring the call as they added President Zelensky. What struck you as odd about that?

A: Same concern. That is, in the normal, regular channel, the State Department operations center that was putting the call together would stay on the line, in particular when you were having a conversation with the head of state, they would stay on the line, transcribe, take notes so that there could be a record of the discussion with this head of state. It is an official discussion. When he wanted to be sure that there was not, the State Department operations center agreed.

[468] *Id.* at 26.

[469] *Id.* at 127.

[470] Kurt Volker Document Production, Bates KV00000036 (Oct. 2, 2019).

[471] *Id.*

[472] Taylor Dep. Tr. at 26.

[473] Kurt Volker Document Production, Bates KV00000027 (Oct. 2, 2019).

[474] Volker Transcribed Interview Tr. at 242-243.

[475] Kurt Volker Document Production, Bates KV00000055 (Oct. 2, 2019).

[476] *Id. at* Bates KV00000027.

Taylor: Are you OK with me briefing Ulrich on these conversations? Maybe you have already?

Volker: I have not—please feel free

Volker: The key thing is to tee up a phone call w potus and then get visit nailed down

Taylor: I agree. Is Ze on board with a phone call?

Volker: Yes—bogdan was a little skeptical, but Zelensky was ok with it. Now we need to get it on potus schedule…

Taylor: The three amigos are on a roll. Let me know when I can help.

[477] Taylor Dep. Tr. at 65-66 ("Kurt told me that he had discussed how President Zelensky could prepare for the phone call with President Trump. And without going into—without providing me any details about the specific words, did talk about investigations in that conversation ... Kurt suggested that President Trump would like to hear about the investigations.").

[478] Morrison-Volker Hearing Tr. at 94.

Q:	In the July 2nd or 3rd meeting in Toronto that you had with President Zelensky, you also mentioned investigations to him, right?
A:	Yes
Q:	And again, you were referring to the Burisma and the 2016 election.
A:	I was thinking of Burisma and 2016.
Q:	And you understood that that what the Ukrainians interpreted references to investigations to be, related to Burisma and the 2016 election?
A:	I don't know specifically at that time if we had talked that specifically, Burisma/2016. That was my assumption, though, that they would've been thinking that too.

[479] Sondland Hearing Tr. at 27.

[480] *Id*. at 43.

[481] *Id*. at 21-22.

[482] Kent Dep. Tr. at 246.

[483] Hill-Holmes Hearing Tr. at 59.

[484] Kent Dep. Tr. at 246-247 ("I do not recall whether the follow-on conversation I had with Kurt about this was in Toronto, or whether it was subsequently at the State Department. But he did tell me that he planned to start reaching out to former Mayor of New York, Rudy Giuliani. And when I asked him why, he said that it was clear that the former mayor had influence on the President in terms of the way the President though of Ukraine. And I think by that moment in time, that was self-evidence to anyone who was working on the issues, and therefore, it made sense to try to engage the mayor. When I raised with Kurt, I said, about what? Because former Mayor Giuliani has a track record of, you know, asking for a visa for a corrupt former prosecutor. He attacked Masha, and he's tweeting that the new President needs to investigate Biden and the 2016 campaign. And Kurt's reaction or response to me at that was, well, if there's nothing there, what does it matter? And if there is something there, it should be investigated. My response to him was asking another country to investigate a prosecution for political reasons undermines our advocacy of the rule of law.").

[485] Kurt Volker Document Production, Bates KV00000036 (Oct. 2, 2019).

[486] *Id*.

[487] *Id. at* Bates KV00000006.

[488] Volker Transcribed Interview Tr. at 308; Kurt Volker Document Production, Bates KV00000018 (Oct. 2, 2019).

[489] Volker Transcribed Interview Tr. at 138.

[490] Sondland Hearing Tr. at 23.

[491] Hill Dep. Tr. at 63.

[492] *Id*. at 63-67, 155.

[493] *Id*.

Q:	Did anything happen in that meeting that was out of the ordinary?
A:	Yes. At one point during that meeting, Ambassador Bolton was, you know, basically trying very hard not to commit to a meeting, because, you know—and, again, these meetings have to be well-prepared. They're not just something that you say, yes, we're going to have a meeting without there being a clear understanding of what the content of that meeting is going to be. ... And Ambassador Bolton is always—was always very cautious and always very much, you know, by the book and was not going to certainly commit to a meeting right there and then, certainly not one where it wasn't—it was unclear what the content of the meeting would be about, what kind of issues that we would discuss that would be pertaining to Ukrainian-U.S. relations. ... Then

Ambassador Sondland blurted out: Well, we have an agreement with the chief of staff for a meeting if these investigations in the energy sector start. And Ambassador Bolton immediately stiffened. He said words to the effect—I can't say word for word what he said because I was behind them sitting on the sofa with our Senior Director of Energy, and we all kind of looked up and thought that was somewhat odd. And Ambassador Bolton immediately stiffened and ended the meeting.

Q: Right then, he just ended the meeting?

A: Yeah. He said: Well, it was very nice to see you. You know, I can't discuss a meeting at this time. We'll clearly work on this. And, you know, kind of it was really nice to see you. So it was very abrupt. I mean, he looked at the clock as if he had, you know, suddenly another meeting and his time was up, but it was obvious he ended the meeting.

[494] Vindman Dep. Tr. at 17 ("The meeting proceeded well until the Ukrainians broached the subject of a meeting between the two Presidents. The Ukrainians saw this meeting as critically important in order to solidify the support for their most important international partner. Ambassador Sondland started—when Ambassador Sondland started to speak about Ukraine delivering specific investigations in order to secure the meeting with the President, Ambassador Bolton cut the meeting short.")

[495] Volker Transcribed Interview Tr. at 310.

[496] Morrison-Volker Hearing Tr. at 23, 73, 103.

[497] Hill Dep. Tr. at 68 ("And Ambassador Sondland said to Ambassador Volker and also Secretary Perry and the other people who were with him, including the Ukrainians, to come down to—there's a room in the White House, the Ward Room, to basically talk about next steps. And that's also unusual. I mean, he meant to talk to the Ukrainians about next steps about the meeting.")

[498] *Id.* ("And Ambassador Bolton pulled me back as I was walking out afterwards and said: Go down to the Ward Room right now and find out what they're talking about and come back and talk to me. So I did go down.").

[499] Vindman Dep. Tr. at 64-65.

Q: And what do you recall specifically of what Sondland said to the Ukrainians—

A: Right.

Q: —in the Ward Room?

A: So that is right, the conversation unfolded with Sondland proceeding to kind of, you know, review what the deliverable would be in order to get the meeting, and he talked about the investigation into the Bidens, and, frankly, I can't 100 percent recall because I didn't take notes of it, but Burisma, that it seemed—I mean, there was no ambiguity, I guess, in my mind. He was calling for something, calling for an investigation that didn't exist into the Bidens and Burisma.

Q: Okay. Ambiguity in your mind is different from what you—

A: Sure.

Q: —actually heard?

A: Right. Correct.

Q: What did you hear Sondland say?

A: That the Ukrainians would have to deliver an investigation into the Bidens.

Q: Into the Bidens. So in the Ward Room he mentioned the word "Bidens"?

A: To the best of my recollection, yes.

Q: Okay . Did he mention 2016?

A: I don't recall.

Q: Did he mention Burisma?

A: My visceral reaction to what was being called for suggested that it was explicit. There was no ambiguity.

...

A: Again, based on my visceral reaction, it was explicit what he was calling for. And to the best of my recollection, he did specifically say "investigation of the Bidens."

...

A   So the meeting that occurred in the Ward Room referenced investigations into the Bidens, to the best of my recollection, Burisma and 2016

[500] Hill Dep. Tr. at 69.

[501] *Id.* at 151-152.

[502] *Id.* at 69-70.

[503] Vindman Dep. Tr. at 31.

Q: Did Ambassador Sondland—were the Ukrainian officials in the room when he was describing the need for these investigations in order to get the White House meeting?

A: So they were in the room initially. I think, once it became clear that there was some sort of discord amongst the government officials in the room, Ambassador Sondland asked them to step out of the room.

Q: What was the discord?

A: The fact that it was clear that I, as the representative—I, as the representative of the NSC, thought it was inappropriate and that we were not going to get involved in investigations.

Q: Did you say that to Ambassador Sondland?

A: Yes, I did.

[504] *Id.* at 18. While not specifically disagreeing with any of the content of the discussion in the Ward Room, Ambassador Sondland generally disputed Dr. Hill and Lt. Col. Vindman's accounts, saying that he did not recall "any yelling or screaming … as others have said." Sondland Hearing Tr. at 23. Neither Dr. Hill nor Lt. Col. Vindman described yelling or screaming in the meetings.

Ambassador Sondland also testified that "those recollections of protest do not square with the documentary record of our interactions with the NSC in the days and weeks that followed." Sondland Hearing Tr. at 23. As an example, Sondland provided text from a July 13 email that he sent—not to Dr. Hill, but to her successor Tim Morrison—which said that the "sole purpose" of the call between President Trump and President Zelensky was to give the former "assurances of 'new sheriff' in town." Sondland Hearing Tr. at 23. The email that Ambassador Sondland provided does not undermine Dr. Hill's or Lt. Col. Vindman's testimony that they objected to Ambassador Sondland's conduct in the Ward Room meeting. The email provided by Ambassador Sondland, however, was sent to Mr. Morrison, not Dr. Hill. Mr. Morrison had not yet started working as NSC Senior Director for Europe and was not at the July 10 meeting.

[505] Vindman Dep. Tr. at 29.

A: So I heard him say that this had been coordinated with White House Chief of Staff Mr. Mick Mulvaney.

Q: What did he say about that?

A: He just said that he had had a conversation with Mr. Mulvaney, and this is what was required in order to get a meeting.

[506] Hill Dep. Tr. at 69-70.

[507] Kurt Volker Document Production, Bates KV00000036 (Oct. 2, 2019).

Taylor: Eager to hear if your meeting with Danyliuk and Bolton resulted in a decision on a call.

Taylor: How did the meeting go?

Volker: Not good—lets talk—kv

[508] *Id. at* Bates KV00000018.

[509] Hill Dep. Tr. at 70-72.

[510] *Id.* at 126-27.

Q: Okay. But what did you understand him to mean by that?

A: Well, based on what had happened in the July 10th meeting and Ambassador Sondland blurting out that he'd already gotten agreement to have a meeting at the White House for Zelensky if these investigations were started up again, clearly Ambassador Bolton was referring directly to those.

[511] *Id.* at 129.

[512] *Id.* at 139. ("I told him exactly, you know, what had transpired and that Ambassador Sondland had basically indicated that there was an agreement with the Chief of Staff that they would have a White House meeting or, you know, a Presidential meeting if the Ukrainians started up these investigations again.").

[513] *Id.*

[514] Id. at 146-147.

[515] *Id.* at 158-159, 161.

Q: What was Mr. Eisenberg's reaction to what you explained to him had and Mr. Griffith had explained to him had occurred the day before?

A: Yeah. He was also concerned. I mean, he wasn't aware that Sondland, Ambassador Sondland was, you know, kind of running around doing a lot of these, you know, meetings and independently. We talked about the fact that, you know, Ambassador Sondland said he'd been meeting with Giuliani and he was very concerned about that. And he said that he would follow up on this.

[516] Vindman Dep. Tr. at 37. ("Sir, I think I—I mean, the top line I just offered, I'll restate it, which is that Mr. Sondland asked for investigations, for these investigations into Bidens and Burisma. I actually recall having that particular conversation. Mr. Eisenberg doesn't really work on this issue, so I had to go a little bit into the back story of what these investigations were, and that I expressed concerns and thought it was inappropriate.").

[517] *Id.* at 36.

[518] *Id.* at 38.

Q: Did he say anything to you, that, all right, I'm going to do anything with it?

A: I vaguely recall something about: I'll take a look into it. You know, there might not be anything here. We'll take a look into it, something of that nature. But—and then he offered to, you know, if I have any concerns in the future, you know, that I should be open—I should be—feel free to come back and, you know, share those concerns.

Q: Did either he or anyone from the legal staff circle back to you on this issue?

A: No.

[519] *Id.* at 39-40.

[520] Taylor Dep. Tr. at 29. ("In the same July 19th phone call, they gave me an account of the July 10th meeting with the Ukrainian officials at the White House. Specifically, they told me that Ambassador Sondland had connected investigations with an Oval Office meeting for President Zelensky, which so irritated Ambassador Bolton that he abruptly ended the meeting, telling Dr. Hill and Mr. Vindman that they should have nothing to do with domestic politics.").

[521] Morrison Dep. Tr. at 12.

[522] House Permanent Select Committee on Intelligence, Opening Statement of Ambassador Gordon Sondland, Department of State, *Impeachment*, 116th Cong. (Nov. 20, 2019) ("2. The call between Zelensky and Potus should happen before 7/21. (Parliamentary Elections) Sole purpose is for Zelensky to give Potus assurances of 'new sheriff' in town. Corruption ending, unbundling moving forward and any hampered investigations will be allowed to move forward transparently. Goal is for Potus to invite him to Oval. Volker, Perry, Bolton and I strongly recommend.").

[523] House Permanent Select Committee on Intelligence, Opening Statement of Ambassador Gordon Sondland, Department of State, *Impeachment*, 116th Cong., at 21 (Nov. 20, 2019).

[524] Sondland Dep. Tr. at 227.

[525] House Permanent Select Committee on Intelligence, Opening Statement of Ambassador Gordon Sondland, Department of State, *Impeachment*, 116th Cong., at 21 (Nov. 20, 2019).

[526] *Id.*

[527] *Id.*

[528] Sondland Hearing Tr. at 27.

[529] Verizon Document Production. It is unclear whether this call occurred before or after Ambassador Sondland spoke with President Zelensky, and it is also unclear whether the White House caller was an Administration official or the President himself.

[530] Kurt Volker Document Production, Bates KV00000037 (Oct. 2, 2019).

[531] *Id.*

[532] Volker Transcribed Interview Tr. at 229-230.

[533] Kurt Volker Document Production, Bates KV00000018 (Oct. 2, 2019).

[534] Volker Transcribed Interview Tr. at 202-203.

[535] *Id.* at 232.

[536] Kurt Volker Document Production, Bates KV00000002 (Oct. 2, 2019).

[537] *Id. at* Bates KV00000018.

[538] Volker Transcribed Interview Tr. at 138-139.

[539] AT&T Document Production, Bates ATTHPSCI_20190930_02705.

[540] Volker Transcribed Interview Tr. at 139.

[541] Kurt Volker Document Production, Bates KV00000018 (Oct. 2, 2019).

[542] *Id. at* Bates KV00000002-KV00000003.

[543] *Id. at* Bates KV00000042.

Volker:	Orchestrated a great call w Rudy and Yermak. They are going to get together when Rudy goes to Madrid in a couple of weeks.
Volker:	In the meantime, Rudy is now advocating for phone call
Volker:	I have call into Fiona's replacement and will call Bolton if needed.
Volker:	But I can tell Bolton and you can tell Mick that Rudy agrees on a call, if that helps
Sondland:	I talked to Tim Morrison. (Fiona's replacement). He is pushing but feel free as well.

[544] *Id.*

[545] Taylor Dep. Tr. at 30.

[546] Kurt Volker Document Production, Bates KV000000 37 (Oct. 2, 2019).

---

547 Taylor Dep. Tr. at 74.

548 Kent-Taylor Hearing Tr. at 68.

549 Taylor Dep. Tr. at 177.

550 Sondland Dep. Tr. at 183.

551 Sondland Hearing Tr. at 17.

552 *Id.* at 18.

553 *Id.* at 19, 17.

554 *Id.* at 27.

555 *Id.* at 26.

556 *Id.* at 27.

557 Taylor Dep. Tr. at 26.

558 Hill-Holmes Hearing Tr. at 25.

559 Hill Dep. Tr. at 420-421.

Q: You've mentioned repeatedly concerns that you had about, in particular, Mr. Giuliani and his efforts. When you read the call transcript of July 25th, the call record, which you must have done just a couple weeks ago, did it crystalize in your head in any way a better understanding of what was transpiring while you were there?

A: In terms of providing, you know, more information with hindsight, unfortunately, yes.

Q: And in what way?

A: The specific references, also juxtaposed with the release of the text messages by Ambassador Volker—you know, what I said before—really was kind of my worst fears and nightmares, in terms of, you know, there being some kind of effort not just to subvert the national security process but to try to subvert what really should be, you know, kind of, a diplomatic effort to, you know, kind of, set up a Presidential meeting.

Q: This may—

A: There seems to be an awful lot of people involved in, you know, basically turning a White House meeting into some kind of asset.

Q: What do you mean by "asset"?

A: Well, something that was being, you know, dangled out to the Ukrainian Government. They wanted the White House meeting very much. And this was kind of laying out that it wasn't just a question of scheduling or having, you know, the national security issues worked out, that there were all of these alternative discussions going on behind.

560 Taylor Dep. Tr. at 174.

561 *Id.*

562 Kurt Volker Document Production, Bates KV00000042 (Oct. 2, 2019).

563 Sondland Hearing Tr. at 53-55.

564 *Id.* at 52-53.

565 Morrison Dep. Tr. at 30-31, 101, 247, 256.

566 *Id.* at 31.

567 *Id.* at 111.

568 Volker Transcribed Interview Tr. at 102-103; Kurt Volker Document Production, Bates KV00000007 (Oct. 2, 2019). In his testimony, Ambassador Volker did not explain to the Committees what he had heard about the July 25 call put him in a position to tell Mr. Giuliani that the "right messages" were, in fact, discussed.

Ambassador Volker testified twice about the readouts that he received of the July 25 call. In his deposition, he told the Committees that he received "the same" readout from both the State Department and Mr. Yermak: that there was a message of congratulations to President Zelensky, that President Zelensky promised to fight corruption and that President Trump repeated the invitation to visit the White House. Volker Transcribed Interview Tr. at 102-103. Ambassador Volker described it as a "superficial" readout. Volker Transcribed Interview Tr. at 19.

In his public testimony, Ambassador Volker repeated that claim: the readouts from Mr. Yermak and Ambassador Volker's U.S. sources "were largely the same, that it was a good call, that it was a congratulatory phone call for the President winning the parliamentary election." Volker-Morrison Hearing Tr. at 74. Ambassador Volker did testify that he "expected" the call to cover the material in his July 25 text message—that the Ukrainians would "investigate/'get to the bottom of what happened' in 2016"—but did not receive anything more than a "barebones" description of what was said. Volker-Morrison Hearing Tr. at 87-88, 75.

If Ambassador Volker is correctly describing the readouts he received, it is not clear what he heard that gave him the basis to tell Mr. Giuliani that "exactly the right messages" were discussed.

569 Williams Dep. Tr. at 37-38.

570 Hill-Holmes Hearing Tr. at 23.

571 *Id*. at 25.

572 *Trump and Putin Share Joke About Election Meddling, Sparking New Furor*, New York Times (June 28, 2019) (online at www.nytimes.com/2019/06/28/us/politics/trump-putin-election html) ("As he sat down on Friday with Mr. Putin on the sidelines of an international summit in Japan, Mr. Trump was asked by a reporter if he would tell Russia not to meddle in American elections. 'Yes, of course I will,' Mr. Trump said. Turning to Mr. Putin, he said, with a half-grin on his face and mock seriousness in his voice, 'Don't meddle in the election, President.'").

573 Morrison Dep. Tr. at 41.

574 Williams Dep. Tr. at 131.

575 *See* Vindman Dep. Tr. at 42, 109; Morrison Dep. Tr. at 41.

576 Vindman Dep. Tr. at 18; Morrison Dep. Tr. at 15.

577 Vindman Dep. Tr. at 42-43; Morrison-Volker Hearing Tr. at 32.

578 Morrison Dep. Tr. at 39; Vindman Dep. Tr. at 45.

579 U.S. Embassy & Consulates in Italy, *Secretary Michael R. Pompeo and Italian Foreign Minister Luigi Di Maio at a Press Availability* (Oct. 2, 2019) (online at https://it.usembassy.gov/secretary-michael-r-pompeo-and-italian-foreign-minister-luigi-di-maio-at-a-press-availability/). Mr. Morrison testified that Dr. Kupperman was not in the Situation Room, but Mr. Morrison was informed after the fact that Dr. Kupperman was listening. Morrison Dep. Tr. at 39-40. Ms. Williams and Lt. Col. Vindman testified that they both believed Dr. Kupperman was present, but neither had a clear recollection. Williams Dep. Tr. at 64; Vindman Dep. Tr. at 45.

580 *See* Transcript, *This Week with George Stephanopoulos*, ABC News (Sept. 22, 2019) (online at https://abcnews.go.com/Politics/week-transcript-22-19-secretary-mike-pompeo-gen/story?id=65778332) (Q: And I want to turn to this whistleblower complaint, Mr. Secretary. The complaint involving the president and a phone call with a foreign leader to the director of national intelligence inspector general. That's where the complaint was launched by the whistle-blower. 'The Wall Street Journal' is reporting that President Trump pressed the president of Ukraine eight times to work with Rudy Giuliani to investigate Joe Biden's son. What do you know about those conversations? A: So, you just gave me a report about a I.C. whistle-blower complaint, none of which I've seen. …").

581 *Pompeo Took Part in Ukraine Call, Official Says*, Wall Street Journal (Sept. 30, 2019) (online at www.wsj.com/articles/pompeo-took-part-in-ukraine-call-official-says-11569865002).

582 The White House, *Memorandum of Telephone Conversation* (July 25, 2019) (online at www.whitehouse.gov/wp-content/uploads/2019/09/Unclassified09.2019.pdf).

583 *Id.*

584 *Id. See* European Union External Action Service, *EU-Ukraine Relations—Factsheet* (Sept. 30, 2019) (online at https://eeas.europa.eu/headquarters/headquarters-Homepage/4081/eu-ukraine-relations-factsheet_en).

585 The White House, *Memorandum of Telephone Conversation* (July 25, 2019) (online at www.whitehouse.gov/wp-content/uploads/2019/09/Unclassified09.2019.pdf).

586 *Id.*; Kent-Taylor Hearing Tr. at 29.

587 The White House, *Memorandum of Telephone Conversation* (July 25, 2019) (online at www.whitehouse.gov/wp-content/uploads/2019/09/Unclassified09.2019.pdf).

588 Vindman Dep. Tr. at 114.

589 The White House, *Memorandum of Telephone Conversation* (July 25, 2019) (online at www.whitehouse.gov/wp-content/uploads/2019/09/Unclassified09.2019.pdf).

590 *See* Office of the Director of National Intelligence, *Assessing Russian Activities and Intentions in Recent U.S. Elections* (Jan. 6, 2017) (online at www.dni.gov/files/documents/ICA_2017_01.pdf).

591 The White House, *Memorandum of Telephone Conversation* (July 25, 2019) (online at www.whitehouse.gov/wp-content/uploads/2019/09/Unclassified09.2019.pdf).

592 *Charges of Ukrainian Meddling? A Russian Operation, U.S. Intelligence Says*, New York Times (Nov. 22, 2019) (online at www.nytimes.com/2019/11/22/us/politics/ukraine-russia-interference.html).

593 The President of Russia, *Joint News Conference with Hungarian Prime Minister Viktor Orban* (Feb. 2, 2017) (online at http://en.kremlin.ru/events/president/news/53806).

594 Hill-Holmes Hearing Tr. at 39-40.

595 *President Trump's Former National Security Advisor 'Deeply Disturbed' by Ukraine Scandal: 'Whole World Is Watching,'* ABC News (Sept. 29, 2019) (online at https://abcnews.go.com/Politics/president-trumps-national-security-advisor-deeply-disturbed-ukraine/story?id=65925477).

596 Hill Dep. Tr. at 234-235.

597 The White House, *Memorandum of Telephone Conversation* (July 25, 2019) (online at www.whitehouse.gov/wp-content/uploads/2019/09/Unclassified09.2019.pdf).

598 *Id.*

599 *Id.*

600 *Id.*

601 *Id.*

602 *Id.*

603 The White House, *Remarks by President Trump before Marine One* (Oct. 3, 2019) (online at www.whitehouse.gov/briefings-statements/remarks-president-trump-marine-one-departure-67/).

604 Hill Dep. Tr. at 400; Kent-Taylor Hearing Tr. at 73; Hill-Holmes Hearing Tr. at 63-64; Yovanovitch Hearing Tr. at 49-50; Morrison-Volker Hearing Tr. at 23.

605 Kent Dep. Tr. at 45.

606 Kent-Taylor Hearing Tr. at 116.

607 Yovanovitch Hearing Tr. at 50.

608 *See* Section I, Chapter 1.

609 Kent Dep. Tr. at 44-50.

610 Morrison-Volker Hearing Tr. at 23.

611 *Id.*

612 *See* Section I, Chapter 1.

613 The White House, *Memorandum of Telephone Conversation* (July 25, 2019) (online at www.whitehouse.gov/wp-content/uploads/2019/09/Unclassified09.2019.pdf).

614 Yovanovitch Dep. Tr. at 192-193.

615 *Id.*

616 Ambassador Volker was the only witness to testify that President Trump's reference to the "prosecutor" during the July 25 call was to Mr. Shokin, not Mr. Lutsenko. *See* Volker Transcribed Interview Tr. at 355. However, Mr. Holmes testified that, on July 26—the day after the call—he spoke with President Zelensky's Chief of Staff Andriy Bohdan who told Holmes that "President Trump had expressed interest during the previous day's phone call in President Zelensky's personnel decisions related to the Prosecutor General's office," which Mr. Holmes understood to refer to Mr. Lutsenko once he saw the July 25 call transcript. Holmes Dep. Tr. at 22, 49. In addition, in a text message to Taylor and Sondland after his July 19 breakfast with Giuliani, Volker emphasized that "Most impt [important] is for Zelensky to say" on the July 25 call "that he will help investigation—and address any specific personnel issues—if there are any." Kurt Volker Document Production, Bates KV00000037 (Oct. 2, 2019).

617 The White House, *Memorandum of Telephone Conversation* (July 25, 2019) (online at www.whitehouse.gov/wp-content/uploads/2019/09/Unclassified09.2019.pdf).

618 *Id.*

619 Hill-Holmes Hearing Tr. at 55.

620 Holmes Dep. Tr. at 49-50.

621 Kent-Taylor Hearing Tr. at 25.

622 Morrison-Volker Hearing Tr. at 19.

623 Hill-Holmes Hearing Tr. at 18.

624 *In-Town Pool Report #6—Ukraine Call*, White House Pool Report (July 25, 2019) (online at https://publicpool kinja.com/subject-in-town-pool-report-6-ukraine-call-1836700221).

625 Vindman Dep. Tr. at 42-43.

626 Vindman-Williams Hearing Tr. at 31-33; Morrison-Volker Hearing Tr. at 34.

627 Vindman Dep. Tr. at 46-47.

628 Taylor Dep. Tr. at 29.

629 Vindman Dep. Tr. at 94.

630 *Id.* at 46-47.

631 Vindman-Williams Hearing Tr. at 28.

632 Vindman Dep. Tr. at 147.

633 Vindman-Williams Hearing Tr. at 28-29.

634 Vindman Dep. Tr. at 96-97.

635 *Id.* at 97-98.

636 Morrison-Volker Hearing Tr. at 29.

637 Morrison Dep. Tr. at 23-24.

638 *Id.* at 41-42, 191-192.

639 *Id.* at 97.

[640] *Id.*

[641] *Id.* at 101.

[642] *Id.* at 41.

[643] *Id.* at 43.

[644] *Id.* at 44.

[645] *Id.* at 16.

[646] *Id.* at 101.

[647] Morrison-Volker Hearing Tr. at 38.

[648] Vindman Dep. Tr. at 121.

[649] *Id.* at 122.

[650] *Id.* at 122-123.

[651] *Id.* at 121.

[652] *Id.* at 123-124.

[653] Morrison Dep. Tr. at 121.

[654] *Id.* at 55-56.

[655] *Id.* at 55-56, 121-123.

[656] *Id.* at 270.

[657] Williams Dep. Tr. at 16, 63.

[658] *Id.* at 149.

[659] Vindman-Williams Hearing Tr. at 34.

[660] Williams Dep. Tr. at 148.

[661] Vindman-Williams Hearing Tr. at 29.

[662] Williams Dep. Tr. at 54, 149.

[663] Vindman Dep. Tr. at 54-55 ("There's one other substantive item in the next paragraph from Zelensky, where it says 'He or she will look into the situation specifically to the company'—it shouldn't be 'the company.' It should be 'to Burisma that you mentioned.' Because I think, you know, frankly these are not necessarily folks that are familiar with the substance. So President Zelensky specifically mentioned the company Burisma.").

[664] Vindman-Williams Hearing Tr. at 61.

[665] Vindman Dep. Tr. at 89.

[666] Williams Dep. Tr. at 68-69.

Q: Okay. When the transcript was made available to the VP's office, do you remember when that occurred?

A: My colleagues—I can't remember the precise time, but before the end of the day that day my colleagues who help prepare the Vice President's briefing book received a hard copy of the transcript from the White House Situation Room to include in that book. I didn't personally see it, but I understood that they had received it because we wanted to make sure the Vice President got it.

Q: On the 25th or 26th?

A: It was on the 25th.

[667] Vindman Dep. Tr. at 139–141.

[668] Kent Dep. Tr. at 163-165.

[669] Holmes Dep. Tr.at 107.

[670] *Id.* at 21-22.

[671] Kent-Taylor Hearing Tr. at 38; Hill-Holmes Hearing Tr. at 26.

[672] Morrison-Volker Hearing Tr. at 74 ("Yes. So I was not on the phone call. I had arrived in Ukraine, and I had had that lunch with Mr. Yermak that we saw on the day of the phone call. I had been pushing for the phone call because I thought it was important to renew the personal connection between the two leaders and to congratulate President Zelensky on the parliamentary election. The readout I received from Mr. Yermak and also from the U.S. side—although I'm not exactly sure who it was on the U.S. side, but there was U.S. and a Ukrainian readout—were largely the same, that it was a good call, that it was a congratulatory phone call for the President winning the parliamentary election. President Zelensky did reiterate his commitment to reform and fighting corruption in Ukraine, and President Trump did reiterate his invitation to President Zelensky to come visit him in the White House. That's exactly what I thought the phone call would be, so I was not surprised at getting that as the readout.").

[673] Holmes Dep. Tr. at 22.

[674] *Id.* at 22, 48-49.

[675] *Id.* at 49.

[676] *Id.* at 49.

[677] *Id.* at 22.

[678] Hill-Holmes Hearing Tr. at 27.

[679] *Id.* at 48-49.

[680] Croft Dep. Tr. at 118-119.

[681] Sondland Hearing Tr. at 25; Kent-Taylor Hearing Tr. at 38.

[682] Morrison-Volker Hearing Tr. at 89-90.

[683] Holmes Dep. Tr. at 64.

[684] Kent-Taylor Hearing Tr. at 38.

[685] Hill-Holmes Hearing Tr. at 27.

[686] *Id.*

[687] *Id.* at 27-28.

[688] *Id.*

[689] *Id.*

[690] Holmes Dep. Tr. at 108.

[691] Hill-Holmes Hearing Tr. at 49.

[692] Sondland Hearing Tr. at 25-26.

[693] Hill-Holmes Hearing Tr. at 28.

[694] *Id.*

[695] *Id.* at 49 ("The restaurant has sort of glass doors that open onto a terrace, and we were at the first tables on the terrace, so immediately outside of the interior of the restaurant. The doors were all wide open. There were—there was tables, a table for four, while I recall it being two tables for two pushed together. In any case, it was quite a wide table, and the table was set. There was sort of a table runner down the middle. I was directly across from Ambassador Sondland. We were close enough that we could, you know, share an appetizer between us, and then the two staffers were off to our right at this next table.").

[696] Hill-Holmes Hearing Tr. at 28.

[697] *Id.*

[698] Holmes Dep. Tr. at 160.

[699] Hill-Holmes Hearing Tr. at 28.

[700] *Id.* at 50.

Q: Now, you said that you were able to hear President Trump's voice through the receiver. How were you able to hear if it was not on speaker phone?

A: It was several things. It was quite loud when the President came on, quite distinctive. I believe Ambassador Sondland also said that he often speaks very loudly over the phone, and I certainly experienced that. When the President came on, he sort of winced and held the phone away from his ear like this, and he did that for the first couple exchanges. I don't know if he then turned the volume down, if he got used to it, if the President moderated his volume. I don't know. But that's how I was able to hear.

[701] *Id.* at 28-29.

[702] *Trump Denies Discussing Ukraine Investigations with Sondland in July Phone Call*, Axios (Nov. 13, 2019) (online at: www.axios.com/trump-denies-ukraine-investigation-sondland-6063f555-2629-4f99-b2f9-fd38739c0548 html).

[703] Sondland Hearing Tr. at 26.

[704] *Id.* at 46.

[705] *Id.* at 26.

[706] *Id.*

[707] *Id.* at 48.

[708] Holmes Dep. Tr. at 25.

[709] *Id.* at 25-26.

[710] Sondland Hearing Tr. at 49-50. Ambassador Sondland opined that, while he may have referred to an investigation that Mr. Giuliani was pushing as an example of an investigation that President Trump cared about, he believed that he would have said "Burisma, not Biden." He testified, however:

Q: But do you recall saying at least referring to an investigation that Rudy Giuliani was pushing? Is that something that you likely would have said?

A: I would have, yes.

Id. at 50.

[711] Sondland Hearing Tr. at 50.

[712] Holmes Dep. Tr. at 67.

[713] *Id.* at 68-69.

[714] Hill-Holmes Hearing Tr. at 30.

[715] *Id.* at 107.

[716] *Id.* at 34.

[717] Holmes Dep. Tr. at 80.

[718] *Id.* at 80-81.

[719] Kurt Volker Document Production, Bates KV00000007 (Oct. 2, 2019).

[720] *Id.*

721 *Id.*

722 *Id.* at Bates KV00000019.

723 Volker Transcribed Interview Tr. at 112.

724 Kurt Volker Document Production, Bates KV00000019 (Oct. 2, 2019).

725 Morrison-Volker Hearing Tr. at 42.

726 *Id.*

727 *Id.* at 20-21.

728 Kurt Volker Document Production, Bates KV00000019 (Oct. 2, 2019).

729 *Id.* at Bates KV00000007.

730 AT&T Document Production, Bates ATTHPSCI_20190930_02786.

731 Kurt Volker Document Production, Bates KV00000007 (Oct. 2, 2019).

732 Sondland Dep. Tr. at 192-193.

733 Kurt Volker Document Production, Bates KV00000007 (Oct. 2, 2019).

734 AT&T Document Production, Bates ATTHPSCI_20190930_02797.

735 *Id.*

736 *Id.*

737 *Id. at* Bates ATTHPSCI_20190930_03326.

738 *Id.*

739 *Id.*

740 *Id.*

741 *Id.*

742 *Id.*

743 *Id.* at Bates ATTHPSCI_20190930_02798.

744 *Id.*

745 *Id.*

746 *Id.*

747 *Id.*

748 AT&T Document Production, Bates ATTHPSCI_20190930_02799.

749 *Id.* at Bates ATTHPSCI_20190930_02801.

750 Kurt Volker Document Production, Bates KV00000019 (Oct. 2, 2019).

751 *Id.*

752 *Id.*

753 *Id.*

754 AT&T Document Production, Bates ATTHPSCI_20190930_02802-03, 02813, 03326, 03719.

755 *Id.* at Bates ATTHPSCI_20190930_03326.

756 *Id.* at Bates ATTHPSCI_20190930_02802.

757 *Id.* at Bates ATTHPSCI_20190930_02803.

[758] *Id.* at Bates ATTHPSCI_20190930_03719.

[759] *Id.*

[760] *Id.* at Bates ATTHPSCI_20190930_02803.

[761] *Id.*

[762] *Id.*

[763] *Id.*

[764] *Id.*

[765] Kurt Volker Document Production, Bates KV00000004- KV00000005 (Oct. 2, 2019).

[766] *Id.* at Bates KV00000004- KV00000005; AT&T Document Production, Bates ATTHPSCI_20190930_02805-06.

[767] Kurt Volker Document Production, Bates KV00000023 (Oct. 2, 2019).

[768] *Id.*

[769] *Id.*

[770] Verizon Document Production.

[771] Kurt Volker Document Production, Bates KV00000042 (Oct. 2, 2019).

[772] Sondland Dep. Tr. at 290; Sondland Hearing Tr. at 100-101.

[773] Kurt Volker Document Production, Bates KV00000042 (Oct. 2, 2019).

[774] Sondland Dep. Tr. at 291.

[775] *Id.*

[776] Kurt Volker Document Production, Bates KV00000019 (Oct. 2, 2019).

[777] *Id.*

[778] *Id.*

[779] *Id.* at Bates KV00000042.

[780] House Permanent Select Committee on Intelligence, Opening Statement of Ambassador Gordon Sondland, Department of State, *Impeachment*, 116th Cong., at 15 (Nov. 20, 2019).

[781] Kurt Volker Document Production, Bates KV00000042 (Oct. 2, 2019).

[782] Sondland Dep. Tr. at 291-292.

[783] *Id.*

[784] House Permanent Select Committee on Intelligence, Opening Statement of Ambassador Gordon Sondland, Department of State, *Impeachment*, 116th Cong., at 14 (Nov. 20, 2019).

[785] Kurt Volker Document Production, Bates KV00000005 (Oct. 2, 2019).

[786] AT&T Document Production, Bates ATTHPSCI_20190930_02816.

[787] House Permanent Select Committee on Intelligence, Opening Statement of Ambassador Gordon Sondland, Department of State, *Impeachment*, 116th Cong., at 22 (Nov. 20, 2019).

[788] Sondland Hearing Tr. at 102.

[789] House Permanent Select Committee on Intelligence, Opening Statement of Ambassador Gordon Sondland, Department of State, *Impeachment*, 116th Cong., at 22 (Nov. 20, 2019).

[790] Sondland Hearing Tr. at 28.

[791] Kurt Volker Document Production, Bates KV00000020 (Oct. 2, 2019).

[792] *Id.* at Bates KV00000007.

[793] AT&T Document Production, Bates ATTHPSCI_20190930_02828.

[794] Volker Transcribed Interview Tr. at 113.

[795] *Id.* at 71-72.

[796] Kurt Volker Document Production, Bates KV00000023 (Oct. 2, 2019).

[797] *Id.*

[798] *Id.*

[799] *Id.*

[800] WhatsApp Security (online at www.whatsapp.com/security/) (accessed Nov. 29, 2019).

[801] Kurt Volker Document Production, Bates KV00000043 (Oct. 2, 2019).

[802] *Id.*

[803] *Id.* at Bates KV00000023 .

[804] *Id.*

[805] Volker Transcribed Interview Tr. at 43-44, 113-114.

[806] House Permanent Select Committee on Intelligence, Opening Statement of Ambassador Gordon Sondland, Department of State, *Impeachment*, 116th Cong., at 5 (Nov. 20, 2019).

[807] Sondland Hearing Tr. at 18.

[808] Volker Transcribed Interview Tr. at 191, 197-198.

[809] *Id.* at 191-192.

[810] *Id.* at 201.

[811] *Id.* at 198.

[812] *Id.* at 197.

[813] *Trump Hasn't Talked to Attorney General About Having Ukraine Investigate Biden, DOJ Says*, CNN (Sept. 25, 2019) (online at www.cnn.com/politics/live-news/trump-impeachment-inquiry-09-25-2019/h_619f3c67775916f27e22898fbed210f2).

[814] *Cleaning Up Ukraine in the Shadow of Trump*, The Financial Times (Nov. 28, 2019) (online at www.ft.com/content/eb8e4004-1059-11ea-a7e6-62bf4f9e548a).

[815] *Id.*

[816] Taylor Dep. Opening Statement at 9.

[817] *Id.*

[818] Volker Transcribed Interview Tr. at 196-197.

[819] Taylor Dep. Opening Statement at 9.

[820] Kurt Volker Document Production, Bates KV00000043 (Oct. 2, 2019).

[821] Volker Transcribed Interview Tr. at 196-197.

[822] Kent Dep. Tr. at 261

[823] *Id.* at 262-263.

[824] *Id.* at 264.

[825] *Id.* at 264-265.

[826] Kurt Volker Document Production, Bates KV00000020 (Oct. 2, 2019).

[827] *Id.* at Bates KV00000043.

[828] *Id.*

[829] *Id.*

[830] Volker Transcribed Interview Opening Statement at 8.

[831] Volker Transcribed Interview Tr. at 44.

[832] Morrison-Volker Hearing Tr. at 21.

[833] Volker Transcribed Interview Tr. at 259-260.

[834] *Id.* at 260.

[835] Morrison-Volker Hearing Tr. at 128.

[836] Kurt Volker Document Production, Bates KV00000043 (Oct. 2, 2019).

[837] Volker Transcribed Interview Tr. at 199-200.

[838] Hill-Holmes Hearing Tr. at 31-32, 68; Sondland Hearing Tr. at 55-57.

[839] Cooper Dep. Tr. at 71.

[840] *Id.* at 62, 66.

[841] *Id.* at 62.

[842] Morrison-Volker Hearing Tr. at 90-91.

[843] House Permanent Select Committee on Intelligence, Opening Statement of Ambassador Gordon Sondland, at 23, *Impeachment*, 116th Cong. (Nov. 20, 2019).

[844] *Id.*

[845] Sondland Hearing Tr. at 104.

[846] House Permanent Select Committee on Intelligence, Opening Statement of Ambassador Gordon Sondland, at 18, *Impeachment*, 116th Cong. (Nov. 20, 2019).

[847] Sondland Hearing Tr. at 44.

[848] *Id.* at 75.

[849] *Id.* at 76.

[850] House Permanent Select Committee on Intelligence, Opening Statement of Ambassador Gordon Sondland, at 23, *Impeachment*, 116th Cong. (Nov. 20, 2019).

[851] Hill-Holmes Hearing Tr. at 30.

[852] *Id.*

[853] Sondland Hearing Tr. at 28.

[854] *Id.* at 106.

[855] Hill-Holmes Hearing Tr. at 31-32.

[856] *Id.* at 31.

[857] Kent-Taylor Hearing Tr. at 40.

[858] Taylor Dep. Tr. at 230.

[859] Kent-Taylor Hearing Tr. at 40.

[860] Hill-Holmes Hearing Tr. at 8.

[861] Kurt Volker Document Production, Bates KV00000020 (Oct. 2, 2019).

[862] Volker Transcribed Interview Tr. at 80-81.

> A: By the time it hit Politico publicly, I believe it was the end of August. And I got a text message from, it was either the Foreign Minister or—I think it was the future Foreign Minister. And, you know, basically, you're just—you're—I have to verbalize this. You're just trying to explain that we are trying this. We have a complicated system. We have a lot of players in this. We are working this. Give us time to fix it.
>
> Q: So anybody on the Ukrainian side of things ever express like grave concern that this would not get worked out?
>
> A: Not that it wouldn't get worked out, no, they did not. They expressed concern that, since this has now come out publicly in this Politico article, it looks like that they're being, you know, singled out and penalized for some reason. That's the image that that would create in Ukraine.

[863] Taylor Dep. Tr. at 34.

[864] *Id.* at 137-138.

[865] *Id.*

[866] Kent-Taylor Hearing Tr. at 174.

[867] *Id.* at 40.

[868] *Id.*

[869] Hill-Holmes Hearing Tr. at 31-32.

[870] *Id.*

[871] *Id.* at 68.

[872] Holmes Dep. Tr. at 58.

[873] Kent-Taylor Hearing Tr. at 40.

[874] *Trump, in August Call with GOP Senator, Denied Official's Claim on Ukraine Aid*, Wall Street Journal (Oct. 4, 2019) (online at www.wsj.com/articles/trump-administration-used-potential-meeting-to-pressure-ukraine-on-biden-texts-indicate-11570205661).

[875] *Id.*

[876] Letter from Senator Ron Johnson to Ranking Member Jim Jordan, House Committee on Oversight and Reform, and Ranking Member Devin Nunes, House Permanent Select Committee on Intelligence (Nov. 18, 2019) (online at www.ronjohnson.senate.gov/public/_cache/files/e0b73c19-9370-42e6-88b1-b2458eaeeecd/johnson-to-jordan-nunes.pdf).

[877] *Id.*

[878] The White House, *Memorandum of Telephone Conversation* (July 25, 2019) (online at www.whitehouse.gov/wp-content/uploads/2019/09/Unclassified09.2019.pdf).

[879] Office of the Director of National Intelligence, *Background to "Assessing Russian Activities and Intentions in Recent US Elections": The Analytic Process and Cyber Incident Attribution* (Jan. 6, 2017) (online at www.dni.gov/files/documents/ICA_2017_01.pdf).

[880] Letter from Senator Ron Johnson to Ranking Member Jim Jordan, Committee on Oversight and Reform, and Ranking Member Devin Nunes, Permanent Select Committee on Intelligence (Nov. 18, 2019) (online at www.ronjohnson.senate.gov/public/_cache/files/e0b73c19-9370-42e6-88b1-b2458eaeeecd/johnson-to-jordan-nunes.pdf).

[881] Sondland Hearing Tr. at 30.

[882] Volker Transcribed Interview Tr. at 251-252; Kent-Taylor Hearing Tr. at 41.

191

[883] Williams Dep. Tr. at 74-77.

[884] *Id.* at 76.

[885] *Id.* at 78-79.

[886] Sondland Hearing Tr. at 30.

[887] *Id.* at 38. *See also* Sondland Hearing Tr. at 57:

A: I don't know exactly what I said to him. This was a briefing attended by many people, and I was invited at the very last minute. I wasn't scheduled to be there. But I think I spoke up at some point late in the meeting and said, it looks like everything is being held up until these statements get made, and that's my, you know, personal belief.

Q: And Vice President Pence just nodded his head?

A: Again, I don't recall any exchange or where he asked me any questions. I think he—it was sort of a duly noted response.

Q: Well, he didn't say, Gordon, what are you talking about?

A: No, he did not.

Q: He didn't say, what investigations?

A: He did not.

[888] *Pence Disputes that Sondland Raised Concerns to Him About Ukraine Aid-Investigations Link*, Wall Street Journal (Nov. 20, 2019) (online at www.wsj.com/livecoverage/gordon-sondland-testifies-impeachment/card/1574268547).

[889] Taylor Dep. Tr. at 190.

[890] *Id.* at 35.

[891] *Id.* at 190-191.

[892] Williams Dep. Tr. at 81.

[893] *Id.* at 82.

[894] *Id.* at 82-83.

[895] *Id.* at 83.

[896] *Id.*

[897] *How a CIA Analyst, Alarmed by Trump's Shadow Foreign Policy, Triggered an Impeachment Inquiry*, Washington Post (Nov. 16, 2019) (online at www.washingtonpost.com/national-security/how-a-cia-analyst-alarmed-by-trumps-shadow-foreign-policy-triggered-an-impeachment-inquiry/2019/11/15/042684a8-03c3-11ea-8292-c46ee8cb3dce_story html).

[898] Hill-Holmes Hearing Tr. at 31.

[899] Sondland Hearing Tr. at 31.

[900] Morrison Dep. Tr. at 134.

[901] *Id.* at 155.

[902] *Id.*

[903] *Id.* at 137.

[904] *Id.* at 182.

[905] *Id.* at 184.

[906] *Id.* at 228.

[907] *Id.* at 154.

[908] Kent-Taylor Hearing Tr. at 42.

[909] *Id.*

[910] *Id.* at 57.

[911] Kurt Volker Document Production, Bates KV00000039 (Oct. 2, 2019).

[912] Kent-Taylor Hearing Tr. at 42.

[913] Taylor Dep. Tr. at 190.

[914] *Id.*

[915] *Id.*

[916] Kent-Taylor Hearing Tr. at 60.

[917] Sondland Hearing Tr. at 59.

[918] *Id.* at 59-60.

[919] Morrison Dep. Tr. at 190-191.

[920] Morrison-Volker Hearing Tr. at 52.

[921] *Id.* at 53-54; Morrison Dep. Tr. at 238.

[922] Kent-Taylor Hearing Tr. at 43-44.

[923] Kurt Volker Document Production, Bates KV00000053 (Oct. 2, 2019).

[924] Kent-Taylor Hearing Tr. at 44.

[925] *Id.*

[926] *Id.*

[927] Sondland Hearing Tr. at 109-110.

[928] *Id.*

[929] *Id.* at 110-111.

[930] Kent-Taylor Hearing Tr. at 45.

[931] *Id.* at 45, 63.

[932] *Id.* at 45.

[933] Sondland Hearing Tr. at 110. Ambassador Volker also testified that Ambassador Sondland used the same analogy to him when discussing the release of the hold on security assistance. Morrison-Volker Hearing Tr. at 96-97.

[934] Kurt Volker Document Production, Bates KV00000053 (Oct. 2, 2019).

[935] Taylor Dep. Tr. at 209.

[936] Kurt Volker Document Production, Bates KV000000053 (Oct. 2, 2019).

[937] Kent-Taylor Hearing Tr. at 54.

[938] *Id.*

[939] *Id.*

[940] *Id.*

[941] Kurt Volker Document Production, Bates KV00000053 (Oct. 2, 2019).

[942] Sondland Dep. Tr. at 217.

[943] Sondland Hearing Tr. at 26 ("Was there a quid pro quo? As I testified previously with regard to the requested White House call and the White House meeting, the answer is yes.").

[944] *Id.* at 41.

[945] *Id.* at 112

[946] *Id.* at 61-62.

[947] Taylor Dep. Tr. at 39.

[948] *Taylor Dep. Tr. at 39.*

[949] Maguire Hearing Tr. at 110; Whistleblower Compl. Appendix 2. Public reporting indicates that "[l]awyers from the White House counsel's office told Mr. Trump in late August about the complaint, explaining that they were trying to determine whether they were legally required to give it to Congress." *Trump Knew of Whistle-Blower Complaint When He Released Aid to Ukraine*, New York Times (Nov. 26, 2019) (online at www.nytimes.com/2019/11/26/us/politics/trump-whistle-blower-complaint-ukraine.html).

[950] Letter from Michael Atkinson, Inspector General of the Intelligence Community, to Chairman Adam B. Schiff and Ranking Member Devin Nunes, House Permanent Select Committee on Intelligence (Sept. 9, 2019) (online at https://intelligence house.gov/uploadedfiles/20190909_-_ic_ig_letter_to_hpsci_on_whistleblower.pdf).

[951] *Id.*

[952] Sondland Hearing Tr. at 118. *See also Witness Testimony and Records Raise Questions About Account of Trump's 'No Quid Pro Quo' Call*, Washington Post (Nov. 27, 2019) (online at www.washingtonpost.com/politics/witness-testimony-and-records-raise-questions-about-account-of-trumps-no-quid-pro-quo-call/2019/11/27/425545c2-0d49-11ea-8397-a955cd542d00_story.html).

[953] Sondland Hearing Tr. at 118.

[954] *Id.* at 73.

[955] Declaration of Ambassador Gordon Sondland, Department of State, at 1 (Nov. 4, 2019). This addendum did not address the July 26 telephone conversation that Sondland had with President Trump, which he only recalled following the testimony of David Holmes on November 15, 2019. Sondland Hearing Tr. at 46.

[956] Declaration of Ambassador Gordon Sondland, Department of State, at 3 (Nov. 4, 2019).

[957] Kent-Taylor Hearing Tr. at 43-44; Morrison Dep. Tr. at 190-191.

[958] Morrison Dep. Tr. at 190-191; Kent-Taylor Hearing Tr. at 43-44.

[959] Sondland Hearing Tr. at 109.

[960] *Id.* at 45, 109.

[961] Kurt Volker Document Production, Bates KV00000020 (Oct. 2, 2019).

[962] *Id.*

[963] Id. at Bates KV00000053.

[964] *Id.*

[965] The White House, *Press Briefing by Acting Chief of Staff Mick Mulvaney* (Oct. 17, 2019) (online at www.whitehouse.gov/briefings-statements/press-briefing-acting-chief-staff-mick-mulvaney/).

[966] *Id.*

[967] *Id.* Ambassador Taylor's testimony contradicted Mr. Mulvaney's statement about the ubiquity of such quid pro quos in American foreign policy. Ambassador Taylor testified that in his decades of military and diplomatic service, he had never seen another example of foreign aid conditioned on the personal or political interests of the President. Kent-Taylor Hearing Tr. at 55. Rather, "[w]e condition assistance on issues that will improve our foreign policy, serve our foreign policy, ensure that taxpayers' money is well-spent." Kent-Taylor Hearing Tr. at 150.

968 There were early concerns raised in the House and Senate about the frozen aid, even before the news became public. On August 9, the Democratic leadership of the House and Senate Appropriations Committees wrote to OMB and the White House warning that the August 3 letter apportionment might constitute an illegal impoundment of funds. They urged the Trump Administration to adhere to the law and obligate the withheld funding. Letter from Vice Chairman Patrick Leahy, Senate Committee on Appropriations, and Chairwoman Nita M. Lowey, House Committee on Appropriations, to Acting Chief of Staff Mick Mulvaney, The White House, and Acting Director Russell Vought, Office of Management and Budget (Aug. 9, 2019) (online at https://appropriations house.gov/sites/democrats.appropriations.house.gov/files/documents/SFOPS%20Apportionment%20Letter%20Lowey-Leahy%20Signed%202019.8.9.pdf). On August 19, the Democratic leadership of the House and Senate Budget Committees wrote to OMB and the White House urging the Administration to comply with appropriations law and the Impoundment Control Act. Letter from Chairman John Yarmuth, House Committee on the Budget, and Ranking Member Bernard Sanders, Senate Committee on the Budget, to Acting Chief of Staff Mick Mulvaney, The White House (Aug. 19, 2019) (online at https://budget house.gov/sites/democrats.budget.house.gov/files/documents/OMB%20Letter_081919.pdf).

969 Letter from Senators Jeanne Shaheen, Rob Portman, Richard Durbin, Ron Johnson, and Richard Blumenthal to Acting White House Chief of Staff Mick Mulvaney (Sept. 3, 2019) (online at www.shaheen.senate.gov/imo/media/doc/Ukraine%20Security%20Letter%209.3.2019.pdf).

970 Id.

971 Letter from Chairman Eliot L. Engel and Ranking Member Michael T. McCaul, House Foreign Affairs Committee to Mick Mulvaney, Director, and Russell Vought, Acting Director, Office of Management and Budget, The White House (Sept. 5, 2019) (online at https://foreignaffairs.house.gov/_cache/files/c/4/c49328c2-941b-4c41-8c00-8c1515f0972f/D1968A9C42455BB3AFC38F97D966857B.ele-mccaul-letter-to-mulvaney-vought-on-ukraine-assistance.pdf).

972 *Trump Tries to Force Ukraine to Meddle in the 2020 Election*, Washington Post (Sept. 5, 2019) (online at www.washingtonpost.com/opinions/global-opinions/is-trump-strong-arming-ukraines-new-president-for-political-gain/2019/09/05/4eb239b0-cffa-11e9-8c1c-7c8ee785b855_story.html).

973 Taylor Dep. Tr. at 37-38.

974 *Id.* at 38.

975 *See* Letter from Senator Christopher Murphy to Chairman Adam B. Schiff, House Permanent Select Committee on Intelligence, and Acting Chairwoman Carolyn Maloney, House Committee on Oversight and Reform (Nov. 19, 2019) (online at www.murphy.senate.gov/download/111919-sen-murphy-letter-to-house-impeachment-investigators-on-ukraine) ("Senator Johnson and I assured Zelensky that Congress wanted to continue this funding, and would press Trump to release it immediately."); Letter from Senator Ron Johnson to Ranking Member Jim Jordan, Committee on Oversight and Reform, and Ranking Member Devin Nunes, Permanent Select Committee on Intelligence (Nov. 18, 2019) (online at www.ronjohnson.senate.gov/public/_cache/files/e0b73c19-9370-42e6-88b1-b2458eaeeecd/johnson-to-jordan-nunes.pdf) ("I explained that I had tried to persuade the president to authorize me to announce the hold was released but that I was unsuccessful.").

976 House Permanent Select Committee on Intelligence, *Three House Committees Launch Probe Into Trump and Giuliani Pressure Campaign* (Sept. 9, 2019) (online at https://intelligence.house.gov/news/documentsingle.aspx?DocumentID=685).

977 Letter from Chairman Eliot L. Engel, House Committee on Foreign Affairs, Chairman Adam B. Schiff, House Permanent Select Committee on Intelligence, and Chairman Elijah E. Cummings, House Committee on Oversight and Reform, to Pat Cipollone, Counsel to the President, The White House (Sept. 9, 2019) (online at https://intelligence.house.gov/uploadedfiles/ele_schiff_cummings_letter_to_cipollone_on_ukraine.pdf).

978 *Id.*

979 *Id.*

980 Letter from Chairman Eliot L. Engel, House Committee on Foreign Affairs, Chairman Adam B. Schiff, House Permanent Select Committee on Intelligence, and Chairman Elijah E. Cummings, House Committee on Oversight and Reform, to Michael R. Pompeo, Secretary of State (Sept. 9, 2019) (online at https://intelligence.house.gov/uploadedfiles/ele_schiff_cummings_letter_to_sec_pompeo_on_ukraine.pdf).

[981] Morrison Dep. Tr. at 245.

[982] *Id.*

[983] Vindman Dep. Tr. at 303.

[984] *Id.* at 304.

[985] Letter from Michael Atkinson, Inspector General of the Intelligence Community, to Chairman Adam B. Schiff and Ranking Member Devin Nunes, House Permanent Select Committee on Intelligence (Sept. 9, 2019) (online at https://intelligence house.gov/uploadedfiles/20190909_-_ic_ig_letter_to_hpsci_on_whistleblower.pdf).

[986] *Id.*; *see also* 50 U.S.C. § 3033(k)(5) (setting forth procedures for reporting of complaints or information with respect to an "urgent concern" to Congressional intelligence committees).

[987] Maguire Hearing Tr. at 14 ("As a result, we consulted with the White House Counsel's Office, and we were advised that much of the information in the complaint was, in fact, subject to executive privilege, a privilege that I do not have the authority to waive. Because of that, we were unable to immediately share the details of the complaint with this committee but continued to consult with the White House counsels in an effort to do so.").

[988] *Id.* at 15-16 ("Because the allegation on its face did not appear to fall in the statutory framework, my office consulted with the United States Department of Justice Office of Legal Counsel. … After reviewing the complaint and the Inspector General's transmission letter, the Office of Legal Counsel determined that the complaint's allegations do not meet the statutory definition concerning legal urgent concern, and found that I was not legally required to transmit the material to our oversight committee under the Whistleblower Protection Act.").

[989] *Id.* at 22-23. *See also CIA's Top Lawyer Made 'Criminal Referral' on Complaint about Trump Ukraine Call*, NBC News (Oct. 4, 2019) (online at www.nbcnews.com/politics/trump-impeachment-inquiry/cia-s-top-lawyer-made-criminal-referral-whistleblower-s-complaint-n1062481) (reporting that the CIA's General Counsel, Courtney Simmons Elwood, informed NSC chief lawyer John Eisenberg about an anonymous whistleblower complaint on August 14, 2019).

[990] Maguire Hearing Tr. at 14, 21-22. On September 26, Acting DNI Maguire testified that he and the ODNI General Counsel first consulted with the White House counsel's office before discussing the whistleblower complaint with the Department of Justice's Office of Legal Counsel:

The Chairman.	I'm just trying to understand the chronology. You first went to the Office of Legal Counsel, and then you went to the White House Counsel?
Acting Director Maguire.	No, no, no, sir. No, sir. No. We went to the White House first to determine— to ask the question—
The Chairman.	That's all I want to know is the chronology. So you went to the White House first. So you went to the subject of the complaint for advice first about whether you should provide the complaint to Congress?
Acting Director Maguire.	There were issues within this, a couple of things: One, it did appear that it has executive privilege. If it does have executive privilege, it is the White House that determines that. I cannot determine that, as the Director of National Intelligence.

Id. at 21-22.

[991] *Trump Knew of Whistle-Blower Complaint When He Released Aid to Ukraine*, New York Times (Nov. 26, 2019) (online at www nytimes.com/2019/11/26/us/politics/trump-whistle-blower-complaint-ukraine html).

[992] *Id.* The Administration repeatedly referenced privilege concerns in connection with the whistleblower complaint. *See, e.g.*, Letter from Jason Klitenic, General Counsel, Office of the Director of National Intelligence, to Chairman Adam B. Schiff, House Permanent Select Committee on Intelligence (Sept. 13, 2019) (noting that "the complaint involves confidential and *potentially privileged* communications by persons outside the Intelligence Community") (emphasis added); Letter from Jason Klitenic, General Counsel, Office of the Director of National Intelligence, to Chairman Adam B. Schiff, House Permanent Select Committee on Intelligence (Sept. 17, 2019) (characterizing subpoena to the Acting DNI for documents as demanding "sensitive and *potentially privileged*"

materials and whistleblower complaint as involving "*potentially privileged* matters relating to the interests of other stakeholders within the Executive Branch") (emphasis added).

However, the White House never formally invoked executive privilege as to the whistleblower complaint. *See* Maguire Hearing Tr. at 20 ("Chairman Schiff: So they never asserted executive privilege, is that the answer? Acting Director Maguire: Mr. Chairman, if they did, we would not have released the letters yesterday and all the information that has been forthcoming.").

[993] Letter from Chairman Adam B. Schiff, House Permanent Select Committee on Intelligence, to Joseph Maguire, Acting Director of National Intelligence (Sept. 10, 2019) (online at https://intelligence.house.gov/uploadedfiles/20190910_-_chm_schiff_letter_to_acting_dni_maguire.pdf).

[994] *Id..*

[995] *See* Letter from Jason Klitenic, General Counsel, Office of the Director of National Intelligence, to Chairman Adam B. Schiff, House Permanent Select Committee on Intelligence (Sept. 13, 2019).

[996] Letter from Chairman Adam B. Schiff, House Permanent Select Committee on Intelligence, to Joseph Maguire, Acting Director of National Intelligence (Sept. 13, 2019) (online at https://intelligence.house.gov/uploadedfiles/20190913_-_chm_schiff_letter_to_acting_dni_re_whistleblower_-_subpoena.pdf).

[997] The White House, *Memorandum of Telephone Conversation* (July 25, 2019) (online at www.whitehouse.gov/wp-content/uploads/2019/09/Unclassified09.2019.pdf).

[998] Vindman Dep. Tr. at 305-06; Morrison Dep. Tr. at 242.

[999] Morrison Dep. Tr. at 242.

[1000] *See, e.g., Id.* at 244; Vindman Dep. Tr. at 306; Williams Dep. Tr. at 147.

[1001] Cooper Dep. Tr. at 68-69.

[1002] Williams Dep. Tr. at 147. Ms. Williams did testify that President Trump's pressure on President Zelensky to open investigations into the Bidens on the July 25 call "shed some light on possible other motivations behind a security assistance hold." Williams Dep. Tr. at 149.

[1003] Sandy Dep. Tr. at 42, 139-140. According to a press report, after Congress began investigating President Trump's scheme, the White House Counsel's Office reportedly opened an internal investigation relating to the July 25 call. As part of that internal investigation, White House lawyers gathered and reviewed "hundreds of documents" that "reveal extensive efforts to generate an after-the-fact justification" for the hold on military assistance for Ukraine ordered by President Trump. These documents reportedly include "early August email exchanges between acting chief of staff Mick Mulvaney and White House budget officials seeking to provide an explanation for withholding the funds after the president had already ordered a hold in mid-July on the nearly $400 million in security assistance." *White House Review Turns Up Emails Showing Extensive Effort to Justify Trump's Decision to Block Ukraine Military Aid*, Washington Post (Nov. 24, 2019) (online at www.washingtonpost.com/politics/white-house-review-turns-up-emails-showing-extensive-effort-to-justify-trumps-decision-to-block-ukraine-military-aid/2019/11/24/2121cf98-0d57-11ea-bd9d-c628fd48b3a0_story.html). The White House has withheld these documents from the Committee, so the Committee cannot verify the accuracy of the reporting as of the publication of this report.

[1004] Sandy Dep. Tr. at 49.

[1005] *Id.* at 42, 44.

[1006] *Id.* at 180.

[1007] Vindman Dep. Tr. at 306.

[1008] Cooper Dep. Tr. at 83.

[1009] *Id.* at 47-48, 58, 112-114; Sandy Dep. Tr. at 34-35, 85-86, 95, 128, 129-131, 133; Morrison Dep. Tr. at 163; Kent Dep. Tr. at 308-309; Reeker Dep. Tr. at 133. News reports indicate that a confidential White House review of President Trump's hold on military assistance to Ukraine has identified hundreds of documents revealing "extensive efforts to generate an after-the-fact justification for the decision and a debate over whether the delay was legal." *White House Review Turns Up Emails Showing Extensive Effort to Justify Trump's Decision to Block Ukraine Military Aid*, Washington Post (Nov. 24, 2019) (online at www.washingtonpost.com/politics/white-house-review-turns-up-emails-showing-extensive-effort-to-justify-trumps-decision-to-block-ukraine-military-aid/2019/11/24/2121cf98-0d57-11ea-bd9d-c628fd48b3a0_story.html). According to "two people briefed on an internal White House review," in August, Acting Chief of Staff Mulvaney "asked … whether there was a legal justification for withholding hundreds of millions of dollars in military aid to Ukraine." *Mulvaney Asked About Legal Justification for Withholding Ukraine Aid*, New York Times (Nov. 24, 2019) (online at www.nytimes.com/2019/11/24/us/politics/mulvaney-ukraine-aid html). Reports indicate that, "[e]mails show [OMB Director] Vought and OMB staffers arguing that withholding aid was legal, while officials at the National Security Council and State Department protested. OMB lawyers said that it was legal to withhold the aid, as long as they deemed it a 'temporary' hold." *White House Review Turns Up Emails Showing Extensive Effort to Justify Trump's Decision to Block Ukraine Military Aid*, Washington Post (Nov. 24, 2019) (online at www.washingtonpost.com/politics/white-house-review-turns-up-emails-showing-extensive-effort-to-justify-trumps-decision-to-block-ukraine-military-aid/2019/11/24/2121cf98-0d57-11ea-bd9d-c628fd48b3a0_story.html). The White House and State Department's obstruction of Congress has prevented the Committee from obtaining any documents on this matter and, therefore, the Committee cannot verify the accuracy of this reporting as of the publication of this report.

[1010] Cooper Dep. Tr. at 80.

[1011] Sandy Dep. Tr. at 146-147.

[1012] *See* Department of Defense, *DOD Budget Materials (FY2011-FY2018)* (online at https://comptroller.defense.gov/Budget-Materials/). In 1974, President Nixon impounded 15-20 percent of a number of specific programs, which prompted the passage of the Impoundment Control Act of 1974. Congressional Research Service, *The Congressional Budget Act of 1974 (P.L. 93-344) Legislative History and Analysis* (Feb. 26, 1975).

[1013] Department of Defense and Labor, Health and Human Services, and Education Appropriations Act, 2019 and Continuing Appropriations Act, 2019, Pub. L. No. 115-245, § 9013 (2018); Sandy Dep. Tr. at 147.

[1014] Continuing Appropriations Act 2020, and Health Extenders Act of 2019, Pub. L. No. 116-59, § 124 (2019).

[1015] Cooper Dep. Tr. at 98.

[1016] *$35 Million in Pentagon Aid Hasn't Reached Ukraine Despite White House Assurances*, L.A. Times (Nov. 19, 2019) (online at www.latimes.com/politics/story/2019-11-19/documents-show-nearly-40-million-in-ukraine-aid-delayed-despite-white-house-assurances).

[1017] *Zelensky Planned to Announce Trump's 'Quo' on My Show. Here's What Happened*, Washington Post (Nov. 14, 2019) (online at www.washingtonpost.com/opinions/zelensky-was-planning-to-announce-trumps-quid-pro-quo-on-my-show-heres-what-happened/2019/11/14/47938f32-072a-11ea-8292-c46ee8cb3dce_story.html).

[1018] *Id.*

[1019] Taylor Dep. Tr. at 40.

[1020] Kent-Taylor Hearing Tr. at 106.

[1021] *Id.*

[1022] Hill-Holmes Hearing Tr. at 33.

[1023] *Id.*

[1024] Taylor Dep. Tr. at 41.

[1025] *Id.* at 217-18.

[1026] *Id.*

[1027] Holmes Dep. Tr. at 30.

[1028] *Zelensky Planned to Announce Trump's 'Quo' on My Show. Here's What Happened*, Washington Post (Nov. 14, 2019) (online at www.washingtonpost.com/opinions/zelensky-was-planning-to-announce-trumps-quid-pro-quo-on-my-show-heres-what-happened/2019/11/14/47938f32-072a-11ea-8292-c46ee8cb3dce_story.html).

[1029] Hill-Holmes Hearing Tr. at 33; *see also Zelensky Planned to Announce Trump's 'Quo' on My Show. Here's What Happened*, Washington Post (Nov. 14, 2019) (online at www.washingtonpost.com/opinions/zelensky-was-planning-to-announce-trumps-quid-pro-quo-on-my-show-heres-what-happened/2019/11/14/47938f32-072a-11ea-8292-c46ee8cb3dce_story.html).

[1030] Kent. Dep. Tr. at 333.

[1031] *Id*. at 329-31.

[1032] *Id*. at 330.

[1033] *Zelensky Planned to Announce Trump's 'Quo' on My Show. Here's What Happened*, Washington Post (Nov. 14, 2019) (online at www.washingtonpost.com/opinions/zelensky-was-planning-to-announce-trumps-quid-pro-quo-on-my-show-heres-what-happened/2019/11/14/47938f32-072a-11ea-8292-c46ee8cb3dce_story.html).

[1034] Hill-Holmes Hearing Tr. at 46-47.

[1035] Williams Dep. Tr. at 156.

[1036] *Id*.

[1037] *Pence Says He's Working to Release Transcripts of His Calls with Ukraine Leader*, Politico (Oct. 9, 2019) (online at www.politico.com/news/2019/10/09/pence-ukraine-zelensky-biden-043684).

[1038] *Pence: I Don't Object To Releasing My Call Transcripts With Zelensky*, Fox Business (Nov. 7, 2019) (online at www.realclearpolitics.com/video/2019/11/07/pence_i_dont_object_to_releasing_my_call_transcripts_with_zelensky.html).

[1039] *Rudy Giuliani's Remarkable Ukraine Interview, Annotated*, Washington Post (Sept. 20, 2019) (online at www.washingtonpost.com/politics/2019/09/20/rudy-giulianis-remarkable-ukraine-interview-annotated/).

[1040] The White House, *Remarks by President Trump and President Duda of Poland Before Bilateral Meeting* (Sept. 23, 2019) (online at www.whitehouse.gov/briefings-statements/remarks-president-trump-president-duda-poland-bilateral-meeting/).

[1041] The White House, *Remarks by President Trump Upon Arriving at the U.N. General Assembly* (Sept. 24, 2019) (online at www.whitehouse.gov/briefings-statements/remarks-president-trump-upon-arriving-u-n-general-assembly-new-york-ny/).

[1042] The White House, *Remarks by President Trump and President Zelensky of Ukraine Before Bilateral Meeting* (Sept 25, 2019) (online at www.whitehouse.gov/briefings-statements/remarks-president-trump-president-zelensky-ukraine-bilateral-meeting-new-york-ny/).

[1043] The White House, *Remarks by President Trump at the Swearing-in Ceremony of Secretary of Labor Eugene Scalia* (Sept 30, 2019) (online at www.whitehouse.gov/briefings-statements/remarks-president-trump-swearing-ceremony-secretary-labor-eugene-scalia/).

[1044] The White House, *Remarks by President Trump and President Niinistö of the Republic of Finland Before Bilateral Meeting* (Oct. 2, 2019) (www.whitehouse.gov/briefings-statements/remarks-president-trump-president-niinisto-republic-finland-bilateral-meeting/).

[1045] The White House, *Remarks by President Trump Before Marine One Departure* (Oct. 3, 2019) (online at www.whitehouse.gov/briefings-statements/remarks-president-trump-marine-one-departure-67/).

[1046] The White House, *Remarks by President Trump Before Marine One Departure* (Oct. 4, 2019) (online at www.whitehouse.gov/briefings-statements/remarks-president-trump-marine-one-departure-68).

[1047] *Id*.

[1048] The White House, *Remarks by President Trump Before Marine One Departure* (Oct. 3, 2019) (online at www.whitehouse.gov/briefings-statements/remarks-president-trump-marine-one-departure-67/). These recent statements by President inviting foreign assistance for his personal political interests are consistent with his statements to George Stephanopoulos of ABC News on June 12, when President Trump indicated a desire to receive dirt on a political opponent provided by a foreign country. *ABC News' Oval Office interview with President Trump*, ABC News (June 13, 2019) (online at https://abcnews.go.com/Politics/abc-news-oval-office-interview-president-donald-trump/story?id=63688943).

[1049] Morrison-Volker Hearing Tr. at 46-47, 91-92.

[1050] Vindman Dep. Tr. at 158-19; Holmes Dep. Tr. at 100; Kent-Taylor Hearing Tr. at 43.

[1051] Kent-Taylor Hearing Tr. at 24.

[1052] Hill-Holmes Hearing Tr. at 46.

[1053] Kent-Taylor Hearing Tr. at 165.

[1054] *Id.*

[1055] *Id.* at 24.

[1056] *Id.* at 55-56.

[1057] *Id.* at 164.

[1058] Kent Dep. Tr. at 329; Morrison-Volker Hearing Tr. at 138-139.

[1059] Morrison-Volker Hearing Tr. at 139.

[1060] *Id.*

SECTION II.

THE PRESIDENT'S OBSTRUCTION OF THE HOUSE OF REPRESENTATIVES' IMPEACHMENT INQUIRY

1.   Constitutional Authority for Congressional Oversight and Impeachment

> *Article I of the Constitution vests in the House of Representatives the "sole Power of Impeachment." Congress is authorized to conduct oversight and investigations in support of its Article I powers. The Supreme Court—and previous Presidents—have acknowledged these authorities.*

Overview

The House's Constitutional and legal authority to conduct an impeachment inquiry is clear, as is the duty of the President to cooperate with the House's exercise of this authority. The Constitution vests in the House of Representatives the "sole Power of Impeachment" as well as robust oversight powers. As the Founders intended, the courts have agreed, and prior Presidents have acknowledged, the House's sweeping powers to investigate are at their peak during an impeachment inquiry of a President. Congress has also enacted statutes to support its power to investigate and oversee the Executive Branch.

Unlike President Donald J. Trump, past Presidents who were the subject of impeachment inquiries acknowledged Congress' authority to investigate and—to varying degrees—complied with information requests and subpoenas. Even so, the House has previously determined that partial noncooperation can serve as a ground for an article of impeachment against a President as it would upend the separation of powers to allow the President to dictate the scope of an impeachment inquiry. When President Richard Nixon withheld tape recordings and produced heavily edited and inaccurate records, the House Judiciary Committee approved an article of impeachment for obstruction.

Constitutional Power of Congress to Investigate—and to Impeach

Article I of the U.S. Constitution gives the House of Representatives the "sole Power of Impeachment."[1] The Framers intended the impeachment power to be an essential check on a President who might engage in corruption or abuse power. For example, during the Constitutional Convention, George Mason stated:

> No point is of more importance than that the right of impeachment should be continued. Shall any man be above Justice? Above all shall that man be above it, who can commit the most extensive injustice? … Shall the man who has practised corruption & by that means procured his appointment in the first instance, be suffered to escape punishment, by repeating his guilt?[2]

Congress is empowered to conduct oversight and investigations to carry out its authorities under Article I.[3] In light of the core nature of the impeachment power to the nation's Constitutional system of checks and balances, Congress' investigative authority is at its zenith during an impeachment inquiry.[4]

As the House Judiciary Committee explained during the impeachment of President Nixon:

> Whatever the limits of legislative power in other contexts—and whatever need may otherwise exist for preserving the confidentiality of Presidential conversations—in the context of an impeachment proceeding the balance was struck in favor of the power of inquiry when the impeachment provision was written into the Constitution.[5]

This conclusion echoed an early observation on the floor of the House of Representatives that the "House possessed the power of impeachment solely, and that this authority certainly implied the right to inspect every paper and transaction in any department, otherwise the power of impeachment could never be exercised with any effect."[6]

The House's "sole Power of Impeachment" is the mechanism provided by the Constitution to hold sitting Presidents accountable for serious misconduct. The Department of Justice has highlighted the importance of the impeachment power in justifying the Department's view that a sitting President cannot be indicted or face criminal prosecution while in office.[7] The Department's position that the President is immune from prosecution has not been endorsed by Congress or the courts, but as long as the Department continues to refuse to prosecute a sitting President, Congress has a heightened responsibility to exercise its impeachment power, if necessary, to ensure that no President is "above the law."[8]

The Supreme Court has recognized that Congress has broad oversight authority under the Constitution to inquire about a wide array of topics, even outside the context of impeachment:

> The power of inquiry has been employed by Congress throughout our history, over the whole range of the national interests concerning which Congress might legislate or decide upon due investigation not to legislate; it has similarly been utilized in determining what to appropriate from the national purse, or whether to appropriate. The scope of the power of inquiry, in short, is as penetrating and farreaching as the potential power to enact and appropriate under the Constitution.[9]

The Supreme Court has made clear that Congress' authority to investigate includes the authority to compel the production of information by issuing subpoenas,[10] a power the House has delegated to its committees pursuant to its Constitutional authority to "determine the Rules of its Proceedings."[11]

The Supreme Court has affirmed that compliance with Congressional subpoenas is mandatory:

> It is unquestionably the duty of all citizens to cooperate with the Congress in its efforts to obtain the facts needed for intelligent legislative action. It is their unremitting obligation to respond to subpoenas, to respect the dignity of the Congress and its committees and to testify fully with respect to matters within the province of proper investigation.[12]

Federal courts have held that the "legal duty" to respond to Congressional subpoenas extends to the President's "senior-level aides" and that the failure to comply violates the separation of powers principles in the Constitution.[13] As one court recently explained:

> [W]hen a committee of Congress seeks testimony and records by issuing a valid subpoena in the context of a duly authorized investigation, it has the Constitution's blessing, and ultimately, it is acting not in its own interest, but for the benefit of the People of the United States. If there is fraud or abuse or waste or corruption in the federal government, it is the constitutional duty of Congress to find the facts and, as necessary, take corrective action. Conducting investigations is the means that Congress uses to carry out that constitutional obligation. Thus, blatant defiance of Congress' centuries-old power to compel the performance of witnesses is not an abstract injury, nor is it a mere banal insult to our democracy. It is an affront to the mechanism for curbing abuses of power that the Framers carefully crafted for our protection, and, thereby, recalcitrant witnesses actually undermine the broader interests of the People of the United States.[14]

Laws Passed by Congress

Congress has enacted statutes to support its power to investigate and oversee the Executive Branch. These laws impose criminal and other penalties on those who fail to comply with inquiries from Congress or block others from doing so, and they reflect the broader Constitutional requirement to cooperate with Congressional investigations. For example:

- ***Obstructing Congress:*** Obstructing a Congressional investigation is a crime punishable by up to five years in prison. An individual is guilty of obstruction if he or she "corruptly, or by threats or force, or by any threatening letter or communication influences, obstructs, or impedes or endeavors to influence, obstruct, or impede" the "due and proper exercise of the power of inquiry under which any inquiry or investigation is being had by either House, or any committee of either House."[15]

- ***Concealing Material Facts:*** Concealing information from Congress is also punishable by up to five years in prison. This prohibition applies to anyone who "falsifies, conceals, or covers up" a "material fact" in connection with "any investigation or review, conducted pursuant to the authority of any committee, subcommittee, commission or office of the Congress, consistent with applicable rules of the House or Senate."[16]

- ***Intimidating and Harassing Witnesses:*** Intimidating witnesses in a Congressional investigation is a crime punishable by up to twenty years in prison. This statute applies to anyone who "knowingly uses intimidation, threatens, or corruptly persuades another person, or attempts to do so, or engages in misleading conduct toward another person," with the intent to "influence, delay, or prevent the testimony of any person in an official proceeding."[17] An individual who "intentionally harasses another person and thereby hinders, delays, prevents, or dissuades" a person from "attending or testifying in an official proceeding" is also guilty of a crime punishable by fines and up to three years in prison.[18]

- ***Retaliating Against Employees Who Provide Information to Congress:*** Employees who speak to Congress have the right not to have adverse personnel actions taken against them. Retaliatory actions taken against Executive Branch employees who cooperate with Congress may constitute violations of this law.[19] Any Executive Branch official who "prohibits or prevents" or "attempts or threatens to prohibit or prevent" any officer or employee of the federal government from speaking with Congress could have his or her salary withheld.[20]

Precedent of Previous Impeachments and Other Investigations

Unlike President Trump, past Presidents who were the subject of impeachment inquiries—including Presidents Andrew Johnson, Richard Nixon, and Bill Clinton—acknowledged Congress' authority to investigate and, to varying degrees, complied with information requests and subpoenas.

For example, President Johnson complied with the House's requests for information. According to a report subsequently adopted by the House Judiciary Committee, "There is no evidence that Johnson ever asserted any privilege to prevent disclosure of presidential conversations to the Committee, or failed to comply with any of the Committee's requests."[21]

Similarly, President Clinton provided written responses to 81 interrogatories from the House Judiciary Committee during the House's impeachment inquiry.[22]

Even President Nixon agreed to let his staff testify voluntarily in the Senate Watergate investigation, stating: "All members of the White House Staff will appear voluntarily when requested by the committee. They will testify under oath, and they will answer fully all proper questions."[23] As a result, numerous senior White House officials testified, including White House Counsel John Dean III, White House Chief of Staff H.R. Haldeman, Deputy Assistant to the President Alexander Butterfield, and Chief Advisor to the President for Domestic Affairs John D. Ehrlichman.[24] President Nixon also produced numerous documents and records in response to the House's subpoenas as part of its impeachment inquiry, including more than 30 transcripts of White House recordings and notes from meetings with the President.[25]

However, President Nixon's production of documents was incomplete. For example, he did not produce tape recordings, and transcripts he produced were heavily edited or inaccurate. President Nixon claimed that his noncompliance with House subpoenas was necessary to protect the confidentiality of Presidential conversations, but the House Judiciary Committee rejected these arguments and approved an article of impeachment for obstruction of the House's impeachment inquiry.[26]

In a letter to President Nixon, Judiciary Committee Chairman Peter Rodino explained that it would upend the separation of powers to allow the President to dictate the scope of an impeachment inquiry:

Under the Constitution it is not within the power of the President to conduct an inquiry into his own impeachment, to determine which evidence, and what version or portion of that evidence, is relevant and necessary to such an inquiry. These are matters which, under the Constitution, the House has the sole power to determine.[27]

Consistent with that long-settled understanding, other Presidents have recognized that they must comply with information requests issued in a House impeachment inquiry. In 1846, for example, President James Polk stated in a message to the House:

It may be alleged that the power of impeachment belongs to the House of Representatives, and that with a view to the exercise of this power, that House has the right to investigate the conduct of all public officers under the government. This is cheerfully admitted. In such a case, the safety of the Republic would be the supreme law; and the power of the House in the pursuit of this object would penetrate into the most secret recesses of the executive departments. It could command the attendance of any and every agent of the government, and compel them to produce all papers, public or private, official or unofficial, and to testify on oath to all facts within their knowledge.[28]

Past Presidents have also produced documents and permitted senior officials to testify in connection with other Congressional investigations, including inquiries into Presidential actions.

For example, in the Iran-Contra inquiry, President Ronald Reagan's former National Security Advisor, Oliver North, and the former Assistant to the President for National Security Affairs, John Poindexter, testified before Congress.[29] President Reagan also produced "relevant excerpts of his personal diaries to Congress."[30]

During the Clinton Administration, Congress obtained testimony from top advisors to President Clinton, including Chief of Staff Mack McLarty, Chief of Staff Erskine Bowles, White House Counsel Bernard Nussbaum, and White House Counsel Jack Quinn.[31]

Similarly, in the Benghazi investigation, led by Chairman Trey Gowdy, President Barack Obama made many of his top aides available for transcribed interviews, including National Security Advisor Susan Rice and Deputy National Security Advisor for Strategic Communications Benjamin Rhodes.[32] The Obama Administration also produced more than 75,000 pages of documents in that investigation, including 1,450 pages of White House emails containing communications of senior officials on the National Security Council.[33]

2.   The President's Categorical Refusal to Comply

President Trump categorically directed the White House, federal departments and agencies, and federal officials not to cooperate with the House's inquiry and not to comply with duly authorized subpoenas for documents or testimony.

Overview

Donald Trump is the first and only President in American history to openly and indiscriminately defy all aspects of the Constitutional impeachment process, ordering all federal agencies and officials categorically not to comply with voluntary requests or compulsory demands for documents or testimony.

On September 26, President Trump argued that Congress should not be "allowed" to impeach him under the Constitution and that there "should be a way of stopping it—maybe legally, through the courts." A common theme of his defiance has been his claims that Congress is acting in an unprecedented way and using unprecedented rules. However, the House has been following the same investigative rules that Republicans championed when they were in control.

On October 8, White House Counsel Pat Cipollone—acting on behalf of President Trump—sent a letter to House Speaker Nancy Pelosi and the three investigating Committees confirming that President Trump directed his entire Administration not to cooperate with the House's impeachment inquiry. Mr. Cipollone wrote: "President Trump cannot permit his Administration to participate in this partisan inquiry under these circumstances."

Mr. Cipollone's letter elicited immediate criticism from legal experts across the political spectrum. He advanced remarkably politicized arguments and legal theories unsupported by the Constitution, judicial precedent, and more than 200 years of history. If allowed to stand, the President's defiance, as justified by Mr. Cipollone, would represent an existential threat to the nation's Constitutional system of checks and balances, separation of powers, and rule of law.

The House's Impeachment Inquiry of President Trump

In January, the House of Representatives voted to adopt its rules for the 116th Congress. These rules authorized House Committees to conduct investigations, hold hearings, issue subpoenas for documents and testimony, and depose witnesses.[34] Significantly, these authorities are similar to those adopted when Republicans controlled the House during previous Congresses.[35]

In April, Special Counsel Robert S. Mueller III, who was appointed by then-Deputy Attorney General Rod J. Rosenstein to investigate Russian interference in the 2016 U.S. Presidential election and potential obstruction of justice by President Trump, issued a two-volume report.[36] In connection with that report, the Committee on the Judiciary began an inquiry into "whether to approve articles of impeachment with respect to the President."[37] The Judiciary

Committee detailed its authority and intent to conduct this investigation in a series of reports, memoranda, and legal filings.[38]

On August 22, Rep. Jerrold Nadler, the Chairman of the Committee on the Judiciary, sent a letter requesting that the Permanent Select Committee on Intelligence, the Committee on Oversight and Reform, the Committee on Foreign Affairs, and the Committee on Financial Services provide "information, including documents and testimony, depositions, and/or interview transcripts" relevant to the "ongoing impeachment investigation relating to President Trump."[39]

In September, the Intelligence Committee, the Oversight Committee, and the Foreign Affairs Committee sent letters requesting documents and interviews from the White House and the Department of State regarding the actions of President Trump, the President's personal agent, Rudy Giuliani, and others to pressure Ukraine to launch investigations into former Vice President Joe Biden and a debunked conspiracy theory alleging Ukrainian interference in the 2016 election.[40]

On September 22, President Trump admitted to discussing former Vice President Biden and his son with the President of Ukraine during a telephone call on July 25.[41]

On September 24, Speaker Pelosi stated publicly that the House Committees were "moving forward" to "proceed with their investigations under that umbrella of impeachment inquiry." She explained that, for the past several months, the House had been "investigating in our Committees and litigating in the courts, so the House can gather 'all the relevant facts and consider whether to exercise its full Article I powers, including a constitutional power of the utmost gravity—approval of articles of impeachment.'"[42]

On September 25, the White House made public a Memorandum of Telephone Conversation of President Trump's call with President Volodymyr Zelensky on July 25. As discussed in detail in Section I, this call record documented how President Trump directly and explicitly asked President Zelensky to launch investigations of former Vice President Biden and the 2016 election.[43]

Following the Speaker's announcement and the release of the call record, the Intelligence Committee, the Oversight Committee, and the Foreign Affairs Committee continued their investigation, requesting documents and information, issuing subpoenas, and conducting interviews and depositions. The Committees made clear that this information would be "collected as part of the House's impeachment inquiry and shared among the Committees, as well as with the Committee on the Judiciary as appropriate."[44]

On October 31, the House voted to approve House Resolution 660, directing the Committees "to continue their ongoing investigations as part of the existing House of Representatives inquiry into whether sufficient grounds exist for the House of Representatives to exercise its Constitutional power to impeach Donald John Trump, President of the United States of America." The resolution set forth the process for holding public hearings, releasing deposition transcripts, presenting a report to the Judiciary Committee, holding proceedings within the Judiciary Committee, and submitting to the House of Representatives "such resolutions, articles of impeachment, or other recommendations as it deems proper."[45]

President Trump's Unprecedented Order Not to Comply

President Trump's categorical and indiscriminate order and efforts to block witness testimony and conceal documentary evidence from the Committees investigating his conduct as part of the House's impeachment inquiry stand in contrast to his predecessors and challenge the basic tenets of the Constitutional system of checks and balances.

Even before the House of Representatives launched its investigation regarding Ukraine, President Trump made numerous statements rejecting the fundamental authority of Congress to investigate his actions as well as those of his Administration. For example, on April 24, he stated, in response to Congressional investigations: "We're fighting all the subpoenas."[46] Similarly, during a speech on July 23, he stated: "I have an Article II, where I have to the right to do whatever I want as president."[47]

When the three investigating Committees began reviewing the President's actions as part of the House's impeachment inquiry, President Trump repeatedly challenged the investigation's legitimacy in word and deed. President Trump's rhetorical attacks appeared intended not just to dispute public reports of his misconduct, but to persuade the public that the House lacks authority to investigate the President and the inquiry is therefore invalid and fraudulent. For example, the President described the impeachment inquiry as:

- "a COUP"[48]
- "illegal, invalid, and unconstitutional"[49]
- "an unconstitutional power grab"[50]
- "Ukraine Witch Hunt"[51]
- "a continuation of the Greatest and most Destructive Witch Hunt of all time"[52]
- "a total Witch Hunt Scam by the Democrats"[53]
- "bad for the country"[54]
- "all a hoax"[55]
- "the single greatest witch hunt in American history"[56]
- "Democrat Scam"[57]
- "just another Democrat Hoax"[58]
- "a fraud against the American people"[59]
- "A Witch Hunt Scam"[60]
- "a con being perpetrated on the United States public and even the world"[61]
- "ridiculous"[62]
- "a continuation of the greatest Scam and Witch Hunt in the history of our Country"[63]
- "Ukraine Hoax"[64]
- "No Due Process Scam"[65]
- "the phony Impeachment Scam"[66]
- "the phony Impeachment Hoax"[67]

On September 26, President Trump argued that Congress should not be "allowed" to impeach him under the Constitution: "What these guys are doing—Democrats—are doing to this country is a disgrace and it shouldn't be allowed. There should be a way of stopping it— maybe legally, through the courts."[68]

A common theme of President Trump's defiance has been his claims that Congress is acting in an unprecedented way and using unprecedented rules. However, the House has been following the same investigative rules that Republicans championed when they were in control and conducted aggressive oversight of previous Administrations.[69]

White House Counsel's Letters Implementing the President's Order

On October 8, White House Counsel Pat Cipollone sent a letter to Speaker Pelosi and the three Committees explaining that President Trump had directed his entire Administration not to cooperate with the House's impeachment inquiry. He wrote:

> Consistent with the duties of the President of the United States, and in particular his obligation to preserve the rights of future occupants of his office, President Trump cannot permit his Administration to participate in this partisan inquiry under these circumstances.[70]

On October 10, President Trump confirmed that Mr. Cipollone was indeed conveying his orders, stating:

> As our brilliant White House Counsel wrote to the Democrats yesterday, he said their highly partisan and unconstitutional effort threatens grave and lasting damage to our democratic institutions, to our system of free elections, and to the American people. That's what it is. To the American people. It's so terrible. Democrats are on a crusade to destroy our democracy. That's what's happening. We will never let it happen. We will defeat them.[71]

Mr. Cipollone's letter elicited immediate criticism from legal experts from across the political spectrum.[72]

Mr. Cipollone wrote a second letter to the Committees on October 18, declaring that the White House would refuse to comply with the subpoena issued to it for documents.[73]

On November 1—after the House had already issued several subpoenas to the White House and other Executive Branch officials for testimony—the Trump Administration issued a new "Letter Opinion" from Assistant Attorney General Steven A. Engel to Mr. Cipollone. The Office of Legal Counsel opinion sought to extend the reach of the President's earlier direction to defy Congressional subpoenas and to justify noncompliance by officials who could not plausibly be considered among the President's closest advisors.

Mr. Engel's opinion asserted that the House's impeachment inquiry seeks information that is "potentially protected by executive privilege" and claimed the Committees' deposition subpoenas are "invalid" and "not subject to civil or criminal enforcement" because the House's long-standing deposition rules do not allow the participation of attorneys from the White House or other government agencies.[74] These claims are without basis and unsupported by precedent.

The Letter Opinion cited statements from previous Presidents and Attorneys General that directly undercut the Administration's position. For example, President James K. Polk, stated that in an impeachment inquiry the House had power to "penetrate into the most secret recesses of the Executive Departments."[75] In addition, Attorney General Robert H. Jackson, who later served on the Supreme Court, stated that "pertinent information would be supplied in impeachment proceedings, usually instituted at the suggestion of the Department and for the good of the administration of justice."[76]

In his letters conveying the President's direction, Mr. Cipollone advanced remarkably politicized arguments and legal theories unsupported by the Constitution, judicial precedent, and more than 200 years of history. These letters effectuated the President's order and campaign to obstruct and thwart the House's exercise of its sole power of impeachment under the Constitution. They are rebutted as follows:

- ***The Impeachment Inquiry is Constitutional:*** According to Mr. Cipollone, "the President did nothing wrong," and "there is no basis for an impeachment inquiry."[77] President Trump has repeatedly described his call with President Zelensky as "perfect."[78] Speaking for President Trump, Mr. Cipollone also asserted that the impeachment inquiry is "partisan and unconstitutional," "a naked political strategy that began the day he was inaugurated, and perhaps even before," and that it "plainly seeks to reverse the election of 2016 and to influence the election of 2020."[79]

  However, as this report details in Section I, Congress found abundant evidence of a scheme directed by the President to solicit foreign election interference by pressing the newly-elected President of Ukraine to announce publicly politically-motivated investigations to benefit President Trump's own reelection campaign. Fundamentally, the Constitutional validity of an impeachment inquiry cannot depend on a President's view that he did nothing wrong or on the political composition of the House. Such an extreme reimagining of the Constitution would render the Article I impeachment power meaningless and provide the President with power the Constitution does not grant him to thwart, manipulate, and stonewall an impeachment inquiry conducted by the House, including by concealing information of his own misconduct.[80] Taken to its logical conclusion, the President's position would eliminate the impeachment power in every year during which a political party other than the President's is in power. Under this approach, the impeachments of President Clinton, President Nixon, and President Andrew Johnson would not have been permitted.[81]

  The purpose of an impeachment inquiry is for the House to collect evidence to determine for itself whether the President may have committed an impeachable offense warranting articles of impeachment. Because the Constitution vests the House alone with "the sole Power of Impeachment," it is not for the President to decide whether the House is exercising that power properly or prudently. The President is not free to arrogate the

House's power to himself—or to order across-the-board defiance of House subpoenas—based solely on his unilateral characterization of legislative motives or because he opposes the House's decision to investigate his actions.

- *The Impeachment Inquiry is Properly Authorized:* According to Mr. Cipollone, the "House has not expressly adopted any resolution authorizing an impeachment investigation" nor has it "delegated such authority to any of your Committees by rule."[82] However, nothing in either the Constitution or the House Rules requires the full House to vote to authorize an impeachment inquiry.[83] The impeachment inquiries into Presidents Andrew Johnson, Nixon, and Clinton all began prior to the House's consideration and approval of a resolution authorizing the investigations.[84] The same is true of many judicial impeachments;[85] indeed, numerous judges have been impeached without any prior vote of the full House authorizing a formal inquiry.[86] Even though Mr. Cipollone's argument is inherently invalid, the House has taken two floor votes that render it obsolete—the first on January 9 to adopt rules authorizing committees to conduct investigations, and the second on October 31 to set forth procedures for open hearings in the Intelligence Committee and for additional proceedings in the Judiciary Committee.[87] Even following passage of House Resolution 660, whereby the House confirmed the preexisting and ongoing impeachment inquiry, the President and the White House Counsel, acting on the President's behalf, have persisted in their obstructive conduct.

- *President Has No Valid Due Process Claims:* According to Mr. Cipollone, "the Committees have not established any procedures affording the President even the most basic protections demanded by due process under the Constitution and by fundamental fairness," and the Committees "have denied the President the right to cross-examine witnesses, to call witnesses, to receive transcripts of testimony, to have access to evidence," and "to have counsel present."[88] Yet, there is no requirement that the House provide these procedures during an impeachment inquiry. The Constitution vests the House with "the sole Power of Impeachment," and provides no constraints on how the House chooses to conduct its impeachment process.[89] Nevertheless, Mr. Cipollone's complaints are unfounded as the House has implemented procedural protections for the President in its exercise of its Constitutional power. House Resolution 660 authorizes procedures to "allow for the participation of the President and his counsel."[90] The Committee Report accompanying House Resolution 660 explains that these protections for the President are part of the Judiciary Committee hearing process and are "based on those provided during the Nixon and Clinton inquiries." These procedures include "that the president and his counsel are invited to attend all hearings; the ability for the president's counsel to cross-examine witnesses and object to the admissibility of testimony; and the ability of the president's counsel to make presentations of evidence before the Judiciary Committee, including the ability to call witnesses."[91]

- *Fact-Finding Was Appropriately Transparent:* According to Mr. Cipollone, the Committees conducted their proceedings "in secret."[92] This argument fundamentally misconstrues and misapprehends the fact-gathering process required at this initial stage of the House's impeachment inquiry. Unlike in the cases of Presidents Nixon and Clinton, the House conducted a significant portion of the factual investigation itself because no independent prosecutor was appointed to investigate President Trump's conduct regarding Ukraine. Attorney General William P. Barr refused to authorize a criminal investigation into the serious allegations of misconduct, and even this decision was limited to possible violations of federal campaign finance laws.[93] The investigative Committees proceeded consistent with the House's rules of procedure and in keeping with investigative best practices, including the need to reduce the risk that witnesses may try to coordinate or align testimony. As the House explained in its report accompanying House Resolution 660:

> The initial stages of an impeachment inquiry in the House are akin to those preceding a prosecutorial charging decision. Under this process, the House is responsible for collecting the evidence and, rather than weighing the question of returning an indictment, the Members of the House have the obligation to decide whether to approve articles of impeachment.[94]

The Committees have released transcripts of all interviews and depositions conducted during the investigation. As these transcripts make clear, all Members of all three Committees—including 47 Republican Members of Congress—had the opportunity to ask questions, and these transcripts are now available to the President and his counsel. These same procedures were supported by Acting White House Chief of Staff Mick Mulvaney when he served as a Member of the Oversight Committee and by Secretary of State Mike Pompeo when he served as a Member of the Benghazi Select Committee. In fact, some of the same Members and staff currently conducting depositions as part of the present impeachment inquiry participated directly in depositions during the Clinton, Bush, and Obama Administrations.[95] The Intelligence Committee also held public hearings with 12 of these witnesses.

- *Agency Attorneys Can Be (And Should Be) Excluded from Depositions:* According to Mr. Cipollone, "it is unconstitutional to exclude agency counsel from participating in congressional depositions."[96] Mr. Cipollone cites no case law to support his position—because there is none. Instead, he relies on a single opinion from the Trump Administration's Office of Legal Counsel and ignores the ample legal authority and historical precedent that clearly support the Committees' actions. For example, the Constitution expressly delegates to Congress the authority to "determine the Rules of its Proceedings,"[97] which includes the power to determine the procedures used for gathering information from witnesses whether via interview, staff deposition, or in a public hearing.[98] The basis for the rule excluding agency counsel is straightforward: it prevents agency officials who are directly implicated in the abuses Congress is investigating from trying to prevent their own employees from coming forward to tell the truth to Congress. The rule protects the rights of witnesses by allowing them to be accompanied in depositions by personal counsel. Agency attorneys have been excluded from Congressional depositions of Executive Branch officials for decades, under both Republicans and Democrats, including Chairmen Dan Burton, Henry Waxman, Darrell Issa, Jason Chaffetz, Trey Gowdy, Kevin Brady, and Jeb Hensarling, among others.[99]

- ***Congress Can Exercise Its Broad Oversight Authority:*** According to Mr. Cipollone, "you simply cannot expect to rely on oversight authority to gather information for an unauthorized impeachment inquiry that conflicts with all historical precedent and rides roughshod over due process and the separation of powers."[100] But, of course, the present impeachment inquiry does neither. Moreover, the Supreme Court has made clear that Congress' "power of inquiry" is "as penetrating and farreaching as the potential power to enact and appropriate under the Constitution."[101] The subject matter of the impeachment inquiry implicates the House's impeachment-specific as well as legislative and oversight authorities and interests. The activity under investigation, for instance, relates to a broad array of issues in which Congress has legislated and may legislate in the future, including government ethics and transparency, election integrity, appropriations, foreign affairs, abuse of power, bribery, extortion, and obstruction of justice. In fact, Members of Congress have already introduced legislation on issues related to the impeachment inquiry.[102] The House does not forfeit its Constitutional authority to investigate and legislate when it initiates an impeachment inquiry.[103] Congress passed sweeping legislative reforms following the scandal over the Watergate break-in and President Nixon's resignation.[104]

- ***"Confidentiality Interests" Do Not Eliminate Congress' Authority:*** According to Mr. Cipollone, the Administration would also not comply with the Committees' demands for documents and testimony because of unspecified Executive Branch "confidentiality interests."[105] There is no basis in the law of executive privilege for declaring a categorical refusal to respond to any House subpoena. In an impeachment inquiry, the House's need for information and its Constitutional authority are at their greatest, and the Executive's interest in confidentiality must yield. Only the President can assert executive privilege, yet he has not done so in the House's impeachment inquiry. Prior to asserting executive privilege, the Executive Branch is obligated to seek to accommodate the legitimate informational needs of Congress, which, as discussed below, it has not done.[106] In any event, much of the information sought by the Committees would not be covered by executive privilege under any theory,[107] and the privilege—where validly asserted on a particularized basis and not outweighed by the legitimate needs of the impeachment inquiry—would protect any legitimate Executive Branch interest in confidentiality.[108]

- ***President's Top Aides Are Not "Absolutely Immune":*** According to Mr. Cipollone, the President's top aides are "absolutely immune" from being compelled to testify before Congress.[109] This extreme position has been explicitly and repeatedly rejected by Congress—which has received testimony from senior aides to many previous Presidents—and by federal courts. In 2008, a federal court rejected an assertion by President George W. Bush that White House Counsel Harriet Miers was immune from being compelled to testify, noting that the President had failed to identify even a single judicial opinion to justify his claim.[110] On November 25, 2019, another federal judge rejected President Trump's claim of absolute immunity for former White House Counsel Don McGahn, concluding: "Stated simply, the primary takeaway from the past 250 years of recorded American history is that Presidents are not kings," and that "Executive branch officials are not absolutely immune from compulsory congressional process—no matter how many times the Executive branch has asserted as much over the years—even if the President expressly directs such officials' non-compliance."[111] Mr. Cipollone's position, adopted by President Trump, has thus been repudiated by Congress and the courts, and is not salvaged by Executive Branch legal opinions insisting upon a wholly fictional ground for non-compliance. In ordering categorical defiance of House subpoenas, President Trump has confirmed the unlimited breadth of his position and his unprecedented view that no branch of government—even the House—is empowered to investigate whether he may have committed constitutional offenses.

In addition to advancing specious legal arguments, President Trump has made no effort to accommodate the House's interests in conducting the impeachment inquiry. For example, the Committees first requested documents from the White House on September 9, but the White House disregarded the request.[112] The Committees made a second request on September 24, but the White House again ignored the request.[113] Finally, on October 4, the Committees transmitted a subpoena for the documents.[114] However, on October 18, the White House Counsel sent a letter stating that "the White House cannot comply with the October 4 subpoena."[115]

Since then, there has been no evidence of a willingness by the President to produce any of the documents covered by the subpoena to the White House. The State Department made passing references to potentially engaging in an "accommodations" process in response to its September 27 subpoena.[116] However, there has been no effort to do so, and departments and agencies have not produced any documents in response to subpoenas issued as part of the House impeachment inquiry. The President also made no apparent effort to accommodate the House's need for witness testimony and instead continued to flatly refuse to allow Executive Branch officials to testify.

3.   **The President's Refusal to Produce Any and All Subpoenaed Documents**

> *Pursuant to the President's orders, the White House, federal departments and agencies, and key witnesses refused to produce any documents in response to duly authorized subpoenas issued pursuant to the House's impeachment inquiry.*

Overview

Following President Trump's categorical order, not a single document has been produced by the White House, the Office of the Vice President, the Office of Management and Budget, the Department of State, the Department of Defense, or the Department of Energy in response to 71 specific, individualized requests or demands for records in their possession, custody, or control. The subpoenas to federal departments and agencies remain in full force and effect. These agencies and offices also blocked many current and former officials from producing records directly to the Committees.

Certain witnesses defied the President's sweeping, categorical, and baseless order and identified the substance of key documents. Other witnesses identified numerous additional documents that the President and various agencies are withholding that are directly relevant to the impeachment inquiry.

The President's personal attorney, Mr. Giuliani, although a private citizen, also sought to rely on the President's order, as communicated in Mr. Cipollone's letter on October 8, to justify his decision to disobey a lawful subpoena for documents.

The White House

On September 9, the Committees sent a letter to White House Counsel Pat Cipollone seeking six categories of documents in response to reports indicating that, "for nearly two years, the President and his personal attorney, Rudy Giuliani, appear to have acted outside legitimate law enforcement and diplomatic channels to coerce the Ukrainian government into pursuing two politically-motivated investigations under the guise of anti-corruption activity."[117] The Committees asked the White House to voluntarily produce responsive documents by September 16.[118] The White House did not provide any response by that date.

On September 24, the Committees sent a follow-up letter requesting that the White House produce the documents by September 26.[119] Again, the White House did not provide any documents or respond by that date.

Having received no response from the White House, then-Chairman Elijah E. Cummings sent a memorandum to Members of the Committee on Oversight and Reform, which has jurisdiction over the Executive Office of the President, explaining that he was preparing to issue a subpoena in light of the White House's non-compliance and non-responsiveness. He wrote:

Over the past several weeks, the Committees tried several times to obtain voluntary compliance with our requests for documents, but the White House has refused to engage with—or even respond to—the Committees.[120]

On October 4, the Committees sent a letter to Acting White House Chief of Staff Mick Mulvaney transmitting a subpoena issued by Chairman Cummings compelling the White House to produce documents by October 18.[121]

As discussed above, on October 8, the White House Counsel sent a letter to Speaker Pelosi and the Committees stating that "President Trump cannot permit his Administration to participate in this partisan inquiry under these circumstances."[122] The White House Counsel also sent a letter on October 18, confirming that "the White House cannot comply with the October 4 subpoena to Acting Chief of Staff Mulvaney."[123]

To date, the White House has not produced a single document in response to the subpoena.[124] Instead, the White House has released to the public only two documents—call records from the President's phone calls with President Zelensky on April 21 and July 25.[125]

Witnesses who testified before the Committees have identified multiple additional documents that the President is withholding that are directly relevant to the impeachment inquiry, including but not limited to:

- briefing materials for President Trump's call with President Zelensky on July 25 prepared by Lt. Col. Alexander S. Vindman, Director for Ukraine at the National Security Council;[126]

- notes relating to the July 25 call taken by Lt. Col. Vindman and Tim Morrison, the former Senior Director for Europe and Russia on the National Security Council;[127]

- an August 15 "Presidential decision memo" prepared by Lt. Col. Vindman and approved by Mr. Morrison conveying "the consensus views from the entire deputies small group" that "the security assistance be released";[128]

- National Security Council staff summaries of conclusions from meetings at the principal, deputy, or sub-deputy level relating to Ukraine, including military assistance;[129]

- call records between President Trump and Ambassador Gordon Sondland, United States Ambassador to the European Union;[130]

- National Security Council Legal Advisor John Eisenberg's notes and correspondence relating to discussions with Lt. Col. Vindman regarding the July 10 meetings in which Ambassador Sondland requested investigations in exchange for a White House meeting;[131]

- the memorandum of conversation from President Trump's meeting in New York with President Zelensky on September 25;[132] and

- as explained below, emails and other messages between Ambassador Sondland and senior White House officials, including Acting Chief of Staff Mick Mulvaney, Senior Advisor to the Chief of Staff Rob Blair, and then-National Security Advisor John Bolton, among other high-level Trump Administration officials.[133]

The Committees also have good-faith reason to believe that the White House is in possession of and continues to withhold significantly more documents and records responsive to the subpoena and of direct relevance to the impeachment inquiry.

The Committees have closely tracked public reports that the White House is in possession of other correspondence and records of direct relevance to the impeachment inquiry. On November 24, for instance, a news report revealed that the White House had conducted a confidential, internal records review of the hold on military assistance in response to the Committees' inquiry. The review reportedly "turned up hundreds of documents that reveal extensive efforts to generate an after-the-fact justification for the decision and a debate over whether the delay was legal."[134]

Office of the Vice President

On October 4, the Committees sent a letter to Vice President Mike Pence seeking 13 categories of documents in response to reports that he and his staff were directly involved in the matters under investigation. The Committees wrote:

Recently, public reports have raised questions about any role you may have played in conveying or reinforcing the President's stark message to the Ukrainian President. The reports include specific references to a member of your staff who may have participated directly in the July 25, 2019, call, documents you may have obtained or reviewed, including the record of the call, and your September 1, 2019, meeting with the Ukrainian President in Warsaw, during which you reportedly discussed the Administration's hold on U.S. security assistance to Ukraine.[135]

The Committees asked the Vice President to produce responsive documents by October 15.[136] On that date, Matthew E. Morgan, Counsel to the Vice President, responded to the Committees by refusing to cooperate and reciting many of the same baseless arguments as the White House Counsel. He wrote:

[T]he purported "impeachment inquiry" has been designed and implemented in a manner that calls into question your commitment to fundamental fairness and due process rights. … Never before in history has the Speaker of the House attempted to launch an "impeachment inquiry" against a President without a majority of the House of Representatives voting to authorize a constitutionally acceptable process.[137]

To date, the Vice President has not produced a single document sought by the Committees and has not indicated any intent to do so going forward.

Witnesses who testified before the Committees have identified multiple additional documents that the Vice President is withholding that are directly relevant to the impeachment inquiry, including but not limited to:

- notes taken by Jennifer Williams, Special Advisor to the Vice President for Europe and Russia, during the call between President Trump and President Zelensky on July 25;[138]

- notes taken by Lt. Gen. Keith Kellogg, National Security Advisor to the Vice President, during the call between President Trump and President Zelensky on July 25;[139]

- materials regarding the July 25 call that were placed in the Vice President's briefing book that same day;[140]

- the memorandum of conversation from Vice President Pence's call with President Zelensky on September 18;[141] and

- briefing materials prepared for Vice President Pence's meeting with President Zelensky September 1 in Warsaw, Poland.[142]

The Committees also have good-faith reason to believe that the Office of the Vice President is in possession of and continues to withhold significantly more documents and records responsive to their request and of direct relevance to the impeachment inquiry.

Office of Management and Budget

On October 7, the Committees sent a letter to Russell Vought, Acting Director of the Office of Management and Budget (OMB), conveying a subpoena issued by the Intelligence Committee for nine categories of documents in response to public reports that the President directed OMB to freeze hundreds of millions of dollars in military assistance appropriated by Congress to help Ukraine counter Russian aggression. The Committees wrote:

> According to multiple press reports, at some point in July 2019, President Trump ordered Acting Chief of Staff and Office of Management and Budget (OMB) Director Mick Mulvaney to freeze the military aid to Ukraine, and Mr. Mulvaney reportedly conveyed the President's order "through the budget office to the Pentagon and the State Department, which were told only that the administration was looking at whether the spending was necessary."[143]

The subpoena compelled Acting Director Vought to produce responsive documents by October 15.[144] On that day, OMB Associate Director for Legislative Affairs Jason Yaworske responded by refusing to produce any documents and reciting many of the same baseless arguments as the White House Counsel:

> [T]he President has advised that "[g]iven that your inquiry lacks any legitimate constitutional foundation, any pretense of fairness, or even the most elementary due process protections, the Executive Branch cannot be expected to participate in

it." ... President Trump cannot permit his Administration to participate in this partisan inquiry under these circumstances.[145]

To date, Acting Director Vought has not produced a single document sought by the Committees and has not indicated any intent to do so going forward.

Witnesses who testified before the Committees have identified multiple additional documents that Acting Director Vought is withholding that are directly relevant to the impeachment inquiry, including but not limited to:

- a June 19 email from OMB Associate Director of National Security Programs Michael Duffey to Department of Defense (DOD) Deputy Comptroller Elaine McCusker regarding the fact that "the President had seen a media report and he had questions about the assistance" and expressing "interest in getting more information from the Department of Defense," specifically a "description of the program";[146]

- a July 12 email from White House Assistant to the President and Senior Advisor to the Chief of Staff Robert Blair to Associate Director Duffey explaining that the "President is directing a hold on military support for Ukraine" and not mentioning any other country or security assistance package;[147] and

- an August 7 memorandum drafted in preparation for Acting Director Vought's attendance at a Principals Committee meeting on Ukrainian security assistance, which included a recommendation to lift the military assistance hold.[148]

The Committees also have good-faith reason to believe that the Office of Management and Budget is in possession of and continues to withhold significantly more documents and records responsive to the subpoena and of direct relevance to the impeachment inquiry.

Department of State

On September 9, the Committees sent a letter to Secretary of State Mike Pompeo requesting six categories of documents in response to reports that "President Trump and his personal attorney appear to have increased pressure on the Ukrainian government and its justice system in service of President Trump's reelection campaign" and "the State Department may be abetting this scheme."[149] The Committees requested that Secretary Pompeo produce responsive documents by September 16. The Secretary did not provide any documents or response by that date.

On September 23, the Committees sent a follow-up letter asking Secretary Pompeo to "inform the Committees by close of business on Thursday, September 26, 2019, whether you intend to fully comply with these requests or whether subpoenas will be necessary."[150] The Secretary did not provide any documents or respond by that date.

On September 27, the Committees sent a letter to Secretary Pompeo conveying a subpoena for documents issued by Rep. Eliot Engel, the Chairman of the Committee on Foreign Affairs, compelling the production of documents by October 4.[151]

Since Secretary Pompeo had failed to respond, the Committees also sent separate letters to six individual State Department employees seeking documents in their possession and requesting that they participate in depositions with the Committees.[152]

On October 1, Secretary Pompeo responded to the Committees for the first time. He objected to the Committees seeking documents directly from State Department employees after he failed to produce them, claiming inaccurately that such a request was "an act of intimidation and an invitation to violate federal records laws."[153] He also claimed that the Committees' inquiry was "an attempt to intimidate, bully, and treat improperly the distinguished professionals of the Department of State."[154]

To the contrary, Deputy Assistant Secretary George Kent, one of the State Department professionals from whom the Committees sought documents and testimony, testified that he "had not felt bullied, threatened, and intimidated."[155] Rather, Mr. Kent said that the language in Secretary Pompeo's letter, which had been drafted by a State Department attorney without consulting Mr. Kent, "was inaccurate."[156] Mr. Kent explained that, when he raised this concern, the State Department attorney "spent the next 5 minutes glaring at me" and then "got very angry." According to Mr. Kent, the official "started pointing at me with a clenched jaw and saying, What you did in there, if Congress knew what you were doing, they could say that you were trying to sort of control, or change the process of collecting documents."[157]

With respect to his own compliance with the subpoena for documents, Secretary Pompeo wrote that he "intends to respond to that subpoena by the noticed return date of October 4, 2019."[158]

Later on October 1, the Committees sent a letter to Deputy Secretary of State John J. Sullivan in light of new evidence that Secretary Pompeo participated on President Trump's call with President Zelensky on July 25. The Committees wrote:

> We are writing to you because Secretary Pompeo now appears to have an obvious conflict of interest. He reportedly participated personally in the July 25, 2019 call, in which President Donald Trump pressed President Volodymyr Zelensky of Ukraine to investigate the son of former Vice President Joseph Biden immediately after the Ukrainian President raised his desire for United States military assistance to counter Russian aggression.

> If true, Secretary Pompeo is now a fact witness in the impeachment inquiry. He should not be making any decisions regarding witness testimony or document production in order to protect himself or the President. Any effort by the Secretary or the Department to intimidate or prevent witnesses from testifying or withhold documents from the Committees shall constitute evidence of obstruction of the impeachment inquiry.[159]

The following day, at a press conference in Italy, Secretary Pompeo publicly acknowledged that he had been on the July 25 call between Presidents Trump and Zelensky.[160]

On October 7, Committee staff met with State Department officials who acknowledged that they had taken no steps to collect documents in response to the September 9 letter, but instead had waited for the September 27 subpoena before beginning to search for responsive records. During that conversation, the Committees made a good-faith attempt to engage the Department in the constitutionally-mandated accommodations process. The Committees requested, on a priority basis, "any and all documents that it received directly from Ambassador Sondland," as well as "documents—especially those documents identified by the witnesses as responsive—related to Ambassador Yovanovitch and DAS [Deputy Assistant Secretary] Kent." The depositions of these witnesses—Ambassador Sondland, Ambassador Yovanovitch, and Mr. Kent—were scheduled for the days shortly after that October 7 meeting. The Department's representatives stated that they would take the request back to senior State Department officials, but never provided any further response.[161]

To date, Secretary Pompeo has not produced a single document sought by the Committees and has not indicated any intent to do so going forward. In addition, the Department has ordered its employees not to produce documents in their personal possession. For example, on October 14, the Department sent a letter to Mr. Kent's personal attorney warning that "your client is not authorized to disclose to Congress any records relating to official duties."[162]

Moreover, the Department appears to have actively discouraged its employees from identifying documents responsive to the Committees' subpoena. Mr. Kent testified in his deposition that he informed a Department attorney about additional responsive records that the Department had not collected, including an email from Assistant Secretary of State for Consular Affairs David Risch, who "had spoken to Rudy Giuliani several times in January about trying to get a visa for the corrupt former prosecutor general of Ukraine, Viktor Shokin."[163] The Department attorney "objected to [Mr. Kent] raising of the additional information" and "made clear that he did not think it was appropriate for [Mr. Kent] to make the suggestion."[164] Mr. Kent responded that what he was "trying to do was make sure that the Department was being fully responsive."[165]

Certain witnesses defied the President's directive and produced the substance of key documents. For example, Ambassador Sondland attached ten exhibits to his written hearing statement.[166] These exhibits contained replicas of emails and WhatsApp messages between Ambassador Sondland and high-level Trump Administration officials, including Secretary Pompeo, Secretary Perry, Acting Chief of Staff Mick Mulvaney, and former National Security Advisor John Bolton.[167] The exhibits also contained a replica of a WhatsApp message between Ambassador Sondland and Mr. Yermak.[168]

Earlier in the investigation, Ambassador Kurt Volker had produced key text messages with Ambassador Taylor, Ambassador Sondland, President Zelensky's senior aide, Andriy Yermak, Mr. Giuliani, and others very soon after the Committees requested them and prior to Mr. Cipollone's letter on October 8 conveying the President's directive not to comply.[169]

The Department also prevented Ambassador Sondland—a current State Department employee—from accessing records to prepare for his testimony. As described above, federal law imposes fines and up to five years in prison for anyone who corruptly or by threats "impedes or endeavors to influence, obstruct, or impede" the "due and proper exercise of the power of inquiry under which any inquiry or investigation is being had by either House, or any committee of either House."[170] Ambassador Sondland explained that the Department's actions directly impeded his testimony:

> I have not had access to all of my phone records, State Department emails, and other State Department documents. And I was told I could not work with my EU Staff to pull together the relevant files. Having access to the State Department materials would have been very helpful to me in trying to reconstruct with whom I spoke and met, when, and what was said. …
>
> My lawyers and I have made multiple requests to the State Department and the White House for these materials. Yet, these materials were not provided to me. They have also refused to share these materials with this Committee. These documents are not classified and, in fairness, should have been made available.[171]

He testified, "I have been hampered to provide completely accurate testimony without the benefit of those documents."[172] Ambassador Sondland also stated:

> Despite repeated requests to the White House and the State Department, I have not been granted access to all of the phone records, and I would like to review those phone records, along with any notes and other documents that may exist, to determine if I can provide more complete testimony to assist Congress.[173]

On November 22, the Department produced 99 pages of emails, letters, notes, timelines, and news articles to a non-partisan, nonprofit ethics watchdog organization pursuant to a court order in a lawsuit filed under the Freedom of Information Act (FOIA).[174] This handful of documents was limited to a narrow window of time and specific people, but it clearly indicates that the Department is withholding documents that are responsive to the Committees' requests.

For example, the Department's FOIA production contains an email from the Office Manager to the Secretary of State to "S_All" sent on March 26 which states that "S is speaking with Rudy Giuliani."[175] It also contains a March 27 email in which Madeleine Westerhout, the Personal Secretary to President Trump, facilitates another phone call between Rudy Giuliani and Secretary Pompeo.[176] These documents are directly responsive to the September 27 subpoena for "all documents and communications, from January 20, 2017 to the present, relating or referring to: Communications between any current or former State Department officials or employees and Rudolph W. Giuliani, including any text messages using personal or work-related devices."[177]

Witnesses who testified before the Committees have identified multiple additional documents that Secretary Pompeo is withholding that are directly relevant to the impeachment inquiry, including but not limited to:

- a cable on August 29 from Ambassador Bill Taylor, at the recommendation of then-National Security Advisor John Bolton, sent directly to Secretary Pompeo "describing the folly I saw in withholding military aid to Ukraine at a time when hostilities were still active in the east and when Russia was watching closely to gauge the level of American support for the Ukrainian Government" and telling Secretary Pompeo "that I could not and would not defend such a policy";[178]

- WhatsApp messages and emails that Ambassador Sondland replicated and provided as exhibits to the Intelligence Committee showing key communications between Ambassador Sondland and high-level Trump Administration officials, including Secretary Pompeo, Secretary Perry, Acting Chief of Staff Mick Mulvaney, and Ambassador Bolton, as well as President Zelensky's senior aide, Andriy Yermak;[179]

- notes and memoranda to file from Mr. Kent, Ambassador Taylor, and others, including Ambassador Taylor's "little notebook" in which he would "take notes on conversations, in particular when I'm not in the office," such as meetings with Ukrainians or when out and receiving a phone call," as well as his "small, little spiral notebook" of calls that took place in the office;[180]

- emails among Philip Reeker, Acting Assistant Secretary of State, Bureau of European and Eurasian Affairs; David Hale, Under Secretary of State for Political Affairs; Mr. Kent; and others regarding the unsuccessful effort to issue a public statement in support of Ambassador Yovanovitch, including the "large number of emails related to the press guidance and the allegations about the Ambassador" from the "late March timeframe."[181]

The Committees also have good-faith reason to believe that the Department of State is in possession of and continues to withhold significantly more documents and records responsive to the subpoena and of direct relevance to the impeachment inquiry.

Department of Defense

On October 7, the Committees sent a letter to Secretary of Defense Mark Esper conveying a subpoena issued by the Intelligence Committee for 14 categories of documents in response to reports that the President directed a freeze of hundreds of millions of dollars in military aid appropriated by Congress to help Ukraine counter Russian aggression. The Committees wrote:

> Officials at the Departments of State and Defense reportedly were "puzzled and alarmed" after learning about the White House's directive. Defense Department officials reportedly "tried to make a case to the White House that the Ukraine aid was effective and should not be looked at in the same manner as other aid," but "those arguments were ignored."[182]

The subpoena required Secretary Esper to produce responsive documents by October 15. On October 13, Secretary Esper stated in a public interview that the Department would comply with the Intelligence Committee's subpoena:

Q: Very quickly, are you going to comply with the subpoena that the House provided you and provide documents to them regarding to the halt to military aid to Ukraine?

A: Yeah we will do everything we can to cooperate with the Congress. Just in the last week or two, my general counsel sent out a note as we typically do in these situations to ensure documents are retained.

Q: Is that a yes?

A: That's a yes.

Q: You will comply with the subpoena?

A: We will do everything we can to comply.[183]

On October 15, however, Assistant Secretary of Defense for Legislative Affairs Robert R. Hood responded by refusing to produce any documents and reciting many of the same legally unsupportable arguments as the White House Counsel:

In light of these concerns, and in view of the President's position as expressed in the White House Counsel's October 8 letter, and without waiving any other objections to the subpoena that the Department may have, the Department is unable to comply with your request for documents at this time.[184]

To date, Secretary Esper has not produced a single document sought by the Committees and has not indicated any intent to do so going forward, notwithstanding his public promise to "do everything we can to comply."[185]

Witnesses who testified before the Committees have identified multiple additional documents that Secretary Esper is withholding that are directly relevant to the impeachment inquiry, including but not limited to:

- DOD staff readouts from National Security Council meetings at the principal, deputy, or sub-deputy level relating to Ukraine, including military assistance;[186]

- an email from Secretary Esper's Chief of Staff, to Laura K. Cooper, Deputy Assistant Secretary of Defense for Russia, Ukraine, and Eurasia, in late July "asking for follow-up on a meeting with the President," including information on whether "U.S. industry [is] providing any of this equipment," "international contributions" to Ukraine, and "who gave this funding";[187]

- fact sheets and other information provided by Ms. Cooper in response to the email request;[188]

- an email sent to Ms. Cooper's staff on July 25 at 2:31 p.m.—the same day as President's Trump's call with Ukrainian President Zelensky—stating that the Ukrainian Embassy was inquiring about the status of military aid, suggesting that Ukrainian officials were concerned about the status of the military aid much earlier than ever previously acknowledged by the Executive Branch;[189]

- an email sent to Ms. Cooper's staff on July 25 at 4:25 p.m. stating that the Ukrainian Embassy and *The Hill* newspaper had become aware of the situation with the military assistance funding;[190] and

- an email received by Ms. Cooper's staff on July 3 at 4:23 p.m. from the Department of State explaining that the Department of State "had heard the CN [Congressional Notification] is currently being blocked by OMB."[191]

The Committees also have good-faith reason to believe that the Department of Defense is in possession of and continues to withhold significantly more documents and records responsive to the subpoena and of direct relevance to the impeachment inquiry.

Department of Energy

On October 10, the Committees sent a letter to Secretary of Energy Rick Perry conveying a subpoena issued by the Intelligence Committee for ten categories of documents in response to reports about his involvement with matters under investigation. The Committees wrote:

Recently, public reports have raised questions about any role you may have played in conveying or reinforcing the President's stark message to the Ukrainian President. These reports have also raised significant questions about your efforts to press Ukrainian officials to change the management structure at a Ukrainian state-owned energy company to benefit individuals involved with Rudy Giuliani's push to get Ukrainian officials to interfere in our 2020 election.[192]

The subpoena required Secretary Perry to produce responsive documents by October 18. On that day, Melissa F. Burnison, the Assistant Secretary of Energy for Congressional and Intergovernmental Affairs, responded by refusing to produce any documents and reciting many of the same flawed arguments as the White House Counsel:

Pursuant to these concerns, the Department restates the President's position: "Given that your inquiry lacks any legitimate constitutional foundation, any pretense of fairness, or even the most elementary due process protections, the Executive Branch cannot be expected to participate in it."[193]

To date, Secretary Perry has not produced a single document sought by the Committees and has not indicated any intent to do so going forward.

Witnesses who testified before the Committees have identified multiple documents that Secretary Perry is withholding that are directly relevant to the impeachment inquiry, including but not limited to:

- a document passed directly from Secretary Perry to President Zelensky in a May 2019 meeting with a list of "people he trusts" that President Zelensky could seek advice from on issues of relating to "key Ukrainian energy-sector contacts," according to David Holmes, the Political Counselor at the U.S. Embassy in Kyiv;[194]

- a June 5 email from Philip Reeker, Acting Assistant Secretary of State, Bureau of European and Eurasian Affairs, to Secretary Perry and others, regarding "Zelenskyy's visit to Brussels, and the critical—perhaps historic—role of the dinner and engagement Gordon [Ambassador Sondland] coordinated";[195] and

- a July 19 email from Secretary Perry in which he states "Mick [Acting Chief of Staff Mick Mulvaney] just confirmed the call being set up for tomorrow by NSC" in reference to a call between President Trump and President Zelensky.[196]

The Committees also have good-faith reason to believe that the Department of Energy is in possession of and continues to withhold significantly more documents and records responsive to the subpoena and of direct relevance to the impeachment inquiry.

Rudy Giuliani and His Associates

On September 30, the Committees sent a letter conveying a subpoena issued by the Intelligence Committee to the President's personal attorney, Rudy Giuliani, compelling the production of 23 categories of documents relating to his actions in Ukraine.[197]

On October 15, Mr. Giuliani's counsel responded to the Committees by stating that Mr. Giuliani "will not participate because this appears to be an unconstitutional, baseless, and illegitimate 'impeachment inquiry.'"[198] He also stated: "Mr. Giuliani adopts all the positions set forth in Mr. Cipollone's October 8, 2019 letter on behalf of President Donald J. Trump."[199]

To date, Mr. Giuliani has not produced a single document sought by the Committees and has not indicated any intent to do so going forward.

On September 30, the Committees sent letters to two of Mr. Giuliani's business associates—Igor Fruman and Lev Parnas—requesting testimony and eleven categories of documents from each.[200] The Committees sought documents from Mr. Fruman and Mr. Parnas related to their efforts to influence U.S. elections.

According to press reports, Mr. Parnas and Mr. Fruman reportedly were "assisting with Giuliani's push to get Ukrainian officials to investigate former vice president Joe Biden and his son as well as Giuliani's claim that Democrats conspired with Ukrainians in the 2016 campaign." Press reports also indicate that Mr. Parnas and Mr. Fruman were involved with efforts to press Ukrainian officials to change the management structure at a Ukrainian state-owned energy company, Naftogaz, to benefit individuals involved with Mr. Giuliani's push to get Ukrainian officials to interfere in the 2020 election.[201]

On October 3, counsel to Mr. Fruman and Mr. Parnas responded to Committee staff, explaining his clients' relationship with Mr. Giuliani and President Trump:

Be advised that Messrs. Parnas and Fruman assisted Mr. Giuliani in connection with his representation of President Trump. Mr. Parnas and Mr. Fruman have also been represented by Mr. Giuliani in connection with their personal and business affairs. They also assisted Joseph DiGenova and Victoria Toensing in their law practice.[202]

With respect to preparing Mr. Fruman's and Mr. Parnas' response, their counsel wrote: "The amount of time required is difficult to determine. [sic] but we are happy to keep you advised of our progress and engage in a rolling production of non-privileged documents."

On October 8, their counsel wrote again to Committee staff, stating:

This is an update. We continue to meet with Mr. Parnas and Mr. Fruman to gather the facts and documents related to the many subjects and persons detailed in your September 30 letter and to evaluate all of that information in light of the privileges we raised in our last letter.[203]

On October 9, their counsel wrote to Committee staff, stating, "Please be advised that Messrs. Parnas and Fruman agree with and adopt the position of White House Counsel pertaining to Democrat inquiry."[204]

On October 10, the Committees transmitted subpoenas compelling Mr. Fruman and Mr. Parnas to produce eleven categories of documents.[205] That same day, their counsel responded:

As I did in my recent letter of October 8, 2019, please be advised we were in the formative stages of recovering and reviewing records on October 9 when Messrs. Parnas and Fruman were arrested by the FBI and locked up in Virginia pursuant to Four Count Indictment by a Federal Grand Jury in the Southern District of New York unsealed on October 10, 2019.

Further, their records and other belongings, including materials sought by your subpoenas, were seized pursuant warrants [sic] by the FBI in several locations on the 9th and 10th of October.[206]

To date, Mr. Fruman has not produced a single document in response to his subpoena and has not indicated any intent to do so going forward.

With respect to Mr. Parnas, he obtained new counsel during the course of the impeachment inquiry. His new attorney has asserted that Mr. Parnas will cooperate with the House's inquiry, stating: "We will honor and not avoid the committee's requests to the extent they are legally proper, while scrupulously protecting Mr. Parnas' privileges including that of the Fifth Amendment."[207]

In contrast to Mr. Giuliani and Mr. Fruman, Mr. Parnas has begun rolling production of certain records in his possession, custody, or control in response to the subpoena, which the Committees are evaluating. The Committees expect Mr. Parnas' full compliance with the subpoena.

4. The President's Refusal to Allow Top Aides to Testify

At President Trump's direction, twelve current or former Administration officials refused to testify as part of the House's impeachment inquiry, ten of whom did so in defiance of duly authorized subpoenas. The President's orders were coordinated and executed by the White House Counsel and others, and they prevented testimony from officials from the White House, National Security Council, Office of Management and Budget, Department of State, and Department of Energy.

Overview

No other President in history has issued an order categorically directing the entire Executive Branch not to testify before Congress, including in the context of an impeachment inquiry. President Trump issued just such an order.

As reflected in White House Counsel Pat Cipollone's October 8 letter, President Trump directed all government witnesses to violate their legal obligations by defying House subpoenas—regardless of their office or position.[208] President Trump even extended his order to former officials no longer employed by the federal government. This Administration-wide effort to prevent all witnesses from providing testimony was coordinated and comprehensive.

These witnesses were warned that their refusal to testify "shall constitute evidence that may be used against you in a contempt proceeding" and "may be used as an adverse inference against you and the President."

Despite the President's unprecedented commands, the House gathered a wealth of evidence of his conduct from courageous individuals who were willing to follow the law, comply with duly authorized subpoenas, and tell the truth. Nevertheless, the President's efforts to obstruct witness testimony deprived Congress and the public of additional evidence.

In following President Trump's orders to defy duly authorized Congressional subpoenas, several Administration officials who, to date, remain under subpoena may have placed themselves at risk of being held in criminal contempt of Congress.[209] These witnesses were warned explicitly that their refusal to obey lawful orders to testify "shall constitute evidence that may be used against you in a contempt proceeding" and could also result in adverse inferences being drawn against both them and the President.[210]

Mick Mulvaney, Acting White House Chief of Staff

On November 5, the Committees sent a letter to Acting White House Chief of Staff Mick Mulvaney seeking his appearance at a deposition on November 8.[211] The Committees received no response to this letter.

On November 7, the Intelligence Committee issued a subpoena compelling Mr. Mulvaney's appearance at a deposition on November 8.[212] On November 8, Mr. Mulvaney's personal attorney sent an email to Committee staff stating that "Mr. Mulvaney will not be attending the deposition today, and he is considering the full range of his legal options."[213]

Mr. Mulvaney's personal attorney provided a letter that was sent on November 8 from Mr. Cipollone, stating that "the President directs Mr. Mulvaney not to appear at the Committee's scheduled deposition on November 8, 2019."[214] Mr. Mulvaney's personal attorney also provided a letter sent on November 7 from Steven A. Engel, Assistant Attorney General at the Office of Legal Counsel of the Department of Justice, to Mr. Cipollone, stating, "Mr. Mulvaney is absolutely immune from compelled congressional testimony in his capacity as a senior advisor to the President."[215]

Mr. Mulvaney did not appear at the deposition on November 8, in defiance of the Committees' subpoena. The Committees met, and Chairman Schiff acknowledged Mr. Mulvaney's absence, stating:

> Neither Congress nor the courts recognize a blanket absolute immunity as a basis to defy a congressional subpoena. Mr. Mulvaney and the White House, therefore, have no legitimate legal basis to evade a duly authorized subpoena. The President's direction to Mr. Mulvaney to defy our subpoena can, therefore, only be construed as an effort to delay testimony and obstruct the inquiry, consistent with the White House Counsel's letter dated October 8, 2019.[216]

Chairman Schiff also explained Mr. Mulvaney's knowledge of and role in facilitating the President's conduct:

> Mr. Mulvaney's role in facilitating the White House's obstruction of the impeachment inquiry does not occur in a vacuum. Over the past several weeks, we have gathered extensive evidence of the President's abuse of power related to pressuring Ukraine to pursue investigations that would benefit the President personally and politically and jeopardize national security in doing so. Some of that evidence has revealed that Mr. Mulvaney was a percipient witness to misconduct by the President and may have had a role in certain actions under investigation. The evidence shows that Mr. Mulvaney may have coordinated with U.S. Ambassador to the European Union Gordon Sondland, Rudy Giuliani, and others to carry out President Trump's scheme to condition a White House meeting with President Zelensky on the Ukrainians' pursuit of investigations of the Bidens, Burisma holdings, and purported Ukrainian interference in the 2016 U.S. Presidential election. In addition, evidence suggests that Mr. Mulvaney may have played a central role in President Trump's attempt to coerce Ukraine into launching his desired political investigations by withholding nearly $400 million in vital security assistance from Ukraine that had been appropriated by Congress. At a White House press briefing on October 17, 2019, Mr. Mulvaney admitted publicly that President Trump ordered the hold on Ukraine security assistance to further the President's own personal political interests rather than the national interest. ...

Based on the record evidence gathered to date, we can only infer that Mr. Mulvaney's refusal to testify is intended to prevent the Committees from learning additional evidence of President Trump's misconduct and that Mr. Mulvaney's testimony would corroborate and confirm other witnesses' accounts of such misconduct. If the White House had evidence to contest those facts, they would allow Mr. Mulvaney to be deposed. Instead, the President and the White House are hiding and trying to conceal the truth from the American people. Given the extensive evidence the Committees have already uncovered, the only result of this stonewalling is to buttress the case for obstruction of this inquiry.[217]

To date, Mr. Mulvaney has not changed his position about compliance with the subpoena.[218]

Robert B. Blair, Assistant to the President and Senior Advisor to the Chief of Staff

On October 24, the Committees sent a letter to Robert B. Blair, an Assistant to the President and the Senior Advisor to Acting Chief of Staff Mulvaney, seeking Mr. Blair's appearance at a deposition on November 1.[219] On November 2, Mr. Blair's personal attorney sent a letter to the Committees stating:

Mr. Blair has been directed by the White House not to appear and testify at the Committees' proposed deposition, based on the Department of Justice's advice that the Committees may not validly require an executive branch witness to appear at such a deposition without the assistance of agency counsel. In light of the clear direction he has been given by the Executive Branch, Mr. Blair must respectfully decline to testify, as you propose, on Monday, November 4, 2019.[220]

On November 3, the Committees sent a letter to Mr. Blair's personal attorney transmitting a subpoena compelling Mr. Blair to appear at a deposition on November 4.[221]

On November 4, Mr. Blair did not appear for the scheduled deposition, in defiance of the Committees' subpoena. The Committees met and Chairman Schiff acknowledged Mr. Blair's absence, stating:

Although the committees requested a copy of the correspondence from the White House and Department of Justice, Mr. Blair's Counsel did not provide it to the Committees. This new and shifting rationale from the White House, like the others it has used to attempt to block witnesses from appearing to provide testimony about the President's misconduct, has no basis in law or the Constitution and is a serious affront to decades of precedent in which Republicans and Democrats have used exactly the same procedures to depose executive branch officials without agency counsel present, including some of the most senior aides to multiple previous Presidents.[222]

Unlike President Trump's directive to Acting Chief of Staff Mulvaney, neither Mr. Blair nor the White House have asserted that Mr. Blair is "absolutely immune" from providing testimony to Congress. To date, Mr. Blair has not changed his position or contacted the Committees about compliance with the subpoena.

Ambassador John Bolton, Former National Security Advisor

On October 30, the Committees sent a letter to the personal attorney of Ambassador John Bolton, the former National Security Advisor to President Trump, seeking his appearance at a deposition on November 7.[223] Later that day, Ambassador Bolton's personal attorney sent an email to Committee staff stating, "As you no doubt have anticipated, Ambassador Bolton is not willing to appear voluntarily."[224]

On November 7, Ambassador Bolton did not appear for the scheduled deposition. On November 8, Ambassador Bolton's personal attorney sent a letter to Douglas Letter, the General Counsel of the House of Representatives, suggesting that, if Ambassador Bolton were subpoenaed, he would file a lawsuit and would comply with the subpoena only if ordered to do so by the court. He referenced a lawsuit filed by another former official, Dr. Charles Kupperman, represented by the same attorney, and stated:

> As I emphasized in my previous responses to letters from the House Chairs, Dr. Kupperman stands ready, as does Ambassador Bolton, to testify if the Judiciary resolves the conflict in favor of the Legislative Branch's position respecting such testimony.[225]

To date, Ambassador Bolton has not changed his position or come forward to testify.[226]

John A. Eisenberg, Deputy Counsel to the President for National Security Affairs and Legal Advisor, National Security Council

On October 30, the Committees sent a letter to John A. Eisenberg, the Deputy Counsel to the President for National Security Affairs and the Legal Advisor at the National Security Council, seeking his appearance at a deposition on November 4.[227] The Committees received no response to this letter.[228]

On November 1, the Committees sent a letter to Mr. Eisenberg transmitting a subpoena compelling his appearance at a deposition on November 4.[229] On November 4, Mr. Eisenberg's personal attorney sent a letter to the Committees, stating:

> Even if Mr. Eisenberg had been afforded a reasonable amount of time to prepare, the President has instructed Mr. Eisenberg not to appear at the deposition. Enclosed with this letter is the President's instruction as relayed by Pat A. Cipollone, Counsel to the President, in a letter dated November 3, 2019. We also enclose a letter, also dated November 3, 2019, from Steven A. Engel, Assistant Attorney General for the Office of Legal Counsel at the Department of Justice, to Mr. Cipollone advising that Mr. Eisenberg is "absolutely immune from compelled congressional testimony in his capacity as a senior advisor to the President." Under these circumstances, Mr. Eisenberg has no other option that is consistent with his legal and ethical obligations except to follow the direction of his client and employer, the President of the United States. Accordingly, Mr. Eisenberg will not be appearing for a deposition at this time.[230]

Enclosed was a letter sent on November 3 from Mr. Cipollone to Mr. Eisenberg's personal attorney stating that "the President directs Mr. Eisenberg not to appear at the Committee's deposition on Monday, November 4, 2019."[231] Also enclosed was a letter sent on November 3 from the Office of Legal Counsel of the Department of Justice to Mr. Cipollone stating:

> You have asked whether the Committee may compel Mr. Eisenberg to testify. We conclude that he is absolutely immune from compelled congressional testimony in his capacity as a senior advisor to the President.[232]

Mr. Eisenberg did not appear for the scheduled deposition, in defiance of the Committees' subpoena. The Committees met and Chairman Schiff acknowledged Mr. Eisenberg's absence, stating:

> Despite his legal obligations to comply, Mr. Eisenberg is not present here today and has therefore defied a duly authorized congressional subpoena. This morning, in an email received at 9:00 a.m., when the deposition was supposed to commence, Mr. Eisenberg's personal attorney sent a letter to the committee stating that President Trump had, quote, "instructed Mr. Eisenberg not to appear at the deposition," unquote. The attorney attached correspondence from White House counsel Pat Cipollone and a letter from the Office of Legal Counsel at Department of Justice. The OLC letter informs the White House that Mr. Eisenberg is purportedly, quote, "absolutely immune from compelled congressional testimony in his capacity as a senior advisor to the President," unquote. …

> Moreover, neither Congress nor the courts recognize a blanket, quote, "absolute immunity," unquote, as a basis to defy a congressional subpoena. Mr. Eisenberg and the White House, therefore, have no basis for evading a lawful subpoena. As such, the President's direction to Mr. Eisenberg to defy a lawful compulsory process can only be construed as an effort to delay testimony and obstruct the inquiry, consistent with the White House counsel's letter dated October 8, 2019. As Mr. Eisenberg was informed, the Committees may consider his noncompliance with the subpoena as evidence in a future contempt proceeding. His failure or refusal to appear, moreover, shall constitute evidence of obstruction of the House's impeachment inquiry and may be used as an adverse inference against the President. The subpoena remains in full force. The committees reserve all of their rights, including the right to raise this matter at a future Intelligence Committee proceeding, at the discretion of the chair of the committee.

> Mr. Eisenberg's nonappearance today adds to a growing body of evidence of the White House seeking to obstruct the White House's impeachment inquiry. To the extent the White House believes that an issue could be raised at the deposition that may implicate a valid claim of privilege, the White House may seek to assert that privilege with the Committee in advance of the deposition. To date, as has been the case in every other deposition as part of the inquiry, the White House has not done so. Mr. Eisenberg's failure to appear today also flies in the face of historical precedent. Even absent impeachment proceedings, congressional committees have deposed senior White House officials, including White House counsels and senior White House lawyers.[233]

Michael Ellis, Senior Associate Counsel to the President and
Deputy Legal Advisor, National Security Council

On October 30, the Committees sent a letter to Michael Ellis, a Senior Associate Counsel to the President and the Deputy Legal Advisor at the National Security Council, seeking his appearance at a deposition on November 4.[234] On November 2, Mr. Ellis' personal attorney sent an email to Committee staff stating:

> [W]e are in receipt of an opinion from the Office of Legal Counsel providing guidance on the validity of a subpoena under the current terms and conditions and based on that guidance we are not in a position to appear for a deposition at this time.[235]

This email followed the November 1 Office of Legal Counsel opinion, discussed above, which sought to extend the reach of the President's earlier direction to defy Congressional subpoenas and provided justification for noncompliance by officials who could not plausibly be considered among the President's closest advisors.

On November 3, Mr. Ellis' personal attorney sent another email to Committee staff stating:

> [O]ur guidance is that the failure to permit agency counsel to attend a deposition of Mr. Ellis would not allow sufficient protection of relevant privileges and therefore render any subpoena constitutionally invalid. As an Executive branch employee Mr. Ellis is required to follow this guidance.[236]

On November 3, the Committees sent a letter to Mr. Ellis' personal attorney transmitting a subpoena compelling his appearance at a deposition on November 4, stating:

> Mr. Ellis' failure or refusal to comply with the subpoena, including at the direction or behest of the President or the White House, shall constitute further evidence of obstruction of the House's impeachment inquiry and may be used as an adverse inference against Mr. Ellis and the President.[237]

On November 4, Mr. Ellis did not appear for the scheduled deposition, in defiance of the Committees' subpoena. The Committees met and Chairman Schiff acknowledged Mr. Ellis' absence, stating:

> Other than the White House's objections to longstanding congressional practice, the committees are aware of no other valid constitutional privilege asserted by the White House to direct Mr. Ellis to defy this subpoena.[238]

To date, Mr. Ellis has not changed his position or contacted the Committees about compliance with the subpoena.

Preston Wells Griffith, Senior Director for International
Energy and Environment, National Security Council

On October 24, the Committees sent a letter to Preston Wells Griffith, the Senior Director for International Energy and Environment at the National Security Council, seeking his appearance at a deposition on November 5.[239] On November 4, Mr. Griffith's personal attorney sent a letter to the Committees stating:

> As discussed with Committee counsel, Mr. Griffith respectfully declines to appear for a deposition before the joint Committees conducting the impeachment inquiry, based upon the direction of White House Counsel that he not appear due to agency counsel not being permitted.[240]

Later that day, the Committees sent a letter to Mr. Griffith's personal attorney transmitting a subpoena compelling his appearance at a deposition on November 5, stating:

> Mr. Griffith's failure or refusal to comply with the subpoena, including at the direction or behest of the President or the White House, shall constitute further evidence of obstruction of the House's impeachment inquiry and may be used as an adverse inference against Mr. Griffith and the President.[241]

On November 5, Mr. Griffith did not appear for the scheduled deposition, in defiance of the Committees' subpoena. The Committees met and Chairman Schiff acknowledged Mr. Griffith's absence, stating:

> Although the committees requested a copy of any written direction from the White House, Mr. Griffith's counsel has not provided any such documentation to the committees. The White House's newly invented rationale for obstructing the impeachment inquiry appears based on a legal opinion that was issued by the Department of Justice Office of Legal Counsel just last Friday, November 1. It is noteworthy and telling that OLC issued this opinion after multiple current and former White House, State Department, and Department of Defense officials testified before the committees, both voluntarily and pursuant to subpoena, all without agency counsel present. The White House's invocation of this self-serving OLC opinion should therefore be seen for what it is: a desperate attempt to staunch the flow of incriminating testimony from the executive branch officials about the President's abuse of power.[242]

To date, Mr. Griffith has not changed his position or contacted the Committees about compliance with the subpoena.

Dr. Charles M. Kupperman, Former Deputy Assistant to the President
for National Security Affairs, National Security Council

On October 16, the Committees sent a letter to Dr. Charles M. Kupperman, a former Deputy Assistant to the President for National Security Affairs, seeking his appearance at a deposition on October 23.[243]

On October 25, the Intelligence Committee issued a subpoena compelling Dr. Kupperman to appear at a deposition on October 28.[244]

Later that day, Dr. Kupperman's personal attorney sent an email to Committee staff attaching a 17-page complaint in federal court seeking a declaratory judgment as to whether he should comply with the subpoena.[245] His counsel wrote:

> Pending the courts' determination as to which Branch should prevail, Dr. Kupperman will not effectively adjudicate the conflict by appearing and testifying before the Committees.[246]

Enclosed as part of the complaint was a letter sent on October 25 from Mr. Cipollone to Dr. Kupperman's personal attorney stating that "the President directs Mr. Kupperman not to appear at the Committee's scheduled hearing on Monday, October 28, 2019."[247] Also enclosed was a letter sent on October 25 from the Office of Legal Counsel of the Department of Justice, to Mr. Cipollone stating that Dr. Kupperman "is absolutely immune from compelled congressional testimony in his capacity as a former senior advisor to the President."[248]

On October 26, the Committees sent a letter to Dr. Kupperman's personal attorneys, stating:

> In light of the direction from the White House, which lacks any valid legal basis, the Committees shall consider your client's defiance of a congressional subpoena as additional evidence of the President's obstruction of the House's impeachment inquiry.[249]

Later that day, Dr. Kupperman's personal attorney sent a letter to Committee staff, stating: "The proper course for Dr. Kupperman, we respectfully submit, is to lay the conflicting positions before the Court and abide by the Court's judgment as to which is correct."[250] On October 27, Dr. Kupperman's personal attorney sent a letter to Committee staff, writing: "If your clients' position on the merits of this issue is correct, it will prevail in court, and Dr. Kupperman, I assure you again, will comply with the Court's judgment."[251]

On November 5, the Committees sent a letter to Dr. Kupperman's personal attorneys withdrawing the subpoena, stating:

> The question whether the Executive Branch's "absolute immunity" theory has any basis in law is currently before the court in *Committee on the Judiciary v. McGahn*, No. 19-cv-2379 (D.D.C. filed Aug. 7, 2019). In addition to not suffering from the jurisdictional flaws in Dr. Kupperman's suit, *McGahn* is procedurally much further along.[252]

On November 8, Dr. Kupperman's personal attorney sent a letter to Douglas Letter, the General Counsel of the House of Representatives, stating that Dr. Kupperman stands ready to testify "if the Judiciary resolves the conflict in favor of the Legislative Branch's position respecting such testimony."[253]

On November 25, the district court in *McGahn* held that "with respect to senior-level presidential aides, absolute immunity from compelled congressional process simply does not exist." The court explained there is "no basis in the law" for a claim of absolute immunity regardless of the position of the aides in question or whether they "are privy to national security matters, or work solely on domestic issues."[254] To date and notwithstanding the ruling in *McGahn* as it relates to Presidential aides who "are privy to national security matters," Dr. Kupperman continues to refuse to testify, and his case remains pending in federal court.[255]

Russell T. Vought, Acting Director, Office of Management and Budget

On October 11, the Committees sent a letter to Russell T. Vought, the Acting Director of OMB, seeking his appearance at a deposition on October 25.[256] On October 21, an attorney at OMB sent an email to Committee staff stating:

> Per the White House Counsel's October 8, 2019 letter, the President has directed that "[c]onsistent with the duties of the President of the United States, and in particular his obligation to preserve the rights of future occupants of his office, [he] cannot permit his Administration to participate in this partisan inquiry under these circumstances." Therefore, Acting Director Vought will not be participating in Friday's deposition.[257]

That same day, Mr. Vought publicly stated:

> I saw some Fake News over the weekend to correct. As the WH letter made clear two weeks ago, OMB officials—myself and Mike Duffey—will not be complying with deposition requests this week. #shamprocess.[258]

On October 25, the Committees sent a letter transmitting a subpoena compelling Mr. Vought's appearance at a deposition on November 6.[259]

On November 4, Jason A. Yaworske, the Associate Director for Legislative Affairs at OMB, sent a letter to Chairman Schiff stating:

> The Office of Management and Budget (OMB) reasserts its position that, as directed by the White House Counsel's October 8, 2019, letter, OMB will not participate in this partisan and unfair impeachment inquiry. ... Therefore, Mr. Vought, Mr. Duffey, and Mr. McCormack will not appear at their respective depositions without being permitted to bring agency counsel.[260]

On November 5, Mr. Vought did not appear for the scheduled deposition, in defiance of the Committees' subpoena. The Committees met and Chairman Schiff acknowledged Mr. Vought's absence, stating:

> On Monday of this week, OMB reasserted its position that, quote, "as directed by the White House Counsel's October 8, 2019, letter, OMB will not participate in this partisan and unfair impeachment inquiry," unquote. OMB argues that the impeachment inquiry lacks basic due process protections and relies on OLC opinion that the committee cannot

lawfully bar agency counsel from depositions. This new and shifting rationale from the White House, like the others it has used to attempt to block witnesses from appearing to provide testimony about the President's misconduct, has no basis in law or the Constitution and is a serious affront to decades of precedent in which Republicans and Democrats have used exactly the same procedures to depose executive branch officials without agency counsel present, including some of the most senior aides to multiple previous Presidents.[261]

To date, Mr. Vought has not changed his position or contacted the Committees about compliance with the subpoena.

Michael Duffey, Associate Director for National Security Programs, Office of Management and Budget

On October 11, the Committees sent a letter to Michael Duffey, the Associate Director for National Security Programs at OMB, seeking his appearance at a deposition on October 23.[262]

On October 21, an attorney at OMB sent an email to Committee staff stating:

Per the White House Counsel's October 8, 2019 letter, the President has directed that "[c]onsistent with the duties of the President of the United States, and in particular his obligation to preserve the rights of future occupants of his office, [he] cannot permit his Administration to participate in this partisan inquiry under these circumstances." Therefore, Mike Duffey will not be participating in Wednesday's deposition.[263]

On October 25, the Committees sent a letter transmitting a subpoena compelling Mr. Duffey to appear at a deposition on November 5, stating:

Your failure or refusal to appear at the deposition, including at the direction or behest of the President or the White House, shall constitute evidence of obstruction of the House's impeachment inquiry and may be used as an adverse inference against the President.[264]

On November 4, Jason A. Yaworske, the Associate Director for Legislative Affairs at OMB, sent a letter to Chairman Schiff stating that, "as directed by the White House Counsel's October 8, 2019, letter," Mr. Duffey will not appear at his deposition.[265]

On November 5, Mr. Duffey did not appear for the scheduled deposition, in defiance of the Committees' subpoena. The Committees met and Chairman Schiff acknowledged Mr. Duffey's absence, stating:

This effort by the President to attempt to block Mr. Duffey from appearing can only be interpreted as a further effort by the President and the White House to obstruct the impeachment inquiry and Congress's lawful and constitutional functions.[266]

To date, Mr. Duffey has not changed his position or contacted the Committees about compliance with the subpoena.

Brian McCormack, Associate Director for Natural Resources, Energy, and Science, Office of Management and Budget

On October 24, the Committees sent a letter to Brian McCormack, the Associate Director for Natural Resources, Energy, and Science at OMB, seeking his appearance at a deposition on November 4.[267]

On November 1, the Committees sent a letter transmitting a subpoena compelling Mr. McCormack's appearance at a deposition on November 4.[268]

On November 4, Jason A. Yaworske, the Associate Director for Legislative Affairs at OMB, sent a letter to Chairman Schiff stating that, "as directed by the White House Counsel's October 8, 2019, letter," Mr. McCormack will not appear at his deposition.[269]

On November 4, Mr. McCormack did not appear for the scheduled deposition, in defiance of the Committees' subpoena. The Committees met and Chairman Schiff acknowledged Mr. McCormack's absence, stating:

> At approximately 11:30 a.m. today, committee staff received via email a letter from the Associate Director for Legislative Affairs at OMB. The letter states that, quote, "As directed by the White House counsel's October 8, 2019, letter," unquote, OMB will not participate in the House's impeachment inquiry. The letter further states that, based on the advice of the Office of Legal Counsel that, quote, "the committee cannot lawfully bar agency counsel from these depositions," unquote, Mr. McCormack will not appear at his deposition today without agency counsel present. As Mr. McCormack was informed, the committees may consider his noncompliance with a subpoena as evidence in a future contempt proceeding. His failure or refusal to appear, moreover, shall constitute evidence of obstruction of the House's impeachment inquiry and may be used as an adverse inference against the President.[270]

To date, Mr. McCormack has not changed his position or contacted the Committees about compliance with the subpoena.

T. Ulrich Brechbuhl, Counselor, Department of State

On September 13, the Committees sent a letter to Secretary of State Mike Pompeo seeking transcribed interviews with Counselor T. Ulrich Brechbuhl and other officials.[271] The Committees received no direct, substantive response to this letter.

On September 27, the Committees sent a letter informing Secretary Pompeo that Mr. Brechbuhl's deposition was being scheduled on October 8, stating:

On September 13, the Committees wrote to request that you make State Department employees available for transcribed interviews. We asked you to provide, by September 20, dates by which the employees would be made available for transcribed interviews. You failed to comply with the Committees' request.[272]

That same day, the Committees sent a letter directly to Mr. Brechbuhl seeking his appearance at a deposition on October 8.[273]

On October 1, Secretary Pompeo sent a letter to the Committees stating, "Based on the profound procedural and legal deficiencies noted above, the Committee's requested dates for depositions are not feasible."[274]

Later that day, the Committees sent a letter to Deputy Secretary of State John J. Sullivan stating that the State Department "must immediately halt all efforts to interfere with the testimony of State Department witnesses before Congress."[275]

On October 2, Mr. Brechbuhl's personal attorney sent an email to Committee staff stating:

> My law firm is in the process of being formally retained to assist Mr. Brechbuhl in connection with this matter. It will take us some time to complete those logistics, review the request and associated request for documents, and to meet with our client to insure he is appropriately prepared for any deposition. It will not be possible to accomplish those tasks before October 8, 2019. Thus, as I am sure that you can understand, Mr. Brechbuhl will not be able to appear on that date as he requires a sufficient opportunity to consult with counsel. Moreover, given the concerns expressed in Secretary Pompeo's letter of October 1, 2019, to Chairman Engel, any participation in a deposition would need to be coordinated with our stakeholders.[276]

On October 8, Committee staff sent an email to Mr. Brechbuhl's personal attorney stating: "The Committees have agreed to reschedule Mr. Brechbuhl's deposition to Thursday, October 17. Please confirm that Mr. Brechbuhl intends to appear voluntarily."[277] On October 9, Committee staff sent an email to Mr. Brechbuhl's personal attorney asking him to "confirm by COB today whether Mr. Brechbuhl intends to appear voluntarily."[278] Later that day, Mr. Brechbuhl's personal attorney sent an email to Committee staff stating, "I am still seeking clarification from the State Department regarding this deposition."[279]

On October 25, the Committees sent a letter to Mr. Brechbuhl's personal attorney transmitting a subpoena compelling Mr. Brechbuhl's appearance at a deposition on November 6.[280]

On November 5, Mr. Brechbuhl's personal attorney sent a letter to the Committees stating:

> Mr. Brechbuhl respects the important Constitutional powers vested in the United States Congress. And, indeed, he would welcome the opportunity to address through testimony

an existing inaccuracy in the public record—the false claim that Mr. Brechbuhl in any way personally participated in the telephone call between President Trump and President Zelensky that occurred on July 25, 2019. However, Mr. Brechbuhl has received a letter of instruction from the State Department, directing that he not appear. The State Department letter of instruction asserts significant Executive Branch interests as the basis for direction not to appear and also asserts that the subpoena Mr. Brechbuhl received is invalid. The letter is supported by analysis from the United States Department of Justice. We are also aware that litigation has recently been initiated in the United States District Court for the District of Columbia that may bear on resolving the significant issues now arising between the Committees and the President. Given these circumstances, Mr. Brechbuhl is not able to appear on November 6, 2019.[281]

On November 6, Mr. Brechbuhl did not appear for the scheduled deposition, in defiance of the Committees' subpoena. The Committees met and Chairman Schiff acknowledged Mr. Brechbuhl's absence, stating:

> The committees requested a copy of the State Department's letter and the Department of Justice analysis, but Mr. Brechbuhl's attorney has not responded. While the letter from Mr. Brechbuhl's attorney provides only vague references to unidentified executive branch interests and a DOJ analysis as the basis for the State Department's blocking of Mr. Brechbuhl's testimony, the Department's latest obstruction of this inquiry appears to be predicated on the opinion issued by the Department of Justice Office of Legal Counsel just last Friday, November 1, well after the subpoena was issued to Mr. Brechbuhl. It is noteworthy and telling that the OLC issued this opinion only after multiple State Department officials testified in this inquiry, both voluntarily and pursuant to subpoena, all without agency counsel present. Indeed, this morning, the third-highest-ranking official at the State Department, Under Secretary David Hale, appeared and has begun testifying in accordance with his legal obligations pursuant to a subpoena.[282]

The Committees sent Mr. Brechbuhl's personal attorney two separate inquiries asking him to provide a copy of the "letter of instruction" that Mr. Brechbuhl claimed to have received from the State Department directing him to defy a congressional subpoena.[283] Mr. Brechbuhl's personal attorney furnished the Committees with a copy of the letter on December 2. The State Department's letter to Mr. Brechbuhl is dated November 4, 2019.[284]

To date, Mr. Brechbuhl has not changed his position or contacted the Committees about compliance with the subpoena.

Secretary Rick Perry, Department of Energy

On November 1, the Committees sent a letter to Secretary of Energy Rick Perry seeking his appearance at a deposition on November 6, stating:

> Your failure or refusal to appear at the deposition, including at the direction or behest of the President or the White House, shall constitute evidence of obstruction of the House's impeachment inquiry and may be used as an adverse inference against the President.[285]

On November 5, an attorney at the Department of Energy sent a letter to the Committees stating:

> Please be advised that the Secretary will not appear on Wednesday, November 6, 2019, at 2:00 pm for a deposition to be conducted jointly by the Permanent Select Committee on Intelligence, the Committee on Foreign Affairs, and the Committee on Oversight and Reform.[286]

To date, Secretary Perry has not changed his position or come forward to testify.

5.   The President's Unsuccessful Attempts to Block Key Witnesses

> *Despite President Trump's explicit orders that no Executive Branch employees should cooperate with the House's impeachment inquiry and efforts by federal agencies to limit the testimony of those who did, multiple key officials complied with duly authorized subpoenas and provided critical testimony at depositions and public hearings. These officials adhered to the rule of law and obeyed lawful subpoenas.*

Overview

Despite President Trump's orders that no Executive Branch employees should cooperate with the House's impeachment inquiry, multiple key officials complied with duly authorized subpoenas and provided critical testimony at depositions and public hearings. These officials not only served their nation honorably, but they fulfilled their oath to support and defend the Constitution of the United States.

In addition to the President's broad orders seeking to prohibit all Executive Branch employees from testifying, many of these witnesses were personally directed by senior political appointees not to cooperate with the House's impeachment inquiry. These directives frequently cited or enclosed copies of Mr. Cipollone's October 8 letter conveying the President's order not to comply.

For example, the State Department, relying on President Trump's order, attempted to block Ambassador Marie Yovanovitch from testifying, but she fulfilled her legal obligations by appearing at a deposition on October 11 and a hearing on November 15. More than a dozen current and former officials followed her courageous example by testifying at depositions and public hearings over the course of the last two months. The testimony from these witnesses produced overwhelming and clear evidence of President Trump's misconduct, which is described in detail in Section I of this report.

Ambassador Marie Yovanovitch, Former
 U.S. Ambassador to Ukraine, Department of State

On September 13, the Committees sent a letter to Secretary of State Mike Pompeo seeking a transcribed interview with Ambassador Marie Yovanovitch and other State Department officials.[287] The Committees received no direct, substantive response to this letter.

On September 27, the Committees sent a letter informing Secretary Pompeo that Ambassador Yovanovitch's deposition was being scheduled on October 2, stating:

> On September 13, the Committees wrote to request that you make State Department employees available for transcribed interviews. We asked you to provide, by September 20, dates by which the employees would be made available for transcribed interviews. You failed to comply with the Committees' request.[288]

Also on September 27, the Committees sent a letter directly to Ambassador Yovanovitch seeking her appearance at a deposition on October 2.[289]

On October 1, Secretary Pompeo sent a letter to the Committees stating:

> Therefore, the five officials subject to your letter may not attend any interview or deposition without counsel from the Executive Branch present to ensure that the Executive Branch's constitutional authority to control the disclosure of confidential information, including deliberative matters and diplomatic communications, is not impaired.[290]

After further discussions with Ambassador Yovanovitch's counsel, her deposition was rescheduled for October 11. On October 10, Brian Bulatao, the Under Secretary of State for Management, sent a letter to Ambassador Yovanovitch's personal attorney directing Ambassador Yovanovitch not to appear for her deposition and enclosing Mr. Cipollone's October 8 letter stating that President Trump and his Administration would not participate in the House's impeachment inquiry. Mr. Bulatao's letter stated:

> Accordingly, in accordance with applicable law, I write on behalf of the Department of State, pursuant to the President's instruction reflected in Mr. Cipollone's letter, to instruct your client (as a current employee of the Department of State), consistent with Mr. Cipollone's letter, not to appear before the Committees under the present circumstances.[291]

That same day, October 10, when asked whether he intended to block Ambassador Yovanovitch from testifying the next day, President Trump stated: "You know, I don't think people should be allowed. You have to run a country, I don't think you should be allowed to do that."[292]

On the morning of Ambassador Yovanovitch's deposition on October 11, the Committees sent a letter to her personal attorney transmitting a subpoena compelling her appearance, stating:

> In light of recent attempts by the Administration to direct your client not to appear voluntarily for the deposition, the enclosed subpoena now compels your client's mandatory appearance at today's deposition on October 11, 2019.[293]

Later on October 11, Ambassador Yovanovitch's personal attorney sent a letter to Mr. Bulatao, stating:

> In my capacity as counsel for Ambassador Marie Yovanovitch, I have received your letter of October 10, 2019, directing the Ambassador not to appear voluntarily for her scheduled deposition testimony on October 11, 2019 before the Committee on Foreign Affairs, the Permanent Select Committee on Intelligence, and the Committee on Oversight and Reform in connection with the House of Representatives's impeachment inquiry. Just this morning, the Ambassador received a subpoena issued by the House Permanent Select Committee on Intelligence, requiring her to appear for the deposition as

scheduled. Although the Ambassador has faithfully and consistently honored her professional duties as a State Department employee—including at all times following her abrupt termination as U.S. Ambassador to Ukraine—she is unable to obey your most recent directive. As the recipient of a duly issued congressional subpoena, Ambassador Yovanovitch is, in my judgment, legally obligated to attend the depositions as scheduled.[294]

Ambassador Yovanovitch participated in the deposition on October 11, in compliance with the Committees' subpoena.[295] During her deposition, Ambassador Yovanovitch's personal attorney confirmed that "she received a direction by the Under Secretary to decline to appear voluntarily."[296]

On November 15, the Committees transmitted a subpoena to Ambassador Yovanovitch compelling her to testify at a public hearing of the Intelligence Committee that same day.[297] Ambassador Yovanovitch complied with the Committees' subpoena and testified at the public hearing. During the hearing, Chairman Schiff acknowledged Ambassador Yovanovitch's compliance, stating:

> Ambassador, I want to thank you for your decades of service. I want to thank you, as Mr. Maloney said, for being the first one through the gap. What you did in coming forward and answering a lawful subpoena was to give courage to others that also witnessed wrongdoing, that they, too, could show the same courage that you have, that they could stand up, speak out, answer questions, they could endure whatever threats, insults may come their way. And so in your long and distinguished career you have done another great public service in answering the call of our subpoena and testifying before us today.[298]

Ambassador Gordon Sondland, U.S. Ambassador to the European Union, Department of State

On September 27, 2019, the Committees sent a letter informing Secretary Pompeo that Ambassador Gordon Sondland's deposition was being scheduled on October 10.[299] That same day, the Committees sent a letter directly to Ambassador Sondland seeking his appearance at the deposition.[300] On October 1, Secretary Pompeo sent a letter to the Committees stating that Ambassador Sondland "may not attend" the deposition.[301]

After further discussions with Ambassador Sondland's personal attorney, his deposition was rescheduled for October 8. On October 7, Mr. Bulatao sent a letter to Ambassador Sondland's personal attorney, stating:

> Based on consultations with the White House, the State Department hereby instructs your client, Ambassador Gordon Sondland, not to appear tomorrow for his voluntary deposition based on the Executive Branch confidentiality interests remaining to be addressed, including, in particular, the Committee's refusal to permit agency counsel to appear.[302]

On October 8, Ambassador Sondland's personal attorney sent an email to the Committees stating:

> I am incredibly disappointed to report that, overnight, the State Department advised that it will direct Ambassador Sondland not to appear before the Committee this morning. While we have not yet gotten written confirmation of that direction, we wanted to advise you of this development at the earliest opportunity. As the sitting US Ambassador to the EU and employee of the State Department, Ambassador Sondland is required to follow this direction. I hope that whatever concerns the Department has can be resolved promptly and that Ambassador Sondland's testimony can be scheduled at the earliest opportunity. I am very sorry for the inexcusably late notice, but we are sharing this with you as soon as it was confirmed to us. Ambassador Sondland is personally disappointed that he will not be able to answer the Committee's questions this morning.[303]

On October 8, the Committees sent a letter to Ambassador Sondland transmitting a subpoena compelling his appearance at a deposition on October 16, stating:

> The Committees have not received any communication directly from the White House or the State Department about this matter. In light of Secretary Pompeo's direct intervention to block your appearance before our Committees, we are left with no choice but to compel your appearance at a deposition pursuant to the enclosed subpoena.[304]

On October 14, the Committees sent a letter to Ambassador Sondland stating:

> We hereby write to memorialize our agreement with your counsel, Mr. Robert Luskin, Esq., to adjourn the date and time of your document production and deposition to October 17, 2019, at 9:30 a.m. at the Capitol, HVC-304.[305]

Ambassador Sondland participated in the deposition on October 17, in compliance with the Committees' subpoena.[306] During the deposition, Ambassador Sondland's personal attorney stated:

> But we also wish to emphasize that it's his belief, and ours, that the Committee should have access to all relevant documents, and he regrets that they have not been provided in advance of his testimony. Having those documents would lead to a more fulsome and accurate inquiry into the matters at hand. Indeed, Ambassador Sondland has not had access to all of the State Department records that would help him refresh his recollection in anticipation of this testimony.[307]

During the deposition, Ambassador Sondland stated:

> I was truly disappointed that the State Department prevented me at the last minute from testifying earlier on October 8, 2019. But your issuance of a subpoena has supported my appearance here today, and I'm pleased to provide the following testimony.[308]

On November 4, Ambassador Sondland's personal attorney transmitted to the Committees a sworn declaration from Ambassador Sondland, which supplemented his deposition testimony and noted that despite "repeated requests to the White House and the State Department," he still had not been granted access to records he sought to review to determine if he could "provide more complete testimony to assist Congress."[309]

On November 20, the Committees transmitted a subpoena to Ambassador Sondland compelling him to testify at a public hearing of the Intelligence Committee that same day.[310] Ambassador Sondland complied with the Committees' subpoena and testified at the public hearing. During the hearing, Ambassador Sondland described the direction he received from the White House:

> Q: Ambassador Sondland, in your deposition, you lamented, quote: I was truly disappointed that the State Department prevented me at the last minute from testifying earlier on October 8, 2019, but your issuance of a subpoena has supported my appearance here today, and I am pleased to provide the following testimony. So it is clear that the White House, the State Department did not want you to testify at that deposition. Is that correct?
>
> A: That is correct.
>
> Q: And since then, you have on numerous occasions during your opening statement today indicated that you have not been able to access documents in the State Department. Is that correct?
>
> A: Correct.
>
> Q: So you have been hampered in your ability to provide testimony to this committee. Is that correct?
>
> A: I have been hampered to provide completely accurate testimony without the benefit of those documents.[311]

George P. Kent, Deputy Assistant Secretary of State, Bureau of European and Eurasian Affairs, Department of State

On September 13, 2019, the Committees sent a letter to Secretary of State Pompeo seeking a transcribed interview with Deputy Assistant Secretary of State George Kent and other State Department officials.[312] The Committees received no direct, substantive response to this letter.

On September 27, the Committees sent a letter informing Secretary Pompeo that Mr. Kent's deposition was being scheduled on October 7.[313] That same day, the Committees sent a letter directly to Mr. Kent seeking his appearance at the deposition on that date.[314] Later that day, Mr. Kent sent an email to Committee staff acknowledging receipt of the Committees' request and copying an official from the Office of Legislative Affairs at the Department of State.[315] On October 1, Secretary Pompeo sent a letter to the Committees stating that Mr. Kent "may not attend" the deposition.[316]

After consulting with Mr. Kent's personal attorney, the Committees rescheduled his deposition for October 15.[317] On October 10, Under Secretary Bulatao sent a letter to Mr. Kent's personal attorney enclosing the White House Counsel's letter of October 8, and stating:

> I write on behalf of the Department of State, pursuant to the President's instruction reflected in Mr. Cipollone's letter, to instruct your client (as a current employee of the Department of State), consistent with Mr. Cipollone's letter, not to appear before the Committees under the present circumstances.[318]

On October 15, the Committees sent a letter to Mr. Kent's personal attorney transmitting a subpoena compelling him to appear at a deposition on that date.[319]

Mr. Kent participated in the deposition on October 15, in compliance with the Committees' subpoena.[320] During the deposition, he stated:

> As you all know, I am appearing here in response to your congressional subpoena. If I did not appear I would have been exposed to being held in contempt. At the same time, I have been instructed by my employer, the U.S. Department of State, not to appear. I do not know the Department of State's views on disregarding that order.[321]

On November 13, the Committees transmitted a subpoena to Mr. Kent compelling him to testify at a public hearing before the Intelligence Committee on that day.[322] Mr. Kent complied with the Committees' subpoena and testified at the public hearing. During the hearing, Mr. Kent described the direction he received from the White House, stating that he "received, initially, a letter directing me not to appear. And once the committees issued a subpoena, I was under legal obligation to appear, and I am here today under subpoena."[323]

Ambassador William B. Taylor, Jr., Chargé d'Affaires for U.S. Embassy in Kyiv, Department of State

On October 4, 2019, the Committees sent a letter to Deputy Secretary of State John Sullivan seeking a deposition with Ambassador William B. Taylor, Jr. on October 15.[324] That same day, the Committees sent a letter directly to Ambassador Taylor seeking his appearance at the deposition.[325]

On October 14, after consulting with Ambassador Taylor's counsel, the Committees sent a letter to Ambassador Taylor stating: "We hereby write to adjourn the date and time of your deposition to Tuesday, October 22, 2019, at 9:30 a.m. at the Capitol, HVC-304."[326]

On October 22, the Committees transmitted a subpoena to Ambassador Taylor's personal attorneys compelling Ambassador Taylor to appear at a deposition on that date, stating:

> In light of recent attempts by the Administration to direct witnesses not to appear voluntarily for depositions, the enclosed subpoena compels your client's mandatory appearance at today's deposition.[327]

Ambassador Taylor participated in the deposition on October 22, in compliance with the Committees' subpoena. During the deposition, Ambassador Taylor's personal attorney stated, in regard to communications with the Department of State:

> They sent us the directive that said he should not appear under I think the quote is under the present circumstances. We told the majority that we could not appear; he'd been instructed not to. We saw the pattern.[328]

On November 13, the Committees transmitted a subpoena to Ambassador Taylor compelling him to testify at a public hearing of the Intelligence Committee that same day.[329] Ambassador Taylor complied with the Committees' subpoena and testified at the public hearing. During the hearing, Ambassador Taylor described the direction he received from the State Department:

> Q: Ambassador, were you also asked not to be part of the deposition?
> A: Mr. Quigley, I was told by the State Department: Don't appear under these circumstances. That was in the letter to me. And when I got the subpoena, exactly as Mr. Kent said, that was different circumstances and obeyed a legal subpoena. So, yes, sir, I'm here for that reason.[330]

Catherine Croft and Christopher Anderson, Department of State

On October 24, 2019, the Committees sent letters to the personal attorney representing two State Department officials, Catherine Croft and Christopher Anderson, seeking their attendance at depositions on October 30 and November 1, respectively.[331]

On October 25, their attorney sent a letter to the Committees acknowledging receipt of the Committees' requests and stating that "we are in the process of contacting the Office of the Legal Advisor of the Department of State in an effort to learn the disposition of that Office with regard to the Committee's request."[332]

On October 28, Under Secretary Bulatao sent letters to the personal attorney for Ms. Croft and Mr. Anderson. Both letters enclosed the White House Counsel's October 8 letter and stated:

> Pursuant to Mr. Cipollone's letter and in light of these defects, we are writing to inform you and Ms. Croft of the Administration-wide direction that Executive Branch personnel "cannot participate in [the impeachment] inquiry under these circumstances."[333]

On October 30, the Committees transmitted subpoenas to the personal attorney for Ms. Croft and Mr. Anderson compelling their appearance at depositions on October 30, stating:

> In light of recent attempts by the Administration to direct witnesses not to appear voluntarily for depositions, the enclosed subpoenas compel your clients' mandatory appearance.[334]

Ms. Croft and Mr. Anderson participated in their depositions on October 30, in compliance with the Committees' subpoenas.[335] During Ms. Croft's deposition, her personal attorney stated:

> On October 28th, 2019, Ms. Croft received a letter through her lawyers from Under Secretary of State Brian Bulatao, in which we were instructed that Ms. Croft cannot participate in the impeachment inquiry being conducted by the House of Representatives and these committees. Under Secretary Bulatao's letter stated that these instructions were issued pursuant to a directive from the Office of White House Counsel. Nonetheless, Ms. Croft has been served with a valid subpoena, and so she is obliged to be here today.[336]

During Mr. Anderson's deposition, his personal attorney stated:

> On October 28th, 2019, Mr. Anderson received a letter, through his lawyers, from Under Secretary of State Brian Bulatao in which we were instructed that Mr. Anderson cannot participate in the impeachment inquiry being conducted by the House of Representatives and these committees. Under Secretary Bulatao's letter stated that these instructions were issued pursuant to a directive from the Office of White House Counsel. Nonetheless, Mr. Anderson has been served with a valid subpoena, and so he is obliged to be here today.[337]

Laura K. Cooper, Deputy Assistant Secretary of Defense for Russia, Ukraine, and Eurasia, Department of Defense

On October 11, the Committees sent a letter to Deputy Assistant Secretary of Defense Laura K. Cooper seeking her attendance at a deposition on October 18.[338]

After consulting with Ms. Cooper's personal attorney, the Committees rescheduled her deposition for October 23.

On October 22, Deputy Secretary of Defense David L. Norquist sent a letter to Ms. Cooper's personal attorney, stating:

> This letter informs you and Ms. Cooper of the Administration-wide direction that Executive Branch personnel "cannot participate in [the impeachment] inquiry under these circumstances" [Tab C]. In the event that the Committees issue a subpoena to compel Ms. Cooper's appearance, you should be aware that the Supreme Court has held, in *United States v. Rumely*, 345 U.S. 41 (1953), that a person cannot be sanctioned for refusing to comply with a congressional subpoena unauthorized by House Rule or Resolution.[339]

On October 23, the Committees sent an email transmitting a subpoena compelling Ms. Cooper to appear at a deposition on that date, stating:

In light of recent attempts by the Administration to direct witnesses not to appear voluntarily for depositions, the enclosed subpoena compels your client's mandatory appearance at today's deposition.[340]

Ms. Cooper participated in the deposition on October 23, in compliance with the Committees' subpoena.[341]

During her deposition, Ms. Cooper stated with regard to the Department of Defense, "They instructed me yesterday not to participate."[342]

On November 20, the Committees transmitted a subpoena to Ms. Cooper compelling her to testify at a public hearing before the Intelligence Committee on that day.[343] Ms. Cooper complied with the Committees' subpoena and testified at the public hearing.[344]

Mark Sandy, Deputy Associate Director of National Security Programs, Office of Management and Budget

On November 5, the Committees sent a letter to Mark Sandy, the Deputy Associate Director of National Security Programs at OMB, seeking his appearance at a deposition on November 8.[345] On November 6, Mr. Sandy responded to confirm receipt of the Committees' letter.[346]

On November 7, an attorney at OMB sent an email to Committee staff stating:

In light of the Committee's rules that prohibit agency counsel from being present in a deposition of an executive branch witness and consistent with the November 1, 2019 OLC letter opinion addressing this issue, OMB has directed Mr. Sandy not to appear at tomorrow's deposition.[347]

After consulting with Mr. Sandy's personal attorney, the Committees rescheduled his deposition for November 16.

On November 16, the Committees sent an email transmitting a subpoena compelling Mr. Sandy to appear at a deposition on that date, stating:

In light of recent attempts by the Administration to direct witnesses not to appear voluntarily for depositions, the enclosed subpoena compels your client's mandatory appearance.[348]

Mr. Sandy participated in the deposition on November 16, in compliance with the Committees' subpoena.[349] During his deposition, Mr. Sandy also testified that the Administration sent his personal attorney an official communication with further direction, stating: "It did direct me to have my personal counsel ask for a postponement until agency counsel could accompany me."[350]

Dr. Fiona Hill, Former Deputy Assistant to the President and
Senior Director for Europe and Russia, National Security Council

On October 9, 2019, the Committees sent a letter seeking Dr. Hill's testimony at a deposition on October 14.[351] On October 13, Dr. Hill's personal attorney informed the White House that she intended to appear at the scheduled deposition.[352] On October 14, the White House sent a letter to Dr. Hill's personal attorney stating that "Dr. Hill is not authorized to reveal or release any classified information or any information subject to executive privilege."[353] Also on October 14, the Committees sent Dr. Hill a subpoena seeking her testimony the same day.[354] Dr. Hill complied and participated in the deposition.[355]

On November 18, Dr. Hill's personal attorney sent a letter to the White House stating that Dr. Hill had been invited to provide testimony at a public hearing on November 21, and stating: "We continue to disagree with regard to the parameters of executive privilege as you articulated it on October 14 and our prior telephone calls."[356] On November 20, the White House sent a letter to Dr. Hill's personal attorney stating that Dr. Hill "continues to be bound by important obligations to refrain from disclosing classified information or information subject to executive privilege in her upcoming testimony before the House Permanent Select Committee on Intelligence."[357] On November 21, the Committees sent Dr. Hill a subpoena seeking her testimony the same day.[358] Dr. Hill also complied with this subpoena and testified at the public hearing.[359]

Lieutenant Colonel Alexander S. Vindman,
Director for Ukraine, National Security Council

On October 16, 2019, the Committees sent a letter seeking Lt. Col. Alexander Vindman's testimony at a deposition on October 24.[360] After discussions with Lt. Col. Vindman's personal attorneys, the deposition was rescheduled to October 29. On October 29, the Committees sent Lt. Col. Vindman a subpoena seeking his testimony the same day.[361] Lt. Col. Vindman complied.[362] In addition, on November 19, the Committees conveyed a subpoena seeking Lt. Col. Vindman's testimony at a public hearing that same day.[363] Lt. Col. Vindman also complied with this subpoena and testified at the public hearing.[364]

Timothy Morrison, Former Deputy Assistant to the President
and Senior Director for Europe and Russia, National Security Council

On October 16, 2019, the Committees sent a letter to Timothy Morrison seeking his testimony at a deposition on October 25.[365] After discussions with Mr. Morrison's personal attorney, the deposition was rescheduled to October 31. On October 31, the Committees sent Mr. Morrison a subpoena seeking his testimony the same day.[366] Mr. Morrison complied.[367] In addition, on November 19, the Committees conveyed a subpoena seeking Mr. Morrison's testimony at a public hearing that same day.[368] Mr. Morrison also complied with this subpoena and testified at the public hearing.[369]

David Hale, Under Secretary for Political Affairs, Department of State

On November 1, 2019, the Committees sent a letter seeking Under Secretary David Hale's testimony at a deposition on November 6.[370] On November 5, Mr. Hale's counsel wrote to the Committees, stating that Mr. Hale would be willing to testify pursuant to a subpoena.[371]

On November 6, the Committees sent Mr. Hale a subpoena seeking his testimony the same day.[372] Mr. Hale complied.[373] In addition, on November 20, the Committees conveyed a subpoena seeking Mr. Hale's testimony at a public hearing that same day.[374] Mr. Hale also complied with this subpoena and testified at the public hearing.[375]

David Holmes, Counselor for Political Affairs at the U.S. Embassy in Kyiv, Ukraine, Department of State

On November 12, 2019, the Committees sent a letter to Political Counselor David Holmes' personal attorney seeking his testimony at a deposition on November 15.[376] On November 15, the Committees conveyed a subpoena to Mr. Holmes' personal attorney seeking his testimony the same day.[377] Mr. Holmes complied.[378] In addition, on November 21, the Committees conveyed a subpoena seeking Mr. Holmes' testimony at a public hearing that same day.[379] Mr. Holmes also complied with this subpoena and testified at the public hearing.[380]

Ambassador P. Michael McKinley, Former Senior Advisor to the Secretary of State, Department of State

On October 12, 2019, Committee staff emailed Ambassador P. Michael McKinley requesting his voluntary participation in a transcribed interview on October 16.[381] On October 14, the Committees sent a letter formalizing this request.[382] On October 16, Ambassador McKinley participated in the scheduled transcribed interview.[383]

Ambassador Philip T. Reeker, Acting Assistant Secretary, Bureau of European and Eurasian Affairs, Department of State

On October 16, 2019, the Committees sent a letter seeking Ambassador Philip T. Reeker's testimony at a deposition on October 23.[384] On October 25, the Committees sent Ambassador Reeker a subpoena seeking his testimony on October 26.[385] Ambassador Reeker complied and testified at the scheduled deposition.[386]

Ambassador Kurt Volker, Former U.S. Special Representative for Ukraine Negotiations, Department of State

On September 13, 2019, the Committees wrote a letter to Secretary Pompeo requesting the testimony of four witnesses, including Ambassador Kurt Volker.[387] On September 27, the Committees sent a follow up letter to Secretary Pompeo, noting that Ambassador Volker's deposition had been scheduled for October 3.[388] On that same day, the Committees sent a letter directly to Ambassador Volker, seeking his testimony at the deposition scheduled for October 3.[389]

On October 1, Secretary Pompeo responded to the Committees, refusing to make Ambassador Volker available on the requested date.[390] On October 2, the Department of State wrote a letter to Ambassador Volker's counsel instructing Ambassador Volker not to reveal classified or privileged information and prohibiting Ambassador Volker from producing any government documents.[391]

On October 2, Ambassador Volker produced copies of text messages in response to the Committees' request.[392] On October 3, Ambassador Volker voluntarily participated in a transcribed interview.[393] In addition, on November 19, Ambassador Volker testified voluntarily at a public hearing.[394]

Jennifer Williams, Special Advisor for
Europe and Russia, Office of the Vice President

On November 4, 2019, the Committees sent a letter to Jennifer Williams seeking her testimony at a deposition on November 7.[395] On November 7, the Committees sent Ms. Williams a subpoena seeking her testimony the same day.[396] Ms. Williams complied.[397] On November 11, Ms. Williams sent a letter to Chairman Schiff to make one amendment to her deposition testimony.[398] In addition, on November 19, the Committees conveyed a subpoena seeking Ms. William's testimony at a public hearing on November 19.[399] Ms. Williams also complied with this subpoena and testified at the public hearing.[400]

6. The President's Intimidation of Witnesses

President Trump publicly attacked and intimidated witnesses who came forward to comply with duly authorized subpoenas and testify about his conduct. The President also threatened and attacked an Intelligence Community whistleblower.

Overview

President Trump engaged in a brazen effort to publicly attack and intimidate witnesses who came forward to comply with duly authorized subpoenas and testify about his conduct, raising grave concerns about potential violations of the federal obstruction statute and other criminal laws intended to protect witnesses appearing before Congressional proceedings. President Trump issued threats, openly discussed possible retaliation, made insinuations about witnesses' character and patriotism, and subjected them to mockery and derision. The President's attacks were broadcast to millions of Americans—including witnesses' families, friends, and coworkers—and his actions drew criticism from across the political spectrum, including from his own Republican supporters.

It is a federal crime to intimidate or seek to intimidate any witness appearing before Congress. This statute applies to all citizens, including federal officials. Violations of this law can carry a criminal sentence of up to 20 years in prison.

This campaign of intimidation risks discouraging witnesses from coming forward voluntarily, complying with mandatory subpoenas for documents and testimony, and disclosing evidence that may support consideration of articles of impeachment.

Ambassador Marie Yovanovitch, Former U.S. Ambassador to Ukraine, Department of State

As discussed above, President Trump removed Marie Yovanovitch as the U.S. Ambassador to Ukraine in May 2019 following a concerted effort by Rudy Giuliani, his associates Lev Parnas and Igor Fruman, and others to spread false conspiracy theories about her. The smearing of the Ambassador was part of the larger campaign undertaken by Mr. Giuliani at President Trump's direction and in his capacity as President Trump's representative. During her deposition on October 11, Ambassador Yovanovitch explained that she felt threatened and "very concerned" after she read President Trump's statements about her during his July 25 call with President Zelensky, including President Trump's claim that "she's going to go through some things."[401]

On November 15, Ambassador Yovanovitch testified at a public hearing that she was "shocked" and "devastated" by the President's statements about her:

I was shocked and devastated that I would feature in a phone call between two heads of state in such a manner, where President Trump said that I was bad news to another world

255

leader and that I would be "going through some things." So I was—it was—it was a terrible moment. A person who saw me actually reading the transcript said that the color drained from my face. I think I even had a physical reaction. I think, you know, even now, words kind of fail me.[402]

Ambassador Yovanovitch was also asked about her reaction to the President's comment that she would "go through some things." She acknowledged feeling threatened, stating: "It didn't sound good. It sounded like a threat."[403]

As Ambassador Yovanovitch was in the process of testifying before the Committee, President Trump tweeted an attack against her. He wrote:

> Everywhere Marie Yovanovitch went turned bad. She started off in Somalia, how did that go? Then fast forward to Ukraine, where the new Ukrainian President spoke unfavorably about her in my second phone call with him. It is a U.S. President's absolute right to appoint ambassadors.[404]

During the hearing, Chairman Schiff asked Ambassador Yovanovitch for her reaction to the President's attacks:

> Q: Ambassador, you've shown the courage to come forward today and testify, notwithstanding the fact you were urged by the White House or State Department not to; notwithstanding the fact that, as you testified earlier, the President implicitly threatened you in that call record. And now, the President in real-time is attacking you. What effect do you think that has on other witnesses' willingness to come forward and expose wrongdoing?
> A: Well, it's very intimidating.
> Q: It's designed to intimidate, is it not?
> A: I—I—I mean, I can't speak to what the President is trying to do, but I think the effect is to be intimidating.
> Q: Well, I want to let you know, Ambassador, that some of us here take witness intimidation very, very seriously.[405]

In response to the President's attacks, Rep. Liz Cheney, Chair of the House Republican Caucus, stated that the President "was wrong" and that Ambassador Yovanovitch "clearly is somebody who's been a public servant to the United States for decades and I don't think the President should have done that."[406] Rep. Francis Rooney, also a Republican, stated: "I don't necessarily think it's right to be harassing or beating up on our professional diplomatic service."[407]

Even after these rebukes, the President continued to attack and threaten Ambassador Yovanovitch. For example, in an interview on November 22, President Trump stated: "This was not an angel, this woman, okay? And there are a lot of things that she did that I didn't like. And we will talk about that at some time."[408]

Lieutenant Colonel Alexander S. Vindman,
Director for Ukraine, National Security Council

On October 29, President Trump tweeted that Lt. Col. Alexander Vindman is a "Never Trumper."[409] When asked by a reporter what evidence he had for his claim, the President responded: "We'll be showing that to you real soon. Okay?"[410] President Trump continued attacking Lt. Col. Vindman during his testimony on November 19, seeking to question his loyalty to the United States. The President retweeted: "Lt. Col. Vindman was offered the position of Defense Minister for the Ukrainian Government THREE times!"[411] Allies of the President also questioned Lt. Col. Vindman's loyalty to the country and amplified the smear.[412]

For his part, Lt. Col. Vindman stated during his testimony:

I want to take a moment to recognize the courage of my colleagues who have appeared and are scheduled to appear before this Committee. I want to state that the vile character attacks on these distinguished and honorable public servants is reprehensible.[413]

Ambassador William B. Taylor, Jr., Chargé d'Affaires for
U.S. Embassy in Kyiv, Department of State

On October 23, one day after Ambassador William Taylor's deposition, the President sent a tweet comparing "Never Trumper Republicans" to "human scum."[414] An hour later, he described Ambassador Taylor in a tweet as a "Never Trumper."[415]

On October 25, the President discussed Ambassador Taylor's testimony with reporters, and again dismissed the Ambassador as a "Never Trumper." After a reporter noted that Secretary of State Mike Pompeo had hired Ambassador Taylor, the President responded: "Hey, everybody makes mistakes." He then had the following exchange about Ambassador Taylor:

Q: Do you want him out now as the top diplomat?
A: He's a Never Trumper. His lawyer is the head of the Never Trumpers. They're a dying breed, but they're still there.[416]

On the morning of November 13, just before Ambassador Taylor and George Kent testified at a public hearing, the President tweeted: "NEVER TRUMPERS!"[417]

Jennifer Williams, Special Advisor for
Europe and Russia, Office of the Vice President

On November 17, two days before Jennifer Williams testified at a public hearing, President Trump sent a tweet attacking her and stating that "she should meet with the other Never Trumpers, who I don't know & mostly never even heard of, & work out a better presidential attack!"[418] During the hearing, Rep. Jim Himes asked Ms. Williams what impression the President's tweet had made on her. She responded: "It certainly surprised me. I was not expecting to be called out by name." Rep. Himes noted that the tweet "surprised me, too, and it looks an awful lot like witness intimidation and tampering, and an effort to try to get you to perhaps shape your testimony today."[419]

Threats of Retaliation

The President suggested that witnesses who testified as part of the impeachment inquiry could face retaliation. For example, on November 16, the President sent a pair of tweets indicating that three witnesses appearing before the impeachment inquiry could face dismissals as a result of their testimony. The President tweeted language he attributed to radio host Rush Limbaugh:

> "My support for Donald Trump has never been greater than it is right now. It is paramountly obvious watching this, these people have to go. You elected Donald Trump to drain the Swamp, well, dismissing people like Yovanovitch is what that looks like. Dismissing people like Kent … and Taylor, dismissing everybody involved from the Obama holdover days trying to undermine Trump, getting rid of those people, dismissing them, this is what it looks like. It was never going to be clean, they were never going to sit by idly and just let Trump do this!" Rush L[420]

Intelligence Community Whistleblower

In addition to his relentless attacks on witnesses who testified in connection with the House's impeachment inquiry, the President also repeatedly threatened and attacked a member of the Intelligence Community who filed an anonymous whistleblower complaint raising an "urgent concern" regarding the President's conduct. The whistleblower filed the complaint confidentially with the Inspector General of the Intelligence Community, as authorized by the relevant whistleblower law. Federal law prohibits the Inspector General from revealing the whistleblower's identity.[421] Federal law also protects the whistleblower from retaliation.[422]

On September 9, the Inspector General notified Congress that this individual had filed a credible complaint regarding an "urgent concern," but that the Acting Director of National Intelligence was withholding the complaint from Congress—contrary to his statutory obligation to have submitted the complaint to the congressional intelligence committees by no later than September 2.[423] On September 13, 2019, the Intelligence Committee issued a subpoena to the Acting Director of National Intelligence for the whistleblower's complaint and other records.[424]

On September 26, the Intelligence Committee received the declassified whistleblower complaint and made it available to the public.[425]

That day, the President issued a chilling threat against the whistleblower and those who provided information to the whistleblower regarding the President's misconduct, suggesting that they could face the death penalty for treason. President Trump stated:

> I want to know who's the person who gave the whistle-blower the information because that's close to a spy. You know what we used to do in the old days when we were smart with spies and treason, right? We used to handle it a little differently than we do now.[426]

In response, the Committees warned President Trump to stop attacking the whistleblower, stating:

> The President's comments today constitute reprehensible witness intimidation and an attempt to obstruct Congress' impeachment inquiry. We condemn the President's attacks, and we invite our Republican counterparts to do the same because Congress must do all it can to protect this whistleblower, and all whistleblowers. Threats of violence from the leader of our country have a chilling effect on the entire whistleblower process, with grave consequences for our democracy and national security.[427]

Yet the President's attacks did not stop. Instead, he continued to threaten the whistleblower, publicly questioned the whistleblower's motives, disputed the accuracy of the whistleblower's account, and encouraged others to reveal the whistleblower's identity. The President's focus on the whistleblower has been obsessive, with the President making more than 100 public statements about the whistleblower over a period of just two months. For example, the President stated:

- "I want to meet not only my accuser, who presented SECOND & THIRD HAND INFORMATION, but also the person who illegally gave this information, which was largely incorrect, to the 'Whistleblower.' Was this person SPYING on the U.S. President? Big Consequences!"[428]
- "I think it's outrageous that a Whistleblower is a CIA agent."[429]
- "But what they said is he's an Obama person. It was involved with Brennan; Susan Rice, which means Obama. But he was like a big—a big anti-Trump person. Hated Trump."[430]
- "The Whistleblower got it sooo wrong that HE must come forward. The Fake News Media knows who he is but, being an arm of the Democrat Party, don't want to reveal him because there would be hell to pay. Reveal the Whistleblower and end the Impeachment Hoax!"[431]
- "But the whistleblower should be revealed because the whistleblower gave false stories. Some people would call it a fraud; I won't go that far. But when I read it closely, I probably would. But the whistleblower should be revealed."[432]
- "I think that the whistleblower gave a lot of false information."[433]
- "The whistleblower is not a whistleblower. He's a fake. … Everybody knows who the whistleblower is. And the whistleblower is a political operative."[434]

In response to a request from Intelligence Committee Ranking Member Nunes to call the whistleblower to testify at an open hearing, Chairman Schiff underscored the danger posed by the President's threats against the whistleblower and why the whistleblower's testimony was now unnecessary:

> The Committee also will not facilitate efforts by President Trump and his allies in Congress to threaten, intimidate, and retaliate against the whistleblower who courageously raised the initial alarm. It remains the duty of the Intelligence Committee to protect whistleblowers, and until recently, this was a bipartisan priority. The

whistleblower has a right under laws championed by this Committee to remain anonymous and to be protected from harm.

The impeachment inquiry, moreover, has gathered an ever-growing body of evidence—from witnesses and documents, including the President's own words in his July 25 call record—that not only confirms, but far exceeds, the initial information in the whistleblower's complaint. The whistleblower's testimony is therefore redundant and unnecessary. In light of the President's threats, the individual's appearance before us would only place their personal safety at grave risk.[435]

Until President Trump's attacks on the whistleblower, Republicans and Democrats were united in protecting whistleblowers' right to report abuses of power and be free from retaliation.[436] For example, Ranking Member Nunes, serving in 2017 as Chairman of the Intelligence Committee, spoke in defense of whistleblowers, stating: "We want people to come forward and we will protect the identity of those people at all cost."[437] He also stated:

As you know, and I've said this several times, we don't talk about sources at this committee. … The good thing is, is that we have continued to have people come forward, voluntarily, to this committee and we want to continue that and I will tell you that that will not happen if we tell you who our sources are and people that come—come to the committee.[438]

Other Republican Members of Congress have opposed efforts to expose the whistleblower. For example, Senator Charles Grassley stated:

This person appears to have followed the whistleblower protection laws and ought to be heard out and protected. We should always work to respect whistleblowers' requests for confidentiality. Any further media reports on the whistleblower's identity don't serve the public interest—even if the conflict sells more papers or attracts clicks.[439]

Senator Richard Burr, the Chair of the Senate Select Committee on Intelligence, affirmed that he would "never" want the identity of the whistleblower revealed and stated, "We protect whistleblowers. We protect witnesses in our committee."[440]

Senator Mitt Romney also called for support of the whistleblower's rights, stating: "[W]histleblowers should be entitled to confidentiality and privacy, because they play a vital function in our democracy."[441]

SECTION II ENDNOTES

[1] U.S. Const. Art. I, § 2, cl. 5.

[2] Statement of George Mason, Madison Debates (July 20, 1787).

[3] *McGrain v. Daugherty*, 273 U.S. 135 (1927) ("We are of [the] opinion that the power of inquiry—with process to enforce it—is an essential and appropriate auxiliary to the legislative function."); *Eastland v. United States Servicemen's Fund*, 421 U.S. 491 (1975) ("the power to investigate is inherent in the power to make laws"); *Committee on the Judiciary v. McGahn*, Case No. 1:19-cv-02379, Memorandum Opinion, Doc. No. 46 (D.D.C. Nov. 25, 2019) ("[T]he House of Representatives has the constitutionally vested responsibility to conduct investigations of suspected abuses of power within the government, and to act to curb those improprieties, if required."). As of this report, an appeal is pending in the D.C. Circuit. No. 19-5331 (D.C. Cir.).

[4] *Cf. Nixon v. Fitzgerald*, 457 U.S. 731 (1982) ("Vigilant oversight by Congress also may serve to deter Presidential abuses of office, as well as to make credible the threat of impeachment."); *Senate Select Committee on Presidential Campaign Activities v. Nixon*, 498 F.2d 725 (D.C. Cir. 1974) (discussing in dicta the "inquiry into presidential impeachment" opened by the House Judiciary Committee regarding President Nixon and explaining, "The investigative authority of the Judiciary Committee with respect to presidential conduct has an express constitutional source."); *In re Report & Recommendation of June 5, 1972 Grand Jury Concerning Transmission of Evidence to House of Representatives*, 370 F. Supp. 1219 (D.D.C. 1974) ("[I]t should not be forgotten that we deal in a matter of the most critical moment to the Nation, an impeachment investigation involving the President of the United States. It would be difficult to conceive of a more compelling need than that of this country for an unswervingly fair inquiry based on all the pertinent information."). In 1833, Justice Joseph Story reasoned—while explaining why pardons cannot confer immunity from impeachment—that, "The power of impeachment will generally be applied to persons holding high office under the government; and it is of great consequence that the President should not have the power of preventing a thorough investigation of their conduct, or of securing them against the disgrace of a public conviction by impeachment, should they deserve it. The constitution has, therefore, wisely interposed this check upon his power." Joseph L. Story, 3 *Commentaries on the Constitution of the United States* § 1501 (1873 ed., T.M. Cooley (ed.)).

[5] House Committee on the Judiciary, *Impeachment of Richard M. Nixon, President of the United States*, 93rd Cong. (1974) (H. Rep. 93-1305).

[6] Statement of Rep. William Lyman, Annals of Congress, 4th Cong. 601 (1796).

[7] Department of Justice, Office of Legal Counsel, *A Sitting President's Amenability to Indictment and Criminal Prosecution* (Oct. 16, 2000) (explaining that a President "who engages in criminal behavior falling into the category of 'high Crimes and Misdemeanors'" is "always subject to removal from office upon impeachment by the House and conviction by the Senate") (online at www.justice.gov/sites/default/files/olc/opinions/2000/10/31/op-olc-v024-p0222_0.pdf).

[88] *Id.* ("Moreover, the constitutionally specified impeachment process ensures that the immunity [of a sitting President from prosecution] would not place the President 'above the law.'"). President Trump's personal lawyers have staked out the more extreme position that the President may not be investigated by law enforcement agencies while in office. For example, President Trump's personal attorney asserted in court that the President could not be investigated by local authorities if he committed murder while in office. *If Trump Shoots Someone on 5th Ave., Does He Have Immunity? His Lawyer Says Yes*, New York Times (Oct. 23, 2019) (online at www.nytimes.com/2019/10/23/nyregion/trump-taxes-vance.html). A federal district court and appeals court rejected this argument. *Trump v. Vance*, 941 F.3d 631 (2nd Cir. 2019) ("presidential immunity does not bar the enforcement of a state grand jury subpoena directing a third party to produce non-privileged material, even when the subject matter under investigation pertains to the President"); *Trump v. Vance*, 395 F. Supp. 3d 283 (S.D.N.Y. 2019) (calling the President's claims of "unqualified and boundless" immunity from judicial process "repugnant to the nation's governmental structure and constitutional values"). The case is currently being appealed.

[9] *Barenblatt v. U.S.*, 360 U.S. 109 (1959).

[10] *McGrain v. Daugherty*, 273 U.S. 135 (1927) ("A legislative body cannot legislate wisely or effectively in the absence of information respecting the conditions which the legislation is intended to affect or change; and where the legislative body does not itself possess the requisite information—which not infrequently is true—recourse must

be had to others who do possess it. Experience has taught that mere requests for such information often are unavailing, and also that information which is volunteered is not always accurate or complete; so some means of compulsion are essential to obtain what is needed."); *Eastland v. United States Servicemen's Fund*, 421 U.S. 491 (1975) ("the subpoena power may be exercised by a committee acting, as here, on behalf of one of the Houses"); *Committee on the Judiciary v. Miers*, 558 F. Supp. 2d 84 (D.D.C. 2008) ("In short, there can be no question that Congress has a right—derived from its Article I legislative function—to issue and enforce subpoenas, and a corresponding right to the information that is the subject of such subpoenas. ... Congress's power of inquiry is as broad as its power to legislate and lies at the very heart of Congress's constitutional role. Indeed, the former is necessary to the proper exercise of the latter: according to the Supreme Court, the ability to compel testimony is 'necessary to the effective functioning of courts and legislatures.'") (citation omitted).

[11] U.S. Const. Art. I, § 5, cl. 2.

[12] *Watkins v. United States*, 354 U.S. 178 (1957).

[13] *See Committee on the Judiciary v. Miers*, 558 F. Supp. 2d 84 (D.D.C. 2008) ("Thus, federal precedent dating back as far as 1807 contemplates that even the Executive is bound to comply with duly issued subpoenas.").

[14] *Committee on the Judiciary v. McGahn*, Case No. 1:19-cv-02379, Memorandum Opinion, Doc. No. 46 (D.D.C. Nov. 25, 2019). As of this report, an appeal is pending in the D.C. Circuit. No. 19-5331 (D.C. Cir.).

[15] 18 U.S.C. § 1505.

[16] 18 U.S.C. § 1001 (also prohibiting making "any materially false, fictitious, or fraudulent statement or representation" or making or using "any false writing or document knowing the same to contain any materially false, fictitious, or fraudulent statement or entry" in connection with a Congressional investigation).

[17] 18 U.S.C. § 1512(b); *See also* 18 U.S.C. § 1515(a) (defining "official proceeding" to include "a proceeding before the Congress").

[18] 18 U.S.C. § 1512(d).

[19] *See, e.g.*, 5 U.S.C. § 2302; 10 U.S.C. § 1034; P.L. 113-126.

[20] P.L. 116-6, § 713 ("No part of any appropriation contained in this or any other Act shall be available for the payment of the salary of any officer or employee of the Federal Government, who ... prohibits or prevents, or attempts or threatens to prohibit or prevent, any other officer or employee of the Federal Government from having any direct oral or written communication or contact with any Member, committee, or subcommittee of the Congress in connection with any matter pertaining to the employment of such other officer or employee or pertaining to the department or agency of such other officer or employee in any way, irrespective of whether such communication or contact is at the initiative of such other officer or employee or in response to the request or inquiry of such Member, committee, or subcommittee.").

[21] House Committee on the Judiciary, *Impeachment of Richard M. Nixon, President of the United States*, 93rd Cong. (1974) (H. Rep. 93-1305).

[22] House Committee on the Judiciary, *Impeachment of William Jefferson Clinton, President of the United States*, 105th Cong. (1998) (H. Rep. 105-830).

[23] The White House, *The President's Remarks Announcing Developments and Procedures to be Followed in Connection with the Investigation* (Apr. 17, 1973). President Nixon initially stated that members of his "personal staff" would "decline a request for a formal appearance before a committee of the Congress," but reversed course approximately one month later. The White House, *Statement by the President, Executive Privilege* (Mar. 12, 1973).

[24] *See, e.g.*, Senate Select Committee on Presidential Campaign Activities, Testimony of John Dean, *Watergate and Related Activities, Phase I: Watergate Investigation*, 93rd Cong. (June 25, 1973); Senate Select Committee on Presidential Campaign Activities, Testimony of H.R. Haldeman, *Watergate and Related Activities, Phase I: Watergate Investigation*, 93rd Cong. (July 30, 1973); Senate Select Committee on Presidential Campaign Activities, Testimony of Alexander Butterfield, *Watergate and Related Activities, Phase I: Watergate Investigation*, 93rd Cong. (July 16, 1973); Senate Select Committee on Presidential Campaign Activities, Testimony of John Ehrlichman, *Watergate and Related Activities, Phase I: Watergate Investigation*, 93rd Cong. (July 24, 1973).

---

[25] *See* House Committee on the Judiciary, *Impeachment of Richard M. Nixon, President of the United States*, 93rd Cong. (1974) (H. Rep. 93-1305).

[26] *Id.*

[27] *Id.* (quoting letter from Chairman Peter W. Rodino, Jr., House Committee on the Judiciary, to President Richard M. Nixon (May 30, 1974)).

[28] H.R. Jour., 29th Cong., 1st Sess., 693 (Apr. 20, 1846).

[29] Senate Select Committee on Secret Military Assistance to Iran and the Nicaraguan Opposition and House Select Committee to Investigate Covert Arms Transactions with Iran, Testimony of Oliver North, *Iran-Contra Investigation: Joint Hearings Before the House Select Committee to Investigate Covert Arms Transactions with Iran and the Senate Select Committee on Secret Military Assistance to Iran and the Nicaraguan Oppositions*, 100th Cong. (July 7, 1987); Senate Select Committee on Secret Military Assistance to Iran and the Nicaraguan Opposition and House Select Committee to Investigate Covert Arms Transactions with Iran, Testimony of John Poindexter, *Iran-Contra Investigation: Joint Hearings Before the House Select Committee to Investigate Covert Arms Transactions with Iran and the Senate Select Committee on Secret Military Assistance to Iran and the Nicaraguan Oppositions*, 100th Cong. (July 15, 1987).

[30] *Committee on the Judiciary v. McGahn*, Civ. No. 1:19-cv-02379, Memorandum Opinion, Doc. No. 46 (D.D.C. Nov. 25, 2019). As of this report, an appeal is pending in the D.C. Circuit. No. 19-5331 (D.C. Cir.).

[31] Committee on Government Reform, Democratic Staff, *Congressional Oversight of the Clinton Administration* (Jan. 17, 2006) (online at https://wayback.archive-it.org/4949/20141031200116/http://oversight-archive.waxman house.gov/documents/20060117103516-91336.pdf) (noting that Republican Dan Burton, Chairman of the Committee on Government Reform, deposed 141 Clinton Administration officials during his tenure).

[32] Select Committee on the Events Surrounding the 2012 Terrorist Attack in Benghazi, *Final Report of the Select Committee on the Events Surrounding the 2012 Terrorist Attack in Benghazi*, 114th Cong. (2016) (H. Rep. 114-848) (noting that the Select Committee interviewed or received testimony from 107 people—none of whom was instructed not to appear—including 57 current and former State Department officials such as Secretary of State Hillary Clinton, Chief of Staff and Counselor to the Secretary of State Cheryl Mills, Deputy Chief of Staff and Director of Policy Planning Jacob Sullivan, and Deputy Chief of Staff for Operations Huma Abedin; 24 Defense Department officials such as Secretary Leon Panetta and General Carter Ham; and 19 Central Intelligence Agency (CIA) officials such as Director David Petraeus and former Deputy Director Michael Morell).

[33] *Id.* (including productions of 71,640 pages of State Department documents, 300 pages of CIA intelligence analyses, 200 pages of Federal Bureau of Investigation (FBI) documents, 900 pages of Defense Department documents, and 750 pages of National Security Agency documents).

[34] *See, e.g.*, House rule X, clause 2(a) (assigning "general oversight responsibilities" to committees); House Rule XI, clause 2(m) (authorizing Committees to "hold such hearings as it considers necessary" and to "require, by subpoena or otherwise, the attendance and testimony of such witnesses and the production of such books, records, correspondence, memoranda, papers, and documents as it considers necessary"); H. Res. 6 (2019) (granting deposition authority to committees); 116th Congress Regulations for Use of Deposition Authority, Congressional Record (Jan. 25, 2019) (establishing procedures for committee depositions).

[35] *See, e.g.*, House Rules (2017); H. Res. 5 (2017); 115th Congress Staff Deposition Authority Procedures, Congressional Record (Jan. 13, 2017).

[36] Special Counsel Robert S. Mueller III, Department of Justice, *Report on The Investigation Into Russian Interference In The 2016 Presidential Election*, Vol. I (March 2019) (online at www.justice.gov/storage/report.pdf); Special Counsel Robert S. Mueller, III, Department of Justice, *Report on The Investigation Into Russian Interference In The 2016 Presidential Election*, Vol. II (March 2019) (online at www.justice.gov/storage/report_volume2.pdf).

[37] *See* H. Res. 430; *see also* H. Rep. 116-105 (2019) (the purposes of the Judiciary Committee's investigation include "considering whether any of the conduct described in the Special Counsel's Report warrants the Committee in taking any further steps under Congress' Article I powers," including "whether to approve articles of impeachment with respect to the President or any other Administration official").

[38] *See* Letter from Chairman Jerrold Nadler, House Committee on the Judiciary, to Chairman Adam B. Schiff, House Permanent Select Committee on Intelligence, Chairwoman Maxine Waters, House Committee on Financial Services, Chairman Elijah E. Cummings, House Committee on Oversight and Reform, and Chairman Eliot L. Engel, House Committee on Foreign Affairs (Aug. 22, 2019) (online at https://judiciary.house.gov/sites/democrats.judiciary.house.gov/files/documents/FiveChairsLetter8.22.pdf).

[39] *Id.*

[40] Letter from Chairman Eliot L. Engel, House Committee on Foreign Affairs, Chairman Adam B. Schiff, House Permanent Select Committee on Intelligence, and Chairman Elijah E. Cummings, House Committee on Oversight and Reform, to Pat A. Cipollone, Counsel to the President, The White House (Sept. 9, 2019) (online at https://intelligence.house.gov/uploadedfiles/ele_schiff_cummings_letter_to_cipollone_on_ukraine.pdf); Letter from Chairman Eliot L. Engel, House Committee on Foreign Affairs, Chairman Adam B. Schiff, House Permanent Select Committee on Intelligence, and Chairman Elijah E. Cummings, House Committee on Oversight and Reform, to Secretary Michael R. Pompeo, Department of State (Sept. 9, 2019) (online at https://intelligence.house.gov/uploadedfiles/ele_schiff_cummings_letter_to_sec_pompeo_on_ukraine.pdf); Letter from Chairman Eliot L. Engel, Committee on Foreign Affairs, Chairman Adam B. Schiff, Permanent Select Committee on Intelligence, and Chairman Elijah E. Cummings, Committee on Oversight and Reform, to Secretary Michael R. Pompeo, Department of State (Sept. 13, 2019) (online at https://oversight.house.gov/sites/democrats.oversight.house.gov/files/2019-09-13.EEC%20ELE%20Schiff%20re%20Ukraine.pdf).

[41] The White House, *Remarks by President Trump Before Marine One Departure* (Sept. 22, 2019) (online at www.whitehouse.gov/briefings-statements/remarks-president-trump-marine-one-departure-66/) ("We had a great conversation. The conversation I had was largely congratulatory. It was largely corruption—all of the corruption taking place. It was largely the fact that we don't want our people, like Vice President Biden and his son, creating to the corruption already in the Ukraine.").

[42] Speaker of the House Nancy Pelosi, *Pelosi Remarks Announcing Impeachment Inquiry* (Sept. 24, 2019) (online at www.speaker.gov/newsroom/92419-0).

[43] The White House, *Memorandum of Telephone Conversation* (July 25, 2019) (online at www.whitehouse.gov/wp-content/uploads/2019/09/Unclassified09.2019.pdf).

[44] *See, e.g.*, Letter from Chairman Elijah E. Cummings, House Committee on Oversight and Reform, Chairman Adam B. Schiff, House Permanent Select Committee on Intelligence, and Chairman Eliot L. Engel, House Committee on Foreign Affairs, to Mick Mulvaney, Acting Chief of Staff, The White House (Oct. 4, 2019) (online at https://oversight.house.gov/sites/democrats.oversight.house.gov/files/documents/2019-10-04.EEC%20Engel%20Schiff%20to%20Mulvaney-WH%20re%20Subpoena.pdf).

[45] H. Res. 660 (2019).

[46] *Trump Vows Stonewall of 'All' House Subpoenas, Setting Up Fight Over Powers*, New York Times (Apr. 24, 2019) (online at www.nytimes.com/2019/04/24/us/politics/donald-trump-subpoenas.html).

[47] *While Bemoaning Mueller Probe, Trump Falsely Says the Constitution Gives Him 'The Right to do Whatever I Want'*, Washington Post (July 23, 2019) (online at www.washingtonpost.com/politics/2019/07/23/trump-falsely-tells-auditorium-full-teens-constitution-gives-him-right-do-whatever-i-want/).

[48] Donald J. Trump, Twitter (Oct. 1, 2019) (online at https://twitter.com/realDonaldTrump/status/1179179573541511176).

[49] *At Louisiana Rally, Trump Lashes Out at Impeachment Inquiry and Pelosi*, New York Times (Oct. 11, 2019) (online at www.nytimes.com/2019/10/11/us/trump-rally-louisiana-lake-charles.html).

[50] Donald J. Trump, Twitter (Oct. 18, 2019) (online at https://twitter.com/realDonaldTrump/status/1185374394350215169) (purporting to quote former Rep. Jason Chaffetz).

[51] Donald J. Trump, Twitter (Sept. 21, 2019) (online at https://twitter.com/realDonaldTrump/status/1175409914384125952).

[52] Donald J. Trump, Twitter (Sept. 24, 2019) (online at https://twitter.com/realDonaldTrump/status/1176559970390806530).

[53] Donald J. Trump, Twitter (Sept. 24, 2019) (online at https://twitter.com/realDonaldTrump/status/1176623010230525953).

[54] The White House, *Remarks by President Trump and President Salih of Iraq Before Bilateral Meeting* (Sept. 24, 2019) (online at www.whitehouse.gov/briefings-statements/remarks-president-trump-president-salih-iraq-bilateral-meeting-new-york-ny-2/).

[55] The White House, *Remarks by President Trump and President Bukele of El Salvador Before Bilateral Meeting* (Sept. 25, 2019) (online at www.whitehouse.gov/briefings-statements/remarks-president-trump-president-bukele-el-salvador-bilateral-meeting-new-york-ny/).

[56] The White House, *Remarks by President Trump in a Multilateral Meeting on the Bolivarian Republic of Venezuela* (Sept. 25, 2019) (online at www.whitehouse.gov/briefings-statements/remarks-president-trump-multilateral-meeting-bolivarian-republic-venezuela-new-york-ny/).

[57] Donald J. Trump, Twitter (Sept. 26, 2019) (online at https://twitter.com/realDonaldTrump/status/1177285017636093953).

[58] Donald J. Trump, Twitter (Oct. 1, 2019) (online at https://twitter.com/realDonaldTrump/status/1179023004241727489).

[59] Donald J. Trump, Twitter (Oct. 5, 2019) (online at https://twitter.com/realDonaldTrump/status/1180482408522629120).

[60] Donald J. Trump, Twitter (Oct. 8, 2019) (online at https://twitter.com/realDonaldTrump/status/1181761045486080002).

[61] The White House, *Remarks by President Trump at Signing of Executive Orders on Transparency in Federal Guidance and Enforcement* (Oct. 9, 2019) (online at www.whitehouse.gov/briefings-statements/remarks-president-trump-signing-executive-orders-transparency-federal-guidance-enforcement/).

[62] Donald J. Trump, Twitter (Oct. 9, 2019) (online at https://twitter.com/realDonaldTrump/status/1181913137483829250).

[63] Donald J. Trump, Twitter (Oct. 9, 2019) (online at https://twitter.com/realdonaldtrump/status/1181969511697788928).

[64] Donald J. Trump, Twitter (Oct. 20, 2019) (online at https://twitter.com/realDonaldTrump/status/1186035686396321793).

[65] Donald J. Trump, Twitter (Nov. 12, 2019) (online at https://twitter.com/realDonaldTrump/status/1194214569591394304).

[66] Donald J. Trump, Twitter (Nov. 24, 2019) (online at https://twitter.com/realDonaldTrump/status/1198733640722718725).

[67] Donald J. Trump, Twitter (Nov. 26, 2019) (online at https://twitter.com/realDonaldTrump/status/1199352977934487553).

[68] The White House, *Remarks by President Trump Upon Air Force One Arrival* (Sept. 26, 2019) (online at www.whitehouse.gov/briefings-statements/remarks-president-trump-upon-air-force-one-arrival-prince-georges-county-md/).

[69] *See, e.g.*, Co-Equal, *Investigative Rules and Practices Followed by House Republicans* (online at www.co-equal.org/guide-to-congressional-oversight/investigative-rules-and-practices-followed-by-house-republicans). *See also* Committee on Government Reform, Democratic Staff, *Congressional Oversight of the Clinton Administration* (Jan. 17, 2006) (online at https://wayback.archive-it.org/4949/20141031200116/http://oversight-archive.waxman house.gov/documents/20060117103516-91336.pdf) (noting that House Republicans conducted hundreds of confidential depositions of both political appointees and career officials without agency counsel present, with one Committee alone conducting over 140 depositions of Clinton Administration officials).

[70] Letter from Pat A. Cipollone, Counsel to the President, The White House, to House Speaker Nancy Pelosi, Chairman Adam B. Schiff, House Permanent Select Committee on Intelligence, Chairman Eliot L. Engel, House Committee on Foreign Affairs Committee, and Chairman Elijah E. Cummings, House Committee on Oversight and Reform (Oct. 8, 2019) (online at www.whitehouse.gov/wp-content/uploads/2019/10/PAC-Letter-10.08.2019.pdf).

[71] *Speech: Donald Trump Holds a Political Rally in Minneapolis, Minnesota*, Factbase Videos (Oct. 10, 2019) (online at www.youtube.com/watch?time_continue=742&v=_y8Al_mGwmc&feature=emb_logo).

[72] Gregg Nunziata, a former legal counsel and senior policy advisor to Senator Marco Rubio, stated: "This letter is bananas. A barely-lawyered temper tantrum." Gregg Nunziata, Twitter (Oct. 8, 2019) (online at https://twitter.com/greggnunziata/status/1181685021926662144). Jonathan Turley, a law professor who has represented House Republicans, stated: "A President cannot simply pick up his marbles and leave the game because he does not like the other players. A refusal to cooperate with a constitutionally mandated process can itself be an abuse of power." *White House Issues Defiant Letter Refusing to Cooperate in Impeachment Proceedings*, Res Ipsa Loquitur (Oct. 9, 2019) (online at https://jonathanturley.org/2019/10/09/white-house-issues-defiant-letter-refusing-to-cooperate-in-impeachment-proceedings/). Preet Bharara, the former U.S. Attorney for the Southern District of New York, stated, "It's one of the worst letters I've seen from the White House counsel's office." George Conway, a prominent conservative attorney, called Mr. Cipollone's letter "a disgrace to the country, a disgrace to the presidency, and a disgrace to the legal profession." He accused the White House of "clearly engaging in obstructionist tactics." *Diagnosing Trump (with George Conway)*, Stay Tuned with Preet Bharara (Oct. 9, 2019) (online at https://cafe.com/stay-tuned-transcript-diagnosing-trump-with-george-conway/). Mr. Conway also stated: "I cannot fathom how any self-respecting member of the bar could affix his name to this letter. It's pure hackery, and it disgraces the profession." George T. Conway, III, Twitter (Oct. 8, 2019) (online at https://twitter.com/gtconway3d/status/1181685229687394307).

[73] Letter from Pat A. Cipollone, Counsel to the President, The White House, to Acting Chairwoman Carolyn B. Maloney, House Committee on Oversight and Reform, Chairman Adam B. Schiff, House Permanent Select Committee on Intelligence Chairman Eliot L. Engel, Chairman, House Committee on Foreign Affairs (Oct. 18, 2019).

[74] Department of Justice, Office of Legal Counsel, *Exclusion of Agency Counsel from Congressional Depositions in the Impeachment Context* (Nov. 1, 2019) (online at www.justice.gov/olc/file/1214996/download).

[75] Department of Justice, Office of Legal Counsel, *Legal Aspects of Impeachment: An Overview* (1974) (quoting President James K. Polk) (online at www.justice.gov/olc/page/file/980036/download).

[76] *Position of the Executive Department Regarding Investigative Reports*, 40 Op. Atty Gen. 45 (1941).

[77] Letter from Pat A. Cipollone, Counsel to the President, The White House, to House Speaker Nancy Pelosi, Chairman Adam B. Schiff, House Permanent Select Committee on Intelligence, Chairman Eliot L. Engel, House Committee on Foreign Affairs Committee, and Chairman Elijah E. Cummings, House Committee on Oversight and Reform (Oct. 8, 2019) (online at www.whitehouse.gov/wp-content/uploads/2019/10/PAC-Letter-10.08.2019.pdf).

[78] *See, e.g.*, The White House, *Remarks by President Trump and President Salih of Iraq Before Bilateral Meeting* (Sept. 24, 2019) (online at www.whitehouse.gov/briefings-statements/remarks-president-trump-president-salih-iraq-bilateral-meeting-new-york-ny/) ("The phone call was perfect."); The White House, *Remarks by President Trump Upon Arriving at the U.N. General Assembly* (Sept. 24, 2019) (online at www.whitehouse.gov/briefings-statements/remarks-president-trump-upon-arriving-u-n-general-assembly-new-york-ny/) ("That call was perfect."); Donald J. Trump, Twitter (Nov. 11, 2019) (online at https://twitter.com/realDonaldTrump/status/1193615188311912449) ("The call to the Ukrainian President was PERFECT.").

[79] Letter from Pat A. Cipollone, Counsel to the President, The White House, to House Speaker Nancy Pelosi, Chairman Adam B. Schiff, House Permanent Select Committee on Intelligence, Chairman Eliot L. Engel, House Committee on Foreign Affairs Committee, and Chairman Elijah E. Cummings, House Committee on Oversight and Reform (Oct. 8, 2019) (online at www.whitehouse.gov/wp-content/uploads/2019/10/PAC-Letter-10.08.2019.pdf).

<sup/> <sup/>

⁸⁰ *See* House Committee on the Judiciary, *Impeachment of Richard M. Nixon, President of the United States*, 93rd Cong. (1974) (H. Rep. 93-1305) (Impeachment Article III: "In refusing to produce these papers and things, Richard M. Nixon, substituting his judgment as to what materials were necessary for the inquiry, interposed the powers of the presidency against the lawful subpoenas of the House of Representatives, thereby assuming to himself functions and judgments necessary to the exercise of the sole power of impeachment vested by the Constitution in the House of Representatives.").

⁸¹ In this case, one Republican Member of the House of Representatives supported impeaching President Trump—Rep. Justin Amash from Michigan. In explaining his support, Rep. Amash noted the importance of upholding Congress' "duties under our Constitution" rather than "loyalty to a political party." After Rep. Amash announced his support for impeachment, President Trump denounced him as a "total lightweight" and a "loser." Rep. Amash subsequently declared that he was leaving the Republican party. *See* Justin Amash, Twitter (May 18, 2019) (online at https://twitter.com/justinamash/status/1129831626844921862); *Trump Calls Representative Justin Amash a 'Loser' Over Impeachment Talk*, New York Times (May 19, 2019) (online at www.nytimes.com/2019/05/19/us/politics/trump-justin-amash-impeachment.html); *Justin Amash: Our politics is in a partisan death spiral. That's why I'm leaving the GOP*, Washington Post (July 4, 2019) (online at www.washingtonpost.com/opinions/justin-amash-our-politics-is-in-a-partisan-death-spiral-thats-why-im-leaving-the-gop/2019/07/04/afbe0480-9e3d-11e9-b27f-ed2942f73d70_story.html).

⁸² Letter from Pat A. Cipollone, Counsel to the President, The White House, to Acting Chairwoman Carolyn B. Maloney, House Committee on Oversight and Reform, Chairman Adam B. Schiff, House Permanent Select Committee on Intelligence, Chairman Eliot L. Engel, Chairman, House Committee on Foreign Affairs (Oct. 18, 2019).

⁸³ Jefferson's Manual of Parliamentary Practice § 603 (stating that "various events have been credited with setting an impeachment in motion," including "facts developed and reported by an investigating committee of the House"). On October 25, 2019, a federal district court affirmed that "no governing law requires" the House to hold a such a vote. *In re Application of the Committee on the Judiciary, United States House of Representatives*, 2019 U.S. Dist. LEXIS 184857 (D.D.C. 2019). More than 300 legal scholars agreed, concluding that "the Constitution does not mandate the process for impeachment and there is no constitutional requirement that the House of Representatives authorize an impeachment inquiry before one begins." *An Open Letter from Legal Scholars on Trump Impeachment Inquiry* (Oct. 17, 2019) (online at www.law.berkeley.edu/wp-content/uploads/2019/10/Open-Letter-from-Legal-Scholars-re-Impeachment.pdf).

⁸⁴ *In re Application of the Committee on the Judiciary, United States House of Representatives*, 2019 U.S. Dist. LEXIS 184857 (D.D.C. 2019).

⁸⁵ *See, e.g.*, 3 Deschler Ch. 14 § 5 (discussing impeachment of Justice William O. Douglas).

⁸⁶ *See, e.g.*, H. Res. 87, 101st Cong. (1989) (impeachment of Judge Walter L. Nixon, Jr.); H. Res. 461, 99th Cong. (1986) (impeachment of Judge Harry E. Claiborne).

⁸⁷ H. Res. 6 (2019); H. Res. 660 (2019). In addition, on June 11, 2019, the House approved House Resolution 430, which, in part, authorized the House Committee on the Judiciary to seek judicial enforcement of subpoenas in the ongoing investigation related to Special Counsel Mueller's report. The resolution granted the Committee "any and all necessary authority under Article I of the Constitution" to seek judicial enforcement. The accompanying report by the House Committee on Rules explained that this authority is intended to further the Judiciary Committee's ongoing investigation, the purpose of which includes assessing whether to recommend "articles of impeachment with respect to the President." H. Rep. 116-108, quoting H. Rep. 116-105.

⁸⁸ Letter from Pat A. Cipollone, Counsel to the President, The White House, to House Speaker Nancy Pelosi, Chairman Adam B. Schiff, House Permanent Select Committee on Intelligence, Chairman Eliot L. Engel, House Committee on Foreign Affairs Committee, and Chairman Elijah E. Cummings, House Committee on Oversight and Reform (Oct. 8, 2019) (online at www.whitehouse.gov/wp-content/uploads/2019/10/PAC-Letter-10.08.2019.pdf). President Trump has also made these claims directly, stating: "we had a great two weeks watching these crooked politicians, not giving us due process, not giving us lawyers, not giving us the right to speak, and destroying their witnesses," and "we weren't allowed any rights." *Speech: Donald Trump Holds a Political Rally in Sunrise, Florida*, Factbase Videos (Nov. 26, 2019) (online atwww.youtube.com/watch?v=zoRcCRULQl8&feature=youtu.be).

[89] Indeed, Mr. Cipollone articulated no basis under the Constitution for his various "due process" demands—and there is no such basis, especially when the House is engaged in a fact-finding investigation as part of its efforts to ascertain whether to consider articles of impeachment. *See* H. Rept. 116-266 (2019).

[90] H. Res. 660 (2019).

[91] H. Rept. 116-266 (2019) ("The purpose of providing these protections is to ensure that the president has a fair opportunity to present evidence to the Judiciary Committee if it must weigh whether to recommend articles of impeachment against him to the full House.").

[92] Letter from Pat A. Cipollone, Counsel to the President, to House Speaker Nancy Pelosi, Chairman Adam B. Schiff, House Permanent Select Committee on Intelligence, Chairman Eliot L. Engel, House Committee on Foreign Affairs, and Chairman Elijah E. Cummings, Committee on Oversight and Reform (Oct. 8, 2019) (online at www.whitehouse.gov/wp-content/uploads/2019/10/PAC-Letter-10.08.2019.pdf).

[93] In a September 25, 2019, statement, a Department of Justice spokesperson stated: "The Attorney General was first notified of the President's conversation with Ukrainian President Zelensky several weeks after the call took place, when the Department of Justice learned of a potential referral. The President has not spoken with the Attorney General about having Ukraine investigate anything relating to former Vice President Biden or his son. The President has not asked the Attorney General to contact Ukraine—on this or any other matter. The Attorney General has not communicated with Ukraine—on this or any other subject. Nor has the Attorney General discussed this matter, or anything relating to Ukraine, with Rudy Giuliani." As to the President's conduct with regard to Ukraine, the Department stated: "In August, the Department of Justice was referred a matter relating to a letter the Director of National Intelligence had received from the Inspector General for the Intelligence Community regarding a purported whistleblower complaint. The Inspector General's letter cited a conversation between the President and Ukrainian President Zelensky as a potential violation of federal campaign finance law, while acknowledging that neither the Inspector General nor the complainant had firsthand knowledge of the conversation. Relying on established procedures set forth in the Justice Manual, the Department's Criminal Division reviewed the official record of the call and determined, based on the facts and applicable law, that there was no campaign finance violation and that no further action was warranted. All relevant components of the Department agreed with this legal conclusion, and the Department has concluded the matter." *Department of Justice* (Sept. 25, 2019) (as emailed by the Department of Justice to the House Permanent Select Committee on Intelligence).

[94] H. Rept. 116-266 (2019) (The report continued: "As previously described, an impeachment inquiry is not a criminal trial and should not be confused with one. The president's liberty is not at stake and the constitutional protections afforded a criminal defendant do not as a matter of course apply. The constitutionally permitted consequences of impeachment are limited to immediate removal from office and potentially being barred from holding future federal office. Moreover, it is the Senate that conducts the trial to determine whether the conduct outlined in the articles warrant the president's removal from office, which requires a 2/3 majority vote. Indeed, given the nature of the ongoing investigation into the Ukraine matter, President Trump has received additional procedural protections. During closed door depositions held by HPSCI and others related to the Ukraine matter, minority members have been present and granted equal time to question witnesses brought before the committees. This is unlike the process in the preceding two presidential impeachment inquiries, which relied significantly upon information gathered by third-party investigators.").

[95] *See* Committee on Government Reform, Democratic Staff, *Congressional Oversight of the Clinton Administration* (Jan. 17, 2006) (online at https://wayback.archive-it.org/4949/20141031200116/http://oversight-archive.waxman house.gov/documents/20060117103516-91336.pdf) (explaining that when Rep. Dan Burton served as Chairman of the Committee on Government Reform, the Committee deposed 141 Clinton Administration officials without agency counsel present—including White House Chief of Staff Mack McLarty; White House Chief of Staff Erskine Bowles; White House Counsel Bernard Nussbaum; White House Counsel Jack Quinn; Deputy White House Counsel Bruce Lindsey; Deputy White House Counsel Cheryl Mills; Deputy White House Chief of Staff Harold Ickes; Chief of Staff to the Vice President Roy Neel; and Chief of Staff to the First Lady Margaret Williams).

[96] Letter from Pat A. Cipollone, Counsel to the President, The White House, to House Speaker Nancy Pelosi, Chairman Adam B. Schiff, House Permanent Select Committee on Intelligence, Chairman Eliot L. Engel, House Committee on Foreign Affairs, and Chairman Elijah E. Cummings, Committee on Oversight and Reform (Oct. 8, 2019) (online at www.whitehouse.gov/wp-content/uploads/2019/10/PAC-Letter-10.08.2019.pdf). On

November 1, 2019, after the House approved H. Res. 660, the Administration continued to press this spurious claim, with the Office of Legal Counsel issuing an opinion asserting that "Congressional committees participating in an impeachment inquiry may not validly compel executive branch witnesses to testify about matters that potentially involve information protected by executive privilege without the assistance of agency counsel." Department of Justice, Office of Legal Counsel, *Exclusion of Agency Counsel from Congressional Depositions in the Impeachment Context* (Nov. 1, 2019) (online at www.justice.gov/olc/file/1214996/download). As discussed in this section, this position is entirely unsupported by judicial precedent and erroneous.

[97] U.S. Const., Art. I, sec. 5, cl. 2.

[98] The regulations that govern House depositions state: "Only members, Committee staff designated by the chair or ranking minority member, an official reporter, the witness, and the witness's counsel are permitted to attend. Observers or counsel for other persons, including counsel for government agencies, may not attend." 116th Congress Regulations for Use of Deposition Authority, Congressional Record, H1216 (Jan. 25, 2019) (online at www.congress.gov/116/crec/2019/01/25/CREC-2019-01-25-pt1-PgH1216-2.pdf).

[99] Committee on Oversight and Reform, *Committee Depositions in the House of Representatives: Longstanding Republican and Democratic Practice of Excluding Agency Counsel* (Nov. 5, 2019) (online at https://oversight.house.gov/sites/democrats.oversight.house.gov/files/Committee%20Depositions%20in%20the%20House%20of%20Representatives_Longstanding%20Republican%20and%20Democratic%20Practice%20of%20Excluding%20Agency%20Counsel.pdf).

[100] Letter from Pat A. Cipollone, Counsel to the President, The White House, to House Speaker Nancy Pelosi, Chairman Adam B. Schiff, House Permanent Select Committee on Intelligence, Chairman Eliot L. Engel, House Committee on Foreign Affairs Committee, and Chairman Elijah E. Cummings, House Committee on Oversight and Reform (Oct. 8, 2019) (online at www.whitehouse.gov/wp-content/uploads/2019/10/PAC-Letter-10.08.2019.pdf).

[101] *Barenblatt v. United States*, 360 U.S. 109 (1959).

[102] *See, e.g.*, S. 2537 (requiring an investigation by the State Department Inspector General into the withholding of aid to Ukraine, directing the President to immediately obligate previously appropriated funds, and authorizing funds to counter Russian influence); H.R. 3047 (providing support to Ukraine to defend its independence, sovereignty, and territorial integrity).

[103] *In re Application of the Committee on the Judiciary, United States House of Representatives*, 2019 U.S. Dist. LEXIS 184857 (D.D.C. 2019), quoting *Trump v. Mazars USA, LLP*, 2019 U.S. App. LEXIS 30475 (D.D.C. 2019) ("Nothing 'in the Constitution or case law ... compels Congress to abandon its legislative role at the first scent of potential illegality and confine itself exclusively to the impeachment process.'").

[104] *See, e.g.*, the 1974 Amendments to the Freedom of Information Act, P.L. 93-502; Ethics in Government Act of 1978, P.L. 95-52; Presidential Records Act of 1978, P.L. 95-591; Federal Election Campaign Act Amendments of 1974, P.L. 93-443.

[105] Letter from Pat A. Cipollone, Counsel to the President, The White House, to House Speaker Nancy Pelosi, Chairman Adam B. Schiff, House Permanent Select Committee on Intelligence, Chairman Eliot L. Engel, House Committee on Foreign Affairs Committee, and Chairman Elijah E. Cummings, House Committee on Oversight and Reform (Oct. 8, 2019) (online at www.whitehouse.gov/wp-content/uploads/2019/10/PAC-Letter-10.08.2019.pdf); Letter from Pat A. Cipollone, Counsel to the President, The White House, to Acting Chairwoman Carolyn Maloney, House Committee on Oversight and Reform, Chairman Adam B. Schiff, House Permanent Select Committee on Intelligence Chairman Eliot L. Engel, Chairman, House Committee on Foreign Affairs (Oct. 18, 2019).

[106] *United States v. American Tel. & Tel. Co.*, 567 F.2d 121 (D.C. Cir. 1977) ("Rather, each branch should take cognizance of an implicit constitutional mandate to seek optimal accommodation through a realistic evaluation of the needs of the conflicting branches in the particular fact situation.").

[107] For example, on November 22, 2019, the Department of State produced to a private party 99 pages of emails, letters, notes, timelines, and news articles under a court order pursuant to the Freedom of Information Act. *State Department Releases Ukraine Documents to American Oversight*, American Oversight (Nov. 22, 2019) (online at www.americanoversight.org/state-department-releases-ukraine-documents-to-american-oversight).

[108] Even if the President were to make a colorable assertion of executive privilege, which he has not, the Supreme Court has held that the privilege is not absolute. In the context of a grand jury subpoena, the Supreme Court found that the President's "generalized assertion of privilege must yield to the demonstrated, specific need for evidence in a pending criminal trial." *United States v. Nixon*, 418 U.S. 683 (1974). Similarly, the D.C. Circuit has held that executive privilege is a "qualified" privilege and that "courts must balance the public interests at stake in determining whether the privilege should yield in a particular case, and must specifically consider the need of the party seeking privileged evidence." *In re Sealed Case*, 121 F.3d 729 (D.C. Cir. 1997). As described above, Congress' need for information during an impeachment inquiry is particularly "compelling." *In re Report & Recommendation of June 5, 1972 Grand Jury Concerning Transmission of Evidence to House of Representatives*, 370 F. Supp. 1219 (D.D.C. 1974) ("[I]t should not be forgotten that we deal in a matter of the most critical moment to the Nation, an impeachment investigation involving the President of the United States. It would be difficult to conceive of a more compelling need than that of this country for an unswervingly fair inquiry based on all the pertinent information.").

[109] *See, e.g.*, Letter from Pat A. Cipollone, Counsel to the President, The White House, to William Pittard, Counsel to Mick Mulvaney, Acting Chief of Staff, The White House (Nov. 8, 2019) (asserting that Acting Chief of Staff Mick Mulvaney "is absolutely immune from compelled congressional testimony with respect to matters related to his service as a senior advisor to the President" and that "[s]ubjecting a senior presidential advisor to the congressional subpoena power would be akin to requiring the President himself to appear before Congress on matters relating to the performance of his constitutionally assigned executive functions").

[110] *Committee on the Judiciary v. Miers*, 558 F. Supp. 2d 53 (D.D.C. 2008) ("The Executive cannot identify a single judicial opinion that recognizes absolute immunity for senior presidential advisors in this or any other context. That simple yet critical fact bears repeating: the asserted absolute immunity claim here is entirely unsupported by existing case law. In fact, there is Supreme Court authority that is all but conclusive on this question and that powerfully suggests that such advisors do not enjoy absolute immunity. The Court therefore rejects the Executive's claim of absolute immunity for senior presidential aides.").

[111] *Committee on the Judiciary v. McGahn*, Case No. 1:19-cv-02379, Memorandum Opinion, Doc. No. 46 (D.D.C. Nov. 25, 2019). As of this report, an appeal is pending in the U.S. Court of Appeals for the D.C. Circuit. No. 19-5331 (D.C. Cir.).

[112] Letter from Chairman Eliot L. Engel, House Committee on Foreign Affairs, Chairman Adam B. Schiff, House Permanent Select Committee on Intelligence, and Chairman Elijah E. Cummings, House Committee on Oversight and Reform, to Pat A. Cipollone, Counsel to the President, The White House (Sept. 9, 2019) (online at https://intelligence.house.gov/uploadedfiles/ele_schiff_cummings_letter_to_cipollone_on_ukraine.pdf).

[113] Letter from Chairman Eliot L. Engel, House Committee on Foreign Affairs, Chairman Adam B. Schiff, House Permanent Select Committee on Intelligence, and Chairman Elijah E. Cummings, House Committee on Oversight and Reform, to Pat A. Cipollone, Counsel to the President, The White House (Sept. 24, 2019) (online at https://intelligence.house.gov/uploadedfiles/2019-09-24.eec_engel_schiff_to_cipollone-wh_re_potus_ukraine.pdf).

[114] Letter from Chairman Elijah E. Cummings, House Committee on Oversight and Reform, Chairman Adam B. Schiff, House Permanent Select Committee on Intelligence, and Chairman Eliot L. Engel, House Committee on Foreign Affairs, to Pat A. Cipollone, Counsel to the President, The White House (Oct. 4, 2019) (online at https://oversight.house.gov/sites/democrats.oversight.house.gov/files/documents/2019-10-04.EEC%20Engel%20Schiff%20to%20Mulvaney-WH%20re%20Subpoena.pdf).

[115] Letter from Pat A. Cipollone, Counsel to the President, The White House, to Acting Chairwoman Carolyn B. Maloney, House Committee on Oversight and Reform, Chairman Adam B. Schiff, House Permanent Select Committee on Intelligence, and Chairman Eliot L. Engel, House Committee on Foreign Affairs, (Oct. 18, 2019).

[116] Email from Bureau of Legislative Affairs, Department of State, to Committee Staff (Oct. 2, 2019).

[117] Letter from Chairman Eliot L. Engel, House Committee on Foreign Affairs, Chairman Adam B. Schiff, House Permanent Select Committee on Intelligence, and Chairman Elijah E. Cummings, House Committee on Oversight and Reform, to Pat A. Cipollone, Counsel to the President, The White House (Sept. 9, 2019) (online at https://intelligence.house.gov/uploadedfiles/ele_schiff_cummings_letter_to_cipollone_on_ukraine.pdf).

[118] *Id.*

[119] Letter from Chairman Eliot L. Engel, House Committee on Foreign Affairs, Chairman Adam B. Schiff, House Permanent Select Committee on Intelligence, and Chairman Elijah E. Cummings, House Committee on Oversight and Reform, to Pat A. Cipollone, Counsel to the President, The White House (Sept. 24, 2019).

[120] Memorandum from Chairman Elijah E. Cummings to Members of the House Committee on Oversight and Reform, Notice of Intent to Issue Subpoenas (Oct. 2, 2019) (online at https://oversight.house.gov/sites/democrats.oversight.house.gov/files/documents/2019-10-02.COR%20WH%20Subpoena%20Memo%20and%20Schedule.pdf).

[121] Letter from Chairman Elijah E. Cummings, House Committee on Oversight and Reform, Chairman Adam B. Schiff, House Permanent Select Committee on Intelligence, and Chairman Eliot L. Engel, House Committee on Foreign Affairs, to Pat A. Cipollone, Counsel to the President, The White House (Oct. 4, 2019) (online at https://oversight.house.gov/sites/democrats.oversight.house.gov/files/documents/2019-10-04.EEC%20Engel%20Schiff%20to%20Mulvaney-WH%20re%20Subpoena.pdf).

[122] Letter from Pat A. Cipollone, Counsel to the President, The White House, to Speaker Nancy Pelosi, Chairman Adam B. Schiff, House Permanent Select Committee on Intelligence, Chairman Eliot L. Engel, House Committee on Foreign Affairs, and Chairman Elijah E. Cummings, House Committee on Oversight and Reform (Oct. 8, 2019) (online at www.whitehouse.gov/wp-content/uploads/2019/10/PAC-Letter-10.08.2019.pdf).

[123] Letter from Pat A. Cipollone, Counsel to the President, The White House, to Acting Chairwoman Carolyn B. Maloney, House Committee on Oversight and Reform, Chairman Adam B. Schiff, House Permanent Select Committee on Intelligence, and Chairman Eliot L. Engel, House Committee on Foreign Affairs (Oct. 18, 2019).

[124] On September 13, the Intelligence Committee issued a subpoena pursuant to its oversight authority to the Acting Director of National Intelligence to compel the production of a complaint submitted by an Intelligence Community whistleblower, as well as other records. The Intelligence Committee issued this subpoena before Speaker Pelosi announced on September 24 that the Intelligence Committee and other committees would be continuing their work under the umbrella of the impeachment inquiry being conducted by the Judiciary Committee. As a result, this subpoena should not be conflated with subpoenas issued as part of the impeachment inquiry. *See* Letter from Chairman Adam B. Schiff, House Permanent Select Committee on Intelligence, to Joseph Maguire, Acting Director of National Intelligence, Office of the Director of National Intelligence (Sept. 13, 2019).

[125] The White House, *Memorandum of Telephone Conversation* (Apr. 21, 2019) (online at http://cdn.cnn.com/cnn/2019/images/11/15/4-21-19.trump-zelensky.call.pdf); The White House, *Memorandum of Telephone Conversation* (July 25, 2019) (online at www.whitehouse.gov/wp-content/uploads/2019/09/Unclassified09.2019.pdf).

[126] Vindman-Williams Hearing Tr. at 31-32.

[127] Vindman Dep. Tr. at 53; Morrison Dep. Tr. at 19-20.

[128] Vindman Dep. Tr. at 186-187; Morrison Dep. Tr. at 166-167.

[129] *See, e.g.*, Cooper Dep. Tr. at 42-43.

[130] Sondland Hearing Tr. at 78-79.

[131] Vindman Dep. Tr. at 36-37.

[132] Holmes Dep. Tr. at 31.

[133] House Permanent Select Committee on Intelligence, Opening Statement of Ambassador Gordon Sondland, Department of State, *Impeachment*, 116th Cong. (Nov. 20, 2019).

[134] The review reportedly uncovered "early August email exchanges between acting chief of staff Mick Mulvaney and White House budget officials seeking to provide an explanation for withholding the funds after the president had already ordered a hold in mid-July on the nearly $400 million in security assistance." The review also reportedly included interviews with "some key White House officials involved in handling Ukraine aid and dealing with complaints and concerns in the aftermath of the call between Trump and Zelensky." *White House Review Turns Up Emails Showing Extensive Effort to Justify Trump's Decision to Block Ukraine Military Aid*, Washington Post (Nov. 24, 2019) (online at www.washingtonpost.com/politics/white-house-review-turns-up-emails-showing-

extensive-effort-to-justify-trumps-decision-to-block-ukraine-military-aid/2019/11/24/2121cf98-0d57-11ea-bd9d-c628fd48b3a0_story.html).

[135] Letter from Chairman Eliot L. Engel, House Committee on Foreign Affairs, Chairman Adam B. Schiff, House Permanent Select Committee on Intelligence, and Chairman Elijah E. Cummings, House Committee on Oversight and Reform, to Vice President Michael R. Pence (Oct. 4, 2019) (online at https://oversight house.gov/sites/democrats.oversight.house.gov/files/documents/2019-10-04.EEC%20Engel%20Schiff%20%20re%20Request%20to%20VP%2010-04-19%20Letter%20and%20Schedule.pdf).

[136] *Id.*

[137] Letter from Matthew E. Morgan, Counsel to the Vice President, Office of the Vice President, to Chairman Elijah E. Cummings, House Committee on Oversight and Reform, Chairman Eliot L. Engel, House Committee on Foreign Affairs, and Chairman Adam B. Schiff, House Permanent Select Committee on Intelligence (Oct. 15, 2019).

[138] Vindman-Williams Hearing Tr. at 61.

[139] Williams Dep. Tr. at 129.

[140] Vindman-Williams Hearing Tr. at 15.

[141] *Id.* at 23-24.

[142] Williams Dep. Tr. at 74-75.

[143] Letter from Chairman Adam B. Schiff, House Permanent Select Committee on Intelligence, Chairman Eliot L. Engel, House Committee on Foreign Affairs, and Chairman Elijah E. Cummings, House Committee on Oversight and Reform, to Acting Director Russell T. Vought, Office of Management and Budget (Oct. 7, 2019) (online at https://intelligence house.gov/uploadedfiles/2019-10-07.eec_engel_schiff_to_vought-_omb_re_subpoena.pdf).

[144] *Id.*

[145] Letter from Jason Yaworske, Associate Director for Legislative Affairs, Office of Management and Budget, to Chairman Adam B. Schiff, House Permanent Select Committee on Intelligence (Oct. 15, 2019).

[146] Sandy Dep. Tr. at 23-26.

[147] *Id.* at 36-41.

[148] *Id.* at 57-60, 62-63.

[149] Letter from Chairman Eliot L. Engel, House Committee on Foreign Affairs, Chairman Adam B. Schiff, House Permanent Select Committee on Intelligence, and Chairman Elijah E. Cummings, House Committee on Oversight and Reform, to Secretary Michael R. Pompeo, Department of State (Sept. 9, 2019) (online at https://intelligence.house.gov/uploadedfiles/ele_schiff_cummings_letter_to_sec_pompeo_on_ukraine.pdf).

[150] Letter from Chairman Eliot L. Engel, House Committee on Foreign Affairs, Chairman Adam B. Schiff, House Permanent Select Committee on Intelligence, and Chairman Elijah E. Cummings, House Committee on Oversight and Reform, to Secretary Michael R. Pompeo, Department of State (Sept. 23, 2019).

[151] Letter from Chairman Eliot L. Engel, House Committee on Foreign Affairs, Chairman Adam B. Schiff, House Permanent Select Committee on Intelligence, and Chairman Elijah E. Cummings, House Committee on Oversight and Reform, to Secretary Michael R. Pompeo, Department of State (Sept. 27, 2019) (online at https://oversight house.gov/sites/democrats.oversight.house.gov/files/documents/2019-09-27.EEC%20Engel%20Schiff%20%20to%20Pompeo-%20State%20re%20Document%20Subpoena.pdf).

[152] Letter from Chairman Adam B. Schiff, House Permanent Select Committee on Intelligence, Chairman Elijah E. Cummings, House Committee on Oversight and Reform, and Chairman Eliot L. Engel, House Committee on Foreign Affairs, to Ambassador Gordon Sondland, Department of State (Oct. 8, 2019) (online at https://oversight house.gov/sites/democrats.oversight.house.gov/files/documents/2019-10-08.EEC%20Engel%20Schiff%20to%20Sondland%20re%20Subpoena.pdf); Letter from Chairman Eliot L. Engel,

House Committee on Foreign Affairs, Chairman Adam B. Schiff, House Permanent Select Committee on Intelligence, and Chairman Elijah E. Cummings, House Committee on Oversight and Reform, to Ambassador William Taylor, Department of State (Oct. 4, 2019); Letter from Chairman Eliot L. Engel, House Committee on Foreign Affairs, Chairman Adam B. Schiff, House Permanent Select Committee on Intelligence, and Chairman Elijah E. Cummings, House Committee on Oversight and Reform, to Counselor T. Ulrich Brechbuhl, Department of State (Sept. 27, 2019) (online at https://intelligence.house.gov/uploadedfiles/20190927_-_eec_engel_schiff_to_brechbuhl_re_individual_deposition_request.pdf); Letter from Chairman Eliot L. Engel, House Committee on Foreign Affairs, Chairman Adam B. Schiff, House Permanent Select Committee on Intelligence, and Chairman Elijah E. Cummings, House Committee on Oversight and Reform, to Deputy Assistant Secretary George P. Kent, Department of State (Sept. 27, 2019); Letter from Chairman Eliot L. Engel, House Committee on Foreign Affairs, Chairman Adam B. Schiff, House Permanent Select Committee on Intelligence, and Chairman Elijah E. Cummings, House Committee on Oversight and Reform, to Ambassador Kurt Volker, Department of State (Sept. 27, 2019); Letter from Chairman Eliot L. Engel, House Committee on Foreign Affairs, Chairman Adam B. Schiff, House Permanent Select Committee on Intelligence, and Chairman Elijah E. Cummings, House Committee on Oversight and Reform, to Ambassador Marie Yovanovitch, Department of State (Sept. 27, 2019).

[153] Letter from Secretary Michael R. Pompeo, Department of State, to Chairman Eliot L. Engel, House Committee on Foreign Affairs (Oct. 1, 2019) (Secretary Pompeo sent identical letters to Chairman Elijah. E. Cummings, House Committee on Oversight and Reform, and Chairman Adam B. Schiff, House Permanent Select Committee on Intelligence, the same day).

[154] *Id.*

[155] Kent Dep. Tr. at 27.

[156] *Id.* at 33-34.

[157] *Id.* at 34-35.

[158] Letter from Secretary Michael R. Pompeo, Department of State, to Chairman Eliot L. Engel, House Committee on Foreign Affairs (Oct. 1, 2019) (Secretary Pompeo sent identical letters to Chairman Elijah. E. Cummings, House Committee on Oversight and Reform, and Chairman Adam B. Schiff, House Permanent Select Committee on Intelligence, the same day).

[159] Letter from Chairman Eliot L. Engel, House Committee on Foreign Affairs, Chairman Adam B. Schiff, House Permanent Select Committee on Intelligence, and Chairman Elijah E. Cummings, House Committee on Oversight and Reform, to Deputy Secretary John J. Sullivan, Department of State (Oct. 1, 2019) (online at https://foreignaffairs.house.gov/_cache/files/4/6/4683bc86-be2a-49fc-9e76-7cdbf669592f/98BEBD8006DE62BA36BEBD175775F744.2019-10-1-ele-abs-eec-to-depsec-sullivan.pdf).

[160] *Pompeo: 'I Was on the Phone Call' with Trump and Ukrainian President*, CNN (Oct. 2, 2019) (online at www.cnn.com/2019/10/02/politics/mike-pompeo-ukraine-call/index html).

[161] Email from Committee Staff to Bureau of Legislative Affairs, Department of State (Oct. 7, 2019).

[162] Letter from Brian Bulatao, Under Secretary of State for Management, Department of State, to Andrew Wright, Counsel to Deputy Assistant Secretary George P. Kent, Department of State (Oct. 14, 2019).

[163] Kent Dep. Tr. at 30-31, 46.

[164] *Id.* at 32.

[165] *Id.* at 35.

[166] House Permanent Select Committee on Intelligence, Opening Statement of Ambassador Gordon Sondland, Department of State, *Impeachment*, 116th Cong. (Nov. 20, 2019).

[167] *Id.*

[168] *Id.* In addition, Dr. Fiona Hill, the former Senior Director for Europe and Russia at the National Security Council, produced calendar entries relating to relevant meetings. Fiona Hill Document Production, Bates Hill0001-Hill0049 (Oct. 13, 2019).

[169] Kurt Volker Document Production, Bates KV00000001-KV00000065 (Oct. 2, 2019).

[170] 18 U.S.C. § 1505.

[171] House Permanent Select Committee on Intelligence, Opening Statement of Ambassador Gordon Sondland, Department of State, *Impeachment*, 116th Cong., at 3-4 (Nov. 20, 2019).

[172] Sondland Hearing Tr. at 160.

[173] Declaration of Ambassador Gordon Sondland, Department of State, at 3 (Nov. 4, 2019).

[174] *State Department Releases Ukraine Documents to American Oversight*, American Oversight (Nov. 22, 2019) (online at www.americanoversight.org/state-department-releases-ukraine-documents-to-american-oversight); *American Oversight v. Dep't of State*, Case No. 19-cv-2934, Doc. No. 15 (D.D.C. November 25, 2019).

[175] Email from Office Manager to the Secretary of State to S_All (Mar. 26, 2019) (online at www.americanoversight.org/wp-content/uploads/2019/11/AO_State_Ukraine_Docs_11-22.pdf).

[176] Email from Madeleine Westerhout to State Department Official, (Mar. 27, 2019) (online at www.americanoversight.org/wp-content/uploads/2019/11/AO_State_Ukraine_Docs_11-22.pdf).

[177] Letter from Chairman Eliot L. Engel, House Committee on Foreign Affairs, Chairman Adam B. Schiff, House Permanent Select Committee on Intelligence, and Chairman Elijah E. Cummings, House Committee on Oversight and Reform, to Secretary Michael R. Pompeo, Department of State (Sept. 27, 2019) (online at https://oversight.house.gov/sites/democrats.oversight.house.gov/files/documents/2019-09-27.EEC%20Engel%20Schiff%20%20to%20Pompeo-%20State%20re%20Document%20Subpoena.pdf).

[178] Taylor Dep. Tr. at 33-34.

[179] House Permanent Select Committee on Intelligence, Opening Statement of Ambassador Gordon Sondland, Department of State, *Impeachment*, 116th Cong., at 20-23 (Nov. 20, 2019).

[180] Taylor Dep. Tr. at 45-46.

[181] Hale Dep. Tr. at 147-148.

[182] Letter from Chairman Adam B. Schiff, House Permanent Select Committee on Intelligence, Chairman Eliot L. Engel, House Committee on Foreign Affairs, and Chairman Elijah E. Cummings, House Committee on Oversight and Reform, to Secretary Mark Esper, Department of Defense (Oct. 7, 2019) (online at https://intelligence.house.gov/uploadedfiles/2019-10-07.eec_engel_schiff_to_esper-dod_re_subpoena.pdf).

[183] *Transcript: Secretary of Defense Mark Esper on "Face the Nation," October 13, 2019*, CBS News (Oct. 13, 2019) (online at www.cbsnews.com/news/transcript-secretary-of-defense-mark-esper-on-face-the-nation-october-13-2019/).

[184] Letter from Robert R. Hood, Assistant Secretary of Defense for Legislative Affairs, Department of Defense, to Chairman Adam B. Schiff, House Permanent Select Committee on Intelligence, Chairman Eliot L. Engel, House Committee on Foreign Affairs, and Chairman Elijah E. Cummings, House Committee on Oversight and Reform (Oct. 15, 2019).

[185] *Transcript: Secretary of Defense Mark Esper on "Face the Nation," October 13, 2019*, CBS News (Oct. 13, 2019) (online at www.cbsnews.com/news/transcript-secretary-of-defense-mark-esper-on-face-the-nation-october-13-2019/).

[186] *See, e.g.*, Cooper Dep. Tr. at 42-43.

[187] *Id.* at 33.

[188] *Id.* at 33-38.

[189] Cooper Hearing Tr. at 13-14.

[190] *Id.* at 14.

[191] *Id.*

[192] Letter from Chairman Eliot L. Engel, House Committee on Foreign Affairs, Chairman Adam B. Schiff, House Permanent Select Committee on Intelligence, and Chairman Elijah E. Cummings, House Committee on Oversight and Reform, to Secretary Rick Perry, Department of Energy (Oct. 10, 2019) (online at https://oversight house.gov/sites/democrats.oversight.house.gov/files/documents/2019-10-10.EEC%20Engel%20Schiff%20to%20Perry-DOE%20Joint%20Cover%20Letter%20re%20Subpoena.pdf).

[193] Letter from Melissa F. Burnison, Assistant Secretary for Congressional and Intergovernmental Affairs, Department of Energy, to Chairman Eliot L. Engel, House Committee on Foreign Affairs, Chairman Adam B. Schiff, House Permanent Select Committee on Intelligence, and Chairman Elijah E. Cummings, House Committee on Oversight and Reform (Oct. 18, 2019).

[194] Hill-Holmes Hearing Tr. at 160.

[195] House Permanent Select Committee on Intelligence, Opening Statement of Ambassador Gordon Sondland, Department of State, *Impeachment*, 116th Cong. (Nov. 20, 2019).

[196] House Permanent Select Committee on Intelligence, Opening Statement of Ambassador Gordon Sondland, Department of State, *Impeachment*, 116th Cong. (Nov. 20, 2019).

[197] Letter from Chairman Chairman Adam B. Schiff, House Permanent Select Committee on Intelligence, Eliot L. Engel, House Committee on Foreign Affairs, and Chairman Elijah E. Cummings, House Committee on Oversight and Reform, to Rudy Giuliani (Sept. 30, 2019) (online at https://oversight house.gov/sites/democrats.oversight.house.gov/files/documents/20190930%20-%20Giuliani%20HPSCI%20Subpoena%20Letter.pdf).

[198] Letter from Jon A. Sale, Counsel to Rudy Giuliani, to Committee Staff (Oct. 15, 2019).

[199] *Id.*

[200] Letter from Chairman Adam B. Schiff, House Permanent Select Committee on Intelligence, Chairman Eliot L. Engel, House Committee on Foreign Affairs, and Chairman Elijah E. Cummings, House Committee on Oversight and Reform, to Igor Fruman (Sept. 30, 2019) (online at https://oversight house.gov/sites/democrats.oversight.house.gov/files/documents/20190930%20-%20Fruman%20Letter%20and%20Doc%20Request%20Schedule.pdf); Letter from Chairman Adam B. Schiff, House Permanent Select Committee on Intelligence, Chairman Eliot L. Engel, House Committee on Foreign Affairs, and Chairman Elijah E. Cummings, House Committee on Oversight and Reform, to Lev Parnas (Sept. 30, 2019) (online at https://oversight.house.gov/sites/democrats.oversight house.gov/files/documents/20190930%20-%20Parnas%20Letter%20and%20Doc%20Request%20Schedule.pdf).

[201] Letter from Chairman Adam B. Schiff, House Permanent Select Committee on Intelligence, Chairman Eliot L. Engel, House Committee on Foreign Affairs, and Chairman Elijah E. Cummings, House Committee on Oversight and Reform, to John M. Dowd, Counsel to Igor Fruman and Lev Parnas (Oct. 10, 2019) (online at https://intelligence.house.gov/uploadedfiles/2019-10-09.eec_engel_schiff_to_parnas_fruman_re_subpoena.pdf).

[202] Letter from John M. Dowd, Counsel to Igor Fruman and Lev Parnas, to Committee Staff (Oct. 3, 2019).

[203] Letter from John M. Dowd, Counsel to Igor Fruman and Lev Parnas, to Committee Staff (Oct. 8, 2019).

[204] Email from John M. Dowd, Counsel to Igor Fruman and Lev Parnas, to Committee Staff (Oct. 9, 2019).

[205] Email from Committee Staff to John M. Dowd, Counsel to Igor Fruman and Lev Parnas (Oct. 10, 2019).

[206] Email from John M. Dowd, Counsel to Igor Fruman and Lev Parnas, to Committee Staff (Oct. 10, 2019).

[207] *Exclusive: Giuliani Associate Parnas Will Comply with Trump Impeachment Inquiry—Lawyer*, Reuters (Nov. 4, 2019) (online at www.reuters.com/article/us-usa-trump-impeachment-parnas-exclusiv/exclusive-giuliani-associate-now-willing-to-comply-with-trump-impeachment-inquiry-lawyer-idUSKBN1XE297). On November 23, 2019, Mr. Parnas' attorney informed the press that "Mr. Parnas learned from former Ukrainian Prosecutor General Victor Shokin that [Ranking Member Devin] Nunes had met with Shokin in Vienna last December." According to the report, "Parnas says he worked to put Nunes in touch with Ukrainians who could help Nunes dig up dirt on Biden and Democrats in Ukraine, according to Bondy." *Exclusive: Giuliani Associate Willing to Tell Congress Nunes Met with Ex-Ukrainian Official to Get Dirt on Biden*, CNN (Nov. 23, 2019) (online at

www.cnn.com/2019/11/22/politics/nunes-vienna-trip-ukrainian-prosecutor-biden/index.html). On November 24, 2019, Mr. Parnas' attorney told press that his client had arranged skype and phone calls earlier this year between Ranking Member Nunes' staff and Ukraine's chief anti-corruption prosecutor, Nazar Kholodnytsky, as well as a deputy in Ukraine's Prosecutor General's office, Kostantyn Kulyk. According to Mr. Parnas' attorney, Ranking Member Nunes had actually planned a trip to Ukraine instead of the calls, but cancelled the trip when his staff realized it would require alerting Chairman Schiff about the travel. *Giuliani Associate Parnas Wants to Testify that Nunes Aides Hid Ukraine Meetings on Biden Dirt from Schiff,* CNBC (Nov. 24, 2019) (online at www.cnbc.com/2019/11/24/giuliani-ally-would-testify-that-nunes-staffers-hid-ukraine-meetings-from-schiff html).

[208] Letter from Pat A. Cipollone, Counsel to the President, The White House, to House Speaker Nancy Pelosi, Chairman Adam B. Schiff, House Permanent Select Committee on Intelligence, Chairman Eliot L. Engel, House Committee on Foreign Affairs Committee, and Chairman Elijah E. Cummings, House Committee on Oversight and Reform (Oct. 8, 2019) (online at www.whitehouse.gov/wp-content/uploads/2019/10/PAC-Letter-10.08.2019.pdf).

[209] *See* 2 U.S.C. §§ 192, 194. Witnesses who received subpoenas that were subsequently withdrawn would not face a similar risk of being held in contempt of Congress.

[210] *See, e.g.*, Email from Committee Staff to Mick Mulvaney, Acting Chief of Staff, The White House (Nov. 7, 2019) ("Your failure or refusal to comply with the subpoena, including at the direction or behest of the President, shall constitute further evidence of obstruction of the House's impeachment inquiry and may be used as an adverse inference against you and the President. Moreover, your failure to appear shall constitute evidence that may be used against you in a contempt proceeding.").

[211] Letter from Chairman Eliot L. Engel, House Committee on Foreign Affairs, Chairman Adam B. Schiff, House Permanent Select Committee on Intelligence, and Acting Chairwoman Carolyn B. Maloney, House Committee on Oversight and Reform, Mick Mulvaney, Acting Chief of Staff, The White House (Nov. 5, 2019) (online at https://oversight.house.gov/sites/democrats.oversight house.gov/files/2019-11-05.CBM%20Engel%20Schiff%20to%20Mulvaney-WH%20re%20Depo%20Notice.pdf).

[212] House Permanent Select Committee on Intelligence, Subpoena to Mick Mulvaney, Acting Chief of Staff, The White House (Nov. 7, 2019).

[213] Email from William Pittard, Counsel to Mick Mulvaney, Acting Chief of Staff, The White House, to Committee Staff (Nov. 8, 2019).

[214] Letter from Pat A. Cipollone, Counsel to the President, The White House, to William Pittard, Counsel to Mick Mulvaney, Acting Chief of Staff, The White House (Nov. 8, 2019) (online at www.whitehouse.gov/wp-content/uploads/2019/10/PAC-Letter-10.08.2019.pdf).

[215] Letter from Steven A. Engel, Assistant Attorney General, Office of Legal Counsel, Department of Justice, to Pat A. Cipollone, Counsel to the President, The White House (Nov. 7, 2019).

[216] Mulvaney Dep. Tr. at 5.

[217] *Id.* at 7-9.

[218] On November 8, 2019, Mr. Mulvaney filed a motion in federal court seeking to join a lawsuit, discussed below, filed by Dr. Charles Kupperman seeking a declaratory judgment as to whether he should comply with the Committees' subpoena. On November 11, 2019, Mr. Mulvaney withdrew his request to join the case. *White House Chief of Staff Mulvaney Drops Bid to Join Kupperman Impeachment Lawsuit*, Washington Post (Nov. 11, 2019) (online at www.washingtonpost.com/local/legal-issues/bolton-and-kupperman-reject-white-house-chief-of-staff-mulvaneys-bid-to-join-impeachment-lawsuit/2019/11/11/cdf40226-04ac-11ea-8292-c46ee8cb3dce_story.html).

[219] Letter from Chairman Eliot L. Engel, House Committee on Foreign Affairs, Chairman Adam B. Schiff, House Permanent Select Committee on Intelligence, and Acting Chairwoman Carolyn B. Maloney, House Committee on Oversight and Reform, to Robert B. Blair, Assistant to the President and Senior Advisor to the Chief of Staff, The White House (Oct. 24, 2019).

[220] Letter from Whitney C. Ellerman, Counsel to Robert B. Blair, Assistant to the President and Senior Advisor to the Chief of Staff, The White House, to Chairman Eliot L. Engel, House Committee on Foreign Affairs,

Chairman Adam B. Schiff, House Permanent Select Committee on Intelligence, and Acting Chairwoman Carolyn B. Maloney, House Committee on Oversight and Reform (Nov. 2, 2019).

[221] Letter from Chairman Adam B. Schiff, House Permanent Select Committee on Intelligence, Acting Chairwoman Carolyn B. Maloney, House Committee on Oversight and Reform, and Chairman Eliot L. Engel, House Committee on Foreign Affairs, to Whitney C. Ellerman, Counsel to Robert B. Blair, Assistant to the President and Senior Advisor to the Chief of Staff, The White House (Nov. 3, 2019); House Permanent Select Committee on Intelligence, Subpoena to Robert B. Blair, Assistant to the President and Senior Advisor to the Chief of Staff, The White House (Nov. 3, 2019).

[222] Blair Dep. Tr. at 6-7.

[223] Letter from Chairman Eliot L. Engel, House Committee on Foreign Affairs, Chairman Adam B. Schiff, House Permanent Select Committee on Intelligence, and Acting Chairwoman Carolyn B. Maloney, House Committee on Oversight and Reform, to Charles J. Cooper and Michael W. Kirk, Counsel to Ambassador John Bolton, Former National Security Advisor, The White House (Oct. 30, 2019).

[224] Email from Charles J. Cooper, Counsel to Ambassador John Bolton, Former National Security Advisor, The White House, to Committee Staff (Oct. 30, 2019).

[225] Letter from Charles J. Cooper, Counsel to Ambassador John Bolton, Former National Security Advisor, The White House, to Douglas N. Letter, General Counsel, House of Representatives (Nov. 8, 2019).

[226] In early November 2019, Ambassador Bolton's personal attorney also informed Committee staff that if the Committees were to issue a subpoena to compel his testimony, he would seek to join the lawsuit filed by Dr. Kupperman. On November 24, 2019, Chairman Schiff stated, "We've certainly been in touch with his lawyer and what we've been informed by his lawyer—because we invited him and he did not choose to come in and testify, notwithstanding the fact that his deputy Fiona Hill and his other deputy Colonel Vindman and Tim Morrison and others on the National Security Council have shown the courage to come in—is if we subpoena him, they will sue us in court." *Schiff Pushes Bolton to Testify But Will Not Go to Court to Force Him*, CNN (Nov. 24, 2019) (online at www.cnn.com/2019/11/24/politics/adam-schiff-house-democrats-impeachment-state-of-the-union-cnntv/index.html).

[227] Letter from Chairman Eliot L. Engel, House Committee on Foreign Affairs, Chairman Adam B. Schiff, House Permanent Select Committee on Intelligence, and Acting Chairwoman Carolyn B. Maloney, House Committee on Oversight and Reform, to John A. Eisenberg, Deputy Counsel to the President for National Security Affairs and Legal Advisor to the National Security Council, National Security Council, The White House (Oct. 30, 2019).

[228] Eisenberg Dep. Tr. at 6 ("Mr. Eisenberg never acknowledged receipt or otherwise responded to the committees' deposition request, nor did any official at the White House.").

[229] Letter from Chairman Eliot L. Engel, House Committee on Foreign Affairs, Chairman Adam B. Schiff, House Permanent Select Committee on Intelligence, and Acting Chairwoman Carolyn B. Maloney, House Committee on Oversight and Reform, to John A. Eisenberg, Deputy Counsel to the President for National Security Affairs and Legal Advisor to the National Security Council, National Security Council, The White House (Nov. 1, 2019); House Permanent Select Committee on Intelligence, Subpoena to John A. Eisenberg, Deputy Counsel to the President for National Security Affairs and Legal Advisor to the National Security Council, The White House (Nov. 1, 2019).

[230] Letter from William A. Burck, Counsel to John A. Eisenberg, Deputy Counsel to the President for National Security Affairs and Legal Advisor to the National Security Council, National Security Council, The White House, to Chairman Eliot L. Engel, House Committee on Foreign Affairs, Chairman Adam B. Schiff, House Permanent Select Committee on Intelligence, and Acting Chairwoman Carolyn B. Maloney, House Committee on Oversight and Reform (Nov. 4, 2019).

[231] Letter from Pat A. Cipollone, Counsel to the President, The White House, to William A. Burck, Counsel to John A. Eisenberg, Deputy Counsel to the President for National Security Affairs and Legal Advisor to the National Security Council, National Security Council, The White House (Nov. 3, 2019).

[232] Letter from Steven A. Engel, Assistant Attorney General, Office of Legal Counsel, Department of Justice, to Pat A. Cipollone, Counsel to the President, the White House (Nov. 3, 2019).

[233] Eisenberg Dep. Tr. at 6-8.

[234] Letter from Chairman Eliot L. Engel, House Committee on Foreign Affairs, Chairman Adam B. Schiff, House Permanent Select Committee on Intelligence, and Acting Chairwoman Carolyn B. Maloney, House Committee on Oversight and Reform, to Michael Ellis, Senior Associate Counsel to the President and Deputy Legal Advisor to the National Security Council, National Security Council, The White House (Oct. 30, 2019).

[235] Email from Paul Butler, Counsel to Michael Ellis, Senior Associate Counsel to the President and Deputy Legal Advisor to the National Security Council, National Security Council, The White House, to Committee Staff (Nov. 2, 2019).

[236] Email from Paul Butler, Counsel to Michael Ellis, Senior Associate Counsel to the President and Deputy Legal Advisor to the National Security Council, National Security Council, The White House, to Committee Staff (Nov. 3, 2019).

[237] Letter from Chairman Adam B. Schiff, House Permanent Select Committee on Intelligence, Acting Chairwoman Carolyn B. Maloney, House Committee on Oversight and Reform, Chairman Eliot L. Engel, House Committee on Foreign Affairs, to Paul W. Butler, Counsel to Michael Ellis, Senior Associate Counsel to the President and Deputy Legal Advisor to the National Security Council, National Security Council, The White House (Nov. 3, 2019); House Permanent Select Committee on Intelligence, Subpoena to Michael Ellis, Senior Associate Counsel to the President and Deputy Legal Advisor to the National Security Council, National Security Council, The White House (Nov. 3, 2019).

[238] Ellis Dep. Tr. at 7.

[239] Letter from Chairman Eliot L. Engel, House Committee on Foreign Affairs, Chairman Adam B. Schiff, House Permanent Select Committee on Intelligence, and Acting Chairwoman Carolyn B. Maloney, House Committee on Oversight and Reform, to Preston Wells Griffith, Senior Director for International Energy and Environment, National Security Council (Oct. 24, 2019).

[240] Letter from Karen D. Williams, Counsel to Preston Wells Griffith, Senior Director for International Energy and Environment, National Security Council, to Chairman Eliot L. Engel, House Committee on Foreign Affairs, Chairman Adam B. Schiff, House Permanent Select Committee on Intelligence, and Acting Chairwoman Carolyn B. Maloney, House Committee on Oversight and Reform (Nov. 4, 2019).

[241] Letter from Chairman Adam B. Schiff, House Permanent Select Committee on Intelligence, Acting Chairwoman Carolyn B. Maloney, House Committee on Oversight and Reform, and Chairman Eliot L. Engel, House Committee on Foreign Affairs, to Karen D. Williams, Counsel to Preston Wells Griffith, Senior Director for International Energy and Environment, National Security Council (Nov. 4, 2019); House Permanent Select Committee on Intelligence, Subpoena to Preston Wells Griffith, Senior Director for International Energy and Environment, National Security Council (Nov. 4, 2019).

[242] Griffith Dep. Tr. at 5-6.

[243] Letter from Chairman Eliot L. Engel, House Committee on Foreign Affairs, Chairman Adam B. Schiff, House Permanent Select Committee on Intelligence, and Chairman Elijah E. Cummings, House Committee on Oversight and Reform, to Dr. Charles M. Kupperman, Former Deputy Assistant to the President for National Security Affairs, National Security Council (Oct. 16, 2019).

[244] Email from Committee Staff to Charles J. Cooper and Michael W. Kirk, Counsel to Dr. Charles M. Kupperman, Former Deputy Assistant to the President for National Security Affairs, National Security Council (Oct. 25, 2019); House Permanent Select Committee on Intelligence, Subpoena to Dr. Charles M. Kupperman, Former Deputy Assistant to the President for National Security Affairs, National Security Council (Oct. 25, 2019).

[245] Compl., *Kupperman v. U.S. House of Representatives et al.*, No. 19 Civ. 3224 (D.D.C. filed Oct. 25, 2019).

[246] Email from Michael W. Kirk, Counsel to Dr. Charles M. Kupperman, Former Deputy Assistant to the President for National Security Affairs, National Security Council, to Committee Staff (Oct. 25, 2019).

[247] Letter from Pat A. Cipollone, Counsel to the President, The White House, to Charles J. Cooper, Counsel to Dr. Charles M. Kupperman, Former Deputy Assistant to the President for National Security Affairs, National Security Council (Oct. 25, 2019).

[248] Letter from Steven A. Engel, Assistant Attorney General, Office of Legal Counsel, Department of Justice, to Pat A. Cipollone, Counsel to the President, The White House (Oct. 25, 2019).

[249] Letter from Chairman Adam B. Schiff, House Permanent Select Committee on Intelligence, Chairman Eliot L. Engel, House Committee on Foreign Affairs, and Acting Chairwoman Carolyn B. Maloney, House Committee on Oversight and Reform, to Charles J. Cooper and Michael W. Kirk, Counsel to Dr. Charles M. Kupperman, Former Deputy Assistant to the President for National Security Affairs, National Security Council (Oct. 26, 2019).

[250] Letter from Charles J. Cooper, Counsel to Dr. Charles M. Kupperman, Former Deputy Assistant to the President for National Security Affairs, National Security Council, to Committee Staff (Oct. 26, 2019).

[251] Letter from Charles J. Cooper, Counsel to Dr. Charles M. Kupperman, Former Deputy Assistant to the President for National Security Affairs, National Security Council, to Committee Staff (Oct. 27, 2019).

[252] Letter from Chairman Eliot L. Engel, House Committee on Foreign Affairs, Chairman Adam B. Schiff, House Permanent Select Committee on Intelligence, and Acting Chairwoman Carolyn B. Maloney, House Committee on Oversight and Reform to Charles J. Cooper and Michael W. Kirk, Counsel to Dr. Charles M. Kupperman, Former Deputy Assistant to the President for National Security Affairs, National Security Council, (Nov. 5, 2019).

[253] Letter from Charles J. Cooper, Counsel to Dr. Charles M. Kupperman, Former Deputy Assistant to the President for National Security Affairs, National Security Council, to Douglas N. Letter, General Counsel, House of Representatives (Nov. 8, 2019).

[254] *Committee on the Judiciary v. McGahn*, Memorandum Opinion (D.D.C. Nov. 25, 2019) ("To make the point as plain as possible, it is clear to this Court for the reasons explained above that, with respect to senior-level presidential aides, absolute immunity from compelled congressional process simply does not exist. Indeed, absolute testimonial immunity for senior-level White House aides appears to be a fiction that has been fastidiously maintained over time through the force of sheer repetition in OLC opinions, and through accommodations that have permitted its proponents to avoid having the proposition tested in the crucible of litigation. And because the contention that a President's top advisors cannot be subjected to compulsory congressional process simply has no basis in the law, it does not matter whether such immunity would theoretically be available to only a handful of presidential aides due to the sensitivity of their positions, or to the entire Executive branch. Nor does it make any difference whether the aides in question are privy to national security matters, or work solely on domestic issues."). As of this report, an appeal is pending in the D.C. Circuit. No. 19-5331 (D.C. Cir.).

[255] *See Kupperman v. U.S. House of Representatives, et al.*, No. 19 Civ. 3224 (D.D.C.). As of this report, the House Defendants' Motion to Dismiss (Nov. 14, 2019), ECF No. 41, remains pending. Although the Committee will not reissue the subpoena to Dr. Kupperman and the court case is moot, he could choose to appear on a voluntary basis to assist Congress in the discharge of its Constitutional responsibilities.

[256] Letter from Chairman Eliot L. Engel, House Committee on Foreign Affairs, Chairman Adam B. Schiff, House Permanent Select Committee on Intelligence, and Chairman Elijah E. Cummings, House Committee on Oversight and Reform, to Acting Director Russell T. Vought, Office of Management and Budget (Oct. 11, 2019).

[257] Email from Jessica L. Donlon, Deputy General Counsel for Oversight, Office of Management and Budget, to Committee Staff (Oct. 21, 2019).

[258] Russell T. Vought, Twitter (Oct. 21, 2019) (online at https://twitter.com/RussVought45/status/1186276793172578306?s=20).

[259] Letter from Chairman Eliot L. Engel, House Committee on Foreign Affairs, Chairman Adam B. Schiff, House Permanent Select Committee on Intelligence, and Acting Chairwoman Carolyn B. Maloney, House Committee on Oversight and Reform, to Acting Director Russell T. Vought, Office of Management and Budget (Oct. 25, 2019).

[260] Letter from Jason A. Yaworske, Associate Director for Legislative Affairs, Office of Management and Budget, to Chairman Adam B. Schiff, House Permanent Select Committee on Intelligence (Nov. 4, 2019).

[261] Vought Dep. Tr. at 10-11.

[262] Letter from Chairman Eliot L. Engel, House Committee on Foreign Affairs, Chairman Adam B. Schiff, House Permanent Select Committee on Intelligence, and Chairman Elijah E. Cummings, House Committee on Oversight and Reform, to Associate Director Michael Duffey, Office of Management and Budget (Oct. 11, 2019).

[263] Email from Jessica L. Donlon, Deputy General Counsel for Oversight, Office of Management and Budget, to Committee Staff (Oct. 21, 2019).

[264] Letter from Chairman Eliot L. Engel, House Committee on Foreign Affairs, Chairman Adam B. Schiff, House Permanent Select Committee on Intelligence, and Acting Chairwoman Carolyn B. Maloney, House Committee on Oversight and Reform, to Michael Duffey, Associate Director of National Security Programs, Office of Management and Budget (Oct. 25, 2019) (online at https://intelligence.house.gov/uploadedfiles/20191025_-_letter_duffey_re_subpoena.pdf); House Permanent Select Committee on Intelligence, Subpoena to Michael Duffey, Associate Director of National Security Programs, Office of Management and Budget (Oct. 25, 2019).

[265] Letter from Jason A. Yaworske, Associate Director for Legislative Affairs, Office of Management and Budget, to Chairman Adam B. Schiff, House Permanent Select Committee on Intelligence (Nov. 4, 2019).

[266] Duffey Dep. Tr. at 7.

[267] Letter from Chairman Eliot L. Engel, House Committee on Foreign Affairs, Chairman Adam B. Schiff, House Permanent Select Committee on Intelligence, and Acting Chairwoman Carolyn B. Maloney, House Committee on Oversight and Reform, to Brian McCormack, Associate Director for Natural Resources, Energy, and Science, Office of Management and Budget (Oct. 24, 2019).

[268] Letter from Chairman Eliot L. Engel, House Committee on Foreign Affairs, Chairman Adam B. Schiff, House Permanent Select Committee on Intelligence, and Acting Chairwoman Carolyn B. Maloney, House Committee on Oversight and Reform, to Brian McCormack, Associate Director for Natural Resources, Energy, and Science, Office of Management and Budget (Nov. 1, 2019); House Permanent Select Committee on Intelligence, Subpoena to Brian McCormack, Associate Director for Natural Resources, Energy, and Science, Office of Management and Budget (Nov. 1, 2019).

[269] Letter from Jason A. Yaworske, Associate Director for Legislative Affairs, Office of Management and Budget, to Chairman Adam B. Schiff, House Permanent Select Committee on Intelligence (Nov. 4, 2019).

[270] McCormack Dep. Tr. at 6.

[271] Letter from Chairman Eliot L. Engel, House Committee on Foreign Affairs, Chairman Adam B. Schiff, House Permanent Select Committee on Intelligence, and Chairman Elijah E. Cummings, House Committee on Oversight and Reform, to Secretary Michael R. Pompeo, Department of State (Sept. 13, 2019).

[272] Letter from Chairman Eliot L. Engel, House Committee on Foreign Affairs, Chairman Adam B. Schiff, House Permanent Select Committee on Intelligence, and Chairman Elijah E. Cummings, House Committee on Oversight and Reform, to Secretary Michael R. Pompeo, Department of State (Sept. 27, 2019) (internal citations omitted) (online at https://oversight.house.gov/sites/democrats.oversight.house.gov/files/documents/2019-09-27.EEC%20Engel%20Schiff%20%20to%20Pompeo-%20State%20re%20Depositions.pdf).

[273] Letter from Chairman Eliot L. Engel, House Committee on Foreign Affairs, Chairman Adam B. Schiff, House Permanent Select Committee on Intelligence, and Chairman Elijah E. Cummings, House Committee on Oversight and Reform, to T. Ulrich Brechbuhl, Counselor, Department of State (Sept. 27, 2019).

[274] Letter from Secretary Michael R. Pompeo, Department of State, to Chairman Eliot L. Engel, House Committee on Foreign Affairs (Oct. 1, 2019) (Secretary Pompeo sent identical letters to Chairman Elijah. E. Cummings, House Committee on Oversight and Reform, and Chairman Adam B. Schiff, House Permanent Select Committee on Intelligence, the same day).

[275] Letter from Chairman Eliot L. Engel, House Committee on Foreign Affairs, Chairman Adam B. Schiff, House Permanent Select Committee on Intelligence, and Chairman Elijah E. Cummings, House Committee on Oversight and Reform, to Deputy Secretary of State John J. Sullivan, Department of State (Oct. 1, 2019) (online at https://oversight.house.gov/sites/democrats.oversight.house.gov/files/documents/2019-10-01%20ELE%20ABS%20EEC%20TO%20DEPSEC%20SULLIVAN.pdf).

[276] Email from Ronald J. Tenpas, Counsel to T. Ulrich Brechbuhl, Counselor, Department of State, to Committee Staff (Oct. 2, 2019).

277 Email from Committee Staff, to Ronald J. Tenpas, Counsel to T. Ulrich Brechbuhl, Counselor, Department of State (Oct. 8, 2019).

278 Email from Committee Staff, to Ronald J. Tenpas, Counsel to T. Ulrich Brechbuhl, Counselor, Department of State (Oct. 9, 2019).

279 Email from Ronald J. Tenpas, Counsel to T. Ulrich Brechbuhl, Counselor, Department of State, to Committee Staff (Oct. 9, 2019).

280 Letter from Chairman Eliot L. Engel, House Committee on Foreign Affairs, Chairman Adam B. Schiff, House Permanent Select Committee on Intelligence, and Acting Chairwoman Carolyn B. Maloney, House Committee on Oversight and Reform, to T. Ulrich Brechbuhl, Counselor, Department of State (Oct. 25, 2019); House Permanent Select Committee on Intelligence, Subpoena to T. Ulrich Brechbuhl, Counselor, Department of State (Oct. 25, 2019).

281 Letter from Ronald J. Tenpas, Counsel to T. Ulrich Brechbuhl, Counselor, Department of State to Chairman Adam B. Schiff, House Permanent Select Committee on Intelligence, Chairman Eliot L. Engel, House Committee on Foreign Affairs, and Acting Chairwoman Carolyn B. Maloney, House Committee on Oversight and Reform (Nov. 5, 2019).

282 Brechbuhl Dep. Tr. at 4-5.

283 Email from Committee staff to Ronald J. Tenpas, Counsel to T. Ulrich Brechbuhl, Counselor, Department of State (Nov. 5, 2019); Email from Committee Staff to Ronald J. Tenpas, Counsel to T. Ulrich Brechbuhl, Counselor (Nov. 22, 2019).

284 Letter from Brian Bulatao, Under Secretary of State for Management, to Ronald J. Tenpas, Counsel to T. Ulrich Brechbuhl, Counselor, Department of State (Nov. 4, 2019.)

285 Letter from Chairman Eliot L. Engel, House Committee on Foreign Affairs, Chairman Adam B. Schiff, House Permanent Select Committee on Intelligence, and Acting Chairwoman Carolyn B. Maloney, House Committee on Oversight and Reform, to Secretary Rick Perry, Department of Energy (Nov. 1, 2019).

286 Letter from General Counsel Bill Cooper, Department of Energy, to Chairman Adam B. Schiff, House Permanent Select Committee on Intelligence, Chairman Eliot L. Engel, House Committee on Foreign Affairs, and Acting Chairwoman Carolyn B. Maloney, House Committee on Oversight and Reform (Nov. 5, 2019).

287 Letter from Chairman Eliot L. Engel, House Committee on Foreign Affairs, Chairman Adam B. Schiff, House Permanent Select Committee on Intelligence, and Chairman Elijah E. Cummings, House Committee on Oversight and Reform, to Secretary Michael R. Pompeo, Department of State (Sept. 13, 2019).

288 Letter from Chairman Eliot L. Engel, House Committee on Foreign Affairs, Chairman Adam B. Schiff, House Permanent Select Committee on Intelligence, and Chairman Elijah E. Cummings, House Committee on Oversight and Reform, to Secretary Michael R. Pompeo, Department of State (Sept. 27, 2019) (internal citations omitted).

289 Letter from Chairman Eliot L. Engel, House Committee on Foreign Affairs, Chairman Adam B. Schiff, House Permanent Select Committee on Intelligence, and Chairman Elijah E. Cummings, House Committee on Oversight and Reform, to Ambassador Marie Yovanovitch, Former U.S. Ambassador to Ukraine, Department of State (Sept. 27, 2019).

290 Letter from Secretary Michael R. Pompeo, Department of State, to Chairman Eliot L. Engel, House Committee on Foreign Affairs (Oct. 1, 2019) (Secretary Pompeo sent identical letters to Chairman Elijah. E. Cummings, House Committee on Oversight and Reform, and Chairman Adam B. Schiff, House Permanent Select Committee on Intelligence, the same day).

291 Letter from Brian Bulatao, Under Secretary of State for Management, Department of State, to Lawrence S. Robbins, Counsel to Ambassador Marie Yovanovitch, Former U.S. Ambassador to Ukraine, Department of State (Oct. 10, 2019).

292 The White House, *Remarks by President Trump Before Marine One Departure* (Oct. 10, 2019) (online at www.whitehouse.gov/briefings-statements/remarks-president-trump-marine-one-departure-69/).

[293] Letter from Chairman Adam B. Schiff, House Permanent Select Committee on Intelligence, Chairman Eliot L. Engel, House Committee on Foreign Affairs, and Chairman Elijah E. Cummings, House Committee on Oversight and Reform, to Lawrence S. Robbins, Counsel to Ambassador Marie Yovanovitch, Former U.S. Ambassador to Ukraine, Department of State (Oct. 11, 2019); House Permanent Select Committee on Intelligence, Subpoena to Ambassador Marie Yovanovitch, Former U.S. Ambassador to Ukraine, Department of State (Oct. 11, 2019).

[294] Letter from Lawrence S. Robbins, Counsel to Ambassador Marie Yovanovitch, Former U.S. Ambassador to Ukraine, Department of State, to Brian Bulatao, Under Secretary of State for Management, Department of State (Oct. 11, 2019) (citations omitted).

[295] Yovanovitch Dep. Tr.

[296] *Id.* at 70.

[297] Email from Committee Staff to Lawrence S. Robbins, Counsel to Ambassador Marie Yovanovitch, Former U.S. Ambassador to Ukraine, Department of State (Nov. 15, 2019); House Permanent Select Committee on Intelligence, Subpoena to Ambassador Marie Yovanovitch, Former U.S. Ambassador to Ukraine, Department of State (Nov. 15, 2019).

[298] Yovanovitch Hearing Tr. at 157-158.

[299] Letter from Chairman Elijah E. Cummings, House Committee on Oversight and Reform, Chairman Eliot L. Engel, House Committee on Foreign Affairs, and Chairman Adam B. Schiff, House Permanent Select Committee on Intelligence, to Secretary Michael R. Pompeo, Department of State (Sept. 27, 2019) (internal citations omitted) (online at https://oversight.house.gov/sites/democrats.oversight.house.gov/files/documents/2019-09-27.EEC%20Engel%20Schiff%20%20to%20Pompeo-%20State%20re%20Depositions.pdf).

[300] Letter from Chairman Elijah E. Cummings, House Committee on Oversight and Reform, Chairman Eliot L. Engel, House Committee on Foreign Affairs, and Chairman Adam B. Schiff, House Permanent Select Committee on Intelligence, to Ambassador Gordon Sondland, U.S. Ambassador to the European Union, Department of State (Sept. 27, 2019).

[301] Letter from Secretary Michael R. Pompeo, Department of State, to Chairman Eliot L. Engel, House Committee on Foreign Affairs (Oct. 1, 2019) (Secretary Pompeo sent identical letters to Chairman Elijah. E. Cummings, House Committee on Oversight and Reform, and Chairman Adam B. Schiff, House Permanent Select Committee on Intelligence, the same day).

[302] Letter from Brian Bulatao, Under Secretary of State for Management, Department of State, to Robert Luskin, Counsel to Ambassador Gordon Sondland, U.S. Ambassador to the European Union, Department of State (Oct.7, 2019).

[303] Email from Robert Luskin, Counsel to Ambassador Gordon Sondland, U.S. Ambassador to the European Union, Department of State, to Committee Staff (Oct. 8, 2019).

[304] Letter from Chairman Adam B. Schiff, House Permanent Select Committee on Intelligence, Chairman Elijah E. Cummings, House Committee on Oversight and Reform, and Chairman Eliot L. Engel, House Committee on Foreign Affairs, to Ambassador Gordon Sondland, U.S. Ambassador to the European Union, Department of State (Oct. 8, 2019); House Permanent Select Committee on Intelligence, Subpoena to Ambassador Gordon Sondland, U.S. Ambassador to the European Union, Department of State (Oct. 11, 2019).

[305] Letter from Chairman Adam B. Schiff, House Permanent Select Committee on Intelligence, Chairman Elijah E. Cummings, House Committee on Oversight and Reform, and Chairman Eliot L. Engel, House Committee on Foreign Affairs, to Ambassador Gordon Sondland, U.S. Ambassador to the European Union, Department of State (Oct. 14, 2019).

[306] Sondland Dep. Tr.

[307] *Id.* at 16.

[308] *Id.* at 17.

[309] Letter from Robert Luskin, Counsel to Ambassador Gordon Sondland, U.S. Ambassador to the European Union, Department of State, to Chairman Adam B. Schiff, House Permanent Select Committee on Intelligence (Nov. 4, 2019); Declaration of Ambassador Gordon Sondland, Department of State (Nov. 4, 2019).

[310] House Permanent Select Committee on Intelligence, Subpoena to Ambassador Gordon Sondland, U.S. Ambassador to the European Union, Department of State (Nov. 20, 2019).

[311] Sondland Hearing Tr. at 160.

[312] Letter from Chairman Eliot L. Engel, House Committee on Foreign Affairs, Chairman Adam B. Schiff, House Permanent Select Committee on Intelligence, and Chairman Elijah E. Cummings, House Committee on Oversight and Reform, to Secretary Michael R. Pompeo, Department of State (Sept. 13, 2019).

[313] Letter from Chairman Eliot L. Engel, House Committee on Foreign Affairs, Chairman Adam B. Schiff, House Permanent Select Committee on Intelligence, and Chairman Elijah E. Cummings, House Committee on Oversight and Reform, to Secretary Michael R. Pompeo, Department of State (Sept. 27, 2019) (online at https://oversight house.gov/sites/democrats.oversight.house.gov/files/documents/2019-09-27.EEC%20Engel%20Schiff%20%20to%20Pompeo-%20State%20re%20Depositions.pdf) (internal citations omitted).

[314] Letter from Chairman Eliot L. Engel, House Committee on Foreign Affairs, Chairman Adam B. Schiff, House Permanent Select Committee on Intelligence, and Chairman Elijah E. Cummings, House Committee on Oversight and Reform, to George P. Kent, Deputy Assistant Secretary of State, Bureau of European and Eurasian Affairs, Department of State (Sept. 27, 2019).

[315] Email from George P. Kent, Deputy Assistant Secretary of State, Bureau of European and Eurasian Affairs, Department of State, to Committee Staff (Sept. 27, 2019).

[316] Letter from Secretary Michael R. Pompeo, Department of State, to Chairman Eliot L. Engel, House Committee on Foreign Affairs (Oct. 1, 2019) (Secretary Pompeo sent identical letters to Chairman Elijah. E. Cummings, House Committee on Oversight and Reform, and Chairman Adam B. Schiff, House Permanent Select Committee on Intelligence, the same day).

[317] Email from Committee Staff to Andrew M. Wright, Counsel to George P. Kent, Deputy Assistant Secretary of State, Bureau of European and Eurasian Affairs, Department of State (Oct. 8, 2019).

[318] Letter from Brian Bulatao, Under Secretary of State for Management, Department of State, to Andrew M. Wright, Counsel to George P. Kent, Deputy Assistant Secretary of State, Bureau of European and Eurasian Affairs, Department of State (Oct. 10, 2019).

[319] Letter from Chairman Adam B. Schiff, House Permanent Select Committee on Intelligence, Chairman Eliot L. Engel, House Committee on Foreign Affairs, and Chairman Elijah E. Cummings, House Committee on Oversight and Reform, to Andrew M. Wright, Counsel to George P. Kent, Deputy Assistant Secretary of State, Bureau of European and Eurasian Affairs, Department of State (Oct. 15, 2019); House Permanent Select Committee on Intelligence, Subpoena to George P. Kent, Deputy Assistant Secretary of State, Bureau of European and Eurasian Affairs, Department of State (Oct. 15, 2019).

[320] Kent Dep. Tr.

[321] *Id.* at 17.

[322] House Permanent Select Committee on Intelligence, Subpoena to George P. Kent, Deputy Assistant Secretary of State, Bureau of European and Eurasian Affairs, Department of State (Nov. 20, 2019).

[323] Kent-Taylor Hearing Tr. at 142-143.

[324] Letter from Chairman Eliot L. Engel, House Committee on Foreign Affairs, Chairman Adam B. Schiff, House Permanent Select Committee on Intelligence, and Chairman Elijah E. Cummings, House Committee on Oversight and Reform, to John J. Sullivan, Deputy Secretary of State, Department of State (Oct. 4, 2019).

[325] Letter from Chairman Eliot L. Engel, House Committee on Foreign Affairs, Chairman Adam B. Schiff, House Permanent Select Committee on Intelligence, and Chairman Elijah E. Cummings, House Committee on Oversight and Reform, to Ambassador William B. Taylor, Jr., Chargé d'Affaires, U.S. Embassy, Kyiv, Department of State (Oct. 4, 2019).

---

[326] Letter from Chairman Adam B. Schiff, House Permanent Select Committee on Intelligence, Chairman Elijah E. Cummings, House Committee on Oversight and Reform, and Chairman Eliot L. Engel, House Committee on Foreign Affairs, to Ambassador William B. Taylor, Jr., Ambassador William B. Taylor, Jr., Chargé d'Affaires, U.S. Embassy, Kyiv, Department of State (Oct. 14, 2019).

[327] Email from Committee Staff to John B. Bellinger, III, and Jeffrey H. Smith, Counsel to Ambassador William B. Taylor, Jr., Chargé d'Affaires, U.S. Embassy, Kyiv, Department of State (Oct. 22, 2019); House Permanent Select Committee on Intelligence, Subpoena to Ambassador William B. Taylor, Jr., Chargé d'Affaires, U.S. Embassy, Kyiv, Department of State (Oct. 22, 2019).

[328] Taylor Dep. Tr. at 83.

[329] House Permanent Select Committee on Intelligence, Subpoena to Ambassador William B. Taylor, Jr., Chargé d'Affaires, U.S. Embassy, Kyiv, Department of State (Nov. 13, 2019).

[330] Kent-Taylor Hearing Tr. at 143.

[331] Letter from Chairman Eliot L. Engel, House Committee on Foreign Affairs, Chairman Adam B. Schiff, House Permanent Select Committee on Intelligence, and Acting Chairwoman Carolyn B. Maloney, House Committee on Oversight and Reform, to Mark J. MacDougall, Counsel to Catherine Croft, Foreign Service Officer, Department of State (Oct. 24, 2019); Letter from Chairman Eliot L. Engel, House Committee on Foreign Affairs, Chairman Adam B. Schiff, House Permanent Select Committee on Intelligence, and Acting Chairwoman Carolyn B. Maloney, House Committee on Oversight and Reform, to Mark J. MacDougall, Counsel to Christopher Anderson, Foreign Service Officer, Department of State (Oct. 24, 2019).

[332] Letter from Mark J. MacDougall, Counsel to Catherine Croft, Foreign Service Officer, Department of State, and Christopher Anderson, Foreign Service Officer, Department of State, to Committee Staff (Oct. 25, 2019).

[333] Letter from Brian Bulatao, Under Secretary of State for Management, Department of State, to Mark J. MacDougall, Counsel to Catherine Croft, Foreign Service Officer, Department of State (Oct. 28, 2019) (bracketed text in original); Letter from Brian Bulatao, Under Secretary of State for Management, Department of State, to Mark J. MacDougall, Counsel to Christopher Anderson, Foreign Service Officer, Department of State (Oct. 28, 2019) (bracketed text in original); *see* Letter from Pat A. Cipollone, Counsel to the President, The White House, to Speaker Nancy Pelosi, Chairman Elijah E. Cummings, House Committee on Oversight and Reform, Chairman Eliot L. Engel, House Committee on Foreign Affairs, and Chairman Adam B. Schiff, House Permanent Select Committee on Intelligence (Oct. 8, 2019) (online at www.whitehouse.gov/wp-content/uploads/2019/10/PAC-Letter-10.08.2019.pdf).

[334] Email from Committee Staff to Mark J. MacDougall and Abbey McNaughton, Counsel to Catherine Croft, Foreign Service Officer, Department of State and Christopher Anderson, Foreign Service Officer, Department of State (Oct. 30, 2019); House Permanent Select Committee on Intelligence, Subpoena to Catherine Croft, Foreign Service Officer, Department of State (Oct. 30, 2019); House Permanent Select Committee on Intelligence, Subpoena to Christopher Anderson, Foreign Service Officer, Department of State (Oct. 30, 2019).

[335] Croft Dep. Tr.; Anderson Dep. Tr.

[336] Croft Dep. Tr. at 12.

[337] Anderson Dep. Tr. at 11-12.

[338] Letter from Chairman Eliot L. Engel, House Committee on Foreign Affairs, Chairman Adam B. Schiff, House Permanent Select Committee on Intelligence, and Chairman Elijah E. Cummings, House Committee on Oversight and Reform, to Laura K. Cooper, Deputy Assistant Secretary of Defense for Russia, Ukraine, Eurasia, Department of Defense (Oct. 11, 2019).

[339] Letter from Deputy Secretary of Defense David L. Norquist to Daniel Levin, Counsel to Laura K. Cooper, Deputy Assistant Secretary of Defense for Russia, Ukraine, Eurasia, Department of Defense (Oct. 22, 2019).

[340] Email from Committee Staff to Dan Levin, Counsel to Laura K. Cooper, Deputy Assistant Secretary of Defense for Russia, Ukraine, Eurasia, Department of Defense (Oct. 23, 2019); House Permanent Select Committee on Intelligence, Subpoena to Laura K. Cooper, Deputy Assistant Secretary of Defense for Russia, Ukraine, Eurasia, Department of Defense (Oct. 23, 2019).

341 Cooper Dep. Tr.

342 *Id.* at 108.

343 Email from Committee Staff to Dan Levin, Counsel to Laura K. Cooper, Deputy Assistant Secretary of Defense for Russia, Ukraine, Eurasia, Department of Defense (Nov. 20, 2019); House Permanent Select Committee on Intelligence, Subpoena to Laura K. Cooper, Deputy Assistant Secretary of Defense for Russia, Ukraine, Eurasia, Department of Defense (Nov. 20, 2019).

344 Cooper-Hale Hearing Tr.

345 Letter from Chairman Adam B. Schiff, House Permanent Select Committee on Intelligence, Acting Chairwoman Carolyn B. Maloney, House Committee on Oversight and Reform, and Chairman Eliot L. Engel, House Committee on Foreign Affairs, to Mark Sandy, Deputy Associate Director of National Security Programs, Office of Management and Budget (Nov. 5, 2019).

346 Email from Mark Sandy, Deputy Associate Director of National Security Programs, Office of Management and Budget, to Committee Staff (Nov. 6, 2019).

347 Email from Jessica L. Donlon, Deputy General Counsel for Oversight, Office of Management and Budget, to Committee Staff (Nov. 7, 2019).

348 Email from Committee Staff to Barbara Van Gelder, Counsel to Mark Sandy, Deputy Associate Director of National Security Programs, Office of Management and Budget (Nov. 16, 2019); House Permanent Select Committee on Intelligence, Subpoena to Mark Sandy, Deputy Associate Director of National Security Programs, Office of Management and Budget (Nov. 16, 2019).

349 Sandy Dep. Tr.

350 *Id.* at 161.

351 Letter from Chairman Eliot L. Engel, House Committee on Foreign Affairs, Chairman Adam B. Schiff, House Permanent Select Committee on Intelligence, and Chairman Elijah E. Cummings, House Committee on Oversight and Reform, to Dr. Fiona Hill, Former Deputy Assistant to the President and Senior Director for Europe and Russia, National Security Council (Oct. 9, 2019).

352 Letter from Lee S. Wolosky, Counsel to Dr. Fiona Hill, Former Deputy Assistant to the President and Senior Director for Europe and Russia, National Security Council, to Michael M. Purpura, Deputy Counsel and Deputy Assistant to the President, The White House, and Patrick F. Philbin, Deputy Counsel and Deputy Assistant to the President, The White House (Oct. 13, 2019).

353 Letter from Michael M. Purpura, Deputy Counsel and Deputy Assistant to the President, The White House, to Lee S. Wolosky, Counsel to Dr. Fiona Hill, Former Deputy Assistant to the President and Senior Director for Europe and Russia, National Security Council (Oct. 14, 2019).

354 Email from Committee Staff to Lee S. Wolosky and Samuel S. Ungar, Counsel to Dr. Fiona Hill, Former Deputy Assistant to the President and Senior Director for Europe and Russia, National Security Council (Oct. 14, 2019); House Permanent Select Committee on Intelligence, Subpoena to Dr. Fiona Hill, Former Deputy Assistant to the President and Senior Director for Europe and Russia, National Security Council (Oct. 14, 2019).

355 Hill Dep. Tr.

356 Letter from Lee S. Wolosky, Counsel to Dr. Fiona Hill, Former Deputy Assistant to the President and Senior Director for Europe and Russia, National Security Council, to Michael M. Purpura, Deputy Counsel and Deputy Assistant to the President, The White House (Nov. 18, 2019).

357 Letter from Michael M. Purpura, Deputy Counsel and Deputy Assistant to the President, The White House, to Lee S. Wolosky, Counsel to Dr. Fiona Hill, Former Deputy Assistant to the President and Senior Director for Europe and Russia, National Security Council (Nov. 20, 2019).

358 Email from Committee Staff to Lee S. Wolosky and Samuel S. Ungar, Counsel to Dr. Fiona Hill, Former Deputy Assistant to the President and Senior Director for Europe and Russia, National Security Council (Nov. 21, 2019); House Permanent Select Committee on Intelligence, Subpoena to Dr. Fiona Hill, Former Deputy Assistant to the President and Senior Director for Europe and Russia, National Security Council (Nov. 21, 2019).

[359] Hill-Holmes Hearing Tr.

[360] Letter from Chairman Eliot L. Engel, House Committee on Foreign Affairs, Chairman Adam B. Schiff, House Permanent Select Committee on Intelligence, and Chairman Elijah E. Cummings, House Committee on Oversight and Reform, to Lieutenant Colonel Alexander S. Vindman, Director for Ukraine, National Security Council (Oct. 16, 2019).

[361] Email from Committee Staff to Michael Volkov and Matt Stankiewicz, Counsel to Lieutenant Colonel Alexander S. Vindman, Director for Ukraine, National Security Council (Oct. 29, 2019); House Permanent Select Committee on Intelligence, Subpoena to Lieutenant Colonel Alexander S. Vindman, Director for Ukraine, National Security Council (Oct. 29, 2019).

[362] Vindman Dep. Tr. (During the deposition, Lieutenant Colonel Vindman stated: "I was subpoenaed to appear here. You know, absent a subpoena, I would believe I was operating under the President's guidance to not appear, but I was subpoenaed and I presented myself." Vindman Dep. Tr. at 232).

[363] Email from Committee Staff, to Michael Volkov and Matt Stankiewicz, Counsel to Lieutenant Colonel Alexander S. Vindman, Director for Ukraine, National Security Council (Nov. 19, 2019); House Permanent Select Committee on Intelligence, Subpoena to Lieutenant Colonel Alexander S. Vindman, Director for Ukraine, National Security Council (Nov. 19, 2019).

[364] Vindman-Williams Hearing Tr.

[365] Letter from Chairman Eliot L. Engel, House Committee on Foreign Affairs, Chairman Adam B. Schiff, House Permanent Select Committee on Intelligence, and Chairman Elijah E. Cummings, House Committee on Oversight and Reform, to Timothy Morrison, Former Deputy Assistant to the President and Senior Director for Europe and Russia, National Security Council (Oct. 16, 2019).

[366] Email from Committee Staff to Barbara Van Gelder, Counsel to Timothy Morrison, Former Deputy Assistant to the President and Senior Director for Europe and Russia, National Security Council (Oct. 31, 2019); House Permanent Select Committee on Intelligence, Subpoena to Timothy Morrison, Former Deputy Assistant to the President and Senior Director for Europe and Russia, National Security Council (Oct. 31, 2019).

[367] Morrison Dep. Tr.

[368] Email from Committee Staff to Barbara Van Gelder, Counsel to Timothy Morrison, Former Deputy Assistant to the President and Senior Director for Europe and Russia, National Security Council (Nov. 19, 2019); House Permanent Select Committee on Intelligence, Subpoena to Timothy Morrison, Former Deputy Assistant to the President and Senior Director for Europe and Russia, National Security Council (Nov. 19, 2019).

[369] Morrison-Volker Hearing Tr.

[370] Letter from Chairman Eliot L. Engel, House Committee on Foreign Affairs, Chairman Adam B. Schiff, House Permanent Select Committee on Intelligence, and Acting Chairwoman Carolyn B. Maloney, House Committee on Oversight and Reform, to David Hale, Under Secretary of State for Political Affairs, Department of State (Nov. 1, 2019).

[371] Letter from Brian A. Glasser, Counsel to David Hale, Under Secretary of State for Political Affairs, Department of State, to Chairman Adam B. Schiff, House Permanent Select Committee on Intelligence, Chairman Eliot L. Engel, House Committee on Foreign Affairs, and Acting Chairwoman Carolyn B. Maloney, House Committee on Oversight and Reform (Nov. 5, 2019).

[372] Email from Committee Staff to Brian Glasser and Cary Joshi, Counsel for David Hale, Under Secretary of State for Political Affairs, Department of State (Nov. 6, 2019); House Permanent Select Committee on Intelligence, Subpoena to David Hale, Under Secretary of State for Political Affairs, Department of State (Nov. 6, 2019).

[373] Hale Dep. Tr.

[374] Email from Committee Staff to Brian A. Glasser, Counsel to David Hale, Under Secretary of State for Political Affairs, Department of State (Nov. 20, 2019); House Permanent Select Committee on Intelligence, Subpoena to David Hale, Under Secretary of State for Political Affairs, Department of State (Nov. 20, 2019).

[375] Cooper-Hale Hearing Tr.

[376] Letter from Chairman Adam B. Schiff, House Permanent Select Committee on Intelligence, Acting Chairwoman Carolyn B. Maloney, House Committee on Oversight and Reform, and from Chairman Eliot L. Engel, House Committee on Foreign Affairs, to Kenneth L. Wainstein, Counsel to David Holmes, Political Counselor at the U.S. Embassy in Kyiv, Ukraine, Department of State (Nov. 12, 2019).

[377] Email from Committee Staff to Kenneth L. Wainstein, Paul J. Nathanson, and Katherine Swan, Counsel to David Holmes, Political Counselor at the U.S. Embassy in Kyiv, Ukraine, Department of State (Nov. 15, 2019); House Permanent Select Committee on Intelligence, Subpoena to David Holmes, Political Counselor at the U.S. Embassy in Kyiv, Ukraine, Department of State (Nov. 15, 2019).

[378] Holmes Dep. Tr.

[379] Email from Committee Staff to Kenneth L. Wainstein, Paul J. Nathanson, and Katherine Swan, Counsel to David Holmes, Political Counselor at the U.S. Embassy in Kyiv, Ukraine, Department of State (Nov. 21, 2019); House Permanent Select Committee on Intelligence, Subpoena to David Holmes, Political Counselor at the U.S. Embassy in Kyiv, Ukraine, Department of State (Nov. 21, 2019).

[380] Hill-Holmes Hearing Tr.

[381] Email from Committee Staff to Ambassador P. Michael McKinley, Former Senior Advisor to the Secretary of State, Department of State (Oct. 12, 2019).

[382] Letter from Chairman Eliot L. Engel, House Committee on Foreign Affairs, Chairman Adam B. Schiff, House Permanent Select Committee on Intelligence, and Chairman Elijah E. Cummings, House Committee on Oversight and Reform, to John B. Bellinger, III, Counsel to Ambassador P. Michael McKinley, Former Senior Advisor to the Secretary of State, Department of State (Oct. 14, 2019).

[383] McKinley Transcribed Interview Tr.

[384] Letter from Chairman Eliot L. Engel, House Committee on Foreign Affairs, Chairman Adam B. Schiff, House Permanent Select Committee on Intelligence, and Chairman Elijah E. Cummings, House Committee on Oversight and Reform, to Ambassador Philip T. Reeker, Acting Assistant Secretary, Bureau of European and Eurasian Affairs, Department of State (Oct. 16, 2019).

[385] Letter from Chairman Adam B. Schiff, House Permanent Select Committee on Intelligence, Chairman Eliot L. Engel, House Committee on Foreign Affairs, and Acting Chairwoman Carolyn B. Maloney, House Committee on Oversight and Reform, to Margaret E. Daum, Counsel to Ambassador Philip T. Reeker, Acting Assistant Secretary, Bureau of European and Eurasian Affairs, Department of State (Oct. 25, 2019); House Permanent Select Committee on Intelligence, Subpoena to Ambassador Philip T. Reeker, Acting Assistant Secretary, Bureau of European and Eurasian Affairs, Department of State (Oct. 25, 2019).

[386] Reeker Dep. Tr.

[387] Letter from Chairman Eliot L. Engel, House Committee on Foreign Affairs, Chairman Adam B. Schiff, House Permanent Select Committee on Intelligence, and Chairman Elijah E. Cummings, House Committee on Oversight and Reform, to Secretary Michael R. Pompeo, Department of State (Sept. 13, 2019).

[388] Letter from Chairman Eliot L. Engel, House Committee on Foreign Affairs, Chairman Adam B. Schiff, House Permanent Select Committee on Intelligence, and Chairman Elijah E. Cummings, House Committee on Oversight and Reform, to Secretary Michael R. Pompeo, Department of State (Sept. 27, 2019).

[389] Letter from Chairman Eliot L. Engel, House Committee on Foreign Affairs, Chairman Adam B. Schiff, House Permanent Select Committee on Intelligence, and Chairman Elijah E. Cummings, House Committee on Oversight and Reform, to Ambassador Kurt Volker, U.S. Special Representative for Ukraine Negotiations, Department of State (Sept. 27, 2019).

[390] Letter from Secretary Michael F. Pompeo, Department of State, to Chairman Eliot L. Engel, House Committee on Foreign Affairs (Oct. 1, 2019) (Identical letters transmitted to Chairman Schiff and Chairman Cummings).

[391] Letter from Marik A. String, Acting Legal Advisor, Department of State, to Margaret E. Daum, Counsel to Ambassador Kurt Volker, U.S. Special Representative for Ukraine Negotiations, Department of State (Oct. 2, 2019).

392 Letter from Margaret E. Daum, Counsel to Ambassador Kurt Volker, U.S. Special Representative for Ukraine Negotiations, Department of State, to Chairman Eliot L. Engel, House Committee on Foreign Affairs, Chairman Adam B. Schiff, House Permanent Select Committee on Intelligence, and Chairman Elijah E. Cummings, House Committee on Oversight and Reform (Oct. 2, 2019); Kurt Volker Document Production, Bates KV0000000-KV00000065 (Oct. 2, 2019).

393 Volker Transcribed Interview Tr.

394 Morrison-Volker Hearing Tr.

395 Letter from Chairman Adam B. Schiff, House Permanent Select Committee on Intelligence, and Acting Chairwoman Carolyn B. Maloney, House Committee on Oversight and Reform, and Chairman Eliot L. Engel, House Committee on Foreign Affairs, to Justin Shur, Counsel to Jennifer Williams, Special Advisor for Europe and Russia, Office of the Vice President (Nov. 4, 2019).

396 Email from Committee Staff to Justin Shur, Counsel to Jennifer Williams, Special Advisor for Europe and Russia, Office of the Vice President (Nov. 7, 2019); House Permanent Select Committee on Intelligence, Subpoena to Jennifer Williams, Special Advisor for Europe and Russia, Office of the Vice President (Nov. 7, 2019).

397 Williams Dep. Tr.

398 Letter from Jennifer Williams, Special Advisor for Europe and Russia, Office of the Vice President, Justin Shur, Emily K. Damrau, and Caleb Hayes-Deats, Counsel to Jennifer Williams, Special Advisor for Europe and Russia, Office of the Vice President, to Chairman Adam B. Schiff, House Permanent Select Committee on Intelligence (Nov. 11, 2019).

399 Email from Committee Staff to Justin Shur and Caleb Hayes-Deats, Counsel to Jennifer Williams, Special Advisor for Europe and Russia, Office of the Vice President (Nov. 19, 2019); House Permanent Select Committee on Intelligence, Subpoena to Jennifer Williams, Special Advisor for Europe and Russia, Office of the Vice President (Nov. 19, 2019).

400 Vindman-Williams Hearing Tr.

401 Yovanovitch Dep. Tr. at 193.

402 Yovanovitch Hearing Tr. at 37-38.

403 *Id.* at 38.

404 Donald J. Trump, Twitter (Nov. 15, 2019) (online at https://twitter.com/realDonaldTrump/status/1195356198347956224).

405 Yovanovitch Hearing Tr. at 46.

406 *The Latest: Ousted Ukraine Ambassador Has Her Say in Hearing,* Associated Press (Nov. 16, 2019) (online at https://apnews.com/2f420045618b4106b6fa7419a3d75b8e).

407 *Impeachment Inquiry Hearing with Former US Ambassador to Ukraine*, CNN (Nov. 15, 2019) (online at www.cnn.com/politics/live-news/impeachment-hearing-11-15-19/h_fb32b149181437e02e5d937c6fc64f35). During a recess in the hearing at which Ambassador Yovanovitch was testifying, a federal jury returned a verdict of guilty against President Trump's longest-serving political advisor, Roger Stone, on seven criminal counts, including witness tampering and obstruction of Congress' investigation into Russian interference in the 2016 election and possible links to President Trump's campaign. Mr. Stone used threats and intimidation to attempt to persuade a witness to withhold information and lie to Congress. He has yet to be sentenced. *See Roger Stone Guilty on All Counts of Lying to Congress, Witness Tampering*, Washington Post (Nov. 15, 2019) (online at www.washingtonpost.com/local/public-safety/roger-stone-jury-weighs-evidence-and-a-defense-move-to-make-case-about-mueller/2019/11/15/554fff5a-06ff-11ea-8292-c46ee8cb3dce_story.html). Mr. Stone was convicted of giving false and misleading statements to the Intelligence Committee, failing to produce and lying about the existence of records responsive to Committee requests, and attempting to persuade a witness to give false testimony to the Committee. Among other acts of witness tampering, Mr. Stone told the witness to "Stonewall it. Plead the Fifth" and to "be honest w fbi" that "there was no back channel." He also called the witness a "rat" and "stoolie" and threatened retaliation. *United States v. Roger Stone*, Indictment, No. 1:19-cr-00018-ABJ (Jan. 24, 2019). Mr. Stone

was convicted of violating 18 U.S.C. § 1505 (obstruction), 18 U.S.C. § 1001 (false statements), and 18 U.S.C. § 1512(b) (witness tampering).

[408] *Fox and Friends*, Fox News (Nov. 22, 2019) (online at www.youtube.com/watch?v=WNqKhRcpktU).

[409] Donald J. Trump, Twitter (Oct. 23, 2019) (online at https://twitter.com/realDonaldTrump/status/1189167309455331328).

[410] The White House, *Remarks by President Trump Before Marine One Departure* (Nov. 3, 2019) (online at www.whitehouse.gov/briefings-statements/remarks-president-trump-marine-one-departure-74/).

[411] Donald J. Trump, Twitter (Nov. 19, 2019) (retweeting Dan Scavino Jr., Twitter (Nov. 19, 2019) (online at https://twitter.com/Scavino45/status/1196860213233684480)).

[412] *See, e.g, Berman Shocked by Republican's Attacks on US War Vet*, CNN (Oct. 29, 2019) (online at www.cnn.com/videos/politics/2019/10/29/duffy-berman-spar-over-vindman-loyalty newday-vpx.cnn) (former Rep. Sean Duffy claiming that Lt. Col Vindman "has an affinity, I think for the Ukraine," that "it seems very clear that he is incredibly concerned about Ukrainian defense," and that "I don't know that he's concerned about American policy"); *see also* Rudy Giuliani, Twitter (Oct. 30, 2019) (online at https://twitter.com/RudyGiuliani/status/1189732605383630850) (claiming that Lt. Col. Vindman was "giving advice to two countries" and stating that "I thought he worked for US").

[413] House Permanent Select Committee on Intelligence, Written Statement of Lieutenant Colonel Alexander S. Vindman, Impeachment, 116th Cong. (Nov. 19, 2019).

[414] Donald J. Trump, Twitter (Oct. 23, 2019) (online at https://twitter.com/realDonaldTrump/status/1187063301731209220).

[415] Donald J. Trump, Twitter (Oct. 23, 2019) (online at https://twitter.com/realDonaldTrump/status/1187080923961012228).

[416] The White House, *Remarks by President Trump Before Marine One Departure* (Oct. 25, 2019) (online at www.whitehouse.gov/briefings-statements/remarks-president-trump-marine-one-departure-72/).

[417] Donald J. Trump, Twitter (Nov. 13, 2019) (online at https://twitter.com/realdonaldtrump/status/1194608482793795584).

[418] Donald J. Trump, Twitter (Nov. 17, 2019) (online at https://twitter.com/realDonaldTrump/status/1196155347117002752).

[419] Vindman-Williams Hearing Tr. at 97.

[420] Donald J. Trump, Twitter (Nov. 16, 2019) (online at https://twitter.com/realDonaldTrump/status/1195727871765073921); Donald J. Trump, Twitter (Nov. 16, 2019) (online at https://twitter.com/realDonaldTrump/status/1195727879780360193).

[421] 50 U.S.C. § 3033(g)(3) (when a complaint is received from a member of the Intelligence Community, "the Inspector General shall not disclose the identity of the employee without the consent of the employee, unless the Inspector General determines that such disclosure is unavoidable during the course of the investigation or the disclosure is made to an official of the Department of Justice responsible for determining whether a prosecution should be undertaken").

[422] 50 U.S.C. § 3234(b).

[423] Letter from Michael K. Atkinson, Inspector General of the Intelligence Community, to Chairman Adam B. Schiff, House Permanent Select Committee on Intelligence, and Ranking Member Devin Nunes, House Permanent Select Committee on Intelligence (Sept. 9, 2019); *see also* 50 U.S.C. § 3033(k)(5)(C) ("Upon receipt of the transmittal from the ICIG, the Director *shall* within 7 calendar days of such receipt, forward such transmittal to the congressional intelligence committees, together with any comments the Director considers appropriate.")

[424] Letter from Chairman, Adam B. Schiff, House Permanent Select Committee on Intelligence, to Joseph Maguire, Acting Director of National Intelligence, Office of the Director of National Intelligence (Sept. 13, 2019).

[425] House Permanent Select Committee on Intelligence, *House Intelligence Committee Releases Whistleblower Complaint* (Sept. 26, 2019) (online at https://intelligence.house.gov/news/documentsingle.aspx?DocumentID=708).

[426] *Listen: Audio of Trump Discussing Whistleblower at Private Event: 'That's Close to a Spy,'* Los Angeles Times (Sept. 26, 2019) (online at www.latimes.com/politics/story/2019-09-26/trump-at-private-breakfast-who-gave-the-whistle-blower-the-information-because-thats-almost-a-spy).

[427] House Permanent Select Committee on Intelligence, *Chairmen Warn President to Stop Attacking Whistleblower and Witnesses to His Misconduct and to Halt Efforts to Obstruct Impeachment Inquiry* (Sept. 26, 2019) (online at https://intelligence house.gov/news/documentsingle.aspx?DocumentID=709).

[428] Donald J. Trump, Twitter (Sept. 29, 2019) (online at https://twitter.com/realDonaldTrump/status/1178442765736333313?s=20).

[429] Donald J. Trump, Twitter (Oct. 4, 2019) (online at https://twitter.com/realDonaldTrump/status/1180123504924151809).

[430] The White House, *Remarks by President Trump Before Marine One Departure* (Nov. 3, 2019) (online at www.whitehouse.gov/briefings-statements/remarks-president-trump-marine-one-departure-74/).

[431] Donald J. Trump, Twitter (Nov. 3, 2019) (online at https://twitter.com/realdonaldtrump/status/1191000516580519937).

[432] The White House, *Remarks by President Trump Before Marine One Departure* (Nov. 3, 2019) (online at www.whitehouse.gov/briefings-statements/remarks-president-trump-marine-one-departure-74/).

[433] The White House, *Remarks by President Trump Before Marine One Departure* (Nov. 4, 2019) (online at www.whitehouse.gov/briefings-statements/remarks-president-trump-marine-one-departure-75/).

[434] The White House, *Remarks by President Trump After Tour of Apple Manufacturing Plant* (Nov. 20, 2019) (online www.whitehouse.gov/briefings-statements/remarks-president-trump-tour-apple-manufacturing-plant-austin-tx/).

[435] Letter from Chairman Adam B. Schiff to Ranking Member Devin Nunes, House Permanent Select Committee on Intelligence (Nov. 9, 2019).

[436] In 2017, every Republican Member of Congress joined a unanimous vote in the House of Representatives to increase penalties for retaliation against whistleblowers. U.S. House of Representatives, Roll Call Vote Approving S. 585, The Dr. Chris Kirkpatrick Whistleblower Protection Act of 2017 (Oct. 12, 2017) (420 yeas, 0 nays) (online at www.govtrack.us/congress/votes/115-2017/h568).

[437] *House Intelligence Chair News Conference*, C-SPAN (Mar. 24, 2017) (online at www.c-span.org/video/?425953-1/paul-manafort-volunteered-intelligence-committee-chairman-nunes).

[438] *Id.*

[439] Office of Senator Chuck Grassley, *Grassley Statement Regarding Intel Community Whistleblower* (Oct. 1, 2019) (online at www.grassley.senate.gov/news/news-releases/grassley-statement-regarding-intel-community-whistleblower).

[440] *Senate Intel Chair Doesn't Want Whistleblower's Identity Disclosed*, The Hill (Nov. 7, 2019) (online at https://thehill.com/homenews/senate/469455-senate-intel-chair-doesnt-want-whistleblowers-identity-disclosed).

[441] *Republicans Break with Trump and Rand Paul on Whistleblower Unmasking*, Politico (Nov. 5, 2019) (online at www.politico.com/news/2019/11/05/rand-paul-trump-whistleblower-065917).

APPENDIX A: KEY PEOPLE AND ENTITIES

Anderson, Christopher J.	Special Advisor for Ukraine Negotiations, Department of State, August 2017-July 2019
Atkinson, Michael K.	Inspector General of the Intelligence Community, May 2018-present
Avakov, Arsen	Ukrainian Minister of Internal Affairs, February 2014-present
Bakanov, Ivan	Head of Security Service of Ukraine, August 2019-present; First Deputy Chief of the Security Service of Ukraine, May 2019-August 2019
Barr, William P.	Attorney General, Department of Justice, February 2019-present
Biden, Hunter	Son of former Vice President Joe Biden
Biden, Joseph R., Jr.	U.S. Vice President, January 2009-January 2017
Blair, Robert B.	Assistant to the President and Senior Advisor to the Chief of Staff, February 2019-present
Bohdan (Bogdan), Andriy	Head of Ukrainian Presidential Administration, May 2019-present
Bolton, John	National Security Advisor, March 2018-September 2019
Brechbuhl, T. Ulrich	Counselor, Department of State, May 2018-present
Bulatao, Brian	Under Secretary of State for Management, Department of State, May 2019-present
Burisma Holdings	Ukrainian energy company
Cipollone, Pat	White House Counsel, December 2018-present
Clinton, Hillary Rodham	Democratic Presidential candidate, November 2016
Cooper, Laura K.	Deputy Assistant Secretary of Defense for Russia, Ukraine, Eurasia, Department of Defense, 2016-present
Croft, Catherine M.	Special Advisor for Ukraine Negotiations, Department of State, July 2019-present; Ukraine director, National Security Council, July 2017-July 2018

CrowdStrike	Cybersecurity company; object of conspiracy theories claiming that CrowdStrike framed Russia in hack of the DNC server in the 2016 U.S. election
Danyliuk (Danylyuk), Oleksandr "Sasha"	Secretary, Ukrainian National Security and Defense Council, May 2019-September 2019
diGenova, Joseph	Attorney allegedly working for President Trump to obtain information from Ukrainian officials on the Bidens
Duffey, Michael	Associate Director, National Security Programs, Office of Management and Budget, May 2019-present
Eisenberg, John	Legal Advisor to the National Security Council and Deputy Counsel to the President for National Security Affairs, February 2017-present
Ellis, Michael	Senior Associate Counsel to the President and Deputy Legal Advisor to the National Security Council, March 2017-present
Elwood, Courtney Simmons	General Counsel, Central Intelligence Agency, June 2017-present
Engel, Steven A.	Assistant Attorney General, Office of Legal Counsel, Department of Justice, November 2017-present
Esper, Mark	Secretary of Defense, Department of Defense, July 2019-present; Acting Secretary of Defense, June 2019-July 2019
Fruman, Igor	Giuliani associate named in indictment unsealed on October 10, 2019
Giuliani, Rudolph "Rudy"	President Trump's agent and personal attorney
Griffith, P. Wells	Senior Director for International Energy and Environment, National Security Council, April 2018-present
Hale, David M.	Under Secretary of State for Political Affairs, Department of State, August 2018-present
Hannity, Sean	Host of *Hannity*, Fox News, January 2009-present
Hill, Fiona	Deputy Assistant to the President and Senior Director for Europe and Russia, National Security Council, April 2017-July 2019
Hochstein, Amos J.	Supervisory Board Member, Naftogaz, November 2017-present

Holmes, David A.	Political Counselor, U.S. Embassy in Kyiv, Ukraine, August 2017-present
Johnson, Ron	Senator from Wisconsin, Chairman, Senate Homeland Security and Governmental Affairs Committee, January 2015-present
Kellogg, Keith	National Security Advisor to the Vice President, April 2018-present
Kenna, Lisa D.	Executive Secretary in the Office of the Secretary, Department of State, June 2017-present
Kent, George P.	Deputy Assistant Secretary of State, Bureau of European and Eurasian Affairs, September 2018-present; Deputy Chief of Mission in Kyiv, Ukraine, 2015-2018
Kholodnitsky, Nazar	Head, Ukrainian Specialized Anti-Corruption Prosecutor's Office, November 2015-present
Klitenic, Jason	General Counsel, Office of the Director of National Intelligence
Kulyk, Kostiantyn	Deputy Head of the Ukrainian Department of International Legal Cooperation of the Prosecutor General's Office, November 2018-November 2019
Kupperman, Charles M.	Deputy National Security Advisor, January 2019-September 2019
Kushner, Jared	Assistant to the President and Senior Advisor, 2017-present
Kvien, Kristina	Deputy Chief of Mission, U.S. Embassy in Kyiv, May 2019-present
Lutsenko, Yuriy	Ukrainian Prosecutor General, May 2016-August 2019
McCormack, Brian	Associate Director for Natural Resources, Office of Management and Budget, September 2019-present; Chief of Staff, Department of Energy, March 2017-September 2019
McKinley, P. Michael	Senior Advisor to the Secretary, Department of State, May 2018-October 2019
McKusker, Elaine A.	Deputy Under Secretary of Defense (Comptroller), Department of Defense, August 2017-present
Maguire, Joseph	Acting Director of National Intelligence, August 2019-present

Manafort, Paul	Chairman, Donald J. Trump presidential campaign, May 2016-August 2016; convicted in August 2018 on two counts of bank fraud, five counts of tax fraud, and one count of failure to disclose a foreign bank account
Morrison, Tim	Deputy Assistant to the President for National Security, National Security Council, July 2019-October 2019
Mueller, Robert S., III	Special Counsel, Department of Justice, May 2017-May 2019
Mulvaney, John Michael "Mick"	Acting Chief of Staff, White House, January 2019-present
Murphy, Chris	Senator from Connecticut, Ranking Member, Subcommittee on Near East, South Asia, Central Asia, and Counterterrorism, Senate Committee on Foreign Relations, formerly Ranking Member, Subcommittee on Europe and Regional Security Cooperation, Senate Committee on Foreign Relations, January 2017-January 2019
Naftogaz	Ukrainian state-owned national gas company
Parnas, Lev	Giuliani associate named in indictment unsealed on October 10, 2019
Patel, Kashyap "Kash"	Senior Director for Counterterrorism, National Security Council, July 2019-present; former Staff, Directorate of International Organizations and Alliances, National Security Council, February 2019-July 2019; former National Security Advisor, House Permanent Select Committee on Intelligence, March 2018-January 2019; former Senior Counsel for Counterterrorism, House Permanent Select Committee on Intelligence, April 2017-March 2018
Pence, Michael R.	Vice President, January 2017-present
Pennington, Joseph	Chargé d'Affaires, of the U.S. Embassy in Ukraine, May 2019
Perez, Carol Z.	Director General of the Foreign Service and Director of Human Services, January 2019-present
Perry, James Richard "Rick"	Secretary of Energy, March 2017-December 2019
Pompeo, Michael	Secretary of State, April 2018-present
Poroshenko, Petro	President of Ukraine, June 2014-May 2019

Portman, Robert	U.S. Senator from Ohio, January 2011-present; Chairman, Permanent Subcommittee on Investigations, Senate Homeland Security and Governmental Affairs Committee, January 2015-present
Purpura, Michael	Deputy Counsel to the President, December 2018-present
Putin, Vladimir	Russian President, May 2012-present
Reeker, Philip T.	Acting Assistant Secretary, Bureau of European and Eurasian Affairs, Department of State, March 2019-present
Rood, John C.	Under Secretary of Defense for Policy, Department of Defense, January 2018-present
Sandy, Mark	Deputy Associate Director for National Security at the Office of Management and Budget, December 2013-present; Acting Director of the Office of Management and Budget, January 2017-February 2017
Sekulow, Jay	Personal attorney for President Trump
Shokin, Viktor	Ukrainian Prosecutor General of Ukraine, February 2015-March 2016
Short, Marc	Chief of Staff to Vice President Mike Pence, February 2019-present
Solomon, John	Author of articles promoting debunked conspiracy theories about the Bidens, Crowdstrike, and the 2016 U.S. election
Sondland, Gordon	U.S. Ambassador to the European Union, July 2018-present
String, Marik	Acting Legal Advisor, Office of the Legal Advisor, Department of State, June 2019-present
Sullivan, John J.	Deputy Secretary of State, Department of State, June 2017-present
Taylor, William B., Jr.	Chargé d'Affaires for the U.S. Embassy in Kyiv, Ukraine, June 2019-present
"Three Amigos"	Secretary of Energy Rick Perry, Ambassador Gordon Sondland, and Ambassador Kurt Volker
Toensing, Victoria	Attorney allegedly working "off the books" for President Trump to obtain information from Ukrainian officials on the Bidens

Trump, Donald J.	U.S. President, January 2017-present
Trump, Donald J., Jr.	Son of President Trump
Vindman, Alexander S.	Director for Ukraine, National Security Council, July 2018-present; Lieutenant Colonel, U.S. Army
Volker, Kurt	U.S. Special Representative for Ukraine Negotiations, Department of State, July 2017-September 2019
Vought, Russell T.	Acting Director, Office of Management and Budget, January 2019-present
Whistleblower	Author of complaint declassified by the Office of the Director of National Intelligence on September 25, 2019
Williams, Jennifer	Special Advisor for Europe and Russia, Office of the Vice President, April 2019-present
Yermak, Andriy	Assistant to the President of Ukraine, May 2019-present
Yovanovitch, Marie L.	U.S. Ambassador to Ukraine, August 2016-May 2019
Zakaria, Fareed	Host, *Fareed Zakaria GPS*, June 2008-present
Zelensky, Volodymyr	President of Ukraine, May 2019-present

APPENDIX B: ABBREVIATIONS AND COMMON TERMS

AntAC	Anti-Corruption Action Center
CDA	Chargé d'Affaires / Acting Ambassador
CIA	Central Intelligence Agency
Chargé d'Affaires	Acting Ambassador
CN	Congressional Notification
COM	Chief of Mission
DAS	Deputy Assistant Secretary
DC	Deputies Committee
DCM	Deputy Chief of Mission
DNI	Director of National Intelligence
DNC	Democratic National Committee
DOD	Department of Defense
DOE	Department of Energy
DOJ	Department of Justice
DOS	Department of State
DSCA	Defense Security Cooperation Agency
EDI	European Deterrence Initiative
ERI	European Reassurance Initiative
FBI	Federal Bureau of Investigation
FMF	Foreign Military Financing
FMS	Foreign Military Sales
FSB	Russian Federal Security Service
IC	Intelligence Community
ICIG	Inspector General for the Intelligence Community
IO	Bureau of International Organizations
IG	Inspector General
Legatt	Legal Attaché
LNG	Liquefied Natural Gas
MEMCON	Memorandum of Conversation
MLAT	Mutual Legal Assistance Treaty
NABU	National Anti-Corruption Bureau of Ukraine
NBU	National Bank of Ukraine
NDAA	National Defense Authorization Act
NSC	National Security Council
ODNI	Office of the Director of National Intelligence
OFAC	Office of Foreign Assets Control
OMB	Office of Management and Budget
OSCE	Organization for Security and Co-operation in Europe
OVP	Office of the Vice President
PAC	Political Action Committee
PC	Principals Committee
PCC	Policy Coordination Committee
PDB	President's Daily Briefing
PDM	Presidential Decision Memorandum

PGO	Prosecutor General's Office
SAPO	Specialized Anti-Corruption Prosecutor's Office
SBU	Security Service of Ukraine
SDN	Specially Designated Nationals and Blocked Persons
SMM	Special Monitoring Mission
SOC	Summary of Conclusions
SVTC	Secure Video Teleconference
TCG	Trilateral Contact Group
UNSCR	United Nations Security Council Resolution
USAI	Ukraine Security Assistance Initiative
USAID	United States Agency for International Development
WHSR	White House Situation Room
YES	Yalta European Strategy

www.ingramcontent.com/pod-product-compliance
Lightning Source LLC
Chambersburg PA
CBHW080407270326

41929CB00018B/2927